CRACKING

The Billy the Kid Imposter Hoax of Brushy Bill Roberts

BY
GALE COOPER

GELCOUR
BOOKS

COVER AND BOOK DESIGN BY GALE COOPER

OTHER BILLY THE KID BOOKS BY GALE COOPER

THE HISTORY

BILLY AND PAULITA: THE SAGA OF BILLY THE KID, PAULITA MAXWELL, AND THE SANTA FE RING

BILLY THE KID'S WRITINGS, WORDS, AND WIT

THE LOST PARDON OF BILLY THE KID: AN ANALYSIS FACTORING IN THE SANTA FE RING, GOVERNOR LEW WALLACE'S DILEMMA, AND A TERRITORY IN REBELLION

THE SANTA FE RING VERSUS BILLY THE KID: THE MAKING OF AN AMERICAN MONSTER

THE CORONER'S JURY REPORT OF BILLY THE KID: THE INQUEST THAT SEALED THE FAME OF BILLY BONNEY AND PAT GARRETT

THE HOAXES

CRACKING THE BILLY THE KID CASE HOAX: THE STRANGE PLOT TO EXHUME BILLY THE KID, CONVICT SHERIFF PAT GARRETT OF MURDER, AND BECOME PRESIDENT OF THE UNITED STATES

THE COLD CASE BILLY THE KID MEGAHOAX: THE PLOT TO STEAL BILLY THE KID'S IDENTITY AND DEFAME PAT GARRETT AS A MURDERER

BILLY THE KID'S PRETENDER JOHN MILLER

THE BILLY THE KID'S BAD BUCKS HOAX: FAKING BILLY BONNEY AS A WILLIAM BROCKWAY GANG COUNTERFEITER

BLANDINA SEGALE, THE NUN WHO RODE ON BILLY THE KID: SLEUTHING A FOISTED FRONTIER FABLE

For Billy Bonney
and William Hudspeth,
victims of the
"Brushy Bill" Roberts
Billy the Kid imposter hoax

COPYRIGHT © 2020 Gale Cooper
All Rights Reserved.

FIRST EDITION

*Reproductions, excerpts, or transmittals
of the author's original text or art in this book
are prohibited in any form whatsoever
without written permission of the author.
Infringers will be prosecuted
to the fullest extent of the law.*

ISBN: 978-1-949626-10-0 HARDCOVER
ISBN: 978-1-949626-11-7 PAPERBACK
LCCN: 2018914425

GELCOUR BOOKS
Albuquerque, NM 87112

ORDERING THIS BOOK:
Amazon.com, BarnesandNoble.com, bookstores

WEBSITE:
GaleCooperBillytheKidBooks.com

YOUTUBE CHANNEL:
Gale Cooper's Real Billy the Kid

Printed in the United States of America
on acid free paper

CONTENTS

PREFACE xvii
AUTHOR'S FOREWORD xviii
ACKNOWLEDGMENTS ix
METHODOLOGY xx

PART I:
HOAXING HISTORY

CHAPTER 1:
BILLY THE KID HISTORY HOAXING

THE HOAX TRIUMVIRATE 3
THE "BRUSHY BILL" HOAX 4
VULNERABLE HISTORY 5

CHAPTER 2:
OBSTACLE OF WILLIAM H. BONNEY'S
CORONER'S JURY REPORT

THE HOAXER'S BUGABOO 9
THE CORONER'S JURY REPORT 10
CONFIRMATION OF CORONER'S JURY
    PRESIDENT MILNOR RUDULPH'S SIGNATURE 15
CONFIRMATION OF THE CORONER'S JURYMEN 16
STATUTE GOVERNING THE CORONER'S JURY REPORT 16
PAT GARRETT'S LETTER TO THE ACTING-GOVERNOR 18
ISSUES COMPLICATING GARRETT'S
    REWARD COLLECTION 20
REWARD NEEDING LEGISLATIVE INTERVENTION 22
REWARD GRANTED TO GARRETT BY
    THE LEGISLATURE 26
GOVERNOR SHELDON'S APPROVAL 28
LATER FINDING OF THE REPORT 29
THE "BRUSHY BILL" HOAX RESPONSE 36

CHAPTER 3:
OBSTACLE OF CORPSE WITNESSES

THE PROBLEM OF REALITY 57
PAT GARRETT WROTE A BOOK 57
DEPUTY POE WROTE A BOOK 59
A.P. "PACO" ANAYA BURIED BILLY AND GOT A BOOK 62

A TOWN IDENTIFIED THE BODY TOO 62
DELUVINA MAXWELL WAS THERE ALSO 63
THE PRESS WAS PROFUSE 64
"BRUSHY" HOAX RESPONSE 66

CHAPTER 4:
OBSTACLE OF THE OUTLAW MYTH
OF BILLY THE KID

FAKING A FAKE BILLY BONNEY 67
THE SANTA FE RING'S OUTLAW MYTH
   OF BILLY THE KID 67
LEW WALLACE'S OUTLAW MYTH OF BILLY THE KID 73
PAT GARRETT'S OUTLAW MYTH OF BILLY THE KID 79
WALTER NOBLE BURNS'S OUTLAW MYTH
   OF BILLY THE KID 83
THE BILLY THE KID MONIKER 85
THE "BRUSHY" HOAX'S RESPONSE 92

CHAPTER 5:
OBSTACLE OF MORE
HISTORICAL PEOPLE AND RECORDS

THE UNKNOWN KEY FIGURES AND DOCUMENTS 93
PUBLIC IGNORANCE AS SALVATION 100

PART II:
THE REAL BILLY BONNEY

CHAPTER 1:
BILLY THE KID HISTORY

REAL HISTORY 103

CHAPTER 2:
BILLY BONNEY'S CHAMPIONS

THOSE WHO REALLY KNEW BILLY 123

CHAPTER 3:
BILLY BONNEY'S CHAMPIONS

SPEAKING THROUGH TIME 129
AFFIDAVIT AND DEPUTIZING 130
DEPOSITION TO FRANK WARNER ANGEL 131
"REGULATOR MANIFESTO" 136
HOYT BILL OF SALE 137

LETTER OF MARCH 13, 1879 TO LEW WALLACE 138
LETTER OF MARCH 20, 1879 TO "SQUIRE" WILSON 139
LETTER OF MARCH 20, 1879 TO LEW WALLACE 139
THE LEW WALLACE INTERVIEW 140
THE "BILLIE" LETTER TO LEW WALLACE 143
LOST GRAND JURY TESTIMONY 144
TESTIMONY AGAINST N.A.M. DUDLEY 144
LETTER OF DECEMBER 12, 1880 TO LEW WALLACE 149
SANTA FE JAIL LETTER: JANUARY 1, 1881 151
SANTA FE JAIL LETTER: MARCH 2, 1881 152
SANTA FE JAIL LETTER: MARCH 4, 1881 152
SANTA FE JAIL LETTER: MARCH 27, 1881 153
LETTER TO ATTORNEY EDGAR CAYPLESS 154
NEWSPAPER INTERVIEWS 155
CONCLUSION 160

PART III:
THE ORIGINAL "BRUSHY BILL" ROBERTS BILLY THE KID IMPOSTER HOAX

CHAPTER 1:
CREATORS OF THE "BRUSHY BILL" IMPOSTER HOAX

"BRUSHY" AND HIS HOAX TEAM 163
OLIVER P. "BRUSHY BILL" ROBERTS 164
WILLIAM VINCENT MORRISON 182
CHARLES LELAND "C.L." SONNICHSEN 192
CREATING THE HOOK AND THE BOOK 204

CHAPTER 2:
"BRUSHY BILL'S" BEGINNING AS BILLY

A PASSEL OF PRETENDERS 205
BETTING ON "BRUSHY" 210
FAKING SPECIAL KNOWLEDGE 210

CHAPTER 3:
DEALING WITH MISMATCH DILEMMAS

THE LITERATE BILLY DILEMMA 219
HOAX RESPONSE TO LITERACY 226

THE BI-LINGUAL BILLY DILEMMA..227
THE LITERATE "BRUSHY" DILEMMA 228
THE SERIAL MURDERER MONSTER DILEMMA..................236
THE HOAX FORMULA 236

CHAPTER 4:
THE BILLY THE KID PARDON PRIZE

PRIMED FOR THE PARDON PRIZE 237
THE PARDON PETITION 239
MORRISON'S "EVIDENCE" PACKET
   FOR "BRUSHY'S" PARDON HEARING 240
PARDON REJECTED BASED ON NO BILLY THE KID
   TO PARDON 248
"BRUSHY'S" PRESS..250
HISTORIAN HENDRON'S ARTICLE
   FILLED-IN THE DISASTER...261
HIDDEN HOAXBUSTING TREASURE 262

CHAPTER 5:
A LIMBO OF LIES

MORRISON RISES FROM THE ASHES.....................................263
A FRENZY OF PROMOTION 268
COURTING HIS PARTNER 272
FIX-UP RESEARCH..273
PITCHING THE HOAX..279
STRATEGIZING PERSONAL PROFIT 285
NO LIMIT TO LIES..286

CHAPTER 6:
THE HOAX BECOMES A BOOK

"BRUSHY'S" BIBLE IS BORN 287
THE FIRST AND WORST DUPE..287
FATE OF THE BOOK 292
FATE OF REAL "BRUSHY" 293
CREATING "BRUSHY'S" NARRATIVE 298

CHAPTER 7:
DEBUNKING *ALIAS BILLY THE KID*

SMOKE AND MIRRORS..299
HOAXING ON THE COVER 300
THE HOAX IN THE TITLE..300

"PUBLISHER'S FOREWORD"	301
A "NOTE TO THE SKEPTICAL"	302
"PROLOGUE"	302
"BRUSHY BILL'S STORY"	307
FAKING LIFE AFTER BILLY'S DEATH	369
FAKE PHOTO SECTION	371
FAKING EVIDENCE FOR "BRUSHY" AS BILLY	373
APPENDICES AND PARTING WORDS	404
SUMMARIZING *ALIAS BILLY THE KID'S* "BRUSHY BILL" IMPOSTER HOAX	405

CHAPTER 8:
MORRISON'S LAST GASPS

A POSTHUMOUS PARDON FOR "BRUSHY"	407
DIGGING UP BILLY	408
CREATING A NEW IMPOSTER HOAX	409

CHAPTER 9:
THE RETURN OF *ALIAS BILLY THE KID*

REPRINTING THE HOAX	413

PART IV:
TRUE-BELIEVERS CONTINUE THE "BRUSHY BILL" HOAX

CHAPTER 1:
WHEN DUPES REPLACE CHARLATANS

"BRUSHY" HOAX EVOLUTION	417
INTRODUCTORY MISINFORMATION	418
FAKING BILLY THE KID HISTORY	419
INTRODUCING THEIR MAN "BRUSHY"	423
EXPANDING A FAKE FAMILY TREE"	425
"BRUSHY" TALKS NONSENSE	430
JAMESON AND BEAN TALK NONSENSE	445
ALLEGED ANALYSES	449
FAKE "FORENSIC" PHOTO-COMPARISON	454
CONSPIRACY THEORIES	459
THE JAMESON-BEAN OUTCOME	464

PART V:
"BRUSHY BILL" GETS TO HOLLYWOOD

CHAPTER 1:
A GREAT STORY

FICTION MEETS FILM...467

PART VI:
THE RETURN OF "BRUSHY" IN THE "BILLY THE KID CASE" HOAX

CHAPTER 1:
CREATION OF THE "BILLY THE KID CASE" HOAX

LEGACY OF "BRUSHY BILL" 471
FAKE NEWS 473
FAKE MURDER CASE 480
HOAX PROGRESSION 481

CHAPTER 2:
"BILLY THE KID CASE" HOAXERS AND HOAX DOCUMENTS

REWRITING "BRUSHY'S" HOAX 487
STARTING GATE BLOCKADES 487
REFUSED EXHUMATION PERMITS..488
LAWMEN'S HOAXING DOCUMENTS 494
ATTORNEY BILL ROBINS III IN ACTION..............................549
PAUL HUTTON'S TV PROGRAM..558
THE U.S. MARSHALS SERVICE REPORT 563
FAKE FORENSIC REPORTINGS..568

CHAPTER 3:
ILLEGAL EXHUMATIONS OF JOHN MILLER AND WILLIAM HUDSPETH

TARGETING JOHN MILLER 585
SETTING UP THE EXHUMATION...586
THE SECRET FRENZIED DIG..587
EXPOSED IN THE PRESS 588
THE DNA TRAVESTY 589
THE CRIMINAL CASE 589
BACK TO CATHERINE ANTRIM...592

CHAPTER 4 :
"BRUSHY" GETS BACK IN THE MOVIES

THE HOAX MAKES THE CANNES FILM FESTIVAL..............593

CHAPTER 5 :
TRYING TO DIG UP "BRUSHY BILL"

HEADING TO TEXAS WITH SHOVELS 595

CHAPTER 6 :
STOPPING THE BRUSHY PARDON

RETURN OF THE PARDON PLOT 567
LAST MINUTE PARDON PETITION..........................600
LEW WALLACE'S REAL DNA...............................608
RIGHT UP TO THE END 612
BITTER "BIG BILL'S" LAST LIE.........................614

CHAPTER 7 :
EXPOSING THE
"BILLY THE KID CASE" HOAX IN COURT

OPEN RECORDS SHOWDOWN 615
SUMMARY OF OPEN RECORDS FIGHT.......................615
THE LAWMEN'S MAJOR HOAX DOCUMENTS
  TO HIDE INCRIMINATING RECORDS 617
FORGING DR. HENRY LEE REPORTS 630
KEY POINTS IN THE JUDGE'S FINAL DECISION
  IN THE OPEN RECORDS LITIGATION 638

CHAPTER 8 :
"BILLY THE KID CASE" HOAX UPSHOT

FAILURE TO MAKE "BRUSHY" BILLY.......................641

PART VII:
THE RETURN OF "BRUSHY'S" TRUE BELIEVER, W.C. JAMESON, AS A HOAXER

CHAPTER 1:
RETURN OF FAKERY IN
BILLY THE KID: BEYOND THE GRAVE

HOAXBUSTING "*BILLY THE KID:
  BEYOND THE GRAVE*" 645

MAKING A BETTER "BRUSHY" 645
THE HOAXBUSTING MOON 647
  CELSA AS OMNISCIENT NARRATOR 647
THE "TRAVELING" ARMORY 648
ATTACKING "BRUSHY'S" DEBUNKING 648
CONCLUSION: THE SAME OLD SCAM
  IN NEED OF NEW BLOOD 652

CHAPTER 2:
MORE FAKERY IN
BILLY THE KID: THE LOST INTERVIEWS

PURE HOAXING 653
UPGRADING THE "BRUSHY" HOAX 654
THE MYSTERY TRUNK AND TAPES 655
TRANSCRIBING THE "BRUSHY" TAPES 657
FAKING "BRUSHY'S" WORDS 658
DISCUSSION 670

CHAPTER 3:
DEFAMING IN *PAT GARRETT:*
THE MAN BEHIND THE BADGE

THE "BRUSHY" HOAX'S HEART OF DARKNESS 671
STAGE SET FOR A MEGAHOAX 672

PART VIII:
"BRUSHY BILL" IN THE *COLD CASE*
BILLY THE KID MEGAHOAX

CHAPTER 1:
THE RETURN OF "BRUSHY"
IN A MEGAHOAX

A BLOATED IMPLODING HOAX 675
THE HOAX IN THE TITLE" 676
"FOREWORD" AND "INTRODUCTION" 676

CHAPTER 2:
FAKING KNOWLEDGE

RETURN OF THE IGNORANCE OF
  THE RETURN OF THE OUTLAW BILLY THE KID 677

CHAPTER 3:
"BRUSHY" BASHING HOAXING

NARRATING NEW HOAXING 689

CHAPTER 4:
FAKING DEATH SCENE DOUBTS

THE MEGAHOAX'S BULL'S EYE 697
FAKING DISCREPANCIES 697
FAKING A MAXWELL BEDROOM DOOR DISCREPANCY 700
FAKING SHOOTING SCENE DOUBTS 707
FAKING THE BODY'S REMOVAL 708
FAKING A "PETE MAXWELL" 709
NOTHING BUT FAKING 712

CHAPTER 5:
FAKING NO INQUEST

HOAXERS VERSUS CORONER'S JURY REPORT 713

CHAPTER 6:
THE RETURN OF THE
"BILLY THE KID CASE" FAKE FORENSICS

RECYCLING THE FAKE JAILBREAK INVESTIGATION 715
RECYCLING THE CARPENTER'S BENCH
    DNA INVESTIGATION 721
RECYCLING "MAXWELL FURNITURE" FORENSICS 722
RECYCLING THE JOHN MILLER EXHUMATION 723
LONGING FOR "BRUSHY'S" "DNA FORENSICS" 724

CHAPTER 7:
THE RETURN OF THE
CONSPIRACY THEORIES

FAKING PLOTS AGAINST THE "TRUTH" 725
SEDERWALL'S CONSPIRACY AGAINST HIMSELF 725

CHAPTER 8:
FORGONE FAKE CONCLUSION

WHEN HOAXERS FOOL THEMSELVES 731

PART IX: SUMMARY AND CONCLUSIONS

CHAPTER 1: A LITMUS TEST FOR CROOKS AND DUPES

THE "BRUSHY BILL" HOAX TODAY 735

ANNOTATED APPENDIX 737

ANNOTATED BIBLIOGRAPHY

RELEVANT 19TH CENTURY HISTORY 745
COMPREHENSIVE REFERENCES 745
HISTORICAL ORGANIZATIONS 745
   SANTA FE RING 745
NEW MEXICO TERRITORY REBELLIONS AGAINST
   THE SANTA FE RING 748
HISTORY OF WILLIAM HENRY BONNEY 751
OTHER HISTORICAL FIGURES (PERIOD) 761
THE ORIGINAL "BRUSHY BILL" ROBERTS
   BILLY THE KID IMPOSTER HOAX 784
THE "BRUSHY BILL" HOAX IN
   THE RETURN OF THE OUTLAW BILLY THE KID 808
JOHN MILLER BILLY THE KID IMPOSTER HOAX 809
"BILLY THE KID CASE" HOAX" 809
W.C. JAMESON'S 21st CENTURY
   "BRUSHY" BACKING BOOKS 832

INDEX 835

PREFACE

Well, I'm back. I'm the old-timer who starts this here author's books; and this one takes me back to 1955 when I was bout 20 and a ranch hand near Lincoln town, where they had them the Lincoln County War that made Billy Bonney famous - though he didn't cotton to the fake fame of being some outlaw Billy the Kid stead of a freedom fighter against the Santa Fe Ring. Anyways, the radio was playing The Platters' '55 song, "The Great Pretender;" going like this: "Oh yes I'm the great pretender, Pretending I'm doing well, My need is such I pretend too much, I'm lonely but no one can tell. Oh yes I'm the great pretender, Adrift in a world of my own."

Well, this here book is about a pretender named "Brushy Bill" Roberts, who lied bout being Billy and not being killed by Pat Garrett on July 14, 1881. His lies were like rustlers' hair brands in Billy's day: just shaved on. In other words, he had nothing.

Now this "Brushy" had hisself a problem, cause if he was Billy he had to know things like Billy; but in his day - the '40's - there was no history books to figer out what to say. So he used old dime novel bullshit - excuse the French - figering nobody knew better.

Well, nothing would have come of it if he hadn't met up with a fella as shady as he was, him being a William V. Morrison - a salesman pretending to be a lawyer - looking to make his fortune. He figered his fortune was "Brushy." So he gave "Brushy" more Billy stories, took him to Lincoln town, and tried to trick the Governor into giving him real Billy's pardon. The Governor, being no fool, said no. So they found them an English teacher named C.L. Sonnichsen, who cottoned to be an historian. He figered they was his ticket. So - to get back to '55 - he wrote them a book that year saying "Brushy" was Billy the Kid. "Brushy was dead by then, which was good, cause he couldn't remember his lines.

Well, that book got "Brushy" a passel of suckers. And new authors fixed-up ol' "Brushy" to match new history books; and he even got a movie. Then a crooked New Mexico Governor figered he could get famous by giving dead "Brushy" that old pardon as Billy.

Well, it added up to needing this book to stop the tomfoolery. But, being fictional myself, I got a soft spot for them like me that's not real, like ol' "Brushy," just pretending his heart out.

                            Vern Blanton Johnson, Jr.
                            Lincoln, Lincoln County, New Mexico

AUTHOR'S FOREWORD

This book is about historical fakery on a level of elaborateness and effort that seems inconceivable, if one does not factor in the profit motive in hijacking the famous history of Billy the Kid. It is fitting, however, that the hoaxing began with just one mentally and vocationally disabled man, relying on his delusions blurred with wishful thinking, while presenting himself as the most famous Old West character he could imagine: Billy the Kid.

He got noticed, then remembered, by ironic coincidence that Billy the Kid history was already layered-over by self-serving fakery. Its quirk was that it was written by enemies with an agenda. First came the outlaw myth of Billy the Kid, created in Billy's lifetime by the Santa Fe Ring to hide its terrorist crushing of Territorial uprisings against its corrupt take-over; with Billy epitomizing the freedom fighters in the Lincoln County War. Concomitantly, Governor Lew Wallace - betraying his pardon bargain to Billy for fear of Ring repercussions to his political future - added his own concealing outlaw myths, enhanced by his literary flair. Pat Garrett joined in with a book, with help of a ghost-writer, to justify his killing of Billy as a law-and-order remedy, while hiding his Ring-backed role in the final solution to that gadfly. By "Brushy Bill's" day, in the first half of the 20th century, attention-seeking old men, like "Brushy," inserted themselves into those tales by parroting that outlaw image.

The emergence of scholarly writers in the second half of the 20th century was no salvation, with their plastering of new discoveries onto the antique armature of outlaw Billy the Kid. The reason came back to the Santa Fe Ring. Undefeated in Billy's day, it persisted ominously in New Mexico's impenetrable corruption to the present. So it was avoided, leaving historian's renditions as preposterous as writing about the Civil War and omitting slavery.

Then things got worse in the 21st century, with a modern Santa Fe Ring self-promoting Governor trying to hijack the history by recycling "Brushy Bill" in a forensic hoax of his own.

It has been my mission to write books presenting the real history and exposing its fakers. This book takes on the pernicious "Brushy Bill" imposter hoax, which epitomizes its promulgators' profiteering motives and destructive results.

Gale Cooper, M.D.
Sandia Park, New Mexico

ACKNOWLEDGMENTS

Overriding is my debt to Billy Bonney, whose cause, courage, intelligence, and joie de vivre are my inspiration.

Special thanks goes to family of Oliver Pleasant "Brushy Bill" Roberts. In 1987, his full brother, Tom Ulce Roberts's, daughter, Geneva Roberts Pittmon, exposed him in a letter to the Billy the Kid Outlaw Gang's founders as a 20 year too young imposter. "Brushy" was also the maternal-side half great-granduncle of Roy L. Haws, whose 2015 book, *Brushy Bill: Proof that His Claim to be Billy the Kid Was a Hoax*, provided "Brushy's" true genealogy as well as exposés by family members: Paul Emerson and Cora Heath. And, using Roberts family interviews, historian, Don Cline, debunked "Brushy" in his 1988 unpublished book, *Brushy Bill Roberts: I Wasn't Billy the Kid*; citing as sources Geneva Pittmon and her sisters, Mary June Roberts and Cordelia Roberts.

Hoaxbusting appreciation goes to New Mexico journalist, Jay Miller, who acted as my open records proxy in my early dangerous days of exposing corrupt Governor Bill Richardson's "Brushy Bill"-based "Billy the Kid Case" forensic DNA hoax.

National Archive records used were from the Civilian Records Branch, the Justice Department, the Department of Interior, and the Secret Service Library Counterfeit Division.

Collections used were the Las Cruces, New Mexico State University Library's Rio Grande Historical Collections' Herman B. Weisner Papers, ca. 1957-1992 and Blazer Family Papers, 1864-1965; the Albuquerque, University of New Mexico Center for Southwest Studies, University Library, Catron Papers; the State of New Mexico Office of Cultural Affairs Historic Preservation Division; the Office of the New Mexico State Historian; the Silver City Museum and Library; the Midland, Texas Nita Stewart and J. Evetts Haley Memorial Library and Historical Center; the Canyon, Texas Panhandle-Plains Historical Museum; the Santa Fe, New Mexico, Fray Angélico Chávez Historical Library; the Indianapolis, Indiana Historical Society's Lew and Susan Wallace Collection; the Springfield, Illinois, Abraham Lincoln Library and Museum's William V. Morrison papers; and the University of Texas El Paso Library's C.L. Sonnichsen papers.

METHODOLOGY

PRIMARY DOCUMENTS: For readers' reference, primary documents are presented; with italics for handwriting, two column newsprint for articles, and in distinctive font for books. Original errors in spelling or punctuation are retained, with "sic" noted where needed.

COMMENTARY: Author's notes and responses are provided in boldface. Boldface is also used to highlight important claims by hoaxers. Underlings and italics are added for emphasis. Page numbers are given for cited text in books, or to refer back to pages in this book itself. And the "Appendix" and "Bibliography" are annotated.

BIBLIOGRAPHY: The hoaxers' prompt sources to coach "Brushy Bill" Roberts's Billy the Kid impersonation are listed bibliographically under the original hoax (Pages 802-808). Later fix-up sources to forge "Brushy's" transcript's "words" to match modern historical findings are listed with their respective hoax manifestations.

PART I

HOAXING HISTORY

CHAPTER 1
BILLY THE KID HISTORY HOAXING

THE HOAX TRIUMVIRATE

In 1949, three very different, equally ambitious men, each faced personal failure. One was a 69 year old, mentally disabled, farm laborer, now on welfare, who was the town laughingstock in Hico, Texas, for telling tall tales of his Old West adventures, while dressed in homemade cowboy outfits. His name was Oliver Pleasant Roberts; but he called himself "Brushy Bill." Another was a traveling salesman and bankruptcy case investigator, 42, who pretended to be a lawyer and flaunted a genetic link to the Old West Maxwell family. His name was William Vincent Morrison. The last had earned a Harvard Ph.D. in 17th and 18th century literature, and, at 47, was an English teacher in a comparatively backwater college of mining and metallurgy, while writing fictionalized books about minor Old West characters. His name was Charles Leland Sonnichsen. Before they met, each knew that the most famous Old West character was Billy the Kid.

Crazy "Brushy" had recently settled on declaring himself to be Billy the Kid. Morrison had used Billy to glamorize his obscure Maxwell family, because in their Fort Sumner, New Mexico Territory mansion Sheriff Pat Garrett had killed him. And Sonnichsen, aping an historian, had interviewed peripheral descendants of Billy's contemporaries to collect hearsay malarkey.

The backdrop was burgeoning scholarly research on Billy the Kid, and emergence of historians in that genre. Their discoveries made the news because of media magnetism radiated by the Kid. One could go from being a non-entity to national publicity.

That fact was not lost on the team of "Brushy," Morrison, and Sonnichsen. In their sights was a publicity-grabbing stunt to get "Brushy" the lost Billy the Kid pardon; then to open markets for TV and movies; which would yield their book: *Alias Billy the Kid*.

THE "BRUSHY BILL" HOAX

Once "Brushy Bill," William V. Morrison, and C.L. Sonnichsen united, they created one of the world's most elaborate, most labor intensive, most destructive, and most enduring historical hoaxes: the "Brushy Bill" Roberts Billy the Kid impersonation. Its corollary of "Brushy's" surviving the Kid's famous shooting death in New Mexico Territory's Fort Sumner on July 14, 1881, was defamation of famous lawman, Pat Garrett, as a liar who concealed killing an innocent victim, not Billy, on that night. And when that hoax's creators died, more took their place.

Its cast of madmen, charlatans, hucksters, forgers, windbags, and wannabes, make a pathetic and unsavory lot; whose eventual championing by a corrupt, self-promoting, 21st century, New Mexico governor gave them access to the world stage. All insulted legitimate historical investigation. That makes this book debunking them a study of lying - from delusional to malicious.

More profoundly, this book is a testament to the real history unknown to "Brushy Bill" and his promoters: a magnificent, Territory-wide, freedom fight against New Mexico Territory's deadly land-grabbing Santa Fe Ring political cabal, that culminated in the Lincoln County War Battle, which made a grass-roots hero of teenaged, charismatic, bi-cultural zealot, Billy Bonney; and marked him for killing as his Ring enemies' mythologized outlaw: Billy the Kid.

Also demonstrated in this exposé is that historical research is both a science and an art of picking and comprehending sources to decipher their meaning, as well as distinguishing facts from erroneous hearsay and tall tales. The historical hoaxers in this book demonstrate how easy it is to camouflage fakery by a flurry of name-dropping and misstatements, coupled with defensive conspiracy theories, to foist fiction on the public.

This book is also shows the intensive labor of hoaxbusting. Everything must be checked, since, at this level of dishonesty, no claimed source can be accepted as accurate, no document is above being forged, fallacious straw-man reasoning and fake conspiracy theories substitute for evidence, and truths are hidden. The conniving promulgators, assembled here, rely on a reader's placing trust in authoritative information beyond their knowledge. But to them, readers are victim-dupes, cynically sold flimflam, disguised as discoveries with attention-grabbing claims.

VULNERABLE HISTORY

From its start, Billy Bonney's true history was corrupted by falsehoods because of Billy's entanglement with the larger cover-up being conducted by the deadly Santa Fe Ring to hide its horrific crimes of the 1870's as it ascended to political and mercantile domination by robbery of millions of acres of Hispanic land grants, malicious prosecutions, massacres, assassinations, and military terrorism. New Mexico Territory became its fiefdom, with monopolized executive, legislative, judicial, and law enforcement powers, and a complicit press.

Billy was part of the Ring's most bloody and most incriminating stain: the Lincoln County War Battle of July 14-19, 1878. The Santa Fe Ring, as victors through perfidy, as real outlaws hiding their villainy, and as facing federal investigation, wrote self-justifying fiction of the events. Thus, arose the outlaw myth that transmogrified the Territory's valiant, grass-roots, freedom fighting against it, into a scourge of mindless outlawry against law and order. And, as brilliant, bi-cultural, political zealot Billy emerged as the people's symbol of defiance by repeatedly testifying against Ringites, and by guerilla attacks on Ringites' property, he became the Ring's symbol of fictional outlawry, with the bestowed moniker, "Billy the Kid." He had to be killed. And he was killed as the last of the freedom fighters, completing rule by fear continuing to the present.

So effective was the Ring's historical expurgation, that the Territorial uprisings against it did not appear in Billy the Kid history until my writings. But the citizens' struggles were preserved in their writings, petitions, exposés, and press.

In 1872, legislators in Santa Fe rose up against the increasing Ring stranglehold, and were suppressed by the Ringite Governor. In 1876, to the southwest, was the Grant County Rebellion, in which citizens wrote a "Declaration of Independence" and tried to secede and join Arizona Territory to escape the Ring. From 1875 to 1877, Ring atrocities escalated to the north, in the Colfax County War, with assassination of the anti-Ring leader and with terrorized citizens' futile exposés to Ring-biased President Rutherford B. Hayes. The people's culminating defeat was the 1878 Lincoln County War, where Ring-beholden troops illegally enabled citizens' murder; and in which Billy Bonney became the hero, and a gadfly emerging as a future threat with his bi-cultural links and potential for eliciting an Hispanic uprising.

Billy's outlawing by the Ring was magnified by his 1879 pardon bargain which he offered to non-Ringite Governor Lew Wallace, involving testimony against the latest Ring murderers. But under Ring pressure, Wallace disreputably reneged on his pardon promise after Billy did testify. Wallace guiltily concealed his moral failure by self-justifying additions to the Ring's outlaw myth of Billy the Kid by blaming him as incorrigible.

By 1882, Sheriff Pat Garrett capitalized on his own fame for killing Billy the year before, by publishing his own outlaw myth rendition in a ghostwritten book. That mold was not broken by the scholarly historians of the latter half of the 20th century, who merely plastered their new findings onto that antique armature.

It has taken my 21st century research, analyses, and books to restore Billy Bonney to his freedom fighter glory, along with his compatriots, in that period when democracy was destroyed by the Santa Fe Ring. Likewise, I have exposed the modern Santa Fe Ring, with its unchanged corrupt cronyism, when it came full circle in the 21st century by joining forces with the "Brushy Bill" hoax to hijack Billy the Kid history for mutual profiteering.

But it was amazing Billy Bonney, when alive and after death, whose fame and own words and writings kept alive the memory of his times until truth could prevail.

EMERGENCE OF HISTORICAL PARASITES

There was a peculiar side-effect of Billy's posthumous fame: the emergence of mentally disturbed, attention-seeking old men, in the second quarter of the 20th century, who claimed to be him. Since Billy was fatally shot in Fort Sumner on July 14, 1881 by Pat Garrett, that necessitated these imposters' second fabrication: accusing Pat Garrett of killing the wrong man and covering it up.

This was also the period in which fascination for Billy's story was so insatiable that his old-timer contemporaries achieved publishing books with their own mundane life stories, simply by adding him. And the most glib Billy the Kid impersonators followed suit by attracting hoaxing, profiteering authors.

The problem fabricating historical parasites faced was insurmountable: scholarly history books about Billy Bonney's life had not yet been written. There was only the old outlaw myth of the 19th century, with its seepage into the early 20th century. So cribbing fake fables was imposters' undoing. But their salvation was an equally benighted public, eager for tales of Billy the Kid.

PUBLICIZED PRETENDERS

Oliver "Brushy Bill" Roberts was the pretender who outdistanced the others because he got an energetic huckster promoter, a publicity hook, and a book. Born in Arkansas in 1879, his delusions and attention-seeking endowed him with multiple famous Old West identities, among them Billy the Kid. His luck was inspiring traveling salesman William V. Morrison, who was also promoting a Jesse James impersonator friend of "Brushy's." Morrison was a hardworking showman. He researched his day's documentation of Billy the Kid. And he saw its publicity hook: Billy's lost pardon for Lincoln County War indictments. Morrison would seek that pardon for "Brushy" from New Mexico's current governor. Though this scheme failed, it kindled public imagination, yielded Morrison's co-authored book on "Brushy," and rippled out over time by getting converts, who peddled the lies and backed conspiracy theories to explain "Brushy's" rejection.

A second Billy the Kid imposter, an Arizonian named John Miller, with no known believers, phlegmatically self-promoted, and got an equally lethargic book author. He was long ignored, but burst into public awareness as one object in the biggest, most elaborate, internationally publicized, and best funded historic-forensic hoax ever perpetrated: the 2003 "Billy the Kid Case." And that case ironically linked him to its real objective: faking proof that "Brushy Bill" was Billy the Kid.

THE "BILLY THE KID CASE" HOAX

The "Billy the Kid Case," so named by its perpetrators, beginning in 2003, was a self-serving publicity stunt of corrupt New Mexico Governor Bill Richardson and his major political donor, an attorney who was a "Brushy Bill" believer.

It was a real murder investigation against Pat Garrett, with modern CSI glamour of DNA matchings from exhumations. The covert intent was anointing "Brushy" as Billy. That it was historically indisputable that Garrett killed Billy, and that no forensically valid, Billy the Kid DNA existed anywhere for DNA matching, were kept secret. The scam's genius was to legitimize exhumations by claiming they were part of a filed "cold case" murder investigation against Garrett for killing the innocent victim. And Lincoln and De Baca County Sheriffs Departments' lawmen became Richardson's agents for that fake investigation.

My fighting that hoax in district courts stopped the exhumations of Billy and his mother, then revealed its DNA fraud. And I wrote exposé books. Without all that, the history of Billy the Kid would have been destroyed, beyond retrieval, by these conscienceless hoaxers. And the original dream of "Brushy Bill," William V. Morrison, and C.L. Sonnichsen to scam everybody would have been fulfilled at last.

THE "COLD CASE BILLY THE KID" MEGAHOAX

In 2018, after a string of "Brushy"-backing books that descended increasingly into fix-ups to fake "Brushy's" match to the historical Billy Bonney, their author, William Carl "W.C." Jameson, partnering with past "Billy the Kid Case" hoaxers, combined the "Brushy Bill" and "Billy the Kid Case" hoaxes in his book: *Cold Case Billy the Kid*. His objective was to cast doubt on recorded history - even including imposter John Miller as a Billy the Kid survivor possibility - to propose once again that his man "Brushy" was actually Billy Bonney, since "history is not as written." So exposing that book's potpourri of hoaxes became the subject of another of my exposé books.

The big picture was that "Brushy Bill" has persisted like an incurable and metastasizing cancer within Billy the Kid history.

CHAPTER 2
OBSTACLE OF WILLIAM H. BONNEY'S CORONER'S JURY REPORT

THE HOAXERS' BUGABOO

All the greedy hopes of Billy the Kid old-timer pretenders went out the window if Billy Bonney was proved dead, since their fable was surviving the Pat Garrett killing. So the Coroner's Jury Report on Billy's legal inquest was fatal to them.

On July 14, 1881, Billy Bonney had a dramatic death scene in the Fort Sumner mansion of the Maxwell family - with the bedroom ambush by Sheriff Pat Garrett in the place Billy felt safest - with hundreds of townspeople seeing his corpse.

At the next day's inquest, a Coroner's Jury Report was generated by six local men, confirming him as the victim of justified homicide. It was then filed correctly: at Santa Fe, with the District Attorney of the First Judicial District, which included Fort Sumner's San Miguel County. And, based on it, Pat Garrett was paid his Billy the Kid reward of $500.

Thus, later Billy the Kid identity thieves' had to deny that Report. So they lied desperately that it did not exist; that there were two reports, both false; that the victim was not Billy the Kid; that the jurymen signers were not real people; that Garrett never got the reward because of no Report; that, on the other hand, Garrett got the reward because of a Santa Fe Ring plot hiding the victim's identity; and that everyone in Ft. Sumner had conspired to hide the victim's identity to let Billy escape. That level of lying in the face of stark reality of eye-witnesses in the hundreds in the death night's public wake, and the Report's having been scrutinized by highest public officials, and still existing for modern viewing, necessitated betting on bottomless public ignorance and gullibility. It was a bet bound to be lost.

THE CORONER'S JURY REPORT

Billy the Kid's imposters' survival hoaxes were over before they started because of the Coroner's Jury Report, in Spanish, for the inquest of July 15, 1881 on the victim fatally shot by Pat Garrett on July 14, 1881. **[Figure: 1]**

It confirmed its proper filing with the District Attorney of the First Judicial District, William:

"To the District Attorney of the First Judicial District of the Territory of New Mexico, Greetings."

It showed proper action by San Miguel County Justice of the Peace Alejandro Segura, as *ex officio* **coroner:**

"[I]mmediately upon receiving said information [of a Fort Sumner murder] I proceeded to the said place and named Milnor Rudulph, Jose Silva, Antonio Saavedra, Pedro Antonio Lucero, Lorenzo Jaramillo and Sabal Gutierres a jury to investigate the case."

The body was identified:

"[The jury] found the body of William Bonney alias "Kid" with a shot in the left breast."

The eye-witness was interviewed:

"[The Jurymen] examined the evidence of Pedro Maxwell [Peter Maxwell, owner of Fort Sumner], which evidence is as follows: 'I being in my bed in my room, at about midnight on the 14th day of July, Pat F. Garrett came into my room and sat down. William Bonney came in and got close to my bed with a gun in his hand and asked me "who is it" and then Pat F. Garrett fired two shots at the said William Bonney and the said William Bonney fell near my fire place and I went out of the room and when I came in again about three or four minutes after the shots the said William Bonney was dead.' "

The jurymen's verdict stated:

"[T]he deed of said Garrett was justifiable homicide."

The recommendation was for merited reward:

"[G]ratitude ... is due to the said Garrett for his deed and [he] is worthy of being rewarded."

THE TRANSLATED CORONER'S JURY REPORT

Territory of New Mexico) Precinct No. 27
County of San Miguel)

To the District Attorney of the First Judicial District of the Territory of New Mexico,

Greetings:

On this 15th day of July, A.D. 1881, I, the undersigned, Justice of the Peace of the above named precinct, received information that a murder had taken place in Fort Sumner, in said precinct, and immediately upon receiving said information I proceeded to the said place and named Milnor Rudulph, Jose Silva, Antonio Saavedra, Pedro Antonio Lucero, Lorenzo Jaramillo and Sabal Gutierres a jury to investigate the case and the above jury convened in the home of Luz B. Maxwell and proceeded to a room in the said house where they found the body of William Bonney alias "Kid" with a shot in the left breast and having examined the body they examined the evidence of Pedro Maxwell, which evidence is as follows:

"I being in my bed in my room, at about midnight on the 14th day of July, Pat F. Garrett came into my room and sat at the end on my bed to talk with me. A little while after Garrett sat down, William Bonney came in and got close to my bed with a gun in his hand and asked me "Who is it Who is it?" and then Pat F. Garrett fired two shots at the said William Bonney and the said Bonney fell near my fire place and I went out of the room and when I came in again about three or four minutes after the shots the said Bonney was dead."

The jury has found the following verdict:

We the jury unanimously find that William Bonney has been killed by a bullet in the left breast in the region of the heart, the same having been fired from a pistol in the hand of Pat F. Garrett, and our verdict is that the act of said Garrett was justifiable homicide and we are unanimous in the opinion that the gratitude of all the community is due to the said Garrett for his deed and is worthy of being rewarded.

      M. Rudulph, President
      Anto Sabedra
      Pedro Anto Lucero
      Jose x Silba
      Sabal x Gutierrez
      Lorenzo x Jaramillo

All which information I put at your disposal.
      Alejandro Segura Justice of the Peace

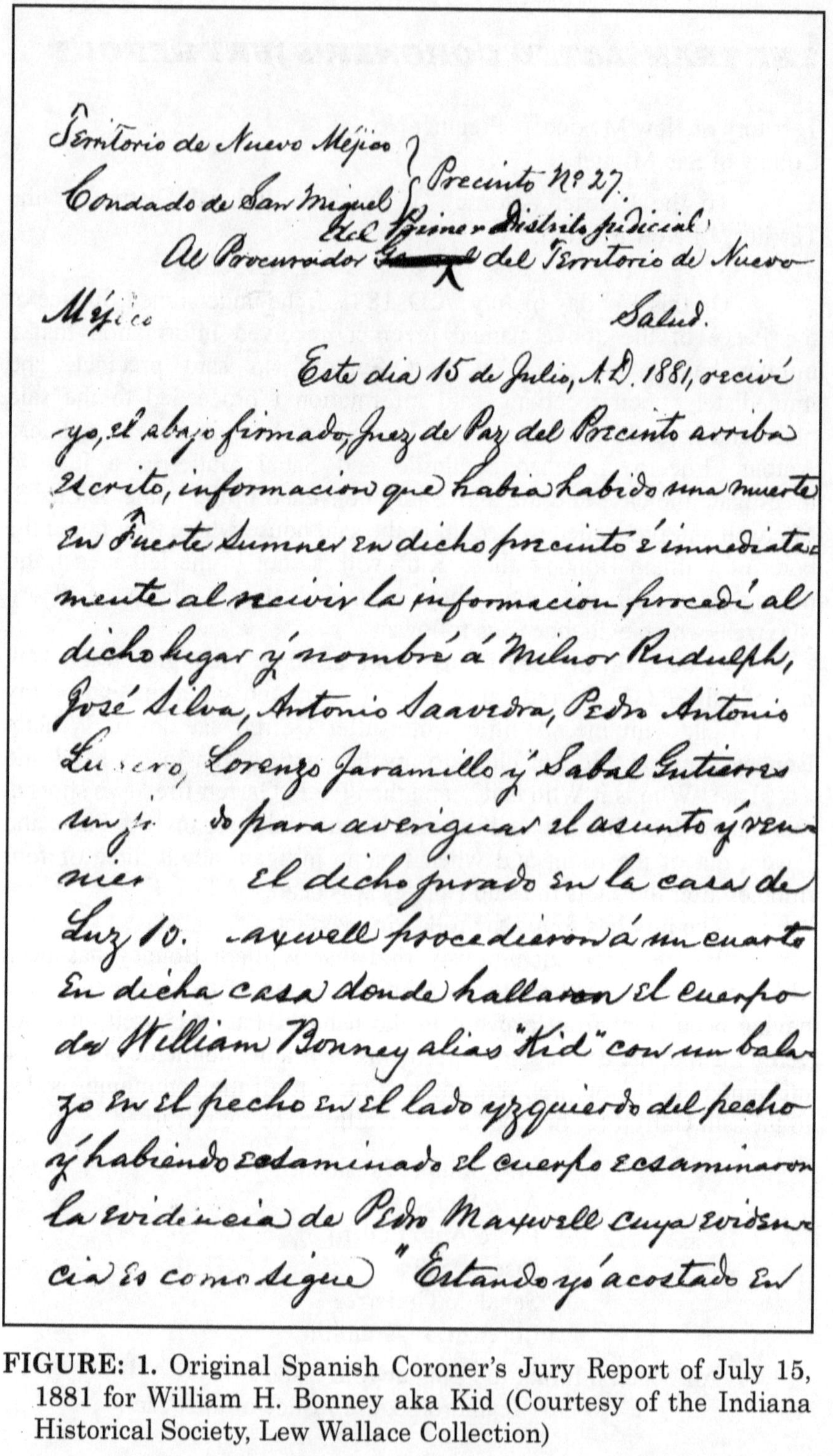

Territorio de Nuevo Méjico) Precinto N° 27.
Condado de San Miguel)
~~Al Procurador~~ Del ~~Juiz~~ r Distrito Judicial
Al Procurador ~~~~ del Territorio de Nuevo
Méjico   Salud.

           Este dia 15 de Julio, A.D. 1881, reciví yo, el abajo firmado, Juez de Paz del Precinto arriba escrito, informacion que habia habido una muerte en Fuerte Sumner en dicho precinto é immediatamente al recivir la informacion procedí al dicho lugar y nombré á Milnor Rudulph, José Silva, Antonio Saavedra, Pedro Antonio Lucero, Lorenzo Jaramillo y Sabal Gutierres un jurado para averiguar el asunto y venier el dicho jurado en la casa de Luz Maxwell procedieron á un cuarto en dicha casa donde hallaron el cuerpo de William Bonney alias "Kid" con un balazo en el pecho en el lado yzquierdo del pecho y habiendo ecsaminado el cuerpo ecsaminaron la evidencia de Pedro Maxwell cuya evidencia es como sigue "Estando yo acostado en

FIGURE: 1. Original Spanish Coroner's Jury Report of July 15, 1881 for William H. Bonney aka Kid (Courtesy of the Indiana Historical Society, Lew Wallace Collection)

mi cama en mi cuarto á cosa de media noche el dia 14 de Julio entró á mi cuarto Pat. F. Garrett y se sentó en la orilla de mi cama á platicar conmigo. A poco rato que Garrett se sentó entró William Bonney y se arrimó á mi cama con una pistola en la mano y me preguntó "Who is it? Who is it?" y Entónces Pat. F. Garrett le tiró dos balazos á dicho William Bonney y se cayó el dicho Bonney en un lado de mi fogon y yo salí del cuarto cuando volví á entrar yá en tres ó cuatro minutos despues de los balazos estaba muerto dicho Bonney."

  El jurado há hallado el siguiente dictámen "Nosotros los del jurado unanimente hallamos que William Bonney há sido muerto por un balazo en el pecho yzquierdo en la region del Corazon tirado de una pistola en la mano de Pat. F. Garrett y nuestro dictámen es que el hecho de dicho Garrett fué homicidio justificable y estamos unánimes en opinion que la gratitud de toda la comunidad es devida á dicho Garrett por su hecho y que es digno de ser recompensado."

       [firma]
       Presidente

   Antº Saavedra
    Pedro Antº Lucero
    José + Silba
    Vidal + Gutierrez
    Lorenzo + Jaramillo

Todo cuya informacion pongo á conocimiento de V.

      Alejandro Seguro
      Juez de Paz

CONFIRMATION OF CORONER'S JURY PRESIDENT MILNOR RUDULPH'S SIGNATURE

A later argument in the evolving "Brushy Bill" hoax was fabricating that Jury President, Milnor Rudulph, was not really present. But one can compare his signature on the Coroner's Jury Report with his signature on his May 18, 1879 letter to Territorial Secretary William G. Ritch. **[FIGURE: 2]** As can be seen, he used Spencerian penmanship, with its extreme flourishes for embellishment, especially for his unique signature.

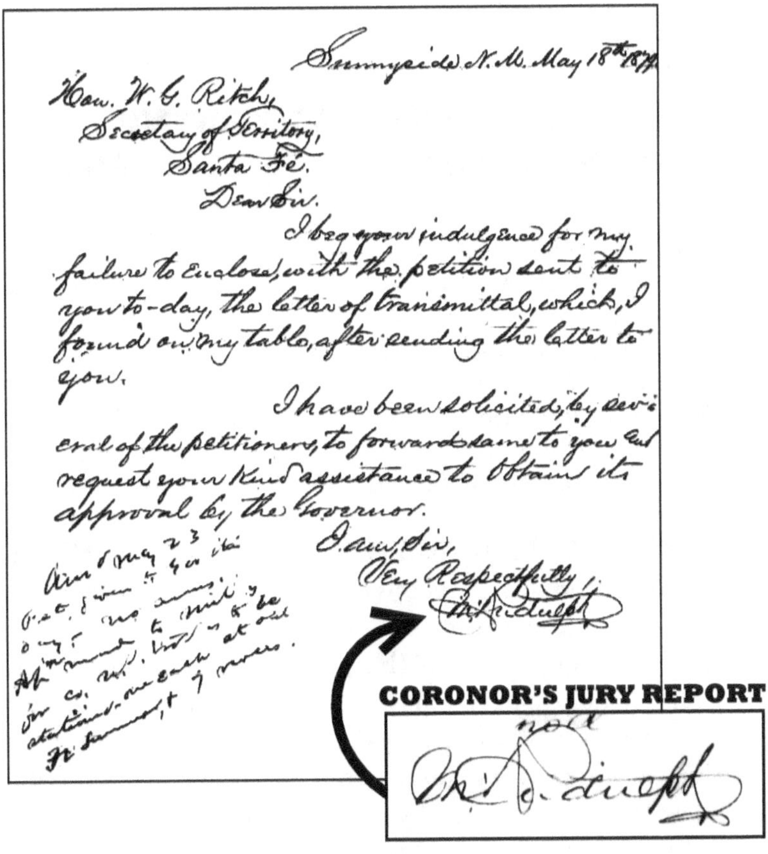

Sunnyside N.M. May 18th 1879

Hon. W. G. Ritch,
Secretary of Territory,
Santa Fe.

Dear Sir.

I beg your indulgence for my failure to enclose, with the petition sent to you to-day, the letter of transmittal, which, I found on my table, after sending the letter to you.

I have been solicited, by several of the petitioners, to forward same to you and request your kind assistance to obtain its approval by the Governor.

I am, Sir,
Very Respectfully,
M. Rudulph

FIGURE: 2. Letter of May 18, 1879 from Milnor Rudulph to Territorial Secretary William G. Ritch to show that his signature as the same as on the Coroner's Jury Report. (Courtesy Territorial Archives of New Mexico Microfilm, Albuquerque Genealogical Library Microfilm)

CONFIRMATION OF THE CORONER'S JURYMEN

Another ploy of the "Brushy" hoax was claiming the Coroner's Jury Report's signers did not exist or were not local men. They were Milnor Rudulph, as President; Antonio Saavedra; Pedro Antonio Lucero; Jose Silba; Sabal Gutierrez; Lorenzo Jaramillo; and Alejandro Segura, as Justice of the Peace.

But checking the census for 1880, the year before they signed, shows all in San Miguel County. At Cabra Arenoso, were Alejandro Segura and Sabal Gutierrez. At Sunnyside, were Milnor Rudulph and Jose Silba. For Fort Sumner, were listed Lorenzo Jaramillo and Antonio Saavedra. At San Miguel, was listed Pedro Antonio Lucero.

STATUTE GOVERNING THE CORONER'S JURY REPORT

The Coroner's Jury Report was written in conformity to Territorial law. Its statute, edited by L. Bradford Prince, Governor from 1889 to 1893, was in *General Laws of New Mexico; Including All the Unrepealed Laws From the Promulgation of the 'Kearney [sic] Code' in 1846, to the End of the Legislative Session of 1880, With Supplement, Including the Session of 1882*. It was under "Article XV, Chapter XL, Constables, Coroners, and Inquests." For Inquests, the Act of January 30, 1867 pertained; stating:

> SECTION 1. It shall be the duty of each justice of the peace within his respective precinct, to inquire into and investigate the cause of death of any human being that shall be found dead in the precinct of said justice of the peace, when it may appear that said death was caused by violence or any other illegal means, and it is hereby made the duty of every justice of the peace, when required so to do, in writing, by any two heads of families and voters in the precinct, to examine and inquire into the cause of death of any human being, be the cause of death what it may.

§ 2. The examination provided for in the foregoing section shall be held over the body of the deceased and with a jury of six men, voters of the precinct, which jury shall be summoned by the constable, verbally, by an order of the justice of the peace to that effect, and the witnesses shall be examined and their attendance compelled as in all other cases before a justice of the peace.

§ 3. Whatever the cause of death of any person shall have been ascertained in the manner prescribed in this act, the verdict of the jury shall be in writing, which shall be signed by the justice of the peace and each one of the jury, **and so recorded in the office of the probate judge of the county in which the inquest was held, and**, and the verdict of the jury shall be in the following form:

"We the undersigned, justices of the peace and jury, who sat upon the inquest held this —— day of ——, 18 —, on the body of (here shall be stated the name of the deceased, if known, and if not, then state 'on the body of a person whose name is unknown'), found in precinct number —, of the county of ——, find that the deceased came to his (or her) death by reason of (here insert the cause of death, and by whom the crime was committed if ascertained)."

A.B., Justice of the Peace
C.Dd., &c.

§ 4. In the absence of the justice of the peace from his precinct, or during the sickness of such justice of the peace, then any justice of the peace of the county may hold such an inquest ...

§ 5. Every justice of the peace who shall hold an inquest as provided for in this act, shall receive from the county treasury of his county the sum of two dollars in full of all his services in such inquest, and the constable shall receive the fees allowed by law to persons in causes before justices of the peace, which fees shall be paid out of the county treasury, and the witnesses shall receive the fees now allowed by law, and the county shall also pay the necessary expenses of the decent interment if the said deceased over which an inquest has been held as herein provided, which shall be allowed by the probate judge.

Thus, Justice of the Peace Alejandro Segura followed proper procedure. By law, he did not retain the Coroner's Jury Report. It was to go to the proper probate judge. But that would be for a decedent's estate or assets. Billy had none.

As will be seen, Segura chose the right disposition for this high-profile killing: the person to whom the Report was addressed: "To the District Attorney of the First Judicial District of the Territory of New Mexico" (whose jurisdiction was Fort Sumner's San Miguel County). That was William Breeden; then also holding the dual appointment of Attorney General. He was the correct prosecutor to assess the killing in light of the Report's verdict of justifiable homicide and deserved reward. Furthermore, this proper procedure was also reported to Acting-Governor William Ritch by Pat Garrett himself.

PAT GARRETT'S LETTER TO THE ACTING-GOVERNOR

On July 15, 1881, the day after the killing, Pat Garrett sent a letter, with enclosed copy of that day's Coroner's Jury Report, to the Territory's Acting-Governor, William Ritch, confirming his killing of Billy Bonney along with its circumstances.

The letter was quoted in July 23, 1881's Las Cruces *Rio Grande Republican* as "Kid the Killer Killed, Wm. Bonney alias Antrim, alias Billy the Kid, Fatally Meets Pat Garrett, the Lincoln County Sheriff." It stated: "Below is given Sheriff Garrett's report as made to Acting-Governor Ritch which contains also the verdict of the coroner's jury [with English translation, but explaining: 'The verdict is given in Spanish in Garrett's report']." The article stated:

William Bonney, alias 'the Kid,' is dead. No report could have caused more general feeling of gratification than this, and when it was further announced that the faithful and brave Pat Garrett, he who had been the mainstay of law and order in Lincoln county, the chief reliance of the people in the dark days, when danger lurked at every hand, has accomplished the crowning feat of his life by bringing down the fierce and implacable foe single-handed, the sense of satisfaction was heightened to one of delight. The following is Sheriff Garrett's official report to the chief executive of the territory.

It is as follows. — Fort Sumner, N.M., July 15. - Fort Sumner, N.M., July 15, '81 - To his Excellency the Governor of New Mexico:

"I have the honor to inform your Excellency that I had received several communications from persons in and about Fort Sumner, what William Bonney, alias the Kid, had been there, or in that vicinity for some time.

"In view of these reports I deemed it my duty to go there, and ascertain if there was any truth in them or not, all the time doubting their accuracy; but on Monday, July 11, I left home, taking with me John W. Poe and T.L. McKinney, men in whose courage and sagacity I relied implicitly, and arrived just below Fort Sumner, on Wednesday, 13th [sic]. I remained concealed near the houses, until night, and then entered the fort about midnight, and went to Mr. P. Maxwell's room. I found him in bed, and had just commenced talking to him about the object of my visit at such an unusual hour, when a man entered the room in stockinged feet, with a pistol in one hand and a knife in the other. He came and placed his hand on the bed just beside me, and in a low whisper, "who is it?" (and repeated the question) he asked Mr. Maxwell.

I at once recognized the man, and knew he was the Kid, and reached behind me for my pistol, feeling almost certain of receiving a ball from his at the moment of my doing so, as I felt sure he had now recognized me, but fortunately he drew back from the bed at noticing my movement, and, although he had his pistol pointed at my breast, he delayed to fire, and asked me in Spanish, "Quien es? Quien es?" This gave me time to bring mine to bear on him, and the moment I did so I pulled the trigger and he received his death wound, for the ball struck him in the left breast and pierced his heart. He never spoke, but died in a minute. It was my desire to have been able to take him alive, but his coming upon me so suddenly and unexpectedly leads me to believe that he had seen me enter the room, or had been informed by someone of the fact; and that he came there armed with pistol and knife expressly to kill me if he could. Under that impression I had no alternative but to kill him or to suffer death at his hands.

I herewith annex a copy of the verdict rendered by the jury called in by the justice of the peace (ex officio coroner), the original of which is in the hands of the prosecuting attorney of the first judicial district."

The verdict is given in Spanish in Garrett's report, and upon being translated is as follows:

"We the jury unanimously say that William Bonney came to his death by a wound in the breast in the region of the heart, fired from a pistol in the hand of Pat F. Garrett, and our decision is that the action of said Garrett, was justifiable homicide; and we are united in opinion that the gratitude of all the community is due to said Garrett for his action, and he deserves to be compensated."

(Signed) M. Rudolph, Foreman,
Antonio Savedra,
Pedro Antonio Lucero,
Sabal Gutierres,
Lorenzo Jaramillo

I am Governor, very respectfully your Excellency's obedient servant,
Pat F. Garrett

THE ISSUE OF NO CULPABILITY

Pat Garrett's letter of July 15, 1881 to Acting-Governor William Ritch confirmed that proper legal procedure had been followed with the original Coroner's Jury Report sent to the District Attorney for the First Judicial District, William Breeden, responsible for San Miguel County, in which was the homicide site of Fort Sumner. Garrett's letter to Ritch had stated: "I herewith annex a copy of the verdict rendered by the jury called in by the justice of the peace [*ex officio* coroner, meaning by virtue of his position or status], **the original of which is in the hands of the prosecuting attorney of the first judicial district.**"

Breeden, also the Territorial Attorney General, would have checked the verdict: "[O]ur verdict is that the action of said Garrett was justifiable homicide." That meant the killing was deemed self-defense, as was subsequently confirmed by prosecutor Breeden by his filing no murder charge against Garrett, and later by his assisting Acting-Governor Ritch in processing Garrett's reward payment.

ISSUES COMPLICATING GARRETT'S REWARD COLLECTION

Garrett's letter to Acting-Governor Ritch also initiated the process of collecting his reward. The Coroner's Jury Report had presented no problem with its conclusion stating: "[W]e are unanimous in the opinion that the gratitude of all the community is due to the said Garrett for his action, and he deserves to be rewarded."

But issuing the reward to Garrett was complicated by two factors: its being considered a **private reward** offered by past-Governor Lew Wallace, and its **not being a capture offer, not a dead-or-alive offer.**

The reward offer, published by Lew Wallace, in his own name, in December 22, 1880's *Las Vegas Daily Gazette*, and May 3, 1881's *Santa Fe Daily New Mexican*, had stated:

> **BILLY THE KID**
> **$500 REWARD**
> I will pay $500 reward to any person or persons who will capture William Bonney, alias The Kid, and deliver him to any sheriff of New Mexico. Satisfactory proofs of identity will be required.
>   LEW. WALLACE,
>   Governor of New Mexico

Its stipulating that William Bonney was to be captured and delivered "to any sheriff of New Mexico," meant alive. To cover that Bonney was now dead (i.e., not deliverable alive), Garrett's letter to Ritch had explained that capture had been impossible, and killing the only option: "**It was my desire to have been able to take him alive, but his coming upon me so suddenly and unexpectedly leads me to believe that he had seen me enter the room, or had been informed by someone of the fact, and that he came there armed with pistol and knife expressly to kill me if he could. Under that impression I had no alternative but to kill him or to suffer death at his hands.**"

And the "Kid the Killer Killed" article showed public agreement; stating: "William Bonney, alias 'the Kid,' is dead. No report could have caused more general feeling of gratification than this, and when it was further announced that the faithful and brave Pat Garrett, he who had been the mainstay of law and order in Lincoln county, the chief reliance of the people in the dark days, when danger lurked at every hand, has accomplished the crowning feat of his life by bringing down the fierce and implacable foe single-handed, the sense of satisfaction was heightened to one of delight."

So death instead of capture presented no problem to all concerned in justifying Garrett's reward.

But the second issue of Lew Wallace's private reward offer presented a more complicated matter for issuing the reward payment to Garrett.

Importantly, the issue of corpse identity never arose, because the it was obviously Billy Bonney by confirmation of the coroner's jurymen and witness, Peter Maxwell.

REWARD NEEDING LEGISLATIVE INTERVENTION

Acting-Governor William Ritch had an impediment in simply issuing the reward's payment: uneasiness about using Territorial funds to cover Lew Wallace's private offer. And Wallace had left the Territory and his governorship in May of 1881, before his term was completed. Lionel Sheldon had been appointed as his replacement, but was away from the Territory. So Ritch, as past Secretary of State under Lew Wallace, became Acting-Governor.

GARRETT'S MEETING WITH RITCH

Garrett, with his attorney, T.B. Catron, met with Ritch on July 20, 1881, as reported by the July 21, 1881 *Santa Fe Daily New Mexican*. Ritch was quoted as "willing to pay the amount, and would be glad to do so," but made clear that the delaying issue was checking the records about the nature of the reward. It stated:

Yesterday afternoon Pat. Garrett; **accompanied by Hon. T.B. Catron** and Col. M. Brunswick, called upon acting-Governor Ritch in regard to the reward offered by ex-Governor Lew Wallace for the Kid. The reward was fixed at five hundred dollars, and the offer was published in the papers. Governor Ritch announced that he was willing to pay the amount, and would be glad to do so, but that he would have to look at the records first. **He was not in the city when the [reward] offer was made, and had never received any notification of it, consequently did not know whether or not it was on record**. In consequence of the state of affairs, the question of the reward was not settled.

LEGAL CONSULTATION OF WILLIAM BREEDEN

So Ritch sought legal advice about the reward from William Breeden. Not only was Breeden the proper prosecutor as District Attorney of the First Judicial District; but he had also received the original of the Coroner's Jury Report, and knew Garrett's killing was in justifiable self-defense. He was also the Territorial Attorney General, and had ultimate authority to advise on proper legality for converting the private reward to a Territorial one.

Ritch recorded his consultation with Breeden in his July 21, 1881 *Executive Record Book 2* entry as: "In the matter of the application by Patrick F. Garrett for a reward claimed to have been offered May-1881 for the capture of Wm Bonney alias 'the Kid.' " It confirmed that Breeden agreed that the reward was a private offer, since Wallace had not filed it with his office or that of the Territorial Secretary (then Ritch himself), converting it to a Territorial offer. Breeden stated: *"In addition, we will add as fact that there was no record whatever in this office or at the Secretary's office of there having been a reward offered as set forth by Attorney General, nor was there any reward or file in said offices of a corresponding reward in any form."* So the issue was converting Wallace's private reward to a Territorial reward.

RITCH'S EXECUTIVE RECORD BOOK ENTRY ON BREEDEN CONSULTATION ON THE REWARD

Ritch's July 21, 1881 *Executive Record Book 2* entry presented Breeden's opinion (here in boldface); stating:

Executive Department
Territory of New Mexico
July 21st 1881

July 20th 1881 Pat F. Garret [sic- throughout] Sheriff of Lincoln County appeared and presented a bill for $500. claiming it as a reward offered on or about the 7th of May 1881 by the late Governor Lew Wallace, for the capture of said Bonny [sic, throughout].

As evidence of said offer having been made the affidavit of publication thereof made by Chas. H. Green [sic – Greene] the editor and manager of the Daily <u>New Mexican</u> was presented with said bill, as also was presented a statement of the proceedings and verdict of a coroner's jury at Fort Sumner in San Miguel County upon the body of the said Bonny, captured as aforesaid, and a statement of Garret directed to this office of his doings in the premises.

Upon examination of said papers it was deemed important that the opinion of the Attorney General be taken thereon and they were at once transmitted to that office. On the following day the papers with the opinion of Hon. Wm Breeden Attorney General were filed.

Said opinion is quite full. We quote the closing paragraphs as sufficient in this connection, to-wit:

"The offer by the Governor, or the notice thereof, which is all there is to show such an offer, is as follows –

Billy the Kid
$500 Reward

"I will pay five hundred dollars reward to any person or persons, who will capture William Bonny, alias the Kid, and deliver him to any Sheriff of New Mexico. Satisfactory proof of identity will be required.

Lew Wallace
Governor of New Mexico"

"This certainly appears to be the personal offer of Governor Wallace, and it seems he did nothing to indicate that it was intended as an executive act on behalf of, and to bind the Territory.

"If the reward should be paid, it is very probable that the Legislature would approve the payment if so desired, and that no objection would be raised, or that it will provide for its payment if it remained unpaid, at the next session thereof;

[AUTHOR'S NOTE: Breeden saw no problem with the Legislature's eventual approving of reward payment.]

but if the Governor [Ritch] should now direct the payment of the claim, he would doubtless expose himself to the charge of misappropriation of the Territorial funds, in case the Legislature should refuse to ratify or approve the payment."

[AUTHOR'S NOTE: So Breeden said if Ritch paid the reward himself *before legislative approval*, it could be criticized as misappropriating funds.]

[AUTHOR'S NOTE: Ritch then added commentary in his own words.]

In addition we will add as a fact that there was no record whatsoever; either in this office or at the [Territorial] Secretary's office of there having been a reward offered as set forth by Attorney General, nor was there any record or file in said offices of a corresponding reward in any form.

[AUTHOR'S NOTE: Ritch confirmed that Wallace had not converted his reward offer into a Territorial offer.]

The opinion of the Attorney General [Breeden] appearing to be consistent with the law and the facts, decision is rendered accordingly and the Governor [Ritch, speaking for himself] declines to allow the reward at this time. <u>Believing however, that Mr Garret has an equitable claim against the Territory for said reward, the action at this office will simply be suspended until the case can properly be represented to the next Legislative Assembly.</u>

       Ritch
       Act Governor NM

[AUTHOR'S NOTE: Ritch confirmed that Garrett's reward was deemed justified by him and Breeden, but had to be converted to a Territorial reward, though that made action in his office "suspended," or delayed in making payment to Garrett until legislative action.]

RITCH'S RECORD OF PRIVATE WALLACE REWARD

To be noted is that William Ritch had recorded Lew Wallace's private Billy the Kid reward offer eight months earlier, when Ritch was Territorial Secretary! This communication confirmed the reward offer, and confirmed that it had to be converted to a Territorial offer to be paid to Garrett with Territorial funds.

Wallace had informed him about the reward by letter on December 13, 1880. That day, Ritch entered it into "Executive Record Book 2" on page 473. Wallace wrote:

       Executive Office
       SANTA FE., N.M.
       Dec. 13   *1880*

Hon. W.G. Ritch
Loc. New Mexico.
Sir:
Be good enough to prepare a draft of proclamation of reward $500. for the capture and delivery of William Bonney, alias the Kid to the Sheriff of the County of Lincoln County.

       Yours, truly,
       Lew Wallace, Governor

Ritch had then written in the "Executive Record Book":

Dec 13 [1880]
Reward
  Territory of New Mexico) Indictment in
     vs   ) Lincoln co. Dist. Court
  William Bonney   ) for murder
   alias "The Kid"
        Executive Office
       Territory of New Mexico
  Whereas William Bonney, alias "The Kid" charged under indictment issued from the District Court in and for the county of Lincoln of the crime of murder committed in said county: And whereas the said William Bonney, alias "The Kid" is a fugitive from justice
       Now Therefore Lewis Wallace, Governor of the Territory, by virtue of the power and authority vested in me by law and believing the ends of justice will be served thereby do hereby offer a reward of five hundred dollars ($500.) for the apprehension and arrest of said William Bonney, alias "The Kid" and for his delivery to the Sheriff of Lincoln County at the county seat of said county.
  In witness Whereof I have set my hand and have caused the great seal of the Territory to be hereto affixed this 13th day of December 1880.
        Lew. Wallace,
        Governor N.M.

By the Governor
 Wm Ritch, Secretary N.M.

REWARD GRANTED TO GARRETT BY THE LEGISLATURE

The actual printed legislative "Act for the Relief of Pat. Garrett," of February 18, 1882, made clear the straightforward process, with the delay being a mere "technicality" of conversion to a Territorial reward; writing: "Garrett is justly entitled to the above reward, and payment thereof has been refused upon a technicality." It stated:

AN ACT FOR THE RELIEF OF PAT. GARRETT
CONTENTS

SECTION 1. Authorizes payment of $500 reward for the arrest of "the Kid."

WHEREAS, The Governor of New Mexico did, on or about the 7th day of May, A.D., 1881, issue certain proclamation in words and figures as follows, to-wit:

"I will pay five hundred dollars reward to any person or persons who will capture William Bonney, alias 'The Kid,' and deliver him to any sheriff of New Mexico. Satisfactory proof of identity will be required."

(Signed)   Lew. Wallace
                              Governor of New Mexico.

AND, WHEREAS, Pat. Garrett was at that time sheriff of Lincoln county, and did, <u>on or about the month of August, 1881</u>, in pursuance of the above reward, and by virtue of a warrant placed in his hands for the purpose, attempted to arrest said William Bonney, and in said attempt did kill said William Bonney at Fort Sumner, in the county of San Miguel, in the Territory of New Mexico, and wherefore, said <u>Garrett is justly entitled to the above reward, and payment thereof has been refused upon a technicality</u>. Therefore

Be it enacted by the Legislative Assembly of the Territory of New Mexico:

SECTION 1. The Territorial Auditor is hereby authorized to draw a warrant upon the Territorial Treasurer of the Territory of New Mexico, in favor of Pat. Garrett for the sum of five hundred dollars, payable out of any funds in the Territorial treasury not otherwise appropriated, in payment of the reward of five hundred dollars heretofore offered by his Excellency, Governor Lew. Wallace, for the arrest of William Bonney, alias "The Kid."

SEC. 2. This act shall take effect and be in force from and after its passage.

Approved February 18, 1882.

GOVERNOR SHELDON'S APPROVAL

And, once returned from traveling, Governor Lionel Sheldon even stated, in his February 14, 1882, letter to the Legislature, that *he* would have paid Garrett's reward outright: *"It is a claim which I think I should have paid if it had not been understood that the matter was to be referred to the legislature before it came into my hands."* (Sheldon had been out of the Territory from July 3, 1881 to August 27, 1881, leaving more timid Ritch in charge). Sheldon wrote:

EXECUTIVE OFFICE,
Territory of New Mexico,
Santa Fe, <u>February 14th 1882</u>

Hon Lewis Baca
    President of the Council
            In the matter of the claim of Sheriff Garrett Lincoln county for the reward offered for the capture of "the Kid" so called, I am of the opinion that he is entitled to payment. He could not technically comply with the terms of the reward because when he met the "Kid" in Maxwell's room it is very certain that one or the other would be killed. It was not a reward the payment of which depended on conviction. The Kid had been convicted and was under sentence to be hanged. Garrett was in pursuit with an intention to capture if it could be done normally but under the circumstances of their meeting capture was pout of the question. It will not do to the technical in this case because men will not be willing to take risks and
proper services in the protection of society against bad men if captious objections are interposed to avoid the discharge of public observations. <u>The case under consideration is too notorious and remarkable to be made a precedent for the refusal to pay for services performed substantially in compliance with the provisions of high authority.</u>
    <u>It is a claim which I think I should have paid if it had not been understood that the matter was to be referred to the legislature before it came into my hands.</u>
                    Very Respectfully
                        Lionel A. Sheldon
                        Governor of New Mexico

Thus, the Coroner's Jury Report for William Bonney ended up getting additional scrutiny and approval by the Acting-Governor, the Territorial Attorney General, the Governor, and the Legislature; with all agreeing that Garrett killed Billy the Kid, and therefore deserved the reward. And the validity of the Coroner's Jury Report itself was never a matter of controversy.

LATER FINDING OF THE REPORT

The proper filing of the Coroner's Jury Report can be traced from its July 15, 1881 sending to Santa Fe to William Breeden - as District Attorney of the First Judicial District and its legal analyst as Attorney General - to its chance finding, in 1932, in stored public records by a government employee.

It had also been indirectly referenced in a 1935 book by a Frank M. King titled *Wranglin' the Past: Reminiscences of Frank M. King*, in his chapter titled "The Kid's Exit." King wrote that Garrett's July 15, 1881 letter to Acting-Governor William Ritch, which cited the Report's copy sent to Ritch, had recently been located in old files of the Secretary of State of New Mexico.

Its modern-day finder, in 1932, was a Harold Abbott, employed in Santa Fe at the State Land Office from 1931 to 1933. He discovered it, with San Miguel County court records, in the state capitol's basement. He made copies of it for himself and others, including his brother George. Harold died in 1937; George in 2006.

So George Abbott lived to see his brother's finding of the Coroner's Jury Report becoming proof against the "Brushy Bill" imposter hoax. On November 30, 1950, the day of "Brushy's" pardon hearing, the *Alamogordo News's* front page declared "Sumner Jury Thought The Kid Had Been Killed." It stated:

Although the perennial controversy over whether the infamous Billy the Kid still lives, has again arisen, at least one Alamogordo man, Frank Phillips, 84, claims personal knowledge of his death in 1881 at the hands of the late Sheriff Pat Garrett, and George Abbott, also of Alamogordo has in his office at the Pioneer Abstract Co., a photostatic copy of the verdict of the coroner's jury which viewed the remains of the late Wm. Bonney

Some twenty years ago, when the late Harold Abbott, brother of George, was an employee of the state land office in Santa Fe, he, with other

employees, were going over some old records in the basement of the state capitol. There they ran across, in the San Miguel court records, the original copy of the coroner's jury, dated July 15, 1881, and written in Spanish. The document covered three pages of which they made photostatic copies.

As the reader will see from the document, translated below, the six men serving on the jury and the Justice of the Peace who empanneled them, seemed convinced that Wm. Bonney, known as "Kid," was quite dead, and that he had been killed by Pat Garrett.

The most recent controversy arose when a firm of El Paso lawyers appealed to Governor Mabry for a full pardon for Wm. Bonney, who claims that the man killed at Fort Sumner by Pat Garrett was another outlaw, and not the Kid at all; that the Kid left the country, assumed the name of ["Brushy Bill"] Roberts, and has lived in Old and New Mexico all this time.

The documentary evidence of the Kid's death is translated as follows:

Territory of New Mexico
San Miguel County
    Precinct No. 27
To the attorney of the 1st Judicial district of the Territory of New Mexico:
Greetings: [The   English Translation followed]

FROM BREEDEN TO HAROLD ABBOTT

One can trace the Coroner's Jury Report's storage in the state Capitol Buildings. First was William Breeden's Palace of the Governors office. Breeden apparently filed it in his capacity as District Attorney for the First Judicial District under San Miguel County court records, as he categorized this Fort Sumner killing in that county.

As Attorney General also, his office was in rooms 5, 6, and 8, according to Clinton P. Anderson in his 1944 *New Mexico Historical Review* article titled "The Adobe Palace." (Anderson, Page 110) **[FIGURE: 3]** Anderson noted that Breeden kept that office till 1889. (Anderson, Page 112)

Next occupying Breeden's office area in that Capitol Building was the State Land Office's Commissioner.

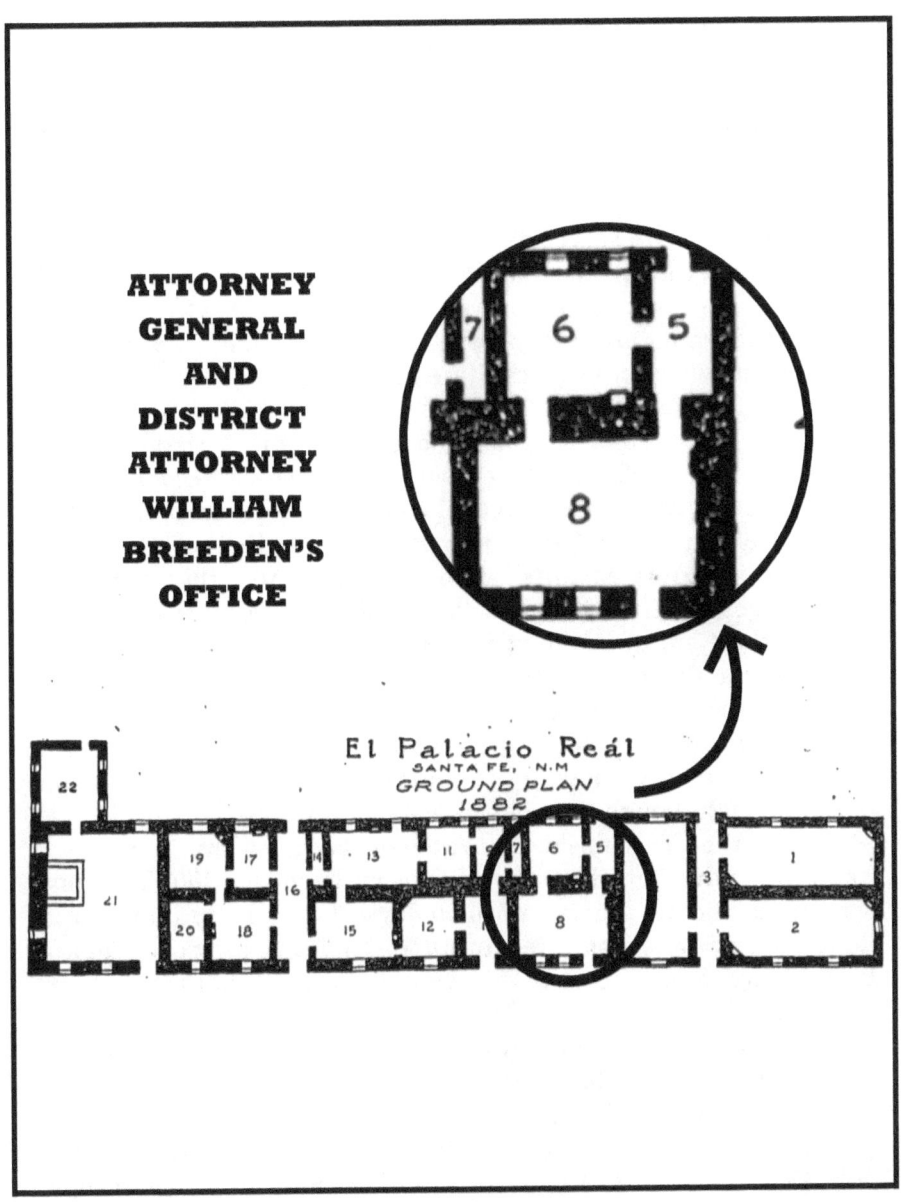

FIGURE: 3. Palace of the Governors in 1882, showing Attorney General William Breeden's office as rooms 5, 6, and 8. (From Clinton P. Anderson's 1944 *New Mexico Historical Review*)

A Jesse Nusbaum's 1909 journal recorded Palace of the Governor's rooms; being published in 1978 by Rosemary Nusbaum, as: *The City Different and the Palace, The Palace of the Governors: It's Role in Santa Fe History*. It stated that "the block of five rooms west of the Historical Society's quarters were occupied by Robert P. Ervin, Commissioner of Lands." (Nusbaum, 86)

Robert P. Ervin served as State Land Commissioner from 1907 to 1918. And though the Palace of the Governors was renovated from Breeden's period to the Ervin one, the general office location stayed the same. And apparently Breeden's old records were stored along with those of the State Land Office.

The office's combined records linked to history of the Capitol Building's relocations. Harold Abbott had stated that in 1932 "he, with other employees, were going over some old records **in the basement of the state capitol**;" so those records presumably related to his Land Office job. But his finding of Breeden's **"San Miguel court records"** with them indicates that they had stayed together since their first Palace of the Governors storage.

But the Capitol Building in Harold Abbott's day was not the one after the Palace of the Governors. From 1850 to 1886 one was under construction, but ending up as the Territorial Courthouse.

In 1886, another building became the Capitol, replacing the Palace of the Governors. But it burned down in six years, on May 12, 1892; though its archives were saved.

Then the Territorial Courthouse became the temporary Capitol Building until another was completed in 1900. That one was used for 66 years, until today's Capitol Building, "the Roundhouse," was dedicated in 1966. And the previous Capitol Building was renamed as the Bataan Memorial Building.

So by Harold Abbott's 1932 finding of the Coroner's Jury Report in the Capitol Building's basement (of the future Bataan Memorial Building), the old Palace of the Governors records might have been moved multiple times. Additionally, Frank M. King had reported in his 1935 book, *Wranglin' the Past*, that Garrett's July 15, 1881 letter to Ritch, with the Coroner's Jury Report copy, was found in old files of New Mexico's Secretary of State. And his offices were also in that Capitol Building, according to a 1932 article in the *Santa Fe New Mexican* titled "Call for Bids."

So the Coroner's Jury Report had provable and correct provenance.

RESURFACING OF HAROLD ABBOTT'S COPY

Harold Abbott's Coroner's Jury Report copy reappeared 19 years later in the February, 1951 edition of *New Mexico Magazine* under "Glimpses of History," in response to "Brushy Bill's" failed pardon attempt, with the reporter writing: "Interest in Billy the Kid - New Mexico's most notorious outlaw - was revived a few weeks ago when an old timer appeared on the scene to claim the identity of the Kid."

The article stated that among the old timer's claims "was an assertion that a coroner's inquest report was not legally on file ... **However, a photostatic copy of the report has been located by New Mexico Magazine in Alamogordo. The photostat is owned by George Abbott, who said his brother had the copy made about 20 years ago.** The report is reproduced on the left. Because part of the copy was badly faded, about a dozed lines were eliminated for this reproduction [in the article]." It concluded: "O.L. Roberts, of Hico, Tex., the man who claimed the identity of Billy the Kid, died late in December of a heart attack, while he was walking along the street in Hico. **He died without being able to make his claim stand.**"

To be noted is that the "Brushy" hoaxers owned this article with its Coroner's Jury Report photostat, since it was in C.L. Sonnichsen's collected papers.

MAURICE G. FULTON RELOCATES THE REPORT

On August 5, 1951, historian Maurice Garland Fulton, having relocated the Report, responded to William V. Morrison's working with C.L. Sonnichsen to write a book on "Brushy." He published an article in *The El Paso Times* titled "Coroner's Report Proves Billy the Kid is Dead, Historian Asserts, Researcher Discovers Document." It had his photostatic copy of the Report, matching the Harold Abbott copy in *New Mexico Magazine,* six months earlier. Fulton had struck at the heart of Morrison's scam which claimed the Report had not been "certified" or "recorded," so was not acceptable; making clear that this was modern procedure and irrelevant to 19th century documents. To be noted is that this article was in Sonnichsen's collected papers - and ignored.

In fact, proved was that public employees had done a good job in keeping San Miguel County legal records together; albeit with State Land Office Records. And the twice found Coroner's Jury Report proves their achievement!

The Fulton article stated:

Billy the Kid is dead. The famed outlaw met death at the business end of Pat Garrett's flaming pistol in July of 1881. So says Col. Maurice G. Fulton, of Roswell, N.M., former custodian of the Lincoln County Museum ...

A 91 year old man, claiming to be the Kid and represented by William V. Morrison of St. Louis, appeared last year before Gov. Thomas J. Mabry of New Mexico and appealed for a pardon [as Billy the Kid and was rejected].

According to Colonel Fulton, "William Bonney, alias Kid, alias William Antrim" could not possibly be alive. He offers, as part of his proof, the coroner's report on the killer's death and a reward believed to be paid to Sheriff Pat Garrett for effecting that death.

Colonel Fulton recently said:

"Morrison's contention that the coroner's report was not 'recorded' is taking the modern practice rather than the older one [about certifying copies]. We are lucky to have a report in this instance, for coroner's jury reports are hard to find, even when they happen to have been made."

Fulton also donated a copy of the Coroner's Jury Report to the Indiana Historical Society, with each of its three pages certified on January 18, 1951 on the back. [FIGURE: 4]

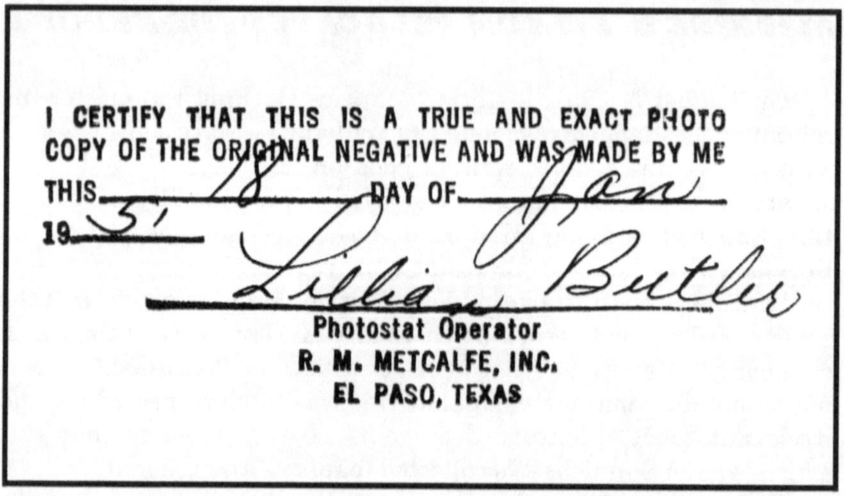

> I CERTIFY THAT THIS IS A TRUE AND EXACT PHOTO COPY OF THE ORIGINAL NEGATIVE AND WAS MADE BY ME THIS _18_ DAY OF _Jan_ 19_51_
>
> _Lillian Butler_
> Photostat Operator
> R. M. METCALFE, INC.
> EL PASO, TEXAS

FIGURE: 4. Certification on January 18, 1951 of Maurice Garland Fulton's Coroner's Jury Report copy donated to the Indiana Historical Society. (Courtesy of the Indiana Historical Society, Lew Wallace Collection).

William V. Morrison referenced Fulton's finding of the Report in a letter of April 12, 1977, to a Lawrence K. Mooney; though he hid Fulton's article and pretended that he had convinced Fulton that its authentication was inadequate. Morrison wrote:

[In 1951] I had engaged the assistance of Colonel Maurice Garland Fulton a retired college professor and noted historian in Lincoln Museum in my search for a purported original coroner jury verdict. **He produced a photostatic copy of the one he had located in Santa Fe and thought to be the original. A friend in the <u>Land Office</u> made two copies; one for Fulton and one that he placed in the Roswell Museum**; but the original had not been recorded in either Santa Fe, or San Miguel County. **[Morrison's fake search]** It was stated – hearsay only – that the killing had occurred at Fort Sumner, San Miguel County, where the Jury Finding should have been recorded. **[Morrison's fake search]** I searched the Coroner's files after it was determined that no recordation had been made among the records in the Clerk's Office, but without avail. **[This is Morrison's fake search. All he had to do was ask Fulton where he found the original in the State Land Office records in Santa Fe.]**

Consequently Fulton agreed eventually that he did not have a copy of an original coroner jury finding, and scrapped it. **[Seeming lie by Morrison]**

Proving that he owned a copy of the Report from Fulton, Morrison formulated an absurd argument against it in that same letter to Lawrence K. Mooney; writing snidely about historian William Keleher:

I had called on the residence of Mr. Keleher requesting a citation to the recordation of his original instrument [claim of the Coroner's Jury Report]. Of course, he had none. He said he **obtained his photostat from a Mr. Abbott at Alamogordo**. Eventually, he agreed with my argument that his copy had no legal effect ...

However, subsequently the Honorable Mr. Keleher, like the Honorable Governor [Mabry], recanted when he produced his Photostat in his book, VIOLENCE IN LINCOLN COUNTY, 1957, University of New Mexico Press, at page 304, and raises a new issue. He asserts **the blank space shown on the first page has been attributed to a rat chewing on a corner of the original**

document. If he looked at the copy in the Roswell Museum [donated by Maurice Garland Fulton] he would have seen that it does not include this rat chewed corner of the original document. **I have a copy of Colonel Fulton's** and it does not bear Keleher's imprint. Perhaps there were many rat holed originals up there.

Fulton's impeccable capability and integrity were unquestionable. Whereas, the old news reporter, Keleher's were not.

So, inadvertently, Morrison added more links to the Report's provenance. Researcher Keleher had gotten his worse-for-wear copy from Harold Abbott himself, unaware that the rat damage had not been on the original - which obviously had been left in its public repository by honest Abbott. In 1951, Fulton had relocated that original Report; and made his own copies, showing that the original was not rat-damaged. But unbeknownst to Morrison, Fulton had certified his copy. **[FIGURE: 4]** And, as deviously omitted by Morrison, it is superimposable with Keleher's copy (except for the tiny rat-nibbled area). It was the same Report, found by Abbott then Fulton!

THE "BRUSHY BILL" HOAX RESPONSE

As can be predicted, the "Brushy" hoaxers desperately lied to attack Billy Bonney's Coroner's Jury Report which was fatal to their scam.

It is important to note that William V. Morrison and C.L. Sonnichsen had a copies of the original Coroner's Jury Report in Spanish, and its English translation, but hectically tried to explain it away. They variously claimed it was not authentic; was written by Pat Garrett himself as a cover-up for either killing no one, or killing an innocent victim; was one of two false reports; was never filed; and was not "certified." And, for lack of it, Garrett's reward was not given; and the Legislature only gave him money because it was Santa Fe Ring-controlled.

That fakery leapt preposterously to claiming that all this proved that Billy the Kid had never been killed - and proved that "Brushy Bill" was the surviving Billy the Kid.

And Morrison repeated these fake claims *ad nauseum* in letters and talks before and after publication of their hoax book, *Alias Billy the Kid*, which presented them also.

CERTIFYING THE REPORT

Morrison obsessively repeated that the obviously existing Coroner's Jury Report was invalid because it was not "certified."

As to the modern notion of "certifying," *Black's Law Dictionary* states that a "certified copy" is: "a duplicate of an original (usu. official) document, certified as an exact reproduction usu. by an officer responsible for issuing or keeping the original." Certification of documents is not customary in historical research, where, instead, location is cited bibliographically.

Nevertheless, for the Coroner's Jury Report, the original met that modern legal standard by being produced by a sworn Coroner's Jury and Justice of the Peace, and sent to the proper official, District Attorney of the First Judicial District William Breeden, who *de facto* certified it as the legal basis of his opinion on the mechanics of issuing Pat Garrett his Billy the Kid reward.

Those technicalities were obviously concealed by Morrison and Sonnichsen. That required ignoring, as "not certified," Harold Abbott's 1932 discovered Report, as repeated in the *Alamogordo News* on the November 30, 1950 day of "Brushy Bill" Roberts gubernatorial pardon hearing as "surviving Billy the Kid."

And it required discounting Maurice Garland Fulton's finding the original Report again in 1951 and making copies; this time sending a certified copy of one to the Indiana Historical Society's Lew Wallace Collection as if thumbing his nose at Morrison. And in Fulton's August 5, 1951 *The El Paso Times* article, "Coroner's Report Proves Billy the Kid is Dead, Historian Asserts, Researcher Discovers Document," Fulton ridiculed the "certified" baloney directly; stating: "Morrison's contention that the coroner's report was not 'recorded' is taking the modern practice rather than the older one."

In response, on August 7, 1951, Morrison indignantly bluffed in double-talk legalese to *The El Paso Times's* Editor; writing:

> With reference to item in your August 5th issue by Col. Fulton on purported death of Billy the Kid ... I wish to state that the item is misleading, and untrue in part.
>
> If Col. Fulton had the proof as contended ... why did he withhold it in November, 1950, when O.L. Roberts petitioned the Executive, Santa Fe, for pardon under terms of an original agreement between Gov. Lew Wallace and petitioner? Roberts had no legal recourse against Fulton's evidence.

Under our democratic from [sic] of government accused, or convicted persons, have the right to ask Courts to set aside judgments for legal reasons. Mr. Roberts was advised that it would be necessary to obtain certified copy of verdict rendered in San Miguel County to prepare petition to set aside the verdict in Court Action.

Due diligence was exercised to obtain certified copy from San Miguel County, but without avail ...

I believe the public should have access to my facts and records since you put the matter at large ... You have raised my issue. I'm ready.

On March 18, 1956, Morrison announced a gimmick by letter to *New Mexico Magazine* Editor Fred Gipson; writing: "I am offering to pay the sum of twenty-five dollars [to anyone] who will **furnish a certified copy of the 'inquest' in the purported death of the Kid**. This is a standing offer, and when you notify me that you have a certified copy from the legal records, I will forward the money to you to be paid to the proper party." Of course, Morrison had known about Fulton's certified copy since 1951, five years earlier!

RESPONSE TO ACTUAL REPORT

During creation of the hoax, Morrison and Sonnichsen got multiple copies of the Coroner's Jury Report; so had to pretend it was not valid. There was the November 30, 1950 reproduction in the *Alamogordo News* of Harold Abbott's 1932 find as "Fort Sumner Jury Thought The Kid Had Been Killed." There was the return of that Report found by Abbott, with its photostatic copy, in the February, 1951 edition of New Mexico Magazine under "Glimpses of History," in response to "Brushy Bill's" failed pardon attempt. That year, saw Maurice Garland Fulton relocating the original Report, as reported in August 5, 1951's *The El Paso Times* as "Coroner's Report Proves Billy the Kid is Dead, Historian Asserts, Researcher Discovers Document;" along with *that Report's* Photostat which was obviously identical to Harold Abbott's photograph 19 years earlier.

That same 1951, which was the year after "Brushy's death, and during Morrison's frenzy of letter-writing denying existence of the Report, historian, Robert N. Mullin sent him yet another copy of it on May 2, 1951; to which Morrison responded with stilted fakery:

This will serve to acknowledge the receipt of ... the transcript copy of the purported coroner verdict in the case of Billy the Kid, for which please accept my thanks.

In my opinion you have a copy of the second purported verdict which was submitted with Garrett's report for the reward money offered by Governor Wallace. Which reward money was suspended upon Garrett filing his application."

[AUTHOR'S NOTE: Morrison is lying, since the apparently translated version locates the original as sent to the District Attorney of the First Judicial District (William Breeden). And "suspended" did not mean denied. Using this report, the payment was merely delayed until it was granted as Territorial through the Legislature (with Morrison having a copy of the Act clearly stating that).]

I showed your transcript to Dr. Sonnichsen. It may be that we will want a photostatic copy of your instrument. I would like to include both purported coroner verdicts in our work. Then attack the validity of each verdict.

[AUTHOR'S NOTE: In fact, *Alias Billy the Kid's* "Appendix" had only the English translation, possibly this one from Mullin, since there existed no "second report."]

All that was left for Morrison to do was to churn out lying letters that the known Report was invalid - with Sonnichsen's apparent approval, since Morrison sent him copies, which are now in Sonnichsen's collected papers. Examples follow.

On March 23, 1955, puffed-up Morrison, anticipating release of *Alias Billy the Kid*, wrote to historian, Carl W. Breihan, calling the Report a "verdict," and writing:

I believe you are mistaken in the fact that you saw the original verdict with the names of the jurors. It is possible that you saw a copy of a purported original, which never existed in fact or in law. Garrett made reference to an original in the hands of the District Attorney, whose successor [about 70 years after the Report!] told me that it was never in that office, and if it had ever been officially made, it would be among the records of the County seat. **[Omitted is that this was incorrect information.]**

I saw a photostatic copy of this purported copy, which indicated **on its face that it was not original. [A copy is obviously not the original; but represents the original.]** Furthermore, this copy of a purported original, which never did appear on record in San Miguel County [**in fact, it appeared as the basis of its recipient, Attorney General William Breeden's, response to Acting-Governor William Ritch to initiate the reward process for Garrett for meeting the reward's requirement by killing Billy Bonney**], was ignored by the Legislative Assembly shortly after it was filed by Garrett in the governor's office [**a lie**]. Therefore, you can understand that the instrument destroyed in Santa Fe [**it was not destroyed**] could not have any legal effect in declaring that the Kid was killed.

Apparently you have not checked all the legal records and probably I should not be giving you this information as it may change your story on the Kid. However, my book is going to disqualify all former writers on the records, and you may as well have it now was later.

FAKING SEARCHES TO CLAIM THE REPORT DID NOT EXIST

Another scam used by Morrison was pretending to seek the Coroner's Jury Report himself in public records - except he looked in places where it never was; then claimed it never existed!

Hidden was that on November 7, 1949, Maurice Garland Fulton had written him about finding the Report; writing:

> Pat Garrett states in his report to the Governor that he filed the official report with the district attorney of the first judicial district. This <u>would likely mean Santa Fe</u>, although San Miguel county was at that time, I believe, in the <u>first</u> judicial district. Shortly after 1881, say about 1883, it became part of a <u>fourth</u> judicial district ....
>
> As I told you, the early documents turn up in the most unlikely places.

Knowing that Santa Fe was the likely location of the Report, Morrison made his request to meaningless Las Vegas instead! He used that dead-end on August 12, 1950 to write to *The El Paso Times's* Managing Editor Bill Latham; stating:

> Colonel Maurice Fulton is one of the N.M. Historians with whom I have come in contact that I have due respect for most of his conclusions ... I think he is mistaken about the purported

Coroner's Report being misplaced. I will admit that many N.M. Records are in bad state of repair, and have been neglected. But I do not think the record was misplaced in San Miguel County, N.M. The Clerk of the Court stated to me that it had never been made a matter of record. Then on July 5th I made a personal inspection, at which time I located old Territorial Records, but not the one in question.

Another example of this scam is Morrison's letter of June 27, 1950, written in his usual stilted legalese of his lawyer imposture, to historian, Eugene Cunningham.
Morrison wrote:

You state that Pat Garrett appended the report of Alejandro Segura, justice of the peace, precinct 27, San Miguel County, containing the verdict of the Coroner's jury he had empanelled, with the claim for the reward, to the territorial Governor's office. I beg to inform you that you are in error with your reference to the verdict.

In recent months a photostatic copy of the purported original verdict was submitted to substantiate the fact that a bonifide verdict did exist. It was set out in Garrett's report that he was attaching a copy of the original Coroner's verdict. However, it was not a certified copy from the record in San Miguel County aforesaid. Therefore, I feel certain that you are making a reference to a copy of the purported verdict.

I ordered a certified copy of the proceedings had in the matter of the Coroner's report from the clerk of the Court, San Miguel County, which order was forwarded to the Clerk of the Court, De Baca County, for attention. The clerk of De Baca County made reference to clerk of Lincoln County and Secretary of State.

All of which clerks of the Courts stated that no such purported Coroner's verdict was a matter of record in their respective Jurisdictions. I have a letter from Secretary of State, Mrs. Alicia Romero, in which she states, "Our records failed to disclose the death record or Coroner's report with reference to William Bonney, alias the Kid, alias William Antrim." in her letter of November 9, 1949, she states, "We also have in our Executive Records a copy of the application by Patrick F. Garrett for the claim of the reward money which was offered, and **upon said application the reward was suspended.**

In view of the above, and other facts, you can understand my conclusion that a bonifide Verdict did not exist ... [I] would seem that a recordation would have been in line, if not necessary or mandatory, to enable Garrett to collect the reward money as prayed in his application ...

I feel certain that you are aware that there were many rumors and statements, at the time of the killing, that Garrett did not kill the kid; that the Kid was seen alive in the vicinity shortly after the purported demise; that he escaped from Fort Sumner to Old Mexico; and many other rumors, and reports. Did not the circumstances, at that time, warrant an investigation while persons responsible for the purported Coroner's verdict were living?

The purported verdict has no bearing on my case, but I was interested to learn why the matter had not been discovered before now.

Another example is Morrison's August 3, 1950 letter to a W.J. Hooten, at *The El Paso* Times, in which he also pretended that the Report was irrelevant to his proving "Brushy" as Billy the Kid, since it did not exist! He wrote: "The Purported Coroner Verdict is no longer of interest in our case. After being informed by the Clerk of the District Court in Las Vegas, San Miguel County, N.M. **[this was a repository for San Miguel County records, but not where Report writer, Alejandro Segura, sent it, as Morrison knew]**, that no such purported instrument was made a matter of record in that jurisdiction, I made a personal check of the records to make sure that no Coroner's verdict was ever made in the death of the Kid." **[As Morrison knew, the Report was sent by Segura to District Attorney William Breeden in Santa Fe, where it was found in his records in 1932 and 1951]**.

On August 9, 1951, Morrison also searched with the wrong District Attorney's office: the modern District Attorney of the Fourth Judicial District, in Las Vegas, New Mexico; writing: "[I]t was called to my attention that your office had possession of the Coroner Verdict rendered in the purported death of Wm H. Bonney, alias Billy the Kid, on July 14, 1881, at Fort Sumner, San Miguel County, Territory of New Mexico. I hereby order a certified copy of said instrument." District Attorney Jose E. Armijo responded in an undated letter, presumably that August of 1951, stating predictably and irrelevantly: "**I am sorry I cannot comply with your request because of the fact that such a record is not now, and never had been, among the records of our office.**"

Morrison used District Attorney Jose E. Armijo's response to claim the Report never existed, as shown in his March 23, 1955 letter to historian, Carl W. Breihan:

> I believe you are mistaken in the fact that you saw the original verdict with the names of the jurors. It is possible that you saw a copy of a purported original, which never existed in fact or in law. Garrett made reference to an original in the hands of the District Attorney, **whose successor [about 70 years after the Report!] told me that it was never in that office**, and if it had ever been officially made, it would be among the records of the County seat. **[Omitted is that this was incorrect information.]**
>
> I saw a photostatic copy of this purported copy, which indicated **on its face that it was not original. [That merely meant it was a copy of the original.]** Furthermore, this copy of a purported original, which never did appear on record in San Miguel County [where it was not filed, being filed in Santa Fe County by its recipient, Attorney General William Breeden], was ignored by the Legislative Assembly shortly after it was filed by Garrett in the governor's office **[a lie]**. Therefore, you can understand that the instrument destroyed in Santa Fe **[it was not destroyed]** could not have any legal effect in declaring that the Kid was killed.
>
> Apparently you have not checked all the legal records ... However, my book is going to disqualify all former writers on the records, and you may as well have it now was later.

In a letter of October 9, 1952, Morrison continued his fake search with Dr. D.B. McKibbin at the University of New Mexico Library; asking: "I am wondering if your old San Miguel County Records contain any Justice of the Peace books **[presumably for Alejandro Segura]**."

Hoaxing Morrison presented his fake conclusion to a George Reid on March 19, 1955; writing: "A few years ago, while checking the legal records on the Kid, it was determined that they never made an official coroner's verdict in the purported killing."

THE TWO CORONER'S JURY REPORTS SCAM

A pivotal scam was Morrison's attempt to discredit the existing Report by citing a rumor that there had been two Coroner's Jury Reports, with neither real.

That contention is presented in a December 18, 1950 letter to historian, Carl W. Breihan, who had written to Andress, Lipscomb & Peticolas - the firm representing "Brushy" for his pardon request - that Billy the Kid was dead. Morrison wrote:

> I take it from the information contained in your letter ... that your opinion that the Kid is dead is based entirely upon hearsay evidence that Pat Garrett killed the Kid. **Neither of the purported Coroner Verdicts** purportedly rendered is the killing was made a matter of record. [sic] Of course, it is also alleged that each Coroner Verdict contained the names of different jurors, and that one Verdict was written in English, while the subsequent verdict was written in Spanish. **If you are relying on one of the Coroner Verdicts, I am wondering which one it might be**. Are you aware of the first that one of your persons identifying the body was never acquainted with the Kid. [He is referring to John W. Poe who was not part of the Coroner's Jury.] ... Neither is there any evidence that anybody identified the body as that of the Kid. **[Lie]**

By his letter of March 24, 1951 to historian, Robert N. Mullin, Morrison used the two report fiction as truth; writing: "**There was definitely two different purported coroner's verdicts rendered in the killing at Fort Sumner in July, 1881.** But there was no record made in either event. Therefore neither one would be legal and valid, since neither one is subject to attack in a Court Proceeding by a party of interest."

A.P. "PACO" ANAYA ORIGINATES THE TWO REPORTS FABLE

The origin of the rumor of two Coroner's Jury Reports was clarified when Morrison was loaned an April 2, 1936 letter from an A.P. Anaya from the editor of *New Mexico Magazine*, George Fitzpatrick. Morrison responded on August 24, 1951:

> First I want to thank you for the loan of the letter from Mr. A.P. Anaya of April 2, 1936 ... **Your file of correspondence with Mr. Anaya bears out my contention that Pat Garrett made his own record of the matter [i.e., that Garrett wrote a Report]**. Also, he made his own record in application for the reward. It is stated that Gov. Wallace did not make an official reward. But an official reward was made by Wallace in his official capacity. I have certified a copy of same today ... I am advising

Dr. Sonnichsen that you will permit us to use your letter with reference to **the first purported verdict by Anaya**, in our publication [*Alias Billy the Kid*].

Anaya, a younger friend of Billy Bonney's, and a Fort Sumner local, who had no access to any official reports and was not on the Coroner's Jury, as an old-timer nicknamed "Paco," sought attention by spouting Billy the Kid malarkey, which was posthumously published, in 1991, as a book titled *I Buried Billy* (See page 389 below)

It was Paco Anaya who apparently originated the two Coroner's Jury Reports fiction in his February 5, 1936 letter to George Fitzpatrick, Editor of *New Mexico Magazine*, to write himself into the history by pretending he was on Billy's coroner's jury. A typed version of Anaya's statement was in Sonnichsen's collected papers. It stated: "[T]here has been many things said in the other stories that are nothing but falsehoods, there are many things said that are just like the report that Pat Garrett gave the court, he lost the report **that we the coroner's jury gave him** and he got Mr. Manuel Avreu [sic - Abreu] to write him another one."

Anaya expanded his fiction in an April 2, 1936 letter to George Fitzpatrick, by fabricating that Milnor Rudulph was not present; that Garrett wrote a first report which Anaya signed as a juryman, but Garrett lost; and that Garrett then wrote a second report with Rudulph as President. The copy of this letter, in Sonnichsen's collected papers, demonstrates Morrison's and Sonnichsen's dishonesty, since they hid that Anaya's letter also confirmed Billy's killing by Pat Garrett and his seeing Billy's body; while they lifted only his fiction of two Reports.

Anaya's translated letter stated:

> I have your letter of April 1st. in which you tell me many things concerning my history ... Concerning the War it was in 1878. It was thus. In which I do not say much of Billy after he went from my Father's Ranch. It is **because he did not return there until the day on which Pat killed him** ... Billy when he left the Ranch of my Father he went to Tom Yerves [Yerby's] Ranch, in the little canyons about 16 miles to the north of Taiban. From there he came to Fort Sumner and he slept in Saval Gutierres' [Gutierrez's] House. And when Governor Otero's book says that Billy was in Don Jesus Silva's restaurant that is not the truth [showing Otero's book was possible prompt for "Brushy's"

Fort Sumner steak restaurant] Don Jesus is living in Fort Sumner and I can prove with him that he never had a restaurant. In Fort Sumner it is true that [Billy] was in the house of Don Jesus Silva late into the day of the 15th [sic] of July about 8 P.M. There were I, my brother Higini and various other persons. And Billy was there from the house of Saval Gutierres [sic] and at this time that Celsa Gutierres [sic] cooked supper for him. And then he went to Don Pedro Maxwell's room. (The fact that Selsa [sic] Gutierres [sic] was cooking supper for Billy and wished some meat was the reason for Billy's going to Maxwell's.) And at this time Pat was in the room. He had been asking where Billy was. **When at this time Billy entered and Pat killed him.** We hear the shots and went to see what was happening and we saw many people, going toward ol Don's room (Pete's). **And there we found that Billy was dead.**

When I have said that Mr. Rudolfo [sic – Rudulph]. He was in Rosiada in 1880. I can prove this. The Ojo de Sunnyside is 10 miles [sic – 7 miles] north of Fort Sumner ...

I have said concerning the Verdict of the Coroner's Jury that the verdict was the same Pat wrote and we signed it. [Report I] It is not in Register. Pat lost the paper and then put Milnor Rudolfo president. [Report II] I say that is not true and prove it.

On January 19, 1952, George Fitzpatrick sent a copy of Anaya's letter to Sonnichsen, with more explanation; writing:

I am attaching a copy of A.P. Anaya's letter with reference to the coroner's jury which returned a report on Billy the Kid. The copy as I received it – his own quaint Spanish and peculiar capitalization and lack of it – and misspellings.

Mr. Anaya had told me that **he and a friend were called as members of the coroner's jury the night the Kid was killed** and that this jury wrote out a verdict **stating simply that the Kid had come to his death as a result of a wound from a gun in the hands of Pat Garrett, officer.** Anaya claimed that this verdict was lost and that Garrett had Manuel Abreu write a more flowery one for filing. New signatures other than Anaya's and his friends appear on the semi-official verdict. Anaya claimed Milnor Rudulph, who signed as "presidente" of the jury, was not a member of the original jury which viewed the body. ...

As far as I can recall, he did not submit any actual evidence of his claim other than his own statement.

This Fitzpatrick letter confirms that Sonnichsen heard directly from him that Anaya had confirmed the death of Billy Bonney - with the addition of his two reports fable. So Sonnichsen, like Morrison, unquestionably and duplicitously hid the confirmation to lift the weird, two report tale for their hoax.

BUILDING ON THE ANAYA FABLE

Morrison presented the scam built on Anaya's fakery in his notes on Pat Garrett's *The Authentic Life of Billy the Kid* (which were in Sonnichsen's collected papers) in his attempts to discredit the Coroner's Jury Report. Seeking discrepancies, he claimed that Garrett's book's wording of the Coroner's Jury Report was not exactly the same as the purported original since the book said: "the fatal wound was inflicted by the said Garrett in the discharge of his official duty as Sheriff," which was not in the original Report, which made Morrison claim that the original Report had been in English and written by Garrett. Morrison then made-up: "The above mentioned clause was probably incorporated in the first purported Coroner's Verdict, which was written in English by Garrett and attested by different jurors than the names appearing on the later verdict offered by Garrett with his report and application which was filed on July 20, 1881, in the Office of the Secretary of State, Santa Fe, N.M." [sic – on July 15, 1881 the original Coroner's Jury Report was sent to District Attorney of the First Judicial District William Breeden].

He then used "Paco" Anaya as the authority: "Mr. Anaya, an alleged witness to the first verdict, stated in writing [the letter to George Fitzgerald] that Garrett's later version of the verdict was not in accord with the first verdict. Mr. Anaya further stated that neither verdict was made a matter of record."

THE SCAM OF MISSTATING THE REWARD

Another attempt to discredit the Report was to fabricate that the difficulties Pat Garrett encountered in collecting the Billy the Kid reward resulted from the Report's not existing.

To be noted, is that, by 1949, Morrison owned copies of the official records pertaining to that reward's collection. (See pages 18-28 above for the records) That can be seen in his November 9, 1949 letter from New Mexico Secretary of State Alicia Romero confirming her enclosing copies from their "Executive Record Book;" stating: "If you desire to have these copies Certified we will be glad to do so." That meant, from 1949, Morrison knew Acting-

Governor William Ritch and Attorney General William Breeden confirmed the Report, the death of Billy Bonney, and the need to convert Lew Wallace's private reward to a Territorial one. But Sonnichsen cited these records in footnotes in *Alias Billy the Kid* as if they substantiated the hoax's fake claims - slyly assuming no one would check them. So it is clear that both Morrison and Sonnichsen willfully lied to hide the information, which was fatal to their scam.

THE "SUSPENDED" REWARD SCAM

Denying the Coroner's Jury Report was entangled with lying about Pat Garrett's receiving the reward for the killing. As already discussed, the governmental records made clear that Garrett's monetary award merely required conversion from Lew Wallace's private offer of $500 to its Territorial payment.

But Morrison and Sonnichsen built a scam using the November 9, 1949 response of New Mexico's Secretary of State Alicia Romero to Morrison's records request to seize on her word "suspended," to fake that it meant the reward had been *stopped for lack of the Coroner's Jury Report*. Having helpfully reviewed the records herself, she had written: "We also have in our executive Records a copy of the application by Patrick F. Garrett for the claim on the reward money which was offered, and upon said application **the reward was suspended.**"

Secretary of State Romero was paraphrasing the July 21, 1881 entry by Acting-Governor William Ritch which concluded: "*The opinion of the Attorney General [Breeden] appearing to be consistent with the law and the facts, decision is rendered accordingly and the Governor [Ritch, speaking for himself] declines to allow the reward at this time. Believing however, that Mr Garret has an equitable claim against the Territory for said reward, the action at this* **office will simply be suspended until the case can properly be represented to the next Legislative Assembly**. (See page 25 above)

So payment of Lew Wallace's reward to Garrett had been "suspended." The *Merriam-Webster* definition of "suspend" is: "to cause to stop temporarily; to defer to a later time on specified conditions." This described correctly holding up Wallace's $500 private reward until the Legislature could convert it to a Territorial reward of $500 - which it did by an Act.

Instead, con-artist Morrison did a switcheroo on "suspended" as if it meant to stop or to halt – as if Garrett should not be rewarded. Morrison then lied that the reward was halted for lack of the Coroner's Jury Report. His scam can be seen in his letter of January 12, 1952 to A.S. Gaylord Jr. at the Santa Fe Museum of New Mexico; stating: "You are probably aware of the fact that Governor Wallace's **reward money was suspended** upon Garrett filing his application for the reward. **It was not paid to Garrett.**"

THE "AUGUST" DATE SCAM

Another angle of the scam was making-up discrepancies to claim they revealed that the Kid's killing never occurred. For that, Morrison and Sonnichsen seized on the Legislative Act's legalese stating that the killing had occurred "<u>**on or about** the month of **August, 1881.**</u>" That involved lying about this quote.

1) **MISQUOTING LEGISLATIVE ACT:** The Act of February 18, 1882, granting Garrett his reward, stated: "Pat. Garrett was at that time sheriff of Lincoln county, and did, <u>**on or about** the month of **August, 1881**</u>, in pursuance of the above reward ... attempted to arrest said William Bonney, and in said attempt did kill said William Bonney at Fort Sumner."

But Morrison and Sonnichsen lied that the Legislature dated the killing **specifically to August of 1881;** so it never happened on July 14, 1881; so Billy was not killed!

This lie can be seen in Morrison's August 8, 1952 Silver City Kiwanis Club talk titled: "He Said He was Billy the Kid." He stated: "[S]ome of you are probably thinking that I am off the beam [about "Brushy's" surviving the shooting]; that Pat Garrett killed Billy the Kid on that certain July 14, 1881, like his purported coroner verdict said; **or you may think he was killed on that certain month of August, 1881, like the Legislative Act said he was killed** ... I know that Garrett never killed the Kid on that certain July 14th, **nor in that certain month of August**, or at any other time. Billy the Kid was never killed by anyone."

Morrison lied more boldly about the reward and the Legislature in his letter of February 23, 1955 to Guy W. Bradford at *The Texaco Star Reporter*. Morrison wrote: "[B]eing very familiar with Garrett's <u>Authentic Life of Billy the Kid</u>, I can prove that Garrett's tale is not authentic in the least. [No one saw] his famous **purported coroner's verdict which was so thoroughly abrogated** [meaning to repudiate, revoke, or overturn] **by the Legislative Assembly** a few months after its purported inception. Did you know that they **substituted** a day in August for the memorable July 14 as the date of the purported killing?"

Morrison amplified the August date scam in an April 12, 1977 letter to a Lawrence K. Mooney; stating: "Certainly, the Special Act of the Territorial Legislature granting Garrett relief [a reward] for **killing the Kid in that month of August 1881** did not constitute a legal declaration of death, **and they ignored a coroner's verdict by changing the date of killing from July 14 to a date in August.**"

2) USING A HEARSAY ARTICLE FOR A VARIATION ON THE AUGUST DATE SCAM: On December 1, 1950, in debunking "Brushy's" pardon hearing and claim of being surviving Billy the Kid, the *Albuquerque Journal* published a hearsay account titled "Old Timer Claims He Helped Bury Billy the Kid." In Sonnichsen's papers as a source, it was windbag malarkey by a non-historical John Doyle Lee, stating:

> At Phoenix, Ariz., a cowboy who claims he used to rustle cattle with the outlaw, said Billy the Kid could not possibly be alive.
>
> "Hell, me and Tom Storey of Phoenix helped bury Billy 69 years ago," said John Doyle Lee, 92 year old resident of Elroy and Phoenix.
>
> Lee said he and Storey arrived in Fort Sumner, in Lincoln County, N.M. shortly after Billy had been shot by Garrett.
>
> "We saw Billy laid out in Pete Maxwell's shop where they built a coffin for him," he asserted. "**We buried him July 16, 1881, two days after he was shot.**"
>
> Lee said he has a "whole passel of affidavits" to prove his association with William Bonney – the Kid.

So Morrison also lied that it was asserted that Billy was *killed* on July 16, 1881; so he claimed the Coroner's Jury Report was a fake by claiming the killing date as July 14, 1881.

SCAM THAT THE LEGISLATURE INTERVENED BECAUSE OF NO REPORT

Another example of hoaxing is in Morrison's letter of June 30, 1954 to historian Philip J. Rasch, which linked the Report and reward. Morrison wrote: "You can understand that **if they had made a legal record of the killing on July 14, it would not have been necessary for them to lobby before the Legislature** the following January to pass a bill to pay the reward money for killing the Kid in August [sic], 1881. There is no legal proof that they killed him at any time."

By his letter of May 9, 1955 to historian, Robert N. Mullin, Morrison effortlessly lied about the Legislative Act for Garrett's reward; stating: "The private legislative act [**it was not "private," being a formal public Act**] granted relief to Garrett for the arrest and not for the killing of Kid. [**Lie. It merely converted Wallace's private reward to a Territorial one, with the killing accepted.**] It is stated that he was killed in the attempted arrest in the month of August [**lie; it says "on or about August"**], which is merely a conclusion of fact and is not evidence. [**Morrison was making-up that the Report did not exist, so there was no "evidence." He is hiding that the granting of the reward was based on the evidence of the Coroner's Jury Report, by then confirmed by Attorney General William Breeden, Acting-Governor William Ritch, and the Legislature.**]"

SCAM OF LEGISLATURE GRANTING REWARD BY SANTA FE RING CONSPIRACY

Morrison and Sonnichsen also contradicted their hoax claim that Garrett was not rewarded, with a conspiracy theory that he was rewarded, but only because the Santa Fe Ring controlled the Legislature, and they wanted him to have the money even though he did not kill Billy the Kid and there was no Report.

In his letter of January 12, 1952 to A.S. Gaylord Jr. at the Santa Fe Museum of New Mexico, Morrison had admitted: "**I was informed** that the Legislature passed an act granting relief to Garrett." [**Note that sly Morrison himself had a copy of the Act.**]

To counter this proof that all legalities had been in order for the reward, since it was awarded, Morrison built a conspiracy theory, as can be seen in his letter of January 29, 1951 to an A.F. Von Blon; stating: "[I]t was alleged at the time of the killing that Garrett did not kill Billy. Under the circumstances, and in view of the fact that a certified copy of the instrument would have established the fact of proof of death when Garrett applied for the reward money offered by Gov. Wallace, why was a record not made in the matter? **I have evidence that Gov. Wallace did not pay the reward money to Garrett, or anyone else.**" [**But this was because he had left the Territory, and his private reward had to be converted to a Territorial one by legislative act; which was done!**]

Morrison added the Santa Fe Ring to the reward conspiracy theory in his October 8, 1952 letter to George Fitzpatrick, Editor of *New Mexico Magazine*. Morrison wrote:

I am firmly convinced that Governor Wallace made only one official reward in the matter of the Kid. I am convinced that this official reward was never paid to anyone.

The reward mentioned in the act for relief of Garrett was certainly never officially made by the governor. **The Santa Fe Ring was responsible for this reward, and the relief granted by the legislature in 1882.**

I an firmly convinced that an official coroner's verdict was never rendered in the purported killing of the Kid. He had never been legally declared dead as some people seem to think. Certainly the legislative act did not constitute a legal declaration of death. This Judicial function was vested in the courts of the Territory.

ADDING THE SCAM OF THE COLT .41

By March 11, 1964, in a letter to a Mike Francis and John McGinnis, Morrison was embellishing his Coroner's Jury Report lies with additional lies about "circumstantial evidence" that Garrett had faked the death scene because he had claimed that dead Billy had a Colt .41. This was intended to mean that the death scene never happened. That came from *The Authentic Life of Billy the Kid*; which stated: "[T]he Kid must have seen or felt the presence of a third person at the head of the bed. He raised quickly his pistol - a self-cocker - within a foot of my breast ... [After the shooting] [w]e examined his pistol - a self-cocker, caliber .41. It had five cartridges and one shell in the chambers, the hammer resting on the shell. But this proved nothing [as to Billy having fired a shot at him], as many carry their revolvers this way for safety. Moreover, the shell looked as though it had been shot some time before [proving Billy fired no shot at him]." (Garrett, Pages 216, 218)

Morrison wrote:

You can rest assured that Garrett did not leave any legal evidence in New Mexico that the Kid was killed on July 14, 1881, or at any other time.

He did, however, leave strong circumstantial evidence that the Kid was not killed, when he alleged, quote, "We examined his pistol – **a self-cocker, caliber .41**," in the right hand and a knife in the left hand, when the dead body hit the floor.

Garrett **knew the Kid was left handed**; Colt's [sic] did not patent the selfcocker until August 1878, long after Garrett, the Kid, and everyone else there, had been accustomed to use of the single action large caliber pistols; and Pat knew the Kid would not fight his last battle with a pistol strange to him.

FAKERY: Everything is false:
1) **The legal evidence of the killing was the Coroner's Jury Report.**
2) **Billy was not left-handed; he was ambidextrous, favoring the right.** This fakery came from Morrison's and "Brushy Bill's" relying on the tintype, without realizing it was right-to left reversed, so Billy's hand cocked at his revolver was his right.
3) **The double-action Colt .41 or "Thunderer," or Colt Model 1877, came out in 1877. A gunman, like Billy, would be adept with different guns, and had a Winchester '73 carbine too.**
4) **Billy was ambushed, and trusted the Maxwell family's protection; and was not anticipating "his last battle." But as the most hunted person in New Mexico, he would have not walked around unarmed. He obviously carried the small, but six shot, Thunderer, as a hide-away back-up (preferable to a derringer with only one or two cartridges). Also, it was Colt's first double-action model, eliminating manual retracting of the hammer, so was faster in firing multiple rounds.**

THE SUMMARIZED REPORT SCAM

Morrison's and Sonnichsen's full-blown Coroner's Jury Report scam is presented in Morrison's May 8, 1961 letter to *Lincoln County News* publisher, Paul Baker, whose copy is in Sonnichsen's collected papers. It stated:

> Historians believe that Pat Garrett filed a certified copy **[Morrison's made-up notion of "certified"]** of a judgment, which was not true. Pat never claimed he did. He merely stated in his petition to recover the reward money that he was attaching a copy of the coroner's report, the original of which was in the office of the Prosecuting Attorney for the First Judicial District **[omitting that the original Report makes that statement]**.

That Prosecuting Attorney's office reported that "such a record is not now, and never has been, among the records of this office ... such a verdict, if it existed, should have been filed in the office of the County Clerk, in an opinion furnished the undersigned. **[This was Morrison's request to the wrong office. Also omitted is that by November 30, 1950, the location of the original was indicated by the *Alamogordo News* article, "Sumner Jury Thought The Kid Had Been Killed," on how Harold Abbott found it; and how August 5, 1951's *The El Paso Times* article, "Coroner's Report Proves Billy the Kid is Dead, Historian Asserts, Researcher Discovers Document," described that Maurice G. Fulton found it again; and by 1957 it had been published in William Kelleher's book, *Violence in Lincoln County*.]**

Garrett's attorneys **[claimed as part of the Santa Fe Ring]** were very astute and cautious in their efforts to have the Kid declared legally dead. You can rest assured that if a legal judgment had been recorded they would have seen to it that it would have been recorded among the legal records. **[This fake conspiracy theory hid that the issue was not the Report, but was merely conversion of Wallace's private reward to a Territorial one before paying Garrett - which Morrison and Sonnichsen knew since they had the records.]** ...

Now I am ready to dispose of the Legislative Act ... [which] sets out very distinctly that the Kid was killed in the month of August instead of Garrett's certain July 14 **[Lie]**... Probably, none of you have heard of this Legislative Act. **[Sly Morrison is betting on that!]**

Morrison also presented the full Coroner's Jury Report scam in his notes on Pat Garrett's *Authentic Life of Billy the Kid*, apparently given to Sonnichsen for writing their book, since it was in Sonnichsen's collected papers. Morrison wrote:

The purported coroner verdicts **[there was just one]** have been a subject of debate through the years **[by then, the Report was known, available, and accepted]**. Which one was the first verdict rendered, if any was rendered in the death of Wm. H. Bonney. Why was the purported verdict never made a matter of record? **[Lie: It was sent to the proper official, District Attorney of the First Judicial District William Breeden.]** Why did not Garrett furnish a certified copy at the time he filed his application for reward to substantiate the fact that he did actually apprehend the Kid? **[He appropriately sent a copy to Acting-Governor William Ritch. Certified copies are a modern concept.]** Why was not a certified copy from the record in San Miguel County, N.M. offered in this authentic history written by Garrett? **[Because certified copies are a modern concept; and there was no dispute about the Report or that he killed the Kid; and it was filed in Santa Fe County.]** Garrett tells his story but offers nothing to support it. Why not? **[Lie: He supports the killing as the one who did it, tells of the witnesses, and has a legal Coroner's Jury Report documenting it.]** Was there a verdict actually existing then? **[Yes.]** There is none existing in our present day. **[Lie.]** A certified copy was not made available, upon request of Wm. H. Roberts ["Brushy"] ... **[Because Morrison was seeking it in wrong places, and refused to recognize the already located Report, even when offered to him by historian Robert N. Mullin.]** There has been much ballyhoo about Garrett killing the Kid down through the years. **[Historic fact]** Statements were made at the time that the Kid had not been killed by Garrett as well as having been made down through the years ... **[Hearsay malarkey by non-historical attention-seekers]** All of this rumor that the Kid was, or was not killed, by Garrett could have been settled once and for all if an actual Judgment did exist through the years. **[The Coroner's Jury Report does exist, and on July 15, 1881, it settled the killing of Billy Bonney as "justifiable homicide."]** It would not have been necessary for the public to rely upon untrue and unsubstantiated history and legend so to call, if a record had been made. **[Lie: The Report had been made.]** Also it might have saved Garrett expense and time in an attempt to collect the reward money offered by Governor Wallace which was never paid. However, Garrett did recover through act of the legislature after considerable expense and unnecessary time. **[Lie: Wallace's reward was eventually paid. Its collection cost Garrett nothing, since it was an administrative technicality to convert Wallace's private reward of $500 to a Territorial one of $500.]** The act of the legislature could have been dispensed with, and Wm H. Roberts would have had his day in Court to have the original judgment set aside. **[The Report had nothing to do with proving "Brushy" was Billy the Kid; but it proved he was not Billy the Kid, since real Billy was killed on July 14, 1881.]**

By Morrison's grandiose March 19, 1955 letter to a George Reid, in which he flaunted the upcoming publication of *Alias Billy the Kid* (and left out Sonnichsen who wrote it!), the Report hoax was crystallized. Morrison wrote:

> A few years ago, while checking the legal records on the Kid, it was determined that they never made an official coroner's verdict in the purported killing.
> I am of the opinion that Garrett didn't kill anyone at that time. I believe that the Kid got away and went into Old Mexico.
> The University of New Mexico Press is in process of publishing **my book**, Alias Billy the Kid.

On December 8, 1951, Morrison had written to an eccentric named Ozark Jack, a notorious teller of Old West tall tales, hoping he would back "Brushy;" and laid out his Coroner's Jury Report lies: "We know that Garrett did not kill the Kid. There is no legal evidence that he killed anybody. Billy the Kid was never declared legally dead. Pat Garrett did not collect the reward money offered by Gov. Wallace. We have the evidence. The other side has nothing to prove their contentions. We are going to let the public have the facts and records made in the case of Billy the Kid. Never before have the records been uncovered."

On this foundation lie, was built the entire "Brushy Bill" imposter hoax's house of cards.

CHAPTER 3
OBSTACLE OF CORPSE WITNESSES

THE PROBLEM OF REALITY

It took the delusional disorders of "Brushy Bill" Roberts, and the sociopathic scorn of public intelligence by his hoaxing promoters, to claim that the most documented death in the Old West never happened. It was not only the Coroner's Jury Report that was their impassable hurdle. A huge number of people saw the corpse, besides the Report's witness, Peter Maxwell; and they documented their experiences. In addition, killing Billy the Kid was a major media event, with national reporting.

PAT GARRETT WROTE A BOOK

The 1881 killing of Billy the Kid had viral fame, inspiring Pat Garrett to ally with his journalist boarder, Ashmun "Ash" Upson, to create his ghostwritten book, issued the following year: *The Authentic Life of Billy the Kid The Noted Desperado of the Southwest, Whose Deeds of Daring and Blood Made His Name a Terror in New Mexico, Arizona, and Northern Mexico.* Though it used that period's popular and lurid dime novel style, and though the history of Billy Bonney had not yet been researched, so was fictionalized, both men knew Billy. Upson had been a border with his family in Silver City; and Garrett, having met Billy in 1878, when both spent time in Fort Sumner, certainly knew the specifics of his own tracking, capturing, jailing, and killing of him. Garrett's lethality was undisputable, as he first killed two of Billy's companions in his attempt to kill him. On December 19, 1880, he and his Texan posse ambushed Billy's group returning to Fort Sumner. Tom O'Folliard was fatally shot. And in the early morning of December 22, 1881, with Billy and his group attempting to escape the Territory and having spent the night in a rock line-cabin at Stinking Springs, Charlie Bowdre emerged first wearing either Billy's hat, or one that looked like it, and was immediately killed by Garrett, as mistaken for Billy. Only then did Garrett settle on capturing Billy for certain hanging trials.

As to Garrett's finally killing Billy, his book described his coming to Fort Sumner with his Deputies John William Poe and Thomas "Kip" McKinney; and, late that moonlit night of July 14, 1881, stationing them on the porch of the Maxwell family mansion, while he went inside to check with the town's owner, Peter Maxwell, in his dark bedroom. The book stated:

> I left Poe and McKinney at the end of the porch, and about twenty feet from the door of Pete's bedroom, while I myself entered it. I walked to the head of the bed and sat down near the pillow and beside Maxwell's head. I asked him as to the whereabouts of the Kid. He replied that the Kid had certainly been about, but he did not know whether he had left or not. At that moment, a man sprang quickly in the door, and looking back, called twice in Spanish, "Quien es? Quien es? (Who comes there?)" No one replied, and he came into the room. I could see he was bareheaded, and from his tread I could perceive he was either barefooted or in his stocking feet. He held a revolver in his right hand and a butcher knife in his left.
>
> He came directly towards me while I was sitting at the head of Maxwell's bed. Before he reached the bed, I whispered, "Who is it, Pete?" but received no reply for a moment. It struck me that it might be Pete's brother-in-law, Manuel Abreu, who had seen Poe and McKinney on the outside and wanted to know their business. The intruder came close to me, leaned both hands on the bed, his right almost touching my knee, and asked in a low tone "Who are they, Pete?" At the same instant Maxwell whispered to me, "That's him!"
>
> Simultaneously the Kid must have seen or felt the presence of a third person at the head of the bed. He raised quickly his pistol – a self-cocker – within a foot of my breast. Retreating rapidly across the room, he cried, "Quien es? Quien es? (Who is that? Who is that?)"

All this happened more rapidly than it takes to tell it. As quick as possible I drew my revolver and fired, threw my body to one side, and fired again. The second shot was useless. The Kid fell dead at the first one. He never spoke. A struggle or two, a little strangling sound as he gasped for breath, and the Kid was with his many victims. (Garrett, Pages 215-216)

Garrett's description matched Peter Maxwell's witness statement to the Coroner's Jury the next day: "I being in my bed in my room, at about midnight on the 14th day of July, Pat F. Garrett came into my room and sat down. William Bonney came in and got close to my bed with a gun in his hand and asked me "who is it" and then Pat F. Garrett fired two shots at the said William Bonney and the said William Bonney fell near my fire place and I went out of the room and when I came in again about three or four minutes after the shots the said William Bonney was dead."

DEPUTY POE WROTE A BOOK

John William Poe, Kentucky-born and a past buffalo hunter, like Pat Garrett, was a Deputy U.S. Marshal and a Deputy Sheriff in Texas. In late 1880, he was hired by the Canadian River Cattlemen's Association to combat rustling centered in New Mexico, and had moved to its White Oaks. He was deputized by Pat Garrett, who was then Lincoln County Sheriff and a Deputy U.S. Marshal, to hunt Billy Bonney following his April 28, 1881 jailbreak in Lincoln while awaiting hanging. After participating in the killing, Poe was elected Lincoln County Sheriff the following year, serving until 1885; then did ranching and later moved to Roswell in the Territory, operating a store and founding both the Bank of Roswell and the Citizen's Bank of Roswell.

Poe's book, *The Death of Billy the Kid*, was first printed as a long article, *The Killing of Billy the Kid*, then as a booklet by an E.A. Brininstool in 1922 and 1923. It was published as a book by Houghton Mifflin in 1933. Though Poe had never met Billy until moments before the fateful encounter, he was the one who had urged Pat Garrett's reconnaissance of Fort Sumner because of Billy's rumored presence there. And his reporting of the shooting gives the multiple victim identifications that left him confident that Billy had been killed. His book stated:

It was probably not more than thirty seconds after Garrett had entered Maxwell's room, when my attention was attracted, from where I sat in the little gateway, to a man approaching me on the inside of and along the fence, some forty or fifty steps away. I observed that he was only partially dressed and was both bareheaded and barefooted, or rather, had only socks on his feet, and it seemed to me that he was fastening his trousers as he came toward me at a brisk walk.

As Maxwell's was the one place in Fort Sumner that I had considered above suspicion of harboring the Kid, I was entirely off my guard, the thought coming into my mind that the man approaching was either Maxwell or some guest of his ... He came on until he was almost within arm's-length of where I sat, before he saw me, as I was partially concealed from his view by the post of the gate.

Upon seeing me, he covered me with his six-shooter as quick as lightning, sprang onto the porch, calling out in Spanish, "Quien es" (Who is it?) – at the same time backing away from me toward the door through which only a few seconds before had passed, repeating his query, "Who is it?" in Spanish several times.

At this I stood up and advanced toward him, telling him not to be alarmed, that he should not be hurt; and still without the least suspicion that this was the very man we were looking for. As I moved toward him trying to reassure him, he backed up into the doorway of Maxwell's room, where he halted for a moment, his body concealed by the thick adobe wall at the side of the doorway, from whence he put out his head and asked in Spanish for the fourth or fifth time who I was. I was within a few feet of him when he disappeared into the room.

After this, and until after the shooting, I was unable to see what took place on account of the darkness of the room, but plainly heard what was said inside. An instant after the man left the door, I heard a voice inquire in a sharp tome, "Pete, who are those fellows on the outside?"

An instant later a shot was fired in the room, followed immediately by what everyone within hearing distance thought were two other shots. However, there were only two shots fired, the third report, as we learned afterward, being caused by the rebound of the second bullet, which had struck the adobe wall and rebounded against the headboard of the wooden bedstead.

I heard a groan and one or two gasps from where I stood in the doorway, as of someone dying in the room. An instant later, Garrett came out ... He stood close by me to the wall at the side of the door ands said to me, "that was the Kid that came in there onto me, and I think I have got him." I said, "Pat, the Kid would not come to this place; you have shot the wrong man.

Upon my saying this, Garrett seemed to be in doubt himself as to whom he had shot, but quickly spoke up and said, "I am sure that was him, for I know his voice too well to be mistaken." This remark of Garrett's relieved me of considerable apprehension, as I had felt almost certain that someone whom we did not want had been killed.

A moment after Garrett came out of the door, Peter Maxwell rushed squarely onto me in frantic effort to get out of the room, and I certainly would have shot him but for Garrett's striking down my gun, saying, "Don't shoot Maxwell ..."

We afterwards discovered that the Kid had frequently been at his house after his escape from Lincoln, but Maxwell stood in such terror of him that he did not dare inform against him.

[Maxwell then got a candle from his mother's room and placed it on the window-sill from the outside.] This enabled us to get a view of the inside, where we saw a man lying stretched upon his back dead, in the middle of the room, with a six-shooter lying at his right hand and a butcher knife at his left. Upon examining the body, we found it to be that of Billy the Kid. Garrett's first shot had penetrated his breast just above the heart. (Poe, Pages 32-41)

Poe's description matched Pat Garrett's as well as the Coroner's Jury Report; which stated: "[The jury] found the body of William Bonney alias 'Kid' with a shot in the left breast."

A.P. "PACO" ANAYA BURIED BILLY AND GOT A BOOK

A.P. "Paco" Anaya was a Fort Sumner friend of Billy's. His 1991, posthumously printed memoir held the truth in his title: *I Buried Billy*. Anaya was one of the 200 Fort Sumner residents who held a candle-light wake for Billy's body on the night of July 14-15, 1881, all having identified him. Real dead Billy ends the imposters' and "Billy the Kid Case" promulgators' hoaxes. Anaya wrote: "I, the writer, and my brother, Higinio Garcia, and several others of those that were there, **dressed Billy with those clothes then we laid him on a high bed ... [A]nd on the next day we buried him.**" (Anaya, Page 132)

A TOWN IDENTIFIED THE BODY TOO

After his jailbreak on April 28, 1881, Billy had chosen Fort Sumner as a destination for two reasons: his secret young lover, Paulita Maxwell, was there; and he felt confident in the protection of the Maxwell family and Fort Sumner's over 200 residents, who had known him since early 1878, and would have been aware of his freedom fighter role. The response of the townspeople to this horrific killing in their midst, was described by John William Poe in his 1933 book, *The Death of Billy the Kid*. Once again, as an outsider, he was surprised. He quickly realized that this boy, who had been presented to him as a despicable outlaw-murderer, was beloved by the primarily Hispanic residents. Poe wrote:

> Within a short time after the shooting, quite a number of the native people gathered around, some of the bewailing the death of their friend, while several women pleaded for permission to take charge of the body, which we allowed them to do. They carried it across the yard to a carpenter shop, where it was laid out on a workbench, the women placing lighten candles around it according to their ideas of properly conducting a "wake" for the dead ...

[The shooting] occurred at about midnight on the fourteenth of July, 1881. We spent the remainder of the night on the Maxwell premises, keeping constantly on our guard, as we were expecting to be attacked by friends of the dead man. (Pages 41-42, 44)

So not only did multiple townspeople identify Billy as the corpse in the night time wake, but they were infuriated enough by his killing to present a risk its perpetrators.

As an aside, the townspeople's response put in perspective the Coroner's Jury Report's statement: "[W]e are unanimous in the opinion that the gratitude of all the community is due to the said Garrett for his deed and is worthy of being rewarded." The Report was written by their President, Milnor Rudulph, the Postmaster of Sunnyside, seven miles north of Fort Sumner. Rudulph was a loyal Ringite who had helped Thomas Benton Catron and the Santa Fe Ring take over the Legislature in 1872 to block anti-Ring bills. His actions contributed to the first of the Territorial, anti-Ring, freedom fights, which I named the 1872 Legislature Revolt. It took Ringite Governor Marsh Giddings's bringing the military into the Legislature's hall, to suppress the legislators, for the Ring to prevail and keep their Ring-biased judges in power to continue malicious prosecutions of their opponents. With Rudulph as President, the frightened juryman had no alternative but to sign a document praising Pat Garrett the day after Ring terrorism had invaded their once safe town.

DELUVINA MAXWELL WAS THERE ALSO

A Navajo woman, Deluvina was bought as a nine year old slave by Lucien Bonaparte Maxwell - owner of the two million acre Maxwell Land Grant, then Fort Sumner. Never emancipated, she was attached to Billy Bonney, and laid wildflowers on his Fort Sumner grave for decades, till her own death.

Her own eye-witness confirmation of Billy's being the corpse was given in a June 24, 1927 interview to historian, J. Evetts Haley, in Fort Sumner. She stated:

> I came here about [1869] and was here when Billy the Kid was killed. Billy the Kid was my compadre, my friend, poor Billy ... Pete Maxwell had told Billy he better go, as

Pat Garrett was coming after him. Billy said he did not care, he was not afraid of Pat Garrett. The night he was killed Billy came in hungry, went down with a butcher knife to get some meat at Pete Maxwell's ... After passing the men outside, he went into Maxwell's room where Garrett was and he shot him. The story is told that I was there and went in with a candle to see if Billy was dead. I did not do it. Pete took a candle and held it around in the window and Pat stood back in the dark where he could see in the room. When they saw he was dead, they both went in ...

Most of the native people (Mexicans) who lived in town went to his funeral ...

I did not see Billy the night after he was killed, **but I saw him the following morning.**

To be noted is that Deluvina's description matched that of John William Poe about Maxwell placing the candle, and the residents' wake to view the body.

THE PRESS WAS PROFUSE

There was also massive, front page, national press about the killing of Billy the Kid; with no reason to fabricate the event; with Billy portrayed as a terrifying outlaw-murderer, whose death was a public relief. Already mentioned, has been the July 23, 1881's Las Cruces *Rio Grande Republican's* "Kid the Killer Killed, Wm. Bonney alias Antrim, alias Billy the Kid, Fatally Meets Pat Garrett, the Lincoln County Sheriff." which quoted from the Coroner's Jury Report itself.

Here are some other Territorial examples:

On July 18, 1881, *The Las Vegas Daily Optic's* headline was: " 'The Kid' Killed! He Meets His Death at the Hands of Sheriff Pat Garrett, of Lincoln County." It gave identification of the body, as confirmed in the correctly cited Coroner's Jury Report: "An inquest was held on his body today [sic] and the verdict of the jury was 'justifiable homicide' and that Pat Garrett ought to receive the thanks of the whole community ... and that he is truly worthy of a handsome reward."

The July 21, 1881 *Santa Fe Daily New Mexican*, in "Garrett Exonerates Maxwell," confirmed Peter Maxwell as a witness to the shooting, and addressed rumors that he had hidden Billy the Kid in Fort Sumner before the killing. Garrett, protecting Maxwell, a possible traitor, was quoted: "[H]e does not think that Maxwell was in with the Kid ... He says that Pete acknowledged that fear kept him from informing on the Kid."

The July 22, 1881 *Las Vegas Daily Gazette*, in "Words of Commendation and Encouragement," stated: "Immediately on the receipt of the news of the killing of Billy 'the Kid' by Sheriff Garrett, prominent citizens of Roswell and the lower Pecos wrote us ... giving [One wrote] The words, 'God bless Pat Garrett for his good work' will escape many a lip."

Here are some national examples.

July 20, 1881's *The Chicago Daily Tribune* had "Account of the Manner in Which 'Billy the Kid' Was Killed, The Kid Killed;" stated: "[Garrett], who had taken advantage of the dim, uncertain light to get his weapon ready for use, brought it to bear on the Kid, shooting him through the heart at the first pull of the trigger. He died in two minutes without uttering a word. The [Las Vegas *Daily*] *Optic* to-night says of the affair: "Billy the Kid" was the terror not only of Lincoln County, but of the whole Territory; a young desperado who has long been noted as a bold thief, a cold-blooded murderer, having, perhaps, killed more men than any person of his age in the world ... All making rejoices ... It is now in order for Pat Garrett to be well rewarded for his services."

The Weekly Gazette (Colorado Springs Gazette) of July 23, 1881 had "Billy the Kid, At Last the Bullet Finds its Billet, New Mexico's Noted Outlaw Shot by a Sheriff." It stated: "The Gazette has positive information this morning from Fort Sumner of the death of 'Billy the Kid.' This noted desperado was killed at Fort Sumner on the Pecos river on the 14th by Pat Garrett, sheriff of Lincoln county."

One July 26, 1881, under "Champion Murderer," the *Fort Wayne Daily Gazette* stated: "The *Daily Optic* to-night give [sic] an interesting account of the killing of William Bonney, alias Billy the Kid, the noted desperado, at Fort Sumner on Thursday night."

That July 26, 1881 was also the *Savannah Morning News's* "Billy the Kid, A Youth With Nineteen Murders to His Account - The Inhabitants of New Mexico Overawed by a Boy of Twenty-One, Who Was Killed at Sight." It stated: "It is said that there was only one man in Lincoln county, Pat Garrett, who had the nerve to meet [Billy the Kid]. Pat was selected for this very purpose, and started on Billy's trail a few weeks ago, meeting with success ... as the telegraph informs us of Billy's death by his hands."

On August 10, 1881 *The New York Sun*, reprinted from the *St. Louis Globe-Democrat* "The Life of Billy the Kid. His Name Was Billy McCarthy, And He Was Born in New York."

That reprint was also in August 12, 1881's *The Lancaster Intelligencer* as "Billy the Kid, His Name Was Billy McCarthy and He was Born in New York, Murdering a Man at the Age of Sixteen - Made a Deputy Constable - Gen. Lew Wallace's Admiration for the Youthful Desperado, Under Sentence of Death - Killing Two Men in Thirty Seconds - The Kid Killed." It stated: "Billy the Kid was rapidly nearing the inevitable close of his blood-stained career ... Deputy Sheriff Pat Garrett with two companions started on his trail, swearing to capture or kill him or die trying ... Shortly before midnight Garrett went to Maxwell's, and had just seated himself in the dark on the side of Maxwell's bed when the door opened, and in walked the Kid ... [He] leveled his pistols, exclaiming: "Quien es? Quien es? But he delay of asking was fatal. Before the words were off his lips Pat Garrett's bullet was through his heart, and 'Billy the Kid,' the terror of New Mexico, lay a gasping, quivering corpse."

"BRUSHY" HOAX RESPONSE

The "Brushy Bill" hoaxers were left with feeble reliance on non-historical hearsay that Billy the Kid had not been killed, and conspiracy theories that everybody who was a witness was in a conspiracy to conceal that the corpse was not Billy Bonney's.

Thus, in C.L. Sonnichsen's collected papers were typed transcripts of hearsay articles denying the killing. One titled "Denies Garrett's Shot Killed Billy the Kid," from the *El Paso Times* of November 10, 1937, had a Taos, New Mexico businessman named Ben Harbert claiming he saw Billy the Kid in Taos after July 14, 1881. He was quoted: "I know Billy and am convinced it was he."

Another article in Sonnichsen's file used to prompt "Brushy" was in the July 22, 1938 *El Paso Herald Post*, titled "Frontiersman Track Report 'Kid' is Alive." (See page 66 below) It featured showman, Pawnee Bill (Gordon W. Lillie), as an "old frontiersman" going to Albuquerque "seeking to verify reports the Kid escaped into Mexico instead of falling under Pat Garrett's gun" (though it had nothing to do with seeking "Brushy" himself).

CHAPTER 4
OBSTACLE OF THE OUTLAW MYTH OF BILLY THE KID

FAKING A FAKE BILLY BONNEY

The irony of the "Brushy Bill" hoax was that he and his team, without realizing, were faking a fake Billy the Kid. In actuality, the person they knew the least about was Billy Bonney himself. In their day, he was a fictional outlaw created by the Santa Fe Ring's and Lew Wallace's self-serving cover-up of the Lincoln County War as a freedom fight. Billy's book-writing killer, Pat Garrett, with his ghostwriter, Ash Upson, in 1882, merely repeated the outlaw myth in hopes of a dime novel-style best seller. The early 20th century only continued the myth in a pseudo-history book by Walter Noble Burns.

So unwitting "Brushy" built his figment of his imagination on other men's figments of their imaginations. He and his team had no idea of real Billy Bonney's identity, motivations, or times. "Brushy" even called himself the hated, Ring-bestowed, outlaw myth moniker: "Billy the Kid." And Sonnichsen and Morrison, equally ignorant, named "Brushy's" book, *Alias Billy the Kid*.

THE SANTA FE RING'S OUTLAW MYTH OF BILLY THE KID

The Ring's outlaw myth is well illustrated in its first national article which began the fame of the outlaw Billy the Kid, and was entirely fiction. It was a December 22, 1880 *New York Sun* article titled "Outlaws of New Mexico, The Exploits of a Band Headed by a New York Youth, The Mountain Fastness of the Kid and His Followers, War Against a Gang of Cattle Thieves and Murderers, The Frontier Confederates of Brockway, the Counterfeiter."

The article stated:

OUTLAWS OF NEW MEXICO.
THE EXPLOITS OF A BAND HEADED BY A NEW YORK YOUTH.

The Mountain fastness of the Kid and his Followers— War against a Gang of Cattle Thieves and Murderers — The Frontier Confederates of Brockway, the Counterfeiter.

LAS VEGAS, New Mexico, Dec. 20.—One hundred and twenty-seven miles southeast of Las Vegas, New Mexico, is Fort Sumner, once the base of operations against the Indians who committed depredations against the stockmen. The fort was abandoned some ten or twelve years ago, owing to the removal of troops further south, toward the border of Mexico. The property was condemned and sold to Pete Maxwell, a well-known ranchman of the section. Since then it has been a depot of supplies for stockmen and a stage station on the postal route to the Pecos Valley and Panhandle, Texas.

Until recently, on almost any fair day, there might have been seen lounging about the store or engaged in target practice four men, all of them young, neatly dressed, and of good appearance. A stranger riding in the little hamlet would have taken them to be a party of Eastern gentlemen who had come into that sparsely settled region in search of sport. Many who have gone into that country have struck up an acquaintance with these men and found them agreeable fellows. These men are the worst desperadoes in the West, and large parties of armed men are now scouring the country in pursuit of them.

For a number of years the people of eastern New Mexico and Panhandle, Texas, have been harassed by a gang who have run off stock, burned ranches, and committed acts of violence and murder. It was only recently that the leaders and organization of the band were discovered. The leaders are Billy the Kid, so called from his youth; Dave Rudabaugh, Billy Wilson, and Tom O'Phallier, the four loungers about Fort Sumner. The Kid is the captain of the gang. Their fastness is about thirty-five miles nearly due east from Fort Sumner, on the edge of the great Staked Plain. In that region there is a small lake called Las Portales. It is surrounded by steep hills, from which flow numerous streams that feed the little lake. This place the robbers selected for their resort partly on account of its hiding places, but mainly on account of the opportunities it afforded them for stock thieving. No matter from what direction the storm came, it drove to the lake the herds of cattle which roam at large in the rich grazing country. There the band built for themselves one of those rude dugouts so common on the Western frontier, two sides formed by the side of the hill, the other two constructed of sod and dirt plastered together, and the whole covered by a thatched roof. Stockades or corrals were built near by in which to put stolen stock. During pleasant weather the members of the gang lounged about Fort Sumner or other stations in that section. When the storm sent cattle scudding over the plains to the haven afforded by the hill-protected lake basin, the gang would hurry to their rendezvous and cut out from the herds the best cattle, driving them into their corral, whence they were later sent to market. Their booty was large, for they had a vast stock to select from, the whole country for a distance of one hundred and fifty miles either way being a rich, continuous pasture. Besides the active members of the band, there were many who had apparently some settled occupation and made themselves useful in disposing of the stolen cattle. In every town of any size within a radius of 150 miles there were butchers who dealt regularly in this stolen stock. When supplies from roving herds ran short the desperadoes would make a raid on herds that were guarded, attacking ranches and killing or diving off the inmates. Besides their station at Las Portales, they had one at Bosque Grande, fifty miles to the southwest, and another at Greathouse's rancho, fifty miles to the north. Whenever they were pursued when running of stock, they had the choice of three places to which to resort.

The people of the surrounding country finally found the existence of this band unendurable. After repeated searches, which failed, owing to the smallness of the pursuing parties, it was resolved to organize several bands, who should cooperate in a campaign, which should end only when the outlaws were driven out of the country, or their capture, dead or alive, was effected. The authorities of the several counties which bordered on the country ranged over by **the Kid's gang** had been repeatedly petitioned to send out a posse of men to hunt them down, but, as Las Portales was on disputed territory, the authorities were never able to settle upon any plan of action. At last the ranchmen took the matter into their own hands, and the first party they sent out succeeded in getting on the track of a detachment of the gang who were hauling material to Las Portales, where they were building large stock yards. Although the party was not successful in capturing the outlaws, they made the outlaws flit about the country in a more lively manner than had been their wont. This showed that nothing could be done by a small force. A guard was always kept out on the numerous peaks about Las Portales, from which outlook; the country for twenty miles either way could be scanned by the outlaws, so that they could easily elude a small party!

The Panhandle Transportation Company, an association of stockmen of western Texas, banded together for mutual protection, commissioned their superintendent, Frank Stewart, a brave fellow, who was just the man for such work, to organize an expedition against the outlaws. The White Oaks, a flourishing mining camp, organized a band of rangers. Still another party of picked men, under the lead of Sheriff Pat Garrett of Lincoln County, who is considered one of the bravest and coolest men in the whole region, joined in the campaign. In the latter part of November Garrett, with a force of fourteen men, made a dash for Bosque Grande, riding all night, and there succeeded in capturing five of the outlaws. One of them was a condemned murderer who had escaped from jail; another of them was a murderer for whose arrest $1,500 had been offered. These are the sort of men who reinforce the band. Las Portales has long been an asylum for fugitives from justice. Bosque Grande (Great Forest) is situated in one of the most fertile regions of the West, and as the rich lands bordering on the Pecos River are the objective point of many who intend to settle in the Territory, it was thought best to rid that region of the outlaws first, in order that none might be deterred from settling there. Precautions have been taken which will prevent this refuge of the band from ever sheltering them again.

It was expected that the two other parties would work with Garrett's band, but the Panhandle party were delayed, owing to scarcity of feed, and the White Oaks Rangers had their hands full in another quarter. The latter party had a brush with the Kid, Rudabaugh, Wilson, and several others at Coyote Spring, near the Oaks camp, and the outlaws succeeded in escaping, although two had their horses shot from under them. The rangers started back for reinforcements and supplies, and then pressed on after the outlaws, coming upon them at their other station at Greathouse's ranch. It was night when the rangers reached the ranch. They threw up earthworks a few hundred yards from the stockade of the ranch, and when the outlaws rose up in the morning they found themselves hemmed in. The rangers sent a messenger to Jim Greathouse, the owner of this ranch, demanding the surrender of the outlaws. Greathouse replied in person. He came out to the camp of the rangers and stoutly asserted that the outlaws had taken possession of his ranch and that he had no power over them nor anything to do with them. It was considered best to hold Greathouse as a hostage, while Jim Carlyle, the leader of the rangers, heeded to the Kid's request for a conference. A long time elapsed and Carlyle did not return. His men began to feel uneasy about him, and dispatched a note to the renegade chief saying that unless Carlyle was given up in less than five minutes they would kill Greathouse. No reply was received. Soon after the rangers saw

Carlyle leap from the window and dash down the hill toward their entrenchments. He had not gone far, however, when they saw the Kid throw half his body through the window, and, taking deliberate aim, brought down poor Carlyle, killing him instantly. A sharp fight followed, but the outlaws succeeded in making their escape, Greathouse also getting away during the confusion. Before leaving for home with the dead body of their leader, the rangers fired everything about the place, and Greathouse concealed some miles away, saw the smoke of his burning property.

The three parties are now engaged in scouting the country, and will not give up the chase till the country is rid of every one of the outlaws. Money and outfits have been freely offered by men who have large interests in that section. **Government officials are now interested in the campaign, for, in addition to their other crimes, the outlaws have put in circulation a large quantity of the counterfeit money manufactured by William Brockway, the forger. The bills were obtained by one of the gang named Doyle who formerly operated in Chicago, and counterfeit $100 bills in large numbers have been put in circulation among the stockmen and merchants in all that region.**

[AUTHOR'S NOTE: This was the fake news that possibly inspired a Steve Sederwall's 2018 hoax that Billy Bonney was a counterfeiter in cahoots with the Brockway gang; with James Doyle being a real Brockway gang member]

The information that enabled the Government officers to discover the handling of counterfeit money by the Kid's gang came from a freighter named Smith. Soon afterward, while Smith was on his way from Las Vegas to Fort Sumner with a load of freight, he was waylaid and murdered by some of the gang.

William Bonney, alias the Kid, the leader of the band, is scarcely over 20 years of age. He is handsome and dresses well. He has a fair complexion, smooth face, blue eyes, and light brown hair. He is about six feet tall and deceptively handsome. A beautiful bay mare, that he has carefully trained, is all that he seems to care for, unless he reserves some affection for his brace of six-shooters and Winchester rifle, which have helped him out of many a tight place. His care of the beautiful mare is well deserved, for many a time has her fleetness which surpasses that of any other horse in the Territory, saved his life. The Kid is an admirable rider, and as he is always expected to be obliged to take flight, he usually rides another horse, leading his pet behind, in order to make the best time possible on a fresh horse. He is considered a dead shot and much of his time is spent in target practice. He was born in New York State, but his parents removed to Indiana when he was quite small, and thence to Arizona. There in the Tombstone District the Kid killed his first man when he was only 17 years old, and was obliged to leave the country. He came to New Mexico, where he has since lived.

About three years ago a difficulty arose in Lincoln County, New Mexico, between the stockmen and the Indian agent on the reservation. The trouble arose in regard to some cattle that had been purchased for the Indians. Nearly every man in the county was under arms, and the troops were called out by Gov. Wallace to quell the disturbance. The Kid was mixed up in the affair, and had some narrow escapes. On one occasion he was hotly pursued and was obliged to take refuge in a house in Lincoln, which was surrounded by sixty solders. To the demand to surrender, he only laughed and shot down a soldier just to show that he was game. The house was set on fire, when the Kid, after loading up his Winchester Rifle, leaped from the burning building and made a dash for liberty. All the while he was running he kept firing from his Winchester, bringing down a number of his pursuers. Bullets whistled over his head, but he made his escape, and leaping on a horse was soon laughing at his pursuers. There is no telling how many men he has killed. He sets no value on human life, and has never hesitated at murder when it would serve his purpose. Gov. Wallace a few days ago offered a reward of $500 for his capture, and prominent citizens would make up a handsome purse in addition.

Billy Wilson is much the same sort of good looking fellow as his chief. He is about the same build, with dark hair and a slight moustache. He left the Ohio home where his people, who are all highly esteemed, still reside, several years ago. After being engaged in the cattle business in Texas for some time, he came to New Mexico. When the excitement broke out over the new camp at White Oaks, he went there and was engaged in the butchering business. He was always considered a smart, energetic fellow, and was well thought of. In some way the Kid persuaded him to join his party, and it was by him that much of the forged paper was put into circulation.

Tom O'Phallier is a Texan and is also a man of good appearance. He has a ruddy, face, and can be an exceedingly agreeable companion. He has been with the band from the first, and has committed many crimes.

Dave Rudabaugh is 36 years old, and was born in New York city, where he lived until about eight years ago. He has raided over southern Kansas, the Indian nations, Texas, southern Colorado, and New Mexico. It would not be difficult to establish charges of murder against him in any or all of those States and Territories. In Colorado, a few years ago he ran off some Government stock, and, while pursued by a detachment of soldiers, he killed a Sergeant and two privates. He once headed an attack on the Las Vegas jail, in order to liberate one of his friends, and shot down a guard who interfered. He is a thorough desperado in look, word, and action, ready at all times for a fight. He thinks no more of putting a bullet through a human brain than through the bull's eyes of the target before which he is continually practicing. He is 5 feet 8 inches tall, and weighs about 180 pounds. He has a swarthy complexion, black hair and beard, and hazel eyes, whose cruel, defiant expression has often been noted.

The career of the band is about run, for they are hotly pursued, and the chances are that before long they will be killed or captured. It is not expected that the Kid or Rudabaugh will be taken alive, as they will fight to the last.

Another example is the Ring's use of the outlaw myth to prejudice potential jurymen for Billy Bonney's April 8, 1881 trial in Mesilla - where jurymen were ignorant of Lincoln County War issues - the Ring had advertised Billy as a danger to Governor Lew Wallace if he was set free by them. On April 2, 1881, *Newman's Semi-Weekly*" ran "The Kid;" stating:

[The Kid] is a notoriously dangerous character, has on several occasions before escaped justice where escape appeared even more improbable than now, and has made his **brags that he only wants to get free in order to kill three men – one of them being** **Governor Wallace.** Should he break jail now, there is no doubt that he would immediately proceed to execute his threat ... We expect every day to hear of his escape and hope that legal technicalities may not be permitted to render escape more probable.

LEW WALLACE'S OUTLAW MYTH OF BILLY THE KID

Even cited by the "Brushy" hoaxers as a source, was Lew Wallace's culmination of his obsessive outlaw myth articles on Billy the Kid, which reversed his betrayal of Billy's pardon, by blaming Billy and making himself the hero. Only Wallace's death in 1905 ended the hypocrisy. Wallace's final, novella-length article appeared, on June 8, 1902, in *New York World Magazine* as:

"General Lew Wallace Writes a Romance of 'Billy the Kid' Most Famous Bandit of the Plains, Thrilling Story of the Midnight Meeting Between Gen. Wallace, Then Governor of New Mexico, and the Notorious Outlaw, in a Lonesome Hut at Santa Fe." In it, Wallace confirmed the pardon bargain as: " 'Testify,' I said ... 'and convict the murderer of Chapman and I will let you go scot-free with a pardon in your pocket.' " As usual, his outlaw Billy the Kid betrays the bargain. This version was incorporated into his *Autobiography*, advertising his life by Billy's far greater fame. It stated:

GENERAL LEW WALLACE WRITES A ROMANCE OF 'BILLY THE KID' MOST FAMOUS BANDIT OF THE PLAINS

Thrilling Story of the Midnight Meeting Between Gen. Wallace, Then Governor of New Mexico, and the Notorious Outlaw, in a Lonesome Hut at Santa Fe.

Gen. LEW WALLACE, author of "Ben Hur," is completing his autobiography, which will be issued in a few weeks.

The most thrilling chapter in this remarkable personal narrative tells of the midnight meeting in a lonely hut between Gen. Wallace, at the time Governor of the Territory of New Mexico, and "Billy the Kid," the most notorious outlaw the far West has ever produced.

From advance sheets of Gen. Wallace's book the following account of this strange rendezvous has been copied and compiled for the Sunday World Magazine. The story has never been printed in any newspaper or magazine before.

The episode occurred in 1879. The outlaw was at the zenith of his wild career. Gen. Wallace conceived the idea that he might gain certain important information by a face-to-face talk with the outlaw. With much difficulty the meeting was finally arranged. It was not without a strong element of danger to both participants, but they trusted each other and the trust was not betrayed.

The Midnight Rendezvous.

On the night of the meeting two men sat, shortly before midnight, silent and expectant, in the hut which had been chosen for the rendezvous, which was on the outskirts of Santa F, N.M.

Their gaze was fastened on the door, and, as the minutes slipped away the tension grew more severe, the silence more oppressive.

One man was the owner of the rude home that stood desolate in the shifting sands of the great mesa.

The other was Gen. Lew Wallace, Governor of New Mexico.

The hands of the clock pointed to 12.

The hush deepened. Suddenly it was broken by the sound of a resolute knock on the door of the cabin.

"Come in," said the Governor of New Mexico.

The door flew open and, standing with his form outlined by the moonlight behind him, was "Billy the Kid." In his left hand he carried a Winchester rifle. In his right was a revolver. The weapons, quick as a flash, covered the two occupants in the room.

"I was to meet the Governor here at midnight. It is midnight: Is the Governor here?"

The light of the candles flickered against a boyish face, yet the man who stood in the doorway was the most notorious desperado in all the West. He had killed scores of men: he was the quarry of every sheriff from the Rio Grande to the bordering foothills that shut in Death Valley.

The Boy Outlaw.

In facial features "Billy the Kid" was a mere stripling. His narrow shoulders were rounded, his posture slightly stooping, his voice low and effeminate. But his eyes were cold and piercing, steady, alert, gray like steel.

Gen. Wallace rose to his feet and held out his hand, inviting the visitor forward for a conference.

"Your note gave the promise of absolute protection," said the outlaw, warily.

"I have been true to my promise," replied the Governor. "This man," pointing to the owner of the cabin, "and myself are the only persons present."

The rifle was slowly lowered, the revolver returned to its leather holster. "Billy" advanced and the two seated themselves at opposite sides of the narrow table.

Gen. Wallace was able to effect an important arrangement with the outlaw, of which he gives the details. In fact, a very friendly understanding was established between the two.

Explaining the purpose of the interview and its result with "Billy," Gen. Wallace says:

"Shortly before I had become Governor of New Mexico, Chapman, a young attorney in Lincoln, had been murdered. Half a dozen men were arrested, accused of the crime. Among them was Jesse James.

While it was more than probable that one or more of the men charged with the murder were guilty, it was impossible to prove the allegation, for the witnesses, filled with terror, fled the country. **When I reached New Mexico it was declared on every hand that "Billy the Kid" had been a witness to the murder. Could he be made to testify?**

"That was a question on the tip of every tongue.

"I had been sent to the Southwest to pacify the territory; here was an opportunity I could not afford to pass by. Therefore I arranged the meeting by note deposited with one of the outlaw's friends, and at midnight was ready to

receive the desperado should he appear. He was there on time – punctual to the second.

"When 'Billy the Kid' stepped to the chair opposite mine, I lost no time in announcing me proposition.

Agrees to the Plan.

" 'Testify,' I said, 'before the Grand Jury and the trial court and convict the murderer of Chapman and I will let you go scot-free with a pardon in your pocket for all your misdeeds.'

[AUTHOR'S NOTE: After 23 years, Wallace confirmed the bargain.]

" 'Billy' heard me in silence; he thought several minutes without reply.

" 'Governor,' said he, "if I were to do what you ask they would kill me."

" 'We can prevent that,'' said I.

"Then I unfolded my plan. 'Billy' was to be seized while he was asleep. To all appearances, his capture was to be genuine. To this he agreed, picking the men who were to effect his capture. He was afraid of hostile bullets and would run no risk. Another stipulation was to the effect that during his confinement he should be kept in irons. 'Billy the Kid' was afraid also of the loss of his reputation as a desperate man."

The plan agreed upon in the cabin on the lonely mesa at midnight was carried out to the letter. "Billy the Kid" was seized the following morning and confined in the Lincoln County jail. It was here that Gen. Wallace, in spite of the fears of the guards, permitted the outlaw to give an exhibition of his skill with the revolver and the rifle. "Billy," standing or riding, using either the one weapon or the other, sent every bullet true to its mark.

"Billy," said the General, "there's some trick to that shooting. How do you do it?"

"Well, General," replied the desperado, "there is a trick to it. When I was a boy I noticed that a man in pointing to anything he wished observed, used his index finger. With long use, unconsciously, the man had learned to point it with unerring aim. When I lift my revolver, I say to myself, 'Point with your finger.' I stretch the finger along the barrel and, unconsciously, it makes the aim certain. There is no failure; I pull the trigger and the bullet goes true to its mark."

"Billy," though at his own request kept in irons, did not remain long confined. One morning the guards led him to breakfast. Returning, the desperado drawled in the feminine voice that was a part and parcel of his character:

"Boys, I'm tired. Tell the Governor I'm tired."

The manacles slipped like magic from his wrists. The guards stood stupefied, and "Billy the Kid," laughing mockingly, walked leisurely from the jail yard, through the gate and across the street. Easily, gracefully, he threw himself into the saddle on the back of a horse standing near at hand and, putting spurs to the animal, dashed away. "Billy" was gone. He had not escaped in the night; he had walked away in the broad light of day, with his guards, heavily armed, standing about him.

"Boys," I'm tired," he said, and looked them straight in the eyes.

They were not in collusion with the desperado; Gen. Wallace satisfied himself of the fact.

But how account for "Billy's" escape?

Hypnotism, some say – hypnotism or that strange something that lurked in the depths of the steel-gray eyes.

The desperado's freedom, however, was not long-lived. He was arrested soon afterward for a series of murders, and was brought again to the Lincoln County Jail. Patrick Garrett was Sheriff. He was probably the one man in New Mexico who did not fear "Billy the Kid." He was his match in every respect – as calm, as desperate, as certain.

Perhaps "Billy" knew this. At any rate he must have considered himself in desperate straits. He sent for Gen. Wallace. The General refused to respond. Then the outlaw sent him a note. The note said:

"Come to the jail. I have some papers you would not want to see displayed."

"I knew what he meant," said Gen. Wallace, reminiscently. "He referred to the note he received from me in response to which he appeared in the hut on the mesa. He was threatening to publish it if I refused to see him. I thwarted his purpose by giving a copy of the latter and a narrative of the circumstances connected with it to the paper published in the town. It was duly printed and upon its appearance a copy was sent to "Billy" in his cell. He had nothing further to say."

Not Daunted By His Sentence.

In the end the desperado was convicted and sentenced to be hanged. When the sentence was read he stood before the trial judge and said:

"Judge, that doesn't frighten me a bit. 'Billy the Kid' was not born to be hung."

He was a thorough fatalist. He believed he bore a charmed life. He believed he would not die until his "time came," and then death was inevitable.

From the court-room "Billy" was led back to the jail. Nine men were put on guard, and he was never allowed a moment from the sight of one of them.

On the day before that set for his execution one man sat in front of Billy while he ate his dinner. During the meal the guard forgot himself and suddenly stooped. "Billy's" quick eye took in the situation in a glance.

With a leap he sprang upon the bending man and dashed his brains out with his handcuffs. He seized the dead guard's revolver and, his steel-gray eyes gleaming, he walked forward deliberately and routed all the other guards, who ran to the assistance of their comrade.

Once more "Billy the Kid" escaped in the full light of day

through the doors of the jail. He forced a blacksmith to break the manacle chains, seized a good horse that stood nearby and rode away.

He called back as he spurred the animal into a gallop: "Tell the judge that I said "Billy the Kid' was not born to be hung."

But "Billy" had forgotten one thing; he had not reckoned on the character of the man who was Sheriff of the county. He had forgotten Patrick Garrett. Garrett shut his teeth hard, like a man who is determined to accomplish his purpose, no matter the obstacles presenting themselves. He set out to take "Billy the Kid," dead or alive.

Garrett received information that "Billy" had gone back to an old fort in the mountains to see his sweetheart. Garrett followed. He lay in wait in the dooryard of the home of "Billy's" love, and finally his vigil was rewarded when he saw the door open one night and a man step out into the white light of the moon.

His hat was off, he was in his stocking feet and he wore only shirt and trousers. He passed out into the night.

Garrett crept to the door and passed in.

He covered the girl's father with his gun.

"Not a word," he said, and slid behind the headboard of the bed.

The Death of "Billy the Kid."

The door opened again and "Billy the Kid" entered. He seemed to scent danger as a camel scents rain; instinct taught him that something was wrong. He cried to the cowering old man in Spanish:

"Who's here?" he asked. "Who's here?"

Garrett raised his revolver; two shots rang out on the quiet air and the room filled with smoke. A form tottered, then crashed to the floor. In the nerveless hand was a smoking revolver; for the first and last time the notorious New Mexican outlaw had missed his aim. Garrett escaped unwounded. But there were two bullet wounds in the body of "Billy the Kid" and both pierced the heart. Garrett's aim was unerring.

To-day there is a little lowly heap of earth located in Las Cruces, N.M. [sic – Fort Sumner] To the curious stranger some idle native may, now and again, point out this little grave and explain, with a certain pride, that Las Cruces possesses the final resting place of the worst bad man that ever infested the Southwestern border. An ancient Mexican, who sometimes shows this grave to visitors, once made the cautious remark regarding its occupant that, had he lived, he would probably have turned out to be a bad man.

"And how old was 'Billy' when he died?" asked one curious stranger.

"Twenty-one, senor," replied the ancient. "He died, almost one might say, before he fully began to live."

"You say he was bad?" remarked another stranger.

"He is said to have killed many men."

"How many? How many, amigo, had this man killed at the time he himself died?"

"He had killed," replied the ancient Mexican, **"twenty-one men, one for each year of his age,** may the saints defend us," said the Mexican.

[AUTHOR'S NOTE: Wallace's 21 men for 21 years is on one of Billy's Fort Sumner gravestones.]

"He was a good man, and very kind to poor people. Yet, had he lived, he might, according to the opinion of some, have turned into a bad man."

Gen. Wallace also tells in his autobiography how and why "Billy the Kid" started on his career of crime:

A Waif of New York City.

"The man whose deeds of blood had drawn upon him the eyes of an entire nation, was born a New York waif. Before he was more than ten years of age he was brought to Indiana, and in Terre Haute and Indianapolis, where he was reared, he was known as William Bonne. In 1876, when he was about seventeen years old, he suddenly left his home, crossed the Mississippi and went to the country of the men of his kind – the frontier of the far West.

"Billy began his career with an oath to kill John Chisum, his first employer when the lad reached the plains. Chisum and the "Kid' had been unable to agree on terms of settlement for a season's work. The result was the lad's fearful vendetta, sworn not only against Chisum, but against all of Chisum's other employees as well.

" 'For each herdsman employed by you whom I kill," Billy sent him word, "I will deduct $5 from our unsquared account. If I kill you,' he added grimly, 'my bill will be receipted in full.'

"Then his bloody career began. It was not long until William Bonne, the waif, reared in the peaceful surroundings of Indiana, became the most feared man in the Southwest. At the same time, he was the most revered, the most adored and the most respected man in the Territory.

"It was the kind of good reward that sometimes comes to bad men."

PAT GARRETT'S OUTLAW MYTH OF BILLY THE KID

For Pat Garrett and his journalist boarder and ghostwriter, Ashmun "Ash" Upson, the motive in churning out a book by 1882, after Garrett's July 14, 1881 killing of Billy Bonney, was to make money with a sensationalistic rendition of the Ring's outlaw myth, with Garrett representing triumph of law and order. Its title said it all: *The Authentic Life of Billy the Kid The Noted Desperado of the Southwest, Whose Deeds of Daring and Blood Made His Name a Terror in New Mexico, Arizona, and Northern Mexico.*

Its publisher was the New Mexican Printing and Publishing Company (which published the Ringite *Santa Fe New Mexican*), and had as its President Ringite Attorney William Breeden, who was also Vice-President of Ring bosses', T.B. Catron's and S.B. Elkins's, Second National Bank of Santa Fe. Breeden was then in law partnership in Santa Fe with Henry Waldo, who was originally in Catron's law firm. And the book's printer was Charles Greene, a Ringite who printed the *Santa Fe New Mexican*.

Read by "Brushy" and his team in its 1927 second edition, Garrett's book was a major influence. It even had a footnote by its historian-editor, Maurice Garland Fulton, adding a brief summary of the Santa Fe Ring, which they lifted for name-dropping for their hoax, without comprehending its actual role in the history.

BILLY THE KID'S CHILDHOOD

Ash Upson had been a border with Billy Bonney's family in Silver City, so had a starting point for fictionalizing. To be noted is that the claim in Garrett's 1882 book, *The Authentic Life of Billy the Kid*, that Billy was born in New York on November 23, 1859, apparently came from Upson's direct knowledge; and might have also come from Garrett's multiple contacts with Billy himself. As Garrett wrote in the book: "I have known the Kid personally since and during ... the Lincoln County War, up to the moment of his death ... At camp-fires, on the trail, on the prairies, and at different plazas, I have listened to [Billy's disconnected recital of events in his early and more recent life." (Garrett, Page xxvi)

That said, the rest of the childhood and early adolescence was elaborate fiction to manufacture their outlaw boy character and conceal their ignorance of his time in Arizona Territory from 1875 to 1877. The book stated:

> **When young Billy was about twelve years of age, he first imbrued his hand in human blood.** This affair, it may be said, was the turning point of his life, for it outlawed him and left him a victim of his worser impulses and passions. **As Billy's mother was passing a knot of idlers on the street, one of the loafers made an insulting remark**

about her. Billy heard it, and quick as thought, with blazing eyes, he planted a stinging blow on the blackguard's mouth. Then springing out into the middle of the street, he stooped for a rock. The brute made a rush for the boy, but as he passed Ed Moulton, a well-known citizen of Silver City, he received a stunning blow on the ear which felled him, while Billy was caught and restrained. However, the punishment inflicted on the offender by no means satisfied Billy. Burning for revenge, he visited a miner's cabin, procured a Sharp's rifle, and started in search of his intended victim. By good fortune, Moulton saw him with the gun and persuaded him to return it.

Some weeks subsequent to this adventure, Moulton ... became involved in a rough-and-tumble bar-room fight at Joe Dyer's saloon ... He had two "shoulder-strikers" to contend with and was getting the best of them [when] the man who had been one of Moulton's "lifters" ... thought he saw an opportunity to take cowardly revenge on Moulton and rushed upon him with a heavy bar-room chair upraised.

Billy ... saw the motion and like lightning darted beneath the chair. Once, twice, thrice, his arm rose and fell. Then rushing through the crowd, his right hand above his head grasping a pocket-knife, its blade dripping with blood, **he went out into the night, and outcast and a wanderer, a murderer self-baptized in blood ... His hand was now against every man, and every man's hand against him.** (Garrett, Pages 5-7)

Garrett's fictional, young, pre-Lincoln County Billy wandered through Arizona and Old Mexico, and was called Billy the Kid. The book stated luridly: "And thus, from one locality to another was the Kid banished by his bloody deeds and violations of the law ... It was his delight to drop down occasionally on some of his old haunts ... pistol in hand, and jeer at those officers of the law ... to watch their trembling limbs and pallid lips as they blindly rushed to shelter. For all knew and feared Billy the Kid." (Garrett, Page 36)

EVIL BILLY THE KID AND HIS GANG

A central theme in Billy Bonney's outlaw myth, was his having a gang; which was in keeping with the large-scale criminality fabricated for him by the Santa Fe Ring. That yielded the fiction that he was a leader in the Lincoln County War, which subsequently misled "Brushy" and his team. To be noted is that, on December 12, 1880, Billy himself denied this fiction to Lew Wallace, writing: *"I noticed in the Las Vegas Gazette a piece which stated that, Billy "the" Kid, the name by which I am known in the Country was the captain of a Band of Outlaws who hold Forth at the Portales.* **There is no such Organization in Existence.** *So the Gentleman must have drawn very heavily on his Imagination ... There is no Doubt but what there is a great deal of Stealing going on in the Territory. and a great deal of the Property is taken across the [Staked] Plains as it is a good outlet but* **so far as my being at the head of a Band there is nothing of it.**"

Garrett wrote:

> **The Kid had a devil lurking in him.** It was a good-humored jovial imp, or a **cruel and bloodthirsty fiend**, as circumstances prompted. Circumstances favored the worser angel, and the Kid fell ... (Garrett, Page xxviii)
>
> To the Kid the killing [by him] of ["Buckshot"] Roberts was neither cause for exultation or grief. He had further bloody work to do ... On their return to Lincoln, the posse [seeking Tunstall's killers] was disbanded, but most of those comprising it **joined forces with the Kid as their accepted leader.** (Garrett, Pages 76-77)
>
> [After the ambush murder of Sheriff Brady] [t]**he Kid and his desperate gang were now outlawed in Lincoln**, yet they haunted the plaza by stealth and always found a sure and safe place of concealment at [Alexander] McSweens ... (Garrett, Pages 84)
>
> [After the lost Lincoln County War] **the Kid gathered together such of his gang as were fit for duty** and took to the mountains south of Lincoln.

WALTER NOBLE BURNS'S OUTLAW MYTH OF BILLY THE KID

Walter Noble Burns, knowing little real history, was a journalist who, like Pat Garrett, hoped to cash in with the outlaw myth of Billy the Kid with dime novel fabrications for his 1926 *The Saga of Billy the Kid*, borrowing heavily from Garrett's 1882 edition of *The Authentic Life of Billy the Kid*.

For the early years, he copied Garrett's fable of 12 year old Billy murdering for his mother's honor; writing:

> **It was at Silver City, when twelve years old, That Billy killed his first man.** His mother with Billy at her side was on her way from home into the business section to do some shopping ... A group of men lounged in front of a saloon, a young blacksmith among them ... As Billy and his mother passed, the smith ... dropped some light remark ... at Mrs. Antrim ... **Billy flamed at once into violent passion and resentment, picked up a stone, hurled it with all his might at the head of the insulter of his mother** ... Unhurt but blazing with anger, the fellow rushed at Billy ... A man named Moulton ... knocked him down with his fist ... [and] for the time being, closed the incident.
>
> On an evening a few weeks later ... [Moulton became embroiled in a bar room brawl] in Dyer's saloon ... Billy Bonney was ... idly observant ...
>
> The blacksmith saw in the situation an opportunity for revenge ... [H]e sprang from his seat, raised his heavy chair high in the air, aiming it at the back of Moulton's head ... [T]he blow failed on its target ... Billy Bonney ... too, saw an opportunity for revenge and also to render assistance to a friend in distress ... **Whipping out his pocketknife, he rushed upon the blacksmith ... Three times the boy struck with his blade** ... [T]he blacksmith, staggering back, clutched at his heart, pitched headlong.
>
> So, for the first time, the wolf cub tasted blood.
>
> [T]he first murder in Billy's long list – was hall-marked by native expertness in deadliness ...

[His soul] seemed plainly no boy's soul, but rather that of a man with a background of crime already achieved; a soul ... charged with heritage of sinister sophistication.

With his victim at his feet, Billy darted out the door ... The boy slipped out into the night. (Burns, Pages 61, 72-75)

Burns magnified Garrett's evil Kid character; writing:

[Billy] placed no value on human life ... He killed a man as nonchalantly as he smoked a cigarette. Murder did not appeal to Billy the Kid as tragedy; it was merely a physical process of pulling a trigger ... In his murders, he observed no rules of etiquette ... As long as he killed a man he wanted to kill, it made no difference to him how he killed him ... He put a bullet through a man's heart as coolly as he perforated a tin can set upon a fence post. He had no remorse ... (Burns, Page 57)

It is impossible now to name twenty-one men that he killed, though, if Indians be included, it is not difficult to cast up the ghastly total. (Burns, Page 61)

Burns magnified Garrett's fiction of Billy as a leader. He wrote:

[After the death of Dick Brewer at Blazer's Mill] Billy the Kid - eighteen years old, if you please - was now the dominant figure in the situation ... [Brewer's] mantle as leader of the McSween fighting forces descended upon the shoulders of Billy the Kid. The prestige of this youthful desperado as fighter and killer was by this time firmly established. His will, backed by his six-shooter, was the law of the land. He ruled by terror, balked at nothing, and was recognized by friends and enemies alike as the personification of deadliness. (Burns, Pages 108-109)

In dime novel tradition, Burns created a morality tale of law and order prevailing over Billy the Kid's outlawry. He wrote:

Billy the Kid's was the Southwest's most famous desperado and its last great outlaw ... His destructive ... career served a constructive purpose: it drove home the lesson that New Mexico's prosperity could be built only upon a basis of stability and peace. After him came the great change for which he involuntarily had cleared the way. Law and order came in on the flash and smoke of the six-shooter that with one bullet put an end to the outlaw and to outlawry. (Burns, Pages 54-55)

THE "BILLY THE KID" MONIKER

A fatal error of "Brushy" and team was calling him Billy the Kid. For real Billy, it would have been an anathema, and symbol of his prejudicial outlawing. As Billy had written to Lew Wallace on December 12, 1880: *"I noticed in the Las Vegas Gazette a piece which stated that, Billy "the" Kid, the name by which I am known in the Country was the captain of a Band of Outlaws who hold Forth at the Portales. There is no such Organization in Existence."*

Its roots went back to when Billy first came to Lincoln County in October of 1877 to work as a ranch hand for John Henry Tunstall, and was just 17; so was nicknamed by the other employees as simply "Kid."

That partial moniker was first used pejoratively by Governor Lew Wallace in a March 31, 1879 letter to Secretary of the Interior Carl Schurz, to hypocritically denigrate Billy, then risking his life to oppose the Ring in his secret sham arrest for their pardon bargain. Wallace, omitting reality, wrote from Lincoln: *"**A precious specimen nick-named "The Kid,"** whom the Sheriff is holding here in the Plaza, as it is called, is an object of tender regard. I heard singing and music the other night; going to the door, I found the minstrels of the village actually serenading the fellow in his prison."*

The complete moniker appeared for the first time on in the Fort Stanton military Court of Inquiry for potential court martial of Commander Nathan Augustus Monroe Dudley for treasonously supporting the Santa Fe Ring side in the Lincoln County War to enable murder of its freedom fighters. Billy was a key prosecution witness, presenting his eye-witness account of seeing Dudley's soldiers firing a volley at him and others fleeing for their lives.

The moniker was presented in that court on May 23, 1879 by the witness, Susan McSween, whose husband, Alexander, had been killed because of Dudley's action. She heard Dudley use the name. It represented the Ring side's start of Billy's outlaw myth. She was testifying about pleading with Dudley to protect her, her sister, and her sister's children; as follows: "*[Dudley] then got very angry and said it was none of my business, that he would send his soldiers where he pleased, that I have no such business to have **such men as Billy the Kid,** Jim French, and others of like character in my house.*"

Testifying himself in that Court of Inquiry on May 28, 1879, Billy Bonney responded about the forming moniker, which still confused him, as follows:

>   Q. by Recorder [Prosecutor]. What is your name and place of residence?
>   Answer. My name is William Bonney. I reside in Lincoln.
>   Q. by Recorder. Are you known or called Billy Kidd, also Antrim?
>   Answer. Yes Sir ...
>   Q. By Col. Dudley [Attorney for Defense]. In addition to the names you have given, are you also known as the "Kid?"
>   Answer. I have already answered that question, Yes Sir, *I am, **but not "Billy Kid" that I know of***.

On December 3, 1880, the Santa Fe Ring began its press campaign against Billy using a leak of Secret Service Agent Azariah Wild's fabricated reports about a counterfeiting and rustling "Kid gang," with Fort Sumner as its headquarters. That day, the Las Vegas *Gazette* published an editorial by editor-owner J.H. Koogler titled "Powerful Gang of Outlaws Harassing the Stockmen," which stated:

> The gang includes forty to fifty men, all hard characters, the off scouring of society, fugitives from justice, and desperados by profession. Among them are men, with whose names and deeds the people of Las Vegas are perfectly familiar, such as **"Billy the Kid,"** Dave Rudabaugh, Charles Bowdre, and others of equally unsavory reputation ... **The gang is under the leadership of "Billy the Kid," a desperate cuss, who is eligible for the post of captain in any crowd, no matter how mean and lawless.**

By his December 12, 1880 letter to Governor Lew Wallace to deny the Ring's press attempt to frame him, Billy was fully aware of the moniker, calling it *"Billy "the" Kid, the name by which I am known in the Country."*

When Lew Wallace placed his first reward notice on December 22, 1880, in the Las Vegas *Daily Gazette*, it was for "Billy the Kid," proving the moniker's assumed universal recognition by then. Wallace wrote:

BILLY THE KID
$500 REWARD

I will pay $500 reward to any person or persons who will capture William Bonney, alias The Kid, and deliver him to any sheriff of New Mexico. Satisfactory proofs of identity will be required.
LEW. WALLACE,
Governor of New Mexico

On the same December 22, 1880 day that Lew Wallace's $500 reward notice for Billy appeared, Billy gained national fame as Billy the Kid in a long *New York Sun* article titled "Outlaws of New Mexico, The Exploits of a Band Headed by a New York Youth, The Mountain Fastness of the Kid and his followers." With text arguably provided to the paper by the Ring, it stated:

The leaders are **Billy the Kid,** so called from his youth; Dave Rudabaugh, Billy Wilson, and Tom O'Phallier, the four loungers about Fort Sumner. The Kid is the captain of the gang ...
William Bonney, alias the Kid, the leader of the band, is scarcely over 20 years of age. He is handsome and dresses well. He has a fair complexion, smooth face, blue eyes, and light brown hair. He is about six feet tall and deceptively handsome. A beautiful bay mare, that he has carefully trained, is all that he seems to care for, unless he reserves some affection for his brace of six-shooters and Winchester rifle, which have helped him out of many a tight place.

On December 27, 1880, the *Las Vegas Daily Gazette*, published an article by Lucius "Lute" Wilcox about Billy's Stinking Springs capture, titled 'The Kid. Interview with Billy Bonney The Best Known Man in New Mexico, The greatest excitement prevailed yesterday when the news was abroad that Pat Garrett and Frank Stewart had arrived in town bringing with them Billy 'the Kid.' " It stated:

With its customary enterprise, the *Gazette* was the first paper to give the story of the capture of **Billy Bonney, who has risen to notoriety under the sobriquet of "the Kid"** ... **"Billy the Kid,"** and Billy Wilson who were shackled together stood patiently while a blacksmith took off their shackles and bracelets to allow them an opportunity to make a change of clothing.

Describing Billy's transport from the Santa Fe jail to Mesilla, on April 3, 1881 the Santa Fe *Daily New Mexican* in "Something About the Kid," stated:

Tony Neis and Francisco Chaves, deputy U.S. Marshals, arrived Thursday night with **Billy, the Kid,** and Billy Wilson ... At Las Cruces an impulsive mob gathered around the coach and someone asked which is **"Billy the Kid."** The Kid himself answered by placing his hand on [his attorney] Judge Leonard's shoulder and saying "this is the man."

On May 3, 1881, after Billy's April 28, 1881 jailbreak, Lew Wallace repeated his Billy the Kid reward notice in the *Santa Fe Daily New Mexican*; writing:

BILLY THE KID.
$500 REWARD.
I will pay $500 reward to any person or persons who will capture William Bonney, alias The Kid, and deliver him to any sheriff of New Mexico. Satisfactory proofs of identity will be required.
  LEW. WALLACE,
Governor of New Mexico

On May 4, 1881, the day after Wallace's second notice, *Santa Fe Daily New Mexican* reported Billy's jailbreak:

The above is the record of as bold a deed as those versed in the annals of crime can recall. It surpasses anything of which **the Kid** had been guilty, so far that his past offences lose much of their heinousness in comparison with it.

By May 16, 1881, Lew Wallace published his *St. Louis Daily Globe-Democrat* article: "The Thugs Territory, Stage Robbers and Cut-Throats Have Things Their Own Way in New Mexico, Gen. Lew Wallace Anxious to Punish Crime that is So Prevalent - A Chapter About "Billy the Kid;" writing:

[T]he Governor gave a very interesting sketch of the life of **"BILLY THE KID,"** the most noted and desperate character in New Mexico, and who was sentenced to be hanged on the 13th inst., but escaped by killing his guards and defying the entire population of Lincoln to take him ... At the appointed time [for their meeting] GOV. WALLACE was at the house, and exactly at 12 o'clock a knock was heard at the door and in walked **"Billy the Kid."**

On June 18, 1881, Wallace published in the Crawfordsville *Saturday Evening Journal* his article titled "**Billy the Kid**, General Wallace Tells Why the Young Desperado of New Mexico Wanted to Kill Him. A Dashing and Daring Career in the Land of the Petulant Pistol;" writing:

Late newspaper accounts of the exploits of **"Billy the Kid,"** the New Mexico outlaw, have made him the chief among frontier desperados and familiarized readers with his depredations and murdering ... Governor Wallace repaired to the meeting place early, and promptly at midnight, a slight knock was heard at the door and upon response in the inside, **"Billy the Kid"** opened the door and walked in.

Billy's July 15, 1881 Coroner's Jury Report alluded to his moniker as follows: "*[T]he above jury convened in the home of Luz B. Maxwell and proceeded to a room in the said house where they found the body of* **William Bonney alias "Kid"** *with a shot in the left breast*

Billy Bonney's killer, Pat Garrett, featured the by now famous moniker to sell his 1882 book: ***The Authentic Life of Billy the Kid: The Noted Desperado of the Southwest, Whose Deeds of Daring and Blood Made His Name a Terror in New Mexico, Arizona, and Northern Mexico.***

A March 1, 1890, *Lincoln County Leader* interview about Billy's 1881 jailbreak by Gottfried Gauss; stated:

> And so **Billy the Kid** started out that evening, after he had shaken hands with everybody around and after having a little difficulty in mounting on account of the shackle on his leg, he went on his way rejoicing.

The December 10, 1893 *San Francisco Chronicle* carried "Lew Wallace's Foe, Threatened by 'Billy the Kid,' The Writing of "Ben-Hur" Interrupted," which stated:

> The Governor's enemy was no less a personage than the illustrious **"Billy the Kid,"** than whom no man had ever excited more terror on the frontier or given better ground for the dread in which he was held.

On January 6, 1894, Lew Wallace gave a "Billy the Kid" interview to the Weekly *Crawfordsville Review* as "Street Pickings;" stating:

> "When I was governor of New Mexico that territory was and had been for years terrorized by bands of daring and murderous outlaws, at the head of whom was the famous border desperado, **"Billy the Kid"** ... "Two months dragged along and one day at Santa Fe we got the alarming news that **"Billy the Kid"** had murdered his two jailors, stolen a horse and had started for Santa Fe with the open threat, 'Now for the governor and now hang.'

For *The Indianapolis Press* on June 23, 1900, Lew Wallace presented "Gen. Wallace's Feud with Billy the Kid, When the General Was Governor of New Mexico and Billy Bonne Was the Most Dangerous Western Outlaw, He Was a Waif and was Reared in Indiana." Wallace stated:

> So long as I live, I will never lose the image of **Billy the Kid,** as I saw him that midnight in old Santa Fe, back in 1879. There he stands in the doorway of the little adobe house, form outlined by moonlight at his back, face illuminated by glow of the little lamp ... "It was not long until **'Billy the Kid'** became the most daring and notorious of desperadoes.

For *New York World Magazine* on June 8, 1902, Wallace presented a long article as "General Lew Wallace Writes a Romance of 'Billy the Kid' Most Famous Bandit of the Plains, Thrilling Story of the Midnight Meeting Between Gen. Wallace, Then Governor of New Mexico, and the Notorious Outlaw, in a Lonesome Hut at Santa Fe;" stating:

Gen. LEW WALLACE, author of "Ben Hur," is completing his autobiography, which will be issued in a few weeks.

The most thrilling chapter in this remarkable personal narrative tells of the midnight meeting in a lonely hut between Gen. Wallace, at the time Governor of the Territory of New Mexico, and **"Billy the Kid,"** the most notorious outlaw the far West has ever produced ...

In facial features **"Billy the Kid"** was a mere stripling. His narrow shoulders were rounded, his posture slightly stooping, his voice low and effeminate. But his eyes were cold and piercing, steady, alert, gray like steel.

In 1906 Billy appeared in Wallace's late-life *Autobiography*, completed by his wife Susan after he died in 1905. She inserted her May 11, 1879 letter to her son Henry to parrot Wallace's outlaw myth of Billy the Kid, writing:

[W]e hold our lives at the mercy of desperados and outlaws, **chief among them Billy the Kid**, whose boast is that he has killed a man fore every year of his life. Once he was captured and escaped and now he swears, when he has killed the sheriff and the judge who passed sentence upon him and Governor Wallace, he will surrender and be hanged.

In the 1930's, old-timer, John P. Meadows, a cattle rancher living in New Mexico from early 1880, gave interviews to historians about having known Billy Bonney, and performed about it on February 26, 1931 in Roswell, New Mexico, in an historical pageant he named "**Days of Billy the Kid** in Story, Song and Dance." Subsequently, Meadows used his "Days of Billy the Kid" act for serialized newspaper accounts in the *Roswell Daily Record* on March 2nd, 3rd, and 4th of 1931. That year, Meadows also typed a 78 page manuscript with information about Billy the Kid.

And from August 8, 1935 to June 25, 1936, the *Alamogordo News* printed almost forty of Meadows's reminiscence articles.

In 1934, George Coe published *Frontier Fighter: The Autobiography of George Coe Who* **Fought and Rode With Billy the Kid**.

In 1955, as an old-timer, "Teddy Blue" Abbott published *We Pointed Them North: Recollections of a Cowpuncher*. He wrote: "The Lincoln County troubles was still going on, and you **had to be either for Billy the Kid or against him**."

THE "BRUSHY" HOAX'S RESPONSE

"Brushy" called himself an outlaw: the sole identity in his day's Billy the Kid image. This yielded awkward attempts to make his fictional Billy not so bad. But, for this outlaw persona, "Brushy" even fabricated more killings: personally shooting Andrew "Buckshot" Roberts and Bob Beckwith. And by his pardon hearing, as Billy Bonney, poor confused "Brushy" declared that he had killed no one at all.

CHAPTER 5
OBSTACLE OF MORE HISTORICAL PEOPLE AND RECORDS

THE UNKNOWN KEY FIGURES AND DOCUMENTS

Furthering discrediting the "Brushy" hoax was his ignorance of key figures in the history, as well as ignorance of its key documents - like depositions, court transcripts, and investigative notes - all not yet readily available or still undiscovered. And that was a disaster when it came to impersonating Billy Bonney.

INVESTIGATOR FRANK WARNER ANGEL

Attorney Frank Warner Angel was sent, in May of 1878, by President Rutherford B. Hayes, via the Departments of Justice and the Interior, to investigate John Henry Tunstall's murder and Territorial corruption. So, left for posterity, left were Angel's 39 depositions and reports: October 4, 1878's *In the Matter of the Examination of the Causes and Circumstances of the Death of John H. Tunstall a British Subject*; October 4, 1878's *In the Matter of the Lincoln County Troubles*; October 3, 1878's *In the Matter of the Investigation of the Charges Against S.B. Axtell Governor of New Mexico*; and October 2, 1878's *Examination of Charges against F. C. Godfroy, Indian Agent, Mescalero, N. M.*

Aware of the Santa Fe Ring, but obstructed in its exposure by the corrupt administration of President Rutherford B. Hayes, frustrated Angel also provided incoming Territorial Governor Lew Wallace with a secret notebook listing people's Ring affiliations; some of which Billy himself would have known.

As to real Billy Bonney, like all Ring victims, he would have been aware of Angel as a ray of hope. And he knowingly risked his life to give Angel his June 8, 1878 deposition to get justice for his beloved employer, John Tunstall. And real Billy would have been angered by Angel's forced cover-up leaving the Ring untouched, except for scapegoated Governor Samuel Beach Axtell.

The problem for "Brushy" and team was that Angel's writings were not discovered until 1956 by historian Frederick Nolan, leaving them big holes in faking life as Billy.

ALEXANDER MCSWEEN

Frank Warner Angel's longest deposition came on June 6, 1878 from Attorney Alexander McSween, and was used for his Tunstall report. Unknown to "Brushy Bill" and his team, it described the Santa Fe Ring's malicious prosecution of McSween by a fake embezzlement case involving proceeds of a life insurance policy of an Emil Fritz. It made clear that McSween was not Tunstall's business partner, so the Ring's attachment of Tunstall's property was malicious prosecution also.

Unaware, "Brushy" team were left with name-dropping and fabricating, even calling Tunstall McSween's partner.

ATTORNEY IRA E. LEONARD

Billy's best friend in a high place was Attorney Ira E. Leonard, widow Susan McSween's attorney against past Commander N.A.M. Dudley for murdering her husband and arson of her home in the Lincoln County War Battle. Leonard, bravely took her case against Dudley right after the Ring murdered her first lawyer: Leonard's office-mate: Attorney Huston Chapman.

Leonard met Billy in March of 1879 when Billy was in his sham arrest in Lincoln for his Lew Wallace pardon bargain; and he witnessed Billy's fulfilling that bargain by testifying in the April, 1879 Grand Jury against Attorney Huston Chapman's murderers. Reporting on Billy's behalf to Wallace in a letter of April 20, 1879, Leonard stated: "*I will tell you Gov. that the prosecuting officer of this Dist. [William Rynerson] is no friend to the enforcement of the law.* **He is bent on going for the Kid & ... is proposed to destroy his testimony & influence.** *He is bent on pushing him to the wall. He is a Dolan [Ring] man and is defending him by his conduct all he can.*"

Leonard also aided the prosecution at Dudley's Fort Stanton Court of Inquiry. So he heard Billy risking his life when volunteering testimony against that past Commander; and consequently became his loyal attorney into 1881.

During Leonard's 1879 litigation against Commander Dudley, he sustained a near assassination by the Ring. Billy, nearby in his Patrón house sham arrest for his pardon bargain with Governor Lew Wallace, was aware of that April 25, 1879 attempt.

Leonard also tried to get Billy a pardon through the Secret Service. He then represented him in his 1881 Mesilla hanging trial, getting Billy's federal indictment for the "Buckshot" Roberts killing quashed; but quitting after a likely Ring death threat; leaving Billy with Ring-biased court-appointed attorneys.

But this central advocate in Billy's life, and all the dramatic events connected to their relationship, were unknown to "Brushy" and team, except for token name-dropping.

COMMANDER NATHAN AUGUSTUS MONROE DUDLEY AND SUSAN McSWEEN

Comparable in magnitude to the Angel reports, is the Court of Inquiry for possible court martial for Fort Stanton's Commander N.A.M. Dudley. It included Billy's own testimony on May 28th and 29th of 1879. Billy's testimony, on his own anti-Ring initiative, in an honest court, would have achieved Dudley's court martial: Billy saw three of his white soldiers shoot at least one volley at civilians, including Billy, escaping the burning McSween house.

Additionally, the foul-mouthed racism of "Brushy Bill" towards Dudley's black troops was belied not only by Billy's lack of it, but by the fact that he would have known that black 9th Cavalrymen, Private James Bush and Sergeant Huston Lusk, had also risked their lives to testify against Dudley.

As will be seen, the Dudley Court of Inquiry transcript had been discovered, but Morrison had decided that, at $100, it was too expensive. (See page 335 below) Instead he apparently got some garbled renditions of a few of its pages for "Brushy" to parrot. And "Brushy" and team, unaware that Billy's testimony was part of his anti-Ring agenda, left "Brushy" making-up that it was part of the pardon bargain with Lew Wallace.

SECRET SERVICE OPERATIVE AZARIAH WILD

As fatal to the "Brushy" hoax as was the Coroner's Jury Report, was "Brushy's" and team's total ignorance that the

Secret Service, a Treasury Department branch, had played a pivotal role in Billy Bonney's life and death. The Secret Service reports of Special Operative Azariah Wild were not made known until Leon Metz's 1974 book, *Pat Garrett: The Story of a Western Lawman.* So missing for the hoax were how Billy was tracked and captured, and how he lost a second chance for a pardon.

By likely Santa Fe Ring intervention with Secret Service Chief, James Brooks, Azariah Wild had been sent to New Mexico Territory from September to December of 1880, ostensibly to track counterfeiters, but, in fact, to eliminate anti-Ring Billy Bonney and his remaining freedom fighting, Regulator compatriots. New Orleans based Operative Azariah F. Wild, was one of 40 in the country. He wrote daily reports; thus, recording information about Billy Bonney in a format like the following; giving the date for the events documented, then the date on which he wrote the report:

U.S. Treasury Department
SECRET-SERVICE DIVISION

New Orleans District

James J. Brooks,
   Chief U.S. Secret Service

Sir: I have the honor to submit the following, my report as _Chief_ Operative of this District for _Monday_ the _29th_ day of _December,_ 18 _79,_ written at _New Orleans, Louisiana,_ and completed at _9_ o'clock A M on the _30th_ day of _December,_ 18 _79_

Wild was duped by Ringmen into believing that Billy headed a counterfeiting and rustling gang. So Wild helped Pat Garrett become both Sheriff of Lincoln County and a Deputy U.S. Marshal to track down Billy. But Billy's attorney, Ira Leonard, proposed to Wild that Billy would testify against the actual counterfeiters in exchange for a pardon. Billy even wrote to Wild confirming the offer, as reported by Wild in his October 8, 1880 report.

Ringites, however, influenced Wild to arrest Billy at the pardon meeting. Canny Billy, however, robbed the mail coach having Wild's reports, discovered the fatal plan, and avoided the meeting. But he lost the second pardon chance.

EMIL FRITZ'S LIFE INSURANCE POLICY CASE

Since "Brushy" and team were unaware of the historical context of Santa Fe Ring's bloody Territorial take-overs, they missed the horror of the Fritz life insurance policy collection, used to maliciously prosecute Attorney Alexander McSween for embezzling to falsely entangle Ring competitor, John Tunstall, by falsely naming him McSween's partner to leave him vulnerable to assassination. Emil Fritz, was the deceased original partner in Lincoln's Ring-backed store called "The House." Billy even had to be restrained from shooting Ringite Sheriff William Brady's deputies attaching property at Tunstall's store. Billy then witnessed Brady's posseman murdering Tunstall with excuse of those attachments. Billy presented this in his June 8, 1878 deposition to Frank Warner Angel.

SHERIFF WILLIAM BRADY

Lincoln County Sheriff William Brady was the Ring enforcer for the Fritz insurance policy case's fake embezzlement charge, with mission to kill Tunstall and McSween. He was such a danger to McSween, that Deputy Adolph Barrier - from McSween's arrest site in Las Vegas for the embezzling case - kept him in personal custody to protect him. And, on April 1, 1878, when McSween was about to return to Lincoln for his Grand Jury trial, the Regulators - including Billy - knew Brady and his deputies would kill him; and ambushed Brady and his deputies to save McSween. It was for the Brady killing that Billy got his hanging sentence.

"Brushy" and team knew none of this; consequently had no idea why Brady was killed.

PAULITA MAXWELL

Another fatal error was "Brushy's" missing the love of Billy's life, Paulita Maxwell, for whom he risked death to return to Fort Sumner after his April 28, 1881 jailbreak, instead of going to Old Mexico. She was the daughter of deceased Lucien Bonaparte Maxwell, past owner of the 2 million acre Maxwell Land Grant and founder of Fort Sumner.

Their love story was confirmed in an unpublished letter by historian, Walter Noble Burns. On June 3, 1926, he wrote to

Jim East, one of Pat Garrett's Stinking Springs possemen: "*I also know that the Kid and Paulita were sweethearts.*" Nevertheless, in his 1926 book, *The Saga of Billy the Kid*, Burns, leery of libel litigation, only wrote: She and Billy the Kid were friends, and the friendship of this goods, pure girl was a gracious influence on his life." (Burns, Page 180)

Also, Jim East's letter of May 20, 1926 to a Judge William B. Burgess gave the scene of captured Billy's parting with Paulita (whose married name was then Jaramillo).Its copy is in Sonnichsen's papers, but its significance was missed, with the scene merely used for prompting a "Brushy" fable about trading his tintype (as Billy the Kid) to an "Indian girl" (lifted from Walter Noble Burns's *The Saga of Billy the Kid*). (See page 349 below) East wrote: "I was much interested in the statement made by Mrs. **Paulita** Jaramillo. At the time of the capture of Billy the Maxwells were living at Fort Sumner, and when we brought the prisoners in Mrs. Maxwell sent the Old Navajo woman over with a request to Captain Garrett to allow Billy to be sent over to her house **so that her daughter Paulita and she could bid him good-bye**. So Garrett detailed Lee Hall and I to guard Billy over – he being shackled to Dave Rudabaugh. Then Mrs. Maxwell asked Lee and I to unlock Billy from Dave and **let Paulita go into another room with him for an affectionate farewell** – but of course we had to refuse, **although all the world loves a lover.**"

THE HOAX'S RESPONSE

After "Brushy Bill" was denounced as an imposter in his November 30, 1950 pardon hearing, William V. Morrison, went into over-drive rationalizing the failure. But not comprehending that ignorance of Paulita was fatal (which was why he failed to coach "Brushy" on it), he wrote on April 14, 1951 to Robert N. Mullin with double-talk: "I must agree that ["Brushy"] did not remember where the town of Fort Sumner was located. Neither did he recall the name of **Pablita Maxwell. Maybe he did not hear about them down through the years** (some seventy odd years) like the rest of them heard. Then again, maybe he was nervous and excited over the intimidation .... Who knows?"

THE SANTA FE RING

Pivotal to New Mexico Territory's 1870's history, and unknown to "Brushy" and team, were the freedom fights against the rapaciously expanding Santa Fe Ring. Its Territorial "boss" was

Thomas Benton Catron; his Washington, D.C. "co-boss" was Stephen Benton Elkins. Billy, who became a political zealot in the fight, would have known the freedom fighting cause.

Tunstall wrote, on April 27, 1877: *"Everything in New Mexico, that pays at all (you may say) is worked by a "ring."* (Nolan, *Life and Death,* of *John Henry Tunstall,* Page. 213)

Alexander McSween's February 23, 1878 letter to just-murdered Tunstall's father, John Partridge; stated: "**[Tunstall] understood well from the U.S. Attorney [Catron] to the lowest magistrate that there was a combination and determination to keep down independence. This combination is known as the "Santa Fe Ring."** (Nolan, *Documentary History of the Lincoln County War,* Pages 206-207)

The day before the start of the Lincoln County War Battle, and five days after outlaw John Kinney was used by Ringite Lincoln County Sheriff George Peppin for horrific massacre of McSween-side Hispanic residents of San Patricio, Billy wrote his July 13, 1878 "Regulator Manifesto" to Catron's brother-in-law, Edgar Walz, managing his Lincoln County Carrizozo cattle ranch, It stated: *"We are all aware that your brother-in-law,* **T.B. Catron sustains the Murphy-Kinney party** *... Steal from the poorest or richest American or Mexican, and the* **full measure of the injury you do, shall be visited upon the property of Mr. Catron**." "Brushy" and team were unaware of massacre or "Manifesto."

On November 14, 1878, soon after arriving in the Territory as Governor, Lew Wallace wrote to his friend Absalom Markland: *"I came here, and found a "Ring" with a hand on the throat of the Territory. I refused to join them, and now they are proposing to fight me in the Senate. Ex Delegate Elkins is head-center in Washington.*

Billy's attorney, Ira Leonard, wrote to Lew Wallace on May 20, 1879 about "The House's" partners: *"They were a part and parcel of the Santa Fe Ring that has been so long an incubus on the government of this Territory."*

"Brushy" and team merely name-dropped the Ring as a bunch of corrupt politicians from the editor's note by historian, Maurice Garland Fulton, in the 1927 edition of Pat Garrett's *The Authentic Life of Billy the* Kid. Fulton wrote:

> Garrett is one of the few writers of the Lincoln County War who has had the frankness and courage to mention

Catron's name in connection with it. [Catron] is the figure that looms up behind the Murphy and Dolan faction. As the president of the powerful First National Bank at Santa Fe, he furnished the money needed by Murphy and Dolan in their business, of course taking mortgages which at the close of the War gave him possession of their store and its stock of goods. Catron was also a cattle raiser, and in some sense a dominating figure in that industry in the western part of the county. **Besides all this he was a powerful member of the clique of politicians and business men called in those days the "Santa Fe Ring," which largely controlled the Territory of New Mexico.** (Garrett, Page 59)

THE BILLY BONNEY TINTYPE

Billy Bonney appears in the flesh, at about age 20, in a full-length tintype photograph, forcing "Brushy" to match-up, and yielding mistakes because he and Morrison were unaware of tintypes' right-to-left reversal. So "Brushy" claimed to be *left handed*, since Billy's *right hand* his cocked over his Colt 44's butt. "Brushy" and Morrison also seized on details: like Billy's *right* ear being pushed by his right-tilted hat brim, to claim that "Brushy's" *left* ear was deformed! Small hands were claimed by "Brushy" to match the fable that Billy escaped the Lincoln courthouse-jail by slipping off his handcuffs; when Billy's actual hand, cocked beside his gun butt, is normal-sized.

PUBLIC IGNORANCE AS SALVATION

"Brushy Bill" Roberts got a hearing only because of public ignorance of Billy the Kid's complex history, and the prevalence of Billy Bonney's outlaw myth, which had proliferated as mainstream books and movies.

PART II

THE REAL BILLY BONNEY

CHAPTER 1
BILLY THE KID HISTORY

REAL HISTORY

Central to debunking the "Brushy Bill" imposter hoax, is Billy Bonney's real history. It is a complex, colorful, traumatic life of a brilliant, charismatic, teenaged, literate, bi-cultural resistance fighter against the Santa Fe Ring; fit amazingly into just 21 years. Most of it was unknown to "Brushy Bill" Roberts. All of it was a problem to the modern "Billy the Kid Case" hoaxers.

* * * * * * * * * * * * *

In a full-mooned, New Mexico Territory night, as bright as day, the 21 year old, homeless youth, Billy Bonney, with trusting stockinged feet, approached the porticoed, two story, Fort Sumner mansion of the Maxwell family, at about a quarter to mid-night.

That day, July 14, 1881, was the third anniversary of the start of the six day Lincoln County War Battle, which had left him branded as the outlaw, "Billy the Kid." But, to himself, he was a freedom fighter: the last Regulator and that bloody War's only participant to be convicted and sentenced to hanging.

That July night, he intended to cut a dinner steak from the side of beef hanging, at the patrón's generosity, on the mansion's north porch. But first he would check in with that patrón and town owner, Peter Maxwell, at his south porch's corner bedroom.

Asleep in that mansion was Billy's secret lover, Maxwell's sister, Paulita, seventeen, and just pregnant with Billy's child. Also there was a never-emancipated Navajo slave, Deluvina; purchased as a child by Peter's and Paulita's fabulously wealthy, deceased father, Lucien Bonaparte Maxwell. Then, the family lived in Cimarron, a New Mexico Territory town in Colfax County, which Lucien had founded on his and his wife's almost two million acre land grant, named after himself.

That was before Lucien was cheated in the sale of that Maxwell Land Grant by unscrupulous lawyers, Thomas Benton Catron and Stephen Benton Elkins, who used their profits to propel their Santa Fe Ring. As Billy knew, their corrupt collusion of public officials still held New Mexico Territory in a stranglehold. Billy, as a hero in the failed Lincoln County War of 1878, had fought that Ring. If he was thinking about his mortal danger, he knew its source was that Ring. If he thought about injustice, its focus would have been his promised pardon withheld by departed Territorial Governor, Lew Wallace.

That July of 1881 day was 2½ months since Billy's jailbreak escape from his scheduled May 13th hanging. He knew that Lincoln County Sheriff Pat Garrett would be in pursuit. Garrett had captured him on December 22, 1880 at Stinking Springs for his hanging trial. And, in Billy's April 28, 1881 escape from Garrett's Lincoln jail, he had shot dead Garrett's deputy guards: James Bell and Robert Olinger. Garrett would kill him on sight.

When first tracking Billy in late 1880, Garrett had also killed Billy's friends, Tom O'Folliard and Charlie Bowdre - missing Billy only by accident in two consecutive ambushes: at Fort Sumner and Stinking Springs. In fact, at the Stinking Springs capture of Billy and his companions, Garrett killed Bowdre by mistaking him for Billy: the target for which the Ring had made him a sheriff.

To be near Paulita, Billy had recklessly chosen return to Fort Sumner, instead of fleeing to Old Mexico, the natural choice given his bi-culturalism. But he relied on the Maxwell family's protection, as well as affection of the townspeople he had known since late 1877. It would take betrayal to bring his death.

Billy's life had been trauma-filled. Possibly illegitimate, he was a second son, born on November 23, 1859, in New York City, as Henry McCarty. Raised in Indiana and Kansas with his brother, Josie, by his mother, Catherine, he became "Henry Antrim" after she married a William Henry Harrison Antrim, in 1873, after they moved to New Mexico Territory. Antrim became a miner; and the family lived in Silver City. He was a rejecting parent, evicting Billy at 14½ to homelessness when Catherine died of tuberculosis in 1874. But Billy's longing for a father remained, and he sometimes used the name "Antrim" for himself.

In Silver City's school, Billy learned Spencerian script. He also became fluent in Spanish; and, atypically, was equally comfortable in Anglo and Hispanic sub-cultures in those racist times. By 1875, 15½ year old Billy spent his last year in Silver City doing petty thievery, and butcher shop and hotel work; while altercations with local boys revealed his violent temperament.

By that September, Silver City Sheriff, Harvey Whitehill arrested him for burglary, and laundry and revolver robbery; his adult accomplice having escaped. Facing ten years hard labor - Territorial statutes making no provision for juveniles - Billy achieved his first dramatic escape: through the jail's chimney. He then fled westward to Arizona Territory's little town of Bonita.

In Arizona, as Henry Antrim, Billy again combined work – as a cook at a small hotel - with crime: stealing military blankets, saddles, and horses; while fatefully developing shootist skills. In 1876, incarcerated at local Fort Grant's guardhouse with his older, thieving accomplice, John Mackie, he escaped through a roof ventilation space. But he defiantly stayed in Bonita, relying on his rustling charges being dropped on a technicality: his first demonstration of risky behavior for his wish to have a "home."

On August 17, 1877, Billy's life again changed horrifically. His argument at Bonita's Atkins Cantina with a bullying blacksmith named Frank "Windy" Cahill, escalated to his fatally shooting that unknowably unarmed man. Billy escaped on a stolen horse. The Coroner's Jury declared him - as Henry Antrim - guilty of homicide, though in absentia; ignoring self-defense. So, at 17, Billy was almost hanged for murder. He escaped back to New Mexico Territory with an alias: "William Henry Bonney" or Billy Bonney. "Bonney" was possibly his mother's maiden name.

In New Mexico Territory, by the next month of September, 1877, Billy attached himself to familiar sociopaths in Jessie Evans's murderous and rustling Santa Fe Ring-affiliated gang. And since all Ringites ended up immune to prosecution and profited financially, intelligent and energetic Billy, unknown to history, would have likely had a wealthy and long life.

But Billy had a conversion. He met a kind, wealthy, newcomer: Englishman, John Henry Tunstall, a Ring competitor. By the next month, October of 1877, Billy left Jessie Evans's gang to become Tunstall's youngest ranch hand. Tunstall's men affectionately nick-named this teenager "Kid." Tunstall became the lost father found; even gifting him, under the Homestead Act, with a ranch on the Peñasco River in partnership with another employee, half-Chickasaw, Fred Waite. That was likely Billy's proudest and most optimistic moment.

Billy had stumbled into a noble cause: ending Ring oppression. His gunman skill now elevated him as a protector of the good. His hair-trigger temper became vehemence for justice. And the town of Lincoln, as well as Tunstall's ranch on the Feliz River, became home. But Billy's tragic destiny was unrelenting. After only 4½ months, this idyllic time ended with Tunstall's Ring murder.

Lincoln, site of the future Lincoln County War Battle, already had sustained Ring abuses through the mercantile monopoly of "The House": a huge, two-story adobe, general store run by its local Ring bosses - Emil Fritz, Lawrence Murphy, James Dolan, and John Riley - for secret partner, Ring boss, Thomas Benton Catron. They bled cash-poor Mexicans and Anglo homesteaders with usurious credit. Redress was impossible, since law enforcement and courts were Ring-controlled. Terror reigned. In 1875, when local rancher, Robert Casey, defeated Murphy in a Lincoln election, he was killed the same day. Three weeks later, Lincoln's anti-Ring, Mexican community leader, Juan Patrón, was shot by Riley; though accidentally surviving as a limping cripple.

Hope began in late 1876 with arrival of English merchant, John Tunstall; persuaded to settle in Lincoln by resident attorney, Alexander McSween, a Ring opponent; but once legal counsel to "The House," and aware of its abuses. Tunstall planned to defeat the Ring by fair mercantile and ranching competition. But that inadvertently put him in direct competition with Catron's own secret monopolistic plans for Lincoln County: use of "The House" for beef and flour contracts to Fort Stanton and the Mescalero Indian Reservation; a Pecos River cow camp fronted by "The House;" and take-over of dying Lawrence Murphy's huge ranch, which he made his Carrizozo Land and Cattle Company, under management of his brother-in-law, Edgar Walz.

By 1877, Tunstall built - just a quarter mile northeast of "The House" - a general store containing his Lincoln Bank. He made Catron's cattle competitor, cattle king John Chisum, that bank's president. And he founded two cattle ranches to wrest from "The House" its beef and flour contracts. He even exposed Ringite Lincoln County Sheriff William Brady's embezzlement of tax money to buy rustled cattle for Catron's cow camp and Carrizozo ranch. So Tunstall and McSween qualified for the Ring's hit list.

Ringmen preferred to kill with guise of legality. So they entangled Tunstall in fabricated criminality, starting with false prosecution of Alexander McSween, then attorney for the estate of "The House's" partner, Emil Fritz, who died intestate in 1874, but had two local siblings and a life insurance policy. The Ring seized on that policy. In 1877, McSween obtained its $10,000 proceeds from its dishonestly withholding New York City insurance company, minus $3,000 to the collections firm - leaving $7,000 minus his fees. Knowing that "the House" was going bankrupt from Tunstall's competition, and wanted that money from Fritz's local heirs, he retained it while seeking other heirs in Germany.

In December of 1877, McSween left on business to St. Louis with his wife and with Tunstall's business associate, John Chisum. The Ring pounced, declaring McSween an absconding embezzler of the Fritz insurance policy money. Ring boss Catron, then U.S. Attorney, issued McSween's warrant for apprehension in Las Vegas, New Mexico. Chisum was jailed too in retaliation for backing Tunstall. On February 4, 1878, McSween had his hearing in Mesilla under Ringite District Judge Warren Bristol (later Billy's hanging judge), who indicted him for embezzling. The intent was McSween's incarceration and killing in Lincoln by its Ringite Sheriff, William Brady. But McSween was saved by the honorable Deputy Sheriff, Adolph Barrier, from his Las Vegas arrest site, who kept him in protective personal custody.

But Judge Bristol had set other traps for assassination of McSween and Tunstall. Bristol's indictment did two things. First, he set McSween's bail at $8,000, with approval only by Ringite District Attorney William Rynerson; who refused all bondsmen to leave McSween open to Sheriff Brady's fatal seizing at any time.

The second was Tunstall's trap. Bristol attached McSween's property to the sum of $10,000 - falsely deemed the embezzled total - as surety if he was convicted at that April's Grand Jury. Then Bristol lied that Tunstall was in partnership with McSween, to attach Tunstall's property also. And Bristol empowered Sheriff Brady to do attachment inventories at their properties. This harassment was intended to provoke Tunstall and his men to violence to justify Tunstall's killing in "self-defense."

But Tunstall merely responded that any man's life was worth more than all he owned. Hardened Billy, with Tunstall just three months, must have been overwhelmed by this novel idealism.

So the Ring urgently grasped the property attachments to fake justified killing; knowing that the April Grand Jury would likely exonerate McSween, ending the Ring's opportunity for prosecution-related killing of Tunstall.

So, on February 18, 1878, when Tunstall sought to transfer his fine horses, which were immune to the attachment, from his Feliz River Ranch to Lincoln, Brady lied that it was theft of attached property, and sent his posse of Deputies, Ring rustlers, and Jessie

Evans's outlaw gang after him and his men, including Billy. Tunstall, becoming isolated, was murdered, his horse slain; with both corpses mutilated. This martyrdom, coupled with more Ring outrages intended to terrorize the citizens into submission, instead triggered the Lincoln County War.

Sheriff Brady refused to arrest the murderers. So anti-Ring Justice of the Peace John "Squire" Wilson issued warrants for James Dolan and his other possemen. For service, he appointed Billy and Fred Waite as Deputy Constables under Town Constable Atanacio Martinez. Billy had already given Wilson an affidavit as to first-hand knowledge of Tunstall's murderers. But Brady shielded them by illegally casting Billy, Waite, and Martinez into Lincoln's pit jail. And he confiscated and kept Billy's Winchester '73 carbine - likely a gift from Tunstall.

Next, "Squire" Wilson defied the Ring by deputizing Tunstall's foreman, Dick Brewer; who, in turn, made Tunstall's men, including now-released Billy, his possemen to serve those murder warrants. Billy, then 18, was still a lawman.

Meanwhile, Attorney Alexander McSween, in mortal danger from Brady and the Ring, went into hiding with Deputy Sheriff Barrier; mostly in the nearby Hispanic town of San Patricio.

By March of 1878, Dick Brewer's posse had captured Tunstall murder possemen, William "Buck" Morton and Frank Baker. They were shot attempting escape. Billy was in the firing group.

At that point, including "Windy" Cahill, Billy Bonney was now involved in three killings.

The Ring hit back. Ringite Governor Samuel Beach Axtell, by illegal proclamation, removed Wilson's Justice of the Peace powers to retroactively outlaw Dick Brewer's posse; then declared Sheriff William Brady to be Lincoln County's only law enforcer.

Enraged, Tunstall's men named themselves "Regulators" after pre-Revolutionary War freedom fighters. Included were Tunstall's men - Billy; Dick Brewer, Fred Waite; John Middleton; Jim "Frenchie" French; farmers, George and Frank Coe; and homesteader, Charlie Bowdre - and Chisum's cattle detective, Frank MacNab. Brewer was made leader. Only one month after Tunstall's death, Billy was being schooled in politics of revolution.

Sheriff Brady's next chance to assassinate McSween was April 1, 1878, when McSween returned to Lincoln for his Grand Jury embezzlement trial. That morning, to save him, Regulators with carbines, and Billy with a revolver, ambushed Brady and his three deputies from behind an adobe corral wall at Tunstall's store. Brady and Deputy George Hindman died. Recklessly, Billy, with Jim French, ran out to retrieve his confiscated Winchester '73 carbine from Brady's body. Both got leg wounds from firing surviving deputy, Jacob Basil "Billy" Matthews. But Billy regained his symbol of father-figure Tunstall. (It is likely the carbine held in Billy's famous tintype two years hence.)

Three days later, on April 4, 1878, Deputy Dick Brewer, seeking Tunstall's stolen horses, led Billy, John Middleton, Fred Waite, Frank Coe, George Coe, and Charlie Bowdre to Blazer's Mill - a privately owned, way station and grist mill within the Mescalero Indian Reservation. Accidently encountered was Tunstall murder posseman, Andrew "Buckshot" Roberts, for whom they had a warrant. Roberts fired his Winchester carbine at Bowdre, who shot him in the belly. Roberts's bullet had hit Bowdre's belt buckle, ricocheted, and wrenched George Coe's revolver, mutilating his trigger finger. Another Roberts shot hit Middleton's chest, though Middleton survived. Then Roberts killed Brewer, later dying himself from Bowdre's wound. Billy had not fired a shot. Roberts had demonstrably resisted arrest murderously, necessitating self-defense response. But Ring boss Catron, as U.S. Attorney, seized on this killing to file his federal indictment against the Regulators, including Billy, claiming the murder site was the Mescalero Reservation, under federal control.

Billy's murder involvement now totaled six men; though only "Windy" Cahill was demonstrably by his hand.

At the April, 1878, Lincoln County Grand Jury, McSween was exonerated for embezzling. He bravely continued his anti-Ring fight, backed by the Regulators; though John Chisum had dishonestly reneged on paying them. Fighting injustice sufficed. And Billy, their hot-headed fearless zealot, was becoming an inspiration - with McSween as his new father substitute.

McSween's lawful tactic was seeking high-level intervention to expose Tunstall's Ring assassination, because murder of a foreign citizen could elicit a Washington, D.C. investigation. He filed a complaint with the British ambassador and President Rutherford B. Hayes, accusing U.S. officials of murdering Tunstall. In response, investigating attorney, Frank Warner Angel, was sent by the Departments of the Interior and Justice. Arriving May 4, 1878, Angel took 39 depositions. Billy, volunteering for one, risked his life and entered the national stage.

Public optimism of Ring defeat grew further when the Lincoln County Commissioners appointed neutral John Copeland as the Sheriff replacing Brady. He even deputized Regulator, Josiah "Doc" Scurlock, to recover Tunstall's stolen horses. Still a lawman, Billy was on Scurlock's posse. And Wilson, ignoring Axtell's proclamation, continued as Justice of the Peace.

Optimism was short-lived. New Regulator leader, Frank MacNab, was murdered in ambush on April 28, 1878 by Ringite Seven Rivers rustlers. By May 28th, because John Copeland forgot to post his tax collecting bond, Governor Axtell, by another proclamation, removed him and appointed as Sheriff, Ringite George Peppin, Brady's deputy, present at Brady's killing.

War fervor built, with furious Regulators and Mexicans calling themselves "McSweens." Billy's affiliation with local, firebrand youth, Yginio Salazar, and Billy's closeness to Hispanic residents of nearby San Patricio and Picacho, had arguably brought them all into the McSween alliance. By April 30, 1878, McSweens were skirmishing with Ring partisans, known as "Murphy-Dolans."

McSween again hid, often in San Patricio. On July 3, 1878, in revenge, Sheriff George Peppin, with John Kinney's Ring-rustler gang from Mesilla, massacred some residents and destroyed their farm animals and property. In response, on July 13th, the "Regulator Manifesto" was sent to Catron's brother-in-law, managing his Carrizozo ranch, threatening retaliation against Catron. Signed "Regulator," it was likely created by Billy.

The Lincoln County War's culminating Battle began the next day: July 14, 1878. McSween, with 60 men - Regulators and Hispanic residents of San Patricio and Picacho - occupied Lincoln. Reflecting McSween's intended peaceful victory was that his wife, Susan, and her sister with five young children, remained in his double-winged house; along with the sister's attorney husband's law intern, Harvey Morris.

McSween's men took strategic positions in houses throughout the mile-long town, most of whose inhabitants had fled. When Seven Rivers rustlers and John Kinney outlaws joined James Dolan and Sheriff George Peppin, Billy; Yginio Salazar; Tom O'Folliard; and San Patricio men - José Chávez y Chávez, Ignacio Gonzales, Florencio Chávez, Francisco Zamora, and Vincente Romero - rushed to McSween's house, joining guard, Jim French.

Though Ring men occupied foothills south of Lincoln, they were held at bay for five days by shooting McSweens, now winning. But Alexander McSween had not realized that Fort

Stanton's new Commander, Lieutenant Colonel N.A.M. Dudley, was beholden to the Ring. McSween was also reassured by the Posse Comitatus Act, passed the month before in Washington, D.C., baring military intervention in civilian disputes.

On July 16th, Dudley began illegal invention by sending to Lincoln, for "fact-finding," 9th Cavalry Private Berry Robinson, who was almost hit in gunfire. On July 18th, James Dolan used Ringite Lincolnite, Saturnino Baca, McSween's tenant, to lie that his wife and children were at risk from the McSweens.

The next day, July 19th, violating the Posse Comitatus Act, Dudley marched on Lincoln with 39 troops - white infantry, black 9th Cavalry, and white officers - two ambulances; a mountain howitzer cannon; and a Gatling machine-gun, that period's most terrifying weapon. Panicked McSweens - except for those in his besieged house - fled north across the nearby Bonito River. Dudley himself threatened McSween with razing his house if any soldier was shot. He then left three soldiers there to inhibit its defenders' shooting from it, and ordered three more to accompany Sheriff Peppin as a shield. Next, by death threats, he forced Justice of the Peace Wilson to write arrest warrants for McSween and his men as attempting murder of Private Robinson to feign reason for his intervention. Then he encamped at the east side of Lincoln.

Empowered by the troops, Sheriff Peppin's outlaw posseman set fire to McSween's house's west wing. His family was evacuated after Dudley refused McSween's wife's plea to save him.

By nightfall, the McSween house conflagration - worsened by an exploding keg of gunpowder for bullet-making - left all trapped in the east wing. At about 9 p.m., escape was attempted into fire-lit shooting Ringites. With Billy ran law intern, Harvey Morris, whom he saw fatally shot. And before Billy escaped across the Bonito River, at the property's rear - to rescue by fellow Regulators - he witnessed Dudley's treasonous crime: three of his white soldiers, imbedded with the assailants, fired a volley at those escaping. Arguably, they had even killed Morris.

Then shot dead were Alexander McSween, Francisco Zamora, and Vincente Romero. Yginio Salazar survived with two bullets in his back. Symbolizing horror, McSween's starving, yard chickens ate the eyeballs of his corpse. Again was Ring murder and mutilation in Lincoln County to gain treacherous victory.

But people were unaware of Ring influence in Washington, D.C. Investigator Frank Warner Angel, after documenting crimes of Governor S.B. Axtell, U.S. Attorney Catron, and Sheriff Brady's posse, was apparently forced to deny that U.S. officials were involved in Tunstall's murder; though Catron had to resign as U.S. Attorney. President Hayes scapegoated Governor Axtell, replacing him with Civil War General Lew Wallace. But Angel secretly sought justice by giving Wallace a notebook listing Ringites, and an exposé on the Santa Fe Ring, printed in 1877.

Though most Regulators fled the Territory, Billy stayed and carried out the Regulator Manifesto's retaliatory rustling with Tom O'Folliard and Charlie Bowdre - who had relocated to Fort Sumner with his wife Manuela. For his stolen stock, Billy used non-Ring outlets: Pat Coghlan in the western part of the Territory; and Dan Dedrick. Dedrick was a counterfeiter and rustler owner of Bosque Grande, a ranch 12 miles south of Fort Sumner. With his two brothers, he also owned a livery stable in White Oaks, a town about 45 miles northwest of Lincoln. That livery was another stock outlet for Billy. Billy also sold rustled horses in Tascosa, Texas; where he wrote a subsequently famous, bill of sale to a friendly doctor, Henry Hoyt, for an expensive sorrel horse - likely dead Sheriff Brady's. He also got money by gambling. He was again a homeless drifter. That would now be permanent.

Amidst public hope, on October 1, 1878, new Governor, Lew Wallace, took office. A high-achieving elitist, he was the son of an Indiana governor; a Civil War Major General; an Abraham Lincoln murder trial prosecutor; author of best-selling novel, *The Fair God*; and was writing *Ben-Hur A Tale of the Christ*. He had sought an exotic ambassadorship, like to Turkey, not governorship of backwater New Mexico Territory. So, to dispatch with Lincoln County "troubles" without confronting the Santa Fe Ring, a month after arriving, he issued, a general Amnesty Proclamation; though excluding those already indicted. Billy had been indicted for the Brady, Hindman, and Robert killings.

There were more sources of hope. The new Sheriff, George Kimbrell - appointed to replace Sheriff George Peppin, who had resigned - was anti-Ring. And McSween's intrepid widow, Susan, had brought an attorney named Huston Chapman to Lincoln to charge Commander N.A.M. Dudley with the Lincoln County War Battle's murder of her husband and arson of her home.

In that atmosphere of legal scrutiny, James Dolan made peace overtures, first to Susan McSween, then to Billy - a proof of that teenager's acknowledged Ring threat. Billy and his Hispanic compatriots could instigate another uprising - as Thomas Benton Catron feared.

The Billy-Dolan peace meeting was fatefully scheduled on the February 18, 1879 anniversary of Tunstall's murder. It ended in calamity. As James Dolan; Billy; Jessie Evans and Jessie's new gang member, Billy Campbell; and Billy's Regulator friends, Tom O'Folliard and Josiah "Doc" Scurlock, walked Lincoln's dark street after the meeting, they encountered Chapman. Dolan and Campbell fired at point-blank range, killing him, then ignited his clothing. Billy was again an eye-witness. And again there was murder and mutilation in Lincoln County.

Chapman's murder forced Governor Wallace to go to Lincoln - after procrastinating for five months after arriving. Once there, he avoided Ring confrontation, using the Ring's concoction of vague trouble-making "outlaws and rustlers." The Ring had also given him a list of Regulators as the "outlaws," with Billy as "the Kid."

Focus on Billy - likely through James Dolan - made Wallace offer the astronomical reward of $1,000 for him. Billy responded with a pardon plea letter, on March 13, 1879, offering Wallace his eye-witness testimony against Chapman's murderers in exchange for annulling his Lincoln County War indictments. It was Billy's bold and calculated risk to negate Ring power over himself.

His articulate letter, in his personalized Spencerian script, led to his March 17, 1879, nighttime meeting with Wallace in Justice of the Peace Wilson's Lincoln house. Evidence indicates that anti-Ring Wilson had also covertly backed Billy's plea. And Billy believed Wallace agreed to his pardon bargain.

To avoid assassination before testifying, Billy requested, from Wallace, sham arrest. (He had already seen Ring murders of John Tunstall, Alexander McSween, Harvey Morris, Francisco Zamora, Vincente Romero, and Huston Chapman.) He was kept in the home of his Lincoln friend, Juan Patrón, the town Jailer. Wallace, housed next door, interviewed him and got his additional letter - intimately signed "Billie" - about Lincoln County War issues.

Billy fulfilled his pardon bargain the next month by testifying in the Grand Jury. He got indictments of Chapman's killers, with James Dolan and Billy Campbell for first degree murder, and Jessie Evans as accessory. But Ringite District Attorney William Rynerson, colluding with Judge Bristol, had Billy's trial venue for his indictments switched from Lincoln to Doña Ana County to guarantee a hanging verdict. Still Wallace issued no pardon.

By that April of 1879, Alexander McSween's widow, Susan, retained Attorney Ira Leonard, Chapman's office-mate from Las Vegas, to prosecute Dudley. So Dudley, likely advised by

Catron, his attorney for past court martials, got defamatory affidavits to ruin her credibility. And he requested a military Court of Inquiry, where he would be defended by Catron's law firm member, Henry Waldo. And on April 25th, the Ring tried unsuccessfully to assassinate Ira Leonard to stop the case.

Wallace, after removing Dudley as Fort Stanton's Commander, testified against him in the 1879 Court of Inquiry, though still not confronting the Ring. Billy, again risking his life, testified also, for his own anti-Ring agenda. He devastatingly reported the three white soldiers firing a volley at him and escaping others: meaning officers; meaning under Dudley's orders; meaning violating the Posse Comitatus Act and justifying court martial, and even hanging. Billy's courage made Ira Leonard take him as client.

By July of 1879, the biased Court of Inquiry exonerated Dudley. And Billy, with no pardon and imminent transport to Mesilla for a hanging trial, exited his bogus jailing.

The Ring recouped. By October of 1879, Susan McSween lost her civil trial against Dudley in Mesilla, to which her venue had been changed by Judge Bristol. That month, Bristol also voided James Dolan's Chapman murder indictment based on no witnesses daring to appear for a trial. Dolan, certain of immunity, had even taken over Tunstall's store. Tunstall's Feliz River ranch was given by the Ring to Dolan, Riley, and Rynerson; and Billy's Peñasco River ranch went to Jacob Basil "Billy" Matthews, head posseman for Tunstall's murder. And there was a more subtle Ring victory: Wallace's humiliating loss in the Court of Inquiry made him shun Lincoln County "troubles" and Billy's pardon.

Billy's future killer, Patrick "Pat" Floyd Garrett, had arrived in New Mexico Territory's Fort Sumner in 1878. Born to an Alabama plantation family, relocated to Claiborne Parrish, Louisiana, when 9½ - and Billy was just born - he had even been willed a slave. After the Civil War, he had drifted to Texas, where he possibly murdered a black man, before becoming a buffalo hunter from 1876 to 1878 with two partners and a kid named Joe Briscoe. Garrett murdered Briscoe, but claimed self-defense to avoid prosecution. On the range, he never met fellow buffalo hunter, John William Poe; but later, his, Poe's, and Billy's histories would merge on the night of July 14, 1881.

In Fort Sumner, tall Garrett met transient kid, Billy Bonney, gambling at Hargrove's or Beaver Smith's Saloons. They were given townspeople's nicknames, "Big Casino" and "Little Casino," for their poker playing and height discrepancies.

The original Fort Sumner was built in 1865 by the U.S. government on desert flatlands east of the Pecos River for soldiers guarding Bosque Redondo: a concentration camp for 3,500 Navajos and 400 Apaches, until their scandalous starvation caused release of the Navajos to their homeland in 1868; the Apaches having already escaped. In 1870, Fort Sumner was purchased by Lucien Bonaparte Maxwell, one of the Territory's richest men. Converting it into a town around its parade ground, and using its thousands of acres for sheep raising, he settled there with his wife, Luz Beaubien; daughters, including Paulita; and son, Peter. Retained was the military cemetery for his family. It would receive Billy's body, to lie beside Pat Garrett's earlier shooting victims: Billy's Regulator pals, Tom O'Folliard and Charlie Bowdre. Maxwell died in 1875, leaving the town to his wife and son, Peter; who became the family's ruin through mismanagement. But when Pat Garrett and Billy Bonney gambled there, Fort Sumner was still thriving.

Lucien Maxwell's wealth was from marrying Luz Beaubien, an heiress of the almost two million acre Beaubien-Miranda Land Grant, and by buying its shares from her siblings. In 1870, he sold it as the Maxwell Land Grant; but was cheated by his attorneys, Thomas Benton Catron and Steven Benton Elkins, who resold it for double the money. That profit fortified their Santa Fe Ring, as they enriched themselves with railroads, banks, and mines. Catron eventually owned six million acres - more than anyone in U.S. history. In the Lincoln County War period, he was Billy's lethal enemy, with the Ring branding him as the murderous outlaw "Billy the Kid" to justify exterminating him. By 1912's New Mexico statehood, Catron became one of its two first senators.

By 1878, before the Lincoln County War, Pat Garrett and Billy Bonney led separate lives, though connected by Fort Sumner's Gutierrez sisters: Juanita, Apolinaria, and Celsa. Billy befriended Celsa, married to her cousin, Saval Gutierrez, a Maxwell sheep herder. Billy's July 14, 1881 death walk would start at their house. Garrett married Juanita, who soon died of a possible miscarriage. In 1880, he married Apolinaria, with whom he had eight children. It was a double marriage with his Fort Sumner, friend, Maxwell's foreman, Barney Mason, later a spy assisting Garrett's capture of Billy.

In 1878, Garrett had struggled with unemployment. At Fort Sumner, he drove a wagon for Peter Maxwell; helped a local hog raiser, Thomas "Kip" McKinney; and bartended at Hargrove's

Saloon. Then came 1880 and the opportunity of his life. For Lincoln County's November election, the Ring needed a compatible Sheriff. To qualify, Garrett moved with his wife, Apolinaria, to that county's town of Roswell; adding, as a boarder, an unemployed journalist named Ashmun "Ash" Upson. In 1882, Upson would ghostwrite Garrett's book about killing Billy the Kid.

By 1880, the Ring's outlaw myth propaganda had advertised Billy's gunman reputation. That almost achieved his killing on January 3, 1880 at Fort Sumner's Hargrove's Saloon. A Texan bounty hunter named Joe Grant tried to shoot him in the back. Saved by Grant's gun's misfiring, Billy retaliated fatally. Obvious self-defense, that killing was not legally pursued.

Billy was now linked to killings of seven men: Frank "Windy" Cahill, William Brady, George Hindman, Andrew "Buckshot" Roberts, William "Buck" Morton, Frank Baker, and Joe Grant.

That 1880, when Billy's now-famous tintype photograph was taken in Fort Sumner, Billy may have heard first whispers of his outlaw myth as a rustler and murderer. The Ring was setting its legal trap for eliminating him, since he refused to flee, and was impossible to kill or capture with his partisan backing.

Apparently using Santa Fe Ring "co-boss" Stephen Benton Elkins's Washington, D.C., connections, the Chief of the Secret Service, James Brooks, was contacted for what would arguably be one of that agency's first political murders. Formed in the Civil War as a branch of the Treasury Department to combat counterfeiting, the Secret Service could pursue other crimes at its discretion, and could provide funding for informers and posses.

The scheme involved co-ordination of Catron's Lincoln minions, with James Dolan initiating the investigation by reporting receipt of four counterfeit $100 bills from local counterfeiters at his Lincoln store (Tunstall's prior store which he had taken over). The Operative would then be fed information by Dolan himself; by Catron's brother-in-law, Edgar Walz, at his Carrizozo ranch; and by Ringite U.S. Attorney Sidney Barnes. And by 1880, the Ring was confident that Governor Lew Wallace's only mission was protecting himself, and would not pardon Billy or interfere with killing him. So Billy and remaining Regulators, Charlie Bowdre and Tom O'Folliard, would be presented as murderous rustlers linked to the counterfeiting gang. The only missing piece was an Operative who was adequately gullible.

By September 11, 1880, Secret Service Special Operative Azariah Wild was sent to Lincoln, and proved an ideal dupe by lazy reliance on his Ringite informers. Though Wild initially recognized that the counterfeit bills Dolan got were from a youth, Billy Wilson, who was linked to the counterfeiter, Dan Dedrick, who was reputed to also have a printing press, he was duped into thinking Billy was involved. In fact, Billy occasionally used Billy Wilson for his retaliative rustling, along with a "Dirty Dave" Rudabaugh, and past Regulators, Tom O'Folliard, Josiah "Doc" Scurlock, Charlie Bowdre, and Jim "Frenchie" French. And Billy used Dan Dedrick and the White Oaks livery stable as an outlet for his rustled stock.

Wild also was tricked into believing that Billy was in the country's largest counterfeiting and rustling gang. By that December, came the Ring's *New York Sun* article, using Wild's leaked reports for "Outlaws of New Mexico, The Exploits of a band headed by a New York Youth, War Against a Gang of Cattle Thieves, Murderers, and Counterfeiters." Now Billy was alias "the Kid." The Ring had launched his national outlaw myth.

But the Ring's plot almost backfired when Azariah Wild was told by Attorney Ira Leonard that his client, Billy Bonney, would testify *against the counterfeiters* in exchange for the pardon not granted by Lew Wallace. It was obvious that in Billy's dealings with Dan Dedrick, he had become aware of the activities. Billy had even gifted Dedrick his tintype, which became famous. And, as with his prior pardon bargain for testifying against Ringites, Billy was willing to convict people doing reprehensible crimes.

On October 8, 1880, Wild wrote in his daily report to Chief James Brooks that he himself would arrange a pardon for Billy in exchange for that testimony. But Wild confided that pardon plan to his Ringite handlers, who convinced this dupe that Billy, staying in Fort Sumner, was actually the leader of the immense rustling-counterfeiting gang! So, in his report for October 14, 1880, Wild wrote that he intended to arrest Billy at the meeting for the pardon bargain. But Billy was cautious. He held up the stagecoach carrying Wild's mail, read that report, and avoided apprehension by avoiding the meeting with Leonard and Wild. So another pardon chance was lost.

The Ring, determined to eliminate Billy, expanded the scheme to getting a Lincoln County Sheriff willing do it. The current Sheriff, George Kimbrell, who had assisted in Billy's sham arrest for the pardon bargain, was a McSween-side sympathizer.

The Ring chose Pat Garrett. Secretly, Wild worked with him to form a dragnet to capture Billy and his "rustler-counterfeiter gang;" while, for the upcoming sheriff's election, Garrett was advertised as a law-and-order man to new gold-rush settlers in White Oaks, unaware of Lincoln County War issues, but a third of Lincoln County's voters.

In the November 2, 1880 election, Pat Garrett got 358 votes to Kimbrell's 141. Wild, convinced by his Ring contacts that Kimbrell protected the "Kid gang," also gave Garrett Territory-wide power for the capture by appointing him Deputy U.S. Marshall. Unaware, Billy would have wrongly thought that Garrett's lawman authority was limited to Lincoln County, not Fort Sumner's San Miguel County, where he stayed.

And unaware of his locally publicized "outlawry," Billy still brought stolen horses to the Dedrick's White Oaks livery.

On November 22, 1880, a White Oaks posse ambushed Billy, Tom O'Folliard, Billy Wilson, Tom Pickett, and "Dirty" Dave Rudabaugh at nearby Coyote Spring, shooting dead two of their horses before Billy's group escaped. Five days later, that posse attacked them again at the way station ranch of "Whiskey" Jim Greathouse, 45 miles northeast of White Oaks; accidentally killing one of their own men, Jim Carlyle, but blaming Billy.

That accusation prompted Billy's only letter of 1880 to Governor Lew Wallace. On December 12th, he wrote, denying his outlawry and murdering of Jim Carlyle. He even described his Robin Hood role of aiding the downtrodden. Wallace never answered. Instead, on December 22nd, he placed a Las Vegas *Daily Gazette* notice: "Billy the Kid: $500 Reward." He would repeat it in the *Daily New Mexican* on May 3, 1881, after Billy's jailbreak. His betrayal of the pardon bargain was complete.

By December of 1880, dreadful days began for Billy. Deputy U.S. Marshall Pat Garrett, backed by Azariah Wild, had assembled Texan posses to ride after Billy, since New Mexicans, to whom he was an anti-Ring hero, refused. Garrett's first ambush was on December 19, 1880, when Billy, Tom O'Folliard, Charlie Bowdre, Billy Wilson, Tom Pickett, and Dave Rudabaugh rode into Fort Sumner. O'Folliard was shot dead. The rest escaped.

Billy's group tried to flee the Territory in a snowstorm; but stopped, about 16 miles from Fort Sumner, on December 21, 1880, at a rock-walled, windowless, shepherds' line cabin at Stinking Springs. There Garrett ambushed them the next morning, killing Charlie Bowdre, whom he mistook for Billy, his intended victim.

The rest surrendered. It would be seven more months before Garrett succeeded in his mission to kill Billy.

And Azariah Wild, his own mission completed, left the Territory, unperturbed that he had found no mass of counterfeit bills, no counterfeiting-rustling gang, and had not even sought Dan Dedrick's alleged printing press.

Garrett transported his prisoners by train, via Las Vegas, New Mexico, to the Santa Fe jail. Billy was held there from December 27, 1880 to March 28, 1881, because the Ring awaited completion of the railroad to Mesilla to impede any rescue. But Billy nearly escaped anyway by tunneling out with fellow prisoners.

From his cell, Billy wrote four unanswered letters to Wallace, in 1881, pleading for his pardon: writing on March 4th: *"I have done everything that I promised you I would, and you have done nothing that you promised me."* On March 2nd, he had threatened: *"I have some letters which date back two years and there are Parties who are very anxious to get them but I will not dispose of them until I see you."* Wallace never got over that audacity or his own guilt, reworking the pardon obsessively till the end of his life in vindictive fictionalized articles on the outlaw "Billy the Kid."

Billy's first Mesilla murder trial, under Ringite Judge Warren Bristol, began on March 30, 1881, with jurors unaware of Lincoln County War issues, and without any Lincolnites daring to be witnesses for his defense. Attorney Ira Leonard represented him for past U.S. Attorney Catron's June 21, 1878 federal indictment, Case Number 411, the United States versus Charles Bowdre, Josiah Scurlock, Henry Brown, William Bonney alias Henry Antrim alias the Kid, John Middleton, Steven Stevens, John Scroggins, Frederick Waite, and George Coe for the murder of Andrew "Buckshot" Roberts. It was first because the Ringites likely considered it air-tight.

But, surprising everyone, Ira Leonard got it quashed as invalid, since the federal government had no jurisdiction over Blazer's Mill, the murder site; because private property, like it, was under Territorial jurisdiction. Its being surrounded by the federally-controlled Mescalero Reservation was irrelevant.

Remaining were only the Brady and Hindman Territorial indictments; and, though Billy been firing in the group of Regulators, he had only a revolver lacking accurate range.

But, suddenly, Ira Leonard withdrew, likely after a Ring threat. That was disastrous for Billy. He got Ring-biased, court appointed attorney, Albert Jennings Fountain, who considered him an outlaw, along with co-counsel John D. Bail, a Ringite Catron friend.

On April 8th and 9th of 1881, was Billy's Brady murder trial. His Spanish-speaking jury, given no translator, heard only prosecution witnesses - including James Dolan. After Judge Bristol's biased instructions (with translator) made Billy's mere presence equal to firing the fatal shot, the jury found him guilty of first degree murder; its sole punishment being hanging. On April 13th, Judge Bristol set Billy's hanging date for May 13th, to limit time for appeal. Billy was to be hanged in Lincoln by its Sheriff, Pat Garrett.

From the Mesilla jail, Billy wrote to Attorney Edgar Caypless - conducting his replevin case against Stinking Springs posseman, Frank Stewart, for stealing his racing mare at Stinking Springs - hoping to get money from her sale to pay for an appeal.

Ironically, the new Lincoln jail, where Billy was incarcerated to await hanging, was in the past "House," which Catron had sold to Lincoln County for its courthouse, with second floor as jail.

On April 21, 1881, Billy arrived to Sheriff Garrett's custody. For Billy's 24 hour guard, Garrett deputized a White Oaks man, James Bell, and a Seven Rivers man, Bob Olinger. Garrett's further precaution was shackling Billy at wrists and ankles, with securing to a floor ring - all to guarantee his hanging death.

But on April 28th, with Garrett away collecting White Oaks's taxes, Billy escaped. He either used a revolver hidden in the outhouse, or seized Bell's. A likely accomplice was caretaker, Gottfried Gauss: Tunstall's past cook, and witness to the Ring's Lincoln County War atrocities. Billy shot Bell dead as the man fled down the jail's stairway to sound alarm.

Deputy Bob Olinger, across the street at the Wortley Hotel lunching with jail prisoners, either heard the shot or was directed to the ambush. Billy waited at the second-floor east window, and killed him with his own Whitney double-barrel shotgun.

Billy then spent hours using a miner's pick, supplied by Gauss, to break his leg chain to enable riding; while gathered loyalist Lincoln townspeople, in passive resistance, did nothing to stop him. He finally rode away on a pony supplied by Gauss.

As of that April 28, 1881 escape, Billy was involved in the killing of nine men; James Bell and Robert Olinger adding to Frank "Windy" Cahill and Joe Grant as Billy's only provable victims.

Of the dead, Billy would have said that Cahill's and Grant's killings were in self-defense; that he was a legal posseman at the group shooting of escaping, arrested, Tunstall murderers, William "Buck" Morton and Frank Baker; that his gun lacked range to hit Sheriff William Brady or Deputy George Hindman, and their killings by the Regulators were to save Alexander McSween from murder by them; that he had not shot Andrew "Buckshot" Roberts - a Tunstall murderer and murderer of Dick Brewer – who fired at his group, and was killed solely by Charlie Bowdre in self-defense; and that Deputy James Bell, after refusing to be tied, had tried to run for help, so was killed to save himself from unjust hanging (and Bell had been on the White Oaks posse, and possibly killed Jim Carlyle, then falsely accused him).

Only Seven Rivers rustler, Bob Olinger, would have been admittedly hated as being in each Lincoln County War period crime - Tunstall's murder, Frank MacNab's ambush murder, and the War's skirmishes and Battle. Billy's rage was so great, that he smashed apart Olinger's shotgun to throw it on his corpse, delaying his own escape.

That count of nine killed men - with only four certain - remained as Billy's final true tally.

Billy's escape route was across the Capitan Mountains to the Las Tablas home of Yginio Salazar. He next went south, possibly intending to go to Old Mexico, and visited rancher friend, John Meadows. But he then reversed northeast to Fort Sumner and Paulita, where he hid in the Maxwells' sheep camps, confident of protection by the Maxwells and townspeople.

Garrett's two deputies for the pursuit of Billy to Fort Sumner - John William Poe and Thomas "Kip" McKinney - did not know Billy. Poe, a buffalo hunter, past Deputy U.S. Marshall in Texas, cattle detective, and recent White Oaks settler, had met Garrett during the Wild-assisted tracking of the "Kid gang." McKinney knew Garrett from their 1878, hog farming days. And they were unaware of the Santa Fe Ring, the Lincoln County War freedom fight, or Billy's role; knowing only outlaw myth propaganda.

Once in Fort Sumner, Garrett, doubting Billy's presence as too foolhardy, was urged by Poe to stay. On July 14, 1881, Poe, a stranger to the townspeople, did reconnaissance in the town; and also checked with Sunnyside postmaster, Milnor Rudulph, seven miles to its north. Poe became convinced Billy was nearby.

That night, he, Garrett, and McKinney planned an ambush in Peter Maxwell's bedroom, with Maxwell as traitor. Unknown accomplices likely directed Billy to Maxwell's bedroom, where Garrett waited, with Poe and McKinney outside to kill Billy if he managed to escape through the door to the porch.

Near midnight, Billy proceeded from the converted barracks house of Celsa and Saval Gutierrez, carrying their butcher knife across the parade ground to cut a dinner steak in light of the almost-full huge moon, hovering at the horizon. He first went toward Maxwell's bedroom; but seeing Poe, asked in Spanish who he was, then entered.

Inside, to Maxwell, in bed as decoy, Billy asked again in Spanish who was there, possibly sensing Garrett in the darkness. Garrett quickly fired two shots; the first was fatal. In terror, Maxwell ran out to the porch, almost getting shot by Poe, primed for back-up killing. Then Garrett returned to the room with Poe and McKinney, and made sure Billy was dead.

The townspeople held a night time wake for Billy in their carpenter's shop. The Coroner's Jury, the next day on July 15, 1881, had as intimidating President, Postmaster Milnor Rudulph, a Ringite who had helped take over the Legislature in 1872 to block anti-Ring bills. The Coroner's Jury Report, in Spanish, was written by Fort Sumner's Justice of the Peace Alejandro Segura, and sent to the District Attorney of the First Judicial District: Ringite William Breeden, T.B. Catron's close friend and also Territorial Attorney General. The frightened juryman had no alternative but to sign the conclusion: "[O]ur verdict is that the deed of said Garrett was justifiable homicide and we are unanimous in the opinion that the gratitude of all the community is due to the said Garrett for his deed and he is worthy of being rewarded."

Ring terrorism was now complete. Silence fell for a generation before any dared contradict the Santa Fe Ring's outlaw mythology of Billy the Kid. And the Santa Fe Ring's role in the history was buried along with Billy Bonney.

CHAPTER 2
BILLY BONNEY'S CHAMPIONS

THOSE WHO REALLY KNEW BILLY

In the 20th century, Billy Bonney's aging Lincoln County War period contemporaries finally felt safe enough to contradict the Santa Fe Ring's outlaw myth propaganda in print. They confirmed his brilliance, charisma, bi-culturalism, and fluency in Spanish. He had a zealot's fervor in the Lincoln County War, in which he was a freedom fighting soldier. None would have seen him as the outlaw as portrayed by "Brushy Bill." And any remaining legitimate witnesses refused William V. Morrison's request for them to sign affidavits attesting to "Brushy" as Billy.

FRANK AND GEORGE COE

John Tunstall's employees, homestead cousins Frank and George Coe, 26 and 21 respectively, nick-named John Tunstall's new, 17 year old, ranch hand, Billy Bonney, as "Kid." By 1878, after Tunstall's murder, the Coes became his fellow Regulators. After the lost Lincoln County War Battle, they fled for their lives to the Territory's northwest, near Farmington.

FRANK COE

Frank Coe wrote about Billy in an unpublished letter to a William Steele Dean, dated August 3, 1926. He emphasized Billy's bi-culturalism, and above-average height (5'6" was average), belying his mythologized "shortness": "[He was] 5ft 8in, weight 138 lb stood straight as an Indian, fine looking a lad as I ever met. He was a lady's man, the Mex girls were all crazy about him. He spoke their language well. He was a fine dancer, could go all their gaits and was one of them. He was a wonder, you would have been proud to know him."

On September 16, 1923, Frank Coe - like Billy, seeing himself as a Regulator soldier – was quoted in the *El Paso Times*: "[Billy] was brave and reliable, one of the best soldiers we had. He ... had a wonderful presence of mind; the tighter the place the more he showed his cool nerve and quick brain."

Frank Coe also related Billy's shootist preoccupation: "He never seemed to care for money, except to buy cartridges with ... and he always used about 10 times as many as any one else."

GEORGE COE

In 1934, George Coe published *Frontier Fighter: The Autobiography of George Coe Who Fought and Rode With Billy the Kid*. He described employer, John Tunstall's, paternal affection for Billy: "Tunstall seemed really devoted to the Kid. One day I was in Lincoln and I asked him about Billy. 'George, that's the finest lad I ever met," he said. "He's a revelation to me every day and would do anything to please me. I'm going to make a man out of that boy yet. He has it in him.' "

George Coe also emphasized Billy's charisma: "Billy came down to the Dick Brewer Ranch on the Ruidoso. He was the center of interest everywhere he went, and though heavily armed, he seemed as gentlemanly as a college-bred youth. He quickly became acquainted with everybody, and because of his humorous and pleasing personality grew to be a community favorite. In fact, Billy was so popular there wasn't enough of him to go around. He had a beautiful voice and sang like a bird. One of our special amusements was to get together every few nights and have singing. The thrill of those happy evenings still lingers – a pleasant memory – and tonight I would give a lot to live through one again. Frank Coe and I played the fiddles, and all of us danced, and here Billy, too, was in demand."

About Lincoln County War fighting, George Coe quoted Billy to show the boy's militant fervor in its freedom fighting: "As for ... giving up to that outfit, we'll die first." Billy himself exhibited that brave bellicosity in his March 20, 1879 pardon bargain letter to Governor Lew Wallace; writing: "*I am not afraid to die like a man fighting but I would not like to be killed like a dog unarmed.*"

George Coe gave a telling anecdote about Billy's teasing bravado which occurred around April 3, 1878 in the lead-up to the

Lincoln County War Battle. It shows how this teenager inspired grown men, and foreshadowed Billy's undaunted and ironic press interviews which he gave after his capture and after his unjust Mesilla hanging trial: "We made a big bonfire, and sat around swapping lies and bragging ... Then we talked about riding into Lincoln and setting in short order all the difficulties that were troubling the people there. We were a brave band as we told it. Our guns, which formed the most important part of our possessions, had been placed carelessly around against nearby trees. Billy sized up the situation and, looking for a little fun and excitement with an inexperienced bunch of greenhorns, he slipped about five or six cartridges out of his belt and tossed them into the fire. In less than a minute they began to go off, and such a mad dash for tall timber you have never seen ... I looked back as I ran, and there stood the Kid with his arms folded, perfectly unconcerned ... "Well, you're a damn fine bunch of soldiers. Run like a bunch of coyotes and forget to take your guns. I just wanted to break you in a little before we met the enemy, and, boys, I'm sure proud of your nerve."

YGENIO SALAZAR

Lincoln County resident, Ygenio Salazar, somewhat younger than Billy, was arguably his best friend. Quoted in Walter Noble Burns's 1926 *The Saga of Billy the Kid*, Ygenio stated: " 'Billy the Kid' ... was the bravest fellow I ever knew. All through the three-days' battle [sic – six day Lincoln County War Battle] he was as cool and cheerful as if he were playing a game instead of fighting for his life." (Fulton, Page 144)

GOTTFRIED GAUSS

German-born Gottfried Gauss, 56 at Billy's great escape from Lincoln's courthouse-jail, was in Billy's Lincoln County history from his October of 1877 arrival as a John Tunstall ranch hand - when Gauss was the cook - through the Lincoln County War period, and to Billy's 1881 jailbreak, when Gauss was the Lincoln courthouse-jail's caretaker and likely accomplice to Billy's escape. His role and name were unknown to "Brushy" and team.

Gauss's anti-Ring stance went back to 1876 when he was employed in the Ring's store called "The House," and was cheated out of his wages and profits from its brewery, which he ran.

Billy himself mentioned Gauss in his June 8, 1878 deposition to Frank Warner Angel as being at Tunstall's Feliz River ranch before Tunstall's murder, as well as during an earlier intimidation there by Sheriff Brady's possemen. Billy's stated: *"The persons at the ranch were R. M. Brewer, John Middleton,* **G. Gauss***, M. Martz, R.A. Widenmann, Henry Brown, F.T. Waite, W*<u>m</u> *McClosky and this deponent."* When Tunstall made his fatal return ride with his men and horses to Lincoln from the ranch, he assigned Gauss to stay. Thus, Gauss witnessed the arrival of Brady's murderous posse. By shared traumas, Gauss was Billy's steadfast friend.

Interviewed on March 1, 1890 for the *Lincoln County Leader* about Billy's 1881 jailbreak, Gauss implied his sympathy. He may even have directed Deputy Bob Olinger to the courthouse's east side, where Billy shot him dead. Gauss stated:

I was crossing the yard behind the courthouse, when I heard a shot fired then a tussle upstairs in the courthouse, somebody hurrying downstairs, and deputy sheriff Bell emerging from the door running toward me. He ran right into my arms, expired the same moment, and I laid him down, dead. That I was in a hurry to secure assistance, or perhaps to save myself, everybody will believe.

When I arrived at the garden gate leading to the street, in front of the courthouse, I saw the other deputy sheriff Olinger, coming out of the hotel opposite, with the four or five other county prisoners, where they had taken their dinner. I called to him to come quick. He did so, leaving his prisoners in front of the hotel. When he had come up close to me, and while I was standing not a yard apart, I told him that I was just after laying Bell dead on the ground in the yard behind. Before he could reply, he was struck by a well-directed shot fired from a window above us, and fell dead at my feet. I ran for my life to reach my room and safety, when Billy the Kid called to me: "Don't run, I wouldn't hurt you – I am alone, and master not only of the courthouse, but also of the town, for I will allow nobody to come near us." "You go," he said, "and saddle one of Judge (Ira) Leonard's horses, and I will clear out as soon as I have the shackles loosened from my legs." With a little prospecting pick I had thrown to him through the window he was working for at least an hour, and could not accomplish more than to free one leg. He came to the conclusion to wait a better chance, tie one shackle to his waistbelt, and start out. Meanwhile I had saddled a small skittish pony belonging to Billy Burt (the county clerk), as there was no other horse available, and had also, by Billy's command, tied a pair of red blankets behind the saddle ...

When Billy went down the stairs at last, on passing the body of Bell he said, "I'm sorry I had to kill him but I couldn't help it."

On passing the body of Olinger he gave him a tip with his boot, saying, "You are not going to round me up again." And so Billy the Kid started out that evening, after he had shaken hands with everybody around and after having a little difficulty in mounting on account of the shackle on his leg, he went on his way rejoicing.

HENRY HOYT

Henry Hoyt was a 24 year old medical doctor, working as a mail rider, when he met Billy Bonney in Tascosa, Texas, three months after the lost Lincoln County War Battle. Billy and fellow Regulators, Charlie Bowdre and Tom O'Folliard, were selling horses, rustled in retaliation from Ringmen.

Billy gifted Hoyt with an expensive horse - likely dead Sheriff Brady's - writing a legally protective bill of sale, dated October 24, 1878. Hoyt admired Billy's intelligence and bi-culturalism.

In his autobiographical, 1929 book, *A Frontier Doctor*, he wrote: "After learning his history directly from himself and recognizing his many superior natural qualifications, I often urged him, while he was free and the going was good, to leave the country, settle in Mexico or South America, and begin all over again. He spoke Spanish like a native and although only a beardless boy was nevertheless a natural leader of men. With his poise, iron nerve, and all-around efficiency properly applied, he could have made a success anywhere."

"Brushy" and team gleaned only the town "Tascosa" on the bill of sale for name-dropping, missing the relationship.

JOHN P. MEADOWS

John P. Meadows knew Billy, and, as an old-timer, wrote articles and gave interviews to historians about him. Meadows's recollections were collected in a 2004 book titled *Pat Garrett and Billy the Kid as I Knew Them: Reminiscences of John P. Meadows*. It gives insight into how Billy had inspired the older men who were his Lincoln County War compatriots. Meadows stated: "When he was rough, he was as rough as men ever get to be, yet he had a good streak in him."

And the first place Billy stopped after his jailbreak on April 28, 1881, was John Meadows's ranch.

Meadows was unknown to "Brushy" and team.

E.C. "TEDDY BLUE" ABBOTT

E.C. "Teddy Blue" Abbott, a cowboy about Billy's age, roving through New Mexico Territory in 1878, and having merely heard of him, recorded Billy's atypical multi-culturalism. This was another fact fatal to "Brushy Bill's" impersonation of Billy, since he could not speak Spanish and was a racist.

In 1955, as an old-timer, "Teddy Blue" Abbott published *We Pointed Them North: Recollections of a Cowpuncher*. Open about his own racism, Abbott reported, as common knowledge, the existence of two sides, with Billy as the Mexican's hero, writing: "The Lincoln County troubles was still going on, and you had to be either for Billy the Kid or against him. It wasn't my fight ... it was the Mexicans that made a hero of him."

Implied in Abbott's recollection is that Billy could have instigated a future a Hispanic revolt against the land-grabbing, Anglo, Santa Fe Ring minority. Ring "Boss," Thomas Benton Catron himself, confirmed that fear of uprisings in a February 10, 1913 *Washington Times* article stating, "Mexicans ... were perfectly equal to starting five new revolutions in five days." And Catron's anxiety connected to the Ring's mission to exterminate Billy by fabricating his outlaw myth as justification for his killing.

CHAPTER 3
BILLY BONNEY IN HIS OWN WORDS

SPEAKING THROUGH TIME

The real Billy Bonney was spectacularly brave, brilliant, and literate; and he left a big paper trail proving all that. Dull-witted, inarticulate, "Brushy Bill" Roberts, was left with an unattainable standard to mimic. And Billy certainly would not have called himself the hated Santa Fe Ring moniker outlawing him for hanging: "Billy the Kid" - which "Brushy" used.

The quantity of written and recorded records by Billy Bonney is incredible for a minor historical figure; explained, in part, by his anti-Ring political activism, which yielded his deposition and court testimonies. Additionally, his unusual charisma made people - including Lew Wallace - save his letters or documents.

So surviving were his 1878 affidavit and deposition on the murder of John Henry Tunstall, and his testimony in the 1879 military Court of Inquiry for possible court martial for Commander N.A.M. Dudley. His pardon bargain letters and interview with Governor Lew Wallace were retained by Wallace when he left the Territory, and were almost the only civilian documents Wallace kept. They ended up in his collected papers, donated to the Indiana Historical Society. Likewise, Dr. Henry Hoyt kept the Bill of Sale that Billy wrote out for him for a sorrel horse. And as big news in his day, Billy had press interviews.

"Brushy Bill's" doltish quotes exist in his writings and Morrison's notes, and interview transcripts; with devastating mismatch of his bad grammar and ignorance of the known documents' information - unless coached with them. But "Brushy's" undoing was that he was impersonating a dime a novel version of an outlaw: an uncouth, unschooled lout, as was expected by their second quarter of the 20th century audiences. The real Billy was beyond his conception.

AFFIDAVIT AND DEPUTIZING

A key factor Billy Bonney's history was his lawman status in pursuing John Tunstall's killers. On February 19, 1878, the day after Tunstall's murder, Billy and Tunstall's foreman, Dick Brewer, gave eye-witness affidavits to Lincoln Justice of the Peace John "Squire" Wilson, to enable his writing arrest warrants. It is the first time Billy's voice is publicly heard. He named Tunstall's killers as Sheriff Brady's possemen: *"James J. Dolan, Frank Baker, Jessie Evans, George Davis, A.H. Mills, W.S. Morton, [William] Moore, George Hindman, [Frank] Rivers, Pantaleon Gallegos, divers other persons unknown."* It yielded Wilson's February 19th legal arrest warrants, stating:

> *Territory of New Mexico)*
> *County of Lincoln   )*
>
> *Be it remembered that before the undersigned Justice of the Peace in and for the County and Territory aforesaid, personally came R.M. Brewer &* **W. Bonney** *who being duly sworn according to law deposeth & saith that at the County and Territory aforesaid on the 18th day of February 1878 in and upon the [presence] of J.H. Tunstall, Robt A. Widenman[n], R.M. Brewer,* **William Boney** *[sic] & John Middleton, then and there in the Peace of the Territory an assault was made with divers deadly weapons to wit with Winchester Guns and Colts Revolvers, and divers other deadly weapons by James J. Dolan, Frank Baker, Jessie Evans, George Davis, A.H. Mills, W.S. Morton, [omitted first name] Moore, George Hindman, [Frank] Rivers, Pantaleon Gallegos, divers other persons unknown and did then and there as affiant believes wounded & killed J.H. Tunstall contrary to the statute in such case made and provided against the Peace & dignity of the Territory.*
>
>

R.M. Brewer
William Bonney.

After Sheriff Brady refused to serve them, Wilson concluded that *"there being then and there no officers to serve such warrant the undersigned as directed by law, in such cases specially empowered Richard H. Brewer to serve the same endorsing such deputation on said last mentioned warrant."* Wilson wrote:

The Territory of New Mexico)
County of Lincoln)

    I, John B. Wilson justice of the Peace in and for precinct N<u>o</u> 1 Lincoln County, New Mexico, do hereby certify that on or about the 19<u>th</u> day of February 1878 **W. Boney** [sic] and R.M. Brewer filed in my office affidavits charging John [James] J. Dolan, J. Conovair, Frank Baker, Jessie Evans, Tom Hill, George Davis, A. [Andrew] L. ["Buckshot"] Roberts, P. [Panteleon] Gallegos, T. Green, J. Awly, A.H. Mills, "Dutch Charley" proper name unknown, R.W. Beckwith, William Morton, [Deputy] George Hindman, J.B. Matthews and others with having murdered and killed one John H. Tunstall at the said County of Lincoln on or about the 18<u>th</u> day of February 1878, that on or about the 20<u>th</u> day of Feby 1878, I secured warrants on said affidavits for the arrest of the parties above named and directed the same to the Constable of for precinct N<u>o</u> one in said County to wit: Atanacio Martines [Martinez].

    That on or about the 20<u>th</u> day of Feby 1878 said warrant was returned "not served" that on or about the said last mentioned day the undersigned issued an alias warrant for the apprehension of the above named persons, and there being then and there no officers to serve such warrant the undersigned as directed by law, in such cases specially empowered Richard H. Brewer to serve the same endorsing such deputation on said last mentioned warrant.

    In testimony whereof I have hereinto set my hand at Lincoln Precinct N<u>o</u> 1 Lincoln County, N. Mexico this 31<u>st</u> day of August 1878.

                           John Wilson, Justice of the Peace

    This enabled Special Constable Dick Brewer to deputize Billy and Fred Waite as Deputy Constables under Lincoln Town Constable Atanacio Martinez to serve the warrants. To block the arresting, Sheriff William Brady then illegally locked them in Lincoln's pit jail, and confiscated Billy's Winchester '73 carbine.

DEPOSITION TO FRANK WARNER ANGEL

    On June 8, 1878, Billy gave his eloquent eye-witness deposition, with characteristic meticulous attention to detail, on John Tunstall's murder, to Investigator for the Departments of Justice and the Interior, Frank Warner Angel, with Lincoln

Justice of the Peace John "Squire" Wilson, as witness. In it, Billy stated information unknown to the imposters: that he had a ranch on the Peñasco River along with another Tunstall employee, Fred Waite; that he knew about the injustice of the case against Tunstall; and that the horses being herded back to Lincoln were exempted from the case's attachments.

Lacking that still-undiscovered deposition, imposters had to fabricate Tunstall's murder scene and its motive.

And proving his Regulator zeal to attain justice, Billy was risking his life by coming to Lincoln after Ringite Governor Samuel Beach Axtell's illegal proclamation outlawing the Regulators, and after receiving his own April Grand Jury indictments for Regulator killings in the Lincoln County War. He then signed the document, as witnessed by Angel and Wilson; which Angel's transcriptionist recorded as follows:

Territory of New Mexico)
County of Lincoln   )
*   )*
William H. Bonney was duly sworn, deposand says that he is a resident of said county, that on the 11th day of February A.D. 1878 he in company with Robt. A. Widenmann and Fred T. Waite went to the ranch of J. H. Tunstall on the Rio Feliz, that **he and said Fred T. Waite at the time intended to go to the Rio Peñasco to take up a ranch** *for the purpose of farming. That the cattle on the ranch of said J. H. Tunstall were throughout the County of Lincoln, known to be the property of said Tunstall; that on the 13th of February A.D. 1878 one J.B. Matthews claiming to be a Deputy Sheriff came to the ranch of said J.H. Tunstall in company with Jesse Evans, Frank Baker, Tom Hill and [Frank] Rivers, known outlaws who had been confined to the Lincoln County jail and had succeeded in making their escape, John Hurley, George Hindman, [Andrew] Roberts and an Indian aka Poncearo the latter said to be the murderer of Benaito Cruz, for the arrest of murderers of whom (Benaito Cruz) the Governor of this Territory offers a reward of $500. Before the arrival of said J.B. Matthews, deputy Sheriff, and his posse, having been informed that said deputy sheriff and posse were going to round up all the cattle and drive them off and kill the persons at the ranch, the persons at the ranch cut portholes into the walls of the house and filled sacks with earth, so that they, the persons at the ranch,*

should they be attacked or murder attempted, could defend themselves, this course being thought necessary **as the sheriffs posse was composed of murderers, outlaws, and desperate characters none of whom has any interest at stake in the County, nor being residents of said County.** That said Matthews when within about 50 yards of the house was called to stop and advance alone and state his business, that said Matthews after arriving at the ranch said that he had come to attach the cattle and property of A.A McSween, that **said Matthews was informed that A.A. McSween had no cattle or property there**, but that if he had he, said Matthews could take it. That said Matthews said that he thought some of the cattle belonging to R. M. Brewer whose cattle were also at the ranch of J.H. Tunstall, belonged to A.A. McSween, that said Matthews was told by said Brewer that he Matthews could round up the cattle and that he, Brewer, would help him. That said Matthews said that he would go back to Lincoln to get new instructions and if he came back to the ranch he would come back with one man. That said Matthews and his posse were then invited by R.M. Brewer to come to the house to get something to eat.

Deponent further states that Robert A. Widenmann told R.M. Brewer and the others at the ranch, that he was going to arrest Frank Baker, Jesse Evans and Tom Hill said Widenmann having warrants for them. That said Widenmann was told by Brewer and the others at the ranch that the arrest could not be made because if it was made they, all the persons at the ranch would be killed and murdered by J.J. Dolan and their party. That said Evans advanced upon said Widenmann, said Evans swinging his gun and catching it cocked and pointed directly at said Widenmann. That said Jesse Evans asked said Widenmann whether he Widenmann, was hunting for him, Evans, to which Widenmann answered that if he was looking for him, he, Evans, would find it out. Evans also asked Widenmann whether he had a warrant for him; Widenmann answered that it was his (Widenmann's) business. Evans told Widenmann, that if he ever came to arrest him (Evans) he, Evans would pick Widenmann as the first man to shoot at, to which Widenmann answered that that was all right, that two could play at that game. That during the talking Frank Baker stood near said Widenmann, swinging his pistol on his finger, catching it full cocked pointed at said Widenmann.

The persons at the ranch were R. M. Brewer, John Middleton, G. Gayss [Gauss], M. Martz, R.A. Widenmann, Henry Brown, F.T.

Waite, Wm McClosky and this deponent. J.B. Matthews after eating started for Lincoln with John Hurley and Ponceano the rest of the party or posse saying they were going to the Rio Peñasco. Deponent started to Lincoln with Robert A. Widenmann and F.T. Waite and arrived at Lincoln the same evening and again left Lincoln on the next day, February the 14th in company with the above named persons, having heard that said Matthews was going back to the ranch of said J.H. Tunstall with a large party of men to take the cattle and deponent and Widenmann and Waite arrived at said ranch the same day.

Deponent states that on the road to Lincoln he heard said Matthews ask said Widenmann whether any resistance would be offered if he Matthews returned to take the cattle, to which said Widenmann answered that no resistance would be offered if the cattle were left at the ranch but if an attempt was made to drive the cattle to the Indian Agency and kill them for beef as he, said Matthews had been heard to say would be done, he, said Widenmann, would do all in his power to prevent this.

Deponent further says that on the night of the 17th of February A.D. 1878 J.H. Tunstall arrived at the ranch and informed all persons there that reliable information had reached him that J.B. Matthews was gathering a large party of outlaws and desperados as a posse and the said posse was coming to the ranch, the Mexicans in the party to gather up the cattle and the balance of the party to kill the persons at the ranch. It was thereupon decided that all persons at the ranch excepting G. Gauss, were to leave and Wm McClosky was that night sent to the Rio Peñasco to inform the posse who were camped there, that they could come over and round up the cattle, count them and leave a man there to take care of them and that Mr. Tunstall would also leave a man there to help round up and count the cattle and help take care of them, and said McClosky was also ordered to go to Martin Martz, who had left Tunstalls ranch when deponent, Widenmann and Waite returned to the town of Lincoln on the 13th of February and asked him said Martz to come to the ranch of said Tunstall and aid the sheriffs posse in rounding up and counting the cattle and to stay at the ranch and take care of the cattle.

Deponent left the ranch of said Tunstall in company with J.H. Tunstall, R.A. Widenmann, R.M. Brewer, John Middleton, F.T. Waite, said Tunstall, Widenmann, Brewer, Middleton and deponent driving the loose horses, Waite driving the wagon. Said Waite took the road for Lincoln with the wagon, the rest of the *party taking the trail with the horses.* **Deponent says that all the horses which he and the party were driving, excepting 3 had been released by sheriff Brady at Lincoln that one of these 3 horses belonged to R.M. Brewer, and the other was traded by Brewer to Tunstall for one of the released horses.**

Deponent further says, that when he and the party has traveled to within about 3 miles from the Rio Ruidoso he and John Middleton were in drag in the rear of the balance of the party as just upon reaching the brow of a hill they saw a large party of men coming towards them from the rear at full speed and that he and Middleton at once rode forward to inform the balance of the party of the fact. Deponent had not more than barely reached Brewer and Widenmann who were some 200 or 300 yards to the left of the trail when the attacking party cleared the brow of the hill and commenced firing at him, Widenmann and Brewer. Deponent, Widenmann and Brewer rode over a hill towards another which was covered with large rocks and trees in order to defend themselves and make a stand. But the attacking party, undoubtedly seeing Tunstall, left off pursuing deponent and the two with him and turned back at the caño in which the trail was. Shortly afterwards we heard two or three separate and distinct shots and the remark was then made by Middleton that they, the attacking party must have killed Tunstall. Middleton had in the meantime joined deponent and Widenmann and Brewer. Deponent then made the rest of his way to Lincoln in company with Robt. A. Widenmann, Brewer, Waite and Middleton stopping on the Rio Ruidoso in order to get men to look for the body of J.H. Tunstall.

Deponent further says that neither he nor any of the party fired off either rifle or pistol and that neither he nor the parties with him fired a shot.

William H. Bonney

Sworn and subscribed before me this eighth day of June A.D. 1878.

John B. Wilson
Justice of the Peace

"REGULATOR MANIFESTO"

On July 3, 1878, during the multiple skirmishes in the Lincoln County War, and leading to the final Battle, there occurred a retaliatory Santa Fe Ring massacre at anti-Ring San Patricio: the Hispanic community which was like bi-cultural Billy's second home. On July 13, 1878, ten days after it, Billy took action: challenging the Ring, in what I named the "Regulator Manifesto." It is the anti-Ring declaration of the Lincoln County War Battle, starting the next day. It is signed only *"Regulator."*

Existing as a copy, it was first attributed to Charles Bowdre by early historian, Maurice Garland Fulton, who claimed implausibly that its recipient, Ring head, T.B. Catron's, brother-in-law, Edgar Walz, recognized Bowdre's handwriting. But I believe it was Billy's production, either dictated to Bowdre, or wrongly attributed to him by Walz. And it heralds Billy's future retaliative guerrilla rustling from Ringites, like Catron and Walz. It stated:

In Camp, July 13, 1878.

Mr. Walz. Sir: - We are all aware that your brother-in-law, T.B. Catron sustains the Murphy-Kinney party, and take this method of informing you that if any property belonging to the residents of this county is stolen or destroyed, Mr. Catron's property will be dealt with as nearly as can be in the way in which the party he sustains deals with the property stolen or destroyed by them.

We returned Mr. Thornton the horses we took for the purpose of keeping the Murphy crowd from pursuing us with the promise that these horses should not again be used for that purpose. Now we know that the Tunstall estate cattle are pledged to Kinney and party. If they are taken, a similar number will be taken from your brother [in-law, Catron]. It is our object and efforts to protect property, but the man who plans destruction shall have destruction measured on him. Steal from the poorest or richest American or Mexican, and the full measure of the injury you do, shall be visited upon the property of Mr. Catron. This murderous band is harbored by you as your guest, and with the consent of Catron occupies your property.

Regulator

HOYT BILL OF SALE

After the lost Lincoln County War, refusing to leave the Territory, like most Regulators, Billy earned money by gambling and retaliatory rustling from Ringites, as threatened in his July 13, 1878 "Regulator Manifesto." He would not have considered himself a common rustler - as he later labeled Seven Rivers rustlers to Governor Lew Wallace in a March 23, 1879 interview.

Billy used non-Ring outlets for stock, and sold horses himself in Tascosa, Texas. There, on October 24, 1878, he "sold" to Dr. Henry Hoyt a sorrel horse - likely Sheriff William Brady's Dandy Dick stolen from Catron's Carrizozo ranch. He priced it high for its bill of sale, which demonstrated legalese he had possibly learned from Alexander McSween; and with proper witnessing by saloon owners, James E. McMasters and George J. Howard. That skill would be used in 132 days to write his first pardon plea letter to Governor Lew Wallace.

Billy's abilities impressed Hoyt enough for him to keep the document. On April 27, 1929, Hoyt sent its copy to Lew Wallace Jr.; writing: "I am one of the very few men living who was well acquainted with that famous outlaw 'Billy the Kid' and for many years supposed I had the only specimen of his handwriting in existence [until learning about the Lew Wallace letters], **a Bill of Sale for a horse he presented me with, and wrote out himself**, to protect me should my ownership ever be questioned, a very important matter in that part of the world at that period. This paper I have preserved all these years."

The Hoyt Bill of Sale stated:

Tascoso Texas
Thursday Oct 24th 1878

Know all persons by these presents that I do hereby Sell and deliver to Henry F. Hoyt one Sorrel Horse Branded BB on left hip and other indistinct Branded on Shoulders for the sum of Seventyfive $ dollars in hand received
W H Bonney

Witness
Jas. E. McMasters
Geo. J. Howard

LETTER OF MARCH 13, 1879
TO LEW WALLACE

On approximately March 13, 1879, Billy began his pardon plea to Governor Lew Wallace, offering eye-witness testimony against Ringite murderers of Attorney Huston Chapman on February 18, 1879 for an exchange, since Wallace's November 13, 1878 Amnesty Proclamation had excluded those indicted, like him. Noteworthy is that Billy asked to *"annuly"* - meaning annul - his indictments for the murders of William Brady, George Hindman, and Andrew "Buckshot" Roberts. That was correct: a pardon is post-sentencing; annulment is before. And Billy's ability to spell even "indicted," contrasts the pretenders' low literacy. He wrote:

To his Excellency the Governor.
General Lew. Wallace
Dear Sir I have heard that You will give one thousand $ dollars for my body which as I can understand it means alive as a witness. I know it is as a witness against those that murdered Mr. Chapman. if it was so as that I could appear at Court, I could give the desired information. but I have indictments against me for things that happened in the late Lincoln County War and am afraid to give up because my Enimies would Kill me. the day Mr. Chapman was murderded I was in Lincoln, at the request of good citizens to meet Mr. J.J. Dolan to meet as Friends. So as to be able to lay aside our arms and go to Work. I was present when Mr. Chapman was murdered and know who did it and if it were not for these indictments I would have made it clear before now. if it is in your power to Annully those indictments I hope you will do so so as to give me a chance to explain. please send me an annser telling me what you can do. You can send annser by bearer.

I have no wish to fight any more indeed I have not raised an arm since Your proclamation. as to my Character I refer to any of the Citizens, for the majority of them are my Friends and have been helping me all they could. I am called Kid Antrim but Antrim is my stepfathers name.
Waiting for an annser I remain
Your Obedient Servant
W.H. Bonney

LETTER OF MARCH 20, 1879
TO "SQUIRE" WILSON

Billy began a flurry of March 20, 1879 letters by writing to Justice of the Peace John "Squire" Wilson to check with Lew Wallace about his planned feigned arrest for his pardon bargain, since many of the men he was supposed to testify against for the Huston Chapman murder had escaped from their Fort Stanton imprisonment. He wrote from his safe-haven:

> San Patricio
> Thursday 20th 1879
> Friend Wilson.
> Please tell You know who that I do not know what to do, now as those Prisoners have escaped. So send word by bearer. a note through You it may be he has made different arrangements if not and he still wants it the same to Send :William Hudgins [Hudgens]: as Deputy, to the Junction tomorrow at three Oclock with some men you know to be all right. Send a note telling me what to do
> WHBonney
> P.S. do not send Soldiers

LETTER OF MARCH 20, 1879
TO LEW WALLACE

Wallace responded to Wilson with arrangements, and enclosed a vague *"note"* for Billy about their *"understanding."* Billy responded with a precautionary scenario for his sham arrest:

> San Patricio
> Lincoln County
> Thursday 20th 1879
> General. Lew. Wallace:
> Sir. I will keep the appointment I made. but be Sure and have men come that You can depend on I am not afraid to die like a man fighting but

I would not like to be killed like a dog unarmed. tell Kimbal [Kimbrell] to let his men be placed around the house and for him to come in alone: and he can arrest us. all I am afraid of is that in the Fort we might be poisoned or killed through a window at night. but You can arrange that all right. tell the Commanding Officer to watch)Let Goodwin(he would not hesitate to do anything there Will be danger on the road of Somebody Waylaying us to kill us on the road to the Fort. You will never catch those fellows on the road Watch Fritzes. Captain Bacas ranch and the Brewery they Will either go to Seven Rivers or to Jicarillo Mountains they will stay around close untill the scouting parties come in. give a spy a pair of glasses and let him get on the mountain back of Fritzes and watch and if they are there there will be provisions carried to them. it is not my place to advise you, but I am anxious to have them caught, and perhaps know how men hide from Soldiers, better than you. please excuse me for having so much to say

and I still remain Yours Truly
W H. Bonney

P.S.
I have changed my mind Send Kimbal [Kimbrell] to Gutieres just below San Patricio one mile, because Sanger and Ballard are or were great friends of Camels [Billy Campbell's] Ballard told me ~~today~~ *yesterday to leave for you were doing everything to catch me. it was a blind to get me to leave tell Kimbal [Kimbrell] not to come before 3 oclock for I may not be there before*

THE LEW WALLACE INTERVIEW

For his sham arrest in Lincoln, Lew Wallace and Billy were housed next door to each other; with Billy in his friend, jailor Juan Patrón's, house, and Wallace at José Montaño's. On March 23, 1879, Wallace interviewed Billy, asking nothing about the Lincoln County War. At this period, Wallace was also collecting information about Territorial outlawry, and Billy seems to have responded to that quest by telling him about the Santa Fe Ring's network of cattle rustlers, who fulfilled the beef contracts for Fort Stanton and the Mescalero Indian Reservation; which were held by the local Ring front, "The House," then controlled by James J. Dolan and John Riley. Noteworthy is Billy's vast fund of local information and geography. The notes stated:

William Bonney ("Kid")
*relative to arrangement
with him.
Notes:*

3-23-1879

<u>Statements by Kid, made Sunday night March 23, 1879</u>

1. There is a cattle trail beginning about 5 miles above Yellow Lake in a cañon, running a little west of north to Cisneza del Matcho (Mule Spring) and continuing around the point of the Capitan Mountains down toward Carrizozo in the direction of the Rio Grande. Frank Wheeler, Jake Owens and Dutch Chris are supposed to have used this trail taking a bunch of cattle over. Vansickle told K. so. They stopped and killed two beavers for Sam Corbett – hush money to Vansickle to whom they gave the beavers. Vansickle also said the Owens-Wheeler outfit mentioning "Chris" Ladbessor using this trail for about a year, but that lately their horses had given out, and of 140 head which they started to work they had only got through with 40. That now they were going to the Reservation to make a raid on the Indian horses to work on.

<u>The Rustlers.</u>

The "Rustlers," Kid says: were organized in Fort Stanton. Before they organized as "Rustlers" they had been with Peppin's posse. They came from Texas. Owens was conspicuous amongst them. **They were organized before the burning of McSween's house**, and after that they went on their first trip down the county as far as the Coe's ranch and **thence to the Feliz where they took the Tunstall cattle**. From the Feliz they went to the Pecos, where some of them deserted, Owens amongst them. (Martin, known to Sam Corbett) was in charge of the Tunstall cattle, and was taken prisoner, and saw them kill one of their own party. On the same trip they burnt Lola Wise's house, and took some horses. Coe at the time was ranching at the house. On this trip they moved behind a body of soldiers, one company, and a company of Navajo Scouts. They moved in sight of the soldiers, taking horses, insulting women. Lorenzo Trujillo (Jus. Peder) Juan Trujillo, Jose M. Gutierres, Pancho Sanchez, Santos Tafoya, are witnesses against them. They stopped on Pecos at Seven Rivers. Collins, now at Silver City, was one of the outfit – nick-named the Prowler by the cowboys. At Seven Rivers. There joined them Gus Gildey (wanted at San Antonio for killing Mexicans) Gildey is carrying the mail now from Stockton to Seven Rivers – James Irvin and

Reese Gobles, (rumored that their bodies were found in a drift down the Pecos) – Rustling Bob (found dead in the Pecos, killed by his own party) – John Selman (whereabouts unknown) came to Roswell while [Captain] Carroll was there –

The R's [Rustlers] stayed at Seven Rivers; which they left on their second trip via the Berenda for Fort Stanton. On their return back they killed Chavez boys and the crazy boy, Lorenzo – and the Sanchez boy, 14 years old. They also committed many robberies. They broke up after reaching the Pecos, promising to return when some more horses got fat.

Shedd's Ranch

The trail used going from Seven Rivers to Shedd's was round the S.W. part of the Guadalupe Mts. by a tank on the right hand of trail: from Shedd's the drives would be over to Las Cruces Jesse Evans, Frank Baker (killed) Jim [James] McDaniels (at Cruces, ranging between Cruces and El Paso) Reed at Shedd's bought cattle from them – also sold cattle to E.C. Priest, butcher in Cruces. "Big Mose" (at Cruces last heard from) and [blank], deserter from cavalry – (went to Arizona)

Mimbres

Used to be called Mormon City – situated 30 miles on the road to Cruces from Silver City south. A great many of what are known as "West Harden gang" are there. Among them Joe Olney, known in Mimbres as Joe Hill; he has a ranch in old Mexico somewheres near Coralitos. He makes trips up in this country: was at Penasco not long ago.

San Nicholas Spring

Is about 18 miles from Shedd's Ranch on the road to Tularosa, left hand road. There's a house at the spring and about 4 or 5 miles from it N.W. is another corral of brush and a spring, situated in a cañon. There Jim [James] McDaniels used to keep stolen Indian horses. McD. one of the Rio Grande posse. Kid says the latter is still used.

The Jones Family

Came from Texas. Used to keep saloon at Fort Griffin. The family consists of the father, Jim Jones, John Jones, boy about 10 years old, a girl about 13, and the mother. Marion Turner lives with the family, and he killed a Mexican man at Blazers Mill "just to see him kick." He had no cattle **when the War started**. The Jones, John and Jim, killed a man named Riley, a partner of theirs, on the Penasco 3 or 4 years ago.

THE "BILLIE" LETTER TO LEW WALLACE

On a likely March 24, 1879, Billy wrote a letter to Wallace about Lincoln County War events. It exists now as a one-page fragment, signed "Billie." I dated and authenticated it in my 2012 book, *Billy the Kid's Writings, Words, and Wit*. It stated:

... on the Pecos. All that I can remember are the So Called Dolan Outfit but they are all up here now. and on the Rio Grande this man Cris Moten I believe his name is he drove a herd of 80 head one Year ago last December in Company with Frank Wheeler Frank Baker deceased Jesse Evans George Davis alias Tom Jones. Tom Hill, his name in Texas being Tom Chelson also deceased, they drove the cattle to the Indian Reservation and sold them to John Riley and JJ Dolan. and the cattle were turned in for Beef for the Indians the Beckwith family made their boasts that they came to Seven Rivers a little over four years ago with one Milch Cow borrowed from John Chisum they had when I was there Year ago one thousand six hundred head of cattle. the male members of the family are Henry Beckwith and John Beckwith Robert Beckwith was killed the time McSween's house was burned. Charles [blank] Robert Olinger and Wallace Olinger are of the same gang. their cattle ranch is Situated at Rock Corral twelve miles below Seven Rivers on the Pecos. Paxton and Pierce are Still below them forty miles from Seven Rivers there are four of them Paxton: Pierce: Jim Raymers, and Buck Powel. they had when I seen them last about one thousand head of cattle: at Rocky Arroyo there is another Ranch belonging to [blank] Smith who Operated on the Penasco last year with the Jesse Evans gang those and the places I mentioned are all I know of this man Chris Moten at the time they stole those Cattle was in the employ of Dolan and Co. I afterwards Seen Some of the cattle at the Rinconada Bonita on the reservation those were the men we were in search of when we went to the Agency. the Beckwith family were attending to their own Business when this War started but G.W. Peppin told them that this was John Chisums War. and so they took a hand thinking they would lose their Cattle in case that he Chisum won the fight. this is all the information I can give you on this point

Yours Respectfully Billie

LOST GRAND JURY TESTIMONY

Billy fulfilled his side of the Lew Wallace pardon bargain by testifying against the murderers of Attorney Huston Chapman - James Dolan, Billy Campbell, and Jessie Evans - in the April 1879 Lincoln County Grand Jury. By doing that, he was also implicating the Santa Fe Ring and risking his life. His testimony achieved those men's murder indictments (James Dolan and Billy Campbell for murder; Jessie Evans for accessory to murder).

That testimony was confirmed in *The Grant County Herald* of May 10, 1879, as reprinted from the Mesilla *Thirty Four*: "At the recent term of court in Lincoln, about 200 indictments were found. Among them, Col. Dudley and George W. Peppin for burning McSween's house, **Dolan and Campbell for the Chapman murder, in which the Kid is the principal witness.**"

TESTIMONY AGAINST N.A.M. DUDLEY

Proof of Billy Bonney's anti-Ring commitment was his testifying against past Fort Stanton Commander N.A.M. Dudley on May 28th and 29th, 1879, since it was not part of his pardon bargain, and it risked his life. But he was seeking justice for Dudley's illegal military intervention in the Lincoln County War Battle, enabling the murders of Billy's compatriots: Alexander McSween, Harvey Morris, Francisco Zamora, and Vincente Romero. Billy twice made the unprotected, nine mile trip from his Lincoln sham custody to the courtroom in the Fort Stanton Adjutant's office for his court appearances.

His Regulator zeal, plus his courage and intellectual brilliance, made him unshakable under Dudley's lawyer's abusive cross-examination. Billy's precise and devastating testimony alone should have yielded a court martial after this interchange: "*How many soldiers fired at you? ... Three ... How many shots did those soldiers fire, that you say shot from the Tunstall building? ... I could not swear to that on account of firing on all sides, I could not hear. I seen them fire one volley ... Were the soldiers which you say fired at you as you escaped from the McSween house on the evening of July 19th last, colored or white? ... White troops.*"

A volley meant the three soldiers fired in unison. That required Dudley's order. "White" meant they were officers. That directly linked Dudley to ordering his soldiers to murder civilians. That was his treasonous Posse Comitatus Act violation. So dangerous was this evidence, that Dudley's lawyer's closing argument devoted a large part to a false attack on Billy.

Noteworthy, is that the Ring had already bestowed his outlaw moniker, "Billy the Kid;" and Billy was still uncertain about it under questioning. His transcript for May 28, 1879 stated:

WILLIAM BONNEY, *a witness being duly sworn, testified as follows.*

Q. by Recorder. What is your name and place of residence?
Answer. My name is William Bonney. I reside in Lincoln.
Q. by Recorder. Are you known or called Billy Kidd, also Antrim?
Answer. Yes Sir.
Q. by Recorder. Where were you on the 19th day of July last and what, if anything, did you see of the movements and actions of the troops in that city, state fully?
Answer. I was in the McSween house in Lincoln, and I saw soldiers come from the post with the sheriff's party, that is the sheriff's posse joined them a short distance below there, the McSween house. Soldiers passed on by and the men dropped off and surrounded the house, the sheriff's party. Shortly after, the soldiers came back with Peppin, passed the house twice afterwards. Three soldiers came and stood in front of the house, in front of the windows. Mr. McSween wrote a note to the officer in charge asking what the soldiers were placed there for. He replied saying that they had business there, that if a shot was fired over his camp, or at Peppin, or at any of his men, that he had no objection to blowing up, if he wanted, his own house. I read the note myself, he handed it to me to read. I saw nothing further of the soldiers until night. I was in the back part of the house. **When I escaped from the house three soldiers fired at me from the Tunstall store, outside corner of the store.** *That's all I know in regards to it.*
Q. by Recorder. Did the soldiers that stood in front of the windows have guns with them while there?
Answer. Yes Sir.
Q. by Recorder. Who escaped from the house with you and who was killed at the time, if you know, while attempting to make their escape?
Answer. Jose Chavez [Chávez y Chávez] escaped with me, Vincente Romero, Francisco Zamora and McSween.
Q. by Recorder. How many persons were killed in that fight that day, if you know, and who killed them, if you know?

Answer. I seen five killed, I could not swear to who killed them, I seen some of them that fired.

Q. by Recorder. Who did you see that fired?

Answer. Robt. Beckwith, John Hurley, John Jones, **those three soldiers, I don't know their names.**

Q. by Recorder. Did you see any persons setting fire to the McSween house that day, if so, state who it was, if you know?

Answer. I did, Jack Long, and there was another man I did not recognize.

Recorder stated he had finished with the witness.
Cross examination.

Q. By Col. Dudley. What were you, and the others there with you, doing in McSween's house that day?

Answer. We came here with McSween.

Q. By Col. Dudley. Did you know, or had you not heard, that the sheriff was endeavoring to arrest yourself and others there with you at the time?

Answer. Yes Sir. I had heard so, I did not know.

Q. By Col. Dudley. Then were you not engaged in resisting the sheriff at the time you were in the house?

Objected to by Recorder. The Court has already ruled that nothing extraneous from the actual occurrence that took place, and Col. Dudley's actions in connection therewith, should be further inquired into ... it cannot be a matter of defense of Col. Dudley or justify his actions however much the parties may have been resisting the sheriff or civil authorities.

Lt. Col. Dudley, by his Counsel, states he does not deem it necessary to make reply to the objection.

Objection sustained.

Q. By Col. Dudley. In addition to the names you have given, are you also known as the "Kid?"

Answer. I have already answered that question, Yes Sir, I am, but not "Billy Kid" that I know of.

Q. By Col. Dudley. Were you not and were not the parties with you in the McSween house on the 19th day of July last and the days immediately preceding, engaged in firing at the sheriff's posse?

Court objects to the question.

Lt. Col. Dudley, by his Counsel, asks, does the Court intend to rule here, that after once gone into this matter of firing into the McSween house by the testimony of this witness, it is not *permissible to show all the circumstances under which this firing took place ...*

Court cleared and closed.

Court opened and its decision announced ...

The Court directs the case to proceed calling attention to its previous rulings which were deemed sufficient by explicit.

Q. By Col. Dudley. Whose name was signed to the note received by McSween in reply to the one previously sent by him to Col. Dudley?

Answer. Signed N.A.M. Dudley, did not say what rank, he received two notes, one had no name signed to it.

Q. By Col. Dudley. Are you as certain of everything else you have sworn to as you are to what you have sworn to in answer to the last proceeding question?

Answer. Yes Sir.

Q. By Col. Dudley. From which direction did Peppin come the first time the soldiers passed with him?

Answer. Passed up from the direction of where the soldiers camped, the first time I saw him.

Q. By Col. Dudley. What direction did he come from the second time?

Answer. From the direction of the [Wortley] hotel from the McSween house.

Q. By Col. Dudley. In what direction did you go upon your escape from the McSween house?

Answer. Ran towards the Tunstall store, was fired at, and there turned towards the river.

Q. By Col. Dudley. From what part of the McSween house did you make your escape?

Answer. The northeast corner of the house.

Q. By Col. Dudley. How many soldiers fired at you?
Answer. Three.

Q. By Col. Dudley. How many soldiers were with Peppin when he passed the McSween house each time, as you say?

Answer. Three.

Q. By Col. Dudley. The soldiers appeared to go in company of threes that day, did they not?

Answer. All that I ever saw appeared to be three in a crowd at a time after they passed the first time.

Q. By Col. Dudley. Who was killed first that day, Bob Beckwith or McSween men?

Answer. Harvey Morris, McSween man, was killed first.

Q. By Col. Dudley. How far is the Tunstall building from the McSween house?

Answer. I could not say how far, I never measured the distance. I should judge it to be 40 yards, between 30 and 40 yards.

Q. By Col. Dudley. How many shots did those soldiers fire, that you say shot from the Tunstall building?

Answer. I could not swear to that on account of firing on all sides, I could not hear. I seen them fire one volley.

Q. By Col. Dudley. What did they fire at?

Answer. Myself and Jose Chavez [Chávez y Chávez].

*Q. By Col. Dudley. Did you not just now state in answer to the question who killed Zamora, Romero, Morris, and McSween that you did not know who killed them, but you saw Beckwith, John Jones, **and three soldiers fire at them**?*

Answer. Yes Sir. I did.

*Q. By Col. Dudley. Were these men, the McSween men, there with you **when the volley was fired at you and Chavez by the soldiers**?*

Answer. Just a short ways behind us.

Q. By Col. Dudley. Were you looking back at them?

Answer. No Sir.

Q. By Col. Dudley. How then do you know they were just behind you then, or that they were in range of the volley?

Answer. Because there was a high fence behind, and a good many guns to keep them there. I could hear them speak.

Q. By Col. Dudley. How far were you from the soldiers when you saw them?

Answer. I could not swear exactly, between 30 and 40 yards.

Q. By Col. Dudley. Did you know either of the soldiers that were in front of the window of McSween's house that day? If so, give it.

Answer. No Sir, I am not acquainted with them.

Redirect.

Q. by Recorder. Explain whether all the men that were in the McSween house came out at the same time when McSween and the others were killed and the firing came from the soldiers and others?

*Answer. Yes Sir, all came out at the same time. **The firing was done by the soldiers until some had escaped.***

Recorder stated that he had finished with the witness.

Q. by Col. Dudley. How do you know if you were making your escape at the time and the men Zamora, Morris and McSween were behind you that they were killed at that time, is it not true that you did not know of their death or the death of either of them until afterwards?

Answer. I knew of the death of some of them, I did know of the death of one of them. I saw him lying down there.

Q. by Col. Dudley. Did you see any of the men last mentioned killed?

Answer. Yes Sir, I did, I seen Harvey Morris killed first, he was out in front of me.

Q. by Col. Dudley. Did you not then a moment ago swear that he was among those who were behind you and Jose Chavez [Chávez y Chávez] when you saw the soldiers deliver the volley?

Answer. No Sir, I didn't think I did. I misunderstood the question if I did. I said he was among them that was killed not behind me.

Witness then withdrew ...

In Billy's second day of testimony on May 29th, he confirmed that Dudley's white officers fired at escaping McSweens, including himself; and that visibility came from the burning McSween house that made the area *"almost light as day."* The transcript stated:

Q. by Court. Were the soldiers which you say fired at you as you escaped from the McSween house on the evening of July 19th last, colored or white?

Answer. White troops.

Q. by Court. Was it light enough so you could distinctly see the soldiers when they fired?

Answer. The house was burning. Made it almost light as day for a short distance all around.

LETTER OF DECEMBER 12, 1880 TO LEW WALLACE

After Governor Lew Wallace betrayed the pardon bargain, Billy was publicly outlawed in lurid press. On December 12, 1880, he wrote to Wallace to deny a December 3, 1880 *Las Vegas Gazette* article by J.H. Koogler, titled "Desperadoe's Stronghold."

Billy's letter made clear that he did not consider himself an outlaw. He wrote: "*I noticed in the Las Vegas Gazette a piece which stated that, Billy "the" Kid, the name by which I am known in the Country was the captain of a Band of Outlaws who hold Forth at the Portales.* **There is no such Organization in Existence. So the Gentleman must have drawn very heavily on his Imagination.**" In addition, the letter shows his self-assured legal knowledge, describing to Wallace that he considered the posse illegal, for lack of proper arrest warrants: "*I asked for their Papers [warrants] and they had none. So I concluded that it amounted to nothing more than a mob.*"

By that December 12th, he had endured Secret Service pursuit, another lost pardon through a possible Secret Service bargain, two White Oaks posse ambushes, and a false murder accusation for Jim Carlyle. Seven days later, Garrett's posse would ambush Billy's group near Fort Sumner, killing Tom O'Folliard, intending to kill him. Ten days away was Billy's Stinking Springs capture, where Garrett would shoot dead Charlie Bowdre when mistaking him for Billy. Billy wrote:

> Fort Sumner
> Dec. 12th 1880
> Gov. Lew Wallace
> Dear Sir

I noticed in the Las Vegas Gazette a piece which stated that, Billy "the" Kid, the name by which I am known in the Country was the captain of a Band of Outlaws who hold Forth at the Portales. There is no such Organization in Existence. So the Gentleman must have drawn very heavily on his Imagination. My business at the White Oaks at the time I was waylaid and my horse killed was to See Judge Leonard who has my case in hand. he had written me to come up, that he thought he could get Everything Straightened up I did not find him at the Oaks & Should have gone to Lincoln if I had met with no accident. After mine and Billie Wilsons horses were killed we both made our way to a Station, forty miles from the Oaks kept by Mr Greathouse. When I got up the next morning The house was Surrounded by an outfit led by one Carlyle, Who had come into the house and Demanded a Surrender. I asked for their Papers [warrants] and they had none. So I concluded that it amounted to nothing more than a mob and told Carlyle that he would have to Stay in the house and lead the way out that night. Soon after a note was brought in Stating that if Carlyle did not come out inside of five minutes they would Kill the Station Keeper)Greathouse) who had left the house and was with them. in a Short time a Shot was fired on the outside and Carlyle thinking Greathouse was Killed jumped through the window. breaking the Sash as he went and was killed by his own Party they thinking it was me trying to make my Escape. the Party then withdrew.

they returned the next day and burned an old man named Spencer's house and Greathouses also

I made my way to this Place afoot and During my absence Deputy Sheriff Garrett Acting under Chisum's orders went to the Portales and found Nothing. on his way back he went by Mr Yerby's ranch and took a pair of mules of mine which I had left with Mr Bowdre who is in Charge of mr Yerby's cattle. he (Garrett) claimed that they were stolen and even if they were not he had no right to Confiscate any Outlaws property.

I had been at Sumner Since I left Lincoln making my living Gambling the mules were bought by me the truth of which I can prove by the best citizens around Sumner. J.S. Chisum is the man who got me into Trouble and was benefited Thousands by it and is now doing all he can against me There is no Doubt but what there is a great deal of Stealing going on in the Territory. and a great deal of the Property is taken across the [Staked] Plains as it is a good outlet but **so far as my being at the head of a Band there is nothing of it** in Several Instances I have recovered Stolen Property when there was no chance to get an Officer to do it.

      one instance for Hugo Zuber Post office Puerto de Luna. another for Pablo Analla Same Place.

if Some impartial Party were to investigate this matter they would find it far Different from the impression put out by Chisum and his Tools.

                    Yours Respect
                          William Bonney

SANTA FE JAIL LETTER: JANUARY 1, 1881

After capture, Billy was kept in the Santa Fe jail, awaiting transport to Mesilla for his hanging trial. On January 1, 1881, four days after arriving, he wrote to Lew Wallace:

Santa Fe
Jan 1st 1881

Gov. Lew Wallace
Dear Sir
I would like to see you for a few moments if You can spare the time.
Yours Respect.
W.HBonney

SANTA FE JAIL LETTER: MARCH 2, 1881

On March 2, 1881, Billy sent his second jail letter, which Wallace considered "blackmail." Billy wrote:

Santa Fe Jail New Mex
March 2nd 1881
Gov. Lew Wallace
Dear Sir
I wish you would come down to the jail to see me. it will be to your interest to come and see me. **I have some letters which date back two years, and there are Parties who are very anxious to get them but I shall not dispose of them until I see you. that is if you will come immediately**
Yours Respect
Wm H Bonney

SANTA FE JAIL LETTER: MARCH 4, 1881

On March 4, 1881, Billy wrote his third jail letter in tragic confirmation of the pardon's betrayal: "*I have done everything that I promised you I would, and You have done nothing that You promised me.*" Billy wrote:

>Santa Fe. In jail.
>March 4th 1881
>Gov. Lew Wallace
>
>Dear Sir
>
>I wrote You a little note the day before yesterday but have received no annser. I Expect you have forgotten what you promised me, this Month two Years ago. but I have not, and I think You had ought to have come and seen me as I requested you to. **I have done everything that I promised you I would, and You have done nothing that You promised me.**
>
>I think when You think the matter over, You will come down and See me, and I can then Explain Everything to You.
>
>Judge Leonard, Passed through here on his way East, in january and promised to come and See me on his way back. but he did not fulfill his Promise. it looks to me like I am getting left in the Cold. I am not treated right by [U.S. Marshal John] Sherman. he lets Every Stranger that comes to See me through Curiosity in to See me, but will not let a Single one of my friends in, not Even an Attorney.
>
>I guess they mean to Send me up without giving me any Show. but they will have a nice time doing it. I am not entirely without friends.
>
>>I shall Expect to See you Sometime today
>>Patiently Waiting
>>I am Very truly Yours, Respect.
>>W<u>m</u> H. Bonney.

SANTA FE JAIL LETTER: MARCH 27, 1881

On March 27, 1881, Billy wrote to Wallace for the last time, emphasizing the pardon bargain, possibly hoping that it would be issued after sentencing in the Mesilla trial. He wrote:

>Santa Fe New Mexico
>March 27th/81
>Gov Lew Wallace
>Dear Sir
>
>for the last <u>time</u> I ask: Will you keep Your promise. I start below tomorrow. Send Annser by bearer.
>
>>Yours Respt
>>WBonney

LETTER TO ATTORNEY EDGAR CAYPLESS

After Billy's unjust hanging sentence for the Regulators' killing of Sheriff William Brady, handed down by Ringite Judge Warren Bristol on April 13, 1881, Billy wanted to appeal. Two days later, on April 15th, he wrote to Las Vegas attorney, Edgar Caypless, whom he had earlier hired on contingency to file his audacious replevin (rustling) suit for recovery of his bay mare from Pat Garrett's posseman, Frank Stewart, who had stolen her at Billy's Stinking Springs capture. Billy hoped to sell her to pay an appeal lawyer, with grounds that his Spanish-speaking jurymen had been deprived of a translator.

Caypless prevailed in the replevin case, but only after Billy's death; and he kept the mare's sales price as fee.

For his last known letter, Billy wrote:

Dear Sir. I would have written before this but could get no paper. My United States case was thrown out of court and I was rushed to trial on my Territorial charge. was convicted of murder in the first degree and am to be hanged on the 13th day of May. Mr. A.J. Fountain was appointed to defend me and has done the best he could for me. He is willing to carry the case further if I can raise the money to bear his expense. The mare is about all I can depend on at present so hope you will settle the case right away and give him the money you get for her. If you do not settle the matter with Scott Moore [to whom Frank Stewart sold the mare] and have to go to court about it either give him [Fountain] the mare or sell her at auction and give him the money. please do as he wishes in the matter. I know you will do the best you can for me in this. I shall be taken to Lincoln tomorrow. Please write and direct care of Garrett, sheriff. excuse bad writing. I have my handcuffs on. I remain as ever

Yours respectfully,
W.H. Bonney

NEWSPAPER INTERVIEWS

Billy Bonney's press interviews occurred after his Stinking Springs capture, and after his Mesilla hanging verdict. He was already nationally famous, and making ironic commentary like in his April 3, 1881's Santa Fe *Daily New Mexican's* "Something About the Kid": "At least two hundred men have been killed in Lincoln County during the past three years, but I did not kill all of them."

On December 27, 1880, the *Las Vegas Daily Gazette* published editor, Lucius "Lute" Wilcox's, article about the Stinking Springs capture and prisoner transport to Las Vegas, titled: 'The Kid. Interview with Billy Bonney The Best Known Man in New Mexico." Billy teased his outlaw myth; stating about onlookers: "Well, perhaps some of them will think me half man now; everyone seems to think I was some sort of animal." Wilcox wrote:

With its customary enterprise, the *Gazette* was the first paper to give the story of the capture of Billy Bonney, who has risen to notoriety under the sobriquet of "the Kid," Billy Wilson, Dave Rudabaugh and Tom Pickett. Just at this time everything of interest about the men is especially interesting, and after damning the men in general and "the Kid" in particular through the columns of this paper we considered it the correct thing to give them a show.

Through the kindness of [San Miguel County] Sheriff Romero, a representative of the *Gazette* was admitted to the jail yesterday morning.

Mike Cosgrove, the obliging mail contractor, who has met the boys frequently while on business down the Pecos, had just gone in with four large bundles. The doors at the entrance stood open, and the large crowd strained their necks to get a glimpse of the prisoners, who stood in the passageway like children waiting for a Christmas tree distribution. One by one the bundles were unpacked disclosing a good suit of clothes for each man. Mr. Cosgrove remarked that he wanted "to see the boys go away in style."

"Billy the Kid," and Billy Wilson who were shackled together stood patiently while a blacksmith took off their shackles and bracelets to allow them an opportunity to make a change of clothing. Both prisoners watched the operation which was to set them free for a short while, but Wilson scarcely raised his eyes, and spoke but once or twice to his compadres. **Bonney on the other hand, was light and chipper, and was very communicative, laughing, joking and chatting with the bystanders.**

"You appear to take it easy," the reporter said.

"Yes! What's the use of looking at the gloomy side of everything. The laugh's on me this time," he said. Then looking about the placita, he asked: "Is the jail at Santa Fe any better than this?"

This seemed to trouble him considerably, for as he explained, "this is a terrible place to put a fellow in." He put the same question to every one who came near him and when he learned that there was nothing better in store for him, he shrugged his shoulders and said something about putting up with what he had to.

He was the attraction of the show, and as he stood there, lightly kicking the toes of his boots on the stone pavement to keep his feet warm, one would scarcely mistrust that he was the hero of "Forty Thieves," romance which this paper has been running in serial form for six weeks or more.

"There was a big crowd gazing at me wasn't there?" he exclaimed, and then smiling continued: "Well perhaps some of them will think me half a man now; everyone seems to think I was some kind of an animal."

He did look human, indeed, but there was nothing very mannish about him in appearance, for he looked and acted like a mere boy. He is about five feet, eight or nine inches tall, slightly built and lithe, weighing about 140; a frank and open countenance, looking like a school boy, with the traditional silky fuzz on his upper lip, clear blue eyes, with a roguish snap about them, light hair and complexion. He is, in all, quite a handsome looking fellow, the only imperfection being two prominent front teeth, slightly protruding like a squirrels' teeth, and he has agreeable and winning ways.

On December 28, 1880, for the *Las Vegas Gazette*, from inside the train to Santa Fe, for "Interview with the Kid," Billy's steely self-control is evident when one realizes it was detained by a mob, either to lynch or to rescue him. The article stated:

We saw him again at the depot when the crowd presented a really war like appearance. Standing by the car, out of one of the windows from which he was leaning, he talked freely with us of the whole affair:

"I don't blame you for writing of me as you have. You have had to believe others' stories, but then **I don't know as anyone would believe anything good of me, anyway,**" he said. "**I really wasn't the leader of any gang.** I was for Billy all the time. About that Portales business, I owned the ranch with Charlie Bowdre. I took it up and was holding it because I knew that at some time a stage line would run there, and I wanted to keep it for a station. **But I found that there were certain men who wouldn't let me live in the country and so I was going to leave.**

We had all our grub in the house when they took us in, and we were going to a place six miles away in the morning to cook it and then light out. I haven't stolen any stock. I made my living by gambling, but that was the only way I could live. **They wouldn't let me settle down; if they had I wouldn't be here today,"** and he held up his right arm on which was the bracelet.

"Chisum got me into all this trouble and then wouldn't help me out. I went up to Lincoln to stand my trial on the warrant that was out for me, but the Territory took a change of venue to Dona Ana, and I knew I had no show, and so I skinned out ...

If it had not been for the dead horse in the doorway I wouldn't be here in Las Vegas. I would have ridden out on my bay mare and taken my chances of escaping. But I couldn't ride over that for she would have jumped back **and I would have got it in the head.** We could have stayed in the house but there wouldn't have been anything gained by that for they would have starved us out. I thought it was better to come out and get a square meal - don't you?"

The prospects of a fight exhilarated him, and he bitterly bemoaned being chained. "If I only had my Winchester, I'd lick the whole crowd" was his confident comment on the strength of the attacking party. He sighed and sighed again for the chance to take a hand in the fight and the burden of his desire was to be set free to fight on the side of his captors as soon as he should smell powder.

As the train rolled out, he lifted his hat and invited us to call and see him in Santa Fe, calling out *"adios."*

Billy's loyal attorney, Ira Leonard, protectively accompanied him on the train ride to Mesilla, via the Rincón depot. From there, they took the stagecoach ride to Las Cruces. With them were guards and prisoner, Billy Wilson, also transported to Mesilla. At Las Cruces, a crowd had gathered to see the famous outlaw, Billy the Kid. The arrival was covered in the April 3, 1881 Santa Fe *Daily New Mexican* in: "Something About the Kid." It stated:

An extract of a letter written by W.S. Fletcher from Mesilla to a gentleman in the city reads about as follows: Tony Neis and Francisco Chaves, deputy U.S. Marshals, arrived Thursday night with **Billy, the Kid,** and Billy Wilson. They met an ugly crowd at Rincon, where some threats were made, but Tony's crowd were too much for them. **At Las Cruces an impulsive mob gathered around the coach and someone asked which is "Billy the Kid." The Kid himself answered by placing his hand on Judge Leonard's shoulder and saying "this is the man."** The Kid weakened somewhat at Las Cruces, where he found quite a number of Lincoln County men, who were to appear against him as witnesses.

[AUTHOR'S NOTE: Billy had no defense witnesses. The prosecution had Ringites James Dolan, Saturnino Baca, and Sheriff William Brady's deputy, Billy Matthews; and subpoenaed Lincolnite, Isaac Ellis.]

He says at least two hundred men have been killed in Lincoln County during the past three years, but that he did not kill all of them. I think twenty murders can be charged against him. He was arraigned yesterday (Wednesday) before the United States court for the murder of Roberts, on the Mescalero Apache reservation, in 1878. Judge Leonard was assigned to his defense. Judge Newcomb gave notice that he had three other indictments for murder against him, and it looks as if he had no show to get off. His counsel asked today for time to send to Lincoln, which was granted, so that his trial will not commence for at least ten days. Billy Wilson's case is before the grand jury. He is charged with passing counterfeit money. He has retained Judge Thornton as his counsel. He seems to have friends here while the Kid has none.

No mails between Rincon and Doña Ana for the past week. Mosquitoes and flies abound and weather hot as blazes.

Billy's articulate response to the hanging verdict was in an April 16, 1881 article in the *Mesilla News*. He summarized Santa Fe Ring injustice: "I think it hard that I should be the only one to suffer the extreme penalty of the law." He called his court "mob law;" ending with facetious "personal advice": "If mob law is going to rule, better dismiss judge and sheriff and let all take chances alike." And he said sarcastically: "Advise persons never to engage in killing." About Lew Wallace's pardon, he said curtly: "Don't know that he will do it." The article stated:

Well I had intended at one time not to say a word on my own behalf because persons would say, "Oh he lied." Newman, editor of the *Semi-Weekly*, gave me a rough deal; he created prejudice against me, and is trying to incite a mob to lynch me. He sent me a paper which showed it; I think it a dirty mean advantage to take of me, **considering my situation and knowing that I could not defend myself by word or act. But I suppose he thought he would give me a kick down hill.** Newman came to see me the other day. I refused to talk to him or tell him anything. But I believe the *News* is always willing to give its readers both sides of a question. **If mob law is going to rule, better dismiss judge and sheriff and let all take chances alike.** I expect to be lynched going to Lincoln. **Advise persons never to engage in killing.**

Considering the active part Governor Wallace took on our side and the friendly relations that existed between him and me, and the promise he made me, I think he ought to pardon me. Don't know that he will do it. When I was arrested for that murder he let me out and gave me freedom of the town, and let me go about with my arms. When I got ready to leave Lincoln in June, 1879, I left. **I think it hard that I should be the only one to suffer the extreme penalty of the law.**

For his secret transport to Lincoln for hanging, to prevent his partisans' rescue, in darkness, on April 17, 1881, Billy was taken by wagon from the Mesilla jail. April 20, 1881's *Newman's Semi-Weekly* reported his departure, with Billy, as usual, joking:

On Saturday night about 10 o'clock Deputy U.S. marshal Robt. Ollinger [sic] with deputy sheriff David Wood and a posse of five men (Tom Williams, Billy Mathews [sic], John Kinney, D.M. Reade and W.A. Lockhart) started for Lincoln with Henry Antrim *alias* the Kid. The fact that they intended to leave at that time had been purposely concealed and the report circulated that they would not leave before the middle of the week in order to avoid any possibility of trouble, it having been rumored that the Kid's band would attempt a rescue. They stopped in front of our office while we talked to them, and we handed the Kid an addressed envelope with some paper and he said he would write some things he wanted to make public. **He appeared quite cheerful and remarked that he wanted to stay until their whiskey gave out, anyway.** Said he was sure that his guard would not hurt him unless a rescue should be attempted and he was certain that it would not be done, unless, perhaps, "those fellows at White Oaks come out to take me," meaning to kill him. **It was, he said, about a stand-off whether he was hanged or killed in the wagon ...** He was hand-cuffed to the back seat of the ambulance. Kinney sat beside him, Olinger on the seat facing him, Mathews on the seat facing Kinney, Lockhart driving, and Reade, Wood and Williams riding along on horseback on each side and behind. The whole party was armed to the teeth and anyone who knows the men of whom it was composed will admit that a rescues would be a hazardous undertaking. Kid was informed that if trouble should occur he would be shot first and the attacking party attended to afterwards.

CONCLUSION

The real Billy Bonney's high intelligence, literacy, and fund of knowledge,- proved by his own writings and recorded words - contrasts the mental dullness and ignorance of information of "Brushy Bill" Roberts, and was his undoing.

PART III

THE ORIGINAL "BRUSHY BILL" ROBERTS BILLY THE KID IMPOSTER HOAX

CHAPTER 1
CREATORS OF THE "BRUSHY BILL" IMPOSER HOAX

"BRUSHY" AND HIS HOAX TEAM

It took the complementary skills of Oliver P. "Brushy Bill" Roberts, William V. Morrison, and C.L. Sonnichsen to create a Frankensteinian Billy the Kid. "Brushy" was crazy enough to think he could play the part; Morrison was willing to research and coach; and Sonnichsen liked posing as an historian vouching for the gambit. Their upshots were a failed pardon attempt for "Brushy" as Billy the Kid; a 1955 book, *Alias Billy the Kid*, promoting him as Billy; and a glut of conspiracy theories to explain the failure of their hoax to prevail over real history. The "Brushy" team's good fortune was that showman P.T. Barnum's supposed dictum held true: "There's a sucker born every minute." So *Alias Billy the Kid* became "Brushy's" subsequent believers' bible. And the hoax was also given new life by a cynical new generation of profiteering hoaxers.

The "Brushy" hoax relied on readers' ignorance of the true history, and their misguided image of Billy Bonney derived from the Santa Fe Ring's outlaw myth publications. The flimflam had two parts: "Brushy" must be Billy because he had special knowledge; and "Brushy" must be Billy because he was illiterate and could not have read-up to get that knowledge. Both were lies. But the biggest lie was hiding that he was born 20 years *after* Billy Bonney. That was the hoax's biggest problem. Another problem, as already discussed, was that the sources for a good impersonation had either not yet been written, or not yet found. Another problem was that "Brushy" had trouble remembering his lines and ad-libbed wildly. And another problem was that people were not as dumb as the hoaxers had hoped.

OLIVER P. "BRUSHY BILL" ROBERTS

By 1950, when Oliver Pleasant Roberts entered the world stage and exited that same year by sudden death, he had limped through an empty life doing farm labor and menial jobs in the mid-West and Texas. Disabled by mental illness and sociopathic personality flaws, he was dependent on his care-taking family and four older wives. What distinguished him from sad masses of others like himself, were aspirations of grandeur which flowered as delusions and fabrications of a having a completely different life and family in which he was, or was with, famous Old West people from twenty years before his birth. He read books to embellish his tall tales; costumed like a movie cowboy as he aged; and spewed aliases, like "Texas Kid," "Hugo Kid," "Rattlesnake Bill," "Kid Roberts," and "Brushy Bill" - his favorite. He also changed his name from Oliver P. Roberts to Oliver L. Roberts. But his greatest creation was himself as "William Henry" Roberts, alias Billy the Kid. But he also claimed to have been Frank James, Jesse James's brother; a Roosevelt Rough Rider; a Buffalo Bill Cody and Pawnee Bill Wild West performer; operator of his own Wild West show; a Pinkerton Detective; a famous bronco rider; a friend of Bell Starr; a Deputy U.S. Marshall; a rancher in Mexico; and an associate of Pancho Villa. Though these tall tales involved travels to Mexico, Argentina, and the Shetland Islands, historian Donald Cline, in his unpublished 1988 *Brushy Bill Roberts: I Wasn't Billy the Kid*, confirmed that "he actually remained in the same locals with or near his family members in east Texas, Arkansas, and Oklahoma" his whole life. (Cline, Pages 35, 51, 55)

Though "Brushy's" ignorance of actual history doomed his Billy the Kid facsimile, his coup de grâce came from his own kin, whose knowledge of his real identity and antics had always hung over his shenanigans like the sword of Damocles.

"Brushy's" full brother, Tom Ulce's, daughter, Geneva Roberts Pittmon, "Brushy's" niece, wrote to Cline on April 27, 1988: "I don't know of any job ["Brushy"] ever held except for farm work and that was not on welfare then." (Cline, Page 110) Being clumsy, "Brushy" got injuries with scars, which he would display and claim as bullet or knife wounds to credulous listeners.

Geneva Pittmon, on February 2, 1988, gave Don Cline a letter to her by her sister, Cordelia (another of Tom's daughters), as an example of their caretaking when "Brushy's" second wife, Mollie Brown, died. Cordelia wrote:

Oliver came to Arkinda [Arkansas] and lived with us until I got ready to go back to Okla. in September 1918 so Oliver decided to go with me. I don't know just how long Oliver stayed in Okla. then but Tom [his brother] and the family moved back to Texas [Canton] and Grandpa and Grandma ["Brushy's parents, Henry Oliver Roberts and Sara Elizabeth Ferguson] stayed in Arkansas. I think Oliver went back to Arkinda and stayed with them until Grandpa got almost down so Tom went and moved them back to Texas with them. Grandpa didn't live long after they got back there [died March 31, 1924] and Grandma only lived a year or so [August 29, 1924]. I don't know what became of Oliver after that but he must have gone back to Oklahoma as he was there when the boys had typhoid. **I was married by then and B.V. was about a year old so Oliver was so much trouble to mother and Dad [his brother Tom] that Mother asked me if I would take and keep him. So we did. He stayed with us most of the summer [of 1925].** (Cline, Pages 61, 103)

On January 28, 1988, another of Geneva Pittmon's sisters provided information for Don Cline, though he did not record her name. She stated about disabled "Brushy's" dependence: "The first Oliver stayed with us was in 1922 or 23. Jim was about 12 then and Jack about 10. They didn't like him because he wanted them to wait on him ... [He stayed again in 1925.] He came back and stayed a few days in 1942 with Jim and Joan. I guess he visited with Mother and Dad [Tom Ulce Roberts and his wife] also ... Raymond, Ruby's second son was staying with Joan and Jim also. He said Uncle Oliver was always telling 'tall tales.'" (Cline, Pages 105, 113)

"BRUSHY'S" REAL FAMILY TREE

For his Billy the Kid impersonation, "Brushy" fabricated a 20 year, time regressed family. But, from 1987 to 2015, his long-suffering Roberts family exposed his hoax, and provided his actual genealogy. As Don Cline wrote in his *Brushy Bill Roberts: I Wasn't Billy the Kid*: "His family has stated they heard all his stories many times." (Cline, Page 14)

Most complete was the actual genealogy presented in a 2015 book by Roy L. Haws, to whom "Brushy" had been a maternal half great-granduncle, titled: *Brushy Bill: Proof That His Claim to be Billy the Kid Was a Hoax*.

GENEVA PITTMON

Tom Ulce Roberts daughter, and "Brushy's" niece, Geneva Roberts Pittmon, born in 1918, knew disabled "Brushy" all her life. Her parents, his main caretakers, had housed him when she was a child. (Haws, Page 55) On December 16, 1987, she exposed him to the founders of the Billy the Kid Outlaw Gang: Marlyn Estes Perez Bowlin and her husband, Joe Bowlin, who ran the Old Fort Sumner Museum at the cemetery where Billy Bonney is buried. She refuted his claim with the genealogy page of the family Bible; concluding *"My uncle was Not Billy the Kid ... He was born Aug 26, 1879."* She also alluded to the growing fakery around his genealogy. She wrote:

Dec. 16, 1987

Dear Sir: the reason you are not finding my family is you don't have the right name. My grandfather was H.O. Roberts - married to ~~Sara~~ *Shara Elizabeth Ferguson on May 14, 1876. Oliver P. Roberts was Brushy Bill's name. I don't know what the P was for. He was born Aug. 26, 1879. I have the family Bible record.*

My husband thinks I should not tell you anything unless I know just what are your interest in my family?

A William A. Tunstill P.O. Box 995 Roswell New Mex 88201 is also writing me asking questions which I have not written. He also has come up with a Ben Roberts and my great grandfather who was from [Kentucky?] and settled near Austin, 1835. I would also like for this to be settled as I know

my uncle Oliver was not Billy the Kid

Mrs Geneva Pittmon

MARY JUNE ROBERTS

Don Cline, for his 1988 book, *Brushy Bill Roberts: I Wasn't Billy the Kid*, on January 28, 1988 interviewed Mary June Roberts, "Brushy's" niece and another daughter of Tom Roberts. She stated: "Grandpa [O.H.] Roberts never fought in any war. Grandma [Sara Elizabeth Ferguson] was his second wife and Oliver's mother. Oliver never had a stepmother." (Cline, Page 11)

CORDELIA ROBERTS

Geneva Pittmon, on February 2, 1988, gave Don Cline a letter to her by her sister, Cordelia (another of Tom's daughters), about denying "Brushy's" Billy the Kid claim. Cordelia wrote: "These people [a "Brushy"-backing author named William Tunstill] seemed to think the story about [Oliver] being Billy the Kid is true and it happened when he was younger and we didn't know anything about it. I told them I don't believe a word of it and I know it didn't happen that way." (Cline, Pages 103-104)

ANOTHER TOM ULCE ROBERTS DAUGHTER

On January 28, 1988, another of "Brushy's" brother, Tom Ulce's, daughters wrote to Geneva Pittmon to forward to Don Cline, though Cline did not record her name. She wrote: "[When Oliver was staying with, Joan and Jim] Raymond, Ruby's second son was staying with Joan and Jim also. He said Uncle Oliver was always telling 'tall tales …' " Grandpa Roberts [H.O. Roberts] never fought in any war. Grandma [Sara Elizabeth Ferguson] was his second wife and Oliver's mother. Oliver never had a step-mother [his faked Elizabeth Ferguson] … I hope this has given enough ammunition to put the entire mess to rest." (Cline, Pages 105, 113)

ROY L. HAWS

In 2015, "Brushy's" relative, Roy L. Haws, published *Brushy Bill: Proof That His Claim to be Billy the Kid Was a Hoax*. He called "Brushy's" fake genealogy an "incredible farce." (Haws, Page 13) Haws stated that the Roberts family had two branches resulting from "Brushy's" father, Henry Oliver Roberts's, two marriages, with "Brushy" resulting from the second. Haws descended from the first marriage. (Pages 19-20) **[FIGURE: 5]** Importantly, Haws exposed that his mother, Eulaine Haws, in the 1980's, had been duped into vouching for a William Tunstill's fake genealogy, which was subsequently used by "Brushy" backers.

Haws stated: "Brushy was … just under two years of age the night Pat Garrett is said to have killed Billy the Kid." (Haws, Page 14) "Brushy's actual birth name was indeed the identity he used throughout life in census, marriage, divorce, death certificates, and all public documents. **His true name was Oliver Pleasant Roberts, son of Henry Oliver and Sara Elizabeth Ferguson Roberts, born August 26, 1879 in Bates, Arkansas.**" (Haws, Page 28)

Haws showed "Brushy's" place on the family tree, and the names he lifted to fabricate his fake family. (Haws, Pages 136-138) "Brushy's" paternal grandfather was Joseph Roberts (1797-1857). His dirt-farmer father was Henry Oliver "H.O." Roberts, born on May 18, 1852 in Rusk County, Texas; dying on March 31, 1924 in Van Zant County, Texas. (Haws, Pages 136-137)

Henry Oliver Roberts's first marriage was to **Caroline Dunn**, who died. **[FIGURE: 5]** They had Samantha Belle (1871) and **Martha Vada** (1872). Next he married **Sara Elizabeth Ferguson** (1856-1924) in 1876 in Arkansas. Their children were Andrew Berry (1877), Mary C. (1878) **Oliver Pleasant "Brushy" (1879)**, John W. (1881), Lonnie V. (1884), Thomas Ulce (1885, father of Geneva Pittmon), Nora (1892), and Joseph Irvin (1895).

Roy L. Haws descended from **Martha Vada Roberts**, the daughter from Henry Oliver's his first marriage. She married Dudley Heath, and had **Vada Bell Heath**. Vada's marriage to a D.L. Goff, yielded **Eulaine Faye Goff.** Eulaine married Leonard Haws, with **Roy L. Haws** the youngest of three sons. Vada Bell Heath next married Joseph Emerson, producing **Paul Emerson** (who knew "Brushy"). **Key was Roy Haws's mother, Eulaine Faye Goff Haws, who was tricked into vouching that her Caroline Dunn branch from Henry Oliver was <u>a different family</u>, which had a man named Oliver <u>L.</u> "Brushy Bill" Roberts, who was not Oliver Pleasant Roberts!**

Henry Oliver Roberts's second marriage was to **Sara Elizabeth Ferguson**, (1856-1924) on May 17, 1876. It yielded eight children. **[FIGURE: 6]** Oliver Pleasant ("Brushy") was their third child, born in Bates, Sebastian County, Arkansas, on August 26, 1879. Their other children were **Andrew Berry (1877), Mary C. (1878), John W. (1881), Lonnie V. (1884), Thomas Ulce (1885; father of Geneva Roberts Pittmon and Cordelia Roberts, who exposed "Brushy"), Nora (1892), and Joseph Irvin (1895).**

Haws also recorded that "Brushy's" four wives, who cared for him, were **Anna Lee** (married 1909, divorced 1910); **Mollie Brown** (married 1912, died 1919); **Luticia Ballard** (married 1929, died 1944); and **Malinda E. Allison** (married 1945, died 1952). To be noted is that "Brushy" was married to Malinda when he died. His possessions went to her son, then to his son, **Bill Allison** - "Brushy's" step-grandson, who ended up playing an inadvertent part in the "Brushy" hoax.

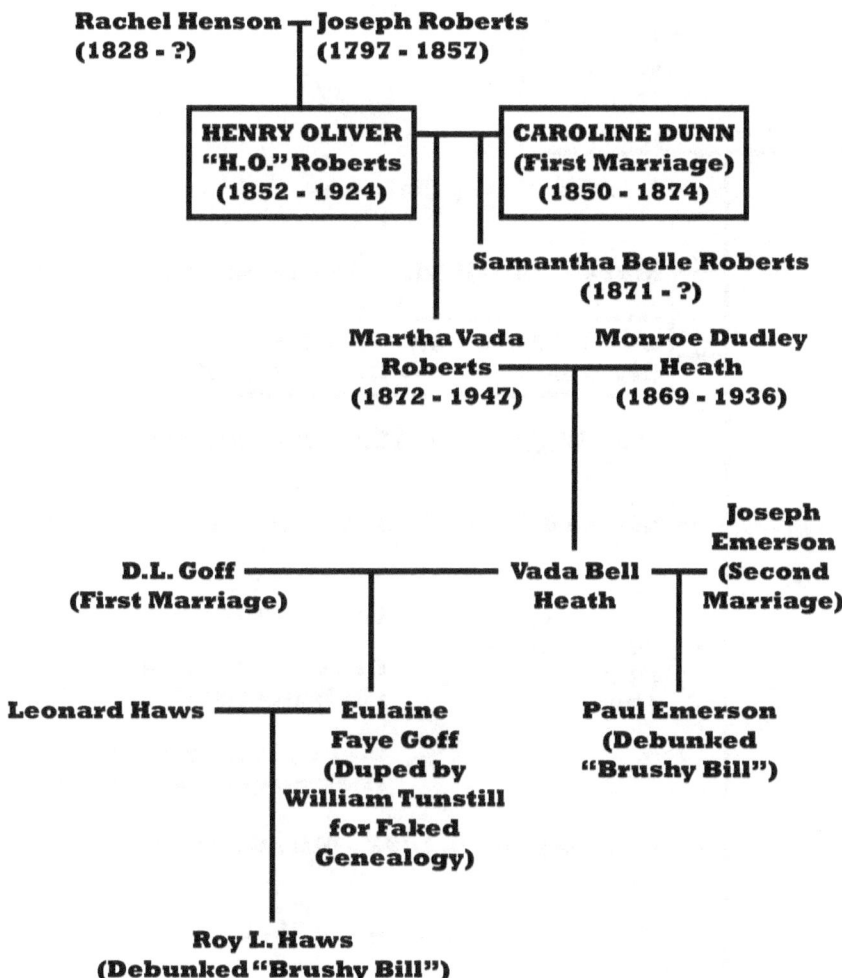

FIGURE: 5. Family tree for "Brushy's" father, Henry Oliver "H.O." Roberts's, first marriage to Caroline Dunn, with descendant debunkers of "Brushy Bill." (Illustrated from information in Roy L. Haws's, 2015 book, *Brushy Bill: Proof His Claim to be Billy the Kid Was a Hoax* and from Don Cline's 1988 manuscript, *Brushy Bill Roberts: I Wasn't Billy the Kid*)

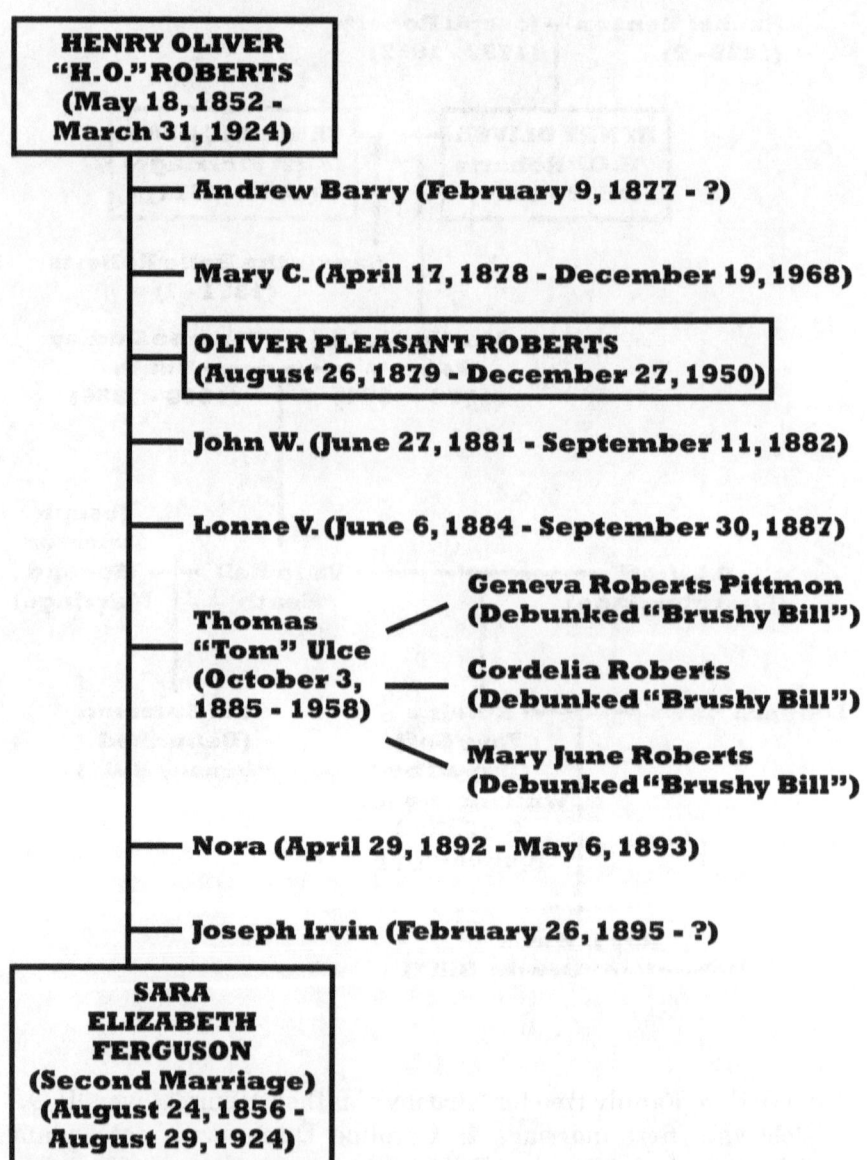

FIGURE: 6. Genealogy of Oliver Pleasant "Brushy Bill" Roberts according to Roy L. Haws and other Roberts family members

PAUL EMERSON AND CORA HEATH

Roy L. Haws added insider perspective in his 2015 book, *Brushy Bill: Proof That His Claim to be Billy the Kid Was a Hoax*, with his chapter titled "What the Family Thought of Brushy." Beside's Geneva Pittmon's December 16, 1987 letter of denial (Haws, Page 52), he quoted an e-mail from his half uncle, Paul Emerson, of Houston, Texas, from Vada Bell Heath's second marriage to a Joseph Emerson (while Haws was descended from her first marriage to D.L. Goff). In about 1946, teenaged Paul Emerson met "Brushy," dressed as a cowboy, and visiting, in Jacksonville, Texas, Martha Vada Roberts Heath - Paul Emerson's grandmother and "Brushy's" half-sister from his father's first marriage to Caroline Dunn. Paul informed Haws that Martha Vada told him "Brushy" was not Billy the Kid. (Haws, Page 53)

Paul Emerson also wrote a letter on August 2, 1986 to "Brushy"-backing author, William Tunstill, informing him that Billy the Kid was killed in 1881, when "Brushy" was about two years old. (Haws, Page 55)

In that same August 2, 1986 letter, Emerson stated that he had found a clipping with Cora Heath's (Martha Vada Roberts Heath's second eldest daughter) writing to Tunstill: "O.L. Roberts was my mother's brother. He was around 75 years of age when he died and he was not Billy the Kid." (Haws, Page 54)

"BRUSHY'S" FAKE AGING

"Brushy's" Billy the Kid imposture necessitated aging himself 20 years. But Roy L. Haws contended that in 1936, he had already aged himself by changing his birth year from 1879 to 1868, while changing his name from Oliver P. to Oliver L. Roberts. Haws found that in the 1930 census, "Brushy," as Oliver Roberts, had given his age as 52, consistent with his 1879 birth. But in the 1940 census, as Ollie Roberts, he became 70 years old, as if born in 1868 - a date he used on documents for the remainder of his life. (Haws, Page 23-24) Haws concluded that this age increase occurred between 1936 and 1940, along with switching the P. to an L. to qualify, by identity fraud, to collect Social Security benefits for those 65 or older, newly offered in Texas in 1936. (Haws, Page 24) subsequently, "Brushy" stuck with the "L." This must have made easier his next leap to birth date of 1859 to match Billy the Kid's.

Don Cline, in his 1988 *Brushy Bill Roberts: I Wasn't Billy the Kid*, said "Brushy" faked other ages. "In 1941 he told the Hico editor [of the *Hico News Review*] he was born in 1867 ... In 1949 he was wire recorded [in Meramec Caverns, Missouri] as stating he was 85 but a year later in the meeting with the Governor of New Mexico he had somehow reached 91 ... He told his last wife he was born in 1868 and this was placed on his death certificate and headstone." (Cline, Page 69)

Haws provided photos of "Brushy's" original, crude, tombstone, matching his benefits fraud and his fourth wife, Malinda Allison's, belief, since he used the L. in 1945 for their marriage document. (Haws, Page 19) It stated: "Ollie L. Roberts Brushy Bill 12-31-1868 - 12-12-1950." (Haws, Page 16)

"BRUSHY'S" REAL TIME-LINE

The real timeline of "Brushy's" claustrophobically dreary, mentally handicapped life was spelled out by Don Cline, in his 1988, *Brushy Bill Roberts: I Wasn't Billy the Kid*. Family interviews revealed that "Brushy" had only lived with relatives or wives in Arkansas, Oklahoma, or Texas, working as a farm laborer, then being on social security benefits, as he descended into delusions of fictional personas. (Cline, Pages 172-177)

On the July 14, 1881 death day of Billy Bonney, "Brushy" was 1 year, 10 months, and 19 days old in Bates Township, Sebastian County, Arkansas; where he was born on August 26, 1879.

In 1900, when he was 21, he was still living with his parents, but now in Hopkins County, Sulphur Springs, Texas. (He gave the census taker his birth date as August of 1879, and parents as H.O. and Sara Elizabeth, and occupation as farm laborer.)

In 1904, the family moved to a farm in Van Zant County, Canton, Texas. From there, "Brushy" went with his brother Tom's family to visit his niece Cordelia (Tom's daughter) in Dibble, Oklahoma and ended up working there for his uncle Ed.

"Brushy" returned to Canton **in 1906, and saw Buffalo Gap (his future faked birthplace) for the first time on the way home**. When his parents moved that year, he stayed in Canton doing farm labor.

In 1909, he married Anna Lee in Canton.

In the 1910 census, as a farm laborer, he **now claimed a Texas birth, and parents from Kentucky, but still birth date of August, 1879**. That year he divorced Anna Lee.

In 1911, still in Canton, he met Mollie Brown, and married her in 1912. They moved to Horatio, Arkansas, where he was a farm laborer. And his brother Tom, with family including daughter Geneva (future Pittmon) moved to nearby Arkinda, Arkansas.

In 1915, Frank James died, and "Brushy" claimed to be him, though James was 36 years older, thus, exhibiting his first known imposture delusion.

In 1918, "Brushy" had many events. He bought a small farm in Sevier County, selling it six months later for a small profit. He and Mollie moved to Polk County, Mena, Texas; where she died of the flu. He returned to live with brother, Tom, in Arkinda, who was displeased with his Frank James imposture. Tom moved back to Canton, and "Brushy" returned to Dibble, Oklahoma, to his niece Cordelia. Cline wrote: "The [Roberts] family believes that Brushy apparently had seen Frank James at one time and became obsessed with him, as he would later with Billy the Kid and others. In 1903 Frank James toured the country with Cole Younger in their ill-fated 'James-Younger Show' which soon faded. Frank retired to the family homestead and by 1912 was selling tours of the James home for a fee until his death in 1915. The family feels Brushy may have made the tour or witnessed the show. He would also incorporate the Youngers into ... his stories." (Cline, Page 59)

Between 1919 to about 1921, "Brushy" lived in Oklahoma and Arkansas with his niece, Cordelia, or his parents.

In 1922, he tried to return to living with Tom in Canton, but was rejected; instead living in Canton with Tom's daughter, **Geneva Pittmon, from 1922 to 1923, and working as a farmhand. With Geneva, "Brushy" added a new persona, claiming to have been a rodeo rider in Madison Square Garden in a period in which he disappeared in 1922**.

In 1924, parents H.O. and Sara Elizabeth were ailing, and Tom brought them back to Canton, where the father died on March 31st and the mother on August 29th.

In 1925, "Brushy" worked for non-family as a farm laborer, but **returned to live with Geneva Pittmon in Canton from 1925 to 1927, though disappearing during 1925 and claiming he had been a rodeo rider in Madison Square Garden.**

In 1929, he married Luticia Ballard, and moved from Canton - to escape town ridicule for his tall tales - to Comanche, where he worked in a turkey processing plant, his last job.

In 1930, he told a Bob Young in Comanche that he was a friend of outlaw James McDaniels, as his delusions expanded.

In 1931, he again moved to escape ridicule, ending up in Gladewater, Texas, and living on welfare. **There he met Dewitt Travis and convinced him he was Billy the Kid, thus, dating that delusion to the 1930's.**

In 1936, he applied for Social Security, and altered his name and birth date.

In 1944, his wife, Luticia Ballard, died.

In 1945, he married Malinda E. Allison, living in Hamilton, then Hico, Texas.

In 1948, Morrison heard of his Billy the Kid claim.

In 1949, "Brushy" went to a convention in Meramec Caverns, Missouri, and vouched for his friend, J. Frank Dalton as being Jesse James. **At the time, "Brushy," at 70, gave his age as 85. That year he told Morrison he was 90.**

In 1950, with Morrison, "Brushy" backed Dalton as Jesse James and failed his own Billy the Kid imposture with Governor T.J. Mabry.

On December 27, 1950, "Brushy" died of a sudden heart attack. He was 71 years, 4 months, and 2 days old.

"BRUSHY'S" PRE-BILLY THE KID PERSONAS

"Brushy" was exhibitionistic and flamboyant in his impostures, even before he was portraying Billy the Kid.

July 25, 1941's *The Hico News Review*, recorded his moving to town as " 'Brushy Bill' Has Come to Hico to Spend the Rest of His Life." It presents a "Brushy" before his Billy the Kid imposture. His fabricated persona was then a 73 year old expert rider - even in Buffalo Bill Cody's show, and sent to South America to "break out" cattle. He had a rancher father named Al Roberts, and once had a ranch in Old Mexico. He had been a lawman for 40 years, including being a State Ranger. And he wanted to be featured in the upcoming Hico Reunion celebration. The article stated:

"Brushy Bill, **arrayed in typical Western regalia** - ten-gallon hat, blue dungarees, boots and all – arrived in Hico the first of the week to make his home here for the rest of his days.

Known formerly as O.L. Roberts **[with made-up L]**, Brushy Bill and his wife came here with their household goods Monday, after having made inquiry beforehand, and have taken up their residence in the home of Mrs. Stanley. They came here from Gladewater, where they have lived since 1931, **and have made their home in East Texas for 40 years [making it since 1901]**. Mr. Roberts possesses a document on City of Gladewater stationery, signed by several officials, attesting to the fact that they have made good citizens in that city and expressing regret at their decision to move.

Son of Al Roberts, known in the early days as Two-Gun Henry [with Morrison he named his father John Henry "J.H." Roberts], Brushy Bill <u>admits to being 73 years old</u> [was actually 62, but this age was to correspond to his Social Security benefits fraud birthdate of 1868; and with Morrison, seven years later, in 1948, he claimed to be 90]. He was on a **Mexican ranch in 1914**, but the Mexican revolution broke things up down there and he and a half-breed Cherokee Indian were the only ones who got out alive. Other escapades retold by him include stories of laying behind his dead horse and using a Winchester to shoot it to a showdown many a time.

In 1899 he represented Texas in the Cheyenne Round-Up as a horse rider, **riding Cyclone**, supposed to have been free from any man's back. He declared that he relieved them of their pocket change and bank accounts too, and when he departed the other attendants said Texas had only one rider, and that was Brushy Bill.

In 1893, on his riding skill he was awarded a trip to South America to break out wild cattle. He says he got the job done and has records to show it. He also claims to have **ridden with Bill Cody in Wild West shows**.

Roberts was **born in Buffalo Gap, in Taylor County [likely why he had to stick with this publicized location for his Billy the Kid imposture]**, and came with his father to a ranch in this section near the Comanche County line. He knew Hico in the early days, he says, and has always wanted to live here although he has been away from this section for 58 years.

"I was an officer of the law first and last for 40 years, I was," he tells his listeners adding that he was a **state Ranger in '91 and '92 under the late Captain McDonald**, stationed along the Mexican border. In '86, '87 and '88 he reports having done **scout duty in the Black Hills of the Dakotas**.

"I don't drink in no shape, form nor fashion," declares the old-timer newcomer, "nor do I dip, chew nor smoke. Yet I don't claim to be a sanctified man, although I try to lead a moral life."

He says he wants to mount the platform at the Hico Reunion and see if he can locate some of his relatives or early friends. [Publicity-seeking]

In March of 1998, an Elreeta Crain Weathers, born in 1935 in Hamilton, County, Texas, and graduating high school in about 1952, recounted her girlhood memories of Hamilton residents' experience of "crazy" "Brushy" in her *Gazeteer of Hamilton County, Texas* blog as "Brushy Bill or Billy the Kid? Oliver L. Roberts." Weathers wrote:

> I don't know anything about the validity of Brushy Bill's claims to his being Billy the Kid ...
> I do remember that he was a wiry little man, whom I thought was crazy. Mother and I would do everything we could do to avoid being trapped by Brushy Bill, as we knew him. In retrospect, I would now classify his behavior as a form of dementia. We did not believe most of his claims and did not like to be the audience for his rantings and ravings. We pitied the other poor souls whom he did trap.
> Roberts would "trap" people between himself and one of the light posts around the square. **Once someone was "trapped", Brushy Bill would begin his tirade about his being Billy the Kid**, displaying his small wrists and explaining how he once slipped out of a pair of handcuffs to escape ...
> His shirts were always constructed [by him or his wife] of brightly colored and patterned fabric ... The diminutive, mustached Mr. Roberts always wore a western hat and tied a red kerchief around his neck. Mr. Roberts died when I was in high school.

One of "Brushy's" strangest impostures was portrayed in a *Dallas Morning News* article of September 18, 1950, by Thomas Turner, titled "Sam Bass' Pistol, Texan Knew Bad Men, Saw Hoss Thieves Hang." In it, "Brushy" oddly contradicts his Billy the Kid impersonation by saying at age 21 he was Dakota's Black Hills and Mexico; though his Billy the Kid pardon hearing with Governor Mabry was upcoming in two months; and his tales for that differed from this interview – including his "father's" name. He stated that his fictional father, James Henry Roberts, was a scout with Kit Carson, and he and Carson had tried to warn Custer about the five Indian tribes against him. But Custer ignored them and lost the battle. Roy L. Haws pointed out that Carson died in 1868, and the Battle of Little Big Horn was in 1876. And there were six tribes. (Haws, Pages 71-72) "Brushy" also stated that he was holding Sam Bass's Colt .45, which he got Belle Starr's daughter, who got it from a "Frank Jackson who grabbed it when Sam was shot by Rangers at Round Rock."

FAKERY: Much like for his Billy the Kid impersonation built with William Morrison since June of 1949, "Brushy" was name-dropping and confabulating history for his revolver.

Sam Bass was a train and stagecoach robber and murderer, born in 1851, and shot by the Texas Rangers on July 19, 1878 in Round Rock, Texas. But wounded Bass escaped; so his gang member Frank Jackson, who escaped with him, did not take his gun at Round Rock. Bass was later found by Williamson County Deputy James Milton Tucker outside Round Rock. Bass died in custody on July 21, 1878.

The name "Jackson" appears lifted from a source that "Brushy" also used for his fake family, and likely because the author's family name was Roberts. It was Dan W. Roberts's popular 1914 book about the Texas Rangers titled *Rangers and Sovereignty*. In it, Dan Roberts has a chapter on Sam Bass. He wrote: ["Bass] didn't believe distributing his patronage to many, as a grave trust, in his line, demanded men of steel nerve. He enlisted Jackson, one named Underwood and a man named Murphy, also Seba Barnes ... [When Murphy was correctly suspected of betraying the gang, Bass would have killed him except] for the intervention of Jackson, who told them they would have to kill him first ... [They went to Round Rock to rob, and also Bass fatally shot a Deputy Sheriff Grimes, and the hidden Texas Rangers emerged and fired at the gang, with Seba Barnes fatally shot] "but [wounded] Bass mounted his horse and fled with Jackson and Underwood ... [And the next morning Sergeant C.L. Neville found Bass dying near a trail.] Jackson and Underwood had left him there, knowing he would die, but Bass told them to go ... Underwood and Jackson were never heard of any more in the state of Texas ... [But a citation from Charles Seringo's [sic] book, 'A Cowboy Detective' mentions a hardcase named Jim T., who some believe is "no other than 'Dad' Jackson of the noted Sam Bass gang." (Roberts, Page 145-151)

The article stated:

SAM BASS' PISTOL
Texan Knew Bad Men, Saw Hoss Thieves Hang
By Thomas Turner

HICO, Hamilton County, Sept. 17. – Brushy Bill Roberts, onetime associate of Belle Starr, Jesse James, and Buffalo Bill, likes to toss a heavy Colt .45-thumb-buster pistol to his visitors while he talks.

Brushy Bill is Hico's best-known character. He says he's ninety. He looks twenty years younger ...

While you fondle the .45 Colt ... Brushy Bill spins a fascinating yarn of his life, in a fast monologue.

"That's one o' Sam Bass' pistols. **Frank Jackson grabbed it when Sam was shot by the Rangers in Round Rock**. He traded it to Belle Starr. She left it to her daughter Pearl Starr when she died ... I traded her a .44 for it. Gave $25 to boot. I wanted that gun."

Bill is part Cherokee Indian, he vows. His mother was half-Cherokee and his father one-quarter Cherokee. Bill swears he was still in the saddle when most old-timers were in front-porch rocking chairs. He still travels, riding in parades, reunions and Western revivals.

In his buckskin jacket, bright shirt, boots, and the big hat a Dallas firm sent him, he looks every inch the former range rider who was once a featured attraction of Buffalo Bill's Wild West Show.

Brushy Bill – his real name, which he distains, is Ollie L. – is the man who appeared on a New York radio show last January to back up the claim of an elderly Missourian, Frank Dalton, that he is Jesse James.

"Shore it's Jesse," he snaps. "I knowed him off and on for most of his life. First time I ever seen him I was about ten. He come to our house wounded. He had a bullet hole in his shoulder you could see through. I watched my mother wrap a rag 'round a stick, put something on it, and swab out the hole ...

Brushy Bill lives out his days in an unpainted house on the outskirts of town, with his fourth wife ... He has envelopes full of photos of the Younger Brothers, the Dalton gang, and the James boys.

To anyone who will listen, he eagerly relates a fabulous career.

Says Brushy:

"I was born in Buffalo Gap in Taylor County, the last hour of 1859. My granddad, Ben Roberts, was with Gen. Sam Houston in the Mexican War ... My dad, J.H. Roberts – everybody called him Wild Henry – come from Kentucky in 1850. He was a scout with Kit Carson – him and Carson tried to warn General Custer he couldn't lick them five tribes of Indians but he wouldn't listen. And they was right."

"We come to this county when I was about seven. Dad taught me to ride horses. I could ride anything you could throw a rope on. He used to win money on me. Boylike, I got mad at him, left home when I was fifteen. Never saw him again. I headed for the Indian territory, Oklahoma now. Near a town called Briartown, I met Belle Starr ... She was wearin' two six-shooters, looked like a man. Her and Jesse James was sweethearts for a while ...

Bill spent several months at Belle Starr's place, he says ... Once he became a member of a gang of horse thieves, unknowingly, but he scooted quick.

In fact, for many years, he made a good, if precarious, living chasing down horse thieves. Part of the time he had a half-breed helper, named Indian Jim. He was wounded twenty-six times and lost thirty horses in scrapes with thieves, he says proudly. He saw many a horse thief at the end of a rope.

He wandered through Texas, Oklahoma, New Mexico and Kansas when still a teenage kid. But he could handle a six-gun, ride anything with four legs, and handle his fists, he says ... **When he was twenty-one he was a guard for a stagecoach in the Dakota Black Hills. He weathered four hold-up attempts. Dakota was too cold, so he headed back south. For seven years, he recalls, he ranched in Mexico.**

[AUTHOR'S NOTE: Importantly, Billy Bonney's age at the shooting, "Brushy" claims he was in Dakota, then moved to Mexico. He has omitted his Billy the Kid imposture!]

"I joined the old Texas Anti-Horse Thieves Association. In 1885 I joined Buffalo Bill's show at Pueblo, Colo., for about a year. Then I went with Pawnee Bill's show ... I come back to Texas and organized my own show. For twenty-five years toured all over the Southwest with it."

Bill settled down in Gladewater during the oil boom. For eighteen years, he thinks, he worked for the city of Gladewater. Then years ago he left there and came back to Hamilton and Comanche Counties.

Still erect, with an athlete's chest, Brushy Bill travels around to parades and sits on the iron cot on his front porch. The folks in Hico are used to his stories and don't pay them much attention any more. But when a stranger comes by, Bill's eyes light up and once again he lives the days of Belle Starr.

A block down the street, you can hear, "Yes, sir, Sam Bass' pistol – while three men like him owned it , it killed fifty-six men, but that's not all ..."

BECOMING BILLY THE KID

Roy L. Haws sought "Brushy's" inspiration for his Billy the Kid imposture; and located a 1949 movie with early cowboy Lash LaRue, titled "Son of Billy the Kid," in which Pat Garrett does not kill Billy, who then becomes law-abiding. (Haws, Page 90)

But Don Cline dated it to his becoming a laughingstock to Hamilton, Texas, locals "Brushy" and Leticia fled to Gladewater, Texas. (Cline, Page 96) There, in the late 1930's or early 1940's, Cline believed, "Brushy" invented his Billy the Kid persona. (Cline, Page 57) And it there that "Brushy" got his first dupes: an oilman named Dewitt Travis and a Robert E. Lee. (Cline, Page 97)

Roy L. Haws stated that when "Brushy" moved to Hico, Texas, in 1949, contrary to what his later backers would claim, he was not secretive about his Billy the Kid claim, using it in his repertoire of tall tales to locals. (Haws, Page 57)

When Leticia died on June 22, 1944, "Brushy" married his fourth wife, widow Malinda E. Allison, on January 13, 1945. (Cline, Page 98) Cline stated she was aware of his Billy the Kid claim. Cline wrote that he had been told by one of her grandsons that: "Since Malinda had been living in Hico she knew Brushy and his reputation well and thus had no preconceived notions about his stories. Evidence of this is when she told her own children never to bring her grandchildren around Brushy as his stories would be a bad influence on them." (Cline, Pages 98, 112)

To Cline, the Roberts family confirmed that "Brushy" had no buck teeth like Billy the Kid. (Cline, Page 98) That his impersonating Billy crossed into delusion is implied by family reports of his fearing that signing his Social Security checks would get him arrested as the Kid; though Cline confirmed that he did sign them. (Cline, Page 96) In Gladewater, "Brushy" got his first converts, a duped wealthy oilman, named Dewitt Travis, and a man named Robert E. Lee. (Cline, Page 97) Both were later used by Morrison for fake affidavits that "Brushy" was Billy the Kid.

"BRUSHY'S" PATHOLOGY

The specifics of "Brushy's" pathology can only be surmised by his dependence on care of family and wives. But his long-winded tall tales match confabulation, a disorder in which absent knowledge is filled in by over-elaborated autobiographical or historical fables. It appears in diseases of memory, like dementias;

and also in psychosis - like claiming to be Napoleon. Would "Brushy" have known he was lying? His benefits fraud proves his sociopathic capacity for willful deceit. But being "Billy the Kid" was delusional. So "Brushy" may have had a schizophrenic or bipolar disorder.

And he collected similarly disturbed, imposter friends. As will be seen, one was a Jesse James imposter; another presented himself as Lincoln County War badman, Jessie Evans. "Brushy's" family member, Roy L. Haws, found a letter "Brushy" had written to a Kit Carson imposter named Oran Ardious Woodman, who called himself "Uncle Kit Carson, Father of Billy the Kid." In a seeming *folie a deux* – two sharing delusion – on April 1, 1949, "Brushy" wrote to Woodman as "your son, O.L. Roberts," about Billy the Kid visiting him in Hico, Texas. (Haws, Pages 113-114) Haws felt that "Brushy" eventually mimicked Woodman's fakery – including altering his birth date, claiming employment by John Chisum, being a Rough Rider, being in Buffalo Bill's and Pawnee Bill's Wild West Shows, and being a Deputy U.S. Marshal in Oklahoma Territory. The difference was Woodman's claim *to know* Billy the Kid, and "Brushy's" eventual claim *to be* him. But "Brushy" incorporated Kit Carson by claiming his fake father, James Henry Roberts, was Carson's friend. (Haws, Pages 116-117)

"Brushy was discovered in 1949 through his imposter network by William V. Morrison; then was coached and promoted by Morrison as a cash cow for a publicity-grabbing gubernatorial pardon and future book and movie deals as Billy the Kid. One can surmise that Morrison, in his greedy urgency, over-taxed this fragile man with high-pressure prompting and exposure to public ridicule with the failed pardon attempt, possibly contributing to his sudden fatal December 27, 1950 heart attack, at 71 years, 4 months, and 1 day – just 27 days after that pardon debacle.

A good summary of "Brushy's" chaotically overlapping fables, and his motivation for creating them, comes from a letter of April 26, 1987 from an Ola Eberhard, one of his believers in Hico, to another of his backers, Bob Hefner, quoted by historian Donald Cline in his 1988 manuscript, *Brushy Bill Roberts: I Wasn't Billy the Kid*. Eberhard wrote: "I have tried my best to get Bill to see and understand how important it is to get things correct about Billy [the Kid] and Jesse James but he just laughs and says, **'Oh well, Ola, people don't pay any mind and will soon forget what they read.' He is more concerned with getting publicity.** So you and I will keep what we discuss so he won't change it." (Cline, Pages 105-106)

WILLIAM VINCENT MORRISON

William V. Morrison, the man who discovered and promoted "Brushy Bill" Roberts, tried to get him a gubernatorial pardon as Billy the Kid, and co-authored the "Brushy"-backing book, *Alias Billy the Kid*, has been excused as a victim of "Brushy's" tomfoolery. Morrison's immunity is unwarranted. Much like farm laborer, "Brushy," he had fictionalized achievements to glamorize his own lackluster life as primarily a traveling salesman.

Born in Kaskaskia, Illinois, Morrison's only brush with fame, was his descent from Pierre Menard and his grandson, Ferdinand Maxwell. Ferdinand was the oldest brother of larger-than-life Lucian Bonaparte Maxwell, owner of New Mexico Territory's, two million acre, Maxwell Land Grant, then owner of Fort Sumner.

In 1975, when Morrison donated his papers to the Abraham Lincoln Library and Museum in Springfield, Illinois, he gave his biography featuring his "heirship," as he called it.

A Hugh W. Maxwell (born in 1777) from Dublin, Ireland, had settled in Kaskaskia, opening a general store. Other store owners were a William Morrison, and a Pierre Menard. They all prospered, and their families intermarried. And Pierre Menard became the first Lieutenant Governor of Illinois.

Hugh Maxwell married Pierre Menard's oldest daughter, Marie Odile in 1810. Their five children included Lucien Bonaparte and Ferdinand (born in 1812). Ferdinand joined the Chouteau trapping expedition on the Platte River in Colorado in 1836; eventually settling in Taos, New Mexico Territory, as an Indian Agent, founding a Masonic lodge, and dying in 1879.

In contrast, his brother, Lucien Bonaparte, joined Fremont's California expedition and amassed a fortune. Lucien settled in New Mexico Territory, where he acquired vast amounts of land, did ranching, and invested in a railroad and bank. And he founded towns: Cimarron, Elizabethtown, and Fort Sumner, where Billy the Kid's intersecting history added to his fame.

So Morrison, born in 1906 in Kaskaskia, descended from less successful, Ferdinand, as his great-great-grandfather. Ferdinand had a daughter named Evelyn (born about 1840). She married a William M. Morrison III in 1859, with their son named William M. Morrison also. This William M. Morrison IV (1859-1939) married a Sophie Hartman in 1884. They named their son Jarrett Morrison (born in 1886). Jarrett married an Afra Link. Their son was William Vincent Morrison himself.

This genetic link to the grand Lucien Bonaparte Maxwell fueled William V. Morrison's longing, just as other Old West celebrities sparked "Brushy's" mania to join the frontier's drama. Billy the Kid became both men's ticket out of detested anonymity. One can see Morrison's jealousy in his false denigration of Lucien Maxwell in a letter on his genealogy that he wrote on April 14, 1951 to historian, Robert N. Mullin. He wrote: "Lucien Bonaparte Maxwell, born in 1818, trapped and scouted for Freemont, settled on the Cimarron in N.M., later became sole owner of the Beaubien-Miranda Land Grant, died in poverty at Fort Sumner, N.M."

Morrison also had a brush with litigating. Pierre Menard's nephew, named Michael S. Menard, married a Catherine Maxwell, a granddaughter of Hugh Maxwell and Pierre Menard, and went to Texas where he founded Galveston. Pierre Menard acquired 2,943 acres of Texas property by financially backing Michael.

Reclaiming Pierre Menard's 2,943 Texas acres for the family involved a suit pursued in 1942 by Morrison and P. Menard Maxwell. They prevailed. Morrison also assisted with restoration of a Pierre Menard portrait, got a statue of Pierre Menard placed on the state house lawn, placed the family documents with the Illinois State Historical Society at the Lincoln Library, and wrote unpublished family histories.

Morrison translated this litigating into impersonating a lawyer, and bombastically badgering opponents of his "Brushy" hoax with stilted intimidating legalese.

IMPERSONATING A LAWYER

Like "Brushy Bill," William V. Morrison was an imposter, his scam being impersonating a lawyer.

His "Family History Sheet," which he wrote on January 2, 1942 for membership in the Missouri Historical Society in St. Louis listed lawyer as his profession (along with salesman and genealogist). [FIGURE: 7] And the biography that he provided to the Abraham Lincoln Library and Museum in Springfield, Illinois, with donation of his papers in 1975 states: "[Morrison] studied law at St. Louis, eventually receiving his law degree from LaSalle Extension University of Chicago, Illinois. He became a lawyer, practicing in St. Louis, until he moved to Texas where he continued to work on family genealogy and eventually filed suit [the implication being as the attorney] to recover Menard lands for the family heirs. He began to do family genealogy in 1925 and eventually used his research to establish

For History

Of the MORRISON Family

Kindly fill in the answers to the questions on this sheet and return to the Missouri Historical Society, Jefferson Memorial, St. Louis.

If you cannot answer all the questions, answer as many as possible, and give addresses of others who may have fuller information. Give names in full, initials are apt to confuse. Give names of children in order of birth when possible, whether living or dead.

Write an account of your own life and that of your father and other ancestors about whom you may have authentic facts. Send copies of obituary notices, old wills and appraisements, ancient letters and manuscripts that would be of interest. Copy all biographical sketches of persons of this family that you find in town and county histories, newspaper clippings, etc., always giving name of book or paper taken from. Photographs, especially of older members of the family, and old homesteads, monuments, relics, etc., will be very acceptable.

Please write in ink by hand, as this is more enduring than typewriter ink. Promptness is important.

Date January 2nd 1942

A

Your name William Vincent V. Morrison P. O. Address 5933 Cote Brilliante, St. Louis, Mo.
Born | full date | Nov. 26, 1906 at or near town of Kaskaskia County of Randolph State Illinois
Married " 1925 " Kaskaskia " Randolph " Illinois
Name of husband or wife Ruth Shields
Born | full date | July 4, 1908 at or near town of   County of Jackson State Illinois
Died "   "   "   "
Name of husband's or wife's Father Patrick Shields
Maiden name of husband's or wife's Mother Mary Gannon
Occupation of yourself (or husband) Lawyer-Salesman-Genealogist Religion Catholic
Politics Democrat   Former residences Kaskaskia, Illinois

CHILDREN

I	Kathleen Marie	When Born	Jan. 25, 1926	Married Whom	Joseph P. Gatti, Jr.
II	Barbara June	"	Feb. 19, 1930	"	O. W. Kuchler
III		"		"	
IV		"		"	
V		"		"	
VI		"		"	

Occupation of yourself (or husband) Lawyer-

*If died unmarried give date of death.

FIGURE: 7. William V. Morrison impersonating a lawyer on his Missouri Historical Society "Family History Sheet." (Courtesy of the Missouri Historical Society Archives, St. Louis, Missouri)

heirship to Pierre Menard when they filed suit for lands in Texas in 1942 against Frost Lumber Industry of Texas, Humble Oil and Refinery, and K. Moore [and prevailed]."

Don Cline, for his 1988, unpublished *Brushy Bill Roberts: I Wasn't Billy the Kid*, researched Morrison's claim in his 1955 book, *Alias Billy the Kid*, that he was a "graduate" "non-practicing attorney." Cline wrote:

> After checking his credentials we discovered he never graduated from a constituted law school nor applied to the Bar Association of any state to practice law ... His hometown was St. Louis where he said he attended law school. St. Louis directories for the years 1940 to 1945 show he listed himself as a sales clerk and a salesman ... Although his book [*Alias Billy the Kid*] states he was working in legal matters in Florida, the Florida Bar Association has no record of him. The book says in 1948 he was working on legal matters for the R.W. Roberts law firm in Beaumont, Texas. He is not listed in their city directory or the Texas Bar Association. He arrived in El Paso in 1950 and city directories beginning in that year until his death in 1978 [sic – 1977] list him mostly as a salesman. Three listings show him as a bankruptcy liquidator and the final, eight years as retired ... [H]e also engaged in real estate after retirement. (Cline, Page 70)

Cline also interviewed employers. Morrison had worked for J.J. Vance Microfilm Service from 1954 to 1955.

Arthur Graves of Car Parts Depot met Morrison in the middle of 1949 when Morrison was in El Paso and made application to him for auto parts salesman. Cline wrote: "**Morrison informed him he was actually a lawyer and that seemed strange to Mr. Graves that he would trade a high-paying profession for a lowly auto parts salesman job.**" Importantly, Morrison gave Graves different versions about "Brushy" than appeared in *Alias Billy the Kid* to match his lawyer impersonation. He told Graves that "Brushy" had come to see him at his St. Louis office (with legal office implied) about getting a pardon; though his book stated that Morrison had traveled to Hico in 1949 seeking "Brushy" as a man claiming to be Billy the Kid. And it was Graves who introduced Morrison to Sonnichsen, because he had taken a course with him at the College of Mines and Metallurgy in El Paso. That meant, at the time of Morrison's pardon quest, he was an auto parts salesman. (Cline, Pages 71-72)

Morrison also worked for a Bill Cardon of Dautrich Realty Company from 1960 to 1970. He told Cline: "**[Morrison] made** statements to the effect that he was a lawyer." At the time, Morrison also worked as a bankruptcy liquidator. (Cline, Page ----)

Exposure of his lawyer imposture by the press at the pardon denial hearing did not deter Morrison's lawyer imposture. Attending the funeral of "Brushy Bill," who had died on December 27, 1950, Morrison appeared as "Brushy's" lawyer for December 30, 1950's *Lubbock Morning Avalanche's* article titled "Brushy Bill Buried But Legend That He Was 'Kid' Lives On." It stated: "Another [mourner] **was Attorney W.V. Morrison** of El Paso. **The attorney said** Brushy Bill did not say he was Billy the Kid until Morrison questioned him. It came up some time ago, said Morrison, when he was running down some land documents. These **led the attorney** to believe the legendary character and Brushy Bill were the same."

Morrison stuck to that intimidating litigious persona for his self-promoting and manipulative communications; though he craftily skirted outright claim. In a letter of November 28, 1955, he alluded to his technique to Carl Breihan; writing: "I enjoy argument and it is my intention to keep the offensive."

To a Texas bookshop owner on January 3, 1950 [sic – 1951] he wrote: "I have several diary books, notes, and pictures which were owned by Brushy Bill. **I represented him and am representing [his wife] Mrs. Roberts** since his death."

To an Eva Jones, on April 4, 1951, he wrote: "**We represented Brushy Bill Roberts** in an action for pardon with Governor Thomas J. Mabry, Santa Fe, N.M., in November 1950. However Billy died before we could continue the action."

On July 23, 1951, he wrote to the N.M. Museum Library's librarian, A.S. Gaylord, that "**my client** ["Brushy Bill"] told me things about certain families in that vicinity [of Roswell]. If you should locate any facts concerning Billy the Kid I would appreciate hearing them."

And he used his stilted legalese to pretend having evidence for "Brushy;" like in his letter of December 12, 1952 to historian, Philip J. Rasch, which stated: "In representing the claim of Billy Roberts we could not accept facts that could not be supported with evidence meeting the legal requirements. Hearsay would not meet the requirements and it was not resorted to. It was necessary for us to obtain certified copies of the records."

He used the words "certified copies" like a bludgeon, whenever a real historian gave him information, by asking if it was "certified." One can see, for example, in his letter of April 1, 1953 to Geraldine S. Mathison, the Clerk of the Doña Ana County District Court, that he wanted copied records to be "certified records." In fact, that merely confirmed the copying; implying no proof about "Brushy" as Billy.

The awkward truth that he was a traveling salesman, and not a lawyer, occasionally surfaced. On January 25, 1954, he wrote as sales manager to Floyd Rigdon, the Publisher of the *Carlsbad Current Argus* in Carlsbad, New Mexico: "**We of Jim Vance Microfilm Company, take this opportunity to thank you** and all members of your fine organization for courtesies, and the great favor of permitting us to display our merchandise at your office." The same day he wrote to Marcus Griffin, Publisher of *Eddy County News*, also in Carlsbad: "**We of the Jim Vance Microfilm Company, wish to thank you for the order on microfilming.**"

In a rare admission, his letter to historian, Carl W. Breihan, on April 19, 1954, revealed his source of income: "At present, I am in charge of sales and production of the local microfilm company. Interesting side line, isn't it?" But three months later, on July 15, 1954, in a letter to Philip Rasch, he reverted to ambiguity; writing: "Usually carry your letters in one of my brief cases, but travel light in Mexico. **I am representing the Microfilm Company** down there as well as two companies of my own in Mexico."

But Mexico was just a sales outlet for Morrison, who signed his letter of November 10, 1954 to purchasing agent, J.C. Careage in Chihuahua, Mexico, as "Sales manager." He wrote: "I take this opportunity to thank you and the members of your fine organization for the splendid cooperation during the demonstration of the Wastman Verifax Printer on our recent visit there." And that November 10th, he thanked a L.D. Gaines of the San Francisco Mines of Mexico, Ltd., also in Chihuahua, and also as a "Sales manager." He wrote: "I hope you will decide to purchase the legal size printer as I am confident it will save much time and expense in your operation."

And his letterhead for a letter to Sonnichsen, on August 20, 1956, listed his services as: "Researches, Appraisals, Estates."

But when Morrison could, he faked being a lawyer, especially for intimidation. On May 18, 1954, he was sent a letter by an Attorney Edward M. Campbell, about a belligerent letter that Morrison had written to a Mrs. Mary Hudson Brothers about her Billy the Kid writing - which exemplified his pattern of viciously bullying lesser researchers in print with his intimidating faked expertise and legalese. Campbell wrote: "**Understand you are a lawyer from St. Louis.** Well, I'm from Paducah, KY, and I certainly don't consider myself an authority on Billy the Kid ... But I certainly don't consider somebody out of St. Louis an authority, either ... [Cited was William Keleher as an authority.] I have been a newspaperwoman for a good many years ... I certainly know how to check sources when I write a story. No doubt you wanted some publicity. Well, this is my answer and Mrs. Brothers' answer to your letter."

Morrison did not stop his harassment. On November 10, 1954, the same day he was writing as a salesman to his Mexico contacts, he again attacked Brothers as a pretend lawyer; writing:

> A friend forwarded to me a copy of Albuquerque Journal, October 17, 1954, wherein appears an article by Nell Campbell stating that you are an authority on Billy the Kid ...
>
> I must take exceptions to that statement, unless sufficient citations can be furnished to prove the contentions in this news article and the false statements made in your little book, Billy The Kid, by Hustler press in 1949 ...
>
> I claim to be an authority on the legal records and the evidence pertaining to the Kid and I can back my claim with legal evidence.
>
> I hope that you can do likewise.

That same November 10th, he wrote to Edward Beverly "E.B." Mann, the duped director of the University of New Mexico Press, which had accepted *Alias Billy the Kid* for publication, apologizing for his delayed answer since he had been in Mexico, but had mailed him microfilm with records on Billy the Kid and "Brushy's" Pardon Petition. He wrote: "Since many hours of hard work were necessary in assembling and writing the manuscript, Alias Billy the Kid, we are quite anxious to see it in print. Especially so, while people are still interested in learning the true facts concerning the Kid and the facts surrounding the filing of **our Petition for Pardon in behalf of Roberts**."

On February 2, 1955, Morrison wrote to Marion H. Borden, connected to the Texas Rangers, hoping he would claim Garrett did not kill Billy; stating: "**When we were representing a man claiming to be Billy the Kid** a few years ago, I made a thorough research into the legal records. I know they never made a legal coroner's verdict in July or August of 1881, when it was reported that the Kid was Killed." But Borden knew judges from Morrison's background, and apparently checked him out; because, on February 9, 1955, Morrison backtracked with double-talk: "I didn't study law with the intention of practicing the profession. Unfortunately, I have never applied for admission to the bar of any State."

By 1955, with his book coming out, bullying Morrison, with his stilted legalese, accused a *Texaco Star* reporter of being a liar if he could not prove that Garrett killed the Kid; writing:

I was reliably informed that you stated in your program that Billy the Kid was killed by Garrett on July 14, 1881.

It is my understanding that your statements made on the program are based upon facts. Therefore, I will gladly pay a reasonable sum of money for citations sufficient for me to obtain certified copies of the records ... [to] substantiate your claims.

On March 5, 1955, Morrison used his job doing collections for bankrupt estates, to mimic a lawyer to Carl W. Breihan; writing: "I have been **working on collection suits** for a bankrupt estate."

In 1966, Morrison wrote with legal-sounding mumbo-jumbo to a Paul Albright of the Associated Press on April 11, 1966, to attack Jarvis Garrett. "It appears that Mr. Patrick F. Garrett, his son, Jarvis, and Walter Noble Burns have done more than the other writers to confuse matters on Kid, when all of them had access to the facts and legal records dug out by the undersigned. Of course, I was not researching for publication of books. **I was engaged to research the legal records inorder [sic] that a client might be able to litigate his legal right in a court of competent jurisdiction.**"

Apparently Morrison's daughter, Barbara J. Kuchler, continued his lawyer hoax after his death. On April 15, 1987, she wrote to the *El Paso Times* editor about an article saying that some Hico, Texas, residents "complied evidence they say proves Billy the Kid was not killed by Garrett and that he spent the last years of his life in Hico as 'Brushy Bill' Roberts and that this was all determined after an 'historical investigation two years ago.' " Calling Morrison a "direct descendant of the famous Lucien Bonaparte Maxwell" - when he had actually descended from his brother, Ferdinand - she wrote:

> To clear up some "facts," in 1948 **a lawyer by the name of William V. Morrison**, was working up some documents ... for inheritance purposes [and learned] Billy was still alive and living in Texas ... Morrison began a correspondence with O.L. "Brushy Bill" Roberts ...
>
> Morrison moved to El Paso where he would be close to the records ... By the summer of 1950 Morrison believed he had what was necessary to obtain a pardon for "Brushy Bill" from the Governor of New Mexico. **Not being a member of the bar, he went to the firm of Andress, Liscombe [sic], and Peticolas** ... With their help he got together a brief ... [But the Mabry meeting] was a "farce" with members of the Garrett family ... newspeople and others present. [Then "Brushy" died] ...Morrison joined with

Dr. C.L. Sonnichsen, who is highly regarded by readers and scholars, in the writing of "ALIAS BILLY THE KID" ...

Because of Morrison's veracity for detail and authenticity inquiries are received frequently from historians, scholars, readers, and writers ...

How do I know all this? I am one of Morrison's daughters.

A year before his death, on April 24, 1990, Sonnichsen was contacted by Don Cline, informing him of his intent to expose "the old fraud," "Brushy Bill." And he related Morrison's lawyer impersonation: "**He had told several employers he was really a lawyer**, which he wasn't, and they wondered why, if a lawyer, he preferred taking such a poor paying job as an auto parts salesman ... Then we turned up his letters at the Missouri Historical Society that **for 39 years he kept telling them he was a lawyer.**" (Cline, Page 73)

Sonnichsen, demonstrating his support for the "Brushy" hoax, ignored this. On June 30, 1988, he had already written to Cline: "I believe, without evidence, that Bill Morrison had a law degree. I have a vague recollection that he told me he earned it in night school in St. Louis. He called himself a non-practicing lawyer. He specialized in bankruptcy cases." (Cline, Page 73)

IMPERSONATING AN HISTORIAN

Important to his "Brushy" hoax, was that Morrison's Menard litigation's research blossomed into his self-image as an historian. A natural huckster, with combined sociopathic personality and striving for attention, he turned his skills to selling his psychological counterpart, "Brushy," as Billy the Kid.

On May 21, 1956, Morrison wrote to a William Kimble, hyping himself as an historian with a legal bent; stating: "My literary partner, Sonnichsen, is a writer of fact and history, which ties in with my theory that history should follow the legal records in any event. Being a member of the Missouri Historical Society, established in 1866 by members of my family, a private institution, The St. Louis Historical Developments Foundation, and local historical societies, I am vitally interested in seeing that true facts are recorded for posterity."

Don Cline had also interviewed Pat Garrett's biographer, Leon Metz, who wrote to him on July 2, 1988 saying that he got to know Morrison when he lived near him in El Paso. Metz stated that

Morrison had also tried to prove "something different about Pancho Villa and (maybe) Jesse James" (Cline, Page 74), names that would later come up in "Brushy's fake biographical "memories."

Morrison was immediately criticized after *Alias Billy the Kid* came out. To historian, Philip J. Rasch, he wrote on May 21, 1955,: "It is your contention that if ["Brushy"] were the Kid he should be able to give us some insight that would straighten out a lot of problems. You say that no where does he give us any. I believe you will see that he did. You say you see nothing in what he said that couldn't have been picked up by 'anyone' who had read a book or two or had been around Lincoln and heard the folklore. That is a broad statement ... I have talked to expert attorneys on evidence, and other men qualified to speak on the whole subject. Frankly, none of them agree with your contention."

AT THE END

Morrison died on August 30, 1977. His September 9, 1977 *El Paso Herald-Post* obituary, with information presumably by his family, stated: "[He was] "a resident of El Paso for 29 years. He had been associated in the George Hervey Real Estate Co. and in Cardon Real Estate Co. for many years. He was also a retired Bankruptcy Referee for the United States District Court. Mr. Morrison was also a member of the Historical Societies in Missouri, Illinois, and El Paso. He is survived by his widow: Ruth Morrison of El Paso. Daughters: Kathleen M. Gatti, of Albuquerque, and Barbara J. Kuchler of El Paso; 4 grandchildren; 2 great grandchildren; 4 brothers and 5 sisters."

Morrison is idolized by "Brushy's" believers as a martyr for the truth; while the reality is that he duplicitously tried to sell "Brushy" as Billy the Kid for his own fame and fortune.

CHARLES LELAND "C.L." SONNICHSEN

Untouched by accusations of hoaxing, was fellow hoaxer, C.L. Sonnichsen, an English teacher and folklorist, who wrote quasi-fictional books on minor Old West characters. He wrote *Alias Billy the Kid*, with Morrison as second author; and his credentials arguably got it a publisher. His quirk was apparently ambition: making a contrarian niche for himself in famous Billy the Kid history. He called himself a "grass-roots historian," as if seeking history from actual participants.

He was born on September 20, 1901 in Fonda, Iowa, with the family moving to Minnesota 15 years later. He got his BA in

English from the University of Minnesota in 1924. He got his masters from Harvard in 1927, and his Ph.D. there in 1931 in English Philology (study of English in historic texts). In 1931, he was hired at the Texas College of Mines and Metallurgy in El Paso, Texas, when it first became a four year institution; later named the University of Texas at El Paso.

As his biographer for his collected papers at the University of Texas, Sarah Ashton, wrote: "[H]e was asked to teach a course in Southwest Literature, which at the time he did not believe to exist, being a seventeenth and eighteenth century English literature man. He accepted though, and began what became a lifelong study of Southwest literature and history." His biographer, Dale L. Walker, in his "Foreword" to Sonnichsen's reprinted 2000 book, *Ten Texas Feuds*, was closer to the truth: "He stayed because college teaching positions were scarce in the Great Depression era and because he was appreciated at the college where doctoral degrees were scarcer than jobs and Harvard doctorates unknown. **"I was a big fish in a little pond," he would later say."**

From 1933 to 1960, Sonnichsen headed the Texas College of Mines and Metallurgy English Department; then became Graduate Dean until 1966, while continuing to teach. In 1936 and 1938, he was also a visiting professor at the university of Texas for classes of well-known folklorist, J. Frank Dobie. He was also on the school's Library Committee, Publications Committee, and editorial Board of the Texas Western Press. Additionally, he was a vice-president and director of the El Paso Historical Society for many years. He retired in June of 1972, becoming, until 1976, Senior Editor for the *Journal of Arizona History*.

Sarah Ashton wrote: "He authored thirty-four books ... mostly on Southwestern history and folklore, and published a great deal of short stories and articles in numerous Southwestern and Western periodicals;" though not mentioned is that his *Alias Billy the Kid* was controversial. In his "Foreword" to Sonnichsen's *Ten Texas Feuds*, Dale L. Walker cited that Sonnichsen's wish to be a writer went back to his University of Minnesota days. Then, in his early days at the University of Texas at El Paso, Sonnichsen boarded with an insurance salesman who fascinated him with tales of Texas's warring families. So he began to document them. Walker wrote: "He became, he said, of the genus *Historianus herbidus*, a grassroots historian, one who 'recognizes that the original researcher was an old plainsman lying in a buffalo wallow standing off a bunch of Comanches - and too bust to write anything down.'"

He was on the editorial boards of *Arizona and the West* and the *Journal of Arizona History*. He was also President of the Texas Folklore Society (1935-1936), President of the Western Literature Association (1966), Sheriff of the El Paso Remuda of the Westerners (1967), President of the Western Writers of America (1977), President of the Western History Association (1966), and on the Executive Council of the Southwestern Literature Association; and had membership in societies for folklore, history, and literature.

He died at 89 on June 29, 1991 after a life of successful self-promotion as a big fish in a little pond. In 1992, his *Arizona Humoresque: A Century of Arizona Humor* was posthumously published. That was appropriate, because he had escaped unscathed after making a mockery of the most important Old West figure he had usurped: Billy the Kid.

MEETING "BRUSHY BILL"

Sonnichsen's meeting with "Brushy" was described by Sonnichsen's admiring biographer, Dale L. Walker, in his 1972 *C.L. Sonnichsen: Grassroots Historian*. In 1949, when he was teaching English in the Texas College of Mines and Metallurgy, Morrison brought "Brushy" to meet him. Sonnichsen liked the act, glossed with Morrison's claim that "illiterate" "Brushy" had inexplicable knowledge of Billy the Kid. And Sonnichsen, as one of the first to witness "Brushy" parroting books and Morrison's prompts, proved he had more hubris than history by thinking "Brushy" sounded like the real deal.

Sonnichsen's biographer, Dale L. Walker, wrote: "Roberts was decked out in a fringed buckskin jacket and a Stetson decorated with meshed horseshoes. After talking to him and Morrison - who had already completed most of the important research spadework - **Sonnichsen too became convinced that the old man was not an absolute fake. He seemed to know too much not at least to have been there during the times and in the places of the unfolding of Billy the Kid's desperate career.**"(Walker, Page 65) Walker quoted flowery Sonnichsen: "Here was a Western Lazarus, risen from the dead with a six-shooter in each hand, who was willing to tell of his experiences behind the veil.

Brushy Bill knew too much to have been an outsider. **He was not a literate man and could not have read up on the subject.** His recollections were too detailed and precise to have come from oral sources. He must have been there, in the flesh, when these things happened." (Walker, Pages 65-66) Recall that Sonnichsen had also taken imposter Morrison at his word that *he* was a lawyer. (Walker, Page 64) That uncritical gullibility combined with his ambition to attain recognition as an historian.

Sonnichsen's first reaction to the scam is presented in *Alias Billy the Kid*, with "Brushy's" spouting that in the Lincoln County War "negro soldiers from Fort Stanton [took] positions on the hillside and joined in the firing that day when the Murphy men burned McSween's house." (*Alias Billy the* Kid, Page 12) But there were never black soldiers there. Demonstrated was Sonnichsen's hubris-gullibility-contrarian muddle.

And canny salesman, Morrison, courted Sonnichsen for his credentials, as seen in Morrison's letter of August 17, 1950 calling him "Dear Friend." (When more secure of their alliance, he would call him "Doc.") Morrison's mission was minimizing the Coroner's Jury Report, while adding cloak-and-dagger of keeping "Brushy" a secret from *The El Paso Times's* Managing Editor, Bill Latham, to appeal to Sonnichsen with its publicity potential for a pardon petition. Morrison wrote:

> I enjoyed our chat again today ...
>
> I have just written to Colonel Fulton. I hope that he finds the original Copy of the Coroner's Verdict. I am no longer interested in it ...
>
> [Bill Latham] has an open mind on the subject [of Garrett killing the Kid]. Latham will probably talk to you on the subject. He asked what you thought on the whole matter. I advised him to contact you ...
>
> I am not adverse to anything you tell him, except the legal action [pardon petition] as discussed with you today. I prefer that you do not admit in writing that you talked with my friend ["Brushy"] ... I have talked quite a bit with Latham, but have never made the admission that Kid is still living. I told him I thought the old man had a just claim with merit, and that I think, in the summation, a preponderance of the evidence will sustain the claimant.
>
> I will keep in touch with you.

In turn, Morrison, in his tireless promotion of himself and "Brushy" as Billy the Kid, also exaggerated his ally, Sonnichsen, as ranking among contemporary Billy the Kid historians. This can be seen in Morrison's May 7, 1954 fawning letter to historian, Philip J. Rasch (a copy of which he sent to Paul Blazer, grandson of Joseph Blazer, whom Morrison was also courting), which stated: "People in the class of you, [Robert] Mullin, **[C.L.] Sonnichsen**, [Maurice Garland] Fulton, etc., represents [sic] the exception in the minority, who desire to see the true facts and records prevail."

Biographer, Dale L. Walker, himself duped by Sonnichsen, in his 1997 *Legends and Lies: Great Mysteries of the American West*, backed the "Brushy" hoax under " 'I'm Billy the Kid,' The Case of 'Brushy Bill' Roberts" (Walker, Pages 111-136). Walker plugged Sonnichsen as "a brilliant Harvard-educated English professor and historian [who] knew about the Lincoln County War and **counted among his friends some of the greatest authorities on it and on Billy the Kid** ... the result was a small but respectable collaborative effort, *Alias Billy the Kid* (1955), a fair and balanced work." (Walker, Page 134) He repeated Sonnichsen's "final word" on "Brushy" as Billy the Kid: "If it were not true, it ought to be." (Walker, Page 136) Walker betrayed the historical ignorance needed to be duped (like calling Sheriff William Brady "James"). And he ignored that Sonnichsen's "greatest authorities" friends, had already condemned his hoax from 1950 onward.

AUTHORING ALIAS BILLY THE KID

Morrison made clear that Sonnichsen authored *Alias Billy the Kid*. Writing on March 15, 1952 to a Dewitt Travis, who was used for an affidavit vouching for "Brushy" in the book, Morrison stated: "Quite some time ago I turned my records and notes over to Dr. Sonnichsen. I did not have the time and money to complete the book like I wanted it. Dr. Sonnichsen took the material and added some from his files. He has done a wonderful job considering what he had to work with. Bill destroyed all the books, papers, and pictures, there at home before he made the trip over here to interview the governor in November, 1950." On the same March 15, 1952, Morrison wrote to "Brushy's" widow, repeating almost verbatim that Sonnichsen wrote *Alias Billy the Kid*.

And Morrison wrote on September 1, 1954 to a Raymond Schleede: "One of our manuscripts has been accepted for publication by the University of New Mexico Press and I promise it will divulge facts and records never before disclosed to the public."

And on September 10, 1954, Morrison wrote to historian, Robert N. Mullin: "Few people realize the guts it took to stick this thing out, plus the hard work my associate, Sonnichsen, put in the manuscript ... I shall never forget the moral support and wonderful send off he gave me at the Rotary Club Meeting here ... A soon as publication date announced, YOU will be the first friend notified."

SONNICHSEN AS FELLOW HOAXER

But was Sonnichsen a true hoaxer or just an incompetent historian? In 1951, for an El Paso Sunland News Bureau press release by reporter, Hawley Richeson, he was quoted: " 'In my opinion, the evidence Morrison turned up indicates that the whole case of the "Kid's" death or survival needs to be re-examined,' Dr. Sonnichsen said. Dr. Sonnichsen, who has authored many books on Southwestern history and lore, said that he expects to commence work on the book sometime this summer." By then, it was clear that the Governor of New Mexico and all legitimate historians had considered "Brushy" to be an imposter. And, as will be seen, Morrison and Sonnichsen had no real evidence to the contrary. Sonnichsen was just engaging in promotion for their hoax with Hawley Richeson.

While pretending not to have taken sides, Sonnichsen actually encouraged new "Brushy"-backers, for years: like hoaxer William A. Tunstill, who fabricated an extensive genealogy for "Brushy" in his 1988 book, "Billy the Kid and Me Were the Same." On April 24, 1987, Tunstill wrote to Sonnichsen:

> Your letter of April 17th at hand as well as a copy of your letter to Mr. Morrison's daughter. Thanks.
>
> In reply must first say that I have not heard a word from Mrs. Barbara Kuckler [the daughter] ... She deals in strange ways that leave me blank.
>
> No, I cannot "BEG" her to write to me ... You did the best you could with what data Mr. Morrison furnished you. This fact I have related to you several times the past six years.
>
> I think she would make a big mistake to merely reprint the old "Alias Billy the Kid" ... As I see it, I must deplete [sic] those items which are in error or incomplete and add the new items which ... offers proof that Brushy Bill Roberts was in fact the real Billy the Kid.

Important in assessing his complicitness, is the test of time. From the 1955 publication of *Alias Billy the Kid*, to his death in 1991, advances in Billy the Kid history confirmed "Brushy's" fakery. But when interviewed for a 1998 book by "Brushy Bill"-backing authors, W.C. Jameson and Frederick Bean, he was unrepentant. According to their book, *The Return of the Outlaw Billy the Kid*, he told them he had been vilified, but had gotten "never one shred of evidence to disprove Roberts' claim." (*The Return of the Outlaw Billy the Kid*, Page 200)

On May 26, 1989, a Robert Dyer, listing himself as a member of the Western Writers of America, Southwest Writers Workshop, and The Billy the Kid Outlaw Gang, tried to determine Sonnichsen's position; writing:

> In the process of compiling my research, I read your book, "Alias Billy the Kid." You appear to have supported the Brushy Bill claim at that time. I heard from a reliable source, however, that you recently told Leon Metz [Pat Garrett's biographer] that you, "wish you'd never written the damn thing."
>
> Did you indeed make the statement ... I've been told that you discovered that you had been duped by Morrison into half-believing the story and that Morrison invented the whole thing. I heard that he led this old, senile, but otherwise harmless old man, Brushy Bill, all over "Billy the Kid Territory" teaching him line and Scripture about the Kid's life, then managed to either convince him that he was the Kid or convince him of the money that could be involved in claiming such fame ...
>
> Can you tell me if any of this is true?

Sonnichsen responded to Dyer on May 30, 1989, with intimidating threat of sensing "character assassination;" and with the glib fence-riding characterizing his public presentation. But his reading recommendations were "Brushy"-backing. He also mentioned that he had been asked to participate in the Lincoln County Heritage Trust's photoanalysis with the Billy the Kid tintype compared to "Brushy," but had declined (and it subsequently proved no match, which he ignored).

He wrote:

> I don't know how much you know about what has been going on in New Mexico and Texas but it is becoming a pretty complicated story and you will need to get hold of Bill Tunstill's **[a major "Brushy"-hoaxer]** book BILLY AND ME WERE THE

SAME [sic], Don Cline's little book on Billy, and several recent articles in magazines before you will be ready to talk. **[Note that no recommendation is made for scholarly historians like William Keleher]** ...

I can answer some of your questions categorically. I never told Leon Metz that I was sorry I wrote the book ... If you read it at all carefully, you will have noted that my last word was, "If he wasn't Billy the Kid, who was he?" **I presented Morrison's evidence, but I did not take sides**.

In the second place, I can assure you that Morrison was a dedicated researcher and in my view an honest man ... **It seems to me that there is some character assassination going on here and I want no part of it** ... What should be a search for the truth is degerating [sic] into eye-gauging and name calling. You can see why I want to keep my distance.

Sonnichsen's actual "Brushy"-backing ambition was exposed in an April 27, 1990 letter from novelist, Frederick Bean, then planning a "Brushy"-backing book (1998's *The Return of the Outlaw Billy the Kid*). Bean reported that he had followed-up on Sonnichsen's advice to contact William Tunstill (the hoaxing "Brushy"-backer) and Donald Cline ("Brushy" opponent). He stated that he had a "final question." Cline had told him that Morrison was a car parts salesman, not a lawyer. Was that true?

On May 6, 1990, Sonnichsen responded to Bean that: "Bill Morrison never said he was a licensed attorney. He spoke of himself as a 'non-practicing lawyer' and he smiled when he said it. I gathered that he had studied law - perhaps in night school in St Louis ... what he did for a living was handling bankruptcy cases. If he was a car-parts salesman, I never knew it ... I see nothing dishonorable about being a used-parts salesman ... Actually, my chief reason for wanting not to be involved in this brouhaha is the disposition on the part of some of the participants to be destructive ... **I hope you can get out of this without getting your fingers burned. I think you are in some danger**." Thus, was demonstrated the sly conspiracy theorizing that characterized Sonnichsen's portrayal of opponents in *Alias Billy the Kid*. And his fake overtone of danger evolved to later "Brushy" hoaxers portraying themselves as martyrs for the truth.

Bean answered on May 9, 1990, that he had decided that Morrison was an attorney, since Webster's Dictionary called an attorney "a person who is legally empowered to act for another;" though he missed that legally empowered means by a law degree and license, proving himself simple enough to be taken in by the hoax. And he gushed fawningly: "Morrison was, as you put it, a furious researcher. The credit for bringing Brushy Bill's story to light is entirely his ... A new generation will be compelled by the story."

This was music to Sonnichsen's ears. He kept, with Bean's other letters in his collected papers, Bean's November 11, 1990 letter. It proved Sonnichsen was aiding publication of Bean's book; sided with Bean's vilifying "Brushy" opponent, Don Cline; and was aware of the photo-analysis done for Bean to contradict one debunking "Brushy" the year before. Contrary to Sonnichsen's claim to doubting Robert Dyer – "I did not take sides" – he certainly did. Bean wrote:

Dear Doc,
Thanks so very, very much for the copy of Arizona History. Read it the minute I got it and found the footnotes about Cline all too accurate. **As graduate in Psy, I'd call Cline a paranoid delusional, openly psychotic type**. Why Sunstone or Creative published him is one of the world's biggest mysteries.

The tip you gave me about Tracy Row was a gem! ... He sounds very much like he wants to do [the book] ... The data from the UT Austin photo study interests him [the bogus Acton photo-comparison study; see pages 457-459] ... **By the way, I did mention your name to him, and I told him I was keeping you posted on the manuscript and photo study** ...

Give my very best to [your wife] lovely Carol ... I hope she is keeping you at your morning walks. Should I hear anything from Tracy Row, I'll let you know.

Best, and keep your fingers crossed.
Fred

Noteworthy is that in Sonnichsen's papers is a letter, dated November 9, 1990, just two days before Frederick Bean's, from historian, Don Cline - who Bean maligned as mad - in which Cline states: "[F]inally located Brushy Bill and his family in Bates, Arkansas, in the 1880 census, confirming his actual birth year of 1879 and birthplace as Arkansas in the 1900 and 1910 census. Morrison, Hefner and Tunstill claimed he has a cousin named 'Ollie L.' and whose parents Henry O. and Sarah Elizabeth Ferguson were Ollie's "parents" and Brushy's 'aunt and cuncle [sic]' and he took Ollie's place in the late 1880s or later as 'their son' ... Yet here he is as Oliver Roberts, born in 1879, living with his "aunt and uncle" H.O. and Sara Ferguson in 1880 when he was 10 months old." This truth was obviously ignored by Sonnichsen when encouraging Bean to back "Brushy."

And Jameson, who stayed in contact with Sonnichsen from 1962, when he was in his English class, till the man's 1991 death, recounted in his 2012 "Brushy"-backing book, *Billy the Kid: The Lost Interviews*, that Sonnichsen told him that he had warned Morrison to be prepared for historians trying to perpetuate the "status quo" of the "legend" – which became "Brushy" hoaxers' standby words used to the present. And Sonnichsen encouraged Jameson to do more work on the man Sonnichsen called "William Henry Roberts" ["Brushy's" made-up name]. (*Billy the Kid: The Lost Interviews*, Pages 29-30) Demonstrated was Sonnichsen's rationalization of "Brushy's" defeat by conspiracy theorizing impervious to facts. That settled whether he was complicit or incompetent. He was both.

But there was more. According to Jameson, Sonnichsen authored *Alias Billy the Kid* using Morrison's notes and taped interviews of "Brushy." (*Billy the Kid: The Lost Interviews*, Pages 28-29) And, without disclosure, he had altered them! As Jameson wrote: "It became clear that Sonnichsen used a relatively small amount of the information ... [and he] heavily edited Roberts' grammar, even adding and deleting words ... In other places, Sonnichsen merely summarized." (*Billy the Kid: The Lost Interviews*, Pages 42) Jameson, thus, guilelessly revealed Sonnichsen's fixing-up of "Brushy" to match Billy Bonney. And, as will be seen, for *Alias Billy the Kid*, Sonnichsen provided his obscure sources as footnotes, apparently confident readers would not check his claims from them. When one does check, revealed is brazen fabrication of their contents. Sonnichsen was, indeed, a hoaxer; smugly posing as a thorn in legitimate historians' side.

THE MAURICE GARLAND FULTON LETTER

Initially, it was beyond conception of Billy the Kid historians that Sonnichsen would stoop so low. So, on February 24, 1952, Maurice Garland Fulton, the then expert on Billy the Kid, and obviously aware of "Brushy's" pardon fiasco, wrote from Roswell, New Mexico, in response to the rumor that Sonnichsen was participating in a "Brushy Bill" book, with the assumption that it was an exposé! It had no effect. Sonnichsen had less ethics and more ambition than Fulton imagined. Sonnichsen's goal was one-upping people - like Fulton! Fulton wrote:

Dear Sonnichsen,

I am glad to hear from you directly about your book. I'll admit I was surprised at your attitude and had fears that you might injure your reputation as a grass roots historian. I would remind you that the masses are highly unintelligent and undiscriminating. They will buy, and be worried, and to finally follow the line of least resistance, which would be to say, "well, mybe [sic] it might be." If you can put it as one of the mysteries of history ... and leave it in that state you might do a good service. But when you go to shifting the wheat from the chafe, you inevitably slant toward one or the other side of the controversy [with possibility of "unethical procedure"] ...

I do not know what your story of Brushy Bill contains, but **I feel that Morrison got much information from his visits to Lincoln and must have coached the old fellow**. I did not meet Morrison until his third trip to Lincoln, when he caught me unawares and talked one Sunday afternoon for about three hours ... **I felt that he did not get from Brushy Bill anything that an old timer who had steeped himself in Billy the Kid lore in books, a sort of specialist in that field**. Morrison at that time had a cock-and-bull story of his having gone to London and of singing before royalty, with Tunstall drawn in ... I left it to him to find individuals who might identify the Kid. I must say that the identifications made of [Severo] Gallegos were weak. He is a Mexican who for 50 cents will tell you the wildest yarns.

When it comes to the question of the escape [from Garrett's shooting], I see no grounds for the idea that ["Brushy"] escaped killing through a plot. You have to postulate a considerable conspiracy to which honest men like John W. Poe become party. ... Garrett was elected, with the approval of Chisum and Capt. Lea. He was the best up to that time ...

[As to the reward for killing Billy the Kid] [t]he legislature met the following January and in February passed legislation that gave Garrett his $500 ...The reward had specified "satisfactory proof of identity required," and the legislature officially accepted it on that ground. I have not found any evidence that there was any difficulty in the legislature. Nor have I found any inclination to disbelief in the fact that it was the Kid ...

Let me hurry to a close. I am not trying to dictate but I hope you will make as clear as daylight and campaign what your position is. The question most frequently asked me was "what does Morrison intend to make out of this effort?" You know that there is an ineradicable element in human beings towards fakery and frauds and impostures. All these devices may be attributed to cupidity in the larger sense. Maybe I should say the desire to get something for nothing ... Rogues and their activities are decidedly interesting ... **The impersonator is of course a sort of forgery ... If your presentation of Brushy Bill would guide people to some thinking about the psychology behind such performances it might serve the world well.** I marvel at the way old timers insist on being Johnny-on-the-spot. Perhaps we need to view it psychiatrically ...

Yours very truly,
Maurice G. Fulton

This postscript is written after some further meditation upon your project ... I will ask that my name not be mentioned, because I see no reason for using it ...

As I have written earlier, I doubt the advisability of your undertaking notes to show the truth and the fiction. I might enjoy the book ... as the old man's story, not as a hoax but showing the public what the inventing is like. **I would very much like to hear his story before he fell in the hands of Morrison, for I am sure Morrison has modified it and made it more in conformity to the standard version.**

Sonnichsen was forewarned. But Fulton did not realize that Sonnichsen was counting on those "highly unintelligent and undiscriminating" masses to succeed with a hoax. And the only psychology in question was Sonnichsen's own.

THE HERVEY CHESLEY LETTER

Two years later, on April 19, 1954, Sonnichsen got another revealing letter from a Hervey Chesley of Hamilton, Texas, acquainted with "Brushy" for years and knowing he was a faker; but not yet realizing that Sonnichsen was one too, since *Alias Billy the Kid* would not be out until 1955. Chesley wrote:

> When you get time or I can see you I would like to know what you wrote about my old friend Brushy Bill Roberts. I knew him about ten years, first met him at Hico, and occasionally chatted with him on the street when he lived there. Short, erect, with too youngist [sic] look for his reputed years and experience, claiming

to be an old Indian scout, gaudily dressed ... He spun out western stories better than you pay for at a newsstand, and if they were maybe more fiction than fact, what is the difference anyway? ... **I thought him a showman and fake** ...

At one time a cousin of mine at Tyler and I could have brought Billy the Kid and Jessie [sic] James together. I was talking to Brushy Bill and he was dealing with Dalton, who Brushy Bill later went to New York and positively identified as Jessie [sic] James. About three years ago at Christmas time a friend of mine from Lubbock came to see me and wanted to know about Brushy Bill, said another friend of ours had just wridden [sic] on a bus with him, and he was on his way to El Paso, and confided in him that he was a half brother to Billie [sic] the Kid. **[Note that Morrison claimed that "Brushy" kept secret his Billy the Kid claims.]** By the time he got to Santa Fe he had metamorphosed into the Kid himself. Understand he broke down on cross examination there. At the very time my friend and I were talking, Brushy Bill was falling dead at Hico with a smile on his face. Those old fellows just had their parting jest and I cant see it did any harm ... Brushy Bill told me when fifteen he tied his pony in Abeline, Kansas **[note that, at 15, Billy Bonney lived in Silver City]**, and about that time the swinging doors of a saloon flew open, people stampeded out, followed by a longhaired man with six shooters, blazing, saying "I'll show you I'm still city marshal!" Said it was his first view of Wild Bill Hickok [sic].

UNDETERRED

Though criticism of *Alias Billy the Kid* occurred, Sonnichsen was undeterred. He partnered with Morrison for the Winter 1959-1960 edition of *Frontier Times* for a long article titled "They Killed Pancho Villa!" Its earliest research by Morrison was probably used to coach "Brushy" for his fictitious association with Villa. **To be noted is that Morrison had taken "Brushy" to Mexico to coach him for the fabrication. On January 31, 1951, Morrison wrote to "Brushy's" widow, Malinda Allison: "The picture of Bill and me [in his storage trunk] was made in Juarez, Mexico, on April 3, 1950, while he was visiting here."**

But the hope had been for another co-authored book, this time on Villa. It was first presented, on January 24, 1956, to their University of New Mexico publisher, E.B. Mann; then to his replacement on January 27, 1958. The book was rejected and never published.

By 1986, Sonnichsen held to his scam, though roundly denounced by historians. As Don Cline wrote to the New Mexico Book League on August 4, 1986 - a copy of which was in Sonnichsen's papers: "I wanted no association with ALIAS BILLY THE KID ... for the fact that both Sonnichsen and Morrison both knew Brushy Bill Roberts was not Billy the Kid but simply one of the many old men seeking a little attention. I also did the background research on Roberts and was amazed to find that was stated in the book is not backed up by the records and sources they claimed, but then, all the historians already knew this. They were simply 'after the buck' and not writing true history."

Interestingly, in a letter of May 29, 1991 to A Stephanie Ricks of the Book of the Month Club, Sonnichsen reported that he had transferred "all rights" to *Alias Billy the Kid* to Morrison before Morrison's 1977 death, and they were inherited by his daughter, Barbara Kuchler, who transferred then to her daughter. Barring an undisclosed financial agreement, implied is that Sonnichsen created the hoax for fame, not fortune.

His biographer, Dale L. Walker, in his "Foreword" to Sonnichsen's *Ten Texas Feuds,* inadvertently summarized Sonnichsen's slip-shod attitude by quoting from Sonnichsen's chapter, "Feud at Mitchell's Bend": "It was so long ago - and there is so little we can know about such things." That vagueness was what Sonnichsen hoped would muffle his fakery and convert his dupes for *Alias Billy the Kid.* He had longed to be a big fish in a big pond. It was fitting that his last public appearance, according to Walker's "Foreword," was in the June 1991 Western Writers of America convention in Oklahoma City. His topic was "The Future of Western Fiction." His contribution of "Brushy Bill's" fiction would endure to blight Old West history to the present.

CREATING THE HOOK AND THE BOOK

The path to a book was long and twisting for the hoaxing trio. But, when first meeting "Brushy," huckster Morrison had already recognized, in his kaleidoscope of identities, one with a publicity hook: he would seek for him, from the Governor of New Mexico, the pardon promised by Governor Lew Wallace to Billy the Kid.

CHAPTER 2
"BRUSHY BILL'S" BEGINNING AS BILLY

A PASSEL OF PRETENDERS

"Brushy Bill" was part of a weird group of Old West pretenders. In *Alias Billy the* Kid, Morrison claimed that, in 1948, when doing probate research for an inheritance, he interviewed a Floridian named Jim Hines, who told him *he* was in Lincoln County War history. So Morrison told Hines that *he* was related to Lucien Maxwell, adding that Billy the Kid had worked for the Maxwells. (Page 3) This was a fitting start to fakery since Billy never worked for the Maxwells. Hines one-upped by sharing that *he* knew Pat Garrett did not kill Billy the Kid, because the Kid now lived in Texas. (Page 3)

Next, Morrison claimed to meet, in undescribed circumstances, a Missourian named J. Frank Dalton, who told him *he* was Jesse James (the J. being for Jesse according to December 8, 1951 letter by Morrison to Carl W. Breihan); knew that Jim Hines was the outlaw, Jessie Evans; and knew Billy the Kid was an O.L. Roberts ("Brushy Bill"), living in Texas. So, in June of 1949, Morrison went to Hico, Texas, to meet "Brushy."

Don Cline, for his 1988 unpublished *Brushy Bill Roberts: I Wasn't Billy the Kid*, wrote that in 1949, when Morrison was an auto parts salesman for Arthur Graves of Car Parts Depot, he took "Brushy" to meet him. "Brushy" told Graves that many old outlaws were living in New Mexico at the same village. They had a get-together once a year for a big party. (Cline, Pages 71-72)

BACKING J. FRANK DALTON AS JESSE JAMES

Morrison had gotten himself a stable of old-timer imposters. His first focus was J. Frank Dalton. Don Cline, in his 1988 *Brushy Bill Roberts: I Wasn't Billy the Kid*, stated that Dalton was

"Brushy's" friend, in Lovington, New Mexico (Cline, Page 14); and, in the 1930's, both claimed to be Billy the Kid. Dalton then switched to "Jesse James." (Cline, Pages 35, 41)

In 1948, attention-seeking "Brushy" had promoted himself and Dalton, as can be seen in a July 8, 1948 article in *The Hinton Record* titled "Jesse James' Friend to Be at Hinton Rodeo July 14-15-16." For it, "Brushy" had a different fake persona as born on January 1, 1867 (subtracting a year from his benefits fraud birth date), and the a son of Al "Wild Henry" Roberts, who fought with the Ross Brigade in 1863 when Ann Parker was captured from the Indians. This Al Roberts also identified Charley Bigelow's body as being Jesse James's to help Jesse escape. And "Brushy" was a past scout, Indian fighter, and bronco rider. The article stated:

"Brushy Bill" Roberts of Hico, Texas, old time friend of Jesse James, will attend the 18th annual Klanla Rodeo July 14, 15, and 16, as a guest of the Hinton Kiwanis Club. "Brushy Bill" **is an 82 year old [the Social Security benefits fraud birth date of 1868 would make him 80, and his real age was a month shy of 69; though the next year he told Morrison he was almost 90] former scout and Indian fighter. He was born January 1, 1867, at Buffalo Gap, Taylor, Texas. "Brushy" is the son of Al "Wild Henry" Roberts, the Indian fighter, who fought with the Ross Brigade in 1863 when [Cynthia] Ann Parker was captured from the Indians.**

"Brushy Bill" was at Guthrie, July 7, visiting with Jesse James, and when interviewed by the press, he stated, as follows, concerning the identity of Jesse James, "I've known him for 69 years, and all this time **I knew that J. Frank Dalton was really Jesse James**.

James used to come to my mother's home whenever he'd get wounded and she would take care of him. My dad, **Al "Wild Henry" Roberts was present to identify the body after Charley Bigelow** who was going under the name of Jesse Howard, was shot and killed.

"He came home and told us all about it, and said he identified Bigelow as Jesse James. He said Jesse's mother knew it wasn't her son, but claimed it was to help Jesse get away."

"Brushy Bill" may be able to teach modern cowboys some of the finer points of bronc riding. **He rode the famous horse, Cyclone** at Cheyenne, Wyoming, in 1889, which horse was supposed to be free from any man's back. Tom Wagonner won $30,000 on "Brushy" for making the ride, and gave "Brushy" $10,000 as a gift after he won the bet.

"Brushy" will appear at the rodeo each night, and any old-timers may visit with him at the rodeo.

Donald Cline stated that in 1950, Morrison himself promoted Dalton as Jesse James, with "Brushy" as a confirming "witness." "Brushy's" relative, Roy L. Haws, in his *Brushy Bill: Proof that His Claim to Be Billy the Kid Was A Hoax*, claimed that Morrison set up a photograph of Dalton as Jesse James with "Brushy" on September 6, 1949. (Haws, Page 111)

On January 13th, Morrison got the two a New York appearance on "We the People" radio show, called "everybody's soap box." Roy L. Haws also cited "Brushy's" September 6, 1949 interview with radio personality Morrey Davidson, titled "The True Jesse James Story," in which "Brushy" called Dalton Jesse James. For that sham, "Brushy" claimed that shot Jesse came to his mother's house in Colorado when he was seven, and she nursed him for six weeks. Then Frank James fetched him. But using "Brushy's" Billy the Kid age dated this to 1866 to 1869, during which real Jesse was robbing banks in Missouri, Iowa, West Virginia, and Texas, and was not wounded. (Haws, Pages 80-81, 140)

The contradictory dates problem was also revealed in Morrison's notes on "Brushy's" statements, which are in the collected papers of C.L. Sonnichsen. An undated page is titled "Brushy Bill Roberts," apparently typed from "Brushy's" original notebooks and notes, with his claim of being a champion rider, and being known to listed men as " 'Hugo Kid' or 'Brushy Bill,' The Outlaw Horse Rider of the World;" with the list including "Frank Dalton, **Known him since 1859."** **["Brushy" had not yet begun his Billy the Kid impersonation and dating!]**

His "We the People" stint landed "Brushy" on his hometown *Hico News Review's* front page for January 20, 1950, in reporter Carolyn Holford's " 'Brushy Bill' Is Back From Gotham." It has no Billy the Kid claim for "Brushy's" Old West personas; but shows the lucrative potential, with the trip being "all expenses paid." That credulous coverage may have emboldened Morrison to abandon his Dalton hoax - with its petition merely seeking a name change to Jesse James - and to switch to a bigger prize of creating "Brushy's" future pardon scam as Billy the Kid. The article stated:

O.L. (Brushy Bill) Roberts returned the first of this week to chat with hometowners about his trip to New York after spending a week as one of the "corroborating witnesses" who are supporting a man known as J. Frank Dalton in his claims to being the real Jesse James.

"Brushy Bill" is well known around Hico as a typical cowboy who dresses in Western regalia.

Roberts gives his birthplace as Buffalo Gap in Taylor County. After living in this section as a boy, he returned to Hico in 1941 "to spend the rest of his life."

He was also a guest of Dalton's last September when he attended a party to celebrate the 102nd birthday of the man at his home in Meramec Caverns, Stanton, Missouri, where Jesse James had a hideout during the Civil War. **He was given both trips with all expenses paid.**

Dalton is one of the many claimants to the title of the notorious outlaw. **He says he has been known since 1882 as J. Frank Dalton, and had a petition in the Union, Mo. Circuit Court to change his name back to Jesse Woodson James.** To support the claim, these witnesses were called to New York, and two of them appeared on a broadcast "We the People" to tell of early recollections of Jesse James.

In telling about his trip, "Brushy Bill" told several people that this man is the real Jesse, and said that he can recognize him from previous meetings.

Among the experiences in his younger days Roberts recounts riding in Wild West shows with Buffalo Bill Cody, breaking wild cattle in South America, serving as a bronc rider in the Cheyenne Roundup of 1899, working on a Mexican Ranch during the Mexican revolution, and doing scout duty in the Black Hills of the Dakotas.

These are only a few of his tales of the "wild west," and he claims to have a collection of documents to authenticate them.

The next month, on February 3, 1950, "Brushy" was again on the *Hico News Review's* front page, in "Cornering Jesse James," still flogging J. Frank Dalton. "Brushy's" media magnetism would not be lost on Morrison, who had been coaching him since 1949 on Billy the Kid history and historic sites. With a big photo of "Brushy" and Dalton, came the short article: "Shown at top of picture is O.L. (Brushy Bill) Roberts of Hico, who, with another crony, lower left, and others, made a recent trip to New York to identify a man claiming to be the real Jesse James. The man known as Frank Dalton passed his 102nd birthday at Hotel Henry Hudson. He said that the man who was killed, thought to be James, was Charles Bigelow."

Interestingly, this J. Frank Dalton as Jesse James hoax had another participant and friend of "Brushy's": an odd-ball Texan from Gladewater, in oil field construction, named Dewitt Travis. Travis was covered in January 12, 1950's *The Whitewright Sun* in "Latest Jesse Tells of $2,000,000 Loot." Travis would later become a backer of dead "Brushy" as having been Billy for *Alias Billy the Kid*. It stated:

Jesse James, that is the latest man to claim he's the notorious outlaw, said today he has $2,000,000 in loot buried near Fort Sill, Oklahoma ...

The latest Jesse said he had been known since 1882 as J. Frank Dalton ... **Dewitt Travis, 61, an oil man, of Longview, Texas, who is helping "Jesse's friends" pay for bringing him to New York and for the petition in Union Mo., Circuit Court to change Dalton's name back to James, said he was "positive" this was the real Jesse**. He said he sat on Jesse's knee as a young boy when the hiding Jesse stayed at the Travis home and had been associated with him for 30 years.

Travis said the James boys kept his mother from starvation during the Civil War and that "Dalton" was always accepted in their home as Jesse James. Travis indicated he believed he could locate Jesse's hidden cache and said the $2,000,000 "will probably be handed back to the government when Jesse dies."

Morrison continued his J. Frank Dalton as Jesse James gimmick while promoting "Brushy" as Billy the Kid. On March 17, 1954, he wrote to a Carl W. Breihan in St. Louis, giving a copy to one of his "Brushy Bill" dupes, Paul Blazer, the grandson to the Lincoln County War figure, Dr. Joseph Blazer. Morrison informed Breihan, that a man named Al Jennings told him "that Dalton was really Jesse ... I would like to study the pictures again, the ones that Mr. [N.H.] Rose [owner of "The Famous N.H. Rose Collection Old Time Photographs"] showed to me, to satisfy my mind whether or not the body they buried could have been Jesse. At that time, we debated the difference of appearance and length and breadth of the face with the heavy dark beard on the purported corpse ... I notice in your book where Homer Croy states that Mrs. James was sent to Missouri by Jesse, Jr., to file a suit against Dalton and that she obtained a judgment. This is the first I have heard of this suit."

The Dalton-"Brushy" scam lived on. An August 9, 1986 letter to the editor of *The Dallas Morning News* by a Ted P. Yeatman; stated: "It never surprises us to see the claims of people like Brushy Bill Roberts ... reappear ... The more they are debunked, the more they surface. Roberts supported J. Frank Dalton's claim to be Jesse James, appearing with him on radio, January 13, 1950 ("We the People") with James Russell Davis of Nashville. Davis then decided to become Cole Younger, and Roberts became Billy the Kid. Dalton's case was demolished in court by no less than the daughter-in-law of Jesse James, Stella James ... The James family descendants ... are as incensed as the Garretts must be ... [But] Western hoaxes sell papers and give those who know better their latest laughs."

BETTING ON "BRUSHY"

The J. Frank Dalton performance apparently awakened Morrison to "Brushy's" showman potential. Already a Hico, Texas, character, he was comfortable parading in his fringed cowboy jacket and declaring his historical delusions. Morrison recognized that all he lacked was information to perform as Billy the Kid.

FAKING SPECIAL KNOWLEDGE

To transform "Brushy" into Billy the Kid, huckster Morrison devised two sound bites: special knowledge exclusive to Billy the Kid, and illiteracy preventing reading-up. There were three hitches: doing enough research for "memories," coaching "Brushy," and having him remember his lines.

Morrison spelled out the special knowledge ploy as a clincher in a June 29, 1955 letter to a William Waters (with a copy sent to Paul Blazer, Joseph Blazer's grandson). Morrison stated: "I will say that I conferred with specialists in the medical and legal professions, and those on other scientific fields, before arriving at my ultimate conclusion [that "Brushy" was Billy]. **I do not believe that it would have been physically and humanly possible for anyone to have located the information and retained it in his mind over such a great period of time as would have been necessary in Roberts' case."**

Morrison must have believed it was the perfect ruse. But he missed its fatal flaw: it depended on the limited and error-filled resources of his day. The give-away would be "Brushy's" repeating tell-tale errors from traceable sources. Conversely, "Brushy" parroting verbatim from Billy's writings of 70 years past, would reveal fakery. But Morrison and Sonnichsen were so confident, that they eventually listed the prompt sources as footnotes in *Alias Billy the Kid*, to pretend that the sources corroborated what "Brushy" had said; thus, inadvertently giving away exactly what "Brushy" had been fed! I called them "source footnotes."

Also, for the impersonation to work, "Brushy" had to remember the mind-boggling complexity and profusion of events and places in the Lincoln County War period if he was to perform as Billy the Kid. His limited intelligence made that task unworkable. Tellingly, when sources ran out, so did "Brushy's" "memories" - or his confabulations took over. So lies were the order of the day, with insolence that no one would notice fakery.

SOURCES FOR THE IMPERSONATION

The unrecognized obstacle for "Brushy" and team was that, in the mid-20th century, key Billy the Kid documents were still undiscovered, and scholarly history books were not yet written. So there were no available records on 1870's New Mexico Territory uprisings against the Santa Fe Ring, which had generated letters, petitions, exposés, articles court transcripts, a federal investigation with depositions and reports, a military court of inquiry, and Secret Service reports; all detailing Billy's world.

Worse for impersonation, was that prevalent in the second quarter of the 20th century were only myths about an outlaw boy named Billy the Kid, who escaped jail by slipping handcuffs, who murdered a man for each of his twenty-one years, and who was killed by a Sheriff named Pat Garrett.

To flesh out details, there existed only quasi-historical books. There were a 1927 reprint of Pat Garrett's 1882, dime novel-style *The Authentic Life of Billy the Kid*; Charles A. Siringo's 1920 *The History of Billy the Kid*; Walter Noble Burns's 1926 *The Saga of Billy the Kid*, based on Garrett's 1882 version; John W. Poe's 1933 *The Death of Billy the Kid*, relying on his memories and Pat Garrett's book; and Sophie Poe's 1936 book, *Buckboard Days*.

Early historians, Robert N. Mullin, Maurice Garland Fulton, and Philip J. Rasch were no salvation, with their groundbreaking research yielding just some historical names and a few big events. And there was a 1926 letter by Pat Garrett's posseman, Jim East, about Billy Bonney's capture.

There were Billy's contemporaries' autobiographies describing him, which lacked accuracy beyond their direct experience. There were Henry Hoyt's 1929 *Frontier Doctor*, George Coe's 1934 *Frontier Fighter: The Autobiography of George Coe Who Fought and Rode With Billy the Kid*, and A.P. "Paco" Anaya's writings, posthumously published in 1993 as *I Buried Billy*.

For Billy himself, there were his pardon bargain letters with Governor Lew Wallace in the Indiana Historical Society, with two more owned by Wallace's grandson, Lew Wallace Jr. And available in the Lincoln Museum in Lincoln, New Mexico, was a copy of his April 15, 1881 letter to an attorney, Edgar Caypless. There was the 1879 military Court of Inquiry for Commander N.A.M. Dudley, which had his testimony, but was too expensive for Morrison to buy. Available were Billy's newspaper interviews, and the Santa Fe Ring's and Lew Wallace's outlaw myth articles.

Unknown were the Secret Service reports of Special Operative Azariah Wild, only discovered decades later by Leon Metz, and used for his 1974 *Pat Garrett: The Story of a Western Lawman*. Since they covered the appointment of Pat Garrett and the tracking and capture of Billy Bonney, ignorance of them left a fatal information gap.

Lincoln, site of the Lincoln County War Battle and Billy's jailing, was largely intact, and Morrison toured "Brushy" there in 1949 for coaching. But lost for trickery was Fort Sumner, including the Maxwell mansion where Billy was killed. And diagrams of the town and house were unavailable. Also, in 1949, Morrison interviewed Lincoln County residents to prompt period "memories."

The tintype of Billy at age 20 was used to fake physical similarities.

Also there was history's junkyard: old-timer windbags spouting malarkey to add themselves to the history of Billy the Kid. They would be the "Brushy" hoax's undoing, since Morrison and Sonnichsen relied on them, and were too incompetent to vet them, so "Brushy" parroted their errors as fake memories.

MORRISON'S MASSIVE RESEARCH

The "Brushy" hoax was labor-intensive. Morrison sought out books, magazines, articles, court filings, executive records, and old-timer interviews. With a con-artists' scorn of readers' intelligence, he betted that the sources would be seen as impressively corroborating "Brushy's" claims, rather than the obvious: they were prompts.

Morrison described his labor to the librarian at the Indiana Historical Society, on October 28, 1950, while copying its Billy the Kid letters. He wrote: "Nearly two years have been consumed in my research, and I can scarcely realize that it has been completed." [To be noted is that Morrison claimed to meet "Brushy" in June of 1949, which would be only 1 year 4 months; leaving the possibility he was researching Billy the Kid after the 1948 leads by Jim Hines and J. Frank Dalton.]

On February 9, 1955, he wrote to a Marion H. Borden: "Not a stone was left unturned during my investigation in behalf of Billy Roberts. In addition to certified copies of the legal records, I have microfilms of all court minute books and most case files pertaining to the Kid and those who were involved in his troubles."

RESEARCH SUMMARIES IN SONNICHSEN'S PAPERS

In C.L. Sonnichsen's collected papers are pages of undated notes by Morrison, in longhand and typing, summarizing research, with annotations showing errors that "Brushy" would parrot. Revealed is the extent of research into esoterica for prompting "Brushy" as to astounding special knowledge.

There are four pages of small handwriting including "Wallace Papers," with lifted quotes from Billy's letters and Wallace's interview of him; the "Mullin Collection," with information about Billy's stealing from a "Chinaman" in Silver City, killing a "Windy, the Blacksmith" in Arizona; an April 4, 1879 letter from Lincoln by a George Taylor to President Hayes (from the Hayes Memorial Library, Fremont, Ohio) quoted as: *"These outlaws [in Lincoln] are the worst characters of the country. Jesse James of the notorious James family of Missouri is one of the leaders among them. Campbell is Jesse James.* "Siringo's book, *Lone Star Cowboy* mentioning Selman. Esoteric newspapers like the *Silver City Independent*, the Las Cruces *Thirty-Four*, the *New Mexico Sentinel* yield esoteric names like Catron's brother-in-law Edgar Walz, outlaw John Selman, shopkeeper Sam Corbet, and getting the Edgar Caypless letter in the Lincoln State Museum in Mesilla about Billy selling his mare to pay Fountain.

Morrison also researched Billy Bonney's indictments and court cases. And in Sonnichsen's papers is Morrison's typed transcript of "Minute Book 'B,' U.S. District Court for the Third Judicial District at Mesilla, Doña Ana County, Territory of New Mexico," which he got from "the Clerk of District Court, Santa Fe, New Mexico." It states that on April 6, 1881, Billy Bonney's indictment for the Andrew "Buckshot" Roberts killing was "quashed (dismissed)," misunderstood by Morrison as acquitted.

As to articles, there was Lew Wallace's June 8, 1902 *New York World Magazine's* article titled "General Lew Wallace Writes a Romance of 'Billy the Kid' Most Famous Bandit of the Plains." Excerpted was its quote: " 'Testify,' I said, before the grand jury **and the trial court** and convict the murderers of Chapman, and I will let you go scot free with a pardon in your pocket for all your misdeeds." Unbeknownst to Morrison, Wallace was writing fiction about Billy going to "trial court." But prompted "Brushy" mouthed that the pardon bargain involved standing trial for Billy's indictments.

There were eight typed pages of Morrison's commentary about Pat Garrett's 1927 edition of *The Authentic Life of Billy the Kid*.

The notes' errors were parroted by "Brushy": that Billy the Kid and his boys bought clothing for Garrett when he arrived in Fort Sumner; that Celsa Gutierrez, related to Garrett by marriage, was Billy's sweetheart; that Billy left Silver City at age 12; that Billy freed a Mel Segura from a jail; and that Barney Mason was Garrett's brother-in-law because they had a double wedding.

Additionally, in Sonnichsen's papers, were eight pages of Morrison's typed commentary about John W. Poe's 1933 *The Death of Billy the Kid*. Attacked is editor Maurice Garland Fulton's confirmation of the Coroner's Jury Report. Morrison wrote: "M.G. Fulton knows that no bonified coroner verdict exists, but he is satisfied for purposes of history, to accept hearsay evidence which cannot be supported by any evidence." This demonstrates the conspiracy theorizing that Sonnichsen would build on himself.

BILLY THE KID'S LETTERS

Morrison's "research" included Billy's Bonney's letters to Governor Lew Wallace. He had first gone to Lincoln, New Mexico, with "Brushy" for coaching and research. As he wrote to librarian Caroline Dunn at the Indiana Historical Society's William Henry Smith Memorial Library in Indianapolis, on October 9, 1950: "While in Lincoln [at the Lincoln Museum] I copied most of the letters in which I am interested. I am enclosing herewith copies for your ... assistance in locating the original to be photostated and certified by your office." The first set of copies was for coaching. The certified copies were for his fake legal presentation at the pardon hearing for "Brushy." He also communicated directly with Lew Wallace Jr. to get a copy of the first pardon bargain letter.

He had urgency, because of his intent to use the letters in the pardon hearing for "Brushy" as Billy. He also wanted a copy of Lew Wallace's "Interview With 'Kid' of March 23, 1879." On October 6, 1950, he sent a Western Union telegram; stating: "URGENT NEED OF PHOTOSTATIC COPIES CORRESPONDENCE BETWEEN GOVERNOR LEW WALLACE AND WM BONNEY BILLY THE KID ALSO GOVERNORS REPORT OF MEETING ON THURSDAY NIGHT MARCH 1879 ADVISE WILL FORWARD CHECK COVER COSTS." By October 25, 1950, he got the $9.78 bill for "17 sheets Photostats, Lew Wallace Collection." On October 28, 1950, Morrison responded to the librarian: "Your documents complete my file on this unusual case ... Being a member of the Missouri Historical Society, St. Louis, Missouri, I appreciate the valuable assistance rendered to research workers by various Historical Institutions. Again I thank you for prompt attention to my requests." But cagy Morrison ignored her request as to the purpose of his research.

On October 30, 1950, Lew Wallace Jr., Lew Wallace's grandson, wrote suspiciously to Morrison:

> Mr. William V. Morrison
> 1312 Arizona,
> El Paso, Texas.
>
> Dear Sir:
> A photostatic copy is being prepared of the letter in my possession from William H. Bonney ("Billy the Kid") to Governor Lew Wallace and will be sent to you when completed.
>
> Miss Dunn of the Indiana Historical Bureau has shown me your correspondence with her, and from it I am not able to understand the purpose for which you desire this Wallace MSS material. In one letter I believe you referred to a legal proceeding and in another to a "case". **I am pleased to cooperate with and assist all bona fide use of this historical data, but, as you can understand, I do not wish it to be used for any advertising, commercial or other purposes of that nature.**
>
> May I therefore ask that you explain what will be done with this material. If we understand correctly that you are collecting evidence for a law suit, I believe it would be of historical value to have a transcript of the proceedings added to the Wallace collection in the Smith Memorial Library.
>
> Very truly yours,
> *Lew Wallace*

By November 10, 1950, still suspicious Lew Wallace Jr. answered Morrison's double-talk, with: "**I do not care to assist any imposter to appear in the role of Billy the Kid.**" Wallace wrote:

> Dear Sir:
> Your letter of November 2 confuses me in some respects. **I cannot understand your reference to work "on the heirship of the father of certain persons" and your discovery that "the party in the interest was the same person as Billy the Kid."** Do you mean that you have proved that some person whom you know is a child or descendant of William H. Bonney?

I am also puzzled as to what you find lacking in proof of the death of Billy the Kid. If only documentary proof is missing, how many others have died in the American frontier without death certificates? In view of the Kid's age he would be some ninety years old in 1950, and it is, of course, possible that a man of ninety years could be alive today, provided that he had not been killed seventy years ago.

I do not care to assist any imposter to appear in the role of Billy the Kid or a child of Billy the Kid. There is plenty of serious work in the world to be done by everybody. Therefore, I would appreciate a clarification of this matter.

Your letter refers to a pardon of the Kid "as promised". **It is my impression (and at the moment of writing I do not have the time to check my memory) that Governor Wallace "promised" William H. Bonney that if he, Bonney, would give himself up <u>and stand trial</u>, Wallace would pardon him, if he were convicted.**

[AUTHOR'S NOTE: This is a quote to remember. Lew Wallace Jr. wrongly added the bargain as <u>to stand trial, and get pardoned if convicted</u>. This error will later appear in "Brushy's" mouth as to his pardon bargain as Billy.]

I do not recall ever having seen an account of the Kid's story in which these conditions were shown to have been fulfilled, although the romanticizers of the Kid's life have intimated a broken pledge and bad faith.

[AUTHOR'S NOTE: Neither Wallace nor Morrison know the pardon bargain details, so neither will "Brushy!"]

The copies of these letters are therefore made available to you on the condition that you will permit me to examine you [sic] use of them in advance of such use in order to determine whether you allege that Governor Wallace broke his promise, and on the further condition that you will justly consider any fair criticism I may be able to make of your interpretation of the facts. Whatever you can prove I shall not object to.

Surely you realize that anyone dealing with history has a responsibility for the truth. I rely on your sense of that responsibility, as I hope you can rely on mine."

This letter does not constitute permission to publish these letters in any form.

Very truly yours,
Lew Wallace

Obviously, Morrison ignored Lew Wallace Jr.'s preaching about "responsibility for truth." He proceeded to the gubernatorial pardon hearing with the Lew Wallace Collection's "certified" Billy the Kid letters a fake "proof" that "Brushy Bill" was Billy the Kid.

PROMPTING "BRUSHY"

Ultimately, all the labor and all the sources came down to "Brushy's" regurgitations. He had to play the part of Billy the Kid. He had been basically a *tabula rasa* for facts. As it would turn out, under pressure, he also had a bad memory for his coached history as Billy. But Morrison would not realize that until too late.

By the November 30, 1950 pardon hearing, Morrison had been coaching "Brushy" since their June, 1949 meeting. He had exposed him to the sources, made tape recordings of his "interviews" with him, and had toured him to Lincoln and its courthouse-jail.

It would take 67 years from "Brushy's" 1950 death, for specifics of "Brushy's" preparation to be revealed. For his 2012 book titled *Billy the Kid: The Lost Interviews*, "Brushy"-believing author, William Carl "W.C." Jameson, related that between the summer of 1949 and December 1950, Morrison had taken notes, and had made eight six-inch tape recorder reels, of his "Brushy" interviews. (Jameson, Page 28) Jameson also confirmed "Brushy's" own notes, kept in "Big Chief writing tablets;" which Jameson's co-author and "Brushy"-believer, Frederick Bean, had located in 1989. (Jameson, Pages 34, 36).

Morrison's prompting was exposed in the pardon hearing. November 30, 1950's *Santa Fe New Mexican's* article, "Billy the Kid Only a Phony It Turns Out," revealed that when "Brushy" forgot any other sheriff besides Brady, this interchange occurred: " 'What's his name?' ["Brushy"] asked, turning to Morrison. 'Garrett,' supplied Morrison."

Obviously, attempt was made by the hoaxers to keep secret the prompting. But W.C. Jameson inadvertently provided insight in his book, *Billy the Kid: The Lost Interviews*. He reproduced portions of "Brushy's" "interview" tapes' transcripts, *which included Morrison's leading questions*. Demonstrated was that "Brushy" lifted their information to confabulate his tales. Jameson failed to recognize that they were rehearsal tapes; so he naively noted that "Brushy" oddly kept repeating things over-and-over! As examples, Morrison asks: "Tell me what you remember about the incident at the Greathouse Ranch where Deputy Jimmy Carlyle was shot and killed, a killing that was attributed to you" (Page 91); or "You rode away and hid out at Stinking Springs then, didn't you? Tell me about the confrontation with Garrett and his posse." (Jameson, Page 97)

One can also picture that, at Morrison's tapings, "Brushy," who could read and write, had in hand the sources which he was parroting. An example is from Billy's March 4, 1881 letter to Lew Wallace, in which he wrote: "*I have done everything that I promised you I would, and you have done nothing that you promised me.*" "Brushy" came up with: "I done everything I promised him to do." (*Alias Billy the Kid*, Page 131)

And Morrison also directed "Brushy's" reading-up and confabulating from afar, as shown in a letter he wrote to "Brushy" on December 18, 1950 (nine days before "Brushy's" sudden death), whose copy is in the Sonnichsen papers. To "Dear Billy," it stated: "This after noon Dr. Sonnichsen's secretary called me and asked if you remember **Clay Allison**. Did you know him? I think you talked about him when we were on a trip in New Mexico. What do you remember about him, if anything?" In fact, Clay Allison was part of Colfax County War history, and had nothing to do with Billy Bonney.

Also, "Brushy" had likely read Pat Garrett's *The Authentic Life of Billy the Kid* and Walter Noble Burns's *The Saga of Billy the Kid* even before meeting Morrison; with Billy already being one of his Old West personas from the 1930's in Gladewater, Texas. What Morrison relied on, was adding his own research, so "Brushy" could mouth masses of details seemingly too hard to study-up, "proving" he was Billy the Kid.

But Morrison miscalculated. The prompt source scam had a big flaw: vast areas of Billy the Kid history lacking any sources in their day. That left "Brushy" relying on confabulations, with his inimitable, garrulous, erroneous, over-elaborated, wild fantasies. And what could be parroted in relaxed privacy of taping, would have to be performed live for the pardon hearing.

CHAPTER 3
DEALING WITH MISMATCH DILEMMAS

"Brushy" had fatal mismatches with Billy Bonney. Besides "Brushy" being 20 years too young - which he made a fake genealogy to conceal - and his knowing no intimate Billy the Kid history - which Morrison tried to remedy by coaching - "Brushy" and team had to face that real Billy was literate and fluent in Spanish. Also, their day painted him as An evil serial murderer.

THE LITERATE BILLY DILEMMA

Billy Bonney's letters were a hurdle for the hoax by proving he was literate and wrote in elegant Spencerian script. [FIGURE: 8 and FIGURE: 9] And he was very articulate, as shown in his Frank Warner Angel deposition (not yet discovered in "Brushy's day), his Court of Inquiry testimony (too expensive for Morrison to buy), and his press interviews.

READING BY BILLY BONNEY

Billy referred to his own ability to read. In his Dudley Court of Inquiry transcript for May 28, 1879, he stated: *"Mr. McSween wrote a note to the officer in charge asking what the soldiers were placed there for ... I read the note myself, he handed it to me to read."* In his letter of December 12, 1880 to Lew Wallace, Billy wrote: *"**I noticed in the Las Vegas Gazette a piece** which stated that, Billy "the" Kid, the name by which I am known in the Country was the captain of a Band of Outlaws."*

WRITINGS BY BILLY BONNEY

Walter Noble Burns, for his 1926 *The Saga of Billy the Kid*, interviewed Billy's fellow Regulator, Frank Coe; who stated: "Billy had a little schooling and **he could read and write as well as anybody else around here.** I never saw him reading any books,

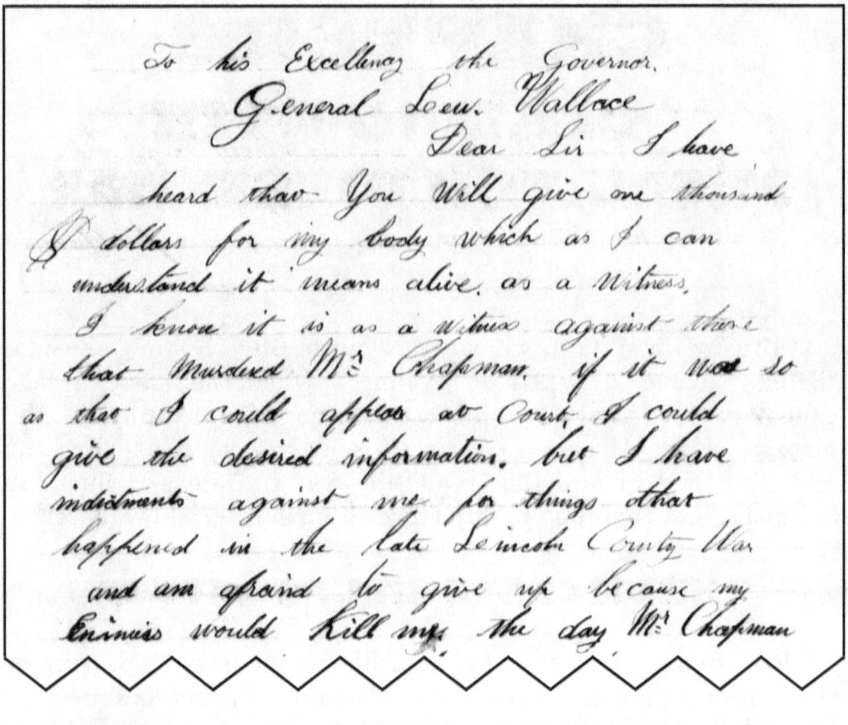

> To his Excellency the Governor.
> General Lew. Wallace
>   Dear Sir I have
> heard that You Will give one thousand
> dollars for my body which as I can
> understand it means alive. as a Witness.
> I know it is as a witness against those
> that Murdered Mr Chapman. if it was so
> as that I could appear at Court I could
> give the desired information. but I have
> indictments against me for things that
> happened in the late Lincoln County War
> and am afraid to give up because my
> Enimies would kill me. the day Mr Chapman

> I have no Wish to fight any more indeed
> I have not raised an arm since Your Proclamation
> as to my Character I refer to any of
> the Citizens. for the majority of them are
> my Friends and have ever been helping me
> all they could. I am called Kid Antrim
> but Antrim is my Stepfathers name.
>   Waiting an answer I remain
> Your Obedient Servant
>   W. H. Bonney

FIGURE: 8. Letter of March 13, 1879 to Governor Lew Wallace, with uniquely modified Spencerian handwriting. (Courtesy of the Indianapolis, Indiana Historical Society, Lew Wallace Collection)

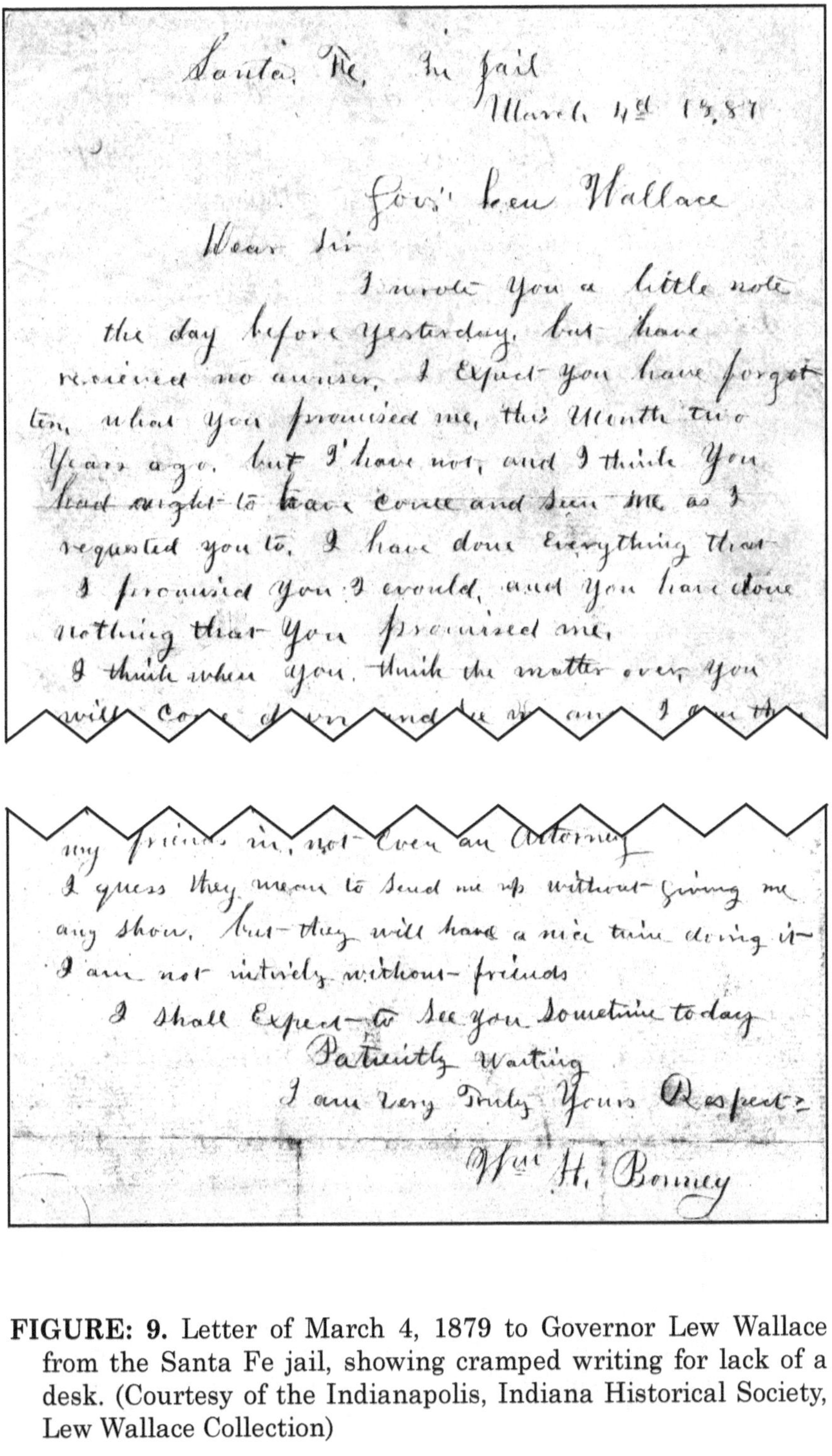

> Santa Fe, In jail
> March 4th 1879
>
> Gov'r Lew Wallace
> Dear Sir
>   I wrote you a little note the day before yesterday, but have received no answer. I expect you have forgotten what you promised me, this Month two years ago, but I have not, and I think You had ought to have come and seen me as I requested you to. I have done Everything that I promised you I would, and you have done nothing that You promised me.
> I think when you think the matter over, you will come down and see me ...
>
> ... my friends in, not even an Attorney. I guess they mean to send me up without giving me any show, but they will have a nice time doing it. I am not intirely without friends
>   I shall Expect to see you Sometime to day
>   Patiently Waiting
>   I am very Truly Yours Respect=
>   Wm H. Bonney

FIGURE: 9. Letter of March 4, 1879 to Governor Lew Wallace from the Santa Fe jail, showing cramped writing for lack of a desk. (Courtesy of the Indianapolis, Indiana Historical Society, Lew Wallace Collection)

but he was a great hand to read newspapers whenever he could get hold of any. He absorbed a lot of education from his newspaper reading. He didn't talk like a backwoodsman. I don't suppose he knew much about the rules of grammar, but he didn't make the common, glaring mistakes of ignorant people. His speech was that of an intelligent and fairly well-educated man." (Burns, Page 67)

And fatal to the "Brushy" hoaxing, was that Billy doing his writing was witnessed by Henry Hoyt for his Hoyt Bill of Sale, whose handwriting matches Billy's other writings. Besides Hoyt, legal witnesses signed it: George J. Howard and James E. McMasters, in whose store Billy wrote it. [FIGURE: 10]

In a letter of April 27, 1927, Henry Hoyt shared that Bill of Sale with Lew Wallace Jr., as well as informing him that he also had a copy of one of Billy's reply letters to Lew Wallace, which Billy had also mentioned to him. Hoyt wrote, with his underlings:

> Incidentally, I am one of the very few men living who was well acquainted with that famous outlaw "Billy the Kid" and **for many years supposed I had the only specimen of his handwriting in existence**, a Bill of Sale for a horse he presented me with, to protect me should my <u>ownership</u> ever be <u>questioned</u>, a <u>very important matter</u> in that part of the world in that period. This paper I have preserved all these years.
>
> Shortly before I wrote you last year I learned of the letter your grandfather [Lew Wallace] wrote to Billy the Kid and the latter's reply, then in the possession of Maurice G. Fulton, of Roswell, N.M., so opened up a correspondance [sic] with him that resulted in his exchanging copies of both letters with me for a copy of the Bill of Sale.
>
> As **I happened to know about this correspondance, both from the Kid and General Wallace**, and mention it in my manuscript, I naturally would like to include these letters in my book [*Frontier Doctor*] – that is to be published this fall by Houghton Mifflin Company of Boston – and am asking your kind permission to do so.
>
> I am enclosing a photo-copy of my souvenir of the Kid – Wm H. Bonney – with my permission to use same for publication at your pleasure. You will find a written and signed by me, statement on the back explaining it. As I do not know if you have a copy of the only picture of Billy in existence or not, I am also sending a

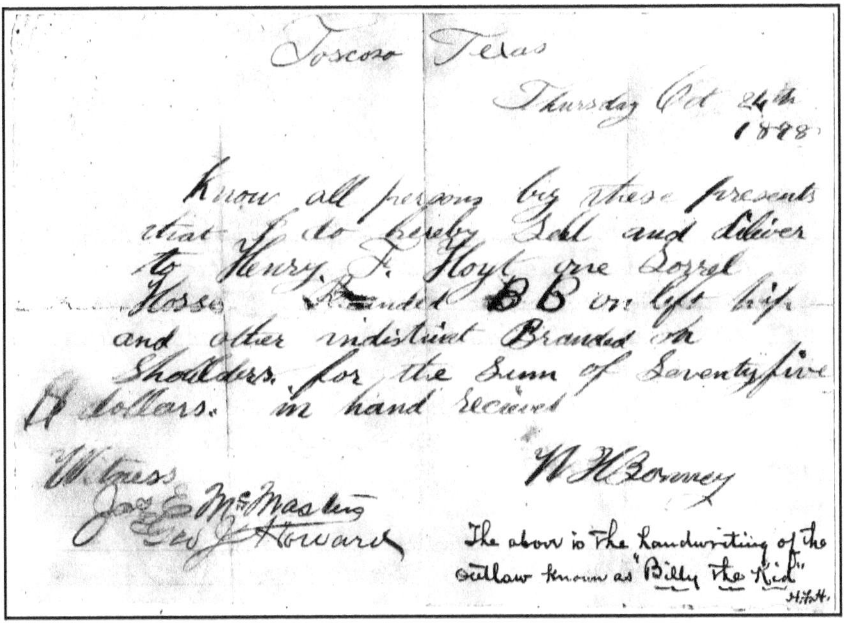

Toscoso Texas

Thursday Oct 24th
1878

Know all persons by these presents that I do hereby Sold and deliver to Henry F. Hoyt one Sorrel Horse Branded BB on left hip and other indistinct Branded on Shoulders. for the Sum of Seventy five dollars. in hand received

W H Bonney

Witness
Jas E McMasters
Geo J Howard

The above is the handwriting of the outlaw known as "Billy the Kid" H.F.H.

FIGURE: 10. Hoyt Bill of Sale, October 24, 1878 (Courtesy of the Panhandle-Plains Historical Museum, Canyon, Texas)

copy of it ... By looking closely you will see a chain crossing his chest. This is a long braided hair chain attached to a ladies gold watch that I presented to Billy for his sweetheart in Fort Sumner, who is still living [Paulita Maxwell].

I presume this had something to do with his later giving me Dandy Dick the best horse he had [thought to have been dead Sheriff Brady's]. You will notice in my note on the back of the bill of sale that it was written <u>before</u> I learned of the letters between he and General Wallace.

Hoyt's handwritten note on the back of the Bill of Sale stated:

Copy of a bill of sale written by Wm H. Bonney – alias "Billy the Kid" Oct 24' 1878 – at Tascosa, Panhandle of Texas, U.S.A., and given to me for my protection in case my ownership of this horse, which Billy had presented to me – was ever questioned. **It is witnessed by Howard & McMasters, owners of the leading store in Tascosa where it was written.** *It is without a doubt the only* **specimen of the handwriting of this famous young outlaw** *now in existence –* **He was 19 years old when he wrote this** *– was killed by the famous gun man, Sheriff Pat Garrett 3 years later ... He was a remarkable character, a natural leader of men, and was largely forced into the life of an outlaw by his circumstances over which he had no control.*   Henry Hoyt
Long Beach California. 1927

Though concealed by Morrison and Sonnichsen, they had samples of "Brushy's handwriting, with some retained in Sonnichsen's collected papers. Poorly educated and intellectually limited, "Brushy" had scrawled cursive handwriting and big childish printing. (See pages 230-231 below) They were no match with Billy's penmanship, making clear the reason to claim his illiteracy to prevent fatal comparison with real Billy's own productions.

But there was worse for "Brushy": Billy had intellectual brilliance and a sophisticated vocabulary, and was even being able to correctly spell indictments in his letter of March 13, 1879 to Lew Wallace, in which he wrote: "*I have* **indictments** *against me for things that happened in the late Lincoln County War.*"

VERBAL SOPHISTICATION

The bigger picture was Billy's grammatical and verbal sophistication, seen in his elegant language in his letters, legal testimonies, and interviews.

His July 3, 1878 "Regulator Manifesto" declared: "*Steal from the poorest or richest American or Mexican, and the full measure of the injury you do, shall be visited upon the property of Mr. Catron.*"

Examples of his skill are in his letters to Governor Lew Wallace. On March 13, 1879, he wrote: "*I have no wish to fight any more indeed I have not raised an arm since Your proclamation.*" On March 20, 1879, he wrote: "*I am not afraid to die like a man fighting but I would not like to be killed like a dog unarmed.*" On December 12, 1880, he wrote: "*There is no such Organization in Existence. So the Gentleman must have drawn very heavily on his Imagination ... if Some impartial Party were to investigate this matter they would find it far Different from the impression put out by Chisum and his Tools.*" On March 4, 1881, he wrote: "*I have done everything that I promised you I would, and You have done nothing that You promised me.*"

He could even use correct legalese as shown in his October 24, 1878 Bill of Sale to Henry Hoyt; which stated: "*Know all persons by these presents that I do hereby Sell and deliver to Henry F. Hoyt one Sorrel Horse.*" And, in his March 13, 1879 letter to Lew Wallace, he wrote: "*if it is in your power to Annully those indictments I hope you will do so so;*" with annulment being the proper action (rather than pardon) before sentencing.

In his May 28, 1879 Dudley Court of Inquiry testimony, he responded meticulously: "*Q. By Col. Dudley. How far is the Tunstall building from the McSween house? Answer. I could not say how far, I never measured the distance. I should judge it to be 40 yards, between 30 and 40 yards.*"

Illustrative also is his December 27, 1880 *Las Vegas Daily Gazette* interview with its editor, Lucius "Lute" Wilcox's, as: 'The Kid. Interview with Billy Bonney The Best Known Man in New Mexico." Billy was quoted: "There was a big crowd gazing at me wasn't there?" he exclaimed, and then smiling continued: "Well perhaps some of them will think me half a man now; everyone seems to think I was some kind of an animal." And in his April 16, 1881 article in the *Mesilla News*, he was quoted: "If mob law is going to rule, better dismiss judge and sheriff and let all take chances alike ... I think it hard that I should be the only one to suffer the extreme penalty of the law."

In contrast, "Brushy" was a loutish, racist, grammatically primitive, country bumpkin. In *Alias Billy the Kid*, Sonnichsen quoted "Brushy's" May 24, 1949 letter to Morrison about hiding his Billy the Kid identity: "I ain't putting out nothing." (Page 59) That book also gives examples: "I done wrong like everyone else did in those days." (Page 5) "I wasn't no outlaw." (Page 8) "If we could have kept them [N-word]s out there at Stanton, we would have whipped Peppin's posse." (Page 30) "He done all he could for me" (Page 39) - trying to repeat Billy's April 13, 1881 letter to Edgar Caypless, which stated: "*Mr. A.J. Fountain was appointed to defend me and has done the best he could for me*." Morrison's recorded June 16, 1949 interview of "Brushy" in Hamilton, Texas, quoted in *Alias Billy the Kid*, has examples: "It made me mad, it did [that people thought Garrett killed the Kid.]" "I done everything I promised him to do [for the pardon]." "I didn't have to testify against Evans and I shouldn't a done it." (Pages 130-131)

CONTENT

The even bigger picture on Billy's literacy was the content of his productions, and the fact that he repeatedly risked his life to testify against Ringites; as is shown in his 1878 deposition to Frank Warner Angel and 1879 testimony in the Dudley Court of inquiry. (see pages 131-135, 144-149 above)

HOAX RESPONSE TO LITERACY

The "Brushy" hoax response was to ignore or conceal everything proving Billy's high literacy except his letters, which were claimed to be written by a "friend." This required hoping no one would not notice that this "friend" was with him, from 1878 to 1881, in Tascoso, Texas; San Patricio; his Lincoln incarceration; and in his *solitary* confinement in the Santa Fe jail.

This "friend" claim was in Morrison's October 3, 1956 letter to an E.B. Fowler that Billy Bonney had not written his letters:

> Since you mention handwriting comparison, you will be interested to know that **we made a scientific study in the laboratory of the leading expert in St. Louis**. We did not have access to the original Wallace letters. We used photo copies, which would be inconclusive in court action. However, it was determined that more than one hand wrote those letters. We were unable to definitely establish that the Kid wrote anything.

Historians accepted all of the writings as being those of the Kid without question, until I raised the issue. Of course, Historians and writers are never interested in legal evidence. It disturbs their findings.

That "leading [handwriting] expert in St. Louis" was a liar or an incompetent. He or she declared that the letters were written by two people, because the 1881 jail letters looked different from the original pardon bargain letters of 1879. But that is explained by their Spencerian script requiring a desk to support the arm - an option not in jail, and resulting in Billy's more cramped jail script.

But, as I showed in my 2014 book, *Billy the Kid's Writings, Words, and Wit*, the alphabet letters were identical. And Billy's idiosyncrasies were repeated in all his writings. He almost never capitalized the first word of a sentence - unless it was coincidentally a name or "I." He also repeated his few misspellings - like "annser" for "answer." His first pardon bargain letter to Lew Wallace of March 13, 1879 states: *"please send me an annser telling me what you can do. You can send annser by bearer ... Waiting for an **annser** I remain Your Obedient Servant W.H. Bonney."* His March 4, 1881 Santa Fe jail letter to Lew Wallace states: *"I wrote You a little note the day before yesterday but have received no **annser**."* His March 27, 1881 Santa Fe jail letter to Lew Wallace states: *"for the last time I ask: Will you keep Your promise. I start below tomorrow. Send **Annser** by bearer."*

The "Brushy" hoax was rightly terrified of a comparison of "Brushy's" handwriting to Billy's.

THE BI-LINGUAL BILLY DILEMMA

Billy was accentlessly bi-lingual, as confirmed by his contemporaries. As Pat Garrett stated in his 1882 *The Authentic Life of Billy the Kid*: **"[Billy] talked Spanish as fluently as any Mexican."** (Garrett, Page 8) Henry Hoyt wrote in his 1929 book, *A Frontier Doctor*: **"He spoke Spanish like a native."** "Teddy Blue" Abbott's 1955 *We Pointed Them North: Recollections of a Cowpuncher* made clear that Billy allied with the Mexican cause; writing: "The Lincoln County troubles was still going on, and you had to be either for Billy the Kid or against him. It wasn't my fight ... **it was the Mexicans that made a hero of him**." And Billy's bi-culturalism may be credited with bringing Hispanic fighters into the Lincoln County War Battle.

"Brushy" did not speak Spanish; and that could not be faked; though his later authors tried. (See pages 646, 650 below) And contrary to real Billy's multi-culturalism, "Brushy" was a crass racist, who called Fort Stanton's black 9th cavalrymen "[N-word]s."

THE LITERATE "BRUSHY" DILEMMA

Another problem was that "Brushy" *was* literate, so fully able to read-up on Billy the Kid for tall tales, instead of being Billy the Kid. As bad, his handwriting did not match real Billy's.

Early on, Morrison and Sonnichsen seemed to miss the pitfalls of "Brushy's" literacy, and did not hide it. Samples of his cursive script and printing are in Sonnichsen's collected papers, and many examples of his literacy were cited.

Historian Don Cline, in his 1988 manuscript, *Brushy Bill Roberts: I Wasn't Billy the Kid*, found that "Brushy" confirmed that he could both read and write in the census of 1910; and had attended school to the fourth or fifth grade before being expelled (for unstated reason). And "he continued writing letters right up to his death." (Cline, Page 56)

That literacy resulted in slip-ups by Morrison and Sonnichsen as they evolved the illiteracy lie, in his lifetime; and after his death, for the 1955 publication of *Alias Billy the Kid*.

In transcripts of his interviews with Morrison in Sonnichsen's papers, "Brushy" references his own prompt notes; stating: "Sixty nine years is a long time to recollect ... **Some I made those notes you saw ...** You mention to me some names I can't recall right now. They are in those books you saw I guess. **I gave you a list of some of these men, I did.**" (Interview in Hamilton, Texas, 6/16/49, Pages 6, 9) About casualties in the Lincoln County War Battle "Brushy" says: "We lost four men, but about eight, or seven of us got away. **I don't remember, but you read my note book.**" (Interview in Lincoln, New Mexico, 8/18/49, Page 2)

Sonnichsen, in his collected papers, also had pages titled "Notes for Brushy Bill Roberts 'The Texas Kid,' " which were typed and had crossed-out dates and ages. One, undated, seems to have Morrison's typed and altered transcript of a "Brushy" note, followed by what looks like Morrison's writing, followed by a scrawled script addition using "i" instead of "I," and with random capitalizing that apparently was "Brushy's" addition. **[FIGURE: 11]** And an undated typed page, signed by Morrison and described as "printed on a third sheet of paper" and signed by

"Brushy" as "Ollie Roberts," appeared to be "Brushy's" pre-Morrison genealogy notes and stated: "My father moved to Idaho 45 years ago living there only a short time when he was killed Then my mother went back to Ky to her people. I went there about 40 years ago but was unable to find her Then I returned t [sic] Ardmore, Okla."
[FIGURE: 12]

On December 18, 1950, Morrison wrote to an Attorney Dennis Zimmerman in Tulia, Texas, whom he was trying to convince that "Brushy" was Billy: "We have handwriting of the Kid <u>as well as handwriting of the claimant.</u>"

In a letter of February 14, 1951 to an Ola Eberhard, Morrison described writings he had on recently deceased "Brushy;" stating: "Billy ["Brushy"] gave me his diary books some months ago."

And on February 22, 1951, he wrote to "Brushy's" widow: "Do you have anything that Billy did write?"

On October 8, 1952, Morrison wrote to a George G. Swett, who apparently analyzed handwriting, that he had made a photostatic copy of the Hoyt Bill of Sale "written by Wm. H. Bonney." Morrison wrote: "I informed Dr. Sonnichsen along the lines discussed at your office with reference to your investigation. He is anxious to include your opinion in our first book **if it is possible to establish a connection between the Photostats and writings of Brushy Bill.**" That meant in 1952, Morrison and Sonnichsen had not yet settled on the illiteracy excuse. Possibly the obvious mismatch of Billy's elegant Spencerian script and "Brushy's" scrawl ended that scam. But indicated is that Sonnichsen was in on the eventual hoaxed illiteracy.

On March 15, 1953, Morrison wrote to a Patience Glennon, daughter of Billy Bonney's Silver City teacher, Mary Richards, requesting copies of Mary's handwriting "to determine if the Kid adopted her style of writing in his early school days."

And on March 29, 1954, Morrison wrote to Paul Blazer, grandson of the Blazer's Mill owner, being careless while trying to convince him of "Brushy's" special knowledge: "Billy's [<u>"Brushy's"</u>] <u>letters to me</u> have been copyrighted in my Petition for Pardon and I will make copies of the ones <u>wherein he wrote his escape to me</u> before we made any trips to this country. He certainly didn't get his story in your country. Amazing, isn't it?"

And "Brushy's" literacy crept accidentally into *Alias Billy the Kid*. Its first footnote states that his account of his life was "assembled from Roberts' **notebooks, correspondence, and** conversation." (Page 14) He is referred to as "**writing an**

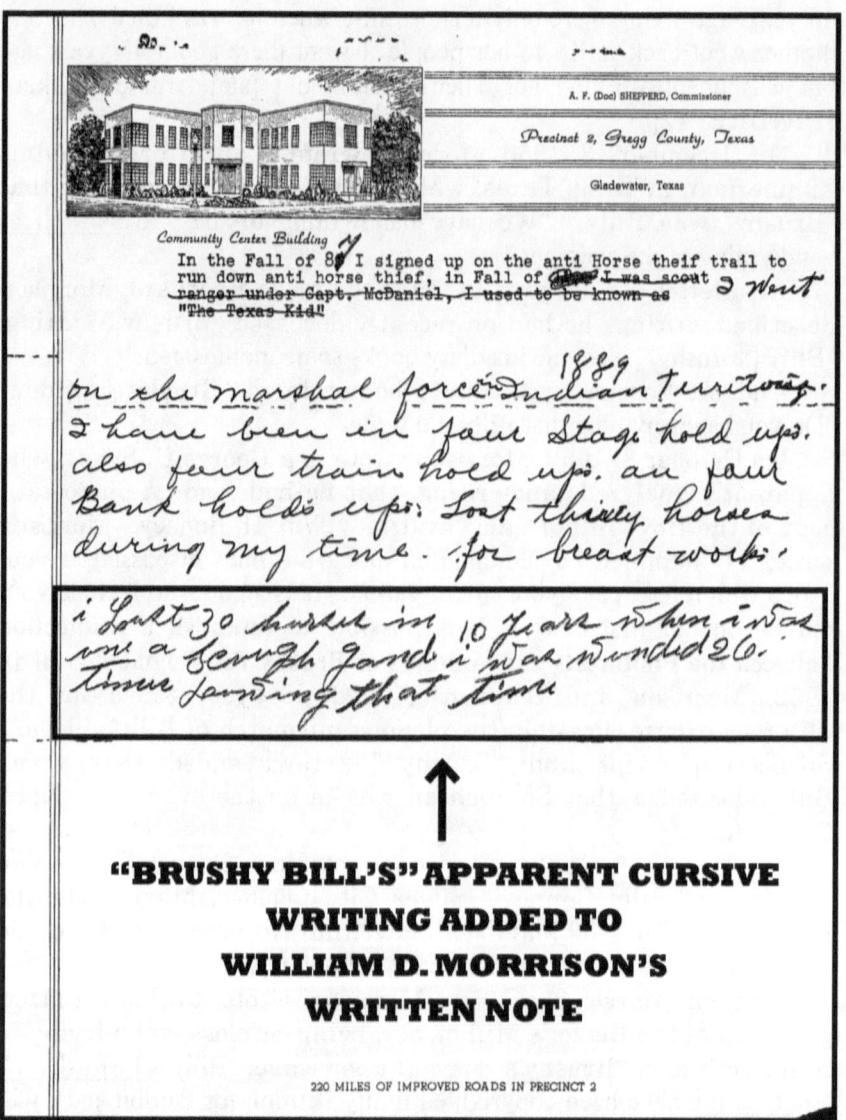

FIGURE: 11. Apparent sample of "Brushy Bill's" cursive writing, along with William V. Morrison's cursive writing and alteration of "Brushy's" dates. (Courtesy of University of Texas at El Paso, C.L. Sonnichsen Papers. MS 141, Box 92, Folder 386)

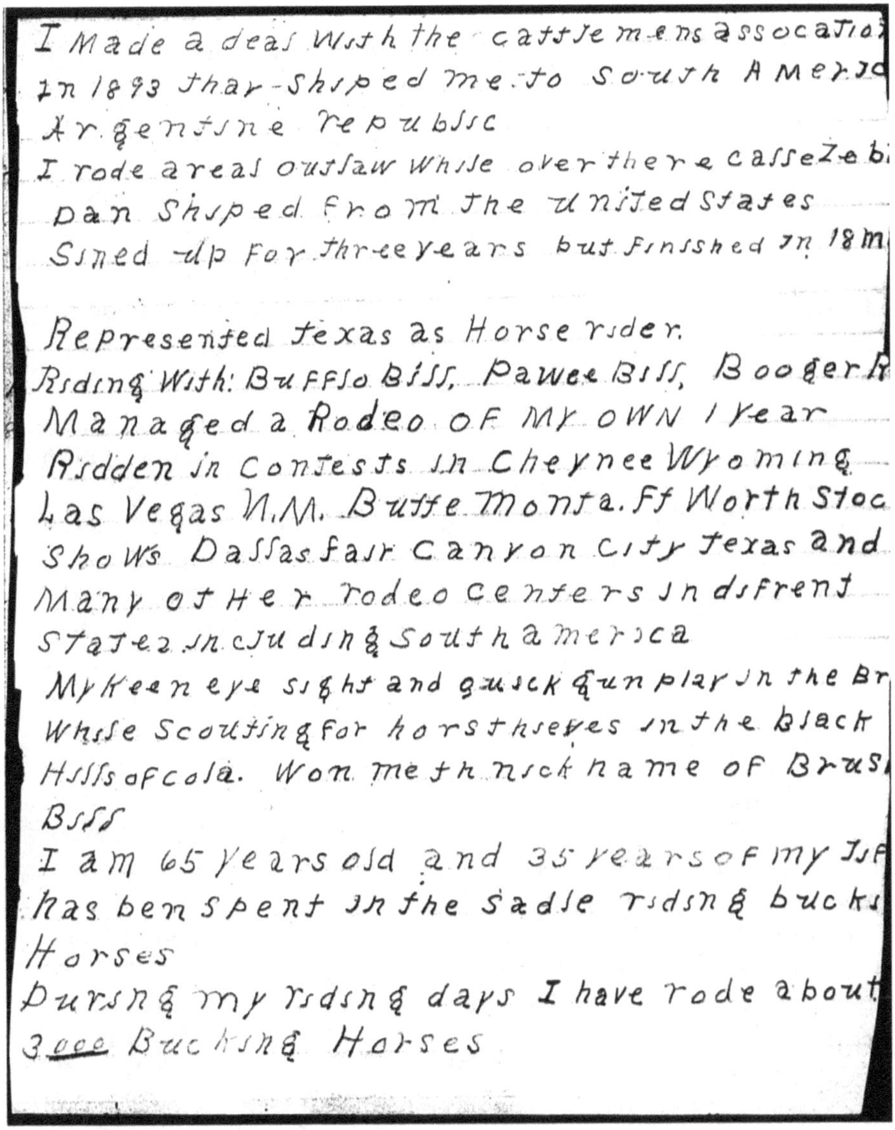

I Made a deal With the cattlemens assocation
In 1893 thay shiped me to South Amerjc
Argentine republic
I rode areal ouslaw while over there calleZebi
Dan Shiped From The United States
Sined up for three years but Finished In 18 m

Represented texas as Horse rider.
Riding With: Buffsio Biss, Pawee Bill, Booger R
Managed a Rodeo oF MY OWN 1 Year
Ridden in Contests in Cheynee Wyoming
Las Vegas N.M. Butte Monta. Ft Worth Stoc
Shows Dallas fair Canyon City texas and
Many other rodeo centers in difrent
States including South america
My Keen eye sight and guick gun play in the Br
Whsle Scouting for horsthseves in the black
Hills of cola. Won me th nick name of Brusi
Bill
I am 65 years old and 35 years of my life
has ben Spent in the Sadle riding bucki
Horses
During my riding days I have rode about
3000 Bucking Horses

FIGURE: 12. Apparent sample of "Brushy Bill's" printed handwriting and pre-Morrison fables. (Courtesy of University of Texas at El Paso, C.L. Sonnichsen Papers. MS 141, Box 92, Folder 386) [Original was printed in reverse from a negative; and has been reprinted as a positive for legibility]

autobiography." (Page 11) **His "notebooks"** "covered practically the entire West," wrote Sonnichsen. (Page 20) And he kept "**copious notes**" on his post-Fort Sumner shooting life. (Page 50) Sonnichsen even quoted **his literate May 24, 1949 letter** to Morrison to show that he was secretive about being Billy. "Brushy" wrote: "She said she had three affidavits that people knew me in 1887 ... These men said I was Billie [sic] the Kid ... I ain't putting out nothing ... I don't like for other people to meddle with my business." (Page 59) And "Brushy" is described as "**writing up his history the way he wanted it told. He set down his story in a series of paper-covered composition books ... and a couple of loose-leaf notebooks. One of the latter is dated 1925.**" (Page 59) Sonnichsen commented: "Roberts' account of these early days is hard to follow." (Page 20) They rambled about roaming through Arizona, Montana, Oregon, Oklahoma Indian Territory, Wyoming, and Nebraska, and Old Mexico; with outlaws, rustlers, Cheyenne and Arapaho Indians, and employed as a bronco buster and ranch worker. And that was before age 17!

Sonnichsen also referred to "Brushy's" three prompt notebooks on Billy the Kid, which he destroyed after the Mabry hearing; writing: "There was a possibility that **he did write down some of the things he was trying to hide.**" (Page 60) Though Sonnichsen rationalized that "Brushy" feared they were evidence that would get him arrested as Billy, more likely was post-pardon failure paranoia that they too revealed that he was an imposter.

Later "Brushy"-backing authors, W.C. Jameson and Frederick Bean, in their 1998 book, *The Return of the Outlaw Billy the Kid*, having seen "Brushy's" notebooks, said he **wrote with a "scrawl," and had bad grammar and misspellings**. (*The Return of the Outlaw Billy the Kid*, Page 204)

And "Brushy's" relative, Roy L. Haws, for his 2015 book, *Brushy Bill: Proof That His Claim to Be Billy the Kid Was a Hoax*, provided a literate letter by "Brushy," dated April 1, 1949, to a tall tale teller named Oran Ardious Woodman, who claimed to be Kit Carson. **"Brushy" wrote: "We are doing fine. Hope this finds you the same. The wind blows every day and its cold – Wheat looks good ... Cattle they are fat.**" (Haws, Page 113)

The secret Parkinson Affidavit of December 1, 1950, which follows, confirmed not only "Brushy's" "**diary books**," but Morrison's aiding its fix-ups to match Billy. It stated: "["Brushy"] admitted that certain alterations had been made by him and Mr. Morrison to correspond with, and represent the true facts as they would be: that certain names and dates had been changed." Even *Alias Billy the Kid* stated that "["Brushy"] had spent time with Morrison correcting his narrative before his death." (Page 11) And Morrison, on April 12, 1977, wrote to a Lawrence K. Mooney, admitting both to "Brushy's" writings and his fix-ups. He stated that after "Brushy's" death, "[w]e started to correct passages in **his memoirs** and **the letters he had sent me**, which were never completed."

So "Brushy" could study-up for the biggest role of his life!

SECRET AFFIDAVIT ON "BRUSHY'S" WRITINGS

In Sonnichsen's collected papers was an astounding, never used, typed template for an Affidavit attesting to "Brushy's" literacy! It concerned a recording of "Brushy" made on December 1, 1950, 26 days before his sudden death. Apparently written by Morrison, it was signed by a non-historical Mrs. S.N. Parkinson on April 18, 1951, described as: "personally acquainted with WM. H. Roberts, also known as Wm. H. Bonney, "Billy the Kid", Texas Kid, Hugo Kid, Brushy Bill Roberts, and O.L. Roberts, who is now deceased." Oddly, written-in is that it was also signed by Kathryn Cuellar, unidentified in the single affiant statement, on April 19, 1951. Importantly, it was made before the writing of *Alias Billy the Kid*, and never heard of again.

It was Parkinson's attesting to hearing, at Morrison's home, contents of Morrison's taped December 1, 1950 interview with "Brushy," and her attesting to seeing "Brushy's" five diaries and his notebooks. **[APPENDIX: 1]**

The Parkinson Affidavit demonstrates that in the early hoax version, "Brushy's" literacy was not hidden. As astounding was the Affidavit's admission that Morrison altered his writings to correspond to Billy the Kid history; with the fake excuse that "Brushy" had hidden his Billy the Kid identity by using wrong dates and names! Obvious, however, is intent to use the tapes as future proof of "Brushy's" "special knowledge" as Billy the Kid. This hoax-demolishing confession was later hidden by Morrison and Sonnichsen. But it proved Morrison's forging of "Brushy's" words!

It also preserves "Brushy's" own pre-Morrison hoax, with fables about other Old West personas, with himself being "Ollie Roberts," "Brushy Bill," "Al Brushy Bill," "the Texas Kid," or "The Out Law Horse Rider." The Parkinson Affidavit stated:

The affiant ... states that she was present, together with Mr. William V. Morrison ... at the residence of William V. Morrison, on December 1, 1950, at which time they witnessed a recording in which William V. Morrison interrogated the said Wm. H. Roberts, alias Wm. H. Bonney, with reference ... to the life and happenings of the said Roberts, alias Bonney, alias Billy the Kid; that **the said Roberts ... admitted the ownership of five certain and definite diary books in the possession of William V. Morrison, which books he identified, and he admitted that certain alterations had been made by him and Mr. Morrison to correspond with, and represent the true facts as they would be: that certain names and dates had been changed** for the reason that the said Roberts had been covering up certain facts during his life time to withhold his true identity through fear of apprehension for crimes he had committed as Wm. H. Bonney, alias Billy the Kid, in New Mexico.

This affiant further states ... that a certain black back, loose leaf note book, titled, "This Book the private life of Brushy Bill was wrote in 1925", and containing thirty-eight sheets of writing script in ink; that there appears near the center of the sheet No. 39, the name, "Brushy Bill Old Scout", which he admitted having written in his own hand; that there appeared on sheet No. 37, the name, "Ollie Roberts, age 76", which was also written by him, and the age "76 years", to cover up his true and correct age in withholding his true identity; that there appeared on sheet No. 35, a list of names including Pawnee Bill, Texas Jack, and Buffalo Bill, with the notation on the bottom thereof, "Yours truly, Brushy Bill", all of which was admittedly written by him; he admitted that he had formerly worked with all of the men whose names appeared thereon.

This affiant further states that the said Wm. H. Roberts identified the following described books as being the original diary books concerning his life; and he identified the following mentioned articles and pictures:

Book No. one. gray back composition, containing 100 pages;

Book No. two, blue back composition, beginning page 101, and including page 199;

Book No. three, blue back composition, beginning with page 200, and including page 294, with the following page no numbered, containing names of people with whom he was acquainted through the years;

Book No. four, blue back composition, titled, "The Life of Ollie Roberts or Brushy Bill or the Texas Kid", containing 128 pages, with changes on the first page from Ollie Roberts to Billy Roberts, and the year of birth from 1869 to 1859; that there appeared on page 84 thereof, the final page of writing, "Signed Al Brushy Bill The Out Law Horse Rider", which he admitted having written in his own hand ...

[Added, with Morrison's obvious prompting and writing for the affidavit, was Billy the Kid history lifted from traceable sources, and calling the Mabry pardon hearing not a "fair trial."]

This affiant further states that the said Wm. H. Roberts, openly admitted to us during this interview and recording on December 1, 1950, that he was "Billy the Kid".

LITERACY REVEALED BY "BRUSHY" HIMSELF

By the time Sonnichsen wrote *Alias Billy the Kid*, the illiteracy claim was settled on. But since Sonnichsen used Morrison's taped interviews of "Brushy," he accidentally forgot to edit out all "Brushy's" quotes about literacy. Parroting real Billy's December 12, 1880 letter to Wallace, "Brushy" had slipped-up and stated: "We went to Las Vegas, where **I read** that Billy the Kid had killed Carlyle." (Page 35) And about Billy's Santa Fe jail letters, "Brushy" stated: "**I wrote to Governor Wallace** to come and talk to me, but he failed to do so." (Page 39)

THE ILLITERACY SOLUTION

"Brushy" and his team settled on illiteracy as the way to claim special knowledge and to deny reading-up.

In transition to the illiteracy claim, there was floated that he hid his handwriting to hide being Billy the Kid! This silliness was in an undated typed note, likely from 1951 and by Morrison (when he was writing to "Brushy's" widow, Malinda Allison Roberts for samples of his writing), and in Sonnichsen's collected papers. It stated: "Little things show how careful ["Brushy"] was not to give himself away. He never wrote in longhand - always printed his brief notes, and got somebody else to write his letters."

At times, Morrison tried to play both sides, as in a letter on January 6, 1956 to a Rick Steinke that "["Brushy"] could not read or write for more then twenty-five years." This claim came without explaining the mysterious loss of literacy at age 65 (calculated with fake age 90)!

In a July 12, 1955 letter to historian, Robert Mullin, (with its copies in Sonnichsen's collected papers and to Paul Blazer), Morrison said "Brushy" "could not read."

Sonnichsen joined in - proving that he was a liar, since he had copies of "Brushy's writings in his collected papers — and revealed why the hoax had settled on illiteracy. He was quoted in Dale L. Walker's 1972 biography of him, *C.L. Sonnichsen: Grassroots Historian*: "['Brushy Bill'] was not a literate man and **could not have read up on the subject**." (Walker, Page 64)

THE SERIAL MURDERER MONSTER DILEMMA

In "Brushy's" day, Billy the Kid was believed to be the cold-blooded murderer, cattle thief, and gang leader of the outlaw myth. Since "Brushy" and team were ignorant of the actual freedom fight against the Santa Fe Ring, with Billy as its hero, they struggled to make "Brushy" palatable as the Kid, and deserving of a pardon. So "Brushy" and team feebly offered that Billy was not so bad, other men in his day were bad too, and after the killing scene he (as "Brushy") led a law-abiding life. Worse, "Brushy" and team did not know why Billy killed anyone, so floated was revenge for Tunstall's killing. Writer Sonnichsen apparently just hoped readers would not dwell on the awkward, monster murderer problem.

THE HOAX FORMULA

From "Brushy's" 1950 death to the 1955 publication of *Alias Billy the Kid*, Morrison and Sonnichsen, crystallized their hoax to an almost 91 year old named William Henry Roberts, who was Billy the Kid because he looked like him, had special knowledge, and was illiterate to prevent reading-up. And there was no proof of the Kid's killing, since there was no Coroner's Jury Report, and Pat Garrett got the reward by Santa Fe Ring corruption. And "Brushy" was opposed by Garrett's family and historians because they refused to admit that they had no proof of Billy the Kid's killing.

But the key secret was that real "Brushy Bill" Roberts would now be surreptitiously fixed-up to create a better "Brushy" to better match real Billy Bonney and new historical research.

CHAPTER 4
THE BILLY THE KID PARDON PRIZE

PRIMED FOR THE PARDON PRIZE

Toward the end of 1950, William V. Morrison's sly stunt paid off: he actually got New Mexico Governor Thomas Jewett Mabry to agree to a pardon interview with "Brushy." Morrison accompanied him bearing the fruits of his labors; as described by Dale L. Walker in his 1997 *Legends and Lies*: "seventeen parcels of legal materials – transcriptions of his interviews, investigative findings, depositions, and several notarized statements from people who had known the Kid and testified that Roberts and the Kid were one and the same." (Walker, Page 132) Then all involved discovered the publicity magic of Billy the Kid: the charade became big news.

The inconvenient truth was that at the scheduled hearing on November 30, 1950, Billy Bonney had been dead for 69 years, 4 months, and 17 days - as impeccably documented.

ABOUT GOVERNOR THOMAS JEWETT MABRY

The make-or-break for William V. Morrison's bid for his own glory depended on the 14th Governor of New Mexico: Thomas Jewett Mabry, an attorney at the tail-end of his term, which was from 1947 to 1951. Born in Carlisle County, Kentucky, three years after Billy Bonney was fatally shot by Sheriff Pat Garrett, Mabry was 66 when facing-off "Brushy Bill." A Chief Justice of the New Mexico Supreme Court from 1939 to 1946, Mabry was able to test evidence. He also had a long career in public service, having also been a state Senator, an Albuquerque City Commissioner, and an Albuquerque District Attorney. And he had integrity and respected the state's iconic Old West history. So he gathered Billy the Kid experts to assist his evaluation.

PUMPING-UP "BRUSHY"

By the time of the pardon petition, "Brushy" had gone through almost a year and a half of Morrison's coaching. Everything would depend on his performance; though Morrison unrealistically bet that his own presentation of Billy Bonney materials indicating that *he* had deserved the original Lew Wallace pardon, coupled with "Brushy's" small hands and thick wrists for shackle-slipping, plus two affidavits of non-historical people claiming "Brushy" was Billy, would do the trick. And he strove to pump-up "Brushy." (To noted is that Morrison always called him Billy; though when asked his name in the eventual hearing he flubbed it as Ollie!)

On August 3, 1950, Morrison wrote to literate Brushy":

My Dear Friend Billy:

... The consensus of opinion in this entire country is swinging in our favor. The Historians of note are beginning to pull in their ears, and the remaining few in quantity and quality, will have nothing to offer by the time we are ready to finish out case. I have been forced to release a few statements, but nothing that will hurt out cause ...

I am sending clipping which you can keep ... Mr. Hooten [of the *El Paso Times*] told me that definitely Garrett killed Billy because a friend of his was told by a friend of Pete Maxwell that Maxwell saw the dead body, etc. From Mr. Hooten's Column in his paper yesterday, it appears like he is not going to make any more statements of facts. He has turned tail now.

I have the affidavit of the old lady [Martile Able] that we talked to in El Paso. She is very sick at present.

I will be in Carrizozo and Lincoln over the weekend.

I hope that both of you [his wife] are well and with best wishes.

                        Your friend,
                [No signature, because this was a copy
                    sent to colluding Sonnichsen, and
                    was in his collected papers]

THE PARDON PETITION

In C.L. Sonnichsen's papers is a draft of the Pardon Petition, apparently by Morrison. The signature line has typed in: "By Andress, Lipscomb and Peticolas, Attorneys for Applicant." And Attorney Ted Andress signed eventually. In a letter of January 2, 1951, Morrison wrote to a John S. Mayfield: "Mr. Andress was recently retained to represent ["Brushy"] in the petition for pardon to Governor Mabry in Santa Fe, N.M."

Noteworthy is the November 15, 1950 final Petition's incorrect description of Billy Bonney's pardon bargain, which was reflected in "Brushy's" own errors about it. On Andress, Lipscomb and Peticolas letterhead, the Pardon Petition stated:

The Honorable Thomas J. Mabry
Governor State of New Mexico
State Capitol
Santa Fe, New Mexico

Honorable Sir:
Application is herewith respectfully made for a full, unconditional pardon for William Henry Roberts, alias William Henry Bonney, alias William H. Antrim, alias "The Kid," alias "Billy the Kid," alias A.L. Roberts, who was wrongfully convicted of murder in Dona Ana Country, Territory of New Mexico, after a change of venue from Lincoln County in April, 1881. After such wrongful conviction and in the desperation brought about by reason of the facts revealed in the enclosed verified statements, affidavits, letters, news articles, etc., Billy the Kid escaped from the Lincoln County jail and has never thereafter been apprehended.

There is a legend that this applicant was killed by Sheriff Pat F. Garrett in July, 1881, at Fort Sumner, San Miguel County, New Mexico, but this legend has no competent evidence and support is wholly improper and untrue. As a matter of fact applicant was not killed by anyone and lived in Old Mexico for many years.

As proved by the attached file of affidavits, statements, letters, etc. Territorial Governor Lew Wallace promised to pardon applicant for all offences committed by him upon his promise to surrender to the Sheriff of Lincoln County, furnish statements to the Governor on general conditions existing in Lincoln County, to testify before the Grand Jury concerning the disturbance in Lincoln County, and in connection with the murder of Houston [sic] J. Chapman, an attorney, on a public street in Lincoln, and to plead to the indictment against him in Lincoln County District Court. The applicant carried out his agreement to the letter, but the promises made to him were never carried out.

Even at this late date it is highly proper and essential that the terms of the original agreement with Governor Lew Wallace, Territorial Governor of New Mexico, be carried out by the Executive of the State of New Mexico and that the full pardon be granted in order that the few remaining days of applicant, now past ninety years of age, may be spent in peace. We are sure that the great amount of work and effort reflected by the enclosed file is readily apparent. Considering the sentence that applicant is under it has been impossible for him to live openly without fear.

> Respectfully submitted,
> William Henry Roberts, also known as
> William Henry Bonney, William H. Antrim,
> "The Kid," "Billy the Kid, A.L. Roberts
>
> By ANDRESS, LIPSCOMB AND PETICOLAS
> *Ted Andress*
> El Paso, Texas
> Attorneys for Applicant

On October 1, 1954, Morrison wrote to editor, E.B. Mann, who had accepted *Alias Billy the Kid* at the University of New Mexico Press: "Ted Andress [was] attorney of record in the Petition for Pardon."

MORRISON'S "EVIDENCE" PACKET FOR "BRUSHY'S" PARDON HEARING

In the years that followed "Brushy's" November 30, 1950 pardon failure, Morrison would complain that all the "evidence" he brought with him to prove that "Brushy" was Billy the Kid had been ignored by Governor Mabry and historical experts with him. That segued to claiming the hearing outcome was unjust.

Examples occurred right after "Brushy's" December 27, 1950 death. Morrison was quoted for December 30, 1950's *Lubbock Morning Avalanche's* article titled "Brushy Bill Buried But Legend That He Was 'Kid' Lives On." It stated: "Gov. T.J. Mabry of New

Mexico recently refused Roberts' plea for a pardon as Billy the Kid. Morrison [pretending to be an attorney] said **the governor did not properly examine documents backing up Brushy Bill's claim**." The January 5, 1951 *Hico News Review* ran "Notorious Character is Buried" using Morrison's claim: "**The governor denied their appeal in spite of evidence consisting of a 17-page brief, a 2-page letter of testimonial from the law firm of Andres, Lipscomb and Peticolas of El Paso, and 22 instruments containing what was presented as documentary proof of the contention that he was, in fact, Billy the Kid.**" Morrison repeated that claim in a August 8, 1952, Kiwanis Club talk in Silver City, titled "He Said He was Billy the Kid;" copies of which were in Sonnichsen's collected papers. Morrison stated: "**Not one person in that [hearing] room asked to see any evidence, or any records.**"

Interestingly, in C.L. Sonnichsen's extensive copies of Morrison's "Brushy" Bill" documents, this "evidence" packet is absent. Morrison, however, sent it to historian, Robert N. Mullin, whom he was courting about "Brushy;" and it is in Mullin's papers at the Nita Stewart Haley Memorial Library in Midland, Texas.

MORRISON'S FAKE "EVIDENCE"

In a letter of July 2, 1988, Pat Garrett historian, Leon Metz, wrote to historian, Don Cline - then preparing his 1988 manuscript, *Brushy Bill Roberts: I Wasn't Billy the Kid* - about Morrison having no valid evidence. Metz wrote: "I met William V. Morrison in the early 1970's when he was living ... not over a mile from my home ... He was a very secretive man ... I never saw any of his papers. I asked him repeatedly about his research papers, and he implied loads of stuff, but I never saw a single sheet. Lately, I have come to suspect ... that he had no extensive files. I'll bet his only papers were copies of correspondence with various New Mexico County Clerks." (Cline, Page 74)

Morrison's "evidence" for the pardon hearing consisted of a "Statement of Facts" and 22 listed "instruments for reference" as "proofs." They are patently absurd, even without the debunking that follows in this book. They were merely copies of Billy Bonney's letters, some New Mexico clerk's statements that they had no Coroner's Jury Report on file, and the documents about Pat Garrett's reward. Nothing linked them to "Brushy." Possibly Morrison was betting on "Brushy's" I'm-Billy-the-Kid act - after two years of coaching - to make these Billy documents look like his own.

"STATEMENT OF FACTS"

A "Statement of Facts" for November 30, 1950 was 21 typed pages, with Morrison's embarrassingly error-filled history of Billy Bonney, to show "Brushy's" "special knowledge." It stated:

In Re: William H. Roberts, alias William H. Bonney

William Henry Roberts **[made-up name of Oliver Pleasant Roberts]**, alias **[made up aliases]** "Kid," alias William Henry Bonney, alias William H. Antrim, alias A.L. Roberts **[another fake name, also used for his father, and subsequently abandoned for the hoax]**, who was born on December 31, 1859 **[not Billy's birth date]**, went to Lincoln County, New Mexico in the summer of 1877. He was employed by Frank McNabb [sic], foreman **[wrong]**, on the John S. Chisum Ranch where he worked for a short period of time **[wrong]**. From Chisum's he went to work on the Maxwell Ranch for the brother of Pete Maxwell **[Maxwell had no brother]** where he became acquainted with Mrs. Maxwell and her children **[Pete was her son]**. He stayed in the Ruidoso Country during the winter of 1877 **[Billy was employed by Tunstall in October of 1877]**, living with the Coe boys. In January of 1878 **[wrong date]** he was employed on a ranch on the Rio Feliz by the owner, John Tunstall.

The history limps through the murder of Tunstall, seen as starting a "Cattle War between the two factions" **[Murphys and McSweens; the Regulators were unknown to him]**. The killing of Brady occurs at an adobe wall at the "McSween Store Building" **[actually Tunstall store]**. "Buckshot" Roberts is killed by "Constable" Brewer's Deputy Bowdry [sic], but no federal indictment No. 411 results. Three day battle **[not called the Lincoln County War]** occurs because Sheriff Peppin harassed the McSween faction, who were in McSween's house and refused to surrender. On the third battle day Fort Stanton Commander Col. Dudley told McSween to stop fighting, but did not tell the Murphy faction. So the Murphy men set fire to his house, and Dudley pointed "his guns" at McSween men in other buildings and told them to leave. And according to testimony in Col. Dudley's Court of Inquiry, Court Martial Proceedings **[it was not a court martial]**, "three of the Negro soldiers were firing with the Murphy faction during the battle. **[Morrison later admitted that the Inquiry cost too much money to buy, so he must** have misheard its contents, and made-up firing black soldiers.] Those killed and those escaped were named. Then a United States Commissioner named Angell **[confusing Justice and Interior Departments' Investigator Frank Warner Angel]** blamed Governor S.B. Axtell for friendship with the Murphy faction. **[There is no Santa Fe Ring.]** Lew Wallace replaces Axtell, issues an Amnesty Proclamation **[retyped in full]**, but Billy the Kid **[not called that yet]** did not qualify because of past indictments. In 1979, the factions represented by Billy the Kid and James Dolan **[it was a personal peace-making attempt]** tried to make peace; but right after, Dolan and his men murdered Attorney Houston [sic] Chapman Mrs. McSween's attorney. So the War started again, and Wallace issued orders to General Hatch to apprehend the Kid as accessory to murder of Chapman. **[wrong]** Then the pardon bargain letters were retyped in full: Billy Bonney's first letter, Wallace's response letter for a meeting at "Squire" Wilson's, Billy's answer to Wallace, Billy's letter to Wilson, and Wallace's interview notes on Billy. "The 'Kid' agreed with Governor Wallace to submit to arrest to Sheriff George Kimbrel [sic]; to testify before the Lincoln County Grand Jury with reference to the killing of Chapman; to give statements on Lincoln County War in general **[wrong]**; to plead to the indictments against him **[wrong]**; to stand trial in District Court in Lincoln County N.M. **[wrong]**. The Governor agreed to pardon him if convicted **[wrong - pardon based only on Chapman testimony]**. Billy testifies in the 1879 Grand Jury and gets indictments of Dolan, Campbell, and Evans. Billy's venue is changed to Dona Ana County. But Billy wanted to be tried in Lincoln, felt betrayed, and left the jail **[wrong scenario]**.

In November of 1880, **[paraphrasing, then giving a retyping of Billy's letter of December 12, 1880 to Lew Wallace]** a posseman named James Carlyle, cornered the "Kid" and his men at the Greathouse Ranch and is killed by friendly fire trying to escape; and the next day his men burned down the ranch thinking Billy was still inside **[wrong]**.

Then Billy steals cattle from Chisum for unpaid Lincoln County War wages. So Chisum, Charles Goodnight **[not part of that history]**, and Captain J.C. Lea, made Pat Garrett Sheriff **[made-up scenario]**. So Garrett got a Texas posse **[with cited source of a 1926 letter by Jim East]**, which killed Tom O'Folliard, then killed Charles Bowdre at "an old stone building" **[unaware of Stinking Springs's name]**, and Billy and others were captured. At the Maxwell house, Mrs. Maxwell asked for Billy to say farewell to her daughter, Paulita **[with the 1926 Jim East letter quoted in full as source; but later forgotten in the hoax, with use of Celsa Gutierrez as the sweetheart by "Brushy"]**. At the meeting the Indian servant gives Billy her scarf in exchange for his tintype **[lifted from not cited Walter Noble Burns's *The Saga of Billy the Kid*.]**

Three of Billy's Santa Fe jail pardon plea letters to Lew Wallace are retyped in full **[with the March 2, 1881 one missing, because Lew Wallace Jr. never gave the copy]**. For the Mesilla trial, Federal indictment No. 411 appears and is quashed, using Billy's April 15, 1881 letter to Edgar Caypless [quoted in full], but not understanding the grounds for quashing, Morrison double-talks it as a "plea to the Jurisdiction of the Court." **[It was quashed based on Blazer's Mill being a private property site in the "Buckshot" Roberts killing; so it was erroneous to call it a federal, instead of Territorial, case.]** Then Billy is convicted and sentenced to hang for Brady's murder.

Billy is transported to Lincoln by named guards **[from an uncited newspaper article]**, and incarcerated on the second floor of the "Murphy Store Building" **[unaware of its nickname "The House" or that it was then the new Lincoln County Courthouse]**. His guards are Bell and Olinger. The escape occurs on April 28, 1881, with no description at all!

Billy ends up in Fort Sumner, and the "Brushy" hoax follows:

> The "Kid" ran upon Sheriff Garrett and the Posse at the Maxwell house on the night of July 14, 1881, and a battle ensued between the 'Kid' and Garrett's deputies in the rear yard of Maxwell's house **[ignoring that Garrett had no posse, just Deputies Poe and McKinney, the ambush killing was in Maxwell's bedroom, and no one in town ever heard this reported gun battle]. [This fake scene was contributed by Sonnichsen for coaching "Brushy." (See pages 366-367 below)]**
>
> The "Kid" was wounded several times, in the moonlit yard [note moonlight, it eventually emerged that "Brushy" called it a dark night, but moonlight was lifted from Poe's *The Death of Billy the Kid*] while Garrett and his men were in the house of Maxwell. He sustained a wound across the top of his forehead which rendered him unconscious. He fell back into the doorway of a Mexican woman's house at the rear of the yard. **[Not knowing the Fort Sumner lay-out, and the buildings being gone in**

Morrison's day, this erroneous location is faked.] The Mexican woman picked him up and took him into her house where she proceeded to dress the wounds. While in the act of dressing the wounds, Celsa Gutierrez, sister-in-law of Pat Garrett, and sweetheart of the "Kid" **[the sweetheart error used throughout the hoax which missed Paulita Maxwell]**, came running into the house to inform the Mexican that Billy's partner **[unnamed Billy Barlow]** had been killed on the back port [sic – porch] of Maxwell's, and they were passing off his body as that of the Kid.

Celsa Gutierrez, upon seeing the "Kid" in a dazed condition, urged the "Kid" to leave for the sheep ranch **[unknown ranch, dropped by later hoax]**. She stated that they were going to kill the "Kid" if they could find him. She further stated that Garrett and his two deputies were in the Maxwell house and would remain there until morning as they were afraid of being mobbed **[Lifted from Poe's book, *The Death of Billy the Kid*, while omitting the fear was from anger that Billy had been killed, since townspeople were holding a wake on his body]**. The "Kid" had many friends in Fort Sumner and vicinity, while Garrett had none. The "Kid" insisted upon going after Garrett [claim later abandoned in hoax], but they persuaded him to return to the sheep ranch before morning. **[This sheep ranch claim appears only in this stage of the hoax, and arose from confusing Billy's having hidden in Maxwell's sheep *camps* after his jailbreak.]**

About August 1st, the "Kid" left for Old Mexico ... **[What follows are "Brushy's" confabulations about living in Old Mexico and Texas under aliases.]**

During a cattle drive to Kansas City in the late 1800's he was arrested in the stock yards, suspected of being Billy the Kid. Having furnished a satisfactory alibi he was released. This was the only time, since his escape from the Lincoln County jail, 1881, that he has been arrested. **[This fiction was abandoned in the later hoax.]**

Morrison's necessary punch line for "Brushy" as Billy was faking no Coroner's Jury Report; stating:

Historical facts and legend indicate that Wm. H. Bonney, alias Billy the Kid **[Billy the Kid was not Billy Bonney's alias]**, was killed by Pat Garrett in the Maxwell house that night in Fort Sumner, San Miguel County, N.M., and that a Coroner's Verdict was rendered. None of which facts, nor legend have been supported by competent evidence. No mention of a purported Coroner's Verdict in the death of Wm. H. Bonney has been made except by Pat Garrett, a party of interest in attempting to collect reward offered by Governor Wallace. **[This was Morrison's make-or-break lie.]** The said purported original Coroner's verdict has not been produced, nor is a certified copy available. **[On that November 30, 1950 hearing day, the *Alamogordo News* published the article on Harold Abbott's 1932 location of the Report in Santa Fe mixed with State Land Office Records and his making copies.]** Therefore said facts and legend are improper and untrue. It has been reported by the County Clerks of San Miguel and De Baca Counties, that no such purported coroner's verdict is a matter of record in their respective jurisdictions **[because it was not there]**. (Photostatic copies of letters attached hereto.) The Secretary of State, Santa Fe, N.M., reported that the records failed to disclose the death record or Coroner's report with reference to the purported death of William H. Bonney **[because it was not there]**. It is also stated that the Executive records disclose a copy of the application by Patrick F. Garrett for the claim on the reward money which was offered, and upon said application the reward was suspended. **[Morrison's scam that Secretary of State Alicia Romero's using "suspended" meant categorical denial of the reward for lack of the Report instead of delay for a legislative act.]** (Photostatic copy of letter attached hereto.)

Missing the irony, Morrison also stated: "None of [Billy's] indictments can be located. They are missing from the Case Files." (Page 17) He forgot his Coroner's Jury Report scam that no records found means no event happened!

And in this flurry of lying and name-dropping, Morrison forgot to say why "Brushy" (as Billy) deserved the pardon!

REFERENCES FOR PETITION

Morrison listed a potpourri of real Billy's documents, the wrong locations where he sought the Coroner's Jury Report to claim it did not exist, and two Affidavits by non-historical people, with no connection to Billy Bonney, attesting to "Brushy's" being Billy. Listed were:

1. Certified copy of Proclamation of Amnesty for Lincoln County disorder of November 15 [sic- 13], 1878, by Governor Wallace.

2. Certified photostatic copies of the documents listed below, originals of which are in the General Lew Wallace Collection of the William Henry Smith Memorial Library of the Indiana Historical Society: **[Billy's letters on the pardon bargain are listed, as well as the Wallace interview of him. His jail letter of March 2, 1881 is missing from the list.]**
3. Certified copy of Change of Venue, from Lincoln County, N.M. to Dona Ana County, N.M.
4. Certified copy of Jury venire in Cause 532, Dona Ana County, N.M.
5. Certified copy of Judge Warren Bristol's Instructions to the Jury.
6. Certified copy of the Jury Verdict of Guilty of Murder in the first degree and assessment of death penalty.
7. Certified copy of Judgment and Sentence of death assessed by the Court.
8. Order dismissing indictment numbered 531 of the criminal docket against William Bonney. **[The Hindman case not pursued. The quashing of Federal indictment No. 411 for the "Buckshot" Roberts killing is missing, accounting for Morrison's ignorance of the reason, and inadequately coaching "Brushy" with Edgar Caypless's letter.]**
9. Certified copy of death warrant for William Bonney.
10. Certified copy of Return on Death Warrant issued by Sheriff Pat F. Garrett, Lincoln Country, in behalf of William Bonney, alias The Kid, alias William Antrim.
11. Transcript of letter from Jim East.
12. Transcript of letter from Walter Noble Burns.
13. Transcript of letter from William Bonney to Edgar Caypless, attorney in Santa Fe.
14. Photostatic copy of letter from W. V. Morrison, dated October 8, 1949, to Clerk of County Court of De Baca County, Fort Sumner, N.M., together with answer of said clerk, Cecil W. Williams. **[Fake search for Coroner's Jury Report]**
15. Photostatic copy of letter from Carmen Armijo, deputy District Court Clerk, Las Vegas, San Miguel County, N.M., dated October 31, 1949, to William V. Morrison. **[Fake search for Coroner's Jury Report]**
16. Photostatic copy of letter from Mrs. Alicia Romero, Secretary of State, Santa Fe, N.M., dated November 9, 1949, to William V. Morrison. **[Fake search for Coroner's Jury Report]**

17. Photostatic copy of letter from Mrs. Alicia Romero, Secretary of State, Santa Fe, N.M., dated November 21, 1949, to William V. Morrison. [**Fake search for Coroner's Jury Report**]
18. Affidavit from Martile Able to Wm. H. Roberts, dated August 1, 1950. [**Fake Affidavit that "Brushy" was Billy**]
19. Affidavit from Mr. Severo Gallegos to Wm. H. Roberts, dated November 11, 1950. [**Fake Affidavit that "Brushy" was Billy**]
20. Copy of letter from W.H. Bonney, March, 1879, to General Lew Wallace, the original of which is in possession of Mr. Lew Wallace [Jr.], Indianapolis, Indiana. [**Missing jail letter of March 2, 1881**]
21. Letter from William E. Brady, grandson of Sheriff William Brady, of whose death Billy the Kid was convicted.
22. Letter from the Attorney General of New Mexico as to the power of the Governor of New Mexico to grant this pardon.

CONCLUSION

If the hearing had looked at Morrison's meaningless packet, it would have ended the charade. As it turned out, "Brushy" was all that was needed to pulverize the scam: he forgot his lines!

PARDON REJECTED BASED ON NO BILLY THE KID TO PARDON

At the November 30, 1950 hearing, Governor Mabry stated: "I am taking no action, now or ever, on this application for a Pardon for Billy the Kid because I do not believe this man is Billy the Kid."

"Brushy's" tale of surviving the Garrett shooting was also clobbered that day by the *Alamogordo News's* publication of Billy Bonney's Corner's Jury Report, with sarcastic front page headline: "Fort Sumner Jury Thought The Kid Had Been Killed." It confirmed that the report had been found in 1932 by a New Mexico state employee, in the State Land Office's basement.

Gathered as experts were Pat Garrett's sons, Oscar and Jarvis Garrett; Arcadio Brady, Sheriff Brady's grandson; Cliff McKinney, Kip McKinney's son; Wilbur Coe, Frank Coe's son; and historians Will Robinson and William Keleher of Albuquerque and J.W. Hendron of Santa Fe.

For them, "Brushy" performed deplorably. The December 1, 1950 *Albuquerque Journal's* " 'Billy the Kid' Bubble Bursts as Gov. Mabry Rejects Oldster's Claim," quoted Oscar Garrett: "Roberts was 'either a deliberate imposter or the victim of a delusion.' "

The November 30th *Santa Fe New Mexican's* "Billy the Kid Only a Phony It Turns Out," reported that "Brushy" "refused to admit to having killed anybody;" forgetting that Billy the Kid's killings were why he was there requesting a pardon! "[A]bout his escape from the Lincoln jail ... he denied he shot either of the two men killed ... His story was that he had been freed by friends." "His story of that night of July 14, 1881 at Fort Sumner was substantially this: **A restaurant was out of meat**. He was asked to go to Pete Maxwell's house and get some. He suspected a trap and declined. However Billy Barlow ...volunteered to go [and got shot]."

November 30th *El Paso Herald Post's* " 'Billy the Kid' Flunks in Talk With Governor," said: "He could not remember Sheriff Garrett's name or any particulars in the Lincoln county war." He claimed "he escaped from the Lincoln County jail at Lincoln earlier in 1881 with the help of some friends. He said he didn't "do any shooting" in the escape, but jumped on a horse and rode to a blacksmith shop three miles away to have the chain shackles removed."

The December 1, 1950 *Albuquerque Journal* reported in " 'Billy the Kid' Bubble Bursts as Gov. Mabry Rejects Oldster's Claim" that "Brushy" "did not remember, without prompting from Morrison, the name of Garrett ... Nor did he remember much about the famous Lincoln County cattle war in which Billy the Kid earned much of his infamous reputation ... He could not recollect the names of the important leaders in the Lincoln County fracas, nor the way the factions lined up ...**At times he referred to Billy the Kid as "he," and at other times used the personal pronoun 'I.'** Roberts said that when he previously escaped from the Lincoln County court house on April 28, 1881, **he shot no one ... Roberts used his right hand** in handling his cane, in drinking water from a glass, in buttoning his jacket and straightening his hat today. Tradition has it that the Kid was left-handed ... Roberts said both he and Barlow worked for John Chisum during the Lincoln County cattle war ...'Me and Billy Barlow,' Roberts declared, 'was as much alike as two blackeyed peas. You couldn't tell us apart' [which explained Barlow being shot instead of him]."

The November 30, 1950 *Santa Fe New Mexican's* "Billy the Kid Only A Phony It Turns Out" demonstrated that "Brushy" did not even know what the pardon was for: "I want to die a free man ... [T]hey'll put up a fine monument over my grave over in Texas. "Why?" Mabry inquired. Roberts said he had spent 10 years as a scout for an anti-horse thief association. That was why."

William V. Morrison was also exposed. The November 30, 1950 *Clovis News Journal's* "Mabry Terms "Billy" Outright Imposter," implied that Morrison was one too; stating: "**William V. Morrison [is] an El Paso salesman. He had previously claimed to be a St. Louis lawyer.**" The November 30, 1950 *Santa Fe New Mexican's* "Billy the Kid Only a Phony It Turns Out," nailed him for prompting. When "Brushy" was asked if he knew another sheriff besides Brady, the reporter recorded: "What's his name?" ["Brushy"] asked, turning to Morrison. "Garrett," supplied Morrison." And December 1, 1950's *Albuquerque Journal's* " 'Billy the Kid' Bubble Bursts as Gov. Mabry Rejects Oldster's Claim" called him "**a traveling salesman**" **from** "**St. Louis;**" and clarified that the law firm supposedly petitioning for the pardon, merely represented Morrison: "El Paso law firm ... said it was acting solely as the legal representative for William V. Morrison, who was seeking the pardon on behalf of the man Morrison claimed was Billy the Kid." And the November 30, 1950 *Santa Fe New Mexican's* "Billy the Kid Only A Phony It Turns Out," brought up profiteering with "Brushy": "Not that I know of," he said when Mabry asked him if **somebody were using him to 'promote something.' "**

So it turned out that people were smarter than Morrison had reckoned, and "Brushy" was dumber than he had realized.

"BRUSHY'S" PRESS

On November 25, 1950, a Sexton Humphreys wrote " 'Pardon Me, I'm Alive,' Says Billy the Kid" as a pardon prelude for the *Indianapolis News*; stating:

'Pardon Me, I'm Alive,' Says Billy the Kid

The 1878 [sic – 1881] death of BILLY THE KID is "nothing but a legend," says an attorney who asks New Mexico Governor THOMAS J. MABRY for a pardon for him. The attorney, Ted Andress, says William Henry Roberts, alias William Henry Bonney, William H. Antrim, the Kid, Billy the Kid and A.L. [sic] Roberts still is alive at an undisclosed address and is now 90. The petition says he surrendered because the territorial Governor, Crawfordsville's LEW WALLACE, of "Ben Hur" fame, promised him a pardon. But the pardon was never given and Billy, under conviction for murdering a sheriff, broke for freedom. The "legend" is that he was killed in the escape attempt [sic], but the petition says that he was only wounded and got to Mexico, that it was a companion that was killed.

From Indianapolis, Indiana, on the November 30, 1850 day of decision, the United Press reported anticipation for *The Indianapolis News* under "Pardon My 6-Shooters. Billy the Kid? Governor to Decide." It stated:

Pardon My 6-Shooters Billy the Kid? Governor to Decide

SANTA FE, N.M., Nov. 30 – A page out of the old West comes to life today when a grizzled old man who claims to be the fabulous outlaw, "Billy the Kid," matches wits with the Governor of New Mexico.

Governor Thomas Mabry will get out of a sickbed to confer with several distinguished historians and "Billy" over his application for a pardon in connection with the 1878 murder of Sheriff William Brady.

It has long been presumed that the legendary gunman was shot to death by Sheriff Pat Garrett July 14, 1881. But periodically since that date "Billys" have come forth to claim ownership of the silver six-guns that killed 21 frontiersmen.

The latest claimant, unseen so far by newspapermen and New Mexico officials, has been both verified and denied by elderly Southwesterners who claim to be former companions of "The Kid."

Mrs. Martile Able, of El Paso, Tex., says he "has the same keen blue eyes" as Billy. Fevero [sic] Gallegos, of Ruidoso, N.M., said he is "still as fast on the draw, despite age."

Both agreed in sworn affidavits that he possesses the same small hands and large wrists, supposedly physical characteristics of the pint-sized outlaw.

However, the aged cowpuncher Ben Cisneros said he "couldn't possibly be Billy the Kid." Cisneros said he "saw Billy in a casket in Ft. Sumner after Sheriff Garrett shot him."

Governor Mabry indicated that he wants to meet the new Billy and decide once and for all if the notorious gunman is still alive, or in a grave near Ft. Sumner, N.M. where hundreds of tourists have gazed on him for many years.

The latest Billy came suddenly to life when an El Paso law firm last week wrote Mabry seeking a pardon, "because the applicant, now past 90 years of age, wishes to spend his remaining years in peace."

The lawyers claimed Billy had not really been killed by Sheriff Garrett, but only wounded. He was then nursed back into health by a Mexican woman, and later escaped to old Mexico where he lived up to now, they said.

Then poured in news of "Brushy's" flop. From Clovis, New Mexico, Mabry's home town, the *Clovis News Journal* of Thursday, November 30, 1950, minced no words, declaring:

"Mabry Terms "Billy" Outright Imposter." It also implied that Morrison was one too; stating: "William V. Morrison [is] an El Paso salesman. He had previously claimed to be a St. Louis lawyer." On the front page, it stated:

MABRY TERMS "BILLY" OUTRIGHT IMPOSTER

SANTA FE. AP - Governor Thomas J. Mabry said Thursday he believes a 91-year-old man who claims to be Billy the Kid is an imposter.

"No action will be taken on his petition for a full pardon for Billy the Kid because I don't believe this man is Billy the Kid," the governor said at the end of a 45 minute interview with the man in the governor's office.

The November 30, 1950 *Santa Fe New Mexican's* article by an Art Morgan was "Billy the Kid Only A Phony It Turns Out." Cowboy dressed "Brushy's" photo was captioned "[He] couldn't remember enough of the youthful outlaw's career to convince the governor and newsmen of his right to the title." The article stated:

Billy the Kid Only A Phony It Turns Out
By Art Morgan

A pardon for Billy the Kid, famous killer of New Mexico's - Lincoln county "war" in the late 70's and early 80's, today was refused by Gov. Tom J. Mabry. The Governor announced his decision after an hour's interview with Ollie or Henry Roberts (address withheld) at the executive mansion this afternoon. Roberts allowed as to how he was the Kid who, historians say, Sheriff Pat Garrett shot to death on the night of July 14, 1881, at Fort Sumner. **"I don't think he is Billy the Kid," the governor said. "I am taking no action, now or ever, on this petition for a pardon."**

In the presence of a group of newspaper reporters, Roberts told Mabry it was not he but a pal, Billy Barlow, whom Garrett killed on that night at Pete Maxwell's house at Fort Sumner. "You couldn't tell us apart," said Roberts. **Instead of a six-shooter, he handled a cane with his right hand. (Tradition, not verified, says the Kid was a southpaw.)**

Roberts recounted convincingly incidents in the Kid's life, when he was doing the talking. However, when Mabry asked pointed questions the answer frequently was: "Sixty-nine years is a long time to remember."

Dressed in a fringed buckskin jacket, levis and boots, Roberts turned once or twice to **William V. Morrison, St. Louis businessman who accompanied him for prompting.**

The Kid is reputed to have slain 21 men in the 21 years of his life. Roberts **refused to admit to having killed anybody.**

Roberts said he didn't know who killed Sheriff William Brady at Lincoln April 1, 1878. Four men were shooting at one another at the time, he said.

"If a man is shooting at you don't you shoot back?" he asked Mabry.

"Well I don't know," said the governor.

"It was a case of dog eat dog," Roberts said.

It was for the Brady killing that the Kid was sentenced to hang.

Questioned about his escape from the Lincoln jail, after the death sentence had been passed, **he denied he shot either of the two men killed in that incident. His story was that he had been freed by friends.**

His story of that night of July 14, 1881 at Fort Sumner was substantially this:

A restaurant was out of meat. He was asked to go to Pete Maxwell's house and get some. He suspected a trap and declined. However Billy Barlow, who was "half-shot," volunteered to go.

Roberts heard shooting and ran to Maxwell's yard. Men shot at him and he shot back. A bullet creased his skull, knocking him out. A Mexican woman who, who lived in the back of the yard, dragged him into her house and revived him. Soon afterward he lit out for the Mexican border.

"I see a mark there," said Mabry when Roberts told of the wound.

Oscar Garrett, Odessa, Tex., and Jarvis Garrett, here on a visit from South America – sons of Pat Garrett – sat in on the meeting.

Asked if he had any questions to ask, Oscar said he wouldn't "dignify the occasion" by asking any.

Roberts insisted on wearing his hat when cameramen took his picture ....

In his youth The Kid supposedly lived with his mother, Kathleen [sic] Antrim, at Silver City. Roberts said today she was not his mother, but his aunt.

He also "corrected" The Kid's biographers on another point. He was not born in New York, but in Buffalo Gap, Tex.

Roberts also knew another sheriff, besides Brady. "What's his name?" he asked, turning to Morrison.

"Garrett," supplied Morrison.

[AUTHOR'S NOTE: This showed "Brushy's" reliance on Morrison's coaching.]

Roberts, replying to Mabry, said he had "a good many girls," Garrett's wife's sister, Celsa Gutierrez, was one of his favorites, he said ...

"Did you ever steal any cattle?" Mabry asked.

Roberts answer was a loud "No."

Introduced to Cliff McKinney, Carlsbad, a mist dimmed

Roberts' bright blue eyes. Roberts was informed McKinney was the son of T.C. (Kip) McKinney, who was with Garrett on that night of July 14, 1881, at Fort Sumner.

Saying McKinney, as well as Garrett, had earlier been a friend of his, Roberts choked up.

"God bless you," he said, clinging to McKinney's hand.

[AUTHOR'S NOTE: This is "Brushy's" confabulation: Garrett and McKinney were not Billy's friends; but "Brushy" shows that he can even fake emotions.]

Roberts said he would be 91 on his next birthday ...

"Not that I know of," he said when Mabry asked him if somebody were using him to "promote something."

[AUTHOR'S NOTE: The profiteering motive was obvious to Mabry.]

"I want to die a free man," he added. "When I do they'll put up a fine monument over my grave over in Texas.

"Why?" Mabry inquired.

Roberts said he had spent 10 years as a scout for an anti-horse thief association. That was why.

[AUTHOR'S NOTE: Roberts demonstrated his chaotic thinking with inability to stick to his Billy the Kid tale, and switched to another of his personas.]

On the front page of the November 30th *El Paso Herald Post*, along with "U.S. Considers Use of A-Bomb," was Vernon Smylie's, " 'Billy the Kid' Flunks in Talk With Governor." It stated:

"Billy the Kid" Flunks in Talk With Governor
by VERNON SMYLIE
Herald-Post Santa Fe Correspondent

SANTA FE, Nov. 30. – Governor Thomas Mabry believes a 91-year-old man who claims to be Billy the Kid is an imposter.

Governor Mabry said he intends to take no action on a request by an El Paso law firm to grant a full pardon to the man.

"In my opinion, the man is not Billy the Kid," the governor said.

Governor Mabry, New Mexico historians and relatives of men who had been historically associated with the Kid, questioned the man in the governor's mansion today.

The man who claims he was the notorious outlaw was represented by **William V. Morrison, an El Paso salesman. He had previously claimed to be a St. Louis lawyer**.

The man gave his name as Ollie Roberts or Henry Roberts. He told the Governor that he used both names.

Roberts said that he did not want to tell his address or any of the details of where he lived for many years.

The petition presented the Governor by the El Paso law firm of Andress, Lipscomb and Peticolas, for a pardon for Billy the Kid maintained Roberts has been living with the Yaqui Indians in Mexico.

Roberts told Governor Mabry that he was born in Buffalo Gap, Texas. Historians say it is a "well determined fact" that Billy the Kid was born in New York.

Roberts said he left home at the age of 14 because "his father was mean to him." He then went to New Mexico, he said.

"The fellow that was killed was named Billy Barlow, Roberts said. "I was with him. We looked like two peas in a pod.

"Billy Barlow drank a heap. I never drank. Couldn't go for that rotgut beer.

"I figured it was a trap at the Maxwell house. I stayed away. It was Barlow that went."

Has Scar on Head

History does not mention Billy Barlow as an associate of the Kid's.

Governor Mabry asked Roberts where he was at the time of the shooting.

"I ran out in the yard," Roberts answered. "Two men started shooting at me. One bullet cut me across the head."

[AUTHOR'S NOTE: There was no "yard;" there was a parade ground with perimeter buildings.]

Roberts paused to show the governor a scar on the top of his head. "I fell into a Mexican woman's yard," he continued. "It wasn't far from the shooting. She doctored my wounds."

Roberts wore a buckskin coat, blue denim pants, cowboy boots and a Western-style hat. He had a loud handkerchief around his neck.

Who Was Pat Garrett?

When he arrived at the governor's mansion, Roberts wanted to lie down. The governor took him to a couch and talked with him privately for about 20 minutes. Then they went to a dining room, where historians and relatives of men involved in the Fort Sumner shooting were waiting.

Governor Mabry and Roberts sat at the dining table. The governor questioned him again for another 20 minutes. Roberts was foggy. **He could not remember Sheriff Garrett's name or any particulars in the Lincoln county war.**

Roberts said that he was married, but that his wife is critically ill. When the governor asked him whether his wife called him Ollie or Henry, Roberts said, "She calls me Billy."

Cliff McKinney, son of Kip McKinney who was at the Maxwell house the night of the shooting, also questioned Roberts.

Son Refuses Questions

Will Robinson, an Albuquerque historian, asked Roberts several questions. Later Robinson said Roberts is not Billy the Kid.

The governor offered to let Oscar Garrett of Odessa, son of Sheriff Garrett, question Roberts, but Garrett said, "I don't intend to dignify this claim with any questions."

Among those present at the interview were Arcadio Brady, grandson of Sheriff Brady of Lincoln County, the man who Billy is charged with having killed, and Jarvis Garrett of Las Cruces, another son of Sheriff Garrett.

Not Like History

The old man said **he escaped from the Lincoln County jail at Lincoln earlier in 1881 with the help of some friends. He said he didn't "do any shooting" in the escape, but jumped on a horse and rode to a blacksmith shop three miles** away to have the chain shackles removed from his body.

History and records reveal, however, that in that escape Billy the Kid killed two guards and shot another.

[AUTHOR'S NOTE: Only guards, James Bell and Bob Olinger, were shot.]

Shot With His Hat On

At one time during the questioning, Roberts pounded on the table and demanded: Don't you dare take any pictures of me with my hat off.

The December 1, 1950 *Albuquerque Journal's* front page had " 'Billy the Kid' Bubble Bursts as Gov. Mabry Rejects Oldster's Claim." Calling Morrison a "traveling salesman," it said "Brushy" flubbed basic questions:

'Billy the Kid' Bubble Bursts as Gov. Mabry Rejects Oldster's Claim

SANTA FE, Nov. 30 (AP) – The bubble burst today for the buckskin-clad vain little man who claims he is 91 years old and is the one and only, the true Billy the Kid.

Governor Thomas Jewett Mabry rejected both the man's claim to being Billy the Kid and his request for a "full and complete pardon so I can die a free man."

For the time being at least, history books will continue to record that Billy the Kid, the West's most notorious juvenile delinquent punk, was shot to death by Sheriff Pat Garrett at Fort Sumner, N.M., July 14, 1881.

At that time the Kid was 21 years old and boasted that he had killed 21 men.

"I am taking no action, now or ever, on this application for a pardon for Billy the Kid because I do not believe this man is Billy the Kid," Governor Mabry said after a 45-minute interview with the aged man, who alternatively referred to himself as Billy the Kid, Billy Roberts, Henry Roberts, and Ollie Roberts.

Pardon Requested

The request for the pardon was first presented to Governor Mabry last week by an El Paso law

firm, which said it was acting solely as the legal representative for William V. Morrison, who was seeking the pardon on behalf of the man Morrison claimed was Billy the Kid.

[AUTHOR'S NOTE: The law firm represented Morrison, not "Brushy," as Morrison would later claim.]

It was Morrison who brought Roberts to today's interview, in the executive mansion where the governor has been confined for the week with a severe cold. Their interview was arranged after Mabry said he would take no action at all on the pardon request until he had a personal interview with the man claiming to be Billy the Kid.

Roberts refused to say where he had been living or is living at the present time and **Morrison, who described himself as a traveling salesman and gave his permanent home as St. Louis**, said Roberts refusal to reveal his permanent address stemmed from a current serious illness of Roberts' wife.

The governor's disbelief was shared by more than a score of newsmen, state historians and descendants of men who figured in the Billy the Kid saga who attended the interview.

That disbelief was nourished on many things:
Couldn't remember
Roberts did not remember, without prompting from Morrison, the name of Garrett.

Nor did he remember much about the famous Lincoln County cattle war in which Billy the Kid earned much of his infamous reputation.

He could not recollect the names of the important leaders in the Lincoln County fracas, nor the way the factions lined up.

At times he referred to Billy the Kid as "he," and at other times used the personal pronoun "I."

Roberts said he was born in Buffalo Gap, in Taylor County, Texas, and that the family later moved to Hamilton County, Texas.

But J.W. Hendron, Santa Fe historian and author of a book about Billy the Kid, says it is a "well-documented fact" that Billy the Kid was born in New York City, Nov. 23, 1859.

Roberts said that when he previously escaped from the Lincoln County court house on April 28, 1881, he shot no one.

History and county records, however, detail that the Kid killed two guards and shot a third in that escape.

[AUTHOR'S NOTE: Billy shot just his two guards: James Bell and Bob Olinger.]

Roberts used his right hand in handling his cane, in drinking water from a glass, in buttoning his packet and straightening his hat today. Tradition has it that the Kid was left-handed.

[AUTHOR'S NOTE: Billy Bonney was ambidextrous; with the left-handedness an error from ignorance of his right to left reversed tintype.]

Garrett Kin Scoffs

Oscar Garrett, of Odessa, Tex., son of the sheriff who history says shot the Kid to death, declined to question Roberts, adding "I don't want to dignify this claim with any questions."

His brother, Jarvis, here on a visit from South America, also scoffed at Roberts's [sic] claim that he was Billy the Kid.

After today's interview, Oscar Garrett declared Roberts was "either a deliberate imposter or the victim of a delusion."

Garrett also said that Roberts's [sic] claim is a "slur on the character of my father and on every pioneer in New Mexico at that time.

Pat Garrett reported to Territorial Governor Lew Wallace that he had killed the Kid and claimed the $500 reward offered for the Kid.

"I have never capitalized on being Pat Garrett's son," Oscar Garrett said. "I just want to see the record kept straight ..."

Balding and extremely sensitive about it, Roberts at one time pounded on the dining room table in the Governor's mansion, where the interview was held, and demanded:

Poses With Hat

"Don't you dare take any pictures of me with my hat off. I won't have pictures taken with my hat off."

He then carefully set his hat on his head, threw back his shoulders, and posed proudly for picture after picture.

Roberts, resplendent in a yellow buckskin jacket and a bright green-figured bandana, declared that the man killed by Pat Garrett was a man named Billy Barlow.

Roberts said both he and Barlow worked for John Chisum during the Lincoln County cattle war.

"Me and Billy Barlow," Roberts declared, "was as much alike as two blackeyed peas. You couldn't tell us apart."

The night he was supposed to have been killed, Roberts said, Barlow wanted him to go to the Pete Maxwell home, where history records Billy the Kid died with his boots on in front of Pat Garrett's blazing guns.

"There was a trap"

"But Barlow drank a heap and he was half shot at the time. He went right into the trap and was killed, not me."

Roberts refused to answer questions about being wounded in gun battles at Mocking Bird Gap and at Stinking Springs. These were put to him by Will Robinson, pioneer New Mexico newsman who is himself past 80 and known as a historian of the Lincoln County war.

Roberts said he was wounded many times and showed a scar on his bald head. He said he got that scar in a gun fight in the Maxwell house. He said he ran to the Maxwell house after he heard shots there. A shot creased his skull and knocked him out.

He said he was treated for that wound by "a Mexican woman and by Celsa Gutierrez." He described Celsa Gutierrez as Pat Garrett's sister-in-law and said she was his (Roberts's [sic]) sweetheart at the time. While he was being treated, he said, Barlow's body was being passed off as his.

"So Much Alike"

"That's because we were so much alike."

Morrison, meanwhile, told newsmen that he first became interested in the Billy the Kid case when he was associated with the R.R. Roberts accounting and law firm in Beaumont, Texas. He said Roberts and the man who claims to be Billy the Kid are distant relatives.

"We are satisfied," Morrison said, "that this man is not an imposter, but is the real Billy the Kid."

Morrison and Roberts headed back to Albuquerque after the interview with the governor. They spent last night at an Albuquerque hotel and came to Santa Fe this morning for the interview.

Morrison would not comment on what he intends to do now in the affair.

AN HISTORIAN'S ATTACK

Historian William Keleher debunked "Brushy" in the December 1, 1950, *Albuquerque Journal, as* "Will A. Keleher, History Student, Sure Kid Was Shot." Keleher later put a photocopy of Billy's Coroner's Jury Report in his book 1957 titled *Violence in Lincoln County: 1869-1881*. The article stated:

Will A. Keleher, History Student, Sure Kid Was Shot

Will A. Keleher, Albuquerque attorney and former newspaperman, was asked what he thought of the Governor's decision to disregard the latest pretender's attempt for recognition. Keleher, who made an extensive study of Billy the Kid's history, said:

"I'm not surprised to learn the death of Billy the Kid was considered once more. If the Kid wasn't killed at Fort Sumner on July 14, 1881, a lot of intelligent people living at the time were badly fooled." He continued:

"A list of the people who knew the facts of the case at that time contains many impressive names. For instance, Sheriff Pat Garrett, who killed him; John W. Poe, a later highly respected banker of Roswell and who, along with Kip McKinney, rode with Garrett's posse; George Coe and Frank Coe, Pete Maxwell, Paulita Maxwell Jaramillo, and Charles Siringo, who later became a famous Pinkerton detective.

"There was also Governor Miguel A. Otero who believed the Kid was the one they buried and Ash Upson, a reporter from the New York Tribune who also investigated the crime.

"Two nationally known writers investigated the death and wrote about it. Emmerson Hough, one time resident of White Oaks, in Lincoln county, had a book called "The Story of the Outlaw," published and Walter Noble Burns, who wrote the "Saga of Billy the Kid."

Other old-timers who knew quite a lot about the days when the 21-year-old outlaw was riding high in Lincoln County, were inclined to agree with Keleher.

The rejection was front page news for December 30, 1950's *Lubbock Morning Avalanche* with "Billy the Kid is Called Imposter by New Mexico Chief." It stated:

'BILLY THE KID' IS CALLED IMPOSTER BY NEW MEXICO CHIEF

SANTA FE, N.M. Nov. 30 (AP) – Gov. Thomas J. Mabry today branded a 91-year-old man claiming to be Billy the Kid an imposter and denied his petition for a pardon.

"No action will be taken on his petition for a full pardon because I don't believe this man is Billy the Kid," the Governor said after a 45-minute interview at the executive mansion.

The decision means that history books will continue to record that the notorious outlaw died at the age of 21 under the flaming guns of Pat Garrett, famous New Mexico sheriff, at Fort Sumned [sic] in 1881.

Giving his name at [sic] Ollie Henry Roberts, the aged man appeared for the unusual interview wearing buckskins and a western hat. He told his story to more than a score of interested persons.

Without prompting from his representative, William V. Morrison of St. Louis, Roberts was unable to recall the name of Sheriff Garrett. He was similarly vague on details of the Lincoln county cattle war, in which his famous reputation was earned.

Roberts differed with the history books on Billy the Kid's birthplace, too. He said he was born at Buffalo Gap, in Taylor County, Texas. Historians say it is a "well documented fact" that the Kid was born in New York City.

Obviously sensitive about his baldness, the claimant at one time during the questioning demanded that no pictures be taken of him with his hat off. But he posed willingly enough with the hat on.

The Governor, ailing with a cold, got out of a sick bed to conduct the interview. It resulted from an appeal by an El Paso, Tex., law firm for a full pardon for the outlaw.

HISTORIAN HENDRON'S ARTICLE FILLED-IN THE DISASTER

Historian J.W. Hendron was at "Brushy's" pardon hearing. On January 5, 1951, he published "No Pardon For Billy" in *Highway Happenings* adding details of the fiasco. In C.L. Sonnichsen's papers, it was and ignored. Hendron, calling "Brushy" the " 'nth' claimant to the title of 'Billy the Kid,' " wrote:

When I arrived, the old man who claimed to be the real Billy the Kid was resting and did not appear for a few minutes. When the Governor gave the word, he arose and walked awkwardly with his cane into the dining room [of the Governor's Mansion] and took a seat at the table.

Governor Mabry, himself well-versed in the pros and cons of Lincoln County history, proceeded to ply the old gentleman with some very pointed and detailed questions. At the onset of the interview it was easy to see that this latest "Billy the Kid' had little conception of the facts about the Lincoln County War.

He gave his name as **Ollie (or Henry) Roberts. [He could not stick to the fabricated William Henry.]** He said that he was **born in Buffalo Gap, Taylor County, Texas** ... (Historians generally agree that Billy the Kid was born in New York City on November 29, 1859.)

Roberts claimed that he had lived in Silver City, N.M., as a boy, and **said that Mrs. Antrim was his aunt** and not his mother ... It is somewhat difficult to understand how a man, even in his 90's, could forget his own mother's name.

He said he **knew nothing of the people involved in the Lincoln County War** ... Roberts said he **knew Sheriff William Brady but did not know who shot him to death on April 1, 1878** ... Even so, Roberts had come to Santa Fe seeking pardon for the murder of Brady. It seems odd that a man would seek pardon for a crime he did not commit ...

[As to the killing of the two guards in Billy's Lincoln jailbreak] [h]e claimed he was handcuffed, shackled, and **chained to a post** and that he had friends who helped him to escape. **He admitted there was shooting at the time but said he didn't know who did it** ...

[E]lderly Roberts claimed he **never stole cattle** – just helped other men get back those that had been stolen from them ...

Ollie Roberts didn't even know where Chisum's ranch was located, and didn't know whether Tunstall was his friend or not ...

The real Billy spent much time in and around Fort Sumner, and Roberts claimed he knew Pete Maxwell and his sister, but **could not remember her name, Paulita. He didn't even know where the town of Fort Sumner was located** ...

[H]ere is how he explains the way he escaped death at Fort Sumner on the night of July 14, 1881. He says he was asked to go to Pete Maxwell's house for some meat. He suspected he was being tricked into something and instead sent Billy Barlow, who was drunk. **When Barlow entered Maxwell's bedroom he was shot by Garrett. [This is noteworthy, because in *Alias Billy the Kid*, "Brushy" is claimed to have said Barlow was shot on the back porch, leaving open that C.L. Sonnichsen simply wrote the alternative death scene himself.]** (See pages 366-367 below) Roberts ran out into the yard [was shot, and dragged into a house by women who dressed his wounds; then escaped to the Mexican border] ...

It is odd that this story of Roberts has never been told before. Everyone in Fort Sumner couldn't keep such a secret this long.

HIDDEN HOAXBUSTING TREASURE

The pardon failure did not end the "Brushy Bill" hoax. But it was last time anyone would be allowed to see incompetent "Brushy Bill's" imposture in action. William V. Morrison and C.L. Sonnichsen had learned their lesson. But that made "Brushy's" hearing's flubs hoaxbusting treasure - before his promoters' surreptitious fix-ups began.

CHAPTER 5
A LIMBO OF LIES

MORRISON RISES FROM THE ASHES

To a legitimate petitioner, exposing of "Brushy" as an imposter by Governor T.J. Mabry and experts would have yielded bowing out. But to a huckster like William V. Morrison the message was hitting pay-dirt. "Brushy's" press was front page. As P.T. Barnum said, "Without promotion something terrible happens: Nothing!" So after the pardon hook, Morrison pushed a "Brushy" book! He even had a writer lined up: C.L. Sonnichsen, unfazed by real historians' ridicule or by real history.

"BRUSHY'S" TIMELY DEATH

Fate provided Morrison with what no con-man can create: luck. "Brushy" died in on December 27, 1950. That embarrassing old fool who said Billy the Kid had *killed no one, forgot Pat Garrett's name*, guessed Fort Sumner's *restaurant was out of steak* on July 14, 1881, and called Billy *he* not *me*, was out of the way.

The *Hico News Review* of January 5, 1951, announced "Notorious Character is Buried." No Roberts family member came. But Morrison was there proclaiming: "There is considerable evidence on both sides of the [Billy the Kid] question;" though he admitted (for the last time) that there was "a noted discrepancy in the reported age of Brushy Bill." The article stated:

In striking contrast to colorful tales of his checkered career on the frontier, the earthly remains of O.L. Roberts lay in Barrow-Rutledge Funeral Chapel last Friday afternoon. Friends gathered to pay their last respects to a departed citizen ... "Brushy Bill," as he called himself, had recounted his last tale about Indian battles and wild horse riding. His robust health had broken suddenly. His heart failed, and he dropped dead at noon Wednesday on the streets he had trod so often with a bearing erect and stalwart. Dressed in Western style ... he had explained a yen for such garb by telling his listeners innocent tales of derring-do while hobnobbing with famous desperados of pioneer days.

In a neat, plain business suit, his body rested before the assemblage ...

[Two of the pallbearers came] from East Texas with lifelong friend, De Witt Travis of Longview, to attend the services. **Another close acquaintance, W.A. Morrison of El Paso, was present to help console the widow, Mrs. Malinda F. Roberts** ...

Burial was in Littleville Cemetery, 20 miles south of Hico. He had made his home [there] in Hamilton at various times.

"Brushy Bill" had recounted often that his place of birth was Buffalo Gap in Taylor County, and the time was <u>December 31, 1868</u>, **stating that he was born on the last day of that year. If correct, that would belie current tales being aired by daily newspapers linking his identity with that of a famous early-day character.** There is considerable evidence on both sides of the question.

On November 30, 1950, he had appeared before the governor of New Mexico, according to his friend, Morrison of El Paso, who said he accompanied him. The governor denied their appeal in spite of evidence consisting of a 17-page brief, a 2-page letter of testimonial from the law firm of Andres, Lipscomb and Peticolas of El Paso, and 22 instruments containing what was presented as documentary proof of the contention that he was, in fact, Billy the Kid.

"**We are not basing our claim on hearsay,**" Morrison **emphatically stated in an interview with the News Review editor, "but on evidence which I have assembled over a period of years. It is taken from official records and affidavits, and will be on file for the proper parties to inspect.**" He stated that he expected to continue his efforts to piece the evidence together, with **Mrs. Roberts' permission, and said he made three trips to Hico and one to Hamilton for interviews with the late Mr. Roberts** during the past year and a half. He went through the background of the case meticulously, and said that his proof was more convincing **than the fact that there was a discrepancy in the reported age of the old man**.

[DeWitt] Travis, who has journeyed here frequently from Longview to visit his old friend, took a similar attitude as to his identity. "I am 62 years old," he stated, "and I have known who Billy was as long as I have known anything. Our fathers fought together in the Civil War, and we have made it a point not to discuss this man's past until just recently."

[AUTHOR'S NOTE: Travis was exposed as "Brushy's" dupe by Don Cline in his book, *Brushy Bill Roberts: I Wasn't Billy the Kid***. (Cline, Page 97)]**

This claim was corroborated by his two companions accompanying him from East Texas for the funeral.

Contradictory claims have been made in statements and letters to the News Review, bearing testimony to the claim that the rustic character known so well in and around Hico was a law-abiding citizen. And there is no evidence here, where he has made his residence for most of the last decade, to support any contention otherwise.

Peace be to his ashes.

RATIONALIZING THE LOST PARDON

Sly Morrison turned "Brushy's" lost pardon into martyrdom, calling the hearing an unfair "memory test." On April 9, 1951, he presented this fakery to a C.G. Killinger; writing:

> Wm H. Roberts, alias Wm H. Bonney, was actually Billy the Kid. We had definite proof, but we were not afforded a legal conference on the evidence. We **submitted to a memory test** in the presence of the McKinney and Garrett families, and the public in general. He did not answer the questions as dictated by historians in a manner to their liking. Therefore, the Governor refused to grant a legal conference on the evidence.
> There was no definite proof that Garrett killed anyone in Fort Sumner. Neither was there any evidence in the interview with Governor Mabry.

On April 3, 1954, to a Carl W. Breihan, then writing a Billy the Kid biography, Morrison floated his Coroner's Jury Report fakery (and sent a copy to loyalist Paul Blazer, who saved it). His rationalization was that no Coroner's Jury Report existed, so "Brushy" had no "legal judgment" to contest in a court (to say he was alive as Billy); so requesting a pardon had been his only option. Then Morrison fabricated a catch-22: Governor Mabry could not pardon him without proof of death! So a legal technicality explained the pardon's refusal! Morrison wrote: "It was most unfortunate that ["Brushy" and I] did not have the opportunity to prove our case in a court of law for the reason that we could not dig up a cause of action. You know that they never made a legal coroner's verdict. Therefore it was not possible to file an action against the non-existent judgment. So, the Pardon was the only legal declaration that could be made. They had no cause of action against Billy Roberts for the reason that there was no proof that Garrett killed anyone in Fort Sumner on July 14, as contended." Morrison added an excuse of "Brushy's" being intimidated: "It is difficult for anyone to realize the intimidation meted out to Billy Roberts that day in Santa Fe, unless they were present during the working over. And no one present had ever seen the Kid about whom they thought they knew so much."

On April 3, 1954, Morrison wrote to historian, Carl W. Breihan, with the same fake claim in his belligerent legalese doubletalk:

> I do not expect you to believe that Billy Roberts was Billy the Kid, although I do not know to what extent you checked the matter. **It was most unfortunate that we did not have an opportunity to prove our case in a court of law for the reason that we could not dig up a cause of action. You know that they never made a legal coroner's verdict. Therefore it was not possible to file an action against a non-existent judgment. So, the Pardon was the only legal declaration that could be made.** They had no cause of action against Billy Roberts for the reason there was no proof that Garrett had killed anyone in Fort Sumner on July 14, as contended.
>
> It is difficult for one to realize the intimidation meted out to Billy Roberts that day in Santa Fe, unless they were present during the working over. And no one present had ever seen the Kid about whom they thought they knew so much.

On April 12, 1954, to historian Philip J. Rasch, Morrison sent his fabricated version of the pardon failure, fishing for allies. This time, Morrison added a conspiracy theory blaming the Santa Fe Ring! He wrote: "I don't believe there was any secret why the Garrett faction opposed a legal hearing. **They were put on notice that there was no legal record or evidence to support the contention that Garrett's Posse had killed anyone on that memorable July 14, 1881**. And probably, that had acknowledged that I conferred with legal authority in New Mexico in an endeavor to prove up their purported coroner's verdict, or the first verdict – not mentioned by the Ring – in an attempt to file suit to then have it set aside. I was advised that it would be impossible to prove up the lost instrument at this late date. Therefore, the idea was abandoned and the Petition for Pardon was the only manner in which to make a declaration. The Santa Fe Ring had failed to make a legal record of the purported killing at the time. However, they did almost everything else in an attempt to collect the $500 reward [presumably for Pat Garrett]."

On April 19, 1954, Morrison wrote again to Rasch, reworking the pardon disaster, and fixating on "Brushy's" little hands, as if proof of identity (for fictional shackle-slipping), while raving with double-talk legalese about the Coroner's Jury Report entangled with conspiracy theorizing and the Santa Fe Ring:

> During out little show or performance, with the Garrett faction doing most of the performing, on that dreadful day in November 1950, in Santa Fe, I was not permitted to interrogate anyone or to produce any evidence – except Billy, who stood through the intimidation, waving those unusually small hands with the large wrists – and no one seemed interested in his peculiar physical makeup, except the Governor. Their only interest was to have him retell the stories and untrue facts and records that had been told to everyone there by someone else. Certainly there was no one there who could have known Billy the Kid ...
>
> After the intimidation, the Governor promised to grant us a legal hearing on the law and evidence ... [but] the Great General Pat Hurley leading the Garrett faction, took the Governor back in the room and changed his mind ...
>
> Thus, the General from Oklahoma, a nephew of John Hurley who had fought against the Kid and pleaded the Governor's Amnesty on his indictments for murder, was there defending the honor of the Santa Fe Ring and the Great Pat Garrett, against an innocent old man who was there to establish a legal right without the benefit of counsel ...
>
> I don't believe there was any secret why the Garrett faction opposed a legal hearing. They were put on notice that there was no legal record or evidence to support the contention that Garrett's Posse had killed anyone on that memorable July 14, 1881 ...
>
> The Santa Fe Ring had failed to make a legal record of the purported killing at the time. However, they did everything else in an attempt to collect the $500.00 reward ...
>
> Then, when it was realized [at the pardon hearing] that we were prepared to submit the law and the evidence to a tribunal, apparently they did not want to join issues ... [W]e were prepared with evidence they had never anticipated. And they did not have a leg to stand on.
>
> If Dr. Sonnichsen saw fit, he could inform you of some of the tactics resorted to after the death of Roberts, in order to prevent the facts and records being made public.

By Morrison's March 7, 1955 letter to a Susie Peters, the Mabry hearing had virtually disappeared, along with "Brushy's" disastrous showing. Now the only problem was "Brushy's" dying before getting justice. Morrison wrote: "The governor refused to grant a hearing on the petition **[lie]** and Roberts died on December 27, 1950, before we had an opportunity to present it to the newly elected Governor, Edwin L. Meecham."

A FRENZY OF PROMOTION

A limbo existed between the pardon failure and any next step. Energetic salesman Morrison filled it with hundreds of letters promoting "Brushy" and giving talks replaying his "Brushy" lies to pave the way for the book Sonnichsen was writing. When its manuscript was done by 1952, Morrison sought a publisher. Morrison also wanted movie deals. And he shamelessly, but futilely, barraged historians - Philip J. Rasch, Robert Mullin, Maurice Garland Fulton, William Keleher, and young Frederick Nolan - in his campaign of bullying persuasion.

Morrison's act, a puffery of bombast, bluff, and belligerence, had set themes. Often couched in stilted legalese of his lawyer imposture, and oozing with his salesman skills, he excused "Brushy's" zero fund of knowledge at the pardon hearing by his being intimidated, being too old for a "memory test," the evidence alone proving Billy deserved the Wallace pardon, affidavits said "Brushy" was Billy, and his small hands and thick wrists for shackle-slipping had been ignored. This flim-flam distilled to claiming "Brushy" should not have had to prove he was Billy the Kid! And only after "Brushy's" death (guaranteeing no more dumb flubs) was Morrison's sales pitch switched to "Brushy's" having "special knowledge" proving he was Billy the Kid.

A good summary of Morrison's desperately dishonest excuses for "Brushy's" failure was in his letter of May 13, 1952 to historian, J.W. Hendron, present in the Mabry hearing and author of its exposé: "No Pardon for Billy." (See pages 261-262 above) Morrison claimed:

1) Nobody who questioned "Brushy" had known Billy the Kid personally. **[Omitted is that "Brushy" lacked basic knowledge available to any questioner with historical information.]**

2) "Brushy's" claim of birth in Buffalo Gap, Texas, is acceptable since there is no proof Billy Bonney was born in New York. **[The New York birth came from those who knew Billy and likely heard it from him: Pat Garrett, Ash Upson, and Lew Wallace.]**

3) "Brushy" was not the " 'nth' claimant," because no one else made the claim "legally." **["Legally" is meaningless. Multiple old-timers, like John Miller, made the pretender claim.]**

4) "Brushy" deserved the pardon for sentence of killing Sheriff Brady because there was a group firing, so he could not be incriminated. **[This leaves out that the Mabry pardon was based on "Brushy's" *being Billy*, not just on whether Billy himself deserved pardon.]**

5) "Brushy" denied killing Deputies Bell and Olinger, because it was not part of his pardon request. And "legal counsel" had told "Brushy" to deny "all charges not legally made against him." **[Fakery to cover-up that "Brushy" forgot his coaching.]**

6) "Brushy" denied stealing cattle as Billy, because he was "human like the rest of us." And others stole cattle but did not admit it. **["Brushy" simply forgot his prompt.]**

7) "Brushy's" knowing neither where Fort Sumner was, nor anything about Paulita Maxwell got Morrison's response: "I must agree that ["Brushy"] did not remember where the town of Fort Sumner was located. Neither did he recall the name of Pablita Maxwell. Maybe he did not hear about them down through the years (some seventy odd years) like the rest of them heard. Then again, maybe he was nervous and excited over the intimidation .... Who knows?" **[These fatal errors had resulted from Morrison's not having taken "Brushy" to Fort Sumner because its buildings were gone; and his not knowing that Paulita was Billy's lover, which resulted in his not coaching "Brushy" on either. And "Brushy's" "memory" had no problem coming up with a wrong "sweetheart": Celsa Gutierrez, on which he had been coached.]**

8) That everyone in Fort Sumner could not keep the secret to the present that Billy was not killed got Morrison's double-talk: "But it is agreed that the Kid was among friends, and Pat Garrett was among people he did not trust. Maybe Garrett did not kill anyone that night. Maybe someone else killed a man. Maybe Garrett was the victim of circumstances. Who knows?" **[Apparently the Billy Barlow as victim scam was still being developed, and vied with no one killed that night.]**

9) "Brushy" was intimidated, and with your being present, Mr. Hendron, "you understood that the foolish memory test could not have established anything conclusive in the matter." **[It was not a "memory test." If "Brushy" was Billy Bonney, he would have had correct knowledge about his life. And if he was too demented to know anything whatsoever, he could not be a claimant. In fact, he did give answers; and they were wrong.]**

10) "Brushy" had small hands and feet, and "historic bullet scars" which were ignored. **[By "historic scars" Morrison was referring to "Brushy's" fictional gun battle injuries from Garrett's fictional posse on July 14, 1881.] [The shackle-slipping, as well as small hands were myth. And Billy had only one "historic" bullet scar: on his upper thigh from Deputy Billy Matthews's shot during the Brady ambush.]** Morrison stated: "You will recall that no one inquired about the small feet, small well shaped hands with large wrists over which hand-cuffs could be removed. Nor the historic bullet scars on his body. Why not? ... Their only interest was to obtain answers to the foolish questions as dictated by historians."

On August 18, 1952, Morrison made a lie-laden, threatening attack on William Keleher, in attempt to intimidate this most substantial opponent at the time of the Mabry hearing, and an anticipated enemy for his fledgling book, *Alias Billy the Kid*, with its manuscript then complete. Morrison was bolstered by a successful talk he had given four days earlier to the Silver City Kiwanis Club, in which he had experienced the ease of duping his naïve audience about his "Brushy" fakery. He wrote:

> Of course, as you probably expected, it was necessary for me to take exception to your opinion given to the Press on November 25, 1950, at the time Wm. H. Roberts was praying a Petition for Pardon in Santa Fe.
> At that time my answer was, "No comment until all the facts and evidence can be presented to the proper tribunal."
> I am making reference to your "indisputable" evidence when you said, "In 1882, the coroner's jury and the state legislature approved a $500 reward to Sheriff Pat Garrett for killing the Kid," which records, as you know, are highly disputable. **[Lie]**
> I do not know to which coroner's jury you refer. You are probably familiar with both of them. **[Lie of two coroner's jury**

reports] And you are probably aware of the fact that neither verdict was officially made, proof of which I have. **[Lie]** However, that is immaterial as the legislature did not recognize either verdict. **[Lie]** The Act of the legislature did not recognize either verdict. **[Lie]** The Act of the legislature specifically sets out that Garrett killed the Kid in that certain month of August instead of that certain July 14th **[Lie. It said "on or about August"]** which is still being relied upon by all of you. Therefore you can understand that your statement cannot be true. You probably made the same mistake as all of them by not looking into the records thoroughly. **[Bluffing]**

In my book I have answered fully regarding your erroneous opinion, by remarking that it could not have been based upon the facts and records made in the matter, and that your remarks were improper, untrue, and prejudicial to the legal rights of the Petitioner ...

Since you are a recognized Historian, I believe you will follow the records cited in my books [anticipated was another just on "Brushy's" pardon] in the event you approach the subject of the Kid in the future.

Near this letter, in Sonnichsen's collected papers, is an undated note, presumably in the August, 1952, time-frame, in oversized scrawl from Morrison to him, revealing the unvarnished con-man in action. Morrison wrote: *"Must give them something to dwarf the Billy the Kid issue so they will remain quiet when the book is published."*

In keeping with his rabid offence strategy, Morrison attacked anyone writing about Billy the Kid, even a novelist named Edwin Corle, with a barrage of letters to anyone connected to him. On July 26, 1953, Corle responded: "The answer to your excited letters about my BILL THE KID can be put into two words, and the words occur on the jacket of the book. They are: "a novel." Your tirades merely indicate your woeful ignorance of what constitutes a novel." And, believing Sonnichsen was more sane, on the same day he wrote to him: "A Mr. William V. Morrison states that you are his friend ... Anyone so emotionally distraught as Mr. Morrison will only become more so if the discussion is prolonged. I have, therefore, made my reply brief, and I enclose herewith a copy of it for your information." But Sonnichsen was relying on Morrison's mental aberrations and aggression to hide his own crass ambitions, as he meticulously filed away Morrison's letters of raving blather.

On August 11, 1953, Morrison continued his insane harassment of Edwin Corle; writing: "I sincerely believe that you can answer my letters more intelligently .... As a rule I have found that you gentlemen shut up before putting up, which I hope is not the case with you. I have no intention of shutting up. Furthermore, I can define words and phrases, and I can prove up my contentions with competent evidence. Can you?"

With visions of his coming book, and profit feeling attainable, Morrison viciously blasted any opponent with his sociopathic rage. On August 9, 1953, he attacked *El Paso Times* correspondent, Georgia B. Redfield, with his fake legalese bludgeon; writing: "This is to notify you that I have read your false statement that was published in this issue today. Therefore, I hereby make demand for sufficient citations to the legal evidence to support your contention that representations in the petition for Billy Roberts were false ... New Mexico is probably the only State in which you could qualify as an historian. My research is performed with a tape recorder and a microfilm machine. Furthermore, I have certified copies from the court records to prove most of my contentions. Can you say the same thing about your methods of research? In addition to my demand for your citations, I would like to have answers to all of the above mentioned questions."

COURTING HIS PARTNER

Salesman Morrison knew that the ticket to his dreams was C.L. Sonnichsen. The book gambit required his flaunted Harvard degree, professorship, and familiarity to historians. Right after "Brushy's" death, Morrison wrote, on December 31, 1950, to Sonnichsen: "Brushy Bill (Billy the Kid) Roberts, died on December 27, 1950, 12:40 O'Clock Noon, Hico, Hamilton County, Texas, at the age of ninety years, eleven months and twenty-seven days." From then on, Morrison's fawning letters would be addressed to "My Friend;" and eventually "Doc" - when he was sure the man was in his court.

By December 27, 1951, they signed an agreement for writing a still untitled "Brushy" book; stating:

> First: Party of the first part [Morrison] agrees to furnish facts, records, and pictures, now in his possession, and pertaining to the life and activities of Wm Henry Roberts, alias Wm Henry Bonney, alias "Billy the Kid", and divers other aliases, for the express intent and purpose of publication.

Second: The party of the second part [Sonnichsen] agrees that the legal title to the aforesaid mentioned facts, records, and pictures, shall remain vested in said party of the first part.

Third: The party of the second part [Sonnichsen] agrees to assemble and compile the aforesaid mentioned material for publication, and assist with the sale thereof.

Fourth: [Expenses to be divided equally]

Fifth: The net proceeds derived from the sale of said publication, or derivatives therefrom, shall be divided equally.

And in Sonnichsen's collected papers was a list of possible titles in what looks like Sonnichsen's handwriting: *"Alias Billy the Kid; Billy the Kid Comes Back; The Return of Billy the Kid; Was This Billy the Kid; A Man Named Roberts, Brushy Bill – or Billy the Kid;* and *He Said he was Billy the Kid.* Number one was the fateful choice.

FIX-UP RESEARCH

Morrison knew the hoax was entering an environment of new scholarly investigations about Billy Bonney that imperiled "Brushy's" confabulations. So he continued research for fix-ups in *Alias Billy the Kid.*

BLAZER FAMILY PAPERS

A key source was Paul Blazer, whom Morrison convinced that "Brushy" was Billy, and who retained all Morrison's communications with his family papers. His grandfather, Joseph Blazer, had owned Blazer's Mill, within the Mescalero Indian Reservation. Joseph was a Lincoln County War period figure, since the killing of Andrew "Buckshot" Roberts occurred at his building housing his office, a post office, and quarters of the Indian Agent Frederick Godfroy. Morrison's letters document his visits with Paul Blazer in Mescalero, New Mexico. From him, Morrison got photographs for scene reconstructions, and errors.

For example, one photo caption reads: "The old Blazer homestead, built in 1869, by Dr. Blazer, burned in 1883. Leased to Godfroy, Indian Agent, with Blazer retaining two rooms at N.W. corner, at rear near tree. The first floor window was cut into a door, and it was from this door that Buckshot Roberts made his brave stand against

13 men, until mortally wounded by the Kid **[wrong]** in April, 1878. Roberts aimed Dr. Blazer's 45-70 Springfield rifle from the door and hit Brewer as his head came up from behind a log at the mill ... killing Brewer instantly."

On April 18, 1952, Morrison, fine-tuning his fakery, wrote to Paul Blazer, "I was very much interested in hearing you say Billy the Kid was ambidextrous." And he sent a copy of this letter to C.L. Sonnichsen. On March 15, 1953, he wrote to a Patience Glennon, daughter of Billy's Silver City teacher, Mary Richards, to follow-up that Richards "knew that [the Kid] was ambidextrous."

BILLY'S FAMILY NAMES

Because Billy's Silver City years were unknown, "Brushy's" team used his confabulations, including a fabricated family.

ANTRIM AND BONNEY NAMES

The main researcher on the family names was then Philip J. Rasch. On December 12, 1952, Morrison wrote him in attempted damage control of "Brushy's" ignorance of them. He wrote:

> I had no interest in the Bonney or Antrim families for the reason that those names did not appear in records of heirship of the Kid **[as "Brushy's" version]. I found no evidence or legal proof that he descended from Mrs. Antrim as her offspring**. The nearest relationship that I was able to prove was that of aunt. If legal evidence is submitted to prove the contrary I shall be pleased to accept it, otherwise I will be forced to accept the heirship as I found it. As a historian I am very much interested in the Antrim and Bonney families and am anxious to learn the results of your research. **I do not believe it will affect my case to a great extent**.

Thirteen days later, on December 25, 1952, Morrison again wrote to Rasch, and included "Brushy's" fake family; writing:

> As previously stated, I have no proof that Antrim married Katherine Dunn or anyone else. However, I still insist that this issue has no particular bearing on my case. **[He is absurdly claiming that "Brushy's" being unaware of the origins and childhood of Billy Bonney is irrelevant to "Brushy's" claim of being Billy!]** The paternal issue was not raised in my petition, and I intend to keep it out. Neither was the issue of childhood days

involved. It was immaterial of the name used by his father. He may have been **McCartney**, Antrim, Bonney, or anything else. I was interested in obtaining a pardon for a man who said he was Billy the Kid, New Mexican Outlaw, and I believe he could have established his claim in law. **[Not without being able to match real Billy, which he failed to do!]** We had legal proof of the allegations made in the petition. If the Governor would have granted a hearing **[he did!]**, I believe that all the angles would have been worked out eventually.

THE McCARTY NAME

"Brushy" had fabricated a variety of names to mimic Billy - like "William Henry" - but the name "Henry McCarty" was newly discovered by Philip Rasch, so unknown to "Brushy."

Equally ignorant Sonnichsen had merely added it in a footnote as "**McCartney**;" writing: "Another story, current in Silver City, says that Billy the Kid was really named McCartney." (*Alias Billy the Kid*, Page 16) That came from Morrison's letter of June 16, 1952 to Roscoe Wilson, author of a 1951 article on "the early days of Billy the Kid in Silver City." Morrison asked: "Mr. Truesdell says that Billy was known as Antrim at the time he lived in Silver City. **I wonder if he ever heard him called "McCartey, or McCartney," at the time?**" (The Silver City years were not fleshed out until 1993, with Jerry Weddle's *Antrim Is My Stepfather's Name: The Boyhood of Billy the Kid*.)

But by his letter of June 30, 1954, to Philip Rasch, Morrison lied to add "McCarty" into dead "Brushy's" repertoire. He wrote:

> It is not too difficult to comprehend that the Kid's name could have been Roberts, or just about anything else, and still he could have been known as McCarty, etc. **I believe that ["Brushy"] did use the name, McCarthy [sic] in Silver City**. Aliases were not too unusual in those times and they do not disturb me.
>
> In view of the fact that he did continue to use aliases, it is possible that he was born William Henry Roberts. And I believe that we could have proved that Billy Roberts, born in Texas, was the same person as McCarty, Antrim, Bonney, if we had been given an opportunity to raise the issue in court during his lifetime.

On July 15, 1954, Morrison continued his mad attempt to persuade Rasch about the McCarty problem with inverted illogic that "Brushy" was the standard to present genealogy! He wrote:

"It is well settled that Billy Roberts would have been competent to testify on his own family history, whereas Garrett, Poe or John Smith would not have been competent to testify on the family history of the Kid."

With *Alias Billy the Kid* already published with the wrong names, Rasch ignored Morrison's rigmarole and used their absence to debunk the hoax.

On June 1, 1955, Morrison wrote to Rash, attacking with his usual, pompous legalese: "I am a dog for evidence, whereas you appreciate news reporters ideas which carry little, if any, weight in the courts ... [Y]ou inferred that [Billy Bonney's] early life had a bearing on Roberts' claim. You did state in your letter of June 14, 1954, by quoting from the affidavit [sic – military pension application of April 2, 1915] of William Antrim in 1915, 'We had no children ... my wife had two boys one died in the eighties & the other I have not heard from in 14teen [sic] years,' which I must contend is not evidence on the Kid's family history." **[It was actually key historical documentation.]**

In that letter, Morrison also slyly corrected Sonnichsen's "McCartney" to "McCarty" to ridiculously minimize that "Brushy" (as Billy) did not know his own birth name or that his mother was Catherine McCarty married to step-father William Antrim! Morrison wrote:

> That footnote on the **McCarty** name in Silver City paper about 1905, is Sonnichsen's baby **[referring to his "McCartney" footnote]** and I am going to talk to him before commenting on the incomplete citation. ["Brushy"] could have used the name or just about any other without affecting my case, but we should have given a complete citation ... [W]e all make mistakes at times. **[Feebly bluffed is that "Brushy" just happened not to mention his own birth name!]**
>
> I am ready, able, and willing to accept your church record [First Presbyterian Church in Santa Fe] on the marriage of Mrs. McCarty to Mr. Antrim ... as sufficient evidence to close this issue. **I had no interest in the record, but I picked it up**.
>
> In view of all the above stated facts and citations, I believe that you will understand that it is impossible for me to admit that "his early history does have a great bearing on whether he was the Kid," as you expect me to. So why look at it? I hope I have satisfactorily disposed of the issue.

And Morrison did research that marriage record. In Sonnichsen's papers is a typed copy of "Santa Fe County, New

Mexico, Book A, Matrimonio, Page 33a" certifying the March 1, 1873 Antrim-McCarty marriage union by Reverend D.F. McFarland; with **Henry McCarty** as witness, along with his brother, Josie McCarty.

The actual marriage certification of March 1, 1873 was in the First Presbyterian Church of Santa Fe. Entered by Reverend David F. McFarland, it stated:

1873
March 1st Mr. William H. Antrim and Mrs Catherine McCarty
Both of Santa Fé New Mexico
by D.F. McFarland
Witnesses
Harvey Edwards, Mrs A. R. McFarland
Miss Katie McFarland, **Henry McCarty**, *& Josie Mc Carty*

That meant that by April 12, 1977 Morrison, concealing Rasch's research, had lied to a Lawrence K. Mooney; writing: "I heard rumors the Kid's name was Henry McCarty but no documentation."

And Morrison had continued his obsessive campaign against Rasch after his June 1, 1955 letter. On June 4, 1955, he continued his letter barrage, having come up with a demand for "legal requirement of evidence;" and writing: "Although, I want to know if your statements from Sheriff Whitehill, Chauncey Truesdell, Anthony Connor, et als, meet the legal requirement of evidence. If they don't, then I will be forced to contend that they established absolutely nothing. You are attacking my statements, evidence, etc., and I believe I should enjoy the same privilege." He added falsely: "you and I have been arguing about evidence, statements, etc., without discussing the kind. I mean that which meets legal requirements. Nothing else sufficed for my purpose in the ["Brushy"] investigation." **[This faked that if Silver City residents knew Billy's name was McCarty, it should be disregarded if they did not swear affidavits!]** Morrison, besides being a liar, had no concept of historical research. He was all sound and fury signifying nothing.

Later, Morrison settled on simply lying, as seen in his seven page, single-spaced letter to young Frederick Nolan, on August 7, 1957 - eight years before Nolan's first major book, 1965's *The Life and Death of John Henry Tunstall*. Sonnichsen had the letter in his papers. Morrison tried to bamboozle Nolan about the McCarty name problem; writing: "**Rasch told me if I could not establish that the Kid's name was McCarty my case must fail.**" He had added: "[Rasch] has not produced one iota of evidence that the Kid's real name - the name conferred at birth - was McCarty, that he was born in New York, or that Mrs. Antrim was the natural mother" - each enough, as Morrison feared, to sink "Brushy." He wrote:

> I notice that Phil Rasch cited his writings in New Mexico Folklore and Historical review to prove his contentions of the incontrovertible facts that the Kid's real name was Henry McCarty ...
>
> I know that Rasch really believes that his works are infallible and incontestable, to which I take exceptions.
>
> For instance, in New Mexico <u>Folklore Record</u> ... **he quotes from the New York Sun that the Kid's real name was McCarty and a New Yorker by birth, which is not evidence in any form. He has not produced one iota of evidence that the Kid's real name** - the name conferred at birth - was McCarty, that he was born in New York, or that Mrs. Antrim was the natural mother.
>
> He told me that he had an affidavit, or some kind of writing [it was Antrim's pension petition of 1896], from Mr. Antrim that the boys were the children of his wife. It is my contention that Mr. Antrim would not be competent to prove up the family history of children born to his wife ...
>
> **Rasch told me if I could not establish that the Kid's name was McCarty my case must fail**.
>
> **My contention was, and it still is, that the only names pertinent to the case were the aliases used in the indictment and judgment; that any names or aliases used prior thereto/ immaterial, irrelevant, and, having no bearing on the issues to bar** ...
>
> If Rasch contends to you that I am in error in correcting his mis-statements, ask him to furnish you with citations to the evidence and I will check them out for you at my own expense ...
>
> Let me know what I can do at this end to unravel the legend.

The outcome of the "McCarty" disaster was that future "Brushy"-backing authors merely dispensed with Morrison's contorted rigmarole and dishonestly inserted the "McCarty" name into "Brushy's" words, as if he had claimed the name himself.

PITCHING THE HOAX

More important than facing critics, was selling the hoax.

TRYING FOR LIFE MAGAZINE

An early Morrison pitch, with copy in Sonnichsen's papers, was his January 2, 1951 letter to Art Liebson at *Life Magazine* - six days after "Brushy" died and 33 days after the lost pardon.

With pompous legalese implying being an attorney, Morrison described his meeting with "Brushy," and floated a peculiar *late-life* illiteracy claim - later changed to simply illiterate - to cover "Brushy's" not reading-up for imposture as: "**He could not read, or write in his late years**, therefore it was necessary for the wife to read and answer his correspondence at his direction." Advertised were the fake Affidavits for him as Billy. The no-Coroner's Jury-Report-ploy was emphasized. For "Brushy's" completely different origins, argued was that Billy's were unknown. The pardon failure appeared as injustice. And physical likeness to Billy was claimed as a clincher. Noteworthy, was using "Brushy's" fabricated name of "William Henry," to match Billy's name. Morrison wrote:

Dear Mr. Leibson:

The file that I submitted on the matter of W.H. Roberts, alias Wm H. Bonney, reflects some of the time spent on the investigation into the facts and records in the matter.

While living in Pensacola, Florida, in 1948, I learned that Billy the Kid was not killed by Pat Garrett, or anyone else. And he was still living a short time before I had met my informant ...

[His meeting with "Brushy" was framed as to assist him in getting the Lew Wallace pardon as Billy the Kid.]

There were many friends who knew him [as Billy the Kid] before and after the purported killing by Garrett. [Recounted is his taking "Brushy" to Lincoln's courthouse-jail.] ...

After receiving notice from clerks of the various Counties, and Secretary of State, Santa Fe, N.M. that they could not furnish a certified copy of a purported coroner verdict in the killing by Garrett, I decided to make a personal check of the old records to satisfy my own mind that it had never been made a matter of record. After weighing all the facts it was decided that no bonifide coroner's Verdict had ever been recorded in the matter. Therefore it is my contention that Pat Garrett did not kill Wm Bonney as reported by Garrett ...

The only evidence that Garrett killed Wm Bonney is based upon hearsay, which can not be supported by competent evidence. The only evidence that Wm Bonney was born in New York City ... The publication of the birth record in the New York Times has proved to be untrue ... Therefore I contend that the History, legend, and erroneous contentions, are improper and untrue ...

After filing the application for pardon with Governor T.J. Mabry, Santa Fe, N.M., we were required to produce the petitioner, which was accordingly done. It is admitted that petitioner could not answer some of the questions propounded to him before the members of the press, historians, and other people, attending the interview. Some of the questions were answered correctly, but they were not answers desired by historians. some of the incidents occurred some seventy odd years ago. Then again it was denied that the petitioner killed the two guards at the time of the escape. Of course, those purported offences were not included in the pardon. No one present at the interview contended to have been present when the incidents occurred in Lincoln County, nor did anyone contend to have known Billy in person.

It is my belief that the evidence and proof submitted with the application for pardon, together with the personal appearance of the man possessing the peculiar physical characteristics known to have been possessed by Wm Bonney, alias Kid, was sufficient to conclusively establish the identity as well as to establish the existence of the agreement between Governor Lew Wallace and Wm Bonney in 1879, at Lincoln, N.M., and the fact that the Governor failed to perform as agreed to upon performance of Wm Bonney, which has been proved ...

It is my belief and contention that facts disclosed in public records are the best evidence for this case... With this thought in mind I decided to release the records in my file to Life Magazine for perusal and consideration in placing the true facts before the reading public.

It is my opinion that Billy the Kid was not killed by Pat Garrett or anyone else. It is also my opinion that Wm Henry Roberts, alias Wm Henry Bonney, alias Kid, alias Billy the Kid, alias Brushy Bill Roberts, alias O.L. Roberts was one and the same person.

       Yours respectfully,
       Wm V. Morrison

KIWANIS CLUB TALK

On August 8, 1952, Morrison gave a Kiwanis Club talk in Silver City, titled "He Said He was Billy the Kid;" copies of which were in Sonnichsen's collected papers. The talk demonstrates developing lies of the *Alias Billy the Kid* manuscript Sonnichsen was writing.

Claimed was Morrison's meeting "Brushy," who pleaded for his help in getting a pardon as Billy the Kid. Claimed, in a clumsy early version of the illiteracy scam, was that " 'Brushy' did not read or write for more than thirty years [for some unstated reason]." And claimed was that Morrison tried to find the Coroner's Jury Report to have a lawyer "have the judgment set aside" based on Billy the Kid being alive. But it could not be found. So they asked for the pardon from Governor Mabry instead. But "Brushy" was intimidated at the hearing and failed the "memory test;" and no one cared about his little hands and big wrists for [fictional] shackle-slipping, or "Brushy's" multiple scars from his [fictional] shoot-out, on July 14, 1881, with "Garrett's posse." And they ignored Morrison's "evidence." (See pages 241-248 above) Then "Brushy" died before he could appeal for pardon with the next governor.

But huckster Morrison declared: "I [had] examined ["Brushy"] thoroughly, and questioned him rigorously until I was firmly convinced that he was Billy the Kid as claimed."

So Morrison would now tell them "Brushy's special knowledge of Silver City: that he came there "in 1868 and left in 1871 [going to Texas and] returning to Silver City in 1874, where his foster mother, Mrs. Antrim, died in the fall." **[Silver City did not exist in 1868. Real Billy was in Silver City from 1873 to 1875; with his real mother, Catherine Antrim dying on September 16, 1874.]** After spending the winter of 1877 "on the Ruidoso," "he joined his old friend, Jesse [sic] Evans, with whom he roamed the streets in Silver City in the early day." The fact that no one in the audience objected to these fictions (including Silver City not having existed in 1868) must have encouraged Morrison and Sonnichsen.

A description followed, with Morrison's capitalizations retained. It was the only time "Brushy's" speaking Spanish was claimed; and added were Native American tongues! Morrison wrote (with his capitalizations): "There he stood before me. As straight as an Indian from whom he DESCENDED. A small, well built man, standing five feet eight inches, weighing 160 pounds. With SMALL feet, SMALL well shaped hands with LARGE WRISTS over which I saw him remove HANDCUFFS. His dancing BLUE EYES were piercing through me ... However, he DID NOT read or write for more than thirty years ... He talked distinctly with a high-pitched voice, speaking SPANISH as well as THREE Indian dialects. He laughed as he talked, and always seemed to be in a good mood."

Fictionalized Lincoln County War history followed. This segued to total fabrications of "large cattlemen" putting Pat Garrett into office, and Garrett's faking the killing of Billy the Kid. The punch line was the no Coroner's Jury Report hoax; with its two versions, a copy submitted by Garrett's attorney which did not get him the reward; and "[t]he governor failed to recognize Garrett's copy in 1881 [and] [t]he legislature refused to recognize it in 1882 ... [and the Act says Garrett killed Bonney] "in the month of August, 1881." That this was all a plot of the Santa Fe Ring was proved by "Garrett's lawyer [having] to go before the legislature to get relief for killing the Kid [because] [t]hey could not produce an official coroner verdict in the purported death of the Kid." So Billy the Kid was not killed. He lived on as "Brushy Bill," got no justice from Governor Mabry, and died in December of 1950.

That the audience was duped was confirmed by Morrison's letter of August 15, 1958 to a Dr. McCain of the Silver City Kiwanis Club, stating: "Glen called today saying the members enjoyed my talk on the 'Kid', which was apparent in their reaction last night. Upon his suggestion, I am enclosing a copy of the speech for your club."

This talk convinced Morrison that he had struck gold. That August 15th, Morrison wrote to Sonnichsen: "Dear Friend": "I wish you could have been there last night to witness the occasion. It was amazing to see their reaction ... I have never seen such an attentive audience ... They want me to visit again ... And you must go along."

The next day, August 16, 1952, the *Silver City Daily Press* published "Kiwanians Hear Writer Support Claims of a Man Who Said He Was Billy the Kid." Declared was: "Morrison, who has written a book, "Alias Billy the Kid," disclaimed the story, generally accepted, that Billy the Kid was killed by Sheriff Pat Garrett in 1881. He said facts to support Roberts story will appear in his first book and in another book to be called "Pardon For Billy the Kid." **[never published]**

EL PASO ROTARY CLUB TALK

Morrison repeated his "Brushy Bill" fakery in a December 3, 1953, El Paso Rotary Club lecture on "Billy the Kid," with Sonnichsen giving the introduction (a copy of which was sent to Paul Blazer).

Morrison stated: "During my talk I hope to dispose of the two purported coroner's verdicts **[lie]**, and I hope to prove, among other things, That: The Kid was not killed by Garrett or anyone else; No official coroner's verdict was rendered; The Kid was a product of the times; Governor Wallace broke his agreement to pardon the Kid after the Kid had performed fully; The Kid's trial was unfair; The Kid lived for many years before appearing and applying for a pardon in 1950, which was refused by Governor Mabry without considering the indisputable records and evidence; At no time did anyone come forward with legal evidence to invalidate Billy Robert's [sic] claim; Billy Roberts was actually Billy the Kid as he claimed to be." Morrison concluded: "Garrett's posse purportedly killed an unidentified man in July or August, 1881 ... In fact, there is no legal evidence in San Miguel County to prove that they killed anyone at that time."

And Sonnichsen was right on board, as shown by Morrison's follow-up letter on December 3, 1953 to him; writing: "Words cannot express my appreciation for the wonderful introduction that you gave me today. It certainly relieved nervous tension that may have been present if I were alone." The two charlatans now had a polished routine: with Harvard professor Sonnichsen vouching for intrepid researcher and lawyer Morrison.

Of course, the "Brushy" hoax rested on claiming that Garrett lied about killing Billy the Kid, and that no Coroner's Jury Report identified William Bonney. Since those claims were fake, Morrison fabricated an absurd and error-filled plot based on the Santa Fe Ring falsifying documents, and giving Garrett the reward money, to hide that he did not kill the Kid and that "Brushy" was Billy.

Later used by Sonnichsen in *Alias Billy the Kid*, this scam can be seen full-blown in Morrison's letter of May 7, 1954 to historian Philip J. Rasch, whom he was trying to convert to "Brushy" belief (and which he copied to Paul Blazer). Morrison wrote:

> [Y]ou can understand that little credence can be placed on those papers controlled by the Ring at that time. I am sure you are probably aware of the fact that Catron was a dominant figure in the Lincoln County War, even though it might not have been written up. Also that Green, Garrett's attorney [sic] in the reward issue [for killing the Kid], was editor of Catron's <u>New Mexican</u> that printed the Government publications. And that Thornton, Catron's law partner, was the member of the legislature that pushed the act for relief of Garrett for killing the Kid in August [this misstates the Act's customary legalese of "<u>on or about the</u>

month of August, 1881," but was seized on for fakery by Morrison and Sonnichsen] and not on that memorable July 14 as Garrett would have you believe. All of this was done in less than a year from the time they claimed the Kid was killed, which they could not prove at the time. And none of it was reported in their paper as it actually happened, Why not? Certainly the Editor, Mr. Greene, knew about it ... In fact, all writers still contend that the killing took place on that memorable July 14, except Sonnichsen and Morrison, who have reproduced the record, the Official Act. Why has it gone untouched all of these years? Certainly they had never intended for old man Roberts to come along seventy years later and dig it out, or did they? ... **Garrett did not kill anybody in the month of July or August 1881.**"

[AUTHOR'S NOTE: Carried away by his lying, Morrison left out "Brushy's" key Billy Barlow tale!]

Soon after the book was released, Morrison presented its made-up claims on June 29, 1955, to William Waters (sending a copy to Paul Blazer): "A man was killed by mistake in July – not in August – by a member of Garrett's posse on the outside - not in Maxwell's house - but excusing Garrett as the killer; he was buried the next day and not on the second day after the killing as reported; he had used an alias, Billy B. Barlow; he had worked on a ranch near Mule Shoe, Texas; was not an outlaw and he had not fought in the war; was a relative of the old Clements family from Texas; Garrett paid for this mistaken murder with his life in 1908, and that Wayne Brezel [sic - Brazel] did not kill Garrett ... I have two objectives in this case. Did Garrett kill anyone that night? Was Roberts Billy the Kid."

On April 17, 1954, sending Paul Blazer a copy, Morrison wrote to Fred Gipson, then editor of *True West* magazine: "Garrett's posse claimed to have killed a man on that memorable July 14, 1881 ... but they left no evidence to support the contention that they had killed anyone at that time. I have the proof." (This had an irony that Morrison, dying in 1977, would not live to see: by 2003, that magazine, under new editor, Bob Boze Bell, participating in the "Billy the Kid Case" hoax, would back "Brushy" and fake forensics, trying to make him Billy the Kid.)

And Morrison was in full, lying, huckster mode with the University of New Mexico Press's sales manager, Eileen Quinn, informing her by letter of December 14, 1954 that among those who would "assist in advertising" *Alias Billy the Kid* were historians William Keleher and Philip J. Rasch, and Gene Autry!

STRATEGIZING PERSONAL PROFIT

By March 17, 1954, Morrison, already imagining big bucks, lied in a letter to a Carl W. Breihan, giving its copy to Paul Blazer. Morrison made-up that "Mr. Wm. Keleher, the attorney-historian-author, in Albuquerque, has definitely decided that my theory is the correct one. He is accepting my records in the case of Billy the Kid." And Morrison could see a golden future: "At present, I am dickering on movie and television rights on my work." And he added something that did not make it to his hoax, but lived on with its descendants: he bemoaned not getting "the opportunity to remove the remains [in the Billy the Kid grave] for scientific investigation."

Morrison's March 28, 1977 letter to Sonnichsen shows how high the two were aiming. Morrison wrote:

> Your letter of February 3, 1954, to me in Los Angeles ... aroused fond memories. You heard from your agent and wanted me to have this information prior to meeting with **Gene Autry and Howard Hughes**. You probably recall that Marcus Griffin [Editor of *New Mexico Magazine*] wrote to Autry about my research, and the trip contemplated out there. Autry had accompanied Wm. S. Hart to New Mexico on his research of the Kid ... We refused to accept the first contract submitted on Alias by UNM Press, urging additional clauses re cancellation and subsidiary rights. **I was still negotiating with Autry on television rights, and averse to sharing the profits equally with the Press**.

On March 31, 1954, Morrison was rejected by Gene Autry via a Mr. Schaefer; after trying to sell his "information on Billy the Kid" to that movie cowboy. And he sent its copies to Sonnichsen and Blazer. And never one to relinquish a great contact, that September 10th, he wrote again to Autry: "Our manuscript, Alias Billy the Kid, has been accepted for publication by the University of New Mexico Press. As soon as I receive a copy of the book, I will forward it to you. I take this opportunity to thank you and Mr. Schaefer for the consideration given my material."

POST-PUBLICATION LIES

After *Alias Billy the Kid* came out in 1955, it was dismissed by historians. So Morrison continued lying, now about its fatal errors. And he attacked its opponents.

To historian, Philip Rasch, he angrily wrote on June 1, 1955: "I make reference to your contention that Roberts or anyone else who read a book or two or who had been around Lincoln and heard the folklore, could have picked up everything in our book ... I am sorry to disappoint you by saying that no one else has concurred in your opinion up to this writing, and that the book is selling exceptionally well." And he faked backing of William Keleher: "[H]e has accepted the legal records as the best evidence" [leaving out that Keleher was "Brushy's" opponent at the time of the pardon hearing, and had also cited the Coroner's Jury Report]. And Morrison floated a conspiracy theory excuse: "Most of the experts have a closed mind."

A June 5, 1955 letter to *New Mexico Magazine* editor George Fitzpatrick, Morrison spelled out his counterattacks: "I am not too much disturbed by misunderstandings as I am on the offensive and plan to stay there. They gave me a tough time when I was on the defensive. I have made my case and it is up to them to bring in their evidence to disqualify my contentions."

NO LIMIT TO LIES

The writing was on the wall for hysterically lying William V. Morrison: historians were still not buying "Brushy's" bullshit. But the salesman in him knew that this tiny handful constituted no market for a book. The market was the vast public, whose ignorance about Billy the Kid could be counted on. That was why he, "Brushy," and Sonnichsen had built the hoax.

CHAPTER 6
THE HOAX BECOMES A BOOK

"BRUSHY'S" BIBLE IS BORN

It took from "Brushy's" 1950 death to 1955 for William V. Morrison and C.L. Sonnichsen to create a manuscript and find a publisher for their "Brushy Bill" hoax as *Alias Billy the Kid*.

On April 6, 1955, exuberant Morrison announced its publication to Paul Blazer: "The book will be reviewed this month and go on sale on May first, then autographing party is scheduled at White House on May 21. Also, television program in El Paso on KTSM as soon as I get there." "Brushy's" own P.T. Barnum was counting on Barnum's maxim: "There's a sucker born every minute."

By April 29, 1956, Morrison was hyping it to a George J. Hayes: "You may or may not know that Dr. C.L. Sonnichsen and I have a book published by the University of New Mexico Press on Billy the Kid. It has been declared by many as the best book on the subject." Though this was wishful hyperbole, *Alias Billy the Kid* would become the bible for benighted "Brushy"-believers to the present.

THE FIRST AND WORST DUPE

It took just one man to lift "Brushy Bill" Roberts's hoax from deserved disappearance, to dissemination. He was Edward Beverly "E.B." Mann, Director of the University of New Mexico Press, the dupe landed by Morrison and Sonnichsen. Flattering himself as a Billy the Kid aficionado, and ignoring Governor T.J. Mabry's verdict and scholarly historians' debunking, in 1954, Mann put the hoax under the aegis of his academic press to become 1955's *Alias Billy the Kid*. On January 7, 1955, smarmy Morrison flattered him; writing: "I certainly enjoyed the visit there and it was very interesting to hear that you are an enthusiast of the Kid as well as being an authority on guns."

Twenty-six years later, ignoring historians' scorn, E.B. Mann still promoted "Brushy" as Billy, in the July, 1981 edition of *Field and Stream's* "Billy the Kid," which used "Brushy" for its history. It demonstrates the ignorance that got this fool fooled. He wrote:

> Billy the Kid – call him Bonney, McCarty, Antrim, or whatever – is the most overrated badman in the Wild West legend. He was nothing more than a teenaged boy ... dragged into a range war by an angry loyalty to his friends ... A deadly little fighting man, yes; a big-time outlaw, no ...
>
> [L]et me offer less known facts of the legend, which, in a long lifetime of gunfighter research, have brought me into contact with that legend.
>
> I once wrote a novel ... titled *Gamblin' Man* ... published by William Morrow & Company in 1934 and is long out of print ... **In my book, Billy was not killed by Pat Garrett that fateful night in Pete Maxwell's house in Fort Sumner – and there are many people, some of them descendants of oldtime New Mexicans who participated in the war, who think that my guess was right!** ...
>
> [I]n 1950, a little man known in Texas as Brushy Bill Roberts, ninety-one years old, confessed that he was Billy the Kid and appealed to the Governor of New Mexico, Thomas Mabry, for pardon for crimes charged against him under that name. Said Brushy Bill, "I want to die a free man."
>
> On November 29 [sic – 30], 1950, I was one of the fifty or more avid witnesses in the Governor's mansion when Brushy Bill and his attorney [William V. Morrison impersonating a lawyer] appeared to plead their case. The little man was sick, and scared. Small wonder that he was scared, confronted as he was by Pat Garrett's lowering sons, Oscar and Jarvis, by clusters of state and local police, by yammering newsmen and flashing cameras. He denied knowledge of, or gave wrong answers to, the questions fired at him; and finally collapsed and had to be carried from the room. The news media made a joke of it, and Governor Mabry denied action on the petition for pardon "because I do not believe this man is Billy the Kid." No one could have believed it based on the little man's performance.
>
> But that was only the beginning of my connection with the Brushy Bill story. In 1954, as director of the University of New Mexico Press, I received a manuscript detailing and documenting that story. Dr. C.L. Sonnichsen, one of the authors, was a respected historian; the other, **William V. Morrison, was a successful Texas attorney** and a veteran student of Western legends. They came with documents they had unearthed, with sheaves of correspondence from many sources, and with literally miles of tape recordings of their discussions with Brushy Bill Roberts. **I was sure then and am sure now that no**

researchers ever dug deeper into the Billy the Kid story, or ever spent more of their own money in so doing, than did Sonnichsen and Morrison.

The book, *Alias Billy the Kid*, was published in 1955. It is an engrossing story, whether you choose to believe it or not. Certainly the Brushy Bill of the tapes was a very different witness than the little man in the Governor's mansion. His memory of names, dates, and events was remarkable, guiding the researchers to proofs of facts never before known, and to documented records refuting "facts" previously accepted by all of the "experts."

[AUTHOR'S NOTE: Mann was tricked by "Brushy's" parroted prompt sources, and too ignorant to recognize that their errors were a give-away of the hoaxing.]

He was the right size, had large wrists and small hands (the better to escape from handcuffs?), and he had a not impossible story (with some supporting evidence) of his life after his escape from New Mexico.

No, he didn't prove his story beyond doubt, but he knew things that made one wonder. As Morrison [sic – Sonnichsen] put it, "If he wasn't Billy the Kid, who was he?"

How did Brushy Bill explain that escape? What happened that night he was supposedly killed? He said that another boy, about his size (a transient in the area), was killed that night and that Garrett, Pete Maxwell, "Tia" Deluvina, and the six-man coroner's jury misidentified the body – Garrett "to get the reward"; the others "to give me a chance to get away."

Brushy Bill made it all seem plausible, though Morrison and Sonnichsen could not find a trace of the man Brushy Bill said was killed. But it was true that neither of the deputies with Garrett that night had ever seen Billy. It was true that Pete Maxwell was Billy's friend, and that Tia Deluvina loved him like a mother. [Omits all the townspeople seeing the body at the wake] It was true too, that every man on the jury was Spanish [unaware of its President, Milnor Rudulph], and that Billy was a folk hero among Spanish people …

Another mystery is Billy's name. Some insist that his real name was McCarty. Others say that his name was Antrim though the date of the McCarty-Antrim marriage [1873] makes that somewhat unlikely).

[AUTHOR'S NOTE: By 1981, Billy's names were common knowledge, except to this fool; and Billy himself had already explained "Antrim" in his letter of March 13, 1879 to Lew Wallace; writing: "*I am called Kid Antrim but Antrim is my stepfathers name.*"]

Still others say his name was William H. Bonney, born in New York City November 23 (or 29?) [29 is made-up], 1859, a son of an earlier marriage (or non-marriage?) [to] Catherine (Katherine? Kathleen?) ["Brushy's faked names] ... Brushy Bill Roberts said, "They'll never find records that I was born in New York!" And so far as I know, they never have.

Certain it is, though, that Bonney was the name Billy bore in New Mexico ...

[The tintype is described with the carbine called a rifle.] That picture has often been printed in reverse **[unaware that tintypes *are* in reverse]**, resulting in a mirror image which makes the boy, from the position of the revolver on his left hip, appear to be left-handed. Never mind that Brushy Bill Roberts said that he was left-handed by preference, but shot equally well with either hand ...

Fractured history followed. [The Lincoln County troubles are called a competition between "Alexander McSween [sic- Tunstall] ... who opened a general store in competition with the Murphy-Dolan business." Used is "Brushy's" tale that Billy "worked for Chisum, for Pete Maxwell, and finally for Tunstall." Tunstall is killed for no reason by "a drunken crew of killers" that hurled Billy into the imbroglio that followed" because - as "Brushy" made-up - revenge was sought. Morton and Baker are killed by Brewer's posse, and "returned ... face-down over their saddles." [They were buried where killed.] "So it was war: war of the ugly guerilla kind that pitted neighbor against neighbor, with politicians in Santa Fe calling the shots and naming the winners." Dick Brewer is killed "in a badly managed fight," Sheriff Brady is killed, George Peppin becomes Sheriff by "appointment from Santa Fe;" and "Billy the Kid was, by common consent, the war chief of that faction." **[Wrong]**

But Billy was a bad leader, as proved by Peppin surrounding the McSween house in Lincoln, filled with his partisans, as were other houses. The fight was "days-long" **[he is unaware of the six day battle]**. "At one point in the days-long battle, a column of U.S. cavalrymen under the command of Lieutenant-Colonel Dudley, three captains, and several lieutenants marched into Lincoln from Fort Stanton" [but did not intervene except for letting Susan McSween leave] and the McSween house was set on fire. Men inside fled and some were killed, including McSween. "Billy was last through that kitchen door. He moved swiftly, picking his way around and over the bodies, a gun blazing in either hand. Billy dived over the back wall into the bushes. Nobody pursued him." **[Escape scene made-up, even unaware of escape across the Bonito River]**

That made Billy an outlaw. "Pat Garrett asked for and got the job of hunting them down." **[Escape was on July 19, 1878. Garrett was elected Sheriff in November of 1880!]** Governor

Lew Wallace offered amnesty to everyone who would " 'go straight. He even carried that offer to Billy in person. Billy said, 'If I laid down my guns, they'd kill me before I could get out of town.' Wallace said, 'If you believe that, I'll give you safe conduct out of the Territory.' Can you hear the boy in you answer that offer? I can! Billy said, "I have as much right here as they do! I won't run!' " **[Made-up]**

[So Tom O'Folliard was killed and Tom Pickett **[made-up]** wounded by Garrett's posse, which chased the remainder to Stinking Springs and killed Charley [sic] Bowdre.] "Two days later, lacking food and water, Billy and his three remaining companions surrendered." **[Surrender was same day as Bowdre's killing: December 22, 1880.]**

Billy was tried for the Brady murder of which he was guilty, though others were too. And Brady and his men had shot at them, which wounded Billy's hip. **[made-up]** And Brady was fighting to avenge the death of his deputies, Morton and Baker. **[made-up; and ignorant of why Brady was killed or of the Regulators]**

Billy was placed in a cell room in the Lincoln County Courthouse, guarded by Bell and Olinger. When Garrett was out of town Billy slipped "his slim hands out of his cuffs [and] snatched Bell's revolver and ordered Bell to lead the way to the armory" [but Bell ran down the stairs and Billy shot him]. Then Billy shot returning Olinger with Olinger's shotgun.

Billy stayed in the Territory, and Garrett sought him in Fort Sumner with two deputies, and went into Peter Maxwell's house to question Maxwell. Billy had gone to Deluvina's house to eat, and she sent him to Maxwell's to get beef hung on a side porch. **[made-up]** When Billy entered Maxwell's room, Garrett shot him. Billy was identified by Deluvina, Peter Maxwell, and Garrett. Garrett also identified Billy's "self-cocker," which Mann questioned since Billy used single-actions and the room was dark. **[This lifts and garbles Morrison's fake argument that Garrett lied about the gun - consequently about the body's identity - which proved both men's ignorance that the Colt .41 "Thunderer" was used as a hide-away. Also Garrett identified the gun in the corpse's hand in the lit room.]**

The coroner's jury is claimed as accepting "the identification of the body" **[fakery: they could identify Billy and had Peter Maxwell's eye-witness statement]** "and signed Garrett's claim for the bounty." **[made-up]**

Deluvina Maxwell was quoted as faking the body as Billy's, because "we wanted to give Billy time to get away." **[Made-up quote. For 40 years, she laid wildflowers on Billy's grave.]**

Mann claimed to interview an unnamed "direct descendant" of an unnamed juryman, who refused to say if Billy was the body. He concluded: "So you decide for yourself. Either way, it's a great story. And, either way, it could be true." Thus, Mann concluded with the credulous stupidity and ignorance it took to fall for the hoax.

FATE OF THE BOOK

The print run for *Alias Billy the Kid* in 1955 was 3,000 books. In 1956, the year after its publication, E.B. Man was fired as Director of the University of New Mexico Press, and replaced by a Roland Dickey. This was announced in a June 14, 1956 *Albuquerque Journal* article: "UNM to Combine 3 Publications Under One Head;" stating: "[The Press] will discharge eight to 10 of the present publications employees, including E.B. Mann, director of the University Press since 1949." It is unclear if *Alias Billy the Kid* had made him dispensable. September 8, 1956's *Albuquerque Journal*, reported, under "Magazine Editor," that Mann had been appointed "managing editor of *Guns* magazine and *Guns Merchandise* magazine." He was touted as contributing "extensively to ... literature on firearms and is the author of numerous Western novels."

By 1976, the University of New Mexico Press chose not to reprint *Alias Billy the Kid*. On December 11, 1976, Morrison wrote to Sonnichsen with an explanatory conspiracy theory involving historical families and historians: "Perhaps there is more than meets the eye in the sudden demise of Alias, and firing of Mr. Mann by the Press [in the past] ... I received his letter ... that his position as Director had been terminated. He asked me to keep a look out for a job in my trips. I performed the research on Alias and did not burden you with the flack. It was my responsibility as I did not want to impair your relationship with their press." Morrison added that "the Garrett faction" and Oscar Garrett had threatened a lawsuit if they published *Alias Billy the Kid*, but Oscar had died, ending it. To address perfidious historians, Morrison groused that, in 1950, William Keleher even ignored his warning that the coroner's "verdict" was not valid, and published it, in 1957, in his book, *Violence in Lincoln County*.

On December 14, 1976, Morrison wrote a long letter about *Alias Billy the Kid's* "sudden death" to Press's Rights and Permissions' Barbara Franklin. He blamed the "Garrett faction" for changing Governor Mabry's mind about pardoning "Brushy," blamed "under currents of politics exercised by the old Santa Fe Ring," and blamed William Keleher for lack of research on the Coroner's

Jury Report and Garrett's reward. He hinted at blaming the Press too: "Roberts died a natural death after so many years; and so had Alias. It went out of print after sale of the initial publication of 3,000 copies. I hope its death was from natural causes without any interference from the Ring." And he added that "true historian," President Harry S. Truman, had hoped another governor would pardon "Brushy."

On March 28, 1977, Morrison, on behalf of himself and Sonnichsen, asked the Press to reprint *Alias Billy the Kid*. Three months later, on June 3, 1977, the new University of New Mexico Press Director, Hugh W. Treadwell, refused, returning the copyright to them.

On September 5, 1977, Sonnichsen wrote to Treadwell informing him that Morrison had died on August 30, 1977; adding: "As you may have guessed, he was the one who was ambitious for a republication of Alias. I think he had some small publisher in mind but I don't know who it was. I do not intend to press the matter myself ... [I once told] the Macmillan editor, 'Old Western books never die. They just get reprinted' ... I have no doubt that some day somebody will want to reprint the book - probably after I am long gone."

The University of New Mexico stayed clear of the book, but not the hoax. Forty-eight years after its press published *Alias Billy the Kid*, in 2003, corrupt New Mexico Governor Bill Richardson got one of its state-funded professors to be his "official historian" for his re-run of the "Brushy" hoax as the "Billy the Kid Case," because no legitimate historian accepted the job.

FATE OF REAL "BRUSHY"

Real "Brushy" in action was never seen again after his pardon fiasco. He had failed the special knowledge trick with his Lincoln County War ignorance, killing of no guards in his jailbreak, forgetting Pat Garrett, and his Fort Sumner steak restaurant for July 14, 1881. The "Brushy" of *Alias Billy the Kid* was a manufactured better "Brushy."

But it took 62 years after *Alias Billy the Kid's* publication, for its fix-ups to be inadvertently revealed. "Brushy"-believer, William Carl "W.C." Jameson, in his 2017 book, *Billy the Kid: The Lost Tapes*, stated that Sonnichsen had used "Brushy's" taped interviews to write *Alias Billy the Kid*. (Jameson, Page 29) But that did not mean that they were all actually "Brushy's" words. Jameson stated that his past co-author, Frederick Bean, had transcribed those tapes in 1989. When Jameson compared Bean's transcript to *Alias Billy the Kid*, he realized: "Sonnichsen used a relatively small amount of the information contained therein. It was also apparent that Sonnichsen, a long-time college professor of English literature, **heavily edited** Robert's grammar, even **adding and deleting** words for clarity. In other places, Sonnichsen merely summarized what Roberts said." (Jameson, Page 42) Jameson missed that this meant that Sonnichsen had dishonestly fixed-up "Brushy" to match Billy!

Of course, Morrison had also tried to make "Brushy" a better "Billy": coaching him with information, touring historic sites, and rehearsing answers on tape. As Jameson naively noted: "[On tape] Roberts related the same event as many as three times ... some contained information others did not. Roberts repeated himself often, sometimes three or four times within only a few minutes." (Jameson, Page 43) This is called practicing one's lines!

ALIAS BILLY THE KID AS FORGERY EVIDENCE

So the last time real "Brushy" was seen by the public was at his November 30, 1950 pardon hearing. And the hoax's fix-ups snowballed with later authors, "upgrading" "Brushy's" "knowledge" with new historical information, cleansing his racism, gentrifying his speech, and even making him bi-lingual! So *Alias Billy the Kid*, still reflecting his fatal ignorance because of his day's primitive sources for coaching, is a baseline for exposing later forged fix-ups of "Brushy's" transcripts.

EXPURGATING "BRUSHY'S" WORST FLUBS

Though the process of editing "Brushy," as described by W.C. Jameson in his 2012 book, *Billy the Kid: The Lost Tapes*, was kept secret by Morrison and Sonnichsen, one can reconstruct it, in part, from "Brushy's" taped statements, Morrison's notes, or confabulations when sources ran out.

In C.L. Sonnichsen's collected papers are some transcript pages and typed notes of "Brushy's" statements titled, by Sonnichsen, "Billy the Kid-Roberts." They reveal out-takes, that did not make it to *Alias Billy the Kid*, when garrulous real "Brushy" headed wildly off the tracks - like with the Mabry hearing's steak restaurant - embarrassingly proving that he certainly was not Billy Bonney. Examples follow:

1) **INTERVIEW JUNE 16, 1949, Page 1**: "I worked for John Maxwell at Fort Sumner a short time." **[It was Peter Maxwell; and real Billy did not work for him.]**

2) **INTERVIEW JUNE 16, 1949, Page 3**: "Jesse James knew Tunstall. He told Jesse about a place in England. Jesse went over there, but didn't buy it. They were friends and I guess that is the reason I liked Tunstall." **[Jesse James was not part of the history.]**

3) **INTERVIEW JUNE 16, 1949, Page 4**: "I got my six shooter off Brady's body too that day [of the ambush]. He took it when he arrested us at Seven Rivers a short time before. We got out on bond but he said he didn't have that one six shooter, a .44 single action with pearl handle grips. But he gave me the .44 with the wooden handles. I got it though when he fell there on the street dead. And I got his cartridge belt too." **[Brady arrested Deputized Billy and Fred Waite in Lincoln, along with Town Constable Atanacio Martinez, on February 20, 1878, with no legal justification, but to block their arresting John Tunstall's murderers. At the time, he confiscated Billy's Winchester '73 carbine, which Billy later retrieved from his corpse. And Brady released them on February 22, 1878, after Tunstall's funeral.]**

4) **INTERVIEW JUNE 16, 1949, Page 5**: "Sellman fought on our side in that cattle business in '78. I knew him in '77. He was always in trouble and my men helped him too ... Hines knew him too." **[John Selman was not part of that history; and Joe Hines was "Brushy's" friend impersonating Jessie Evans.]**

5) **INTERVIEW JUNE 16, 1949, Page 6**: "Jesse James almost killed Peppin. He didn't want to get mixed up in the war though ... Jesse was in Lincoln when Chapman was killed. Dalton can tell you the same thing." **[Made-up; and J. Frank Dalton was "Brushy's" friend impersonating Jesse James]**

6) **INTERVIEW AUGUST 18, 1949, Page 3**: "Then General Wallace was sent out here by the president of the U.S., McKinley." **[The President was Rutherford B. Hayes.]**

7) **UNDATED INTERVIEW NOTE OR TYPED FROM "BRUSHY'S" OWN NOTES:** "In the spring of 1891 I got a job catching Shetland Ponies on Shetland Island belonging to England. Took along five cow hands and we caught 100 head. Queen Victoria was Queen of England at that time. We were guarded by English Soldiers while there. We all had on buckskin suits. She invited us over to England

as she wanted to see a Texas Cowboy. We had a nice time over there for four days dancing and feasting all the time." **["Brushy" being way off the rails.]**

8) **TYPED NOTE WITH TYPED SIGNATURE: "BRUSHY BILL ROBERTS" and titled "1940."** Written before Morrison's coaching, it had a different fake genealogy, with grandfather named Benjamin Franklin Roberts, and a non-abusive father named Al Roberts, who was an Indian fighter and Civil War hero. It also stated: "I commenced with Buffalo Bill in 1885 ... I rode with Pawnee Bill in the Wild West Show. Also I rode with Bud Schnell's Wild West Show. The Miller Brothers Wild West Show, which came from the 101 Ranch ... I rode with Bugger Red in his Wild West Show ... During the time I owned my own show I had some of the best riders in the World, but many times in conversation they would remark, 'The old boss can beat any of us ...' Buffalo Bill was the first man to put up a Wild West Show. Pawnee Bill was next. Brushy Bill was the next man to put up a Wild West Show. I put one up in 1895, and I followed the Wild West Business 25 years before I quit. We were the first three men to put up a Wild West Show, and I am the only one living out of the three." **[Subsequently Sonnichsen had the father as abusive John Henry "J.H." Roberts, and shortened the absurd list to only Buffalo Bill and Pawnee Bill.]**

PROMPTS OF BILLY'S LETTERS AND ARTICLES

The partial transcripts of Morrison's taped "Brushy" interviews in Sonnichsen's collected papers also reveal "Brushy's" near-verbatim repeating of real Billy's letters to fake special knowledge, leaving the possibility he was reading from Morrison's Lincoln Museum copies while confabulating. Newspaper articles were used in the same way. Sonnichsen later hid that transparent cheating by selective quoting. Examples follow:

1) **INTERVIEW AUGUST 18, 1949, Page 4**: "I heard the Governor offered a thousand dollars for me to come in and testify. I wrote and told him that I would come in and testify if he would annul those indictments against me." **[Billy's letter to Lew Wallace of March 13, 1879 stated:** *"I have heard that You will give one thousand $ dollars for my body which as I can understand it means alive as a witness ... if it is in your power to Annully those indictments I hope you will do so so as to give me a chance to explain."***]**

2) **INTERVIEW AUGUST 18, 1949, Page 6**: "While we were [at Greathouse's] we were surrounded by a posse, surrounded by a posse we was. They sent in Carlyle to get us to surrender. He had no warrant. I just told him it amounted to mob violence and we didn't intend to be mobbed, not just yet anyhow. His posse had Greathouse with them. When they commenced shooting out there Carlyle got scared and he jumped out the window. As he went through the window they shot him down without warning. They thought it was me making my escape, but they got fooled that time. We were going to make Carlyle ride out with us after dark. They left and we got out that night. The next day they came back and burned down the house thinking we were inside." [Billy's letter to Lew Wallace of December 12, 1880 stated: *"After mine and Billie Wilsons horses were killed [at Coyote Spring] we both made our way to a Station, forty miles from the Oaks kept by Mr Greathouse. When I got up the next morning The house was Surrounded by an outfit led by one Carlyle, Who had come into the house and Demanded a Surrender. I asked for their Papers [warrants] and they had none. So I concluded that it amounted to nothing more than a mob and told Carlyle that he would have to Stay in the house and lead the way out that night. Soon after a note was brought in Stating that if Carlyle did not come out inside of five minutes they would Kill the Station Keeper)Greathouse) who had left the house and was with them. in a Short time a Shot was fired on the outside and Carlyle thinking Greathouse was Killed jumped through the window. breaking the Sash as he went and was killed by his own Party they thinking it was me trying to make my Escape. the Party then withdrew. they returned the next day and burned an old man named Spencer's house and Greathouses also."*]

3) **INTERVIEW AUGUST 18, 1949, Page 8**: "We planned to ride out after dark and started to lead the horses inside the doorway [at Stinking Springs]. They shot a horse and he fell dead in the doorway. My mare wouldn't jump over a dead horse so we gave up on the idea. <u>I had intended to ride my mare out on her side like the Cheyenne Indians taught me in my boyhood days. I would have ridden out shootin [sic] if that dead horse had not fell over in the opening.</u>" [Used was a December 28, 1880, *Las Vegas Gazette* interview of captured Billy, who was quoted: **"If it had not been for the dead horse in the doorway I wouldn't be here in Las Vegas. I would have ridden out on my bay mare and taken my chances**

of escaping. But I couldn't ride over that for she would have jumped back and I would have got it in the head." This also shows "Brushy's" erroneous confabulating, as underlined, to expand information - like being taught to ride by Indians. But he was unaware that the narrow doorless opening in the rock house had no room for riding sideways to support his fiction.]

CREATING "BRUSHY'S" NARRATIVE

C.L. Sonnichsen cobbled together "Brushy's" narrative from "Brushy's" pre-Morrison multi-persona fabrications and genealogy, and from his coaching from sources and tours of historic sites, as they appeared in "Brushy's" own writings and Morrison's tape recordings and notes.

As claimed by "Brushy"-believer, W.C. Jameson in his 2012 book titled *Billy the Kid: The Lost Interviews* - who also interviewed Sonnichsen - from the summer of 1949 to December of 1950, Morrison took notes on "Brushy's" statements, and recorded eight six-inch reels of taped interviews; which Sonnichsen got to write *Alias Billy the Kid*. (Jameson, Page 23)

Morrison's "interviews" with "Brushy" that are cited in *Alias Billy the Kid*, are those of May 24, 1949 at an uncertain location; June 16 and 17, 1949, in Hico, Texas; and on August 18, 1949, at Carrizozo and Lincoln. (Footnote 5, Page 21) (In a July 12, 1955 letter to historian, Robert Mullin, the date is given as August 19, 1949, rather than August 18th). An April of 1950 trip throughout New Mexico is also cited, in which Morrison took "Brushy" to get supposedly verifying affidavits of his being Billy the Kid from non-historical people. (Pages 70-72) Carrizozo was clarified later in *Alias Billy the Kid* as having the courthouse for Morrison, with "Brushy," "to go through the records;" but the date of that endeavor was changed to "August, 1950." (Page 40) Morrison also referred to "later expeditions" with "Brushy" to Lincoln. (Page 45)

Alias Billy the Kid's sheer quantity of information, from the sheer quantity of labor by "Brushy," Morrison, and Sonnichsen, was intended to amaze a reader as impossible to have been faked. But, as will be seen, it was all just smoke and mirrors.

CHAPTER 7
DEBUNKING
ALIAS BILLY THE KID

SMOKE AND MIRRORS

After the failed pardon, the *Alias Billy the Kid* book was William V. Morrison's next chance to fake "Brushy Bill" Roberts as Billy the Kid. With accomplice, C.L. Sonnichsen, as writer, the new hook was that "Brushy" had special knowledge unique to Billy the Kid, and unavailable to him from books an illiterate. Sonnichsen edited Morrison's research and "Brushy's" interview quotes and notes (since "Brushy" was literate). Intended was that massed names, places, and events would appear as memories, "proving" he was Billy. Sonnichsen's taunt made its cover: "Was he Billy the Kid? If not, who was he?"

But the hoax unravels when "Brushy's" "special knowledge" is shown as lifted from publications and in footnoted sources, with give-aways being parroted errors. And, for lack of information, "Brushy's" filled-in confabulations are wrong. Some errors are fatal: ones real Billy would never make. Also, physical match was faked; and only Billy's outlaw myth was used for identity. The result is a surrealistic mélange of historical names and basic events jumbled with "Brushy's" fictions, with no evidence that he was Billy Bonney. Worse, revealed is the authors' falsifying documents, fixing-up "Brushy's" words, faking conspiracy theories, and presenting false affidavits to bamboozle readers.

The 136 page book, with photographs, has: "Publisher's Foreword;" a note "To the Skeptical;" "Prologue;" "Brushy Bill's Story;" "evidence" in "The Tangled Web," "Be He Alive, Or Be He Dead, and "In Black and White;" "Epilogue;" and "Appendices," mixing real Billy's documents with some on "Brushy."

The book fails. Its errors are total - with one so fatal that it would lay bare the hoax's *modus operandi* when future "Brushy"-believing authors, new hoaxers, and my research would reveal that terrible, telling, and terminating mistake - right at the death scene that was intended to clinch "Brushy" as Billy Bonney.

HOAXING ON THE COVER

Before one even opens *Alias Billy the* Kid, one encounters shameless lying on the back dust jacket's biographies - presumably provided by the authors to fake expertise.

Morrison floats his lawyer imposture as: "**Attorney** William V. Morrison knew that many famous and notorious men ... are said to have survived long after they were presumed dead ... [After he found evidence that Billy the Kid was living as Brushy Bill Roberts] **he traced all legal documents on the case, and represented Brushy Bill when he sought pardon in New Mexico.**" English teacher Sonnichsen poses as an historian: "Since 1931, when he took his Ph.D. at Harvard, C.L. Sonnichsen has been a dweller in and student of the Southwest ... [and his name is] **highly regarded by readers and scholars alike as a contributor to Southwestern lore and letters.**"

THE HOAX IN THE TITLE

The title inadvertently distilled the chicanery into four words: *Alias Billy the Kid*. Unknown to "Brushy," Morrison, and Sonnichsen, Billy the Kid was not real Billy's alias.

SOURCE ERROR: The mistake is lifted from an *Alias Billy the Kid* source footnote: a 1943 *Frontier Times Magazine* article titled "A Story of 'Billy the Kid,' " which reproduced an August 10, 1881 article, from the *Laredo Times*, titled "Killing of 'Billy the Kid.' " The apocryphal article stated: "Information from Lincoln County is that <u>William Bonney, alias, 'Billy the Kid</u>," who escaped from Lincoln jail on April 30 last, while under sentence of death, has added three more victims to his already large list." In truth, that moniker was only used in outlaw myth press - like this example.

And real Billy objected to it in his December 12, 1880 letter to Lew Wallace; stating: "*I noticed in the Las Vegas Gazette a piece which stated that, <u>Billy "the" Kid, the name by which I am known in the Country</u> was the captain of a Band of Outlaws who hold Forth at the Portales. There is no such Organization in Existence. So the Gentleman must have drawn very heavily on his Imagination.*"

"PUBLISHER'S FOREWORD"

Though not signed, the "publisher" giving the foreword is apparently E.B. Mann, revealing inadvertently how he was duped. He gave a quote: "Was Billy the Kid really shot to death by Sheriff Pat Garrett on that July night in 1881, or was someone else the victim?" Cited bizarrely as his source is a "Southwestern writer [who] stated the case for Brushy Bill Roberts." (Page vii) He is named as J.W. Hendron.

FAKERY: J.W. Hendron's "No Pardon For Billy" appeared in January 5, 1951's *Highway Happenings*. His "case" for "Brushy," was that he was *not* Billy the Kid. (See pages 261-262 above) Hendron wrote: "At the onset of the [Mabry] interview it was easy to see that this latest "Billy the Kid' had little conception of the facts about the Lincoln County War." Sly Morrison, who had attacked Hendron in print and by letters for opposing "Brushy," may have provided Hendron's out of context quote, for lack of any historian backer.

The dupe "publisher" declares that the rumor of Billy the Kid's survival persists. And, though other famous dead people also have rumored survival, "[Brushy"] was "one of very few claimants whose claims have been subjected to careful, expert, extensive examination while he was still living." (Page viii) **[False]** Added is that the book might not convince skeptics, but "readers of the manuscript have been amazed by what Brushy Bill knew: things never printed; things even in contradiction to the accepted stories, since proved to have been the way Brushy Bill told them. (It was generally believed, for example, that there was a federal charge outstanding against Billy the Kid. Brushy Bill said the case was 'thrown out of court.' The legal records, when found, proved Brushy Bill's statement." (Page viii)

THE HOAX IN A NUTSHELL: Presumed dupe, E.B. Mann, was ignorant of "Brushy's" prompt source of the April 15, 1881 letter of Billy Bonney to Attorney Edgar Caypless – copied by Morrison from the Lincoln Museum - which stated: "*My United States case was thrown out of court and I was rushed to trial on my Territorial charge.*"

A "NOTE TO THE SKEPTICAL"

Signed by Sonnichsen and Morrison for March 10, 1955, this introduction claims the book's intent "is to let Brushy Bill tell his own story, without addition or subtraction ... and throw light on it [with] correspondence, eye-witness testimony, and official records. No attempt is made to highlight, select, or color Bill's statements." (Page ix) **[Lie]**

They call themselves "[h]is editors, one a lawyer **[lie]** and the other a college professor **[of English, not history]** ... [who] would not willingly participate in deception. **[Brazen lie!]**. (Page ix] Misleadingly thanked to name-drop historical experts are Robert N. Mullin, Maurice Garland Fulton, Oscar Garrett (with aside that they denied Brushy's" claim). (Page x)

"PROLOGUE"

The 12 page "Prologue" recites Morrison's original hoax hook: "Brushy" wanting Billy the Kid's pardon; and it repeats his fakery that "Brushy" failed the Mabry pardon hearing by being rattled by press, hostile experts, and historical family members; and because Morrison's written "brief" (the fake evidence packet) was ignored. Then "Brushy" died before getting justice from another governor. (Pages 1-3, 5, 9-11)

Sonnichsen falsely advertises Morrison as "**a graduate lawyer** with a good nose for evidence." Added is that Morrison was "a member in good standing of the Missouri Historical Society ... [and] direct descendant of Ferdinand Maxwell, brother of the famous Lucien Bonaparte Maxwell." (Page 3)

Given is Morrison's tale of locating "Brushy." In 1948, he finds a Floridian Jim Hines, who, as a past Lincoln County War participant, told him that Billy the Kid had not been killed by Pat Garrett, and now lived in Texas. (Page 3) Next, Morrison met a Missourian named "Dalton," claiming to be Jesse James, who told him Billy the Kid was "O.L. (Brushy Bill) Roberts" living in Hamilton, Texas. (Pages 3-4) **[This trail of oldster Old West imposters is a good test for reader credulity.]** So Morrison tried to find this Billy the Kid.

PHYSICAL MATCH

Morrison found "Brushy" in June of 1949. He was impressed that "Brushy" looked younger than 90; was slim and short; was left handed; had a protruding left ear; had large wrists and small hands (and did a handcuff slipping trick); and was toothless - to dispense with having no buck-teeth. (Page 4,6)

FAKERY AND SOURCES: "Brushy" was 69 and right handed. His Billy the Kid handcuff-slipping came from Billy's apocryphal jailbreak tales. His left-handedness and funny left ear claims came from imitating the right-to-left reversed tintype, as well as lifting from Walter Noble Burns's 1926 book, *The Saga of Billy the Kid*, which fictionalized Billy's death walk from the same tintype error; stating: "So the Kid started out for the meat ... the butcher knife in his right hand and, naturally enough, <u>as he was left-handed, his forty-one caliber double-action revolver in its scabbard on his left side</u>." (Burns, Page 281)

Morrison absurdly thought small hands and thick wrists was a clincher. In his April 19, 1954 letter to historian, Philip J. Rasch, now in the Blazer family papers, attacking the pardon hearing, wrote: "Billy ["Brushy"], who stood there through the intimidation, waving those <u>unusually small hands with large wrists</u> – and no one seemed interested in his peculiar physical makeup."

Real Billy had no evidence of "small hands," as shown by his regular-sized right hand seen in his tintype.

But used was Pat Garrett's *The Authentic Life of Billy the Kid*, which stated that "Billy was ... about five feet, seven and a half inches high, straight as a dart. He weighed about a hundred thirty-five pounds ... [He wore] a neat boot on his small, shapely foot ... <u>His hand was small and his wrist large</u>; so it was difficult to keep a pair of handcuffs on him." (Garrett, Page 116) And, for the great escape, Garrett/Upson fabricated that, after killing Bell, Billy "ran to the window at the south end of the hall, from which he saw Bell fall; <u>then slipping his handcuffs over his hands</u> he threw them at [Bell's] body." (Garrett, Page 201)

Lew Wallace's outlaw myth articles on Billy the Kid repeated the fable by hiding that Billy was in sham jailing in Lincoln, and merely walked out after Wallace never gave the promised pardon. In *New York World Magazine* on June 8, 1902, Wallace published "General Lew Wallace Writes a Romance of 'Billy the Kid' Most Famous Bandit of the Plains," which stated: "**The manacles slipped like magic from his wrists.** The guards stood stupefied, and "Billy the Kid," laughing mockingly, walked leisurely from the jail yard."

That myth was also used for the great escape, Russ Kistler's *Las Vegas Daily Optic* of June 15, 1881 published "The Land of the Petulant Pistol, 'Scenes' where Life and Land are Cheap ... Billy the Kid as a Killer;" stating: "**[Billy] had worked his bracelet off** and snatched the officer's pistol."

Walter Noble Burns, copying Garrett's book, used it for his 1926 *The Saga of Billy the Kid;* writing: "**His hands and feet were remarkably small.**" (Burns, Page 59)

A 1935 book by a Frank M. King, titled *Wranglin' the Past: Reminiscences of Frank M. King*, also lifting the myth for the jailbreak; stated: "After the Kid had killed [Bell], he slipped the handcuffs off over his extremely small hands." (King, Page 170)

Examining willingly striped-down "Brushy," Morrison found 26 scars claimed from bullets and knives. Real Billy had one scar. For that, "Brushy" says one on his hip "was from the time I ran into the street in Lincoln to take the **guns** off the body of Sheriff Bill Brady. Billy Matthews **ran behind an adobe wall** and fired. His shot went through the flesh of this hip and then hit **Wayte** [sic]." (Page 5) "Fred and I jumped the wall ... I pulled my pearl-handled .44 off his body." (Page 27)

FALSE: This was a failed special knowledge trick.

In fact, it was Billy and the Regulators who ambushed Brady *from behind an adobe wall*. Jacob Basil "Billy" Matthews, a Deputy Sheriff, next fired at them from *inside the Cisneros house* when Billy ran out with companion Jim "Frenchie" French - not Fred Waite - to retrieve his Winchester '73 carbine from Brady's body. The carbine had been confiscated after John Tunstall's murder by Brady in a brief illegal arrest of Billy - though "Brushy" fabricated a retrieved "pearl-gripped .44 revolver."

Ambidextrousness, a known Billy trait, is claimed, but ruined by "Brushy's" claiming to favor the left (Page 6), repeating his tintype reversal error.

THE SPECIAL KNOWLEDGE SCAM

To select for the credulous and historically ignorant, Sonnichsen dangled some of "Brushy's" special knowledge tricks. But their errors merely revealed his mismatch with Billy, his failed confabulations around known names and events, and his use of prompt sources. Examples follow:

INARTICULATE "BRUSHY": When "Brushy" is quoted, he reveals the mismatch with Billy: **"I done wrong like everyone else in those days."** (Page 5) An unschooled rustic matched 1950's readers' Billy the Kid expectation; but was incompatible with the actual literate and articulate freedom fighter Billy Bonney, who objected to being called an outlaw.

FAKING MURDER TRIAL SUBPOENA KNOWLEDGE: "Brushy" states that his hanging trial witnesses lacked subpoenas. (Page 7) In fact, the subpoena of Lincoln resident and prosecution witness, Isaac Ellis, still exists. Furthermore, as a defendant, real Billy would not have that information, which apparently reflected Morrison's prompting "research" failure to find subpoenas.

SOURCING A LEW WALLACE ARTICLE FOR A QUOTE: About facing the murder trial with no Governor Wallace pardon, "Brushy" states: " 'But they didn't hang me, they didn't ... **I wasn't born to hang.**' " (Page 7) That quote was lifted from a Lew Wallace article, available at the Indiana Historical society, titled "Gen. Wallace's Feud with Billy the Kid, When the General Was Governor of New Mexico and Billy Bonne Was the Most Dangerous Western Outlaw;" stating: "He was convicted for murder and sentenced to be hanged. When the sentence was read, he arose in court and said: "Judge, that doesn't frighten me the least bit. **Billy the Kid was not born to be hung.**'... [When he escaped] [he] called back as he spurred the animal into a gallop: **'Tell the judge that I said Billy the Kid was not born to be hung.'**

SOURCING A BILLY LETTER FOR A QUOTE: About the Garrett posse chase-down, "Brushy" is quoted: "I was never afraid to die like a man fighting, but I did not want to be shot down like a dog without a chance to fight back." (Page 8) That was lifted from Billy's March 20, 1879 letter to Governor Lew Wallace; stating: *"I am not afraid to die like a man fighting but I would not like to be killed like a dog unarmed."*

BILLY THE KID AS AN ALIAS: Claimed are "Brushy's" "aliases": "Ollie L. Roberts, Brushy Bill Roberts, Rattlesnake Bill, Texas Kid, Hugo Kid, William Antrim, William Bonney, **Billy the Kid**." (Page 9) But Billy Bonney never used Billy the Kid as an alias; being called just "Kid" by friends. And William Antrim was Billy's actual name after his mother's marriage.

ADMITTING LITERACY: Though the hoax rested on the illiteracy claim, "Brushy's" ability to read and write breaks through. So, trying to show he had enough "Brushy" quotes after his death, Sonnichsen admitted: "["Brushy"] made some attempts at writing his autobiography." (Page 11)

THE FAKED SHOOTING NEGRO SOLDIERS: "Negro" soldiers from Fort Stanton are described by "Brushy" as taking "positions on the hillside and joining in the firing that day when the Murphy men burned McSween's house." (Page 12) This is wrong. During the Lincoln County War Battle on July 19, 1878, the only day troops were present in the fighting, only Sheriff George Peppin's white possemen attacked McSweens from the south foothills. And the only soldiers that fired on McSweens were three white ones, as Billy himself testified in the military court of inquiry against their commander. Furthermore, to hide "Brushy's" racism, Sonnichsen changed "[N-word]" to "negro" - accidently retained later. And Negro Fort Stanton soldiers came from Walter Noble Burns's 1926 *The Saga of Billy the Kid*. (Burns, Page 122)

SOURCING A BILLY LETTER FOR THE JIM CARLYLE KILLING: "Brushy's" claim that Jim Carlyle's fellow possemen, not Billy, killed Jim Carlyle in the Greathouse Ranch encounter (Page 12), was lifted from Billy's December 12, 1880 letter to Lew Wallace; which stated: "*Short time a Shot was fired on the outside and Carlyle thinking Greathouse was Killed jumped through the window. breaking the Sash as he went and was killed by his own Party they thinking it was me trying to make my Escape.*" Morrison, with "Brushy" in tow, got it from the Lincoln Museum.

FABRICATING THE DEATH/SURVIVAL SCENE: For surviving the Fort Sumner shooting of Billy the Kid, "Brushy" made-up a "battle" with Pat Garrett's shooting possemen. (Page 6) That scene is key to cracking the "Brushy" hoax - but it would take decades for later "Brushy"-believing authors to reveal the Sonnichsen/Morrison fix-up of what "Brushy" actually said about that night. Sonnichsen added that Pat Garrett's son, Oscar, claimed that survival story accused his father, and all involved in the shooting, to have conspired to lie. Sonnichsen opined smugly: "It may be so." (Page 13)

BACKING "BRUSHY"

Sonnichsen wrote that Morrison, convinced "Brushy" was Billy, took him to historic sites, while "Brushy" recounted his tales. Morrison then moved to El Paso for further researching; and engaged the Andress, Lipscomb, and Peticolas law firm there to prepare "Brushy's" pardon petition. (Pages 7-8)

Sonnichsen gave his own meeting with cowboy-costumed "Brushy," and his amazement that he knew "negro soldiers from Fort Stanton [shot from the foothills] when the Murphy men burned McSween's house." **[Wrong]** He added that he was "a hobbyist in Southwestern history and folklore." (Pages 11- 12)

"BRUSHY BILL'S STORY"

Alias Billy the Kid, purporting to be a first-person account, lacked intimate information for autobiography. But for "Brushy Bill's Story," "Brushy" was on the firing line for a life tale of 44 pages. And, as discussed, there were unsolvable impasses. "Brushy" and team were ignorant about Billy Bonney's early years, why the Lincoln County War was fought, or that Billy was a zealot hero in grass-roots anti-Ring uprisings. So "Brushy's" confabulations were a necessity to minimize Billy's outlaw myth of being a serial killer-rustler. So that delusional, grammatically impaired, cowboy obsessed, lying, racist, old-timer, not only demonstrated no match for Billy, but also became a caricature insulting the historical figure he was miming.

Sonnichsen mixed short "Brushy" quotes with damage-controlling paraphrasing and narration. Footnotes pretend to corroborate "Brushy's" statements, but were actually his prompt sources, as revealed by "Brushy's" parroting their errors. Photographs, mixed real Billy's with "Brushy's." As discussed above, hidden is that this was a secretly fixed-up, better "Brushy." And, forgetting the illiteracy claim, to feign authenticity, the first footnote states: "What follows is assembled from Roberts' **notebooks, correspondence**, and conversation." (Page 14)

FAKING A FAMILY

To be Billy Bonney, "Brushy" needed two decades of aging and a fictionally back-dated family to match. His genealogy, mostly by "Brushy" himself, proved his cunning sociopathy. Only after his death, and continued publicizing of his hoax, did his embarrassed Roberts family relatives reveal his actual August 26, 1879 birth date - in contrast to Billy Bonney's on November 23, 1859.

But the fact that in the mid-20th century, real Billy's known history started in 1877 (at his age of 17-18), enabled "Brushy" and team to get away with faking a family.

And, as discussed, "Brushy" had already added 10 years to his life, and the middle initial "L" (instead of "P") for his Social Security benefits fraud. Ten more years were added to be Billy. So when "Brushy" met Morrison, he was 80 year old Oliver L. Roberts for his benefits checks, but was William Henry Roberts, and 90 years old, for Morrison as Billy the Kid.

PROMPTS: William V. Morrison's prompts for "Brushy" were implied in his letter of April 23, 1951 to Mrs. I.A. Adams in Lindsay, Oklahoma; stating: "I have been working on a family history of the Roberts family for several years."

Fake genealogy may also have been surreptitiously added after "Brushy's" death for *Alias Billy the Kid*, since Morrison wrote on the same day to a Tom Roberts that he had also been getting information from a J. Henry Roberts of Richland Springs, Texas, to "finish my history as soon as possible" (the manuscript of *Alias Billy the Kid* was then being written); and stated: "It is interesting to hear that you are a member of the old Roberts family. I am enclosing a memorandum on the family for you to fill in and return to me ... I would like to finish my history as soon as possible." On May 4, 1951, Morrison wrote to J. Henry Roberts: "Dr. C.L. Sonnichsen, Professor of English, Texas Western College, is helping with my research. After all of the questionnaires are in my file we plan to talk to the various branch members of the Roberts Family."

On April 16, 1951, J. Henry Roberts responded irritably that: "In regard to O.L. Roberts I don't know a thing about his people ... and Pat Garrett did kill the Kid. The Kid's grave is in Fort Sumner there is no doubt about that [O.L. Roberts] was not the kid."

Not the illiterate as claimed for his hoax, "Brushy" had himself researched a fake family for his impersonation. From Walter

Noble Burns's quasi-fictional 1926 *The Saga of Billy the Kid*, he apparently lifted wrong information that Billy Bonney's parents were named "**William H. and Kathleen Bonney.**" (Page 14) (Burns, Page 70) He, thus, wrongly thought "Bonney" was a family name. In truth, Billy's father was a McCarty, and his mother was Catherine - with unknown maiden name. "Bonney" was an alias devised by Billy in 1877 from unknown inspiration.

"Brushy" contributed: "I was born at Buffalo Gap [Texas] on December 31, 1859" (Page 14) as William Henry Roberts.

FAKING: "Brushy" was born on August 26, 1879 in Bates, Sebastian County, Arkansas, as Oliver Pleasant Roberts. William Henry was Billy Bonney's name.

According to historian, Don Cline's 1988 manuscript, *Brushy Bill Roberts: I Wasn't Billy the Kid*, "Brushy" learned of the old town of Buffalo Gap in about 1906, when he first went to west Texas. He later saw it many times when visiting his half-sister, Samantha Belle Roberts, in Carlsbad, New Mexico. Additionally, his Jesse James imposter friend, J. Frank Dalton, lived in Lovington, New Mexico, on the way from Buffalo Gap. And it was old enough for his fake December 31, 1859 birth. (Cline, Pages 14, 57)

FAKING: The added age for birth date 1879 was obvious to those acquainted with him, including his last wife, Malinda Allison; and made Morrison admit at his funeral, as reported in the *Hico News Review* of January 5, 1951, that there was "noted discrepancy in the reported age of Brushy Bill." And Malinda Allison picked "Brushy's" benefits fraud date of December 31, 1868 as his tombstone birth date!

To account for real Billy's being born in New York City, "Brushy" responded that he told that to "the Coe boys" when he first came to New Mexico because he was like "the James boys and Belle Starr," who also came to Lincoln under assumed names. (Page 15) And mouthing a prompt - or just a later write-in by sly Sonnichsen - was added: "[T]hey have no proof on record that Billy the Kid was born in New York." (Page 15)

FACT: Billy Bonney's real birth location and date came credibly from Ash Upson, ghostwriter of Pat Garrett's *The Authentic Life of Billy the Kid*. (Garrett, Page 1) Journalist Upson likely learned them when boarding with Billy's family in Silver City. In addition, Garrett himself knew

Billy, and may have been told by him about the New York birth. And Lew Wallace, who got to know Billy for their pardon bargain in 1879, consistently wrote that he was born in New York in his later articles about Billy the Kid. That gains credence, since Billy also told Wallace about his subsequently confirmed family sojourn in Indiana (to appeal to Wallace, who was from that state).

Then "Brushy" launched into his own great creation: his fictitious Roberts family, interwoven with some of Billy Bonney's family names. [FIGURE: 13] (See pages 165-171 above for his real family tree.)

Since pure fiction is hard to write, and this fiction needed knowledge of the Civil War, "Brushy" twisted his own family names, changed geography, and used sources. To add drama, he also reworked his first, fake, benign, benefits fraud family - devised before he met Morrison.

Now there was a Texas Army of the Revolution grandfather named **Ben Roberts,** born in 1835, from Kentucky, who moved to Nacogdoches, Texas. Pre-Morrison, in "Brushy's" own signed notes titled "1940" - and apparently retyped by Morrison and in Sonnichsen's collected papers - "Brushy had named him "Benjamin Franklin Roberts;" and stated: "He fought in the Mexican War under Sam Houston in 1836." Now he fought as a Confederate under Ross, joined Quantrill, then became a cowboy. (Page 14)

POSSIBLE SOURCE: For his unpublished 1988 *Brushy Bill Roberts: I Wasn't Billy the Kid*, historian, Don Cline, found "Brushy's" possible source for grandfather Ben: 1914's popular *Rangers and Sovereignty*, by Texas Ranger Capitan Dan W. Roberts. (Cline, Page 15) Dan W. Roberts wrote: "[I] was born in the state of Mississippi ... on October 10th, 1841. [My] father, <u>Alexander Roberts</u> ["Brushy's" possible grandfather Ben], came to Texas in 1836, and <u>helped the Texans fight the battles of the Republic for nearly four years</u>, being in many engagements with the enemy." (Dan W. Roberts, unnumbered page, "Biographical Sketch")

THE PRE-MORRISON FATHER: In "Brushy's" notes titled "1940," he called his fake and heroic father Al Roberts and "Wild Henry, the Indian Fighter" from Nacogdoches, Texas. "Brushy" stated: "[He] began to fight Wild Indians in 1853. When the Civil War broke out he joined Ross' brigade in 1861. He fought

"BRUSHY BILL'S" FAKE FAMILY AS MADE-UP WILLIAM HENRY ROBERTS

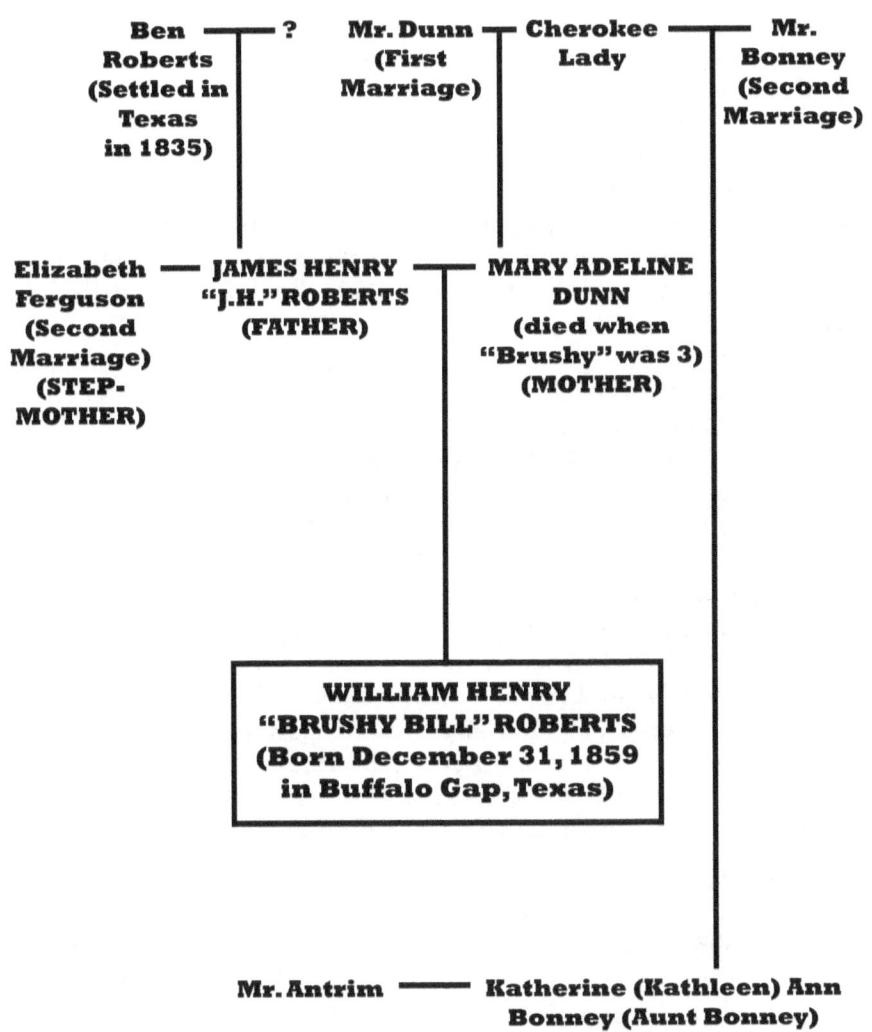

FIGURE: 13. "Brushy Bill" Roberts's fabricated family tree complied from *Alias Billy the Kid*

under Ross in the Civil War Days. He was with Ross's Brigade in 1863 when they captured Cynthia Ann Parker from the Indians. After the Civil War he was a Ranger under Ross."

In fact, General Lawrence Sullivan Ross's Brigade was a famous Texas Confederate cavalry unit. Ross himself had been an Indian fighter. Later a state senator, governor, rancher, and president of the Agricultural and Mechanical College of Texas, Ross was never a Texas Ranger for fake Al Roberts to serve under.

And the famous Cynthia Ann Parker was a white woman kidnapped at age 10 by Comanches in 1836, living with them for 24 years and marrying a chieftain; with one of their three children becoming the last free Comanche Chief, Quanah Parker. In about 1860, she was brought back by the Texas Rangers, not Ross's Brigade. But she identified as Comanche, finally going on a hunger strike and dying in 1871. She had nothing to do with Lawrence Sullivan Ross. But this early fake genealogy demonstrated "Brushy's" own technique of name-dropping while confabulating events to include himself or his fake kin.

To be noted is that "Brushy," for a July 25, 1941 pre-Morrison interview with *The Hico News Review*, when just settling in Hico, Texas, was still using Al Roberts as his fake father's name. (See pages 174-175 above)

"Brushy's" relative, Roy L. Haws, in his 2015 book, *Brushy Bill: Proof that His Claim to be Billy the Kid was a Hoax*, believed that "Brushy" fabricated this family from an unrelated Roberts family with names Ben and James Henry, in Nacogdoches, Texas, though matching none of "Brushy's" other claims. (Haws, Page 32)

For Morrison, "Brushy" made a new father, possibly realizing that "Wild Henry" was a strange name for an *Al* Roberts. He became John Henry "J.H." "Wild Henry" "Two Gun" Roberts, from Kentucky, a monstrously abusive rancher. (Page 14) [His name used "Brushy's" real father's: **Henry** Oliver "H.O." Roberts.] His fictional mother was **Mary Adeline Dunn** from Kentucky. (Page 14)

BETRAYAL OF HIS PARENTS: One should not miss ingrate "Brushy's" mean-spirited sociopathic betrayal of his actual kind-hearted parents and relatives, who saved him from life as a mentally ill street person or hobo, as he callously transmogrified them to brutes or to deaths for his fables. Don Cline, in his 1988 *Brushy Bill Roberts: I Wasn't Billy the Kid*, stated that "Brushy," aged 45, attended his real father, Henry Oliver Roberts's funeral, with other family members, in Canton, Texas, in 1924. (Cline, Page 78) And Cline, having interviewed family members, emphasized that Henry Oliver was "an honest, hard-working farmer who dearly loved his family and provided for them in an excellent manner. He never abused "Brushy" or any of his offspring. As far as is known ... he didn't own or carry a gun." Unstintingly, he had bought land, cleared and plowed it, and then sold it to start again in a new location. He brought his family, including "Brushy," to east Texas between 1882 and 1884. (Cline, Page 91)

THE FAKE DUNN FAMILY: For fictional mother, Mary Adeline Dunn, "Brushy" lifted the Dunn name from his father's first wife, Caroline Dunn.

For his "1940" notes family, "Brushy" had a fictitious Cherokee woman, married to a Mr. Dunn, since her only name given was "Mrs. Dunn." Their daughter was Mary Adeline Dunn. Cherokee Mrs. Dunn remarried a Mr. Bonney, to yield Mary Adeline Dunn's half-sister: a Katherine or Kathleen Bonney - to add "Bonney," because "Brushy" thought it was real Billy's family name.

In *Alias Billy the Kid's* photographs, is one titled "Frontier Mother: Mary Adeline Dunn, wife of J.H. Roberts and mother of William H. Roberts ["Brushy"]." It was identified by "Brushy's" relative, Roy L. Haws, in his 2015 *Brushy Bill: Proof That His Claim to Be Billy the Kid Was a Hoax*, as actually being "Brushy's real mother, Sara Elizabeth Ferguson Roberts, married to his real father, Henry Oliver Roberts! (Haws, Pages 27, 31)

"Brushy" had J.H. Roberts and Mary Adeline Dunn settle in Buffalo Gap, Texas, where he was born on December 31, 1859 as William Henry Roberts. Then evil J.H. Roberts, a Civil War Confederate, **[when his real father, H.O. Roberts, was actually nine]**, joined William Quantrill. (Page 14)

Mary Adeline Dunn dies when "Brushy" was three. **[His real mother, Sara Elizabeth Ferguson died in 1924, when he was 45.]** So her half-sister, Katherine (Kathleen) Ann Bonney ("Aunt Bonney"), in 1862, came from Oklahoma Indian Territory to rescue him from his mean father, and take him to Trinidad, Colorado, then Santa Fe.

THE FAKE "AUNT BONNEY" PHOTO: A photograph in the book is captioned as "Katherine Ann Bonney ... Billy the Kid's aunt." The sly dishonesty of Morrison and Sonnichsen is revealed, since this picture, in their day, was alleged to be of Billy's mother, Catherine Antrim. But, as shown by historian, Frederick Nolan, the photo was a hoax, and was an unknown woman. (See page 314 below) So, the implication that "Brushy" himself identified the picture as "Aunt Bonney," is another example of hoax underpinnings.

Alias Billy the Kid has an alleged picture of "Katherine [sic] Antrim," described by Morrison to Philip J. Rasch in a November 10, 1952 letter; with "Brushy's" fake claims. He wrote: "A copy of the picture [of Katherine Bonney, foster mother of the Kid] is included in our book, wherein it is stated that it is the picture of the half-sister of Mary Adeline Dunn Roberts who was the mother of Kid. They were daughters of Mrs. Dunn, a Cherokee Indian woman ... [H]istorians have accepted as fact, without research on the subject, that Mrs. Bonney [sic – Catherine McCarty Antrim] was the Kid's mother and that he was born in New York. Neither contention can be supported with competent evidence."

Trying to mimic Billy Bonney's history, had "Brushy" taken by "Aunt Bonney" to Silver City in the 1860's, where she married a man named Antrim. And, for unstated reason, "Brushy" was passed as their son. (Pages 14-16) It appears that Sonnichsen had added that she was "later Mrs. Antrim" (unaware of the William Henry Harrison Antrim name), and added the footnote about a Silver City rumor about Billy being called "McCartney" - missing how fatal the unknown McCarty name was to "Brushy's tale. (Page 16)

FAKERY: "Brushy" and team were ignorant of real Billy's mother's name of "Catherine McCarty Antrim;" or that she died when he was 14½; or that he was not in Silver City until 1873, or that he departed Silver City in 1875 after breaking jail for robbery and burglary.

For his unpublished 1988 *Brushy Bill Roberts: I Wasn't Billy the Kid*, historian, Don Cline pointed out that being taken to Silver City in 1861 or 1862 by "Aunt Bonney" made no sense, since it was formed in 1871! (Cline 19)

Meanwhile, evil J.H. Roberts, back from the Civil War, had married an **Elizabeth Ferguson**, and had James Roberts, six years younger than "Brushy." (Page 16)

SOURCE: "Brushy" lifted his real mother's name: Sara Elizabeth Ferguson, his real father's second wife.

For unstated reason, "Brushy" leaves Silver City in 1872 **(real Billy did not arrive there till 1873)** to return to his father and second wife, staying two years, and being called "Kid Roberts." (Page 16) "Brushy" rides with his father on cattle drives on the "old Chidam" trail (fixed-up by Sonnichsen to Chisholm). (Pages 16-17) Then his evil father almost beat him to death with a cow whip, so he ran away in "May of 1874" for Indian Territory **(when real Billy was still in Silver City)**. (Page 17)

Then "Brushy" returned to "Aunt Bonney" in Silver City, though she died in a few months - apparently still in 1874 – in attempt to match her death to real Billy mother's. (Pages 18-19)

FAKERY: Real Catherine Antrim died September 16, 1874.

MORRISON'S FAKE FAMILY TREE SUMMARY: Morrison presented "Brushy's" fake family tree in a January 2, 1951 letter to John S. Mayfield of The Mayfield Library; writing: "O.L. (Brushy Bill) Roberts was the person claiming to be Billy the Kid ... He was born William Henry Roberts. He later assumed the name of William Henry Bonney, and many other aliases. However, he was always known as Billy Bonney, Billy Roberts, Brushy Bill, which facts indicate that his actual name was William. The name of Ollie was assumed when he was on the dodge. It represented the name of his cousin who was killed in Indian Territory."

This "cousin Ollie" scam appears in *Alias Billy the Kid*, and was possibly created by Morrison, Sonnichsen, and "Brushy," after Morrison apparently discovered "Brushy's" real family tree, making him too young to be Billy the Kid. So invented was that he, as older Billy the Kid named William Henry Roberts, had assumed the identity of a dead younger cousin named Ollie L. Roberts to hide being the famous outlaw; and used the name for the rest of his life. The fable was that "cousin Ollie" ran away from home in 1884 and was killed in 1892. When "Brushy," as William Henry Roberts (son of fictional J.H. Roberts and Mary Adeline Dunn), took Ollie's possessions to Ollie's parents (actually his own) in Sulphur Springs, Texas, they *mistook him* for their son, Oliver "Ollie" Roberts ("Brushy's real name); and took him in. So he assumed Ollie's identity, though much older.

That fake genealogy was expanded by a hoaxer named William A. Tunstill for his "Press Release" for his 1988 "Brushy"-backing book, *Billy the Kid and Me Were the Same*. As historian, Donald Cline, wrote to Sonnichsen on November 9, 1990, unaware that Sonnichsen was in on the scam: "Morrison ... and Tunstill claimed ["Brushy"] has a cousin named 'Ollie L.' and whose parents Henry O. and Sarah [sic] Elizabeth Ferguson were Ollie's "parents [though they were "Brushy's" actual parents]. Tunstall also duped a real Roberts family member named Eulaine Haws into backing this genealogy. (See pages 167-168 above; and Figure: 14, page 429 below.) Her son, Roy L. Haws exposed his mother's victimization his 2015 book: *Brushy Bill: Proof That His Claim to be Billy the Kid Was a Hoax*.

FAKING EARLY ADOLESCENCE

Not till 1993, would Billy Bonney's early adolescence be known from Jerry Weddle's *Antrim Was My Stepfather's Name*, filling in Billy's dramatic and traumatic Silver City and Arizona years. So necessity mothered invention by "Brushy's" confabulations.

THE 12 YEAR OLD MURDERER DILEMMA

Knowing his day's claim that Billy Bonney left Silver City at 12, "after committing his first murder," "Brushy," minimizing Billy as a killer, used it just for his departure age. (Page 16)

PROMPT SOURCES: Age 12 came from Pat Garrett's *The Authentic Life of Billy the Kid*, and Walter Noble Burns's *The Saga of Billy the Kid*, using Garrett's book.

Garrett stated: "When young Billy was about twelve years of age, he first imbrued his hand in human blood ... As Billy's mother was passing a knot of idlers on the street, one of the loafers made an insulting remark about her. Billy heard it, and quick as thought, with blazing eyes, he planted a stinging blow on the blackguard's mouth [and subsequently fatally stabbed him]." (Garrett, Page 5) Burns stated: "It was at Silver City, when twelve years old, that Billy killed his first man." (Burns, Page 72)

FAKING EARLY ADOLESCENT YEARS

Since Billy's early adolescence was an historical vacuum, "Brushy" made-up being in Texas from 1872 to 1874 with his father and working for outlaw, Belle Starr, who introduced him as "Texas Kid" to the James and Younger gangs. (Pages 17-18)

FAKERY: Don Cline, in his 1988 manuscript *Brushy Bill Roberts: I Wasn't Billy the Kid*, stated that Myra Belle Shirley Reed took the name Bell Starr in 1880; and was not in Oklahoma in 1874. (Cline, Page 32)

After fake "Aunt Bonney" dies in his brief visit to Silver City in 1874, "Brushy" made-up a hectic return to Indian Territory; being a cattle rustler; and going to Kansas's Dodge City, the Black Hills of South Dakota, Arizona, Montana, Oregon, Wyoming, and Nebraska, where he was a "bronco buster." (Pages 19-20) Sonnichsen, stating that the accounts came from "Brushy's" "notebooks" **[contradicting illiteracy]**, added, without irony at the obvious fakery, "Roberts' account of these early days is hard to follow ... they covered practically the entire West." (Page 20)

MISSED REAL HISTORY: "Brushy" missed Billy's crisis-filled Silver City years. Moving there in 1873 with his mother and stepfather, William Henry Harrison Antrim, he was cast out to homelessness by Antrim at her tuberculosis death in 1874. In September of 1875, he fled to Arizona Territory from Silver City's jail, where he was held for stealing revolvers and clothes from a Chinese laundry, escaping to avoid 10 years in prison with hard labor - there being no juvenile exception in the Kearny legal code.

"Brushy," having no idea of why Billy went to Arizona, stated that in April of 1877 he, as Billy, returned there from being a Nebraska bronco buster, to work at "the <u>Gila ranch</u>." (Page 21)

PROMPT SOURCE'S ERROR: *The Saga of Billy the Kid* made-up that, in Arizona, Billy worked on various cattle ranches and for various cattle outfits [including] <u>Gila</u> River villages (Burns, Page 76); from which "Brushy" faked a "<u>Gila ranch</u>." And *The Authentic Life of Billy the Kid* also stated that Billy was in Arizona. (Garrett, Page 8)

A source footnote cites a 1929 *The Texas Monthly* magazine article by a Ramon F. Adams, titled "Billy the Kid's Lost Years: Cyclone Denton Tells of Bonney's Life as a Cowboy in Arizona." Adams interviewed "Cyclone" Denton, who made-up that he "knowed Billy," when they worked together at the "Gila Ranch" in Arizona.

MISSED REAL HISTORY: Unknown to "Brushy" and team was the dramatic real history. Billy was in Arizona from September of 1875 to August of 1877 as Henry Antrim. He was first refused employment at Hooker Ranch, but got a job as a cook in the Hotel de Luna in Bonita. From there, he also stole Fort Grant's horses and tack, with an adult accomplice, John Mackie. In March of 1877 he was held, with Mackie, at Fort Grant for the thievery, but escaped, and stayed in Bonita. On August 17, 1877, in an altercation with blacksmith, Frank "Windy" Cahill, Billy fatally shot him in likely self-defense. But Cahill was unarmed, and the Coroner's Jury declared it unjustified homicide, meaning likely hanging. Billy escaped back to New Mexico Territory, assuming a self-created alias: William Henry "Billy" Bonney.

ATTEMPTED FIX-UP: In a letter on January 11, 1955 to a J.C. Dykes, Morrison tried a fix-up, though wrong. It was not in the *Alias Billy the Kid*. "Roberts told us about the killing in Arizona, but he said that no indictment was voted against him."

In "Brushy's" fiction, he simply leaves the Gila ranch to go to Mesilla, New Mexico Territory, where he encounters Lincoln County War badman, Jesse [sic- Jessie] Evans, whom he says he knew in about "1870 or 1871" in Silver City. (Page 21)

PROMPT SOURCE'S ERRORS: Neither real Jessie nor real Billy were in Silver City then, and Billy only rode with outlaw Jessie Evans and his boys in September of 1877.

The "Jesse" misspelling came from *The Authentic Life of Billy the Kid*, which sourced "Brushy's" tale in its own fiction: "During the latter portion of Billy's residence in Silver City, he was the constant companion of Jesse Evans, a mere boy but as dangerous as many an older ... desperado ... This youthful pair made themselves well known in western Texas, northern and eastern Mexico, and along the Rio Grande in New Mexico, by many deeds of daring crime." (Garrett, Pages 5, 20)

Morrison, may have directly prompted "Brushy" with that Garrett source error. On June 16, 1952, he followed up on the misinformation with a Roscoe Wilson, author of a

1951 article on "the early days of Billy the Kid in Silver City." Morrison wrote: "I am wondering if Mr. Truesdell recalls incidents about Jesse [sic] Evans in Silver City. Jesse and Billy were pals there, and left Silver City together on one occasion."

"Brushy" then confabulated going with Jessie Evans to Old Mexico, then joining a "Mel Segura" in Chihuahua State, and breaking Segura from jail at San Elizario. (Page 21)

PROMPT SOURCES' ERROR: The fictional Melquiadez Segura (whom "Brushy" familiarized as "Mel"), with the named locations, was lifted from *The Authentic Life of Billy the Kid*, where Garrett/Upson filled in their own big historical vacuum with a long-winded tale of Billy in Mexico with Segura; stating: "In Sonora ... [Billy] established a coalition with a young Mexican gambler named Melquiadez Segura which lasted during his stay in the Republic ... [There, Billy murdered a monte dealer named José Martinez, escaped with Segura, settled in Chihuahua City, and possibly murdered again. Then Billy left Segura and joined up with Jesse [sic] Evans, and they planned to go to the Pecos River to join outlaws.] A day or two before they were ready to start [Billy] received information that his old partner, Segura, was in the vicinity of ... San Elizario, Texas [where Billy went to join him] ... [But] Segura had been arrested and locked up in the jail of that town ... [So Billy went there and captured the jailer.] The door of the room in which Segura was confined was quickly opened ... [Billy then freed Segura.] They soon left the San Elizario jail and its inmates far behind." (Garrett, Pages 15-16, 31-34)

The Saga of Billy the Kid copied the fable; writing: "Billy slipped across the border [from Arizona] into old Mexico. While knocking about Sonora, he fell in with Melquiadez Segura, a young gambler as ready as he for any escapade ... [After murdering a Mexican, with Segura, Billy returned to New Mexico] parted from Segura ... [and] met Jesse Evans, a few years older than himself ... These two scapegrace men-at-arms wandered together through the border country, rustling stock occasionally [and gambling]." (Burns, Pages 78-79)

FAKING RETURN TO NEW MEXICO TERRITORY

For his 1877 fakery, "Brushy," gets back with Jessie Evans, goes to Mesilla, and meets up with "**Jimmy McDaniel [sic], Billy Morton, and Frank Baker.**" (Page 21)

PROMPT SOURCE'S ERROR: The names and scenario are lifted from *The Authentic Life of Billy the Kid's* fictions, as Billy and Jesse [sic] Evans join outlaws: "Among this party of cowboys were James McDaniels, William Morton, and Frank Baker, all well known from the Rio Grande to the Pecos." (Garrett, Page 30)

"Brushy" name-dropped a **Tom O'Keffe** to put himself into real Billy's crossing of the Guadalupe Mountains with him, adding a "fight" with Apaches, to get to the Pecos River settlements of real Billy's 1877 history. (Pages 21-22)

PROMPT SOURCES' ERRORS: The name "Tom O'Keffe" came from *The Authentic Life of Billy the Kid*, which also fabricated a fight with Indians, with Billy killing one. (Garrett, Page 37-47) And *The Saga of Billy the Kid* repeated the tale, calling the encounter with Apaches "a running battle." (Burns, Pages 82)

A source footnote gave Eve Ball's article, "Billy Strikes the Pecos," from the 1949-50 *New Mexico Folklore Record* (likely from folklorist Sonnichsen). It too had a fight, and claim that Apaches "struck."

In fact, O'Keffe, alone, was ambushed by Apaches, who stole Billy's horse, leaving Billy on foot for the crossing.

"Brushy" was also thrown by the word "Mountains" in Guadalupe Mountains; and made-up that his feet got cut up by "mountain brush." That error was also lifted from Garrett-Upson, who wrote: "More than once clambering up that mountain-side the Kid ... trusted his whole weight to his 'sinewy hands' and more than once did he dare 'an unsupported leap into air.' Safely the Kid reached the top of the peak [of the Guadalupe Mountains]." (Garrett, Pages 46, 48) And *The Saga of Billy the Kid* repeated the error and fictionalized: "When his horse was shot under him, Billy scrambled up a steep hillside, dodging among giant boulders and working gradually to the top of the ridge." (Burns, Page 82)

In fact, the Guadalupes, in this region, are just a flat, gradually sloping, sparsely vegetated, flat, limestone plain down to the Pecos River. Billy's real difficulties were no source of water and foot injuries from his boot soles wearing out in the 40 mile, three day crossing.

FAKING LINCOLN COUNTY HISTORY

FAKING EARLY EMPLOYMENT

At the Pecos River, lacking sources, "Brushy" just name-drops; stating: "**Jim and John Jones** were working for **Chisum**, so I went to work for them - I think up at **Bosque Grande**. Frank McNab [sic - MacNab] was foreman ... I worked for **Maxwell** for a short time at **Bosque Redondo**." (Page 22)

FAKERY: The Jones boys did work for Chisum prior to 1877; but, in late 1877, they had a Roswell store with their father, Heiskell. MacNab, no foreman, was a cattle detective with consortium Hunter and Evans, which had bought John Chisum's herd. Bosque Grande was Chisum's original ranch, south of Fort Sumner; and was not connected to Billy until 1879 or 1880, when Billy sold rustled stock to its new owner, Dan Dedrick (to whom he gave the famous tintype). By then, John Chisum was living near Roswell at his South Spring River Ranch. And Billy never worked for the Jones family, Chisum, or the Maxwells. Bosque Redondo was the name of the Apache and Navajo concentration camp connected to Fort Sumner in the 1860's, before Lucien Maxwell bought the Fort and surrounding land in 1870 to make Fort Sumner as a town.

"Brushy" also said he went on a Chisum cattle drive to Dodge City in the fall of 1877, going up "the Loving Trail ... [or] the Goodnight Trial... This was the time we had the tintype made at the end of the cattle trail in Dodge City."

Sonnichsen added a footnote stating that "Brushy" went with Morrison to visit Sam and Bill Jones, where they showed him a photograph. He told them it was made in Dodge City, and pointed out a man he said was himself. He was given a copy, and Morrison and Sonnichsen cut out that one man to use as a young photo of "Brushy" for the book.

322

FAKERY: "Brushy" was unaware that the name was the Goodnight-Loving Trial. And in the fall of 1877, real Billy rode in September with Jessie Evans and his gang, then was hired in October as a Tunstall ranch hand.

The photograph was of the Seven Rivers boys, with the one "Brushy" said was himself being Marion Turner. And Sam and Bill Jones refused to sign Morrison's pre-written affidavit to trick them into swearing "Brushy" was Billy. (See pages 372, 376-377 below)

Then "Brushy" said he worked with Jessie Evans at "Murphy's Seven Rivers camp that winter [of 1877] (Page 22).

PROMPT SOURCE'S ERROR: The source footnote is Charles Siringo's 1920 largely fictitious book, *History of Billy the Kid*, which lifted from Pat Garrett's *The Authentic Life of Billy the Kid*. It stated: "McDaniels, Morton and Baker ... persuaded [Billy] to join the Murphy and Dolan outfit, and become one of their fighting cowboys. This he agreed to do and was put on the pay-roll at good wages." (Siringo, Page 32)

And real Billy never worked for Dolan's Pecos River Cow Camp (which was not at Seven Rivers, but south of it).

As to Jessie Evans, "Brushy" made-up that they were "like brothers," "roamed New Mexico, Arizona, Texas, and Old Mexico together," and he "tried to spring him from jail in Stockton one time after they killed Chapman." (Page 23)

PROMPT SOURCE MISREADING: The source footnote was August, 1880's Adjutant General's files in the Austin, Texas, State Library's August 26 and September 5, 1880 reports by a Lieutenant C.L. Nevill about intercepting a letter by his Fort Davis, Texas, prisoner, Jessie Evans (killer of Texas Ranger George Bingham that July), to Billy Antrum" alias Kid, asking for rescue. So Billy got no letter, and no rescue occurred. All this was unrelated to Chapman's murder, a year before, on February 18, 1879. And the "they" killing Chapman, included Jessie himself!

In reality, Billy Bonney rode with Jessie Evans and his boys only in September of 1877 before joining Tunstall.

"Brushy" then makes-up arguing with Jessie, going to the "Coe's," and "stopping at Tunstall's **to get something to eat**." (Page 23) Tunstall hires him. And "Brushy" dropped names he thought were Tunstall employees, including unrelated ones from Billy's 1880 history: Dave Rudabaugh, Tom Pickett and Wilson (missing first name of Billy). (Page 24)

PROMPT SOURCE FOOTNOTE: George Coe's 1934 autobiography, *Frontier Fighter*, is parroted: "[W]ith kindly feeling [Tunstall] was drawn to the boy and invited him to lunch." (Coe, Page 49)

The erroneous addition of Rudabaugh and Wilson may be explained by Morrison's typed note about a *Las Vegas Gazette* prompt article of November 30, 1880, listing them in Billy the Kid's "gang," and found in Sonnichsen's collected papers; stating: "Last week, three of the crowd, Dave Rudabaugh, 'Billy the Kid' and Billy Wilson went to the Oaks to dispose of some of their surplus stock."

MISSED REAL HISTORY: "Brushy" and team were unaware that Tunstall was ranching on the Peñasco, as well as the Feliz River. So missed was real Billy's proudest moment: being gifted with a Peñasco River ranch by Tunstall - as Billy described in his June 8, 1878 Frank Warner Angel deposition, unavailable to these hoaxers. Found by historian Frederick Nolan, it was cited in 1956 in his article, "Sidelight on the Tunstall Murder" - a year after *Alias Billy the Kid* was published.

FAKING LINCOLN COUNTY TROUBLES

Ignorant of causes of the Lincoln County War, "Brushy" and team were left only with name-dropping and claiming mercantile competition of John Tunstall and the Murphy and Dolan enterprise in a cattle war or "great cattle feud." (Pages 24, 50)

PROMPT SOURCES' ERROR: The cattle war cause was the going formula in "Brushy's" day, to reduce the uprising against the Santa Fe Ring to a local business conflict. That it was Morrison's direct prompt was revealed in his December 3, 1953 speech to the El Paso Rotary Club (with C.L. Sonnichsen giving the introduction): "This private [Lincoln County] war was created by friction between the Murphy-Dolan and Tunstall-McSween-Chisum factions, each of which was wresting trade from the other. The Murphy faction was controlled by the Santa Fe Ring, which was backed by politicians from the governor on down, and including the county officers."

Morrison lifted that prompt from *The Saga of Billy the Kid*, which called it an "ugly local feud" between "A.G. [sic – L.G.] Murphy," who had "virtual lock on the cattle business in Lincoln County," and cattleman, John Chisum." (Burns, Page xxiii). So, without understanding, "Brushy" and team inserted the Ring as simply on the Murphy side.

Used also for prompting was *The Authentic Life of Billy the Kid*, where Garrett, avoiding the Ring, used a cattle war; writing: "The principles in this difficulty were on one side John S. Chisum, called the Cattle King of New Mexico, with Alexander A. McSween and John H. Tunstall as important allies. On the other side were the firm of Murphy & Dolan, merchants in Lincoln, the county seat, backed by nearly every small cattle owner in the Pecos Valley. This latter faction was supported by Thomas B. Catron, United States Attorney for the Territory ... and a considerable cattle owner in the Pecos region ... This bloody war originated about as follows: The smaller cattle owners in the Pecos Valley charged Chisum with monopolizing as a right all this vast range of grazing country [along the Pecos]." (Garrett, Pages 52-53)

"Brushy" added: "The Murphy bunch had the backing of the Santa Fe Ring, which included Tom Catron, U.S. District Attorney, and his brother-in-law. Of course, they were not out in the open with it, but during the cattle war Old Tom took over the Murphy-Dolan property. All the politicians belonged to the Santa Fe Ring, even judges and attorneys." (Page 25) After that, "Brushy" used the Ring merely to claim things were unfair in those days.

PROMPT SOURCES: "Brushy's" incorrect addition of brother-in-law came from reading that Edgar Walz, Catron's brother-in-law, managed his Carrizozo cattle ranch. But Walz was not a Ring head.

The 1927 edition of Garrett's book added Maurice Garland Fulton's note about the Santa Fe Ring as involved. (Garrett, Page 59) And *The Saga of Billy the Kid* stated that the Murphy side had "the patronage of politicians and businessmen in Santa Fe." (Burns, Page xxiii). So Santa Fe Ring was used for mindless name-dropping.

"Brushy" erroneously calls McSween Tunstall's partner. (Page 24)

PROMPT SOURCE ERROR: This fatal error was lifted from *The Authentic Life of Billy the Kid*; which stated: "Tunstall was an Englishman who only came to this country in 1876. He had ample means at his command and <u>formed a partnership with McSween at Lincoln [for a mercantile house and bank]</u> ... <u>He had also, in partnership with McSween, invested considerably in cattle</u>." (Garrett, Pages 52-53) The partnership error was also in *The Saga of Billy the Kid*; which made-up: "Tunstall and McSween ... were soon close friends. When Tunstall proposed that they enter <u>into a business partnership</u> and open a general merchandise store in Lincoln, which he consented to finance in major part, McSween agreed with enthusiasm." (Burns, Page 41)

In fact, they were not partners. That was a Santa Fe Ring lie to link Tunstall to its malicious prosecution of McSween for the fake charge of embezzling the Fritz life insurance money. By lying about a partnership, the Ring could attach Tunstall's property for harassment or murder. As Billy would have known, the Lincoln County War resulted from outrage at Tunstall's abuse, while *not being McSween's partner*.

Then, using the cattle conflict theme, "Brushy" confabulated that McSween had worked for Murphy to prosecute "Chisum's cowboys for cattle rustling," but quit when he learned Chisum was only taking back cattle Murphy rustled from him! (Page 24)

PROMPT SOURCE: This mistake was confabulated from *The Authentic Life of Billy the Kid*; which stated: "McSween was a successful lawyer at Lincoln and was often retained by Chisum and who had other pecuniary interests with the Pecos Valley Cattle King." (Garrett, Page 52)

In fact, McSween quit as attorney for "The House" because of disgust at their corruption.

"Brushy" states Tunstall's men were paid by Chisum to steal back his cattle from Murphy (Page 24) in a conflict in which "each accused the other of cattle stealing." (Page 25)

PROMPT SOURCE'S ERROR: This was lifted from *The Saga of Billy the Kid's* wrongly stating that Chisum employed McSween as an attorney to prosecute Murphy's cattle thieves. (Burns, Page 38)

"Brushy" adds that the Ring's head, Tom Catron, took over the Murphy-Dolan property during that "cattle war." (Page 25)

PROMPT SOURCE: This was lifted from Maurice Garland Fulton's note in Pat Garrett's *The Authentic Life of Billy the Kid*; stating: "[Catron] furnished the money needed by Murphy and Dolan in their business, of course taking mortgages which at the close of the War gave him possession of their store and its stock of goods." (Garrett, Page 59)

"Brushy" states the Fritz insurance policy conflict was about McSween's law fee. And he says Murphy attached Tunstall's property because of the partnership with McSween. (Page 25)

PROMPT SOURCE'S ERRORS: Relying on the erroneous partnership, "Brushy" guessed the conflict was McSween's fee, and guessed Murphy as the litigant against McSween.

In fact, the embezzlement case was by Fritz's brother and sister as the life insurance policy's beneficiaries, not Murphy. That error was lifted from *The Saga of Billy the Kid*; which stated: "Murphy had sworn out an attachment against the McSween-Tunstall store with purpose to collect the old debt he alleged against Fritz." (Burns, Page 46)

MISSED REAL HISTORY: "The Fritz insurance policy conflict" was the Ring's false accusation of McSween for embezzling its proceeds, with entanglement of Tunstall by falsely claiming their partnership.

Real Billy, knowing the injustice to Tunstall, was so enraged that, on February 10, 1878, he almost shot at Sheriff William Brady's deputies doing the property attachment at Tunstall's store.

FAKING JOHN TUNSTALL'S MURDER AND IMMEDIATE AFTERMATH

John Tunstall's murder is threadbare, since "Brushy" and team lacked real Billy's eye-witness deposition about it, or even knowledge that the deposition had occurred! "Brushy" has a posse, but it is headed by **"Billy Morton"** (Page 25), not correct Chief

Deputy Jacob Basil "Billy" Matthews; and Billy is not present - though he was, in reality. And "Brushy" makes up that Tunstall was herding horses to Lincoln to "surrender them until the case was cleared up," and was killed "in cold blood." (Page 25),

PROMPT SOURCE'S ERROR: The "Billy Morton" mistake was lifted from *The Authentic Life of Billy the Kid's* stating: "William S. Morton (said to have had authority as deputy sheriff) with a posse of men composed of cowboys from the Rio Pecos started out to attach some horses which Tunstall and McSween claimed." (Garrett, Pages 60-61)

The fatal error of not knowing that Billy was present as a witness also came from *The Authentic Life of Billy the Kid's* stating: "Before night the Kid was appraised of his friend's death." (Garrett, Page 61).

MISSING REAL HISTORY: "Brushy" and team had no idea of the big picture. Tunstall's horses were not part of the embezzlement case attachment, so Tunstall was merely transferring them from his Feliz Ranch to Lincoln. His action was used as an excuse for Ringite Brady's posse to complete their mission of assassinating him – as real Billy knew and saw. And also missed by "Brushy" and team was the terrorist intent: with Tunstall's horse shot dead also, with Tunstall's hat mockingly put on its head.

For the aftermath, "Brushy" has attempted arrest of the murderers, and attending Tunstall's funeral (as Billy); stating: "We buried his body behind the Tunstall store." (Page 26)

PROMPT SOURCE'S ERRORS: Billy at the funeral, and the wrong site of the grave, were lifted from *The Saga of Billy the Kid*; which stated: "They buried Tunstall ... <u>back of the McSween store</u> [it was Tunstall's store] ... <u>Billy the Kid was in the little group that stood beside the grave</u> as the body was returned to the earth." (Burns, Page 49)

MISSED REAL HISTORY: Fatally missed are key events for real Billy: the day after Tunstall's assassination, he gave an affidavit to Justice of the Peace John "Squire" Wilson identifying the murderers, and was deputized for their apprehension along with Fred Waite. So Ringite Sheriff Brady shielded the murderers by illegally jailing deputized Billy and Fred Waite, from February 20 to 23, 1878, to block their serving the murderers' warrants. That was why Billy was not at Tunstall's funeral, but was in the pit jail.

Also missed is the outrage at the Ring's murder of Tunstall that galvanized citizens to form the Regulators and led to the Lincoln County War.

And Tunstall's grave was on property to the east of his store. Behind his store was just a corral.

Unaware of the Regulators, "Brushy" thinks Billy simply sought revenge for "this dirty deed." (Page 26)

PROMPT SOURCE ERROR: The revenge motive is lifted from *The Authentic Life of Billy the Kid*; which stated: "His rage was fearful [at Tunstall's death]. Breathing vengeance ... from that day to the hour of his death his track was blazed with rapine and blood ... The Kid had become a monomaniac on the subject of revenge for the death of Tunstall." (Garrett, Pages 61, 78) It was also in *The Saga of Billy the Kid*: "With the murder of the Englishman, the Kid threw himself into the feud to avenge his friend's death. There seems no reason to attribute any other motive to him." (Burns, Page 51)

MISSED REAL HISTORY: Unaware of the anti-Ring freedom fight, early writers - like Garrett and Burns - made-up the revenge motive, which "Brushy" lifted. In reality, Tunstall's martyrdom made Billy a political zealot, yielding his personally fighting the Ring by his deposition, his pre-Lincoln County War Battle "Regulator Manifesto," his Grand Jury testimony against murderers of Attorney Chapman, and his Court of Inquiry testimony against Commander Dudley's Lincoln County War intervention.

Pursuit is of "Billy Morton, the leader of the mob, and [Frank] Baker." (Page 26) "Brushy" adds wrongly that they had been "good pals of mine," when he worked with them at Murphy's cow camp. (Page 26)

MISSED REAL HISTORY: "Brushy," unaware of the Regulator movement, has Morton and Baker pursued for revenge. And real Billy never worked at the Cow Camp.

On the ride back to Lincoln, captives Morton and Baker are killed trying to escape; and "Brushy" says that the way back to Lincoln was "the north road over the mountains." (Page 26)

FAKERY: "Brushy" guessed that getting to Lincoln needed crossing over the Capitan Mountains, being ignorant of the military road around their eastern terminus that was actually used by Billy and the other Regulators. "Brushy" likely got that mistake from his Morrison tour, where the east to west range looks like a barrier to Lincoln town.

FAKING THE MURDER OF SHERIFF BRADY

"Brushy," unaware of Brady's motive, guessed: "Sheriff Brady was gunning for me with warrants for cattle stealing." (Page 27)

PROMPT SOURCE'S ERROR: "Brushy" apparently reworked, equally wrong, *The Authentic Life of Billy the Kid's*: "Sheriff Brady held warrants for the Kid and his associates charging them with the murders of Morton, Baker, and Roberts." (Garrett, Page 78) *The Saga of Billy the Kid* merely built on Garrett's fiction: "Billy the Kid, by whose hand Morton and Baker had died, was the special target of Sheriff Brady's wrath ... So the Sheriff sought personal vengeance against the Kid." (Burns, Page 102)

Further confabulating, "Brushy" added: "[Brady] had caught us at Seven Rivers a short time before he arrested us. He took my six-shooter, a .44 single action with pearl handles." (Page 27) A footnote gives the gun taking source as George Coe's *Frontier Fighter*, but adds that Coe said it was a Winchester.

MISSED REAL HISTORY: "Brushy" was fatally unaware of deputized Billy's arrest in Lincoln by Brady before Tunstall's funeral, with confiscation of his Winchester '73 carbine, and just used the Coe source to confabulate an arrest and taken revolver. Further fatal error was Seven Rivers, where the Regulators would not have gone, since it was the stronghold of the Ringite Seven Rivers boys.

"Brushy" and team had no idea why Brady was ambushed.

NO PROMPT SOURCE HELP: *The Authentic Life of Billy the Kid* merely stated: "There was apparently no motive for [killing Brady] except that Brady harassed the Kid and his followers." (Garrett, Note B, Page 82)

MISSED REAL HISTORY: "Brushy" and team were unaware of the anti-Ring Regulators, with Billy as a member. Their motive in killing Brady that April 1, 1878 was to save Alexander McSween from murder, when he arrived later that day for his upcoming Grand Jury trial on the embezzlement case. Brady had murdered Tunstall just 42 days before; and, with three deputies, was proceeding to McSween's arrival point at the east of Lincoln town.

The ambush has Brady accompanied by Hindman (no first name) and Billy Matthews, called the County Clerk. (Page 27)

PROMPT SOURCES' ERROR: Wrongly calling Matthews a Clerk was lifted from *The Saga of Billy the Kid*; which stated: "Sheriff Brady, Deputy Sheriffs George Hindman and 'Dad' Peppin, and <u>Circuit Court Clerk Billy Matthews</u> foregathered in front of Murphy's store in Lincoln ... on the morning of April 1, 1878." (Burns, Page 102) Billy Matthews was a Deputy, as real Billy stated in his own deposition to Investigator Frank Warner Angel about Tunstall's murder.

"Brushy" states he was aiming for Billy Matthews, so should not have been accused of Brady's murder. (Pages 27-28).

PROMPT SOURCE ERROR: The source footnote was an alleged Pat Garrett statement that Billy would have tried to get Matthews, from a 1936 fictionalized book by Miguel Otero, titled *The Real Billy the Kid*. The same fiction was in *The Saga of Billy the Kid* as: "[Billy was disappointed that] "he had 'failed' to get Matthews." (Burns, Page 105)

Knowing Billy had taken a gun from Brady's corpse, "Brushy" calls it a "pearl-handled .44." (Page 27)

PROMPT SOURCES' ERROR: The retrieval comes from *The Saga of Billy the Kid*, where Walter Noble Burns made-up that Billy took "Brady's rifle and six-shooter, both new and brightly furbished." (Burns, Page 106) Burns copied *The Authentic Life of Billy the Kid*, which stated that Billy and his fellows went out to steal guns. (Garrett, Page 80)

In reality, Billy retrieved his own Winchester '73 carbine, which Brady had confiscated in his illegal arrest before Tunstall's funeral; and likely a gift from Tunstall.

Knowing from sources that an adobe wall was involved in the ambush, "Brushy" mistakenly said Billy Matthews was shooting from behind one when hitting himself, as Billy, and Fred Wayte (sic - Waite) when they ran out to retrieve the gun. (Pages 27-28)

FAKING AND SOURCE'S ERROR: In fact, Matthews, having escaped the ambush, shot from inside the Cisneros house; and <u>Billy had run out from behind the adobe wall</u> of Tunstall's corral, accompanied by Jim "Frenchie" French.

The Waite error, along with its misspelling, was lifted from *The Saga of Billy the Kid*; which stated: "[Billy] and <u>Wayte</u> [sic] vaulted over the wall and walked out into the road where Brady lay ... Billy Matthews, from the Mexican house in which he had found refuge, opened fire. His first shot cut through the flesh of the Kid's hip and <u>wounded Wayte</u> [sic] in the thigh." (Burns, Page 106)

MISSED REAL HISTORY: Lack of sources made "Brushy" miss the drama of the actual carbine retrieval in which Jim "Frenchie" French was shot through the thigh, got the bullet removed by town doctor Taylor Ealy using a poker, and was hidden by Billy under floorboards in Tunstall's store until the Regulators could get him out of town.

FAKING THE "BUCKSHOT" ROBERTS KILLING

Unaware of the Regulator movement, "Brushy" sticks to a "cattle war" for the "Buckshot" Roberts killing at Blazer's Mill. He fabricates a back-story of "Buckshot" arguing with himself, as Billy, and Charlie Bowdre at a his house in San Patricio, followed by Billy Matthews shooting at them. (Page 28)

PROMPT SOURCE: The "argument" of Billy and Bowdre with "Buckshot" Roberts seems confabulated by "Brushy" using a statement in *The Saga of Billy the Kid*: "Billy the Kid and Bowdre had a brush with Roberts in the neighborhood of San Patricio on the Ruidoso. Roberts is said to have fired on them without warning ... The details of this fight are vague." (Burns, Page 94)

MISSED REAL HISTORY: In reality, Billy had no house in San Patricio, though he spent time there. "Brushy" likely got the idea from *The Authentic Life of Billy the Kid's* calling it "a favorite resort for the Kid." (Garrett, Page 85) It was also the location that Billy wrote on his March 20, 1879 pardon bargain letter to Wallace.

More subtly, if "Brushy" had a house there, he would have known about the massacre there that inspired real Billy's "Regulator Manifesto" and the Lincoln County War Battle itself: the July 3, 1878 murdering of San Patricio's men, women, and children by Ringite Sheriff George Peppin, using John Kinney's rustler gang as his "posse"

So "Brushy" claims that after the argument at his San Patricio house, "Buckshot's" shooting at them was "the reason I was trying to kill him at Blazer's" for revenge. (Page 28)

PROMPT SOURCE'S ERROR: This was cribbed from fiction in *The Authentic Life of Billy the Kid*; which lacked knowledge of the historic event. It had everyone on horseback, and stated: "[Billy's] hunger for vengeance was by no means satiated" [when the group led by Dick Brewer went to arrest "Buckshot" Roberts]. [So Billy decided to kill him himself.] "The Kid was as quick as his foe [Roberts shot at him] and his aim more accurate; the bullet from the rifle went crashing through Robert's body, inflicting a mortal wound." (Garrett, Pages 74-75)

MISSED REAL HISTORY: "Brushy" and team were unaware that "Buckshot" Roberts was on Tunstall's murder posse, and that the Regulators' having a murder warrant on him resulted in the Blazer's Mill encounter in their attempt to arrest him.

In the actual confrontation, everyone was on foot at Dr. Joseph Blazer's office building, with their horses corralled at a distance. Billy did not fire at all. "Buckshot" was killed by Charlie Bowdre's single shot to his belly.

Missed is "Buckshot's" carnage with his Winchester: shooting Bowdre's belt buckle, maiming George Coe by that ricocheting bullet, shooting John Middleton in the chest, and ended with killing Dick Brewer.

Noteworthy is that *The Authentic Life of Billy the Kid* also falsely had Billy replace Brewer as leader (but, unaware of the Regulators, called them a "squad"), stating: "With Brewer dead, the command of the squad by common consent was conferred upon the Kid." (Garrett, Page 76) In actuality, Chisum's cattle detective, Frank MacNab became the next Regulator leader.

FAKING THE LINCOLN COUNTY WAR BATTLE

The Lincoln County War Battle gets a big Sonnichsen plug: "**The three-day battle in Lincoln, July 17, 18, and 19, 1878**, was the end of the struggle for the McSween faction. It was a bloody business, and Brushy Bill Roberts described it as if every detail had been burned into his memory with a branding iron." (Page 29)

PROMPT SOURCES' ERROR: The Battle was from the 14th to 19th, so it was six days long. The source was *The Authentic Life of Billy the Kid's* Chapter XII being "The Desperate Three Days' Fight in Lincoln" (Garrett, Page 94); and *The Saga of Billy the Kid*'s chapter: "The Three Day Battle" (Burns, Page 114). Neither gave dates.

MISSED REAL HISTORY: The Battle's immediate precipitant was Ringite Sheriff Peppin's San Patricio massacre of July 3rd, to punish Hispanic residents for backing the Regulators, resulting in the majority of McSween-side fighters being Hispanic and from nearby San Patricio and Picacho.

Unaware of the freedom fight, "Brushy" stuck to a "cattle war," claiming the Murphy store stole cattle from Chisum, and "we'd get them back from him." He stated that Chisum had promised to pay the men "$500 apiece to fight for them." (Page 29)

PROMPT SOURCES' ERROR: The aped sources were *The Authentic Life of Billy the Kid*: "[Billy and his companions] said that Chisum owed them $600 each, for services rendered during the War." (Garrett, Page 118) And its version is in *The Saga of Billy the Kid*. (Burns, Page 177)

The source footnote is a 1943 *Frontier Times* magazine's "A Story of Billy the Kid," reprinting an August 10, 1881 *Laredo Times* article titled "Killing of 'Billy the Kid.'" It stated: "[After killing some Chisum cowboys after the War, Billy said to one,] "I want you to live and take a message to old John Chisum for me. Tell him during the Lincoln County War he proposed to pay me $5 a day for fighting for him. I fought for him, and never got a cent. Now I intend to kill his men wherever I meet them, giving him credit for $5 every time I drop one."

That article was, in turn, cribbed from Lew Wallace's June 18, 1881 Billy the Kid outlaw myth article in the Crawfordsville *Saturday Evening Journal* as "Billy the Kid, General Wallace Tells Why the Young Desperado of New Mexico Wanted to Kill Him. A Dashing and Daring Career in the Land of the Petulant Pistol." It stated: "**[Billy] worked for John Chisum, the cattle dealer, in the late Lincoln county trouble, and claiming he has never received the promised $5 per day for his services, he is hunting down and killing Chisum's herdsmen, and giving their employer credit for $5 for each man killed.**"

Then "Brushy" gave a threadbare error-filled version of the Lincoln County War Battle. (Pages 29-31)

PROMPT SOURCE PROBLEM: The fabrication lacked sources detailed enough for faking a first person narrative.

MISSED REAL HISTORY: Missed from Dudley's July 19, 1878 march into Lincoln was his intentionally terrifying Gatling gun and howitzer cannon - which caused flight of all the McSween men, except those trapped in his besieged house (including Billy)! Missed is that trapped in the house were Susan McSween, her sister, and her sister's five young children. Missed was the exploding keg of gunpowder that demolished the front of the McSween house after it was set on fire by Peppin's men.

For the intervention of Commander Dudley, racist "Brushy" stated: "On the last day, Colonel Dudley rode into town with those [N-word] soldiers. He demanded that McSween stop the fighting." Then "Brushy" gave his black shooting soldiers statement that was a "special knowledge" clincher claimed by publisher, E.B. Mann, and Sonnichsen: "[S]ome of his [N-word] soldiers were up on the side of that hill firing on us with the Murphy men." (Page 30)

PROMPT SOURCE: "Brushy" had no special knowledge about Dudley having black troops. *The Saga of Billy the Kid* stated: "Two squadrons of Negro cavalry, with ... Colonel Dudley in command, were soon moving at double-quick on the road to Lincoln." (Burns, Page 122) But Walter Noble Burns was unaware of Dudley's white infantrymen and white officers, in addition to the black 9th cavalry.

LACK OF PROMPT SOURCE: Morrison inadvertently revealed why he had lacked a prompt source for the Dudley intervention: it was too expensive to buy!

On May 21, 1955, after *Alias Billy the Kid* was out, Morrison wrote with defensive belligerence to historian, Philip J. Rasch, who had ridiculed it: "You say it wasn't so that the negro soldiers were fighting with Peppin's men, but you do not cite evidence to support it. I would like to have it. Otherwise, I am not going to say 'it is so.' " Then Morrison revealed his impediment to Rasch: "Apparently you have a copy of the Court of Inquiry Proceeding. <u>They quoted me around $100 for copy, which was too expensive for my use</u>. I located other evidence to prove that [Billy] testified before court. [Apparently Morrison got a page from the transcript with Billy giving the order of people escaping the burning McSween house, which "Brushy" had imitated.]

By August 2, 1955, Morrison attacked Rasch; writing: "I should point out that you are extraordinarily presumptuous in assuming that everyone has knowledge of facts contained in the Court of Inquiry Proceedings. When was this published? I believe that you will agree that less than one millionth of one percent of the readers have read it ... <u>It seems peculiar that, up to this writing, you are the only one contending to have legal evidence to controvert mine</u>." Morrison was well aware that it had testimony by Billy Bonney of which he was unaware, so had not coached "Brushy." This was the vulnerability of the hoax: one fatal error could bring it down. But he had been betting on "less than one millionth of one percent of the readers have read it."

Morrison's sociopathic rage came out in his letter of August 21, 1955 to Sonnichsen, in which he called confrontational Rasch a "rat."

SOURCE REVEALED: To Robert N. Mullin, on March 24, 1951, in a double-talk letter, with usual stilted legalese, Morrison revealed his error-filled source and misconceptions with which he had coached "Brushy" for the Lincoln County War Battle confabulations about "shooting [N-word] soldiers." Morrison wrote: "In briefing the issues [Morrison conceals his "briefing" source, which was obviously a defective few pages of the actual Court of Inquiry transcript] on the Lincoln County War reference was made to the Court Martial Proceedings [wrong], or Court of Inquiry, against Colonel N.A.M. Dudley. Dudley was acquitted, but the fact remains that the testimony by Kid, and others, was not rebutted on certain issues [double-talk for lacking actual content]. Therefore we considered it competent in establishing certain facts in which we were interested. <u>Billy ["Brushy"] told me that negro soldiers under Col. Dudley were fighting with Murphy men. The testimony in Inquiry sets out that three Negro Soldiers were firing with murphy [sic] Men against the McSween Men.</u>"

One can now trace "Brushy's prompt error by the number "three" used for firing soldiers. Morrison used his defective transcript of Billy's actual testimony about <u>three firing soldiers</u>, but it apparently lacked the part that they were <u>white</u> - meaning officers. So Morrison and "Brushy" extrapolated from Fort Stanton having a black 9th Cavalry to erroneously fill in the race of the shooting soldiers.

MISSED REAL HISTORY: Real Billy had testified on May 29, 1879: *"How many soldiers fired at you? ... Three ... How many shots did those soldiers fire, that you say shot from the Tunstall building? ... I could not swear to that on account of firing on all sides, I could not hear. I seen them fire one volley ... Were the soldiers which you say fired at you as you escaped from the McSween house on the evening of July 19th last, colored or white? ... White troops."*

Key is volley - which meant the three white officers fired in unison, requiring Dudley's order, making Dudley responsible for firing on civilians in violation of the Posse Comitatus Act. Morrison - and "Brushy" - had missed the punch-line of "white troops!" (See pages 144, 149 above)]

AN EDITED-OUT "BRUSHY" FLUB: The Battle scene may have also been sparse because "Brushy's" confabulations were so glaringly wrong that Sonnichsen did not use them in *Alias Billy the Kid*.

An example was in a Morrison letter of April 14, 1951 to Robert N. Mullin; stating: "[T]he Murphy Store Building [note that "Brushy" was unaware of its nick-name, "The House"] ... was the fortress from where the Murphy men fired on the McSween house. It was a very important land mark in ["Brushy's] memory."

This reveals that Morrison's prompt source error came from *The Saga of Billy the Kid*; which stated: "Came a crash of rifles from the Murphy clan <u>shooting from the windows of the Murphy store</u> and hotel. The balls thudded against the adobe walls of the McSween house and tore ragged holes through the window shutters." (Burns, Page 117)

In fact, there was no firing from "The House," which was not also a hotel," and which was at the far west end of town; and McSween's house was at the town's center. So no shooting came from "The House." When they could, Sheriff Peppin's posse fired from the south foothills, before attaining the advantage from Dudley's troops on July 19th, then directly surrounding the burning McSween house.

Next fabricated by "Brushy" was: "Some of the Murphy men were just across the river, which ran past the north of the house." (Page 31) "Brushy" added that they escaped through the burning house's kitchen. (Page 31)

PROMPT SOURCES' ERRORS: In fact, there were never Murphy-side assailants at the Bonito River. That was lifted and misstated from *The Saga of Billy the Kid*; which made-up: "[James Dolan, Andy Boyle, Old Man Pearce, and Charlie Hall] plunged down the embankment behind the hostelry [Wortley Hotel?] and, hidden from the road, went at a run across the bottoms of the Bonito. Up the embankment they scrambled in the rear of the McSween house [to set it on fire]." (Burns, Pages 124-125)

The kitchen escape came from *The Authentic Life of Billy the Kid;* which stated: "When night set in, the defenders of the house had but one tenable room left, the kitchen at the back of the house." (Garrett, Page 100) "Brushy" also had *The Saga of Billy the Kid* as a source for the house's lay-out (Burns, Page 128), and for the kitchen escape: "One room remained - the kitchen ... With the roof blazing over their heads, the Kid and his men prepared for a dash for safety ...   He threw open the back door." (Burns, Pages 136-137)

"Brushy" added that when they escaped, "Bob Beckwith and some of them [N-word]s started to come in." (Page 31)

FAKERY AND RACISM: Dudley's black cavalrymen were not in the fighting.

"Brushy" claimed that when Beckwith was entering, he, as Billy, shot him dead. (Page 31)

PROMPT SOURCES' ERROR: "Brushy's" falsehood that Billy shot Bob Beckwith was lifted from *The Authentic Life of Billy the Kid*, which stated: "Robert W. Beckwith ... passed around the corner of the main building in full view of the kitchen doorway ... The Kid shot but once, and Beckwith fell dead, the ball entering near the eye." (Garrett, Page 101) And *The Saga of Billy the Kid*, having fabricated that Billy was last to leave the burning house, wrongly timed it to after McSween's killing. So Burns wrote: "Fire poured from the muzzles of [Billy's] forty-fours in continuous streaks. Bob Beckwith, slayer of McSween, fell dead across the wall, his rifle clattering on the ground." (Burns, Page 140)

MISSED REAL HISTORY: In fact, Sheriff Peppin's posseman, Bob Beckwith, was killed by friendly fire after Alexander McSween's men, including Billy, had already escaped. Beckwith was serving a warrant on cornered McSween, when Peppin's possemen opened fire on McSween, accidentally killing Beckwith in friendly fire.

To be noted is that *Alias Billy the Kid's* having Billy shooting Beckwith was debunked by historian, Philip J. Rasch; to whom Morrison responded with a double-talked fix-up on June 1, 1955: "I want it understood that Roberts did not <u>believe</u> that his shot killed Beckwith. He merely <u>thought</u> that it did." Evaded is that Beckwith was actually shot after Billy's escape; and "Brushy" was just name-dropping.

"Brushy" then gave the order of escaping people from the burning McSween house. (Page 31)

PROMPT SOURCE: Morrison's March 24, 1951 letter to Robert N. Mullin revealed use of the defective transcript of the Court of Inquiry to prompt "Brushy" about of escaping people, which, Morrison boasted was unknown to "[h]istorians." Morrison wrote: "Billy ["Brushy"] told me that he was the first man to leave the burning McSween Building that night. The testimony [in the Court of Inquiry] <u>definitely establishes the sequence</u> with which the McSween men left the burning building. It states that Billy accompanied by another man left at the same time with the other men following. Of course, Historians would like for us to believe that Billy was the last man to leave the building."

Morrison's prompt appeared to be a bad copy of the Dudley Court of Inquiry's testimony page for Billy on May 28, 1879; stating: "*Q. by Recorder. Who escaped from the house with you and who was killed at the time, if you know, while attempting to make their escape? Answer. Jose*

Chavez [Chávez y Chávez] escaped with me [source for "Brushy's" "accompanied by another man"], *Vincente Romero, Francisco Zamora and McSween."*

MISSED REAL HISTORY: Morrison's few Court of Inquiry transcript pages apparently lacked real Billy's testimony on May 28, 1879: *Q. by Recorder. Explain whether all the men that were in the McSween house <u>came out at the same time</u> ... A. [A]ll came out at the same time. The firing was done by the soldiers until some had escaped."*

Also missed because Morrison could not afford a Court of Inquiry copy, was Billy's punch-line that should have gotten Dudley court martialed for Posse Comitatus Act violation, if the court was not corrupt: that he saw three white soldiers embedded with Sheriff Peppin's possemen treasonously firing a volley at himself and the other McSween civilians as they escaped! (See page 144 above)

"Brushy" added: "[Chavez] and I ran toward Tunstall's store, was fired at, and then turned toward the river." (Page 31)

PROMPT SOURCE: Lifted from real Billy's May 28, 1879 Dudley Court of Inquiry testimony, was Billy's answer to the escape route: *"<u>Ran towards the Tunstall store, was fired at, and there turned towards the river</u>."*

Racist "Brushy" concluded: "If we could have kept them [N-word]s out there at Stanton, we would have whipped Peppin's posse." (Page 30)

MISSED REAL HISTORY: Real non-racist Billy would have correctly blamed Dudley, not his troops.

And Billy would have known that, like himself, Dudley's black 9th Cavalrymen, Private James Bush and Sergeant Huston Lusk, on May 30-31, 1879, (the day after Billy's own Court of Inquiry testimony) had risked *their* lives to testify *against* Dudley as ordering them to accompany Sheriff George Peppin; and, thus, prevent McSween's defenders from firing as he walked through town for fear of hitting a soldier and getting retaliative fire from Dudley's Gatling gun and howitzer. This tactic enabled possemen's setting fire to McSween's house. All this violated the Posse Comitatus Act forbidding military intervention in civilian conflicts, as Bush and Lusk testified.

FAKING THE HUSTON CHAPMAN MURDER

"Brushy's" problem with the murder of Susan McSween's attorney, Huston Chapman, was both lack of sources and erroneous coaching by Morrison.

Morrison's ignorance about the murder is evident in his El Paso Rotary Club talk on December 3, 1953. Thinking Billy the Kid was a leader in the War, he stated: "The Kid and James J. Dolan, **surviving leaders of the two factions**, had gathered in Lincoln to arbitrate. At the close of a favorable agreement, attorney Chapman, representing the widow of McSween, was killed by Dolan's men." So "Brushy" stated in *Alias Billy the Kid*, "In the winter of '79 we got together with Dolan and Evans and agreed to stop fighting each other." (Page 33)

"Brushy added: "When we came out of the saloon that night in Lincoln we run into Chapman, the lawyer for Mrs. McSween. Campbell and Dolan killed him in cold blood. **I was standing there with them and saw who killed him.** (Page 33)

PROMPT SOURCE: Used for wording, was Billy's letter of March 13, 1879 to Lew Wallace; stating: "*I was present when Mr. Chapman was murderded and know who did it.*"

PROMPT SOURCE'S ERROR: "Brushy's" omission of Jessie Evans as one of the killers came from *The Authentic Life of Billy the Kid*'s calling Jessie just a witness (Garrett, Page 113); when, in fact, real Billy testified against Jessie and got him indicted as accessory to Chapman's murder.

FAKING THE WALLACE PARDON BARGAIN

"Brushy" and team had no idea of the pardon bargain Billy Bonney made with Lew Wallace: which was exchanging his Grand Jury testimony against Huston Chapman's murderers for Wallace's annulling his Lincoln County War murder indictments for William Brady, George Hindman, and "Buckshot" Roberts.

"Brushy" began with: "**I was standing there with them and saw who killed [Chapmen] ... I heard that Governor Wallace had offered a thousand dollars for me if I would come and testify. I wrote him back that I would come in if he would annul those indictments against me.**" (Page 33)

PROMPT SOURCE: Used is real Billy's letter of March 13, 1879 to Wallace; stating: "*I have heard that You will give one thousand $ dollars for my body which as I can understand it means alive as a witness. I know it is as a witness against those that murdered Mr. Chapman. if it was so as that I could appear at Court, I could give the desired information ... I was present when Mr. Chapman was murderded and know who did it ... if it is in your power to Annully those indictments I hope you will do so so as to give me a chance to explain.*" In fact, Wallace had merely offered the thousand dollar award for Billy's capture as a local outlaw. It was Billy who proposed the testifying against Chapman's murderers as a pardon bargain to get his Lincoln County War indictments annulled.

PROMPT SOURCES' ERROR: "Brushy" and team wrongly thought that Wallace initiated the pardon bargain. That mistake was lifted from *The Saga of Billy the Kid*; which stated: "Governor Wallace determined to have a personal interview with Billy the Kid and use his power of persuasion to induce him to leave off fighting and lawlessness and settle down to useful citizenship." (Burns, Page 152)

Another source faking Wallace as initiator was Wallace's own outlaw myth article, used as a footnote elsewhere in the book. It was his June 8, 1902 *New York World Magazine* article titled: "General Lew Wallace Writes a Romance of 'Billy the Kid' Most Famous Bandit of the Plains: Thrilling Story of the Midnight Meeting Between Gen Wallace, Then Governor of New Mexico, and the Notorious Outlaw, in a Lonesome Hut in Santa Fe." Wallace lied: "**When I reached New Mexico [to be Governor] it was declared ... that "Billy the Kid" had been a witness to the murder. Could he be made to testify? That was a question on the tip of every tongue. I had been sent to the Southwest to pacify the territory; here was an opportunity I could not afford to pass by. Therefore I arranged the meeting by note deposited with one of the outlaw's friends, and at midnight was ready to receive the desperado should he appear.**"

For Billy's first pardon meeting with Wallace, "Brushy" and team floated the special knowledge trick, with "Brushy's" confabulation: "We didn't meet like they say we did in the daytime at Patron's." (Page 34)

PROMPT SOURCE'S ERROR: This wrong meeting site was lifted from *The Saga of Billy the Kid's* fabrication: "Governor Wallace sat with General Hatch, Juan Patron, and a group of army officers on the porch of the Ellis House." (Burns, Pages 152-153)

MISSED REAL HISTORY: The meeting was on March 17, 1879, at night, at the Lincoln house of Justice of the Peace John "Squire" Wilson.

"Brushy" made-up the bargain: "He promised to pardon me if I would stand trial on my indictments in district court in Lincoln, testify before the grand jury in the Chapman case, and testify against Dudley ... in his court-martial trial at Stanton." (Pages 33-34)

PROMPT SOURCES' ERROR: "Brushy's" mistakes of Billy needing to "stand trial" and to "testify against Dudley" came from Morrison's wrong prompting, as seen later in his December 3, 1953 El Paso Rotary Club talk: "The governor met the Kid in Lincoln and agreed to pardon the Kid if convicted on his indictments, provided, that: The Kid submit to arrest; plead to his indictments in Lincoln County ... District Court; testify before the Grand Jury; furnish statements in general; and to cooperate fully with the governor."

And Morrison lifted his errors from sources, as follows:

1) The standing trial error came from *The Saga of Billy the Kid*, which fabricated Lew Wallace stating: "I want you to surrender ... and stand trial on whatever charges may be brought against you ... I will pardon you if the verdict goes against you. But I want you first to stand trial like a man." (Burns, Pages 156-157)

2) The Dudley testifying error was elaborated from *The Authentic Life of Billy the Kid*: "The Kid was a witness before the court of inquiry which convened at Fort Stanton in April, 1879 [sic – May, 1879], to investigate Col. Dudley's activities with his soldiers during the three days' fight in Lincoln." (Garrett, Note A, Page 126)

MISSED REAL HISTORY: Dudley's Court was not a court martial, just an inquiry as to possible future court martial. And Billy testified against Dudley on his own initiative.

"Brushy" continued by name-dropping in utter ignorance. He cited the grand jury, but, thinking Billy was on trial, said that Attorney Ira Leonard was not there to represent him. (Page 34)

PROMPT SOURCE'S ERROR: Billy needed no lawyer. He was a prosecution witness against Chapman's murderers. The error came from the Morrison-Sonnichsen misreading of the 1879 Grand Jury minutes, which had Billy's name, so they guessed he was a defendant, and coached "Brushy" as to that. Those minutes are cited in the *Alias Billy the Kid* source footnote accompanying "Brushy's" error.

Adding even worse error, "Brushy" name-drops that the Court appointed Colonel Fountain to represent him. (Page 34)

FAKERY: This is a fatal error about the 1879 Lincoln County Grand Jury. In fact, Albert Jennings Fountain was Billy's court appointed lawyer in April of 1881 in his Doña County hanging trial in Mesilla after Billy's attorney, Ira Leonard, withdrew after a likely Ringite death threat after he got Billy's "Buckshot" Roberts indictment quashed.

FAKING THE PURSUIT PERIOD

Lack of sources left "Brushy" and team with a vacuum for most of 1880. So fatally missed were Billy's surviving a murder attempt, his second pardon chance, his pursuit by the Secret Service, and details of his pursuit by Pat Garrett.

UNAWARE OF NEAR-KILLING BY JOE GRANT

A big event missed by "Brushy" and team was Billy Bonney's January 3, 1880, near killing by Texan bounty hunter, Joe Grant, in Fort Sumner's Hargrove's Saloon.

Grant's gun misfired, and Billy killed him in self-defense. It was not legally pursued, but, for almost-killed real Billy, it was a memorable event!

Though the Joe Grant incident is in *The Authentic Life of Billy the Kid* (Garrett, Pages 120-122), it was hard to follow and mixed together with Grant's threatening John Chisum's bother before taking a shot at Billy.

And, at the time of the "Brushy" coaching, Philip J. Rasch, was newly documenting Billy's killings, including Frank "Windy" Cahill and Joe Grant, and the information appeared unknown to "Brushy's" team.

Later, Morrison, nervous about the fatal mistake of Joe Grant's omission in *Alias Billy the Kid*, lied defensively to fledgling historian, Frederick Nolan, on August 7, 1957: "[Rasch] contends the actual records shows [sic] that Henry [Antrim] killed F.P. Cahill, **Joe Grant**, J.W. Bell and Robert Ollinger [sic]. **Whereas there is no record to prove that anyone killed Joe Grant,** and the legal records of Lincoln County prove that he misspelled Olinger's name."

UNAWARE OF PURSUIT BY SECRET SERVICE AND A SECOND PARDON BARGAIN CHANCE

Fatally missed by "Brushy" and team for lack of its source, were the catastrophic events in Billy's life, which led to his death: his pursuit by the Secret Service, resulting in his capture by Pat Garrett as a Deputy U.S. Marshal.

From September to December of 1880, Secret Service Special Agent Azariah Wild was assigned to New Mexico Territory to pursue counterfeiters. Manipulated by the Santa Fe Ring, Wild falsely accused Billy of being the leader of a gang of rustlers and counterfeiters. To capture or kill Billy, Wild implemented the election of Pat Garrett as Lincoln County Sheriff, made him a Deputy U.S. Marshal for Territory-wide jurisdiction, and paid for spies to locate Billy. Also, Wild initially intended to give Billy a pardon, in exchange for his testifying against the counterfeiters. But Ring influence made Wild plan to arrest Billy at their meeting; which Billy learned by stealing Wild's reports from the mail coach. So he avoided the meeting, but lost the second pardon chance. Arguably, without Wild, Billy would have avoided capture, trial, jailbreak, and Fort Sumner killing by Garrett.

"Brushy" and team could have read Pat Garrett's unclear reference to Azariah Wild in *The Authentic Life of Billy the Kid*; which stated: "In October [1880], **Azariah F. Wild, a detective in the employment of the Treasury Department,** hailing from New Orleans, La., visited New Mexico to glean information in regard to the circulation of counterfeit money, some of which had certainly been passed in Lincoln County. Mr. Wild sent for me to come to Lincoln to confer with him and assist in working up these cases ... [Wild gave] me authority to act in the manner according to my judgment." (Garrett, Pages 139-140) No mention is made of the Secret Service; and Wild was not a Detective. As a Special Operative, he had extraordinary power. So Garrett did not give enough information for "Brushy's" team to red flag the information so he could build a tale.

Wild's role was not known until over twenty years later, in the 1970's, when Pat Garrett's biographer, Leon Metz, discovered Wild's daily reports to the Secret Service in the National Archives for his 1974 book, *Pat Garrett: The Story of a Western Lawman.* (Metz, Pages 58-66)

FAKING THE JIM CARLYLE KILLING

The only available source for 1880 was real Billy's December 12, 1880 letter to Lew Wallace about Jim Carlyle's killing at the Greathouse Ranch ambush. So "Brushy" parroted it: "We went to Las Vegas where I read that Billy the Kid had killed Carlyle. I wrote to Governor Wallace and told him that I did not kill Carlyle. That his own men killed him. But I got blamed for that killing too." (Pages 35-36)

PROMPT SOURCES: Billy's letter is given as the source footnote. To be noted is that "Brushy" confabulated being in Las Vegas from Billy's writing that he read about his faked gang in the *Las Vegas* Gazette. Billy wrote: *"I noticed in the Las Vegas Gazette a piece [about Billy "the" Kid having an outlaw gang ... As to Carlyle] a Shot was fired on the outside and Carlyle thinking Greathouse was Killed jumped through the window. breaking the Sash as he went and was killed by his own Party they thinking it was me trying to make my Escape."*

This fakery reveals how early Morrison's prompting had been. It appeared in an August 18, 1949 interview, in Sonnichsen's collected papers (See page 297 above), which had "Brushy stating: "When they commenced shooting out there Carlyle got scared and he jumped out the window. As he went through the window they shot him down without warning. They thought it was me making my escape, but they got fooled that time."

Cited also is another prompt footnote: Maurice Garland Fulton's article in *The New Mexico Folklore Record's* 1949-1950 volume, titled "Billy the Kid in Life and Books," in which Fulton called the Carlyle killing unsolved.

Since the location of the Greathouse Ranch was unknown until the 1980's, "Brushy" *forgets* where it was! He stated: "That has been a long time to recollect." (Page 35) And, lacking a prompt source, he omitted Billy's Coyote Spring ambush by the White Oaks posse immediately before the ambush at Greathouse's ranch.

FAKING KNOWLEDGE ABOUT PAT GARRETT

Unaware that the Secret Service backed Pat Garrett for Sheriff, "Brushy" and team make-up that he was backed by John Chisum. To feign special knowledge about Garrett, "Brushy" claims that, <u>as a buffalo hunter, Garrett killed his partner in an argument</u> about dividing buffalo hides. (Page 36)

PROMPT SOURCE'S ERROR: Cited was a prompt footnote March 8, 1936 *Alamogordo News* article by old-timer, John Meadows, titled "My Association with Pat Garrett, Pioneer Peace Officer of N.M., As Told By John P. Meadows To A Representative of the Alamogordo News," which made-up that buffalo hunter, Garrett killed his partner, "Glenn" [sic]. Meadows, claiming he had been a buffalo hunter in the "Knox camp;" stated: "One morning one of Garrett's men drove in early ... He told Mr. Knox he wanted Knox and his men to go over to the Garrett camp, as <u>Garrett had shot and killed his partner that day</u> ... [A]s I remember, this was his story: <u>Garrett and his partner fell out over a rather trivial matter</u>. The partner, Glenn, made at Garrett with an ax ... Garrett ran ... [He] grabbed [his] gun up and called to Glenn: 'Glenn, you stop where you are or I'll kill you' ... Glenn came on threateningly ... The latter blazed away ... and killed Glenn instantly."

First of all, real Billy would not have known. And Garrett did not kill his partner, Willis Skelton Glen. His 1876 murder was of Joe Briscoe, a teenager with their hunting group. It was discovered in 1890, when Glenn wrote in a manuscript, titled *Pat Garrett As I Knew Him on the Buffalo Ranges*, that he killed Briscoe in depressive irritability, but successfully claimed self-defense.

Noteworthy, however, is that "Brushy" denied a friendship with Garrett, saying he "turned coat" after first being helped by Billy when he arrived in Fort Sumner. (Page 36) That would be a problem, decades later, for "Billy the Kid Case" hoaxers' fabricated Garrett's "friendship" as key to "Brushy's" July 14, 1881 "survival.

FAKING THE CAPTURE AND TRANSPORT

Ignorant of Lincoln County War issues, the Ring's role, or the Secret Service-backed election of Pat Garret, "Brushy" and team did not know why he pursued Billy. "Brushy" wrongly guessed the Jim Carlyle murder (Page 36); when it was for the murder indictments for the Brady, Hindman, and Roberts.

FAKING THE KILLING OF TOM O'FOLLIARD

For Garrett's December 19, 1880 ambush of Billy and his friends entering Fort Sumner, with killing of Tom O'Folliard, "Brushy" made-up that he, as Billy, was not present; stating: "As we rode in, I took another road, thinking they might be watching for us." (Page 36) He also faked special knowledge that Kip McKinney was there, and was O'Folliard's cousin. (Page 37)

UNLISTED PROMPT SOURCES: Name-dropped Kip McKinney was not present; he was only Pat Garrett's Deputy in Fort Sumner for Billy Bonney's killing.

The erroneous hearsay that O'Folliard and McKinney were cousins arose from both being from Uvalde, Texas; and from a female cousin of McKinney's marrying a possible family member of O'Folliard; though, according to Frederick Nolan, O'Folliard's genealogy is uncertain.

The unlisted prompt source was Morrison's use of a January, 1934 article by a Jack Shipman in *Voice of the Mexican Border* magazine, "Brief Career of Tom O'Folliard Billy the Kid's Partner," which had O'Folliard's unsubstantiated genealogy. On December 6, 1949, Morrison followed-up the article by interviewing Shipman's wife, who claimed: "McKinney was a cousin of Tom."

Also available was a 1935 old-timer windbag book by a Frank M. King, titled *Wranglin' the Past: Reminiscences of Frank M. King*, which used the cousin claim; stating: "T.C. McKinney's full name was Thomas Christopher McKinney, but was known to his intimates as 'Kip" ... Kip was also a cousin of Tom O'Folliard, who was one of the main supports of Billy the Kid until Pat Garrett killed him at Fort Sumner some time before the Kid was put out of business." (King, Page 173)

A further prompt was likely misreading of Pat Garrett's vague connecting of O'Folliard and McKinney in his *The Authentic Life of Billy the Kid* in O'Folliard's death scene; stating: "[O'Folliard] also asked [Barney] Mason to tell McKinney to write to his grandmother in Texas and inform her of his death." (Garrett, Page 173) That did not mean that McKinney was present or that he and O'Folliard were cousins. It simply meant that they knew each other, and McKinney could get a message back to O'Folliard's family.

FAKING THE STINKING SPRINGS CAPTURE

For the Stinking Springs capture, "Brushy" stated that it took "a couple of days in the snow" to reach the rock house. (Page 37)

FAKERY: Unaware of the Fort Sumner area, "Brushy" wrongly exaggerated the distance to Stinking Springs, which was only about 16 miles.

For the ambush there, "Brushy" had shot Charlie Bowdre erroneously die beside the rock house's horses. Then he had Garrett shoot dead a horse they were leading inside. (Page 37)

PROMPT SOURCES: A source footnote elsewhere gives Bell Hudson's 1949 fictionalized book *Billy the Kid*, which stated: "Bowder [sic] fell in the doorway, to be dragged into the hut by his companions." (Hudson, Page 34) Thus, Bowdre's death walk and fall into the ravine with the posse was missed.

For the shot horse in the doorway, used was *The Authentic Life of Billy the Kid*, with Garrett stating: "[J]ust as the horse was fairly in the door opening, I shot him dead, partially barricading the outlet." (Garrett, Page 179) Another was cited in a source footnote, erroneously listing Lew Wallace's June 8, 1902 *New York World Magazine* article, "General Lew Wallace Writes a Romance of 'Billy the Kid' Most Famous Bandit of the Plains." However, the correct prompt article was actually the December 28, 1880 interview of Billy by the *Las Vegas Gazette*. In it, Billy says: "If it had not been for the dead horse in the doorway I wouldn't be here in Las Vegas. I would have ridden out on my bay mare and taken my chances of escaping. But I couldn't ride over that for she would have jumped back and I would have got it in the head."

FAKING A SCENE AT THE MAXWELLS' MANSION

"Brushy" creates an elaborately confabulated post-capture scene in which Garrett stopped at Fort Sumner with his captives. "Brushy" name-drops Garrett's posseman, Jim East, as taking him, as Billy, into the Maxwell house at the request of Mrs. Maxwell's "Indian servant;" and calls East "a friend of mine from Tascosa, Texas." He adds that, at this time, he traded the Billy the Kid tintype in his pocket to that servant in exchange for her scarf (which he showed to Morrison). (Page 38)

PROMPT SOURCE: "Brushy" lifted <u>Tascosa, Texas</u>, from Billy's October 24, 1878 Hoyt Bill of Sale. It had nothing to do with Jim East.

PROMPT SOURCES' ERROR: In Sonnichsen's papers, was Morrison's and "Brushy's" undated, full-blown, scarf fiction built on missing the point of Jim East's description of Billy's Maxwell house meeting. It is titled "Note on Scarf," and stated: "Maxwell's Indian Servant had just finished weaving a multi-colored scarf ... She was wearing it on the cold day in December when Mrs. L.B. Maxwell sent her over to request P. Garrett to being Billy the Kid over to her house for a farewell before the journey to jail in S. Fe. with the prisoners ... The Servant ... noticed that [Billy] appeared cold. She offered her scarf to make him more comfortable ... In return Billy removed a tintype from his pocket giving it to her in return for the scarf. The tintype had been made in Ft. Sumner by a roving photographer a short time before. (Doc. I have a description and snap shot of this scarf if you want it.)"

And the non-historical scarf trade was a lifted fiction from *The Saga of Billy the Kid*; stating: "When Billy was locked up in the Fort Sumner calaboose after his capture at [Stinking Springs], Deluvina went to visit him. It was a cold winter's day and, as the little jail was unheated, Deluvina came home and got a heavy scarf she had knitted and took it to her hero. In return for this kindness, the Kid gave her his only photograph which he had carried around in his pocket." (Burns, Page 195) The actual tintype was given by Billy in 1880 to counterfeiter, Dan Dedrick, who took it to California, and willed it to his family. Its provenance was so iron-clad that collector Bill Koch paid $2.3 million for it in 2010.

The *Alias Billy the Kid* prompt footnote, described as from Sonnichsen, was the May 20, 1926 letter by Garrett's posseman, Jim East, to a W.H. Burgess, about the meeting, stating that the Maxwells tried to get Billy unshackled from fellow prisoner, Dave Rudabaugh, to get him alone for a supposed farewell, but to help him to escape.

MISSED REAL HISTORY: Jim East was not real Billy's friend, being only Garrett's posseman. And Morrison's letter of April 14, 1951 to historian, Robert N. Mullin, confirms that Mullin had provided the letter. Morrison wrote: "Thanks for your offer to furnish photostatic copies of the original letters from Jim East."

The intent of the cited Jim East letter of May 20, 1926 to Judge William B. Burgess was to give the scene of captured Billy's parting with Paulita Maxwell (whose married name was Jaramillo in 1926), which East witnessed as a posseman. Its copy is in Sonnichsen's papers, but was merely used for "Brushy's" scarf confabulation. East wrote:

> I was much interested in the statement made by Mrs. Paulita Jaramillo. At the time of the capture of Billy the Maxwells were living at Fort Sumner, and when we brought the prisoners in Mrs. Maxwell sent the Old Navajo woman over with a request to Captain Garrett to allow Billy to be sent over to her house so that her daughter Paulita and she could bid him good-bye. So Garrett detailed Lee Hall and I to guard Billy over – he being shackled to Dave Rudabaugh. Then Mrs. Maxwell asked Lee and I to unlock Billy from Dave and let Paulita go into another room with him for an affectionate farewell – but of course we had to refuse, although all the world loves a lover.

Sonnichsen's and Morrison's incompetence in reading documents is demonstrated by *Alias Billy the Kid's* footnote citing Walter Noble Burns's June 3, 1926 letter to Jim East about that Maxwell house incident. Sonnichsen's take was only: "Burns omitted the incident because it made Paulita out to be Billy's sweetheart, and Paulita (then living) objected." (Page 38) In fact, Burns confirmed that Billy and Paulita were lovers, but stated his publisher's concern; writing: "<u>I also know that the Kid and Paulita were sweethearts</u> - at least I heard that story on most good authority many times. But I was unable to write it frankly because my publishers were afraid any such statement might lay them open to a libel suit." But Morrison's and Sonnichsen's missing of Paulita's significance led to prompted "Brushy's" fatal confabulating Celsa Gutierrez as his sweetheart.

FAKING THE SANTA FE JAIL STAY

For the Santa Fe jail stay, "Brushy" just paraphrased Billy's jail letters; like: "I wrote to Governor Wallace to come and talk to me, but he failed to do so." (Page 39)

PROMPT SOURCES: The source footnote cited Billy's Santa Fe jail letters. January 1, 1881's said: "*I would like to see you for a few moments if You can spare the time.*" March 4, 1881's said: *I wrote You a little note the day before yesterday but have received no annser. I Expect you have forgotten what you promised me, this Month two Years ago. but I have not, and I think You had ought to have come and seen me as I requested you to.*"

MISSED REAL HISTORY: Lacking a source, "Brushy" fatally missed dramatic history: Billy almost escaped the Santa Fe jail! He and his cellmates' almost tunneled out, but were betrayed by fellow cellmate, Edward "Choctaw" Kelly. That resulted in Billy's being placed in solitary confinement on February 28, 1881, in a windowless cell, until transport to Mesilla for his trials.

FAKING THE MESILLA HANGING TRIALS

Billy's Mesilla hanging trial gets color from Billy's April 15, 1881 letter to Attorney Edgar Caypless, which had duped *Alias Billy the Kid's* publisher, E.B. Mann as special knowledge, and had been parroted by "Brushy" as: "In April I pleaded to the federal indictment and it was thrown out of court." But that was all "Brushy" and team knew.

PROMPT SOURCE PROBLEM: Billy's April 13, 1881 letter to one of his attorneys, Edgar Caypless; stated: "*My United States case was thrown out of court and I was rushed to trial on my Territorial charge.*"

But that letter did not describe the circumstances. And *The Authentic Life of Billy the Kid* merely said erroneously: "[T]he outcome of the trial was that the Kid was acquitted." (Garrett, Page 189) *The Saga of Billy the Kid* was even more confused, listing the victim as Indian Agency Clerk, Morris Bernstein (not a Billy indictment), and stating Billy was acquitted for lack of witnesses. (Burns, Page 220)

The "Brushy" team's ignorance is revealed in Morrison's December 3, 1953 El Paso Rotary Club talk; stating: "**The Kid's Federal Indictment had been dismissed, on plea to the jurisdiction of the court, on April 6, 1881.**" This doubletalk hid that Morrison had no idea what had happened. The date was actually March 30, 1881, the

Attorney was Ira Leonard, the case was "Buckshot" Roberts's killing, and the indictment was quashed because U.S. Attorney T.B. Catron had claimed the federally-controlled Mescalero Indian Reservation as its site. But the real site was Territorially-controlled private property of Joseph Blazer. So it was quashed as not a federal case, but a Territorial one.

"Brushy" also lifted from the Caypless letter to claim court appointment of A.J. Fountain as Billy's lawyer, adding with his usual bad grammar: "**He done all he could for me.**"(Page 39)

PROMPT SOURCE: Billy's letter stated: *"Mr. A.J. Fountain was appointed to defend me and <u>has done the best he could for me</u>."*

MISSED REAL HISTORY: For lack of a source, the key event in Billy's Mesilla trials was fatally missed: his trauma that his loyal attorney, Ira Leonard, abruptly quit, after likely Ring death threat, after he got the "Buckshot" Roberts indictment quashed.

One can trace the error to Morrison's ignorance about Leonard impairing his "Brushy" prompting. His March 17, 1954 letter to *Arizona Highway's* editor, Raymond Carlson, while boasting about himself as a great researcher using "modern methods of digging out true facts for posterity," he stated: "[U]ntil my research uncovered the actual records, every writer, including a New Mexico attorney-author [William Keleher], insisted that Ira E. Leonard represented the Kid at his trial in Mesilla. Mr. Burns went so far as to quote the eloquent plea to the jury by Leonard, when <u>Leonard was not even there</u>." Morrison gave its copies to historian, Carl W. Breihan, and to Paul Blazer.

A story about Billy's famous bay racing mare is then mutilated by the team's ignorance. "Brushy" confabulated: "They didn't sell my mare up at Scott Moore's in Las Vegas. He was a friend of mine, but now he said I owed him money to board." (Page 39)

PROMPT SOURCE MISUNDERSTANDING: A source footnote references Billy's April 15, 1881 letter to Attorney Edgar Caypless, with Billy's quote: *"The mare is about all I can depend on at present so hope you will settle the case right away and give him [Fountain] the money you get for her. If you do not settle the matter with Scott Moore and* *have to go to court about it either give him [Fountain] the mare or sell her at auction and give him the money."*

The *"settle the matter with Scott Moore"* stimulated "Brushy's" confabulation of paying "board." In reality, Garrett's posseman, Frank Stewart, stole the mare from Billy at the Stinking Springs capture, and had illegally sold her to Scott Moore, owner of luxurious Moore's Hotsprings Hotel in Las Vegas, New Mexico Territory. Billy wanted to sell her to pay for an appeal attorney after Ira Leonard's withdrawal from his case - as Billy described in the Caypless letter; writing: *"[Fountain] is willing to carry the case further if I can raise the money to bear his expense."*

Also unknown to "Brushy" and team is why Billy contacted Caypless: he was Billy's attorney for his replevin (rustling) case against Frank Stewart for that mare.

For the Brady trial, "Brushy" merely calls it "**crooked**," because he and his team had no idea of its issues. So he confabulated that he wanted "Hank Brown" as a defense witness, but Pat Garrett would not get him. (Page 39)

PROMPT SOURCES: A source footnote for a "crooked" trial is Maurice Garland Fulton's article in *The New Mexico Folklore Record's* 1949-1950 volume titled "Billy the Kid in Life and Books." In it, Fulton argued that the trial was unjust, and that, by comparison, James Dolan, murderer of Attorney Huston Chapman, had gotten his case dismissed by intervention of T.B. Catron and his law firm.

Another possible source for a "crooked" trial and lack of defense witness was a 1935 book by a Frank M. King, titled *Wranglin' the Past: Reminiscences of Frank M. King*, stating: "[[I]n Judge Warren H. Bristol's court] <u>Billy's witnesses had all either been killed or were afraid to appear in court to testify.</u> The prosecution had a bunch of the Murphy gunmen to swear against him ... The Kid didn't have a chance and he knew it. He had often said he would never be given a fair trial in a New Mexico court where the Murphy-Dolan influence was strong. I myself, have often wondered how a jury could have found the Kid guilty of murdering Brady, when a battle was going on and others were firing at the time. The Kid claimed he didn't shoot Brady."

MISSED REAL HISTORY: Henry (not "Hank") Newton Brown was not a viable witness; he was a fellow Regulator, also indicted for Brady's killing; and had fled the Territory.

If real Billy had a wish-list for witnesses in his defense, he would have wanted John "Squire" Wilson, the Lincoln County War period Justice of the Peace who knew that Brady was a Ringite who had refused to arrest Tunstall's murderers and had necessitated the Regulator movement to get justice; himself deputizing Billy to serve arrest warrants. Billy would have also wanted Juan Patrón, the Hispanic community leader and jailor, in whose house he stayed for the sham arrest, who had formed a Citizen's Committee to protest Brady's shielding of Tunstall's killers. And he would have wanted subpoenaed prosecution witness, Isaac Ellis, cross-examined as to the Lincoln County War skirmishes against McSween's men, in which Ellis provided his Lincoln house as refuge.

"Brushy" confabulated that the Brady trial lasted a week, when it was just two days, April 8-9, 1881.

PROMPT SOURCE: But the prompt footnote of Doña Ana County Court Minutes let "Brushy" correctly give the sentencing day as April 13th, with hanging set for May 13th.

FAKING TRANSPORT TO THE LINCOLN JAIL

A good example of "Brushy's almost verbatim parroting of a prompt source to fake special knowledge is his description of being transported, as Billy, from the Mesilla jail to the Lincoln jail. (Page 79) Possibly because the cribbing was so extreme, a "corroborating" footnote was hidden.

"Brushy" stated: "**John Kinney ... sat on the back seat beside me. Billy Matthews ... sat across and facing Kinney. Deputy U.S. Marshal Bob Olinger ... sat beside Matthews facing me ... Dave Woods and a couple of other guards rode horseback, one on each side, and the other rode behind the ambulance. They told me if anyone attacked they would kill me first then catch the other fellows. We left Mesilla a little before midnight so no one would know where we were ... It took about five days to make the trip to Fort Stanton, where Garrett picked me up and took me to the jail in Lincoln.**" (Page 40)

PROMPT SOURCES: The lifting was from an April 15, 1881 *Newman's Semi-Weekly* article; stating:

> On Saturday night about 10 o'clock Deputy U.S. marshal Robt. Ollinger [sic] with deputy sheriff David Wood and a posse of five men (Tom Williams, Billy Mathews [sic], John Kinney, D.M. Reade and W.A. Lockhart) started for Lincoln with Henry Antrim *alias* the Kid. The fact that they intended to leave at that time had been purposely concealed and the report circulated that they would not leave before the middle of the week in order to avoid any possibility of trouble, it having been rumored that the Kid's band would attempt a rescue. They stopped in front of our office while we talked to them, and we handed the Kid an addressed envelope with some paper and he said he would write some things he wanted to make public. He appeared quite cheerful and remarked that he wanted to stay until their whiskey gave out, anyway ... It was, he said, about a stand-off whether he was hanged or killed in the wagon ... **He was hand-cuffed to the back seat of the ambulance. Kinney sat beside him, Olinger on the seat facing him, Mathews on the seat facing Kinney, Lockhart driving, and Reade, Wood and Williams riding along on horseback on each side and behind.** The whole party was armed to the teeth and anyone who knows the men of whom it was composed will admit that a rescues would be a hazardous undertaking. **Kid was informed that if trouble should occur he would be shot first and the attacking party attended to afterwards.**

That scenario was lifted from *The Authentic Life of Billy the Kid*, and was used by "Brushy" for the destination of the transport. Garrett stated: "[Billy] was brought from Mesilla to Lincoln by Deputy Robert W. Ollinger [sic] and Deputy Sheriff David Woods of Dona Ana County, and turned over to me by them at Fort Stanton, nine miles west of Lincoln." (Garrett, Page 189; Note D, Page 196)

FAKING THE GREAT ESCAPE

The next big event was escape from the Lincoln County courthouse-jail. "Brushy's" rendition reveals Morrison's coaching with known information, touring "Brushy" in Lincoln; and getting input from old-timer, Lincoln County resident, Severo Gallegos. Morrison later used Gallegos's windbag malarkey for an Affidavit that "Brushy" was Billy. (See pages 378-380 below) Added are staged histrionics of "Brushy's" crying at the upsetting courthouse-jail, and identifying old-style shackles. (Page 49)

Alias Billy the Kid first stated that Morrison took "Brushy" to Lincoln and that courthouse-jail on August 18, 1849, during their Carrizozo courthouse records research; but later changed the date when describing the jailbreak, to taking Brushy" in "August, 1950." (Page 40) That is noteworthy because Morrison-Sonnichsen fix-ups will later be apparent. Here the issue is just that in 1949 or 1950 Morrison toured "Brushy" to prepare for his pardon hearing. And Morrison also described "later expeditions" of taking "Brushy" back to Lincoln; so the coaching was intense. (Page 45)

FAKING THE COURTHOUSE-JAIL

For the courthouse-jail, "Brushy" says its second floor was changed - though it matched Billy's day - adding that in 1881 there were no outside stairs to the upstairs balcony. (Page 42)

PROMPT SOURCE: The lack of external stairs to the second floor balcony came from *The Authentic Life of Billy the Kid*; which stated: "[A]t the south-west corner of the building was a door leading to a small hall and broad staircase, which was the only means of access to the second story." (Garrett, Page 190) And "Brushy" saw the new stairs himself in his Lincoln tour.

"Brushy" makes-up the armory as directly across from Garrett's north-end office along the north to south hall. (Page 42)

FAKERY: The armory was actually at that front-to-back hall's opposite south end. Opposite Garrett's office, across the hall, was a room which had held the Tularosa Ditch War prisoners during Billy's imprisonment. It connected westward to the long Masonic Hall room of the past Murphy-Dolan "House."

FAKING KILLING OF THE DEPUTY GUARDS

Basic information about Billy's guards, Bob Olinger and James Bell, is given. For the escape, "Brushy" used both of the popular scenarios. Gor the gun-placed-in-outhouse one, "Brushy" wrongly identified an accomplice as **Sam Corbett** (sic). (Page 43)

PROMPT SOURCE ERROR: To be recalled first, is that in the Mabry hearing, "Brushy" denied killing the guards!

The prompt footnote for the incorrect Sam Corbet name was a July, 1936 *Frontier Times* interview of a Leslie Traylor of Galveston, Texas, titled "Facts Regarding the Escape of Billy the Kid." As a Billy the Kid history buff, he visited Lincoln and Fort Sumner in 1933 and 1935, collecting old-timers' hearsay for escape scenarios. He got the "Sam Corbet" name from a Francisco Salazar, "who came to live in Lincoln after Billy escaped" and married a Saturnino Baca daughter. Salazar said he was told by his brother-in-law, Bonificio Baca, "that Sam Corbett left the gun in the jail latrine for the Kid, that when the Kid and Bell went to the jail latrine during the mid-day, when Ollinger [sic] had the other prisoners across the street for their mid-day meal, the noted desperado secured the gun and concealed it on his person, and on returning to the guard room the Kid was naturally in the lead, and as he ascended the stairway he quickly turned around and shot Bell through the heart, who was near the top of the stairway."

In Sonnichsen's collected papers, in Morrison's handwrittten multi-page listing of sources, are referenced July 17, 1938 *New Mexico Sentinel* articles titled "Sam Corbet Writes of the Slayings" and "Tunstall's Father Learns of the Raids," about Corbet's eye-witness experience of the Lincoln County War Battle. "Brushy" may have lifted the Corbett name from them.

In fact, Sam Corbet was just John Tunstall's past shopkeeper. Billy's likely accomplice was Gottfried Gauss, the building's caretaker, and Billy's anti-Ring friend.

"Brushy" then abandoned the hidden gun version, and claimed his shackle-slipping trick to free a cuff to strike Bell; then shooting Bell as he ran down the stairs. (Page 44) Olinger is then shot from the window in the known scenario.

FAKING CUTTING LEG SHACKLE CHAIN

For releasing the leg shackles, "Brushy" said: "I told [Old Man] Goss [sic] to cut this chain between my legs. He tried to cut it with a saw. I told him to get the ax and cut it ... I held a .44 on him. He cut the chain as I stood over a rock." (Pages 44-45)

FAKERY AND PROMPT SOURCE: Not knowing the name of Billy's friend of four years, Gottfried Gauss, or that he was the likely escape accomplice, "Brushy" confabulated him as an enemy needing a pointed gun to force assistance.

The chain-breaking being outside was lifted from *The Saga of Billy the Kid*, and retained its erroneous spelling as "Old Man Goss." (Burns, Pages 240, 251)

That fable also came from Morrison's October 11, 1949 interview with Lincoln old-timer Severo Gallegos, who was referenced in a prompt footnote as stating: "Goss, the jail cook, cut the chain on the leg irons." (Page 45) Gallegos, as will be seen, was a windbag liar, who also used *The Saga of Billy the Kid* for his fakery! (See pages 359-360 below)

Knowing Billy went out on the balcony, "Brushy" has him threatening the people: "I called out that if anyone was looking for a six-foot grave, that they should follow me." (Page 45)

PROMPT SOURCE ERROR: "Brushy" was apparently inspired by *The Saga of Billy the Kid's* violent fiction in which Billy can see dead Olinger from that porch (though it faced north and Olinger lay at the east side of the building), so "[Billy] raised the shotgun ... and took deliberate aim ... The dead man seemed to jump at the nine buckshot drove home between the shoulder blades." (Burns, Page 250)

MISSED REAL HISTORY: In a fatal error, "Brushy" missed that, in reality, Billy asked Gottfried Gauss for a miner's pick, which was handed up by Gauss to the balcony. Billy then took hours using it by himself, <u>inside the courthouse</u>, to break the leg chain. Meanwhile, he periodically went out on the balcony to address assembled Lincolnites, telling them he was standing pat against the world. No one tried to stop him. Though the Lincoln County War had been lost, this was one way the people could still save their hero.

FAKING THE ESCAPE HORSE

"Brushy" gives an elaborate escape horse tale: "Goss [sic] caught the horse behind the jail in the pasture. He and the **Gallegos boy** saddled the horse and took him to the front of the jail ... I went back downstairs and out the front of the jail, where the horse was tied. I jumped for the saddle, but slid off the other side hanging to the rope. The **Gallegos kid went down the road and took a rope off a yoke of steers in the field and tied it to my saddle.** I got on the horse and rode out of Lincoln." (Page 45)

PROMPT SOURCES' ERROR: The source footnote for the horse fable and meaningless "rope" is Morrison's October 11, 1949 interview of then 84 year old windbag, Severo Gallegos, which Sonnichsen quoted: "Billy called to me [through the upstairs window] to help catch that horse back there. Goss [sic] ... then caught the horse in the yard. He led the horse up and I helped saddle him. Then Goss took the horse around to the front and into the street, where he was tied. Billy ... got on the horse. The horse started to buck, and Billy fell off and held to the rope. He told me to go down the road and get the rope from Prisciano, who had a rope tied over the horns of the cow near Dad Peppin's place ... I tied it around the neck of the horse and threw it on the saddle horn." (Page 45)

Gallegos was garbling a fictionalized mention of himself in *The Saga of Billy the Kid*, in which he and another child, "Miguel Luna," were portrayed as playing marbles on the street and witnessing Billy's escape; and a Manuel Blandano as giving Billy a rope to picket the escape pony. (Burns, Pages 262-263)

Severo Gallegos was a known Lincoln County eccentric, aggrandizing himself with tall tales of Billy the Kid. In his August 6, 1948 *Ruidoso News* interview with reporter Mary Nell Taeger, he also gave the horse scene, which Morrison may also have lifted from it. Gallegos was claimed as having "**a prominent part in the escape of Billy the Kid and remembers every incident as if it were yesterday instead of sixty years ago ... [After Billy shot "George, the jailor" [sic - Bob Olinger] Billy yelled to me saying 'Severo, don't run ... come help Gus (the cook in the jail) get a horse and saddle from the corral ... I ... caught the horse ... a fine big one ... black with a white nose ... took him back to Billy ... walking to** the horse we had saddled he mounted ... that horse started bucking ... hadn't been ridden while he was in jail ... then Billy called to me 'Severo, see that man in the field plowing with the steers ... and the rope around their horns ... go get it!' I ran to the field ... asked for the rope ... brought it back to the Kid he threw it around the neck of the horse ... the saddle horn ... and was off into Ventura Canyon."

Another source for the escape plus rope fable was *The Saga of Billy the Kid*; quoting old-timer, Miguel Luna: "I was a little boy ... and was spinning tops with Savero [sic] Gallegos in the front of Larue's store. When I heard the shot that killed Bell, I stood looking at the courthouse wondering what it meant. I saw Ollinger [sic] run across the street and the Kid lean out the window ... and shoot him down. Savero [sic] Gallegos and I ... saw old Goss [sic] chasing Billy Burt's pony in the jail pasture. Then we saw the Kid bucked off ... As he rode out of town, he met Manuel Baldano ... <u>Manuel had a new rope and Billy asked him for it to use in picketing his pony ... [But Manuel refused.] So [Billy] threw a gun down on the boy and got the rope</u>. He tossed Manual a dollar as he galloped away." (Burns, Pages 262-263)

MISSED REAL HISTORY: Contrary to the fake "rope" tales, the actual escape event had a different dramatic object: a red blanket. And the actual horse was Court Clerk Billy Burt's white pony. Billy realized that his severed, rattling leg chains might spook the pony, so he had Gauss wrap the blanket over the saddle. However, that proved slippery, and when Billy was mounted, the horse bucked, and Billy slid off. Then Billy remounted and rode away.

And, as stated, Severo Gallegos, was later used by Morrison for an Affidavit that "Brushy" was Billy the Kid.

FAKING THE ESCAPE ROUTE

Billy's escape route was uncertain, so "Brushy" had no script, except that the Capitan Mountains were crossed. "Brushy said: "[I] walked over the mountain. My guns began to get heavy and I hung one of them in the fork of a tree." (Page 46)

PROMPT SOURCE: *The Saga of Billy the Kid's* fable stated Billy was "weighed down" by guns stolen from the armory, and "traveling over the mountain roads [on foot] was wearying," so he "lightened his load by hiding one of his six-shooters in the <u>forks of a juniper tree</u>." (Burns, Page 256)

MISSED REAL HISTORY: Billy had escaped on County Clerk Billy Burt's pony, which he had promised to return. So for most of the escape route he was mounted. Only after he released the pony, presumably near his Las Tablas destination, was he was on foot.

Used then is known information that Billy went to his friend Yginio Salazar (Page 46); except it is spelled "Higinio," a mistake Yginio's bi-lingual, literate friend, real Billy, would not make.

And "Brushy's" confabulated scene with Ygenio makes-up why Billy did not go to Old Mexico. Unaware of Billy's sweetheart, Paulita Maxwell, that made him choose Fort Sumner to be with her, "Brushy" fabricated that he wanted to stay to kill John Chisum, Barney Mason and Pat Garrett. (Page 46) But name-dropping Barney Mason was out of place, since he appeared later in the history as a spy helping Garrett determine that Billy was in Fort Sumner for the resulting ambush killing.

FAKING THE FORT SUMNER STAY

When "Brushy" gets to Fort Sumner, sources ceased; so he confabulated around known names; claiming to stay at the home of Charlie Bowdre's widow. (Pages 47, 48)

PROMPT SOURCE ERROR: *The Saga of Billy the Kid* fictitiously used Manuela Bowdre for a Pat Garrett scene; writing that Garrett told John W. Poe: "[A]s long as we're here [in Fort Sumner] ...we might as well try watching Charlie Bowdre's old home ... Manuela Bowdre, Charlie Bowdre's widow, still lives there ... and if the Kid's in there parts, he's probably hiding there." (Burns, Page 277)

In fact, Manuela Bowdre had left Fort Sumner after Garrett killed Charlie on December 22, 1880.

Sticking with revenge for being in Fort Sumner, "Brushy" confabulated his going to Chisum's South Spring River Ranch to kill him, but finding only a "Mexican cowboy." (Page 47)

PROMPT SOURCES: Chisum as antagonist used Billy's December 12, 1880 letter to Lew Wallace; stating: *"if Some impartial Party were to investigate this matter* *they would find it far Different from the impression put out by <u>Chisum</u> and his Tools."*

Used also was Lew Wallace's June 8, 1902 *New York World Magazine* article, "General Lew Wallace Writes a Romance of 'Billy the Kid' Most Famous Bandit of the Plains; stating: ""**Billy began his career with an <u>oath to kill John Chisum</u> ... Chisum and the "Kid' had been unable to agree on terms of settlement for a season's work.**"

A source footnote elsewhere gives Bell Hudson's 1949 fictionalized book *Billy the Kid*, which stated: "Old John S. Chisum ... heard that Billy the Kid was on the loose again, and he was one of the main ones threatened." (Hudson, Page 47)

In reality, a ride to Chisum's ranch would have been 78 miles of exposure each way (and real Billy was actually hiding in sheep camps near Fort Sumner to be with Paulita).

"Brushy" also faked seeking Barney Mason to kill him. The quote was: "I left [Chisum's] looking for **Barney Mason. He started to ride up to the camp where I was staying. When I came out, he left mighty quick.**" (Page 47)

PROMPT SOURCE: The source footnote, almost quoted verbatim by "Brushy," is Bell Hudson's 1949 fictionalized book *Billy the Kid*. "Brushy" lifted its tale of Barney Mason seeking the "$5,000 reward for the scalp of Billy the Kid," and stopping at the non-historical Cureton Brothers ranch, where Jim Cureton joined him. "<u>They rode together most of the day, when from the top of a hill they saw a sheep camp tent ... Barney grew very nervous as they drew near, and when Billy the Kid walked out [he]</u> rode away as fast as he could go." (Hudson, Page 47) This is a good example of Sonnichsen's incompetence as an historian by inability to distinguish obvious fakery.

Confabulating around name-dropping, "Brushy" gets into trouble. He states that Pat Garrett and Barney Mason "were related by marriage" (Page 47); mixing-up that, as friends, they had celebrated a double marriage.

"Brushy," on a name-dropping roll, also states: "I knew Celsa and Pat's wife [name not given], **who were sisters to Saval Gutierrez**, before Pat came to this country. **Celsa was one of my sweethearts** when I was in Fort Sumner. **Her brother Saval,** lived in Fort Sumner ... [Saval] went up to Cañaditas and got Celsa for me. **She wanted to go to Mexico with me.**" (Page 47)

THE FATAL SIBLINGS ERROR AND PROMPT SOURCE: This fatal error concerns a married couple so well known to real Billy that he began his death walk from their house: Saval and Celsa Gutierrez.

"Brushy's" "sisters-to-Saval" error nicely reveals hoax underpinnings. Knowing from *The Saga of Billy the Kid* that Saval Gutierrez was Garrett's *brother-in-law* (Burns, Page 279), "Brushy's" lying got into trouble because of the coincidence that both Celsa and Saval had the last name of Gutierrez. So he guessed they were siblings. In fact, they were *married cousins*. And Saval was Garrett's brother-in-law *by Garrett's marriage* to two of Celsa's sisters: first Juanita, who died, then Apolinaria. "Brushy" made the lie worse by fabricating Celsa as his sweetheart, who wanted to run off with him - with Saval facilitating!

The siblings error also provides a good example of Morrison's coaching with his own mistake that "Brushy" then confabulated around. On March 19, 1955, Morrison wrote to historian, Robert N. Mullin: "I believe the records in San Miguel, and De Baca Counties will indicate that Saval, Celsa, and Apolinari [sic], were children of Delores Gutierrez. However, I am not certain at this writing just where I located the records. It was on our [his and "Brushy's] first trip to New Mexico at the time I was checking records and testing Robert's [sic] information. Billy Roberts told me they were and I thought it would be common knowledge in that country ... Celsa was definitely the sweetheart of the Kid."

"Brushy" also says he hid out at the Yerby Ranch, where, he claims, Yerby kept horses and mules for him when Charlie Bowdre worked there. (Page 48)

PROMPT SOURCE: Used was Billy's December 12, 1880 letter to Lew Wallace; stating *"During my absence Deputy Sheriff Garrett Acting under Chisum's orders went to the Portales and found Nothing. on his way back <u>he went by Mr Yerby's ranch and took a pair of mules of mine which I had left with Mr Bowdre who is in Charge of Mr Yerby's cattle</u>."* But that was not a hide-out. Thomas Yerby held some of Billy's rustled stock when Charlie Bowdre worked there; but Yerby was not Billy's friend.

FAKING A DEATH SCENE

Then comes the make-or-break Fort Sumner death scene. Its title is "Death by Moonlight." (Page 48)

SOURCES: **For the bright moonlight, John W. Poe's 1933** *The Death of Billy the Kid*, stated: "[T]he moon was shining very brightly." (Poe, Page 28) *The Saga of Billy the Kid* said: "**The Kid's figure** stood out clearly in the moonlight." (Burns, Page 281) It added: "<u>Coming out of the bright moonlight</u>, the Kid could hardly see his hand in front of him [in Maxwell's dark bedroom]." (Burns, Page 283)

The historical death scene had three famous elements: bright moonlight; Billy walking to the Maxwell house to cut himself a steak from the hanging side of beef at its north porch; and his going into Peter Maxwell's bedroom at the southeast corner, where Pat Garrett fatally shot him in ambush." (Page 48)

But for his survival as Billy, "Brushy" audaciously abandoned the historical record, and confabulated a different scene to explain his survival as Billy the Kid. As will be seen, he not only created the necessary innocent dead victim, Billy Barlow, mistaken for himself (as Billy the Kid); but also completely changed the circumstances and location. So he had Barlow killed on the Maxwell house's "back porch" by Garrett's "posse" - not necessarily by Garrett - and had himself wounded by that "posse's" barrage of gunfire in the house's "yard." As will be seen, his prompt source was a shocker. Also, Sonnichsen drastically abbreviated his wild confabulations for the entire scene to just 50 lines! They only appeared, in full, years later, with "Brushybelievers" and hoaxers who had access to his transcribed tape recording. (See pages 536-538 below)

PROMPT SOURCE FOR GARRETT'S "POSSE" ERROR: Garrett did not have a posse for the killing. He was accompanied by his deputies John William Poe and Thomas "Kip" McKinney. The error was lifted from *The Saga of Billy the Kid*; which fabricated: "So westward out of Lincoln rode Sheriff Garrett and his posse, gaunt, hawkeyed men ... their quarry a slender youth, five feet eight in his boots." (Burns, Page 267) And there was no historical shoot-out.

POSSIBLE SOURCES FOR BILLY BARLOW: Barlow is non-historical. "Brushy's" family member, Roy L. Haws, in his 2015's *Brushy Bill: Proof That His Claim To Be Billy the Kid Was a Hoax,* found the name in a 1930's song called "Cutty Wren." (Haws, Page 91) It was also in a popular Southwestern ballad called "Billy Barlow," derived from an old English version. (Haws, Page 90) In Sonnichsen's collected papers was also a July 24, 1963 letter from a Tom Swan, about a "Billy Barlow" song collected by John A. Lomax; with lyrics: " 'Let's go hunting,' says Risky Rob, 'Let's go hunting,' says Robin to Bob, 'Let's go hunting,' says Dan'l to Joe, 'Let's go hunting,' says Billy Barlow."

"Brushy" spends the day at the house of Garrett's "brother-in-law, Saval Gurierrez." "Garrett and his posse" arrive at night when he and Billy Barlow were **at a dance**. He, Barlow, and "the girls" rode into town, and were warned by Jesus Silva (dropped name of Peter Maxwell's foreman) about Garrett. At midnight, the dance girls left. (Page 48)

FAKING: The absurd dance scene appears to be "Brushy's" confabulation, missing the dire necessity of Billy's hiding-out as the country's most-hunted man.

"Brushy," building on his brother-in-law mistake about Saval Gutierrez, states he believed Garrett would visit Saval, so he decided to spend the night with Billy Barlow at Jesus Silva's house. He has Silva cooking a meal for him and Barlow; but Barlow wanting "fresh beef," which necessitated one of them going to get it at "Maxwell's." (The Mabry hearing's local steak restaurant has been purged!) Sensing a "trap," "Brushy" lets Barlow go, stating: "I thought that Garrett might still be in town, and I wanted to meet him in daylight so I could beat him to it." (Page 49)

GARRETT AS THE ADVERSARY: To be noted again is Brushy's" formulation of Garrett as a death-dealing adversary. The later "Brushy"-backing "Billy the Kid Case" hoax would hide that formulation, and fake the death scene escape as based on Garrett colluding to kill Billy Barlow instead of "Brushy," as Billy, because Garrett was "Brushy's" friend.

Hearing shots, "Brushy" stated that he ran "through the gate into Maxwell's **back yard** in **the bright moonlight** and started shooting at shadows along the house." But he discovered "[o]ne of **their first shots had <u>killed my partner on the back porch</u>**." (Page 49)

SHOCKING PROMPT SOURCE FOR THE ERROR: First of all, real Billy was by himself in the Fort Sumner house of Saval and Celsa Gutierrez, when he went to get meat, carrying their butcher knife. And there was no shooting posse, just Garrett in the southeast front bedroom, and his two deputies outside it. And, to be noted, is that "Brushy" does not necessarily claim Garrett as Barlow's killer,

And shockingly revealed accidentally is *why* "Brushy" confabulated Barlow as shot on the back porch: "BRUSHY" CREATED HIS BARLOW SHOOTING SCENE FROM C.L. SONNICHSEN'S PROMPT, proving it was charlatan Sonnichsen who invented the hoax's key lie!

It went like this: Sonnichsen used a hearsay source stating Barlow was shot *outside the bedroom*. But Sonnichsen wrongly thought Maxwell's bedroom was at the *back porch*. So to be *shot outside the bedroom*, meant to Sonnichsen being *shot at the back porch*. That is why he coached "Brushy" to put Barlow there (or told Morrison, who was doing the coaching).

The footnote gives Sonnichsen's source as *his own* April 15, 1944 interview of Jack Fountain, the son of Albert Jennings Fountain (Billy's Mesilla trials' second attorney). Jack told Sonnichsen that Pat Garrett had told him that Billy was at the "house of a woman across the street" and went to get the beef. And the beef was in a "little outer room" beside Peter Maxwell's bedroom. From that outside spot, according to Jack, Billy asked Peter, in his bedroom, who was there, and was told, "Nobody." Jack said, "Garrett, in the room, had a perfect target of Billy outside the room. So he shot him dead." (Page 49) Sonnichsen - proving his ignorance of the layout - added that there are many versions[of the killing], but this is best, since it "places the victim outside Maxwell's bedroom." To be noted is that the tale is obviously apocryphal, but Jack still confirmed the victim was Billy. It was Sonnichsen who dishonestly modified it for "Brushy's" fable of an innocent victim.

Proved also is that Sonnichsen was doing shoddy, conspiracy theory-oriented research about Billy the Kid *five years before partnering with Morrison!*

Jack's fake descriptions are give-aways for old-timer malarkey. The actual side of beef hung on the cool north porch, on the *opposite side of the house* from Maxwell's southeastern corner bedroom. Neither beef nor bedroom were at a "back porch." And there was no house "across the street." The Maxwell mansion faced a large parade ground with buildings around its perimeter. And there was no "posse": just Garrett's two deputies. And no one of the over 200 witnesses ever reported a gun battle.

Morrison himself responded to Frederick Nolan on August 7, 1957, lying with his pompous legalese to support the preposterous scene; writing: "["Brushy's"] contention that the wrong man was killed on Maxwell's porch was verified by McKinney, and can not be controverted by any kind of evidence."

Also, neither "Brushy," nor his team, nor Jack Fountain, knew Fort Sumner's layout. And when "Brushy" and Morrison visited in 1949, there were no buildings left. So "Brushy" confabulated that when he heard shots he ran through a gate into Maxwell's back yard (to stick to the Jack/Sonnichsen back porch fable) and shot at "shadows along the house."

Continuing with his anonymous shooters, and in "the yard," "Brushy" confabulated himself as shot by the "posse" through the mouth, his left shoulder, and across his forehead. He stumbles "into the gallery of an adobe behind Maxwell's yard fence," where a Mexican woman pulls him inside. (Page 49)

A GLITCH IN "BRUSHY'S" FABLE: If the phantom posse had already killed Billy the Kid (as Barlow), why were they shooting at random man, "Brushy?"

PROMPT SOURCES' ERRORS: Used for the "yard" fakery, was Morrison's interview of John "Squire" Wilson's grandson, G. Wilson (with "Squire" Wilson in Lincoln having had no way of knowing anything about the Fort Sumner killing). In a letter to G. Wilson on August 7, 1950, Morrison cited his telling him: "John Poe told Garrett that he killed the wrong man, and that the Kid was still <u>outside in the yard</u>."

And, Walter Noble Burns, unaware of Fort Sumner's lay-out, also made up a yard; writing in *The Saga of Billy the Kid*: "They carried the body <u>across the Maxwell yard</u> into a deserted carpenter's shop." (Burns, Page 285)

That absurd "yard" shoot-out, unreported by Garrett, Poe, McKinney, and the entire town, later presented an headache to the hoaxers. But glib con-artist Morrison took it on by spouting nonsense and changing the subject in a letter of January 6, 1956 to a Rick Steinke; writing:

> It may seem strange that no mention was made of the fight in Maxwell's yard, but even stranger things than that have occurred in Garrett's activities. Remember, Garrett was in enemy territory, whereas the Kid was at home. Garrett may have been a victim of circumstances the same as the time he slipped up on Oliver Lee in an attempt to kill him. Many of these facts are little known.

REAL HISTORY: What is known, is that the scene never occurred, and was one of "Brushy's" glaring fatal errors, not only for the innocent victim fable, but for his global ignorance of the Fort Sumner setting.

Then Celsa Gutierrez enters the Mexican woman's house to tell "Brushy" that they were passing-off Barlow's body as his, and "they would not leave Maxwells for the night ... [because] [t]hey were afraid of being mobbed." (Page 50)

PROMPT SOURCE: In reality, Celsa's statements about Garrett and his deputies would have been unknown to her.

They are lifted from John W. Poe's 1933 *The Death of Billy the Kid*": "We spent the remainder of the night on the Maxwell premises, keeping constantly on our guard, as we were expecting to be attacked by friends of the dead man." (Poe, Page 44)

But the key that would tumble the "Brushy" hoax's house of cards was something easy to overlook. Following the "**Death by Moonlight**" chapter title, "Brushy" had been quoted for the shooting scene: "I ran through the gate into Maxwell's back yard **in the bright moonlight**." (Page 49) Moonlight was correct. But it would take 43 years to recognize how irrevocably fatal that night's moonlight had been to Brushy's," Sonnichsen's, and Morrison's hoax.

FAKING LIFE AFTER BILLY'S DEATH

For life after the shooting, "Brushy" added more delusional personas. "Illiteracy" was abandoned, with Sonnichsen's claim that he used "Brushy's" "copious notes." (Page 50) Also his jobs - like a Pinkerton detective - needed literacy. So Sonnichsen kept a straight face while recording "Brushy's" absurdly peripatetic jobs across the globe to 1950 in "From Then Till Now." (Pages 51- 58)

THE CRAZY CAVALCADE OF IDENTITIES

Being "Billy the Kid" did not fill "Brushy's" empty self. After the death scene, he added his delusional pre-Morrison personas. Sonnichsen included them, betting on readers' missing their preposterous profusion and contradictory dates. (Pages 51- 58)

"Brushy" first goes to El Paso, Texas; then Mexico; then, in 1882, to Grand Saline, Texas, where he "dressed like an Indian" and drove a salt wagon; then returned to Mexico in 1883; returning that year to Texas as the "Texas Kid" to work at a cattle company. He claimed he was arrested on a cattle drive in Kansas City as Billy the Kid, but freed by friends. He then, for "three or four years" he broke horses, went to the Black Hills of South Dakota to guard stage lines, and was named "Brushy Bill" for riding in brushy hills. He then rode for Buffalo Bill Cody on his North Platte, Nebraska, ranch. In 1888, he became a Pinkerton detective, joined the Anti-Horse Thief Association to pursue Texas horse thieves; and worked four years for Judge Parker in Fort Smith, Arkansas. **[But Don Cline, in his 1988** *Brushy Bill Roberts: I Wasn't Billy* **the Kid, stated that "Brushy" was not listed as in the Pinkertons. (Cline, Page 41, 51-54)]** In 1892, he he became a Deputy U.S. Marshal pursuing train robbers, and encountered the Dalton gang, who knew he was Billy the Kid. In 1889 he won $10,000 in the cowboy roundup in Cheyenne, Oklahoma, riding a horse named Cyclone; then moved to Oklahoma City. In 1890, he became a left-handed boxer in Cincinnati, Ohio, then a bronco rider in Mexico, before going to Fort, Worth, then Sulphur Springs, Texas. In 1893, as a bronco rider, he went to Argentina to break horses. In 1894 he caught ponies in the Shetland Islands; returned to Indian Territory where he shot dead an attacking Creek Indian; and became a marshal again, serving three years [making it 1894 to

1897]. During the three years, he also rode in Wild Bill's and Pawnee Bill's Wild West shows. But from 1895 to 1897, he also ranched in Old Mexico as "the Hugo Kid." In 1898, he was a Roosevelt Rough Rider, and went to Cuba, where a Lieutenant Cook recognized him as the "Texas Kid," and he became a scout and was put in charge of the horses. But he was accused of shooting four officers and was discharged. In 1899, "Brushy" went back to Old Mexico, but President Diaz seized his ranch in a 12 day shoot-out. From 1902 to 1904, he made his own Wild West show **[though his own notes said he had it for 25 years]**. In 1904, he moved to Canton, Texas, then back to Indian Territory as a horse trader. In 1907, he returned to Mexico and made another ranch called the Three Bar. In 1910 he joined the Mexican revolution and rode with Pancho Villa as a captain **[a possible Morrison prompt, since he was researching a future book on Villa]**, before escaping to Brownsville, Texas, in 1914. But, in 1912, he also married Mollie Brown in Texas, making ranches in Oklahoma and Arkansas and working in oil fields. They moved at unstated date to Gladewater, Texas, at its oil strike, and worked as a plainsclothesman against bank robbers. Widowed in 1919, he married a Lucinda Ballard in 1925; remarrying a Melinda (sic) Allison 1944, the year Lucinda died.

Sonnichsen concluded by providing "Brushy's" quote for the hoped-for Mabry pardon: "I've been a good useful citizen and I think I deserve a break." (Page 58) In 54 years, it would resurface in the mouth of a "Brushy"-backing "Billy the Kid Case" hoax attorney. claiming to speak for Billy the Kid, as not killed by Pat Garrett, and as deserving a pardon for having "led a long and law-abiding life."

FAKERY: "Brushy's" actual, dreary, family-dependent time-line is presented above. (See pages 172-174)

"Brushy's" relative, Roy L. Haws, checked his claimed jobs from 1888 to 1893, and found he flubbed by adding long durations to each job, forgetting they were in just a five year period. (Haws, Pages 73-74)

In the already mentioned *Dallas Morning News* article of September 18, 1950, by Thomas Turner, titled "Sam Bass' Pistol, Texan Knew Bad Men, Saw Hoss Thieves Hang" (see pages 176-179 above), "Brushy" also claimed to have joined Buffalo Bill's Wild West Show in 1885 for a year, then went with Pawnee Bill's show, before forming his own for touring the Southwest for 25 years.

Haws found that Pawnee Bill's Show only began in 1888. If "Brushy" stayed a year, that would put "Brushy's" own show from 1889 to 1914, contradicting his other listed employments. And for this period, he had also claimed he ranched in Mexico from 1907 to 1914, fought with Pancho Villa in 1910, and married twice and divorced once in Texas from 1909 to 1912. (Haws, Pages 74-75) "Brushy" also claimed that in 1898 he enlisted as a Roosevelt Rough Rider. For that experience, Haws found that that "Brushy" made-up a Lieutenant Cook who recognized him as Billy the Kid; made-up four officers shot in the back; made-up training the military's horses, when it was an unmounted cavalry without horses; and claimed being in Cuba for two months, when the Rough Riders arrived on June 22, 1898, and fighting ended on July 1, 1898's Battle of San Juan Hill. Haws added that during this Spanish American War, "Brushy" was still living with his parents in Sulphur Springs, Texas. (Haws, Pages 76-77)

FAKE PHOTO SECTION

Since "Brushy" was not Billy, *Alias Billy the Kid's* 16 pages of photos are surrealistic; but summarize the book's lies and ignorance in captions. Used is the hoax's formula: mixing together Billy Bonney's and "Brushy's" documents to fake identity.

For example, the photo used for "Katherine Ann Bonney" was accepted in "Brushy's" day as Billy's mother, Catherine McCarty Antrim. It was referenced in a source footnote in the book as from Maurice Garland Fulton's article in *The New Mexico Folklore Record's* 1949-1950 volume titled "Billy the Kid in Life and Books;" where it was called "Mrs. Antrim, [Billy the Kid's] mother." But, unknown to the "Brushy" hoaxers and to Fulton, it was a fake - though amusingly vouched for by "Brushy" as his Silver City "Aunt Bonney!" According to Frederick Nolan's *The West of Billy the Kid:* "The original was owned by the George Griggs family, who exhibited it at their Billy the Kid Museum. It was called the Kid's mother sometime in the late 1930's, when Eugene Cunningham, author of the book, *Triggernometry*, identified it as such to photographic collector Noah H. Rose in order to obtain from Rose another photograph ... he eventually confessed that he had no idea who the woman was."

Another woman's photo is labeled "Frontier Mother," and captioned as "Brushy's" mother, Mary Adeline Dunn, married to J.H. Roberts. "Brushy's" relative, Roy L. Haws identified her, in his 2015 *Brushy Bill: Proof that His Claim to Be Billy the Kid Was a Hoax*, as his real mother: Sara Elizabeth Ferguson Roberts, married to his father Henry Oliver "H.O." Roberts. (Haws, Page 29)

A Seven Rivers boys tintype is labeled as having been identified by "Brushy" as being taken in Dodge City in fall of 1877; and captioned that Bill and Sam Jones identified him in it as Billy the Kid. That is a lie. An earlier footnote in the book admitted that in "Brushy's" July of 1950 visit to the Jones brothers (a Morrison trip seeking Affidavits claiming he was Billy, and refused by the Jones boys), it was *"Brushy" who told them* that one figure was himself as Billy the Kid, and was given a copy. (Page 22) And the person "Brushy" called himself, as Billy, was actually Marion F. Turner, identified by Eve Ball; and cited in Frederick Nolan's 1998 *The West of Billy the Kid*. (See pages 375-377 below for Morrison's attempted fake Jones brothers' Affidavit)

An historical photo of Fred Waite, misspelled as Wayte, and called the man who was shot with Billy at the Brady killing - when the shot companion was actually Jim "Frenchie" French.

A page had a Billy the Kid tintype drawing, with a photo of the scarf "Brushy" claimed he got for trading it to an "Indian girl."

Other photographs are a hodgepodge of Tom O'Folliard; Charles Bowdre with wife; a revolver of "Brushy's;" a non-historical revolver claimed taken from Billy "when he surrendered to Garrett" (though it is not authenticated); the town of Lincoln; the Lincoln courthouse; the Maxwell mansion; Fort Sumner's barracks; and "Brushy" on a horse at 30; and an unsubstantiated horse-head charm captioned as an Anti-Horse Thief badge.

Then there is a five photo collage, supposedly of "Brushy," labeled "A Study in Ears;" though the one on the upper left is Marion Turner (not "Brushy"), cut from the Seven Rivers boys' photo, but labeled as "Brushy" at 17. In the center is a boy labeled as "Brushy" at 14, lacking sign of buck teeth. The bottom left crayon drawing, labeled as "Brushy" at 27, looks like the 14 year old, but with a handle-bar mustache. The top right is gray-haired "Brushy," called 55 years old. The bottom right is of "Brushy" labeled as 85 (with the 20 year added fix-up). Its point is a "protruding left ear," based on faking the reversed tintype's *right* ear, pushed forward by real Billy's rakishly tilted hat brim.

FAKING EVIDENCE FOR "BRUSHY" AS BILLY

Having failed to convince experts and historical families in the Mabry pardon hearing, having provided no evidence in *Alias Billy the Kid* that "Brushy" was Billy the Kid, and having belied their own claim of his illiteracy as blocking studying-up, Sonnichsen and Morrison resorted to rationalizations, hearsay, lies, and conspiracy theories in chapters: "The Tangled Web," "Black and White" and "Epilogue."

"THE TANGLED WEB": FAKING PROOF

Sonnichsen and Morrison offer fake rationalizations, lies, and no valid evidence that "Brushy" was Billy Bonney; as follows:

"Brushy's" notebooks' giving a too young age, mixed-up events, and not mentioning Billy the Kid history prove he was hiding his true identity as Billy the Kid. (Pages 59-60) [In fact, proved is that he wrote the notebooks before he made-up his Billy the Kid persona and fake age. Also, Sonnichsen admitted that "Brushy" destroyed three notebooks, which may have had Billy the Kid information, after the Mabry hearing. So Sonnichsen made-up that "Brushy" knew they proved he was Billy, and did not want to be jailed without a pardon. (Page 60) More obvious, is that they were his collected Billy the Kid prompts, and he feared they, like the failed pardon hearing, revealed him as an imposter.]

"Brushy's" knowledge proved he was Billy the Kid. (Page 60) [In fact, "Brushy" had no special knowledge beyond his prompt sources, whose errors he replicated.]

Brushy" got the name Ollie Roberts by impersonating his cousin, Ollie Roberts, to hide being Billy the Kid. (Pages 60-61) ["Brushy" *was* Ollie Roberts, as shown by his relative, Roy L. Haws, in his 2015 *Brushy Bill: Proof that his Claim to be Billy the Kid Was a Hoax*. As discussed, Haws pointed out that "Brushy's" lie required H.O. Roberts and Sara Elizabeth Roberts ("Brushy's" real parents, not uncle and aunt), in 1892, mistaking a 33 year old man ("Brushy" with his 20 year addition to be Billy the Kid age) for their 13 year old son, Ollie, ("Brushy's actual age in 1892).] (See pages 315-316 above)]

Pawnee Bill knew "Brushy" was Billy the Kid, as proved in a June 22, 1938 El Paso *Herald* article. (Page 62) [That is a lie. That tiny, 30 line, article, titled "Frontiersmen Track Reports 'Kid' is Alive," was one in a flood of early 20th century Billy the Kid fables. It said merely that Major Gorden W. (Pawnee Bill) Lillie of Pawnee, Oklahoma, and other members of the National Frontiersmen's Association were "seeking to verify reports the Kid escaped to Mexico instead of falling under Pat Garrett's guns." It had nothing to do with Pawnee Bill knowing "Brushy" or his claim. Pawnee Bill was a Wild West showman, in brief partnership with "Buffalo Bill" Cody - both lifted by "Brushy" for his fake personas.]

"Brushy" claimed that a Tom Waggoner, Judge Parker, a man named Longwell, a Tex Moore, John Selman, Jesse [sic] Evans, Tom Pickett, and people in general from Montana to Missouri knew he was Billy the Kid. (Pages 62-63) ["Brushy's" confabulations are not evidence, nor is there evidence that these men knew him or claimed him as the Kid.]

"BE HE ALIVE, OR BE HE DEAD": FAKING SHOOTING SURVIVAL

For this chapter, Sonnichsen and Morrison faked evidence that Billy Bonney had not been shot, and that "Brushy" was vouched for by old-timers as surviving Billy the Kid. As Sonnichsen made-up: "[T]he ones with most deeply rooted doubts about Billy's demise ... were likely to be real old-timers, or people who had known the Lincoln county for a long time." (Page 65)

Offered were just rumors that the Kid was not killed, and five fake Affidavits, largely written by Morrison, (and presented in full in the "Appendix").

MEANINGLESS SURVIVAL RUMORS

Meaninglessly presented are hearsay tales by non-historical people, some unnamed, and not connected to the shooting event.

A woman from Seven Rivers claimed Billy had dinner at her house three days after the Garrett shooting. Another woman living in "Peñasco country" from 1887 to 1889, claimed Billy was known to be hiding there. A man in the Whipple, Arizona, Veterans' Hospital heard that Garrett killed a Mexican boy instead in a plot with Billy. And a Manuel Taylor told someone that Garrett killed a young cattle detective instead of Billy. (Pages 65-67)

Hearsay articles of survival were cited. (Pages 67-69) A June 23, 1926 El Paso *Herald* was quoted as to someone in Alamogordo hearing that George Coe did not believe Billy was killed, and people in Lincoln did not believe it either. Dishonestly omitted is the title: "**Billy the Kid, Alive Is Ridiculed by Oldtimers**;" its actual gist being that the killing was historically verified, and Garrett and the Fort Sumner residents knew Billy and identified him when "the body lay in state for several hours." The parts Sonnichsen lifted were to illustrate ridiculed claims.

Reused was the Pawnee Bill 1938 "Frontiersmen Track Reports 'Kid' Is Alive" El Paso *Herald* article (carelessly dated as 1937) claiming that people were searching for Billy as alive; and having nothing to do with "Brushy."

And an April, 1933 *New Mexico Magazine* article, by Wilbur Smith "The Amigo of Billy the Kid," claimed that Billy's friend, Ygenio Salazar, believed he had not been killed. (Page 69) That is true. But Ygenio, as an old-timer, thought a school teacher from Mexico, who had visited him, was Billy the Kid. But Ygenio was unreliable, sadly being a morphine addict from the pain of the two bullets left in his back from the Lincoln County War Battle.

And Sonnichsen threw-in any preposterous claim. For example a C.C. McNatt of Alamogordo, "who was in the vicinity of Lincoln when the Kid was supposed to have been killed ... recalls that settlers there at the time doubted the story of the Kid's demise." (Page 67) In fact, Lincoln was 150 miles from the Fort Sumner killing, and the claim is not even McNatt's; it was hearsay from equally fantasizing others who told random man McNatt.

FAKING SURVIVAL AFFIDAVITS

An even more dishonest thrust was inducing five people, with no connection to real Billy Bonney, to sign meaningless Affidavits that "Brushy" was Billy the Kid. Three came from people met when Morrison took "Brushy" on an April of 1950 tour to New Mexico and Texas; and two were by friends of "Brushy's." They are printed in full in *Alias Billy the Kid's* "Appendix;" and, as will be seen, Morrison wrote them in part or in full for signing.

FAILING TO DUPE HISTORICAL FAMILIES

People with credible contact with Billy Bonney refused to give Morrison Affidavits. On July 2, 1950, Morrison took "Brushy" to meet Sam and Bill Jones, brothers of John and Jim Jones - who are erroneously claimed to have worked with Billy at Chisum's ranch. When shown a photograph of four Seven Rivers boys, "Brushy" identified Marion Turner as himself. The Jones brothers refused to sign affidavits, stating correctly that "Brushy" gave "no conclusive proof." (Page 72)

But Morrison had tried to get Bill and Sam Jones to sign his pre-written Affidavits. Morrison's letter of July 4, 1950 to Sam Jones - with a nearly identical one on the same date to Bill Jones - reveals "Brushy's" confabulated knowing them. It is a good example of Morrison in full con-artist mode. He wrote:

> Although our time was very limited Sunday we certainly enjoyed the visit with all of you. Billy ["Brushy"] just keeps talking about it. He was sure glad to be able to talk to you and Mr. Bill Jones. He says that Bill looks like his father.
>
> [Bill Jones's letter differed only in the first paragraph: "It was certainly a pleasure to be able to meet you in person an [sic] Billy ["Brushy"] has told me about you and your family ever since I have known him. He was most anxious to get to see you."]
>
> We have not been able to find anyone else who knew him in the old days. We certainly need your help to get the pardon. You and your brother are the best we could ever hope to get. **I have typed a short form which will serve our purpose**. I hope you can see your way clear to help him ... You do not have to say anything about Garrett if you don't want to ...
>
> I have spent almost two years of my time, plus many hundreds of dollars of my own money in behalf of him. He was a friend of my old family. [This uses his Maxwell descent coupled with claiming Billy Bonney knew the Maxwells.] I feel it is my duty to continue for him if I can get the affidavits. The records and evidence are in my files. All I need are Affidavits.
>
> I am sending photostatic copies of letters showing that **Garrett did not collect the reward on the report he filed with Governor Wallace [sic]. Also, that there is no Purported Coroner's Verdict on file in the state of New Mexico**.
>
> I promised you we would not file a suit in the matter as there is nothing showing that Garrett killed him ... The affidavit is only for purposes of identification of Billy. I believe you know him ...
>
> Thanking you for this great favor in behalf of Billy, and hoping [sic] that I have your affidavit when I get back to El Paso next week,
>
>   Most respectfully yours,
>   [unsigned copy in Sonnichsen's papers]

The outrageous, enclosed affidavit to trick the Jones brothers was worth its weight in gold to Morrison if signed. It stated:

> This affiant further states that William Henry Roberts, alias Wm Antrim, alias Wm Bonney, alias Billy the Kid, alias Brushy Bill Roberts, alias O.L. Roberts, on July 2, 1950, while visiting with him here in Carlsbad, N.M., that he compared old pictures in his album from the time he was 14 years of age up through the various years to the present time with an old picture in my collection, **which pictures show a marked resemblance**; that we **talked over many things that happened in the old days**; that I noticed that he had the same blue eyes, prominent nose, large ears, small feet, **small hands with large wrists over which he slipped the hand cuffs in the old days**; he no longer had the large front teeth, is nearly white haired, but he still stands straight as he used to stand, and talks and laughs much the same as he always did.
>
> **This affiant further states that to the best of his knowledge, information, and belief Wm H. Roberts, alias Wm H. Antrim, alias Wm H. Bonney, alias Billy the Kid, alias Brushy Bill Roberts, alias O.L. Roberts, is one and the same person as O.L. Roberts who visited here in Carlsbad.** And further affiant says nothing.

Morrison repeated his scam with the George Coe family, and failed. On April 18, 1951, to an Elzet Perry Jr., he wrote:

> While talking to Mary Neal a couple of weeks ago, she informed me that you are a grandson of George Coe, who rode with Billy the Kid. You are aware of the fact that we represented a party claiming to be Billy the Kid in an action for Pardon on November 15 [sic], with Governor Mabry ... We are still researching on the subject.
>
> Mrs. George Cole, El Paso, Texas, stated to me that your grandfather and her husband were friends. She further stated that they knew Billy was not killed by Garrett. I am wondering if Mr. Coe mentioned to you, during his life time, that he had seen Billy the Kid after the purported demise. Of course, this would be only hearsay, but that is the only kind of evidence submitted by opposing parties. There has been no legal evidence offered that Billy the Kid ... was killed by Garrett.
>
> If it is convenient I would like to talk to you in Ruidoso during my next trip there.

AFFIDAVIT OF SEVERO GALLEGOS

Made-up by Sonnichsen as "one of the best prospects" (Page 70), 82 year old Severo Gallegos, signing his Affidavit on November 11, 1950, was the only affiant from Lincoln County. Morrison had included his Affidavit in "Brushy's" pardon hearing "evidence packet." Morrison had first interviewed Gallegos in Ruidoso, New Mexico, on October 11, 1949, for his fable of getting a rope for Billy's escape horse, which "Brushy" later parroted as a memory. (Page 45) Gallegos, living in Lincoln at the time of Billy's escape, was 11 or 12 years younger than Billy (giving birth dates of 1867 or 1868), and had no direct contact with him; but, as an old-timer, he fabricated tales inserting himself into the history.

It should be noted that Billy was barely in Lincoln himself for child Gallegos to see. Billy's employment with John Tunstall lasted only 4½ months, with Billy mostly at his Feliz River ranch, before Tunstall's murder by the Ring. After the murder, Billy was imprisoned by Sheriff William Brady in Lincoln's pit jail from February 20-22, 1878. Outlawed soon after with the other Regulators, Billy only came secretly to Lincoln on June 8, 1878 to give his deposition to Frank Warner Angel on Tunstall's murder. From March to June of 1879, Billy was held in Juan Patrón's Lincoln house in his sham arrest for his Governor Lew Wallace pardon bargain to await his Grand Jury testifying - none of which were known to Gallegos.

Gallegos proved that he was a self-aggrandizing windbag in an interview he gave to a Mary Nell Taeger for a two-part article in the *Ruidoso News* titled "Severo Gallegos Tells His Story of His Family's Friend 'Billy the Kid,' " on July 30 and August 6, 1948. Apparently Morrison found it, then found Gallegos for the prompt source interview on October 11, 1949. (Page 45) But the article, which Morrison did not cite, destroyed Gallegos's credibility.

In the July 30th part, Gallegos garbled *The Saga of Billy the Kid* to claim Billy told him and his family that, at age 13, he killed his step-father for abusing his mother, which resulted in his being jailed. Then Gallegos wildly fabricated, unaware of the Lincoln County War, capture by Pat Garrett, or Billy's Mesilla hanging trial. He had child Billy escape that jailing for step-father murder to come to Ruidoso (which did not yet exist), make friends with Frank and George Coe, hide in caves, and befriend Gallegos's family. His family then saved Billy from a posse in San Patricio, while Severo hid Billy's horse. Then Gallegos said his father killed a man, was put in Lincoln's jail, and Billy promised to rescue him.

The August 6th part completes the lies. Gallegos has Billy, dressed as a woman, enter the jail, tie the jailor, and release his father and all the other prisoners from behind "iron bars" (though the courthouse-jail had no cells). His Billy, in hiding again for unclear reasons, is captured in the Gallinas Mountains (in the northwest, where Billy never was), escapes by killing a Deputy Sheriff Johnnie Hurley (made-up), then is surrounded in a fortress-like stone house in the mountains (garbling of Stinking Springs) where he surrendered and was put in jail in Lincoln. Then Gallegos inserted himself into Billy's escape, first as playing marbles with friends (from the reference to himself in *The Saga of Billy the Kid*) seeing Billy kill "jailor George" (sic-Robert Olinger), and seeing Billy breaking "every one [of the armory guns] over a big rock in the yard." (This is a garbling of Billy smashing Olinger's Whitney double barrel shotgun after shooting the man, then throwing the pieces out the second floor window at the corpse.)

Then Gallegos gave his horse-rope tall tale, which Morrison fed to "Brushy" to parrot: "Billy yelled to me saying, "Severo ... come help Gus (the cook in the jail) [sic - Gauss] get a horse and saddle from the corral ... I went to the corral ... caught the horse ... a fine big one, black with a white nose [in truth, Gauss brought County Clerk Billy Burt's pony]... took him back to Billy. Right then Billy came out with every gun in the jail ... the one he killed George with too ... he broke every one over a big rock in the yard ... [Mounting the horse it] started bucking ... then Billy called to me 'Severo, see that man in the field plowing with the steers ... and the rope around their horns ... go get it.' I ran to the field ... asked for the rope ... brought it back to the Kid ... he threw it around the neck of the horse ... the saddle horn ... [this maneuver makes no sense] and was off across the field into Ventura Canyon." Following this horse lie, Gallegos claimed that "Gus" [sic - Gauss] took him upstairs in the courthouse and found a dead jailor on the steps. [In fact, shot Deputy Bell got to the back door; from there, Gauss dragged him outside.]"

As to getting Gallegos to sign the Affidavit, Morrison applied pressure. (Pages 70-71) First meeting "Brushy," Gallegos refused, saying correctly that "Brushy" was too young. So Morrison told the attention-craving old-timer that he would take him back if he identified "Brushy" as Billy. That time, Gallegos - who in reality had never been up close to Billy or spoken with him - identified him by "small brown spots" in his eyes, by "Brushy's" standing straight, and talking like Billy. His Affidavit repeated his lies from his *Ruidoso News* interview articles (Pages 117-118), with added ones. He claimed Billy was an expert shootist - though he had no proof that "Brushy" was. He also made-up that he brought

Billy food in the Lincoln jail. In fact, Hispanic Gallegos, if legitimate, was the obvious person to address "Brushy" in Spanish. He did not. And "Brushy" would have failed that test.

And concealed was that Gallegos was certain of Billy the Kid's killing, stating in his *Ruidoso News* interview: "We always knew he was dead ... he would have come to see my brother Chavez ... they were always such amigos."

Morrison continued to court Severo Gallegos after the lost pardon, writing to him on December 18, 1950, that he was sending him cigars and money for his children to buy candy. To explain the pardon failure to him, Morrison lied: "They gave Billy ["Brushy"] a memory test. It is not possible to remember things for sixty nine years when you have been trying to get away from them ...They could not have answered them if they had not been reading about them ... Billy has not been reading about them ... Why would he remember all of them? We have just started now."

On June 21, 1951, he wrote to Gallegos: "I plan to be in Ruidoso on Saturday June 30, or Sunday July 1. I would like to talk to you and make a recording with you about what you know about Billy the Kid."

All of this courting and lying apparently came to nothing. On January 6, 1956, Morrison wrote to a Rick Steinke that "Severo Gallegos had repudiated his affidavit to the press." So Morrison reported to Steinke that he had re-interviewed him, and he repudiated his repudiation! Morrison's conclusion was that the press was unreliable - not Gallegos!

AFFIDAVIT OF MARTILE ABLE

Morrison, posing as "Brushy's" lawyer, took him to El Paso, Texas, to meet 89 year old, non-historical bedfast, Martile Able, who claimed she and her deceased husband, John Able, had been the Kid's friends. She knew no history, stating only that: "Billy would come to our house [of indeterminate location] when he was on the dodge." (Pages 71, 119-120) Her Affidavit stated that she and her husband were Texans, who lived on a ranch near Carlsbad, New Mexico [no date given, and where Billy never was]. Then they returned to Texas. She also claimed they knew Billy in Pecos, Texas [where he never was], and he visited them [location unstated] up to 1902. She said photos of young "Brushy" looked like her "Billy" in 1880 in Pecos, Texas. Unsurprisingly, "Brushy" then told her tales of Pecos life! This tomfoolery resulted in her meaningless August 1st, 1950 Affidavit. Morrison took it in his "evidence packet" for "Brushy's" pardon hearing.

AFFIDAVIT OF JOSÉ B. MONTOYA

In Carrizozo, New Mexico, Morrison and "Brushy" met with 80 year old, non-historical José B. Montoya, who had been previously interviewed by Morrison. For his July 3, 1950 Affidavit, he claimed he had **seen Billy at a bullfight in Juarez, Mexico, in 1902**. He added that an unnamed man in El Paso had also told him Billy had been seen there. (Page 72)

Like Severo Gallegos, Montoya made up that he knew Billy in Lincoln, that Billy stayed with his family in the Capitan Mountains, and had his own fake tale of throwing quarters in the air while Billy shot them. He added some commonly known Lincoln County history unrelated to Billy. Like the other affiants, he declared "Brushy" to be Billy without any cited examples of proof except that "he looks the same." (Page 122)

Don Cline, in his 1988 manuscript, *Brushy Bill Roberts: I Wasn't Billy the Kid*, from Roberts family interviews, stated that **in 1902 "Brushy" was "living with his family in west Texas, which is verified by census reports."** (Cline, Page 153)

AFFIDAVIT OF DEWITT TRAVIS

The last two meaningless Affidavits were by people who merely were "Brushy's" friends, and backed his tall tales.

DeWitt Travis, 63, born on March 26, 1888 in Van Zant County, Texas, and nine years younger than "Brushy," was an oilman from Gladewater, Texas. Morrison had already used him to vouch for Morrison's other imposter, J. Frank Dalton, as Jesse James. (See pages 174, 205-209 above) Travis also swore that he knew "Brushy" all his life. When "Brushy" died on December 27, 1950, Travis went to the funeral. The December 30, 1950 *Lubbock Morning Avalanche's* article titled "Brushy Bill Buried But Legend That He Was 'Kid' Lives On;" stated: "Among the mourners was Dewitt Travis of Longview, who said he'd known "Brushy" 60 years and knew he was the Kid."

But historian, Don Cline, in his 1988 manuscript, *Brushy Bill Roberts: I Wasn't Billy the Kid*, stated that Travis had not met "Brushy until 1930 or 1931 when "Brushy" moved to Gladewater, Texas. Cline also pointed to Travis's claim that his and "Brushy's" fathers fought together in the Civil War, though "Brushy's" actual father was just nine years old when it began. (Cline, Page 165) Travis also claimed his mother was friends with "Brushy's" mother. Travis backed "Brushy's" multiple personas and demonstration of shackle-slipping. (Pages 124-125)

It appears that Morrison rewrote and prompted Travis's December 12th, 1951 Affidavit, during the year it took to create it. On March 30, 1951, Morrison wrote to Travis: "If possible, I would like to complete affidavit for you, if you would give me more facts about Billy ["Brushy]. I would like to have all you can give me about him."

On April 9, 1951, Travis responded: "You fix up the affidavit and send it to me for my approval ... If I can add anything of interest I will do so." That letter also proved that Travis merely repeated tales told him by "Brushy. He wrote: "Bill ran away from home when he was about 14 years old and knew where he was going when he joined Belle Starr in Oklahoma. She darkened his skin and called him William Bonney to hide him from his real Dad. He was about 17 when he was in New Mexico. Belle Starr even visited him there with him unknown to the public of course." On May 2, 1951, Travis added to the tale; writing to Morrison: "[When "Brushy" ran away at 14] [h]is family was living on the Leon River in Hamilton County at the time. His mother thought he drowned in the Leon River. Bill went directly to the camp of Belle Starr in Oklahoma. There she stained his skin and dressed him as a Cherokee Indian and gave his name as William Bonney from Brooklyn so that his father, "Two Gun Roberts" could find no trace of him through the "Outlaw grapevine" when he hynted [sic] for him." This malarkey was omitted by Morrison for the Affidavit.

On April 23, 1951, Morrison wrote to Travis: "I jotted down some facts concerning the affidavit on Brushy Bill. Check it over and add what you want to and send it back for final typing." And, on May 4, 1951, Morrison prompted Travis; writing: "Billy ["Brushy"] told me that your father and his father served under Quantrill in the Civil War. Do you want to add this fact to the affidavit? It might strengthen the relationship between you and Brushy Bill."

In his affidavit, Dewitt Travis also cited "Brushy's" multiple scars, citing "Brushy's" tales about being shot by Garrett's posse on July 14, 1881, and while taking a gun from Brady's corpse.

But Travis inconveniently told a truth which he actually knew. He stated that "Brushy" had big "eye teeth" like "tusks," that were removed by a dentist. (Pages 74, 124) Eye teeth are the canines. Real Billy had protruding incisors, the front teeth. That was enough to sink "Brushy!"

Travis had made those teeth clear to Morrison in a letter of January 25, 1951, stating: "About Bill's teeth – the two eye teeth were so very big until they looked like tushes [sic – tusks], they bothered him an awful lot so he had a Dr. Cruz in glade water [sic] take them out ... Taking Bill's teeth out made him a lot harder to identify. Bill was a better looking man after his teeth were taken out than he was before – for they really ruined his looks." [**Billy Bonney did not have tusk-like canine teeth, and his prominent incisors (front teeth) were not seen as impairing his looks. A December 27, 1880** *Las Vegas Daily Gazette* **article stated in "The Kid. Interview with Billy Bonney The Best Known Man in New Mexico":** "**He is, in all, quite a handsome looking fellow, the only imperfection being two prominent front teeth, slightly protruding like a squirrels' teeth."**]

What was wrong with Dewitt Travis that made him form a *folie a deux* with "Brushy" - meaning two people sharing the same delusion? One cannot be certain, but the same phenomenon occurred with another Billy the Kid imposter, John Miller, who died in Arizona in 1937. His friend, Herman Tecklenburg, was included in the 1993, Miller-backing book, *Whatever Happened to Billy the Kid?*, by Helen Airy. Knowing no Billy the Kid history, Tecklenburg stated that he knew John Miller in Fort Sumner as Billy the Kid; and was later his "most trusted friend." (Page 42)

On August 9, 1944, Tecklenburg, then a janitor, but claiming to have been a cowpuncher and Indian hunter, was interviewed for the *Gallup Independent* by a Wesley Huff, as: "Did Garrett Kill Billy the Kid? Herman Tecklenburg Says No; Billy Lived on Ranch at Ramah 35 Years Ago and Visited Him." Tecklenburg stated in the article that he had come from Germany in 1869, when he was 14, and met Billy the Kid in Fort Sumner. He stated: "They shot somebody over in Fort Sumner, and they buried him there and put an end to the hunt for Billy the Kid. But it wasn't Billy they shot. He and his Mexican wife escaped over into Old Mexico ... [Later] he was ranching it down near Ramah. They all knew of him down there as Billy the Kid, but never spoke of it for fear of getting him in trouble. He was a prince. Big shots made him out to be an outlaw because they couldn't handle him. Down at Ramah he was known as John Miller."

Jim Johnson, in his 2006 book, *Billy the Kid, His real Name Was* ... found that Tecklenburg was born in Germany on June 9, 1869, arriving in America **on June 5, 1884**. (Johnson, Page 4) So, in 1880 and 1881, he was in Germany, not Fort Sumner.

AFFIDAVIT OF ROBERT E. LEE

The last affiant was 76 year old Robert E. Lee from Baton Rouge, Louisiana. (Pages 126-129) He was among "Brushy's" Old West impersonator friends, and took "Brushy's" word that he was the Kid. Lee stated the last time he had seen "Brushy" was in "New York City in January, 1950 ... at the Jesse James Press

Conference [when Morrison was passing off J. Frank Dalton as Jesse James, and also using Lee's friend, Dewitt Travis]." Lee may have been another of the "witnesses" cited by the press, as vouching for Dalton as Jesse James.

On July 5, 1950, Robert E. Lee signed his Affidavit. Morrison wrote to him on July 10, in Baton Rouge, Louisiana: "Upon my arrival here [El Paso, Texas] I found your affidavit, for which please accept my thanks. I know that Billy ["Brushy"] will be grateful when I notify him that I have it."

Lee's Affidavit summarized "Brushy's" tales and aliases. Lee also claimed that he himself had worked at Buffalo Bill's ranch and at his Wild West Show as his bodyguard; and that "Brushy" had worked there in 1893 as a rider in the show. Lee stated Buffalo Bill had fought Indians with "Brushy's" father, and had known "Brushy's" mother and the Roberts family in Texas. Lee provided his own tall tale that he had met "Brushy" in 1889 near Fort Selden, New Mexico, where, as Billy the Kid with his "band of thieves," "Brushy" rescued him from kidnappers.

FAKING ADDITIONAL SPECIAL KNOWLEDGE

Still flogging the special knowledge trick, Sonnichsen added one from "Brushy's" Affidavit-seeking trip with Morrison. When passing Santa Fe's Palace of the Governors, "Brushy" was reported (apparently from Morrison's notes) to say that he had been taken there from the jail "so people could make fun of me." (Page 73) Brushy" added: "[The governor "wouldn't come down to the jail here and talk to me ... [H]e forgot how I helped him and wouldn't come down here to talk to me. He thought I was helpless and they were going to hang me." (Page 73)

PROMPT SOURCES: "Brushy" was parroting Billy's being on display, but missed that it had occurred in his Santa Fe jail cell. The prompt was real Billy's letter of March 4, 1881 to Lew Wallace which stated: "*I am not treated right by [U.S. Marshal John] Sherman. he lets Every Stranger that comes to See me through Curiosity in to See me, but will not let a Single one of my friends in, not Even an Attorney.*" It also stated: "*I Expect you have forgotten what you promised me, this Month two Years ago. but I have not, and I think You had ought to have come and seen me as I requested you* to ... *I guess they mean to Send me up without giving me any Show. but they will have a nice time doing it. I am not entirely without friends*."

Another prompt was a brief February 10, 1881 *Santa Fe New Mexican* article about U.S. Attorney John Sherman taking curiosity-seekers to the jail to view Billy.

"IN BLACK AND WHITE" FAKING SUSPICION OF GARRETT AND CORONER'S JURY REPORT

Make-or-break for the "Brushy" hoax was proving that Pat Garrett did not kill Billy the Kid. But he said he did; and the Coroner's Jury Report proved it. So faked was Garrett's being a liar, and the Report's not existing. And the lies by Sonnichsen and Morrison end any doubt that they were willful hoaxers. But Sonnichsen's lead-in was that they would ignore "rumor, hearsay, and legend" and concentrate on "what had been set down in black and white regarding the windup of the Kid's career." (Page 76)

BILLY AS A GOOD GUY

As lead-in to denying Billy Bonney's killing, Sonnichsen invented a formula that would become the mantra of "Brushy Bill" hoaxing: history is not as written. As he declared: "[Morrison] found more and more indication that the Billy the Kid story **had not been well and truly told**." (Page 76)

As evidence, Sonnichsen proclaimed Billy the Kid was actually a good guy - though that was irrelevant to whether he was killed on July 14, 1881, got a Coroner's Jury Report, or was "Brushy Bill."

Cited as evidence was that Billy was not a Silver City murderer according to a December 8, 1948 *New Mexico Magazine* article and a March 22, 1932 Silver City *Independent* article from Robert Mullin's papers about interviews with resident, Louis Abraham, who said Billy had really "robbed a Chinaman and was put in jail;" which Sonnichsen calls "petty theft." (Page 77)

PROMPT SOURCES: Revealed is that these were sources for "Brushy's" "special knowledge" claim that he had not committed murder, as Billy, at age 12 (as had been claimed in *The Authentic Life of Billy the Kid*). (See page 316 above) But the sources failed to completely give Billy's very dire

circumstances, which Sonnichsen made-up as "petty theft." It was robbery and burglary, with penalty - if Billy had not escaped through the jail chimney - of thirty-nine stripes to his bare back and 10 years hard labor - with no exceptions for juveniles in the Territorial Kearny Code.

Cited as evidence is that Billy did not murder "Buckshot" Roberts, or a Mescalero Indian Agency clerk named Morris Bernstein, or Jim Carlyle. (Pages 77-78)

Claimed is that Billy deserved the Wallace pardon, though Sonnichsen did not know the bargain; claiming Billy submitted to arrest, agreed to stand trial in Lincoln for Brady's murder, and testified in "two trials" (presumably the Chapman case and Dudley Court of Inquiry). Then he made-up that Billy's change of trial venue to Mesilla made him leave jail, because the pardon deal was *just for standing trial in Lincoln*. (Pages 80-81)

PROMPT SOURCE MISSTATEMENT: The source footnote is Lew Wallace's June 8, 1902 *New York World* **outlaw myth article titled "General Lew Wallace Writes a Romance of 'Billy the Kid'," which does not say that.**

Claimed as evidence is that Billy was a victim. Against him were the Santa Fe Ring - with name-dropped officials District Attorney Rynerson and Judge Warren Bristol - and mean press - like Simon Newman's article in his *Semi-Weekly*, with listed source as Garrett's book. The Brady murder trial is called unfair, because enemies testified, it was not proved Billy shot Brady, and the judge forced the verdict of first degree murder. (Page 78-82)

FAKERY: Sonnichsen was unaware that the correct defense was that that the Regulators (of which "Brushy," he, and Morrison were unaware) had to kill Brady to stop his murdering Alexander McSween, returning to Lincoln within the next few hours.

Claimed is that Garrett's death warrant for Billy was useless *after* Billy's jailbreak, as if that meant Garrett had "no papers" to arrest Billy on July 14, 1881; though, admittedly, none were needed. (Page 82)

Sonnichsen concluded: "**what can be found in black and white about ... the shooting in Pete Maxwell's house [leads to] a most peculiar fact: THERE IS NO ACTUAL PROOF OF THE DEATH OF BILLY THE KID.**" (Page 82)

LYING: Claiming that history is not written, is not proof that the Coroner's Jury Report was invalid. But that is the scam that Sonnichsen now launched.

SCAM OF PAT GARRETT'S AUTHORITY

Faking discrepancies to fake history is not as written, Sonnichsen began with making-up that Pat Garrett, as Sheriff of Lincoln County, had no authority in San Miguel County; so had illegally "stepped out of his own bailiwick when he entered [Fort Sumner's] San Miguel county." He made-up that Garrett should have turned-over Billy to local sheriff, Hilario Romero, but he did not because they were feuding. (Page 82) Presumably, this was to show that Garrett was capable of acting illegally (to segue into claiming he also faked the killing and Coroner's Jury Report).

WRONG: Sonnichsen was ignorant that Garrett was also made a Deputy U.S. Marshal by the Secret Service in late 1880. So he was not confined to Lincoln County for his "bailiwick," was not beholden to San Miguel County Sheriff Romero, and had Territory-wide authority. (Later "Brushy" hoaxers, for fix-up, would quibble erroneously about the *correctness* of his Deputy U.S. Marshal appointment, as is debunked on pages 694-696 below.)

Morrison used that misinformation on December 3, 1953, two years before *Alias Billy the Kid's* publication, by defaming Garrett in his El Paso Rotary Club talk, which was introduced by Sonnichsen. He stated: "Garrett had made a trip into [San Miguel County] Sheriff Romero's jurisdiction in an attempt to capture the Kid. Garrett's posse purportedly killed an unidentified man there in July or August, 1881. But, did they call in Sheriff Romero and turn the matter over to him? There's no legal evidence that they did. In fact, there is no legal evidence in San Miguel Court to prove they killed anyone at that time."

Morrison repeated the Romero fakery in a February 9, 1955 letter to a J.T. O'Brien; in which he wrote:

> During my investigation a few years ago, when we filed a Petition for Pardon in behalf of a man claiming to be Billy the Kid, it was determined that a legal record was not made in San Miguel County to prove that they had killed anyone on July 14, 1881, as claimed by Garrett.
>
> Therefore, I do not believe that Garrett killed anyone at that time. It may be that a member of his posse killed a man

by mistake [the Billy Barlow fiction]. <u>However, they did not notify Mr. Romero, who was the legally qualified sheriff of San Miguel County. They failed to leave any evidence that anyone had been killed.</u>"

SCAM OF NO CORONER'S JURY REPORT

Sonnichsen then came to the "Brushy" hoax's heart: denying the "black and white" proof of the July 15, 1881 Coroner's Jury Report confirming that Garrett killed Billy Bonney, with the body identified and the killing determined as self-defense homicide, deserving reward.

Attacking irrefutable evidence proved that Sonnichsen was a charlatan capitalizing on Morrison's lies. Sonnichsen knew about the found original Report, and even had its photostat in the 1951 Fulton article in his papers. Additionally, in 1949, Morrison had gotten copies of the reward collection's documents from Secretary of State Alicia Romero, as he confirmed, on October 8, 1952, to an Attorney Henry G. Morris; writing: "I checked the Executive records in Secretary of State's Office with reference to the reward propositions. I am fully convinced that I have certified copy of the only official reward made by Gov. Wallace."

So available to Sonnichsen (who footnoted it in *Alias Billy the Kid*) was the *Executive Record Book* entry by Acting-Governor William Ritch, which also quoted the original Report's recipient, William Breeden, to explain reward payment as delayed *only* by need to convert it from private to Territorial. And Morrison also had the Legislative Act granting the reward solely based on resolving that technicality. (See pages 18-28 above) Since Sonnichsen referenced the documents, he, presumably, read them.

But Sonnichsen lied that the Report never existed, was "two" invalid versions, Morrison could not find it, and its irregularity prevented Garrett from getting his reward. Thus, he claimed, Billy Bonney had not been killed; and Billy Barlow was killed instead.

In *Alias Billy the Kid's* "Appendix," he placed the translated Coroner's Jury Report as: "Report of the Coroner's Jury (translation of a Photostat copy of a **purported original which was never filed in San Miguel County).**" (Pages 108-109)

FAKERY: Typical of Sonnichsen's trickery is sarcasm – like "purported original," in lieu of presenting real proof. To be noted, is that, after publication of *Alias Billy the Kid*, William Keleher, in his 1957 *Violence in Lincoln County:*

1869-1881, printed a photostatic copy of the original Spanish Report, with its English translation. But Sonnichsen never recanted his misinformation.

SCAM OF TWO-CORONER'S JURY REPORTS

To discredit the Report, Sonnichsen, repeating Morrison's lies, alleged two coroner's juries generating no "official record." (Page 83) His cited source was windbag, A.P. "Paco" Anaya, writing malarkey to George Fitzpatrick, Editor of the *New Mexico Magazine*, that a first report had been lost and that Garrett forged one with different jurymen's names. (See pages 44-47 above)

Sonnichsen's intent was to call Garrett a liar, since Garrett had paraphrased the Report in his *The Authentic Life of Billy the Kid*; stating: "On the following morning, the alcade, Alejandro Segura, held an inquest over the body, M. [Milnor] Rudolph of Sunnyside being foreman of the coroner's jury. Their verdict [in the Report] was that William H. Bonney came to his death from a gunshot wound, the weapon being in the hands of Pat F. Garrett; and that the fatal wound was inflicted by the said Garrett in the discharge of his official duty as sheriff and that the homicide was justifiable." (Garrett, Page 219)

LYING: Hoaxing Sonnichsen selectively quoted from Anaya's letter for *Alias Billy the Kid*. But, in his collected papers, he had Anaya's complete April 2, 1936 letter to George Fitzpatrick, which, besides faking that he had been on the coroner's jury for Billy, confirmed that the victim *was Billy*; stating: "Pat was in the room. He had been asking where Billy was. When at this time <u>Billy entered and Pat killed him</u>." (See page 46 above) And, on January 19, 1952, George Fitzpatrick sent a copy of Anaya's letter *to Sonnichsen himself* (which is in Sonnichsen's collected papers), adding: "Mr. Anaya had told me that he and a friend were called as members of the coroner's jury <u>the night the Kid was killed</u> and that this jury wrote out a verdict stating simply that <u>the Kid had come to his death as a result of a wound from a gun in the hands of Pat Garrett, officer</u>. (See page 46 above)

In 1991, the year of Sonnichsen's death, Anaya's family published his manuscript titled *I Buried Billy*, which stated: "I, the writer, and my brother, Higinio Garcia, and several others of those that were there, <u>dressed Billy with those clothes then we laid him on a high bed</u> ... [A]nd on the next day we buried him." (Anaya, Page 132) But beyond that, Anaya knew no history, his book being just fabrications to insert himself - including his two coroner's juries fable – into events to which he would not have been privy.

SCAM OF NON-FILING OF THE REPORT

To pretend the Report never existed, Sonnichsen lied that it was never filed; ergo Garrett made-up the killing. Building on Anaya's faked two Reports, he wrote: "What happened to the second purported death certificate? Garrett stated in his report [sic – letter] to the governor [sic – Acting-Governor] that he filed it with the district attorney of the first judicial district. **This should have meant that it was deposited in Las Vegas, the county seat of San Miguel County**, but no such document could be found there." And Sonnichsen cited the "Appendix" with Morrison's requests to the wrong locations. (Pages 83-84)

LYING: Sonnichsen was giving misinformation:

1) <u>Garrett did not say in his July 15, 1881 letter to Acting-Governor William Ritch that he filed the Report</u> with "the district attorney of the first judicial district." What Garrett wrote was: "I herewith **annex a copy** of the verdict rendered by the jury called in by the justice of the peace (ex officio coroner), **the original of which is in the hands of the prosecuting attorney of the first judicial district**." (See page 19 above) Garrett gave the location, not that *he* sent it there.

The Report was really sent by Justice of the Peace Alejandro Segura, as Sonnichsen knew, since he put the translated Report in the "Appendix." Segura began by addressing its recipient: "To the District Attorney of the First Judicial District of the Territory of New Mexico, Greetings."

2) <u>Sending the Report to the district attorney of the first judicial district did not mean it went to Las Vegas</u>. This repeated Morrison's scam of seeking it in the wrong location of Las Vegas to claim it was never filed.

In reality, sending the Report to the District Attorney of the First Judicial District meant sending it to William Breeden *in Santa Fe*. Sonnichsen and Morrison were scamming, since they knew that the Report had been found *in Santa Fe*, in Breeden's records, in 1932 by State Land Office employee, Harold Abbott, and in 1951 by Maurice Garland Fulton. (See pages 29-36 above.)

SCAM OF NO CORONER'S JURY REPORT CAUSING NO REWARD ISSUED

Sonnichsen made-up that Garrett could not collect his reward because no Report existed to prove he had killed Billy the Kid.

SCAM OF WALLACE'S REWARD REFUSED

Sonnichsen claimed that **Garrett's lawyer, Charles W. Green [sic]**, applied for the "governor's reward."

WRONG AND USED FOR HOAXING: Both Sonnichsen and Morrison manufactured a fake conspiracy theory about Garrett getting the reward *without a Coroner's Jury Report*. Charles W. Greene's name was lifted from Acting-Governor Ritch's documentation for the fakery.

Charles W. Greene was not Garrett's lawyer. He ran a printing company. His name was lifted from Acting-Governor Ritch's July 21, 1881 *Executive Record Book* entry citing evidence that the reward offer had actually been made. Greene *gave an affidavit* confirming the reward as existing *by his having been its printer*. Ritch stated: "*As evidence of said [reward] offer having been made the affidavit of publication thereof made by Chas. H. Green [sic – Greene] the editor and manager of the Daily New Mexican was presented with said bill.*" That the *Santa Fe New Mexican*, which ran that reward notice on May 3, 1881, was a Ring-biased paper is irrelevant.

Beyond the affidavit, Greene did not assist Garrett in the reward collection process.

Morrison had devised this hoax earlier, as can be seen from his letters. Morrison had lifted the Greene misinformation from an editorial note by Maurice Garland Fulton in John W. Poe's 1933 book, *The Death of Billy the Kid*, stating: "Pat Garrett with the aid of his lawyer, Charles W. Green [sic], made a very full presentation of his claim, and submitted the coroner's verdict in support of it."

On May 19, 1952, Morrison wrote to historian, J.W. Hendron, "Brushy's" pardon hearing opponent, lying that Greene forged the Report for Garrett's reward, then "lobbied" the Legislature to grant it! The letter is in Sonnichsen's collected papers. In it, Morrison built a conspiracy theory about lawyer Greene, which Sonnichsen used. Morrison wrote:

I will insist that Garrett employed a member of the Santa
Fe Ring to represent him in the matter [of the reward]. Mr.
<u>Greene</u>, Editor of the Santa Fe New Mexican, publisher of
official documents for the Territory, <u>acted as attorney for
Garrett in the unsuccessful attempt to collect the reward from
the Governor</u> ... [LIE: The reward was successfully collected]

Furthermore, I will say that Greene used everything in his
power to further Garrett's claim. <u>I believe Greene made his
purported coroner verdict upon which all of you are relying
[i.e.; Greene wrote the Coroner's Jury Report]</u>. And which
copy (not certified) <u>failed to stand up.</u> [LIE: It was written by
Justice of the Peace Alejandro Segura and confirmed by
Attorney General William Breeden, Acting-Governor William
Ritch, and the Legislature to grant Garrett the reward.] I do
not believe the original verdict ever existed in fact, nor in law,
proof of which I can produce. [LIE: Morrison was referring to
his fake attempts to find the Report.]

The only logical conclusion would be that if an original
verdict existed at the time, <u>Mr. Greene would have seen to it
that all legal requirements would have been complied with,
and he would have used it instead of resorting to the more
expensive method of lobbying in the legislature</u> to collect an
amount that may not have defrayed the cost of the venture.
[LIES: There was no "lobbying" in the Legislature for lack of
a Report; there was merely a technicality of converting
Wallace's private reward to a Territorial one. And there was
no cost to Garrett. The process was a Territorial procedure, so
payment would be by public funds.]

In Sonnichsen's collected papers, is an undated note
signed "W.V.M.," giving Morrison's Greene fakery: "Chas W.
Green [sic], editor and manager of the Daily New Mexican, acted as
attorney for Garrett in filing for the reward if my recollection is
correct ... It is my opinion that Garrett made his own record [forged
the Coroner's Jury Report] with the aid of Chas W. Green [sic]."

Morrison continued his Greene hoax on March 27, 1953,
to a Peter Hertzog of "The Press of the Territorian"
(retained in Sonnichsen's collected papers); which stated:
"<u>Garrett's attorney, Mr. Charles W. Green</u> [sic], editor of Santa Fe
New Mexican, a ring paper, <u>attempted, but failed, to collect
Governor Wallace's reward money without offering a certified copy
of a legal record to prove Garrett's claim</u>. They had included a copy
of what they said was a copy – not certified – of a purported original

Court Record in the hands of the prosecuting attorney, whereas it should have been recorded among the legal records of San Miguel County. Mr. Green [sic], Catron and Thornton, et als [sic], were leaders of the Santa Fe Ring - the most astute attorneys in the Territory."

Sonnichsen stated that Green [sic] submitted a copy of the report signed by Milnor Rudulph and jurymen to the "**secretary of the territory** on July 20 [sic], 1881." (Page 84)

MISINFORMATION: Everything is wrong:
  1) The copy of the report was not submitted to the "secretary of the territory." On July 15, 1881, it was submitted by Garrett to Acting-Governor Ritch. Garrett wrote: "**To his Excellency the Governor of New Mexico: [Concerning my killing of William Bonney, alias the Kid] I herewith annex a copy of the verdict rendered by the jury called in by the justice of the peace (ex officio coroner), the original of which is in the hands of the prosecuting attorney of the first judicial district.**"
  2) The Report copy was not submitted on July 20, 1881. It was submitted in Garrett's letter to Ritch on July 15, 1881 – its day of writing.
  3) Sonnichsen identified Garrett's submission (through erroneously by Green [sic]) as: "the report signed by Milnor Rudulph and jurymen," to link it to his other claims of something "curiously" inappropriate going on. This was Sonnichsen's clumsy version of Morrison's more extreme hoaxing about the Report being forged by Greene.

Sonnichsen continued: "Then another curious thing happened. Acting-Governor W.G. Ritch would not validate Garrett's claim and refused to approve payment. As a result, Garrett never collected the $500 offered by Governor Wallace for apprehension of the Kid." The source footnote was the *Executive Record Book*. (Page 84)

LYING: Everything is misleading; and Sonnichsen knew it, since he used, as his footnote, the *Executive Record Book*, with Ritch's July 21, 1881 communication with Breeden, which contradicted his fakery. Sonnichsen obviously bet that readers would not check it themselves, and would think this footnote backed his statements.

Noteworthy is that this is sly lying by tricky wording and omitting facts, to make it seem as if Ritch refused payment, so Garrett never got the reward. The intent was to segue to saying the basis of denial was lack of the Coroner's Jury Report; ergo, lack of proof of any killing. (But Sonnichsen, proving his low cunning, was actually just stating just that Ritch could not approve the claim *right away*, so Garrett did not get *Wallace's* $500 reward - omitting Garrett's getting its $500 Territorial conversion from the Legislature! Here are the deceptions:

1) "[A]nother curious thing happened." Nothing "curious" (i.e.; irregular) happened at any stage in reward collection.

2) "Ritch would not validate Garrett's claim." Validation was not the issue. Ritch *delayed action*, on advice of Breeden, so the legislature could convert Wallace's private reward to a Territorial one. Ritch wrote: *"Believing however, that Mr Garret has an equitable claim against the Territory for said reward, the action at this office will simply be suspended until the case can properly be represented to the next Legislative Assembly."*

And Ritch, after meeting with Garrett on July 20, 1881, backed his being rewarded, as was reported by the July 21, 1881 *Santa Fe Daily New Mexican* that he was "**willing to pay the amount, and would be glad to do so,** but that he would have to look at the records first. He was not in the city when the offer was made, and had never received any notification of it, consequently did not know whether or not it was on record [meaning properly entered by Wallace as a Territorial offer]."

3) Ritch "refused to approve payment." Ritch did not refuse approval. He delayed (or "suspended") payment to await conversion of the reward from private to Territorial. As he wrote in the *Executive Record Book* on July 21, 1881: "*The opinion of the Attorney General [Breeden] appearing to be consistent with the law and the facts, decision is rendered accordingly and the Governor [Ritch, speaking for himself] declines to allow the reward at this time. Believing however, that Mr Garret has an equitable claim against the Territory for said reward, the action at this office will simply be suspended until the case can properly be represented to the next Legislative Assembly.*

4) **As a result, Garrett never collected the $500 offered by Governor Wallace for apprehension of the Kid.**" The key in this lying trick is the *Wallace offer*. It is technically true that Garrett was not immediately paid for Wallace's

private reward; but it was still Wallace's intended $500, that the Legislature granted with Territorial funds.

SCAM OF NO EXISTING REPORT BLOCKING REWARD

Building a fake conspiracy on the fake claim of Ritch denying the reward, Sonnichsen called Ritch's delay in payment "turning down Pat's application;" and, with usual sarcasm, claimed Ritch's reason was "strange and wonderful." He quoted Ritch: "[T]here was no record whatever, in this office or at the Secretary's office of there having been a reward offered as set forth by Attorney General, nor was there any reward or file in said offices of a corresponding reward in any form." (Pages 84-85)

Sonnichsen hissed snidely: "This is truly amazing;" and gave Ritch's forgotten December 13, 1880 *Executive Record Book* entry, made when he was Secretary of State. (See pages 25-26 above), Sonnichsen's intent was to fake that Ritch knew about the reward, so his saying there was no record of it meant he was lying. And if he was lying, there must have been a motive.

FAKERY: Calling the discrepancy of Ritch's forgetting his eight months earlier recording of Wallace's reward, was crooked Sonnichsen's entry point into a conspiracy theory, which not only hid Ritch's misstatement as mere oversight; but also hid all the actual pertinent records by Ritch and others explaining the reward and its eventual payment. Sonnichsen's scam was to imply that his not claiming his old entry was premeditated.

Building conspiracy theories on made-up discrepancies is a hallmark of Sonnichsen's and Morrison's hoaxing, and was replicated by all later "Brushy" hoaxers.

From this oversight by Ritch of having forgotten his own entry, lying Sonnichsen leapt to his fraudulent goal: **"One possible explanation would be Ritch's knowledge of the shaky character of the purported death certificate – a document which cannot now be, and perhaps never could have been, produced."** (Page 85)

LYING: To be recalled, is that Sonnichsen had the Records he was misrepresenting. Here are his lies:

1) Ritch was not "turning down Pat's application;" he was merely delaying payment for Territorial approval.

2) Ritch's writing that *"[T]here was no record whatever, in this office"* in his *Executive Record Book* entry of July 21, 1881, merely meant he forgot his own entry, eight months earlier, on December 13, 1880, about Wallace's reward offer. And, even with his entry, the issue of its being Wallace's private offer remained. All this had nothing to do with the Coroner's Jury Report.

And Sonnichsen hid that Ritch, in his *Executive Record Book* entry of July 21, 1881, used the Coroner's Jury Report as evidence justifying the reward; writing: "<u>*also was presented a statement of the proceedings and verdict of a coroner's jury at Fort Sumner in San Miguel County upon the body of the said Bonny, captured as aforesaid.*</u>"

And Sonnichsen hid Ritch's quote of Breeden's opinion that the reward would be approved *"without objection"* once it was converted to Territorial by the Legislature. The Coroner's Jury Report was not an issue. Breeden stated:

> *This certainly appears to be the personal offer of Governor Wallace ...*
>
> "<u>*If the reward should be paid, it is very probable that the Legislature would approve the payment if so desired, and that no objection would be raised, or that it will provide for its payment if it remained unpaid, at the next session thereof;*</u> *but if the Governor [Ritch] should now direct the payment of the claim, he would doubtless expose himself to the charge of misappropriation of the Territorial funds, in case the Legislature should refuse to ratify or approve the payment.*"

Using Breeden's opinion, Ritch concluded: "*The opinion of the Attorney General [Breeden] appearing to be consistent with the law and the facts, decision is rendered accordingly and the Governor [Ritch, speaking for himself] declines to allow the reward at this time.* <u>*Believing however, that Mr Garret has an equitable claim against the Territory for said reward, the action at this office will simply be suspended until the case can properly be represented to the next Legislative Assembly.*</u>" (See page 25 above)

3) <u>Ritch's delaying payment had nothing to do with "shaky character of the purported death certificate</u>." The Coroner's Jury Report, as Sonnichsen well knew from having read all the relevant documents, had nothing at all

to do with the delay in paying Garrett his reward. Furthermore, crooked Sonnichsen slipped in his own lies of the Report's having a "shaky character," and being "purported," instead of reality of its being validated by Ritch, Breeden, the Legislature, later historians, and impeccable provenance.

SCAM OF REWARD AS A SANTA FE RING CONSPIRACY

Believing he tricked readers that the reward was withheld by Acting-Governor William Ritch for lack of the Coroner's Jury Report, Sonnichsen then tackled the fact that it had been paid by the Legislature. His scam was claiming that the corrupt Santa Fe Ring controlled the Legislature, so it hid that *no report or proof of death existed*! For this, Sonnichsen made a conspiracy theory that the Santa Fe Ring used the Legislature to pay Garrett's reward **to get around Ritch's objection to paying it.** (Page 85 -86)

For his conspiracy theory, Sonnichsen started with Morrison's hoax of Charles-Greene-as-Garrett's-reward-collecting-lawyer. He added that as "editor of the Santa Fe *New Mexican* [Greene was] an important Ring man."

Next came Sonnichsen's claim that Ritch was a friend of Governor Wallace and "in opposition to the Ring." **So Ritch and Wallace "did not want Garrett to get his money ... for some reason."** Also, **"the attorney general (who advised against paying the reward)" did not want Garrett paid**. So these were the good guys opposing payment to Garrett for an unproved killing lacking a Coroner's Jury Report.

On the other side were Ring members who "had been Murphy-Dolan sympathizers opposed to McSween and Billy the Kid." So they were the bad guys.

Sonnichsen, from this fakery, concluded: **"That may explain ... why Charles W. Greene asked the legislature to do what Ritch would not or could not do."** And the committeemen for the bill for granting Garrett relief included "T.B. Catron ... the Big man of the Santa Fe Ring." **The Legislature "was heavily loaded with Ring supporters ... [So there] was no trouble to get an act passed giving Garrett the money the governor had promised to pay."** The legislative Act is referenced in a source footnote. (Page 86)

LYING: Sonnichsen, having no comprehension of the Ring beyond name-dropping it from Maurice Garland Fulton's footnote in *The Authentic Life of Billy the Kid*, willfully created a fiction about Garrett being rewarded without the Coroner's Jury Report existing. Here are his lies:

<u>1) Charles W. Greene was not Garrett's lawyer</u>, as already stated.

<u>2) Ritch and Wallace were not acting in opposition to the Ring</u>.

Ritch, in fact, was a Ringite; as Lew Wallace was warned in Investigator Frank Warner Angel's 1878 secret notebook for him, listing Ringites. The entry stated: "***Ritch W.G. Santa Fe Sec Territory, Axtel [sic] man, otherwise reliable***." Governor S.B. Axtell was a central Ringite.

Also, Ritch's *Executive* Book entry made clear that <u>he backed the reward</u>. As he said after meeting with Garrett on July 20, 1881, and was quoted the next day in the *Santa Fe New Mexican*, he was "<u>willing to pay the amount, and would be glad to do so</u>," but delayed to check the records as to the nature of the reward.

Wallace, though not a Ringite, had refused to oppose the vindictive Ring to protect his own political future. And, by the time of Garrett's reward request, he had been out of the Territory and his governorship since May of 1881, and played no part in the reward process. But it should not be missed that <u>Wallace was the one *who offered the reward*</u> for Billy the Kid – as he published on December 22, 1880 in the *Las Vegas Gazette*, and on May 3, 1881 in the *Santa Fe New Mexican*!

And Sonnichsen, faltering in his fiction, admitted he had no idea why Ritch or Wallace would oppose payment, fudging it as "for some reason!"

<u>3) The attorney general did not advise against paying the reward</u>. The Attorney General was William Breeden. As quoted in Ritch's *Executive Record Book* entry of July 21, 1881, Breeden advised delay for conversion of the reward from private to Territorial. Ritch quoted him: "*<u>If the reward should be paid, it is very probable that the Legislature would approve the payment if so desired, and that no objection would be raised, , or that it will provide for its payment if it remained unpaid, at the next session thereof;</u>* but if the Governor [Ritch] should now direct the

payment of the claim, he would doubtless expose himself to the charge of misappropriation of the Territorial funds [since the offer was Wallace's private one]."

4) Charles W. Greene did not ask "the legislature to do what Ritch would not or could not do." He merely printed the May 3, 1881 reward notice in the *Santa Fe New Mexican*, and gave an affidavit to that effect. And Ritch did not oppose the reward. He awaited legislative conversion of it to a Territorial reward so he could pay it - and did.

5) The Legislature being "heavily loaded with Ring supporters [including T.B. Catron]" had nothing to with the simple technicality of its converting Pat Garrett's justified reward to a form which allowed its payment. The Legislative Act of February 18, 1882, granting Garrett the reward, stated that fact directly: "AND, WHEREAS, Pat. Garrett ... in pursuance of the above reward ... attempted to arrest said William Bonney, and in said attempt did kill said William Bonney ... wherefore, said Garrett is justly entitled to the above reward, and payment thereof has been refused upon a technicality [being conversion to Territorial]."

To be noted is the Legislature also confirmed that: "Pat. Garrett ... did kill said William Bonney;" which validated the Coroner's Jury Report received by District Attorney of the First Judicial District/Attorney General William Breeden.

MISSING REAL HISTORY: Sonnichsen was unaware that the Ring wanted Billy dead as an anti-Ring zealot. So using Sonnichsen's argument of a Ring-biased Legislature, the reality would have been wanting Garrett to get his reward because they had proof, by the Coroner's Jury Report, that he had killed hated opponent, Billy Bonney!

To pretend that the Legislature gave the reward *but had no Coroner's Jury Report*, Sonnichsen imitated Morrison's fakery about its imprecise mentioning of **August** in a date range for the killing of Billy the Kid. Sonnichsen wrote: "It is interesting to note that the act credits Garrett with killing William Bonney 'on or about the month of August, 1881.' " (Page 86) Mentioning August, when the killing was in July, Sonnichsen contended, meant there was no Coroner's Jury Report to provide the correct date. That leapt to: there was no killing of Billy the Kid. (Page 86)

MORRISON'S VERSION OF THIS AUGUST DATE SCAM: Master con-artist, Morrison, did this scam better than Sonnichsen. He omitted the "on or about," and lied that the Legislature said the killing was <u>in August</u>. And, since Garrett said it was in July, it proved that Garrett lied. And the reason Garrett lied was that he killed no one.

An example is Morrison's August 8, 1952 Silver City Kiwanis Club talk titled: "He Said He was Billy the Kid." He stated: "[S]ome of you are probably thinking that I am off the beam [about "Brushy's" surviving the shooting]; that Pat Garrett killed Billy the Kid on that certain July 14, 1881, like his purported coroner verdict said; or you may think he was killed <u>on that certain month of August, 1881, like the Legislative Act said he was killed</u> ... I know that Garrett never killed the Kid on that certain July 14th, nor in that certain month of August, or at any other time. Billy the Kid was never killed by anyone."

LYING: This hoaxing by Sonnichsen and Morrison repeats the scam technique of faking a discrepancy to deny an event – in this case, the creation of the Coroner's Jury Report for William Bonney on July 15, 1881.

MISSING REAL HISTORY: Legal documents back then used "on or about" with a date range.

Ritch used that legal language in his *Executive Record Book* entry of July 21, 1881; writing: "*July 20th 1881 Pat F. Garret [sic] Sheriff of Lincoln County appeared and presented a bill for $500. claiming it as a reward offered <u>on or about the 7th of May 1881</u> by the late Governor Lew Wallace, for the capture of said Bonny [sic].*" That gave wiggle room in an era when there were no computers for quick research! In this case, Ritch wiggled around the <u>true date of Wallace's second reward notice being May 3, 1881</u> in the *Santa Fe Daily New Mexican*. And the vagueness did not prove - as by Sonnichsen's fake illogic - that no reward had been offered!

The Legislative Act of February 18, 1882 itself repeated Ritch's wording to confirm the reward offer, stating: "WHEREAS, The Governor of New Mexico did, <u>on or about the 7th day of May, A.D., 1881,</u> issue certain proclamation in words and figures as follows, to-wit: 'I will pay five hundred dollars reward to any person or persons who will capture William Bonney, alias 'The Kid' ...' "

So there was nothing suspicious about the Legislature's continuing the same legal language for the July 14, 1881 killing date as: "AND, WHEREAS, Pat. Garrett was at that time sheriff of Lincoln county, and did, <u>on or about the month of August, 1881</u>, in pursuance of the above reward ... attempted to arrest said William Bonney, and in said attempt did kill said William Bonney at Fort Sumner."

Furthermore, when Governor Lionel Sheldon returned, he wrote, on February 14, 1882, to the Legislature, that *he would have paid the reward outright: "It is a claim which I think I should have paid if it had not been understood that the matter was to be referred to the legislature before it came into my hands."* (See page 28 above)

CONCLUDING WITH FAKE "DOUBTS"

Sonnichsen, using his lies about no Coroner's Jury Report and Garrett's reward being granted without it, claims foul play occurred in 1881 because no one expected "Brushy Bill's" appearance in the future to question it! (Page 86) That craziness segued to irrelevant "doubts" as to Billy Bonney's guilt and sentence, and the governor's right to withhold his pardon. From this nonsense, he concludes that Billy's death and burial are also in doubt! So Sonnichsen exclaimed: "['Brushy' deserved] his day in court in order that his representatives could produce whatever was down in black and white for or against him." (Page 86) That left out that "Brushy" had his "day in Court" in the Mabry hearing, and deservedly lost.

Proved, however, in black and white, was that Sonnichsen was an incompetent charlatan trying to insert himself into the famous history of Billy the Kid, as well as to trump his naysayer historian colleagues. And, though he failed, his lies and conspiracy theories, in this chapter, became gospel to the next generation of "Brushy"-believers, and fodder for later "Brushy" hoaxers.

MISSING REAL HISTORY: Contrary to Sonnichsen's lies about no Coroner's Jury Report existing, the Report actually ended up being scrutinized and validated by the Acting-Governor, the Territorial Attorney General, the Legislature, and the Governor; who all agreed that Garrett killed Billy the Kid, and therefore deserved the reward.

"EPILOGUE": RECYCLING FAKERY

The "Epilogue" continued the attempt to fake evidence for "Brushy" as Billy the Kid. (Pages 87-90)

First, Sonnichsen tried maudlin sympathy for "Brushy." He made-up that he had been brave to admit to being Billy the Kid, because they might have hanged him for the 1878 Brady killing. And it was touching that he tried to die a free man. (Page 88)

MISSED REAL HISTORY: "Brushy" was not Billy Bonney, so is just pathetic by being a mentally ill imposter.

More to the point, if "Brushy" had been Billy, New Mexico's statute of limitations on murder had run out in 1888. Though he had been sentenced and escaped, it would mitigate against execution. Likewise, there was no need for a pardon if prosecution possibility had expired.

Abandoning the soap opera, Sonnichsen tried yet another conspiracy theory. Admitting that the survival claim required a "hard to swallow" cover-up conspiracy by Pat Garrett, John W. Poe, and Fort Sumner residents from July 14, 1881 to the present, Sonnichsen backs it; claiming they would have protected Billy. (Page 89) As proof, he quotes John W. Poe's 1933 *The Death of Billy the Kid*: "[I]f the object of my visit had been known, I should have stood no chance for my life whatever." (Page 89)

FAKERY: Sonnichsen hides Poe's stated belief in that book that only a few rough local Americans were in sympathy with the Kid, "while the remainder [of the town of 200-300 people] stood in terror of him" (Poe, Pages 18-19), which removed the 100% needed for Sonnichsen's conspiracy.

More importantly, Sonnichsen hid Poe's documenting of Billy's corpse being taken for the night time wake, and profuse identifications by townspeople – all fatal to the "Brushy" hoax. Poe wrote: "Within a short time after the shooting, quite a number of the native people had gathered around, some of them <u>bewailing the death of their friend</u>, while several women <u>pleaded for permission to take charge of the body, which we allowed them to do</u>. They carried it across the yard to a carpenter shop, where <u>it was laid out on a workbench</u>, the women placing lighted candles around it according to their ideas of properly conducting a '<u>wake' for the dead</u>." (Poe, Page 41-42)

Then Sonnichsen pretended to sort out motives to explain "Brushy's" survival as Billy. Pat Garrett, he wrote, might have been "fooled by the resemblance between Billy ["Brushy"] and his 'partner' [Billy Barlow];" but, he wrote, Garrett knew Billy too well for that. And he wrote that the reward was too small to be worth Garrett's lying.

So Sonnichsen concluded that the Santa Fe Ring was the explanation. Why? Sonnichsen wrote: "Billy was the hottest political potato in New Mexico," which made some people want him alive, some want him dead and some want him to go away." So what? Sonnichsen ventured: "Perhaps Garrett, in imminent danger of mob violence, went along with the fiction which allowed Billy to get away and start a new life." Then "politicians" [presumably Ringite] made him "stick to his story" because they "were glad to be rid of the inconvenient outlaw." (Page 90)

DOUBLE-TALK NONSENSE: Sonnichsen had no idea of how to complete his conspiracy theory. So he grasped Poe's quote in his *The Death of Billy the Kid:* "We spent the rest of the night on the Maxwell premises, keeping constantly on guard, as we were expecting to be attacked by friends of the dead man" (Poe, Page 44) - and pretended that the mob risk extended after the night of the killing. More importantly, Sonnichsen missed that the fear of mob violence in Fort Sumner on July 14, 1881 _was because Billy had been killed_! But dim-witted Sonnichsen was claiming the reverse: that Garrett "went along with the fiction" of Billy's killing to escape danger to himself of "mob violence."

Inserting the Ring to his failing fiction, Sonnichsen had them forcing Garrett to lie that Billy was dead, because that made them rid of him. But that joins the Ring to Sonnichsen's bulging conspiracy of people hiding that Billy was alive. And that meant they were *not* rid of him. As discussed already, Sonnichsen was unaware of the Ring's determination to have Billy killed. They would have been the first to attack Garrett for hiding Billy's survival, and *their* vindictive "violence" was inescapable!

Sonnichsen's conclusion rehashed the special knowledge scam: "The original fact remains unaltered. Brushy Bill knew too much to have been an outsider." Rerun was his being illiterate and unable to read-up. Added was that his "memories" were too detailed for just hearing about events. "He must have been there, in the flesh, when these things happened." Sonnichsen concluded his hoaxing with the quote beloved and put on the cover by duped publisher E.B. Mann: "If Brushy Bill Roberts wasn't Billy the Kid, then who was he?" (Page 90)

MISSED REAL HISTORY: Who was "Brushy?" Answer: One of the 2.5 billion people on the planet in 1950 who were not Billy the Kid.

APPENDICES AND PARTING WORDS

Alias Billy the Kid's "Appendices" reveal more of its sources: Wallace's Amnesty Proclamation, Billy Bonney's change of venue, documents on Billy's Mesilla trial, Wallace's Death Warrant, the translation of Billy's Coroner's Jury Report, letters to Morrison from incorrect New Mexico District Courts denying possession of the Coroner's Jury Report, Lew Wallace's reward offer, Pat Garrett's reward claim, and the five fake Affidavits in verbatim claiming "Brushy" as Billy. (Pages 91-131)

The book ends with Sonnichsen's final special knowledge trick by reprinting "Brushy's" June 16, 1949 Morrison interview in Hamilton, Texas (Pages 130-131), which proved that he and Morrison had wisely limited providing "Brushy's" own words, because his gab was just fatal errors; as follows:

FICTION: "Brushy" said, "Jesse [sic - Jessie] Evans knew that Garrett didn't kill the Kid." **["Brushy" made that same third-person mistake in the Mabry hearing, by saying "he" for Billy, instead of "me."]**

FACT: The outlaw, Jessie Evans, would have known nothing of the sort. In 1881, he was in jail in Huntsville, Texas; and absent from New Mexico Territory since his March, 1879 escape from his Fort Stanton incarceration for the Huston Chapman murder.

FICTION: "Brushy" said: "Jim East, I knew him too. He was a friend of mine."

FACT: Jim East was a Pat Garrett posseman, hunting down Billy, and at his Stinking Springs capture - not Billy's friend. "Brushy" was confabulating around Walter Noble Burns's own fiction in *The Saga of Billy the Kid* in which he has Billy wanting to give East a gun because he was a nice man. (Burns, Page 216)

FICTION: About Lew Wallace, "Brushy" concludes awkwardly: "I done everything I promised him to do."

FACT: Real Billy's prompt-letter of March 4, 1881 to Wallace said elegantly: *"I have done everything that I promised you I would, and you have done nothing that you promised me."*

SUMMARIZING *ALIAS BILLY THE KID'S* "BRUSHY BILL" IMPOSTER HOAX

In the end, *Alias Billy the Kid* only proves a pig's ear cannot make a silk purse, and even the best con-men are only as good as their snare. Coaching from available sources, hoaxing authors William V. Morrison and C.L. Sonnichsen manipulated Oliver Pleasant Roberts, a mentally disabled septuagenarian, with pre-existing grandiose delusions of Old West personalities, including Billy the Kid, into parroting pseudo-memories to pass as Billy Bonney. The three men's motive was self-aggrandizement. The corollary of their hoax was defamation of Sheriff Pat Garrett as an unpunished murderer of an innocent victim, instead of the Kid.

Hiding damning evidence of the Coroner's Jury Report and multiple identifications of dead Billy, the hoax fabricated "Brushy's" 20 year age enhancement with time-regressed genealogy, and feigned special knowledge and illiteracy to hide reading-up.

The failure was demonstrated by "Brushy's" lack of special knowledge separate from coaching, with its parroted source errors; and with erroneous confabulations when prompts were absent. There was no match with real Billy's birth, family history, literacy and letters, and Spanish fluency. Missing was intimate information from real Billy's life: his Peñasco River Ranch; deputizing, the Regulators; the San Patricio massacre; the Lincoln County War freedom fight against the Ring; his deposition, pardon bargain, and court testimonies; his near killing by Joe Grant, the Secret Service pursuit with possible second pardon; his anti-Ring guerrilla rustling; and his true-love, Paulita Maxwell.

As to "Brushy's" authors, William V. Morrison was a con-artist promoter, devising the hoax; prompting, touring, and rehearsing "Brushy" as Billy; and generating fake identity Affidavits. C.L. Sonnichsen was a slipshod amateur historian, hoaxing "Brushy's" words, adding fake conspiracy theories, and hiding debunking evidence; to seek fame with the apparently cynical attitude that history was nothing but "myth" anyway.

The scam worked. Morrison sent *Alias Billy the Kid* to past President Harry S. Truman (1945-1953), and proved the hoax was destined for the big-time. On May 19, 1955, Truman responded (and Morrison sent copies to Sonnichsen and Paul Blazer)

Dear Mr. Morrison:

I can't tell you how much I appreciate the Number 1 copy of ALIAS BILLY THE KID. I read it from cover to cover and it is one of the most interesting documents I have ever come across. I have read a great many of the things written about him and other Westerners, including the great and the desperadoes and this book is the most satisfactory arrangement with supporting documents that I have ever seen.

It is too bad that the old man who called himself "Billy the Kid" could not have lived long enough to see another Governor of New Mexico. He might have obtained a just decision.

That Number 1 copy pleases me immensely. You can be sure it will be placed in my Library when it is finished. I am hoping to have a whole section devoted to Western Lore.

Sincerely yours,

Harry S. Truman

Duped Truman responded to Morrison's letter of May 23rd, writing: "I certainly would like a copy of the [micro]film to which you refer to place in the [Presidential] Library. I hope to have quite a collection of Western lore when the building is complete and ready for occupancy."

It would take 48 more years before a corrupt aspirant to that Presidency would revive the hoax to publicize himself. And he would follow Truman's prophesy of being another Governor of New Mexico; and his hook would be a pardon for "Brushy Bill" as Billy the Kid. But first, Morrison kept hoaxing to the end, and "Brushy" accumulated a duped following.

CHAPTER 8
MORRISON'S LAST GASPS

A POSTHUMOUS PARDON FOR "BRUSHY"

Once William V. Morrison saw *Alias Billy the Kid* on track for a publisher, he returned to his original stunt: a pardon for "Brushy" as Billy; albeit now posthumous (all the better for elimination of incompetent "Brushy's" faux pas).

And he contemplated a new book: *Billy the Kid Petition for Pardon*. On January 23, 1953, he described it to the executive editor of the *New York Post,* Paul Sann. It seems Morrison intended to be the author. He wrote:

> My last manuscript, Billy the Kid Petition For Pardon, has not been submitted to anyone yet. However, publication arrangements will be handled by me in the event that some one becomes interested ... It includes all instruments; letters between the Kid and Wallace; and the letters of Walter Noble Burns, Jim East and Judge Wm. Burgess, which should be of interest to students of history. **The probability of filing a petition for posthumous pardon is being considered at present.**

Morrison kept pardon petition attorney, Ted Andress, in the loop; writing to him on January 28, 1958:

> I have an opportunity to submit my manuscript on the pardon to a publisher in Denver. However, since I talked with Tio Sam Myres last week, I have given more thought to an application for posthumous pardon.
>
> Tio, having talked with Governor Mecham about the pardon shortly after the death of Brushy Bill, is of the opinion that the governor would make a close study of evidence and records made in the whole matter ...
>
> It is established that a valid contract had been entered into by and between the governor and the Kid for a legal consideration ...

The evidence in the records prove that the governor had defaulted after the Kid had performed under the terms of the contract.

This scam omitted that Billy Bonney may have deserved a pardon, but that was irrelevant to deranged imposter "Brushy."

DIGGING UP BILLY

Morrison also wanted to dig up the Billy the Kid grave, omitting that "Brushy's" claim was that Billy Barlow looked identical to him, as Billy the Kid. So the remains should also physically match "Billy the Kid," in those pre-DNA matching days!
Morrison filled Sonnichsen in on May 24, 1961:

> On May 30, I go to New Mexico on oral motion for the Posthumous Petition For Pardon and am attempting to complete the scientific investigation on the remains of those three graves [the Billy the Kid gravesite].
>
> I have asked my M.D. brother in St. Louis to assist with an impartial anthropologist and ballistic expert from that Police Department. No more of those New Mexico Politicians in anything I do up there.

But by 1962, exhumation of Billy the Kid's gravesite was blocked in the case of another apparent hoaxer named Lois Telfer, presenting herself as Billy's kin, and wanting to move his body to Lincoln for a publicity stunt. She was denied based on the body's uncertain location in the three-grave site, and possible disruption of the other remains. Even Morrison had been peripherally involved in her case.
In May 8, 1961 letter to Paul Baker, publisher of the *Lincoln County News*, he wrote:

> [I]t is apparent that the Chairman of Lincoln County Commissioners has established the heirship of Kid from Thomas Bonney, a common ancestor of Miss Lois Telfor [sic], who came to America in 1634; or that Miss Telfor [sic] can establish the fact that she is the nearest kin of the Kid ... I hope they have not resorted to that fraudulent ... copy of the New York Times announcing the purported birth of William Bonney in that city on November 23, 1959.

Adding to the irony of two competing fraudsters, was that on January 30, 1962, an Assistant District Attorney named John Humphrey, representing De Baca County (the location of the Billy the Kid grave in renamed San Miguel County) in opposition to Lois Telfer, contacted Morrison *as a Billy the Kid expert* to check her genealogy claims! And Morrison responded, on February 8, 1962, with information showing that he was aware of the McFarland marriage certificate, and Josie Antrim (whom he obscured as a "half-brother, brother, or cousin"). And he called Catherine Antrim the "mother." All this was unknown to "Brushy" and disqualified him as Billy. Billy Morrison wrote:

> In my opinion the [genealogy] chart is incomplete. I fail to find any mention of the **Kid's half-brother, brother, or cousin**, whichever the other child proves to be. There is no doubt that the **mother** entered Colorado and New Mexico with two children. The **marriage to Wm. H. Antrim recorded in the legal records in Santa Fe** is sufficient proof as the two boys were there then.
> Granting the plaintiff's [Telfer's] contention ... the Kid died sometime in 1881, he would have left surviving the other boy who lived for many years subsequent to this time. She would have to dispose of this issue in proving she is next of kin ...
> There is no legal proof that Katherine [sic] McCarty (Bonney) died in September 1874 in Silver City, New Mexico, as contended by plaintiff.
> It is my firm belief that, at this late date, it would be almost impossible for Lois Telfer to establish her heirship in this case.
> [That segued to his pushing his "Brushy" as Billy hoax.]

CREATING A NEW IMPOSTER HOAX

By 1962, Morrison had been subjected to years of ridicule and debunking of his "Brushy" hoax. So, like the incorrigible con-artist huckster he was, he repackaged it for his new dupe: Attorney John Humphrey, then opposing the Lois Telfer case. Apparently impersonating a lawyer, Morrison explained with his stilted legalese double-talk that he had only sought "Brushy's" pardon to establish the "heirship" of a man he was representing claiming to be "William Campbell" [the Billy Campbell who murdered Huston Chapman with James Dolan and Jessie Evans] by recycling Jim Hines, whom he had first claimed as Jessie Evans]. So his "new" version of the "Brushy" case was presented:

In 1949 I was unable to find legal evidence in your State that Kid was killed by Garrett in either July or August 1881. In fact, we briefed issues in support of a lost instrument [claim of no Coroner's Jury Report] ... I believe it was determined that the foreman of Garrett's version of the jury, Milnor Rudolph [sic], was away from New Mexico on July 14, 1881. It was our intention to proveup the lost instrument [making up that the Coroner's Jury Report was lost] in order to be able to file an action to have it set aside for legal reasons available to our client at that time.

After filing the Petition for Pardon, the late Oscar Garrett, son of Pat, threatened suit in El Paso against the Petitioner ... Therefore, the last chance of litigating the issues folded ...

We were ready to offer proof that our client was one and the same person that had been tried in the Territorial Court of your State, and that the Kid, under various aliases, was not killed as alleged ... [But] our client could not get into court to prove his claim.

At that time I was attempting to establish heirship of a man known in New Mexico Outlaw days as William Campbell. It was necessary to produce him and the Kid in Court, to which they would not agree, until pardons had been obtained for them for offenses in New Mexico ...

We were confronted with all kinds of inadmissible evidence at a hearing before Governor Mabry, which, no doubt, along with other pressure used against us, prevented our client from obtaining a legal hearing on the law and evidence that he was entitled to receive.

In 1955, Morrison had already toyed with a fantastical variant of this Hines-Campbell hoax to include Jesse James. On February 24, 1955, he wrote to historian, Carl W. Breihan:

In the beginning of my research, I had numerous interviews with an old timer, Joseph L. Hines [called Jim in the *Alias Billy the Kid* version, where he is Jessie Evans], in Florida.

I have reason to believe that [he and his brother] were related to the James family; Joe [Hines] robbed with Jesse James; **that Hines was known as Wm. Campbell in Lincoln County; fought with the Murphy faction; and that he and another prisoner were removed from Fort Stanton jail by Jesse James and that Campbell (Hines) was placed on a cattle drive, which eventually took him to California.**

On March 19, 1955, Morrison floated this hoax to historian, Philip J. Rasch, stating he had secret information on William Campbell obtained in 1949, and might interview him again if he was living. He wrote:

> At the time I interviewed [Hines], I was not interested in Campbell ... I thought he was just another old man claiming to have participated in Lincoln County War.
> I have formed an opinion that Campbell was not Jesse James, but a relative of the family ...
> I was working on this heirship at the time I run [sic] into Roberts, who claimed to be Billy the Kid. They were old time friends.
> It is my belief that the James boys and Belle Starr were in Lincoln County during those troublesome times.

He continued to build this hoax with his usual faked evidence, as seen in a March 5, 1956 letter to historian, Carl W. Breihan; stating: "Governor Wallace and others thought that Jesse James was Wm. Campbell in Lincoln County. Although I have no legal proof at this time, I believe Hines was Campbell." But that meant abandoning another of his imposters: J. Frank Dalton also a "Jesse James." So Morrison wrote: "At this time, I am not capable of expressing an opinion on the Dalton issue."

Used for this hoaxing were misstated Lew Wallace outlaw myth articles, in which Wallace dramatically substituted famous Jesse James for unknown Jessie Evans. One, published on June 18, 1881 in the Crawfordsville *Saturday Evening Journal*, was "Billy the Kid, General Wallace Tells Why the Young Desperado of New Mexico Wanted to Kill Him. A Dashing and Daring Career in the Land of the Petulant Pistol." Wallace stated: "A young lawyer named Chapman was murdered in Lincoln county, and for this were arrested **four men, among whom was the notorious Jesse James**, under one of his many names."

Another of his outlaw myth articles was in *New York World Magazine* on June 8, 1902, as "General Lew Wallace Writes a Romance of 'Billy the Kid' Most Famous Bandit of the Plains, Thrilling Story of the Midnight Meeting Between Gen. Wallace, Then Governor of New Mexico, and the Notorious Outlaw, in a Lonesome Hut at Santa Fe." "Shortly before I had become Governor of New Mexico, Chapman, a young attorney in Lincoln, had been murdered. Half a dozen men were arrested, accused of the crime. **Among them was Jesse James**."

This "Brushy"-Hines-Campbell-James concoction died a natural death, and did not appear in later incarnations of the "Brushy" hoax. And William V. Morrison's own death in 1977 saved the "Brushy" hoax from Morrison's increasingly obvious ridiculousness - as had "Brushy's" own fortuitous death in 1950 saved it from his obvious ignorance.

CHAPTER 9
THE RETURN OF
ALIAS BILLY THE KID

REPRINTING THE HOAX

In 2015, Creative Texts Publishers, in Barto, Pennsylvania, reprinted *Alias Billy the Kid* in apparent take-over of its expired copyright, which implied that William V. Morrison's, heirs had abandoned it. Used was the original, Halloween orange and black cover, with new fakery on its back; stating:

> In 1948 a childhood friend of Billy the Kid was still living and led investigators to man [sic] in Texas known as William H. "Brushy Bill" Roberts. After initially denying it, Roberts finally agreed to confess his identity on the condition the investigator could help him obtain a pardon so he could die a free man. Over the course of several months, Mr. Roberts provided many astonishing proofs that he was the Kid of legend **[untrue]**, including physical evidence **[misstating faked physical resemblance]** and firsthand knowledge of many aspects of the Kid's life **[there were none]**. In addition, the investigator assisted Roberts with finding living acquaintances of Billy the Kid who signed sworn affidavits stating that Roberts was teh [sic] man they knew was the notorious outlaw **[untrue]**.

And, trolling for new dupes, that back cover quoted the past big fish: past President Harry S. Truman, writing about it being too bad that "Brushy" did not live long enough to seek a pardon from another Governor of New Mexico.

And with ignorance need to back this travesty, Creative Texts missed that there had actually been a New Mexico Governor corrupt enough to back "Brushy" 12 years before their publication.

PART IV

TRUE-BELIEVERS CONTINUE THE "BRUSHY BILL" HOAX

CHAPTER 1
WHEN DUPES REPLACE CHARLATANS

"BRUSHY" HOAX EVOLUTION

Hoaxes evolve from charlatan creators to dupes. In 1998, 43 years after *Alias Billy the Kid* came out, "Brushy" got true-believer authors: William Carl "W.C." Jameson, a country music performer, and, now deceased, Frederic Bean, a novelist, published *The Return of the Outlaw Billy the Kid*, dedicated to Sonnichsen and Morrison. Jameson stated: "This amazing story captivated me such that for the next twenty-eight years I investigated it at every opportunity." (Page vii) Both wrote: "We believe the case for William Henry Roberts as Billy the Kid is stronger than the case against it." (Page 207)

Converted by the special knowledge trick, they wrote: "Roberts' recollections of people, places, and events were too 'detailed and precise' for a semiliterate man to have come from sources other than from personal experience." (Page 165) Though the main scholarly books had been published by then; their faith was immune to facts. "Brushy" was gospel.

To them, missing was just more "proof." So they would add "scientific" photo-comparisons of "Brushy" with Billy the Kid's tintype. They would expand Sonnichsen's conspiracy theories. But key to their starry-eyed strategy was letting "Brushy" speak for himself through Morrison's interview tapes. (Page vii) Not till Jameson's 2012 book, *Billy the Kid: The Lost Interviews*, was it explained that Bean got them in 1989 from "Brushy's" last wife's grandson, Bill Allison, made their transcript, then returned them. As Jameson wrote: "I was convinced I was looking at the words of the outlaw, Billy the Kid." (*The Lost Interviews*, Page 43)

Uncensored "Brushy" was bad for their mission, but great for hoaxbusting. As Jameson guilelessly reported in *Billy the Kid: The Lost Interviews*, Sonnichsen had *"heavily edited"* "Brushy" from those tapes. (*The Lost Interviews*, Page 42) (Sonnichsen knew that "Brushy" in the raw was what Governor Mabry saw in the pardon hearing - along with his Fort Sumner steak restaurant!) But even in *Alias Billy the Kid*, Sonnichsen had left untouched some of "Brushy's" atrocious grammar and racism (the "[N-word]s" on the foothills), since they fit the crude 1950's image of Billy the Kid.

But Sonnichsen's admitted editing was apparently corrupting, inspiring Jameson's and Bean's own dishonest fix-ups. To better match Billy, they added new historical names - like "Regulators" - unknown to "Brushy;" but faked by them as if they were his words. And they used a 1988 book by a William Tunstill, titled *Billy the Kid and Me Were the Same*, to add more fake genealogy.

Nevertheless, *The Return of the Outlaw Billy the Kid* froze "Brushy" in the amber of their adoration for all to see. And what was revealed, by comparing their text to *Alias Billy the Kid's*, were the sly fix-ups in that book and theirs. Real "Brushy" was disappearing, and trickery was emerging, making their book hoaxbusting treasure. And, as Jameson descended to overt rewrites in later books, he would hide this revealing one.

INTRODUCTORY MISINFORMATION

For the "Prologue," the hoax's holy of holies were rolled out: the corpse was not Billy the Kid; Garrett lied; and the pardon hearing was unfair. So Pat Garrett is misrepresented as **"thinking"** he shot the Kid; Poe as saying he "**shot the wrong man;**" Garrett as ordering Poe and McKinney to guard the closed bedroom door to **prevent viewing of the body**; and Poe as wondering why Garrett said the body was Billy the Kid. (Pages x-xi) The pardon hearing is faked as presenting compelling evidence that "Ollie L. Roberts" was Billy the Kid. (Page xi)

The "Introduction" recites the hoax's lies: "Brushy" knew "more than most scholars." (Page 4) And salesman Morrison is called a "graduate lawyer" (Page 3) and an "attorney." (Page 4)

FAKERY: They knew Morrison was no lawyer. In his 2012 book, titled *Billy the Kid: The Lost Interviews*, Jameson stated that on March 8, 1985 - 13 years *before The Return of the Outlaw Billy the Kid* - he interviewed deceased Morrison's daughter who told him Morrison was a paralegal, with a degree from mail-order college LaSalle, in Chicago, Illinois; and did work related to wills,

bankruptcy, and taxes. And Jameson called him a "glorified law clerk." (*Billy the Kid: The Lost Interviews*, Page 32) By his 2016 *Pat Garrett: The Man Behind the Badge,* on its page 85, Jameson called Morrison a "paralegal investigator."

The "Shadows of Doubt" chapter has their claims. To Jameson and Bean, since "Brushy" *was* Billy the Kid, but was called an imposter by historians, there must be conspiracies to hide truth; as evidenced by his special knowledge trick, coupled with illiteracy blocking studying-up. Then they lie that he "stunned researchers" by his knowledge of Billy the Kid's life, looked just like him, had scars like him, and his genealogy proved the source of the name "Bonney." (Pages 13-15) Actually proved is only that they had bought the "Brushy" hoax hook, line, and sinker; and were abandoning scruples to do anything to get converts.

FAKING BILLY THE KID HISTORY

"The 'Accepted' History of Billy the Kid" chapter is called history "that gained acceptance among a fraternity of historians." (Page 18). Where it differed from "Brushy's" was historians' misinformation! But this supposed fraternal history is just a chaos of errors, including some of "Brushy's" own from *Alias Billy the Kid*. Jameson's and Bean's utter historical ignorance shows why they fell prey to the "Brushy" hoax.

There is a fictional early adolescence, with Billy at 14 sent to a New York Children's Aid Society to live with a William E. Antrim, who marries a woman named Catherine (no last name). He moves with her and her son, Joseph, to Silver City, where she died of T.B. There is Billy's Chinese laundry theft and his Arizona "Windy" Cahill killing - though with Billy erroneously arrested - before getting to his Tunstall job, erroneously as a hired gun, in Lincoln County. There, actually dead Emil Fritz is at the Murphy-Dolan store; and Murphy, rather than the Ring, controlled Sheriff William Brady. This goulash of name-dropping and misinformation, can be seen in the example below:

> At one point, Murphy retained lawyer McSween to collect on a $10,000 life insurance policy on partner Fritz, who died while on a trip to Germany. McSween collected the money but refused to hand it over to Murphy. Under

orders from Murphy, Sheriff Brady attempted to seize some of Tunstall's cattle as partial payment.

Tunstall decided he needed to confer with Brady and arranged an appointment with him in Lincoln. On 18 February 1878 John Tunstall, riding a buckboard and accompanied by several of his hired gunmen, including Billy the Kid, headed for Lincoln. As they approached the town of Ruidoso, the gunmen spotted a flock of turkeys and set off in pursuit. Seconds later, a group of men led by Jesse [sic] Evans rode up to Tunstall in the wagon and shot him dead.

Tunstall's hired hands, led by Dick Brewer, vowed vengeance and organized themselves into a vigilante group they called the Regulators. (Pages 20-21)

Here are the mistakes:

Murphy did not hire McSween as an attorney. McSween was hired to collect the life insurance of deceased Emil Fritz by his siblings, the Administrators, Charles Fritz and Emilie Scholand.

McSween only collected part of the money, the rest was kept by the New York City law firm, Donnell and Lawson, as fee for their collection services from the life insurance company.

McSween refused to hand over the money to James Dolan, not Murphy. Murphy was dying of alcoholism. The money was for Fritz's heirs; not Dolan. Dolan separately litigated falsely to get it, but his claim was rejected by Probate Judge Florencio Gonzales. McSween kept the money while searching for other eligible heirs in Germany as probate law required.

Sheriff Brady did not attempt to seize Tunstall's cattle as partial payment. The mistake is "payment." The Ring made a malicious prosecution case again McSween, with Tunstall added falsely as his business partner. The embezzling complaint against McSween was filed February 4, 1878; with the Grand Jury not until that April. To guarantee the alleged $10,000 in question until the trial's outcome, a Writ of Attachment (meaning appraisal) of both men's property was made to ensure the sum existed in kind to pay the debt if McSween lost. Tunstall's cattle were for the Writ's appraisal, not payment.

Tunstall did not head to Lincoln on February 18, 1878 to confer with Sheriff Brady. Knowing that his cattle would be attached that day at his Feliz River ranch, and that his horses were exempted, he was merely taking them to Lincoln. But it was used as an excuse for Ringite Brady to murder him, ahead of the upcoming Grand Jury's likely exonerating of him and McSween.

Tunstall did not ride on a buckboard. Tunstall was on horseback with his men. His horse was killed with him.

Tunstall's men were not gunmen per say. They were his ranch hands at his Feliz and Peñasco River properties. Billy himself had been given a Peñasco River ranch, along with Fred Waite, as part of Tunstall's plan for mutual ranching along those rivers to the Pecos River. At this stage, there was no overt fighting. Tunstall was building his business.

They were not approaching the town of Ruidoso. It did not exist then.

The murder did not occur at a wagon. Tunstall was attacked on his horse (according to real Billy's own deposition!).

The Regulators were not an outlaw vigilante group. After Tunstall's murder, his men were deputized by Justice of the Peace John Wilson to arrest his murderers, because Lincoln County Ringite Sheriff William Brady was shielding them. After being illegally outlawed by Ringite Governor S.B. Axtell, in his March 9, 1878 Proclamation, they continued their legal mission to make arrests, calling themselves Regulators.

Vowed vengeance was not the Regulator cause. They were part of grass-roots uprisings in New Mexico Territory in the 1870's against the Santa Fe Ring's corrupt and terrorist take-overs.

Total misinformation continued. Sheriff Brady's murder is described as for "vengeance," rather than the Regulators' saving McSween from murder by him later that day. (Page 21) The Regulators' Blazer's Mill killing of "Buckshot" Roberts is attributed to seeking "sanctuary" there; when it was a Ring stronghold, no "sanctuary;" and they were there seeking stolen Tunstall stock. (Page 21) McSween is wrongly claimed as overseeing Tunstall's businesses. (Page 21) The Lincoln County War is merely a cowardly McSween barricading himself in his Lincoln house with Regulators to await an attack by Dolan. Sheriff Peppin requests McSween's surrender (for what is unclear), and a five day battle occurs, involving Fort Stanton soldiers. On July 19th, Peppin's deputies set fire to McSween's house and the occupants flee. McSween is killed and Billy the Kid becomes the Regulators' head. (Pages 22-23) **[Wrong]** The Dolan peace meeting becomes one with Jesse [sic] Evans instead; and ends with Evans's and Dolan's murdering Huston Chapman, wrongly called Susan McSween's attorney *to prosecute the Dolan faction* - instead of Commander Dudley. (Page 23) **[Missed is additional murderer, Billy Campbell, as Billy testified.]**

Things only got worse. Everything was wrong. Lew Wallace is upset by the Murphy-Dolan beef contracts and Chapman murder, so meets with Billy to break up "the corrupt faction." Wallace promises pardon only for the Brady killing if Billy testifies about the Chapman murder. **[The actual pardon was to be for Brady, Hindman, and Roberts indictments.]** Billy testified and got Evans and Dolan indicted but District Attorney Rynerson jailed Billy. (Page 23) **[Billy was already in sham arrest in 1879 the pardon bargain. He was not jailed by Rynerson.]** The made-up Rynerson jailing is confused with Billy's Santa Fe jailing in 1881, so Billy is portrayed as writing his jail letters to Wallace, then escaping jail. (Page 23) **[The jail letters were in 1881, and Billy did not escape in 1879: he walked out of a sham arrest.]** Unrelated incidents in 1879 and 1880 get mixed up. Billy's departure (called an escape) from the sham Patrón house arrest (on June 17, 1879), is called "a short time later" to his "January 10 [sic -3], 1880" killing of Joe Grant. And that killing is attributed to "an argument," (Page 23) **[It was just a gunslinger attempt by "Texas Joe" Grant, to shoot Billy in the back.]** Pat Garrett's 1880 election as sheriff leads to the White Oaks posse attacking Billy and his group in the Greathouse ranch with the killing of Jim Carlyle with Billy blamed. (Page 24) **[The Secret Service is missing.]** That ambush makes Billy hide in Fort Sumner and enables Garrett's ambush of him and his "gang," with Tom O'Folliard killed. (Page 24) For the Stinking Springs capture, shot Charlie Bowdre, mistaken for Billy, falls dead at the rock house (Page 24) **[instead of staggering into the ravine]**. Billy's Mesilla trial is only for the Brady killing and on April 26th (Page 25) **[it was on April 8-9, 1881; and left out is "Buckshot" Roberts's case]**. Judge Warren Bristol is called a Murphy-Dolan man (Page 25), **[when he was a Ringite]**. Billy's courthouse-jail escape has a gun hidden in the outhouse, with Bell shot on the stairs during Billy's return. The Olinger killing and Billy's use of a pickax to break the leg chains is given. (Page 25) Billy's destination of Fort Sumner has town owner, Peter Maxwell, betraying him to Garrett because of "the outlaw's affections for his servant girls!" (Pages 25-26) **[Made-up.]**

For a July 14, 1881, Maxwell bedroom shooting of Billy, (Page 26), Billy starts in Celsa Gutierrez's house; though she is called one of Maxwell's "servant girls." Billy goes to the side of beef on the porch where deputies Thomas McKinney and John Poe, are "**lurking in the dark.**" Then he enters the bedroom. **[This is not "accepted" history. It is "Brushy's" parroting of Sonnichsen's fake back-porch-bedroom-and-side-of-beef construct, which caused "Brushy" to confabulate that Billy Barlow was shot on the back porch. (See pages 366-367 above) Noteworthy too is "Brushy's" error about "the dark." Here, Jameson's and Bean's ignorance will be a boon for hoaxbusting: they are unaware of the bright moonlight! So when it comes to "Brushy's" own quotes, they will not do fix-ups if he sticks to "the dark!!!"**

INTRODUCING THEIR MAN "BRUSHY"

Jameson and Bean used the original "Brushy" hoax's name of William Henry Roberts. They state that others claimed to survive Garrett's shooting, but only "Brushy" had "intimate and confounding Lincoln County War connections" (Page 27); and other old-timers believed he was Billy the Kid. (Page 28)

Morrison enters as a probate attorney; a Missouri Historical Society member; a descendant of Ferdinand Maxwell (brother of Lucien Maxwell, and uncle of Peter Maxwell); and expert on Billy the Kid history. He meets a Joe (not Jim) Hines, who was Jessie Evans, who tells him Billy the Kid was living in Texas. He meets another unnamed old-timer in Missouri. **[His being J. Frank Dalton as Jesse James from the original hoax is omitted, likely because real Jesse was proved to be in his Kearney, Missouri, grave by DNA testing in 1995, ending Dalton's imposter scam.]** This Missourian knew Billy the Kid was O.L. Roberts of Hamilton, Texas. So in June of 1949, Morrison went there to meet him. (Pages 28-29)

That meeting presents the *Alias Billy the Kid* tricks that duped Jameson and Bean: fake physical similarities; shackle slipping; and supposed "incredible knowledge of New Mexico history," while too illiterate to study-up. (Page 33) So Morrison believes "Brushy" was Billy and deserved a pardon. And when Morrison took "Brushy" to sites, he had knowledge unknown to historians. So, if not Billy, he was his compatriot! (Page 34)

C.L. Sonnichsen appears as "a noted Southwestern historian," who joined Morrison to write 1955's *Alias Billy the Kid*. (Page 34)

Claimed is that in 1950, the Governor refused "Brushy's" pardon request, because Billy the Kid "researchers" and Pat Garrett's descendants called him an imposter; while Morrison and Sonnichsen knew "Brushy" was telling "one of the most amazing stories of all time." (Page 34)

Updated "Brushy" is called "semi-literate" to encompass his jottings for Morrison. They quote his saying about Billy's letter of March 13, 1879 to Lew Wallace: "I had a friend who spelled it out in a letter for me, what I wanted from Governor Wallace." (Pages 56-57) And real Billy's Spanish fluency is hidden.

FAKERY: As discussed, that lie broke-down with identical writing; witnesses seeing Billy write; and writing in multiple situations, including solitary confinement in jail.

To this recitation of *Alias Billy the Kid* gospel, Jameson and Bean added their true-believer twist. They were sure that the solution to converting readers was to let them hear "Brushy" talk; unaware that this was the fiasco Morrison and Sonnichsen had labored to prevent by sly editing of his alleged words! But, through them, "Brushy" would speak from "actual tape recordings made by Morrison." Then, strangely, they say those words came to them from "transcriptions given by Roberts' step-grandson" "Bill Allison," rather than Jameson's later claim of being made by Bean from "Brushy's" tapes *provided by* Allison. (Pages 35, 37)

LYING: For some reason, Bean's getting the original tapes from Allison, then *transcribing them himself* - as Jameson claimed in his 2012 *Billy the Kid: The Lost Interviews* - here had Allison doing the transcribing. As will be seen, fabricating and misstating are part of the Jameson-Bean style. In fact, by the *Lost Interviews* book, the existence of *The Return of the Outlaw Billy the Kid* - with its accidental revelations of hoax-revealing truth - would be hidden.

To be noted is that it remains unclear how Allison got the tapes. As of 1955, they were in Morrison's possession, as he wrote on July 12, 1955 to Robert N. Mullin: "You know it will be most enjoyable for me to play back the tapes when you are this way ... I shall never forget the thrill I enjoyed at the time you asked to play them back on important statements made by Roberts."

EXPANDING A FAKE FAMILY TREE

Geneva Pittmon's 1987 letter was a disaster for the "Brushy" hoax; with her being his niece and knowing his parents were H.O. Roberts and Sara Elizabeth Ferguson, and that his August 26, 1879 birthday made him a baby at Billy's fatal shooting.

Jameson and Bean tackled that crisis of truth in the chapter "Birth and Genealogy." It was a fix-up using hoaxer, William A. Tunstill's, 1988 book, *Billy the Kid and Me Were the Same*. (Pages 37-39) Tunstill's underhanded solution had been to claim that Geneva Pittmon's Oliver P. was not *their* "Brushy," who was Oliver L. And Oliver L. came from a different Roberts family, was born in Buffalo Gap, Texas, on December 31, 1859, and had the relatives "Brushy" had claimed.

Countering Pittmon's Roberts family Bible, was *another family Bible* from a **Martha Vada Roberts Heath**, and "genealogical papers" from a **Eulaine Haws** of Tyler, Texas. (Pages 90-91)

Tunstill's background as a Fort Worth junior high school principal, now operating a one-man "Western History Research Center" was in February 12, 1989's *Houston Chronicle's* "A Texas Town's Brush With Billy the Kid," was given by Don Cline calling "Brushy" "an imposter and windy old coot." The article was in C.L. Sonnichsen's papers, with Sonnichsen cited as "an Arizona historian, [who] wrote *Alias Billy the Kid*, a speculative book based on material Morrison had gathered from Brushy Bill."

HOAXING: It would take till 2015, 17 years after their book, for "Brushy's" Roberts family relative, Roy L. Haws, to publish his book, *Brushy Bill: Proof His claim to Be Billy the Kid Was a Hoax*, proving that that there were not two Roberts families. "Brushy" was his maternal half great-grand-uncle. <u>Martha Vada Roberts Heath</u> was his great-grandmother, and <u>Eulaine Haws</u> was his mother!

As discussed, the Roberts family had two branches from Henry Oliver "H.O." Roberts's two marriages. (See pages 168-170 above) <u>Martha Vada Roberts</u> was H.O.'s daughter from his first marriage to Caroline Dunn; so half-sister to "Brushy," from H.O.'s second marriage to Sara Elizabeth Ferguson. Martha Vada Roberts married Dudley Heath; their daughter, Vada Bell Heath, married D.L. Goff. Their daughter, <u>Eulaine</u>, married Leonard Haws becoming <u>Eulaine Haws</u>, Roy L. Haws's mother. (Haws, Page 137) And there was no separate family "Bible."

Haws revealed that Tunstill conned his mother, Eulaine. Haws wrote: "After reviewing numerous pieces of correspondence between Mr. Tunstill and my mother, I now realize that she mistakenly aided Mr. Tunstill by acknowledging the false genealogy provided her. In the early 1980's, Mr. Tunstill communicated often with her over a period of five years [and] successfully convinced my mother of the validity of his false Roberts family genealogical creations." (Haws, Page 41)

Haws presented Eulaine's notes on her first phone contact by Tunstill, who got her to confirm that she was Eulaine Haws, with grandmother Martha Roberts Heath. Tunstill then told her she was a cousin to Brushy Bill Roberts who was Billy the Kid. And she admitted that she helped Tunstill for five years, even designing his fake Roberts family tree which he used in a 1990 press release. (Haws, Pages 42, 45)

Haws accused *The Return of the Outlaw Billy the Kid* of perpetuating that fake genealogy. (Haws. Pages 39, 47)

Tunstill kept Sonnichsen in touch with his hoax. In Sonnichsen's papers is a letter to Tunstill from duped Eulaine Haws, dated February 5, 1983 in big childish script (with her underlinings). She wrote:

Dear Mr. Tunstill,
 Thanks for your picture. I have no idea where a picture of <u>Oliver Pleasant Roberts</u> might be found.

[AUTHOR'S NOTE: "Brushy" and team never used Oliver Pleasant, calling him William Henry. Eulaine accidentally revealed the single family tree of Geneva Pittmon!]

My brother has all of my mother's old pictures, but I don't remember any of grandmother's family. I will continue to try to find one, however. Just maybe!
 In searching through mother's (<u>Vada Heath</u> Emerson) book I came across these pages that might be of help to you. I'm glad I have been of a little help in <u>your search for the truth</u>. I knew my grandmother & grandfather (Martha Vada Roberts & ~~Monroe~~-Nathan Augustus Monroe Dudley Heath) very well. When I was young I lived a while with my grandfather and later I lived next door and helped tend to my grandmother until she died. I had the luck to meet Uncle Tom

[Roberts, "Brushy's" full brother from H.O. Roberts's second marriage] & Aunt Manty. They stayed with us for 2 weeks one summer. <u>I heard the story about one of my grandmother's brothers being lost for a long time. I never heard any connection with Billy The Kid,</u> however. It is all very interesting. <u>My mother always said there was a "criminal streak" in her family, but I always thought it was the Heath side.</u> My boys now laugh and ask, "What kin are we to Billy The Kid? What shall I tell them?

I teach school (4th grade) and believe I would really like a job like you have. More power to you! If I can ever be of more help, I will be happy to help.

*Sincerely,
Eulaine Haws*

Sonnichsen directly aided Tunstill's fakery by manipulatively writing, on March 23, 1987, to deceased Morrison's daughter, Barbara J. Kuckler [sic - Kuchler] - who, in 1981 had refused to share information with Tunstill:

I think this would be in accord with your father's wishes. As you know, he was anxious to have our book reprinted and that was why I agreed to let him renew the copyright in his own name. He never succeeded in finding a publisher but he did not want his research to be lost, and neither did I. If he were alive, I am sure he would be delighted to talk to Mr. Tunstill ...

Mr. Tunstill believes that your father was right in his assumptions about Brushy Bill and has followed the trail with considerable success. He says that everything brushy bill [sic] said checks out.

As your dad's friend and partner, I think my recommendations should carry some weight and I hope you or your daughter will reconsider.

Kuchler did not respond, so Tunstill wrote to Sonnichsen, proving Sonnichsen's six years of backing Tunstill's hoaxing: "No, I cannot "BEG" her to write me, as I feel she has no interest ... You did the best you could with the data Mr. Morrison furnished you. This fact I have related to you several times the past six years."

Jameson and Bean likely believed Tunstill's fake genealogy was real. They wrote: "The origin of the name Bonney has long eluded and confused Billy the Kid researchers ... Roberts had an answer, and his claims have subsequently been supported by a genealogy taken from the family Bible of the late Texas resident **Martha Vada Roberts Heath.** Heath was the daughter of Henry Oliver Roberts (brother to James Henry Roberts ["Brushy's claimed father]) and Caroline Dunn (sister to Mary Adeline Dunn). According to **genealogy records provided to the authors by Heath descendants and researcher William A. Tunstill,** William Henry Roberts' aunt Catherine Bonney (b. 1829) was the daughter of a man named Bonney (first name unknown) and an unnamed wife." (Pages 89-91)

This fakery shows Tunstill's fix-ups of names to match Billy's family. **[FIGURE: 14.]** So Jameson and Bean wrote: "Following the death of Bonney, the wife married William Dunn and the two begat Mary Adeline, Catherine Bonney's half-sister. The Heath genealogy shows Catherine Bonney first married a man named Michael McCarty, who died in the War Between the States. They had a son, Joseph. Catherine subsequently married William Antrim in Santa Fe in 1873." (Page 91)

Their diagram of the family tree is labeled: "Genealogy of William Henry Roberts (Billy the Kid) reconstructed from information **taken from the family Bible of the late Martha Vada Roberts Heath as well as from Heath family papers**." (Page 90) Its having the names **Bonney, McCarty, and Antrim** is claimed as the source of names used by Billy the Kid. (Page 91)

HOAXING: The dishonest fix-ups are corrected spelling of "Catherine" for Aunt Katherine Bonney; and adding Michael McCarty (last name of Billy's father), son Joseph (like real Billy's brother), and marriage to William Antrim, correctly in Santa Fe and in 1873 (to match Billy's mother's marriage). All this had been unknown to "Brushy;" and, in fact, disproved him by his ignorance.

THE FAKE MYSTERY BIBLE: It took 19 years - until Jameson's 2012 *Billy the Kid: The Lost Interviews* - for the tale of this fake "Heath Bible" to unfold; albeit altered. There, Jameson said Frederick Bean got it in "Brushy's" trunk from his step-grandson, Bill Allison.

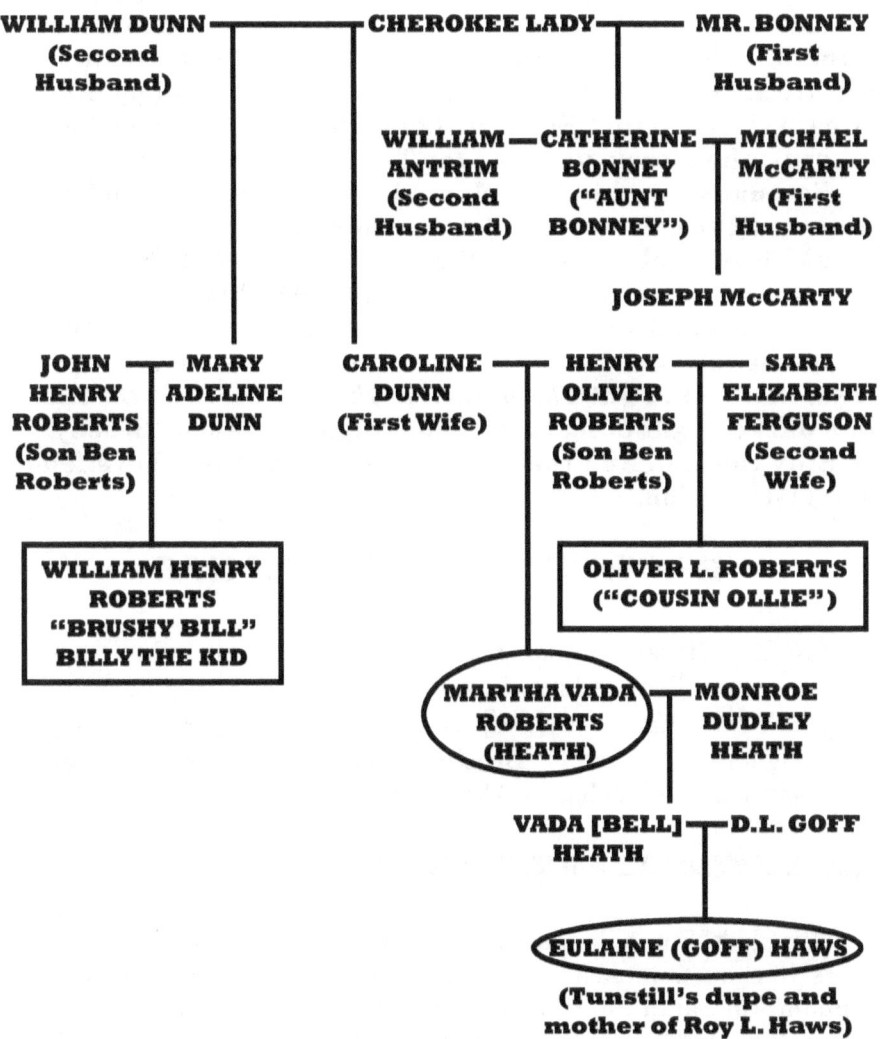

FIGURE: 14. Fake "Brushy Bill" family tree by William A. Tunstill; derived from notes for his 1988 *Billy the Kid and Me Were the Same,* and used by Frederick Bean and W.C. Jameson for the faked genealogy claiming Martha Vada Roberts Heath and Eulaine Haws were from a different Roberts family.

Importantly, "Brushy" never claimed having a family Bible. And he did not use "McCarty," unknown in his day. Sonnichsen's *Alias Billy the Kid* footnote merely stated: "Another story, current in Silver City, says that Billy the Kid was really named <u>McCartney</u>." (*Alias Billy the Kid*, Page 16)

And think about it. How could this Bible, with William Tunstill's <u>1988</u> fake genealogy, be found in <u>1989</u> by Bean in the trunk belonging to "Brushy," who died in <u>1950</u>? And "Heath descendant" Eulaine Haws did not give genealogy records; she merely vouched for Tunstill's fakery.

So unanswered is who planted or made-up this modern forgery (if it exists at all) in the claimed "Brushy"-Allison trunk? Frederick Bean was the trunk's alleged 1989 finder, and would have known about the 1987 Pittmon family Bible claim and the 1988 Tunstill family tree fakery. This leaves Bean and Jameson as the "Bible's" possible creators. If so, that would put *The Return of the Outlaw Billy the Kid* in a darker light of malicious hoaxing to advance "Brushy" as Billy the Kid. And their belief in "Brushy" may have felt like justification.

"BRUSHY" TALKS NONSENSE

Finally, "Brushy" talks, but not entirely in his own words. Jameson and Bean admit "inserting important historical and geographical references [for] clarity." (Page 37) Fortunately, their ignorance leaves "Brushy's" key errors and reveals Morrison's and Sonnichsen's *Alias Billy the Kid* fix-ups.

EARLY TRAVELS WITH "BRUSHY"

"Brushy's" Aunt Bonney, now Catherine instead of Katherine, takes him on unnamed travels until marrying Antrim - now as William - in Santa Fe in correct 1873, with moving to Silver City, where "Brushy" has a fake friendship with Jesse [sic] Evans. At age 12, for no reason, he leaves Silver City to return to his Roberts family for two years, being called "Kid" Roberts because he was small. Fleeing abusive father, "Wild Henry" Roberts father, he becomes "Texas Kid," travels the mid-west, works with Belle Starr, encounters Jesse James and the Youngers, and returns to Silver City for Aunt Bonney's dying. (Pages 39-41)

FAKING THE LINCOLN COUNTY PERIOD

"Brushy's confabulations, plus fix-ups to match real history, have him go, in 1877, to Arizona work *near* the Gila *River* [fixed-up from the Gila *Ranch*, but still wrong], where he encounters Jesse [sic] Evans and Lincoln County War outlaws. (Page 41)

He then crosses the Guadalupe Mountains on foot to Seven Rivers where he joins Jim and John Jones herding cattle for John Chisum, then works for Pete Maxwell at Bosque Redondo [actually the 1860's Apache and Navajo concentration camp before Lucien Maxwell bought it to found Fort Sumner]. (Page 41) Then he works for Frank Coe near the Ruidoso River, then for Jesse [sic] Evans, then for the Tunstall Ranch on the Feliz River; where a worker is Dave Rudabaugh [from 1880]! (Page 42)

For the Lincoln County War period, everything is wrong; but with the let-"Brushy"-speak policy, his ignorance is now shown. **And the dishonest fix-up is adding the Regulators**. (Page 45) The conflict is about supplying beef to the Mescalero Indian Reservation. Tunstall and McSween are partners owning a Lincoln store competing with Murphy and Dolan. They accused each other of cattle stealing, but the Murphy side was backed by Santa Fe Ring and by Sheriff Brady. (Pages 42-43)

"Brushy" stated: "I remember how it all started ... Lawyer McSween had been hired by the Murphy bunch to prosecute some of the Chisum cowboys for rustling cattle, but when he found out the Chisum boys were only taking back Chisum cows that were stolen by Murphy's men, [McSween] switched sides and joined up with John Tunstall. The Murphy-Dolan Ring operated a store where they sold supplies to the ranches, and then John Tunstall came along and opened his own store. That's where the trouble really started, between the two stores. McSween formed a partnership with Tunstall when he worked the case for Emil Fritz." (Page 43)

FAKERY: Everything is wrong. McSween represented the Fritz estate. He had no partnership with Tunstall. He had been a Murphy-Dolan lawyer, but for their mercantile business. The "Murphy bunch" were themselves stealing Chisum's cattle for their beef contracts. McSween was not working for Murphy and Dolan when Tunstall came; having quit in opposition to their corruption. The Fritz life

insurance money case was unrelated to Tunstall. It was being done by McSween before his arrival; but was made the Ring's embezzlement case to attack McSween and enable Tunstall's murder. There was no "Murphy-Dolan Ring;" though adding Ring was an attempted fix-up. "The House" was a front for T.B. Catron's Santa Fe Ring.

MAULING THE FRITZ INSURANCE POLICY CASE

Next proved is that "Brushy" had mauled the Emil Fritz life insurance money case far worse than Sonnichsen had revealed. "Brushy" stated: "There was a settlement when Fritz died and the Murphy-Dolan Store claimed that Fritz owed a bill of goods. McSween got the settlement money and the Murphy bunch claimed it, so they rode over to Mesilla and got a court order in the form of a **writ that would give them some of the goods in McSween's and Tunstall's store and a herd of blooded horses out at Tunstall's ranch.**" (Page 44)

FAKERY AND FIX-UP: Everything is wrong. It was an embezzlement case against McSween by Fritz's New Mexico heirs claiming he kept Emil Fritz's life insurance proceeds. Dolan made a *separate* case to get the money by claiming Fritz owed it to "The House;" but lost in probate court. The "writ" was for property attachment on McSween; with Tunstall falsely added as his partner, to attach his property too.

And "Brushy's" quote is a fixed-up from *Alias Billy the Kid*, in which he stated: "Tunstall had a herd of fine horses of his own. He decided that he would drive the horses over to Lincoln and surrender them until the case was cleared up." (*Alias Billy the Kid*, Page 25) And that was wrong too!

MAULING TUNSTALL'S MURDER

"Brushy" makes-up Tunstall's murder: "We sat on our horses off in some brush watching when Dolan and his boys rode up on Tunstall [and killed him] ... I swore that day at the funeral that I would make them pay for the dirty deed." (Pages 44-45)

FAKERY: Everything is wrong. And real Billy gave the facts in his Angel deposition. Billy and the others fled at the posse, and did not see the killing. And Billy was not at Tunstall's funeral, having been jailed by Sheriff Brady.

MAULING THE MORTON AND BAKER KILLING

To pursue Tunstall's killers, added are the Regulators, unknown to "Brushy." For the Morton and Baker killing, "Brushy" stated that, after capture, they went toward Lincoln, by "**the north road, over the mountains**." And he alone shoots them. (Page 47)

FAKERY: This is wrong. "Brushy" made-up the route from his Morrison Lincoln tour, thinking the east to west Capitan Mountains were a barrier to cross to the town. He was unaware of the military road, skirting the Capitan's. And all the Regulators shot escaping Morton and Baker.

MAULING THE BRADY KILLING

The Sheriff Brady killing uses "Brushy's" confabulation that he pursued Billy, for "cattle theft." The fix-up has "Brushy," as Billy, was arrested for that crime, and his "pearl-handled .44" confiscated, before he was released on bond. (Page 47)

FAKERY: Everything is wrong. Brady was not after Billy for cattle theft; the illegal arrest detained deputized Billy, Fred Waite, and Town Constable Atanacio Martinez to block their warrants on Tunstall's murderers; confiscated was a Winchester '73 carbine; and there was no bond.

The Brady ambush uses "Brushy's" made-up aiming for Billy Matthews, and going with Fred Waite [fixed-up from "Wayte"] to retrieve his "pearl-handled .44." And shooting Mathews [sic] hits them from "behind an adobe wall down the street." (Page 49)

FAKERY: This is all wrong. As discussed, "Brushy" had no idea why Brady was ambushed. There were no warrants on Billy. The gun taken was a Winchester '73 carbine. The Regulators were behind an adobe wall. Billy Matthews fired from the Cisneros house. And the motive was saving McSween from murder by Brady when he entered Lincoln later that day in anticipation of his Grand Jury Trial.

MAULING THE "BUCKSHOT" ROBERTS KILLING

More "Brushy" confabulations are revealed: that "Buckshot" Roberts "was worse than any of them;" that he raided San Patricio with "Murphy's gang;" that "Brushy" "shot it out" with "Buckshot;" and that the incident ended with Bowdre shooting "Buckshot." (Page 50)

FAKERY: This is all wrong. Missed is that "Buckshot," resisting arrest for his warrant as a Tunstall murder posseman, first shot at Bowdre, then was shot by Bowdre in self-defense. No one else shot him.

MAULING THE LINCOLN COUNTY WAR BATTLE

The Lincoln County War has fix-ups of adding "Regulators" to escort McSween into Lincoln; adding two more days to "Brushy's" three day War; and using "black," or no mentioned skin color, instead of "Brushy's" "[N-word]" soldiers. Added is "Brushy's" error that Mrs. McSween asked for aid from Dudley "[w]hile the house was burning." (Pages 52) And, for the escape, "Brushy" says the men crossed the *Peñasco* River - not the *Bonito* River. (Page 52)

FAKERY: Confirmed are "Brushy's" wrong confabulations. Fix-ups fake that he knew about the Regulators, knew length of the battle (though they are wrong too, since it was six days), and was not a crude racist. And "Brushy's" ignorant name-dropping is revealed by the crossing of the *Peñasco* - a 100 miles south of the crossed *Bonito* River! And there is still no idea why the battle was fought.

FAKING THE LEW WALLACE PERIOD

MAULING THE CHAPMAN MURDER

Huston Chapman's murder has grammatically impaired "Brushy's" "Me and Tom were standing right there and saw the whole thing." (Page 56) But what "Brushy" "saw," was: "**Mrs. McSween and her lawyer, Chapman**, walk up to Evans and Dolan and Campbell [and kill him]." (Page 56)

FAKERY AND FIX-UP: This is wrong. Chapman was alone. And real Billy testified to the correct scene, getting Dolan, Campbell, and Evans indicted!

And proved is the Morrison-Sonnichsen fix-up of this fatal Susan McSween gaffe! Their book's "Brushy" said: "When we came out of the saloon that night ... we run into Chapman, the lawyer for Mrs. McSween." (*Alias Billy the Kid*, Page 33) And Sonnichsen fixed-up "Brushy's" grammar to: "I was standing there with them and saw the whole thing." (*Alias Billy the Kid*, Page 33)

MAULING THE PARDON BARGAIN

For the Wallace pardon bargain, "Brushy's" confabulation had worse errors than revealed in *Alias Billy the Kid*. Jameson and Bean claimed: "Governor Wallace had **offered a thousand dollars to the outlaw** if he would turn himself in and testify about the illegal activities of the Dolan faction." (Page 56) "Brushy" was quoted: "One day a fellow brought word that Governor Wallace had offered a thousand dollars if I would come in and **give myself up for the murder of Chapman**." (Page 56) Then added was the requirement to "testify about the murder of Chapman." (Page 56) "Brushy" did not even know what indictments were to be annulled, making up that "[t]hey had fresh warrants out on us for rounding up [Chisum's] cattle [as owed payment]. (Page 57)

FAKERY AND FIX-UP: This is all wrong. Proved is that "Brushy" did not know the pardon bargain; even claiming that he, as Billy, was accused of Chapman's murder.

This proves complete fix-up by Sonnichsen-Morrison. Their book's quote was: "I was standing there with them and saw who killed [Chapmen] ... I heard that Governor Wallace had offered a thousand dollars for me if I would come and testify. I wrote him back that I would come in if he would annul those indictments against me." (*Alias Billy the* Kid, Page 33) So it was Sonnichsen-Morrison who had lifted from Billy's pardon plea letter of March 13, 1879, not "Brushy." It stated: "*I was present when Mr. Chapman was murderded and know who did it and if it were not for these indictments I would have made it clear before now. if it is in your power to Annully those indictments I hope you will do so so as to give me a chance to explain.*"

Next faced was Billy's letter to Wallace in light of "Brushy's" claimed "illiteracy." "Brushy" says: "I had a friend who spelled it out in a letter for me, what I wanted from Governor Wallace." (Pages 56-57)

FAKERY: This proves that "Brushy" had participated in the illiteracy scam by getting it onto the Morrison rehearsal tapes, while both he and Morrison knew, from his notebooks and letters, that he was not illiterate. But they knew he could not have written with Billy's beautiful script or articulateness, and had to do a cover-up.

Jameson and Bean hide "Brushy's" confabulation that the Wallace pardon meeting was at Juan Patrón's house in the daytime (*Alias Billy the* Kid, Page 34), instead of "Squire" Wilson's. Their "Brushy" quote proves their fix-up: "We shook hands on it before Tom and I **left Squire Wilson's that night**." (Page 58) [And real "Brushy" would have said: "Tom and me!"]

But they retain "Brushy's" ignorance of the deal: "The governor promised to pardon me if I would stand trial on my indictments in Lincoln. I also agreed to testify against Dudley at his court-martial hearing at Fort Stanton, and testify before the grand jury in the Chapman case." (Page 58)

FAKERY: Standing trial on indictments and testifying against Dudley were not part of the bargain.

Kept are "Brushy's" errors that Wallace promised to appoint his personal attorney, Ira Leonard, to defend Billy for indictment trials; that Leonard did not come; that Albert J. Fountain was appointed by the court; that the bargain was to stand trial in Lincoln; and that the change of venue meant Wallace reneged on the deal, causing "Brushy" to leave before testifying. (*Alias Billy the Kid*, Page 34)

But a fix-up has "Brushy" correctly testifying against Chapman's murderers. (Page 58)

FAKERY: "Brushy's" error of garbling the pardon's 1879 Grand Jury with the 1881 Mesilla trial with Fountain is confirmed, as are Jameson's and Bean's dishonest fix-ups.

Given is "Brushy's" quote for Wallace's broken promise at the time of the Grand Jury: "They pinned the whole affair [Brady shooting] on me because they wanted to get rid of Billy the Kid. The governor broke his word to me. I did what I promised I would do, but he didn't keep his promise to me." (Page 59)

FAKERY: Revealed is that "Brushy" mixed-up the 1879 pardon deal (with Billy's Lincoln County Grand Jury testimony), with Billy's letter of March 4, 1881 from the Santa Fe jail, about his upcoming Mesilla hanging trials, and needing the pardon. He wrote: "*I have done everything that I promised you I would, and you have done nothing that you promised me.*" And the Brady shooting defendants were all the Regulators, not just Billy.

MANGLING THE JIM CARLYLE KILLING

Unaware of why Billy was being pursued and of Secret Service participation, "Brushy" faked the "Murphy bunch" who had **deputized a "James Carlyle** ... to head up the posse and hunt us down" as cattle rustlers. Then he fabricated the Greathouse Ranch ambush, with Carlyle telling Billy: "I wear a badge and that's all I need to bring you in." Then Carlyle is killed in friendly fire. And "Brushy" flees to Las Vegas. (Pages 60-61)

FAKERY: In truth, Jim Carlyle, was just a White Oaks posseman, under actual deputy, Will Hudgens.

The rest was lifted from Billy's December 12, 1880 letter to Wallace about Carlyle's killing by fellow possemen.

But revealed is how "Brushy" built on his prompts. As to Carlyle, Billy had written: *"When I got up the next morning The house was Surrounded by an outfit led by one Carlyle, Who had come into the house and Demanded a Surrender."* "Brushy," reading *"led by one Carlyle,"* confabulated the quote about wearing a badge. And "Brushy's" made-up a flight to Las Vegas came from lifting that town name from that letter's quote: *"I noticed in the Las Vegas Gazette a piece which stated that, Billy "the" Kid ... was the captain of a Band of Outlaws.*

FAKING PAT GARRETT KNOWLEDGE

For the chapter "Enter Garrett," repeated is "Brushy's" faked of special knowledge as: "Garrett] had come over from Texas after he had shot his partner in an argument over some buffalo hides." (Page 61) Missed was the actual Joe Briscoe killing. And "Brushy" had no idea of why Garrett pursued Billy; guessing: "[W]ith this killing of Carlyle tacked on me, [Garrett] had an excuse to come after me." - when it was for the Brady, Hindman, and Roberts indictments. (Page 61)

FAKING BILLY'S CAPTURE AND JAILING

For Garrett's killing of Tom O'Folliard, "Brushy" falsely includes, in the tracking posse, a Deputy Tip [sic] McKinney, as O'Folliard's cousin. And after the capture, "Brushy" claimed he spoke with Tip [sic] McKinney about Tom O'Folliard's death. (Page 63)

FAKERY: Nothing is true. As discussed, Kip McKinney was not present at the ambush or Stinking Springs, and was not O'Folliard's cousin. But revealed is the Morrison-Sonnichsen fix-up of "Brushy's <u>Tip</u> McKinney to <u>Kip with</u>: "His cousin, Kip McKinney, one of Garrett's posse, wouldn't give Tom a drink." (*Alias Billy the Kid*, Page 37)

The Stinking Springs capture has a fix-up that Billy and his group were Regulators. (Pages 62-63)

FIX-UP ERROR: "Brushy" and team did not know about the Regulators. But adding them was wrong. The Regulators disbanded two years earlier. Besides Billy and Charlie Bowdre, the others were just petty criminals.

"Brushy" describes shot Bowdre's being mistaken for him: "Charlie wore a **big hat like mine**." (Page 62)

FUTURE FAKERY: As Jameson's hoaxing increased in later books, "big hat" would fix to "sombrero" to match Billy.

"Brushy's" post-capture scene at the Maxwell house had been worse than *Alias Billy the Kid* had let on. "Brushy" flubbed his Jim East prompt letter; saying: "Mrs. Maxwell asked them to unchain me from Rudabaugh so I **could go in the other room to be with the Indian girl** [for tintype exchange fable]!!!" (Page 63)

FIX-UP: Sonnichsen had faked "Brushy's" quote; writing: "After we went in the house, Mrs. Maxwell asked them to cut me loose from Rudabaugh <u>so I could go into another room with her daughter</u>." (*Alias Billy the Kid*, Page 38)

For the Santa Fe jailing, three letters to Governor Wallace are mentioned as unanswered - there were four; but Morrison had been unable to find the one of March 2, 1881.

MANGLING THE MESILLA TRIALS

For Mesilla, the "Buckshot" Roberts case is omitted.

FIX-UP: Oddly, this was the case Morrison and Sonnichsen used for "Brushy's" special knowledge as: "In April I pleaded to the federal indictment and it was thrown out of court. Judge Leonard represented me on this indictment. He got it thrown out by the judge." (Page 39) This leaves open that this quote was shockingly created by them for their book, since it was not in the transcript used by Jameson and Bean as being "Brushy's" actual quotes!!!

The Brady trial reproduces "Brushy's" errors but now includes "Brushy's" near verbatim repeat of his prompt source: "**Even Pat Garrett admitted to Miguel Otero that he doubted I ever fired a shot at Brady because it was more likely that I would have tried to get Matthews, since I hated him.**" (Page 67)

HOAXING REVEALED: Demonstrated is "Brushy's" use of prompt sources for rehearsal tapings. He was parroting a source footnote in *Alias Billy the Kid*, which quoted from Miguel Otero's fictionalized 1936 book, *The Real Billy the Kid*; and stated: "Pat Garrett told Miguel Otero that he 'doubted if the Kid had even fired at Brady because it was more likely that he would have tried to get Matthews, whom he hated." (*Alias Billy the Kid*, Page 28) Sonnichsen caught the obvious prompt, and edited it out for *Alias Billy the Kid*. But naïve Jameson and Bean put it back!

SILENCING "BRUSHY" FOR THE GREAT ESCAPE

For the Lincoln jailing and escape, Jameson and Bean just summarize, using the Severo Gallegos escape horse and rope fable. Fixed-up is Goss, to "Godfrey Gauss" [though it was Gottfried]; and Higinio Salazar is Ygenio. (Page 69)

Retained are errors of "Brushy" staying with Charlie Bowdre's widow [who had left Fort Sumner], and at "Yerby's," where Billy did not stay. (Page 72) Barney Mason is still wrongly Garrett's brother-in-law, though merely with a double marriage with Garrett. Celsa Gutierrez is still Garrett's sister-in-law, wanting to marry "Brushy;" and her husband, Saval, is still thought to be her brother because of the shared Gutierrez name. (Pages 71-72)

"BRUSHY'S" DEATH SCENE

To Jameson and Bean, the death scene was the holy grail. So their faith in "Brushy's" words, plus their historical ignorance, presented him in the raw, like at his Mabry hearing fiasco. These words would not be seen again as Jameson wised-up and fixed-up in his later "Brushy"-backing books. The sources for "Brushy's" words were listed as "notes in the possession of Roberts' stepgrandson Bill Allison, paraphrased from tapes and transcriptions made by Morrison, and from [*Alias Billy the Kid.*](Page 75); and "tape recordings made of William Henry Roberts' account of the event by William V. Morrison." (Page 101)

The inverted reality illogic was to present death scene events from Pat Garrett's and John W. Poe's books, with "Brushy's" totally different version, to prove that Garrett and Poe were lying!

The death scene is in three chapters: "William Henry Roberts' Story Part I: 1859-1881's" "Shooting in Fort Sumner" (Pages 72-73); "William Henry Roberts' Story Part II: 1881-1950" (Page 75); and "Quien es? A Reexamination of the Shooting in Fort Sumner." (Pages 101-133)

THE FIRST DEATH SCENE

In chapter "William Henry Roberts' Story Part I: 1859-1881's" "Shooting in Fort Sumner" (Pages 72-73), the brief death scene used *Alias Billy the Kid*, repeated its errors, and added fix-ups.

During the day "Brushy" and Barlow visit Sabal Gutierrez - with fatal brother-in-law-of-Garrett error. After going to a dance, "Brushy" and Barlow return to Fort Sumner, with two women, one now fixed-up to be Celsa Gutierrez - with the fatal girlfriend-of-"Brushy" error. The four stop at Jesus Silva's house, where Silva tells them Garrett is in town; and the women leave. Silva started to cook a meal for "Brushy" and Barlow, but claimed lack of meat. **As fix-up, inserted is Sonnichsen's back-porch prompt from Jack Fountain: Silva says there is "a side of beef hanging near Maxwell's bedroom."**

Barlow, shirtless [a weird addition] and in stockinged feet volunteered to get the meat. Fixing-up omitted "Brushy's" ignoble claim to have refused himself to walk into a trap. Pistol shots are heard by "Brushy" and Silva. "Brushy" rushes out to "Maxwell's backyard" to fire "pistols" at "shadows moving near the house." **"Brushy" is "easily seen in the moonlit yard**," and shot at by "the lawmen."

He is wounded, stumbles to an adobe house where a Mexican woman pulls him and staunches his head wound. Celsa enters to say "the sheriff and his men killed Billy Barlow and were passing the body off as the Kid's." In the morning, she brings him his horse. His friend, Frank Lobato, joins him, and they ride off.

A BRIEF POST-DEATH SCENE

In chapter "William Henry Roberts' Story Part II: 1881-1950," the post-death scene departure, reveals the authors' ignorance by getting the date of the day after the death scene very wrong: "After riding out of Fort Sumner in the early morning of 15 April 1881 [sic - !], the Kid, along with Frank Lobato, stayed in one sheep camp after another." (Page 75)

DEATH SCENE IN "BRUSHY'S" WORDS

The chapter "Quien es? A Reexamination of the Shooting in Fort Sumner" (Pages 101-133) was to let "Brushy's" words contradict Garrett's and Poe's books. Then misinformation was given to deny the Coroner's Jury Report and the burial. Finally, the authors did what they called an "Analysis."

"BRUSHY" VERSUS GARRETT AND POE

In bizarre juxtaposition, are given Garrett's and Poe's quotes from their books, and "Brushy's" entirely different confabulation. This is supposed to show that Garrett and Poe were lying, since, in the world of Jameson and Bean, "Brushy" knew the truth.

1) Garrett wrote that he saw a man, who turned out to be Billy, wearing a broad-brimmed hat, rise from the ground and proceed to the Maxwell house. Poe did not cite the scene.

"Brushy" stated: "It was a dark night, but there was enough moonlight to make shadows" when he and Billy Barlow went to Jesus Silva's house, because "Pat's wife was a sister to my friend, Saval Gutierrez" [the sister error], who warned him that Garrett was after him. (Pages 105-106)

2) Poe stated that he and McKinney stayed outside the house, while Garrett "entered Maxwell's room through the open door." Added is that Poe and McKinney could not recognize the Kid or Maxwell, though McKinney could, being a local hog raiser.

"Brushy" was quoted: "I had this crazy feeling that he hadn't ought to go, like someone whispered in my ear that ... there might be some trouble out there ... but he went out anyway." (Page 109)

3) Garrett, sitting beside Maxwell's pillow, is told Billy might have left the town. Poe said that about 30 seconds after Garrett entered a youth approached, and he thought him a guest. The youth pointed his revolver, asking, "Quien es?" and backed into

the door after Poe tried to reassure him. Garrett says the youth entered, holding a butcher knife and revolver, came close to the bed asking Maxwell "Quien es?" He fired two shots, the first killing Billy. Poe stated that he heard the youth ask Maxwell who the men were outside, then what was thought to be three shots, then gasps of someone dying. (Pages 110-111)

"Brushy" hearing a shot, says; "I pulled one of my .44's and ran through the door, trying to see in the dark. Two more shots came from the shadow beside the Maxwell house. I couldn't find a target to shoot at. It was too dark to see." (Page 112)

4) Garrett says Maxwell ran out and he told Poe and McKinney not to shoot him. Poe says he told Garrett that the Kid would not come there, and he shot the wrong man; though Garrett said he was sure. And when Maxwell ran out he almost shot him. (Page 112)

"Brushy" hearing a shot, says; "I ran toward Maxwell's back porch [got hit by a bullet in the jaw and] [f]rom the corner of my eye I saw a body lying on the back porch ... I knew it had to be Barlow. My partner had walked right into a trap, the trap had likely been set for me. [And it was impossible to check on Barlow because] [t]oo many guns were shooting at me." He ran to a back yard fence, was shot in the shoulder "with echo of gunshots all around," shot back, jumped the fence, landed in an ally, was shot across the forehead, kept running as he "heard them shouting to each other behind me [in an argument]," could not see because of pouring blood, a door opened in a shack because "all the shooting woke everybody up," and a Mexican woman pulled him inside. (Pages 113-114) [This showed ignorance of Fort Sumner's layout, back porch shooting of Barlow from Sonnichsen's prompt, and the massive gunfight that no one ever reported.]

5) Garrett wrote that he told his companions he shot the Kid, and told them it was not the wrong man. They examined the body shot above the heart, and examined his .41 caliber self-cocker. Poe said Maxwell got a candle and put it on the outside of the window so they could look in and saw a man on the floor. When they were inside the room, Billy was identified. (Pages 114-115)

"Brushy" says he watched the woman loading his Colts, asked the woman to get his horse, and blacked out. (Page 115)

6) Poe says soon after the shooting, native women asked for the body and took it to a carpenter's shop for a wake for the dead. And they stayed at Maxwell's for the night being afraid of being attacked by Billy's friends. (Pages 115-116)

"Brushy" says when he awoke, Celsa, "another of Saval's sisters .. [who] had been a sweetheart of mine" was there. [The sister and sweetheart errors.] Celsa says the attackers stayed in the house because "[t]hey are afraid to come out in the dark. They think some of your friends will shoot them." [She says that she sent for Frank Lobato to get him his horse.]"

"Brushy" "quotes" Celsa: "Pat is telling everyone you are dead. They took the body of your friend inside the house and they say it is yours. Some men from the town have already been sent to dig a grave by lantern light ... Your partner looks very much like you in the dark except for his beard ... Pat says they will bury the body in the morning. If the coffin is closed, who will guess that you are not inside it?" (Pages 116-117)

FIX-UPS: Jameson and Bean apparently created a pseudo-Celsa to mouth a new Barlow hoax (with a beard), when, in fact, real Celsa would not know anything. And, in *Alias Billy the Kid*, "Brushy" only used her to give the basic hoax: "Celsa came running in and said that they had killed Barlow and they were passing off his body as mine." (Page 50)

But this new omniscient Celsa adds taking the body inside to match the historical scene; and adds Barlow with a beard to match a fake corpse identification used by Jameson and Bean and discussed below. (See page 647)

When leaving with Lobato, "Brushy" says he decided that "Garrett realized his mistake and was **making a try at collecting the reward** that was out on me." (Pages 116-117)

FIX-UP: Added was "Brushy's" mouthing the conspiracy theory of hiding the corpse's identity. to get the reward. In *Alias Billy the Kid*, he just says: "I pushed my .44's into the scabbards and rode out of town with Lobato."

FUTURE HOAXING: Remember this technique of putting hoax fictions in character's mouth. In a later Jameson book, it would forge "Brushy's" as quoting another character to add information to match hoax claims and to present conspiracy theories. (See page 670 below)

ACCIDENTALLY LETTING "BRUSHY" REVEAL HIS HOAXBUSTING MOON PROBLEM

Jameson and Bean were too historically ignorant to protect "Brushy" from his most fatal error: his moon problem. So they inadvertently reveal what Morrison and Sonnichsen had worked so hard to hide by a fake chapter title and forged "Brushy" quotes.

The chapter "William Henry Roberts' Story Part I: 1859-1881," just naively uses *Alias Billy the Kid's* death scene summary to mindlessly repeat: "Billy, **easily seen in the moonlit yard**, immediately drew return fire from the lawmen." (Page 73)

But hoaxbusting treasure was in the chapter "Quien es? A Reexamination of the Shooting in Fort Sumner" (Pages 101-133) where "Brushy" finally speaks. **And he says July 14, 1881's night was dark!** But, in reality, the near-full moon, hovering at the horizon, made it light as day!

Incriminatingly, "Brushy's" dark night was **not in *Alias Billy the Kid*.** Sonnichsen had faked quoting "Brushy" in the chapter he titled "Death **By Moonlight**." It stated: "I ran through the gate into Maxwell's back yard **in the bright moonlight**." (*Alias Billy the Kid*, Page 49)

So Jameson and Bean first naively copied that as "Brushy" being "**easily seen in the moonlit yard**." (Page 73) And, quoting from Poe's book, they kept the moonlight: "**Under a full moon, according to Poe**, they waited until eleven o'clock." (Page 104)

But, unaware of the moon's significance, they left it untampered when quoting "Brushy's" own transcript: "[After hearing the shot from Pete Maxwell's place] I pulled one of my .44's and ran through the door, **trying to see in the dark**. Two more shots came from the shadow beside the Maxwell house. **I couldn't find a target. It was too dark to see**." (Page 112) "Brushy" stuck to darkness with: "emptying my six-shooter at the shadow where I saw the muzzleflash." (Page 113) He had the Celsa character say his attackers were: "**Inside the Maxwell house ... They are afraid to come out in the dark. They think some of your friends will shoot them**." (Page 116) And he used darkness to explain Barlow's killing: "Garrett knew by now that he'd **killed the wrong man in the dark**." (Page 117) So he had Celsa say: "[T]hey say [the body] is yours ...**Your partner looks very much like you in the dark**." (Page-117)

CRACKING THE "BRUSHY BILL" IMPOSTER HOAX: "Brushy's" dark night moon error proved that he was not in Fort Sumner on the night of July 14, 1881, and that Sonnichsen-Morrison had dishonestly fixed-up his fatal error for their hoax. And by Jameson's next books, he too would add bright moonlight, proving his descent to hoaxer.

JAMESON AND BEAN TALK NONSENSE

Jameson and Bean next take on the impassable hurdles.

JAMESON-BEAN VS CORONER'S JURY REPORT

Jameson and Bean lie that Justice of the Peace Alejandro Segura "asked Milnor Rudolph [sic] to assemble a coroner's jury and assume the role of foreman." (Page 118)

WRONG: Segura appointed the jurymen, as he wrote in the Coroner's Jury Report: "On this 15th day of July, A.D. 1881, I, the undersigned, Justice of the Peace ... received information that a murder had taken place in Fort Sumner ... and immediately ... proceeded to the said place and named Milnor Rudolph, Jose Silva, Antonio Saavedra, Pedro Antonio Lucero, Lorenzo Jaramillo and Sabal Gutierres a jury to investigate the case."

They claim that the "body still lay on the floor" according to Charles Frederick Rudulph. (Page 118)

WRONG: Charles Frederick Rudulph was Milnor Rudulph's son, who claimed he came along when Milnor was on the Coroner's Jury. He then wrote *Los Billitos: The Story of Billy the Kid and his Gang*," published in 1980.

Charles Frederick did not say that the body was on the floor for the coroner's jury. His book states: "[The Coroner's Jurymen] met over the Kid's body and with no argument or dissent unanimously agreed on the following report given below. [The Coroner's Jury Report was provided in English.]" (Rudulph, Pages 252-253)]

Missed is that his book confirmed that Billy's body was identified by Garrett, Peter Maxwell, Deluvina Maxwell, Luz Maxwell, townspeople, and the coroner's jury – whom he calls "six honorable men [who] affixed their signatures and

marks to the post mortem of William Bonney, 'Billy the Kid.'"
(Rudulph, Pages 253-254)

Jameson and Bean then repeat the Morrison-Sonnichsen fakery, writing: "For reasons never completely explained, this coroner's jury report never made it into the official records of San Miguel County." (Page 118)

WRONG: This was Morrison's scam of searching for the Report in wrong locations to claim it did not exist. (See pages 40-43 above)

JAMESON-BEAN VS BURIAL

Jameson and Bean write merely that "the body of the man killed by Sheriff Pat Garrett was prepared and dressed [for burial]," hiding that it was in the night time wake where Billy was further identified by townspeople. Described is burial beside Tom O'Folliard and Charles Bowdre. (Pages 118-119)

Then they make a new hoax: that the body did not match Billy. Claiming Billy's **obituary** appeared, on July 28th [sic] in the Silver City *Grant County Herald*, as "Exit the Kid," they quote its "editor" S.M. Ashenfelter: "Since his escape from the Lincoln County jail [the Kid] has allowed his beard to grow, and has stained his skin brown to look like a Mexican." (Page 119)

FAKERY: This hoax came from C.L. Sonnichsen, who, behind-the-scenes, coached "Brushy"-backers. And the Ashenfelter source was typical of the junk he used as "proofs." Jameson's and Bean's Bibliography cites their June 25, 1991 interview with him in Oklahoma City, Oklahoma, when he apparently gave them this concoction.

In fact, Singleton M. Ashenfelter, owner of *The New Southwest and Grant County Herald*, did not write an obituary, but merely a dime novel-style article on July 23, 1881 titled "Exit 'The Kid: The Fugitive Murderer Hunted Down and Killed by Sheriff Garrett." Ashenfelter, in Silver City, was 250 miles from the burial, so he faked his swarthy, bearded, "outlaw" Billy for his public. (The Billy the Kid tintype was then unknown.) Ignorant, he even said the shooting was "near" Fort Sumner, the Deputy was John W. Coe, and Billy was 24! He lifted Pat Garrett's quotes from July 23, 1881's Las Cruces *Rio Grande Republican's* "Kid the Killer Killed, Wm. Bonney alias

Antrim, alias Billy the Kid, Fatally Meets Pat Garrett, the Lincoln County Sheriff." To be noted is that Ashenfelter was a Ringite, which prejudiced his Lincoln County War portrayal. His lurid article stated:

The vulgar murderer and desperado known as "Billy the Kid" has met his just deserts at last. He was shot and killed in the house of Pete Maxwell, <u>near Fort Sumner</u> [wrong], at midnight Thursday, the 14th instant, by Sheriff Pat Garrett, of Lincoln County. He was a native of New York City, of Irish Parentage, and his real name was William McCarthy [wrong], although he had been known as Henry Antrim, Billy Bonney, and other aliases. He lived in this city for some years with his mother, Mrs. Antrim, who has since died, and began his criminal life by acts of petty larceny. He escaped from jail here and grew from bad to worse. He was mixed up in the Lincoln County war, and was one of the most fearless of all those who participated in that trouble. One incident that still can be recalled by many is an index to his dare-devil career, was his escape from the McSween mansion in Lincoln during the Lincoln War. The general facts of his desperate career are well-known, and will not be recounted here. Despite the glamour or romance thrown around his dare-devil life by sensation writers, the fact is he was a low down vulgar cut-throat, with probably not one redeeming quality. The circumstances of his "taking oil" were as follows: He had openly threatened Sheriff Pat Garrett's life. Hearing of his whereabouts the Sheriff with John W. Coe and Kip McKinney proceeded to his rendezvous. At midnight Garrett found the desperado's bed empty, the moonlight streaming through the open door and windows. After posting Coe and McKinney as guards outside Garrett walked into the room. He saw Mr. Maxwell lying on the bed in the S.E. corner of the room and Garrett took a seat at the head of the bed. He asked Mr. Maxwell if he knew the whereabouts of the man he was searching for. Mr. Maxwell informed him that he was in the neighborhood. At the left of the bed, on the same side as the door, was a window. The moonlight streamed in through the open window, but by sitting at the head of the bed Garrett was able to partially hide himself in the shadow. He was talking with Mr. Maxwell when someone came to the door. The figure advanced to the bed with a butcher knife in his hand. Garrett did not recognize the midnight visitor, who kept on advancing till he stood at Mr. Maxwell's bedside and near by Garrett. He put his hand on the supposed sleeper to rouse him, and on Maxwell's rising up he asked, having noticed the strange figure, "who is that!" The Sheriff knew the voice instantly, but not till then did he have any idea that the fellow whom he was after was so near by. Receiving no answer to his query, Billy jumped away from the bed, at the same time drawing his self-cocking revolver. He had not got far from the bed when Garrett, who is always cool, no matter how trying the circumstances, rose up and fired. The shot struck "the Kid" in the heart and he fell on his back, a dead man.

<u>Since his escape from Lincoln jail he had allowed his beard to grow, and had stained his skin to look like a Mexican.</u> He had been to the house of a friend that night for meat, and that explains the knife in his hand. He was comely in appearance, about 5 ft. 7 1/2 in. tall, slight, muscular figure, blue eyes, that had a searching look, and mirrored in their piercing intensity, when he was aroused, the devilish spirit within him. The story that he killed "his first man" for insulting his mother is a fabrication. Although only in his twenty-fourth year he had been guilty of many murders.

Also, Jameson and Bean forgot that this hoax contradicted "Brushy's" construct that Barlow looked just like him (as beardless and fair), so was shot as him.

LIFE AFTER BILLY'S DEATH

For "Brushy's" life after Billy's death, "Brushy's" quotes are abandoned, and given our *Alias Billy the Kid's* peripatetic travels and Wild West name-dropping. (Pages 76-77)

The Mabry pardon fiasco is rationalized as "Brushy" being rattled by reporters, being scared by historical family members and alleged armed guards; being old; and being rejected because his answers "conflicted with accepted notions." (Page 83) Recycling Morrison's original double-talk, they claim the pardon was refused "without a legal hearing." (Page 84)

The chapter "Tracking William Henry Roberts" tries to validate the tales, but they conclude that his aliases made the quest impossible. (Page 93) They conclude slyly: "[W]e were unable to disprove any of Roberts' contentions." (Page 100)

ALLEGED ANALYSES

Jameson and Bean fake investigating in chapters, "Quien es? A Reexamination of the Shooting in Fort Sumner," (Pages 101-133) and "Evidence For and Against William Henry Roberts as Billy the Kid." (Pages 135-163).

FAKING DEATH SCENE ANALYSIS

In chapter, "Quien es? A Reexamination of the Shooting in Fort Sumner," (Pages 119-133), Jameson and Bean dishonestly state that the death scene's only witnesses were Pat Garrett and Pete Maxwell; and "Maxwell ... contributed very little relative to describing what actually took place in the room." (Page 119)

FAKERY: Hidden is Maxwell's Coroner's Jury Report witness statement: "'I being in my bed in my room, at about midnight on the 14th day of July, Pat F. Garrett came into my room and sat down. William Bonney came in and got close to my bed with a gun in his hand and asked me "who is it" and then Pat F. Garrett fired two shots at the said William Bonney and the said William Bonney fell near my fire place and I went out of the room and when I came in again about three or four minutes after the shots the said William Bonney was dead.' "

Then, faked are absurd discrepancies between Garrett's and Poe's accounts, to claim Billy was never shot. (Pages 119-125)

1) Garrett describes the figure in the orchard, Poe does not.

2) Garrett heard Billy speak in the peach orchard **[he said he could not make out the voices]**, and heard him speak in the room, so this was a contradiction about voices.

3) Garrett claimed a man sprang to the door; Poe said they backed in **[which was a matter of perspective, because part of the wall blocked Poe's vision of the door.]**

4) Garrett did not recognize Billy in the dark room, but Maxwell did. **[Garrett hesitated just 30 seconds before shooting him dead.]**

5) Garrett heard Billy was there in a letter from a local rancher, but Poe said Garrett did not believe Billy was around. **[That meant Garrett could not believe it.]**

6) Poe doubted killing of the right man. **[The body subsequently had profuse identifications.]**

7) Poe said that through the lit window, he saw the body on its back; but Miguel Otero's book, *The Real Billy the Kid*, had Jesus Silva's say the body was face down. **[Otero, writing fiction, published the book in 1936, 55 years after the event.]**

8) Poe said the body was taken to the carpenter's shop, but Charles Frederick Rudulph said the Coroner's jury met the next morning "with the body still lying on the floor." **[This is a lie. His book stated: "[The Jurymen] <u>met over the Kid's body</u> and with no argument or dissent unanimously agreed on the following report given below." (Rudulph, Pages 252-253)]**

9) Garrett and Poe said Billy had a .41 caliber pistol, when he used .44's. **[This uses Morrison's fakery. The answer was that a .41 Colt Thunderer was a six-chambered hide-away gun. Billy was not expecting an ambush in the safe town.]**

10) If the man said "Quien es?" how could he be Billy Barlow? **[Sonnichsen's lying input to Jameson and Bean is revealed by their stating he said Barlow was "half Mexican," apparently misstating the Ashenfelter article, "Exit the Kid," which only had a tale of Billy in a Mexican disguise.]**

11) If Billy was Anglo, why would he speak to Maxwell in Spanish? **[It was his disguise, and both were bi-lingual.]**

12) Why was Billy asking questions instead of shooting? **[Because he had no idea it was an ambush.]**

13) Cited is Sonnichsen's April 15, 1944 interview quoting Jack Fountain about the back porch shooting. **[As discussed, Jack's malarkey was built on thinking the side of beef was beside Maxwell's door. And his given quote shows his pure fiction, even claiming that Pat Garrett told him the reward on Billy was $10,000! And Jameson and Bean omit that he did not doubt that the victim was Billy.]**

FAKING EVIDENCE THAT "BRUSHY" WAS BILLY

In "Evidence For and Against William Henry Roberts as Billy the Kid" (Pages 135-163), Jameson and Bean try to mimic a real investigation as to "Brushy's" being Billy the Kid by claiming physical similarities, "Brushy's" "revelations," anecdotal evidence, and identification Affidavits. But they first conclude: "There exists a great deal of evidence that leads to conclusion for some that William Henry Roberts was, in fact, Billy the Kid." (Page 135) [But even the "William Henry" was fake!]

FAKING PHYSICAL SIMILARITIES

Parroted are *Alias Billy the Kid's* fake "physical similarities."

Cited that "Dewitt Travis in an affidavit of identification" said that "Brushy" had "two protruding front teeth" "until they were removed by a Gladewater, Texas, dentist. (Page 136)

MISSTATEMENT: The Travis Affidavit in *Alias Billy the Kid* stated: "["Brushy" had peculiarly shaped teeth with two large teeth protruding outward from under the lower lip and a large tusk on each side of his upper jaw [which were extracted in Gladewater, Texas]." (*Alias Billy the Kid*, Page 124) But it appears that Morrison added the "two large teeth protruding outward from under the lower lip" to match Billy.

In actuality, Travis wrote to Morrison on January 25, 1951, while Morrison was writing that Affidavit: "About Bill's teeth – the two eye teeth were so very big until they looked like tushes [sic – tusks], they bothered him an awful lot so he had a Dr. Cruz in glade water [sic] take them out." So Travis really said that "Brushy" had abnormal canine teeth.

Claimed is that "Brushy's" prominent ears matched Billy's [though that came from the tintype's right ear being pushed out by the tilted hat brim]. (Page 136) They remove Morrison's gaffe about a funny "left" ear [from the tintype's right one]. (Page 136)

FAKING "BRUSHY'S" "REVELATIONS"

True-believers, Jameson and Bean then presented alleged examples of "Brushy's" special knowledge "revelations."

First, they call "Brushy" a "semiliterate [who] could barely read" (Page 137); and repeat his confabulation: "I had a friend who spelled it out in a letter for me, what I wanted from Governor Wallace." (Pages 56-57) But aware of his notebooks and letter to Morrison from *Alias Billy the Kid*, they add that he had "barely legible scrawl." (Page 137) **[But that made him literate and not a match for Billy's elegant handwriting!]**

For evidence were "Brushy's" claims about Lincoln, knowledge of "shooting black soldiers," citing the federal versus territorial indictment for the Mesilla trial, and the Affidavits; along with dishonest fix-ups in attempt to hide his errors and racism.

LINCOLN TRIP REVELATIONS

Lincoln "revelations" are about just two sites in that town: the old Lincoln County courthouse-jail and the McSween house.

FAKING THE COURTHOUSE-JAIL

For the courthouse-jail, given is "Brushy's" report of well-known later addition of stairs to the second-story balcony. (Page 138) Repeated is his wrong location of the armory as opposite Garrett's office (now with a diagram!). (Pages 138, 141) For the escape, is "Brushy's" shackle-slipping and striking Deputy Bell. (Pages 146-147) Given is the Severo-Gallegos-Kid-helping-escape fable (Page 150); and "Brushy's" parroting of Morrison's interview with Yginio Salazar's adopted daughter who told him that Yginio cut-off Billy's shackles. (Page 151) So there are no revelations.

FAKING THE McSWEEN HOUSE

For McSween house, claimed is: "Roberts' intimacy with the layout of the McSween house and yard could only have come from personal experience." (Page 144) To be noted is that after the Lincoln County War Battle arson, the house is gone.

"Brushy" claimed a kitchen window, a corral fence, and a woodpile; which is called "amazing." (Page 143)

Added are his fake attacking "Murphy men ... just across the river" - where no attackers were. (Page 142) Then there his parroting of Billy's Dudley Court of Inquiry testimony about escaping people (Page 145) - but missing Billy's key testimony of shooting white soldiers. There were no revelations.

FAKING THE SHOOTING BLACK SOLDIERS

For the escape, "Brushy's" racism is fixed-up: "We opened the back door and looked out just as **Bob Beckwith and some of them [N-word]s started to come in**" (*Alias Billy the Kid*, Page 31) to: "We opened the back door and looked out just as **Bob Beckwith with some of those soldiers tried to rush us.**" (Page 142)

Then ignorant Jameson and Bean gush that Fort Stanton's soldiers were black was unknown until "Brushy" reported it. (Page 144) They missed "Brushy's" prompt source: *The Saga of Billy the Kid*. It stated: "Two squadrons of Negro cavalry, with ... Colonel Dudley in command, were soon moving at double-quick on the road to Lincoln." (Burns, Page 122) And they were unaware that

"Brushy" missed that black soldiers rode horses, missed white infantrymen and officers, a Gatling gun, and a howitzer cannon; and thought that the black soldiers fired from the south foothills. There were no revelations.

FAKE REVELATION OF FEDERAL VERSUS TERRITORIAL INDICTMENTS

Repeated is "Brushy's" parroting of Billy's April 15, 1881 letter to Attorney Edgar Caypless about his federal indictment thrown out of court, then being tried for his Territorial charge. (Page 145) This is no revelation.

FAKE REVELATION OF THE JIM CARLYLE KILLING

Repeated is "Brushy's" parroting of Billy's December 12, 1880 letter to Lew Wallace about the Jim Carlyle killing. (Page 148) There is no revelation.

FAKE REVELATION OF THE INDIAN GIRL AND SCARF

Repeated is "Brushy's" confabulation about trading the Billy the Kid tintype for a scarf from an Indian girl at the Maxwell house (Page 148) - as lifted from Walter Noble Burns's fable in his 1926 *The Saga of Billy the Kid*. This is no revelation.

FAKE EVIDENCE FROM ANECDOTES

Anecdotes, or hearsay, are not evidence in law or historical investigation. But Jameson and Bean present an absurd list of them, thinking they link "Brushy" to Billy; as follows:

1) Once, on a Hico, Texas, street, a mother called to her child, "Billy!" And Roberts turned. (Page 152) **[Jameson and Bean forgot that *they and he* claimed his name was both "Brushy Bill" and "*William* Henry"!]**

2) In 1990, the grandson of a Pinkerton detective, said, in 1945, his grandfather called out to "Brushy": "Bonnie [sic] ... you're under arrest." (Pages 153-154) **[This proves that in 1945 there were at least two Texas eccentrics.]**

3) In 1983, a Texan wrote a letter saying that Garrett's blind daughter told him Pat did not shoot Billy. (Page 154) **[This is why hearsay is meaningless.]**

4) Yginio Salazar is cited as believing Billy was not killed. (Page 154) That is true. But he had no first-hand knowledge. His belief came from a visit he got years later from a teacher from

Mexico - not "Brushy." That unnamed man disappeared. By then, Yginio was an unreliable morphine addict, from pain of the two, Lincoln County War bullets, still in his back.

5) In 1948, someone told someone in Las Cruces, New Mexico, that Billy was not shot by Garrett, because he saw him in Mexico in 1914. He knew Billy, he said, when they lived in Silver City from 1868 to 1871. (Page 155) **[Billy lived in Silver City from 1873 to 1875.]**

FAKE AFFIDAVITS THAT "BRUSHY" WAS BILLY

Alias Billy the Kid's five Affidavits by non-historical people are repeated, and are still meaningless. (Pages 155-161)

IGNORING CONTRARY EVIDENCE

Jameson and Bean end with "Evidence Against William Henry Roberts as Billy the Kid," and claim: "The only available evidence for Billy the Kid being shot and killed in Fort Sumner on 14 April 1881 is the word of Pat Garrett." (Page 161) Their foregone conclusion is: "[T]he case "for Roberts being Billy the Kid is considerably stronger than the case against." (Page 162)

FAKE "FORENSIC" PHOTO-COMPARISON

Jameson's and Bean's jewel in their crown for "Brushy" was proving he was Billy the Kid with modern science. To them, that meant their 1990 "Photo-Comparison Study" using "computer technology" - which, they enthused, replicated the CIA, FBI, Interpol, and Scotland yard - to compare a photos of "Brushy" from *Alias Billy the Kid* to the correctly named Dedrick-Upham Billy the Kid tintype. (Page 165) The resulting silly study would ultimately yield Jameson's empty boast, in a 2003 *True West* magazine article about "Brushy" being Billy, that "history needed to be rewritten." (See page 483 below) For it, they used a Dr. Scott T. Acton, at the Department of Electrical and Computer Engineering and the Laboratory for Vision Systems and Advanced Graphic Laboratory at the University of Texas; and claimed no expertise for him.

THE HERITAGE TRUST TINTYPE STUDY

Jameson and Bean had a starting-gate problem. A year before their study, one was done by the Lincoln County Heritage Trust: the Lincoln, New Mexico, museum which, at that time, housed the Billy the Kid tintype. It was headed by world-famous forensic anthropologist, Clyde Snow, along with a Thomas G. Kyle of the Los Alamos National Laboratory, and historical experts. The tintype was compared to over 150 alleged photographs of Billy the Kid, with a control of 100 photographs of random men.

The Heritage Trust study was reported in *The Dallas Morning News* on April 22, 1990 by a Michael Haederle as "Experts in photographic studies unable to picture Hico man as Billy the Kid." In C.L. Sonnichsen's papers, it stated:

For 40 years, a few dedicated amateur historians have argued that the legendary Billy the Kid really didn't die at the hands of Pat Garrett in 1881 in Fort Sumner, N.M.

Instead, they said, the Kid lived out his life under another name – Ollie L. "Brushy Bill" Roberts – and died of a heart attack in the Central Texas town of Hico 69 years after the Fort Sumner shooting.

It would be a great story, at least around Hico, if true.

It's not, according to new studies.

Forensic experts, basing their finding on the first results of a pair of sophisticated computer studies, have concluded that "there isn't a very good chance Brushy Bill was Billy the Kid," said Bob Hart, director of the Lincoln County Heritage Trust.

As to be expected, die-hard believers in the Brushy Bill story scoff at the ... findings ...

The Heritage Trust commissioned the studies in 1988, seeking to authenticate nearly 30 photographs said to be of Billy the Kid, as well as to separate fact from fiction regarding one of the Old West's most enduring figures.

The Brushy Bill claim, which has been outlined in several books, has been especially persistent, Mr. Hart said. "Traditional historians had not been able to quiet the claims of the Brushy Bill advocates," he said.

The scientific evidence, in his opinion, should lay those claims to rest ...

[T]he trust-commissioned computer studies of old photographs of Brushy Bill and the Kid found few facial similarities between the two men. In fact, one study showed that 40 convicted felons chosen at random from the Chicago Police Department files looked more like Billy the Kid than did Brushy Bill, Mr. Hart said ...

Clyde Snow, a Norman, Okla., forensic anthropologist, who has been a consultant to the studies, concluded that there was virtually no chance Brushy Bill could have been the Kid, Mr. Hart said.

Meanwhile, Thomas Kyle, a photo enhancement specialist at the Los Alamos National Laboratory, conducted his study of the Brushy Bill and Billy the Kid photos and came to a similar conclusion. Dr. Kyle found the Kid's chin and ears were quite different from Brushy Bill's, making it unlikely they were the same person.

Thomas G. Kyle himself published "Computers, Billy the Kid, and Brushy Bill: The Verdict is In" in July, 1990's *True West* magazine. He wrote:

> The Lincoln County Heritage Trust [LCHT], of Lincoln, New Mexico, is using the only known photograph of Billy the Kid to determine the authenticity of a stack of other pictures said to be of Billy. Computers are playing a role in resolving decades-old debates about some of those photographs. I was asked to help in the computer studies have made new discoveries about the LCHT photograph. **Comparisons of that photo with one of Brushy Bill Roberts, who claimed to be Billy the Kid, have demonstrated that Roberts and the Kid were two different people** ...
>
> The accompanying array of photos illustrates some differences in the faces of Billy the Kid and Brushy Bill Roberts ... Lines between the pupils of Billy's and Brushy's eyes demonstrate ... Brushy's eyes are almost level with the top of his ears. Billy's eyes are well above the top of his ears ...
>
> The horizontal line that passes just under Brushy's nose passes well below Billy's nose. Such a significant difference cannot be explained by the tilt of Billy's head ...
>
> Two identical white boxes are drawn on Billy's and Brushy's chins. The top of the box is positioned at the horizontal dip in the chin ... and low enough to be unaffected by Brushy's missing teeth. **The box was sized to extend down to the bottom of Billy's chin. The same box comes far below Brushy's chin because Brushy's chin is smaller. The gap is almost large enough to show Brushy's Adam's apple. That proves that the chins are different and that Brushy Bill Roberts and Billy the Kid were not the same person.**
>
> **The ears have even greater differences than the chins**. With age, the lobes of the ear become larger, but the rest of the ear remains unchanged ... **Brushy's ears were somewhat triangular while Billy's were round to square, a second proof that they were different people**.
>
> Other discrepancies can be found between the faces, but

they are not so striking as the differences between the chin and the ears ... [I]f one fellow had three eyes and the other two, there would be little need to look for other disparities before deciding they were different people.

Jameson and Bean, of course, opposed this study. They attacked Kyle as in an "economic" conspiracy to maintain the historical "status quo." And they got mean: saying that, for him, the whole thing had been "more like a hobby." Finally, they declared that ears should not have been used! (Page 166-172)

THE ACTON STUDY

Jameson and Bean enthuse about Dr. Scott Acton's "state of the art facilities," and inventory his equipment. Thus, revealed is his old computer system from 1972 and 1976, and unimpressive 92% success rate. And Acton is cited bizarrely as consulting with his school's "Psychology Department [to determine a] method for scientific comparison of facial structure!" (Page 174)

Jameson and Bean give Acton's quote that "the similarity between the facial structure of Roberts and the man in the ... tintype is indeed amazing." (Page 178) What was amazing, was how he reached his conclusion.

His clowning began with "mouths." He used old "Brushy's" death-year picture (*Alias Billy the Kid*, Page 173); though tintype Billy was about 20, and *Alias Billy the Kid* had young "Brushy" photos (which looked nothing like Billy). Acton's chosen "Brushy" had a fish-tail mustache *covering his mouth*! Nevertheless, Acton's "mouth breadth" measurements, give tintype Billy an "80" and "Brushy" an "82." (Page 175) But Billy's "mouth" was also fake, since Acton did a "restoration of the Dedrick-Upham photograph of Billy the Kid." (Page 177) It has black blemishes on the mouth. Acton used them to stretch real Billy's small mouth. And Acton's "Brushy" "restoration" used his mustache shadow to fake a long straight mouth (since none was visible). (Page 176) These faked mouths gave his "amazing" "80 to 82" match!

Wisely, Scott Acton abided by the "Jameson-Bean law," and omitted "Brushy's" ears, unlike Billy's. Though, in Acton's doctored picture, Billy's missing left ear is added, along with added rolled rims on both ears - to emulate "Brushy's!"

This leaves one with an opinion of Dr. Scott Acton, identical to Jameson's and Bean's opinion of Thomas Kyle.

But they conclude that Acton proved "a very close match" between "Brushy" and Billy. (Page 179)

THE ACTON REPORT LETTER

Frederick Bean kept C.L. Sonnichsen informed about the Scott Acton study, since a report dated August 30, 1990 from Acton to Bean is in Sonnichsen's collected papers. Illustrated is Acton's fakery, inadequacy, and willful intent to contradict the Lincoln County Heritage Trust (which he calls "LCHT). Acton wrote:

> In your letter you addressed two problems, the buck teeth and the round ears ... The young Roberts is definitely closing his mouth tightly, and the old Roberts is definitely toothless. The ears remain a mystery ... [T]he poor quality and dubious history of the LCHT tintype (was it doctored?) **[note the ignorance of the excellent provenance and the fake accusation of doctoring, which he himself did]** make me doubt the ear difference as absolute proof that O.L. was not Billy the Kid.
>
> We will concentrate on facial features ...
>
> The final and most important experiment is the computerized pattern recognition system. The fundamental research and design of the system used was by Townes (1976) and Kaya, Kobayashi (1972). Their systems are proven for a 92% success rate in face recognition. **[Confirmed are the old programs.]**
>
> Questions:
>
> How can we account for the dental problems of Billy the Kid, present in both the LCHT photo and the newspaper description? **[Apparently Acton is referring to the December 27, 1880 *Las Vegas Daily Gazette* article by Lucius "Lute" Wilcox about the Stinking Springs capture and prisoner transport to Las Vegas titled 'The Kid. Interview with Billy Bonney The Best Known Man in New Mexico;" which stated: "He is, in all, quite a handsome looking fellow, the only imperfection being two prominent front teeth, slightly protruding like a squirrels' teeth."]** Can we assume the younger Roberts photo is authentic? ...
>
> Conclusions:

The similarity between the facial structure of O.L. Roberts and the man in the LCHT tintype is indeed amazing. The main sources of error are the bizygomatic breadth and the mid-lip to lower chin distance ... [T]he ocular distances, the mid-lip to nose distance, and the nose length are almost exactly the same for Roberts and the LCHT tintype ...

[The] jaw width was not used due to the difficulty encountered in locating the endpoints using the computer. **[Note that Billy's big jaw was his defining feature, and lacked by "Brushy" young or old. So now jaw is added to ignore no ear match.]** ....

The photos used are shown: an unsubstantiated child claimed to be "young Henry McCarty," "old Roberts" [with mouth obscured by fish-tail mustache], "LCHT image of Billy," and "young Roberts." **[The photo with old "Brushy" with hidden mouth, was ridiculously included for measuring "mid-lip to chin distance," mid-lip to nose distance," and "mouth breadth."]**

[Most dishonest is Acton's "Figure 5" labeled: "An attempted restoration of the LCHT photo. I need to restore the photo in order to make valid comparisons of the images. This is not the final restoration." In fact, the head is reversed from the tintype to overlap old "Brushy's" pose, the ears are rounded – with the missing one added – to match "Brushy's," the entire face appears top-to-bottom shortened to reduce the big jaw, the mouth is elongated, and big white buck teeth are added.]

CONSPIRACY THEORIES

Jameson and Bean attack the philistines who denied their truth - that "Brushy" was Billy the Kid - by expanding the Morrison-Sonnichsen gospel of conspiracy theories.

CONSPIRACY OF HISTORIANS

Historians calling "Brushy" an imposter elicits Jameson's and Bean's accusations that they want to maintain the *status quo*, refuse to admit to being wrong, and perpetuate myth and misinformation. (Pages 15, 185-186) They state: "There exists a confederacy of Billy the Kid researchers and writers, an informal alliance composed of a number of adherents to the prevailing and accepted theories regarding the death of the outlaw ... The alliance dismissed Roberts ... The truth is, however, their efforts were never supported by valid scientific and historical research." (Pages 15-16) So they will give the readers examples to prove that plot against "Brushy."

CONSPIRACY OF GARRETT

Obviously the key person to denounce is Pat Garrett, who knew Billy, killed him, and wrote a book about it.

FAKING DEATH SCENE SUSPICION

So Jameson and Bean lie that the only evidence that Garrett killed Billy "was the word of Pat Garrett." (Page 14) "None of the so-called facts relating to the death of Billy the Kid at the hands of Pat Garrett have ever been supported by concrete, or even competent evidence." (Page 125) For proof, they make-up discrepancies between Garrett's and Poe's books, as discussed above. (Pages 449-450) And Poe is called colluding.

Cited are Morrison's claims that an unnamed cousin of McKinney said Garrett killed someone else and kept it secret (Page 125); that McKinney's grandson told him that "the Kid got away" (Page 125); and that Attorney Ted Andress in the pardon law firm was called by an unnamed man who said he would testify that McKinney told Garrett in a saloon in Uvalde, Texas, "that he had not killed anyone that night." (Page 126)

The duo conclude predictably: "[N]o credible evidence exists to indicate what actually occurred in Pete Maxwell's bedroom around mid-night on 14 July 1881. Or who was killed." (Page 126)

FAKING GARRETT AS DISHONEST

They claim the history of Billy the Kid is "flawed" and "suspect" because it is based on Pat Garrett's 1882 book, *The Authentic Life of Billy the Kid*, which contained errors and proved he was a "liar." (Pages 182, 187-188, 197)

FAKERY: The history is not based on Garrett's 1882 dime novel-style book. Jameson and Bean merely phobicly avoided real history books and original documents - like Billy's own writings and words, and depositions of participants - that prove "Brushy's" total mismatch.

They try character assassination, claiming: Garrett was "overrated," "never succeeded in anything," and "was a man of questionable veracity and integrity." (Page 197-198) And, since he was "an aspiring political figure," he wanted to keep secret killing the wrong man. (Pages 125, 189)

MEANINGLESS: Garrett's personality had nothing to do with whether he killed Billy. And they made-up that he lacked integrity and killed the wrong man.

CONSPIRACY OF THE CORONER'S JURY

Jameson and Bean make-up conspiracies to deny the fatal Coroner's Jury Report, starting with a lie: '[T]he inquest has ... been shrouded in confusion and mystery." (Page 126)

CONSPIRACY OF MILNOR RUDULPH

Jameson and Bean sought suspicion about Jury President, Milnor Rudulph. So, for John Poe's July 14, 1881 going to Sunnyside's Postmaster, Milnor Rudulph, to ask about Billy, they portray him as "a friend of the Kid." (Page 102) Poe's observing that he was "nervous out of fear of the Kid," to them meant he was "protective of the Kid" against lawmen, and gave misleading information. (Page 189) Or maybe he and Garrett had plotted to make the Kid seem "officially dead." (Page 191) So Jameson and Bean conclude that he was part of a conspiracy to hide Billy's survival to let him go free. (Page 190)

FALSE: As discussed, Rudulph was an Ringite, who in 1872, as Speaker of the House, assisted the Ring's take-over of the Legislature to block anti-Ring bills; thus, precipitating what I named the 1872 Legislature Revolt: the first anti-Ring uprising. Rudulph was Billy's enemy, and likely feared reprisal from him for betrayal. And he not have known that incognito stranger Poe was a lawman.

CONSPIRACY OF CORONER'S JURYMEN

Jameson and Bean conclude: "There is, in fact, no legal proof of the death of Billy the Kid." (Page 129)

But their "proof" of no proof was absurd and fabricated! They claim the inquest was fast. (Page 126) **[Why not?]** They claim Garrett did not put the body on public display. (Page 126)

[A lie? Their own book "posed" statement about townspeople's carpenter's shop wake, in which 200 who knew Billy saw his body.] They wanted the body photographed. (Page 126). [By whom? Rural people in 1881 did not have cameras.] They recycled Sonnichsen's A.P. Anaya malarkey of two coroner's jury reports. (Pages 126-127) [But Anaya was an old-timer windbag liar, who had no access to knowing about any report; and they were apparently unaware that he also claimed he buried Billy.] They claimed: "To date, no one has ever seen the document." (Page 127) [Its photostatic copy is in William Keleher's 1957 *Violence in Lincoln County*, cited in their own Bibliography!] They questioned spelling of the signers' names, and make-up that the report was a forgery by Garrett. (Page 128) [But Garrett, as the homicide suspect, would have had no access to writing the report.] They claimed that the Report "never made it to the official records of San Miguel County," and "Justice of the Peace Segura never made an entry regarding the report in his own books." (Page 118) [This was the Morrison-Sonnichsen hoax of concealing that the original Report was sent by Segura to Santa Fe to District Attorney of the First Judicial District William Breeden. And it involved hiding the Report's finding by Harold Abbott in 1932 and Maurice Garland Fulton in 1951.] Added is that Morrison was told there was no filed report in an August 14, 1951 letter from District Attorney Jose E. Armijo. (Page 128) [That was Morrison's scam of looking in Las Vegas instead of Santa Fe.] They claim the Coroner's Jury Report found by Maurice Garland Fulton was "challenged" and "unverified." (Page 128) [The only deniers were hoaxing Morrison and Sonnichsen! And Fulton had his copies certified.]

CONSPIRACY OF BURIAL

Jameson's and Bean's foregone conclusion was: "There has long been uncertainty relative to whose remains, if anyone's, is buried at the Fort Sumner site." (Page 132) But the uncertain gravesite location in Fort Sumner's cemetery is irrelevant to Billy Bonney's killing and burial there.

Claimed is that the body was seen only by Garrett, Poe, McKinney, "and two or three other people." (Page 130) [This omits Peter Maxwell, Deluvina Maxwell, over 200 townspeople in the night time wake, and the Coroner's Jury president, five jurymen, and Alejandro Segura.]

Leon Metz, Garrett's biographer, is misrepresented as saying in his *Pat Garrett: The story of a Western Lawman*, that Garrett could have passed off the body. (Page 130) **[Metz's book confirmed that Garrett killed Billy.]**

They repeat Grant County journalist S.M. Ashenfelter's fake dark, bearded corpse description in his July 23, 1881 *The New Southwest's* "Exit 'The Kid'." (Page 119) So, ridiculously, with what they call "scientific style," they cite a book on sexual maturity (with "SMR's – Sexual Maturity Ratings") to compare Ashenfelter's corpse to fair beardless Billy, to show that he could not change from fair to dark-skinned and bearded. So the body was not his. (Page 131) **[They forgot that Billy Barlow was *their* victim, and "Brushy" said *they* looked the same!]**

Hearsay tales follow about non-historical people claiming a Mexican that looked like Billy had been shot, or a Maxwell hired hand was shot, or that the wagon carrying the casket had an "armed guard" so no one could see the body. (Pages 132-133)

The uncertain location of the Fort Sumner Billy the Kid grave is called suspicious (Page 132), rather than mere neglect. And Yginio Salazar of Lincoln is fabricated as being a pallbearer and not knowing the gravesite. (Page 133) **[Admitting the site uncertainty is important, because the later "Billy the Kid Case" hoax, involving Jameson, would claim its location was certain - to justify exhuming Billy the Kid! Remember the Jameson-Bean quote: "Billy the Kid's current gravesite is not even authentic." (Page 132)]**

CONSPIRACY OF GARRETT'S REWARD

Jameson and Bean lifted Sonnichsen's *Alias Billy the Kid* fabrications that Garrett was denied the Billy the Kid reward money because of lack of a Coroner's Jury Report, lack of proven corpse identity; and was paid by the Ringite Legislature, who proved dishonesty by calling the killing in August. (Pages 14, 117, 129) **[This hid the innocuous truth that payment was delayed only by need to convert departed Lew Wallace's private reward into a Territorial one by legislative act. (See pages 20-28 above)]**

MOTHERS OF ALL CONSPIRACY THEORIES

The book ended with conspiracy theories, which claimed:

Fort Sumnerites were in a conspiracy. They tricked Garrett into thinking he killed Billy, to protect Billy. (Page 189)

FAKERY: This needs Garrett unable to recognize Billy. But Garrett knew him well.

All of New Mexico is in a conspiracy. The reason was "tourism." If Billy was a Texan, "millions of dollars each year" would be lost. (Page 191) So, Governor Mabry colluded with the historians and descendants to call "Brushy" an imposter for economic reasons. (Pages 192-193)

IRONY: In five years, corrupt Governor Bill Richardson would back "Brushy" for his "Billy the Kid Case" hoax.

The Lincoln County Heritage Trust was in a conspiracy. Its photo-analysis denying a match of "Brushy" to Billy was a lie by its director, Bob Hart, to protect his job and tourism. (Page 195)

FAKERY: Hidden is the sophisticated Dr. Clyde Snow investigation finding no photo-match for "Brushy."

TV's "Who Was Billy the Kid" on "Prime Time Live" (date not given) was a conspiracy. Presenter, Sam Donaldson admitted tourism value of Billy the Kid, lived in Lincoln County, and had no one on the program to back "Brushy." (Pages 196-197)

FAKERY: "Brushy" was not part of the history.

THE JAMESON-BEAN OUTCOME

Jameson's and Bean's exertions only proved that "Brushy" was undergoing a dishonest transformation. From pardon-"Brushy" killing no one, forgetting Pat Garrett, and claiming a Fort Sumner steak restaurant, to *Alias*-"Brushy" with his racist "[N-word]s" and Lincoln County cattle war; he had become *Return*-"Brushy," with a new genealogy with McCarty and Catherine Antrim, knowing about Regulators, and being cleansed of racism and bad grammar. But *Return*-"Brushy" was permitted quotes, so he spouted his tale of the dark and moonless night of July 14, 1881 that would destroy them all.

PART V

"BRUSHY BILL" GETS TO HOLLYWOOD

CHAPTER 1
A GREAT STORY

FICTION MEETS FILM

In Hollywood's world of make-believe, fact and fiction can be blurred without guilt, with claimed objective of entertainment, and real objective of getting rich. "Brushy Bill" was a perfect fit, once recognized by a screenwriter with adequate indifference to truth. That was how "Brushy's" fabrications became mainstream, misleading the public far beyond the capability of his hoaxers and true-believers.

When gauging a good story, one has to admit that "Brushy Bill's" fantasy tale hit an archetypal nerve. There is defying of death after a life of daring-do; then continuing a life of daring-do. There is the wish-fulfilling discovery that an ordinary old coot was the most famous outlaw of them all. But it took Hollywood 40 years to notice; so dead "Brushy" and dead William V. Morrison saw not a penny. But C.L. Sonnichsen had one year of life left to see the fruits of his lying.

The 1990 movie, "Young Guns II" was by screenwriter, John Fusco. His "Brushy," as Billy the Kid, is spared death by Pat Garrett because they are friends. This man-to-man friendship, so strong that Garrett would murder an innocent victim so Billy could live free, was as moving as it was fake. Not only did real Garrett kill real Billy, but they were not friends. And real Garrett had twice tried to kill real Billy before the capture; and accidentally killed Tom O'Folliard and Charlie Bowdre instead. And there is no doubt that Garrett would have hanged Billy in Lincoln, if he had not escaped the jail.

John Fusco's fakery got him more than box office success. "Brushy Bill" true-believers and future "Billy the Kid Case" hoaxers were poised to make him their hero: like the second coming of William V. Morrison. So he was sought out at the 2003 start of the "Brushy Bill"-based "Billy the Kid Case" hoax, and interviewed for that hoax's promoting, glossy, *True West* magazine's August/September edition.

Staff writer, Janna Bommersbach, used Fusco for her article titled: "Digging up Billy. If Pat Garrett didn't kill the Kid, who's buried in his grave?" The answer was supposed to be "a stranger" - or even Billy Barlow - and John Fusco was positioned for that punch line. Instead, apparently satiated by his $44 million profit, he was frustratingly honest, saying that he did not believe "Brushy" was Billy; but his movie had made a lot of money!

So traveling salesman, pseudo-lawyer, con-man William Morrison, had been right all along: "Brushy" was a great product. And John Fusco became the hoax's actual beneficiary. Though believing actual Billy the Kid history, he took the show-business option of making-up whatever he wanted - even out-Brushying "Brushy." Fusco arguably did more damage to Billy the Kid history than all the hoaxers combined. And he gave them a hook that "Brushy," Morrison, C.L. Sonnichsen, W.C. Jameson, and Frederick Bean had missed: a bromance.

So his "Young Guns II" fiction has an old "Brushy Bill" narrating his story to a young historian. Emilio Estevez is Billy, a leader of an outlaw gang, known as the Regulators. Cattle king John Chisum, pays Pat Garrett to kill Billy. As Billy's super-friend, Garrett only pretends to do the deed. So Billy rides off to life as "Brushy Bill."And the public thought Fusco's fiction was fact.

The lesson was not lost on W.C. Jameson and the "Billy the Kid Case" hoaxers that the formula of "Pat did not kill Billy" was now a proven bonanza. And there was another hook as good as the special knowledge trick. It was the bromance trick to explain the killing of the innocent victim. They were poised for the hoax's encore - Fusco or no Fusco. All they needed was a governor as indifferent to the truth as Fusco had been. Then the best publicity hook of all could be offered again: the gubernatorial pardon of Billy the Kid.

PART VI

THE RETURN OF "BRUSHY" IN THE "BILLY THE KID CASE" HOAX

CHAPTER 1
CREATION OF THE "BILLY THE KID CASE" HOAX

LEGACY OF "BRUSHY BILL"

In the years after the failed Governor T.J. Mabry pardon hearing, two things were proved: the "Brushy" hoax was a money-maker and media magnet (think "Young Guns II"), but it was historically ridiculous. So it took special people to do its re-run: self-serving sociopaths. True-believers, like W.C. Jameson, were rolled out for saccharine sincerity; while the perpetrators conducted thug history by might makes right.

Morrison's ghost hovered with its pardon hook. His May 19, 1955 letter from duped past president Harry S. Truman, was prescient; stating: "It is too bad that the old man who called himself "Billy the Kid" could not have lived long enough to see another Governor of New Mexico. He might have obtained a **just** decision." Truman was right about a future Governor; he just erred about **"just."** The scam was a perfect match for corrupt Governor Bill Richardson; seeking national publicity for a presidential run; and seeking pay-to-play for a Texan, "Brushy"-believer, political donor.

And master promoter Morrison had already invented another hook: digging up Billy the Kid based on scientific-sounding mumbo-jumbo for identity proof. As Morrison had written on February 9, 1955 to a Marion H. Borden: "I studied with photographers, handwriting experts, pathologists, ballistics experts, and other specialists, in anticipation of exhuming the remains in Fort Sumner in the event that a court order could be obtained."

Right after his *Alias Billy the Kid* came out, Morrison wrote to a William Waters on June 29, 1955 (sending a copy to his fan, Paul Blazer): "You say, " 'shouldn't we pay a little more attention to the body buried in the grave,' and I agree with you. **We should pay a lot of attention to the body buried.** If we could have found a cause of action to get into court, one of the first orders would have been to exhume the remains. In the absence of a coroner's verdict [his fake claim], **we did not have the necessary cause of action**. I am giving serious thought to a plan that may enable a legal exhumation. **If so, I firmly believe that a scientific investigation would determine that it was not the body of the Kid** ... This will not prove Roberts' claim, but it will prove that the Kid was not killed by Garrett."

Exhumation remained Morrison's dream. On May 8, 1961, he wrote to *Lincoln County News* publisher, Paul Baker: "It was our intention to exhume the three [Billy Bonney, Charlie Bowdre, and Tom O'Folliard] ... to determine, which, if any, actually represented the cadaver of Kid ... At the time of the purported demise of Kid, and ever since, reports were made that the Kid was not killed as alleged; the two purported coroner verdicts have been, and always will be, highly controversial issues ... and there has been evidence that Kid lived for many years after the purported slaying."

But Morrison, just a traveling salesman, could not think his way around the legal obstacle of "[no] necessary cause of action." Digging up human remains needs a reason overriding sanctity of a grave, and needs someone with legal standing: the right to make a case in a court - usually kin of the deceased.

The brilliant and devious solution likely came from Richardson's potential recipient of "Brushy's" Billy the Kid crown: a law partner in a multi-million dollar personal injury firm: Bill Robins III. The second category able to breech the moral barrier of exhumation is law enforcement - if exhumation is needed to solve a crime. That fit the "Brushy" hoax claim that Pat Garrett murdered an innocent victim, Billy Barlow, and was never punished because of his cover-up. SO A REAL MURDER CASE AGAINST GARRETT COULD GET IN THE GRAVE!

The next hurdle involved conscience: violating a grave for no reason, and lying that there was no statute of limitations for murder in New Mexico. But with Santa Fe Ring politics unbroken from the days of Billy the Kid, morally deficient, profiteering lawmen to file that murder case were readily available. It was named by them "The Billy the Kid" case.

Then came the next hook, possibly a group effort by the growing cabal: to claim modern DNA forensics would prove Billy the Kid was not in his Fort Sumner grave, by matching those remains with his mother's in Silver City. That both graves were just tourist markers, did not faze these reprobates who intended to fake the DNA results to get whatever match they desired. That, of course, necessitated a "forensic" expert in the mold of W.C. Jameson's and Frederick Bean's man who photo-matched "Brushy" to Billy. So they got notorious Dr. Henry Lee. And complicit judges for exhumation permits were recruited by Richardson's appointments of them just for the case.

The fraudulent forensics was to tie in the loose end of the pardon - fake matching of DNA from Billy's mother to "Brushy" (though he said she was not *his* mother) to make him Billy; then pardoning him for having led a long and law-abiding life. And his history would supersede the real history, while Governor Richardson would become the first American governor to hand his state's iconic history to another state for personal gain.

It looked like the perfect crime - and crime it was, because intended was wanton desecration of graves. And after generations of helplessly facing impenetrable Ring corruption, New Mexican's could be counted on to do nothing.

But there was an unanticipated problem: me. I had moved to New Mexico in 1999 to write a novel on Billy the Kid, Paulita Maxwell, the Lincoln County War, and the Santa Fe Ring. Its first draft was then completed, and had used over 40,000 pages of archival documents and books. I knew the history. As an M.D, psychiatrist doing forensic consulting in murder cases, I had access to the most sophisticated DNA experts in the country. I knew the science. And I had recognized the magnificence of the unsung freedom fight, of which Billy Bonney was an inspirational hero. To protect the true history, I was willing to take the risk against these dangerous bullies.

I blocked it by litigation against its illegal exhumations. And I blocked it by open records litigation revealing its DNA frauds. And I exposed it in my 2014 book: *Cracking the Billy the Kid Case Hoax: The Strange Plot to Exhume Billy the Kid, Convict Sheriff Pat Garrett of Murder, and Become President of the United States.*

FAKE NEWS

The "Billy the Kid Case" hoax entered at a stratospheric level. On June 5, 2003, Governor Bill Richardson announced his scam to the world in a front page *New York Times* article titled "122 Years Later, The Lawmen Are Still Chasing Billy the Kid." Its irresponsible reporter, Michael Janofsky, mouthed that Richardson was simply doing an investigation about pardoning Billy the Kid. But Richardson's "experts," unbeknownst to the public, were just "Brushy"-believers and complicit lawmen.

So Janofsky wrote that Richardson was seeking **"evidence to a long-held alternative theory that Garrett shot someone other than the Kid and led a conspiracy to cover up his crime;"** and that a Jannay Valdez, owner of a "Billy the Kid ["Brushy Bill"] Museum" in Canton, Texas, said: **"I'm absolutely convinced that Garrett killed someone else and that Brushy Bill was the Kid." Listed lawmen were Lincoln County Sheriff Tom Sullivan, and his Deputy, Steve Sederwall, filing the murder case against Pat Garrett**; as well as a Texas law firm for the case [**Attorney Bill Robins III**]. Richardson's spokesman [Billy Sparks] stated **"the state would assist by clearing any legal hurdles to gain access to the mother's body."** With feigned CSI glamour, Janofsky concluded that if "Brushy" was not a match, they could check John Miller. As to the pardon, Janofsky wrote that Governor Lew Wallace had promised it. Hidden was that "Brushy" was discredited since 1950, and that Billy the Kid's and his mother's graves were just tourist markers without valid remains for DNA. The article stated:

LINCOLN, NEW MEXICO – For more than 120 years, Pat Garrett has enjoyed legendary status in the American West, a lawman on a par with Wyatt Earp, Bat Masterson, even Matt Dillon. As sheriff here in Lincoln County in 1881, Garrett is credited with shooting to death the notorious outlaw known as Billy the Kid, a killing that made Garrett a hero. For years, a patch bearing his likeness has adorned uniforms worn by sheriff''s deputies here.

But now, modern science is about to interrupt Garrett's fame in a way that some say could expose him as a liar who covered up a murder to save his own skin and reputation.

Officials in New Mexico and Texas are working out plans to exhume and conduct genetic tests on the bodies of a woman buried in New Mexico who was believed to be the Kid's mother and a Texas man known as Brushy Bill Roberts, who claimed to be the Kid and died in 1950 at the age of 90. If test results suggest that the two were related, it would add new evidence to a long-held alternative theory that Garrett shot someone other

than the Kid and led a conspiracy to cover up his crime.

Such skepticism is hardly uncommon. Disputes over major events in the Old West have engaged historians almost since they happened. The debate over Billy the Kid is one of the longest-running.

Beyond renewing interest in the Kid saga, the possibility that testing could enlarge Garrett's reputation or destroy it has even caught the fancy of Gov. Bill Richardson of New Mexico, who has offered state aid for the investigation and a possible pardon that an earlier New Mexico governor had once promised the Kid for a murder he committed.

"The problem is, there's so much fairy tale with this story that it's hard to nail down the facts," said Steve Sederwall, the mayor of Capitan, N.M., who is working with Lincoln County's current sheriff, Tom Sullivan, to resolve the matter. "All we want is the truth, whatever it is. If the guy Garrett killed was Billy the Kid, that makes him a hero. If it wasn't, Garrett was a murderer, and we have egg on our face, big time."

No matter what the genetic testing may show - and it might not show much of anything – it is hard to overstate the prominence of Garrett and the Kid in Western lore, especially here in southeastern New Mexico where their lives converged during and after the gun battles for financial control of the region that were known as the Lincoln County War. The Kid's notoriety grew after he and friends on one side of the conflict killed several men in an ambush, including Garrett's predecessor, Sheriff William Brady. For that, the Kid was hunted down, captured by Garrett, found guilty of murder and taken to the Lincoln jail, where he was placed in shackles to await hanging. He was only 21.

Today the tiny town of Lincoln, population 38, is a memorial to what happened next. More than a dozen buildings, including one that housed the jail, have been preserved as a state monument that attracts as many as 35,000 visitors a year.

Historians generally agree that the Kid, born Henry McCarty and known at times as William H. Bonney, escaped after it became apparent that Gov. Lew Wallace had reneged on a promise to pardon him in exchange for information about another killing in the county war. On April 28, 1881, the Kid managed to get his hands on a gun, kill the two deputies assigned to watch him and leave the area on horseback.

But then the stories diverge, providing fuel for two major theories of where, when, and how the Kid's life ended.

The version embraced here and supported by numerous books and Garrett relatives is that the Kid made his way to a friend's ranch in Fort Sumner, about 100 miles northeast of Lincoln. The ranch owner, Pete Maxwell, was also a friend of

Garrett and somehow got word to Garrett that the Kid was in the area. After arriving, Garrett posted two deputies at the door.

As the Kid approached on the night of July 13 [sic], he spoke a few words in Spanish to the deputies, who did not recognize him. But Garrett, waiting inside, knew the voice. When the Kid walked in, Garrett turned and shot him in the heart.

William F. Garrett of Alamogordo, N.M., who is Garrett's grand-nephew, said years of research, including conversations with his cousin Jarvis, the last of Garrett's eight children, convinced him there is "no question about it" that his great-uncle killed Billy the Kid at Maxwell's. Jarvis died in 1991 at the age of 86.

"He was hired to get the Kid, and he got the Kid," Mr. Garrett said in an interview. "uncle Pat was a person of integrity who did his job. He was a law abider, not a law breaker."

But just as the story of Garrett as hero has flourished over the years, so have others, including the tale of Brushy Bill of Hico, Tex. His trip to New Mexico in 1950 to seek the pardon he said he was denied nearly 70 years before gave new life to an alternative possibility, that Garrett had not killed the Kid at all, but a drifter friend of the Kid's named Billy Barlow.

This story holds that Garrett and the Kid may have been in cahoots for some reason and that Garrett had stashed a gun at the outhouse at the jail that the Kid used to kill the deputies and escape. Even if only part of that is true, it would strongly suggest that Garrett killed the wrong man.

Speaking with the same person as Garrett's great-nephew, Jannay P. Valdez, curator of the Billy the Kid Museum in Canton, Tex., said he had no doubt that Garrett killed someone else and that Brushy Bill was the Kid. "I'm absolutely convinced," he said here on Monday after meeting with Mr. Sederwall to discuss theories and how to begin the kind of genetic testing that has been used to ascertain lineage of other historical figures like Thomas Jefferson and Jessie James. "I'd bank everything I have on it."

As longtime friends, Mr. Sederwall and Sheriff Sullivan decided they wanted to settle the matter once and for all but could do so only through scientific analysis. To justify the effort that would require much of their time and, perhaps at some point, taxpayer money, they needed an official reason. So in April, they opened the first-ever investigation into the murders of the two deputies shot in the Kid's escape, James W. Bell and Robert Olinger, to examine what happened at the jail and Maxwell's ranch.

[AUTHOR'S NOTE: The murdered deputies and Garrett's not killing Billy were connected by claiming Garrett helped the murder.]

As Mr. Sederwall said, "There's no statute of limitations on murder."

[AUTHOR'S NOTE: This his New Mexico's statute of limitations.]

The goal now, he said, is to compare genetic evidence of Catherine Antrim, believed to be the Kid's mother, who died of tuberculosis in 1874 and is buried in Silver City, N.M., and of Brushy Bill, who lived out his life in Texas. A Dallas firm [sic Houston] has agreed to help, and a spokesman for governor Richardson said the state would assist by clearing legal hurdles to gain access to the mother's body.

The Kid was buried at Fort Sumner, N.M., although the whereabouts of the grave are uncertain; he has no known living relatives. Mr. Valdez said he had already secured permission to exhume the body of Brushy Bill, who is buried 20 miles from Hico in Hamilton, Texas.

But solving the mystery might not be so simple. For one thing, Mr. Valdez said he was certain that the woman buried in Silver City was but "a half aunt." And even if tests disqualify Brushy Bill as Billy the Kid, other "Kids" have emerged over the years, including a man named John Miller, who died in 1937 and is buried in Prescott, Ariz. Mr. Sederwall said that efforts would be made to exhume his body as well.

The investigators conceded that much is riding on their quest. Sheriff Sullivan, a tall, strapping man who carries a turquoise-handled .357 magnum on his right hip, said he, like so many others in the West, revered Garrett for gunning down the Kid. The uniform patch with Garrett's likeness was his design. Now, the legend is threatened.

"I just want to get to the bottom of it," said Sheriff Sullivan, who is retiring next year. "My integrity's at stake. So's my department's. So's what we believe in and even New Mexico history. If Garrett shot someone other than the Kid, that makes him a murderer and he covered it up. He wouldn't be such a role model, then, and we'd have to take the patches off the uniforms."

On June 10, 2003, Richardson held a press conference, with a press release. Present were key hoaxers: Lincoln County's Sheriff Tom Sullivan and Deputy Steve Sederwall; De Baca County's Sheriff Gary Graves; Attorney for exhuming the mother, Sherry Tippett; and University of New Mexico professor Paul Hutton, appointed by Richardson as "historical advisor." Richardson revealed that Lincoln County Sheriff's Department murder case against Pat Garrett had been flied as No. 2003-274, and promised was forensic DNA matching to establish a pardon. It stated:

State of New Mexico
Office of the Governor

Bill Richardson
Governor
For immediate release
6/10/03

Contact: Billy Sparks
telephone number

GOVERNOR BILL RICHARDSON ANNOUNCES STATE SUPPORT OF BILLY THE KID INVESTIGATION

SANTA FE – Governor Bill Richardson today outlined how the state of New Mexico will support the investigation efforts to investigate the life and death of Billy the Kid.

Governor Richardson delivered the following remarks during a news conference today in the State Capitol:

This is an important day in the history of New Mexico and the American West. I am announcing my support and the support of the state of New Mexico for the investigation into the life and death of Henry McCarty, also known as William Bonney. To millions around the world, he was called Billy the Kid. How he captured the world's imagination is well worth exploring. His life, though ended at the age of 21, is part of what makes New Mexico and an American West, unique.

My goal is to shed new light on old history.

I am pleased to be joined here by Lincoln County Sheriff Tom Sullivan, Capitan Mayor Steve Sederwall, De Baca County Sheriff Gary Grays [sic - Graves]. Grant County Attorney Sherry Tippett, University of New Mexico History Professor, Doctor Paul Hutton and State Police Major Tom Branch.

Let me tell you how this all came about.

Last month I was contacted by Lincoln County Sheriff, Tom Sullivan and Capitan Mayor, Steve Sederwall, to support reopening the case. Case number 2003-274 seeks to answer key questions that have lingered for over 120 years surrounding the life and the death of Billy the Kid.

This episode in the history of New Mexico and the history of the old west is both fact and legend and continues to stir the imagination and interest of people all over the world.

By utilizing modern forensic, DNA and crime scene techniques, the goal of the investigation is to get to the truth. In the process, the reputation of Pat Garrett, still a hero in Lincoln County law enforcement, hangs in the balance. **The question is did Sheriff Garrett kill Billy the Kid at Fort Sumner, New Mexico on July 14. 1881?**

This investigation will also seek to shed new light on the events surrounding the escape of Billy the Kid from the Lincoln County Jail on April 28, 1881. The shooting of Deputies J.W. Bell and Bob Olinger by Billy the Kid has never been officially investigated. Where did Billy get his gun and what really happened?

I have contacted the national Labs, Los Alamos and Sandia and have been assured that they will volunteer their support in this effort. Los Alamos Lab can assist us by providing ground penetrating radar, DNA expertise and technical forensic assistance. Sandia Labs will allow their experts to volunteer their time to help us uncover the facts.

The State Police will help supervise the investigation and crime scene analysis of the evidence uncovered in the investigation.

I have also asked University of New Mexico Professor of History and Executive Director of the Western History Association, Doctor Paul Hutton, to serve as our historical advisor. Dr. Hutton has served as President of the Western Writers of America and has won several national honors for his works on western history.

I intend to hold hearings at Fort Sumner, Lincoln, Silver City and Mesilla. I will appoint a defense counsel and a prosecutor to present the evidence. **[Never done.]**

As Governor, I will examine the events surrounding the alleged offer of a pardon to Billy the Kid by former New Mexico Governor Lew Wallace. I will evaluate the evidence uncovered and make a decision.

There is no question that this story deserves our attention and that the history of New Mexico and the American West is important to all of us. If we can get to the truth we will. I have total confidence in the team you see here today to conduct a professional, honest and exhaustive investigation of the facts and report back to me and to the rest of the world what really happened here in New Mexico.

The benefits to our state and to the history of the West far outweigh any cost we may incur. I expect the actual cost to be nominal. Just since this investigation was announced, it has sparked news articles about New Mexico and Lincoln County from New York to London to India. Getting to the truth is our goal. But, if this increases interest and tourism in our state, I couldn't be happier.

I understand that Movie Producer Ron Howard has donated the cabin used in shooting his movie "The Missing", being shot in Santa Fe, to Silver City. The cabin is a replica of a Billy the Kid era home. The cabin will be delivered to Silver City this week.

The potential benefit from this investigation to all of New Mexico is already being felt and is well worth the effort.   #30#

Proved was Richardson's scorn of the public, since no relevant DNA existed in the tourist marked graves of Billy and his mother. Also insurmountable, was the 1963, already discussed, Lois Telfer exhumation case which blocked exhumation of Billy the Kid based on uncertain gravesite and risk to other remains.

FAKE MURDER CASE

Also, there was no real murder to investigate. Billy's Coroner's Jury, on July 15,1881, had declared: *"our verdict is that the deed of said Garrett was justifiable homicide."* So this was ignored. Instead, Richardson and cohorts used the "Brushy" hoax's murder by Garrett of the innocent victim to claim a cold case investigation to see if the victim lay in the Fort Sumner grave.

Then, by lying that there was no statute of limitations for murder, they had filed murder case No. 274-2003 against Garrett in the Lincoln County Sheriff's Department (where Garrett had been Sheriff) and Case No. 03-06-136-01 in the De Baca County Sheriff's Department (for Fort Sumner's Billy the Kid grave). Billy's DNA was to be compared with his mother's DNA in Silver City, to see if he matched her. Hidden was that New Mexico's Office of the Medical Investigator (OMI) refused exhumation permits based on no valid DNA available from either grave.

And **DNA of the mother (though there was none) of the mother would also be matched to "Brushy," in his Hamilton, Texas, grave (hiding that he denied she was his mother). If "Brushy" matched mom, then *he* was Billy the Kid; and, by extrapolation, the Fort Sumner remains could not be Billy, so they were the innocent victim, and Garrett was a murderer.** So slyly slipped in "Brushy" just looked like part of their murder case, instead of its purpose. And since there would be no real DNA anyway, they planned to claim any matchings they wanted with their complicit forensic expert.

But what about the pardon? Hoax Attorney, Bill Robins III, gave the link in the Grant County District Court in his January 5, 2004 "Pre-Hearing Brief" petitioning to dig up Catherine Antrim. Speaking for Billy as his client (though a corpse is not a client) he claimed "Billy" had and interest in "his legacy." Then Robins slipped in "Brushy." He stated that **if "Brushy's" DNA matched the mother's in Silver City, *he* would deserve Richardson's gubernatorial pardon as Billy the Kid for having led a long and law-abiding life.**

THE CAST OF HOAXERS

Richardson's fellow hoaxers were in the self-serving mold of Morrison and Sonnichsen. Besides Attorney Robins, there was state-salaried University of New Mexico history professor, Paul Hutton, appointed by Richardson as the official historian, and writer-producer of its hoax-promoting History Channel program. Its lawmen were Lincoln County Sheriff Tom Sullivan, who deputized for the case the Mayor of Capitan, Steve Sederwall. After Sullivan's tenure, his Undersheriff, Rick Virden, was elected Sheriff; and he deputized both Sullivan and Sederwall to continue it under him. Lincoln County Attorney Alan Morel hid the hoax from the County Commissioners. In De Baca County, Sheriff Gary Graves participated. And Ted Hartley, the District Court Judge there, like Henry Quintero in Grant County for the mother's grave, had just been appointed by Richardson to back the exhumation of Billy the Kid there. And the U.S. Marshals Service Historian in Washington, D.C., David Turk, participated. Editor-in-Chief of the *Albuquerque Journal*, Kent Walz, publicized the hoax and blocked rebuttals. And Editor-in-Chief of the glossy Old West magazine, *True West*, Bob Boze Bell, backed the hoax and promoted "Brushy." W.C. Jameson appeared in Professor Hutton's documentary to push "Brushy" as Billy. By 2005, Arizona Governor Janet Napolitano paved the way for illegally exhuming John Miller in her state-controlled cemetery in Prescott. For that foray, a Dave Tunnell, friend of Deputy Sederwall, pretended forensic expertise. And for a forensic expert for DNA fakery, they enlisted Dr. Henry Lee, of O.J. Simpson trial infamy, and detested by colleagues as a publicity hound doing sleazy "show-biz" forensics. But the "star quality" of this shady gang intimidated opponents and dazzled national press.

HOAX PROGRESSION

The "Brushy Bill"-based "Billy the Kid Case" hoax was arguably the most elaborate historical fraud ever perpetrated. And Governor Bill Richardson's megalomaniacal determination to win resuscitated it every time I legally blocked its schemes. The progression, thus, became increasingly absurd, desperate, and ultimately criminal. And it ironically replicated the old Santa Fe Ring, which had been intrinsic to real Billy's own history, as if in a rerun to obliterate him once again.

FROM FAKERY TO FELONIES

Few New Mexicans dared to oppose Richardson's hoax. It fell to me to stop the steamrolling behemoth. I hired attorneys to block the exhumations of Billy and his mother through honorable mayors standing for their towns of Silver City and Fort Sumner. By 2004, we won based on no valid graves, opposition of the OMI, historic certainty that Pat Garrett killed Billy the Kid, and the Telfer precedent case blocking the Fort Sumner exhumation. That had no effect on the "Billy the Kid Case" hoaxers. They merely fabricated a new source of "DNA."

In 2004, they announced they had the carpenter's bench on which shot Billy had been laid out. This changed their hoax, which originally had Billy (as "Brushy") not shot, and the corpse on the bench as the "innocent victim" or Billy Barlow. Ignored too, was that there was no proof that the bench was the real one. Their bench surfaced in 1926, 45 years after Billy's killing, for a Billy the Kid tourist display by a teenaged Maxwell family member.

Nevertheless, the hoaxers claimed Billy *was* laid out, but *played dead*, while bleeding on the bench. Then Garrett added the murdered innocent victim as Billy left as "Brushy." The hoaxers were pushing their luck with public stupidity. And "Brushy" lacked this crazy scenario. But the key was "bled on the bench."

Dr. Henry Lee, was willing to say that the bench's rust stains (expected on a carpenter's bench) looked like blood to him. So he tested for the "blood DNA of Billy the Kid." But the test he used was for iron, so it would be positive for rust, as well as blood. And even if it was the actual carpenter's bench, and even if it had recoverable DNA after 124 years, there existed no proven DNA of Billy the Kid (called reference DNA) to test it against to validate its being *Billy's DNA*. In other words, they had nothing.

But Lee found blood anywhere he was directed. The lawmen had him investigate the Lincoln courthouse to make-up that he found the blood of Deputy Bell at the top of the stairs, instead of the bottom, so Garrett had lied about the murder. That was used to claim that Garrett was Billy's accomplice in the escape. And, as such a good friend, he also killed the Fort Sumner victim so Billy could escape again. And ignored was that "Brushy" had no such bromance in his hoax. And the press reported this junk.

Helpful Dr. Lee also made-up a "crime scene" from unsubstantiated furniture provided to him by the hoaxers. Examining a bed headboard, he claimed Garrett had lied that his second shot went through it, since there was no bullet hole. Lee omitted that there was also no headboard! It was just a frame around air, with no place for a hole. That was also to call Garrett a liar; thus, a likely murderer!

Then Lee "examined" what he called a washstand, finding two holes in it. Though it was not in actual history of the shooting, he fabricated that the holes were from a bullet shot by Garrett crouching on the floor and shooting over his back! He claimed that proved that Garrett had lied about the scene, and had been a crawling chicken. It was not forensics. It was fraud.

By then, the hoax's official historian, Paul Hutton, had written and co-produced, with Bill Kurtis Productions, 2004's History Channel "Investigating History: Billy the Kid," about the "mystery" of the killing of Billy Bonney. It included - beside's narrator Hutton's fakery and ignorant mangling of actual history - almost all the "Billy the Kid Case" hoaxers, including Richardson and Robins. W.C. Jameson even appeared to back "Brushy."

Jameson had already participated, in November of 2003, in hoaxing Editor-in-Chief Bob Boze Bell's *True West* magazine for "Was Brushy Bill Really Billy the Kid? Experts face off over new evidence." in a "debate" with Pat Garrett's biographer, Leon Metz. For it, Jameson parroted Morrisonisms, and waved Scott Acton's fake photo-comparison plus "Brushy's" made-up name. He stated: "[S]upporters of the historical status quo assert Roberts was a fraud, yet to date they have provided no logical, definitive proof ... Roberts was an illiterate man, yet he was astonishingly intimate with the people, geography, architecture and events of Lincoln County, New Mexico, in the late 1870s-early 1880s – an intimacy that could have come only from being present and involved ... After Roberts' image was compared to the only known photograph of Billy the Kid, one researcher [Acton] concluded that William Henry Roberts was, in all likelihood, Billy the Kid ... [so] history needed to be rewritten."

The obvious direction was to "Brushy's" grave. But I had warned Hamilton officials about the hoax and its having no valid DNA for matchings, so no exhumation of "Brushy" was permitted.

But, by then, the hoaxers were desperate for any DNA; and Bill Kurtis's cameras were poised for another production. The only available victim was Billy the Kid imposter, John Miller, underground in Arizona, with corrupt Governor, Janet Napolitano indifferent to violating graves for a publicity stunt. And Dr. Rick Staub, the director of Dr. Henry Lee's regular DNA processing lab, Orchid Cellmark, in Texas, was eager to collect bones with himself on camera. So wanton desecration of graves and grave robbing joined the "Billy the Kid Case" hoax's repertoire. Under Lincoln County Sheriff Rick Virden, the perpetrators were his Deputies Tom Sullivan and Steve Sederwall. Concealed from authorities was that they had no carpenter's bench DNA of Billy the Kid to compare with any remains to justify any exhumation - besides the fact that John Miller was not Billy the Kid, and never claimed their playing-dead-carpenter's-bench-bleeding for DNA scenario.

Then it got worse. Knowing they risked indictments, they behaved with extreme secrecy, rushing a backhoe into the Arizona cemetery, and working into the night with flashlights. Then it got worse. There were no grave markers. So they descended to barbaric depths, plowing into one grave, collapsing its coffin and grabbing bones. In doubt that they were in the right grave, they demolished the adjoining one. Skulls, femurs, a pelvis, and other bones from both graves, were horrifically dismembered for Rick Staub's bone bags. Deputy Steve Sederwall even posed for a trophy photo with a skull. It made it into a New Mexico paper.

Miller's dead neighbor, the random desecrated man, was named William Hudspeth. (Imagine that he was your beloved relative, now with demolished remains and destroyed grave.)

Following these atrocities, the hoaxers claimed to have gotten John Miller's DNA for matching with carpenter's bench "DNA;" and that he had buck teeth, like Billy the Kid. But, at that point, they had a problem besides felonious desecrations and grave-robbing. Faking a forensic investigation, they had hired an Arizona forensic anthropologist named Dr. Laura Fulginiti. She dutifully wrote a report including both exhumations. And she denied that John Miller's skull had buck teeth. It had no teeth! So Bill Kurtis had ended up filming a crime scene.

By 2006, a duped French film maker, with visions of Young Guns II, had filmed the Lincoln County lawmen in New Mexico, and had gotten Chris Kristopherson (Sam Pekinpaugh's Billy the Kid from his movie "Pat Garrett and Billy the Kid") as narrator. It made the Cannes Film Festival. And she got an award, and brought over Deputies Sullivan and Sederwall to celebrate.

The hoax was out-of-control. I had to do something before it destroyed the history. So I made a RICO case with the FBI against Richardson and his colluding public officials. In 1970, Congress passed that Racketeer Influenced and Corrupt Organizations Act to enable prosecution of criminal cabals. But corrupt New Mexico U.S. Attorney, David Iglesias, (removed later for shielding Richardson in other cases) blocked the FBI.

Meanwhile, the Arizona prosecutor yielded to corrupt pressure of Governor Janet Napolitano, and covered up the criminality for the Miller exhumation and hid William Hudspeth.

I also reported Dr. Henry Lee to the American Academy of Forensic Sciences (AAFS) Ethics Committee as perpetrating a hoax. They shielded him.

CALLING THE DNA BLUFF IN COURT

It was left to me to stop the destruction of the history of Billy the Kid. In 2006, under the open records act, I demanded the Lincoln County lawmen's DNA records from the carpenter's bench, the courthouse floorboards, and the bones of John Miller and William Hudspeth. Rick Virden was then Sheriff, with Tom Sullivan, and Steve as his Deputies for the "Billy the Kid Case." For intimidation, complicit Lincoln County Attorney Allan Morel, with the lawmen, then reported me to the U.S. Marshals Service as a terrorist - presumably to their fellow hoaxer there: its historian, David Turk! And they also claimed they had no DNA records at all!

In 2007, I hired a law firm to litigate, under open records law, against the lawmen for the DNA records. So these hoaxers rewrote the hoax again. Since only public officials are required to turn over public records, **they claimed that they had done the case as private hobbyists.** Of course, "private hobbyists" do not operate out of sheriff's departments and cannot dig up graves.

But five sets of my apparently pressured attorneys tried to throw my case, as the hoaxers stonewalled, and the judge permitted it. I finally went *pro se*, and won; though the lawmen hid their DNA records throughout. But I discovered that they had forged reports as Dr. Lee's to trick the court that the case was their private hobby. So the judge ordered them to turn over to me Lee's actual report. And it made no conclusion about obtaining the DNA of Billy the Kid. And I got the hidden results of the bench/Miller/Hudspeth DNA extractions and matchings from my co-plaintiff, who, in 2012, subpoenaed them from Orchid Cellmark Lab. They showed that no DNA from the carpenter's bench for matching. And the only other DNA collected came from random man, William Hudspeth! Had this not been exposed, this was the "DNA" that would have been used to fake "Brushy Bill" as Billy the Kid - and no one would have realized the scam! But the corrupt New Mexico press covered-up the outcome.

Then the corrupt state appellate courts removed all monetary penalties to the lawmen - and it was almost a million dollars owed to me. But the hoaxers' attorneys pocketed a half-million taxpayer dollars in fees for hiding the DNA records, which had been available for cost of postage at the time of my request.

THE FAKE PARDON THRUST

By 2010, Governor Richardson's governorship was ending; and he still wanted to win. So he played his last card: pardoning Billy the Kid, which he linked to his "investigation" that "Brushy" was Billy, and deserved a pardon for his long and law-abiding life.

Huckster William V. Morrison's dream was about to come true. As he wrote on May 8, 1961 to Paul Baker, the *Lincoln County News's* publisher: "[W]e have been considering filing a petition for pardon posthumously; wherein evidence would be incorporated to prove beyond doubt ... that Kid performed his contractual obligations to the letter; and that Governor Wallace refused and failed to perform his, especially to pardon the Kid if convicted."

In July of 2010, anticipating this "Brushy" hoax maneuver, I contacted Pat Garrett's family. His grandson, Jarvis Patrick "J.P." Garrett (from his son Jarvis, who had been in Governor Mabry's hearing) took action, getting a family meeting with Richardson and demanding he sign an agreement (written by me) that he would not claim Pat Garrett killed an innocent victim.

But it was not over. Richardson simply followed Morrison's angle of the Lew Wallace bargain; using a Randy McGinn to file a pardon petition as an "amateur historian" (and hide that she was his attorney for a big pay-to-play corruption case). That was on December 14, 2010, with Richardson having just 17 days left in office. So I contacted Lew Wallace's great-grandson, William N. Wallace, a past *New York Times* reporter. He threatened Richardson with a law suit for defaming his family name.

On the 31st, Bill Richardson told the waiting press that he had come to his decision. He lied that his "investigation" had revealed that Billy the Kid was an outlaw, so he could not pardon him!

But the "Billy the Kid Case" did not end. W.C. Jameson gave its hoaxer's a new platform in his 21st century books. And they recycled the "Billy the Kid Case" hoax as faked "private investigators" of a cold case. So I exposed them in my 2019's *The Cold Case Billy the Kid Megahoax: The Plot to Steal Billy the Kid's Identity and Defame Sheriff Pat Garrett as a Murderer*

CHAPTER 2
"BILLY THE KID CASE" HOAXERS AND HOAX DOCUMENTS

REWRITING "BRUSHY'S" HOAX

The "Billy the Kid Case" hoaxers attempted to keep secret their "Brushy Bill" thrust. But their profuse press and legal documents for fake DNA claims and illegal exhumation attempts, which reveal the attempt to make "Brushy Bill" Billy the Kid revealed it. And also revealed was that the mismatch. Now Catherine Antrim was claimed as "Brushy's" mother, and Pat Garrett was Billy's best pal, risking hanging as an accomplice to murdering the deputy guards in Billy's jailbreak, shooting him in a plot for him to play dead on the carpenter's bench (to leave DNA), them murdering the innocent victim as grave-filler.

STARTING GATE BLOCKADES

The "Billy the Kid Case" was a forensic DNA fraud to call Pat Garrett a murderer. It intended to match DNA from Billy the Kid's grave to his mother's DNA; with no match meaning a stranger was in his grave; ergo, Garrett killed Billy Barlow. "Brushy's" DNA would also be matched to the mother's DNA to prove she was his mother; ergo, he was surviving Billy.

Reality was the blockade. The Coroner's Jury Report proved that Garrett killed Billy the Kid. There was no innocent victim. New Mexico's Statute of Limitations for prosecuting him for murder had run out in 1891. The graves were just tourist markers. "Brushy" denied Catherine Antrim as a mother. The 1962 Lois Telfer case blocked access to the Fort Sumner grave. And the OMI refused to issue exhumation permits for a publicity stunt. None of this fazed the hoaxers.

REFUSED EXHUMATION PERMITS

The New Mexico Office of the Medical Investigator (OMI) clearly documented their refusal to issue exhumation permits for Catherine Antrim's or Billy Bonney's exhumations based on uncertain gravesites and risk of disturbing other remains.

Governor Richardson had anticipated a problem. Its head, Dr. Ross Zumwalt, and its forensic anthropologist, Debra Komar, were ethical. Since the OMI was part of the University of New Mexico Health Sciences Center, Richardson used his recent appointee, University of New Mexico President David Harris, remove their attorney to obstruct their opposition.

And the hoax's Silver City attorney, now deceased Sherry Tippett, working for Richardson, met with the OMI staff, then lied to Richardson through Richard Gay, his Assistant to the Chief of Staff, in her July 11, 2003 "Memorandum RE: Exhumation of Catherine Antrim." She lied: "This is a summary of the work I have performed to date on the exhumation of Catherine Antrim from Memory Lane Cemetery in Silver City … **Research conducted by Dr. Debra Komar, of the Office of Medical Investigations [sic] (OMI) now indicates that the body of Mrs. Antrim can be moved without disturbing any other bodies in the cemetery.**"

Tippett lied again about permission in her October 3, 2003 Grant County Case No. MS 2003-11 "In the Matter of Catherine Antrim, Petition to Remove Remains" for Judge Henry Quintero. Importantly, in this first exhumation petition, she made clear the lawmen's titles and that the case was against Pat Garrett for murder. (The hoaxers would later deny both.) Tippett wrote:

PETITION TO EXHUME REMAINS

Comes now **Petitioners Tom Sullivan, Sheriff of Lincoln County, Steve Sederwall, Deputy Sheriff of Lincoln County, and Gary Graves, Sheriff of De Baca County**, by and through their attorney, Sherry J. Tippett, hereby Petitions this Court to enter an Order directing the New Mexico Office of Medical Examiners [sic- Investigator] (hereinafter "OMI") to disinter the remains of Catherine Antrim for the purpose of obtaining DNA samples. This petition is made in conjunction with investigation No. 2004-274 [sic] filed in Lincoln County and case number 03-06-136-01 filed in De Baca County, **for purpose of determining the guilt or innocence of Sheriff Pat Garrett in the death of William Bonney aka "Billy the Kid."**

Catherine is the undisputed mother of William Bonney. Catherine Antrim is buried in Silver City, NM at the Menorial [sic] Lane Cemetery ...

In the case at hand, there is no known direct descendant of Catherine Antrim or William Bonney alive today.

Section 24-14-23 C NMSA (1978) states that a permit for disinterment and reinterment shall be required to disinterment [sic] of a dead body or fetus except as authorized be regulation or otherwise provided by law. This statute further states that the permit shall be issued by the state registrar or state medical investigator to a licensed funeral service practitioner or direct disposer. Dr. Debra Komar, Forensic Anthropologist with the OMI has performed a significant amount of research on the burial history and exact location of the remains of Catherine Antrim including visiting Memorial [sic] Lane Cemetery and performing records research in both New Mexico and Arizona. **Dr. Komar is confidant that Mrs. Antrim's remains can be exhumed without disturbing the remains of other bodies laid to rest in Memorial [sic] Lane Cemetery.** Disturbance of any other remains is unacceptable to the OMI staff. Dr. Komar is a world renowned Forensic Anthropologist who has previously worked for the united nations in the exhumation of mass buries [sic] in eastern Europe. Several meetings have taken place between the Petitioners, counsel of Record and OMI Director and Forensic staff as well as UNM Counsel Angela Martinez. **All parties are in agreement that an Order should be entered by this court prior to exhumation.**

The Petitioner respectfully requests this Order be entered as soon as possible to begin the exhumation by early to mid November. The coordination of several public and private agencies will be necessary to complete the exhumation.

> Respectfully submitted,
> Sherry J. Tippett
> Attorney for Petitioners

In fact, multiple remains were at risk, since the Antrim gravesite overlapped 12 burials. And one grave was contiguous: Donna Jenice Amos's, from 1989. And its tire-track rutted desecration by the hoaxers' first film crew had outraged the decedent's sister, Joani Amos-Staats, who joined her own Petition to Silver City's Petition in Opposition - the case I had made. So all this was concealed by the hoaxers.

RESPONSE OF THE OMI

Sherry Tippett's failing, besides perjury, was underestimating the OMI. In response to Richardson's gagging attempt, Dr. Ross Zumwalt hired a private attorney, William Snead. Snead filed the OMI's January 12, 2004 response implying Tippett's lying.

Snead stated: "**Contrary to the statements contained in the petition [of Sherry Tippett], Debra Komar, Ph.D., the forensic Anthropologist referred by petitioner, does not believe that Ms. Antrim's remains can be exhumed without disturbing the remains of other bodies** also interred in Memory Lane Cemetery … **Contrary to the petition, the Office of Medical Investigators does not agree that an order should be entered allowing exhumation.** After a detailed and scientific investigation described in the affidavits [of Drs. Zumwalt and Komar] attached hereto, it is the scientific opinion of the OMI that any such attempted exhumation has very little possibility of contributing any information to the petitioner's alleged investigation, threatens the disturbance of unrelated burials, is a very great waste of public resources and a distraction of the OMI from its mandated work."

OPPOSITION AFFIDAVITS

Snead presented the January 9, 2004 Affidavits of Dr. Ross Zumwalt and Dr. Debra Komar.

Zumwalt concluded that the mother's remains were not necessarily in her gravesite; that that comparison with Billy the Kid remains was useless because the site was not confirmed; that comparison with "Brushy Bill" made no sense because mitochondrial DNA only shows descent from the mother, and he claimed a different mother; that other remains would be disturbed; and that permission would not be granted.

He stated: "[I]f the purpose of exhuming Catherine Antrim is to provide a "known" standard for DNA testing, **the fact that she cannot be positively identified [because her unverified remains were moved from another location in 1877] renders all DNA tests suspect** … If attempt is made to exhume the supposed body of Catherine Antrim from the burial site with her name, it is probable with a reasonable degree of scientific probability that the remains of other individuals will be disturbed. The burial site with Catherine Antrim's name is Plot D-27 at Memory Lane Cemetery. **This plot is the resting place of twelve (12) other known individuals** [who might be disturbed or confused with her remains] … **If the purpose of the exhumation of the remains of**

Catherine Antrim is to compare her DNA to the remains of the believed Billy the Kid, those remains are not likely to be obtained in my opinion. Based upon research performed by the OMI, the exact location of the Billy the Kid grave is not known, in my opinion, to a reasonable degree of scientific probability ... **If the purpose of extracting mtDNA [mitochondrial DNA] from the supposed remains of Catherine Antrim is to obtain a sample to compare against Brushy Bill Roberts in Texas, such a comparison, in my opinion, is also scientifically flawed. Based on research to date, I am unaware that Mr. Roberts ever claimed to be the biological child of Catherine Antrim.** Thus, a test between his mtDNA and the putative remains of Catherine Antrim would have no scientific basis to a reasonable degree of scientific probability ... Based on the fact that DNA testing of the putative remains of Catherine Antrim would have no probative value and the fact that an exhumation would likely disrupt other burial sites, **an exhumation of Catherine Antrim is scientifically unsound in my opinion.**"

Komar's Affidavit, repeated Zumwalt's contentions.

THE KOMAR DEPOSITION

On January 20, 2004, Dr. Debra Komar gave a 224 page deposition for the Sixth Judicial District Court Case No. MS 2003-11, "In the Matter of Catherine Antrim" to one of my attorneys fighting the exhumations. Present were hoax attorneys, Sherry Tippett and Bill Robins III. In the deposition, Komar was described as "a world-renowned forensic anthropologist who has previously worked for the United Nations in the exhumation of mass burials in Eastern Europe." (Komar, Page 11)

She highlighted that "Billy the Kid is not buried in an isolated situation, but that he shares his burial with two other individuals" (Pages 17-18); and "there seems to be disagreement as to the placement of the bodies [of Tom O'Folliard, Charles Bowdre, and Billy Bonney] relative to each other; and some disagreement as to the placement of those bodies within the cemetery." (Komar, Page 22)

As to Silver City's Catherine Antrim remains, Komar described their relocation from within the city limits to outside them; with added problem of disruptive flooding. (Komar, Pages 24-25) She explained that the man, who purchased the original in-town cemetery, had his workers move remains to an undocumented location in Memory Lane Cemetery. (Komar, Pages 25, 27-28) Komar stated: "We know she's been moved. We know there's been flooding. We know when she was moved, it was in a completely uncontrolled set of circumstances. And therefore, to hold her up as some sort of standard [for DNA identification] becomes scientifically unacceptable." (Komar, Page 38) Added was that her current plot overlapped 12 other individuals. (Komar, Page 52)

As to Fort Sumner's Billy the Kid grave, where flooding "literally washed bodies out of the ground" (Komar, Page 45), there was "not a specific place where we would put a shovel in the ground ... [because of uncertain location and] remains themselves may no longer still be there." (Komar, Page 69)

As to "Brushy," who denied being Catherine Antrim's son, Komar said: "[Y]ou might as well compare his [mitochondrial] DNA to mine. It would mean as much." (Komar, Page 77)

She concluded: **"So if you ask the opinion of myself and the Office of the Medical Investigator why is this being done or what scientifically valid conclusions can be drawn from it, I can't find any**." (Komar, Page 81)

Attorney Bill Robins III cross-examined her about Catherine Antrim, claiming absurdly to be "defending Billy the Kid." (Komar, Page 97) Ignoring the impasse, he questioned meaninglessly about soil samples, the original grave marker, and how long DNA lasted. Dr. Komar responded: "[W]e're arguing that we can't do that .. given that we can't then prove it's Catherine Antrim." (Komar, Page 139) "If the purpose of using Catherine is to provide [DNA] identification for someone else that must be, for a forensic standard, based on positive identification to begin with." (Komar, Page 142) "We don't exhume historical people for the sake of doing it." (Komar, Page 143) Robins even revealed the secret agenda by asking about matching Catherine to "Brushy." (Komar, Page 149) Komar responded that he denied she was his mother, and mitochondrial DNA gives false positives merely from being white Europeans (Komar, Page 150), which would not prove "Brushy" as Billy. She stated: "DNA won't conclusively prove what you are trying to say." (Komar, Page 152)

As to Billy the Kid, the same problems applied, plus history of removal of a soldier's body from the cemetery's military past, with the chance that Billy's body was accidentally removed! (Komar, Pages 70-72) So the following interchange occurred:

ROBINS QUESTION: You don't think Billy the Kid is buried at Fort Sumner, do you?
KOMAR ANSWER: I don't know. I have reason to suspect perhaps not. (Komar, Page 144)

This repeated her Affidavit that "[b]ased upon research performed by the OMI, the exact location of the Billy the Kid grave is not known." **The hoaxers would later cite this out of context to lie that she said Billy the Kid was buried elsewhere; ergo, he was "Brushy Bill" buried in Hamilton, Texas!**

In fact, she merely referred to her earlier statement about Billy: "**[T]he remains may no longer still be there. Even if they were buried there at one point**" (Page 69) since there was information that his remains might have been stolen, that past digging in the area revealed no remains (Komar, Page 70), or a 1904, gravedigger, Willie E. Griffin, removing soldiers remains to relocate to Santa Fe's National Cemetery, may have taken Billy! (Komar, Page 71-72)

Questioned meaninglessly Attorney Sherry Tippett, Dr. Komar responded that since they were proposing exhumations for a criminal investigation, that, of necessity, involved the OMI; and the OMI demanded scientific validity. Komar stated: "**There is a big difference in the level of standard and what's expected if something is done as an academic versus a criminal investigation. If you want to continue to call it a criminal investigation, it mandates the involvement of our office.**" (Komar, Pages 201-202)

Attorney William Snead concluded Komar's deposition with the OMI's position: **"We're opposed to the principle of digging someone up where it's not going to lead to scientifically probative evidence."** (Komar, Page 203)

THE HOAXERS' RESPONSE TO OPPOSITION

The "Billy the Kid Case" hoaxers simply ignored the OMI. Richardson counted on his recently appointed, corrupt judges in Silver City and Fort Sumner, Henry Quintero and Ted Hartley respectively, to grant him the exhumations in this obvious pay-to-play. And that is what they tried to do.

But the hoaxers, recognizing more push-back than they had anticipated, replaced bumbling Attorney Sherry Tippett with Attorney Bill Robins III himself.

But the law firm I hired, using the Mayors of Silver City and Fort Sumner to protect their cemeteries, stopped the digging which would have fraudulently claimed whatever Governor Richardson wanted, and would have made "Brushy" Billy the Kid.

LAWMEN'S HOAXING DOCUMENTS

Governor Richardson enlisted two Sheriff's Departments to conduct his hoax. To attack past Lincoln County Sheriff Pat Garrett, he got now deceased Lincoln County Sheriff Tom Sullivan, who deputized the Mayor of Capitan, Steve Sederwall, as an accomplice.

For assault on Fort Sumner's Billy the Kid grave, Richardson got De Baca County Sheriff Gary Graves.

But Grant County Sheriff, Raul Holguin, proved incorruptible. On August 29, 2006, Holguin told me that, in 2003, Sheriff Graves pressured him to join. Holguin said, "I was appalled. It was clearly a publicity stunt. [Catherine Antrim] deserved to lie in peace."

Lincoln County Sheriff Tom Sullivan opened murder Case No. 2003-274, and De Baca County Sheriff Gary Graves filed its counterpart as Case No. 03-06-136-01. And his deputy, Steve Sederwall, later claimed authorship of their major documents, including Case 2003-274's "Probable Cause Statement," accusing Pat Garrett of murdering the innocent victim.

And Sullivan's Undersheriff, Rick Virden, assisting from the start, became the next Sheriff, deputized Sullivan and Sederwall. He achieved the illegal exhumation of John Miller and random man William Hudspeth, and attempted to dig up "Brushy Bill."

"MAYOR'S REPORT" OF STEVE SEDERWALL

Steve Sederwall announced the "Billy the Kid Case" murder case in his May, 2003, *Capitan Village Hall News* "Mayor's Report," beating the Governor by a month, and before the hoaxers hid their "Brushy" focus. So he promoted "Brushy," even claiming that Billy Barlow was in the Fort Sumner grave. He also announced a sub-investigation of the murder of Deputy James Bell by Billy the Kid. This report came to his constituents in their monthly water bill. Its showmanship proved him a successor of huckster, William V. Morrison. His "Mayor's Report" stated:

... On April 28, 2003, at five minutes after noon, one of our citizens, Sheriff Tom Sullivan fired two shots in Lincoln, New Mexico. The floor under my feet shook at each report of his pistol. The gun smoke hung in the air just as in a western novel would describe it. As I heard the shots a cold chill ran down my back knowing that J.W. Bell heard the shots that killed him.

A 122 years before, just minutes after twelve, noon, on April 28, 1881, two lawmen lay dead, in the yard of the courthouse in Lincoln, New Mexico, from gunshot wounds. Quicker than it took New Mexico breeze to clear the gunsmoke, history was clouded with the myth of the shooting and escape of William H. Bonney a.k.a. Billy the Kid from the make-shift jail where he awaited the date with the hangman.

Sheriff Sullivan and I have opened a case into that shooting in 1881. As part of the investigation Sheriff Sullivan fired off two rounds from a .45 Long Colt to see if the shots could be heard from the Wortley Hotel. To our surprise the black powder rounds loaded for us by Virgil Hall could be heard in nearly every part of town.

This investigation came about after Sheriff Sullivan and I talked about a man by the name of Brushy Bill Roberts. In 1950 Roberts ["Brushy Bill"] came to the Governor of New Mexico with his attorney [sic - William Morrison, not an attorney]; saying he was Billy the Kid. He said that Pat Garrett shot a man by the name of Billy Barlow and buried his body claiming to be that of Billy the Kid. Roberts said he lived out a life within the bounds of the law under an assumed name and wanted a pardon that was promised to him by Governor Wallace.

On the surface of this story [Brushy Bill Roberts's] you would say "so what?" But if you look at this man's claim he is saying our Sheriff Pat Garrett is a murderer. Garrett knew the Kid and killed someone else. What this says also is that Pete Maxwell who said the body is of The Kid is a co-conspirator in a murder. There is no statute of limitations on Murder [sic], so the Lincoln County Sheriff's Office has opened a case to pursue the investigation. If Brushy Bill Roberts is Billy the Kid then history changes. But if he is lying, we need to clear Garrett's name.

[AUTHOR'S NOTE: Murder cases are not done to clear someone's name; and the expired Statute of Limitations is hidden.]

I feel this investigation will put a positive light on the county, our town and the state in whole. Tom Sullivan and I have been in touch with the Governor's office and he is behind us. People who are conducting DNA on victims of the World Trade Center have agreed to complete DNA tests for us on remains of persons believed to be Billy the Kid. We have a filmmaker creating a made-for-TV story about this investigation. We have recruited some of the best investigators in the country from other states to assist in this investigation. The Sheriff and I feel this should not only clear up a 122-year-old mystery but also bring money into our village ...

Tom Sullivan and I know it is a crazy idea but won't it be fun.

PROBABLE CAUSE TO PROSECUTE GARRETT

For the real murder case to justify exhumations, Steve Sederwall, as Lincoln County Deputy Sheriff, wrote the "Probable Cause Statement" - intending to establish, with probability, Garrett's murdering of the innocent victim.

The December 31, 2003 "Probable Cause Statement for Case No. 2003-274" is 11 pages of single-spaced footnoted text with double-talk, lies, and mock erudition. It is signed by Sederwall and Sheriff Tom Sullivan. Attorney Bill Robins III may contributed, since he used its wording a month in a November 19, 2003 *Albuquerque Journal* article by a Louie Fecteau titled: "No Kidding: Governor Taps Lawyer for Billy." Robins stated: "[I]t was hard to tell who the good guys were." The Probable Cause Statement has: "[I]t was hard to tell who the good guys were." Also, hoaxer, U.S. Marshals Service Historian David Turk, provided fake research. And some claims came from hoax participant, W.C. Jameson's, 1998 *The Return of the Outlaw Billy the Kid*.

It had two thrusts. First were fake "suspicions," fake DNA claims of matchings of Billy the Kid and his mother, and fake post-death sightings. Second was a sub-investigation of Billys jailbreak murder of his deputy guards, making-up Garrett's motive of friendship by claiming him as the escape's accomplice, and claiming that proved he would later murder to save Billy. Ignored was no historical friendship.

An addendum was a fake affidavit by a Homer Overton, swearing that Garrett had not shot the Kid.

The upshot is that the "Probable Cause Statement" presented no evidence that Garrett did not kill the Kid. But its labor in production take one's breath away. Apparently, expecting no opposition, it was to assuage their complicit judges' consciences.

Later, through my open records investigations, I discovered their first version of a probable cause statement which overtly backed "Brushy," had victim Billy Barlow, and quoted "Brushy" for the death scene as the authority. (See pages 522-545 below)

LINCOLN COUNTY SHERIFF'S DEPARTMENT
CASE # 2003-274
Probable Cause Statement

In the struggle dubbed the "Lincoln County War" investigators [Sullivan and Sederwall] soon learned that nothing was as seemed.

[AUTHOR'S NOTE: For lack of any evidence, this is the familiar "suspicion" used by the "Brushy" hoax.]

As they poured through the volumes of information, documents, paperwork, reports, county records, books and examined newly discovered evidence, it became apparent no clear lines could be drawn as to who was working with or for whom. What first appeared to be clear quickly became clouded as new information was uncovered,

[AUTHOR'S NOTE: No new evidence is ever presented.]

it's difficult to judge who the "good guys" and the "bad guys" were. One would think that the Lincoln County Sheriff''s Department would be on the side of the law. However, it was a duly sworn posse of Lincoln County Deputies that shot and killed John Tunstall, in what investigators in clean conscience can only cauterize [sic] as an unprovoked murder.

[AUTHOR'S NOTE: Tunstall's murder is irrelevant. It occurred when William Brady was Sheriff of Lincoln County; and was 3½ years before Garrett killed the Kid. Of course, Brady's dishonesty is irrelevant to Garrett as a murderer.]

Evidence shows that posse-men, Hill and Morton

[AUTHOR'S NOTE: Error: Tom Hill was not Brady's official posseman; he was in Jessie Evans's outlaw gang. Brady, in writing, swore he used no known outlaws on that posse.]

committed murder when "*Hill called to him* (Tunstall) *to come up and that he would not be hurt; at the same time both Hill and Morton threw up their guns, resting their stocks on their knees; that after Tunstall came nearer, Morton fired and shot Tunstall through the breast, and then Hill fired and shot Tunstall through the head ...*" [1]([1]Deposition of Albert Howe, Angel Report) Although these deputies were acting under the color off the law they were not acting within the law. This behavior permeates the Lincoln County War and investigators will not make judgments on that behavior but rather uncover the facts and present the facts without varnish.

[AUTHOR'S NOTE: Repeating that lawman can be dishonest, is irrelevant to proving Garrett a murderer.]

No one from the Governor to the District Attorney to the Sheriff of Lincoln County is beyond suspicion of deception and covering up the true facts in this case.

[AUTHOR'S NOTE: Vague "suspicion" is irrelevant to Garrett.]

This can be seen in a number of examples. In a letter to Riley and Dolan of the Murphy-Dolan faction from District Attorney W. L. Rynerson of the 3rd Judicial District, the attorney clearly demonstrates he himself plays a part in the hostile actions when he writes, "*Shake that McSween outfit up until it shells out and squares up and then shake it out of Lincoln. I will aid to punish the scoundrels all I can.*"[2] ([2]Rynerson letter to Riley and Dolan, Feb. 7 [sic], 1878, University of Arizona Special Collection)

[AUTHOR'S NOTE: Error: The letter is dated February 14, 1878; is about murdering Tunstall; and is irrelevant to Garrett.]

When investigators began to look at the murder of Deputy Sheriff J.W. Bell and Deputy Robert Olinger on April 28, 1881, it was found that much of the information we now know as "history" came from Pat F. Garrett's book, "The Authentic Life of Billy the Kid" published in 1882.

[AUTHOR'S NOTE: Wrong: Bell/Olinger eye-witness murder information was not claimed by Garrett, who was away at White Oaks; but was from, Gottfried Gauss, the caretaker.]

Investigators learned that much of this history is flawed for the reason historian Robert Utley writes: "*Although not many copies of the Authentic Life were sold, it nevertheless had a decisive impact on the Kid's image. More than any other single influence, the Garrett-Upson book fed the legend of Billy the Kid. As the legend blossomed, writers turned to the Authentic Life for details. Ash Upson's fictions became implanted in hundreds of " histories" that followed. For more than a century, only a few students thought to question the wild fantasies that flowed from Ash's imagination. In the evolution of the Kid's image, the Authentic Life is a book of enormous consequence.*"[3] ([3]Robert M. Utley. Billy the Kid a short and violent life. University of Nebraska Press, 1989.)

[AUTHOR'S NOTE: Utley is merely describing evolution of the legend, not history. And Garrett's book confirms his shooting of Billy. All subsequent scholarly historians, including Utley, confirmed that Garrett fatally shot Billy the Kid.]

On March 23 [sic – 17], 1879, Governor Lew Wallace met with William Bonney (Kid) in Lincoln. In this meeting it is demonstrated that Wallace convinced the Kid that it would be to his advantage to work for the government.

[AUTHOR'S NOTE: Wrong. Billy proposed to Wallace, by a letter of about March 13, 1879, to give eye-witness Grand Jury testimony against the murderers of Huston Chapman in exchange for Wallace's annulling his Lincoln County War indictments. But a straw man argument is being set up.]

The Kid becomes, what would be referred to in today's terminology as a "Confidential Informant." In Governor Wallace's hand we read "Statements made by Kid, Made Sunday night March 23, 1879."[4] ([4]Statements by Kid, Lew Wallace Collection, Indiana Historical Society Library) It was through this meeting Wallace devised a plan and attempted to deceive when he and the Kid entered into an agreement where by the Kid would appear to have been arrested.

[AUTHOR'S NOTE: Saying there was an attempt "to deceive" is a misleading switcheroo. The hoaxers have admitted to Billy's confidential informant status. The arrest plan was devised by both Wallace and Billy to prevent Billy's being killed before his Grand Jury testimony against Chapman's murderers. The hoaxers, however, are still pumping the irrelevant claim that everyone was deceptive. Of course, that claim is irrelevant to their Garrett as murderer fakery.]

The Kid later talks of this and says he was allowed to wear his guns and he left when he wanted to leave.

David S. Turk, Historian for the United States Marshals Service has discovered other such deceptions in his study of official records.

[AUTHOR'S NOTE: Referring to "other such deceptions" is fake. Turk's "other deceptions" are never given. And Turk, an active "Billy the Kid Case" hoaxer, contributed his own fake Probable Cause Addendum to the hoax. (See pages 564-568 below)]

It is commonly believed

[AUTHOR'S NOTE: Fakery: It is a *known*.]

that Lincoln County Sheriff Pat F. Garrett arrested the Kid in December of 1880 in Stinking Springs near Fort Sumner. But the records show that Garrett was elected in November of 1880 and did not take office until January of 1881.[5] ([5]Lincoln County Commissioners Records, November 8, 1880).

[AUTHOR'S NOTE: This leads to the "Brushy" hoax's claim that he did not have proper authority to capture Billy.]

He went to Fort Sumner as a Deputy United States Marshall, but even that Commission and authority are now questioned. Secret Service Special Operative Azariah F. Wild of New Orleans writes in his daily logs *"I this day went to Lincoln to meet Capt. Lea & Garrett who are to organize the Posse Comatatus (sic) to make a raid on Fort Sumner to arrest counterfeiters."*[6] ([6]Report of Azariah F. Wild, November 11, 1880, Record Group 87, National Archives) Garrett shot and killed Charles Bowdre and Tom O'Folliard during the chase and arrested the Kid. Later, Secret Service Special Operative Azariah F. Wild writes to his superior and admits he was deceptive in his commission of Garrett. *"I will respectfully state that I applied to Marshall Sherman to appoint P.F. Garrett as a Deputy Marshall to which he paid no attention. I was in great need of Mr. Garrett [sic – Mr. Garrett's aid] at that time and took one of the Commissions Sherman sent to John Hurley (he having sent two) and substituted P.F. Garrett the very man who has rendered the Government such a valuable service in killing and arresting these men who I was in pursuit."*[7] ([7]Report of Azariah F. Wild, January 4 [sic -3], 1881, Record Group 87, National Archives)

[AUTHOR'S NOTE: This is a fake attempt to cast doubt on Garrett's commission and Wild's veracity. In fact, Wild, needing Garrett's aid, requested paperwork from U.S. Marshal John Sherman, and erroneously received two for John Hurley. So he crossed out Hurley's name on one, and added Garrett's. It was not done secretly, since Wild put it in his daily report to his Secret Service Chief, James Brooks. And it was accepted. To be noted, is that Sederwall recycled this fabrication in W.C. Jameson's 2018 book titled *Cold Case Billy the Kid*.]

No one in 122 years has been able to speak with clear certainty where the gun came from that William Bonney used to kill Deputy J.W. Bell.

[AUTHOR'S NOTE: A switch to the sub-investigation begins to fake Garrett as Billy's escape accomplice.]

With the information investigators have seen they question Garrett's involvement in the Kid obtaining a weapon.

[AUTHOR'S NOTE: No such information is ever given. There are just fake "what-ifs": *If* Garrett was Billy's friend, he would give him an escape gun. *If* he gave an escape gun, he would later kill the innocent victim so Billy could escape again.]

It would go to reason that if the body in Fort Sumner is anyone other than William Bonney then Garrett no doubt had a hand in allowing the Kid to escape on July 14, 1881.

501

[AUTHOR'S NOTE: This is fakery. No one says anyone but Billy was buried. It is just hoaxing.]

If the body at Fort Sumner is anyone other than William Bonney, then Garrett, whether by accident or design, is responsible for homicide of the person resting in that grave.

[AUTHOR'S NOTE: Here are more meaningless "what ifs."]

If it is not Bonney in the grave at Fort Sumner it would also go to reason that Garrett would be looked at as a suspect in furthering the escape of the Kid on April 28, 1881 when the two Lincoln County Sheriffs were murdered.

[AUTHOR'S NOTE: Here is the switcheroo. Now the fake "what-ifs" are used as fact: that Garrett helped Billy escape. THIS FAKERY IS THE HOAXERS' SOLE PROBABLE CAUSE FOR GARRETT AS A MURDERER. In fact, no evidence has been given; and none exists. And Pat and Billy were not friends.

[AUTHOR'S NOTE: What follows next is built on the hoaxers' lying that: (1) they established Garrett's murder motive; and (2) they established need to check Billy's grave for Garrett's "innocent victim."]

Although the investigation will deal with what happened in the Lincoln County court house on April 28, 1881, this writing will deal with the alleged shooting of William Bonney at Fort Sumner on the night of July 14, 1881.

[AUTHOR'S NOTE: Do not let this fast-one slip by. The deputy murders "sub-investigation" at the courthouse consisted merely of: (1) firing a gun inside to test if it could be heard across the street; and (2) bringing in forensic consultant, Dr. Henry Lee, whose finding of "blood" on the upstairs hallway floorboards was a hoaxer lie. Lying more, the hoaxers said the "blood" was Bell's. Olinger was left out. Also left out is that this "investigation" has nothing to do with the gun used to shoot Bell. And, even if it did, that would have nothing to do with whether Garrett gave it to Billy, or whether Garrett murdered an innocent victim 2½ months later. The "upstairs blood," though irrelevant, will be debunked later with the rest of the fake forensic claims.]

[AUTHOR'S NOTE: At this point, the hoaxers abandon the deputy murders and the Garrett murder motive. But they pretend that they: (1) established Garrett's Billy friendship; (2) Garrett's escape weapon involvement; (3) Garrett's murder motive; and (4) Garrett's murder of the innocent victim.]

This writing will set forth probable cause as to why investigators question who is in the grave in Fort Sumner and seek DNA from Catherine Antrim.

[AUTHOR'S NOTE: Probable cause of Garrett as a murderer has not been established. But this double exhumation is the hoaxers' goal.]

[AUTHOR'S NOTE: What follows is the hoaxers' attempt to fake that someone other than William Bonney was shot by Garrett. It is back to "what-ifs": *If* **there was any inconsistency in reporting of events around the murder, something is "suspicious;" ergo, Garrett killed someone else. But the hoaxers only use "Brushy" hoax "inconsistencies."]**

The detractors of this investigation hold up the statements of Lincoln County Sheriff Pat F. Garrett, Deputy Sheriff John W. Poe, and the Coroner's Jury report as proof it is William H. Bonney that Sheriff Garrett shot and killed on July 14, 1881 and that the Kid is buried in Ft. Sumner.

[AUTHOR'S NOTE: Hidden are the multiple corpse identifications. Later, in this document, in slip-ups, the hoaxers accidentally present more of them!]

Historian Philip J. Rash [sic - Rasch] tells the story history puts forth about the shooting of the Kid in the following manner:

Garrett led them to the mouth of Taiban Arroyo, arriving after dark on 13 July. When Brazil failed to appear, Poe, who was unknown in the area, agreed to ride into fort Sumner the next morning to see what he could learn. Finding the inhabitants suspicious and uncommunicative, he proceeded to Sunnyside, about seven miles north, to visit Milnor Rudolph, the postmaster and an old friend of Garrett's. Rudolph was nervous and evasive. He denied all knowledge of the Kid's whereabouts, but Poe was sure he was concealing something.[8] (*[8] Poe, John W. The Death of Billy the Kid. New York: Houghton Mifflin Company, 1933) There is a curious story that while the officer was on the way to Sunnyside, John Collins (Abraham Gordon Graham), a former member of Billy's gang, headed to Lobato's camp to warn the outlaw that officers were in the vicinity. On the way he met the Kid, bound for Fort Sumner. "Billy," he warned, "don't go down there. I just saw Poe, and no doubt Pat Garrett and a posse are around town looking for you."*

[AUTHOR'S NOTE: Recall that Poe was unknown to the locals; so this irrelevant hearsay further lacks credibility.]

The Kid merely laughed and answered, "Oh, that's O.K. I'll be alright," and rode on, leaving Collins badly puzzled."[9] ([9]Ben Kemp. *Dead Men, Who Rode Across the Border.* Unpublished. No date.)

That night Poe rendezvoused with Garrett and McKinney at La Punta de la Glorietta [sic], four miles north of Fort Sumner. Poe's report of both his failure to learn anything definite and his suspicions that there was so much smoke there must be some fire only increased the sheriff's skepticism. After some discussion he commented that the Kid was a frequent visitor to the house of Celsa Gutierrez (sister of Pat's wife Polineria [sic] Gutierrez) and suggested that they watch her home. Their vigil proved fruitless. As midnight approached Garrett and Poe decided that there was only one other possible source of information - Peter Maxwell, the town's most prominent citizen.

The officers arrived at his home about 12:30 AM on Friday, the 15th [sic]. Pat instructed Poe and McKinney to wait outside while he went in to talk to Maxwell. Sitting down on the edge of the bed, he asked in a low voice whether the Kid was on the premises. Maxwell became very agitated, but answered that he was not. At that point a bare headed, bare footed man in his shirt sleeves, carrying a butcher's knife in his left hand and a revolver in his right sprang through the door and asked Maxwell who the two men outside were.

Maxwell whispered, "That's him."

[AUTHOR'S NOTE: Note the hoaxer slip-ups in presenting this source: (1) *This* Garrett cannot recognize Billy, though they claimed he and Billy were such good friends that Garrett killed for him; and (2) Maxwell identifies the victim as Billy!]

Sensing a third person in the room, the intruder backed toward the door, at the same time demanding, "Quien es? Quien es?"

Pat jerked his gun and fired twice.[10] [11] ([10]*Las Vegas Daily Optic*, July 18, 1881. [11]*Santa Fe Daily New Mexican*, July 21, 1881) As the man fell Maxwell plunged over the foot of the bed and out the door, closely followed by the sheriff. Maxwell would surely have been shot by Poe if Garrett had not struck the latter's gun down saying, "Don't shoot Maxwell." He added, "That was the Kid that came in there onto me, and I think I have got him."

[AUTHOR'S NOTE: This is Peter Maxwell's second dead Billy identification; and is not contradicting Garrett's statement.]

Poe was not so sanguine. "Pat," he answered, "the Kid would not come to this place, you shot the wrong man." All was quiet inside. After some persuasion Maxwell brought a tallow candle and placed it on the outside of the window sill. By its light the body of a man could be seen

Deluvina Maxwell, a Navajo servant, entered the room, examined the body, and found that it was indeed the Kid's.

[AUTHOR'S NOTE: This is a third identification of Billy! And Deluvina knew him, as he hoaxers later confirm themselves. She also reported his killing in a June 24, 1927 interview by J. Evetts Haley. And Poe's quote, in his 1933 book, *The Death of Billy the Kid***, expressed initial disbelief of Billy's coming there – and he did not know him. It does not disprove the victim.]**

Garrett's first shot had struck him in the left breast just above the heart; the second had gone wild. Later it was learned that Billy had been staying at the house of Juan Chavez.

[AUTHOR'S NOTE: A fourth Billy identification!]

Becoming hungry, he had gone to Maxwell's to slice a steak from a yearling Pete had killed that morning.

The corpse was taken to a carpenter's shop and laid on the work bench.

[AUTHOR'S NOTE: The carpenter's bench would later became the hoaxers' focus for faking DNA claims.]

Fearing an assault from Billy's friends, the officers remained awake and on guard the rest of the night. However, it passed without incident.

[AUTHOR'S NOTE: The townspeople join the list confirming the body as Billy's, and are called "Billy's friends." Note also that Garrett does not try to conceal the "secret" body of the supposed innocent victim of his "murder."]

When morning came, Justice of the Peace Alejandro Segura convened a jury, with Rudolph as president.

[AUTHOR'S NOTE: The Justice of the Peace convened the Coroners Jury. Later the hoaxers will switch this fact.]

They rendered a verdict that William Bonney, Alias "Kid," had been killed by Garrett and were "unanimous in the opinion that the gratitude of the whole community is due the said Garrett for his act and that he deserves to be rewarded".

[AUTHOR'S NOTE: Note that the job of a Coroners' Jury was to identify the body. They did. Billy was known to them. The hoaxers already quoted historian Philip Rasch saying Rudolph was nervous when interviewed by Poe - indicating he knew Billy, and knew he was in the area. Crucial also is that the Coroner's Jury declared the killing justifiable homicide. That closed the case legally. Re-opening it is double jeopardy.]

That afternoon Jesus Silva and Vincente Otero dug a grave for the outlaw in the old military cemetery.[12] ([12]Philip Rasch. *Trailing Billy the Kid* by Philip J. [sic - Rasch] Outlaw-lawman research series Volume 1, University of Wyoming, Laramie, Wyoming, 1993.)

On face value this looks to be the truth. However, if you study the statements of the eye witness [sic] and the documents they do not match up and both can not be true.

[AUTHOR'S NOTE: This is to fake "inconsistencies."]

Deputy John Poe says the following:

It was understood when I left my companions in the morning that in case of my being unable to learn any definite information in Fort Sumner, I was to go to the ranch of Mr. Rudolph (an acquaintance and supposed friend of Garrett's) whose ranch was located some seven miles north of Fort Sumner at a place called "Sunnyside," with the purpose of securing from him, if possible, some information as to the whereabouts of the man we were after. Accordingly I started from Fort Sumner about the middle of the afternoon for Rudolph's ranch,

[AUTHOR'S NOTE: Remember "in the middle of the afternoon." It will later be switched to Poe leaving for Rudulph's at night.]

arriving there sometime before night. I found Mr. Rudolph at home, presented the letter of Introduction which Garrett had given me, and told him that I wished to stop overnight with him.[13] ([13]Poe, John W. Billy the Kid. Privately published by E.A. Brininstool. Los Angeles, CA.)

[AUTHOR'S NOTE: With this unpublished, Brininstool source - and reasonable assumption of its unavailability to readers – the hoaxers are about to construct a fake argument.]

In this part of Deputy Poe's statement he tells us he was sent to Rudolph's ranch by Garrett because Rudolph was *"an acquaintance and supposed friend of Garrett's,"* that the ranch was located seven miles north of Ft. Sumner, at Sunnyside. Poe also tells Rudolph he is going to spend the night at the ranch.

[AUTHOR'S NOTE: The fakery here is leaving out part of the quote. Brininstool information is as follows: There was no "Brininstool book." Poe wrote his account, including the Rudulph episode, for Charles Goodnight in 1917. In 1919; and an Edward Seymour in New York contacted Goodnight for information on the Kid. Goodnight referred him to Poe. Poe sent his account of Billy's death to Seymour, who sent it to Brininstool, who published it in British *Wild World Magazine*, in December of 1919, later making it a brochure. It was also used in in Poe's 1933 book, *The Death of Billy the Kid*, which the

hoaxers earlier cited. **On its page 22, Poe states he declined the invitation to spend the night. But the hoaxers omitted its pages 25-26. There, Poe states:** "Darkness was now approaching, and I said to Mr. Rudulph that inasmuch as myself and my horse were by this time pretty well rested, having had a good meal, I had changed my mind, and instead of stopping with him, would saddle up and ride during the cool of the evening to meet my companions. This I accordingly did, much, I thought, to the relief of Rudulph." **So there was no inconsistency]**

In Sheriff Garrett's statement he gives about the same facts of where he was headed and how far it was from Ft. Sumner. Garrett differs with Poe in one area when he says he "arranged with Poe to meet us that night at moonrise" rather then spend the night with Rudulph, as can be seen below:

[AUTHOR'S NOTE: This is to fake Garrett as making contradictions. But Poe *did not* spend the night. The hoaxers merely hid Poe's quote saying that he did not spend the night.]

I advised him (Poe) *also, to go to Sunnyside, seven miles above Sumner, and interview M. Rudolph Esq. In whose judgment and discretion I had great confidence. I arranged with Poe to meet us that night at moonrise, at La Puenta de la Glorietta, four miles north of Fort Sumner.*[14] ([14]Garrett, Pat F. The Authentic Life of Billy the Kid. University of Oklahoma Press, Norman. Oklahoma. 2000)

[AUTHOR'S NOTE: That was it: the hoaxers' alleged inconsistency: whether Poe did or did not spend the night at Milnor Rudulph's! But both Poe and Garrett agree that Poe did not. There was no inconsistency. Nevertheless, this hoaxer flimflam is later repeated on the same subject.]

Deputy Poe then gives his account of when he says he first saw the Kid when he writes:

I observed that he was only partly dressed, and was both bare-headed and bare-footed - or rather, had only socks on his feet, and it seemed to me that he was fastening his trousers as he came toward me art a very brisk walk.

As Maxwell's was the one place in Fort Sumner that I considered above suspicion of harboring "The Kid," I was entirely off my guard, that thought coming into my mind that the man approaching was either Maxwell

[AUTHOR'S NOTE: This quote dovetails with Poe's question about the correct man, since he could not identify Billy. Also note Poe's lack of alarm. It will be misstated by the hoaxers.]

or some guest of his who might have been staying there. He came on until he was almost within arm's length of where I sat before he saw me, as I was partly concealed from his view by the post of the gate. Upon his seeing me he covered me with his six-shooter as quick as lightening, sprang onto the porch, calling out in Spanish, "Quien es?" (Who is it?), *at the same time backing away from me toward the door through which Garrett only a few seconds before had passed, repeating his query, "Quien es?" in Spanish several times. At this I stood up and advanced toward him, telling him not to be alarmed: that he should not be hurt, and still without the least suspicion that this was the very man we were looking for.*

This statement raises many questions with investigators. Poe says he sees a man *"partially dressed, and was bare-headed and bare-footed - or rather, had only socks on his feet, and it seemed to me that he was fastening his trousers as he came toward me art a very brisk walk."* Then the man covers him with his six shooter. Where did the man put the *"six-shooter"* when he was *"fastening his trousers"*?

[AUTHOR'S NOTE: This is an accidentally hilarious hoaxer contrivance of the impossibility of doing two things at once! Actually, one can hold a revolver and button one's pants. And Billy was a gunman and ambidextrous, so even more able! Amazingly, this silliness would be repeated by Sederwall for W.C. Jameson's 2018 book, *Cold Case Billy the Kid*.]

He did not stop and lay it down because Poe says he *"he came toward me art a very brisk walk."*

[AUTHOR'S NOTE: Triple tasking!]

Another question that investigators struggle with is would it not go without saying Poe would have had a description of the Kid as he ventured into Ft. Sumner to scout around and gather information. It is beyond reason that he would go searching for a man without at least having a description of the man for whom he was searching?

[AUTHOR'S NOTE: It is not beyond reason. Garrett was not an experienced lawman. And Poe's task was not to search for Billy, but to find out from locals about Billy's whereabouts.]

In a town of about 200 people, many of which were Hispanic would Poe be unable to recognize the Kid from this description as he claims?

[AUTHOR'S NOTE: What description? It seems Poe had none. Also, this is racist. Many people of Hispanic background could be as fair as Billy.]

Deputy Poe continues his statement with these words:

As I moved toward him trying to reassure him, he backed up into the doorway of Maxwell's room, where he halted for a moment, his body concealed by the thick adobe wall at the side of the doorway, from whence he put his head out and asking in Spanish for the fourth or fifth time who I was. I was within a few feet of him when he disappeared into the room.

When the Kid asks Poe who he is in Spanish and has his pistol pointed at the deputy, what is Deputy McKinney doing at this time? Why is he not shouldering his rifle, and at least deploying to the side to cover his partner Deputy Poe from this very real threat? Today the shooting policy for police officers is tight and narrow: in 1881 a shooting policy was non-existent. Investigators believe the deputies had to have a description for whom they were searching. With a threat such as Poe describes, a man with a gun, added to the description of the most wanted man in New Mexico, there would have been cause for both deputies to have fired on the suspect.

[AUTHOR'S NOTE: Here comes fakery. Who says Poe had the description, or thought the gun was a threat? Back then, most men were armed. Poe even shows lack of alarm by reassuring the stranger. This fakery was repeated by Sederwall for W.C. Jameson's 2018 book, *Cold Case Billy the Kid*.]

Even if the deputies chose not to fire, would they have allowed the man who was threatening their lives with a gun

[AUTHOR'S NOTE: Note this switcheroo from a fake claim of alarm at "threatening their lives," to making it a fact.]

to walk in on the unaware Sheriff in the dark? If they chose to allow the man with a gun to walk in on the Sheriff would these seasoned lawmen

[AUTHOR'S NOTE: Kip McKinney was just a hog farmer.]

not at least have warned the Sheriff of the danger?

[AUTHOR'S NOTE: No danger is established.]

In Garrett's statement he relates the following:

From his step I could perceive he was either barefooted or in his stocking feet and held a revolver in his right hand and butcher knife in his left.

He came directly towards me. Before he reached the bed, I whispered, "Who is it Pete?"

[AUTHOR'S NOTE: If Garrett cannot recognize Billy, there goes the hoaxers' best-buddies-murder-plot case centerpiece! Note also that Maxwell provides another Billy identification!]

But I received no response for a moment. It struck me that it might be Pete's brother-in-law, Manuel Abrea, who had seen Poe and McKinney and wanted to know their business. The intruder came close to me, leaned both hands on the bed, his right and almost touching my knee, and asked in a low tone: "Who are they, Pete?" At the same moment Maxwell whispered to me, "That's him!" Simultaneously the Kid must have seen, or felt, the presence of a third person at the head of the bed. He raised quickly his pistol, a self cocker, within a foot of my breast. Retreating rapidly across the room he cried: "Quien es? Quien es? (Who's that? Who's that?) All this occurred in a moment. Quickly as possible I drew   my revolver and fired, threw my body aside, and fired again. The second shot was useless: The Kid fell dead ..."

Investigators find it hard to believe that Garrett could see a 6 inch knife in the Kid's hand.

[AUTHOR'S NOTE: That night had a bright moon. When Billy opened the door, a held weapon would have been visible.]

Yet the Kid could not see a six foot, five inch man.

[AUTHOR'S NOTE: It was dark inside. Garrett was 6'4". Note that at this half-way point in the Probable Cause Statement, with killing done, nothing indicates the victim was not Billy.]

Deputy Poe talks about what happened after the shooting of the Kid. He writes:

Within a very short time after the shooting, quite a number of the native people had gathered around, some of them bewailing the death of their friend,

[AUTHOR'S NOTE: From Poe's *The Death of Billy the Kid*, comes this hoaxer slip-up: These people, who can recognize Billy, will later be given his body to lay out.]

while several women pleaded for permission to take charge of the body, which we allowed them to do. They carried it to the yard to a carpenter's shop, where it was laid on a workbench, the women placing candles lightened around it, according to their ideas of properly conducting a "wake" for the dead.

[AUTHOR'S NOTE: By this point, there are profuse eye-witness identifications of Billy!]

Investigators keep Deputy Poe's statement in mind as they studied the Coroner's Jury Report:

Greetings:

On this 15th day of July, A.D. 1881, I, the undersigned, Justice of the Peace of the above named precinct, received information that a murder had taken place in Fort Sumner, in said precinct, and immediately upon receiving said information I proceeded to the said place and named Milnor Rudolph, Jose Silva, Antonio Sevedra, Pedro Antonio Lucero, Lorenzo Jaramillo and Sabal Gutierres a jury to investigate the case and the above jury convened in the home of Luz B. Maxwell and proceeded to a room in the said house where they found the body of William Bonney alias "Kid" with a shot in the left breast and having examined the body they examined the evidence of Pedro Maxwell, which evidence is as follows: "I being in my bed in my room, at about midnight on the 14th day of July, Pat F. Garrett came into my room and sat down. William Bonney came in and got close to my bed with a gun in his hand and asked me "who is it" and then Pat F. Garrett fired two shots at the said William Bonney and the said William Bonney fell near my fire place and I went out of the room and when I came in again about three or four minutes after the shots the said William Bonney was dead."

[AUTHOR'S NOTE: This is a definitive Jury, plus Maxwell , making identifications of the victim as William Bonney.]

The jury has found the following verdict: We the jury unanimously find that William Bonney has been killed by a shot on the left breast near the region of the heart, the same having been fired with a gun in the hand of pat F. Garrett and our verdict is that the deed of said Garrett was justifiable homicide and we are unanimous in the opinion that the gratitude of all the community is due to the said Garrett for his deed and is worthy of being rewarded.

M. Rudolph, President   *Anto, Sevedra(signature)*
Pedro Anto. m. Lucero (signature)
Jose Silba (x)   *Sabal Gutierrez (x)*   *Lorenzo Jaramillo (x)*

All said information I place to your knowledge.

                 Alejandro Segura Justice of the Peace (signature)

[AUTHOR'S NOTE: This is a legally binding document confirming victim identification. To reopen the case is double jeopardy. Further confirmation of jurymen's certainty, is that no murder indictment was later made with the District Attorney of the First Judicial District Attorney against Garrett.]

Investigators remembered Deputy Poe's statement and Sheriff Garrett's statement as to where Poe had been that night.

[AUTHOR'S NOTE: The hoaxers hope readers believed their fake contention that Poe spent the night at Rudulph's. What follows is more fakery to manufacture "inconsistencies."]

Earlier that evening

[AUTHOR'S NOTE: The time was afternoon, as quoted by the hoaxers earlier, and tagged by me to prepare for this switcheroo where they need night for their fake argument.]

Garrett had dispatched Deputy Poe to interview M. Rudolph in Sunnyside, seven miles north of Fort Sumner. Poe says he left Rudolph and rode to meet Garrett and McKinney. All records show that the shooting took place about midnight and Historian Philip I. Rash [sic] sets the time at 12:30 AM on July 15th. If this were true then the time does not allow for the statement of Poe and the coroner's jury report to both be true.

[AUTHOR'S NOTE: Their hoaxers' time switcheroo is done to discredit the Coroner's Jury Report: their bugaboo. But, even if granted them, it does not work because of the length of the ride. Poe could cover the 7 miles to Sunnyside in 1½ hours. Puenta de la Glorietta was 4 miles north of Fort Sumner on the way. So Poe's return journey to meet his companions was only 3 miles, or about 45 minutes: easy to meet them by evening: a fact he and Garrett confirmed. No time inconsistency exists.]

If, after the shooting, Garrett had to get some order to the scene, locate a rider to ride to Sunnyside to get Rudolph,

[AUTHOR'S NOTE: The above Coroner's Jury Report clearly states that the appointment - and contacting - of Rudolph was a legal duty performed by the appropriate official: Justice of the Peace, Alejandro Segura; certainly not Garrett, then a suspect as to his legality in Billy Bonney's killing.]

and the rider then had to get his horses [sic] caught, saddled and ready to go all of which would take the better part of an hour,

[AUTHOR'S NOTE: Timing here is faked. Maxwell had a stable and workers. A horse could be readied quickly.]

the time would be 1:30 am.

[AUTHOR'S NOTE: The hoaxers are faking time "inconsistency. Yet they know that the Coroner's Jury met sometime during daytime of the 15th. There was no need for extreme urgency; and no evidence that it occurred.]

It would take a rider who was in shape, on a good horse, and riding fast, an hour and a half to cover the seven miles to Rudolph's ranch, putting the time at 2:30 am. Adding an hour for the rider to wake Rudolph up and for Rudolph to catch his horse and saddle the horse the time would be 3:30 am. If Rudolph was in good shape, on a good horse it would be another hour and a half on the return trip to Fort Sumner putting the time at 4:30 am. Add another hour to put together a jury, and the time is now 5:30 am. This is if everyone worked smoothly.

In the jury's report we find the words:

... a jury to investigate the case and the above jury convened in the home of Luz B. Maxwell and proceeded to a room in the said in said house where they found the body of William Bonney alias "Kid"...

Either the jury found the Kid in the Maxwell's home, or he was not given to the women to put on the carpenters workbench as Poe says, or the jury report is deceptive.

[AUTHOR'S NOTE: The hoaxers hope they convinced readers of that conclusion to fake an inconsistency. But there was enough time to carry the corpse from the Maxwell house, across about 300 yards of parade ground, to the carpenter's shop. In the morning, it could be returned to the Maxwell's house for the jurymen. This fakery was recycled by Sederwall for W.C. Jameson's 2018 book, *Cold Case Billy the Kid*.]

Deputy Poe also says:

The next morning we sent for the justice of the peace,

[AUTHOR'S NOTE: Here is undone the fakery of the night riding by giving this quote about the next morning.]

who held an inquest over the body, the verdict of the jury being such as to justify the killing, and later, on the same day, the body was buried in the old military burying ground at Fort Sumner.

If the Kid's body was taken to the carpenter shop then the jury did not find the body at Maxwell's house as stated and makes investigators wonder why they would lie in the report.

[AUTHOR'S NOTE: This fabrication leads to a "lie" accusation, though nothing indicates that the body was not brought to the house from the carpenter's shop. But the hoaxers are still trying to discredit the Coroner's Jury Report by fake "contradictions;" though, of course, that is irrelevant to establishing the victim's identity.]

Deputy Poe says something else that raised investigators suspicions when he writes about the shooting itself:

[AUTHOR'S NOTE: This switcheroo distracts from the sly misstatements slipped past. And though the hoaxers never say what is "suspicious" in Poe's quote – which is merely repeating Garrett's description - they are setting the stage for their fake "investigation" to be described next.]

An instant later a shot was fired in the room, followed immediately by what everyone within hearing distance thought was two shots fired, the third report, as we learned afterward, being caused by the rebound of the second bullet which had struck the adobe wall and rebounded against the headboard of the wooden bedstead.

[AUTHOR'S NOTE: Let us take stock now. Nothing so far indicates a victim other than profusely identified Billy Bonney. Nor are there any "contradictions." Later, when exhumations were blocked, the hoaxers contradicted this document: stating Billy *was* shot, laid out on the carpenter's bench, but *played dead* to bleed as a source of DNA, before evil Garrett switched him with the murdered innocent victim!]

[AUTHOR'S NOTE: Note that the second bullet hit the headboard. But the hoaxers will do fake forensics on a washstand instead! So next is a faked CSI-style investigation.]

On August 29, 2003, Deputy Sederwall of the Lincoln County Sheriff's Department

[AUTHOR'S NOTE: Sederwall calls himself a deputy; years later, when hiding the case's DNA documents from my open records case, he would lie that he did the case as his "hobby!"]

located the carpenter bench where the Kid's body was placed on July 14, 1881.

[AUTHOR'S NOTE: Error: earliest morning of July 15th]

On September 13, 2003, investigators located all the furniture that was in Pete Maxwell's bedroom the night of the shooting, July 1881.

[AUTHOR'S NOTE: Though this information is irrelevant to the claim of whether Billy was Garrett's victim, this Maxwell furniture - including the carpenter's bench - became pivotal to the survival of the hoax after exhumations were blocked. But the furniture's connection to the historical scenes is not iron-clad. The Maxwell family sold Fort Sumner at public auction on January 15, 1884 to Lonny Horn, Sam Doss, Daniel Taylor and

John Lord in partnership with the New England Cattle Company, which transferred its operations there. The Maxwell house (with the fateful bedroom) was torn down about 1887, and some of the timber was used to build the Pigpen Ranch south of Melrose, New Mexico.

Peter Maxwell died in 1898, Luz Maxwell in 1900. One of their daughters, Odile Maxwell married a Manuel Abreu, and settled outside the town. Odile may have taken family furniture. In about 1925, Odile's and Manuel's then 15 year old daughter, Stella, made a little "Billy the Kid Museum" in a shack to cater to tourists. She labeled some furniture and a carpenter's bench as from that history. It closed in 1936. In about 1940, she and her husband, Kenneth Miller, displayed the furniture in their Santa Rosa, New Mexico gas station. Later in the decade, they moved to Albuquerque, but stored the furniture until bringing what remained to their converted back-yard chicken coop in 1959. In old age, Stella told historian, Richard Weddle, that she had gotten the carpenter's bench from a local man. Her youngest son, Mannie Miller, showed it to the hoaxers; not her family. Mannie died March 20, 2011; and it was sold to a collector. So all one can say is that about 44 years after Billy's killing, Stella Abreu assembled some alleged Billy the Kid-related furniture for profit.]

Among these items is the headboard of the bed that was in Maxwell's room that night. There is no bullet hole in the headboard.

[AUTHOR'S NOTE: That finding, though irrelevant to the victim, is part of the hoaxers fake forensics and was created to contradict Poe's eye-witness statement that the headboard was hit. The fakery omitted mention that Stella Abreu's museum's headboard was just a frame around a huge opening of the missing headboard. There is no place for a bullet hole!]

In a statement made by Deluvina Maxwell she says the following:

... There was a washstand with a marble top in Pete Maxwell's bedroom, which Garrett had seen in the moonlight and shot at, thinking it was Bonney trying to get up.

[AUTHOR'S NOTE: This is a faked Deluvina quote. Its footnote states: "[15]Deluvina Maxwell's story as related to Lucien B. Maxwell grandchildren, unpublished." This is just hearsay, without a source or date. It is being used to fake legitimacy of the hoaxers' claim that the washstand was shot by Garrett.]

It was an old Spanish custom that the night before the burial of a person, people would take turns staying with the body and reciting prayers. William Bonney had a proper funeral. The people took turns and stayed through the night.

[AUTHOR'S NOTE: Another body identification as Billy!]

He was buried in the old government cemetery in Fort Sumner. For many years Deluvina left flowers on his grave in the summer time.[15]

[AUTHOR'S NOTE: This third person statement again shows the quote was not Deluvina. But she did lay flowers on the grave for decades, proving the body was Billy's!]

Deluvina lends credibility to the story of the Kid's body being laid on the carpenter bench.

[AUTHOR'S NOTE: Here is a hoaxer slip that ends their case: Billy's corpse on bench! And it ends "Brushy's" hoax too! To get out of that problem, the hoaxers later fabricated that Billy was just "playing dead!"]

In the items investigators located on September 13, 2003 was that wash stand.

[AUTHOR'S NOTE: This washstand is unsubstantiated as from Pete Maxwell's bedroom - as is the rest of the furniture from Stella Abreu's Billy the Kid Museum. And this washstand is implausibly toy-sized. Furthermore, eye-witness Poe said the headboard was hit. But what follows is a fake "crime scene investigation" using the unsubstantiated washstand.]

The was stand was dark in color and 29 1/2 inches wide, with a splash board on the back that measured 5 inch at the middle and tapered down to the ends in a decorative curve. From front to back the wash stand measured 16 inches. It stood 29 inches with three drawers with rusted locks on each drawer. There was what appeared to be a bullet hole through the stand.

Deputy Sederwall removed a .45 caliber pistol round from his deputy weapon and noticed the round was just a little bit bigger than the hole. The night of the shooting Sheriff Garrett was shooting a Colt Single Action Army Revolver, Serial Number 55093, caliber .44/40.[16] ([16]Typed letter from P.F. Garrett dated April 16, 1906. James H. Earl Collection, from County Clerk's office, El Paso, Texas.)

[AUTHOR'S NOTE: Note that there is no bullet, just holes. Claiming .44/40 ammunition is fakery to match Garrett's known weapon's caliber. Actually, there is no link to Garrett or to Maxwell's bedroom. There is even no link to anyone being shot, since accidental discharges happened in New Mexico where owning guns was common from the 19th century to the present - the time frame for "shooting" the tiny washstand!]

The bullet pierced the left side of the washstand, both sides of the drawer and exited out the right side of the stand.

The bullet struck the left side of the stand 22 1/4 inches on the center up from the bottom and 6 1/2 inches on the center of the back of the stand. The bullet exited to the right side 20 1/2 inches on the center up from the bottom and 6 1/2 inches on center from the back of the washstand. On the inside of the left side panel the wood was somewhat splintered indicating that was where the bullet entered the stand. On the right side panel the outside of the panel was splintered indicating the exit of the bullet.

The owner of the washstand, whose name investigators do not wish to release at this time

[AUTHOR'S NOTE: The hoaxers later named Mannie Miller.]

says it was inherited along with the bed from Maxwell's bedroom. The discovery of this evidence makes Deluvina's statement believable.

[AUTHOR'S NOTE: Historically real or not, the furniture examination is irrelevant to Garrett's victim's identity.]

Many questions remain. Why would the coroner's jury report and the eye witness reports be so at odds?

[AUTHOR'S NOTE: They are not at odds. The hoaxers simply made up some "discrepancies." But the hoaxers were heading to additional fakery, once again to attack the Coroner's Jury Report that undid their hoaxing.]

A hint can be found in a document discovered in July of 1989 by Joe O. Bowlin.

[AUTHOR'S NOTE: This is a low blow to a dead man. Joe Bowlin, with his wife Marlyn, founded the Billy the Kid Outlaw Gang to "preserve, protect, and promote the history of Billy Bonney and Pat Garrett." This hoax would have been anathema to Joe Bowlin. What follows misstates a book Bolin published posthumously for its old-timer author, A.P. "Paco" Anaya.]

The document is a story, according to Louis Anaya of Clovis, New Mexico as told to his father, Paco Anaya, a friend of Billy the Kid.

[AUTHOR'S NOTE: Note the admitted friendship of "Paco" Anaya and Billy. It will catch the hoaxers in another slip-up about the victim being Billy.]

This story was translated from Spanish and then printed in book form. In this transcript you will find the following:

Also, I will have to tell you a lot in reference to the reports that Pat Garrett made about the sworn declaration that appears in the records of the Secretary of State and more, concerning what he said about the

Coroners Jury that investigated the death of Billy the Kid when Pat killed Billy.

In this report, I find that the Coroners Jury that investigated the death of Billy the Kid when he was dead is not part of the same report that acted as a Coroners Jury, neither the form or the verdict of the Coroners Jury. The verdict is recorded in the office of the Secretary of State in Spanish, and they (the jury) are not the same men. There are two that did not even live in Fort Sumner.[17] ([17]Anaya, A.P. *I Buried Billy*. Creative Publishing Company. 1991.)

Paco Anaya goes on to list the members of the Jury that he remembered holding the inquest over the body. They are not the same as the jury report as is held up as proof that Garrett killed the Kid.

[AUTHOR'S NOTE: This is the "Brushy" hoax's two coroner's jury reports malarkey from "Paco" Anaya, who told it in his April 2, 1937 letter to George Fitzpatrick of *New Mexico Magazine*. It was published posthumously in his 1991 book, *I Buried Billy*. It was recycled in "Brushy" hoax books that followed, including W.C. Jameson's *Cold Case Billy the Kid*]

One of the differences is Illeginio Garcia [sic - poor legibility - unclear spelling] as the Jury President and not M. Rudolph.

Paco Anaya says that Garrett wrote the first version in English himself. Anaya says that Garrett later came back and wrote another report in Spanish with the help of "Don Pedro Maxwell and Don Manuel Abrea," [sic - Abreu] Maxwell's brother-in-law.

This makes the investigators ask, if Garrett wrote the verdict is that why the words are found, "...*we are unanimous in the opinion that the gratitude of all the community is due to the said Garrett for his deed and is worthy of being rewarded"?*

It should be noted that in the Coroners Jury Report that Garrett puts forth

[AUTHOR'S NOTE: Note the switcheroo. Garrett did not "put forth" the Coroner's Jury Report. It was a legal document done by authority of Justice of the Peace, Alejandro Segura. Garrett was the *subject* of their investigation. The document was available to him after he was cleared, to send its copy to Acting-Governor William Ritch. It surely was not available to humble citizen Anaya. But the hidden punch line is that Anaya's posthumously published, 1991 book was titled *I Buried Billy*, with his confirming the body as Billy Bonney's.]

it is interesting to note that two of those listed were in Garrett's wedding, Sabal Gutierrez is his brother-in-law, and Garrett admits in his statement that Rudolph is a close friend.

[AUTHOR'S NOTE: Note the lie. Garrett did not pick the jurymen; the Justice of the Peace did. All the fakery has done nothing to show that Garrett murdered anyone but Billy.]

[AUTHOR'S NOTE: Next is the hoaxer' last try: using fellow hoaxer, David Turk, for useless hearsay and his fancy title.]

David Turk, Historian for the United States Marshal's Service has pointed out other documents

[AUTHOR'S NOTE: Only one document is presented; though Turk came to New Mexico in December of 2003, possibly to assist in writing this Probable Cause Statement.]

bringing into question Garrett's involvement in the Kid's escape.

[AUTHOR'S NOTE: Note the switcheroo. Who said Billy escaped? He was dead.]

Mr. Turk has produced a Works Progress Administration, Federal Writer's Project interview where the following statement was taken:

> The people around Lincoln

[AUTHOR'S NOTE: The killing was 150 miles from Lincoln; and Turk's old-timer reports are useless hearsay. He also supplied the hoax with his own slip-shod and pretender-oriented booklet titled "U.S. Marshals Service and Billy the Kid."]

say Garrett didn't kill Billie (sic) the Kid. John Poe was with Garrett the night he was supposed to ... said that he didn't see the man that Garrett killed.

[AUTHOR'S NOTE: Besides the fact that Poe's statements all refer to seeing the victim, Poe did not know Billy.]

> I can take you to the grave in Hell's High Acre, an old government cemetery, where Billie (sic) was supposed to be buried and show you the grave.
> The cook at Pete Maxwell's was always putting flowers on the grave and praying at it. This woman thought a lot of Billie (sic), but after Garrett killed the man at Maxwell's home her grandson was never seen again

[AUTHOR'S NOTE: No "grandson" was part of this history.]

and Billie (sic) was seen by Bill Nicholi an Indian scout. Bill saw him in Mexico.[18] ([18]Frances E. Tolly [Totty], comp. "Early Days in Lincoln County," Charles Remark Interview. February 14, 1938, Works Progress Administration, Federal Writer's Project, Folklore-Life Histories, Manuscript Division. Library of Congress.)

[AUTHOR'S NOTE: So this sole "evidence" that Garrett did not kill Billy is old-timer malarkey 57 years later, by someone unconnected to the event, and titled as "folklore."]

[AUTHOR'S NOTE: Next comes the conclusion pretending they proved their contentions.]

Discovering the headboard of Maxwell's bed that does not have a bullet hole in it, as Deputy Poe says it did, leads investigators to question if Poe was in fact in the room after the shooting of William Bonney as he said.

[AUTHOR'S NOTE: Omitted is that the headboard is just an empty frame. And claiming if it was not shot, Poe was not in the room" is absurd; and also irrelevant to victim identity.]

However, the discovery of the Maxwell wash stand with the bullet hole through it indicates someone was shot in Maxwell's room on the night of July 14, 18821.

[AUTHOR'S NOTE: Why? A shot washstand does not mean a shot person - or anything at all about who Garrett shot.]

The question remains as to who is in William H. Bonney's grave at Fort Sumner.

[AUTHOR'S NOTE: No question remains. This is all fakery.]

Investigators believe with the conflicts of Sheriff Pat F. Garrett and Deputy John Poe and the fact that these statements are at odds with the Jury Report as shown above,

[AUTHOR'S NOTE: This is fakery. The "conflicts" do not exist; and had nothing to do with whom Garrett shot.]

coupled with the evidence discovered by deputies,

[AUTHOR'S NOTE: There has been no legitimate evidence.]

probable cause exist [sic] to warrant the court to grant investigators the right to search for the truth in criminal investigation 2003-274 through DNA samples obtained from Catherine Antrim.

[AUTHOR'S NOTE: Without any probable cause of a murder, the hoaxers, contrived their objective: exhumation of Billy and his mother.]

[AUTHOR'S NOTE: Signatures follow; typed and written.]

Steven M. Sederwall: Deputy Sheriff, Lincoln County (12/31/03)

Tom Sullivan: Sheriff Lincoln County (12/31/03)

THE OVERTON AFFIDAVIT

Attached to the "Probable Cause Statement" was a two page, typed, old-timer affidavit prepared for Sheriff Tom Sullivan by a Homer Overton in the mold of the fake identity Affidavits used by William V. Morrison for *Alias Billy the Kid.*. To be noted is that Overton is lying, for whatever reason. It should be noted that Pat Garrett's widow, Apolinaria Gutierrez Garrett, died in 1936, four years *before* Overton's alleged conversation with her in 1940 (b.1861 - d.1936)! She is buried in the Masonic Cemetery in Las Cruces, New Mexico, where Pat Garrett also lies.

Overton's windbag malarkey includes fabrications of a Pat Garrett report to Texas Rangers, a corpse with blasted face, and, of course, Garrett's murder of someone other than Billy the Kid.

Overton's claims also insult Pat Garrett's widow's reverential protection of Garrett's legacy. After Garrett's death in 1908, she even legally fought and reclaimed from a saloonkeeper his revolver used to kill Billy the Kid. She was the last person in the world to tell random, 9 year old child, Homer Overton, that Pat had not shot the Kid - even if she had not been four years dead! Homer Overton wrote:

December 22, 2003

Tom Sullivan
Lincoln County Sheriff
P.O. Box 278
Carrizozo, NM 88301

Tom,

It was good talking to you on the phone and, as promised, I am sending this letter as promised to present this Statement of Facts.

Fact: I was born in Pecos, Texas in the year 1931 and lived there until the later [sic] part of 1941. In the summer of 1940, I was invited to spend the summer with Bobby Talbert and his mother, who had moved from Pecos to Las Cruces, New Mexico earlier that year.

[AUTHOR'S NOTE: Time specificity of Overton's age plus the date fixes Overton in Las Cruces in 1940 – not earlier.]

The time I spent there was wonderful, but one thing happened that summer that made the summer unforgettable.

Bobby's next door neighbor was a lady who introduced herself as Mrs. Garrett, the widow of Pat Garrett. Mrs. Garrett would invite us over to have iced tea with mint leaves in it, and told us stories about her life with Pat. I recall her having a parrot that had belonged to Pat which she said was very old. She told us some parrots live to be over 100 years.

That afternoon, she brought out a gun to show us and said it had belonged to Pat. As I recall, the gun appeared to be a Colt single action revolver. At that point I asked her if that was the gun used to kill Billy the Kid. At this point she got an unusual look on her face and stated that she was going to tell us something we would have to promise to keep a secret, and never to tell anyone. We both promised, and until this day I have never told anyone but my immediate family.

Mrs. Garrett proceeded to tell us the following facts concerning her husband and Billy:

Mrs. Garrett said, "Pat did not shoot Billy". She said there was a very close relationship between Pat and Billy, almost like a father and son relationship. She further stated that the night Pat was supposed to kill Billy, that they were in Ft. Sumner and had made a plan to make it look like Pat killed Billy so Billy could go to Mexico and live with no one looking for him any more. She said that Pat had seen a drunk Mexican lying in the street on his way to talk to Billy. So they planned to use the Mexican and claim that he was in fact Billy the Kid. She didn't state if the Mexican was dead or not, but said that they shot him in the face so he couldn't be recognized. They dressed him in Billy's clothes and Pat signed a paper for the Texas Rangers stating that he had killed Billy the Kid and that this was his body. The Mexican was then buried in Fort Sumner and identified as Billy.

Mrs. Garrett struck me as being very sincere when she told us this and she stated that she had never told anyone before. I have kept this secret for sixty-three years and feel it is time to disclose this story. I hope it will be helpful to you in your quest to find the truth about Billy, as I believe what Mrs. Garrett told us that day was the absolute truth.

All that I have told you is as I recall it related to me sixty-three years ago when I was nine years old. It made such an impression on me that I have remembered it in detail these sixty-three years.

Sincerely,
Homer D. Overton
AKA: Homer D. Kinsworthy
CONTACT INFORMATION

Witnessed by: Jerry Raffee, NOTARY
on December 27th 2003

SEAL AFFIXED

ABANDONED PROBABLE CAUSE STATEMENT

A document which the lawmen hoaxers hid, and I got by my open records litigation against them, revealed the "Brushy Bill" core of the "Billy the Kid Case" hoax. Likely created around April of 2003, it is a draft of a never-used "Probable Cause Statement" for Pat Garrett as the murder suspect. "LATEST" is handwritten on its front page, as if drafts were attempted. It was titled: "Lincoln County Sheriff's Office, Lincoln County New Mexico, Case: William H. Bonney, a.k.a. William Antrim, a.k.a. The Kid, a.k.a. Billy the Kid: An Investigation into the events of April 28, 1881 through July 14, 1881 - seventy-seven days of doubt." I nick-named it the "Seventy-Seven Days of Doubt Document." Typed-in for future signatures are: "Tom Sullivan: Sheriff, Lincoln County Sheriff's Office; and Steven M. Sederwall: Deputy Sheriff, Lincoln County Sheriff's Office."

Its intent was promoting "Brushy Bill" as Billy the Kid. "Brushy's" "survival" as Billy the Kid is the "evidence," or probable cause, for Garrett's not having killed Billy. So, according to the fledgling "Billy the Kid Case" hoax, Billy Barlow was their corpse in Billy's Fort Sumner grave - and intended recipient of their hoax's "high-tech, modern, CSI, DNA forensics."

The "Seventy-Seven Days of Doubt" version is pure conspiracy theory where "Brushy" is king; with John Miller fleetingly referenced for "survival suspicion." And with ignorance matching W.C. Jameson and Frederick Bean, it uses "Brushy's" unscreened quotes as proof. In fact, either Jameson himself, or his *The Return of the Outlaw Billy the Kid* may have been the quote's source. So **"Brushy's" fatal mistake of the *dark night* of the July 14, 1881 killing scene appears again, as it was in *The Return of Billy the Kid*;** after having been altered to "bright moonlight" by in original Sonnichsen-Morrison scam for *Alias Billy the Kid*.

But its actual author is unclear. The person was unaware of the history, for example, calling Paulita (Peter Maxwell's sister), his "teenage daughter." Mere guesses for authoring are amateur Attorney Bill Robins III, since needed was a "Brushy"-believer. Or it could have been W.C. Jameson (since he had the "Brushy" transcript); or David Turk, who also contributed his own "Brushy"-oriented report.

Importantly, the "Seventy-Seven Days of Doubt Document" lets uncensored "Brushy" talk, giving another window into his mad and florid confabulated death scene. The document stated:

LINCOLN COUNTY SHERIFF'S OFFICE
LINCOLN COUNTY, NEW MEXICO

Case: *William H. Bonney,* a.k.a. William Antrim,
a.k.a. The Kid, *a.k.a.* Billy the Kid

An Investigation into the events of April 28, 1881 through July 14, 1881 - seventy-seven days of doubt.

Just minutes after twelve, noon, on April 28, 1881, two lawmen lay dead, in the yard of the courthouse in Lincoln, New Mexico, from gunshot wounds. In less time then [sic] it took the New Mexico breeze to clear the gunsmoke, history was clouded with the myth of the shooting and escape of William H. Bonney, a.k.a. Billy the Kid from the makeshift jail, where he awaited a date with the hangman.

The following is a thumbnail sketch of the most widely excepted [sic] account of the events of the escape, capture and shooting death of William H. Bonney a.k.a. Billy the Kid.

The Last Days of William H. Bonney

On August 17, 1877, in George Atkin's cantina near Camp Grant, Arizona, William H. Bonney, who answered to "The Kid" found himself in an altercation with Francis P. "Windy" Cahill over cards or Cahill's woman, no one is quite sure as newspapers report both. It's reported that Windy Cahill called The Kid a "pimp", and in response The Kid dubbed Cahill a "sonofabitch". Infuriated, Cahill reportedly grabbed the Kid and The Kid shoved his pistol into Cahill's stomach, sending a hot round into his belly. With Cahill on the floor, The Kid fled on a stolen horse. Cahill died the next day. A coroner's jury headed by Miles Wood found the shooting by The Kid to be *"criminal and unjustifiable"*. The Kid now being a bona fide outlaw drifted across the line into New Mexico's Lincoln County where he signed on as a cowboy working for London born rancher John Tunstall.

Tunstall and his lawyer friend Alexander McSween had decided to challenge the chock-hold [sic] monopoly L.G. Murphy & Company had on Lincoln County. Murphy and his associates, with the backing of the "Santa Fe Ring" ran Lincoln County as they pleased and verticality [sic] unchecked until Tunstall's challenge. The Santa Fe Ring, with their powerful political and financial backing and through Murphy controlled the sheriff, maintained a buddy-buddy relationship with the military and appropriated by means both legal and illegal most of the government money out of the Mescalero Apache Indian Agency near Fort Stanton. When Tunstall wouldn't back down and his challenge became to [sic] powerful for the Murphy faction to turn their heads to, Tunstall was killed. His death on February 18, 1878 fanned the spark that raged into the white-hot flame that became the famed and bloody Lincoln County War.

As history goes Bonney was insignificant as a man, but there exist [sic] no better example of how legends of the west are born and continue to grow. By participating in a number of bloody shootouts, included [sic] the assassination of Lincoln County Sheriff William Brady and one of his deputies, on April 1, 1878, Bonney was catapulted from his status of an unknown drifter to the undisputed leader of the Tunstall-McSween faction and into history becoming bigger the [sic] life.

[AUTHOR'S NOTE: Though starting when Bonney was 17½ (not his last days!), the intent is to feign historical knowledge, but fails. Billy was never the leader of the Tunstall-McSween faction. The fakery intentionally blurs history and "legend," to pretend that actual history *was* legend, to segue to the fakery that history was not as written. But all this is irrelevant to any probable cause of Pat Garrett murdering an innocent victim.]

After newly elected Lincoln County Sheriff Pat Garrett captured Bonney at Stinking Springs, east of Fort Sumner, just before Christmas 1880, Bonney was held in the jail in Santa Fe for several months and then taken to La Mesilla, New Mexico for trial.

The Dona Ana County, District Court records reveal on April 13, 1881, William H. Bonney was convicted of the April 1, 1878 murder of Lincoln County Sheriff William Brady. United States District Judge, Warren Henry Bristol, of the Third Judicial District, sentenced Bonney to be confined in Lincoln County until Friday, May 13, 1881. Looking down from the bench, the judge proclaimed, *"between 9 a.m. and 3 p.m., William Bonney, alias Kid, alias William Antrim, be taken from such prison to some suitable and convenient place of execution within said county of Lincoln, by Sheriff of such county and that then and there, on that day and between the aforesaid hours thereof, by the sheriff of said county of Lincoln, he, the said William Bonney, alias Kid, alias William Antrim, be hanged by the neck until his body be dead."*

On April 21, 1881, Bonney was transported back to Lincoln under heavy guard. Because Lincoln had no adequate jail Bonney was incarcerated in the upstairs of the old Murphy-Dolan store, recently bought by the county to be used as the courthouse. A staircase led up to a hallway that ran north to south across the middle section of the building. The room ahead and to the left of the hallway was being used as the sheriff''s office. Off the sheriff''s office, with access only through the sheriff''s office was the room where Bonney was confined.

With no bars on the windows of this room, Sheriff Garrett had special leg shackles made, and Bonney was chained to the hardwood floor at all times. In addition, Garrett assigned Lincoln County Sheriffs Deputy J.W. Bell and Deputy United States Marshall [sic] Bob Olinger, to guard the prisoner twenty-four hours a day. On the floor Bonney's guards drew a chalk line across the center of the room, a line which Bonney was forbidden to cross or he would be shot by the guards.

On Wednesday, April 27, 1881 Sheriff Pat Garrett left Lincoln on a tax-collecting mission to White Oaks, New Mexico. Just after twelve, noon, the next day, Thursday, April 28, Deputy United States Marshall [sic] Olinger escorted all the prisoners with the exception of Bonney to the Wortley Hotel, across the street from the courthouse, for their midday meal, leaving Deputy Sheriff Bell in charge of Bonney.

No eye witness record can be found of the escape of Bonney with the exception of the following statement made by the courthouse caretaker Gottfried Gauss, published in the *Lincoln County Leader* on January 15, 1890, nearly a decade later.

I was crossing the yard behind the courthouse, when I heard a shot fired then a tussle upstairs in the courthouse, somebody hurrying downstairs, and deputy sheriff Bell emerging from the door running toward me. He ran right into my arms, expired the same moment, and I laid him down, dead. That I was in a hurry to secure assistance, or perhaps to save myself, everybody will believe.

When I arrived at the garden gate leading to the street, in front of the courthouse, I saw the other deputy sheriff Olinger, coming out of the hotel opposite, with the four or five other county prisoners, where they had taken their dinner. I called to him to come quick. He did so, leaving his prisoners in front of the hotel. When he had come up close to me, and while I was standing not a yard apart, I told him that I was just after laying Bell dead on the ground in the yard behind. Before he could reply, he was struck by a well-directed shot fired from a window above us, and fell dead at my feet. I ran for my life to reach my room and safety, when Billy the Kid called to me: "Don't run, I wouldn't hurt you – I am alone, and master not only of the courthouse, but also of the town, for I will allow nobody to come near us." "You go," he said, "and saddle one of Judge (Ira) Leonard's horses, and I will clear out as soon as I have the shackles loosened from my legs." With a little prospecting pick I had thrown to him through the window he was working for at least an hour, and could not accomplish more than to free one leg. He came to the conclusion to wait a better chance, tie one shackle to his waistbelt, and start out. Meanwhile I had saddled a small skittish pony belonging to

Billy Burt (the county clerk), as there was no other horse available, and had also, by Billy's command, tied a pair of red blankets behind the saddle ...

When Billy went down the stairs at last, on passing the body of Bell he said, "I'm sorry I had to kill him but I couldn't help it." On passing the body of Olinger he gave him a tip with his boot, saying, "You are not going to round me up again." And so Billy the Kid started out that evening, after he had shaken hands with everybody around and after having a little difficulty in mounting on account of the shackle on his leg, he went on his way rejoicing.

There are numerous theories about the killing of Deputy J.W. Bell. One is that he was coming up the stairs when shot. Another theory is Bell was running down the stairs and was at the bottom of the stairs and heading to the doorway when Bonney shot him. Garrett's testimony seems to be the most solid. Garrett says, *"Bell was hit under the right arm, the bullet passing through his body and coming out under the left arm. The ball had hit the wall on Bell's right, caromed passed through his body, and buried itself in an adobe (wall) on the left. There was no other proof besides the marks on the walls."*

Garrett later said of Olinger, that he was *"hit in the right shoulder, breast and side. He was literally riddled by thirty-six buckshot."* Each pellet weighed four grams - nearly a quarter pound of lead in all hit Olinger.

It's hard to determine how many shots were fired at Bell from Bonney's pistol. In the 1920's Maurice G. Fulton saw the building and states there were *"any number of bullet holes".* Fulton had a photograph taken in the 1930's prior to the restoration, which shows three.

With only two people on the stairway that day numerous versions of what happened have been brought forth, and debated. One theory in the Kid's escape is that he slipped his irons, which were double the usual weight, over his small wrists and hands. He turned on Bell striking the deputy over the head with the irons and grabbing the deputy's pistol. This theory could have come from the following article.

In the *Grand County Herald's,* May 14, 1881 edition an article appeared quoting an "anonymous bystander" as testifying about the Kid's escape. *He had at his command eight revolvers and six guns. He stood on the upper porch in front of the building and talked with the people who were in Wortley's, but he would not let anyone come towards him. He told the people that he did not want to kill Bell but, as he had to. He said he grabbed Bell's revolver and told him to hold up his hands and* surrender; that Bell decided to run and he had to kill him. He declared he was "standing pat" against the world; and while he did not wish to kill anybody, if anybody interfered with his attempt to escape, he would kill him.

In this statement the "anonymous bystander" claims Bonney says he took Bell's pistol from him and used it to kill the deputy. In Garrett's book *The Authentic Life of Billy the Kid*, Garrett writes this about the escape:

From circumstances, indications, information from Geiss (also spelled Gauss – the courthouse caretaker) and the Kid's admissions, the popular conclusion is that:
At the Kid's request, Bell accompanied him down stairs and to the back corral. As they returned, Bell allowed the Kid to get considerably in advance. As the Kid turned on the landing of the stairs, he was hidden from Bell. He was light and active, and with a few noiseless bounds, reached the head of the stairs, turned to his right, put his shoulder to the door of the room used as an armory (thought locked, this door was well known to open by a firm push), entered, seized a six-shooter, returned to the head of the stairs just as Bell faced him on the landing of the staircase, some twelve steps beneath, and fired. Bell turned, ran out into the corral and towards the little gate. He fell dead before reaching it. The Kid ran to the window at the south end of the hall, saw Bell fall, then slipped his handcuffs over his hands, threw them at the body, and said: "Here, damn you, take these, too."

Garrett's account seems to have to [sic] many holes to be taken as truth in this matter. At the beginning of Chapter XXII, where this account is found Garrett begins, *On the evening of April 28, 1881, Olinger took all the other prisoners across the street to supper, leaving Bell in charge of the Kid in the guard room.* It is a known fact that the escape did not happen in the evening as Garrett writes but just after noon.

Frederick Nolan, in his commentary notes at the side of the page in this book, points out the following: *The "popular" conclusion set forth here - that Bell would have allowed the Kid latitude and time he needed to perform these maneuvers - has already been examined. That he could have moved "noiselessly" when wearing manacles and leg irons defies belief. And would Billy have waited until after killing Bell before he "slipped his handcuffs over his hands?" Either the Kid struck Bell over the head with his handcuffs, grabbed Bell's gun and killed him with it, or, far more plausibly, someone hid a pistol in the outhouse privy, which Billy retrieved and, when they got inside, killed Bell with it.*

When Garrett describes The Kid shooting Olinger he says that ... *Olinger appeared at the gate leading into the yard, as Geiss appeared at the little corral gate and said, "Bob, The Kid has killed Bell." At the same instant the Kid's voice was heard above: "Hello, old boy," said he. "Yes, and he's killed me too," exclaimed Olinger, and fell dead with eighteen buckshot in his right shoulder and breast and side.*

It is doubtful that Olinger would have time to say the words that Garrett contributes [sic] to him before the Kid cut him down, making Garrett's account difficult to be taken as true accounting of the events.

[AUTHOR'S NOTE: Though lacking crafty finesse of the final Probable Cause Statement, this author likewise uses Garrett's ghostwritten, dime-novel-style book to try to discredit him. But it remains irrelevant to Garrett as a murderer.]

Garrett also says about The Kid in his account – *He took deliberate aim and fired the other barrel, the charge taking effect in nearly the same place as the first; then breaking the gun across the railway of the balcony, he threw the pieces at Olinger, saying: "Take it, damn you, you won't follow me any more with that gun."*

This doubtful this happened. [sic] The account of The Kid breaking Olinger's shotgun on the balcony is not found elsewhere. Added to the fact that Olinger's shotgun was a Whitney, serial number SN903, and is now on loan to the *Texas Ranger Hall of Fame* in Waco, Texas from the James H. Earl Collection; the shotgun is in tact [sic].

[AUTHOR'S NOTE: Wrong. Deputy Bob Olinger's Whitney double-barreled shotgun there is broken at its waist, and repaired, at some unknown time, by a wrapping of copper wire. Its curator at the Texas Ranger Museum, attesting to the description, is Don Agler. This is another irrelevant attempt to discredit Garrett.]

The version which seems the more popular, is that Bonney, retrieved a pistol that had been hidden in the outhouse by a "friend." History has theories but no firm answers to the identity of the "friend" who put the pistol in the outhouse.

[AUTHOR'S NOTE: Wrong. This seems to be a confusion of the Bell killing with Olinger's, for which the Whitney was used.]

After the Kid shot and killed both of his guards he gather [sic] weapons, and left Lincoln about 3 p.m. on a stolen horse. The Kid's whereabouts from the date of his escape until just before his death, as nearly every aspect of the case, is still debated. The Kid later showed up in Ft. Sumner, New Mexico. **Pete Maxwell's teenage daughter, Paulita,**

[AUTHOR'S NOTE: Wrong. Paulita was Peter Maxwell's sister. Also, using Paulita contradicts the "Brushy" hoax which used Celsa as the sweetheart and the John Miller hoax using his wife, Isadora, ending them as Billy contenders!. But revealed is the writer's historical ignorance.]

was supposedly in love with the Kid and he with her, which seems to be the most likely motive for him to return to Ft. Sumner.

On the night of July 14, 1881, after searching the area around Ft. Sumner Lincoln County Sheriff Pat Garrett and his deputies John Poe and Thomas C. "Kip" McKinney were about to ride back to Lincoln. Before leaving they thought it a good idea to check with Pete Maxwell. In Garrett's account of this he takes credit for wanting to check with Maxwell before giving up the chase, Deputy Poe differs with Garrett. In Deputy Poe's account written in 1919 we see the events through his eyes.

Garrett seemed to have but little confidence in our being able to accomplish the object of our trip, but said that he knew the location of a certain house occupied by a woman in Fort Sumner which the Kid had formerly frequented, and that if he was in or about Fort Sumner, he would most likely be found entering or leaving this house some time during the night. Garrett proposed that we go to a grove of trees near the town, conceal our horses, then station ourselves in the peach orchard at the rear of the house, and keep watch on who might come or go. This course was agreed upon, and we entered the peach orchard about nine o'clock that night, stationing ourselves in the gloom or shadow of the peach trees, as the moon was shining very brightly. We kept up a fruitless watch here until some time after eleven o'clock, when Garrett stated that he believed we were on a cold trail; that he had very little faith in our being able to accomplish anything when we started on the trip. He proposed that we leave the town without letting anyone know that we had been there in search of the Kid.

I then proposed that, before leaving we should go to the residence of Peter Maxwell, a man who up to that time I had never seen, but who, by reason of his being a leading citizen and having a large property interest should, according to my reasoning, be glad to furnish such information as he might have aid us [sic] in ridding the country of a man who was looked on as a scourge and curse by all law-abiding people.

Garrett agreed to this, and there-upon led us from the orchard by circuitous by-paths to Maxwell's residence, which was a building formerly used as officers' quarters during the days when a garrison of troops had been maintained at the fort. Upon our arriving at the residence (a very long, one-story adobe, standing end to the flush with the street, having a porch on the south side, which was the direction from which we approached, the premises all being enclosed by a paling fence, one side of which ran parallel to and along the edge of the street up to and across the end of the porch to the corner of the building).\, Garrett said to me, "This is Maxwell's room through the open door (left open on account of the extremely warm weather), while McKinney and myself stopped on the outside. McKinney squatted on the outside of the fence, and I sat on the porch.

It should be here that up to this moment I had never seen Billy the Kid, nor Maxwell, which fact in view of the events transpiring immediately afterward, placed me at an extreme disadvantage.

It was probably not more than thirty seconds after Garrett had entered Maxwell's room, when my attention was attracted, from where I sat at the little gateway, to a man approaching me on the inside of and along the fence, some forty or fifty steps away. I observed that he was only partially dressed and was both bareheaded and barefooted, or rather had only socks on his feet, and it seemed to me that he was fastening his trousers as he came toward me at a very brisk walk.

As Maxwell's was the one place in Fort Sumner that had considered above suspicion of harboring the Kid, I was entirely off my guard, the thought coming to my mind that the man approaching was either Maxwell or some guest of his who might be staying there. He came on until he was almost within arm's length of where I sat, before he saw me, as I was partially concealed from his view by the post of the gate.

Upon seeing me, he covered me with his six-shooter as quick as lightening, sprang onto the porch, calling out in Spanish "Quien es" (Who is it?) - at the same time backing away from me toward the door through which Garrett only a few seconds before had passed, repeating his query, "Who is it?" in Spanish several times.

At this I stood up and advanced toward him, telling him not to be alarmed, that he should not be hurt; and still without the least suspicion that this was the very man we were looking for. As I moved toward him to reassure him, he backed up into the doorway of Maxwell's room, where he halted for a moment, his body concealed by the thick adobe wall at the side of the doorway, form [sic] whence he put his head and asked in Spanish for the fourth time who I was. I was within a few feet of him when he disappeared into the room.

After this, and until after the shooting, I was unable to see what took place on account of the darkness of the room, but plainly heard what was said on the inside. An instant after the man left the door, I heard a voice inquired in a sharp tone, "Pete, who are those fellows on the outside?"

An instant later a shot was fired in the room, followed immediately by what anyone within hearing distance thought were two shots. However, there were only two shots fired, the third report, as we learned afterward, being caused by the rebound of the second bullet, which had struck the adobe wall and rebounded against the headboard of a wooden bedstead.

I heard a groan and one or two gasps from where I stood in the doorway, as of someone dying in the room. An instant later, Garrett came out, brushing against me as he passed. He stood by me close to the wall at the side of the door and said to me, "That was the Kid that came in there onto me, and I think I got him". I said, "Pat, the Kid would not come to this place; you have shot the wrong man".

Upon saying this, Garrett seemed to be in doubt himself as to whom he had shot, but quickly spoke up and said, "I am sure it was him, for I know his voice to [sic] *well to be mistaken". This remark of Garrett's relieved me of considerable apprehension, as I had felt almost certain that someone whom we did not want had been killed.*

The next day Billy the Kid was buried in Fort Sumner. Or was it the Kid in the grave?

[AUTHOR'S NOTE: Poe's initial uncertainty about Billy's identity, is this writer's only "evidence" of victim identity doubt. Omitted are all witnesses, the Coroner's Jury, and Poe's acceptance.]

What Happen [sic] to William H. Bonney a.k.a. Billy the Kid?

Soon after the shooting in Maxwell's home on July 14, 1881, the rumor took life that Garrett shot the wrong man and that he knew he shot the wrong man but covered it up.

[AUTHOR'S NOTE: This "Seventy-Seven Days Document" is transparently tailored to fit the pretenders.]

Some even say that Garrett had an empty coffin buried the next day in Fort Sumner. Some say Garrett wrote the book *The Authentic Life of Billy the Kid*, in which he demonizing [sic] Billy the Kid, to prop up his waning popularity that was being eroded by the rumor that he killed The Kid in less than a fair fight or that he did not kill The Kid at all.

[AUTHOR'S NOTE: These contentions, without sources, appear made-up, and are not evidence.]

To this day the rumor still has life that Billy the Kid never died that night.

[AUTHOR'S NOTE: Nothing has been presented to support that "rumor."]

Most everything we know about William H. Bonney a.k.a. Billy the Kid is what is know [sic] about him in during the last three years of his life. The date and place of his birth, who his father was, where he lived, as a child is still a mystery. Most of what we do know and what we call history is flawed by myth. Even where he is buried is the subject of controversy these 122 years later.

[AUTHOR'S NOTE: This "what-if" illogic tries to make Bonney's death uncertain, by manufacturing "uncertainties" in his earlier history.]

In England is a grave with the name William H. Bonney on the headstone, where is it said [sic] Billy the Kid is buried. The story is that the Tunstall family, in apparition [sic] of his help and loyalty to John Tunstall, brought the Kid back to England where he lived a long life dying of old age.

[AUTHOR'S NOTE: This is so bizarre, it seems a delirium, rather than an argument. It does indicate the author lacks ability to sort fact from fiction.]

[AUTHOR'S NOTE: The case for Garrett's murder of an innocent victim ends here without proof; and segues to the pretenders.]

John Miller

[AUTHOR'S NOTE: At this preliminary stage - years before the hoaxers needed John Miller's exhumation to keep their hoax afloat - he was of minimal interest; their focus being "Brushy Bill." This disinterest is reflected in the following cursory text - and its negative presentation was kept secret when the hoaxers headed with backhoe to John Miller's grave, suddenly claiming *he* was Billy the Kid.]

Helen Airy posthumously published a book, in 1991, by Sunstone Press entitled *What* [sic- Whatever] *Happened to Billy the Kid*. In this book the claim is made that a John Miller who died on November 7, 1937, at six-thirty in the evening, in the Pioneer [sic] Home in Prescott, Arizona and was buried in the Prescott Pioneer home cemetery [sic], was Billy the Kid. In Airy's book Miller is quoted as saying, *"there was a Mexican shot and buried in the coffin that is supposed to be the Kid."*

In her book *What* [sic- Whatever] *Happened to Billy the Kid* these accounts are found:

Page 162 paragraph 2 - *Ann Storrer of Belen writes: "My father, Charlie Walker, grew up around Fort Sumner during the early 1900's. A Mexican he used to work for told him that he saw Billy the Kid at the bullfights in Mexico long after he was supposed to be dead. The rumor around Fort Sumner was that Pat Garrett and Bill [sic] the Kid were good friends and Garrett tried to stop everyone from killing Billy. My father believed there was never a body in the grave.*

Page 162 paragraph 3 and 4 - *Arleigh Nation of Albuquerque supplied the Following story; "A man by the name of Trujillo, who died in 1935 at the age of ninety-five told Nation he worked for Pete Maxwell at the time Billy the kid was supposed to have been killed. He said the day before the shoot-out they dressed up an Indian, who had died the night before, to look like the Kid. The Indian was buried in the grave that was said to have been the Kid's.*

Nation, who is a Billy the kid Buff, also said a neighbor of his who lived in Lincoln, Mrs. Syd Boykin, told him that the kid stayed as [sic] her home in Lincoln many times after he was supposed to have been dead.

Airy states that a John Collins claimed to have been a friend of Billy the Kid. Collins says that he helped bury the corpse of the man Garrett killed on July 14, 1881, and it was not Billy the kid.

Arley Sanches interviewed Nadine Brady, of Adelino, New Mexico, and whose grandfather was Sheriff William Brady, who was shot by the Kid, for a story, which appeared in the *Albuquerque Journal* on September 8, 1990. Nadine says one old timer told her Garrett didn't shoot Bonney. He told her Garrett and Bonney were friends and Garrett invented a story to help his friend escape. A wanderer was killed and buried, and Garrett told everyone he had shot Billy the Kid.

Airy says Frank Coe, a friend of Billy the Kid during the Lincoln County War, believed to the day of his death that Billy was still alive, and spent a great deal of time tracing reports that he had been seen.

The El Paso Herald Post, June 29, 1926 reported a story that a "government official" re[ported that "Billy the Kid and Garrett framed an escape" from Lincoln, New Mexico. The government official claimed the Kid was still alive in this article.

The El Paso Times, July 26, 1964, reported that retired Immigration and Naturalization Service Inspector, Leslie Traylor of San Antonio, Texas claimed Billy the Kid was a man named Henry Street Smith. Traylor said he traced Smith and believes him to be buried under the name of John Miller who died in 1935 in Prescott, Arizona.

[AUTHOR'S NOTE: The writer does not back Miller as Billy. And no death scene is given, that being the purpose of a murder case probable cause statement! In fact, Miller just said an Indian friend mistaken for him was shot, and he was not even there.]

William Henry Roberts a.k.a. Brushy Bill Roberts

[AUTHOR'S NOTE: Next is the attempt to establish Oliver "Brushy Bill" Roberts as Billy the Kid. Noteworthy is use if his fake "William Henry" from *Alias Billy the Kid*. Though he surfaced throughout the hoax, it was pretended to be for "survival suspicion," not the case's goal. The very fact that this "Seventy-Seven Days of Doubt Document" was kept secret, indicates hiding of that motive. Apparently, it was intended to have that conclusion arise from the fake forensic DNA matchings. But the effusions that follow here show the "Brushy" bias as well as access to the transcript of "Brushy's" Morrison interviews. And the contradiction of his non-bench death scene, presented in detail below, was not yet anticipated; since the hoaxers expected the Billy and mother exhumations to go through, followed by a faked match to "Brushy." So switching to the bench scenario for "blood DNA" was unanticipated.]

Before Sheriff Pat Garrett could clean his pistol the bogus Billy the Kid's began to crop up everywhere. Some were too ridiculous to take notice of and some convinced a few people but were forgotten with the passage of time. Out of all the men to come forward to claim they are Billy the Kid the one that caused the most stir and gained national and even worldwide attention was Brushy Bill Roberts.

To this day Roberts' claim is being taken seriously by many. In Hamilton, Texas, where William Roberts is buried there stands a sign that proclaims that his grave is "The Authentic Grave Site of Billy the Kid." A plaque states that he spent the last part of his life attempting to get a "promised pardon" from the New Mexico Governor. Just weeks before Roberts death he and his attorney [sic - William Morrison, not an attorney] approached the Governor of New Mexico and asked for a pardon for the Kid, who Roberts claimed to be. Dubious of Roberts claims the Governor granted no pardon.

[AUTHOR'S NOTE: This "Brushy" pardon focus exposes the otherwise inexplicable linking of DNA matchings to pardon in the hoax. But the intent was making "Brushy" Billy the Kid by the fake match, leading to pardoning him for his alleged long and law-abiding life.]

The story goes that in 1948, William V. Morrison was working as an investigator for a law firm. Morrison was a graduate attorney [sic - Morrison was not an attorney] and it was said that he had a "good nose for evidence". He was a member of the Missouri Historical Society and a descendant of Ferdinand Maxwell, the brother of Lucien Bonaparte Maxwell and uncle of Pete Maxwell. Because of this, Morrison possessed a keen interest in New Mexico history.

During this time Morrison was sent to Florida to investigate an inheritance claimant by the name of Joe Hines. Hines' brother, in North Dakota, had passed away and Hines claimed to be the sole inheritor of some property. As Morrison interviewed the old man the story did not match with the facts Morrison possessed. After more questions Joe Hines told Morrison his name, Hines, was an alias. Hines claimed his real name was Jesse [sic] Evans and he was a survivor of the Lincoln County War.

[AUTHOR'S NOTE: This is the pure "Brushy" hoax, straight from *Alias Billy the Kid*. Indicated is that the writer was a true-believer, like Bill Robins III or W.C. Jameson, or an opportunistic copier, merely seeking publicity and profit from winning.]

Morrison being proud of his ancestral connection to New Mexico history mentioned to Hines (Evans) that Billy the Kid worked for the Maxwells at one time

[AUTHOR'S NOTE: Morrison's fake claim about Billy.]

and added that the Kid was shot and killed in Maxwell's house on July 14, 1881. To that Hines replied, "Garrett did not kill the Kid on July 14, 1881, or any other time." Hines went on to say, "In fact Billy was still living in Texas last year. The reason that I know is that a friend of mine, now living in California stops over to visit with me here every summer. He and Billy and me are the only warriors left of the old Lincoln County bunch.

[AUTHOR'S NOTE: Besides the total fakery, real outlaw-murderer-rustler Jessie Evans would not have called himself a Lincoln County War "warrior."]

Later that year Morrison became acquainted with another man in Missouri who said he knew who all the parties were and gave Morrison an address of a man named O.L. Roberts who lived in Hamilton, Texas. In June of 1948 Morrison drove to Hamilton, Texas and met Roberts. On their first meeting Roberts told Morrison that the Kid was his half brother and was still alive in Old Mexico. The next day Morrison came back to Roberts home and Roberts sent his wife to a neighbor's house saying he and Morrison had business to discuss.

After Mrs. Roberts left the house Morrison claims Roberts pointed his finger at him and said, "Well, you've got your man. You don't need to look any farther. I'm Billy the Kid. But don't tell anyone. My wife doesn't know who I am. She thinks my half brother is Billy the Kid, but he died in Kentucky many years ago. I want a pardon before saying anything about this matter. I don't want to kill anyone anymore, but I'm not going to hang." Morrison goes on to write that Roberts told his story and tears coursed down his cheeks, as he said, "I done wrong like everyone else did in those days. I want to die a free man. I do not want to die like Garrett and the rest of them, by the gun. I have been hiding so long and they have been telling so many lies about me that I want to get everything straightened out before I die. I can do it with some help. The good Lord left me here for a purpose and I know why He did. Now will you help me out of this mess."

Morrison wanted proof that Roberts claims were true and knew the scars the Kid would have on his body. Morrison had Roberts strip and from the scars on Roberts' body Morrison was convinced that he was talking to the true William H. Bonney.

Roberts tells Morrison in detail how he escaped death at the hands of Sheriff Pat Garrett the night of July 14, 1881. In a statement Roberts records the following:

[AUTHOR'S NOTE: To follow are "Brushy's" words from pages 105-117 of W.C. Jameson's and Frederick Bean's 1998 *The Return of the Outlaw Billy the Kid.* **Jameson later claimed Bean had transcribed Morrison's "Brushy" tape recordings, as lent to him in 1989 by "Brushy's" step-grandson, Bill Allison.]**

[AUTHOR'S NOTE: Do not miss the attempted validation of "Brushy," whose words are "evidence" in *a real law enforcement case* **proving Garrett was a murderer, since** *he* **survived; ergo, Garrett** *must have murdered innocent Billy Barlow.***]**

I rode into Fort Sumner from Yerby's a few days before Garrett and his posse rode in. When they rode in that day, I had spent the day with Garrett's brother-in-law, Saval Gutierrez. Nearly all the people in this country were my friends and they helped me. None of them liked Garrett. **It was dark that night***, but there was enough moonlight to make shadows. Me and my partner Billy Barlow, rode up to Jesus Silva's house when we reached Fort Sumner. We had been staying at the Yerby Ranch laying low for a while. Word was all around that Pat Garrett and a posse were after me. Pat's wife was a sister to my friend Saval Gutierrez, and Saval told me that Pat was after me, that he heard it from his sister.*

Things were mighty hot in Lincoln County for me right about then, but I wasn't running from it. I meant to have a talk with Pat Garrett and set things straight between us if I could. We used to be friends ... We hid our horses in the barn and walked up to Jesus' back door. Barlow was nervous about being in Fort Sumner with me and I couldn't blame him much. Jesus came to the back door when I tapped on it with the barrel of my six-shooter. When he saw that it was me, he grinned and let us in. I told Jesus we were hungry. We'd been out in the hills all day, scouting around Fort Sumner for any sign of Garrett and his posse. "I have nothing but cold frijoles, compadre," Jesus whispered as he closed the door. Barlow made a sour face. "I want some meat," he said, "we have been living on beans and tortillas all week. Ain't you got any beef?

According to Roberts statement Jesus Silva told Barlow that Pete Maxwell had some meat hanging on his porch. Barlow wanted to get the beef to cook but Roberts told him it was too dangerous and they should not move from the house. Barlow would not listen. According to Roberts statement Barlow took a butcher knife and left the house to head to Maxwell's to get the beefsteak. While Roberts and Jesus were lighting the wood stove they hear [sic] gunfire in the direction of Pete Maxwell's place. Roberts' statement goes on to describe the following events:

I pulled one of my .44's and ran through the door, trying to see in the dark. Two more shots came from a shadow beside the Maxwell house. I couldn't find a target to shoot at. It was too dark to see. I ran toward Maxwell's back porch. I heard another gunshot and felt something hit me in the jaw. I stumbled and kept on running with a broken tooth rolling around my tongue. I tasted blood and spit the mess out of my mouth as I started emptying my six-shooter **at the shadow where I saw the muzzleflash**. *From the corner of my eye I saw a body lying on the back porch ... I knew it had to be Barlow.*

My partner had walked right into a trap, and the trap had likely been set for me. I pulled my other .44 and ran toward the porch to check on Barlow, but I ran into a wall of gunfire. I knew I wasn't going to make it to my partner. Too many guns were shooting at me. I didn't have a chance. I turned for a fence across the back of Maxwell's yard and dove for it when a bullet caught me in the left shoulder. I jumped over the fence and landed hard on the far side, with the echo of gunshots all around me, ringing in my ears. I staggered into an alley that ran behind the house, firing my .44 over my shoulder until it clicked empty. My mouth and shoulder were bleeding and I lost track of where I was, but I knew I had to get away from Maxwell's before they killed me. I heard a shout and another gunshot. Something passed across my forehead like a hot branding iron. I was stunned. I lost footing and **fell on my face in the darkness**. *I knew I was hurt bad and wondered if I would make it out of this scrape alive.*

I forced myself up again, wiping the blood from my eyes with my shirtsleeve as I stumbled headlong down the ally. I didn't know how bad the head wound was, only that it was bleeding and I couldn't see. It wouldn't matter if the found me in the alley just then, they were bent on killing me, to be sure. If I fell again I knew they'd find me and finish the job, so I kept running down the ally as hard as I could, barely able to see where I was going. I heard them shouting to each other behind me, arguing over something, but I was too woozy to think about what they were saying and too frightened to care. The gunshot to my head had knocked me senseless. I kept on staggering and running down the alley, trying to get away. Blood was pouring into my eyes; I couldn't see a thing. I ran past a little adobe shack down the alley from Pete Maxwell's. I supposed all the shooting woke everybody up, because a door opened just a crack when I ran behind the adobe and I could see a lantern light spilling from the doorway across the alley.

I stumbled toward the light not knowing what else to do. I needed help and the open door was the only place I could find, hurt like I was. A Mexican woman pulled me inside. She saw the blood on my face and threw her hands over her mouth. She closed the door quickly and helped me to a chair. I sleeved the blood from my eyes, watching her, loading my Colts.

In Roberts' statement he identifies the woman as Celsa Cutierriz [sic - Gutierrez] who he had known previously. Ms. Cutierriz [sic] helped Roberts and kept him at her home that night. Roberts says that later Ms. Cutierriz [sic] had Frank Lobato saddle his horse and bring it around in the alley so he can [sic] escape. Before Roberts was able to leave Ms. Cutierriz [sic] told him it was rumored about Fort Sumner that Sheriff Garrett was telling everyone he had killed the Kid.

Roberts says, *I started puzzling over what Celsa told me. Garrett was trying to pass off Barlow's body as that of Billy the Kid. I wondered how he figured to get away with it. Garrett knew by now that he'd killed the wrong man in the dark. Billy Barlow looked a lot like me, the same general description, with blue eyes like mine. But in the daylight, a lot of folks who knew me would know they had the wrong body. I couldn't figure it, unless Garrett realized his mistake and was making a try at collection [sic] the reward money that was out on me anyway ...*

Roberts says it was 3 a.m. when Celsa brought his horse up to the house. He says he left with Frank Lobato. Roberts stayed in a camp south of Fort Sumner until his wounds healed and the first of August he rode to El Paso, Texas.

[AUTHOR'S NOTE: "Brushy's" hoaxing has been debunked earlier, but his dialogue shows the relentless floridness of his confabulations and imagination. Noteworthy for the "Billy the

Kid Case" hoaxers, however, is that his death scene with back-porch-Barlow points to an early phase of their own faking, where they were not yet concealing the major discrepancies between his "death scene" tale and their own.]

Questions About the Case

There seems [sic] to be problems with every account of the escape of Billy the Kid from the make shift [sic] jail in Lincoln and the shooting at Fort Sumner by Pat Garrett. In every account there remain questions as to what really happened.

[AUTHOR'S NOTE: The above used the hoaxers' fakery of "vague, though unfounded, suspicions" instead of actual evidence - which they lacked. What follows are fake "what-ifs" to make unwarranted leaps to hoaxed conclusions – called by the writer "Questions." It represents the writer's last chance to fake a link of Garrett to a "probable cause" of murder.]

[AUTHOR'S NOTE: For clarity, the illogical transitions are put in boldface. The breath-taking leap of the scam is seen when the "what-ifs" of the outhouse version, lead to a fake, implied accusation that Garrett reported the gun from armory version to hide that *he* was the pistol-giving "friend."]

1. In the historical account of the escape of Billy the Kid, from the courthouse in Lincoln, **it's believed** that a "friend" placed a pistol in the outhouse for Billy to use in his escape. The identity of the "friend" who placed the pistol in the outhouse has gone nearly unasked. **If** this version is true, and a "friend" left a pistol in the outhouse to aid in Bonney's escape that "friend" is a coconspirator to the murder of Bell and Olinger. This "friend" also should have been charged with two counts of homicide but remained at large. **Why** didn't Sheriff Garrett pursue the question of the idenenty [sic] of the "friend" who hid the pistol? Garrett says the Kid took the pistol from the armory. **If** the story of the pistol in the outhouse is true did Garrett have a reason to say it was from the armory?

2. **If** Roberts account and claim about the night of July 14, 1881, is to be believed then Lincoln County Sheriff Pat Garrett was not the hero that history portrays him as. Instead, he becomes a murderer who killed Billy Barlow and covered up that killing and passed off Barlow's body as that of Billy the Kid. With the sign in at [sic] Brushy Bill's grave site claiming to the [sic] grave site of Billy the Kid they are in short saying Pat Garrett lied. Did Garrett lie?

[AUTHOR'S NOTE: This earliest version of the "Billy the Kid Case" hoax relies heavily on "Brushy;" later discrepancies between the evolving hoax and "Brushy's" tales would be concealed by the hoaxers. Here, certainty of winning without bearing scrutiny, apparently yielded a devil-may-care attitude.]

[AUTHOR'S NOTE: This earliest version of the hoax is unabashedly vicious in accusing Garrett of heinous crimes. Later, under scrutiny, the hoaxers would lie that the case was to protect Garrett's honor against "others" who had accused him!]

3. **If** Roberts claims are believed, it beings up other questions? [sic] He claims in his statement when talking about Pat Garrett, *"we use* [sic] *to be friend"* [sic]. **If** Garrett and Roberts were friends did Garrett and Garrett [sic] allowed The Kid out of friendship to escape from Fort Sumner, *did he also* arrange his escape from Lincoln? Did Garrett question why **his friend, the Kid**, with all the others involved in all the killing was the only one to be convicted and sentenced to hang? The Kid **mentions this** in an interview that was published in the *Mesilla News* on April 15, 1881 when he said, *Think it hard that I should be the only one to suffer the extreme penalties of the law."*

[AUTHOR'S NOTE: Here, "Brushy" is the authority, with "what-ifs" that fabricate Garrett as Billy's "friend" and "accomplice." Also lied is that Billy's mention had anything to do with Garrett, rather than to his own sense of injustice.]

4. **Did** Garrett arrange having the pistol put in the outhouse by the "friend" **and is this** why he did not search for the coconspirator to the murder of the two lawmen? **If this is the case then** Garrett is also a coconspirator in the murder of those two lawmen.

[AUTHOR'S NOTE: More meaningless "what-ifs."]

5. In the Lincoln County Courthouse Caretaker Gauss' statement he quotes Bonney as saying about Bell, *"I'm sorry I had to kill him but couldn't help it."* This statement must raise the question did Bonney, when he produced the pistol he retrieved from the outhouse

[AUTHOR'S NOTE: Sly switcheroo from "what-ifs" to using the outhouse as a fact.]

order Bell to surrender? Did Bell panic and instead of throwing up his hands, turn and run causing Bonney to shoot him?

[AUTHOR'S NOTE: This parrots the historically accepted version. Later in the hoax, for fake forensics, it would be switched to Billy striking Bell with a shackle to cause "blood" on the hallway.]

6. Other questions come to mind in this investigation, some about Gauss. It should be noted that Gauss had worked with Tunstall, so had Bonney. Gauss and Bonney shared the same table as they took meals, slept on the

same floor and spent a great deal of time together when Bonney was in the courthouse under guard. It goes to reason that Gauss was sympathetic towards Bonney. With that in mind it could be pointed out that there were a number of things missing from Gauss's account. Gauss made no reference to how Bell was killed, and leaves out the fact that Bonney used Olinger's own shotgun to kill him. If Bonney retrieved a pistol from the outhouse it had to be prearranged with Bonney and the "friend" as to what date and where to place the pistol in order for Bonney to find it. Since Gauss spent so much time with Bonney would he not have heard something about the plot?

[AUTHOR'S NOTE: This is failed hoaxing! With Gauss as the accomplice, Garrett is innocent - undoing the scam!"]

7. Since the caretaker Gauss worked outside it is not outside the realm of possibility that he saw who put the pistol in the outhouse?

[AUTHOR'S NOTE: The historical reality of Gauss being the accomplice never made it to the final hoax.]

8. It is known that Bonney ate his meals at the courthouse and the only time he was allowed to leave was to use the outhouse. Bell and Olinger took turns escorting the prisoners to the hotel for lunch, leaving the other in charge of Bonney. Bonney as well as the others would have known that Olinger would be escorting the prisoners to lunch that day. Bonney was aware that out of the two guards Bell was the one to make his escape move on since Bell was easy going and seemed to get along with him. Bonney also knew that Olinger had killed men in the past and had threatened to kill him. **Had Garrett and the Kid discussed this and chose Bell** as the deputy for Bonney to make his move thinking Bell would just give up giving the Kid an hour to escape while Olinger was eating?

[AUTHOR'S NOTE: "What-if" blather with a fake conclusion.]

9. If Garrett was part of the plot for the Kid's escape **is that why** he rode to White Oaks on a "tax collecting" trip, to give himself an alibi?

[AUTHOR'S NOTE: More 'what-if" fakery.]

10. **If Garrett were part of the plot to allow the Kid to escape he would have reason to chase the Kid. He could not afford for the Kid to tell of his involvement in the two killings of the lawmen. Garrett also has a weak link in the plot, that being the "friend" who put the pistol in the outhouse. If Roberts' story is true, is Billy Barlow the one who put the pistol in the outhouse under orders of Garrett?** In Roberts' accounting he shows up at Fort Sumner with no one but

Barlow. Did he meet Barlow after he rode out of Lincoln and move on [sic] to Fort Sumner?

[AUTHOR'S NOTE: The culmination of "what-if" fakery.]

11. If Garrett shot Billy Barlow in the dark, by mistake, on July 14, 1881, and Barlow was the only one who could tell the story of Garrett's involvement other than the Kid, would Garrett not know the Kid would run to keep from hanging?

[AUTHOR'S NOTE: This incoherent reverie, appears to contradict the Pat-Billy friendship on which this hoax relies.]

12. In Deputy John W. Poe's statement as he lays out the shooting in Maxwell's house on July 14, 1881, he says "... Garrett came out, brushing against me as he passed. He stood by me close to the wall at the side of the door and said to me, That was the Kid that came in there onto me, and I think I got him.' I said, "Pat, the Kid would not come to this place; you have shot the wrong man.' Upon my saying this, Garrett seemed to be in doubt himself as to whom had shot ..." Did Garrett kill the wrong man by mistake and cover it up?

[AUTHOR'S NOTE: The writer forgot that backing "Brushy" means no bedroom murder scene – but a Barlow-on-back-porch one. Also forgotten is that "Brushy's" scene had enough gunfire to rival the Alamo.]

[AUTHOR'S NOTE: Similar to the final "Probable Cause Statement," this "question" hides the multiple identifications of Billy, following this moment of doubt in a darkened room.]

13. Most researchers and historians have accepted without much question, the statement that Billy the Kid was born Henry McCarty, in New York on November 23, 1859. It should be noted that the first time this information comes to light is in Pat Garrett's book *The Authentic Life of Billy the Kid*.

[AUTHOR'S NOTE: Wrong. This was outlaw myth press in Billy's lifetime, while he was pursued by Garrett and Secret Service Agent Azariah Wild. It was in "Outlaws of New Mexico. The Exploits of a Band Headed by a New York Youth. The Mountain Fastness of the Kid and His Followers - War Against a Gang of Cattle Thieves and Murderers." December 27, 1880. *The Sun*. New York. Vol. XLVIII, No. 118, Page 3, Columns 1-2.]

In the book the evidence for this claim is sited [sic] to have come from a birth announcement that appeared in the New York Times on November 25, 1859. In 1950 William Morrison the attorney **[AUTHOR'S NOTE: Morrison was not an attorney]** for William (Brushy Bill) Roberts claims he asked the *New York Times* about the announcement and the Times replied that no information about birth announcements appeared in that issue. A ghostwriter by the name of Marshall Asmon [sic - Ashmun] Upson is credited with writing Garrett's book. It might also be worth mentioning the date November 23, is the birth date of Marshall Asmon [sic - Ashmun] Upson. Is it by chance that Upson and the Kid have the same birthday or by design?

[AUTHOR'S NOTE: Irrelevant, but a clumsy manufacturing of fake "suspiciousness," instead of evidence.]

14. As stated above most believe Billy the Kid was born in New York. This information also appeared for the first time in Garrett's book. [AUTHOR'S NOTE: See *New York Sun* 1880 article reference above.] It is also believed that Billy the Kid was shot and killed in 1881 at the age of 21. However, according to the United States Bureau of Census, 1880 census, Fort Sumner, San Miguel County, William Bonney says differently. Between June 17 and 19, 1880, while taking census records at the Fort, Lorenzo Labadie, a former Indian Agent, noted the vital statistics of one William Bonney, who was living next to Charlie Bowdre and his wife Manuela, leaving us to believe this to be the William Bonney of Lincoln County fame. What is interesting about the entry is that he gave his age as twenty-five, and his place of birth not New York but Missouri.

[AUTHOR'S NOTE: Irrelevant, but clumsy fake "suspiciousness." Also, it is thought that Manuela Bowdre gave the interview and the incorrect information.]

The attorney Morrison asked Roberts why Garrett would say he was born in New York. Roberts told him that is what the told the "Coe boys" when he first came to New Mexico. Roberts went on to say he never saw New York until he was a grown man.

[AUTHOR'S NOTE: Morrison was not an attorney.]

[AUTHOR'S NOTE: Irrelevant, since "Brushy" was not Billy.]

Conclusion

If history is correct and William H. Bonney a.k.a. Billy the Kid was shot and killed by Lincoln County Sheriff Pat Garrett on July 14, 1881, at the house of Pete Maxwell in Fort Sumner, and was buried the next day in Fort Sumner, then Brushy Bill Roberts is a fake and nothing more than a story teller of the first order.

[AUTHOR'S NOTE: Again, this early document points to "Brushy" as Billy; which would later be more hidden.]

However, if it is not the body of William H. Bonney buried in Fort Sumner then Lincoln County Sheriff Pat Garrett killed the wrong man on July 14, 1881. He covered up that killing with help from others such as Pete Maxwell. If it is not Bonney buried at Fort Sumner then Garrett is a murderer and Maxwell is a knowing coconspirator to that homicide.

[AUTHOR'S NOTE: This is an early hoax attempt at a conspiracy theory. Instead of the "Garrett friendship," is presented "Brushy's" accidental killing of the innocent victim version. And Maxwell is added as a cover-up conspirator, without motive or evidence – or truth.]

If Brushy Bill Roberts were William H. Bonney then one would have to assume that the body in the grave is that of Billy Barlow as Robert's claims. If that is true Sheriff Garrett could quite possibly be a coconspirator of the double murder of two lawmen that occurred during the Kid's escape from Lincoln.

[AUTHOR'S NOTE: This illogical jump even leaves "Brushy" behind, since he never claimed Garrett as a jailbreak accomplice, or a "friendship" with Garrett to explain not being killed on July 14, 1881 to enable escape.]

The Lincoln County Sheriff''s Department believes, with the unanswered question as to who is buried in Fort Sumner

[AUTHOR'S NOTE: This is fakery. The victim is not doubted.]

there remains serious doubt as to what involvement Sheriff Pat Garrett played in the escape of Billy the Kid from Lincoln that resulted I the deaths of two lawmen.

[AUTHOR'S NOTE: This is fakery. There is no evidence that Garrett assisted the jail escape of Bonney, though it is an early version of the final "Probable Cause Statement's" fake Deputy Bell killing investigation.]

If the body of William H. Bonney is buried in Fort Sumner the claims of William Roberts'' and others alleging to have been Billy the Kid are unfounded and the name of Pat Garrett is cleared of any wrong doing in this incident. It is the duty of the Lincoln County Sheriff''s Office to clear this mystery and possible crime off the books of history in a professional manner and to allow the guilt to fall where it belongs.

[AUTHOR'S NOTE: The imposters are easily debunked without exhumations. And no one is accusing Garrett, except imposters and hoaxers – and without basis.]

Billy the Kid's mother is buried in Silver City, New Mexico. To exhume her body could provide the DNA to solve this 122-year-old mystery. Her DNA would hold the key to the true answer as to where William Bonney is buried and if Pat Garrett was a murderer or a Sheriff doing his duty.

If those in Hamilton, Texas believe Roberts is in fact Roberts [sic] this DNA should prove their claim. If he is not the town of Hamilton, Texas needs to take down the signs that the grave of Roberts is "The Authentic Grave Site of Billy the Kid." However, if Roberts is William Bonney then history should be rewritten showing what really happened in Lincoln County and Fort Sumner.

If Bonney is buried in Fort Sumner the History stands and the name of Sheriff Pat Garrett would be cleared and he did not kill some incendet [sic] person in Fort Sumner and would appear he had no hand in the escape of William Bonney from Lincoln and the death of Olinger and Bell.

Lincoln County Sheriff, Tom Sullivan and the Lincoln County Sheriff's Office believe it our duty to put this mystery to rest after 122 years of doubt. Since these questions continue to nag at our conscience, and since there is no statute of limitations on Murder we feel this investigation should answer the question of "is Pat Garrett a murderer?" or a Sheriff doing his duty and wrongly accused of a crime?

[AUTHOR'S NOTE: No probable cause has been established to implicate Pat Garrett of murdering the innocent victim - the purpose of this document. But much evidence was revealed that the "Billy the Kid Case" hoax was a modernized version of the "Brushy Bill" hoax.]

In Pat Garrett's book *The Authentic Life of Billy the Kid* he pens these words - *"Again I say that the Kid's body lies undisturbed in the grave - and I speak of what I know."*

It is the intention of the Lincoln County Sheriff's Office to prove one way or the other if these words are true.

Tom Sullivan: Sheriff
Lincoln County Sheriff's Office

Steven M. Sederwall: Deputy Sheriff
Lincoln County Sheriff's Office

Date

EXHUMATION PETITIONS AS LAWMEN

The hoaxing lawmen, Sheriffs Tom Sullivan and Gary Graves, and Deputy Steve Sederwall filed the exhumation petitions for Case No. 2003-274, with the necessity of their "murder case" against Pat Garrett justifying exhumations, for lack of kin.

Though they would later lie that they had been hobbyists to evade my open records requests, a good example of their lawman status was their exhumation petition of July 26, 2004 for Billy the Kid by their attorney, Mark Acuña. It was titled "County of De Baca, State of New Mexico, Tenth Judicial District. In the Matter of William H. Bonney A/K/A 'Billy the Kid.' Cause No. CV-04-00005." In it, Acuña called them "law enforcement officers" 13 times in his mere five page filing, to back their exhumation right. Acuña wrote:

PETITIONER'S [sic] RESPONSE TO
THE VILLAGE OF FT. SUMNER'S MOTION TO DISMISS

COME NOW Petitioners Sullivan, Sederwall and Graves by and through their attorneys of record The Jaffe Law Firm (Mark Anthony Acuña, Esq.) and for their response to the Village of Fort Sumner's Motion to Dismiss sate as follows:

INTRODUCTION

Tom Sullivan, Steve Sederwall and Gary Graves are law enforcement officers. Prior to the filing of the Petition for Exhumation of the Remains of Billy the Kid, a.k.a. William H. Bonney, **Sullivan, Sederwall, and Graves acting in their capacity as law enforcement officers initiated Investigation No. 2004 [sic] –274 filed in Lincoln County and Case No. 03-06-136-01 filed in De Baca County**. The principle purpose of opening the investigation and the case was to determine the guilt or innocence of sheriff Pat Garrett in the death of Billy the Kid.

[AUTHOR'S NOTE: The fact that Case No. 2003-274 was a murder investigation against Pat Garrett would later be hidden by the hoaxers – both by calling the case only an investigation of Billy the Kid's jailbreak shootings of the deputy guards, or calling the whole case their "hobby."]

Initially, as part of their on-going investigation, **Sederwall, Sullivan, and Graves, in their capacity as law enforcement officers** petitioned the Sixth Judicial District Court for exhumation of the remains of

Billy the Kid's mother, Katherine [sic] Antrim. As a part of the on-going investigation, the Petition to Exhume Katherine [sic] Antrim was intended to obtain DNA samples for purposes of comparing those DNA samples with DNA samples that were hoped to be obtained upon the exhumation of the remains of what are thought to be that of Billy the Kid. After filing of the Petition to Exhume the remains of Katherine [sic] Antrim, a second petition was filed in the Tenth Judicial Court for purposes of the exhumation of Billy the Kid's remains and for purposes of obtaining DNA samples to compare with those samples obtained from the remains of Katherine [sic] Antrim. Sederwall, Sullivan, and Graves, all joined in on the Petition to Exhume the remains of Billy the Kid as Co-Petitioners and in their capacity as **law enforcement officers** engaged in an on-going investigation.

Petitioners assert that they maintain standing in the instant action as **law enforcement officers** engaged in the investigation of criminal violations, namely, the alleged killing of Billy the Kid by the legendary Sheriff, Pat Garrett. Moreover, Petitioners assert that as **law enforcement officers** they are duly authorized to investigate the death of Billy the Kid to determine 1) the guilt or innocence of sheriff Pat Garrett, and 2) to determine whether or not foul play was involved if there were violations of criminal statutes or laws. Acting in their capacity as **law enforcement officers** on behalf of the public and the public's best interest, Petitioners further assert that they are the real parties in interest to this suit and, therefore, maintain proper standing to prosecute these claims.

ARGUMENT

Petitioners are Law Enforcement Officers Currently Conducting Active Investigations Regarding the Death of <u>Billy the Kid and, therefore, they have Standing.</u>

New Mexico Rule of Civil Procedure 1-017 states in pertinent part that "every action shall be prosecuted in the name of the real party in interest ... for a party authorized by statute may sue in that person's own name without joining the party for whose benefit the action is brought; and when a statute of the state so provides, an action for the use or benefit for another shall be brought in the name of the state."

Moreover, Section 29-1-1 states impertinent [sic] part that ...

"It is hereby declared to be the duty of every Sheriff, Deputy Sheriff, Constable and every other peace officer to investigate all violations of the criminal laws of the state which are called to the attention of any such officer or which he is aware, and it is also declared the duty of every such officer to diligently file a complaint or information, if the circumstances are such to indicate to a reasonably prudent person that such action should be taken, and it is also declared his duty to cooperate with and assist the Attorney General, District Attorney or other prosecutor, if any, if any in all reasonable ways ... Failure to perform his duty in ant material way shall subject such officer to removal from the office and payment of all costs of prosecution."

In the instant case, Petitioners Sullivan, Sederwall, and Graves acting in their capacity as **law enforcement officers** pursuant to Section 29-1-1, were not only authorized to commence the investigation into the death of William H. Bonney, a.k.a. Billy the Kid, but were duty-bound to fulfill their responsibilities as **law enforcement officers** to investigate the circumstances surrounding the death of Billy the Kid. Indeed, Petitioners initiated the investigations into the death of Billy the Kid based upon inconsistent and incongruous facts and information surrounding the death of Billy the Kid and raising suspicion as to the truth of the circumstances surrounding the killing of Billy the Kid. Under the circumstances, Petitioners had a duty to investigate or be subject to removal of office subject to Section 29-1-1.

Furthermore, pursuant to Rule 1-017, Petitioners acting in their capacity as **law enforcement officers**, are real parties in interest to the instant causes of action. Plaintiffs are authorized by statute, that is, Section 29-1-1, to being this action in their own names on behalf of and for the benefit of the public in their capacities of investigating **law enforcement officers**.

CONCLUSION

Therefore, based upon all the foregoing, it is clear that the Petitioners acting in their capacity as **law enforcement officers** and engaged in an active investigation regarding the death and alleged killing of Billy the Kid by Sheriff Pat Garrett, and of standing in this case and are real parties in interest.

Wherefore, Petitioners respectfully request that the court issue its order denying the Village of Ft. Sumner's Motion to Dismiss as against Petitioners; that the court allow Petitioners to remain in the instant action and for such other further and proper relief as the Court deems just and proper."

      Respectfully submitted by:
      The Jaffe Law Firm
      Mark Anthony Acuña
      Attorneys for Petitioners Sullivan,
        Sederwall & Graves

ATTORNEY BILL ROBINS III IN ACTION

The *New York Times* article of June 5, 2003 foreshadowed key hoax participant, Attorney Bill Robins III, under a "Dallas" law firm connected to Governor Richardson. In fact, Robins was second partner in a Houston one; with reported, yearly, multi-million dollar personal injury, product liability, and medical malpractice settlements. He and his firm, Heard, Robins, Cloud, Lubel & Greenwood LLC, also were Richardson's major political donors for his gubernatorial runs and his intended presidential bid in 2008. Robins apparently felt above the law, and made a mockery of the courts for their "Billy the Kid Case."

Calling himself a Billy the Kid historian on his website when the "Billy the Kid Case" began, Robins appeared to be a "Brushy"-believer. And if "Brushy" being Billy was to be Robins's pay-to-play prize, contemplate this: Mad "Brushy" may have risen to a king-maker - or president-maker!

It also seemed likely that Robins was responsible for the legal creativity of achieving exhumations by a real murder case, using "Brushy" as evidence for the survival claim, and using the pardon hook as the goal - thus, finally overriding past Governor Mabry.

His first public entry in the Billy the Kid Case was to take over from Silver City attorney, Sherry Tippet. And he did not hide "Brushy." On November 19, 2003, an AP internet article for Silver City, titled "Lawyer Appointed to Represent Dead Outlaw," quoted him: "Robins says he's excited to represent the Kid. His first duty as Billy's lawyer will be to intervene in the Silver City case to exhume the body of Billy's mother, Catherine Antrim. DNA testing is supposed to show whether Antrim was related to Ollie "Brushy Bill" Roberts. If Antrim is related to Roberts, that would mean Billy the Kid is buried in Hico [sic - Hamilton], Texas - not Fort Sumner."

After replacing Tippett, Robins led the exhumation attacks on both the mother's and Billy's graves. To counter the absolute legal obstacles of the 1962 Lois Telfer case's blockade on exhuming Billy the Kid and the OMI's opposition to both exhumations, on January 5, 2004, he filed his "Billy the Kid's Pre-Hearing Brief" in Grant County to go after Catherine Antrim first.

But an attorney needs a client to appear in a court. The client Robins chose proved his scorn of the law, the public, and the sanctity of graves. **His client was the dead Billy the Kid, "co-petitioner" with the lawmen for his own exhumation!** This, of course, ignored that a corpse has no legal standing in a court of law. But for complicit judges, Henry Quintero in Silver City and Ted Hartley in Fort Sumner, Robins "channeled Billy," and spoke for him without their objection! And "Billy," of course, wanted his mother and himself dug up to protect his "legacy." And, as will be seen, the "legacy" Billy was "protecting" was that an innocent victim, not himself, had been **killed on July 14, 1881 on a "dark and moonless night"** (the fatal "Brushy" moon error that gave away Robins's "Brushy" thrust). And "Billy" claimed he had led a long and law-abiding life, so deserved a pardon (Robins's second give-away for his "Brushy" thrust).

SPEAKING FOR BILLY THE KID IN SILVER CITY

Robins channeled dead Billy on January 5, 2004, before Judge Henry Quintero for "In the Matter of Catherine Antrim, Billy the Kid's Pre-Hearing Brief." It revealed, for the first time, how the hoax linked DNA matching to pardoning. Faked matchings would claim an innocent victim in Billy's grave; and the mother would match "Brushy." Richardson would then pardon "Brushy" as Billy. As Robins wrote: "**Should the DNA extracted from Ms. Antrim confirm that one of the potential Kids ["Brushy"] was in fact Billy the Kid, undersigned counsel will be able to make an even stronger argument for pardon by citing to the long years of law abiding life.**"

So Bill Robins III's outrageous Brief had his client, dead Billy the Kid, as a co-petitioner for exhumation of his own mother, joining petitioner Sheriffs Sullivan and Graves, and Deputy Sederwall, and as backing the pretenders as legitimate. Robins wrote: "[T]he very question of [Billy the Kid's] life and death will be impacted by the results of the Petitioners' [lawmen's] investigation [into the Garrett murder and DNA]." The Brief stated:

B. *The Planned Request For Pardon Confers Standing Here*

Undersigned counsel intends to ask Governor Richardson that he pardon Billy the kid for the murder conviction of Sheriff Brady on several known bases including the fact that then Territorial Governor Lew Wallace reneged on his promise to pardon the Kid. There were at least two individuals that laid claim to Billy the Kid's identity years after his alleged shooting by Garrett. **Both of them apparently led long and peaceful and crime-free lives** ...

The reasons that the exhumation is sought is to disinter the remains of Billy the Kid's mother for the extraction of Mitochondrial DNA.

As such, Ms. Antrim presents the only source of such DNA. Should the exhumation be denied, Billy the Kid will be forever denied the opportunity to make use of modern technology to shed light on his life and death. **Should the DNA extracted from Ms. Antrim confirm that one of the potential Kids was in fact Billy the Kid, undersigned counsel will be able to make an even stronger argument for pardon by citing to the long years of law abiding life.**

Convinced he was above law or decency this smug rogue presented the following examples of fakery in his "Billy the Kid's Pre-Hearing Brief;" writing:

(1) COMES NOW, Bill Robins, III and David Sandoval, of the law firm of Heard, Robins, Cloud, Lubel & Greenwood, LLC, and on the behalf of the estate of William H. Bonney, aka "Billy the Kid."

[AUTHOR'S NOTE: The first claim is representation of Billy's "estate." First of all, Billy had no estate - meaning posthumous property for probate court. Secondly, property has nothing to do with exhuming his mother. Thirdly, this cover of something that sounds legal - like an estate - will next be switched to Billy talking for himself through Robins. Note that Attorney Sandoval was present to provide the New Mexico law license which Robins lacked, making him complicit in the hoax.]

(2) This is an interesting proceeding in that the relief sought here is not exclusively judicial. "[N]ormally a district court would not become involved in such matters unless a protesting relative or interested party files an injunction or takes some other legal action to halt the autopsy or disinterment,"

[AUTHOR'S NOTE: Robins's Brief is not "judicial" at all. It is pseudo-historical rambling with an irrelevant idea of a pardon. And its legal citations are all irrelevant filler.]

(3) Petitioners [Lincoln County Sheriff Tom Sullivan and his Deputy, Steve Sederwall] should thus be commended for bringing this Court into the picture.

[AUTHOR'S NOTE: Robins is trying to legitimize fellow hoaxers. Note also their law enforcement titles.]

(4) As will be shown clearly, Billy the Kid's interests are real, legitimate, proper for consideration, and we respectively ask the Court to recognize them as such.

[AUTHOR'S NOTE: Segueing into speaking for Billy, Robins does a switcheroo from "estate" to "interests." But a dead person has no interests, being dead - meaning legally non-existent.]

(5) To the extent that the Court remains concerned with the presence of Billy the Kid in this litigation, it is a matter that can be more properly addressed pursuant to legal requirements of standing and intervention, which the discussion below shows the Kid satisfies.

[AUTHOR'S NOTE: This is now the switcheroo point for Billy himself entering the courtroom. Robins even claims that Billy has "standing," meaning the legal right to be present in court.]

(6) The governor has the "power to grant reprieves and pardons." Undersigned counsel intends on seeking a pardon for Billy the Kid. Certainly Governor Richardson is within his inherent appointment power to hire counsel to advise him on the merits of such a pardon.

[AUTHOR'S NOTE: Tricky Robins omits that pardon advising gives him no legal justification to be in this court seeking exhumation of Catherine Antrim. He has no real client.]

(7) Counsel's appointment here is in the nature of an appointment as a public defender

[AUTHOR'S NOTE: Now cagy Robins makes up that he was appointed by Richardson as a "public defender" for Billy. But only the judge can legally appoint an attorney for an indigent client in court - and, obviously, the client has to be alive.]

(8) Billy the Kid's interest here is his legacy. As noted in previous briefing the very question of his life and death will be impacted by the results of the Petitioners' investigation.

[AUTHOR'S NOTE: Here, dead Billy has "told" channeling Robins that *he* cares about "his legacy." Besides being absurd, that is not what "interest" means: which is legal justification for a case, not sentimentality of an historical nature.]

(9) Undersigned counsel intends to ask Governor Richardson that he pardon Billy the kid for the murder conviction of Sheriff Brady on several known bases including the fact that then Territorial Governor Lew Wallace reneged on his promise to pardon the Kid.

[AUTHOR'S NOTE: The pardon issue, though irrelevant to exhuming Catherine Antrim, is here segueing into "Brushy Bill" territory with "several known bases" that will apply to "Brushy" and not to Billy Bonney.]

(10) There were at least two individuals that laid claim to Billy the Kid's identity years after his alleged shooting by Garrett. Both of them apparently **led long and peaceful and crime-free lives.**

[AUTHOR'S NOTE: Here is the jump to "Brushy." And the "several known bases" for pardon are his long, peaceful, and crime-free life. The second pretender, John Miller, was added by the hoaxers to obscure their "Brushy" focus.]

(11) The reasons that the exhumation is sought is to disinter the remains of Billy the Kid's mother for the extraction of Mitochondrial DNA. As such, Ms. Antrim presents the only source of such DNA. Should the exhumation be denied, Billy the Kid will be forever denied the opportunity to make use of modern technology to shed light on his life and death.

[AUTHOR'S NOTE: Now Billy is himself in court, pleading, through Robins's mouth, for modern technology to help him. But do not miss the greater absurdity: this is a pretender argument by channeled "Brushy," wanting *his* life and death vouched for as Billy the Kid. And "Brushy's" real problem is hidden by Robins: mitochondrial DNA only proves a mother relationship; "Brushy" *denied* she was his mother!]

(12) Should the DNA extracted from Ms. Antrim confirm that one of the potential Kids was in fact Billy the Kid, **undersigned counsel will be able to make an even stronger argument for pardon by citing to the long years of law abiding life.**

[AUTHOR'S NOTE: <u>This was the sentence that proved to me that the "Billy the Kid Case was a "Brushy Bill" hoax, along with its plot by claiming a match by faking DNA, then pardoning "Brushy" as Billy the Kid.</u>

(13) This Court has allowed the intervention of the Town of Silver City in this matter. The municipal politicians there have apparently authorized the Town's Mayor to oppose the exhumation. Billy the Kid acknowledges the existence of case law that accords standing to the owners of the cemetery concerned in such proceedings.

[AUTHOR'S NOTE: Do not miss that speaking, channeled, dead Billy Bonney even has legal expertise on "case law" about court standing!]

(14) What is of interest here, is that such standing is often given to the cemetery owner because it may be the only entity that can represent the wishes of the deceased, an element typically considered in whether to order an exhumation ...

As expected, the Mayor here opposes the exhumation and is positioned to present evidence in support of its objection. Whether or not that truly represents the interests of Ms. Antrim can never be known. Given the identity of the decedent and the time that has passes since her death, the Mayor cannot possibly have any direct evidence of Ms. Antrim's wishes. As such, the evidence that is presented by the Mayor can be viewed as best, supposition, or at worst, utterly unreliable.

[AUTHOR'S NOTE: Do not miss the bizarreness of this argument. The Mayor, whose legal duty is to protect remains in a cemetery under his authority, according to Robins, needs to mind-read corpse Catherine to find out if *she* wants to be dug up. But Attorney Robins, the channeler, is about to come to the rescue and speak for the dead woman also!]

(15) One is left to question why such a party with such a remote interest and lack of express knowledge about the decedent's wishes is conferred standing while the interests of Billy the Kid go unheard if this Court denier him standing. Allowing such a party to appear and present evidence while denying the same opportunity to a party that has been appointed to represent the interests of the decedent's son does not seem prudent nor fair

[AUTHOR'S NOTE: This argument is so crazy that a reader might be tempted to rationalize that it cannot be as crazy as it sounds. It is. Attorney Robins is saying that dead Billy has more credibility to let his wishes be known than the live Mayor, whose obligation it is to protect the cemetery. And Robins can speak for the exact wishes of the dead, unlike the more supernaturally limited Mayor.]

(16) 1st Factor Public Interest, Billy the Kid's name is forever tied to New Mexico and to that of another legendary figure of the Old West, Sheriff Pat Garrett. **A commonly held version** of history paints a picture of an ambush in which Garrett killed the Kid in Ft. Sumner where most believe the Kid still lies at rest. **This version has been questioned. It is the investigation into whether Garrett killed the Kid that has prompted these investigators to seek exhumation.**

[AUTHOR'S NOTE: This is pure "Brushy Bill" hoaxing. Only "Brushy's" believers question Pat Garrett's killing of Billy. Since "Brushy" was not Billy, there is no "public interest," meaning public value in the case. There are only the self-serving motives of the hoaxers, and the "Brushy" goal of puppeteer Robins.]

(17) 2nd Factor, the Decedents wishes. In spite of Silver City's position to the contrary, we simply do not know what the decedent's wishes would be. Given the present circumstances, however, where her

remains could possibly provide critical evidence to be used by modern day advocates to clear her son's name, one might easily surmise that Silver City's dogged attempt to resist exhumation would not be appreciated by Ms. Antrim.

[AUTHOR'S NOTE: Now Robins is channeling Billy's mother enough to know that Silver City's blocking her exhumation would "not be appreciated" by her! For Robins, she is a "Brushy"-believer too! And she is angry! And corrupt Judge Henry Quintero never objected to Robins's making a mockery of his court. He was just basking in his undeserved Richardson appointment for a desired judgeship.]

(18) 3rd Factor, Surviving Relatives Wishes. There are no relatives of Ms. Antrim currently before the Court ... The closest party currently before the Court is in fact Billy the Kid as represented by the undersigned counsel. As is apparent from the arguments set forth in this brief, the kid's [sic] interests would be furthered by the exhumation.

[AUTHOR'S NOTE: Here is Robins channeling dead Billy again to say that he wants his mother dug up as part of his agenda!]

(19) Billy the Kid believes that the evidence adduced at the exhumation hearing will certainly support an order of exhumation here.

[AUTHOR'S NOTE: Robins has crossed into the "Exorcist" movie's territory. He has disappeared. Only dead Billy is talking now through Robins's mouth. And *he* is "Brushy." The creepy thought is that Robins might not be faking. He may really think he *is* "Brushy Bill" incarnate.]

20) The foregoing has established that the undersigned counsel may legally and properly appear in these proceedings on behalf of, and to represent the interests of Billy the Kid.

[AUTHOR'S NOTE: Robins has established nothing whatsoever to justify his being in court as a channeler of dead Billy; nor has he established any reason for exhumations. But he has proved New Mexico's intractable corruption of collusive cronyism.]

(21) Respectfully submitted this 5th day of January, 2004.
Heard, Robins, Cloud, Lubel & Greenwood, L.L.P.

Bill Robins III
David Sandoval
Address and Telephone Numbers
ATTORNEYS FOR BILLY THE KID

SPEAKING FOR BILLY IN FORT SUMNER

On February 26, 2004, Attorney Robins, with Attorneys David Sandoval and Mark Acuña, filed the "Tenth Judicial Court of De Baca County Case No. CV-2004-00005, Petition for the Exhumation of Billy the Kid's Remains." Dead Billy is listed as a co-petitioner with the hoax's lawmen: "Gary Graves, Sheriff of De Baca County, Tom Sullivan, (Sheriff) and Steve Sederwall (Deputy Sheriff) of Lincoln County, New Mexico. (hereinafter the 'Sheriff-Petitioners')."

For digging up Billy, Robins used hoaxer style of vague suspicion, like: "This was also a time whose history was not accurately nor completely written." Or, as he made-up: "For generations now, the life of Billy the Kid has been the subject of historical debate. Perhaps the most significant lingering question involves whether Billy the Kid was indeed shot by Sheriff Pat Garrett in an ambush."

"Brushy Bill" made his expected grand entrance under Section "IV. Historical Background." with introduction of the pretenders. Robins stated: "The debate has been sparked at various times in the past by at least two individuals who laid claim to his identity. **Ollie "Brushy Bill" Roberts** resided in Hico, Texas and claimed to be Billy the Kid. John Miller, in Arizona also died still claiming he was Billy the Kid. Co-Petitioners are in the initial phases of pursuing exhumations of these individuals as well."

"Brushy" is plugged with Robins's true-believer stance of repeating as fact his "dark night" confabulation for the Fort Sumner shooting scene's actual bright moonlight; and by adding the pardon as deserved by "Brushy" for have led a law-abiding life after the shooting. So Robins wrote that the "ambush [was on] **one dark night** in Ft. Sumner;" and he claimed that the question that needed to be answered was **"whether the Kid went on to live a long and peace-abiding life elsewhere**."

To justify exhumation, Robins called the July 14, 1881 killing of Billy the Kid an "historical quandary" - but it was only a "quandary" for "Brushy" believers! He stated: "The investigation ["Billy the Kid Case"] has renewed questions as to whether Billy the Kid lies buried at the fabled grave-site in Ft. Sumner. Allowing the exhumation of the remains at Ft. Sumner grave site for extraction of DNA to be compared with that of Ms. Antrim's will likely finally provide definitive answers to this **historical quandary**."

Robins's brazen lying is clear. As he well knew, the month before, on January 9, 2004, the OMI had issued the Affidavits of

Drs. Ross Zumwalt and Debra Komar stating the graves' DNA was invalid for matchings. And Robins himself had participated in Komar's deposition of January 20, 2004, in which she said the same thing; and added that, for "Brushy," was further invalidation, since he denied Catherine Antrim was his mother. Obvious is that Robins knew that the hoax intended to fake results, since real ones were impossible.

FOILING THE EXHUMATION SCHEME

The hoaxers were no match for the law firm which I had brought in to represent the Mayors of Silver City and Fort Sumner. They made clear that there was neither forensic nor historical justification for the exhumation.

But Silver City Judge Henry Quintero apparently colluded with Bill Robins III to get the hoaxers to Billy the Kid's Fort Sumner grave. On February 24, 2004, Robins filed "In the Matter of Catherine Antrim: Billy the Kid's **Brief on the Question of Ripeness**;" arguing that Billy should be dug up first; because *his* DNA would justify digging up his mother.

So Quintero promptly - on April 2, 2004 - declared the mother's exhumation **not ripe** - meaning not ready - in his "Sixth Judicial District Court, State of New Mexico, County of Grant. No. MS 2003-11, In the Matter of Catherine Antrim. Decision and Order." He wrote: **"[The Court] finds that the Decision should be entered on ripeness for judicial review of exhumation of Catherine Antrim's remains ... Due to substantial uncertainty surrounding the recovery of the Kid's remains, only if the Petitioners are successful in locating the Kid's burial site and collecting his DNA may they again petition this Court for a review of Catherine Antrim's matter."** [Note that later the hoaxers would lie that Quintero had meant digging up "Brushy" as "Billy."]

It was a desperate time, knowing that Fort Sumner's Ted Hartley was a corrupt Richardson tool. I even flew in Frederick Nolan to testify. But my work on another front paid off. Brave Lincoln County Commission Chairman Leo Martinez, whom I had versed on the hoax, confronted the lawmen. Coincidentally, their fellow hoaxer, De Baca County Sheriff Gary Graves was facing recall for unrelated crimes. Sheriff Sullivan did not want to risk that himself, with his retirement at stake. So the lawmen gave up. On September 24, 2004, their attorney, Mark Acuña, filed "Tenth Judicial District Court, State of New Mexico, County of De Baca.

No. CV-04-00005. In the Matter of William H. Bonney aka 'Billy the Kid.' Stipulation of Dismissal With Prejudice." That meant they could not come back to exhume Billy Bonney.

That was not as good as it sounded. The hoaxers already had a new scheme, and had found a forensic expert to back them if TV cameras were rolling. Just needed was rewriting the hoax.

PAUL HUTTON'S TV PROGRAM

Appointed by Governor Bill Richardson as the hoax's official historian, University of New Mexico teacher, Paul Hutton, was listed in the Lincoln County Sheriff's Department file in the lawmen's "Contact List for "William H. Bonney Case # 2003-274" as a main "investigator." And he repeated the University of New Mexico's responsibility for the "Brushy" hoax; with its press having published *Alias Billy the Kid* 48 years earlier.

Hutton made the hoax's key media contacts: Bill Kurtis of Bill Kurtis Productions, and forensic expert, Dr. Henry Lee. As Steve Sederwall stated in his June 26, 2012 deposition in my open records litigation: "[T]he way I met Bill Kurtis was through Paul Hutton. Paul Hutton wanted me to be on some investigative history ... I said, "You know, I'm looking at bringing Henry Lee out here ... Tell Kurtis I'll let him film it if he wants to, or whatever, if he can get Henry out here." So [Hutton] jumped on it." Sederwall also said in my litigation's January 21, 2011 Evidentiary hearing: "I got a call from Paul Hutton, a historian up in Albuquerque, teaches at the University. He was writing a deal for Bill Curtis [sic]. He wanted us [Sederwall and Sullivan] to interview with Bill Curtis [sic] ... Paul and I were friends ... So Curtis [sic] contacted us and wanted to know if he could follow the investigation ... That's when Bill Curtis [sic] got involved, and **Curtis [sic] paid to bring Dr. Lee to New Mexico.**" [Transcript 1/21/11, pp. 164, 168].

"INVESTIGATING HISTORY: BILLY THE KID"

In 2004, Hutton wrote and co-produced with Bill Kurtis, the first in the hoax's anticipated fake TV documentaries on Billy the Kid Case" exhumations. It was the History Channel's "Investigating History: Billy the Kid. It united all the hoaxers as its talking head participants. They declared the hoax's tenets and backed 'Brushy" with *Alias Billy the Kid* as their source.

THE PROGRAM'S OVERVIEW

For his travesty, Hutton had Richardson as an "historical investigator" assembling "experts" as a "pardon team" for Billy the Kid. They were fellow hoaxers: Sheriff Tom Sullivan, Deputy Steve Sederwall, *True West* magazine Editor-in-Chief Bob Boze Bell; and "Brushy's" believers, Bill Robins III and W.C. Jameson.

Hutton narrated, as *Alias Billy the Kid's* cover loomed: "Over the years that story has gained some credence." W.C. Jameson states that the "Coroner's Jury Report was never found," and there was "no evidence jurymen saw the body." Steve Sederwall adds, "If "Brushy Bill" is Billy the Kid, it comes down to this ... Garrett had to have let him escape in Fort Sumner."

As to the pardon, Hutton states: "New Mexico Governor Bill Richardson is ready to make things right." Then, Richardson says: "I might pardon him." But *that* will be based on [Attorney Bill] Robins's "investigation."

Knowing about the blocked Garrett murder case exhumations, sly Hutton switched the case to a "homicide investigation" to see if Billy the Kid "deserved" a pardon.

Faking hoaxers' expertise, Hutton had Sheriff Sullivan "discover" that Billy was promised a pardon; had himself and Bob Boze Bell as "historians on the "Governor's pardon team;" and had Bill Robins III doing pardon legalities. Deputy Sederwall is a Capitan Mayor wondering if "Brushy" was Billy. And Richardson declares his commitment to "science," "tourism," and New Mexico.

THE PROGRAM'S "BRUSHY" FAKERY

Hutton's presentation, based on the "Brushy Bill" and "Billy the Kid Case" hoaxes, seeks to cast doubt on the Fort Sumner death scene; to make Pat Garrett a liar; and to denigrate legitimate historians. The film starts with Billy approaching a dark Maxwell house (no bright moonlight), while Hutton intones: "This is one of the most controversial moments in the history of the Old West: history's version of the last seconds of Billy the Kid ... Pat Garrett fires into the darkness ... Billy the Kid is dead when he hits the floor - or is he?" He then doubts a successful shot in the dark; and sneers: "The story is almost too good ... that the Kid ... would come strolling into this room unarmed and right into the hands of the law enforcement official ... is just too bizarre." **[But Billy was armed, and was likely sent to the ambush, since he was just going to the opposite side of the house to cut a steak.]**

Concealing all corpse identifications, Hutton calls the killing "a mystery;" quotes Poe's initial doubt, as if denying corpse identity; calls the killing "Garrett's version;" and lies that eye-witness, Pete Maxwell, never gave his version." He concludes that it was "unlikely" that Billy the Kid was shot.

Alias Billy the Kid is then backed by Hutton, with Jameson's denying the Coroner's Jury Report, and Sederwall's pronouncing that Garrett let Billy "escape in Fort Sumner."

Hutton proclaims: "Some suggested that it was more likely that Pat Garrett, Billy's friend, let him go ... burying someone else in his place" **[hoaxing friendship and "innocent victim"]**. Bob Boze Bell (subtitled as "Editor, True West Magazine") sneers that: "Friends of Pat Garrett conducted what they called an autopsy. But there were no photographs." He adds that they said Garrett deserved the reward. **[Jurymen were not his friends, they identified the body as Billy's, and nobody had a camera.]** Boze Bell says Garrett did the killing in "secrecy," and buried the body the next day. **[There was no secrecy. The body had a vigil and legal inquest.)**

Hutton calls history "Garrett's version;" says that the only eye-witness was Pete Maxwell, "who was never interviewed" **[hiding Maxwell's Coroner's Jury testimony, and the townspeople's corpse vigil]**, and lies that Poe "contradicted" Garrett's statement. **[Poe was merely initially unsure that Garrett had shot Billy, whom he could not recognize.]**

Hutton's "history" is pure "Brushy" hoax. He says Billy's mother died when he was 12 **[actually 14½]**; and outlaw, Jessie Evans, was Billy's "old side-kick" **[Billy rode with Jessie one month, September of 1877, before being hired by John Tunstall.]** He says John Tunstall and Alexander McSween were in partnership in Tunstall's Lincoln store **[there was no partnership]**; and says the James Dolan House filed a civil case against Tunstall. **[The case was against McSween, was filed by the Fritz heirs for criminal embezzlement; and Tunstall's property was attached by false claim of partnership with McSween]** Hutton says that after Tunstall's murder, Sheriff William Brady was shot in revenge **[when he was actually ambushed by the Regulators to prevent his murdering McSween later that day when he returned to Lincoln]**; and says "only" Billy was charged with Brady's shooting **[when the murder defendants included all the shooting Regulators]**.

For the Lincoln County War, he says the McSweens lost by being "divided up" in the town **[when they were strategically well placed, held the town for five days, and lost only because of military intervention – which Hutton omits]**.

As to the pardon, Hutton is clueless. He calls Governor Lew Wallace's Amnesty Proclamation "for everyone;" **[when Billy was excluded with those indicted]**. He thinks Billy's testimony in the 1879 Grand Jury *failed* to indict Dolan for the Chapman murder because the district attorney was Dolan's friend. **[Thus, missed was the reason real Billy had deserved pardon: for achieving the indictments of Dolan, Campbell, and Evans!]**

Hutton says Lew Wallace made Garrett Sheriff **[Garrett was backed by the Santa Fe Ring and Secret Service]**; and says he wanted to be sheriff to get the $500 reward **[when it was offered over a month *after* he was elected]**.

About the Stinking Springs capture, he wrongly says it was the day after Garrett's ambush of Billy's group at Fort Sumner **[which was December 19, 1880; with capture on the 22nd]**.

As to Billy's jail letters to Wallace, he says they were written in Lincoln's courthouse-jail **[not the correct Santa Fe jail]**.

But the most egregious and most damaging part of Paul Hutton's TV fraud is his "Billy the Kid Case" hoax re-enactment with Garrett, as Billy's accomplice to murdering Deputies Bell and Olinger, by placing the revolver in the outhouse. No one had accused Garrett of this horrific crime before the "Billy the Kid Case" hoax. And despicable charlatan Hutton contaminated public awareness irrevocably real by his TV scene.

Ongoing errors continue in re-enactment scenes. For example, after Brady is shot, Billy runs out to steal *Brady's* Winchester carbine; when he was retrieving his own confiscated gun.

Hutton announces that the "investigation" will solve if Billy was really killed by Garrett and if Governor Richardson should pardon him. Sullivan appears as a "researcher" who discovered that Wallace reneged on his promise to pardon Billy "which could have ended the Lincoln County War." **[So *he* "discovered" the famous Wallace pardon promise! But *he* called it connected to the Lincoln County War - the year before!]** Hutton intones: "New Mexico Governor Bill Richardson is ready to make things right." Richardson declares: "I might pardon him." But he wants truth "through science." Bill Robins, as the attorney seeking pardon evidence, says Billy "should never have been charged."

Sullivan, with his sheriff's badge, says he tried to settle the matter, but was "opposed by tourism interests" in Silver City and Fort Sumner, which he calls "obstruction of justice." Billy Sparks, Richardson's spokesman, says: "People want to prevent any truth that is not their truth." A Dennis Erickson, Ph.D. Science Policy Advisor *in Richardson's Office*, says there are ways of locating graves through "ground-penetrating radar." **[Hidden is OMI blockage, irrelevance of radar, and uncertain gravesites.]**

Richardson says: "I might pardon him." But *that* will be based on Robins's "investigation." He adds: "When I traveled around the world, there was curiosity about the wild West and I know that's tourism, that's economic development for us." **[Hidden is his pay-to-play intent to give that history to Texas!]**

In conclusion, "Investigating History: Billy the Kid" was "Billy the Kid Case" hoaxing, with its "Brushy" pardon thrust.

HOAXING PERSONAL INNOCENCE

Ignoring evidence, by June 20, 2006, Paul Hutton denied any connection to the "Billy the Kid Case" or to being its "historian." Answering my inquiry proxied through journalist, Jay Miller, he wrote: "I was never the 'state historian' (as *True West* put it) on this project and had absolutely nothing to do with the production of any written materials on it outside of some initial talking points I emailed the governor's office before the first press conference ... As to my work on the History Channel and how I came to any conclusions in the Billy the Kid program, that is really none of your business." And he called the "Billy the Kid Case" a "positive effort to promote our state nationally."

There was actually no doubt about Hutton's being the hoax's historian. Jay Miller had also contacted Hutton's mentor: historian, Robert Utley. No confidentiality was requested, so Miller e-mailed me Utley's September 16, 2004 answer: "I am truly disappointed in your governor ... he should be held accountable for the dumb things he is doing in the Billy dustup. When his aid tried to enlist me as 'historical advisor,' I told him to tell Richardson to stay out of this or he would get in deep doodoo. So they got Paul Hutton, my protégé, who loves the outrageous." When I spoke with Utley himself in November of 2005, he bemoaned that betrayal of historical ethics by the man he called his "protégé": Paul Hutton.

In fact, Hutton continued to milk his hoax participation. Still faking, he validated the carpenter's bench. He then made a Billy the Kid show in the Albuquerque Museum of Art and History featuring it by claiming its fake "blood."

THE U.S. MARSHALS SERVICE REPORT

A shocking and secret "Billy the Kid Case" participant was Washington, D.C., based U.S. Marshals Service Historian David Turk, involved in the hoax from its 2003 start, and coming to New Mexico to help the hoaxers destroy Pat Garrett's reputation. To put his participation in perspective, as the Marshals Service Historian, he was attacking its most famous Old West Deputy U.S. Marshal as a murderer of an innocent victim, with "Brushy Bill" as a possible surviving Billy the Kid.

Turk was the only historian backing Case 2003-274 in its "Probable Cause Statement;" with his fake "proof" being an old-timer's hearsay claim about a post-death Billy the Kid sighting. Also, since the Statement's footnotes were obscure National Archive documents on microfilm (like Azariah Wild's Secret Service reports), Turk may have provided them.

Later, in the forensic scam being conducted by Dr. Henry Lee with an old carpenter's bench, Turk used his title as expertise to fake its "validation." He was also present, in 2004, at Lee's fake forensic investigation of the Deputy Bell killing at the Lincoln courthouse (where Turk was misrepresented as an actual U.S. Marshal). He was also acknowledged for his assistance in the 2018 "Brushy"-backing book, *Cold Case Billy the Kid* by W.C. Jameson.

Turk must have known he was a subversive, hiding his participation in the "Billy the Kid Case" from my open records investigations. But, on June 22, 2005, a William E. Bordley, Associate General Counsel/FOIPA Officer, did respond that Turk had been in New Mexico from December 5, 2003 to December 9, 2003 (when the "Probable Cause Statement" was being written), and had gone to Silver City, Lincoln, Las Cruces, Santa Fe, Ruidoso, Albuquerque, and Tijeras.

More importantly, on August 24, 2005, a Mavis DeZulovich FOI/PA Liaison, Office of Public Affairs for the U.S. Marshals Service, responded: "Mr. Turk is not the author of the Lincoln County Sheriff''s Department Probable Cause Statement 2003-274. **However, mention is made in that document to information contained in a research report authored by Mr. Turk entitled: "The U.S. Marshals Service and Billy the Kid."** That was how I learned about his own report for the case. But he hid it as being "in revisions."

February of 2007 brought hope. Turk had published "Billy the Kid and the U.S. Marshals Service" in "Billy the Kid Case" hoax-promoting *True West* magazine! I got it. It proved his "revisions" were expurgations, being just about U.S. Marshals in the Lincoln County War period. But there was a clue. After giving the usual death scene, Turk spouted the familiar "Brushy Bill" script: that Pat Garrett was the sole witness, there was an innocent victim, and Billy survived. He wrote: "That traditional account [of the killing] - as told by Garrett himself (with the help of a ghostwriter) in the *Authentic Life of Billy, the Kid* - **has been questioned many times over the years with some accounts suggesting that the Kid got away to live another day or decades, and others indicating that somebody else besides the Kid died in Maxwell's bedroom.**" Apparently he was a "Brushy"-believer!

GETTING TURK'S ACTUAL SECRET REPORT

Finally, on September 3, 2008, the Turk mystery was solved - as a part of my open records litigation against the hoaxer lawmen. For Sheriff Rick Virden's September 8, 2008 deposition, we subpoenaed his file for Case 2003-274. Though expurgated of DNA records, its last 26 pages were Turk's actual *The U.S. Marshals Service and Billy the Kid*!

Its date was December 2003: the signing date of the "Probable Cause Statement!" It was titled: "United States Marshals Service Executive Services Division: Research Report, Submitted by David S. Turk." Page one gave me what I wanted: "Research Report: The U.S. Marshals Service and Billy the Kid. **To Be Added in its Present Entirety, with Exhibits, to Lincoln County, New Mexico Case # 2003-274.**" It backed the hoax premise of Pat Garrett as murdering of an innocent victim.

It had a cover page, 9 pages of text; bibliographic "Endnotes;" and "Exhibits" consisting of a Turk article titled "How much did it cost to find Billy the Kid?"; a "National Police Gazette" May 21, 1881 article on Billy's escape; and a May 30, 1881 letter from Attorney Sidney Barnes (one of Billy's Mesilla prosecutors) about Billy's Mesilla trial and his later escape. (Turk's general and irrelevant information on U.S. Marshals is omitted here.)

The only parts of Turk's report in the "Probable Cause Statement" are his Frances E. Totty WPA quote about "Billie" being seen after the death date; and his "Endnote" sources, like Secret Service Operative Azariah Wild's reports. But Turk had been right about hiding it. It revealed him as disreputable and subversive incompetent.

Research Report:
The U.S. Marshals Service and Billy the Kid

Submitted by David S. Turk, Historian
December 2003

"Research Report: The U.S. Marshals Service and Billy the Kid. To Be Added in its Present Entirety, with Exhibits, to Lincoln County, New Mexico Case # 2003-274."

Purpose of Research [Page 1]

There is renewed interest in examining the crimes and final resting place of William H. Bonney, also known as Henry Antrim, Henry McCarty, or Billy the Kid.

[AUTHOR'S NOTE: The only "renewed interest" was from the "Billy the Kid Case" hoax and loony conspiracy theorists.]

Two Sheriff's' Offices in New Mexico reopened an investigation, with the approval of the Governor of New Mexico. In September 2003 Steve Sederwall, Mayor of Capitan, and Deputy Sheriff, Lincoln County, New Mexico, contacted me on research matters relating to the Lincoln County War.

[AUTHOR'S NOTE: Turk claims Sederwall as contact.]

Given the integral role of the U.S. Marshals Service, and the dual roles between our two institutions during the time of Billy the Kid, and further that Pat Garrett was a Deputy U.S. Marshal during the pursuit of the Kid, and that another Deputy U.S. Marshal (and Lincoln County officer), Robert Olinger, was shot and killed by the Kid during his escape, it is relevant to the agency's historical interest to research those portions of the case pertinent to it to ensure accuracy.

[AUTHOR'S NOTE: The report gives no information to doubt conventional history. It does not "ensure accuracy!"]

The primary investigation of Lincoln County, New Mexico State No. 2004-274 [sic] is being conducted by Lincoln County Sheriff Tom Sullivan, De Baca County Sheriff Gary Graves, and Steve Sederwall, but the following findings add significantly to the data being collected in revisiting Billy the Kid.

[AUTHOR'S NOTE: No reason is given for "revisiting Billy the Kid," except hearsay death rumors 56 years after the event.]

Overview of Research Focus [Page 1]

The following research relates to the prominent roles of the U.S. Marshals Service in the Lincoln County War ... Finally, there is a study on the deaths of Deputy Marshal Olinger and Lincoln County Officer J.W. Bell, followed by Billy the Kid's subsequent escape. The Works Progress Administration interviewed several Lincoln residents during the late 1930's in this regard ...

[AUTHOR'S NOTE: The oddness of this statement is easy to miss; but each part is irrelevant to the others. Out of nowhere, will come Turk's "suspicions" that the Kid was not Garrett's murder victim.]

Deputy U.S. Marshal Garrett and His Agency Status [Page 4]

[AUTHOR'S NOTE: This page, about Garrett's U.S. Marshal status has Secret Service Agent Azariah Wild's praise of Garrett to his Chief. All is irrelevant to Garrett's murder victim.]

Key Event: Billy the Kid's Escape and the Deaths of Bell and Olinger [Page 8]

On April 28, 1881, [sic - missing word] made his famous escape from Lincoln. Accounts of the events were recalled later by witnesses. A contemporary news account from *The National Police Gazette* dated May 21, 1881, followed a generally accepted recollection pattern with some minor inconsistencies. Deputy U.S. Marshal Olinger and guard J.W. Bell ... were holding the Kid in the jail. Olinger dined at a local establishment, and during his absence the shackled prisoner hit Bell with handcuffs. He then grabbed Bell's revolver and shot him in the chest ... Just as he [Olinger] entered a small gate leading through the jail fence, the Kid shot him with a double-barreled gun, filling his breast of shot and killing him.

[AUTHOR'S NOTE: Note that the *National Police Gazette*, published in New York, was merely a dime novel tabloid, and not a legitimate historical source. Also, Turk presents Billy the Kid's escape without Garrett's participation.]

Differing Accounts on Death of Billy the Kid [Pages 8 - 9.]

Deputy U.S. Marshal and Lincoln County Sheriff Pat Garrett pursued Billy the Kid for several months after the deaths

[AUTHOR'S NOTE: About 2 ½ months.]

of Deputy Olinger and J.W. Bell. The end of the chase appeared to be at Pete Maxwell's ranch on July 15 [sic], 1881.

[AUTHOR'S NOTE: This is "Brushy" hoax-style sly innuendo of "suspicion" without evidence. And the date was July 14, 1881.]

What occurred at the Maxwell Ranch fueled speculation over the precise outcome. There appears [sic] to be many questions to answer.

[AUTHOR'S NOTE: This is full-blown, hoax conspiracy theory, with vague "suspicion." No evidence is given.]

According to the WPA interview of Francisco Trujillo in May 1937, Garrett was negotiating capture of the Kid with Pete Maxwell himself. Josh Brent's father was one of the Sheriff's deputies, stating that Garrett said "that he sure hated to kill the boy, but he knew it was either his life or the boy's life."

[AUTHOR'S NOTE: The "Billy the Kid Case" hoaxers omitted this hearsay from the Statement. But, as a hoax connoisseur, I say they missed a great hoax quote – even though it is groundless! It was a chance to fake the Pat-Billy friendship.]

Yet another resident stated,

> The people around Lincoln say Garrett didn't kill Billie [sic] the Kid. John Poe was with Garrett the night he was supposed to ... [sic] said that he didn't see the man that Garrett killed. Ican [sic] take you to the grave in Hell's Half Acre, a old government cemetry [sic], where Billie [sic] was supposed to be buried to show you the grave.
>
> The cook at Pete Maxwell's was always putting flowers on the grave and praying at it. This woman thought a lot of Billie [sic], but after Garrett killed the man at Maxwell's home her grandson was never seen again and Billie [sic] was seen by Bill Nicoli? And indian scout. Bill saw him in old Mexico.

[AUTHOR'S NOTE: This hearsay was put in the "Probable Cause Statement" with attribution to Turk.]

The recollections took a legendary bent, even extending to events that occurred after those at the Maxwell ranch. Josh Brent stated that Garrett told his father that after he killed the Kid, "that a fellow from the east wrote him and said that he would pay $5000.00 for the trigger finger of the boy."

[AUTHOR'S NOTE: This is irrelevant pseudo-historical filler.]

Other Related Fact [Page 9.]

A sidelight from this period was the debunking of one widely-held story that Billy the Kid killed twenty-one men by the age of twenty-one. U.S. Attorney Barnes stated in a letter to the Attorney General, dated May 30, 1881, that while the Kid "has killed fifteen different men & is only twenty one years of age."

[AUTHOR'S NOTE: Barnes, one of Billy's Mesilla prosecutors, who had no way of knowing the specifics.]

So U.S. Marshals Service Historian David Turk was a "Billy the Kid Case" hoaxer, abusing the prestige of his federal title.

FAKE FORENSIC REPORTINGS

My blocking the exhumations of Billy Bonney and his mother, along with Fort Sumner and Silver City Mayors, caused the "Billy the Kid Case" hoaxers to rewrite the hoax! Version One had Billy *not shot* by his friend, Pat Garrett, who killed an innocent victim instead. But now, with no "DNA" from Billy and his mother, the hoaxers needed any "DNA" to achieve digging up "Brushy."

So hoax Version Two arose (without admission), to use the only object they had possibly connected to Billy history: the carpenter's bench. Claimed was that it had shot Billy's blood, from which they could get his DNA! Since Billy was *not shot* in Version One, and the body on the bench was the innocent victim, the hoaxers rewrote the hoax. Now Billy *was shot* by friend Garrett, just to *play dead* and bleed on the bench (for future DNA recovery); then was replaced, by Garrett, with the murdered innocent victim.

The bench had already been claimed in the December 31, 2003 "Probable Cause Statement": "On August 29, 2003, Deputy Sederwall of the Lincoln County Sheriff's Department located the carpenter bench where the Kid's body was placed on July 14, 1881."

Now the hoaxers had two needs: verifying the bench; and finding a sleazy enough, name recognition "forensic expert" to play along with faking DNA to desecrate graves for a publicity stunt. They got both. Fellow hoaxers, Paul Hutton and David Turk, made-up that the bench was real. And limelight-seeking Dr. Henry Lee got on board to claim, blood, DNA, and anything else they wanted.

THE INVALID CARPENTER'S BENCH

The carpenter's bench was forensically invalid, since it cannot be proven as the real one. As discussed, the hoaxers found it in the Albuquerque converted chicken coop of Stella Abreu Miller's son. And she got it from a local man for her 1925-1936 Fort Sumner Billy the Kid Museum, according to historian, Jerry Weddle, who interviewed her in her old age. (See page 514 above)

By 1936, Stella's museum, with its furniture alleged from Peter Maxwell's bedroom, closed. But it was recorded in a May 31, 1937, *Clovis, New Mexico Evening News-Journal* article by Dee Blythe as "Billy the Kid Landmarks Fast Vanishing: Historic Spots Hard to Find; Markers Needed." With photos, it stated:

"Nearby [a post office] is the house of Manuel Abreu and Mrs. Stella Miller, children of Mrs. Odelia Abreu, youngest of the daughters of Pete Maxwell. They have treasured quite a few relics of the old days, particularly with reference to Billy the Kid, but these relics are all jumbled together into one small room of the house. The collection includes the carpenter's bench on which Billy the Kid's body was laid to cool, the bed beside which Pat Garrett sat talking to Pete Maxwell that fateful night; a rifle once owned by the Kid; a washstand that was struck by Garrett's second shot; the lamp Deluvina Maxwell held to see if the Kid was dead ... Last year, for awhile these relics were on display in a building on highway 60 in Fort Sumner; but the arrangement was unsatisfactory and they were brought back to their out-of-the-way resting place." Assumedly, this history came from Stella; so noteworthy is her made-up inclusion of the washstand as shot; adding likelihood to the carpenter's bench being bogus.

In 1959, 22 years after Stella's museum closed, her son, Manuel "Mannie" Miller, in Albuquerque since 1944, took her museum's contents to store in his back-yard converted chicken coop. And their storage from 1944 to 1959 involved high temperatures and flooding, eliminating blood preservation.

In 2011, after Mannie Miller's death, I met his nephew, Kenny Miller, Stella's grandson, the new caretaker. He showed me the objects. They included Stella's sign about "outlaw" Billy the Kid – indicating her reliance on myth. Pandering to tourists, it said: "FOR YOUR INFORMATION THIS MUSEUM IS OWNED BY THE NIECE AND NEPHEW OF PETE MAXWELL. IT WAS IN HIS HOME WHERE BILLY THE KID WAS KILLED BY SHERIFF PAT GARRETT WE WILL ASSURE AND NOT MISREPRESENT ANY ONE WHO IS INTERESTED IN THE SOUTH-WEST AND ITS NOTORIOUS OUTLAW BILLY THE KID. THERES NOT JUST ONE OR TWO ANTIQUES BUT SEVERAL THINGS OF INTEREST DATED BACK 18-81 AND TERRITORIAL DAYS."

But Kenny Miller told me the key truth: the family has no doubt that Pat Garrett killed Billy the Kid.

But claiming "blood" - not necessarily *real* blood - was the hoaxers' only bench concern. So they faked it. On August 14, 2004, for the *Lincoln County News,* reporter Doris Cherry's "Forensics 101 for 'Billy," quoted Sederwall: "The bench has been in the Maxwell family descendents since 1881 and has been stored out of weather, protecting the blood evidence ... **Only once was the blood exposed to the elements, when a family member who took the bench without family approval returned it to the Maxwell family home in Fort Sumner and left it outside to get rained on once.** So the odds of finding blood evidence were very good."

The "rained on" part was bad for blood! It got worse. For an October 6, 2005 *RuidosoNews.com* article, hoax loyalist, Julie Carter, wrote "Follow the Blood: In the Billy the Kid Case, Miller Exhumed." She stated: "The Maxwell compound and everything in it was reportedly washed away in a flood of 1906. The photo of the bench was taken in 1926 by historian Maurice Fulton ... Since 1959, they [Maxwell family] had stored the historical furniture and household items in an old chicken coop." The "washed away" in a 1906 flood, and unknown location from 1881 to 1926 were also bad! And added was the gap from Fulton's 1926 photo, to transport in 1959 to Mannie Miller's back yard chicken coop.

For "validation," hoaxer Paul Hutton "authenticated" it. Then, in 2007, for his Albuquerque Museum of Art and History Billy the Kid show, with curator, Deb Slaney, he labeled it as having "human blood." U.S. Marshals Service Historian David Turk gave another fake authentication. On August 8, 2006, via Jay Miller, my Freedom of Information Act request to Turk's agency asked how he could authenticate it. On August 31, 2006, Nikki Cedric at Public Affairs answered: "Mr. Turk ... has seen the said workbench; *however, he did not state that any particular person was on the bench. This is for the lab to determine.* The bench does match descriptions given in other sources and he believes it to be the one described."

So on April 19, 2006, hoax-backing reporter, Julie Carter, in *RuidosoNews.com*, reported in "Digging up Bones": "UNM History professor Paul Hutton and U.S. Treasury [sic - Marshals Service] historian Dave Turk have both authenticated the bench."

But no amount of hoaxer lying could change that the bench was forensically useless for "Billy the Kid's DNA."

Nevertheless, the lawmen hoaxed wildly. Steve Sederwall falsely declared: "Dead men don't bleed." So his shot Billy survived, but bled on the bench! Hoax loyalist reporter, Julie Carter, for her October 6, 2005, *RuidosoNews.com* article "Follow the Blood: In the Billy the Kid Case, Miller Exhumed," quoted Sederwall's whoppers: "Whoever was laid on that, whether it was Billy the Kid or not," said Sederwall, "he left his DNA." The investigators said the amount of blood found on the bench indicated that whoever was on that bench must have been still alive. **"Dead men don't bleed," explained Sederwall. "and we witnessed a large amount of blood."** The hoaxers were back in business with a new hoax and exhumation hopes.

DR. LEE WAS THE PERFECT DNA MATCH

Deputy Steve Sederwall had contacted Dr. Henry Lee through fellow hoaxer, Paul Hutton; as Sederwall testified in his June 26, 2012 deposition for my open records litigation: "Paul Hutton wanted me to be on some investigative history ... I said, "You know, I'm looking at bringing Henry Lee out here ... Tell Kurtis I'll let him film ... if he can get Henry out here." So [Hutton] jumped on it."

Henry Lee jumped on it too, getting the flood of publicity that accompanies media magnet, Billy the Kid; and that Lee craves for what his scornful colleagues call his "show-biz forensics." And he had national name recognition by helping O.J. Simpson walk free in his 1996 murder trial. As to reputation for veracity, that was another story.

Prosecutor, Vincent Bugliosi, in his book, *Outrage: The Five Reasons Why O.J. Simpson Got Away With Murder*, called Henry Lee "nothing short of incompetent." Bugliosi was avoiding "liar." An example from *Outrage* was Lee's testifying that "crime-scene" shoe "imprints" on murder victim Nicole Simpson's walkway did not match O.J. Simpson's incriminatory, "size-12 Bruno Magli bloody shoe prints" - also at the scene. But the smaller "prints" Lee used, according to Bugliosi, had been hardened into the concrete during its laying "ten years earlier!"

Helpful Dr. Lee resurfaced for the 2007 murder trial defense for music impresario, Phil Spector; accused, and ultimately convicted, of fatally shooting actress, Lana Clarkson. But Attorney Sara Caplan - in Spector's first defense team - testified to the judge, Larry Paul Fidler, that, at the crime scene, Lee bottled dead Clarkson's torn-off fingernail, which indicated possible struggle - not Spector's defense's claim of her committing suicide. Then that fingernail disappeared. Judge Fidler declared destruction of evidence. The CNN.com AP headline of May 25, 2007 was: "Famed expert's credibility takes a hit at Spector trial."

Lee's involvement in a 2016 documentary, "The Case of JonBenet Ramsey," accusing her nine year old brother, Burke Ramsey of murdering her, resulted in Burke's $750 million defamation suit, which included Lee. On January 5, 2019, Dailymail.com reporter Maxine Shen wrote: "CBS and the brother of JonBenet Ramsey settle their $750m defamation lawsuit to the 'satisfaction of both parties.' " It stated: "Beyond CBS and the documentary production company Critical Content, LLS, Burke's lawsuit named **forensic scientist Henry Lee** and forensic pathologist Werner Spitz among several others who appeared in the broadcast."

So Henry Lee was the perfect "expert" to keep secret that no verifiable DNA of Billy the Kid existed on the planet - and find some. He sham-tested for "blood" wherever he was pointed; and made up crime scene scenarios however he was directed - as long as Bill Kurtis Productions kept filming.

Lee was part of the "Billy the Kid Case" hoaxers' team from 2004 onward; even acknowledged in 2018's *Cold Case Billy the Kid*. He was funded by Bill Kurtis, who wrote to Sederwall; stating: "This letter is provided as official verification that Kurtis Productions, LTD located in Chicago, Illinois paid all expenses for Dr. Henry Lee and his participation in the making of the documentary *Investigating History: Billy the Kid*. Dr. Lee was flown to New Mexico on July 30, 2004 and departed on August 1, 2004 at the expense of Kurtis Productions, LTD."

Lee's joining the "Billy the Kid Case" was announced by hoax-backing *Albuquerque Journal* reporter, Rene Romo. On August 2, 2004, Romo splashed, "Forensic Expert on Billy's Case: Questions Remain on Outlaw's Fate" Romo declared: "Dr. Henry Lee, one of the nation's leading forensic scientists ... has added the Billy the Kid slaying to his case files ... "This is an extremely interesting case of some historical importance,' Lee said in an interview ... 'That's why I agreed to spend some of my own time to work with them ... **It's basically a worthwhile project and legitimate**."

So famous Dr. Lee called the "Billy the Kid Case" "a worthwhile project and legitimate." What else was the public to think?

Lee's profit motive was further elucidated in the August 12, 2004 *Lincoln County News* article by Doris Cherry: "Forensics 101 for 'Billy." She quoted Sheriff Tom Sullivan: "Along with Sullivan and Lee were a crew from Curtis [sic] Production Company filming for the History Channel and Court T.V. **Dr. Lee also has a show produced by Curtis [sic] Production**."

So Billy the Kid DNA exhumations and "matchings" were to be churned out by Lee and Kurtis for their enterprise.

But the public was fed a different bill of goods via the hoaxers. By April 13, 2006, deceived reporter, Leo W. Banks of the *Tucson Weekly*, in "The New Billy the Kid?" had Lee pleading; as in: "Everybody wants a piece of the Kid, even a celebrity like Henry Lee ... when he heard about the Kid dig-up efforts, **he called Sederwall to volunteer his services**."

The "Billy the Kid Case" hoaxers plugged Lee extravagantly. Rene Romo's August 2, 2004 *Albuquerque Journal* article even used their "Probable Cause Statement's" complicit historian: "You're getting the top guy ... I think that will go a long way to finding out what happened in Lincoln," said **David S. Turk**, historian with the U.S. Marshals Service ... who is cooperating on the case."

Added was that a Calvin Ostler, a Utah Medical Examiner - would participate. Unmentioned, was that Ostler was Lee's business partner. So Lee-Turk-Ostler did ricochet validation, without public awareness that they were all in cahoots for trash "documentaries" by Bill Kurtis and Professor Paul Hutton - all doing their job for Governor Bill Richardson.

DR. LEE'S "BENCH BLOOD OF BILLY THE KID"

By the time Dr. Henry Lee arrived on the scene, it was clear that no valid DNA existed for the Billy the Kid Case." That means "reference DNA," with 100% certainty of being from the person in question. It is *the only valid DNA valid for identity matching*.

The carpenter's bench "blood DNA' was worthless, because it could not be "reference DNA." It would be like a random fingerprint, with no fingerprints existing of the individual in question to compare with it.

But legitimate DNA forensics were not Dr. Henry Lee's worry. His worry was *DNA film footage*. Anything claiming a link to Billy the Kid sufficed. The bench was just fine for Dr. Lee. And when Lee looked at the bench, unsurprisingly, he found "blood."

Rene Romo's August 2, 2004, *Albuquerque Journal's* "Forensic Expert on Billy's Case" gave this new hoaxed finding: "**Lee, assisted by Calvin Ostler ... performed tests on the bench that Sederwall believes to be the one on which the Kid's body was laid out after Garrett gunned him down. Preliminary results indicated trace evidence of blood**, but, without further testing, it is not certain whether the blood was human, Lee said."

In fact, blood was not certain! I had seen the bench. It had some rust-colored discolorations - unsurprising on a carpenter's bench.

By August 12th, reporter Doris Cherry, for her *Lincoln County News*, "Forensics 101 for 'Billy,' " wrote: "Dr. Lee proved the good odds by utilizing a laser to bore into the wood of the bench to take samples and he took scrapings from the top and underneath of the bench. '**Then he swabbed it with the chemical that changes color to indicate the presence of blood,'** Sullivan said."

The hoaxers were just hoaxing. Lee, as his report which I got after years of open records litigation against the record-hiding lawmen, was merely using Luminol, a non-specific chemical that fluoresces with iron-containing substances. Besides blood, it lights up for rust, paints, and cleaning agents - all more likely on a carpenter's bench than blood. **And no other testing would *ever* be done** by that hoaxing group to verify blood - or to connect it to Billy Bonney (which was impossible).

Next the hoaxers got carried away. Romo's **"trace,"** in his August 2, 2004, "Forensic Expert on Billy's Case," started bleeding like stigmata. In Doris Cherry's "Forensics 101 for Billy," Sullivan said Lee "**found a lot of blood.**" For Julie Carter's "Follow the Blood," **Sederwall said: "We witnessed a large amount of blood;"** and he lied that it proved "**an upper chest wound.**" By April 13, 2006, "blood" was almost dripped from the bench. Leo Banks of the *Tucson Weekly*, in "The New Billy the Kid," gave **Sederwall saying the bench was "saturated!**"

Obviously the hoaxers hid Lee's actual report. But after five years of open records litigation against the lawmen, on January 31, 2012, I got it. At 25 pages, it was dated February 25, 2005, and titled "Forensic Research & Training Center Forensic Examination Report." Its header listed "Requested by: Lincoln County Sheriff's Office, New Mexico; Investigation History Program, Kurtis Production." "Local Case No." was "2003-274." The "Report To:" was Steve Sederwall, Lincoln County Sheriff's Office, New Mexico." Recorded for the "forensic investigation team" were: "Calvin Ostler, Forensic Consultant, Riverton, Utah;" "Tom Sullivan, Sheriff, Lincoln County, New Mexico;" "Steve Sederwall, Deputy Sheriff, Lincoln County;" and "David Turk, US Marshall [sic], United States Marshall [sic] Service." The carpenter's bench was "Item # 1 Workbench." Lee concluded:

> After a detail examination of the evidence and review of all the results of field testing, the following conclusion was reached.
> 1. Brownish dark stains were observed on different areas of the workbench. These areas were subjected to chemical presumptive blood tests. Some of those samples give a positive

reaction. These results indicate the presence of Heme or Peroxidase like activity with those stains testing positive, **which suggest that those stains could be bloodstains**. Further DNA testing could reveal the nature and identity of these blood-like stains.

Lee had proved himself a "Billy the Kid Case" hoaxer by omitting more likely rust. And his lab, Orchid Cellmark, does not test for blood anyway. And finding DNA would not even connect it to those stains, since no controls were done for DNA from non-stained areas. Nor were controls taken from people at his testing to check for *their* contaminating DNA (think sneeze!). Lastly, Lee was lying that "[f]urther DNA testing could reveal the nature and identity of these blood-like stains." There was no reference DNA of Billy the Kid, of any kin, to compare with any DNA found - the only way of claiming "bench DNA' as Billy's.

"BLOOD OF BILLY THE KID" GETS A DNA LAB

Next, Dr. Henry Lee had to turn his fake "blood of Billy the Kid" into fake "DNA of Billy the Kid." So he sent his bench swabbing and scraping specimens to Orchid Cellmark Lab.

Reporter, Doris Cherry, in her August 12, 2004, "Forensics 101 for 'Billy' " stated: "Each swab and all scrapings from the bench were sealed in preparation to shipping to the Orchard Selmark [sic - Orchid Cellmark] Lab in Dallas. Sullivan said Dr. Lee uses the lab for most of his work, and the lab is also famous for its forensic work to determine DNA of the 9-11 victims."

Kept secret was that Orchid Cellmark does not test for blood; that objects in a human environment pick up human DNA; that no controls were done; and, of course, no reference DNA existed. Soon, the rightfully nervous hoaxers called the lab's name "secret."

In fact, Orchid Cellmark had "secrets." On August 9, 2004, I had contacted its then director, Mark Stolorow, explaining the "Billy the Kid Case" hoax. He was amused. On August 18th, we spoke again. Stolorow was defensive. Orchid Cellmark, he told me, was under a "gag order" on the case. Dr. Lee was now in charge!

Three months later, Orchid Cellmark was caught faking DNA computer data on another case. November 18, 2004's "TalkLeft.com" reported it as: "Fraud alleged at Cellmark, DNA Testing Firm." It stated: "This is shocking to the forensic community which has always believed that raw data cannot be electronically manipulated." It concluded: "Bottom line: A lot of defendants will be seeking retesting by an independent lab when the prosecution is relying on results by Cellmark." That scandal reduced Orchid Cellmark to one lab in Farmers Branch, Texas.

Mark Stolorow was replaced as Orchid Cellmark's director by Dr. Rick Staub. Unlike Stolorow, he seemed indifferent to scandal. As will be seen, his lab found no DNA at all in Henry Lee's bench specimens. **But the hoaxers claimed they yielded DNA of Billy the Kid for doing exhumations based on it!** Dr. Lee and Dr. Staub never objected. Staub came to Arizona with his bone bags to parts of John Miller back to Texas. After all, Bill Kurtis Productions was filming; and he in it.

LEE ATTACKS GARRETT, A WASHSTAND, AND A HEADBOARD

Dr. Henry Lee's knew he was "investigating" bad guy murderer, Pat Garrett. So he attacked him with fake forensics. Lack of a crime scene to investigate - with the Maxwell house torn down in about 1887, left just Stella Abreu's "museum" furniture.

"Probable Cause Statement" had introduced a "washstand" from Stella Abreu's museum to fabricate that Garrett lied that his second shot hit Maxwell's headboard. In his 1933 *The Death of Billy the Kid*, Poe had reported that: "[A] shot was fired in the room, followed immediately by what everyone within hearing distance thought were two other shots. However, there were only two shots fired, the third report, as we learned afterward, being caused by the rebound of the second bullet, which had struck the adobe wall and **rebounded against the headboard of a wooden bedstead**." So, by fake "what-if" reasoning, the lawmen claimed that *if* Garrett lied about hitting the washstand, he lied about the corpse's identity!

For the washstand, they gave their fake "Probable Cause Statement" Deluvina Maxwell quote: *"There was a washstand with a marble top in Pete Maxwell's bedroom, which Garrett had seen in the moonlight and shot at, thinking it was Bonney trying to get up."* **[This hid it as hearsay from Lucien Maxwell's "grandchildren," in an uncited source. (See page 514 above) And hidden was Deluvina's confirming dead Billy on June 24, 1927 to historian, J. Evetts Haley: "I came here about [1869] and was here when Billy the Kid was killed ... I did not see Billy the night after he was killed, but I saw him the following morning."]**

But all that was important was having the washstand. As the "Probable Cause Statement" said: "On September 13, 2003, investigators located all the furniture that was in Pete Maxwell's bedroom the night of the shooting, July 1881. **In the items investigators located on September 13, 2003 was that wash stand.**"

This supposed "washstand" is a little wooden box, the size of a toy! **[FIGURE: 15]** Lee's measurements were: 28¾" x 16", x 30" high. It had no marble top. But it had two holes. So Lee used it to fabricate a crime scene based on existing room, no authenticated furniture, disregard of the historical record, and the its tiny height. Hoax-helping reporter, Rene Romo, presented Lee's "washstand" fakery in his August 2, 2004 *Albuquerque Journal*'s "Forensic Expert on Billy's Case." stating:

> Lee and the investigators [Sullivan, Sederwall, and Calvin Ostler] also examined a washstand that was purportedly struck by a bullet when Garrett shot the Kid in a bedroom of the outlaw's friend, Pete Maxwell, in Fort Sumner ... Lee and the investigators used laser technology Saturday to determine the trajectory of the bullet as it entered the left side of the washstand and exited the right at a downward angle. Given the washstand's likely location in the room, the investigation has already cast some doubt on Garrett's account of the fatal shooting, Sederwall and [Calvin] Ostler said.
>
> 'The evidence we are seeing does not corroborate the popular legend,' Ostler said. 'Something's askew' ...
>
> **One simple explanation that Lee offered is that Garrett may have shot defensively at the Kid as he fled and struck the washstand from the side instead of head on. Garrett's official story may have omitted that embarrassing detail. "You don't want to paint yourself as a chicken," Lee suggested**.

In his February 25, 2005 "Forensic Research & Training Center Forensic Examination Report" for "Item # 2 Washstand," Lee wrote: "The angles produced in the examination tell us two things: First, the bullet was fired from no more than 41" from the floor given the reported limitations of the room. The room was reported to be 20' by 20'; the maximum distance is assumed to be 20'. If the firearm was a maximum of 41" off the floor it is unlikely that the shooter was standing. It is more likely the shooter was kneeling, squatting, or close to the floor. Second, the horizontal angle is such that if the Washstand was positioned so that the back was against the wall, the shot could not have been fired from more than approximately 40 inches from the Washstand, because the wall would have been in the way. The angle of trajectory intersects

Item # 2 Washstand

This Washstand measures approximately 28 ¾" long by 16" deep by 30" tall. Figure 6 is a sketch diagram of the washstand. This washstand is made of wood with a black color finish on it.

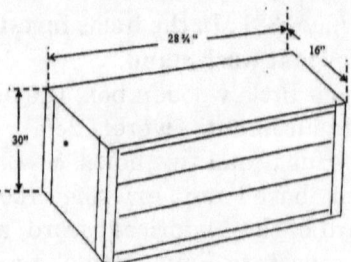

Figure 6, Washstand

Photograph # 3 shows the left side panel of the washstand and photograph # 4 depicts a view of the
Visual examination of the external s
holes, one single hole in each end of
examination of these holes indicates
bullet holes.

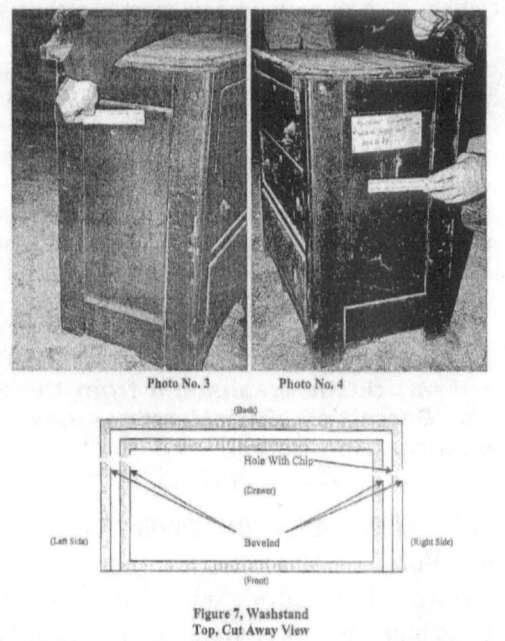

Photo No. 3   Photo No. 4

Figure 7, Washstand
Top, Cut Away View

Figure 7 is a cut away diagram of the washstand. This diagram depicts the relative locations of the two holes on the side panels of the washstand.
The hole on the left side panel is round and well defined. The hole on the right side panel is chipped and beveled. The left side panel hole is consistent with a bullet entrance hole.

FIGURE: 15. "Washstand" from Stella Abreu's Billy the Kid Museum, from Dr. Henry Lee's forensic report 1926-1936

the back plane of the Washstand at approximately 45 3/16", and no more than 46". Lee's conclusion reflected his well-known caution about putting his lies in writing: "Two bullet holes were located on the side panels of the Washstand. The hole on the left side panel is consistent with a bullet entrance hole while the hole on the right side panel is consistent with a bullet exit hole. However, it is not possible to determine when those bullet holes were produced at this time."

The lawmen also gave Lee Stella's museum's headboard. Important for their fake argument of Garrett as a liar, was claiming it had no bullet hole as claimed by him and Poe. So that is what Lee gave them.

Lee's February 25, 2004 report titled "Forensic Research & Training Center Forensic Examination Report" - which I got during the open records litigation against the hoaxing lawmen - under its topic, **"Item # 2 Headboard;"** stated: **"No bullet hole and no observable damage, no sign of bullet ricocheted type of defects were found on the Headboard. No blood or biological materials were observed on the Headboard."**

Lee omitted that the "headboard" is just a rim around a huge hole. **[Figure: 16]** There was no place for the bullet strike! So Lee lied to Rene Romo for his August 2, 2004 *Albuquerque Journal*'s "Forensic Expert on Billy's Case" by stating: "The evidence we are seeing does not corroborate the popular legend."

Deputy Steve Sederwall was soon spouting Dr. Lee's Garrett-is-a-liar fable in Julie Carter's October 2005, "Follow the Blood": "Using high-tech lasers and other modern crime scene methods, investigators learned that the shooting of the Kid in Pete Maxwell's bedroom was not in the way history has portrayed it. Tests indicate that Garrett fired his second shot from the doorway while on his knees and with his left hand on the floor, firing back over his shoulder ... Being blinded by his first shot, it appears he was in a great hurry to get out of the room and fell to the floor.' He [Sederwall] added: 'To find the furniture from Maxwell's bedroom was great. But to have Dr. Lee recover usable evidence was truly a historical find.' "

LEE'S DEPUTY KILLING "INVESTIGATION"

Next on Dr. Henry Lee's agenda for the hoaxers (and presumably for future TV viewing) was Billy Bonney's April 28, 1881 jailbreak killing of Deputy James Bell: the "Billy the Kid Case" hoax's sub-investigation in its "Probable Cause Statement" to defame Garrett as being Billy Bonney's escape accomplice and a liar about the killing of Deputy James Bell.

FIGURE: 16. Headboard without its center from Stella Abreu's Fort Sumner Billy the Kid Museum, 1926-1936 (Courtesy of Kenny Miller)

Lee's job was to manufacture "suspicion" about Garrett. He used Garrett's report from Gottfried Gauss that Billy shot Bell as the man ran down the stairway; and that he found Bell dying at the bottom, and dragged him out the back door.

At the courthouse on August 1, 2004, Lee tested for "blood" on upstairs floorboards and a wall. Of course, he found "blood."

Lee's original report of February 25, 2005, titled "Forensic Research & Training Center Forensic Examination Report" had this "investigation" under "Examination of Lincoln County Court House." Listed as present were "Calvin Ostler, Forensic Consultant, Riverton, Utah;" "Tom Sullivan, Sheriff, Lincoln County, New Mexico;" "Steve Sederwall, Deputy Sheriff, Lincoln County;" and "David Turk, US Marshall [sic], United States Marshall [sic] Service;" and Bill Kurtis of Bill Kurtis Productions for TV footage.

He called the staircase "repainted," when it was *replaced* in the 1980's. His photo of the "target area" showed big brown drips on the wall under the stairway. Not only do they like rusted water from a broken pipe or leaking roof, but the upstairs hall has nothing to do with the historical shooting.

To test those stains, Lee used O-tolidine: like Luminol, a non-specific chemical test for iron-containing compounds - like rust or blood. So cagy Lee called the drips *"blood-like* stains;" and stated they merit "presumptive blood tests." So, in his report's "Conclusions," he stated: "[T]hose stains could be bloodstains." Omitted is that for the amount of dripping, a massacre was needed on the second floor.

And, as an expert, Lee should have asked if there were Bell remains or Bell kin for "reference DNA" to establish if "blood" was Bell's. The answer is: no remains and no kin. Nevertheless, hoaxing Lee concluded: "Various stains were observed on the surface and underside of the floorboards. Chemical tests for the presence of blood were positive with some of these stains. These results indicate presence of Heme or Peroxidase like activity with those stains tested positive, which suggests that those stains could be bloodstains. **Further DNA testing could reveal the nature and identity of those blood-like stains.**"

The day after Lee's fake "investigation," on August 2, 2004, in the *Albuquerque Journal's* "Forensic Expert on Billy's Case," the hoaxers' mouthpiece, Rene Romo, reported the find of Deputy Bell's "blood!" Romo wrote: "Lee and the investigators Sunday afternoon also found several positive indications of blood residue below floor-boards at the top of a stairwell in the old Lincoln County courthouse. Such evidence could support Sederwall's theory that **the Kid fatally shot deputy J.W. Bell there, at the top of the stairs,** in his infamous escape from the Lincoln County jail. **That version would also contradict Garrett's account that the Kid, at the top of the stairs, shot Bell who was at the bottom of the stairwell.**"

Lincoln County News reporter Doris Cherry followed with her August 12, 2004 "Forensics 101 for 'Billy' ": "**Sullivan said that after studying the courthouse and the shooting he contended Bell was really killed at the top of the stairs, not near the bottom of the stairs as legend has it.**" Omitted is that this was based on no blood, no original stairway, and no connection to Bell!

HIDING LEE'S RECORDS AND LAB RESULTS

The lack of any DNA for continuing their hoax, did not faze the hoaxers. What they wanted was lack of Dr. Lee's DNA records availability to expose their hoaxing! So they hid his Orchid Cellmark DNA extraction results, while fabricating DNA claims.

And Lee played hide-the-ball like the hoaxers. On May 1, 2006, he answered my proxy's open records request by saying he wrote a report, but it was with the Sheriff's Department:

Dear Mr. Miller [my proxy journalist]:

In response to your letter dated March 27, 2006 regarding Forensic Consultation in the New Mexico Billy the Kid Case. To set the record straight, **the Lincoln County Sheriff's Department contacted me**. They requested a forensic expert to perform preliminary identification and scene reconstruction. This was a pro bono forensic consultation case. **[AUTHOR'S NOTE: Bill Kurtis Productions was paying him, and anticipated a documentary with him in it.]** We examined a wooden bench, and floorboards at the courthouse.

I completed my examination of the evidence and submitted my report to the Lincoln County Sheriff's Department. If you want a copy of the report, you should contact the Lincoln County Sheriff's Department directly.

Since **I did not conduct any DNA testing on the evidence** and the Lincoln County Sheriff's Department sent samples directly to a private laboratory for analysis **[AUTHOR'S NOTE: Lee is concealing Orchid Cellmark Lab]**, I am sorry but I do not have answers to your questions regarding DNA.

Sincerely,
Dr. Henry Lee

Henry Lee was unaware that past Orchid Cellmark Lab Director Mark Stolorow had told me the "Billy the Kid Case" was under Lee, and that Lee had put the results under gag order! There was no wonder that the hoaxers hid the records. They not only exposed their faked claims, but also would eventually reveal the criminality of their exhumations by proving no DNA existed to justify them. It was just a publicity stunt.

LEE'S SECRET DNA RESULTS AND HOAXER LIES

Ultimately, by open records litigation and subpoena of Orchid Cellmark Lab, on April 20, 2012, I got the 133 pages of Lee's DNA records. They laid bare the hoaxing.

October 15, 2004's "Laboratory Report, Forensic Identity, Mitochondrial Analysis, Results and Conclusions" for its Case 4444-001B-004B (for Case 2003-274) for **THE CARPENTER'S BENCH SHOWED LEE'S SPECIMENS HAVING NO DNA! THE HOAXERS' CLAIM TO HAVE BENCH-BLOOD-DNA OF BILLY THE KID FOR DNA MATCHINGS WAS A LIE!** [APPENDIX: 2] And they knew it by October 15, 2004. There was no justification to dig up anyone at all in their "investigation!"

And Lee's Deputy Bell shooting courthouse investigation - already fake since there was no Bell reference DNA to compare with any other DNA - likewise yielded **no valid DNA from Lee's floorboard specimens**, as reported in that October 15, 2004 "Laboratory Report, Forensic Identity, Mitochondrial Analysis, Results and Conclusions." One specimen yielded no DNA, and his second specimen showed a useless **"mixture of two or more mitochondrial profiles.** Consequently no sequence data are reported." The conclusion was: "[P]rofiles are therefore inconclusive." **And even if there had been valid floorboard DNA, there was no Bell DNA with which to compare it.**

Nevertheless, for years the lawmen hoaxers lied that the *carpenter's bench* had "DNA" from two individuals (taken to mean Billy and the innocent victim, like Billy Barlow). Steve Sederwall, eventually testified in my open records litigation on January 21, 2011 and February 4, 2013, that they had needed "$50,0000" to separate mixed DNA, so had not proceeded! That was a lie too.

In fact, DNA expert and President of San Francisco's Lexigen, Dr. Simon Ford stated: "Mixed DNA results are very common in forensic casework," and the meaning of "two or more ... profiles," **merely means "at least two;"** not that there *are two*. For sorting, needed is reference DNA of the individuals." [But Bell's DNA was not available.] Dr, Ford added: "[B]ased on DNA technology alone, there is no way of knowing from which kind of cell a particular DNA profile originated **[meaning DNA results cannot prove that blood was the source].**

As to a $50,000 cost, Dr. Ford stated: "Most labs charge about $1,000 for testing an evidence sample ... Some labs have a surcharge of between $300 and $500 for "difficult" samples, such as bone or tissue. The interpretation ... is usually included in the cost of the testing."

BIG PICTURE FOR LEE'S FAKED FORENSICS

Even if the hoaxers had gotten DNA from Lee's specimens, they had no reference DNA of Billy or Bell to claim it as theirs. But the lie that they had Billy the Kid's carpenter's bench "DNA" would become the basis for digging up John Miller (with added William Hudspeth), and for trying to dig up "Brushy Bill."

CHAPTER 3
ILLEGAL EXHUMATIONS OF JOHN MILLER AND WILLIAM HUDSPETH

TARGETING JOHN MILLER

By 2005, the hoaxers had accomplished nothing. They were desperate to keep the hoax alive and Bill Kurtis filming. The Sheriff was now Rick Virden. On November 25, 2005, he wrote on departmental letterhead to my journalist proxy, Jay Miller:

Dear Mr. Miller,

We are interested in the truth surrounding Billy the Kid and are continuing the investigation, utilizing volunteers that have investigative experience **and at no cost to Lincoln County**.

[AUTHOR'S NOTE: With my investigation, the hoaxers lied about the massive taxpayer cost.]

Tom Sullivan and Steve Sederwall are Deputies with the Lincoln County Sheriff's Department.

Tom Sullivan and Steve Sederwall belong to the Reserve Deputy Unit.

Tom Sullivan and Steve Sederwall are assigned to investigate the shootings of William H. Bonney and Deputies Bell and Olinger.

As you acknowledge in your letter, there is an ongoing investigation being conducted. When the investigating officers conclude their investigation, I will gladly avail to you all of the information you request in case # 2003-274.

R.E. Virden
Lincoln County Sheriff

From the 2003 start of their "Billy the Kid Case," the hoaxers had John Miller half-heartedly in their sights, as was seen in their already-cited "Seventy-Seven Days of Doubt" initial draft of a "Probable Cause Statement" for their Lincoln County Sheriff's Department Case No. 2003-274. There, Miller's brief presence was for "survival suspicion," and as a foil for "Brushy Bill."

By 2005, John Miller was the only option for action. They hid his 10 years too old death certificate proof from his Arizona Pioneers' Home Cemetery, which author, Jim Johnson, also published in his 2006 book, *Billy the Kid: His real Name Was ...* It gave Miller's birth as in Fort Sill, Texas in December, 1850 and death at 87 on November 7, 1937 at 6:30 PM. The cause of death was a "fracture of the neck of the right femur and bronchopneumonia." (Johnson, Page 7) **[Remember that broken hip. It would become key in their hoax.]**

The hoaxers also hid that Miller had no playing-dead-on-the carpenter's-bench scene - and even denied be*ing present* on July 14, 1881 for his tale that Garrett killed his Indian friend mistaken for him. Nonetheless, scorning their audience as idiots, the hoaxers waved their flag of bleeding-playing-dead-Billy-on-the-bench-DNA from famous forensic expert Dr. Henry Lee - though it was non-existent. So there was no basis, by history or by DNA, to justify his exhumation. So the hoaxers hid that too, but proceeded with great secrecy.

But they had an ace up their sleeve. Governor Richardson's contact with Arizona's corrupt Governor Janet Napolitano.

SETTING UP THE EXHUMATION

On March 13, 2006, a year after digging up John Miller, the hoaxers faked legitimacy for an internet article by a Robert Struckman titled "Bitterroot man hopes to uncover the truth about Billy the Kid." Used was Dave Tunnell, a newly emerged hoaxer, and Sederwall's friend, posing as their Arizona forensic expert and a John Miller believer. Deputy Tom Sullivan also became a Miller-believer for Leo Banks's, April 14, 2006 *Tucson Weekly* article; stating: "Helen Airy's book triggered it for me ... I read it and thought, 'We have another Billy the Kid.' " For the Struckman article, Sullivan was interviewed: "What if the DNA matches the wooden bench? 'We'll change history. I don't know. Arizona would have the real Billy the Kid,' " Sullivan said." And he claimed they had gotten permission to dig up John Miller.

The hoaxers were using a perceived loophole in Arizona exhumation law: the **supervisor of a state cemetery** could approve an exhumation *to identify remains*. The simple statutory intent was to ensure correct grave markers - not to investigate a deceased person's delusional claims of being someone else.

But Dave Tunnell - Sederwall's friend according to the police report I got from the Prescott Police Department detective when the bunch were being criminally investigated - posed as a forensic expert seeking to exhume Billy the Kid-John Miller to dupe the supervisor of the Arizona Pioneers' Home Cemetery site of Miller's grave, Jeanine Dike. He called himself a Ph.D., though his internet site listed him as "President of "Forensitec - Forensic Psycholinguistic Patterning," a "doctoral learner in General Psychology," and the "World's Foremost Authority in Forensic Language Analysis." This apparently meant he read psychology books and identified liars (ironic given his hoax participation). But Supervisor Dike got bamboozled by Tunnell and Sederwall and got them a backhoe.

THE SECRET FRENZIED DIG

John Miller's eternal rest ended on May 19, 2005, when the hoaxers secretly and violently backhoed his grave and coffin, frenetically grabbing bones into the night, and handing them to on-site Orchid Cellmark Lab Director, Dr. Rick Staub, who, with them, was being filmed by Bill Kurtis Productions.

Present with them was moonlighting, Maricopa County, forensic anthropologist, Dr. Laura Fulginiti, who had been nervously added to bolster their zero forensic credibility. An apparent dreamboat, she took their word about "permission," and noticed nothing amiss by their frenzied digging (to get away quickly). She even shrugged off plowing into the adjacent grave, in what would become the "Billy the Kid Case's" greatest secret. Thus, exhumed, torn apart, and stolen for Rick Staub's bone bags was also random man, William Hudspeth. But there was an unforeseen problem with Laura Fulginiti: she was honest, and dutifully recorded everything they did.

Deputy Steve Sederwall added official documentation. I got it from the Prescott Police Department detective after the exhumation was a matter of criminal investigation. It revealed perpetrators and witnesses. Signed by Sederwall on Sheriff Rick Virden's official form, it stated:

LINCOLN COUNTY SHERIFF'S DEPARTMENT
SUPPLEMENTAL REPORT

Case # : 2003-274
Date: Thursday, May 19, 2005
Subject: Exhumation of John Miller
Location: Arizona Pioneers' Cemetery, Prescott, Arizona
Report By: Steven M. Sederwall

On Thursday, May 19, 2005, at approximately 1:00 pm the following met at the Arizona Pioneers' Cemetery at Prescott, Arizona.

Investigators:

Steven M. Sederwall, Lincoln County Deputy Sheriff

Following Sederwall, was Tom Sullivan as "Sheriff of Lincoln County, Retired," then Dale Tunnell as an "Arizona State Investigator." In line was "**Dr. Rick Staub, Orchid Cell Mark** [sic], DNA," proving the lab head himself was there for the bones.

Other "Investigators" were listed as Mike Poling, Yavapai County Sheriff's Deputy [who merely arrived to give Dr. Fulginiti, specimens from another case, but was added to fake presence of Arizona authority; and was later claimed as doing the exhumation!]; Laura Fulginiti, Forensic Scientist; Kristen Hartnett, Archeologist; Misty Rodarte, Pioneers' Administrator.

"Others Present," included Pioneers' Home staff, Tom Sullivan's wife, and Bill Kurtis Productions' cameramen.

Sederwall posed with a trophy skull of Miller or Hudspeth for Julie Carter's, October 6, 2005 *RuidosoNews.com* article, "Follow the Blood: In the Billy the Kid Case, Miller Exhumed."

Subsequently, the Case 2003-274 lawmen perpetrators denied any participation in the exhumation.

EXPOSED IN THE PRESS

The hoaxers got their first skeptical reporter: *Tucson Weekly's* Leo W. Banks. In his April 13, 2006 article "The New Billy the Kid?" he reported that the graves were unmarked, so they simply guessed. And unsure they got Miller, the dup up the adjoining man. The secret of William Hudspeth was out.

Not until my open records litigation, with subpoena of Orchid Cellmark Lab's records, was graves' ravishment made apparent.

Its January 26, 2009's Case No. 4444 (for Case 2003-274) "Laboratory Report, Forensic Identity, Mitochondrial Analysis: Evidence Received," confirmed **John Miller in the "South Grave,"** and **William Hudspeth in the "North Grave."** Stolen and destroyed for no reason were: Miller's "skull and mummified brains," "pelvis," "left femur;" and Hudspeth's "mandible and teeth," and "right femur." Even part of Miller's shattered casket was taken. There was not much left in the graves.

And Bill Kurtis Productions was filming all along. But this time he documented a crime scene. I was told the rumor that he subsequently destroyed or hid his footage.

THE DNA TRAVESTY

Of course, the Orchid Cellmark records were hidden by the hoaxers and Dr. Rick Staub. But my open records litigation, with subpoena of Orchid Cellmark Lab's records, gave the results.

Dr. Rick Staub had told Leo Banks, for his April 13, 2006 *Tucson Weekly* article "The New Billy the Kid?" **that the only DNA came from random man, William Hudspeth.**

But by 2009, Orchid Cellmark claimed DNA from Miller also; implying a fix-up - like November 18, 2004's "TalkLeft.com" as "Fraud alleged at Cellmark, DNA Testing Firm." Its January 26, 2009 report stated Miller's left femur yielded DNA; and Hudspeth's teeth yielded inconclusive mixed results, and his femur yielded DNA. Since they had no Billy the Kid DNA for matching, this meant they had nothing but a crime.

THE CRIMINAL CASE

The Arizona gambit left an incriminatory paper trail for felonious desecration of remains and grave-robbing.

An Arizona citizen, amateur historian, David Snell, started the ball rolling. Hearing the rumor of intended exhumation at the Arizona Pioneers' Home Cemetry, he kept checking until he observed its unmarked, open field rutted with tracks. On March 11, 2006, he made a formal complaint to Yavapai County Attorney, Shiela Polk; stating: "I feel it is my duty to report to you that grave robbers are plying their trade in Yavapai County. There individuals' crimes are being committed openly, knowingly, and with contempt for state and county law regarding exhumations."

On April 12, 2006, reporter Joanna Dodder in *The Daily Courier* of Prescott, printed "Officials Could Face Charges for Digging Up Alleged Billy the Kid." She quoted David Snell: "This is some kind of good ol' boy back-slappin' beer-drinkin' crusade ... He's [Billy's] buried in Ft. Sumner, where he's always been."

Imperiled, Sullivan and Sederwall flaunted their law enforcement case against Garrett. Dodder wrote: "Former Lincoln County Sheriff Tom Sullivan said he and the others plan to compare DNA from Miller's bones with DNA from blood that came from a bench on which Billy the Kid lay after Lincoln County Sheriff Pat Garrett shot him on July 14, 1881, in   Ft. Sumner, N.M. ... Sullivan and former Capitan, N.M., mayor Steve Sederwall **now are commissioned as Lincoln County deputies**, Sullivan said. They are in the midst of a 3-year-old investigation into whether Billy the Kid actually is buried in Ft. Sumner ... Sullivan and his fellow former lawmen are on a mission to find the real Billy using modern-day technology."

For Rene Romo's, November 6, 2005, *Albuquerque Journal* article titled "Billy the Kid Probe May Yield New Twist," they reran their lie that the case was to *protect Pat Garrett*! Romo wrote: "Sederwall acknowledges that what started out as an effort to defend the honor of Garrett against claims that the famous Lincoln County sheriff did not kill the Kid may have taken a new direction."

Cornered, the hoaxers transformed to martyrs for the truth. And to save themselves, they ditched "Brushy Bill." Miller became their man. Hoax-backing reporter, Julie Carter's, October 6, 2005 "Follow the Blood" *Ruidoso News* article quoted Sederwall: "**In the light of the evidence, we see that the history of Billy the Kid will change**. Those with monied interest in history remaining the same will not be happy ... As a cop I know when people fight to keep you from looking at something, they are always trying to hide something. The Lincoln County War is still going on."

But for Rene Romo's November 6, 2006's *Albuquerque Journal's* "Billy the Kid Probe May Yield New Twist," Sederwall, hedging his bets, was quoted: "If that Miller] DNA matches the work bench, I think the game is over ... **If not,"** he said, **"investigators will try to obtain permission to exhume the remains of Roberts, who is buried in Hamilton, Texas**."

FAKING JOHN MILLER'S SKELETON

Without time to fake DNA matching of Miller to bench, and facing arrest, the desperate lawmen acted. Keeping secret William Hudspeth, they proclaimed that John Miller's skeleton had matched Billy the Kid! They were giving Arizona the Kid!

Hoax-backing Romo wrote in his November 6, 2006 "Billy the Kid Probe May Yield New Twist": "Sederwall ... said Miller's skeletal remains were intriguing. **He said Miller had buck teeth, like the Kid, and an old bullet wound that entered his upper left chest and exited through the scapula.**" And Joanna Dodder, for her April 12, 2006 *The Daily Courier,* quoted Sullivan: "**A shoulder bone from Miller's grave already indicates damage consistent with that of a gunshot wound that The Kid suffered ... The skeleton's protruding teeth and small stature also are consistent with Billy** ... Since Garrett was friends with The Kid, he might have shot him and then let him escape."

But there was a problem: Dr. Laura Fulginiti. She had documented the actual findings in her June 2, 2005 report: "Re: Exhumation, Pioneer Home Cemetery, Prescott, Arizona for "Dale L. Tunnell, Ph.D. [sic], Forensitec." I got its copy from the Prescott Police Department. She had researched John Miller, and knew he died of a broken hip. That let her identify the man in the south grave as him. So the north grave had William Hudspeth. Investigative reporter, Leo Banks, in his April 13, 2006, *Tucson Weekly's* "The New Billy the Kid?" had researched the "Billy the Kid Case," and called the roving extravaganza "airship Billy." He called Miller "Hip Man," and Hudspeth "Shoulder Man," because Fulginiti told him that the buck teeth and bad shoulder, claimed by the hoaxers, were Hudspeth's. Not only was it his right shoulder, but there was no bullet injury. And Miller's skull was toothless. When confronted by Banks, Sullivan and Sederwall were left clumsily lying that hired forensic expert Fulginiti was wrong. But these liars were simply lying.

THE CRIMINAL INVESTIGATION

Necessary was blocking the grave robbing crimes. Yavapai County's honest Prescott City Prosecutor Glenn Savona declared that the "internal management" statute did enable Jeanine Dike to give permission, taking remains out of state to Texas was illegal, and no court order came from Yavapai County Community Health Services or family permission. He pointed to felonies.

So the hoaxers got out of Yavapai County. They lied that specimen-delivering Deputy Mike Poling, who had lent his metal detector, was responsible for the exhumation! That meant that Yavapai County might have to prosecute *him*: making a conflict of interest. So the case was transferred to Maricopa County, apparently more reliably corrupt.

So Maricopa County opened Case No. 2006020516, but against Dike and Tunnell! Unaware of the set-up, from June 9, 2006 to October 17, 2006, I supplied the assigned Prosecutor, Deputy Attorney Jonnell Lucca, with hoax information, hoaxer names, lack of DNA to justify any exhumation, and no way around random man William Hudspeth. Nevertheless, she wrote to me on October 17, 2006: "Dear Dr. Cooper: This letter is to inform you that the Maricopa County Attorney's Office has **declined to file charges against Jeanine Dike and Dale Tunnell** as there is no reasonable likelihood of conviction in this case. There is no further information regarding the decision. Thank you for your interest in the case." And she hid William Hudspeth. She had folded under the corrupt influence of Richardson and Napolitano.

I owned a telling e-mail (given by its Lincoln County recipient) dated May 16, 2006 by gloating Sederwall, feeling immune. It was signed with a smiley face symbol and "Steve." He stated:

> Well **we have the governor reaching out to the Arizona [sic- missing word, Prosecutor?]** to stop this investigation. They thought we had the DNA [sic - illegible word follows] and they tried to get the FBI to get John Millers bones back with a warrant and get the DNA. They think we are going to announce that John Miller is the kid in France [an upcoming secret trip promoting the hoax]. We will not give them a break. They are now trying to get is [sic - us?] worked up about grave robbery charges. But being good cops we have all the docs that show the state of Arizona did the dig not us. How funny. if [sic] they do something stupid and file on us we sue and Arizona well [sic] be the state of Tom and Steve.

BACK TO CATHERINE ANTRIM

So confident were the hoaxers, that they planned another try at digging up Catherine Antrim. For Julie Carter's October 6, 2005 *Ruidoso News* article, "Follow the Blood," Sullivan lied that Silver City Judge Henry Quintero backed them: "A judge in Silver City told the investigators to come back if they had enough evidence to warrant the need for Catherine Antrim's ... DNA. With the DNA results from the blood on the table **and soon the results of Miller's DNA**, investigators will likely take the judge up on that offer ... The officials in Ft. Sumner and Silver City thought we would just roll over and play dead. We didn't and this case is far from over."

That bravado translated into going after "Brushy" himself. But first, they would make an astounding announcement.

CHAPTER 4
"BRUSHY" GETS BACK IN THE MOVIES

THE HOAX MAKES THE CANNES FILM FESTIVAL

In 2006, the hoaxers had been keeping a huge secret. The John Miller exhumation was merely a warm-up of their fake forensics. They were well on their way to crowing "Brushy" as Billy the Kid. They had secretly completed a movie with a French film crew - with Tom Sullivan as Sheriff William Brady - and with narration by Kris Kristofferson, who had played Billy the Kid in the Sam Peckinpah movie, "Pat Garrett and Billy the Kid." It was to be a rerun of 1990's "Young Guns II" by John Fusco.

Of all the "Billy the Kid Case" hoax's dupes, the biggest was French film-maker, Anne Feinsilber. Inspired by the hoaxers', June 5, 2003, *New York Times* article, "122 Years Later, The Lawmen Are Still Chasing Billy the Kid." with its quote of "Brushy" believer, Jannay Valdez, ("I'm absolutely convinced that Garrett killed someone else and that Brushy Bill was the Kid"), Feinsilber created a nearly million dollar film, "Requiem for Billy the Kid," about "the mystery of the murder of Billy." And "Brushy Bill" Roberts hovered as "Billy as a murder scene escapee."

Feinsilber's film went on to be screened at the 2006 Cannes Film Festival and won an award.

I learned about this disaster to legitimate history just before Tom Sullivan and Steve Sederwall departed to be honored guests at the Festival. Sederwall had referred to it in his May 16, 2006 e-mail: "They think we are going to announce that John Miller is the kid in France." In fact, Governor Richardson planned to name them Ambassadors from New Mexico to announce DNA matchings implying "Brushy" as Billy. Through a contact, I managed to block Richardson's move. So they kept their mouths shut about DNA. But they still went to France.

REQUIEM FOR REAL HISTORY

Anne Feinsilber's "Requiem for Billy the Kid" got wide publicity; and it gave the "Billy the Kid Case" hoaxers the chance to disseminate misinformation about their own endeavor.

On May 21st, from *Variety* magazine, came the review of "Requiem for Billy the Kid" by a Todd McCarthy. He said:

> With Sam Peckinpah's Billy, Kris Kristofferson re-enlisted to portray the Kid delivering his account of what happened between him and Pat Garrett in 1881, pic goes on a photogenic search for the "truth" about the young killer. Seems there has always been a rumor that Billy escaped and lived to a ripe old age, and Tom Sullivan, who was sheriff of Lincoln County when pic was shot in the fall of 2004, describes his efforts to exhume the body of Billy's mother for DNA, efforts shot down by a judge whose motives Sullivan describes as baldly financial.

A May 25th review by Dave McCoy of MSN Movies, as "L 'Ouest Américain," wrote: "Feinsilber follows up on a rumor that Pat Garrett shot the wrong man and Billy the Kid actually isn't buried where it's said he is."

Feinsilber's damage was further evidenced on a May 6, 2006 Internet version of *The Hollywood Reporter* in reviewer, Ray Bennett's, "Bottom line: A story well told." He wrote:

> History has it that **Sheriff Pat Garrett, a reformed villain,** gunned down William Bonney, also known as Billy the Kid, at Fort Sumner, where his grave has a much-visited marker. Some say, however, that **the friendship between Garrett and Bonney** led the lawman to let the outlaw go and another man's body lies beneath his headstone. **Could Billy the Kid have lived to see two world wars and driven a car?** Feinsilber sets out to discover the truth and she finds several people in New Mexico whose grandparents were said to have known Bonney. Competing factions would like to exhume the bodies of Billy and his mother Catherine, who died of tuberculosis when Billy was 14, in order to prove once and for all when he died. Such myths fuel tourism, however, and the mystery has remained unsolved.

With this hoax victory, Pat Garrett became a "reformed villain," the friendship between Garrett and Billy was real, a stranger's body likely lay in Billy's grave, the exhumation would have solved the questions, but the "mystery" was being left unsolved to "fuel tourism." And "Brushy" was in the running.

CHAPTER 5
TRYING TO DIG UP "BRUSHY BILL"

HEADING TO TEXAS WITH SHOVELS

After Arizona and France, the next step was back to "Brushy" in 2007. But Richardson had no corrupt Texas contact. Hamilton's mayor and town council refused exhumation of "Brushy Bill."

That Texas onslaught, like the Arizona one, was under Sheriff Rick Virden, with his Deputies, Tom Sullivan and Steve Sederwall. And they had another hurdle, compliments of me. In 2006, was my American Academy of Forensic Sciences Ethics Complaint against Dr. Henry Lee for hoaxing. Though the unethical Ethics Committee covered-up, Lee apparently stopped the hoaxers' using his name for the carpenter's bench DNA scam. So they could claim no DNA for matching with "Brushy's!"

Nevertheless, Virden tried, writing that year on his official stationery to Mayor Roy Rumsey, misspelling his name, but using lawman clout to try and get the job done. Virden wrote:

> Hamilton Texas
> Mayor Roy Ramsey
>
> Mayor Ramsey,
>
> This letter will inform you that Tom Sullivan and Steve Sederwall are both commissioned deputies with the Lincoln County New Mexico Sheriff's Department.
>
> They have been investigating case # 2003-274. Their investigation has been funded by them personally and has been conducted on their own time.
>
> Mr. Mayor, should you have any questions please do not hesitate to contact me.
>
> R.E. Virden
> Lincoln County Sheriff

Virden's double-talk was trying to cover all hoax bases. The "funded by them personally," came from my years of open records exposure of their tax-dollar squandering. And, "their own time" was part of their new switcheroo that it was not a law enforcement case at all, but their private hobby! That scam was to hide the DNA records from me, since turn-over was only legally demanded of public officials, not private citizens. That left Virden absurdly telling Rumsey that he was sending his deputies for his New Mexico murder case - which was really a hobby - but those deputies could dig up "Brushy," though his jurisdiction was Lincoln County, New Mexico; and certainly not Texas!

Mayor Rumsey did not have to decipher this craziness, since I had already told him that the circus was coming to town. Deputy Steve Sederwall met with him. Rumsey told me that he told Sederwall: "If 'Brushy Bill' is Billy the Kid, I'm Pancho Villa."

Rumsey added for the press in a May 5, 2007 *Houston Chronicle* article titled "DNA could solve the mystery of Billy the Kid": "Roberts was 'just a big windbag who went around telling stories. Few people, if anybody, believed him."

Sederwall had floated the hoax's new spin. The *Roswell Daily Record*, using a Stephenville, Texas, article, wrote on May 2, 2007, "Billy the Kid Exhumation a Possibility." "Sederwall said if DNA is allowed to be obtained from Roberts, investigators will pursue exhuming the body of Catherine McCarty Antrim, who researchers have confirmed was Billy the Kid's mother." (Omitted is that this was blocked by Judge Quintero.)

On May 4th, for the hoax-backing *Albuquerque Journal's* "Manhunt for Real Billy the Kid Goes On: Deputy hopes DNA will finally reveal outlaw's true identity." Sederwall again blew smoke. "Those (Hamilton City) people want to know, they are not afraid ... You talk to Fort Sumner and they want to pull pistols on us. You talk to Hamilton City and they're like, 'Sure, we'd like to know.' "

On May 10, 2007, Hamilton's Town Council unanimously opposed exhumation; even though Texas's own "Brushy Bill" believer, Jannay Valdez - still pitching after his stint for Richardson for the June 5, 2003 *New York Times* - spoke for it.

But what if the hoaxers had gotten "Brushy's bones? Even Henry Lee might have returned with that lure. (Some old-timer could claim: "Didn't Gramps say that Billy the Kid had vomited on his saddle?") And Orchid Cellmark's Dr. Rick Staub, could have "matched" Billy-vomit-DNA to "Brushy"-bones-DNA. Then there could be another TV show, and Bill Robins III could get the faked "Brushy" pardon. But, so far, I had kept the hoaxers at bay.

CHAPTER 6
STOPPING "BRUSHY'S PARDON

RETURN OF THE PARDON PLOT

By 2010, 55 years after duped past President Harry S. Truman declared to William V. Morrison that "Brushy" "might have obtained a just decision ... under another New Mexico Governor," Governor Bill Richardson proved himself to be the one. Except his pardon would come from sewer of New Mexico corruption, not justice. This megalomaniac wanted to win at last. The hoaxers' fulfilled dream of "Brushy" as Billy the Kid was neigh.

I had a dilemma. Real Billy had deserved the Lew Wallace pardon. But Richardson would pardon "Brushy," with a hoaxed claim of having justified it by forensic "DNA." With world-wide press, he would permanently destroy Billy's history. So I had to stop what I most wanted: the pardon of Billy the Kid.

In July of 2010, I contacted the Garrett family. Most proactive was Jarvis Patrick "J.P." Garrett, Pat's grandson from the second marriage of Pat's youngest son, Jarvis (who had testified against "Brushy" in the Mabry hearing).

We had to act fact. On July 11, 2010 India's *Press Trust of India Hindustan Times* and Pakistan's *Daily Express*, fed hoax claims, printed "Billy the Kid 'to be pardoned.' " It stated:

> Billy the Kid was 19th century America's most infamous frontier outlaw who killed 21 men in Lincoln County War. Now, the Wild West's "Robin Hood" may get a posthumous pardon, 129 years after he was supposedly gunned down by Sheriff Pat Garrett, a media report said. Experts and historians believe the outlaw may not have been the man who died in Fort Sumner, New Mexico, on July 14, 1881, in a shoot-out that has become part of frontier folklore and material for Hollywood producers.
> **Instead, many now believe Garrett, a lawman who is ranked alongside Wyatt Earp, accidentally killed the wrong man and lied to cover up his mistake.**

On hearing reports of his death, it is thought the Kid, born Henry McCarty, but also known to have used the names Henry Antrim and William H Bonney, retired as a gunslinger and fled to Texas where he outlasted both world wars and died, at the ripe old age of 90, in 1950.

Now, the myth surrounding the gambler, cattle rustler and outlaw, who has no known family survivors, could be laid to rest at last as forensic experts want to exhume the body of the man buried in Hamilton under the assumed name of Ollie "Brushy Bill" Roberts, the *Daily Express* reported.

Above the grave is a monument that unequivocally identifies Roberts as Billy the Kid. And, if it proves to be accurate, New Mexico Governor Bill Richardson has pledged that he will grant a formal pardon to the fugitive of many names, the report said.

He said: "The evidence that will clinch this will be if genetic tests match samples from another grave in Silver City, New Mexico, we believe contains the body of Billy the Kid's mother Catherine Antrim."

On Saturday, July 24, 2010, came Richardson's front page *Albuquerque Journal* salvo by hoax-backing Rene Romo as: "Gov. Weighs Pardon for Billy the Kid." Romo gave only Richardson's lies, without warning of state history destruction:

RUIDOSO- The history of Billy the Kid is fueled with enduring debates: Was he a hero fighting for justice in a corrupt landscape? Or was he a scoundrel, unworthy of respect, who sank to the level of his enemies?

It might seem politically questionable for Gov. Bill Richardson, on his way out of office, to wade into the debate, but the governor appears to be doing just that. And think of the field day his critics will have if the governor pardons a serial cop killer ...

After the Lincoln County War, Gov. Lew Wallace offered to pardon the Kid if he testified about heinous crimes. The Kid did, but Wallace never held up his end of the bargain, and the outlaw subsequently killed two Lincoln County deputies in his infamous escape from the Lincoln County jail ...

Richardson first talked about a pardon back in 2003 during a press conference in Santa Fe to announce the Lincoln County Sheriff's Department had opened an investigation into the Kid's slaying on July 14, 1881, by Sheriff Pat Garrett.

The idea, investigators said, was to try to refute, by DNA evidence, claims by several men, such as John Miller and Brushy Bill Roberts, widely regarded as imposters who professed to be the Kid after the historical record said the outlaw had been killed. Those claims, the thinking went, cast doubt on Garrett's character, and modern forensic tools could lay the stories to rest.

[AUTHOR'S NOTE: The hoax was again spun as to clear Pat Garrett's name.]

In any event, publicity about a new investigation was said to be good for New Mexico tourism.

[AUTHOR'S NOTE: Giving Texas the history was not good for tourism!]

But critics lambasted the case. Officials in Silver City and Fort Sumner fought off legal efforts to dig up the remains of the outlaw's mother and the Kid himself in the hunt for DNA. They said the investigation just fed doubts about established history and undermined the value of Billy's Fort Sumner grave as a tourist site.

[AUTHOR'S NOTE: Romo hides that there was no DNA.]

There are even disagreements about whether a pardon would boost state tourism today.

"Leave him (Billy the Kid) alone," said former Mayor Juan Chavez. "As far as pardoning, what good will it do now? He's dead."

The investigation has since ground to a halt, beset by lawsuits and the rebuffed attempt to dig up the remains of Brushy Bill.

[AUTHOR'S NOTE: "Lawsuits" meant my litigation for their fake DNA records. Romo also hides that "Brushy's" exhumation was blocked by no DNA to justify it.]

But I had prepared a letter for the Garrett family to give to Richardson, and leaked it to Santa Fe AP reporter Barry Massey, who interviewed them, writing his July 30, 2010, article which started the salvation of the true history. Titled: "Billy the Kid to be Pardoned, 130 Years Later? Lawman's Grandchildren Outraged; "Would You Issue a Pardon For Someone Who Made His Living As A Thief?" (Obviously, the Garretts were not fans of Billy the Kid!) It had the first mention of me: "Gale Cooper, an amateur historian who lives near Albuquerque, said a pardon by Richardson would be the 'culmination of the hoax that contended Pat Garrett was a nefarious killer and Billy was not buried in his grave.' Cooper has written a book, 'MegaHoax,' to debunk claims that Garrett killed someone other than the Kid."

By August 4, 2010, in his Executive Office, Richardson met with the Garretts, and signed their petition (prepared by me) to promise not to pardon "Brushy" as Billy the Kid. (He had told the family that he would not meet with them if they brought me.)

But devious Richardson apparently thought he could circumvent that guarantee by citing the Lew Wallace pardon promise, and pardon "Brushy" for his long law-abiding life.

LAST MINUTE PARDON PETITION

In his zero hour, Richardson concocted a new twist for his hoax. He secretly enlisted his own attorney, Randy McGinn, who had defended him in a huge pay-to-play Grand Jury trial in which he had been indicted, then saved in a cover-up in 2009 by Attorney General Eric Holder, under apparent behest of President Barack Obama. She posed as a random amateur historian.

On December 14, 2010 - only seventeen days to December 31, 2010's end of Richardson's term, McGinn, on her Albuquerque law firm's official letterhead of McGinn, Carpenter, Montoya & Love, had hand-delivered to Richardson her six page, error-filled "Application for Pardon for Henry McCarty, aka William Bonney or Billy the Kid." The Petition stated:

PARDON APPLICATION FOR HENRY McCARTY, AKA WILLIAM BONNEY and BILLY THE KID

General information:
Applicant Name: Henry McCarty, aka Billy the Kid, William H. Bonney, Henry Antrim, Kid Antrim, Billito, El Chivato
Date of Birth: Precise dob unknown, circa 1859 Soc. Security No. N/A
Address/City/State/Zip Code: Deceased. Buried in Fort Sumner, New Mexico
Home Phone #:   N/A   Work Phone #:   N/A
Dept. of Corrections Inmate #:   N/A
Education: Through the age of 16 [sic-15½] in Silver City, New Mexico
Employment:
    1874   Age 15-16 [14½- 15½] – After his mother's death, worked as a hotel employee, Silver City, N.M. for room and board and for landlord who said he was the only employee who never stole anything.**[Also worked at butcher shops]**
    1875-1877   Seasonal ranch hand in Arizona Territory at various ranches **[Wrong. A cook and petty rustler]**.

1877-2/18/78   Ranch hand for John Tunstall at the Rio Feliz Ranch in Lincoln County, N.M., until Mr. Tunstall was killed **[remained an employee]** by a "posse" of armed men sent by Sheriff William Brady on February 18, 1878 March, 1878 Member of a posse called "the Regulators" to capture and arrest the men who murdered John Tunstall. Arrest warrants for the killers issued by Justice of the Peace John Bautista Wilson were withdrawn by Governor Samuel B. Axtell.

Crime location:
List conviction: <u>Only one of the 6-7 suspected shooters to be tried and convicted of murder in the shooting death of Sheriff William Brady on April 1, 1878, as Brady walked down the streets **[one street]** of Lincoln, New Mexico with 3 other men to inform the assembled grand jurors **[Wrong. No jury was in session that day]** that the grand jury investigation into the death of John Tunstall was canceled **[was delayed]** and would not occur that day. One other man, George Hindman, was also shot and died. Present to testify as witnesses before the grand jury about the killing of John Tunstall were some of the Regulators, John Middleton, Fred Waite, Frank McNab **[MacNab]**, Henry Brown, Jim French, William Bonney and Rob Widenmann **[they were there to kill; they were not testifiers]**.

Although 5 men were ultimately indicted for the killing of John Tunstall by the Grand Jury which re-convened **[convened]** on April 13, 1878 – Jesse **[Jessie]** Evans, Miguel Segovia, Frank Rivers, James J. Dolan, and Billy Matthews – none of these men were ever tried or convicted. Nor was any other person ever tried and convicted of any of the dozens of killings which occurred during the Lincoln County War between February, 1878 and March, 1879 **[Lincoln County War was February 18, 1878 to July 19, 1878]**.</u>
Sentence: <u>Death by hanging. Date sentenced: April 13, 1881   </u>
Date(s) probation/parole ended: N/A Shot by Sheriff Pat Garrett on July 13, 1881 **[July 14, 1881 ... she missed the famous date in the history!!!]**
List additional conviction(s) on the lines below:
<u>None. However, killed 2 men, deputies Jim **[James]** Bell and Bob Olinger, during his escape from custody on April 28, 1881, while awaiting imposition of the death sentence at the jail on the second floor of the Lincoln County courthouse. Shot dead by Sheriff Pat Garrett before he could be tried on those crimes. **[omits the other murders]**</u>

Questions:
Have you met all sentencing requirements? <u>N/A   </u>
Are you requesting restoration of firearm privileges? <u>No</u> State reasons __

Additional attachments:
1. Factual Statement of historical basis for gubernatorial pardon and clemency.

Randi McGinn, Pardon Applicant   *December 14, 2010*

<u>**Factual Basis to Pardon Billy the Kid**</u>

A promise is a promise and should be enforced. It is particularly important to enforce promises and deals made by government officials, law enforcement officers or the governor of a state made in exchange for a citizen risking his life to testify against a criminal who committed murder.

Such a promise was made by New Mexico Governor Lew Wallace **[Billy was tricked]** to the man known in New Mexico as William Bonney, aka Billy the Kid, at the end of the Lincoln County War **[a year later]**. Mr. Bonney kept his end of the bargain by testifying before a grand jury against the men who murdered attorney Huston Chapman on February 18, 1879. Governor Wallace did not keep his end of the deal **["deal" may have been a "trick"]**, which was to pardon Mr. Bonney for all outstanding charges, including the impending indictment related to the death of William Brady **[indictments were for "Buckshot" Roberts, William Brady, George Hindman]**. This injustice should be corrected.

On February 18, 1879, the anniversary of the murder of John Tunstall, Mr. Bonney's former employer and mentor, both sides in the year-long Lincoln County War **[the War was 6 months]** met to negotiate a truce **[the Dolan-Billy meeting was just a peace meeting between *them*]**. The new governor, Lew Wallace, who replaced the old, corrupt governor, Sam Axtell, on October 2 **[sic- October 1st]**, 1878, had issued an amnesty proclamation on November 13, 1878, which pardoned all offences committed during the Lincoln County War, except for those with pending prosecutions. With an indictment pending against him for the April 1, 1878 deaths of Sheriff Brady and Mr. Hindman **[and the April 4, 1878 murder of "Buckshot" Roberts]**, William Bonney was one of the few Lincoln County residents who was not given retroactive amnesty for the dozens of killings which had been committed during the conflict **[no McSweens got amnesty]**.

Both sides of the Lincoln County War – those on the Dolan/Murphy "House" side and those from the Tunstall/McSween/Chisum side – met after the Governor's amnesty proclamation to negotiate a treaty. **[Made- up. The February 18, 1879 meeting was of Dolan and thugs with Billy and friends.]** The prime mover behind the meeting, the person who wanted peace in Lincoln County, was William Bonney, who sent a letter to the other side proposing a truce. **[Made-up. Dolan proposed it following pressure from Susan McSween's lawyer, Huston Chapman, who was threatening litigation against Commander Dudley. Billy was important as arguably representing the Hispanic faction in the War.]** At the meeting, the parties agreed that the fighting would end and none of the parties would testify against any of the others, on pain of death. Unfortunately, after the written treaty was signed **[Made-up]**, Jesse **[Jessie]** Evans and Jimmy Dolan broke out whiskey to celebrate and, in short order, there were 20 **[Made-up]** armed, drunken cowboys **[Dolan was a merchant, Evans and Campbell were outlaws]** stumbling down Lincoln's one street. The only sober one was William Bonney, who did not drink alcohol.

Into this drunken celebration walked a one-armed lawyer named Huston Chapman, who was coming back from a neighbor's house **[Representing Susan McSween, he was walking from her house to Juan Patrón's, where he was staying]**. He was confronted on the street by drunken Billy Campbell, from the Murphy/Dolan House **[Campbell was in Jessie Evans's outlaw gang]**, who pulled out his pistol, pressed it to Chapman's chest **[Wrong. Dolan did that]**, and demanded that he "dance." When Chapman refused, he was shot from the front by Mr. Campbell and from behind by Jimmy Dolan. **[Wrong. Dolan shot first. Campbell fired as Chapman fell. The shots were from the front.]** He was set on fire and burned in the street where he lay.

The death of the lawyer, Chapman, finally convinced Wallace to travel to Lincoln, which he did two weeks after the shooting. Although the federal troops at the Governor's disposal were quickly able to capture Campbell, Dolan and accomplice Jesse **[Jessie]** Evans, and hold them in the fort, he could not find anyone to testify against them. It was then that the Governor received a letter from W.H. Bonney stating that Mr. Bonney had been present and was an eyewitness to the shooting of the lawyer, Chapman, and, despite the risk of death, was willing to testify against the killers if the Governor would annul the pending charges against him, including the indictment for the murder of Sheriff Brady **[Billy asked only for annulling his indictments from the Lincoln County War.]**.

Governor Wallace wrote back to Mr. Bonney and asked to meet him at a private residence, indicating that: "I have the authority to exempt you from prosecution if you will testify to what you say you know." **[This is no promise; just confirmation of authority.]**

Mr. Bonney came to the private, nighttime meeting. **[Justice of the Peace John Wilson was present.]** At that meeting, after representing that he had the power to give him absolute protection, Governor Wallace promised Mr. Bonney that, if he testified fully against Billy Campbell and the other shooters before the grand jury meeting in 2-3 weeks, "In return for your doing this, I will let you go scot free with a pardon in your pocket for all your misdeeds." **[Made-up. The conversation is unknown. The quote is taken Wallace's 1902 outlaw myth in *New York World Magazine*, titled "General Lew Wallace Writes a Romance of 'Billy the Kid' Most Famous Bandit of the Plains." It is fiction- even stating that the meeting occurred in Santa Fe.]**

Several hours after this meeting and agreement **[typical hoaxer style of first making up information, later presenting it as true. McGinn – or whoever wrote this – has not proved any pardon agreement]**, Jimmy Dolan, Jesse **[Jessie]** Evans and Billy Campbell "escaped" from the Fort Stanton guardhouse. **[Only Evans and Campbell escaped. The date was the next day: March 18th. Dolan was released legally, by habeas corpus, on April 13th.]** After the escape, Mr. Bonney wrote another letter to Justice of the Peace John Wilson, where the governor was staying **[Wallace was staying in the Montaño family home to the east of Wilson's; the meeting was in Wilson's]**, asking him to find out whether, now that the prisoners had escaped, the governor was still interested in their deal. **[Billy did not cite a "deal." Billy's total letter stated:** *"San Patricio Thursday 20th 1879 Friend Wilson. Please tell You know who that I do not know what to do, now as those Prisoners have escaped. So send word by bearer. a note through You it may be he has made different arrangements if not and he still wants it the same to Send :William Hudgins: as Deputy, to the Junction tomorrow at three Oclock with some men you know to be all right. Send a note telling me what to do WHBonney P.S. do not send Soldiers"]* Governor Wallace responded:

> The escape makes no difference in arrangements. To remove all suspicions of understanding, I think it better to put the arresting party in charge of Sheriff Kimball, who shall [sic - will] be instructed to see that no violence is used. This will go to you tonight.

[AUTHOR'S NOTE: Wallace had crossed out, in his own unused draft, *"I will comply with my part if you will with yours;"* **taking no chances by putting a "promise" in writing. So he actually wrote:** *"The escape makes no difference in arrangements.* ~~I will comply with my part if you will with yours~~. *To remove all suspicions of* ~~arrangement~~ *understanding, I think it better to put the arresting party in charge of Sheriff Kimball, who will be instructed to see that no violence is used. This will go to you tonight.*]

Mr. Bonney wrote back **[edited for grammar and punctuation]**:

> Sir. I will keep the appointment I made but be sure and have men come that you can depend on. I am not afraid to die like a man fighting but I would not like to be killed like a dog unarmed. Tell Kimbal to let his men be placed around the house and for him to come in alone: and he can arrest us All I am afraid of is that in the Fort we might be ... killed through a window at night. But you can arrange that all right ... It is not my place to advise you, but I am anxious to have them caught, and perhaps know how men hide from soldiers better than you.

Based on the plan devised with Governor Wallace to protect the safety of their eyewitness, Sheriff George Kimball **[Kimbrell]** made a mock arrest of Mr. Bonney on March 23, 1879 **[March 22, 1879]**. Shortly thereafter, Mr. Bonney kept his word and testified before the grand jury which, with an eyewitness, indicted Billy Campbell, Jimmy Dolan and Jesse **[Jessie]** Evans for the murder of lawyer Huston Chapman.

Despite his promise **[no promise has been proven]**, Governor Wallace returned to Santa Fe without granting William Bonney a pardon. After getting the testimony he needed for the indictment, the local District Attorney William L. Rynerson did not enforce the governor's promise **[the pardon had to filed; Wallace never did that]** and immediately pressed the prosecution of his eyewitness, William Bonney, even changing venue out of his hometown, Lincoln, where he was well liked by much of the citizenry. Mr. Bonney was out of jail at the time the indictments were returned in another county and was never pursued by Sheriff Kimball **[Kimbrell]**, who knew firsthand of the Governor's broken promise. **[Made-up. Kimbrell favored the McSween side, including Billy. There is no evidence he was privy to a pardon promise - only the fake arrest.]** Over the next 21 months, while the local and national press gave him the catchy nickname, Billy the kid, and built him into a Western legend, Mr. Bonney started a small ranch near Portales, New Mexico. **[Made-up. In Billy's December 12, 1879 letter to Wallace, Billy states:** *"I had been at Sumner Since I left Lincoln making my living Gambling..."*] **[Missed is Wallace's scornful March 31, 1879 letter to Secretary of the Interior Carl Schurz, showing no pardon intent when Billy was in the fake arrest:** *"A precious specimen nick-named "The Kid," whom the Sheriff is holding here in the Plaza, as it is called, is an object of tender regard. I heard singing and music the other night; going to the door, I found the minstrels of the village actually serenading the fellow in his prison."*]

On December 13, 1880 **[December 22, 1880 in the** *Las Vegas Gazette***]**, Wallace announced a reward of $500 for the capture of the man now known as Billy the Kid. By December 24, 1880 **[December 22, 1880]**, Sheriff Pat Garrett and his posse had tracked William Bonney to Stinking Springs, near Ft. Sumner, where he was captured and taken into custody.

On January 1, 1881, William Bonney wrote the governor from jail asking him to come and see him. When there was no response to the request or a second note on March 2, he wrote a third letter on March 4, 1881 **[with grammar again corrected]**:

> *Dear Sir:*
>
> *... I expect you have forgotten what you promised me, this month two years ago, but I have not, and I think you had ought to have come and seen me as I requested you to. I have done*

everything that I promised you I would, and you have done nothing that you promised me.

... I am not treated right by (his jailor) **[U.S. Marshal John Sherman's name is given by Billy, not his jailor's]**. *He lets every stranger that comes to see me through curiosity in to see me, but will not let a single one of my friends in, not even an attorney. I guess they mean to send me up without giving me any show ...*

There was no response to that or a fourth letter. By that time, because the story of "Billy the Kid" had captured public attention and there was pressure not to pardon an "outlaw," the governor did not keep his promise.

One month later, on April 8, 1881, Mr. Bonney was put on trial for the murder of Sheriff Brady with a recently appointed public defender, Colonel A.J. Fountain, who had just quit his job as a newspaper editor. He was convicted on April 13, 1881 **[April 9, 1881]** and sentenced to death **[April 13, 1881]**.

The Old West wasted no time in carrying out death sentences and there was no appeal. **[Billy tried to get an appeal.]** Three days after his sentence, Mr. Bonney was moved to Lincoln to be hanged. There, he was held in custody in the building owned by "the House" **[Catron had taken over "The House's" defaulted mortgage]**, the powerful business faction behind the killing of his former boss, rancher John Tunstall. Shortly before he was to be executed, On April 28, 1881, while Sheriff Pat Garrett was out of town, William Bonney escaped, in the process killing 2 deputies, Jim **[James]** Bell and Bob Olinger, who were left to guard him.

On July 13, Sheriff Pat Garrett carried out the death sentence **[Even missed is the famous date of July 14, 1881!]** when he tracked Mr. Bonney to where he was hiding at the Maxwell house **[There is no evidence that Billy was hiding there]** near Ft. Sumner **[in Fort Sumner – even missed is the famous death scene location]** and shot him. William Bonney was dead at 22 **[Even famous age of 21 is missed!]**.

Submitted by: Randi McGinn   December 14, 2010

Sources of Historical Information:
Joel Jacobsen, *"Such Men as Billy the Kid"*
Frederick Nolan: *"The Billy the Kid Reader," The West of Billy the Kid"*
Mark Lee Garner, *"To Hell on a Fast Horse"*
Pat F. Garrett's, *"The Authentic Life of Billy the Kid"* (additional author –
    Frederick Nolan
Interview with Drew and Elise Gomber
Review of Historical records, visits to scene and museums

THE McGINN PARDON SWITCHEROO TRICK

Billy Bonney deserved the pardon, as I presented in my 2017 *The Lost Pardon of Billy the Kid: An Analysis Factoring in the Santa Fe Ring, Governor Lew Wallace's Dilemma, and a Territory in Rebellion.*

But Randi McGinn was not in the realm of real history. She was doing a bait and switch trick. The only "investigation" Richardson backed since 2003 was the "Billy the Kid Case" hoax. No analysis of the actual pardon bargain had been done. The "Billy the Kid Case" was just a "Brushy" pardon scam, as its attorney, Bill Robins, had made clear in his January 5, 2004, "In the Matter of Catherine Antrim, Billy the Kid's Pre-Hearing Brief" before Judge Henry Quintero: "**Should the DNA extracted from Ms. Antrim confirm that one of the potential Kids ["Brushy"] was in fact Billy the Kid, undersigned counsel will be able to make an even stronger argument for pardon by citing to the long years of law abiding life.**"

PRESS RELEASE FOR PARDON PETITION

On December 16, 2010, Richardson released McGinn's fake pardon thrust. He added another ploy: calling it a "limited pardon" for only the Brady killing. And he and McGinn shape-shifted to Old West history aficionados. It stated:

> SANTA FE – Governor Bill Richardson today announced his office has received a formal petition for the pardon of Billy the Kid which he will consider and make a decision before the end of the year. Governor Richardson is seeking input on the petition and has set up a website and email address where history buffs, experts, and other interested parties and the general public can weigh in on its merits.
>
> The petition centers around the widespread belief that Territorial Governor Lew Wallace promised Billy the Kid a pardon in return for damning testimony The Kid gave during a murder trial. The petition is narrow in scope and does not argue for a blanket pardon of all of Billy the Kid's activities …
>
> "As someone who is fascinated with New Mexico's rich history, I've always been intrigued by the history of Billy the Kid and, in particular, the alleged promise of a pardon he was given by Territorial Governor Lew Wallace,"   Governor Richardson said.

"I will diligently review this new petition and all the facts available regarding an agreement between Billy the Kid and Governor Wallace before rendering any decision" ...

Independently, nationally prominent trial attorney Randi McGinn was designated to review both the history and prior petitions to ascertain whether there was sufficient basis for the matter to be seriously considered. Ms. McGinn, a New Mexico resident and western history enthusiast, agreed to undertake this voluntarily and at no cost to taxpayers. After concluding her review, Ms. McGinn submitted a formal petition on December 14, 2010 ...

"I hope that it will spark renewed interest in New Mexico's history and how the days of Billy the Kid and the Lincoln County War helped shape our state," Richardson added.

LEW WALLACE'S REAL DNA

Richardson's mistake, when trying to trick the Garrett family, was forgetting that there might be more, real, living, Old West DNA in the form of Wallaces. Lew Wallace and his wife Susan had one son: Henry. Henry had two sons, one having died in World War II. The other, Lew Wallace Jr., had a son, William N. Wallace, and two daughters.

After the McGinn petition, I located Lew Wallace's great-grandson, William N. Wallace, the last male descendant. With trepidation, I phoned. Everything depended on him.

William N. Wallace, an author and retired *New York Times* journalist in his 80's, was imperious (as was probably Lew himself); but was indignant about the insult to "the General," as he called his ancestor. By December 16, 2010, he wrote his letter to Richardson, using my historical talking points, a copy of Richardson's August 9, 2010 letter to the Garrett family, and the McGinn Petition. He wrote:

Governor Richardson –

Your imminent action – issuing a pardon to William H. Bonney, aka Billy the Kid – does not sit well with me, the great grandson of General Lew Wallace and his only remaining male heir. Such action would declare Lew Wallace to have been a dishonorable liar.

Your proposed deed, based on an alleged "broken" promise of then Governor Wallace, is without any rational reasoning. There is no concrete evidence that Governor Wallace ever made any such pardoning promise to Billy the Kid.

The petition filed on this matter lacks any credible supporting evidence. Also, its source, Attorney Randi McGinn, has meager qualifications and possible conflicts of interest in my opinion. Is one to believe that Ms. McGinn thought up this petition all by herself out of her compassion for someone who may have taken as many as 22 lives in federal territories two centuries back? It is not a petition. It is a deceit.

Lew Wallace was an American hero of his time. His honors are many. His statue is one of the just 100, two for each state, in the National Statuary Hall of the United States Capitol, his representing the state of Indiana.

You may have walked across that impressive rotunda. New Mexico's representatives there are Chavez and Pope, each of who would make far more effective objects of tourism enhancement than the questionable pardon of Billy-the-Kid, a convict. Your other motives in issuing the pardon are unclear to me.

Why would a retiring governor choose to defame a distinguished predecessor 130 years later?

By your intended action, you desecrate, defile, debase and dishonor an American hero in favor of a convicted murderer.

Furthermore such an action may have no legal standing because New Mexico, at the time of Governor Wallace, was a territory, not a state, and thus under federal jurisdiction.

I intend to make public my views. (My distribution list is competitive.)

My background: Yale University Bachelor of Arts degree (major in American history); New York City Journalist, 1949-1999 (*New York Times*, 1964-1999); published author of 11 books.

William N. Wallace

REPORTER MASSEY WRITES AGAIN

Santa Fe AP reporter, Barry Massey, covered the William N. Wallace letter on August 21, 2010 William N. Wallace as: " 'Billy the Kid' pardon effort draws Wild West showdown." Massey wrote:

SANTA FE, N.M. (AP) — New Mexico Gov. Bill Richardson has stirred up a historical hornet's nest with his talk of pardoning the Old West outlaw Billy the Kid.

The latest to come out against it is a descendant of the territorial governor who once met with the Kid but never granted him clemency 130 years ago.

William N. Wallace, great-grandson of Civil War Gen. Lew Wallace, said he sees no solid historical foundation for Richardson to offer a posthumous pardon for the Kid, also known as William H. Bonney and Kid Antrim.

"There was nothing in my lifetime knowledge of Gen. Lew Wallace, my great grandfather, that ever suggested that he intended to give William H. Bonney ... a pardon," the 86-year-old Wallace said in a telephone interview from his home in Westport, Conn.

Richardson is considering a pardon to make good on an alleged promise by Gov. Wallace to provide some form of clemency for the Kid in exchange for his testimony about killings during the Lincoln County War ...

The historical record surrounding the supposedly promised pardon - like many events during New Mexico's turbulent frontier days - is ambiguous and open to conflicting views.

There's no written documents "pertaining in any way" to a pardon in the archive of Wallace's papers maintained by the Indiana Historical Society, according to staff members who sent an e-mail and letter to Richardson last week.

"If Gen. Wallace did not intend to give William H. Bonney a pardon, there is no reason why Gov. Richardson should consider giving William H. Bonney, a murderer, a pardon," said Wallace's great-grandson, a retired New York Times sports writer.

Descendants of Sheriff Pat Garrett - the lawman who shot and killed the Kid on July 14, 1881 - met with Richardson earlier this month to oppose a pardon. The governor told them he accepts historical accounts of the Kid's death.

Richardson has made no decision, said chief of staff Eric Witt. Before the governor would issue any pardon, Witt said, he'd start a formal inquiry and solicit comments from historians and others. The governor's term runs through Dec. 31.

Wallace went to New Mexico in 1878 to help bring an end to the violence of the Lincoln County War. After arriving, he offered general amnesty to those involved in the bloodbath unless they already were under indictment.

That excluded the Kid, who faced murder charges, including for killing a Lincoln County sheriff.

A tantalizing part of the pardon question is a clandestine meeting that Wallace had with the Kid in Lincoln in March 1879.

Letters written by the Kid leave no doubt the Kid wanted Wallace to at least grant him immunity from prosecution if he agreed to testify about killings he had witnessed.

The letters suggest the Kid was looking for a way out of a life of crime. Wallace, in arranging the meeting, responded to the Kid: "I have authority to exempt you from prosecution if you will testify to what you say you know."

The Kid delivered on his testimony. But Wallace never granted any form of clemency, even after the Kid was later convicted of murder and sentenced to hang.

As the Kid awaited his execution in 1881 - and as Wallace prepared to leave New Mexico to become ambassador to Turkey - the Las Vegas, N.M., Gazette asked the outgoing governor about prospects that he would spare the Kid's life.

Wallace replied, "I can't see how a fellow like him should expect any clemency from me."

The Kid escaped from the Lincoln County jail but Garrett tracked him to a ranch near Fort Sumner, N.M.

In the early 1900s, a few years before Wallace died, a pardon for the Kid resurfaced in newspaper articles in which Wallace described his secret meeting with the Kid. Wallace, by then, had achieved literary fame as the author of the historical novel, "Ben Hur."

Wallace's great-grandson questions the accuracy of the newspaper accounts, saying a number of facts are wrong. They describe the meeting between Gov. Wallace and the Kid, for instance, as taking place in Santa Fe rather than Lincoln.

"I am smelling a rat right off the bat," William Wallace said.

Doug Clanin of Anderson, Ind., who retired after serving as editor of the Wallace papers for the Indiana Historical Society, said Gov. Wallace became quite famous and in his later years was adept at "improving on old stories" as he entertained audiences on a lecture circuit.

Historian Frederick Nolan, who lives in London and has written extensively about the Lincoln County War, said in an e-mail that "there does not seem to me to be the slightest doubt that Wallace indeed made some kind of promise to the Kid" and that was at least immunity from prosecution, which could have set aside two indictments for murder.

As for a posthumous pardon, Nolan said, "Speaking for myself, I'd sort of like to see the Kid pardoned because - at the time the 'arrangement' was made - he surely merited at least as much consideration as all the others who took advantage of Wallace's amnesty. But the moment passed and so, I think, did the Kid's entitlement to a whitewash."

On September 16, 2010, William N. Wallace e-mailed me: "Ms. Cooper - Barry Massey of the AP has ready from me a reaction quote should Gov. Richardson go ahead with the pardon, a condemning quote. Massey has informed the governor's staff that he has the quote and will use it."

Richardson, unaccustomed to intimidation, had to weigh consequences of his scam. He wanted a political life after December 31, 2010. Was the hoax worth his future?

RIGHT UP TO THE END

December 27, 2010 was the rumored date for Richardson's pardon announcement. But it had only uncertain press. For "CBS News," Edecio Martinez wrote: "Billy the Kid to be Pardoned 130 Years Later?" It pressured Richardson; stating: "Descendants of Old West lawman Pat Garrett and New Mexico Territorial Gov. Lew Wallace are outraged that Gov. Bill Richardson is considering a pardon for Billy the Kid, saying Wallace never offered a pardon, and a petition seeking one is tainted because it comes from a lawyer with ties to Richardson." So Randi McGinn shape-shifted for the reporter from amateur historian to a lawyer seeking weird work - no longer *pro bono*, but for pay: "McGinn said her only tie to the administration is that she volunteered to look into the pardon issue for a fee."

So my exposing her had worked. But could a man with no conscience be stopped?

On December 29, 2010, AP writer, Mark Guarino, wrote: "Outgoing New Mexico Gov. Bill Richardson is considering a pardon for celebrated outlaw Billy the Kid. An informal e-mail poll shows support. But time is running out." For this article, official hoax historian, Paul Hutton resurfaced to back pardoning (omitting his 2004 "Investigating History: Billy the Kid" in which "Brushy" was the "Billy" to be pardoned).

On December 29, 2010, Richardson floated his partial pardon scam via a Glen Levy at TIME NewsFeed.com as "Will Billy the Kid Be Pardoned? Governor Has Until Friday." For it, Richardson's Deputy Chief of Staff Eric Witt - a talking head in Hutton's hoax 2004 History Channel program - stated: "We're not offering a blanket pardon for everything he did."

December 30, 2010 brought FoxNews.com's Kelly David Burke's "Billy the Kid Pardon?" Missing the irony, he wrote that Richardson - with only one day to go - says: "I want to see "some concrete evidence ... on whether ... the pardon promise, potentially a promise by Governor Lew Wallace, was valid and documented."

Left with only drama of time running out, on December 30, 2010, Richardson, through his spokesperson, Alarie Ray Garcia, gave his press release titled "Governor Richardson to Announce his decision on Billy the Kid Pardon Request Tomorrow." Deflecting fall-out to Randi McGinn's "request," it stated: "Governor Bill Richardson will announce his decision regarding a pardon of Billy the Kid tomorrow, Friday, December 31st live on "ABC Good Morning America." The announcement is expected at approximately 7:10 am ET/5:10 am MT."

On December 31, 2010, Jessica Hopper reported for "ABC Good Morning America": "Gov. Bill Richardson: 'I've Decided Not to Pardon Billy the Kid.' " Her article proved that my fear of his using the pardon to validate his eight year "Billy the Kid Case" hoax had been correct. But he kept his mouth shut about "Brushy." Hopper wrote:

> In 2003, Richardson, a history buff, first said he would consider pardoning the famous outlaw. He finally made up his mind today. **"It was a very close call. I've been working on this for eight years. The romanticism appealed to me to issue a pardon,** but the facts and the evidence do not support it and I've got to be responsible especially when a governor is issuing pardons," Richardson said. **Richardson said that Billy the Kid's decision to continue to kill after the pardon wasn't granted to him impacted his decision.**

After my Garretts-Wallace onslaught, I pictured that historically ignorant Richardson asking around: "What's my excuse for no pardon? Oh! The Kid killed deputy guards? I'll use that."

On December 31st, FoxNews.com printed: "Richardson Declines to Pardon Outlaw Billy the Kid." It built on my input to J.P. Garrett and William N. Wallace; stating from J.P. that "Richardson appointed McGinn's husband to the state Supreme Court;" and from William N. Wallace that: "McGinn has 'meager qualifications' and possible conflict of interest."

Again, on December 31st, Kathryn Watson of *The Washington Times* headlined: "Alas, no pardon for Billy the Kid: New Mexico's Richardson says close call." For her, Richardson was a "history buff" reacting to the deputy killings. With hypocrisy lost to all but me, Richardson intoned: "We should not neglect the historical record and the history of the American West."

The *Los Angeles Times*, with a Rick Rojas, gave Richardson's final spin: "No Pardon for Billy the Kid. New Mexico Gov. Bill Richardson Says." 'The romanticism appealed to me ... but the facts and evidence did not support it.' " Richardson had "Albuquerque lawyer Randi McGinn" fall on her sword with an ungranted "pardon petition." She claimed no regrets, and spookily channeled Bill Robins III: "It's great being Billy the Kid's lawyer."

BITTER "BIG BILL'S" LAST LIE

By January 1, 2011, loser Richardson took out his rage on Billy the Kid for *New York Times* reporter, Marc Lacey's "For 2nd Time in 131 Years, Billy the Kid is Denied Pardon." Richardson stated: "If one is to rewrite a chapter as prominent as this, there had better be certainty as to the facts, the circumstances and the motives of those involved," Mr. Richardson said in announcing that he would not tamper with the history **of a man whose life was spent 'pillaging, ravaging and killing the deserving and the innocent alike.'"**

Billy himself might answer Richardson - his worst enemy since Santa Fe Ring bosses of his day - as he did a *Mesilla News* reporter on April 16, 1881, three days after his hanging sentence: "I think it a dirty mean advantage to take of me, considering my situation and knowing that I could not defend myself by word or act. But I suppose he thought he would give me a kick down hill."

I would add: "Billy had dodged his most dangerous bullet yet."

CHAPTER 7
EXPOSING THE "BILLY THE KID CASE" HOAX IN COURT

OPEN RECORDS SHOWDOWN

Cleverly making the "Billy the Kid Case" a real murder investigation to dig up graves, the hoaxers forgot it meant that its public official lawmen were subject to open records law.

By 2006, I took over my records requests from my journalist proxy, Jay Miller. It took me seven years to get records available the day I started. During litigation, five sets of my *own* attorneys tried to throw my case. Then I went *pro se* and won. But the judge and the state's high courts blocked the statute's penalty to the lawmen. The system was rigged for crooks to protect crooks.

But I got what I wanted: proof of no valid DNA, meaning illegality of their exhumations. And I got more than I wanted: facing head-on the terrifying thuggery of the empowered lawmen.

SUMMARY OF OPEN RECORDS FIGHT

Since the "Billy the Kid Case" hoaxers rewrote the hoax every time I blocked them, I realized the only way to end their scam was to expose their DNA fakery by getting their actual DNA documents. From 2004 to 2006, they had refused my proxy, Jay Miller, all documents by claiming that, as part of an ongoing murder case, they were immune to turn-over. This was fakery, because the exception was to prevent a suspect from escaping; and Pat Garrett, dead since 1908, was going nowhere. **(But remember the criminal investigation claim.)**

In 2006, I began my own open records requests to the custodian, Sheriff Rick Virden. He used Lincoln County Attorney

Alan Morel, to respond. They tried intimidation of reporting me as a terrorist! So I got a lawyer in 2007 to do the requests.

Through Morel, Virden lied to my lawyer that he had no records at all for Case 2003-274, and claimed Tom Sullivan and Steve Sederwall had them. Through Morel, they lied that the case was their private hobby, was immune to the public records act, and the records were their "trade secrets." They also lied that Case 2003-274 was just an investigation into Billy the Kid's killing of his deputy guards - which had no DNA records.

Improper withholding of public records triggers litigation, so, in October of 2007, my lawyer filed "Sandoval District Court Case No. D-1329-CV-2007-1364, Gale Cooper et al v. Rick Virden, Lincoln County Sheriff and Custodian of the Records of the Lincoln County Sheriff's Office; and Steven M. Sederwall, Former Lincoln County Deputy Sheriff; Department; and Thomas T. Sullivan, Former Lincoln County Sheriff and Former Lincoln County Deputy Sheriff.

Demanded were the DNA records of Case 2003-274: Dr. Henry Lee's carpenter's bench and courthouse floorboards investigation; the exhumed remains of John Miller and William Hudspeth, and Orchid Cellmark Labs' DNA extractions from the bench, floorboards, Miller, and Hudspeth and its matchings of Miller and Hudspeth DNA to alleged bench DNA. My lawmen defendants - with unlimited tax dollars to pay for attorneys as public officials (while claiming to be hobbyists) - got two law firms, who split the case for apparent double billing (Virden with one, Sullivan and Sederwall with another).

Though the judge eventually declared them public officials and ordered records turn-overs, the lawmen ignored him. Virden claimed he did not know how to get them. Sullivan and Sederwall said they were private. And, contrary to a legitimate court, the judge did not hold them in contempt; instead, permitting years of stonewalling, as five sets of my lawyers tried to throw the case.

Then things got worse. The hoaxers did turn over Lee reports; except they forged them to look like their private investigation to trick the judge! I caught them; so the judge again demanded turn-over. So, after five years, I got Lee's single report. But that was just his specimen recoveries. So my co-plaintiff used an attorney outside the public records act to subpoena the records. Orchid Cellmark turned over 133 pages proving no usable DNA.

Then things got worse. The last of my attorneys betrayed my case, forcing me to go *pro se* and fight alone. I prevailed. But the judge removed all monetary penalties for wrongful records withholding, to punish me by blocking my deserved near million dollars. But he did sanction them for the forgeries of Lee's reports.

I appealed. The corrupt Court of Appeals and Supreme Court not only backed no penalties for the lawmen, but removed the one for forgeries. This Santa Fe Ring-style corruption was epitomized by Charlie Daniels, Chief Justice of the Supreme Court. He was appointed Richardson; a major Richardson political donor; and husband of Attorney Randi McGinn: who did the hoax's fake "Pardon Petition" for Richardson.

To stymie the usual Santa Fe Ring-style cover-up expurgation, I put the major filings on my GaleCooperBillytheKidBooks.com website. And I published two exposé books reproducing the documents: 2012's *Billy the Kid's Pretenders, Brushy Bill and John Miller*; and 2014's *Cracking the Billy the Kid Case Hoax: The Strange Plot to Exhume Billy the Kid, Convict Sheriff Pat Garrett of Murder, and Become President of the United States*.

THE LAWMEN'S MAJOR HOAX DOCUMENTS TO HIDE INCRIMINATING RECORDS

My records requests and litigation exposed the "Brushy" thrust and hoaxers' profound dishonesty. Examples follow.

"INVESTIGATION MEMORANDUM"

On June 22, 2007, hoax-backing Lincoln County Attorney Alan Morel attached to his refusal of records turn-over for Sheriff Virden, a June 21, 2007 document by Deputies Sullivan and Sederwall titled "Memorandum, Subject: Billy the Kid Investigation," addressed to "Rick Virden, Lincoln County Sheriff." It was signed by the three lawmen. It was seven footnoted pages, plus 11 Attachments. It fabricated a conspiracy against them of Governor Richardson Bill Robins III, historians, the OMI's Debra Komar, Silver City and Fort Sumner mayors, Jay Miller, and me. And it overtly promoted "Brushy," as if spitefully revealing the case's secret. It concluded with Sullivan and Sederwall resigning as Deputies, and keeping the records as private property. And it did not change the public nature of the records these crooks hid.

"MEMORANDUM: BILLY THE KID INVESTIGATION"

This June 21, 2007 "Memorandum" is on the level of the "Probable Cause Statement" for labor-intensive fakery.

To: Rick Virden, Lincoln County Sheriff
From: Steven M. Sederwall & Thomas T. Sullivan
Subject: Billy the Kid Investigation
Date: Thursday, June 21, 2007

On April 28, 2003 we began a quest for the truth, looking into the *"escape of William Bonney and the double homicide of James Bell & Robert Olinger.* [Footnote 1: Lincoln County Call sheet pulled by Sheriff Sullivan April 28, 2003.] We chose this as a private venture and did not want to burden the county financially. The idea was to being modern science and police investigation methods to uncover the truth of the escape of the Kid and murder of our deputies. We had planned to file a report with the Sheriff at the end of the investigation, a report which the public could then access if they so desire.

[AUTHOR'S NOTE: The Deputy killing sub-investigation is called the whole case; and that is called a hobby.]

At the beginning of the investigation, it became known that career law enforcement officers were investigating a century old cold case involving Billy the Kid and the case began to generate a great deal of press.

[AUTHOR'S NOTE: Lie. Publicity came from claiming Pat Garrett did not kill the Kid, Richardson's press, and real murder investigation with Case Number 2003-274.]

With the enormous amount of publicity generated by the investigation Governor Bill Richardson was prompted to call a press conference. On Tuesday, June 10, 2003 he told the world of his intentions; *"I am announcing my support and the support of the state of New Mexico for the investigation into the life and death of Henry McCarty, also known as William Bonney"*.

[AUTHOR'S NOTE: This is fake time inversion; Richardson's article and press conference created the publicity.]

He told the roomful of reporters, *"By utilizing modern forensics, DNA and crime scene techniques, the goal of the investigation is to get to the truth. In the process, the reputation of Pat Garrett, still a hero to Lincoln County law enforcement hangs in the balance. The question is did Sheriff Garrett kill Billy the Kid at Fort Sumner, New*

Mexico on July 14, 1881" The Governor went on to say, *"If we can get to the truth we will."*

[AUTHOR'S NOTE: This contradicts the first claim of the deputy investigation. And they are blaming Richardson.]

On September 1, 2003, the Governor, behind the scenes, supported the investigation, by instructing Billy Sparks to hand Sheriff Sullivan three checks, from private backers, totaling $6,500.00. [Footnote 2: Three checks handed to Sheriff Sullivan in Governor's office by Billy Sparks] Standing at the threshold of the Governor's office, Sparks said, *"The governor wants to insure this investigation goes forward."*

[AUTHOR'S NOTE: They exposed Richardson's secret bribery by printing the donor checks in Attachment 2 to Case 2003-274 and the "Billy the Kid Investigation," with improper write-offs as "charity."]

The Governor also asked investigators to contact Ft. Sumner and get them *"on board."* On Friday, June 13th, Sederwall drove to Ft. Sumner and spoke with Mayor Raymond Lopez. Lopez liked the idea of worldwide attention on his village and felt it would help boost tourist dollars. He handwrote a note to the Governor, on Ft. Sumner letterhead saying, *"Mr. Steve Sederwall and I have talked and feel that we are on the same page on this Billy the Kid deal. He'll bring the information to you on the talk we had."* [Footnote 3: Handwritten note by Mayor Raymond Lopez on Ft. Sumner letterhead]

At the time investigators did not know if DNA could be obtained from a grave after 100 years, so after the Governor's news conference Sederwall met with Dr. Debra Komar an investigator with the New Mexico Office of the Medical Investigator's office. During this meeting Dr. Komar said considering the terrain, topography and climate of Silver City she judged chances of obtaining DNA from Catherine Antrim would be somewhere in the ninety percent range. Dr. Komar said she would begin investigating the graves. She and her boss were excited about working on this historical investigation.

[AUTHOR'S NOTE: Switch is to the Garrett murder and the mother's grave. They are hiding Dr. Komar's OMI affidavit and deposition of invalid DNA in both graves.]

On June 17th, 2003, something happened that shocked the investigators. In a Ft. Sumner grocery store, Ft. Sumner's ex-mayor, David Bailey approached De Baca County Sheriff Gary Graves and told him the Billy the Kid investigation *"had to stop."* Bailey said that if the Sheriff's [sic] were to exhume the grave of the Kid there would be a problem. Bailey said, *"You do not know what you are going to find but I do."*

On Friday, October 10, 2003, investigators were in Grant County District Court requesting a court order to exhume the body of Catherine Antrim, who is known as William H. Bonney's mother. Investigators wanted to obtain her DNA. Attorneys for Silver City and Ft. Sumner opposed the exhumation, so the judge scheduled a hearing on the matter, set for August of 2004.

[AUTHOR'S NOTE: This hides that exhumations were part of Case 2003-274, where they were lawmen petitioners with De Baca County Sheriff Gary Graves for Fort Sumner.]

The same day in a special meeting of the town of Silver City, Councilman Steve May objected to the exhumation by saying, *"Who cares? Who cares if it's Billy the Kid buried in Fort Sumner or if it's Brushy Bill in Texas? We might regret this if the DNA shows it's not Billy the Kid. We could shoot ourselves in the foot."*

Fear quickly spread through the "Billy the Kid" community. Anyone with an interest to protect, museum owners, authors, and entire towns became afraid of what the investigation would uncover and how it would affect their livelihood. The newspapers were full of their fears, libelous accusations and paranoia.

[AUTHOR'S NOTE: Blocked exhumations are faked as a "afraid-of-the-truth-conspiracy;" while hiding the OMI's permit refusals, and my attorneys' arguing that there was no historical basis to claim Garrett did not kill the Kid.]

"What will happen if no DNA from that grave matches DNA from the Silver City site? How do we explain that? Might it be better to leave well enough alone?" – **Jay Miler, syndicated columnist, *Inside the Capital* [sic], July 25, 2003.**

"I think it would have a truly negative impact if that's not Billy the Kid over there (Fort Sumner) – **Silver City Councilman Steve May, Silver City Sun News, October 11, 2003.**

"This is an industry for us," Lopez said. *"It's no different from Intel, or Sandia Labs, or Kirkland Airforce Base. It's that big for us. We don't have much to live off other than the legend, so we have to protect it."* – **Fort Sumner Mayor, Raymond Lopez, November 18, 2003, MSNBC News.**

The investigation has the *"potential to destroy the existing legend and mystery and folklore surrounding Billy the Kid, badly damage the state's tourism industry, and severely impact the economy of the state, and damage the reputation of the Governor's Office."* – **Letter to New Mexico Governor Bill Richardson signed by the Silver City Town Counsel [sic], June 21, 2004.**

[AUTHOR'S NOTE: This was Silver City's citizens' petition, ignored by Governor Richardson, while he pursued his "Brushy Bill" as Billy the Kid plot.]

Silver City and Fort Sumner face a loss of part of their Billy the Kid legend if DNA analysis is unable to show a match between bones dug up in the two communities." ?" – **Jay Miler, *Inside the Capital* [sic], July 2, 2004.**

"And if bodies are exhumed and no matching DNA is found, as the Office of the Medical Investigator predicts, the effect on these communities will be considerable, especially on Fort Sumner." – **Jay Miler, *Inside the Capital* [sic], September 19, 2004.**

The comments were published nearly daily. Their words told us they feared the Kid was not buried in Ft. Sumner. Most of the history of the escape of the Kid as well as his alleged killing by Garrett was built on a foundation set forth in Garrett's book. Historian Robert Utley pointed out in his book, *Billy the Kid a short and violent life:* "Although not many copies of the Authentic life were sold, it nevertheless had a decisive impact of the Kid's image. More than any other single influence, the Garrett-Upson book fed the legend of Billy the Kid. As the legend blossomed, writers turned to the Authentic life [sic] for the authentic details. Ash Upson's fictions became implanted in the hundreds of 'histories' that followed.

[AUTHOR'S NOTE: This reruns the Utley misquote from the "Probable Cause Statement," where he is not talking about scholarly history, but growth of the Billy the Kid legend.]

Investigators were searching for the truth in this story and the fact that Garrett was not truthful in his accounts was not brought to the table by investigators but historians themselves. Just as Utley voiced Garrett was not truthful, in an August 8, 2000 interview with the Associated Press, Historian Frederick Nolan made the statement that Garrett's version of the Kid's death *"may have been the biggest lie of all."*

[AUTHOR'S NOTE: This misstates Nolan's comment on Garrett's book's dime novel style, while backing that he killed Billy. They knew he condemned their hoax, but were faking that he called Garrett's report of the killing a lie.]

Yet when it became know [sic] investigators planned to use science, fear prompted the only thing that could be done to protect the books, museums, throw insults, such as, *"The three sheriffs trying to dig up Billy and his mother are a slippery bunch of varmits."* [sic] – **Jay Miler, *Inside the Capital*** [sic], **August 9, 2004.**

It was from there that the campaign to discredit the investigation and investigators was launched. Even Nolan saying that Garrett lied, feared his repeated version of the history was being questioned wrote an editor of the *Ruidoso News*. He said, *"This project is a complete and utter nonsense, and I Wouldn't be at all surprised if Sheriff Sullivan and Mayor Sederwall are already wishing they'd never got started on this benighted project."* The next day Nolan garnered more press by appearing on CCN *Live Saturday* with Frederika Whitfield, talking ill of the investigators.

As the unchecked fear spread, investigators were trying to make contact with Dr. Komar at the OMI's office but she refused to return the calls. We were advised by the girl answering the phone that she had instructions not to send our calls to Dr. Komar. The girl stated that Dr. Komar had "lawyered up" and we would have to talk to her attorney. We had never heard of a medical investigator retaining an attorney to deal with investigators.

[AUTHOR'S NOTE: This omits the OMI's blockade based on forensically useless DNA. The hoaxers fabricate a "conspiracy against truth" by the OMI in what follows.]

We didn't understand until January 20, 2004, when Bill Robins an attorney appointed by the Governor for the Kid, deposed Dr. Komar. She was asked by Robins, on page 144 lines 7 – 10 of the record, *"You don't think Billy the Kid is buried at Fort Sumner, do you?"* Dr. Komar replied, *"I don't know. I have reason to suspect perhaps not."*

[AUTHOR'S NOTE: As discussed above (see page 492-493), they took Komar's response out of context about the Billy's body possibly not being present because of flooding, or accidental removal with soldiers' bodies.]

It was at this point we believed Dr. Komar had discovered information, maybe some of the same information we had, about the Kid's grave. We wondered if the fear of harming New Mexico's tourist industry had caused the state to apply pressure to Dr. Komar and told her not to talk to us, in hopes this case would die and the myth would live.

[AUTHOR'S NOTE: Their "conspiracy" involves Komar and "the state;" though she merely confirmed no valid DNA available in Fort Sumer. But the hoaxers want to *claim she knew Billy was buried elsewhere as "Brushy!"*]

Since doctor Komar had obtained a lawyer and refused to talk, we wrote a letter to the OMI's office under the *New Mexico Open Records Act* asking for Dr. Komar's records. Unlike our part of the investigation, it was government money that financed her studies and paid her trips to gain information, which we reasoned would make the records public.

[AUTHOR'S NOTE: They were harassing Komar to make her to say Billy was never buried in Fort Sumner.]

After nearly 5 months of letters back and forth to the OMI's office we were provided with only a list of who was buried in Silver City. We knew that Dr. Komar had more records than the state admitted because she had stated this fact when deposed by Robins. We pointed out the state had paid for her trips and we knew there was more information, we received a response saying, *"The remainder of the material requested in your public records act request is in the possession of Dr. Komar, a faculty member of the University of New Mexico, and constitutes her intellectual property under federal copyright law and the University of New Mexico's Intellectual Property Policy."* [Footnote 5: Letter from Salvatore J. Giammo, Director of Public Affairs HSC Custodian of Public Records, address to Sullivan and Sederwall, dated April 12, 2007]

It became clear the state was hiding information and was not going to share it with investigators. The nagging question remained, what was the information and why did the state feel a need to hide it?

[AUTHOR'S NOTE: Fabricated is something "hidden." The hoaxers knew the OMI's Affidavits and Komar Deposition confirmed invalid DNA in the Billy and mother graves.]

Friday April 2, 2004, the judge in Silver City came out with a surprise ruling, not waiting for the August hearing; his ruling startled investigators would have to provide the court with DNA from Fort Sumner before he would allow the investigators to obtain DNA from Catherine Antrim.

[AUTHOR'S NOTE: This fakes that Komar caused the 2004 case transfer to Fort Sumner; not the truth that Judge Quintero colluded with Attorney Bill Robins III to call the case "not ripe" – meaning he wanted them to get Billy's Fort Sumner DNA before they could dig up the mother.]

What no one realized was that by September 20, 2003, we had located the workbench on which Garrett claimed to have laid the Kid's body. Through our discussions with the CSI experts we felt the Kid's DNA could be obtained from that bench. We also knew historians, from as far back as the 1920's, knew the grave was not located behind the "museum and gift shop" as Ft. Sumner had led tourist [sic] to believe. [Footnote 6: Notes entitled "Bonney Grave, Ft. Sumner", by Fulton found in the Robert N. Mullin Collection, Haley Memorial Library] We also knew that digging into that empty grave would be fruitless.

[AUTHOR'S NOTE: The hoaxers are lying about Billy's grave not being in Fort Sumner's cemetery to make their hoax switch to the fake bench as a DNA source. And they hide that the bench was part of Case 2003-274, not their private hobby; and that it yielded no DNA.]

Without contacting us and immediately after the judge ruled, Attorney Bill Robins filed to exhume the Kid in Ft. Sumner. The fight was on again with the village of Ft. Sumner filing motions to block Robins' attempt to look in their grave. On Wednesday July 22, 2004, Billy Sparks of the Governor's office called Sederwall at home. Sparks asked if the investigators would *'pull out of Fort Sumner"* and if so the Governor would consider it a *"personal favor."* Sparks said Silver City and Ft. Sumner were putting a great deal of pressure on the Governor to stop the dig because they feared it would destroy their tourism.

[AUTHOR'S NOTE: Besides surprising biting of the hands that had fed them, this fabricates the Fort Sumner withdrawal reason. It occurred after County Commissioner Leo Martinez threatened Sullivan with recall if he continued the hoax. And they well knew of Robins's filing, since they were its lawmen petitioners!]

Sederwall called Mayor Lopez and attempted to talk to him about the issue and tell him it was not our desire to harm tourism in New Mexico. When Sederwall identified himself Lopez shouted, *"fuck you!"* and hung up. This was the last time any of the investigators talk [sic] to Mayor Lopez.

[AUTHOR'S NOTE: This may be thug Sederwall's reworking his original threat to Lopez as: "Get your head out of your ass. We're getting this done whether you want it or not."]

That Friday we called our attorney and told him attorney Robins had filed the case on our behalf and we wanted to withdraw it.

Which he did and we sat back quietly as Ft. Sumner was shorn in the press throwing a party where Frederick Nolan declared it a victory for "truth."

[AUTHOR'S NOTE: Omitted is that the Fort Sumner case had proceeded for months under their attorney, Mark Acuña, that Robins was Billy's, not their, attorney, and they withdrew days before the September 27, 2004 Hearing because of Leo Martinez's and press exposure.]

During the investigation the village of Fort Sumner, the town of Silver City and the city of Hamilton, Texas, in an effort to protect tourism, fought the investigation so DNA could not be recovered.

In the case of Hamilton, Texas, Brushy Bill Roberts died under the name of Oliver L. Roberts and his date of birth, on his official death certificate sets out he was born on December 31, 1868 [Footnote 7: Death certificate of Ollie L. Roberts], which would make the man 12 years old in 1881 when the Kid shot and killed James Bell and Robert Olinger.]

[AUTHOR'S NOTE: This lie that Hamilton had a tourism conspiracy, conceals that digging up "Brushy" was refused by its County Commissioners based on the hoaxers' refusing to provide DNA records to prove they had anything for its justification (which they did not have).]

Roberts died a pauper and was buried at county expense and above his grave was placed a homemade marker of cement. [Footnote 8: Old Tombstone of Ollie L. Roberts] However, the investigators found a new tombstone on a grave located in the middle cemetery [sic] on the first row, in a very prominent place. We wondered if that grave is empty and there only for tourists. We wondered if the man was in fact buried in the back of the cemetery.

The new marker was donated and placed by the owner of the Billy the Kid Memorial Museum in Hamilton. [Footnote 9: New Tombstone for "Henry William Roberts"] Roberts name has changed from Ollie L. Roberts as listed on his death certificate and old tombstone to *Henry W. Roberts* on the new tombstone. As well, his date of birth has changed from December 31, 1868, to December 31, 1859. This would make him 21 in 1881 rather than 12 and would coincide with the history of Billy the Kid.

On May 20, 2005 [sic- May 19, 2003], the only body to be exhumed who claimed to be Billy the Kid was that of John Miller. The state of Arizona exhumed Mr. Miller and the samples were received by Dr. Rick Staub of Orchid Cellmark labs in Dallas for recovery of DNA.

[AUTHOR'S NOTE: This reworks their Arizona exhumation fiasco as "the state did it." And concealed is the horrific desecration and grave-robbing of William Hudspeth. And omitted, of course, is that they did the exhumations for Case 2003-274 under their official titles, while claiming Dr. Lee's fake bench DNA for matching.]

Investigators agree the investigation of Billy the Kid has garnered more press and has been more troublesome than any thing we have encountered in the past. Countless letters have been written to the Village of Capitan, Orchid Cellmark, Dr. Henry Lee's office, Lincoln County, the Lincoln County Sheriff, Lincoln Counties [sic] Attorney, the New Mexico Attorney General, the United States Marshal's [sic], newspapers, magazines and to investigators in an attempt to disrupt or stop the investigation. The majority of these letters were written by Dr. Gail [sic] Cooper or Jay Miller.

[AUTHOR'S NOTE: Now the conspiracy against the truth turns to me and Jay Miller, leaving out that the "letters" were open records requests for their fake DNA records. It is also a lead-in, at this early stage of open records requesting, to claim that the requesting is legal harassment – as fellow hoaxer Attorney Alan Morel had threatened in past attempt to stop Jay Miller's requests.]

Miller weighed into the fight the first time on June 6, 2003 with an article accusing Governor Richardson of attempting to get publicity for the state for the investigation. Had Jay Miller read the press release, he would know that Governor Richardson admitted that fact up front.

Miller wrote letter after letter requesting files and documents concerning the financing of the investigation **but there were no records as it was privately funded by law.** Yet, Miller continued to write letter after letter. In a two month period, Jay Miller wrote the United States Marshals office, the Lincoln County Sheriff, the Lincoln County Attorney, James Jimenez, New Mexico Secretary Department Finance and Administration, the New Mexico Governor, and countless others complaining about Sederwall and Sullivan and each rambling letter, required a response. At one point he complained to the Attorney General Sederwall was *'impersonating a police officer.'*

[AUTHOR'S NOTE: They are misstating the open records requests, as I know, since I wrote them! The issue was that they had no grounds for withholding the records; and murder investigations are not privately funded!]

The attacks did not center only on Sederwall and Sullivan but on anyone who dared look at the Billy the Kid Case. When Ft. Sumner heard Sheriff Gary Graves was part of the investigative team a campaign began attacking his career. On November 30, 2003 Mayor Ramon [sic] Lopez Mayor of Ft. Sumner was quoted in the paper saying Sheriff Graves was trying to start a "war" with the city over the grave of Billy the Kid. In the end, the Mayor and Ft. Sumner successfully removed Sheriff Gary Graves from office. Sheriff Graves became the first sheriff in New Mexico to be removed by a recall vote and the last sheriff taken out by Billy the Kid.

[AUTHOR'S NOTE: This lies that Gary Graves's recall for malfeasance and misfeasance, unrelated to the Billy the Kid Case, was because of it. And Mayor Lopez did not participate. It was a citizens' group that got the necessary signatures, after Graves had stolen a prisoner's money and had repeatedly terrorized residents.]

Both the village of Ft. Sumner and the City of Hamilton, Texas own a grave marked "Billy the Kid" to draw in tourist dollars. The fact remains that a man can have but one grave. Since it is a governmental entity that owns both graves and both governments have fought to keep investigators obtaining DNA from their grave that would prove where Bonney rests, it would go to reason one or both, of these governmental agencies are guilty of perpetrating fraud against the public.

[AUTHOR'S NOTE: Omitted for this fake tourism conspiracy theory, was that they had no DNA of Billy the Kid to match with any remains. And their whole case was a hoax.]

On February 9, 2007, Sederwall and Jay Miller had lunch together in Santa Fe. Without hesitation Sederwall answered any and all questions Miller posed. Miller explained what encouraged him to fight the investigators in the Billy the Kid Case. Miller said he was born in Silver City and knew *"a lot of people up there."* He said he had received a telephone call from someone in Silver City, he chose not to identify, and the caller wanted his help to stop the investigation and the exhumation of the Kid and his mother. Miller said he began to produce the newspaper articles and the massive amount of letters knowing that we would have to answer each of them. He said that a Dr. Gail [sic] Cooper was involved and wrote most of the letters.

Miller admitted if the investigation continued it would jeopardize tourism in both Silver City and Ft. Sumner. The meeting was pleasant and as the men parted company they shook hands. Miller walked away but stopped, turned and said of Catherine Antrim, *"you know she's not in that grave don't you?"*

Even though Ft. Sumner and Hamilton know, in their hearts, Billy the Kid can have only one grave, they continue to fight the discovery of the truth and continue the fraud in the name of commerce. The Governor bending to the pressure from Ft. Sumner and Silver City turned his back on his promise to find the truth. This past week another letter, requiring an answer, came to the Sheriff requesting the information we have gathered in this investigation. **We have been told the letter from Dr. Gail [sic] Cooper's attorney is her attempt to gain the information we have spent years gathering to add to a book she is attempting to sell.**

[AUTHOR'S NOTE: Now revealed is their new tactic for withholding the DNA documents: by calling them proprietary "research," or private property immune to open records law, which is for public officials' public documents - like those of a filed Sheriff's Department murder case like 2003-274! Also, the accusing of me as wanting to get their information for a book I am writing, is intended to mean that they had made spectacular new findings that I wanted to steal to use myself! That came from the open records "trade secret" exclusionary clause they would later misuse in litigation. In fact, that clause is intended for private businesses doing work for the state; and needing to protect their unrelated proprietary information in cases of open records litigation when records have to be revealed. It did not apply to the hoaxers, who were straight-forward public officials, generating public records.]

We will continue our investigation. Later, we shall make the decision if and when we will release the information. Now, we choose to put an end to the harassment and political pressure by tendering our resignations as Deputies of Lincoln County Sheriff''s Department, effective this date.

[AUTHOR'S NOTE: Quitting as its Deputies in 2007, does not convert Case 2003-274's records from public to private, which is the scam they are trying to perpetrate. Nevertheless, throughout my open records litigation, they would call themselves private hobbyists with trade secrets.]

Respectively Submitted,
Steven M. Sederwall, Thomas T. Sullivan [written and typed]

"MEMORANDUM ATTACHMENTS"

Provided was a hodge-podge irrelevant to justifying records withholding, but revealing the Case's "Brushy Bill" direction.

ATTACHMENT 1: "Lincoln County Call sheet requested by Sheriff Tom Sullivan on April 28, 2003 as 'Follow up investigation Escape of William Bonney and double homicide of James Bell & Robert Olinger" **[Faking that Bell's killing was Case 2003-274]**

ATTACHMENT 2: "Checks handed to Sheriff Sullivan in the State Capital [sic] by Billy Sparks"

ATTACHMENT 3: "Handwritten letter by Mayor Raymond Lopez to Governor Bill Richardson on Village of Fort Sumner letterhead"

ATTACHMENT 4: ""Statement by DeBaca County Sheriff Gary Graves dated July 20, 2003"

ATTACHMENT 5: "Letter from the Office of Public Affairs of the OMI's office"

ATTACHMENT 6: "Notes by Historian Marcie [sic - Maurice] Fulton found in the Robert N. Mullin collection, indicating that "what Ft. Sumner claims is the Kid's grave is not possible" **[But their hoax claimed it as a valid DNA source!]**

ATTACHMENT 7: "Brushy Bill Roberts Certificate of Death showing his name and date of birth has been changed to fit the history of the Kid" **[But their case tried to make him Billy!]**

ATTACHMENT 8: (photo) "Original headstone of Ollie L. Roberts in Hamilton, Texas Cemetery"

ATTACHMENT 9: (Photo) "New Headstone put up by the owner of the Billy the Kid Memorial Museum, dates and name has changed. Sederwall on the right and Lucas Speer on the left, note the plastic tube under Sederwall's arm directing tourist [sic] to the museum"

ATTACHMENT 10: (Copy) "Flyer found in plastic tube affixed to Brushy Bill's grave in Hamilton, Texas"

ATTACHMENT 11: (Photocopies) "Commission cards of Deputy Steven M. Sederwall and Deputy Thomas T. Sullivan from the Lincoln County Deputy Sheriff office"

[AUTHOR'S NOTE: Contradicting their "private hobbyist" ploy!]

FORGING DR. HENRY LEE REPORTS

The hoaxers knew the requested Dr. Henry Lee report on his carpenter's bench investigation was fatal to their case. I knew they had it from Lee's May 1, 2006 letter to Jay Miller stating he "examined a wooden bench, and floorboards at the courthouse," and that he had "submitted my report [single] ... to the Lincoln County Sheriff's Department." (See page 582 above) So the lawmen first claimed that they never got it. Since open records law includes records *not in direct possession*, the judge ordered turn-over.

But unbeknownst to me and the judge, that started their frenzy of forging Lee reports to cover-up their two big lies: (1) that they were private hobbyists; (2) that they had the "blood-DNA" of Billy the Kid from the bench for DNA matching.

As it would turn out, Lee's report exposed their lying. But at the start, that was not known, and forgeries were inconceivable.

THE FIRST FLOORBOARD REPORT

On February 18, 2010, my then attorney called me to say that he had received *the* Lee report from Steve Sederwall's lawyer, Kevin Brown. But it turned out to be an unrequested, nine page, official-looking report, dated February 25, 2005, about Lee's checking the courthouse floorboards for the blood of Deputy Bell. It was titled: "Forensic Research and Training Center Forensic Examination Report: Examination of Lincoln County Courthouse. Forensic Examination Report"

Its header stated: "Date of Request: May 22, 2004; Requested By: Steve Sederwall, and Bill Kurtis Productions; "Report To: Steven M. Sederwall. On Sunday, August 1, 2004, the forensic investigation team examined the old Lincoln County Court House in Lincoln, New Mexico. Present at the scene were Steve Sederwall, Tom Sullivan, David Turk, Bill Kurtis, and Gary Wayne Graves. The target area of examination is located on the top landing of the stairs of the old courtroom." **No mention was made of Case 2003-274! No one had an official title! And the case was done for Steve Sederwall!**

Its "Results and Conclusions" section stated: "Various stains were observed on the surface and the underside of the floorboards. Chemical tests [with O-Tolidine] for the presence of blood were positive with some of those stains. These results indicate the presence of oxidas [sic - oxidase] activity with those stains tested positive, which suggests those stains could be bloodstains. Further DNA testing could reveal the nature and identity of that blood like stains [sic - on grammar]."

Signers were: "Dr. Henry C. Lee, Chief Emeritus, Connecticut State Forensic Laboratory, Distinguished Professor, University New Haven" and "Calvin D. Ostler, Forensic Consultant, Crime Scene Investigator" (Lee's business partner).

I told my attorney to return the report unrequested. But I thought it odd that no one had lawmen titles - as if backing the private hobby claim.

A FLOORBOARD REPORT AS EXHIBIT F

On March 9, 2010, my attorney held a Presentment Hearing before the judge to report that no requested records had been turned over. Sheriff Virden lied through his attorney that he was not "required to produce documents that we are not in possession of."

Sederwall lied through his Attorney, Kevin Brown, that Lee's report met my request. Brown said: "**I will state to the Court, the document which I have here, which I would mark as an exhibit ... is the only document that Sederwall received.**" It was marked **Exhibit F**. It was part of the court record, but not shown to me. *But it seemed obvious that it was the same floorboard report I had already been given and rejected.*

FLOORBOARD REPORT AGAIN

On April 6, 2010, my attorney faxed me Virden's turn-over of the same floorboard report that was already given to me by Attorney Brown on February 18, 2010. Virden's Narvaez Law Firm attorney's cover letter stated: "Attached is the Forensic Examination Report from Dr. Lee ... Please be advised that this report was never in Lincoln County's possession, and the only reason we have a copy of it is because Mr. [Kevin] Brown provided it to us."

THE CARPENTER'S BENCH REPORT

On November 10, 2010, with my all-day Evidentiary Hearing looming, Steve Sederwall shockingly pulled another Dr. Lee report out of a hat - this time, the carpenter's bench report!

Its cover letter was to my attorney from his lawyer, Kevin Brown (keeping a straight face after telling the judge that Sederwall had *only one* report). It stated: "Enclosed please find a copy of another report dated February 25, 2005 which deals with the examination of furniture by Dr. Lee."

Oddly, it looked different from the floorboard report, having ornate font in its title. One would assume a standard presentation by an expert. **And it lacked any "Results and Conclusions" section - a forensic report's purpose!** It was titled: "Forensic Research & Training Center Forensic Examination Report, Examination of furniture from Pete Maxwell's of July 15, 1881." It was 16 pages, and signed by Lee and Calvin Ostler. Its header had no law enforcement information; and the "Requested by" section was expanded to "Steve Sederwall, Capitan, New Mexico, paid for by Investigating History Program, Kurtis Production."

Its "Introduction" stated: **At the request of Steve Sederwall of Lincoln County, New Mexico, Bill Kurtis and Jamie Schenk of Kurtis Production**, Dr. Henry Lee went to New Mexico on July 31, 2004 to assist in the re-investigation of the case of Billy the Kid. The forensic investigating team participating in re-investigation consist the [sic] following individuals: [listed as] **Steve Sederwall, Investigator; Tom Sullivan, Investigator; Dr. Henry Lee, Chief Emeritus of the Connecticut State Police Forensic Laboratory; Calvin Ostler, Forensic Consultant, Riverton, Utah; Kim Ostler, Crime Scene Assistant, Riverton, Utah; David Turk, U.S. Marshall [sic], United States Marshall Service [sic]. In addition, Mike Haag, Firearm examiner from Albuquerque Police Department Crime Lab, also provided valuable technical assistance in the investigation**. The forensic investigation team arrived at the Manny [sic - Mannie] Miller residence, located at (address removed), Albuquerque, New Mexico, at 18:20 hours on Saturday, July 31, 2004. Upon arrival we were presented with three pieces of evidence: a **worktable**, a washstand, and a headboard. Investigator Sullivan, Investigator Sederwall, and members of Bill Kurtis Productions had removed the three pieces of evidence from a storage building at the rear of the residence. Each item was inspected visually and macroscopically."

Listed were three separate investigations titled: "Item #1 Workbench," "Item # 2 Washstand," "Item # 3 Bed Headboard."

WORKBENCH: For the carpenter's bench, Lee's testing for "blood" on the top was listed on page 6 as by Phenopathlien and Ortho-tolidine. And page 9 listed testing the underside of the bench with Luminol. (All are merely for iron compounds - like blood or rust.) And it had something fatal on page 9; stating: "Swab samples of area number '3' and area number '4' were collected for DNA testing. Two swabs were taken from each area and placed in two separate swab boxes, one box was labeled for area number '3' and one box was labeled for area number '4'. **These two samples were transferred to Lincoln Sheriff Department.** In addition, scraping samples were also taken from these two areas. These samples were placed in two evidence envelopes **and were transferred to Lincoln Sheriff Department."** [**AUTHOR'S NOTE: When I did get Orchid Cellmark's evidence envelopes by 2012 subpoena, they were, indeed, labeled as for Case 2003-274**]

WASHSTAND: This had its photograph and had diagrams of the supposed bullet holes for the trajectory.

HEADBOARD: With no photograph or diagram, it merely stated: "A piece of headboard was examined. No bloodlike stains was observed. No bullet hole was found. No evidence of damage was noted." [This omitted that the headboard was just a big hole.]

This report was strange as lacking law enforcement titles, while being sent to the Lincoln County Sheriff's Department. There was no way to imagine that this just represented careless forging to prove the private hobbyists claim.

FLOORBOARD REPORT AS EXHIBIT F AND CARPENTER'S BENCH REPORT AS EXHIBIT E

For my January 21, 2011 Evidentiary Hearing, Attorney Kevin Brown, for Sullivan and Sederwall, still calling them "hobbyists" with trade secret DNA results, **dramatically handed over to the judge the bench report as Exhibit E and the supposedly same floorboard report as Exhibit F.** And he pretended that Orchid Cellmark's DNA extraction and matching results were Sullivan's and Sederwall's private "trade secrets."

THE LEE TURN-OVER REPORTS' SHOCKER

As mentioned, my own attorneys kept trying to throw my case; which necessitated my replacing them. Having gotten rid of the attorney who got the floorboard and bench reports, I met with my new attorneys to review the old attorney's boxes of files.

As a layman, I could pay for court transcripts; but only an attorney could get copies of the defense Exhibits. So this was my first time to see them. For the January 21, 2011 Evidentiary Hearing, I was struck by defense Exhibit E (for carpenter's bench) and Exhibit F (for floorboards).

I have near-photographic memory. **I exclaimed, "This Exhibit F floorboard report is completely different from the one Sederwall turned over on February 18, 2010, and gave to Virden's attorney on April 6, 2010!"** It had a different title font, which matched the ornate one on the bench report's title (which Sederwall turned over on November 10, 2010, and then gave to the Court as Exhibit E). I thumbed through Exhibits E and F. Now *neither* had a "Results and Conclusions" section - though that first turned-over Lee floorboard report had one!

From my papers I took out that first Lee floorboard report to show these new attorneys the alterations made on the Exhibit F floorboard report given to the court. Noted were:

1) The "Requested by" phrase on the face of each report was different. The first turn-over had Steve Sederwall and Bill Kurtis Productions requesting the Report, while Exhibit F had: "Steve Sederall, Capitan, New Mexico, paid for by Investigation History Program, Kurtis Production."

2) The introductory paragraph had been changed in Exhibit F to add descriptions of those present.

3) Photograph's reference numbers had been changed, the text changed, and some of it deleted.

4) Diagram's reference numbers had been changed.

5) The "Results and Conclusions" were deleted.

When I laid them out together, I realized that the Lee and Ostler signatures were superimposable - cut and pasted onto the reports. **SO THE DEFENDANTS WERE FORGING DR. LEE REPORTS!** Since 2010 Sederwall had been nervously re-working them, while faking turn-over compliance. **In fact, no real records at all had been turned-over by the lawmen!**

THE AUTHENTIC LEE REPORT

On February 23, 2012 the judge ordered: "Defendant Sederwall is to produce all original Reports received from Dr. Henry Lee with his original signature on them." On January 31, 2012, my attorney and I met in Attorney Kevin Brown's office. Brown kept a straight face as he gave another "only one report." This one had a different font, was 25 pages. Dated February 25, 2005, it was titled "Forensic Research & Training Center Forensic Examination Report;" and had the all investigations combined in one report - just as Lee had informed Jay Miller.

Its sections were: "Item #1 Workbench," "Item # 2 Washstand," "Item 3 (now labeled) A piece of Headboard," Item # 4 "Examination of Lincoln County Court House," and "Results and Conclusion."

Its heading and "Introduction" **had case number and law enforcement titles expurgated from the others**. It stated:

Requested By: **Lincoln County Sheriff's Office, New Mexico**
Investigating History Program, Kurtis Production
Local Case No. 2003-274
Date of Report: February 25, 2005
Report to: **Steve Sederwall**
Lincoln County Sheriff's Office, New Mexico

Introduction

At the request of **Steve Sederwall of Lincoln County Sheriff's Office, Lincoln County**, Bill Kurtis and Jamie Schenk of Kurtis Production, [sic – and] Dr. Henry Lee went to New Mexico on July 31, 2004 to assist in the re-investigation of the case of Billy the Kid. The forensic investigation team participating in re-investigation consist [sic –of] the following individuals:

Dr. Henry Lee, Chief Emeritus of the Connecticut State Police Forensic Laboratory
Calvin Ostler, Forensic Consultant, Riverton, Utah
Kim Ostler, Crime Scene Assistant, Riverton, Utah
Tom Sullivan, Sheriff, Lincoln County New Mexico
Steve Sederwall Deputy Sheriff, Lincoln County New Mexico
David Turk, US Marshal, United States Marshall [sic] Service

In addition, Mike Haag, Firearm examiner from Albuquerque Police Department Crime Lab, also provided valuable technical assistance in the investigation.

The forensic investigation team arrived at the Manny [sic] Miller residence, located at [address given here, not removed like in Exhibit E version], Albuquerque, New Mexico, at 18:20 hours on Saturday, July 31, 2004. Upon arrival we were presented with three pieces of evidence: a worktable, a washstand, and a headboard. The three pieces of evidence had been removed from a storage building at the rear of the residence by **Sheriff Sullivan, Deputy Sederwall**, and members of Bill Kurtis Productions. Each item was inspected visually and macroscopically. The following were found [with findings given].

This report confirmed Lee's giving his samples to the Lincoln County Sheriff's Department. **And it had the "Results and Conclusion" section, which showed that cagy Lee had only claimed "blood-like" stains to hide rust. THERE WAS NO CLAIM OF BLOOD!** The "Results and Conclusion" stated:

> After a detail [sic] examination of the evidence and review of all the results of field testing, the following conclusion [sic] was reached.
>
> 1. Brownish dark stains were observed on different areas of the workbench. These areas were subjected to chemical presumptive blood tests. Some of those samples give a positive reaction. These results indicate the presence of Heme or Peroxidase like activity with those stains testing positive, which suggest that those stains could be bloodstains. Further DNA testing could reveal the nature and identity of these blood-like stains.
>
> 2. Two bullet holes were located on the side panels of the Washstand. The hole on the left panel is consistent with a bullet entry hole while the hole on the right side panel is consistent with a bullet exit hole. However, it is not possible to determine when those bullets were produced at this time. The angles produced in examination tell us two things:
>
> First, the bullet was fired from no more than 41" from the floor given the reported limitations of the room. The room is reported to be 20' by 20'; the maximum distance is assumed to be 20'. If the firearm was a maximum of 41" off the floor it is unlikely that the shooter was standing. It is more likely that the shooter was kneeling, squatting, or close to the floor.
>
> Second, the horizontal angle is such that if the Washstand was positioned so the back was against the wall, the shot could not have been fired from more than approximately 40 inches from the Washstand, because the wall would have been in the way. The angle of trajectory intersects the back plane of the Washstand at approximately 45 3/16", and no more than 46".
>
> 3. No bullet hole and no observable damage, no sign of bullet ricocheted type of defects were found on the Headboard.
>
> 4. The floor boards on the 2nd floor stair landing area of the court house have been repaired. Different types of wood and nails were used on this area.

5. Various stains were observed on the surface and underside of the floor boards. Chemical tests for the presence of blood were positive for some of those stains. These results indicate the presence of Heme or Peroxidase like activity with those stains tested positive, which suggests that those stains could be bloodstains. Further DNA testing could reveal the nature and identity of those blood-like stains.

The motive for forgeries was obvious: hiding the law enforcement case to fake a private hobby; and hiding no blood or DNA to fake legitimacy of the Arizona exhumations.

For his June 26, 2012 deposition, incorrigible rogue Sederwall, when asked by my attorney, "Did you make up that report?" answered: "No, I did not make up the report. **The report has been massaged, it's been changed, it's been worked on. That's what's been done.**" (Deposition Sederwall, 6/26/12; p. 561)

THE JUDGE'S RULING ON THE FORGERIES

For his May 15, 2014 "Findings of Fact and Conclusions of Law and Order of the Court," the judge ruled on Sederwall's forgeries; though the penalty for them that he awarded to me was later removed by the corrupt appellate courts to shield the lawmen of any and all penalties; though forgeries were not denied. For his "Findings of Fact," the judge wrote:

> **Findings of Fact ...**
> 26. In his June 26, 2012 deposition Sederwall admitted to: removing law enforcement information from later Lee reports; called the twenty-five (25) page Lee report he first received from Lee as original; and admitted to knowing that the Orchid Cellmark client was Calvin Ostler [to request the records].
> 29. At an Evidentiary Hearing conducted on December 21 [sic – 18], 2012 and February 4, 2013 ... [w]itness Seterwall [sic], still calling Case 2003-274 his private hobby, admitted to altering the first Lee report's header to remove Case 2003-274 information; and admitted to creating the other report versions given to the Court and lacking law enforcement information ...
> **Conclusions of Law ...**
> 27. Defendants' conduct in providing altered records as discussed in Findings of Facts 25, 26, and 29 and Conclusions of Law 18 is wanton, willful, and in bad faith.

KEY POINTS IN THE JUDGE'S FINAL DECISION IN THE OPEN RECORDS LITIGATION

The District Court judge ruled on May 15, 2014 in his "Findings of Fact and Conclusions of Law and Order of the Court." Exposing the hoaxers under "Findings of Fact" were:

4. The matter in controversy is for enforcement of the New Mexico Inspection of Public [Records] Act, Section 14-2-1 et seq. NMSA 1978 (IPRA) and concerning the Defendants' **refusal to turn over requested DNA records of Lincoln County Sheriff's Department Case No. 2003-274, "Billy the Kid Case"** ...

5. **Case 2003-274 is a murder case, filed in 2003 in the Lincoln County Sheriff's Department by Sheriff Tom Sullivan (hereinafter Sullivan) and his commissioned Deputy Steve Sederwall (hereinafter Sederwall) to be solved by forensic DNA acquisitions and matching, and accusing the suspect Pat Garrett of murdering an innocent victim instead of Billy the Kid**; with a **sub-investigation of Billy the Kid's double homicide of Deputies James Bell and Robert Olinger.**

6. From 2003 to 2004, Case 2003-274's New Mexico exhumation attempts on Billy the Kid and his mother for matching DNA were legally blocked so no DNA was obtained.

7. In 2004 Billy the Kid's DNA was allegedly obtained for Case 2003-274 by Dr. Henry Lee (hereinafter Lee) from an old carpenter's bench on which Billy the Kid [was] laid after being shot. Lee's specimens were sent for DNA processing to Orchid Cellmark Lab (hereinafter Orchid Cellmark) in Texas.

8. In 2005 newly elected Lincoln County Sheriff Rick Virden (hereinafter Virden) deputized Sullivan and Sederwall to continue Case 2003-274 by **exhuming Billy the Kid's identity claimants John Miller and "Brushy Bill" Roberts for DNA match** with Lee's bench DNA to solve the Garrett murder.

9. On May 19, 2005, for Case 2003-274, John Miller and William Hudspeth were exhumed in Arizona and their bones were taken to Orchid Cellmark for DNA extractions and for DNA matching to the carpenter's bench DNA.

10. From April 24, 2007 to June 26, 2007 Plaintiff Cooper made IPRA [open records] records requests from Sheriff Virden for Case 2003-274 ... Requested records were for:

A. Lee's DNA recoveries from the carpenter's bench;
B. Orchid Cellmark's DNA extractions from Lee's specimens;
C. Orchid Cellmark's DNA extractions for the two Arizona bodies; and
D. Orchid Cellmark's DNA matchings for the carpenter's bench [DNA] to the bodies [DNA].

11. **In the request phase, no records were given and their denials were improper** ...

12. The case at hand [litigation] for enforcement of IPRA [open records] was filed on October 15, 2007 ...

16. On November 20, 2009 Partial Summary Judgment was issued ... declaring the records requested were public, were created in official capacities, and should be turned over ...

21. At a September 23, 2011 Presentment Hearing Cooper alerted the Court of the discrepancies in the Lee reports [which had been forged] ...

23. On January 31, 2012 Sederwall turned over a twenty-five (25) page "original" Lee report combining the courthouse floorboard and the carpenter's bench. **Its header identified Lee's work as for Case 2003-274.**

24. On March 20, 2012 [Cooper's co-plaintiff] subpoenaed the Orchid Cellmark records for Case 2003-274, receiving one hundred thirty-three (133) pages on April 20, 2012. The records included DNA results from Lee's specimens and from the two exhumed Arizona bodies ...

27. In his June 27, 2012 deposition Virden admitted to: waiting three (3) years into litigation to write record requests to Lee and Orchid Cellmark; not requesting from Lee the report when Lee wrote back that he had one; and not trying to find out the client's name after Orchid Cellmark wrote back that it was required to send Virden the requested records ...

Exposing the hoaxers under "Conclusions of Law" were:

1. Section 14-2-5 NMSA 1978 states, "The intent of the legislature in enacting the Inspection of Public Records Act is to ensure as the policy of the State of New Mexico, that all persons are entitled to the greatest possible information regarding the affairs of government and the official acts of public officers and employees" ...

4. Without statutory justification, no requested records were produced by the Defendants.

5. **The requested records exist, and have been recoverable from the time of the request phase** ...

10. Virden was obligated to recover records from it [sic- his] deputy agents [Sullivan and Sederwall] ...

11. ... Virden's [claiming] lack or [sic - of] knowledge of records is disingenuous, since his deputies admitted to records possession, his Case 2003-274 file showed DNA investigations and recovery options, Lee responded to Virden and Lee had the record, and Orchid Cellmark responded to Virden that it had the records ...

13. **As public officials ... Sullivan and Sederwall had to provide records as, "an integral part of the routine duties of public officers and employees."**

14. As commissioned deputies ... along with Virden, [Sullivan and Sederwall] were "responsible for the denial of records." As Virden's deputies, they were his agents. ...

15. Sullivan and Sederwall said they were hobbyists and the records were private property. Sullivan's and Sederwall's argument of being "unsalaried "reserve deputies" is irrelevant to the records responsibility ...

16. In their June 21, 2007 "Memorandum" to Virden, Sullivan and Sederwall admitted to having Case 2003-274 records, but called them private property, while at the same time resigning their public official positions as deputies. Furthermore, from 2010 to 2012, Sederwall offered Case 2003-274 records for sale on his own billythekidcase.com website ... [and Sederwall admitted to willfully "altering Lee reports by rewritings to remove the original law enforcement information in Lee's "first" report sent to him as Lincoln County Deputy Sheriff" ...

19. **The Defendants' actions and/or inactions in responding to Plaintiff's IPRA requests are in violation of IPRA law and subject to sanctions** ...

26. **Defendants' conduct in not providing the requested records enumerated in Findings of Fact 10, is willful, wanton, and in bad faith.**

27. Defendants' conduct in providing altered records ... is wanton, willful, and in bad faith ...

The judge ordered: "Judgment be entered in favor of Plaintiff Cooper against Defendants."

CHAPTER 8
"BILLY THE KID CASE" HOAX UPSHOT

FAILURE TO MAKE "BRUSHY" BILLY

The "Billy the Kid Case" hoax failed to make "Brushy Bill" Billy the Kid; despite the sewer of corruption on which it floated. Failed were Governor Bill Richardson, Attorney Bill Robins III, Professor Paul Hutton; lawmen, Tom Sullivan, Gary Graves, and Steve Sederwall; U.S. Marshals Service Historian David Turk; enabling reporters, judges, attorneys, and prosecutors; and the bottomless tax-dollar funded budget for the case and for fighting me in courts. Achieved was the wanton destruction of the graves and remains of John Miller and William Hudspeth for a publicity stunt; and creation of two documentaries disseminating its lies: 2004's "Investigating History: Billy the Kid," and 2006's "Requiem for Billy the Kid."

The "Billy the Kid Case's" unchecked cronyism and corrupt shielding of fellow conspirators, had became just another chapter in New Mexico's Santa Fe Ring racketeering going back to 1866.

Damaged was the legacy of famous Sheriff Pat Garrett by conducting a baseless murder case against him; and damaged was Billy the Kid history by disseminating fraudulent claims. Demeaned were the Lincoln and De Baca County Sheriff's Departments by conducting a fraudulent investigation. Mocked was forensic science by fake investigations. Scorned was the dignity of courts by having Billy the Kid's corpse as a petitioner for his mother's exhumation, and by tricking the open records judge with forged forensic reports.

Most importantly for the future of the "Brushy Bill" hoax, the perpetrators were unpunished, unrepentant, and unexposed. They were left only with the unsatiated monetary greed and glory-seeking that had first united them as co-conspirators. There was eyeing of a comeback.

As to Oliver Pleasant "Brushy Bill" Roberts, he failed to get the Billy the Kid crown, but he got another incarnation. There had been Pardon-"Brushy" with his Fort Sumner steak restaurant. There had been *Alias*-"Brushy" with his crude grammar, racism, and dime novel "memories." There had been *Return*-"Brushy," gentrified, with a new family tree and Bible, and posthumously updated Billy the Kid history. And now there was "Billy the Kid Case"-"Brushy," in a bromance with Pat Garrett that stimulated murder of an innocent victim, and in a conspiracy with Garrett to be shot so that he could play dead on the carpenter's bench to bleed for future DNA.

The problem was that "Brushy's" hoax was degenerating to depths of ridiculousness that would challenge the credulity of his necessary dupes.

PART VII

THE RETURN OF "BRUSHY'S" TRUE-BELIEVER, W.C. JAMESON, AS A HOAXER

CHAPTER 1
RETURN OF FAKERY IN *BILLY THE KID: BEYOND THE GRAVE*

HOAXBUSTING "BILLY THE KID: BEYOND THE GRAVE"

W.C. Jameson was in the "Billy the Kid Case" hoax. His transcript of "Brushy's" Morrison tapes was used in its first "Probable Cause Statement" as the "Seventy-Seven Days of Doubt Document." In November of 2003, he "debated" Pat Garrett's biographer, Leon Metz, with "Brushy" claims for Editor-in-Chief Bob Boze Bell's *True West* magazine's "Was Brushy Bill Really Billy the Kid? Experts face off over new evidence" And, in 2004, he backed "Brushy" for Paul Hutton's History Channel documentary: "Investigating History: Billy the Kid."

And exposure to the hoaxers had an effect. By his 2005 *Billy the Kid: Beyond the Grave*, he ramped up clandestine fix-ups of "Brushy" for a new millennium of dupes.

MAKING A BETTER "BRUSHY"

Billy the Kid: Beyond the Grave is a surreptitious fix-up of Jameson's 1998 *The Return of the Outlaw Billy the Kid*. He was still relatively naïve. That makes it great for hoaxbusting; and it has his last accidental exposure of the fatal moon error.

While rehashing *The Return of the Outlaw Billy the Kid*, Jameson did fix-ups to hide "Brushy's" blunders, attacked mounting proofs that "Brushy" was not Billy, blamed opposition on tourism interests, and concluded that "Brushy" was Billy the Kid. Since his fix-ups contradicted his 1998 *The Return of the Outlaw Billy the Kid*, he hid its existence.

FIXING-UP MORRISON, HIS TALES, THE FAILED MABRY PARDON, AND SONNICHSEN

William V. Morrison, no longer faked as a lawyer, is a "paralegal." He finds "Brushy" through Jim Hines (as Jesse [sic] Evans); but J. Frank Dalton has his Jesse James claim hidden because real James was validated by DNA in 1995. The Mabry hearing is called unjust, though rocking "the world of Western American outlaw and lawman history." And C.L. Sonnichsen becomes a noted Billy the Kid historian. (Page 51)

FIX-UPS AND NEW ERRORS FOR "BRUSHY"

Billy the Kid: Beyond the Grave repeats past "Brushy" fakery, with "physical similarities;" the Billy Barlow shooting; a post-shooting multi-persona life; special knowledge tricks; fake Acton photo-match; the fake Affidavits, with new fake claim that "Lincoln County War veterans" identified him as the Kid; and the conspiracy theories claiming a hidden corpse identity.

Added is more **genealogy from the fake "Roberts family Bible"** from "Brushy's" wife Malinda; with added genealogical records from "Brushy's" step-grandson, Bill Allison. (Pages 6, 54) They add the names Bonney, Antrim, and McCarty.

FIX-UPS: As discussed, this "Bible" appears to be a forgery from 1989. (See pages 655-657 below) And genealogy faker, William Tunstill, is in the Bibliography for his 1988 *Billy the Kid and Me Were the Same*, **which faked records from Eulaine Haws, "Brushy's" real relative, as from a different Roberts family. (See pages 428-429 above)**

Added was a new lie: that "Brushy's" being from Texas gave "facility with Spanish" (Page 54); though he had none.

"Brushy," called by his made-up "William Henry Roberts," still lacks Billy's Silver City and Arizona years. For the Tunstall period, a fix-up adds the name "William Antrim" (Page 26); though it was actually when Billy started using Bonney. For the Lincoln County War Battle, "Brushy's" "[N-word]" racism is cleansed away. **An accidental reveal is "Brushy's" error that Pat Garrett was Sheriff Kimball's [sic] deputy *before* being elected sheriff** (Page 35); when, in fact, Garrett was deputized by Kimbrell after the election. The Santa Fe jailing is missing. The Lincoln jailing begins on April 6, when it was April 21, 1881, and ends with the "Brushy's" unchanged jailbreak tales.

For Fort Sumner, "Brushy's" fatal Celsa-Saval siblings error is fixed-up to making her Saval's wife, and Saval Garrett's brother-in-law by marriage; though retained is "Brushy's" tale of planning to leave with her! (Page 41) For "Brushy's" post-Billy-shooting life, Jameson fixes-up by meaningless updating.

THE HOAXBUSTING MOON

Hoaxbusting value of *Billy the Kid: Beyond the Grave*, is epitomized by still naïve Jameson's repeating of the fatal moon error. Like "Brushy," he backs logic of accidental killing of Billy Barlow, mistaken as "Brushy," **because it was so dark**.

So, from "Brushy's" original transcript, Jameson wrote: "**William Henry Roberts recalled that the night was dark but there was enough moonlight to make shadows.**" (Page 57) And after "Brushy was shot, Jameson quoted from the transcript: "**I lost my footing and fell on my face in the darkness.**" (Page 61) And from the transcript came "Brushy's" stating: "**Garrett knew by now that he killed the wrong man in the dark.**" (Page 64)

This dark night matched Jameson's *The Return of the Outlaw Billy the Kid*, and the transcript in the "Seventy-Seven Days of Doubt" Probable Cause Statement.

But Jameson, in his upcoming alliance with "Billy the Kid Case" hoaxers, would never again reveal "Brushy's" moon error. But it was too late. **Every time he and his hoaxing partners added bright moonlight for "Brushy" tales about July 14, 1881's night, it branded them as hoaxers.**

CELSA AS OMNISCIENT NARRATOR

Claiming "Brushy's" quote, Jameson faked a pseudo-Celsa Gutierrez's omniscient description of the shooting aftermath; one real Celsa could not know. Pseudo-Celsa stated that Garrett and his deputies were afraid to leave Maxwell's house because Billy's friends would shoot them; Garrett set a trap expecting Billy's visit; Garrett killed Barlow but passed him off as Billy, except he had a beard; Garrett had the grave dug by lantern light; and Deluvina was crying to pretend Billy was shot. So pseudo-"Brushy" stated that he realized that Garrett was hiding the corpse identity to collect the reward. (Pages 63-64)

THE "TRAVELING" ARMORY

"Brushy's" faked armory location in Lincoln's courthouse red-flagged Jameson's hoaxer transformation. In *Billy the Kid: Beyond the Grave* it is still wrongly across the hall from Garrett's office as "Brushy" had confabulated, though with an added unlabeled room beyond it. Jameson gave its fake diagrams in figures 24 and 25. (See page 671 below for Jameson's hoaxing a corrected location.)

FIX-UP: The second floor "diagram" fixes-up "Brushy's" misconception that one room - which he called the armory - was opposite Garrett's office. But Jameson learned there were *two* adjoining rooms. So he added a room. This is important, because once Jameson became a full hoaxer, forging "Brushy's" words, he would move the armory down the hall to its correct location, far from Garrett's office!

ATTACKING "BRUSHY'S" DEBUNKING

Jameson tried to counter some of "Brushy's" debunking that followed the Mabry pardon rejection and *Alias Billy the Kid*, concluding that all were wrong; as follows:

1) **NO HANDWRITING MATCH:** Claimed is that "Brushy's" handwriting could not be compared with Billy's, because **Billy's was unknown**. Made-up is that since Billy had little education, he did not write his known letters. An alleged handwriting expert, Howard Chandler, is cited to claim Billy's letters were "written by at least two men" who were "law clerks." (Page 108)

FAKERY: Billy's verbal sophistication and his writing all his letters, is presented above. (See pages 129-160)
Jameson's "expert" was confused by Billy's 1879 pardon bargain letters looking different from his 1881 Santa Fe jail letters. But he gave the explanation in his April 15, 1881 letter to Edgar Caypless: *"excuse bad writing. I have my handcuffs on."* And brilliant Billy's high literacy seemed like a law clerk's to the inadequate "expert!"
And "Brushy's" non-matching handwriting is known. Jameson (with Frederick Bean) called it a "scrawl." (*The Return of the Outlaw Billy the Kid*, Page 204) And, in 2012, Jameson described "Brushy's" trunk, from step-grandson,

Bill Allison, which had his three Big Chief writing tablets, which Bean said had his bad handwriting in pencil. (*Billy the Kid: The Lost Interviews*, Pages 35-36)

2) "BRUSHY" WAS OLIVER P. ROBERTS: Jameson denies Geneva Pittmon's December 16, 1987 letter (omitting her name); by claiming he could not be Oliver P. because he was born on August 26, 1879 in Arkansas, and "Brushy" was born on December 31, 1859 in Texas! Claimed is the alternate Roberts family with names McCarty, Antrim, and Bonney. (Page 108)

WRONG: True-believer Jameson cannot accept the logical response to the Pittmon letter: "Brushy" was 20 years too young to be Billy the Kid! And it would be 10 years until "Brushy's" relative, Roy L. Haws, published *Brushy Bill: Proof That His Claim to Be Billy the Kid Was a Hoax*, proving no separate Roberts family or different Roberts family Bible.

3) NO RECORD OF WILLIAM HENRY ROBERTS IN LINCOLN COUNTY: Jameson claims "Brushy" used the aliases William Bonney, Henry McCarty, and Henry Antrim. (Page 109)

FAKE FIX-UP: In *Alias Billy the Kid*, the least tampered "Brushy" hoax version, "Brushy" does not claim the aliases Henry McCarty and Henry Antrim, unknown to him and his team. As will be seen, Jameson, in his 2012 *Billy the Kid: The Lost Interviews*, claimed the latter two were in "Brushy's" trunk's Roberts family Bible, which is debunked for that book. (See pages 655-657 below)

4) "BRUSHY" WAS LEFT-HANDED; BILLY WAS NOT: Jameson, learning Billy was not left handed, says "Brushy" was actually ambidextrous, like Billy the Kid. (Page 109)

FAKE FIX-UP: For *Alias Billy the Kid*, "Brushy" and Morrison used the Billy the Kid tintype's right-to-left reversal to fake "Brushy" as left-handed. (*Alias Billy the Kid*, Page 6) In the Mabry hearing, "Brushy" was observed to favor his right. And Morrison may have fixed-up his book, because, on April 18, 1952, he wrote to Paul Blazer, "I was very much interested in hearing you say Billy the Kid was ambidextrous." And by a March 15, 1953 letter to a Lou Blachley, he wrote: "Roberts was ambidextrous, but preferably left-handed."

5) POE AND McKINNEY CONCURRED THAT GARRETT KILLED BILLY THE KID ON JULY 14, 1881: Jameson claims that Poe, who did not know Billy, eventually concurred; but McKinney did not. (Page 109)

FAKERY: Poe and McKinney were irrelevant, since Billy was identified by Pat Garrett, Peter Maxwell, Deluvina Maxwell, about 200 townspeople, and the official Coroner's Jury inquest for their Report of July 15, 1881. As to McKinney, Jameson merely used Morrison's double hearsay account in a June 29, 1855 letter to a William Waters, claiming that McKinney's cousin had said that McKinney had told relatives that *he* McKinney had "killed the man in Maxwell's bedroom 'by mistake and that the Kid got away.'" (Pages 70-71) That this McKinney fakery does not match "Brushy's" fake back-porch-Barlow account is ignored by Jameson.

6) BILLY BARLOW IS NON-HISTORICAL: You guessed it: Jameson says Billy Barlow was an alias. (Pages 109-110)

FAKERY: "Brushy's" entire killing scene is fake. Barlow is irrelevant, as well as non-existent.

7) ROBERTS COULD NOT SPEAK SPANISH: Jameson says "Brushy" lived in Mexico, so he spoke Spanish. And Morrison and Sonnichsen claimed "passable" Spanish. (Page 110)

FAKERY: "Brushy" made-up being in Mexico. And one of the many reasons "Brushy" failed his Mabry pardon hearing was *that he could not speak Spanish*. And, the least tampered source, *Alias Billy the Kid*, does not claim his Spanish speaking. And real Billy spoke more than "passable" Spanish. In his 1929 book, *A Frontier Doctor*, Henry Hoyt wrote: "[Billy] spoke Spanish like a native."

For his 2006 "Brushy"-debunking *Billy the Kid: His Real Name Was...*", author Jim Johnson noted that in "Brushy's" tale of being on his ranch in Old Mexico in 1899, he claimed "old Diaz seized everything," and fifty Mexican soldiers came to take his stock. So "Brushy" and his friends send an interpreter to talk to them. Johnson says bi-lingual Billy would not have needed an interpreter. (Johnson, Page 71)

8) NO RECORD OF "BRUSHY" WITH ROUGH RIDERS: Of course, Jameson claims he used an alias. (Page 110)

FAKERY: The Rough Rider fakery was addressed in 2006 by Jim Johnson in his *Billy the Kid: His Real Name Was...* The problem was more than an alias. "Brushy" had no first person knowledge. (Johnson, Pages 69-71) According to Johnson, "Brushy" did not know the transport specifics to Cuba; the Lieutenant Cook "Brushy" mentioned did not exist; and the "two months" of war "Brushy" confabulated were just June 22, 1898 to July 1, 1898. "Brushy" claimed being in charge of the horses, but there were *none*. It was a "dismounted cavalry unit." "Brushy" claimed a battle with "four officers shot in the back." There was no such battle. And "Brushy" left out the famous "charge up San Juan Hill!"

9) DON CLINE DISPUTED ANTI-HORSE THIEF ASSOCIATION EXISTENCE: Jameson said it did exist. (Page 110)

FAKERY: Existence would not prove "Brushy" was a member. And "Brushy" had bigger Don Cline problems. Jameson seemed unaware of Cline's 1988 manuscript titled *Brushy Bill Roberts: I Wasn't Billy the Kid*. Cline, as discussed above, saw the entire "Brushy" endeavor as a scam abusing a mentally ill man.

10) BILLY THE KID HAD BUCK TEETH: Jameson says "Brushy's" "incisors" (meaning front teeth) were extracted in 1931. (Page 110)

FAKERY: This was Morrison's fakery added to the Dewitt Travis Affidavit. Travis actually reported that "Brushy" had tusk-like canine teeth, pulled by a dentist.

11) THE DEATH SCENE ACCOUNTS OF PAT GARRETT AND JOHN W. POE AGREE: Jameson says they *did not* agree because of "discrepancies." (Page 110)

FAKERY: This repeats the hoax's faked "discrepancies" and hiding profuse identification of the body.

12) MORRISON WAS A FRAUD BY CLAIMING TO BE A LAWYER: Jameson says that he just claimed to be an attorney, not a lawyer; and they are not the same, since an attorney is a "person legally appointed to conduct business for another." He assed that Morrison took paralegal correspondence courses at LaSalle College in Chicago. (Page 111)

FAKERY: Jameson was hiding that in his 1998 *The Return of the Outlaw Billy the Kid*, he advertised Morrison as both: calling him a "graduate lawyer" on page 3, and an "attorney" on page 4.

Jameson's "attorney" definition is made-up to hide Morrison's compulsive self-aggrandizing lying; which, of course, created his "Brushy" hoax.

The Free Dictionary of legal terms states: "[Lawyer] is synonymous with attorney." Morrison, neither an attorney nor a lawyer, was a fraud.

Morrison's impersonating a lawyer was pervasive and continuous. (See pages 183-190 above)

13) **THE LINCOLN COUNTY HERITAGE TRUST PHOTOANALYSIS FOUND NO MATCH OF "BRUSHY" TO BILLY THE KID:** Like in his 1998 *The Return of the Outlaw Billy the Kid*, Jameson accused Dr. Thomas Kyle of an inaccurate study. Jameson's conspiracy theory blames "the [Lincoln County Heritage] Trust" having a "vested interest" in "Brushy" not being Billy to protect "tourist interests." (Page 113)

FAKERY: Omitted is that the study was done under the world-famous forensic anthropologist Clyde Snow; and "Brushy" showed no match to Billy Bonney's tintype image.

CONCLUSION: THE SAME OLD SCAM IN NEED OF NEW BLOOD

By his 2005 *Billy the Kid: Beyond the Grave* W.C. Jameson seemed to have hit a wall as to the number of times he could repeat the same "Brushy" tales and conspiracy theories; with some fix-ups to modernize the fakery. And evidence was piling up, striking at the heart of "Brushy's" claims. Jameson needed help.

By 2006, he got it, by accidentally meeting "Billy the Kid Case" hoaxer, Steve Sederwall. Though their hoaxes did not match beyond a death scene's sparing of the Kid, the mantra of "history is not as written" must have appealed to him.

So Jameson hit the big leagues of hoaxing; and, replicating his response to the "Brushy"-Morrison-Sonnichsen scam, he was awed, enamored, duped, and corrupted. The means to make "Brushy" Billy became justified by the ends to make him Billy.

CHAPTER 2
MORE FAKERY IN *BILLY THE KID: THE LOST INTERVIEWS*

PURE HOAXING

In 2012, came W.C. Jameson's *Billy the Kid: The Lost Interviews*. It was intentionally misleading: as if based on newly found, convincing, "lost interviews" for "Brushy Bill." In fact, they were just Morrison's 1949-1950 taped interviews used by Sonnichsen to write *Alias Billy the Kid*; and that Frederick Bean found in 1989, and were quoted from his transcript in *The Return of the Outlaw Billy the Kid*. As Jameson wrote in the "Acknowledgments": "Fred Bean ... located and transcribed the long-lost interview tapes, subsequently turning the transcriptions over to me." The change was in Jameson. He was now in league with hoaxers.

In his 2018 book, *Cold Case Billy the Kid*, Jameson stated that he first met Steve Sederwall in 2006 at a book signing for this 2005 *Billy the Kid: Beyond the Grave*. Tellingly, he enthused in its second edition "Preface" about him as "a dogged and determined retired federal investigator ... separating truth from legend ... who treated ... Billy the Kid-related events as historic cold cases ... [and got] information and facts heretofore unknown but entirely supportive of the revelations and contentions offered in this book." Of course, the "Billy the Kid Case" is unmentioned.

On the surface, the book follows *The Return of the Outlaw Billy the Kid's* let "Brushy" speak for himself formula. But that book is now hidden; and the quotes are by a pseudo-"Brushy," mouthing newly discovered facts and conspiracy theories!

And the bibliography has modern sources for its "prompting" upgrades. But absent are the works disproving "Brushy;" like: Frederick Nolan's 1992 *The Lincoln County War: A Documentary*

History for actual events; like Jerry Weddle's 1993 *Antrim is My Stepfather's Name's* on the Silver City and Arizona years; and like niece, Geneva Pittmon's fatal family Bible letter.

To be noted is that the publisher is Creative Texts Publishers of Barto, Pennsylvania; which then picked up the copyright of *Alias Billy the Kid* for its republishing in 2015.

UPGRADING THE "BRUSHY" HOAX

For the "Foreword," a Daniel A. Edwards, as author of *Billy the Kid: An Autobiography*, claims "Brushy" was Billy the Kid. He adds that the Mabry hearing was "treacherous," To him, Jameson is a savior with his 2004 *Billy the Kid: Beyond the Grave;* and "federal investigator" Steve Sederwall is praised for "extensive forensic studies" on Billy the Kid "crime scenes." So Edwards wants to end the "lie" about the death of Billy the Kid.

Jameson's "Preface" now unabashedly reveals the hoax's dark heart: defamation of Pat Garrett. He is called "dishonest, a debtor, an adulterer, a drunk, an inveterate gambler, and a liar" to claim his murdering an innocent victim and covering it up.

The "Brushy" hoax is updated for knowledgeable readers. His "illiteracy" is only in a fake quote: "I don't rightly know what the history books say ... Malinda reads me stuff ... She helps me write letters to my friends too." (Page 85) And the bi-lingual Billy obstacle is hidden.

Made-up is that evidence had accumulated proving he was Billy; only Garrett identified the corpse; there was no "inquest;" the swarthy bearded body was not Billy [using Singleton Ashenfelter's fake description (see pages 446-448 above)]; burial hid the corpse; and people saw live Billy after the burial.

Morrison is called a "paralegal;" but the book begins slyly with Daniel A. Edwards's "Foreword" stating: "In 1950, **a young lawyer named William V. Morrison**, shook up the world." Given is Morrison's finding "Brushy," his slipping shackles trick; and his scars reduced to just Billy's hip one.

The new Jameson lies more freely. He claims that Morrison introduced "Brushy" to "veterans of the Lincoln County War" who "immediately recognized" him as Billy the Kid. (Page 11) There were none. He was faking the fake Affidavits of non-War participants in *Alias Billy the Kid*. And, this time around, they are hidden to block checking.

"Brushy's" Billy Barlow killing is awkwardly fixed-up to add the Ashenfelter corpse, by calling him identical to fair "Brushy" except for dark skin and beard! And he is now killed vaguely "near Pete Maxwell's bedroom," with aftermath of "Brushy" being wounded and helped by two women and Frank Lobato.

"Brushy's" later multi-identity life is now fabricated as: "All of the claims have been investigated and verified." (Page 13) And the Mabry hearing is called unjust. Repeated are the well-worn conspiracy theories to explain historians' rejection; and New Mexico is blamed for a conspiracy to protect tourism. The fake Acton study is again touted.

Fakery from his *Billy the Kid: Beyond the Grave* is added with its "new" family Bible, with McCarty, Bonney, and Antrim - with Jameson lying that "Brushy" used the names himself.

THE MYSTERY TRUNK AND TAPES

For this book, the mystery truck, first mentioned in Jameson's 2005 *Billy the Kid: Beyond the Grave*, got a bigger role of holding the interview tapes and family Bible (unknown to "Brushy").

THE ORIGINAL TRUNK: Just a month after "Brushy's" death, on January 31, 1951, Morrison wrote to "Brushy's" widow about the trunk and its contents; stating: "I don't want you to worry about those things in the trunk ... When you get the things out you can put the negatives of the pictures he had in the envelope and mail them to me ... Then you can put the rest of the things in a cardboard box and send them to me ... I would like to have all the Newspaper clippings and magazine clippings of his riding days ... If you want to send the letters I wrote to him you can send them ... You should keep the things I copied for him. Also, you should keep the copy of the petition for pardon. You can send the Marshal Badge and I will have a copy made." In a letter of February 14, 1951 to a Ola Eberhard, Morrison wrote: "Mrs. Roberts just sent me some of Billy's papers, etc., and some of them concern the James [sic] and Daltons. Billy gave me his diary books some months ago." <u>There is no Roberts family Bible, which Morrison would, obviously, have mentioned</u>. Nor did he mention multiple other items now claimed by Jameson.

The sequence of this current trunk's changing contents is suspicious. In the *Beyond the Grave* book, Jameson said Frederick Bean simply learned of it in the 1980's (now made specifically

1989) from "Brushy's step-grandson Bill Allison, Malinda Allison's son's son. (*Beyond the Grave,* Page 84) Omitted is that Bean had used its tape recordings to make the transcript for their 1998 *The Return of the Outlaw Billy the Kid.* And it was claimed to have the Roberts family Bible "in the possession of ["Brushy's"] wife Melinda [sic]," as validating Aunt Bonney by having a "Catherine" [fixed-up from Katherine] Bonney. (*Beyond the Grave,* Page 54)

But for their 1998 *The Return of the Outlaw Billy the Kid,* nine years after Bean allegedly got that trunk with "Brushy's Bible," there was no mention of one. In that book, the alternate Bible is claimed to be owned by "the late Texas resident Martha Vada Roberts Heath," called "the daughter of Henry Oliver Roberts (brother to James Henry Roberts) and Caroline Dunn (sister to Mary Adeline Dunn)." (*The Return,* Pages 89-91) And the new genealogy (including the name "McCarty," unknown to "Brushy") was attributed to "[Martha Vada Roberts] Heath descendants" and "researcher " William Tunstill. (*The Return,* Page 91)

FAKERY: Tunstill's fake genealogy adding Billy Bonney's family names is discussed above. (See pages 425-429)

Jameson states that he had failed to get tapes from Morrison's daughter in 1985 and 1994. In 1994, he learned that his future co-author, Frederick Bean, had gotten Morrison's materials in 1989 from Bill Allison, of Temple, Texas; who had contacted Bean to say his grandfather was Billy the Kid. (Pages 35-36)

Jameson claimed Bean opened this trunk like archeologist Howard Carter opening the sealed lost tomb of Tutankhamen. "Bean unlatched the trunk lid ... within were a jumble of objects ... Bean lifted them out one by one." (Page 36) According to Jameson, Bean found three Big Chief writing tablets with bad handwriting in pencil; the five Affidavits from the Morrison book; various photos of Roberts, with one claimed to be aunt Catherine [fixed-up] Bonney **[possibly the fake Katherine Antrim picture in Morrison's book]**; an alleged Spanish War Service medal; an alleged Anti-Horsethief Association badge; two alleged "incisors" described as extracted by a dentist in Gladewater, Texas **[misstating Dewitt Travis's claimed extracted canine teeth]**; a .44 caliber revolver; and eight six-inch reels of tape, labeled as Morrison interviews; and the alternate Bible with Bonney, McCarty, and Antrim. (Pages 37-38)

THE TRUNK-BIBLE MYSTERY: But "Brushy" and team mentioned no Bible.

Jameson dated its find to 1989 by Bean, meaning before they wrote *The Return of the Outlaw Billy the Kid*. But, in that book, they claimed the alternate Bible belonged to Martha Vada Heath Roberts.

And its genealogy corresponded to William Tunstill's 1988 fakery in *Billy the Kid and Me Were the Same*. It seems clear that this Bible, if it exists at all, was a forgery using Tunstill. But its creator is uncertain.

But implied is forgery and planting evidence in the desperate drive to fake "Brushy" as Billy the Kid.

TRANSCRIBING THE "BRUSHY" TAPES

Jameson stated that Bean was lent Morrison's taped "Brushy" interviews by Bill Allison; and transcribed those not too deteriorated, making no copies. Bean apparently strove for accuracy; as Jameson wrote: "even spelling words as Roberts mispronounced them." (Page 40) Jameson reported Bean's true-believer awe: reporting that "Brushy" spoke as if personally involved in events. (Page 42) Jameson, however, admitted that revealed was that Sonnichsen had "heavily edited" "Brushy's" grammar, and added words for *Alias Billy the Kid*. (Page 42) That would make Bean's transcript the more accurate one.

Now deceased Bean ultimately gave Jameson his transcript. As Jameson wrote: "I was convinced that I was looking at the words of the outlaw, Billy the Kid." (Page 43) It was used for their 1998 *The Return of the Outlaw Billy the Kid* and the "Billy the Kid Case's" "Seventy-Seven Days of Doubt Document's" death scene - both with the dark moonless night error.

But, by 2012, Jameson admitted to altering the transcript by "corrections;" eliminating "Brushy's" repeating himself many times in "only a few minutes;" adding politically correct words; and "blended elements" of narrations. (Pages 43-44)

FORGING A TRANSCRIPT: So Jameson was forging the transcript and destroying evidence in order to fake "Brushy" as Billy - as had C.L. Sonnichsen.

In fact, a transcript is an identical copy, and a potential legal document. The *Merriam-Webster Dictionary* defines it as a "usually typed copy of dictated or recorded material," or "a reproduction of an original work." *Black's Law Dictionary* calls it an "official record ... copy." The whole point is its being *exactly the same as its original source*.

And forgery, in *Duhaime Legal Dictionary*, is "[t]he making of a false document knowing it to be false with intent that it should be used or acted on as genuine."

In fact, "Brushy's" bad grammar, racism, and historical errors *are* evidence that he was not Billy. And "repeating himself" was rehearsal for his special knowledge trick.

Jameson has merely created a work of fiction which proved his cross-over from true-believer to hoaxer.

FAKING "BRUSHY'S" WORDS

The transcript's format, as Jameson now revealed, is Morrison asking leading questions to set up "Brushy's" confabulating. But now Jameson fixed-up "Brushy's" responses. Still, his historical ignorance left many error-filled confabulations, and his additions are wrong or discovered after "Brushy's" day, and absent in "Brushy's" quotes in *Alias Billy the Kid* and *The Return of the Outlaw Billy the Kid*. So Jameson's forgeries stand out.

FORGING "BRUSHY" AS BILLY THE KID

Attempt is made to fix-up "Brushy" and his quotes.

1) Though not in *Alias Billy the Kid* - when "Brushy" and team would certainly have used it - the Bible from the mystery trunk is now used for his date of birth as December 31, 1859, and for his fake genealogy. (Page 45)

2) "Brushy" calls himself "William Henry Roberts," but says: "I mostly used names from some of my relatives like Antrim and McCarty and Bonney." (Page 45)

FAKING THE TRANSCRIPT: The "Brushy quote using historical names is added from the fake Bible.

Sonnichsen's footnote, proving "McCarty" was unknown to them, stated: "Another story, current in Silver City, says Billy the Kid was really named McCartney. See the *New Mexico Magazine* for December, 1948, reprint of an interview with H.H. Whitehill." (*Alias Billy the Kid*, Page 16)

And "Brushy" did not use McCarty, Antrim, and Bonney as his aliases. Antrim and Bonney were merely tacked on to his fake aunt Kathleen for name-dropping.

3) "Brushy" says about the Fritz life insurance policy case: "They [Murphy side] had a lot of trouble about McSween's law fee too. <u>McSween got the settlement money and the Murphy bunch claimed it. They rode over to Mesilla and got a court **order in the form of a writ** that would give them some of the goods in McSween's and Tunstall's store and a herd of blooded horses out at Tunstall's ranch. Sheriff William Brady was given the papers and he served them on McSween, padlocking the store until it was settled</u>." (Pages 64-65)

FAKING THE TRANSCRIPT: Added is everything underlined. Besides making "Brushy" sound like an attorney, it has information unknown to him and his team, who were unaware of specifics in the Fritz insurance case's legal maneuvers (and Jameson is wrong also).

Alias Billy the Kid stated: "They had a lot of trouble about McSween's law fee. Finally Murphy got a judgment or attachment against McSween and started to pick up partnership property of Tunstall's. We turned the cattle over to the law. Tunstall had a herd of fine horses of his own. He decided that we would drive the horses over to Lincoln and surrender them until the case was cleared up." (*Alias Billy the Kid*, Page 25)

4) "Brushy" says: "Tunstall was a good man. He had been good to me and treated me like a gentleman." (Page 66)

DISHONESTLY RECYCLED QUOTE: For his 2018 book, *Cold Case Billy the Kid*, Jameson attributed this quote to real Billy Bonney, hiding that it was "Brushy's!"

5) "Brushy" says: "Dick Brewer was a foreman at the Tunstall Ranch, so it was up to him what we would do about the way they shot John. That day at the funeral we asked Brewer how we ought to go about settling the score." (Page 68)

FAKING THE TRANSCRIPT: Not in *Alias Billy the Kid*, this is made-up and wrong. Brady, responsible for arrests, refused So Tunstall's men became Regulators, and Justice of the Peace John Wilson gave them arrest warrants. And

Billy *was not at Tunstall's funeral.* He was jailed by Brady, who confiscated his Winchester '73 carbine.

6) "Brushy" says: "We'd have won that war, too, if those (black) soldiers of Dudley's had been kept out." (Page 78)

FAKING THE TRANSCRIPT: Racist "Brushy" actually said: "We'd have won the war too, if those [N-word] soldiers of Dudley's had been kept out." (*Alias Billy the Kid,* Page 29)

7) "Brushy" says: "The real battle broke out when we took over Montoya's house across the street from the tower." (Page 78)

TRANSCRIPT FIX-UP: *Alias Billy the Kid* had "Montaña's house." (*Alias Billy the Kid,* Page 30) Both names are wrong. It was José Montaño's house - as real Billy knew.

8) "Brushy" says: "They started firing on us as we rode in that day, so we fought back at them. The battle lasted three days. It was July, and on the 19th, on the last day, Colonel Dudley rode into town with those (black) soldiers." (Pages 78-79)

FAKING THE TRANSCRIPT: In *Alias Billy the Kid*, racist "Brushy" had no date; stating: "They started firing on us as we rode in that day, so we fought back at them. On the last day, Colonel Dudley rode into town with those [N-word] soldiers." (*Alias Billy the Kid,* Page 30)

9) "Brushy" says: "If we could have kept them (black) soldiers out at Stanton, we could have whipped Peppin's posse all right." (Page 79)

FAKING THE TRANSCRIPT: Racist "Brushy" said: "If we could have kept them [N-word] soldiers out at Stanton, we could have whipped Peppin's posse." (*Alias Billy the Kid,* Page 30)

10) "Brushy" says: "[Dudley] said that he did not have the authority to interfere, but some of his (black) soldiers was up on the side of the hill firing at us with the Murphy men." (Page 79)

FAKING THE TRANSCRIPT: Racist "Brushy" actually said: "Dudley's] [N-word] soldiers was up on the side of that hill firing at us with the Murphy men." (*Alias Billy the Kid*, Page 30)

11) "Brushy" says: "We opened the back door and looked out just as Bob Beckwith and some of them (black soldiers) tried to rush us, started to come in." (Page 80)

FAKING THE TRANSCRIPT: Racist "Brushy" said: "We opened the back door and looked out just as Bob Beckwith and some of them [N-word]s started to come in." (*Alias Billy the Kid*, Page 31)

12) "Brushy" says: "**Folliard [sic]**, Salazar, and the rest of our boys started through." (Page 81)

FAKING THE TRANSCRIPT: Rewriting Tom O'Folliard's name would not be explicable until Jameson's 2018 *Cold Case Billy the Kid* where it was Steve Sederwall's absurd claim that he discovered the name, when he was just seeing a census taker's misspelling. But this revealed that Sederwall was behind-the-scenes for this book.

In fact, this name discredited "Brushy," who always used "O'Folliard;" stating: "O'Folliard, Salazar, and the rest of our boys started through." (*Alias Billy the Kid*, Page 31)

13) "Brushy" says: "We didn't know it then, but the fight we lost at McSween's was the turning point for us in the war. With McSween and Tunstall dead, we didn't have a way to make a living. We drifted down to San Patricio for a while, but there were warrants out for us and we had to stay on the dodge. I was bitter about what they'd done to McSween and Tunstall." (Page 81)

FAKING THE TRANSCRIPT: This complex explanation of the War was not in *Alias Billy the Kid*; appearing made-up.

14) "Brushy" is quoted about "the winter of '79," being with Tom "Folliard" and meeting with J.J. Dolan and Jesse Evans "to talk about things," with a "fellow named Campbell along;" and that with "Tunstall and McSween dead, Tom and I didn't have much of a stake in things." And they shake hands. (Page 86)

FAKING THE TRANSCRIPT: *Alias Billy the Kid* had no Dolan initials or "Folliard." "Brushy" merely stated:

"In the winter of '79 we got together with Dolan and Evans and agreed to quit fighting each other." (*Alias Billy the Kid*, Page 33)

15) "Brushy" says: "When we walked out of the saloon, we parted company. Just down the street, **I saw Mrs. McSween** and her lawyer, Chapman, walk up to Evans, Dolan, and Chapman." (Page 86)

INADVERTENT REVEAL OF SONNICHSEN'S FIX-UP: This is likely real. Jameson's ignorance leaves in this fatal error of Susan McSween at the Chapman shooting. Dishonest Sonnichsen had done his own fix-up for *Alias Billy the Kid*; writing: "When we came out of the salon that night in Lincoln we run into Chapman, the lawyer for Mrs. McSween. Campbell and Dolan killed him in cold blood. I was standing there." (*Alias Billy the Kid*, Page 33)

16) "Brushy" has a long quote of Governor Wallace wanting to "clean" up the Lincoln mess, "looking into cattle contracts controlled by the Catron Ring up in Santa Fe," and wanting to stop "crooked dealings." So he tells Tom he wants a meeting with Wallace to see "if he is on the level," and to testify "about the murder of Chapman." Wallace agrees, and "Brushy" states: "I sent word back that I would come in if he would annul those indictments against me. I had a friend who spelled it out in a letter for me, what I wanted from Governor Wallace." (Page 87)

FAKING THE TRANSCRIPT: This is not in *Alias Billy the Kid*, where "Brushy" said: "I heard that Governor Wallace had offered a thousand dollars for me if I would come and testify. I wrote and told him I would come in if he would annul those indictments." (*Alias Billy the Kid*, Page 33) And inserted is the hoax's fakery of someone writing for him.

"Brushy," his team, and Jameson were unaware of the pardon bargain, so Jameson left "Brushy's" errors of "standing trial on my indictments," "testifying against Dudley" at a "court martial," and testifying against Chapman. (Pages 88-89) The pardon bargain was just for the Chapman murder testifying.

17) "Brushy" is quoted about the arranged arrest with Sheriff Kimbrell, with long text about testifying in a "board of Inquiry in Colonel Dudley's case," then being told his trial would be in Mesilla, and leaving because that was a switch from Lincoln. Omitted is the Chapman murder testimony. (Pages 89-90)

FAKING THE TRANSCRIPT: This is not in *Alias Billy the Kid*, where "Brushy" mixes-up Ira Leonard and Albert Jennings Fountain, gets Dolan "and his men" indicted, and testifies in the "Dudley trial." (*Alias Billy the Kid*, Page 34)

The quote is made-up for fix-ups of the Leonard-Fountain errors, and correcting to Dudley's "board of Inquiry." But ignorant Jameson cut out "Brushy's" claim of getting Chapman case indictments: the pardon's punch line! Instead, Jameson has "Brushy" exiting jailing before testifying; thus, breaking the bargain himself!

18) "Brushy" says: "Deputy Sheriff Kip McKinney, Tom's own cousin and one of Garrett's posse, wouldn't give Tom a drink of water." (Page 96)

FAKING THE TRANSCRIPT: *Alias Billy the Kid* stated: "His cousin, Kip McKinney, one of Garrett's posse, wouldn't give Tom a drink." (*Alias Billy the Kid*, Page 37) Fix-up to "Deputy Sheriff" fails, since McKinney was just deputized by Garrett for the Fort Sumner killing of Billy.

19) "Brushy" says: "I had known McKinney some time before all the difficulties ... It turned out he was just another coward like the rest of them Murphy men and Garrett men. I learned years later that McKinney never lived down riding with Garrett, that it left a bad taste in his mouth for the rest of his life." (Page 96)

FAKING THE TRANSCRIPT: This is not in *Alias Billy the Kid*. It is made-up to defame Garrett.

20) "Brushy" says about the Bowdre shooting: "Charlie wore a large sombrero like mine when he stepped out the door that morning and I figured they must have thought Charlie was me." (Page 97)

FAKING THE TRANSCRIPT: *Alias Billy the Kid* stated: "He wore a large hat like mine. They thought it was me."

(*Alias Billy the Kid,* Page 37) Added is "sombrero" and polished grammar. More subtly, "Brushy" was unaware of Billy's bi-culturalism, of which the sombrero was part.

21) "Brushy" says: "While I was [in the anta Fe jail] I had a letter sent to Governor Wallace asking him to come and talk to me." (Page 101)

FAKING THE TRANSCRIPT: *Alias Billy the Kid* stated: "I wrote to Governor Wallace to come and talk to me." (*Alias Billy the Kid,* Page 39) Fixed-up is "Brushy's" gaffe revealing that he could write.

22) "Brushy" says: "I pleaded to the federal indictment. It was for killing Buckshot Roberts and I never did. It was thrown out of court." (Page 102)

FAKING THE TRANSCRIPT: *Alias Billy the Kid* stated: "I pleaded to the federal indictment and it was thrown out of court." (*Alias Billy the Kid,* Page 39) A fix-up is adding "Buckshot" Roberts, unknown to "Brushy" and team.

23) Answering a Morrison question about arrests for the Brady killing, a long text garbles previous pardon bargain misinformation about "Judge Leonard" not being "there like the governor promised," "Colonel Fountain" being appointed as attorney, being before "the grand jury that brought in indictments" against Dolan and Chapman, testifying at Fort Stanton, being threatened with Mesilla trial, Judge Bristol being a "Murphy sympathizer and friend of Tom Catron at the head of the Santa Fe Ring," having to be a Mason to stand a chance, and leaving Lincoln's jail. (Pages 104-105)

FAKING THE TRANSCRIPT: This was not in *Alias Billy the Kid*. It is a rewrite of "Brushy's" (or Sonnichsen's) garbling of the 1979 pardon bargain trials and the 1881 Mesilla trial.

24) "Brushy" goes on about Peppin's Mesilla trial testimony being unfair; his trying to shoot Matthews, not Brady; Pat Garrett saying Governor Otero said Billy the Kid never shot at Brady; and nobody knowing who killed Brady; but he, as Billy, was blamed for his "reputation." (Pages 104-105)

FAKING THE TRANSCRIPT: This is not in *Alias Billy the Kid* for the Mesilla trial. It is made-up from that book's

footnote about Otero's fake claim about Matthews. It is a fix-up to show the Brady trial as unjust. But, like for "Brushy" and his team, Jameson is too ignorant about that Regulator killing to make a correct argument.

25) "Brushy" says about transport to Lincoln: "John McKinney, who fought against me in the war, sat on the back seat." (Page 106)

FAKING THE TRANSCRIPT: *Alias Billy the Kid* stated: "John Kinney, who fought against me in the war, sat on the back seat." (*Alias Billy the Kid*, Page 40) It is not clear if Jameson wrongly fixed-up the correct "Kinney" name, or if "Brushy" had mixed-up his name-dropping, and had been corrected with an earlier Sonnichsen fix-up.

26) "Brushy" says for the jailbreak: "I could lay my thumbs flat against my palms and the irons would slide right off ... (Page 109) The date for my execution was only a few days away. I knew I had to make a break." (Page 111)

FAKING THE TRANSCRIPT: This is not in *Alias Billy the Kid*. It adds an error: from the jailbreak on April 28, 1881 to hanging date of May 13, 1881 was over two weeks, not a few days. Billy escaped seven days after arriving.

27) "Brushy" says when escaping: "[O]ld man Gauss and someone else was standing near Bell's body." (Page 113)

FAKING THE TRANSCRIPT: This is fixed-up from the *Alias Billy the Kid's* "Goss." (*Alias Billy the Kid*, Page 44)

30) "Brushy" says about cutting his leg irons: "It was 'ol Cipio Salazar. He was cousin to Ygenio ... Ol' Cipio had a time of it, he did." (Page 116)

FAKING THE TRANSCRIPT: *Alias Billy the Kid* stated only: "I got on the horse and rode out of Lincoln to the west and up the canyon to the home of a friend, who cut the bolts in my leg irons." (*Alias Billy the Kid*, Page 45)

This fake quote uses Sonnichsen's footnote, which stated: "Mrs. Bernardo Salazar, adopted daughter of Higinio [sic - Ygenio], told Morrison on October 11, 1949, that Higinio's [sic] cousin, Sepio Salazar, was the one who cut the bolts." (*Alias Billy the Kid*, Page 45)

FIX-UPS OF THE FAKE DEATH SCENE

For the death scene, Jameson has his pseudo-"Brushy" mouth Sonnichsen-Morrison conspiracy theories and "Billy the Kid Case" hoax claims. These are examples:

1) "Brushy" has a long passage before the Fort Sumner shooting saying he wanted to "have a talk with Mr. Pat Garrett" to set things "straight between us" because "[w]e used to be friends before the Lincoln County War." (Page 121)

FAKING THE TRANSCRIPT: This was not in *Alias Billy the Kid*. It fabricates the "Billy the Kid Case" hoax friendship. "Brushy" had accidental killing of Billy Barlow when Garrett was *trying to kill him*.

2) "Brushy" says about the shooting: "I pulled one of my .44's and ran through the door, trying to see in the dark. I ran through the gate into Maxwell's back yard **into the bright moonlight**. Two more shots came from a shadow beside the Maxwell house. I started shooting at the shadows along the house." (Page 124)

EXPOSING JAMESON AS A HOAXER BY HIS FORGED TRANSCRIPT: "Brushy's" fatal error was making-up a dark night for July 14, 1881, as Jameson revealed in his 1998 *The Return of the Outlaw Billy the Kid*. So now correcting "Brushy's" words to bright moonlight is a red flag for hoaxing. Sonnichsen did it in *Alias Billy the Kid*. (See pages 364, 366, 368) Now Jameson did it.

3) "Brushy" is quoted about Maxwell's beef: "Silva said if one of us would go over to Maxwell's and get beef, he would cook it for us. He said Maxwell had one on his back porch hanging from a rafter hook, killed on the day before ..." (Page 123) "[After hearing shots] [f]rom the corner of my eye I saw a body lying on the back porch. A candle was lit in the alcove where the beef was hung and I knew it had to be Barlow." (Page 124)

**FAKING THE TRANSCRIPT: In *Alias Billy the Kid* and *The Return of the Outlaw Billy the Kid*, says only: "One of their shots had killed my partner on the back porch." (*Alias Billy the Kid*, Page 49; *The Return of the Outlaw*, Page 113)

The quote is faked for the back porch location of the shooting from Sonnichsen's prompt source footnote of his

April 15, 1944 interview with Jack Fountain about the side of beef as beside Maxwell's bedroom.

4) "Brushy" is "quoted" for a two page description of being shot and running down a long "alley" behind the Maxwell house to an "adobe shack." (Pages 125-126)

FAKING THE TRANSCRIPT: This is not in *Alias Billy the Kid*; which only stated: "I stumbled into the gallery of an adobe behind Maxwell's yard fence." (*Alias Billy the Kid*, Page 49)

5) "Brushy" says about his rescue that when he came to he saw "another woman in the room ... She was another of Saval's sisters, named Celsa, and she had been a sweetheart of mine at one time." (Page 127)

FAKING THE TRANSCRIPT: This is not in *Alias Billy the Kid* at this location, but was "Brushy's" Celsa-Saval-sibling mistake which was given earlier in the book.
Jameson's ignorance limited his fix-ups.

6) "Brushy" says: "Celsa confirmed what I had guessed. Garrett and a posse had been laying for me over at Maxwell's. They knew Pete and I were friends and that I'd stop by to see him if I was in this country. Me and Barlow rode into town late and I figured Mrs. Maxwell was already in bed by the time we got there. I aimed to talk to Pete in the morning." (Page 128)

FAKING THE TRANSCRIPT: This is not in *Alias Billy the Kid*. Jameson was unaware that Billy hid in Maxwell's sheep camps; so he had "Brushy" just visit "the country."

7) "Brushy" gives Celsa's long quote explaining the plot to hide that the body was Barlow's; and "Brushy's" ruminating about Garrett doing it to get the reward.

PAST FAKING THE TRANSCRIPT: This is not in *Alias Billy the Kid*, which stated: "Celsa came running in and said they had killed Barlow and they were passing off his body as mine." (*Alias Billy the Kid*, Page 50) This had been made-up for omniscient pseudo-Celsa in *The Return of the Outlaw Billy the Kid*. (See page 647 above)

To be noted is mismatch with the "Billy the Kid Case" hoax's friend Garrett, purposefully shooting *him* to play dead on the bench (to leave blood for DNA); and Billy sneaking off while Garrett put the murdered victim there.

8) "Brushy" says in answer to a Morrison question about Garrett's claim of killing Billy the Kid: "I wondered how he figured to get away with it. I had lots of friends in town. Would they go along with Garrett's ploy. Garrett knew by now he had killed the wrong man in the dark ... [Barlow looked like me] [b]ut in daylight, a lot of folks who knew me would know they had the wrong body. I couldn't figure it, unless Garrett was making a try at collecting the reward ... [He] was out of his bailiwick in San Miguel County. Hilario Romero was sheriff there ... Sheriff Romero would have to appoint a coroner's jury to sign the death certificate, not Garrett ... [T]hey would have trouble rounding up a coroner's jury that didn't know what I looked like." (Pages 130-131)

FAKING THE TRANSCRIPT: This is not in *Alias Billy the Kid*. This is made-up to put the hoax's fake conspiracy theories in pseudo-"Brushy's" mouth: Garrett hid the corpse identity to collect the Billy the Kid reward; Garrett was out of his jurisdiction in Sheriff Romero's San Miguel County; no Coroner's Jury had been called, since it was Sheriff Romero's responsibility; and the jurymen could not recognize Billy the Kid.

9) "Brushy" states that there was another reason for Garrett being in trouble: that Barlow had a .41 double action revolver, which he would not use because they jam. (Page 131)

FAKING THE TRANSCRIPT: This is not in *Alias Billy the Kid*. It builds on Jameson's 1998 *The Return of the Outlaw Billy the Kid* where he used the Colt .41 to claim Garrett lied about dead Billy having one.

This fake discrepancy was lifted from Morrison. He used it in his January 23, 1955 letter to George Fitzparick, Editor of *New Mexico Magazine*; stating: 'In all my research I failed to find any evidence that they used anything except the old reliable .44 & .45 single-actions in that country at that time. Furthermore, Garrett knew quite well that the Kid fired only the large caliber, single-actions, like the rest of the law and lawless."

In fact, the Colt .41 Thunderer was a smaller revolver that still had six bullets. It was an ideal hide-away.

10) "Brushy" ruminates about Garrett digging a grave the night of the killing to hide that the body was Barlow's, since killing Billy the Kid would have made him famous and he would have showed off the body. And he claims gravedigger Jesus Silva, who knew him, kept secret the body's identity. (Pages 131-132)

FAKING THE TRANSCRIPT: This is not in *Alias Billy the Kid*. It is faked to set up conspiracy theorizing about Garrett hiding the corpse's identity for personal gain.

11) "Brushy" says: "**It crossed my mind that Garrett might be trying to help me. We'd been friends once,** back when he first came to this country." (Page 132) "Brushy's" confabulation for special knowledge that Garrett had been a buffalo hunter who killed a partner over hides is inserted here as proof of "friendship." "Brushy" continues that, as Lincoln County Sheriff, Garrett had to pursue him, but wonders if "he saw his chance to let me get away clean and make a fresh start for myself.'" (Pages 132-133)

EXPOSING JAMESON AS A COMPLICIT "BILLY THE KID CASE" HOAXER BY HIS FAKED TRANSCRIPT: This is not in *Alias Billy the Kid* - except for the wrong prompt source quote about Garrett's buffalo hunter murder used in another context. (*Alias Billy the Kid*, Page 36. (See page 346 above)

This is Jameson's attempt to make "Brushy" fit the "Billy the Kid Case" hoax based of the Garrett friendship motive for the innocent victim killing to let Billy go free.

But it contradicts "Brushy's" description of Garrett's effort to kill him as Billy the Kid. As Jameson's own "Brushy" text quoted: "My partner walked right into the trap, and the trap had likely been set for me ... I knew I had to get away from Maxwell's before they killed me." (Pages 124-125)

12) "Brushy" is quoted that Garrett could keep the corpse identity secret because the only people who knew it was not him were Celsa, Jesus Silba, the Mexican woman who took him in, and a Frank Lobato; and they would keep a secret.

FAKING THE TRANSCRIPT: This is not in *Alias Billy the Kid*. It is made-up pseudo-"Brushy" mouthing conspiracy theories to back the "Brushy" hoax's lies of hiding the night vigil and the Coroner's Jury Report.

13) "Brushy" gives a flashback of a **Frank Lovato** having checked Fort Sumner and reporting to him that Barlow's body had been taken to the carpenter's shop wrapped in a sheet to hide its identity; Poe could not recognize him, so could not identify the body; Garrett sealing the house to hide the body; and a "coroner's jury was appointed to sign the death certificate so Garrett could file for the reward." "Brushy" adds that there were two coroner's jury reports, with the first lost and Garrett making people sign a second with different signers; that Milnor Rudulph was not the real president, and never saw the body. He adds that Garrett succeeded by putting Barlow in Billy the Kid's grave and taking the fake report to Santa Fe to get his reward. (Pages 134-135)

EXPOSING JAMESON AS AN ACTIVE HOAXER AND COMPLICIT WITH THE "BILLY THE KID CASE" HOAX BY HIS FAKED TRANSCRIPT: This is not in *Alias Billy the Kid*. It fakes omniscient Lobato to match the "Billy the Kid Case" hoax's carpenter's bench scenario by putting sheet-hidden Barlow on it, and having the coroner's jury shield Garrett. It adds Morrison-Sonnichsen's two coroner's jury reports by "Paco" Anaya.

This is now out-of-control hoaxing and forging. And it ridiculously requires sheepherder, Frank Lobato, to know insiders' information about a cover-up of the innocent victim. And, if real Lobato had found it out, it would only prove general gossip among townspeople, and no postulated conspiracy of them to keep the secret!

At this point, Jameson's "transcript" goes on to "Brushy's" faked life after the death scene, and is irrelevant to Billy Bonney.

DISCUSSION

In *Billy the Kid: The Lost Interviews*, W.C. Jameson created a fictionalized, grammatically-sophisticated, politically correct, more historically savvy pseudo-"Brushy," intended to fake a better match with real Billy and the "Billy the Kid Case" hoax. Added contrivance was having pseudo-"Brushy" mouth the hoax's conspiracy theories. This is active hoaxing. This is a forged transcript. And, since hoaxer-forger Steve Sederwall's input was implied, he may have assisted surreptitiously. But, from now on, Sederwall would be revealed as in the driver's seat for this dupe.

CHAPTER 3
DEFAMING IN *PAT GARRETT: THE MAN BEHIND THE BADGE*

THE "BRUSHY" HOAX'S HEART OF DARKNESS

W.C. Jameson's 2016 *Pat Garrett: The Man Behind the Badge* brought to the forefront the malicious core of the "Brushy Bill" and "Billy the Kid Case" hoaxes: the defamation of Pat Garrett as a heinous murderer of an innocent victim. And, though not a co-author, Steve Sederwall was Jameson's acknowledged source: "Intrepid investigator Steve Sederwall turned over more stones and found more pertinent information and evidence regarding Pat Garrett ... Billy the Kid, and others than all the so-called experts put together." (Page 223) The multiple hoaxes in this book are debunked in my 2019 *The Cold Case Billy the Kid Mehahoax: The Plot to Steal Billy the Kid's Identity and Defame Sheriff Pat Garrett as a Murderer*. But its fake "investigations" apparently appealed to Jameson as proof that "history is not as written."

Amusingly, right from the start, wised-up Jameson took no more chances with "Brushy's" fatal "dark night" moon error, which the more honest version of himself had exposed in his 1998 *The Return of the Outlaw Billy the Kid*. He now officiously announced July 14, 1881's moon was full three nights earlier, in waning phase, with 87 percent brightness! (Page x) Also fixed-up was the correct armory location in the Lincoln courthouse.

Jameson also used his forged transcripts of Morrison's 1949-1950 taped "Brushy" interviews from his 2012 *Billy the Kid: The Lost Interviews*. His pseudo-"Brushy" now mouths the conspiracy theories. The "Brushy" hoax was bloating into the monstrosity that would emerge in two more years, in his 2018 collusion with "Billy the Kid Case" hoaxers for his book: *Cold Case Billy the Kid*.

More ludicrous is that in faking Pat Garrett's history, Sederwall supplied information that "Brushy" did not know - like the Secret Service investigation involving Billy Bonney, or a fabrication that Billy was a Brockway gang counterfeiter; thereby canceling "Brushy" out as a Billy the Kid contender!

Given free rein, Sederwall rolled out new hoaxes. He made-up that the death scene participants lied because they described a outside door to Maxwell bedroom, but it had no such door! He made-up that Pete Maxwell became a cattle company cook and told someone that Billy the Kid was not shot by Garrett!

Dr. Henry Lee reappears for fake forensics - done for Sederwall personally, with his assistants as Tom Sullivan, Kim [sic – Calvin] Ostler, and David Turk (as from the U.S. Marshals Service, but with "Historian" hidden to fake him as a Marshal), and Mike Haag (as a firearms examiner) - and with the "Billy the Kid Case" hidden. (Pages 206-207) But, this time around, Sederwall faked Lee's fakery! Lee's crouching chicken Garrett and shot washstand scam gets addition of a fake room diagram.

The exhumations for DNA become Sederwall's own investigation that was blocked by tourist interests. (Page 97)

Relegated to the "Appendix," "Brushy's" tale is given. (Pages 203-205, 215-216) William V. Morrison is a "paralegal;" and C.L. Sonnichsen as "a noted author, historian, and folklorist" from Harvard. There is no pardon hearing! *Alias Billy the Kid* gives "remarkable evidence," but get hostile response from historians, including death threats, to keep the "status quo." Subsequent research is said to have prove that "Brushy's" genealogy had the names Antrim, McCarty, and Bonney; that his photo matched the Billy the Kid tintype; that his transcribed tapes (ala *Billy the Kid: The Lost Interviews*) proved the special knowledge trick, since he was illiterate. Ergo, "Brushy" was Billy the Kid. And his fantastical life after the Fort Sumner shooting scene was exactly as he told it.

STAGE SET FOR A MEGAHOAX

Jameson was poised to release the "Billy the Kid Case" hoaxers for a rerun in harebrained hope that their counter-historical claims would point to "Brushy" as Billy. But all he was about to achieve was becoming the author of a megahoax; once again a dupe for the same kind of charlatans as huckster William V. Morrison, and historian wannabe, C.L. Sonnichsen.

PART VIII

"BRUSHY BILL" IN THE *COLD CASE BILLY THE KID* MEGAHOAX

CHAPTER 1
THE RETURN OF "BRUSHY" IN A MEGAHOAX

A BLOATED IMPLODING HOAX

Sixty-eight years after "Brushy" and William V. Morrison failed to trick honorable Governor Thomas Jewett Mabry with their Billy the Kid imposter hoax, and 15 years after corrupt Governor Bill Richardson tried to trick the public with his "Billy the Kid Case" rerun of that imposter hoax, W.C. Jameson fused them, added more hoaxing, and created a megahoax in his 2018 *Cold Case Billy the Kid: Investigating History's Mysteries.*

The book incorporated "Billy the Kid Case" hoaxers. Its "Acknowledgements" cite: Gary Graves, Dr. Henry Lee, Rick Staub, Tom Sullivan, Dale Tunnell, and Dave Turk. (Page 181) Sullivan's death in 2013, proves the long association. Featured is Steve Sederwall, as his book's major contributor. (Page 181) As Jameson gushed: "[H]is aggressive investigations into a variety of Billy the Kid-related events ... differed, sometimes dramatically, from established history." (*Cold Case*, Page v) Jameson advertised him as a "cop" with an "investigative agency." (Page vi) Here, at last, was a partner for the Morrison-Sonnichsen history-is-not-as written trick.

But Jameson missed that "Brushy's" special knowledge trick was squelched in the ballooning megahoax, with Sederwall manufacturing fakery faster than he had forged Dr. Henry Lee reports. And "Brushy" would have been unaware of this new Billy the Kid, who was a counterfeiter William Brockway's gang, a murderer of an informant on him, in a mail theft conspiracy, and a partner of Jesse James. I exposed the hoaxing in my 2019 *The Cold Case Billy the Kid Megahoax: The Plot to Steal Billy the Kid's Identity and Defame Sheriff Pat Garrett as a Murderer.*

THE HOAX IN THE TITLE

Like with *Alias Billy the Kid*, which was not Billy's alias; *Cold Case: Billy the Kid* had no cold case! There was just "Brushy's" fable that Pat Garrett accidentally killed Billy Barlow, and hid it; and the "Billy the Kid Case's" lie that Garrett murdered an innocent victim to save Billy and did a cover-up.

"FOREWORD" AND "INTRODUCTION"

Jameson dated his first meeting with Steve Sederwall to 2006. (*Billy the Kid: Beyond the Grave*, Page ----) In that year, the illegal John Miller exhumation was exposed, the hoaxers were feted at the Cannes Film Festival, and I began my open records investigation of the "Billy the Kid Case." That year, Sederwall had not yet resigned as a Lincoln County Deputy Sheriff in order to pretend he did Case 2003-274 as a private hobby. To him, Jameson must have seemed like a dupe made in heaven. So he shape-shifted for Jameson to a "private detective" (Page x) "investigating western cold cases," with emphasis on Billy the Kid, since 1998. (Pages vi-vii) And the only whiff of me was Jameson's acceptance of Sederwall's martyr for the truth scam. As Jameson wrote: **"[H]e was once hauled into court by one of the rabid embracers of the status quo."** (Page x)

And, though the "Brushy" hoax did not match the "Billy the Kid Case" hoax, with its Garrett bromance and Billy-playing-dead-and-bleeding-on-bench, Jameson was in no position to quarrel with his new larger-than-life hero; who used fancy words like "crime scene" and "Deoxyribonucleic acid – DNA;" which Jameson called Sederwall's "investigation kit." (Pages vii-viii)

So Jameson's lead-in quotes C.L. Sonnichsen's biographer Dale L. Walker's *Legends and Lies:* "All history is a mystery" (Page viii) Jameson added that the "published" history of Billy the Kid is "fraudulent." The truth would now come from his mouthing of Sederwall; who, according to himself, had done the whole (unnamed) "Billy the Kid Case" himself, while thwarted by politicians - "up to and including the Governor of New Mexico" - panicked by *his* findings as risking tourism! (Page xviii)

CHAPTER 2
FAKING KNOWLEDGE

RETURN OF THE IGNORANCE OF *THE RETURN OF THE OUTLAW BILLY THE KID*

For this book, Billy the Kid history is still stuck in antique historical ignorance, with new surreptitious fix-ups and errors. Scholarly books are called "legend." (Page xiv) Added are "crime scene investigations" by Steve Sederwall (Page 11); while narrator Jameson informs readers that Sederwall uses "tells" - a "cop term" to find "suspicious discrepancies." (Page xvi)

FAKING EARLY YEARS

Jameson claims that Billy the Kid's origins were unknown (Page 1) as proof that "Brushy" filled them in.

HOAXING: By 2018, "Brushy" had been debunked by his Roberts family members as 20 years too young.

FAKING TUNSTALL PERIOD

For the Tunstall period (Pages 4-10) Lawrence Murphy's beef and mercantile monopoly and Santa Fe Ring involvement are attributed to competition with John Chisum. Arriving Tunstall is claimed to have partnered with another *Englishman*, Alexander McSween. [WRONG: McSween as British is a new error. He was born in Canada in 1843. And there was no "partnership." Tunstall was *falsely* named as his partner by Ringite Judge Warren Bristol, to enable malicious prosecution of him, along with McSween, with intent of forcing their flight or killing them.]

Tunstall's alliance with Chisum is cited. Using "Brushy's" fake history, Murphy is claimed as making a legal case against

Tunstall [WRONG: the Emil Fritz heirs, not Murphy, made a legal case], allowing him to seize Tunstall's store goods and horses [WRONG: the property was attached as part of the Fritz case, unrelated to Murphy, and the horses were immune]. To avoid problems, Tunstall decided to deliver the horses himself to Lincoln. [WRONG: Tunstall was innocently taking the immune horses back to Lincoln.] On the way, Fred Waite, driving a wagon, separated from the group. [FIX UP: "Brushy" had Tunstall driving the wagon.] Tunstall is killed by a posse. [CONCEALED: The Frank Warner Angel report is cited in a fix-up; but hidden is Billy's deposition on Tunstall's murder for it, likely because Billy's high literacy eliminated coarse-spoken "Brushy."] The murder is blamed on the "Murphy-Dolan faction." [WRONG: It was a Santa Fe Ring assassination, which is why it precipitated the Lincoln County War freedom fight.]

Jameson introduced Sederwall by claiming the murder *was not investigated*, so Sederwall can fabricate his "suspicions."

FAKERY: The crime scene had been investigated by the trackers, which included law enforcement official, Probate Judge Florencio Gonzales, who also gave the findings in his June 8, 1878 deposition to Frank Warner Angel. Concluded was murder, and the Coroner's Jury concurred.

Sederwall's "crime scene investigation" with a metal detector yielded a old rifle casing, which he made-up as from the bullet that killed Tunstall! He cited the Frank Warner Angel files, likely from fellow hoaxer with easy access to the National Archives, U.S. Marshal's Service Historian David Turk. He also used an alleged Tunstall autopsy report, without given source, and allegedly by Fort Stanton Assistant Post Surgeon Daniel Appel. He excerpted quotes as to the wounds. (Page 14)

FLAWED EVIDENCE: Sederwall seemed unaware that Appel was unreliable because of his Ring bias, shown in his July 1, 1878 deposition to Frank Warner Angel, which fabricated Tunstall attacking possemen, while maddened by venereal disease, forcing them to shoot him in self-defense. Also missed was that Alexander McSween countered the bias by getting an opinion from town doctor, Taylor Ealy, who reported his beaten face and coup de grâce wound. This is why the Coroner's Jury declared murder.

Sederwall also cited a few words of what he called "testimony provided by Billy the Kid," omitting that they were from Billy's deposition on June 8, 1878 to Frank Warner Angel.

"BRUSHY" BASHING: "Brushy" and team were ignorant of the deposition, it being discovered in 1956 by Frederick Nolan. So "Brushy" never to give it as Billy.

Sederwall then used the unspecified "autopsy report" to make-up bullet trajectories to claim a cover-up by the Sheriff's posse and Judge Florencio Gonzales. (Pages 21-22)

MISSED EVIDENCE: Anti-Ring Florencio Gonzales's June 8, 1878 Angel deposition showed he was *blocking cover-up of Tunstall's Ringite assassination by Brady*. Gonzales was a Tunstall-McSween ally from San Patricio.

Sederwall then claimed *he* discovered that Tunstall was murdered; that William Morton was the murderer; that the sheriff's pose was acting unlawfully; and did a cover-up!

FAKED DISCOVERY: All that may have been news to Jameson and Sederwall - but, with addition of more killers, this is conventional history of Tunstall's assassination!

FAKED AFTERMATH OF TUNSTALL MURDER

Naming his chapter "The Law Gets in the Way of Truth," Jameson continued faking suspicions about written history. (Pages 24-27) Cited were cover-ups of Brady's posse's killing of Tunstall. Dishonest fix-ups added Billy's being deputized, and his illegal arrest by Sheriff Brady.

"BRUSHY" BASHING: Billy's deputizing and arrest are damning to "Brushy," since they were unknown to him.

FAKED REVENGE MOTIVE

In this chapter, Jameson makes a bizarre and duplicitous switcheroo - without telling the reader. "Brushy's" confabulations are used as Billy Bonney's quotes! So Jameson wrote: "Billy the Kid stated, 'He had been good to me and treated me like a gentleman. I lost the best friend I ever had when they killed him.' " (Page 28) In *Alias Billy the Kid*, "Brushy stated: "Tunstall was a good man. **He had been good to me and treated me like a** gentleman. I lost the best friend I ever had when they killed him. I swore that day that I would make them pay with their lives for this dirty deed." (*Alias Billy the Kid*, Page 26)

Jameson also presented "Brushy's" guess that the aftermath to the Tunstall killing was revenge. Added is that Justice of the Peace Wilson - called a "judge" – helped the revenge. **[But Wilson was not a judge, and his agenda, like the Regulators', was anti-Ring, which included arresting responsible Ringites.]**

Known history of the Morton Baker, and McCloskey killings, yields a Sederwall "investigation." (Pages 32-34) As expected, without a verified killing site in the open plain east of the Capitan Mountains, Sederwall found spent cartridges. He gives versions of the killings, from Regulator Frank "McNab" [sic - MacNab], James Dolan, a Lucius Dills, and Pat Garrett.

FLAWED "CRIME SCENE INVESTIGATION": With fake "what-if" reasoning, Sederwall ruminates *if* Morton and Baker had their hands tied, they could not snatch McCloskey's gun and kill him or ride a horse. This silliness yields the conclusion that they were killed in revenge by Billy the Kid. But this is just fantasizing.

BILLY THE KID AS A GOOD GUY

The original "Brushy" hoax painted "Brushy," as Billy, as a victim of injustice, deserving a pardon. That theme is in Jameson's chapter "The Evolution of an Outlaw." (Pages 35-40)

That formulation is correct, but neither "Brushy," nor his hoaxers knew the outlaw myth came from the Santa Fe Ring. So Jameson blamed Pat Garrett for Billy's outlaw reputation, calling him a "politician and constant self-promoter" with his *Authentic Life of Billy the Kid*. He also blamed Governor S.B. Axtell for his Proclamation outlawing the Regulators. To show Axtell as bad, he called him a past governor of Utah, "removed from that position for corruption." (Pages 37-38)

WRONG AND "BRUSHY" BASHING: First of all, this debunks "Brushy," who knew nothing of the Regulators.

And Jameson confused Utah Governor Axtell's transfer to New Mexico, in 1875, to replace deceased Marsh Giddings as Governor, with Axtell's removal in late 1878, after the Lincoln County War, for corruption, with replacement by Lew Wallace.

Made-up is that Axtell outlawed the Regulators because Angel exposed his debt to Murphy, Dolan, and Riley of "The House."

WRONG: In fact, the $1800 loan through John Riley, when Axtell assumed office, was his Ring bribe.

Jameson parlays this feeble foray into historical analysis to attack all historians by stating that they do not "probe for facts, and attempt to uncover the truth." (Page 40)

"BRUSHY" BASHING: "Brushy" knew none of this stuff.

FAKING THE SHERIFF BRADY KILLING

The Sheriff William Brady killing, called "the pivotal event of the Lincoln County War," is in "Blood and Mud." (Pages 41-51) Actually, the pivotal event was Tunstall's killing, which yielded the Regulator movement. **That ambush now has fix-ups of Billy running out to retrieve "something," along with Jim French, instead of "Brushy's" Fred Wayte [sic].** Questioning if the "something" was Billy's "rifle" [sic - carbine] or arrest warrants for Alexander McSween, Jameson slips in "a revolver" as a "something," to add unnamed "Brushy's" fakery. And fixed-up is that Billy Matthews shot Billy and French **[instead of "Brushy's" shot Wayte [sic]]**.

Claimed is lack of investigating of the Brady-Hindman killings until "cop" Sederwall's. (Pages 43-51) But, like for "Brushy's" team, the motive for Brady's murder is unknown. Sederwall used Francisco Trujillo's 1937 WPA fake hearsay from the "Probable Cause Statement" (see page 567 above) that McSween told Billy to stop Brady from arresting him. "Brushy" had guessed: "Sheriff Brady was gunning for me with warrants for cattle stealing." (*Alias Billy the Kid*, Page 27)

So Sederwall did a "crime scene" investigation, deciding killing in town was a bad way to keep a secret; weather was too bad for socializing; it was better to kill Brady coming from his ranch (which he boasts "cops" call a "kill zone"). **So Sederwall claimed the Regulators were there to testify in the Grand Jury.** And, when it was delayed, they got angry at Brady for "obstructing justice;" so abruptly killed him. This was apparently an attempted defense as to a "crime of passion," as opposed to more legally blameworthy premeditation.

FLAWED ANALYSIS: Oddly, Sederwall used Attorney Randi McGinn's error from her Pardon Petition: that the Regulators were "[p]resent to testify as witnesses before the grand jury about the killing of John Tunstall" (See page 601 above); possibly indicating that he wrote the fake Petition for her.

In fact, the Regulators were outlawed by Governor S.B. Axtell's March 9, 1881 Proclamation. To come to Lincoln that April 1, 1878, risked their lives, indicating their desperate motive. And it was to kill Brady before he killed returning McSween later that day. And that would have been the correct murder defense: killing to save a life.

Sederwall also faked discovery of "discrepancies," stating reports that Brady and Deputies were on foot were false because it is unpleasant to walk in the mud; and Brady was old. Also, they were described as walking abreast, but *only horses walk abreast*! So he fabricated a scene with Brady falling off his horse when being shot. And he cited a witness stating that "he saw "Brady 'fall into a sitting position.' " (Pages 49-50)

FAKERY: This is too silly for words. Nevertheless, here goes. The street was unpaved; walking on mud was a part of Old West life. The word "abreast," means side by side, or shoulder to shoulder - like Brady and the Deputies walked.

And Sederwall built his fakery on confusing shot Brady with shot George Hindman's "fall into a sitting position."

And it bashes "Brushy" for knowing none of it.

Added to his horseback scenario was Sederwall's fantasy that, in the escape, Billy stole Brady's horse. He then claimed that Billy sold Brady's horse to Henry Hoyt in the Bill of Sale.

FAKE INVESTIGATION: Sederwall built on his own fakery that horses were involved, then used meaningless "what-ifs": *If* Billy stole the horse, he could have sold it to Hoyt in Tascosa, Texas. But this sale of an expensive sorrel for $75, on October 24, 1878, merely lifts conventional history of sale of Brady's sorrel horse Dandy Dick. But it was 206 days after the Brady killing. The horse was likely stolen by Billy from Catron's or Charles Fritz's ranch.

BASHING "BRUSHY": "Brushy" is bashed since his rendition of the Brady ambush had no ridden horses or horse stolen by himself as Billy. (*Alias Billy the* Kid, Page 27)

FAKING "BUCKSHOT" ROBERTS'S KILLING

Jameson claimed the Regulators' Blazer's Mill killing of "Buckshot" Roberts furthered Billy the Kid's reputation, so Sederwall would investigate the truth of what actually happened. The chapter is "The Shooting at Blazer's Mill." (Pages 52-55)

First presented is conventional history, though missing the key event: "Buckshot" *shot first* while resisting arrest, hitting Charlie Bowdre's cartridge belt buckle, then being shot by him.

But "Brushy's" tale had left a problem. Unaware of the Regulators, he accounted for the shooting by confabulating an earlier argument with himself, Charlie Bowdre, and "Buckshot; followed by his own revenge shooting of "Buckshot" as Billy. (*Alias Billy the Kid*, Pages 27-28; using Pat Garrett's *The Authentic Life of Billy the Kid* fiction, Pages 74-75) So a scenario was needed to make Billy the killer. That was left to "cop" Sederwall.

Admitted by Sederwall is that the Blazer's Mill building for the scene no longer exists. And the only "evidence" he had was three letters by Joseph Blazer's son, A.N. Blazer, to historian, Maurice Garland Fulton, claiming he had been an eye-witness to the April 4, 1878 shootings at age 13. His three letters' dates make them 52 years and 5 days after the scene, 53 years and 20 days after the scene, and 59 years, 4 months, and 23 days after the scene. He made-up that "Buckshot" arrived **at night, and in minutes there was shooting**. He also related that his sister had told him that Billy, returning to Lincoln after the hanging trial, had breakfast at Blazer's Mill, and told her that **he shot Roberts through the door in the room into which he had retreated**. Windbag A.N. Blazer even described the bullet wound as just above the left hip and a little up.

Using A.N. Blazer's malarkey, Sederwall made-up a "crime scene," with Billy sliding and falling on the boards on the way to the room and firing through the door from a prone position! Sederwall claimed corroboration from the no longer existing door with its unprovable bullet hole!

FLAWED ANALYSIS: Sederwall merely used an old-timer's hearsay malarkey as revealed by the made-up wound. In fact, "Buckshot" had a single abdominal one from Charlie Bowdre, as documented in U.S. Attorney Thomas Benton Catron's June 21, 1878 federal indictment of the Regulators - including Billy - for the killing.

Sederwall concluded his history is not as written scam by stating that "Buckshot" Roberts and Dick Brewer were buried **in the same grave.** So he did what he called "on-site examination;" and found two markers.

FAKING DISCREPANCIES: Sederwall mixed-up the burial issue in this known tourist site. There are two graves, but uncertainly marked as to which was which.

FAKING THE LINCOLN COUNTY WAR BATTLE

The Lincoln County War chapter is titled "The Burning of the McSween House." (Pages 56-67) For it, Jameson presented names and events unknown to "Brushy;" thus, inadvertently discrediting his man, who confabulated a "three day" "cattle war."

With fix-ups from modern history books, the Frank Warner Angel files, and Dudley Court of Inquiry, it was revealed by Jameson as Steve Sederwall's "analysis of the 'war.'" (Page 67)

But the Jameson-Sederwall duo, like "Brushy" and team, did not know that the War was a six month freedom fight against the Santa Fe Ring, that it began at Tunstall's assassination, had multiple skirmishes, and culminated in a six day battle in Lincoln. They did, however, did add more days to "Brushy's" three.

In the Jameson-Sederwall fantasy, the Regulators ride into Lincoln on July 14, 1878 because they had warrants to arrest Tunstall's killers and to protect McSween.

WRONG: In fact, it was Alexander McSween's culminating show-down with the Ring, its local bosses at "The House," Ringite Sheriff George Peppin, and the Ring's allies of Seven Rivers boys and John Kinney's outlaw gang. It was his intention, with his 60 Regulator and Hispanic backers, to take the town peacefully. The immediate precipitant was the July 3, 1878 Ring massacre at San Patricio.

Adrift, the duo create a bizarre fiction that the battle resulted from squabbling about trespassing on some McSween land in town, saying McSween got angry that Peppin's posseman were on his land in an old stone tower called the Torreon; and McSween also blamed Saturnino Baca, his tenant in a house on that land, and sent him an eviction notice. Claimed is that Baca, an "ex-sheriff," knew the law, so he sent for his friend, Fort Stanton Commander Dudley. And Dudley sent Post Surgeon Daniel Appel, who tried to negotiate as "a peacemaker," but the possemen would not leave the Torreon because it gave them "an advantage." So, according to the clueless duo, "the Regulators dug in for war."

WRONG: In the Battle's first day of July 14th, the Torreon was of no advantage, since McSween's men were positioned along Lincoln's street to prevent attackers ascending the south foothills to shoot down at them. Saturnino Baca, McSween's tenant, but a Lincoln settler since 1867, was a rare Hispanic Ringite; and McSween knew it. In a political alliance with T.B. Catron since 1868, Baca was also a hay supplier to "The House" in its earliest days in Lincoln in 1873, and a Murphy ally. And he had been a Probate Judge, not Sheriff. Lincoln's first Sheriff was Brady. And on the Battle's first day, Baca was not yet actively involved. And Appel did not come to town until later, as a Ring-biased fact-finder, not peacemaker.

The duo thought shooting began when Deputy Jack Long tried to serve warrants on McSween for attempted murder. (Page 58)

WRONG: Gunfire began with entry of Ringite Seven Rivers boys, joining the Peppin posse. That caused McSween's men, including Billy, to rush to his house as protectors.

As to McSween's evicting Baca, it occurred on July 15th, for his assisting Sheriff Peppin's possemen at the Torreon. Baca used that eviction notice for his pre-planned Ringite plot to evade the Posse Comitatus Act that barred military intervention in civilian matters, as passed the month before. The plot was to use its exception allowing intervention if women and children were in danger. So traitor to his people, Baca, wrote to Dudley that his pregnant wife and many children were in danger of McSween, and requested troops.

As to Ringite Post Surgeon Daniel Appel's coming to Lincoln, it was on July 15th, and he was a fact finder for Dudley, seeking an excuse to attack. Appel's presence made the cease fire that enabled Deputy Jack Long to go the McSween house with a fake warrant.

But writing fiction, the duo next had departing failed "peacemaker" Daniel Appel encounter the John Kinney gang, whom they call "Seven Rivers Warriors" [confusing Kinney from Mesilla with the Seven Rivers boys]. They add Jessie Evans, and say that Appel convinced Kinney to go to Lincoln [when Kinney and his gang from Mesilla were already there for a pre-planned attack - along with Seven Rivers boys from the Pecos valley].

For the next day [of uncertain date, but with information compatible with July 16th], the duo have Sheriff Peppin station men on the south foothills to shoot at "McSween's snipers." Claimed is that Peppin then requested a howitzer from Dudley.

FLAWED: Here the duo missed a crucial point. McSween's plan for a peaceful take-over was working. The south foothills were unattainable, with his men able to fire at any attempted ascent. That was why Peppin tried to get military intervention by a claim that violated the Posse Comitatus Act - arming a civilian posse against civilians.

The duo then garble the next incident of July 16th. They state that Dolan and Kinney wrote Dudley making up that McSweens had fired on his soldier in town. And that made Dudley come.

WRONG: In fact, that July 16th, responding to Peppin's cannon request, Dudley sent 9th Cavalryman Private Berry Robinson as a fact-finder. Robinson was then likely fired upon by the Dolan side, was uninjured, and returned to Fort Stanton. The Dolan side claimed Robinson was attacked by McSweens, but Dudley hesitated to act.

For that same July 16th, the duo have McSween-side Fernando Herrera shoot Charles Crawford, a Peppin posseman on the south foothills; with good Surgeon Appel suddenly appearing in town to "risk his life" to give him aid - though Crawford died.

WRONG: The actual date was July 17th. And Appel was back in another fake fact-finding mission, now with past Fort Stanton Commander George Purington, and five soldiers, with the excuse of Berry Robinson's shooting. Dudley feared to act, but was Ring-beholden, since T.B. Catron had represented him for two prior court martials. It was in that context, that Appel - not risking his life because McSweens would not shoot at soldiers - picked up dying Charles Crawford. But the crucial big picture missed by the duo was that it was now the fourth day of McSween's occupation, and he was holding the town.

For July 18th, the duo have McSween side's Ben Ellis shot in the neck, though it occurred the day before. They then describe town doctor [Taylor] Ealy, going to assist Ben, making clear that Mrs. Ealy was there too. And an unidentified "Sue Gates" accompanies her to get water.

WRONG: The duo was unaware that there were also two young Ealy children. And there were also women and children in McSween's house. The missed *big picture is women and children*. It was Dudley's obligation, under the Posse Comitatus Act, to protect them.

For the 19th, the duo had Dudley arrive at Lincoln with troops. Avoiding "Brushy's" racism, they avoid races! A fix-up adds Dudley's Gatling gun, howitzer, ammunition load, and provisions - proving the "Brushy" and team's ignorance!

The duo pretend they discovered Dudley's "lying" about protecting women and children. And they had Dudley pointing a cannon at McSween's front door. (Page 65)

WRONG: The cannon was pointed at José Montaño's house. Thus, the duo missed the key point: Dudley's intentional terrorism, which McSween's men to flee, leaving him and his men besieged in his house.

Now possessing the Dudley Court of Inquiry transcript, likely from fellow "Billy the Kid Case" hoaxer U.S. Marshals Service David Turk, the duo cite Billy's testimony. But his testifying to three soldiers stationed at McSween's house by Dudley, is misunderstood as: "an attempt to draw fire."

WRONG: In fact, the key point that Billy was making was that the soldiers were stationed there to inhibit those inside from shooting to give Peppin's men the advantage.

For the burning of the McSween house, the duo have Peppin order his posse to commit arson, with Andy Boyle as the fire-setter, though unaware he was a Seven Rivers boy.

WRONG: There were more fire setters as proved by the May 23, 1879 testimony of Susan McSween at the Dudley Court of Inquiry. She stated: " *[O]n my way to [Dudley's] camp I saw [Sebrian] Bates, he being a colored servant of mine ... just in the act of picking up some lumber. At the time I saw* three of Murphy's men *... I then asked what they were doing, they said ... [t]hat Peppin and Col. Dudley had sent them to carry lumber to our house to set it on fire ... I then begged them not to do so."*

The duo describe the nighttime escape from the kitchen. They state that the "**Kid said they had to jump over the body of Harvey Morris,** then ran towards the Tunstall Store and then turned towards the river." (Page 66)

WRONG: Jumping over Morris's body is invented here; and is not in "Brushy's" own quote copying Billy's testimony on running towards the Tunstall store and river (*Alias Billy the Kid*, Page 31), or Jameson's 1998 book (*Return of the Outlaw Billy the Kid*, Page 54), or in real Billy's testimony. It opens the possibility that Jameson simply published whatever Sederwall made-up.

FLAWED: Missed was Billy's key testimony about the three white soldiers firing at them; meaning Dudley ordered soldiers to attack civilians.

The duo then give the killing of McSween and shooting of Yginio [now corrected from "Brushy's Higinio] Salazar.

FLAWED: Missed are the murders of McSween-side Vincente Romero and Francisco Zamora. Even the friendly fire shooting of Ring-side Bob Beckwith is omitted.

Unaware of the Battle's cause, the duo conclude feebly that Billy the Kid and his companions were disappointed because they did not get a chance to serve the warrants for Brady's murder, and had failed to protect McSween! And they floated the hoax's point that authorities cannot be trusted. Jameson narrated Sederwall's conclusion that "more violations of the law were committed by the men responsible for law enforcement than by those who were identified as outlaws." That was to imply that lawman Garrett did not kill Billy the Kid either!

"BRUSHY" BASHING: All this was irrelevant to Garrett not killing Billy, or "Brushy" being Billy. Even worse, the duo had discredited "Brushy" by demonstrating that his confabulations had missed almost all of the Battle's people and events. Poor Jameson had even permitted omission of the jewel in "Brushy's" special knowledge tricks: black ("[N-word]") soldiers on the foothills shooting down at the burning McSween house!

CHAPTER 3
"BRUSHY" BASHING HOAXING

NARRATING NEW HOAXING

Steve Sederwall had clearly hijacked W.C. Jameson's book to showcase his own hoaxing, with a "Brushy"-be-damned attitude. These elaborate hoaxes are just summarized here, but are debunked in my 2019 books: *The Cold Case Billy the Kid Megahoax: The Plot to Steal Billy the Kid's Identity and Defame Sheriff Pat Garrett as a Murderer* and *The Billy the Kid's Bad Buck's Hoax: Faking Billy Bonney as a William Brockway Gang Counterfeiter.*

THE BILLY THE KID AS COUNTERFEITER HOAX

The chapter, "Counterfeit Money" (Pages 68-84), recycles a Sederwall hoax faking Billy the Kid as a Secret Service-pursued crook, in cahoots counterfeiter, William Brockway, in a national rustling-money laundering racket; as a conspirator in mail coach robberies, and as a murderer of an informer on his criminality.

Jameson missed that this scam demolished his man "Brushy," who, as Billy, not only had no idea of these activities; but also made him, as Billy, so despicably evil that a pardon was unthinkable. Possibly, mesmerized narrator Jameson thought Sederwall's theme was still just history is not as written.

In fact, Sederwall's trick was simple: tracking the New York Brockway gang's counterfeit bill distributions nationally, then faking links to Billy Bonney. Like C.L. Sonnichsen's fraud about Pat Garrett's reward money, it relied on readers having no access to obscure cited documents, which are either old timers' malarkey or wildly misstated archival records to support the hoaxing.

Sederwall first presented his hoax in 2010 and 2015 articles. The first, titled "Counterfeit Bank Note Rewrites Chapter of Billy the Kid," was on July 16, 2010 by "Billy the Kid Case" hoax-backing reporter, Julie Carter, in the *Ruidoso News*. Cited as a fellow researcher was fellow "Billy the Kid Case" hoaxer, David Turk. It had a picture captioned: "Counterfeit bank note passed in Lincoln County by Billy the Kid and his gang. William Brockway ... printed it from the plate the Secret Service recovered the day before Thanksgiving in 1880." Claimed was that the $100 bill came from Secret Service archivist, Michael Sampson. I called him. He told me that he had told Sederwall that there were **no notes in the files from the Azariah Wild investigation. So Sederwall accepted a random bill, then made up its claim.** The Billy the Kid link to Brockway was made-up by fictionalizing that the Brockway gang laundered money by buying rustled cattle; and Billy was a rustler, so he was rustling as one of their money-launderers. But Billy had no connection to that gang, and Brockway did not money-launder. Being garbled was Azariah Wild's report about his spy, Barney Mason, disclosing counterfeiter, Dan Dedrick's plot to buy cattle with bad money, and resell them for good money. There was no rustling. The Brockway link was fabricated from Pat Garrett's statement in *The Authentic Life of Billy the Kid* that Billy sold rustled stock to "Colorado beef buyers." (Garrett, Page 118) Since the national Brockway gang had members in Colorado, Sederwall made-up that Colorado meant that Billy sold to them! Added was that a freighter named Smith" had reported Billy's counterfeiting to Wild, so vengeful Billy killed him. This fakery used a December 22, 1880 outlaw myth article in the *New York Sun* titled "Outlaws of New Mexico, The Exploits of a Band Headed by a New York Youth." It stated: "The information that enabled the Government officers to discover the handling of counterfeit money by the Kid's gang came from a freighter named Smith. Soon afterward, while Smith was on his way from Las Vegas to Fort Sumner with a load of freight, he was waylaid and murdered by some of the gang." In fact, Sam Smith was killed by Apaches in April of 1880, five months before Wild arrived. Made-up also was that Billy conspired with the mail carrier to steal Wild's reports. This came from a December 27, 1880 *Las Vegas Daily Gazette* article by Lucius "Lute" Wilcox about the Stinking Springs capture, in which mail contractor (not deliverer), Mike Cosgrove gave Billy a suit. Sederwall made-up that this was to get Billy alone and plead for secrecy about their conspiracy! In fact, Billy just robbed the mail coach once, during his pardon negation.

Five years later, Sederwall expanded his counterfeiting fiction in fellow "Billy the Kid Case" hoaxer and editor, Bob Boze Bell's *True West* magazine of June, 2015, as "Billy Bonney's Bad Bucks: Did the Kid Travel the Counterfeit Trail?" For it, Sederwall proclaimed: "With all we know about Billy the Kid, most do not know that he was part of a counterfeiting ring." A counterfeit bill photo was used, this time of $5.00 **[Brockway made $100]**, captioned: "Both sides of an actual counterfeit bill from the New Mexico ring" **[made-up]**. Repeated was his 2010 fakery, with addition that **Billy was in counterfeiting cahoots with Jesse James**. Concealed was that the source was a possible 1879 sighting of Billy *eating a meal* with James in a Las Vegas, New Mexico, hotel, as reported by Henry Hoyt in his 1936 book, *Frontier Doctor*. And Hoyt stated that Billy told him he was not doing business with James. (Hoyt, Pages 110-113) Furthermore, James was not a counterfeiter. For faking Billy's rustling as money-laundering, Sederwall used an undisclosed old-timer malarkey book by a Jim (Lane) Cook, who he made-up as Tom O'Folliard's cousin in a scheme with Billy to steal Chisum's cattle, and sell them to a Brockway gang member for counterfeit money, which would be laundered by Cook in a Kansas bank. The hidden book was Cook's fictional 1936 *Lane of the Llano*. And, as would be seen when Sederwall elaborated this hoax in *Cold Case Billy the Kid*, besides the money-laundering scheme making no sense, it was used Cook's tale of doing the Chisum rustling with Billy and Tom, driving the cattle to Kansas to sell, then depositing the money in the *Master's Bank* in Kansas, and withdrawing $9000 to pay Billy. But Sederwall changed it to fabricate the cattle being sold to a Brockway gang member for bad money, which was deposited by Cook in a Confederate-biased *Mastin Bank* in *Kansas City*, which was in cahoots with the Brockway gang and would give Cook good bills for Billy. Sederwall slyly switched Cook's tale's *Master Bank* to the *Mastin Bank* – because it was actually connected to a Brockway bill pusher [though unconnected to Billy]. The conclusion was that Garrett as not break the New Mexico counterfeiting ring, because Brockway had been arrested earlier in New York.

Three years later, Sederwall recycled and elaborated all this complex flimflam in *Cold Case Billy the Kid* in a pinnacle of his con-artistry. Of course, "Brushy" and team had made no mention of any of this.

THE "FOLLIARD" NAME PLUS COUSIN HOAX

Jameson had used Sederwall's "**Folliard**" name hoax without elaboration in his 2012 *Billy the Kid: The Lost Interviews*. (See page 661 above) As discussed, that eliminated "Brushy," who consistently called his Billy the Kid friend, Tom **O'Folliard**!

But Jameson announced: "As a result of genealogical records and census records, detective Steve Sederwall learned [Tom O'Folliard's] **real name was Thomas O. Folliard**." (Page 82) Corrupted Jameson then quoted pseudo-"Brushy," to pretend "Brushy" used the name when talking about "the winter of '79 [and] **being with Tom Folliard**." (Page 86)

HOAXING: "Brushy" stated: "In the winter of '79 we got together with Dolan and Evans and agreed to quit fighting." (*Alias Billy the Kid*, **Page 33) He always used "O'Folliard."**

Sederwall's "discovered" genealogy has Tom's father as a "Tom Folliard," coming from Ireland and marrying "Sarah Cook;" and having Tom after "two and a half years." (Page 82) They then died of small pox in Monclova, Coahuila, Mexico. John Cook (called Sarah's uncle) then took Tom to Uvalde, Texas. Cited as evidence is that "[t]he Uvalde census for 1870 lists 'Thomas Folliard, 9 years old," and other family members. Claimed as Sarah's parents were David Cook and Eliza Jane Cook; and that "[t]his would make Eliza Jane Cook, the woman who raised him, Tom's grandmother. Eliza Jane's married name was McKinney; she was Kip McKinney's cousin. Kip McKinney and Tom Folliard were related." (Pages 82-83)

Sederwall also claimed that the genealogy proved that "Folliard" was Kip McKinney's cousin - a claim made-up by "Brushy" about O'Folliard. Sederwall had already floated this faked genealogy in his 2015 "Billy the Kid's Bad Bucks" hoax, in which he made-up that a "Lane Cook" was Tom O'Folliard's cousin [leaving out that he was just the old-timer author Jim (Lane) Cook of 1936's *Lane of the Llano*, and the Cook name was coincidental].

HOAXING: This is not a real genealogical investigation coordinating census reports, obituaries, and other kinship records. Sederwall just lifted from unsubstantiated sources; since O'Folliard's real genealogy is uncertain. Worse, Sederwall made-up information.

Only one relevant record exists, tentatively linked to Tom O'Folliard: the 1870 census on September 26, 1870 in Zavalla County, Uvalde, Texas, used by Sederwall.

Frederick Nolan cited it in his 2011 publishing of a 1940 manuscript by a Frank Clifford, titled *Deep Trails in the Old West: A Frontier Memoir*. But Nolan critiqued it as problematically listing Tom's age as 9 in 1870, which contradicted other claimed birthdays of 1854 and 1958. Also, the name used is "Folliard," making it not him or misspelled. Nolan concluded: "[A] lot more work needs to be done before we have anything remotely like an acceptable biography." (*Deep Trails*, Nolan, Page 276)

But Sederwall used and misstated a January, 1934 article by a Jack Shipman in *Voice of the Mexican Border* magazine, "Brief Career of Tom O'Folliard Billy the Kid's Partner," giving an Irish immigrant father named Tom O'Folliard. From it, Sederwall lifted Tom's birth "two and a half years" after his parents' marriage. Shipman claimed, without proof, that Tom was raised by John Cook and his sister, Margaret Jane Cook, till she married; then his living with John, till his marriage in 1875. Then Tom was with grandmother, "Mrs. David Cook." (Shipman, Page 216)

Also, Philip J. Rasch's 1995 *Trailing Billy the Kid* (in *Cold Case Billy the Kid's* Bibliography) had "The Short Life of Tom O'Folliard," using Shipman's article. Rasch's Tom is born in Uvalde, Texas, to "Irish immigrant" Tom O'Folliard, and Sarah Cook; moves to Mexico, with the parents dying. Sarah's brother, John Cook, takes him to Uvalde to his sister Margaret Jane Cook, until her 1873 marriage. Then Tom lives with John Cook, until his marriage to "a Miss McKinney" in 1875; when he went to grandmother, "Mrs. James Cook." (Rasch, Page 77)

But these sources' Irish father was Tom O'Folliard. So Sederwall made-up "Folliard" to match the census's misspelled "Folliard" to fabricate his "Folliard" discovery. And he made-up that the son's middle initial was "O," as: Thomas O. Folliard! (Page 82)

That "Folliard" is not O'Folliard's name, is proved by the obvious: all his contemporaries used O'Folliard. Even Operative Azariah Wild, who tracked him in the "Wilson & Kid gang," wrote in his report completed on October 18, 1880: *"Thomas O'Falliard: [Came] [f]rom Texas here."*

Pat Garrett, who knew and killed him, wrote in *The Authentic Life of Billy the Kid*: "[After the shooting] Mason came around the building just as O'Folliard was returning, reeling in his saddle." (Garrett, Page 172)

Sederwall made-up that Eliza Jane's married name was McKinney, when it was her *maiden name*, with *married name* Cook. And he made-up that she and David Cook were O'Folliard's grandparents.

Also, Sederwall used "Brushy's" claim that Kip McKinney was his cousin, though he reduced it to "relative." "Brushy's" original prompt source had been the 1935 book by Frank M. King, titled *Wranglin' the Past: Reminiscences of Frank M. King*; stating: "Kip was also a cousin of Tom O'Folliard." (King, Page 173) Another prompt, was Garrett's O'Folliard death scene; stating: "He also asked [Barney] Mason to tell McKinney to write to his grandmother in Texas and inform her of his death." (Garrett, Page 173) But that did not mean cousins, or even relatives.

Linking of Cook and McKinney families was explained in Frederick Nolan's note in Frank Clifford's *Deep Trials in the Old West*: On April 4, 1875, Tom's uncle, John Enoch Cook married <u>Elizabeth Francis McKinney, a cousin of Kip McKinney</u>. Also, Tom's uncle, David Cook, had married, as second wife, <u>Eliza Jane McKinney Cook</u>. Nolan noted that possibly Eliza's father was a Collin McKinney, possibly Kip McKinney's grandfather, through Collin's son, Thalis McKinney. That would make her Kip's aunt. <u>None of this made Tom and Kip cousins, but might explain dying Tom's knowing Kip could contact his Cook family</u>.

THE GARRETT'S NO AUTHORITY HOAX

Hoaxing that Pat Garrett illegally tracked Billy originated with C.L. Sonnichsen for *Alias Billy the Kid*. Sederwall used it in his 2003 "Probable Cause Statement for Case 2003-274." He now expanded it by claiming that Secret Service Operative Azariah Wild had faked Garrett's Deputy U.S. Marshal commission by crossing out the name, "John Hurley" on papers from Santa Fe's U.S. Marshal John Sherman. Concluded was that "sheriff-elect" and Lincoln County Deputy Garrett only had authority in Lincoln County. (Pages 80-81)

FAKE INVESTIGATION: For his history is not as written scam, Sederwall misstated Wild's appointment of Garrett to head posses tracking the "Wilson and Kid gang."

Garrett's biographer, Leon Metz, in his 1974 *Pat Garrett: The Story of a Western Lawman*, gave the circumstance: "Since United States marshals and deputy marshals were too frightened to help him, Wild ... compiled a list of brave citizens ... Among them ... [was] Pat Garrett ... [He] wrote [U.S. Marshal] Sherman saying that these men would do the work if Sherman would simply sign United States deputy marshal commissions for all of them. Sherman happily complied, sending everything the Treasury man asked for, except that he mistakenly dispatched two commissions for Hurley and none for Garrett. Wild rectified this error by scratching Hurley's name from one of the papers and substituting Garrett's."

Sederwall hid that Wild informed Secret Service Chief James Brooks of this on January 3, 1881; and, as one of only 40 Special Operatives in the country, he had power to make appointments and pursue investigations as he chose - including capturing and killing suspects. He had already reported his difficulty getting warrants and commissions on October 13, 1880, informing Chief Brooks that *"Marshal Sherman ... is a drunkard and inefficient."* Also, Lincoln County citizens refused to go after Billy, as he reported on October 29, 1880. Garrett was one of the few willing to help, as Wild reported to Chief Brooks on November 11, 1880.

What Sederwall lifted out of context, was that Wild, back in his New Orleans home base, was complaining about U.S. Marshal Sherman's sloppy paperwork. Wild's January 3, 1881 report stated:

> *I am disposed to believe U.S. Attorney Barnes will and has done all he could, but he had a man as Marshal who is but little or no assistance to him, and in fact I will state that had I gone there and found no U.S. Marshal I would have accomplished my work sooner and I believe more satisfactory to the government and to myself.*
>
> *I will respectfully state that I appealed to Marshal Sherman to appoint P.F. Garrett as Deputy Marshal to*

which he paid no attention. <u>I was in great need of Mr. Garrett's aid at that time and took one of the Commissions Sherman sent to John Hurley (he having sent two) and substituted the name of P.F. Garrett the very man who has rendered the Government such valuable service in killing and arresting these men who I was in pursuit.</u>

So Garrett's Deputy U.S. Marshal appointment was proper. Chief Brooks acceptance confirmed its legitimacy.

In addition, further debunking Sederwall's fabricated illegal appointment, is Wild's commendation letter for him, included in his report to Chief Brooks of January 25, 1881. Wild wrote:

> *Patrick F. Garrett Esq.*
>   *Sheriff of Lincoln County*
>   *New Mexico*
>
> *Dear Sir:-*
>   *Your letter dated Lincoln NM January 10th 1881 just received and noted.*
>
> *1st Allow me to congratulate you, and your men for the success in bringing up, arresting and killing the worst band of outlaws in the United States ...*
>
> *Your services to the Government have been of too great value to go unpaid or be treated in a miserly manner.*
>
> *I have properly represented you and the services performed by you and your men to the Departments to which I belong, at Washington, and will continue to aid you all that is in my power until you are fully paid ...*
>
>   *Very Respectfully*
>   *Azariah F. Wild*
>   *Operative*

Garrett himself referenced his Deputy U.S. Marshal appointment in his 1882 *Authentic Life of Billy the Kid*: "[Bob] Olinger and myself were both commissioned as deputy United States marshals and held United States warrants for the Kid and Bowdre for the killing of ["Buckshot"] Roberts on an Indian Reservation." (Garrett, Page 145)

CHAPTER 4
FAKING DEATH SCENE DOUBTS

THE MEGAHOAX'S BULL'S EYE

The Jameson-Sederwall duo (presumably assisted by the acknowledged additional hoaxers) present their hoax's make-or-break July 14, 1881 death scene in chapters "Shooting at Fort Sumner" (Pages 131-134) and "Discrepancies." (Pages 135-163)

Concealed is that "Brushy's" tale was totally different from the "Billy the Kid Case's." Concealed also, is zero evidence supporting either hoax; and profuse evidence debunking them. So the duo rely on fake "discrepancies" and fake "investigations."

FAKING DISCREPANCIES

Discrepancies are faked using Pat Garrett's 1882 *Authentic Life of Billy the Kid* and John W. Poe's *The Death of Billy the Kid*, to pretend they proved events did not occur. So the duo conclude that this "incident [shooting in the bedroom] as the two lawmen described it never took place." (Page 141) Examples follow:

1) DEPUTIES OUTSIDE: The duo claim it was suspicious for Garrett to enter the Maxwell's bedroom, while leaving his deputies outside, because it was too careless for searching for "the most dangerous outlaw in New Mexico." (Page 138)

FAKING EVIDENCE: Omitted is that Garrett did not believe that Billy was in Fort Sumner, and was merely checking with Maxwell. Omitted is another possibility: that a trap was being set, with Billy being sent to Maxwell's bedroom for ambush. In that case, it was strategic to have the deputies outside in case Billy escaped out of the room.

2) **IN SOX AND BUTTONING PANTS:** The approach of the stranger, in sox and buttoning his pants, is tackled by "cop" Sederwall (Page 139), recycling this absurdity from his (concealed) Case No. 2003-274's "Probable Cause Statement" about it being too hard to hold a gun and a knife and button your pants; plus gravel would hurt your sensitive stockinged feet! (See page 507 above)

FAKING EVIDENCE: Billy apparently could multi-task! And apparently he could tackle gravel too!

3) **SPEAKING SPANISH:** Sederwall cogitated that if approaching Billy said, "Quien es?" and non-Spanish-speaking Poe responded in English to reassure him, then bi-lingual Billy would have reverted to English. So Sederwall concluded that left just two possibilities: it was not Billy, or Poe lied! (Page 140)

FAKING EVIDENCE: Omitted is that hunted Billy was speaking Spanish to a stranger as a disguise. Also, he likely used the language commonly, as he would with bi-lingual Peter Maxwell in the next a moment. And it worked! Poe thought he was a Maxwell worker. Sederwall's two "possibilities" are absurd.

Noteworthy is ongoing demolition of "Brushy" as Billy; here arguing based on being bi-lingual. "Brushy" was not.

4) **LETTING BILLY ENTER THE BEDROOM:** Sederwall claimed it was unimaginable that two deputies let a man with a knife and a gun walk into the bedroom with Garrett, without shouting a warning. And he imagines that Billy would have been more cautious, or even shot the deputies. (Pages 140-141)

FAKING EVIDENCE: Fantasizing is not evidence.

In fact, neither Poe nor McKinney knew Billy, and thought he was a worker. Billy's gun was attributed to strangers alarming him. And none of the lawmen were expecting Billy to turn up at Maxwell's house, so were not alarmed. As Poe stated in his book: "As Maxwell's was the one place in Fort Sumner I considered above suspicion of harboring the Kid, I was entirely off my guard." (Poe, Page 34)

As to Billy being incautious, he was known for fearlessness. That is how he ended up in Fort Sumner, instead of hightailing it to Old Mexico after his jailbreak. And Fort Sumner had strangers passing through. It is absurd to think that he would automatically shoot them!

5) ENTERING THE BEDROOM: Garrett's statement that the person "sprang quickly into the door" is contrasted with Poe's Billy backing to the door, to claim Billy never entered! (Page 132)

FAKING EVIDENCE: The manner of entering is merely vantage. In his 1933 book, Poe described Billy as "<u>backed up into the doorway of Maxwell's room, where he halted for a moment, his body concealed by the thick adobe wall at the side of the doorway</u>." (Poe, Page 35) So Poe could not have seen Billy's final turn to enter face-forward as Garrett saw.

6) THE VICTIM'S IDENTITY: After the shooting, Maxwell is presented as running out; Garrett as doubtful, saying, "<u>I think I have got him;</u>" and Poe being doubtful. (Page 133)

FAKING: Garrett did not say, "I think I have got him." In his book, he was certain: "I told my companions that <u>I had got the Kid</u>. They asked if I had not shot the wrong man. <u>I told them I made no mistake</u>, for I knew the Kid's voice too well." He explained the Deputies' doubt: "Seeing a bareheaded, bare-footed man, in his shirt sleeves, with a butcher knife in his hand, and hearing his hail in excellent Spanish, they naturally supposed him to be a Mexican and an attaché of the establishment, hence their suspicion that I had shot the wrong man." (Garrett, Page 217)

The quote is from Poe: " '<u>I think I have got him</u>' ... I said, 'Pat, the Kid would not come to this place; you have shot the wrong man ...' Upon my saying this, Garrett seemed to be in doubt himself as to whom he shot, but quickly spoke up and said, 'I am sure that was him.' " (Poe, Pages 37-38) And Poe confirmed: Upon examining the body, we found it to be that of Billy the Kid." (Page 41)

7) POST-SHOOTING SCENES: The scene is given of "native people" taking the body "to a carpenter shop where it was laid out on a workbench." Poe's quote about fear because of "friends of the dead man" is given. (Page 134) Sederwall says it is suspicious that Garrett would let women take the body of such a famous outlaw, or that he would "cower" in Maxwell's house. To him that means Garrett was a bad leader - or worse. (Page 134)

FAKING DOUBT: Sederwall's fantasies are not evidence.

FAKING A MAXWELL BEDROOM DOOR DISCREPANCY

Sederwall's hoax of Maxwell's bedroom having no outside door - first used in *Pat Garrett: The Man Behind the Badge* (see page 672 above) - is to destroy the historical death scene in one fell swoop, since all participants recounted it. A diagram is given and labeled "Floor plan of the Maxwell house," and has no door. And the building is called a one-story adobe. (Page 137) **[FIGURE: 17]**

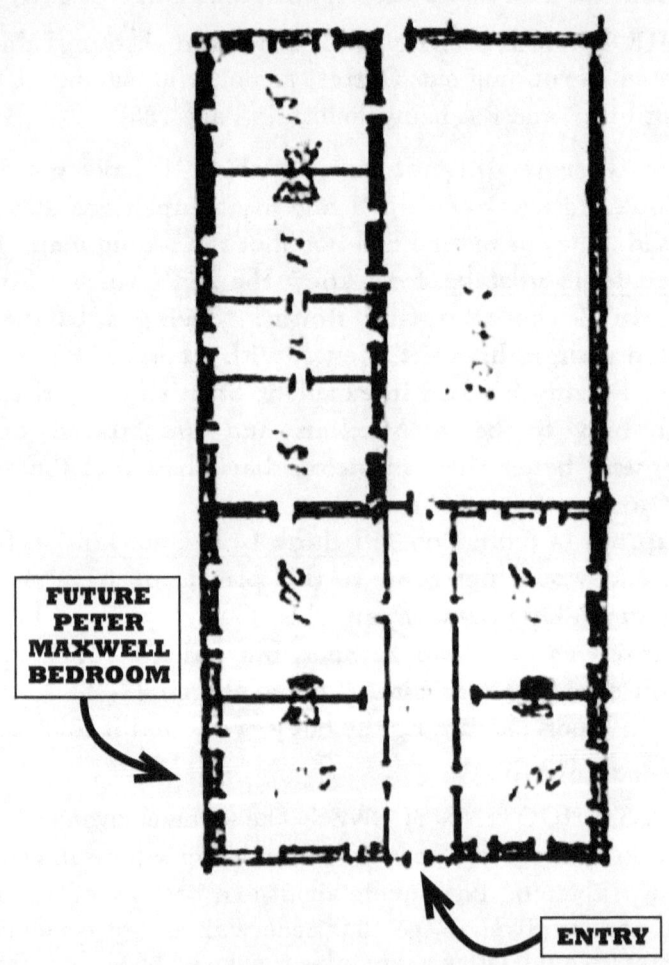

FIGURE: 17. Falsely used by the hoaxers as "Floor plan of Maxwell house" from the "National Archives" (Page 137); this diagram is from the National Archives as "Commanding Officer's Quarters, Fort Sumner, New Mexico Territory;" and its copy, so labeled, is at the Fort Sumner State Monument.

To indicate that Garrett lied about the door, the hoaxers state: "Garrett wrote, '[Billy] 'stepped onto the porch and entered Maxwell's room through the open door left open on account of the extremely warm weather.' " (Page 131) And Poe's witnessing Billy enter through that door is cited as to his lying also. (Page 140) So the duo conclude that both men lied about the scene to conceal that Billy the Kid was never shot.

FAKED INVESTIGATION: The claimed "floor plan" is not Maxwell's bedroom, but is the original Fort Sumner Commanding Officer's quarters for the Bosque Redondo Indian Reservation from 1863 to 1868. Since its sources in the National Archives and at Fort Sumner State Monument label it as such, the hoaxers are faking its identification.

Omitted is that in 1870, when Lucien Maxwell bought Fort Sumner, he rebuilt it as his family home. As Robert Mullin wrote on the back of his Maxwell house photo: *"Pete Maxwell's House Fort Sumner ... Originally 1 Story Flat Roof, Officers Quarters. 2nd Floor Added By Maxwell."*

The actual Maxwell house floor plan shows the outside door. [Figure: 18] And the Maxwell house photograph, also shows that door in Maxwell's bedroom. [Figure 19]

And the Garrett quote is faked. He actually wrote: "When we reached the porch in front of the building, I left Poe and McKinney at the end of the porch, and about twenty feet from the door of Pete's bedroom, while I myself entered it." (Garrett, Page 215)

The quote is actually distorted from Poe's book; stating: "'You fellows wait here while I go in to talk to [Maxwell].' Thereupon he stepped onto the porch and entered Maxwell's room through the open door (left open on account of the extremely warm weather), while McKinney and myself stopped on the outside." (Poe, Page 31)

Also, Poe described the further role of that door to the outside when he almost shot Maxwell: "A moment after Garrett came out of the door, Pete Maxwell rushed squarely onto me in a frantic effort to get out of the room." (Poe, Page 38) This contradicts the hoaxers' fakery that the participants had to walk through the house to get to the bedroom.

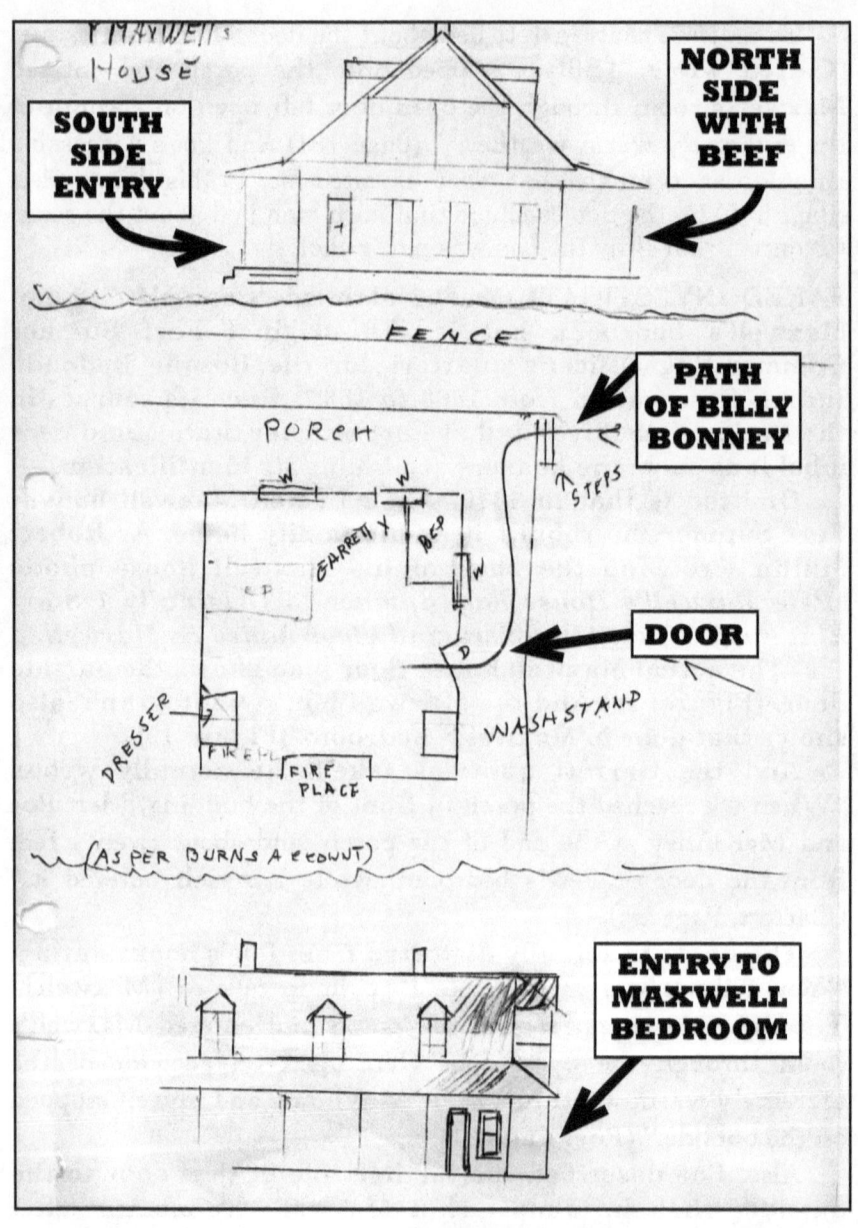

FIGURE: 18. Diagrams by Maurice Garland Fulton of the Maxwell's house, with Peter Maxwell's bedroom, and Billy Bonney's entry through its outside door. (Courtesy of the Midland, Texas, Haley Library, Robert N. Mullin Collection)

FIGURE: 19. Photograph of the Maxwell house showing Peter Maxwell's bedroom with an outside door. (Courtesy of the Midland, Texas, Haley Library, Robert N. Mullin Collection)

SOURCE FOR FAKE DOOR INVESTIGATION: This "investigation's" no door claim was lifted from an undated article by an unknown author (erroneously named as Gregory Scott Smith) titled "The Death of Billy the Kid: A New Scenario?" now in the Fort Sumner State Monument files. It used John L. McCarty papers of an October 22, 1942 interview titled "Kid Dobbs Interviews: An Interview with Garrett H. 'Kid' Dobbs at Farmington, New Mexico, on September 12, 1942, with Mel Armstrong and John McCarty, Thursday Morning, October 22, 1942, In the Presence of Mrs. Dobbs and Pat Flynn. J.D. White, Amarillo, Heard Part of the Final Statements of this Interview Re. Billy the Kid's Death."

Garrett H. "Kid" Dobbs merely spouted old-timer windbag malarkey. His fabrication, with the usual claim of knowing Billy the Kid, began with: "Billy told me ... he came from San Francisco, California, and had killed a chinaman out there for insulting his mother." Here is Dobbs's Lincoln County War Battle: "Once when a friend of Billy the Kid was killed, Billy went to Chisholm [sic] and volunteered to lead the Chisholm party at war ... They made a fight and Murphy's men set fire to McSwain's [sic] house ... Billy had killed four of Murphy's men during the fight ... [During the escape] McSwain [sic] was killed by Murphy. Mrs. McSwain [sic] yelled for her trunk in the house and Tom O'Folliard went back in and got it but burnt his whiskers."

For the death scene, Dobbs's fakery continued:

> Billy was hiding out in Pete Maxwell's house ...
>
> Maxwell wrote Garrett a letter saying he would turn over Billy to him. Garrett thought it might be a trick to trap him for Billy. **Pat had Frank Poe and Jim McIntosh, two deputies with him.** [Note ignorance of even of the famous deputies.] He told them he was afraid this was a trap and wasn't going up there until he spoke with Maxwell ... Garrett wrote a note to Maxwell and sent it to him by a Mexican boy telling him to meet them at the Mexican plaza 6 miles below Fort Sumner ...
>
> Garrett told Pete if it was a trap he would kill him too. He told Pete he was coming up that night.
>
> They arrived ay Maxwell's early before Billy came in from his daylight hiding and [Pat] told his deputies to bed down in one corner of Maxwell's yard. Pat went in to the house and waited in Maxwell's bedroom.

When Billy came in that night he saw the men in the yard and asked the cook who they were. The cook said they were some of Pete's sheepherders ...

In the meantime Maxwell had told the cook not to save any cold meat ... so the Kid would have to fix his own supper.

Billy asked the cook where the knife was ... Garrett could hear every word in the bedroom.

Then the Kid asked where the meat was and the cook said he guessed it was in the meat box. The Kid told him it wasn't. The cook told Billy it must be in Pete's bedroom then as Pete had brought some new meat out from town. [Note that Dobbs did not even know that Fort Sumner *was* the town.]

<u>The Kid had the knife in his left hand and started to the bedroom to get some meat. [Note that Billy walks through the house to get to the bedroom.] There was a broken-rock walk way just large enough for two to pass in the hall way from the kitchen to the bedroom. There was a dining room between the kitchen and bedroom. Garrett could hear the Kid coming on those rocks. He was sitting on the foot of the bed</u> [The interviewer here explains that the hall "ran east and west; and Pete's room was on the west] ...

It was warm weather and the bedroom window was open ... The door opened and Billy saw Pat move off the bed. Billy said: Como estes? (What's that) ...

Garrett ... fired and as Billy fell he fired over Pat's head and the bullet went in the ceiling ... Pat's shot went under Billy's heart ...

Pat and Pete ... told me how it happened many times as did the deputies.

For "The Death of Billy the Kid: A New Scenario?" the unknown author used this junk and added his/her ignorant research by attaching the National Archives floor plan. It was called "the original layout of the officers' quarters buildings, one of which became the Maxwell house [provided to show no outside door]. Taken in conjunction with the Dobbs interview [Billy walking through the house], it raises a whole new series of questions as to exactly how Billy the Kid was killed on that July night in 1881." This author was unaware that Lucien Maxwell rebuilt the house as two stories and added the outside door to what would be Peter's bedroom. (And the equally ignorant hoaxers used that diagram for *Cold Case Billy the Kid*.) So the ignorant author concluded:

"We can posit an alternative scenario, based partly on what Dobbs said and partly on common sense. If the Kid was really after a hunk of steak he would have gone to the kitchen or the 'cool box' either in the storage or dining area or even outside in the courtyard, because it beggars belief that Maxwell would have a side of beef hanging in his bedroom. However, if the Kid was either going to or just leaving [his lover] Paulita either from the room next to Dona Luz - which would then require him to use the hallway just as Dobbs describes it – or alternatively from one of the two rooms on the northern side of the house, he would as he reached the front (eastern) doorway [believed by Smith, and used by the hoaxers, as the only entrance] – either from the inside or out – have seen the two strangers and acted just as Poe and Garrett described – skipping through the door [here an inside door] into Pete's bedroom to find out who they were – and Garrett was there waiting for him."

PAST FAKE DOOR GAMBIT: Sederwall had given this fake "evidence" for the no door scam for fellow "Billy the Kid Case" hoaxer and editor, Bob Boze Bell, for Bell's August, 2010's *True West's* "Caught with his Pants Down? Billy the Kid vs Pat Garrett, One Door Closes."

For it, Sederwall was a "retired lawman" giving "CSI" evidence that Billy was in Paulita's bedroom, "across from Pete's, when he heard two men (Poe and McKinney) talking outside." Using Dobbs's no outside door, Sederwall has Billy enter the bedroom from the hall. And his "CSI" proof is none other than hoaxing Dr. Henry Lee's Case 2003-274 fake washstand forensics, with Sederwall making-up his own version that "laser lines up perfectly with the hole [sic] in the washstand" if Garrett shot Billy, then ran out the inside door, and on his knees fired back in, hitting the washstand!

So Bob Boze Bell concluded: "[C]onventional wisdom is often misinformed, which I found out when Gregory Smith [the erroneously listed author of the article] discovered the original 1863 floor plans ... Apparently, windows, not doors, were located alongside these rooms. Lucien ... might have created doorways when he and his family moved in. Yet if Pete's room did not have an outside door, historians will certainly be forced to look at the event with new eyes."

<u>To be noted is that opportunistic faker Sederwall here backs the victim being Billy Bonney!</u>

FAKING SHOOTING SCENE DOUBTS

The historical Maxwell bedroom shooting scene is given. Then doubts are presented about Garrett's claims. (Pages 142-143)

OMITTED EXPLANATIONS: Garrett's description may have been tempered by shielding Peter Maxwell from complicitness in the ambush. Implied is that Garrett hid in the dark room, with his deputies outside to shoot in case Billy escaped. This is supported by Poe's book, in which he described almost shooting Maxwell when he ran out the door. (Poe, Page 39) It would have only occurred if Poe anticipated an escaping Billy, and was prepared to shoot him. And Poe reported the danger from Billy's partisans: "We spent the remainder of the night on the Maxwell premises, keeping constantly on our guard, was we were expecting to be attacked by friends of the dead man." (Poe, Page 44)

Another possibility is in Frederick Nolan's 1992 *The Lincoln County War: A Documentary History*. "Garrett found the Kid in bed with Paulita Maxwell and shot him *in flagrante delictu*; the authored version [given by Garrett] ... was then cooked up to protect the girl's reputation." (Nolan, Page 425)

Questioned are whether two or three shots were fired.

OMITTED EVIDENCE: Poe gave the explanation: "An instant later a shot was fired in the room, followed immediately by what everyone within hearing distance thought were two other shots. However, <u>there were only two shots fired</u>, the third report, as we learned afterward, being caused by the rebound of the second bullet, which had struck the adobe wall and rebounded against the headboard of a wooden bedstead." (Poe, Pages 36-37) Garrett also heard three reports and thought Billy fired one to his two. But Billy's revolver showed no firing. Garrett stated: "We searched long and faithfully – found <u>both my bullet marks</u> but no other." (Garrett, Page 218) And Maxwell testified for the Coroner's jurymen: *"Pat F. Garrett <u>fired two shots</u> at the said William Bonney and the said William Bonney fell near my fire place."*

Then, added are "Brushy" hoax's claims that Garrett had "high political ambitions," so he covered-up killing an innocent victim; and "there is disagreement on whether the body of the slain man was inside or outside the room." (Page 143; and *Alias Billy the Kid*, Page 49)

FAKING EVIDENCE: Garrett was not politically ambitious, and the killing was in the bedroom. And the "Brushy" hoax is not evidence.

Omitting that the second bullet hit Maxwell's headboard, given is Dr. Henry Lee's fake washstand forensics, with Garrett shooting from the floor. Then a Homeland Security "expert" is used to claim physiologic alterations in a shooter causing "fight or flight mode," to confirm Lee's crawling Garrett and to say Garrett lied by reporting differently. Also claimed is that Garrett lied by leaving out the washstand. (Pages 144-146)

HOAXING: The "Billy the Kid Case" hoax's fake washstand investigation is not evidence. And Poe had confirmed that: "[T]he second bullet, which had struck the adobe wall ... [had] rebounded against the headboard of a wooden bedstead." (Poe, Pages 36-37)

FAKING THE BODY'S REMOVAL

To hide the multiple body identifications, taking Billy's body to the carpenter's shop is minimized. Instead, a quote is used from Garrett's July 15, 1881 "letter to the territorial governor": "It was my desire to have been able to take him alive, but his coming upon me so suddenly and unexpectedly led me to believe that he had seen me enter the room, or had been informed by someone of the fact, and that he had come there armed with pistol and knife expressly to kill me if he could." (Page 147)

Seeking a discrepancy, claimed was that Poe said the room was too dark to see. Added was that there was no outside door, so Poe had to go through the house to get to the bedroom. (Page 147)

FAKING EVIDENCE: Hiding identifications of the corpse as Billy's, and faking no bedroom door is merely hoaxing.

And Garrett's letter of July 15, 1881 to Acting-Governor William Ritch (as reprinted in the Las Cruces *Rio Grande Republican* as "Kid the Killer Killed" (see pages 18-20 above)) not only had the shooting scene, but gave the Coroner's Jury Report's body identification.

Next was quibbling about the body being face-up or down, with Jesus Silva, quoted from Miguel Otero's fictional **1936** book, *The Real Billy the Kid,* as face down. So the duo questioned whether Silva entered first (Page 148) (and Jameson forgot that "Brushy" had no bedroom scene!).

FAKING EVIDENCE: With Billy shot from the front, he would be thrust backwards, landing supine. And the hoaxers admit the room was next lit, and the body examined. And it could have been turned over then.

The Jesus Silva story came from an *Alias Billy the Kid* prompt footnote: a July, 1936 *Frontier Times* interview of a Leslie Traylor of Galveston, Texas, titled "Facts Regarding the Escape of Billy the Kid." Traylor, a history buff, interviewed old-timers in Lincoln and Fort Sumner in 1933 and 1935; including Silva. He wrote: "Silva said he was at home when he heard the shot, and they sent for him, that when he arrived they were afraid to go into the room, and as he knew the Kid well and was not afraid, he went in with a light and found him dead, lying face downward with a pistol in one hand and a butcher knife in the other." So the real issue is not face-up or down, but that Jesus Silva was yet another witness identifying the corpse as Billy Bonney's!

And Miguel Otero was a meaningless hearsay source, who wrote his book 55 years after the shooting!

FAKING A "PETE MAXWELL"

Peter Maxwell, as key testifier in the Coroner's Jury as to dead Billy, received Sederwall's fake attack. Used was a 1978 article by a "Bundy Avants" [sic] (unreferenced) titled "The Bundy Avants [sic] Story," with his claim that years after the shooting, Maxwell told him Billy was not shot, Poe was not there, the body was a Mexican, and Garrett hid it all. (Page 136)

FAKE EVIDENCE: The Bundy Avant article is from a May-June, 1978 *True West* magazine interview with old-timer Avant, spouting malarkey. In 1894, as a child, he came with his cattle ranching family from Texas to Roswell, New Mexico; then moved to Capitan, when he was eight; then White Oaks in 1905 for farming. Avant's Billy the Kid-related tall tales begin with George Coe, who, he made-up, told him he had retrieved murdered John Tunstall's body. Name-dropping, Avant faked John Chisum's brand as the "Long S," when it was the "Long Rail." He babbled that "Colonel Henry Fountain" was a family friend; when Fountain's name was Albert Jennings, and his little son, murdered with him, was Henry.

For his Peter Maxwell fabrication, <u>Avant had himself meeting an old man named "Pete," a cook at a ranch near the San Andres Mountains</u>. This pseudo-Pete says: "I've takin a likin' to you" ... I sensed he had something on his mind which had bothered him for a long time and he felt he had found someone to confide in." Avant says the man told him he was Pete Maxwell, and would tell Avant a secret, if he promised not to tell it "to a living sole as long as I'm alive." Pete then tells him, "Billy is not dead; I can take you to where he lives and has a nice family ... I'll tell you how it was ... There was no light in the house and Pat and I were in the dark when we heard someone come in. We both thought it was Billy. So when the man came in and sensed someone else was there beside me, he said, 'Quien es?' and Pat just fired. We heard the man fall. But when we struck a match and looked at him, we saw it was not the Kid ... Pat was pretty well shook up, as he didn't want it said he had killed the wrong man. It was a Mexican and we decided he was a drifter who would never be missed ... I agreed to keep quiet, too, as I could see it would give Billy a chance to slip away and start a new life, which he had been talking of doing." Avant says it must be true, because Maxwell would know.

In fact, Peter Maxwell lived near Fort Sumner until his death on June 21, 1898. [FIGURE: 20] His death, as a "Las Vegas" item, in June 28, 1898's *The Albuquerque Citizen*; stated: "**By parties arriving from Fort Sumner it was learned Saturday that Peter Maxwell died at his home near that place , an the morning of the 21st, and was buried on the following day. He leaves a wife and one child. Peter Maxwell was the son of Lucien B. Maxwell, the original owner of the celebrated Maxwell land grant lying in Colorado and New Mexico. Peter Maxwell is well remembered in Las Vegas, where he was a frequent visitor in years past.**" Also, the coarse vernacular Avant faked for pseudo-Pete is unlike that sophisticated and bi-lingual man born to Hispanic aristocracy and Lucien Bonaparte Maxwell's prominent Menard family.

FIGURE: 20. Peter Maxwell's house near Fort Sumner, where he lived after the town was sold; discrediting Bundy Avant's claim that Maxwell worked as a cook in a San Andres Mountains cow camp. (Courtesy of the Midland, Texas, Haley Library, Robert N. Mullin Collection)

Avant continued his lies with meeting John W. Poe at Roswell at a later date. Poe asks him what he thought of Garrett, and Avant "didn't think too highly of him." This pseudo-Poe, who was not present at the killing scene, tells Avant that he had been Garrett's deputy when Garrett killed Billy in Fort Sumner, but since "Pat Billy, and I were good friends at one time," he wanted to pay his last respects [with Avant unaware that Poe had never met Billy until moments before the killing]. So Poe used two horses to ride to Fort Sumner that night. Avant says Garrett then refused to let Poe see the body; so Poe suspected foul play and turned in his badge. Avant concluded: "This made the second time in a period of three years that I had been told by two men, who of all people should know the facts, that Billy was not killed by Pat Garrett." (Avant, Pages 47-48)

This Bundy Avant fakery replicated garrulous Billy the Kid fakery of old-timer Severo Gallegos, featured in the original "Brushy" hoax; and old-timer Homer Overton's fake Affidavit used as evidence in 2003 by then "Billy the Kid Case" hoaxer, Sheriff Tom Sullivan, for an addendum to Case No. 2003-274's "Probable Cause Statement." (See pages 520-521 above) It showed that the Jameson-Sederwall duo relied on the same junk as "evidence."

An interesting aside is that Avant described having "a little white pony called Billy Barlow" (Avant, Page 12), showing the prevalence of the name "Brushy Bill" picked for his own death scene confabulation.

NOTHING BUT FAKING

The Jameson-Sederwall fakery, though adding more hoaxing to the original chicanery, added not a stitch of evidence to prove Pat Garrett did not kill Billy the Kid. And abandoning "Brushy's" back-porch-Billy-Barlow-shot-fetching-meat contrivance actually ended "Brushy's" run. One is left wondering what the hoaxers were trying to accomplish, besides the well-worn, hollow, meaningless, and failed history-is-not-as-written mantra of their respective hoaxes; along with Sederwall showing off his fake "investigations" and hijacking the "Billy the Kid Case" as his own.

CHAPTER 5
FAKING NO INQUEST

HOAXERS VERSUS CORONER'S JURY REPORT

To face the fatal July 15, 1881 Coroner's Jury Report, the Jameson-Sederwall duo had only faked discrepancies, fake "investigations," and fake conspiracy theories.

Recycled was Sederwall's "Billy the Kid Case" hoax's "Probable Cause Statement," with his fake time discrepancies to fabricate that the Jury never convened. (See pages 511-513 above)

The body's location is questioned because the Report said: *"[T]he above jury convened in the home of Luz B. Maxwell and proceeded to a room in the said house where they found the body of William Bonney alias "Kid."* Since the body was taken to the carpenter's shop, the location is called a lie. (Page 149)

FAKERY: It is obvious that, after that wake, the body was returned to the Maxwell house for the inquest.

Claimed is: Justice of the Peace Segura "instructed Rudolph to assemble a coroner's jury and serve as foreman." (Page 149)

WRONG: Segura appointed Rudulph and the five jurymen; as he stated in the Coroner's Jury Report: *"I, the undersigned, Justice of the Peace ... immediately upon receiving said information I proceeded to the said place and named Milnor Rudulph, Jose Silva, Antonio Sevedra, Pedro Antonio Lucero, Lorenzo Jaramillo and Sabal Gutierres a jury to investigate the case."*

The Report's stating "gratitude of the community" was owed Garrett, is called "suspicious" by Sederwall, because Fort Sumner people were angry at the killing, not grateful. (Pages 150-151)

FALSE INTERPRETATION: Sederwall seems unaware that President Milnor Rudulph was a Ringite. (See page 63

above) He would have praised Garrett for stamping out the last anti-Ring rebel. And the jurymen, presumably terrified by this killing, would not have dared to object.

The Report's existence is next "doubted" by claiming its not being filed in San Miguel County; "Paco" Anaya claiming two reports; the inquest being speedy; William Keleher's photocopy in Spanish [in his 1957 *Violence in Lincoln County*] as the "second coroner's report;" his English translation meaning the victim spoke English; and that some signers misspelled names. So the duo doubt that the jurymen even saw the body. (Pages 150-151)

HOAXING EVIDENCE: This just repeats "Brushy" hoax fakery (see pages 36-47 above), with an update referring to the Report's English translation in William Keleher's book.

As to viewing the body, the Coroner's Jury Report confirmed it performed the inquest's legal duties: interviewing witness Peter Maxwell, identifying the body as Billy Bonney's, examining the wound, and concluding that the homicide did not require prosecution as being justifiable self-defense.

For their conclusion, the Jameson-Sederwall duo rely on their own fakery; and, of course, state that Garrett killed an innocent man, rushed through the inquest process to hide the body of the non-Billy victim by burial, and wrote the "second" [i.e., real] Coroner's Jury Report himself. And 'cop' Sederwall intones meaninglessly that "somebody (or somebodies) are lying." (Pages 151 -152)

CHAPTER 6
THE RETURN OF THE "BILLY THE KID CASE" FAKE FORENSICS

RECYCLING THE FAKE JAILBREAK INVESTIGATION

Hiding that courthouse forensics were for Lincoln County Sheriff's Department Case 2003-274's "Probable Cause Statement," Steve Sederwall made them his *personal investigation* in Jameson's chapters: "Escape" (Pages 95-101), "Lincoln County Courthouse Crime Scene Investigation" (Pages 102-111), and "An Escape Plot." (Pages 112-119). And his fellow hoaxers were rewritten as his assistants. He even recycled his forged Dr. Henry Lee floorboard report, as cited in the "Bibliography." Of course, based on the Pat and Billy bromance, it damned "Brushy" by his ignorance of it. But Jameson missed that.

Instead of unsavory reality, readers got Jameson's adulating: "Steve Sederwall revealed elements of this gripping event that had long escaped the notice of earlier researchers and writers." (Page 95) Jameson also gave the "William Henry Roberts aka Billy the Kid" to add shackle-slipping. And he makes-up that the hole on the descent stairway from the fatal bullet was made by Maurice Garland Fulton with a "hand-drill." (Pages 100-101)

He claims Garrett never did an "investigation" (Page 101), as lead-in for Sederwall's "applying modern crime-solving and investigative techniques" to the Bell "crime scene." (Page 102). Sederwall claimed friend Garrett gave Billy the gun to kill Deputy Bell, proving the loyalty which made Garrett kill the innocent victim in Fort Sumner 77 days later to help Billy escape again.

For this go-around, Sederwall rolled out fake "suspicions" as proof of Garrett's colluding with Billy; as follows:

1) It was "suspicious" that Garrett described the scene, since he was away at White Oaks collecting taxes. **[But Garrett made clear he was recounting the escape from eye-witnesses.]**

2) It was "suspicious" that Garrett said the armory door could be opened by a "firm push." **[Concealed is that in *The Authentic Life of Billy the Kid* Garrett was just saying that "Lincoln did not then have a jail that would hold a cripple." Prisoners were just held on the courthouse's second floor and chained to steel rings in the floor. That is why he kept Billy guarded and with extra shackles.]**

3) It was "suspicious that Garrett blamed Bell and Olinger. **[Why not? They were the responsible guards.]**

Sederwall said he would "remedy the situation" of Garrett's "lying." And his own lying embellishment of the original hoax were out-of-control. On August 4, 2002, he leads lawmen and Dr. Henry Lee to the courthouse. (Page 104) Admitted is that the stairway was replaced. **[Omitted is that the shooting of Bell had occurred on it - so there was no longer an evidence source!]** Stated is that the second floor floorboards were exposed for Lee to do "presumptive blood tests" with o-Tolidine, called a test for blood [hiding it was for any iron-containing compound, like rust]. Sederwall portrays Lee as swabbing the flooorboards, and **quotes him as saying: "Positive for blood."** (Page 105) Sederwall added: **"The tests showed positive reactions for blood in several areas on the landing ... Lee's conclusion was that 'chemical tests for the presence of blood were positive with some of [the floorboard] stains."** (Page 105)

LYING: Sederwall fabricated the quote and conclusion. And he hid that no Bell "reference DNA" existed to see if it was Bell's "blood;" and that Orchid Cellmark Lab, which got Lee's specimens, does not test for blood.

JAMESON AS INADVERTENTLY COMPLICIT: Dupe Jameson cited Sederwall's forged Dr. Lee report in his Bibliography under "Reports" with yet another faked title and a new made-up date as "Forensic Examination Report (Lincoln County Courthouse), May 22, 2004." Lee's actual and sole report was dated February 25, 2005, and cited only need for testing possible blood-like stains. (See pages 574-575 above)

Sederwall next lied that blood was confirmed; it was Bell's because his was the only bloodshed in the courthouse's history; and it was a "significant amount." (Pages 105-106; 110) He then made-up that Garrett must have lied because he did not mention so much blood on the second floor. (Page 106)

Sederwall the quoted Gauss's hearing a "tussle upstairs, somebody hurrying down the stairs," and Bell coming out to him - which is conventional history. But Sederwall claimed this proved Bell was "upstairs," since he ran down. (Page 106)

FAKERY: Running down the stairway, has nothing to do with proving bleeding on its top.

Sederwall then pretended that Sophie Poe, Sheriff John Poe's wife, in her 1936 book, *Buckboard Days*, claimed blood <u>on the second floor</u> when she lived in the courthouse. (Page 106) Then he then made-up that her writing that Bell fell "to the bottom of the stairs" meant she saw blood from the top to the bottom. Then he claimed Garrett lied by not describing that too.

LYING: In reality, Sophie Poe commented on stairway blood, while forgetting that Bell was heading down, not up, when shot. She stated: "The back stairway ... which I had to travel many times during the day, was still stained with blood, a grim reminder of the day ... when Billy the Kid had shot and killed his guard, James W. Bell. Bell had been climbing those stairs and his body had fallen to the bottom of them." (Sophie Poe, Page 205) The place she referenced is preserved for tourists as a bullet crater on the wall half-way down the stairway, to the right of a descent.

Sederwall faked "discrepancies" in Garrett's account; questioning slipped handcuffs, and ruminating about how to wipe yourself in the latrine if your hands were cuffed behind your back [which was never claimed for Billy]. (Pages 107-108)

FAKE ANALYSIS: Omitted is that Garrett might not have been given the true manner of escape, especially if Billy's likely accomplice, Gottfried Gauss, gave the information. and obviously concealing a plot.

Sederwall then gave the gun-left-in-the-outhouse version, and ruminated about why Billy did not shoot Bell then. And he gave the known scenario that Billy wanted to take Bell prisoner, not kill him. But he added Bob Olinger to that plan. And he made-up scenes of Billy's confronting Bell with the gun, and wounding Bell's head [usually seen as Billy's attempt to subdue him to enable tying-up]. But Sederwall faked Bell's head's blood as being on the floorboards for Dr. Lee's fake forensics! (Pages 108-110)

By then, Sederwall had blood pouring. So he made-up that Lee had said "Bell lost a great deal of blood." (Page 110)

THEN CAME THE WHOLE POINT OF JAMESON'S BOOK: FUSING THE "BRUSHY" AND "BILLY THE KID CASE" HOAXES INTO A MEGAHOAX: SEDERWALL QUOTED "BRUSHY" HIMSELF FOR AN ESCAPE SCENARIO TO GO WITH FOR HIS FAKE FORENSICS! Sederwall has "Brushy" ask to go to the latrine. While Bell goes to get the key, he slips out of his handcuff, hits and stuns returned Bell on the head, grabs his gun and key, and wants to be taken to the armory. On the way there, Bell runs for the stairway, pauses at the hall on top of the stairs so "copious amounts of blood" can fall. Then Billy's fatal bullet ricochets on the wall. So Sederwall says this explains the "blood" he and "his investigative team" found "a century and a quarter later."(Page 111)

FABRICATING "BRUSHY'S FABRICATION: This, at last, unites two liars: "Brushy" confabulating himself as Billy; and Sederwall fabricating himself as a valid investigator.

But Sederwall faked "Brushy's" tale. "Brushy" had Olinger leaving himself and Bell in the east room where Billy was kept. Bell goes to Garrett's office to the west to get the key. "Brushy" slips his shackle, and when Bell returns, he stated: "I hit him in the back of the head. He tumbled over on the floor ... [NOTE: "Brushy" said <u>he hit Bell in the east room, not the hallway.</u>] I told him to walk through [Garrett's] office and unlock the armory door." (*Alias Billy the Kid*, Pages 43-44) Then "Brushy" has Bell's flight down the stairs, and the shot hitting the wall, as "Brushy" would have seen himself on his Morrison tour.

Key, is that "Brushy" never claimed that Pat Garrett played a part in this escape.

This fakery leads to accusing Garrett of "perfidy;" to segue into sneering: "[H]e may have been more involved in the Kid's escape than we have been led to believe." (Page 112)

A BAD FIT OF HOAXES: Since the "Brushy" hoax is a bad fit for the "Billy the Kid Case" hoax, contradictions like this arise: "Brushy" did not claim Garrett helped his escape, or that Garrett killed Billy Barlow to save him. But the "Billy the Kid Case" hoax, and now Sederwall, used the Bell killing to fake Garrett's friendship for Billy, for a future murder motive for Garrett.

Faking evidence of Garrett's perfidy, Sederwall used usual fake "what-ifs," to ask: What if Garrett had been away collecting taxes on purpose? (Pages 113-114)

WRONG: Tax collecting was required. When new Sheriff John Copeland neglected filing his tax collecting bond, on May 28, 1878, Governor S.B. Axtell issued a removal Proclamation and replaced him with George Peppin.

Since Garrett reported the escape horse as Court Clerk Billy Burt's, Sederwall tried a history-not-as-written trick to claim the horse was Garrett's. The source was a Gorgonio Wilson, who stated in an August 7, 1955 (!) *El Paso Times* article, when 89, that Billy called him from a window to saddle *Garrett's horse* for him. And a non-historical Robert Corn's daughter said her father said Billy used *Pat's horse*. And in 1977, a Ygenio Salazar relative claimed *Garrett's horse*. (Page 116-117) So Sederwall concluded that sharing his horse meant Garrett and Billy were friends.

FLAWED EVIDENCE: The Wilson horse story hides that the escape was witnessed by Lincoln's townspeople, and no legitimate witness reported Garrett's horse being used. And, if it was stolen, Garrett would have reported it. Also, he would have ridden his horse to White Oaks for his tax collecting, so it would not have been there.

And it is crucial to note that this scam demolished "Brushy" as Billy, for lack of a Garrett horse tale. His he had child Severo Gallegos getting Billy a rope for the horse, <u>which he called Ira Leonard's</u>. Worse, Gallegos, just made a liar by Sederwall, was "Brushy's" *only eye-witness Lincolnite* to give a him a "Brushy"-as-Billy Affidavit! And, marble-playing on the street, Gallegos was really someone who could have recognized Garrett's horse!

Next, Sederwall presented known scenarios of Gauss's involvement in the escape, and of the Kid's going to the outhouse to get the gun; but rejected them as "lies." (Pages 117-118)

FAKE ANALYSIS: No evidence is given that Gauss lied.

Omitted are likely motives for Gauss's willingness to risk his life by hanging as a murder accomplice of Billy's deputy killings. In fact, Gauss, was bitterly anti-Ring. He had first been employed in running the brewery for "The House" in its sutler store beginnings, and had been cheated out of his wages. As anti-Ring, John Tunstall's, cook, he would have met Billy by October of 1877, and had been present at every subsequent Ring atrocity. He was at Tunstall's Feliz River ranch when Brady's murderous posse came looking for Tunstall, then murdered him. He knew about Governor S.B. Axtell's Proclamation outlawing the Regulators, and might even have been at Tunstall's store during the Regulator's Brady ambush. And he would have been outraged at the murder of Alexander McSween in the Lincoln County War Battle. He would have believed Billy's hanging sentence was unjust, since all the Ring murderers had been shielded from penalties. And he was now courthouse caretaker, positioned to intervene. Also, he was above suspicion, because Pat Garrett was a late entry to Lincoln County, and would have been unaware of his partisanship. And is obvious that Gauss and Billy would have used the outhouse plan when Garrett was out of town - as Garrett could have stopped them.

To bolster his fakery of Pat Garrett as Billy's accomplice, Sederwall relied on his usual "what ifs;" now so bizarre they knock your sox off: What if Garrett made up that Billy was a bad outlaw to build himself up as a hero by contrast? What if Garrett blamed his deputies for incompetence to remove responsibility from himself? What if, on purpose, he did not seal off the town to further investigate the deputy killings? (Pages 118-119)

Jameson added "Brushy" hoaxing that Garrett sought "higher political office" he had to convince citizens he was competent, so he lied. (Page 119) The Jameson-Sederwall duo conclude: "The evidence clearly shows that Garrett lied. The evidence is highly suggestive of [his] possible role in the escape plot."

FAKERY: All this fakery is irrelevant to Garrett not killing Billy, or "Brushy" being Billy. And much of it demolished "Brushy's" special knowledge claim by his ignorance of the tales.

RECYCLING THE CARPENTER'S BENCH DNA INVESTIGATION

Jameson pretending it was proved that Pat Garrett killed an innocent victim (Pages 153-154), lets Steve Sederwall call Fort Sumner an active crime scene. (Page 154)

HOAXING: Fort Sumner was not a crime scene after the Coroner's Jury decision of July 15, 1881; stating that *"[T]he deed of said Garrett was justifiable homicide."*

With the "Billy the Kid Case" hidden, Sederwall, as sole "investigator," presents its carpenter's bench hoax, with additions. The bench is called an **important source of "bloodstains from the slain intruder"** (Page 155) - a new name for the innocent victim - **as a source of DNA.**

The bench is claimed as a Maxwell family possession (Pages 155-159), though it was never bench's location. Hilariously, for evidence is used Bundy Avant's malarkey of meeting "Pete Maxwell in the San Andres Mountains (See page 709-712 above); so Sederwall makes-up that Maxwell gave the furniture away after being reduced to "cooking for 'wagon outfits!' " It ends up in Stella Abreu's "museum," with Sederwall tracing it to Mannie Miller's Albuquerque converted chicken coop. (Pages 158-160)

Sederwall portrays Dr. Henry Lee as contacted by him, and as finding that "**a number of locations" on the bench's top and bottom tested positive for blood** by "presumptive blood test reagents phenolphthalein and o-tolidine." **Sederwall attributes the "blood" to "two different human beings;" claiming future separation would identify the "slain intruder."** (Page 163) A Lee report is not cited, but one is in the Bibliography as: "Lee, Dr. Henry. Forensic Examination Report (Examination of Furniture From Pete Maxwell's of July 15, 1881) 22 May 2004." (Page 187)

LYING: Sederwall made-up that he was a private investigator for the bench, that it had blood, and that there was a "slain intruder." Lee's sole report of February 25, 2005 merely noted "blood-like" stains; and Orchid Cellmark Lab did not test for blood, and got no DNA. [APPENDIX: 2] The invalid mixed sample was for courthouse floorboards.

The cited Lee report appears to be one of Sederwall's forged ones, with the date changed to May 22, 2004. The one given to me and the Court was titled "Forensic Research and Training Center Forensic Examination Report: "Examination of furniture from Pete Maxwell's of July 15, 1881," and dated February 25, 2005.

BASHING "BRUSHY": This fakery contradicted "Brushy's" death scene with shot-Billy-bleeding-on-the-bench.

RECYCLING "MAXWELL FURNITURE" FORENSICS

Sederwall, as sole "investigator," next had Dr. Henry Lee examine the headboard and the washstand.

HOAXING THE HEADBOARD

Sederwall reminds the reader that Deputy Poe had said Garrett's second shot rebounded from the wall and hit the Maxwell's headboard. But he states that Lee found "nothing resembling the impact of a bullet, even a scratch." So Poe is called a liar. (Pages 160-161) No mention is made of Lee's report, but the Bibliography cites "Lee, Dr. Henry. Forensic Examination Report (Examination of Furniture From Pete Maxwell's of July 15, 1881) 22 May 2004." (Page 187)

HOAXING: The headboard fragment, is just an empty frame, missing the place for bullet damage to be seen.

The Lee report in the Bibliography appears to be one of Sederwall's forged ones, with the date changed to May 22, 2004. The one Sederwall first presented to me was his fake "Forensic Research and Training Center Forensic Examination Report: "Examination of furniture from Pete Maxwell's of July 15, 1881," dated February 25, 2005. Its second forged version, with different font and deleted "Results and Conclusions," went to the Court as Exhibit E.

Lee's, actual report of February 25, 2005 had stated dishonestly: "No bullet hole and no observable damage."

This is pure hoaxing by both Sederwall and Lee; as well as records forgery, as found by the Court, for Sederwall.

IRRELEVANT: All this fakery had nothing to do with Garrett not killing Billy, or "Brushy" being Billy.

HOAXING THE WASHSTAND

Sederwall repeated, as his own investigation, Dr. Henry Lee's fake washstand forensics with the fake bullet trajectory and Garrett shooting from the floor. (Pages 161-163) No report is mentioned, but the Bibliography cites: "Lee, Dr. Henry. Forensic Examination Report (Examination of Furniture From Pete Maxwell's of July 15, 1881) 22 May 2004." (Page 187)

HOAXING: The washstand is not historically connected to the death scene. And Lee faked Garrett's crouched position from the toy-sized washstand. (See pages 576-579 above)

The Lee report cited in the Bibliography appears to be one of Sederwall's forged ones, with date changed to May 22, 2004. It was given to me with a "Results and Conclusions" section absent.

Lee's actual report of February 25, 2005 was non-committal; stating: "Two bullet holes were located on the side panels of the Washstand ... However, it is not possible to determine when those bullet holes were produced at this time [meaning anytime from the 1880's to the 1900's]."

IRRELEVANT: All this was irrelevant to Garrett not killing Billy, or "Brushy" being Billy.

RECYCLING THE JOHN MILLER EXHUMATION

Duped W.C. Jameson, show-casing anything Steve Sederwall claimed, did not flinch when he presented "Brushy" blasphemy that dead John Miller matched Billy the Kid, in what he called his private investigation! (Page 165) And dug-up dismembered, random man, William Hudspeth, was obviously concealed. Also concealed is that Miller was almost 10 years older than Billy, knew no history, died of a broken hip, and was toothless.

His exhumation is claimed to have been done on May 9, 2005 [sic – May 19] by an unnamed "forensic anthropologist" and "authorized by the state of Arizona."(Page 165)

HOAXING: Hidden is "Lincoln County Sheriff's Department Supplemental Report for Case # 2003-274 for exhumation of John Miller." (See page 588 above) Hidden is having no Billy the Kid DNA for identity matching.

Sederwall stated: "The right scapula of John Miller manifested a round hole. The anthropologist observed that it appeared to be a bullet hole that had healed [and the bullet entered the upper chest and exited his back]." He added that "Miller's right front incisor was placed somewhat in front of his left front incisor." So he was shot Billy the Kid. (Page 165)

LYING: Sederwall recycled his fakery to reporter, Rene Romo, in November 6, 2006's *Albuquerque Journal's* "Billy the Kid Probe May Yield New Twist." Romo wrote: "**Sederwall ... said Miller's skeletal remains were intriguing. He said Miller had buck teeth, like the Kid, and an old bullet wound that entered his upper left chest and exited through the scapula.**" Hidden, is that the hoaxers' forensic expert, Dr. Laura Fulginiti, reported Miller having no teeth, and no bullet-damaged scapula. Hidden is that the teeth and not bullet-damaged healed *right* scapula were William Hudspeth's. (See page 591 above)

Sederwall then claimed he got DNA from Miller's remains "sufficient to conduct a test." (Page 165)

HOAXING: Hidden was having no Billy the Kid DNA to compare with Miller's. Hidden was no need for DNA matching, since Miller had no historical match to Billy.

MYSTERY: It is inexplicable that "Brushy"-believing Jameson put this Miller-backing hoax in his book.

LONGING FOR "BRUSHY'S" "DNA FORENSICS"

After 165 pages, Jameson finally got to extol "Brushy's" special knowledge and the fake photoanalysis match. (Pages 165-167) And he wished Sederwall could have settled the "controversy" by matching DNA from the Fort Sumner grave, to the bench to make "Brushy" Billy. (Page 167)

TRUE-BELIEVER BEFUDDLEMENT: Proved was that Jameson still clung to the standard "Brushy Bill" imposter hoax, and had missed that it was contradicted by the "Billy the Kid Case" hoax's claims which he put in his book. There was no "Brushy" on the bench for DNA!

CHAPTER 7
THE RETURN OF THE CONSPIRACY THEORIES

FAKING PLOTS AGAINST "TRUTH"

For duped W.C. Jameson, the only explanation for the blockade of Billy's and his mother's graves for exhumations was a conspiracy. He wrote: "As expected, [those] who claimed to be historians, who were defensive of the status quo and were also clearly concerned about their own reputations as 'experts,' have been reluctant to embrace a number of Sederwall's findings that contradict the legend." (Page 168) To it, he added New Mexico's governor and city officials [who] "fought to keep the legends and myths of Billy the Kid and Pat Garrett alive." (Page 168)

So he presented Steve Sederwall's culminating fable of being a lone crusader, seeking truth.

SEDERWALL'S CONSPIRACY AGAINST HIMSELF

For his chapter "Politics v. Truth," Jameson gave Sederwall a platform to attack fellow hoaxers and aggrandize himself. (Pages 168-171) For this fiction, Sederwall secretly recycled June 21, 2007's "Memorandum," which he, as a Deputy, with Deputy Tom Sullivan, wrote for my open records case to hide "Billy the Kid Case" records. (See pages 617-629 above). But Jameson presented Sederwall's astounding fable; as follows:

As Mayor of Capitan, who happened to be a "reserve" deputy in the Lincoln County Sheriff's Department, Sederwall went to Santa Fe with Sheriff Tom Sullivan for unstated reason. There, also for unstated reason, they met with Governor Bill Richardson and his communications director, Billy Sparks.

Sparks immediately whisked Sederwall away to the "parking garage" to tell him that "Fred Nolan had called the governor" and said the carpenter's bench was not real, and Richardson wanted Sparks to "talk with Sederwall about the situation." So all turned to Sederwall for help.

Since the bench was just located, Sederwall suspected that a spy had gotten to Nolan in England. Since history professor, Paul Hutton, had been present, that spy must have been him! And, by chance, Hutton was Richardson's Billy the Kid legend history advisor! So there were a lot of politicians, employees, and sycophants in bed together! (Pages 169-170)

So Sparks, still in the garage, needed Sederwall's help; since Fort Sumner officials, like Mayor Raymond Lopez, were upset that their "cash cow" would be ruined. (Page 170) And people feared carpenter's bench DNA would upset the legend. Sederwall, then still an idealist, thought Richardson would back the truth. But Sparks made clear that the governor had thought that Sederwall would merely "drive around, ask some questions, talk to the newspapers, and proudly declare that everything associated with the Billy the Kid legend was correct." But now it looked like intrepid Sederwall would do a DNA analysis that could "ruin the Billy the Kid legend." So idealist Sederwall abruptly realized, right in that garage, that this was all about politics and money, not truth! (Pages 170-171)

Billy Sparks then asked him to change *his* focus to a pardon for Billy the Kid. Sederwall, smelling a rat, got Sparks to admit the truth. The truth was that Sederwall's **"photograph and details about the ongoing investigation were showing up in 'every paper on the planet. [H]e was getting more publicity than Governor Richardson."** And they were afraid that Sederwall would find out that Pat Garrett had not killed Billy the Kid. And they wanted to hide this outcome. (Page 171)

Still in that fateful garage, Sederwall asked Sparks if the governor wanted to back out. Sparks said that Richardson wanted to be President of the United States, and wanted the publicity; and his attorney, Bill Robins III would file for the pardon for Billy the Kid "using Sederwall's investigations." So Sederwall could get "cop fun," and tourist dollars would flow in. Except they were now afraid of Sederwall's carpenter's bench. (Page 172)

Worse, Sparks knew about Sederwall's investigations into John Miller and "William Henry Roberts" as potential Billy the

Kid's, as also risking the history. And Sparks admitted that they actually did not know where Billy the Kid was buried. (Page 172) **So Sederwall realized that he was doing such a good job as an investigator that they wanted him to stop, because it could interfere with Richardson being President of the United States.** (Page 172) Then Sederwall made clear his extreme danger, since everything depended on him. Sparks shared a "heads-up": "they [unnamed] have you in their crosshairs and before this is over ... [y]ou guys are going to feel the heat." (Page 172)

Sederwall later learned that his opponent was Fort Sumner Mayor Raymond Lopez, who had tried to get Richardson to stop his investigation. Evidence was that when Richardson's attorney, Bill Robins III, filed in Grant County to exhume Catherine Antrim to get her DNA **for Sederwall**, Lopez rushed there to stop officials from getting access. Lopez feared her DNA "would not match the DNA from the workbench." (Pages 172-173)

FAKERY: In truth, Mayor Lopez had gone to Silver City to just to sit in on a Catherine Antrim exhumation hearing.

Sederwall then made up a Silver City Town Council meeting about the threat of *his* getting the mother's DNA; with fear he would show that Billy the Kid was not buried in New Mexico; and that "Brushy Bill" Roberts was Billy the Kid. So Sederwall realized they too feared truth, and it was all for money. (Page 173)

Then the ruling of Grant County District Judge Henry Quintero, postponing exhumation of the mother, was quoted: "Only if the petitioners are successful in locating the Kid's burial site and collecting his DNA, may they petition this court for a review of Catherine Antrim's matter."

Sederwall claimed that meant Judge Quintero knew the plan was to compare the mother's remains with Miller and "Brushy Bill," and also k new Fort Sumner's grave would be blocked; **so he wanted Sederwall to dig up Billy wherever he was buried!** (Pages 173-174)

FAKERY: Sederwall misstated Judge Quintero's ruling of April 2, 2004, for "Sixth Judicial District Court, State of New Mexico, County of Grant. No. MS 2003-11, In the Matter of Catherine Antrim. Decision and Order."

Quintero called the case "not ripe," meaning not ready for decision, until Billy the Kid's remains in Fort Sumner yielded DNA for matching to justify digging up the mother. Complicit Quintero was responding to Attorney Bill Robins's filing six days earlier on February 24, 2004: "In the Matter of Catherine Antrim: Billy the Kid's Brief on the Question of Ripeness. Case No. MS 2003-11. Sixth Judicial Court, Grant County;" and to Robins's, David Sandoval's, and Mark Acuña's February 26, 2004's "Tenth Judicial Court of De Baca County, Case No. CV-2004-00005, In the Matter of William H. Bonney, aka 'Billy the Kid.' Petition for the Exhumation of Billy the Kid's Remains." Sederwall also faked that Quintero's order meant digging up any "Billy" - like "Brushy" or John Miller - for DNA.

Sederwall next made-up that Attorney Bill Robins III *then* filed for Fort Sumner's Billy the Kid exhumation, as if to purposefully interfere with Judge Quintero wanting Sederwall to dig up Miller and Roberts first. And Sederwall claimed surprise that his name had been included as a lawman exhumation petitioner by Robins. (Page 174)

FAKERY: To fake a conspiracy, Sederwall reversed the filings. In fact, first came the Robins filings on February 24 and 26, 2004 for Fort Sumner's exhumation. Then, on April 2, 2004, Judge Quintero ordered that exhumation before the mother could be dug up.

Also, Sederwall's "surprise" at his name on the petition is silly, since he was on all the petitions as a Deputy, along with Sheriffs Tom Sullivan and Gary Graves.

Sederwall claimed that three days before the Fort Sumner hearing, Billy Sparks called him and told him to drop the exhumation petition in Fort Sumner; and that it needed his permission because he was a listed petitioner. He gave permission, and then claimed the Fort Sumner politicos had a party to celebrate the news. (Page 174)

FAKERY: Sederwall hid that the Fort Sumner exhumation petition was actually withdrawn by Sheriff Tom Sullivan to prevent his recall as threatened by Lincoln County Commissioner Leo Martinez.

Also, the party was hosted by Fort Sumner for my victorious law firm, Frederick Nolan, Mayor Raymond Lopez, and local citizens, like Billy the Kid Outlaw Gang founder, Marlyn Bowlin.

Sederwall next fabricated the response of the OMI for this figment of his imagination. He claimed that he then told Billy Sparks that he had reason to believe that Billy the Kid was not buried in Fort Sumner, and there was no body in its grave. (Pages 174-175) For proof, he stated that Governor Richardson had assigned the state medical investigators office to the case. And he, Sederwall, gave them his theories and plans. Then, state medical investigator, Debra Komar, investigated the Fort Sumner grave and the Arizona grave of John Miller. After that, she refused his calls. (Page 175)

So Sederwall concluded that this proved Komar found something in Fort Sumner or Arizona, and **"the state of New Mexico wanted it covered up"** from **"the public."** He said he was determined to find the truth. So on January 20, 2004, Komar appeared in court under a subpoena, to give a deposition. He stated that her going to Fort Sumner's cemetery upset local officials. And he stated that she had testified that she had been prevented from contacting him, and her attorney in the deposition prevented her from telling him what she found. (Pages 175-176) **He concluded that her refusing to speak to him meant she "found something that would negate the legend of Billy the Kid if the information were released."** (Page 176) He then lifted quotes from her deposition out of context: To the question, "You don't think Billy the Kid is buried at Fort Sumner, do you?" she said: "I don't know. I have reason to suspect perhaps not." (Page 176)

FAKERY: Sederwall is making-up the OMI investigation, and Debra Komar's testimony; and implying falsely that he obtained her deposition by subpoena.

In fact, the OMI investigation was not requested by Richardson, who had tried to block it, since the OMI opposed exhuming Billy and his mother as forensically useless for DNA. (See pages 488-493)

The OMI did not evaluate the grave of John Miller, it being in another state, and not part of the New Mexico exhumation petitions it was opposing.

As discussed, Debra Komar, as the OMI's forensic anthropologist, gave a January 9, 2004 Affidavit opposing the exhumations.

And Komar's deposition on January 20, 2004 was subpoenaed by my law firm. (See pages 491-493 above) She was cross-examined by Attorney Bill Robins III; and concluded: "So if you ask the opinion of myself and the Office of the Medical Investigator why is this being done or what scientifically valid conclusions can be drawn from it, I can't find any." (Deposition, Page 81)

Sederwall recycled this fakery from his June 21, 2007 "Memorandum," which lifted her response to Attorney Robins out of context: "ROBINS QUESTION: You don't think Billy the Kid is buried at Fort Sumner, do you? KOMAR ANSWER: I don't know. I have reason to suspect perhaps not." (Komar, Page 144) The point was that Billy's remains might no longer be there after flooding and accidental removal with relocated soldiers. But Sederwall faked that she meant Billy was never buried there, but was buried in Texas as "Brushy" or Arizona as John Miller! (See page 492 above)

Sederwall concluded his fable with a claim that a David Bailey, a past Fort Sumner Mayor, had told De Baca County Sheriff Gary Graves that "Sederwall's investigation" had to be stopped, because he knew what was in the Billy the Kid grave, because he and a companion, on June 17, 2003, had dug it up and found nothing. And they had hidden their excavation by shoveling into adjoining graves. So Sederwall's concluding punch line was that there were no remains at the marked gravesite. (Page 177)

FAKERY: This merely proved the site's uncertainty.

But the story does not hang together. The Billy the Kid grave is surrounded by a thick-barred locked, iron cage, and its surface is covered with concrete. There are no adjoining graves to shovel into. And Marlyn Bowlin, then running the Old Fort Sumner Museum at the cemetery, checked the graves daily, and would have seen the massive disruption needed for David Baily's crime.

MEANINGLESS EVIDENCE: Stating that no remains were available proves nothing. And Jameson forgot that he stated the same thing in *The Return of the Outlaw Billy the Kid*! (See page 463 above)

JAMESON'S DUPED BEFUDDLEMENT: It is inexplicable that Jameson backed this conspiracy theorizing, after he participated himself in the "Billy the Kid Case" hoax and knew that Richardson had been backing "Brushy."

CHAPTER 8
FOREGONE FAKE CONCLUSION

WHEN HOAXERS FOOL THEMSELVES

W.C. Jameson, bedazzled by the fake forensics of the "Billy the Kid Case" hoaxers, and impressed by the flimflam "investigations" of "cop" Steve Sederwall, believed that, in this rerun with his *Cold Case Billy the Kid*, "Brushy" was finally home free, as he declared in his "Conclusion." (Pages 178-180) Smugly, he wrote: "The historians got it wrong." But he despaired of convincing them because they refused to admit being wrong; and the state of New Mexico suppressed the truth. He concluded hysterically: "[Steve Sederwall] will turn to dust ... [t]he truth he uncovered ... will remain, will endure." (Page 180)

In fact, neither Jameson, Sederwall, nor their back-up team of other hoaxers in the wings, had given any evidence whatsoever to indicate that "Brushy" had been Billy Bonney, or that history was not as written. The "Billy the Kid Case" hoax had fared no better, though Steve Sederwall had repeated its lies as truths - while audaciously absconding with the entire case as his own!

OUTCOME: By firing every bit of ammunition he had, and showing it was all blanks, W.C. Jameson inadvertently discredited the Billy the Kid pretender hoaxes of "Brushy Bill" and John Miller, as well as exposing the reprehensible hucksters who had sought to profit from riding the coattails of famous Billy the Kid.

PART IX

SUMMARY AND CONCLUSIONS

CHAPTER 1
A LITMUS TEST FOR CROOKS AND DUPES

THE "BRUSHY BILL" HOAX TODAY

Seventy years ago, mad, exhibitionistic, sociopathic Oliver Pleasant "Brushy Bill" Roberts and his hoaxing accomplices parasitized Billy the Kid history. To the present, that hijacking has attracted glory-seeking profiteering rogues in the same mold. In the process, "Brushy" himself, with his coarse grammar, offensive racism, parroted antiquated outlaw myth, and cowboy confabulations, was eradicated by his promoters' fix-ups, forgeries, fictions, and fake forensics, leaving only a pseudo-"Brushy, who would have been unrecognizable to that original fraudster.

In the wake, are the astoundingly labor-intensive productions of scoundrels to create just smoke and mirrors. The outcome is a congregation of pathetic wannabes, offering nothing real, and trolling for dupes - just like their man "Brushy," who longed to be someone special, like Billy the Kid.

The extreme complexity of the hoaxing, which was intended camouflage of its fakery, required meticulous exposing of each false claim and of each flawed misinformation source. But one could say that it all came down to the inescapable near-full moon of Billy Bonney's light-as-day killing night of July 14, 1881. "Brushy" guessed "darkness," undoing his entire hoax in one word. And his scurrilous hucksters forged his word as "brightness," undoing their secret hoaxing in one word.

Added is decades of 20th and 21st century scholarly research, leaving that error-laden scam beyond possibility of reworking.

All that makes the "Brushy Bill" hoax a litmus test for profiteering charlatans and historically imbecilic dupes. Now there are no other alternatives for backing "Brushy Bill" as Billy the Kid.

ANNOTATED APPENDIX

APPENDIX: 1. Never used, secret, Parkinson Affidavit template, apparently written by William V. Morrison, and in C.L. Sonnichsen's papers, revealing "Brushy Bill" Roberts's literacy, and summarizing the hoax's claims; with hand-written end note stating it was signed by a Mrs. S.N. Parkinson on April 18, 1951, and a Kathyrn Cuellar on April 19, 1951.

STATE OF TEXAS) ss.
COUNTY OF EL PASO)

Before me, the undersigned authority, on this day personally appeared, who upon her oath, deposes and says:

That her name is _____, that she is of lawful age, that she was personally acquainted with Wm. H. Roberts, also known as Wm. H. Bonney, "Billy the Kid", Texas Kid, Hugo Kid, Brushy Bill Roberts, and O.L. Roberts, who is now deceased."

The affiant further states that she was present, together with Mr. William V. Morrison and _____ at the residence of William V. Morrison, at which time they witnessed a recording in which William V. Morrison interrogated the said Wm. H. Roberts, alias Wm. H. Bonney, with reference to the meeting with Governor T.J. Mabry, Santa Fe, N.M., on the preceding day, with reference to the life and happenings of the said Roberts, alias Bonney, alias Billy the Kid; that the said Roberts acknowledged certain facts of his family history and lifetime happenings; **that he also admitted the ownership of five certain and definite diary books in the possession of William V. Morrison, which books he identified, and he admitted that certain alterations had been made by him and Mr. Morrison to correspond with, and represent the true facts as they would be: that certain names and dates had been changed for the reason that the said Roberts had been covering up certain facts during his life time to withhold his true identity through fear of apprehension for crimes he had committed as Wm. H. Bonney, alias Billy the Kid, in New Mexico.**

[AUTHOR'S NOTE: Confirmation that Morrison had worked with "Brushy" to change his earlier writings to better match Billy the Kid dates and names.]

[AUTHOR'S NOTE: Confirmation of "Brushy's" literacy follows.]

This affiant further states that the said Wm H. Roberts identified a certain sheet of paper that had been removed from a book that had been subsequently misplaced; that the letters "O.L.R.", and the year 1951 appeared at the top of the sheet, which had attached thereto at the bottom thereof, a heading of the El Paso Times, Tuesday, April 4, 1950, with the hand printed letters, "O.L. Roberts"; that **the said Wm H. Roberts admitted that all the above printing had been made by him**; that a certain black back, loose leaf note book, titled, "This Book the private life of Brushy Bill was wrote in 1925", and containing thirty-eight sheets of writing script in ink; that there appears near the center of the sheet No. 39, the name, "Brushy Bill Old Scout", **which he admitted having written in his own hand**; that there appeared on sheet No. 37, the name, "Ollie Roberts, age 76", **which was also written by him, and the age "76 years", to cover up his true and correct age in withholding his true identity**; that there appeared on sheet No. 35, a list of names including Pawnee Bill, Texas Jack, and Buffalo Bill, with the notation on the bottom thereof, "Yours truly, Brushy Bill", **all of which was admittedly written by him**; he admitted that he had formerly worked with all of the men whose names appeared thereon.

This affiant further states that the said Wm. H. Roberts identified the following described books as being the original diary books concerning his life; and he identified the following mentioned articles and pictures:

Book No. one. gray back composition, containing 100 pages;
Book No. two, blue back composition, beginning page 101,
 and including page 199;
Book No. three, blue back composition, beginning with page 200, and including page 294, with the following page no-numbered, containing names of people with whom he was acquainted through the years;
Book No. four, blue back composition, titled, "The Life of Ollie Roberts or Brushy Bill or the Texas Kid", containing 128 pages, with changes on the first page from Ollie Roberts to Billy Roberts, and the year of birth from 1869 to 1859; that there appeared on page 84 thereof, the final page of writing, "Signed Al Brushy Bill The Out Law Horse Rider", which he admitted having written in his own hand.

The said W. H. Roberts identified a certain old scarf as being the same scarf which was given to him in Fort Sumner, N.M., IN December, 1880, by a Navajo Indian woman, and he stated that he had given the Indian woman a tintype picture of himself, copies of which have been made by many person's through the years;

[AUTHOR'S NOTE: This is fictional scarf tale is lifted from Walter Noble Burns's 1926 book, *The Saga of Billy the Kid*.]

He further stated that Sheriff Pat Garrett took a forty-four, single action, colt six shooter from him at the time of the arrest at Stinking Springs in December, 1880; that he never fired anything smaller than a forty-four caliber pistol; that Garrett took a forty-one, double action six shooter from the body of the man purported killed in Fort Sumner and passed as the body of Wm H. Bonney on July 14, 1881;

[AUTHOR'S NOTE: At this early hoax version, Morrison made up that Garrett's writing, in *The Authentic Life of Billy the Kid*, that he took a Colt .41 from Billy's body, proved that it could not have been Billy Bonney, but was Billy Barlow, because "Brushy," as Billy, only used a larger caliber Colt. Later in the hoax, the faked discrepancy was used to claim simply that Garrett lied about the gun, so he lied about the killing. In fact, Billy would have had a small Colt .41 as a hide-away weapon.]

that he always fired the rifle with his left hand, that he fired six-shooters with either hand;

[AUTHOR'S NOTE: Left handedness came from misinterpreting the right-to left reversal in the Billy the Kid tintype, where Billy is holding his Winchester '73 carbine (not rifle) on the tintype's left. The either hand claim, came from Morrison's learning that Billy was ambidextrous.]

that he cross fired six shooters, and that he fanned the trigger at times.

[AUTHOR'S NOTE: "Brushy" embellished with cowboy movies.]

[AUTHOR'S NOTE: What follows are faked pictures, some of which made it into *Alias Billy the Kid*.]

This affiant further states that the said Roberts identified picture No. 1, as representing a copy of the original tintype, made in the fall of '77 on the Chisum [sic] Trail in Dodge City, depicting four men, one of which had been admitted by the owners, Jones of Carlsbad, N.M., as being the picture of "Billy the Kid," said copy having been given to Roberts by Mr. Sam Jones;

[AUTHOR'S NOTE: This is Morrison's lie; since the Jones Brothers, Sam and Bill, refused to make an affidavit for "Brushy;" and it was "Brushy" who looked at their photo of Seven Rivers boys, and claimed that Marion Turner was himself as Billy the Kid.]

Picture No. 2, copy of a picture made at Fort Smith, Arkansas, representing him and a cousin, the name of which is withheld, and made when he was about 13 years of age; Picture No. 3, copy of a picture made in Butte, Montana, at the age of 27 years, representing him when he was riding the Anti Horst Thief trail; Picture No. 4, copy of picture made in Brownsville, Texas, at the time he came out of the Mexican Revolution, in 1914; Picture No. 5, copy of a picture made in Texas, at age 85, representing him; Picture No. 6, copy of tintype taken from his family album from Kentucky, representing his mother, Mary Adeline Roberts; Picture No. 7, copy of picture of Mrs. Antrim [**actually drawing of his real mother Sara Ferguson Roberts**], a half-sister of his mother, who took him at the time of the death of his mother, and proceeded to act as his foster mother.

[AUTHOR'S NOTE: What follows is the rationalization of "Brushy's" pardon failure.]

This affiant further states that the said Wm H. Roberts, alias "Billy the Kid", described the interview with Thomas J. Mabry, Governor, at Santa Fe, N.M., on the preceding day, with reference to obtaining a pardon for offences submitted against the Territory of N.M., as promised by Lew Wallace, Territorial Governor, in 1879; that during the interview he was fearful of apprehension by the State Officers and the Sheriff of Carlsbad, all of whom were present; that he was so nervous and excited during the interview with the Governor that he could not think, nor recollect coherently, until queried about the kind and type of teeth he had in Lincoln County days, date of extraction, etc., which facts he explained to the group of historians, news reporters, private individuals, relatives of Garrett and McKinney, etc.; that was when the Governor introduced the Sheriff of Carlsbad among the people present in the room, his nervousness grew to the extent that he thought the Sheriff would arrest him if the State Officers did not as he had previously admitted to the Governor that he previously visited in Carlsbad several months before the interview; he thought that some of the officers would put hand cuffs on him as soon as he would start to leave the conference table for passing through Carlsbad; he said that the Governor promised him a private interview, but that when he entered the Mansion he saw several people; that he was introduced to two sons of former Sheriff Pat Garrett, a son of Kip McKinney, said McKinney having been a member of Garrett's posse in December, 1880 [**wrong**], when they killed Tom O'Folliard, a cousin of Kip McKinney [**wrong**], that he saw many news-reporters and photographers, none of whom were supposed to be present; that he did not expect to be intimidated by the above mentioned persons as he was promised a private interview by Governor Mabry; that he did not think that he had received a fair trial at the interview.

[AUTHOR'S NOTE: What follows is Billy the Kid history to fake "Brushy's" "special knowledge."]

The affiant further states that the said Wm H. Roberts described the trip from the jail to Mesilla, N.M. to the jail in Lincoln, N.M. and the escape from the Jail in APRIL, 1881, as follows:

"About three days after I was sentenced to hang for the murder of Sheriff Bill Brady, by Judge Bristol, they put me in an old gray ambulance, handcuffed, with my leg irons chained to the bottom of the ambulance and we started to Fort Stanton. There were three guards riding inside the ambulance with me. one guard beside me, one sat right around in front of me and another guard sat along side the other one. There were about three guards riding on the outside. One guard was riding each side and one was riding behind. There may have been a guard riding in front of the ambulance, but I am not certain. That has been a long time ago." "Sheriff Garrett picked me up at Fort Stanton. Olinger went with me from Fort Stanton and Garrett made him a guard to watch over me in the jail in Lincoln. They put me in the Murphy Store Building [unaware it was called "The House"] on the second floor. I was in handcuffs, and my leg irons were locked to the floor with a chain. Olinger and Bell guarded me. The only time I was taken from the building was when they took me downstairs to the toilet. I was there about a week when I made an escape by killing Bell while Olinger took some prisoners across the street for lunch at noon time. The sun was shining and it was not in the evening like they say it happened. [Made-up. The escape started at noon.] After Olinger left for lunch I told Bell that I had to go to the toilet. He said, 'he didn't know', but he went into the other room and got the key to unlock the chain at the floor on the leg irons. As bell was standing over to unlock the chain, I slipped the handcuff from my right hand and hit him over the head with my left hand. He fell over and came up looking down the barrels of his own guns. [Note two guns taken] I told him to unlock the armory room at the end of the hall as I was going to lock him in there until Olinger got back. As soon as he stepped out into the hall he began to run toward the stairway. My leg irons had a fourteen inch chain between them and I could not run. I slid across the floor of the hall and fired my left hand pistol down the stairway which was to my left. [It would have been to his right.] I fired one shot that struck him near the shoulder [actually shot sideways through chest] as he ran down the steps. He fell over near the bottom of the steps and I knew he was done. I went back inside Garrett's office where Olinger put his shot gun when he went to lunch. I remembered that this morning Olinger had told me that I was going to get all 44 between my shoulders if I tried to escape. I told him that he might get them before I get them. I went over to the east window and aimed the gun down the window. Olinger came out of the Hotel and ran over to the jail. As he walked under the window I yelled for him to look up that I did not want to shoot him in the back. I wanted him to know that he was getting his own buckshot. When he looked up I fired the barrel into his chest and he fell over dead. Then I fired the other barrel into his dead body. I wanted to fulfill his promise. He shot the Jones boy in the back and promised to shoot me in the back. There was nothing to him. That was the happiest moment of my life. Bell was all right. He treated me like any other prisoner, but he forced me to kill him. I never killed a man unless he had to be killed. They were still trying to kill me. I was no outlaw". I was no outlaw. W, H. Roberts further mentioned that he had operated a ranch in Old Mexico in 1899, and again during the Revolution; that he and his men rode with Carrunza's soldiers, after joining forces with Pancho Villa; that he rode out of Mexico into Brownsville, Texas, in 1914, with one horse, saddle, Winchester, and a 36-40, single action colt's pistol, which he displayed at this interview, on December 1, 1950.

[AUTHOR'S NOTE: What follows is the "Brushy" hoax's Fort Sumner death scene.]

This affiant further states that the said Wm H. Roberts, openly admitted to us during this interview and recording on December 1, 1950, that he was "Billy the Kid", N. M. outlaw; that he had escaped the fight with Sheriff Garrett's posse on the night of July 14, 1881, at Maxwell's house in Fort Sumner, N.M., with serious injuries; especially a large scalp wound across the top of his head, the scar thereof still being prominent; that he mentioned several other wounds; that he had been shot across the first knuckle joint on the forefinger of right hand, which scar is readily discernable.

[AUTHOR'S NOTE: What follows is the "Brushy" hoax's faked physical match to Billy Bonney, including small hands and thick wrists for fictional shackle-slipping, and a protruding left ear to match the misinterpreted tintype's right-to-left reversed *right* ear protruding from the tilted hat brim.]

This affiant further states that the said Wm H. Roberts, alias Wm H. Bonney, alias Billy the Kid, was an unusual type man, standing about five feet, eight inches in height, well built and muscular, standing very erect, walking with a lively step, with small feet, **small well shaped hands with large wrists**, large ears with the <u>**left**</u> **ear protruding farther from the head than the right ear**, long straight nose with high cheek bones, piercing blue eyes, and laughing a great deal as he talked; that after due consideration, the affiant is of firm belief that the above mentioned Wm H. Roberts was the same person as the New Mexican Outlaw, Wm H. Bonney, alias "Billy the Kid", of Lincoln County notoriety in the 1880's [sic], and further this affiant says nothing.

_____
Affiant

[Blank notary public information is typed in for El Paso, Texas]

[Written in is] "*This affidavit executed by Mrs. S.N. Parkinson on Apr-18-1951- ack by Toleth Rogers – N.P.*
and
Kathyrn Cuellar on Apr 19-51 ack – by R.D. Petty NP"

APPENDIX: 2. NO DNA FROM CARPENTER'S BENCH: Orchid Cellmark's October 15, 2004's "Laboratory Report, Forensic Identity, Mitochondrial Analysis, Results and Conclusions" for its Case 4444-001B-004B (for Case 2003-274's bench results).

[AUTHOR'S SUMMARY: Lee's carpenter's bench underside swabbings and shavings were labeled as evidence numbers 4444-001B, 4444-002B, 4444-003B, and 4444-004B. "Results" showed the specimens "failed to yield amplifiable DNA." "Conclusions" recorded: "no mitochondrial [DNA] sequence data were generated."

LABORATORY REPORT - FORENSIC IDENTITY – MITOCHONDRIAL ANALYSIS

CASE DATA:

Referring Agency: Calvin D. Ostler
Cellmark Case #: FOR 4444B
Agency Contact: Calvin D. Ostler
Report Date: October 15, 2004

1. Evidence Received:

Accession #	Sample Description	Receipt Date/ Method of Delivery
4444-001A	Wood shavings "Lincoln County Courthouse #1"	8/4/04 - FedEx
4444-002A	Wood shavings "Lincoln County Courthouse #2"	
4444-001B	Swabbing from "underside of bench #3"	
4444-002B	Swabbing from "underside of bench #4"	
4444-003B	Wood shavings "underside of bench #3"	
4444-004B	Wood shavings "underside of bench #4"	

DR. HENRY LEE'S CARPENTER'S BENCH SAMPLES:
4444-001B
4444-002B
4444-003B
4444-004B

2. **Results:**

Sequence data obtained from the swabbing from the underside of the bench (4444-001B) are inconclusive. As a result, no data from this sample are reported.

The swabbing from the underside of the bench (4444-002B) and wood shavings from the underside of the bench (4444-003B and 4444-004B) were extracted according to accepted mitochondrial extraction protocol; however, the swabbing and wood shavings (4444-002B, 4444-003B, 4444-004B) failed to yield amplifiable DNA. Therefore, no sequence data were generated for comparison to a reference specimen.

Procedures used in the analysis of this case adhere to the standards adopted by the DNA Advisory Board on DNA analysis methods.

3. **Conclusions:**

Sample 4444-001B provided an inconclusive mtDNA profile; therefore, no conclusions can be reached with regard to the origin of this sample.

Samples 4444-002B, 4444-003B and 4444-004B did not provide sufficient human mitochondrial DNA for sequencing. Since no mitochondrial sequence data were generated, no conclusions with regard to this sample can be reached.

4. **Disposition of Evidence:**

All evidence received in this case will be returned to the submitting agency.

Orchid Cellmark has maintained complete chain of custody documentation from receipt of evidence to disposition.

NO DNA RECOVERED:

3. Conclusions

Sample 4444-001B provided an <u>inconclusive mtDNA profile</u>; therefore, no conclusions can be reached with regard to the origin of this sample.

Samples 4444-002B, 4444-003B and 4444-004B did not provide sufficient human mitochondrial DNA for sequencing. Since <u>no mitochondrial sequence data were generated</u>, no condlusions with regard to this sample can be reached.

---

5. **Case Review:**

The individuals below have reviewed the results and conclusions described in this report.

Joseph Warren
Forensic Supervisor

Rick W. Staub, Ph.D.
Laboratory Director

Kristina Paulette
Forensic Analyst

S I G N E D under oath before me this 15th day of October, 2004.

Notary Public

ANNOTATED BIBLIOGRAPHY

RELEVANT 19th CENTURY HISTORY

COMPREHENSIVE REFERENCES

Nolan, Frederick. *The War: A Documentary History*. Norman: University of Oklahoma Press. **1992**.

_____. *The West of Billy the Kid*. Norman: University of Oklahoma Press. **1998**.

HISTORICAL ORGANIZATIONS (PERIOD)

SANTA FE RING, 19th CENTURY

MODERN SOURCES

Cleaveland, Agnes Morley. *No Life for a Lady*. Boston: Houghton Mifflin. 1941.

_____. *Satan's Paradise: From Lucien Maxwell to Fred Lambert*. Boston: Houghton Mifflin Company. 1952.

Cleaveland, Norman, *Colfax County's Chronic Murder Mystery*. Santa Fe: New Mexico. The Rydel Press. 1977.

_____. *A Synopsis of the Great New Mexico Cover-up*. Self-printed. 1989.

_____. *Some Comments Norman Cleveland May Make to the Huntington Westerners on Sept. 19, 1987*. Unpublished.

_____. *Some Highlights of William R. Morley's Contribution to the Pioneer Development of the Southwest*. Self-printed. No Date.

_____. *The Great Santa Fe Cover-up*. Based on a Talk given Before the Santa Fe Historical Society on November 1, 1978. Self-printed. 1982.

Cleaveland, Norman and George Fitzpatrick. *The Morleys - Young Upstarts on the Southwest Frontier*. Albuquerque, New Mexico: Calvin Horn Publisher, Inc. 1971.

Cooper, Gale. *The Santa Fe Ring Versus Billy the Kid: The Making of An American Monster*. Albuquerque, New Mexico: Gelcour Books. 2018.

Klasner, Lilly. Eve Ball. Ed. *My Girlhood Among Outlaws*. Tucson, Arizona: The University of Arizona Press. 1972. Klasner, Lilly. Eve Ball. Ed. *My Girlhood Among Outlaws*. Tucson, Arizona: The University of Arizona Press. 1972. (**John Chisum's in jail write-up about Santa Fe Ring injustices to himself**)

Lamar, Howard Robert N. *The Far Southwest 1846 – 1912: A Territorial History*. New Haven and London: Yale University Press. 1966. (**Chapter 6 covers the Santa Fe Ring**))

Meinig, D. W. *The Shaping of America. A Geographical Perspective on 500 Years of History. Vol. 3. Transcontinental America 1850 - 1915*. New Haven and London: Yale University Press. 1998. (**Pages 127 and 132 are on the Santa Fe Ring.**)

Montoya, María E. Translating Property. The Maxwell Land Grant and the Conflict Over Land in the American West, 1840-1900. Berkeley and Los Angeles: University of California Press. 2002.

Naegle, Conrad Keeler. *The History of Silver City, New Mexico 1870-1886*. University of New Mexico Bachelor of Arts thesis. Pages 30-60. Unpublished. 1943. Collection of the Silver City Museum, Silver City, New Mexico. (**Grant County rebellion**)

_____. "The Rebellion of Grant County, New Mexico in 1876." *Arizona and the West: A Quarterly Journal of History*. Autumn, 1968. Volume 10. Number 3. Tucson, Arizona: The University of Arizona Press. 1968. Pages 225-240. (**Grant County rebellion against Santa Fe Ring**)

Newman, Simeon Harrison III. "The Santa Fe Ring." *Arizona and the West.* Volume 12. Autumn 1970. Pages 269-288.

Otero, Miguel A. *My Life on the Frontier, 1882-1897: Incidents and Characters of the period when Kansas, Colorado, and New Mexico were Passing Through the Last of their Wild and Romantic Years.* New York: The Press of the Pioneers. 1935. Pages 232-233. (Quoted by Victor Westphall, *Thomas Benton Catron and His Era.* Page 188*)* (**Quote: "the 'Santa Fe Ring,' the real machine controlling the political situation in New Mexico."**)

Pearson, Jim Berry. *The Maxwell Land Grant.* Norman: University of Oklahoma Press. 1961.

Taylor, Morris F. *O.P. McMains and the Maxwell Land Grant Conflict.* Tucson, Arizona: The University of Arizona Press. 1979. (**Traces origins of the Santa Fe Ring**)

Theisen, Lee Scott. "Frank Warner Angel's Notes on New Mexico Territory, 1878." *Arizona and the West: A Quarterly Journal of History.* Winter 1976. Volume 18. Number 4. Pages 333-370. (**About the Angel notebook given to Lew Wallace and listing names of Santa Fe Ring members**)

Westphall, Victor. *Thomas Benton Catron and His Era.* Tucson, Arizona: University of Arizona Press. 1973. (**Ring-denier, who cites sources exposing the Ring**)

CONTEMPORARY SOURCES (CHRONOLOGICAL)

A.C.L. Editorial. "New Mexico, A Sorry Showing for a Would-be State, Tweed's Disciples Preying on the Populace, How the Territorial Ring is Run, Why the Territory Should Not Be Made a State. **March 13, 1876.** *The Boston Daily Globe.* Volume IX, Number 62. Newspaperarchive.com.

No Author. "A Contemplated Political Change." Grant County *Herald.* **September 16, 1876.** Quoted by Conrad Keeler Naegle in *The History of Silver City, New Mexico 1870-1886* doctoral thesis. Pages 39-40. (**Listing reasons to escape the Ring by annexing to Arizona Territory**)

Wallace, Lew. "Our mutual friend, M. Hinds, who will hand you this ..." Letter to A.H. Markland. **November 14, 1878.** Indiana Historical Society. Lew Wallace Collection. M0292. Box 3. Folder 17. (**Ring tries to remove him as governor**)

Leonard, Ira E. "When you left here I promised to write you concerning events transpiring here ..." Letter to Lew Wallace. **May 20, 1878 [sic - 79].** Indiana Historical Society. Lew Wallace Collection. M0292. Box 4. Folder 10. (**Quote: "Santa Fe ring ... so long an incubus on the government."**)

Wallace, Lew. "I have the honor to inform you that the Legislature of this Territory adjourned ..." **February 16, 1880.** Letter to Carl Schurz. Indiana Historical Society. Lew Wallace Collection. M0292. Box 4. Folder 14. (**Key documentation of Catron as head of the Santa Fe Ring, and Wallace's Ring opposition**)

No Author. "White Cap's Proclamation." *Las Vegas Optic.* March 12, 1880. (**Manifesto against land-grabbing Catron and the Ring**)

No Author. "The Santa Fe Ring is the most corrupt combination that ever cursed any country or community." Las Cruces *Thirty-Four Newspaper.* **October 27, 1880.** From Victor Westphall, *Thomas Benton Catron and His Era.* Page 186. (**Article on Santa Fe Ring abuses urging voters to oppose Ring candidates**)

No Author. "The Ring must soon discover that the time has passed in New Mexico when men can be herded like so many sheep ..." *Albuquerque Daily Democrat.* **March 4, 1884.** (Quoted by Victor Westphall, *Thomas Benton Catron and His Era.* Page 191.) (**About Santa Fe Ring control of appointments to legislature**)

No Author. *Santa Fe Weekly New Mexican Review.* **March 13, 1884.** *Santa Fe Weekly New Mexican Review.* (**Accusation of Catron and the Ring of controlling grand juries and bribery**)

Valdez, Jose and Enrique Mares. "Scorching Letter, The Knights of Labor Send a Communication to Powderly! Politicians Arraigned! The Boldest Document Ever Issued in the Territory." **August 18, 1890.** *Las Vegas Democrat.* Volume 1. Center for Southwest Studies. Thomas B. Catron Papers, MSS 29, Series 102, Box 8, Folder 4. (**Gives history of Santa Fe Ring with T.B. Catron as head**)

EXPOSÉS OF (CONTEMPORARY)
COMPLAINT ABOUT TO PRESIDENT RUTHERFORD B. HAYES

Matchett, W.B. and Mary E. McPherson. " W.B. Matchett and Mary E. McPherson 'Make certain charges against the U.S. Officials in the Territory of New Mexico.' " Letter to President Rutherford B. Hayes. Received and filed **May 1, 1877**. Interior Department Papers 1850-1907; Appointments Division and Subsequent Actions. Microfilm File Case Number 44-4-8-3. Record Group 48. Microfilm No. M750. Roll 1. National Archives and Records Administration. U. S. Department of Justice. Washington, D.C. (**Sent to President Rutherford B. Hayes and Secretary of the Interior Carl Schurz.**)

McPherson, Mary and W.B. Matchett. "To the President. Please make the enclosed a part of the evidence in the case of "Charges Against New Mexican Officials" Letter to President Rutherford B. Hayes. **May 3, 1877.** McPherson, Mary E. Letters and Petitions to President Rutherford B. Hayes re: Removal Governor Axtell and the Santa Fe Ring. Interior Department Papers 1850-1907; Appointments Division and Subsequent Actions. Microfilm File Case Number 44-4-8-3. Record Group 48. Microfilm Roll M750. National Archives and Records Administration. U.S. Department of Justice. Washington, D.C. (**Addendum to their May, 1877 "Certain Charges Against U.S. Officials in New Mexico Territory."**)

_____. "The Secretary of the Interior, Sir – Accompanying please find copy of charges, &c., against S.B. Axtell, Governor, and Other New Mexican Officials ..." "Charges Against New Mexican Officials." Letter to Secretary of the Interior Carl Schurz. **May 5, 1877.** McPherson, Mary E. Letters and Petitions to President Rutherford B. Hayes re: Removal Governor Axtell and the Santa Fe Ring. Interior Department Papers 1850-1907; Appointments Division and Subsequent Actions. Microfilm File Case Number 44-4-8-3. Record Group 48. Microfilm Roll M750. National Archives and Records Administration. U.S. Department of Justice. Washington, D. C.

_____."*In the Matter of Charges vs. Gov. S.B. Axtell and Other New Mexico Officials. Submitted to the Departments of the Interior and Justice.* **August, 1877.** Printed as a 31 page booklet. No publisher listed. Indiana Historical Society. Lew Wallace Collection. M0292. Box 3. Folder 20. (**About the Santa Fe Ring, Catron, and Elkins; in Lew Wallace's personal possession**)

McPherson, Mary. "Please place before the Attorney General ..." Letter to President Rutherford B. Hayes. **August 23, 1877.** Interior Department Papers 1850-1907; Appointments Division and Subsequent Actions. Microfilm File Case Number 44-4-8-3. Record Group 48. Microfilm No. M750. Roll 1. National Archives and Records Administration. U. S. Department of Justice. Washington, D.C.

Springer, Frank. Deposition to Investigator Frank Warner Angel for the Departments of Justice and the Interior. **August 9, 1878**. Frank Warner Angel report titled *In the Matter of the Investigation of the Charges Against S.B. Axtell Governor of New Mexico.* October 3, 1878. Interior Department Papers 1850-1907; Appointments Division and Subsequent Actions. Microfilm Case File No. 44-4-8-3. Record Group 48. Microfilm Roll M750. National Archives and Records Administration. U.S. Department of Interior. Washington, D.C.

(SEE: Thomas Benton Catron)

NEW MEXICO TERRITORY REBELLIONS AGAINST THE SANTA FE RING (CHRONOLOGICAL)

LEGISLATURE REVOLT (1872)

No Author. *Journal of the House of Representatives of the Territory of New Mexico, Session of 1871-1872.* Santa Fe: A.P. Sullivan. 1872. Pages 144-154. (**Confirms troops used by Ring to suppress the Legislature Revolt of 1872**)

No Author. "Our Own Dear Steve, How Elkins Made His Influence Felt in New Mexico – The Ring in Which a Judge Figured – Politics in 1870. *Las Vegas Daily Optic.* **September 2, 1884.** (Reprinted from the *Omaha Herald*) Front Page. Volume V, Number 258, Column 4. Newspaperarchive.com. (**Exposing the Ring in the 1872 Legislature Revolt with Catron's and Elkins's corrupt alliance with Judge Joseph Palen**)

GRANT COUNTY REBELLION (1876)

MODERN SOURCES

Naegle, Conrad Keeler. *The History of Silver City, New Mexico 1870-1886.* University of New Mexico Bachelor of Arts thesis. Pages 30-60. Unpublished. 1943. Collection of the Silver City Museum, Silver City, New Mexico.

_____. "The Rebellion of Grant County, New Mexico in 1876." *Arizona and the West: A Quarterly Journal of History.* Autumn, 1968. Volume 10. Number 3. Tucson, Arizona: The University of Arizona Press. 1968. Pages 225-240. (**Rebellion against Santa Fe Ring**)

CONTEMPORARY SOURCES (CHRONOLOGICAL)

No Author. "Diario del Consejo der Territorio de Neuvo Mejico, Session de 1871-1872." *Santa Fe New Mexican.* **January 8, 1872.** Santa Fe: A.P. Sullivan. 1872. Pages 144-154. New Mexico Supreme Court Library. Santa Fe, New Mexico. (**A Ring expurgated document, with a copy found in 1942 by Conrad Naegle; confirming troops used by Ring to suppress Territorial legislature**)

No Author. "Diario del Consejo der Territorio de Neuvo Mejico, Session de 1871-1872. Las Cruces *Borderer.* **January 24, 1872.** Pages 110-113. (**Don Diego Archuleta, President of the Council, gives speech objecting to troops in legislature**)

No Author. "Ring influence [in the Territorial legislature is] being actively used against every measure that tends to do justice" [in Grant and Doña Ana Counties]." *Grant County Herald.* **August 8, 1875.** Quoted by Conrad Keeler Naegle in *The History of Silver City, New Mexico 1870-1886,* doctoral thesis. Page 39.

No Author. "A Contemplated Political Change." *Grant County Herald.* **September 16, 1876.** Quoted by Conrad Keeler Naegle in *The History of Silver City, New Mexico 1870-1886* doctoral thesis. Pages 39-40. (**Listing reasons to escape the Ring by annexing to Arizona Territory**)

No Author. [Grant County should not] "sort o' wait and hear from Santa Fe ... before taking action." Tucson *Arizona Citizen.* **September 23, 1876.** Quoted by Conrad Keeler Naegle in *The History of Silver City, New Mexico 1870-1886* doctoral thesis. Page 41. (**Arizona encourages escape from Santa Fe Ring**)

No Author. Grant County *Herald.* **September 23, 1876.** (**Need for school system stressed.**)

No Author. Grant County *Herald.* **September 30, 1876.** (**"Annexation Meeting" announced**)

No Author. "Proceedings of Grant County Annexation Meeting." Grant County *Herald.* **Saturday October 7, 1876.** Page 2. Columns 1 and 2. Collection of the Silver

City, New Mexico, Museum. (**Anti-Santa Fe Ring "Grant County Declaration of Independence" published**)
No Author. Grant County *Herald*. " 'Petition to Remove Judge Bristol. We the undersigned citizens of the Third Judicial District of the Territory of New Mexico, without regard to party, would respectfully request and petition for the removal of Judge Warren Bristol ...' " No date. **1876 or 1877**.(Quoted in "W.B. Matchett and Mary E. McPherson 'Make certain charges against the U.S. Officials in the Territory of New Mexico.' " Letter to President Rutherford B. Hayes. Received and filed May 1, 1877. Interior Department Papers 1850-1907; Appointments Division and Subsequent Actions. Microfilm File Case Number 44-4-8-3. Record Group 48. Microfilm No. M750. Roll 1. National Archives and Records Administration. U.S. Department of Justice. Washington, D.C.) (**Anti-Santa Fe Ring article**)

(SEE: Santa Fe Ring; Thomas Benton Catron; Stephen Benton Elkins)

COLFAX COUNTY WAR (1877)

MODERN SOURCES

Caffey, David L. *Frank Springer and New Mexico: From the Colfax County War to the Emergence of Modern Santa Fe*. Texas A and M. University Press. 2007.
Cleaveland, Norman. *The Morleys - Young Upstarts on the Southwest Frontier*. Albuquerque, New Mexico: Calvin Horn Publisher, Inc. 1971.
Dunham, Harold H. "New Mexican Land Grants with Special Reference to the Title Papers of the Maxwell Grant." *New Mexico Historical Review*. (January 1955) Volume 30, Number 1. Pages 1 - 23.
Keleher, William A. *The Maxwell Land Grant. A New Mexico Item*. Albuquerque, New Mexico: University of New Mexico Press. 1964.
Lamar, Howard Roberts. *The Far Southwest 1846 - 1912. A Territorial History*. New Haven and London: Yale University Press. 1966.
Montoya, María E. *Translating Property. The Maxwell Land Grant and the Conflict Over Land in the American West, 1840-1900*. Berkeley and Los Angeles, California: University of California Press. 2002.
Murphy, Lawrence R. *Lucien Bonaparte Maxwell. Napoleon of the Southwest*. Norman: University of Oklahoma Press. 1983.
Pearson, Jim Berry. *The Maxwell Land Grant*. Norman: University of Oklahoma Press. 1961.
Poe, Sophie. *Buckboard Days*. Albuquerque, New Mexico: University of New Mexico Press. 1964.
Taylor, Morris F. *O.P. McMains and the Maxwell Land Grant Conflict*. Tucson, Arizona: The University of Arizona Press. 1979.

CONTEMPORARY SOURCES (CHRONOLOGICAL)

No author. "Anarchy at Cimarron." *Santa Fe Weekly New Mexican*. **November 16, 1875**. (**Ringite backing of Axtell's use of troops in the Colfax County War**)
No Author. Report on murder trial for Franklin Tolby. Pueblo, *Colorado Chieftain*. **May 25, 1876**. Quoting *Daily New Mexican*, May 1, 1876. From Morris F. Taylor. *O.P. McMains and the Maxwell Land Grant Conflict*. Tucson, Arizona: The University of Arizona Press. 1979. Page 49. (**Ring-biased jury instructions by Judge Henry Waldo to protect Ring murderers of Tolby**)
No Author. "Rejoicing at Cimarron," "Axtell's Head Falls at Last," "General Lew. Wallace Appointed Governor." *Cimarron News and Press*. **September 6, 1878**.
No Author. *Santa Fe Weekly New Mexican*. **September 21, 1878 and October 19, 1878**. (**Ring-biased accolades for removed Gov. Axtell**)

(SEE: Santa Fe Ring; Thomas Benton Catron)

LINCOLN COUNTY WAR (1878)

MODERN SOURCES

Cramer, T. Dudley. *The Pecos Ranchers in the Lincoln County War.* Orinda, California: Branding Iron Press. 1996.

Fulton, Maurice Garland. Robert N. Mullin. Ed. *History of the Lincoln County War.* Tucson, Arizona: The University of Arizona Press. 1997.

Jacobsen, Joel. *Such Men as Billy the Kid. The Lincoln County War Reconsidered.* Lincoln and London: University of Nebraska Press. 1994.

Keleher, William A. *The Fabulous Frontier: Twelve New Mexico Items.* Albuquerque, New Mexico: The University of New Mexico Press. 1962.

_____. *Violence in Lincoln County 1869-1881.* Albuquerque, New Mexico: University of New Mexico Press. 1957.

Mullin, Robert N. Re: Frank Warner Angel Meeting with President Hayes. August, 1878. Binder RNM, VI, M. Midland, Texas: Nita Stewart Haley Memorial Library and J. Evetts Haley History Center. (Unpublished).

Nolan, Frederick W. *The Life and Death of John Henry Tunstall.* Albuquerque, New Mexico: The University of New Mexico Press. 1965.

Rasch, Philip J. *Gunsmoke in Lincoln County.* Laramie, Wyoming: National Association for Outlaw and Lawmen History, Inc. with University of Wyoming. 1997.

_____. Robert K. DeArment. Ed. *Warriors of Lincoln County.* Laramie: National Association for Outlaw and Lawmen History, Inc. with University of Wyoming. 1998.

Utley, Robert M. *High Noon in Lincoln. Violence on the Western Frontier.* Albuquerque, New Mexico: University of New Mexico Press. 1987.

Wilson, John P. *Merchants, Guns, and Money: The Story of Lincoln County and Its Wars.* Santa Fe, New Mexico: Museum of New Mexico Press. 1987.

CONTEMPORARY SOURCES (CHRONOLOGICAL)

No Author. "Brady Inventory McSween Property." **February, 1878**. Herman B. Weisner Papers, ca. 1957-1992. New Mexico State University Library at Las Cruces. Rio Grande Historical Collections. Accession No. Weisner Ms 0249. Box 10. Folder M15. Folder Name. "Will and Testament A. McSween."

No Author. "Amnesty for Matthews and Long in the Third Judicial Court April Term 1879." **April, 1879**. Herman B. Weisner Papers, ca. 1957-1992. New Mexico State University Library at Las Cruces. Rio Grande Historical Collections. Accession No. Ms 0249. Box 1. Folder 4. Folder Name. "Amnesty."

No Author. "Charges against Jessie Evans and John Kinney." Doña Ana County Civil and Criminal Docket Book. **August 18, 1875 to November 7, 1878**. Herman B. Weisner Papers, ca. 1957-1992. New Mexico State University Library at Las Cruces. Rio Grande Historical Collections. Accession No. Ms 0249. Box 13. Folder V 3. Folder Name. "Venue, Change Of."

No Author. "Dismissal of Cases Against Dolan, Matthews, Peppin, October 1879 District Court." **October, 1879**. Herman B. Weisner Papers, ca. 1957-1992. New Mexico State University Library at Las Cruces. Rio Grande Historical Collections. Accession No. Ms 0249. Box 13. Folder V3. Folder Name: "Venue, Change Of."

No Author. "Killers of Tunstall. February 18, 1879." Herman B. Weisner Papers, ca. 1957-1992. New Mexico State University Library at Las Cruces. Rio Grande Historical Collections. Accession No. Ms 0249. Box 12. Folder T1. Folder Name: "Tunstall, John H."

No Author. "Lincoln County Indictments July 1872 - 1881." Herman B. Weisner Papers, ca. 1957-1992. New Mexico State University Library at Las Cruces. Rio Grande Historical Collections. Accession No. Ms 0249. Box 8. Folder L11. Folder Name. "Lincoln Co. Indictments."

Ealy, Mrs. Taylor. Ed. Haniel Long. "New Mexico Writers: The Lincoln County War Part 1. *The New Mexico Sentinel.* **October 5, 1937.** Volume 1, Number 45, Page 8. New York Public Library. (**Eye-witness of Lincoln County War; describes mutilation of John Tunstall's face**)

_____. Ed. Haniel Long. "New Mexico Writers: The Lincoln County War Part 2. *The New Mexico Sentinel.* **October 12, 1937.** Volume 1, Number 46, Page 6. New York Public Library. (**Eye-witness of Lincoln County War**)

Corbet, Sam. "Sam Corbet Writes of Slayings." *The New Mexico Sentinel.* **July 17, 1938.** Volume 2, Number 33. Angelo State University Library. West Texas Collection, New York Public Library. (**Eye-witness of Lincoln County War**)

_____. "Tunstall's Father Lears of the Raids." *The New Mexico Sentinel.* **July 17, 1938.** Volume 2, Number 33. Angelo State University Library. West Texas Collection, New York Public Library. (**Sam Corbet's letter as eye-witness of Lincoln County War**)

HISTORY OF WILLIAM HENRY BONNEY (WILLIAM HENRY McCARTY, HENRY ANTRIM, AKA BILLY THE KID)

BIOGRAPHICAL SOURCES

Abbott, E.C. ("Teddy Blue") and Helena Huntington Smith. *We Pointed Them North: Recollections of a Cowpuncher.* Norman, Oklahoma: University of Oklahoma Press. 1955. (**Billy the Kid's multi-culturalism, Page 47.**)

Anaya, A.P. "Paco." *I Buried Billy.* College Station, Texas: Creative Publishing Company. 1991.

Ball, Eve. *Ma'am Jones of the Pecos.* Tucson, Arizona: The University of Arizona Press. 1969.

Bell, Bob Boze. *The Illustrated Life and Times of Billy the Kid.* Cave Creek, Arizona: Boze Books. 1992. (Frank Coe quote about the Kid's cartridge use, Page 45.)

Bell, Bob Boze. *The Illustrated Life and Times of Billy the Kid.* Second Edition. Phoenix, Arizona: Tri Star-Boze Publications, Inc. 1996.

Burns, Walter Noble. *The Saga of Billy the Kid.* Stamford, Connecticut: Longmeadow Press. 1992. (Original printing: 1926, Doubleday.)

_____. *"I also know that the Kid and Paulita were sweethearts."* Unpublished letter to Jim East. **June 3, 1926.** Robert N. Mullin Collection. File RNM, IV, NM, 116-117. Nita Stewart Haley Memorial Museum, Haley Library. Midland, Texas.

Coe, George with Doyce B. Nunis, Jr. Ed. *Frontier Fighter. The Autobiography of George Coe Who Fought and Rode With Billy the Kid.* Chicago: R. R. Donnelley and Sons Company. **1984.**

Cooper, Gale. *Billy the Kid's Writings, Words, and Wit.* Gelcour Books: Albuquerque: New Mexico. 2012.

_____. *Billy and Paulita: The Saga of Billy the Kid, Paulita Maxwell, and the Santa Fe Ring.* Gelcour Books: Albuquerque: New Mexico. **2012.**

_____. *The Lost Pardon of Billy the Kid: An Analysis Factoring in the Santa Fe Ring, Governor Lew Wallace's Dilemma, and a Territory in Rebellion.* Gelcour Books: Albuquerque: New Mexico. 2017.

_____. *The Santa Fe Ring Versus Billy the Kid: The Making of an American Monster.* Gelcour Books: Albuquerque: New Mexico. 2018.

Garrett, Pat F. *The Authentic Life of Billy the Kid The Noted Desperado of the Southwest, Whose Deeds of Daring and Blood Made His Name a Terror in New Mexico, Arizona, and Northern Mexico.* Santa Fe, New Mexico: New Mexico Printing and Publishing Co. 1882. (Edition used: Edited by Maurice Garland Fulton. New York: The Macmillan Company. 1927)

Hoyt, Henry. *A Frontier Doctor*. Boston and New York: Houghton Mifflin Company. 1929. **(Describes Billy's superior abilities. Pages 93-94, including fluency in Spanish.)**

Jacobsen, Joel. *Such Men as Billy the Kid. The Lincoln County War Reconsidered*. Lincoln and London: University of Nebraska Press. 1994.

Kadlec, Robert F. *They "Knew" Billy the Kid. Interviews with Old-Time New Mexicans*. Santa Fe, New Mexico: Ancient City Press. 1987.

Keleher, William A. *The Fabulous Frontier: Twelve New Mexico Items*. Albuquerque, New Mexico: The University of New Mexico Press. 1962.

_____.*Violence in Lincoln County 1869-1881*. Albuquerque, New Mexico: University of New Mexico Press. 1957.

Koop, W.E. *Billy the Kid: The Trail of a Kansas Legend*. Self Published. **1965**.

McFarland, David F. Reverend. *Ledger: Session Records 1867-1874. Marriages in Santa Fe New Mexico.* "Mr. William H. Antrim and Mrs. Catherine McCarty." March 1, 1873. Santa Fe, New Mexico: First Presbyterian Church of Santa Fe.

Meadows, John P. "Billy the Kid to John P. Meadows on the Peñasco, May 1-2, 1881." *Roswell Daily Record*. **February 16, 1931**. Page 6.

_____. "Story of Billy the Kid, His Life and Death, as Told Here by John Meadows, Friend of the Kid." *Roswell Daily Record*. **March 2, 1931**. Page 6. **(With quote on Billy's roughness)**

_____. "Oldtimer, Friend of the Billy the Kid, Tells of the Kid's Capture After Many Killings." *Roswell Daily Record*. **March 3, 1931**. Page 6.

_____. "Oldtimer Pays Tribute to Sheriff Pat Garrett in Final Chapter of Billy the Kid." *Roswell Daily Record*. **March 4, 1931**. Page 6.

_____. Ed. John P. Wilson. *Pat Garrett and Billy the Kid as I Knew Them: Reminiscences of John P. Meadows*. Albuquerque: University of New Mexico Press. 2004.

Mullin, Robert N. *The Boyhood of Billy the Kid*. Monograph 17, Southwestern Studies 5(1). El Paso, Texas: Texas Western Press. University of Texas at El Paso. 1967.

Poe, John W. *The Death of Billy the Kid*. (Introduction by Maurice Garland Fulton). Boston and New York: Houghton Mifflin Company. 1933.

_____. "The Killing of Billy the Kid." (a personal letter written at Roswell, New Mexico to Mr. Charles Goodnight, Goodnight P.C., Texas) July 10, 1917. Earle Vandale Collection. 1813-946. No. 2H475. Center for American History. University of Texas at Austin.

Rakocy, Bill. *Billy the Kid*. El Paso, Texas: Bravo Press. 1985.

Rasch, Phillip J. *Trailing Billy the Kid*. Laramie, Wyoming: National Association for Outlaw and Lawman History, Inc. with University of Wyoming. 1995.

Russell, Randy. *Billy the Kid. The Story - The Trial*. Lincoln, New Mexico: The Crystal Press. 1994.

Siringo, Charles A. *The History of Billy the Kid*. Santa Fe: New Mexico. Privately Printed. 1920.

Tuska, Jon. *Billy the Kid. His Life and Legend*. Westport, Connecticut: Greenwood Press. 1983.

Utley, Robert M. *High Noon in Lincoln. Violence on the Western Frontier*. Albuquerque, New Mexico: University of New Mexico Press. 1987.

_____. *Billy the Kid. A Short and Violent Life*. Lincoln and London: University of Nebraska Press. 1989.

Weddle, Jerry. *Antrim is My Stepfather's Name. The Boyhood of Billy the Kid*. Monograph 9, Globe, Arizona: Arizona Historical Society. 1993.

No Author. "The Prisoners Who Saw the Kid Kill Olinger." April 28, 1881. Herman B. Weisner Papers, ca. 1957-1992. New Mexico State University Library at Las Cruces. Rio Grande Historical Collections. Accession No. Ms 0249. Box 30 T. Folder 8.

WORDS OF (CHRONOLOGICAL)

SPENCERIAN PENMANSHIP

Spencer, Platt Rogers. *Spencerian Penmanship*. New York: Ivison, Phinney, Blakemont Co. **1857.**

_____. *Spencerian System of Practical Penmanship*. New York: Ivison, Phinney, Blakemont Co. **1864.** (Reprinted by Milford, Michigan: Mott Media, Inc. 1985.)

Cooper, Gale. *Billy the Kid's Writings, Words, and Wit*. Albuquerque, New Mexico: Gelcour Books. **2012.**

HOYT BILL OF SALE

Bonney, W H. "Know all persons by these presents ..." Thursday, **October 24, 1878.** Collection of Panhandle-Plains Historical Museum, Canyon, Texas. Item No. X1974-98/1. (**Hoyt Bill of Sale**)

LETTERS TO LEW WALLACE

Bonney, W H. "I have heard you will give one thousand $ dollars for my body which as I see it means alive ..." **March 13(?), 1879.** Fray Angélico Chávez Historical Library, Santa Fe, New Mexico. Lincoln County Heritage Trust Collection. (AC481).

_____. "I will keep the keep the appointment ..." **March 20, 1879.** Indiana Historical Society. M0292.

_____. "... on the Pecos." ("Billie" letter fragment). **March 24(?), 1879.** Indiana Historical Society. Lew Wallace Collection. M0292. Box 4. Folder 7.

_____. "I noticed in the *Las Vegas* Gazette a piece which stated that 'Billy the Kid' ..." **December 12, 1880.** Indiana Historical Society. Lew Wallace Collection. M0292.

_____. "I would like to see you ..." **January 1, 1881.** Indiana Historical Society. Lew Wallace Collection. M0292.

_____. "I wish you would come down to the jail and see me ..." **March 2, 1881.** Fray Angélico Chávez Historical Library, Santa Fe, New Mexico. Lincoln County Heritage Trust Collection. (AC481).

_____. "I wrote you a little note day before yesterday ..." **March 4, 1881.** Indiana Historical Society. Lew Wallace Collection. M0292.

_____. "For the last time I ask ..." **March 27, 1881.** Indiana Historical Society. Lew Wallace Collection. M0292.

(SEE: Lew Wallace response letters to)

LETTER TO SQUIRE WILSON

Bonney, W H. "Friend Wilson ..." **March 18, 1879.** Indiana Historical Society. Lew Wallace Collection. M0292. (**For pardon negotiation with Lew Wallace**)

LETTER TO EDGAR CAYPLESS

Bonney, W H. "I would have written before ..." **April 15, 1881.** Copy in William Kelleher's *Violence in Lincoln County;* originally reproduced in Griggs *History of the Mesilla Valley*. (**Original lost**)

REGULATOR MANIFESTO LETTER

Regulator. "Mr. Walz. Sir ..." Letter to Edgar Walz. **July 13, 1878.** Adjutant General's Office. File 1405 AGO 1878. (Quoted in Maurice Garland Fulton, *History of the Lincoln County War*. Tucson: University of Arizona Press. 1975. Pages 246-247.)

DEPOSITION OF

Bonney, William Henry. Deposition to Frank Warner Angel. **June 8, 1878.** Frank Warner Angel report, Pages 314-319 from *In the Matter of the Examination of the Causes and Circumstances of the Death of John H. Tunstall a British Subject.* Report filed October 4, 1878. Angel Report. Records of the Justice Department. Record Group 60. Class 44 Litigation Files. Container 21. National Archives and Records Administration. U.S. Department of Justice. Washington, D.C. or Angel Report in Interior Department Papers 1850-1907; Appointments Division and Subsequent Actions. Microfilm File Case Number 44-4-8-3. Record Group 48. Microfilm No. M750. Roll 1. National Archives and Records Administration. U.S. Department of Justice. Washington, D.C.

COURT TESTIMONY OF

Rynerson, William. "The Grand Jurors for the Territory of New Mexico taken from the body of the good and lawful men of the County of Lincoln ..." Indictments of the April, Lincoln County Grand Jury. **April 28, 1879.** Herman B. Weisner Papers, ca. 1957-1992. New Mexico State University Library at Las Cruces. Rio Grande Historical Collection. Accession No. Ms 0249. Box 4/39. Folder E-Z. Folder Name: "Jessie Evans Accessory to Murder." **(Billy's testimony for pardon bargain)**

Bonney, William Henry. Testimony in Court of Inquiry for N.A.M. Dudley. **May 28-29, 1879.** *Proceedings of a Court of Inquiry in the Case of Lt. Col. N.A.M. Dudley (May 2,1879 – July 5, 1879).* File No. QQ1284. (Boxes 3304, 3305, 3305A); Court Martial Files 1809-1894. Records of the Office of the Judge Advocate General - Army. Record Group 153. Old Military and Civil Branch. National Archives and Records Administration. Washington, D. C.

Waldo, Henry. "Then was brought forward William Bonney, alias "Antrim," alias "the Kid," a known criminal of the worst type ..." Closing argument on Billy Bonney's testimony in Court of Inquiry for N.A.M. Dudley. **July 5, 1879**. *Proceedings of a Court of Inquiry in the Case of Lt. Col. N.A.M. Dudley (May 2,1879 – July 5, 1879).* File No. QQ1284. (Boxes 3304, 3305, 3305A); Court Martial Files 1809-1894. Records of the Office of the Judge Advocate General – Army. Record Group 153. Old Military and Civil Branch. National Archives and Records Administration. Washington, D. C.

INTERVIEW WITH LEW WALLACE OF

Wallace, Lew. "Statements by Kid, made Sunday night **March 23, 1879.**" (Cover sheet reads: "Fort Stanton, March 20, 1879. William Bonney ("Kid") relative to arrangement with him." Indiana Historical Society. Lew Wallace Collection. M0292. Box 4. Folder 6.

NEWSPAPER INTERVIEWS BY

Wilcox, Lucius "Lute" M. (city editor, owner, J.H. Koogler). "The Kid. Interview with Billy Bonney The Best Known Man in New Mexico." *Las Vegas Gazette.* **December 27, 1880. (Mentions that Billy Bonney has squirrel-like incisors)**
_____. Interview, at train depot. *Las Vegas Gazette.* **December 28, 1880.**
No Author. "Something About the Kid." *Santa Fe Daily New Mexican.* **April 3, 1881.**
   (Billy's quote: "two hundred men have been killed ... he did not kill all.")
No Author. "I got a rough deal ..." *Mesilla News.* **April 15, 1881.**
Newman, Simon N. Ed. Interview with "The Kid." *Newman's Semi-Weekly.* **April 15, 1881.**
_____. Departure from Mesilla. *Newman's Semi-Weekly.* **April 20, 1881.** Pages 1, 3. https://chroniclingamerica.loc.gov/ **(Reporting for April 16th, listing the transport guards and their positions in the vehicle)**

FEDERAL INDICTMENT OF

Catron, Thomas Benton. "Case No. 411. The United States vs. Charles Bowdry [Bowdre], Doc Scurlock, Henry Brown, Henry Antrim alias "Kid," John Middleton, Stephen Stevens, John Scroggins, George Coe and Frederick Waite." **June 21, 1878.** Herman B. Weisner Papers, ca. 1957-1992. New Mexico State University Library at Las Cruces. Rio Grande Historical Collections. Accession No. Ms 0249. Box 1. B-Folder 4. Name: Andrew Roberts Indictment.

GENERAL LETTERS ABOUT

Kimbrell, George. "I have the honor to request that you will furnish me a posse ..." Letter to Lieutenant Millard Filmore Goodwin. **February 20, 1879.** Indiana Historical Society. Lew Wallace Collection. Box 4, Folder 3. (**For pursuit of William Bonney and Yginio Salazar**)

Goodwin, Millard Filmore. ""I have the honor to submit the following report regarding my duties performed ..." Letter to Fort Stanton Post Adjutant John Loud. **February 23, 1879.** Indiana Historical Society. Lew Wallace Collection. Box 4. Folder 3. (**Assisting pursuit of William Bonney and Yginio Salazar**)

Dudley, Nathan Augustus Monroe. "I enclose herewith report of 2nd Lieut. M.F. Goodwin ..." Letter to Acting Assistant Adjutant General at Headquarters. **February 24, 1879.** Indiana Historical Society. Lew Wallace Collection. M0292. Box 4, Folder 3. (**Documents military pursuit of William Bonney**)

Leonard, Ira. "The air is filled tonight with 'rumors of wars ... Letter to Lew Wallace. **April 20, 1879.** Indiana Historical Society. Lew Wallace Collection. M0292. Box 4. Folder 9. (**About DA Rynerson: "He is bent on going for the Kid"**)

East, James H. "Jim." "I wish to say that I appreciate your courtesy ..." Letter to William B. Burgess. **May 20, 1926.** C.L. Sonnichsen Papers, MS 141. C.L. Sonnichsen Special Collections Department. University of Texas El Paso Library. Box 92. Folder 386. (**About Paulita Maxwell as Billy's lover**)

Hoyt, Henry F. "This time it is me who is apologizing for the long delay in answering ..." (Letter to Lew Wallace Jr.) **April 27, 1927.** Indiana Historical Society. Lew Wallace Collection. M0292. Box 14, Folder 11. (**About having a sample of Billy's handwriting in his Bill of Sale**)

_____. "Copy of a bill of sale written by Wm H. Bonney ..." Letter to Lew Wallace Jr. **April 27, 1927.** Indiana Historical Society. Lew Wallace Collection. M0292. Box 14, Folder 11. (**Calls Billy Bonney "a natural leader of men"**)

SECRET SERVICE REPORTS ABOUT

Wild, Azariah F. "Daily Reports of U. S. Secret Service Agents, Azariah F. Wild." Microfilm T-915. Record Group 87. Rolls 308 (July 1, 1879 - June 30, 1881) National Archives and Records Department. Department of the Treasury. United States Secret Service. Washington, D. C.

LEW WALLACE WRITINGS TO AND ABOUT

WALLACE'S LETTERS TO (CHRONOLOGICAL)

Wallace, Lew. "Come to the house of Squire Wilson ..." Letter to W H. Bonney. **March 15, 1879.** Indiana Historical Society. Lew Wallace Collection. M0292. Box 4. Folder 6.

_____. "The escape makes no difference in arrangements ..." Letter to W.H. Bonney. **March 20, 1879.** Indiana Historical Society. Lew Wallace Collection. M0292. Box 4. Folder 6.

WALLACE'S LETTERS ABOUT (CHRONOLOGICAL)

Wallace, Lew. "I have just ascertained that 'The Kid' is at a place called Las Tablas ..." Letter to Edward Hatch. **March 6, 1879.** Indiana Historical Society. Lew Wallace Collection. Box 9, Folder 10. **(Written on dead John Tunstall's stationery)**

_____. "I beg to submit to you a list of persons whom it is necessary, in my judgment, to arrest ..." Letter to Henry Carroll. **March 11, 1879.** Indiana Historical Society. Lew Wallace Collection. M0292. Box 4. Folder 5. **(Sherman outlaw list with "The Kid" – William Bonney)**

_____. "I enclose a note for Bonney." Letter to John "Squire" Wilson. **March 20, 1879.** Indiana Historical Society. Lew Wallace Collection. M0292. Box 4. Folder 6.

_____. "My time has been so constantly occupied in getting my work into operation ..." Letter to Carl Schurz. **March 21, 1879.** Indiana Historical Society. Lew Wallace Collection. M0292. Box 4. Folder 7. **(Progress report with multiple enclosures; one listing "The Kid -William Bonney in anti-outlaw campaign of "taking the head off the evil.")**

_____. "To day I forwarded a telegram to you, with another to the President ..." Letter to Carl Schurz. **March 31, 1879.** Indiana Historical Society. Lew Wallace Collection. M0292. Box 4. Folder 7. **(Mention of "precious specimen nicknamed 'The Kid' ")**

REWARD NOTICES FOR

Wallace, Lew. "Be good enough to prepare a draft of proclamation of reward $500 for the capture and delivery of William Bonney, alias the Kid ..." Letter to Territorial Secretary William Ritch. **December 13, 1880.** Herman B. Weisner Papers, ca. 1957-1992. New Mexico State University Library at Las Cruces. Rio Grande Historical Collections. Accession No. Ms 0249. Box W3. Folder 13. Folder Name: "Wallace, Gov. N.M." From Lew Wallace Papers. New Mexico State Records Center. Santa Fe, New Mexico. **(Wallace's first reward for Billy the Kid)**

_____. "Billy the Kid: $500 Reward." *Las Vegas Gazette.* **December 22, 1880.**

_____. "Billy the Kid. $500 Reward." **May 3, 1881.** *Daily New Mexican.* Volume X, Number 33, Page 1, C 3.

REWARD POSTERS FOR

Greene, Chas. W. "To the New Mexican Printing and Publishing Company." **May 20, 1881.** Indiana Historical Society. Lew Wallace Collection. M0292. Box 4, Folder 17. **(Printer's bill to Lew Wallace for Reward posters for "Kid")**

_____. "I enclose a bill ..." Letter to Lew Wallace for "Kid" wanted posters. **June 2, 1881.** Indiana Historical Society. Lew Wallace Collection. M0292. Box 4, Folder 18.

DEATH WARRANT FOR

Wallace, Lew. "To the Sheriff of Lincoln County, Greeting ..." **April 30, 1881.** Indiana Historical Society. Lew Wallace Collection. M0292. Box 9, Folder 11.

CORONER'S JURY REPORT FOR

Rudulph, Milnor, Pedro Lucero, Jose Silba, Sabal Gutierrez, Lorenso Jaramillo. Coroner's Jury Report for William Bonney alias "Kid." **July 15, 1881.** Original in Spanish. Indiana Historical Society. Lew Wallace Collection. M0292. Box 9. Folder 11. **(Certified photocopy donated by Maurice Garland Fulton in 1951 of Spanish Coroner's Jury Report, July 15, 1881 - matches photo in William Kelleher's *Violence in Lincoln County*, Pages 306-307)**

_____. Coroner's Jury Report for William Bonney alias "Kid." **July 15, 1881.** English translation. The Mullin Collection, RNM, VI, J - Legal Papers and

Documents. Midland, Texas: Nita Stewart Haley Memorial Library and J. Evetts Haley History Center.

_____. Coroner's Jury Report for William Bonney alias "Kid." **July 15, 1881.** English translation. William A. Keleher. *Violence in Lincoln County 1869-1881.* Pages 343-344.

Ritch, William G. "In the matter of the application by Patrick F. Garrett for a reward claimed to have been offered May-1881 for the capture of Wm Bonney alias "the Kid." *Executive Record Book Number 2.* July 25, 1867-November 8, 1882. **July 21, 1881.** Pages 533-535. New Mexico Secretary of State Records. Collection 1971-001, Series 1; Records of the Secretary of the Territory. (Accessed from Albuquerque Public Library Microfilm, Territorial Archives of New Mexico, Roll 21.) **(Presentation of Garret's bill for the reward and demonstrating that Acting-Governor Ritch agreed with the reward, and citing the Coroner's Jury Report's identification of William Bonney)**

No Author. *Executive Record Book Number 2.* July 25, 1867-November 8, 1882. **July 21, 1881.** Pages 533-535. New Mexico State Records Center and Archives, Santa Fe. New Mexico Secretary of the State Records Series 1. Records of the Secretary of the Territory. **(About granting Garrett's reward, citing copy of Coroner's Jury Report)**

No Author. "Kid the Killer Killed, Wm. Bonney alias Antrim, alias Billy the Kid, Fatally Meets Pat Garrett, the Lincoln County Sheriff." Las Cruces *Rio Grande Republican.* **July 23, 1881.** Page 2. Volume 1, Number 10. NewspaperArchive.com. **(Copy of Pat Garrett's letter to Acting-Governor William Ritch confirming that the original Coroner's Jury Report was sent to District Attorney of the First Judicial District, and copy of it was included in this letter to the Governor)**

King, Frank M. *Wranglin' the Past: Reminiscences of Frank M. King.* "Chapter xix, The Kid's Exit." Pasadena, California: Trail's End Publishing Company. **1935 and 1946. (Describes recent location of Pat Garrett's report to the Governor about the killing of Billy the Kid, with confirmation of Coroner's Jury Report, Page 171)**

Rudulph, Milnor. Coroner's Jury Report for William Bonney alias "Kid." **July 15, 1881.** Indiana Historical Society. Lew Wallace Collection. M0292. Box 9. Folder 11. Accession Number 1951.0104 from Maurice G. Fulton. **(Photostatic copy of original Spanish Coroner's Jury Report, certified on January 18, 1951, donated by Maurice Garland Fulton - matches photo in William Kelleher's *Violence in Lincoln County* copy; identifying the body of Billy Bonney)**

No Author. "Fort Sumner Jury Thought the Kid Had Been Killed." *Alamogordo News.* **November 30, 1950.** Volume 53, Number 48. .NewspaperArchive.com. **(Harold Abbott's finding the Coroner's Jury Report in 1932)**

No Author. "Glimpses of History." **February, 1951.** *New Mexico Magazine.* Volume 29, Number 2, Pages 26, 54. **(Reprinting the Harold Abbott Coroner's Jury Report copy)**

No Author. "Coroner's Report Proves Billy the Kid is Dead, Historian Asserts, Researcher Discovers Document." **August 5, 1951.** *The El Paso Times.* Number 217, Page 13. **(Maurice Garland Fulton finds and publishes its copy)**

Keleher, William A. *Violence in Lincoln County 1869-1881.* Albuquerque, New Mexico: University of New Mexico Press. **1957. (Photocopy of Spanish Coroner's Jury Report, July 15, 1881. Pages 306-308; Keleher's English translation, Pages 343-344)**

CONFIRMING SIGNERS OF REPORT

Rudulph, Milnor. " I beg your indulgence for ..." Letter to William G. Ritch. **May 18, 1879.** Albuquerque and Bernalillo County Public Library. Genealogical Center.

MS. Territorial Archives of New Mexico Microfilm. Roll 99. Image 10. (**Rudulph's signature matches his signature on the Coroner's Jury Report.**)

No Author. **Census 1880 for Alejandro Segura and Sabal Gutierrez**. Place: *Cabra Arenoso, Fort Sumner, San Miguel, New Mexico*; Roll: *803*; Page: *434B*; Enumeration District: *037*. Ancestry.com and The Church of Jesus Christ of Latter-day Saints. *1880 United States Federal Census* [database on-line]. Lehi, UT, USA: Ancestry.com Operations Inc, 2010. 1880 U.S. Census Index provided by The Church of Jesus Christ of Latter-day Saints © Copyright 1999 Intellectual Reserve, Inc. Original data: Tenth Census of the United States, 1880. (NARA microfilm publication T9, 1,454 rolls). Records of the Bureau of the Census, Record Group 29. National Archives, Washington, D.C. (**Confirmed as local residents**)

No Author. **Census 1880 for Milnor Rudulph and Jose Silva**. Place: *Sunnyside, Fort Sumner, San Miguel, New Mexico*; Roll: *803*; Page: *435C*; Enumeration District: *037*.Ancestry.com and The Church of Jesus Christ of Latter-day Saints. *1880 United States Federal Census* [database on-line]. Lehi, UT, USA: Ancestry.com Operations Inc, 2010. 1880 U.S. Census Index provided by The Church of Jesus Christ of Latter-day Saints © Copyright 1999 Intellectual Reserve, Inc. Original data: Tenth Census of the United States, 1880. (NARA microfilm publication T9, 1,454 rolls). Records of the Bureau of the Census, Record Group 29. National Archives, Washington, D.C. (**Confirmed as local residents**)

No Author. **Census 1880 for Lorenzo Jaramillo and Antonio Saavedra**. Place: *Fort Sumner, San Miguel, New Mexico*; Roll: *803*; Page: *436A*; Enumeration District: *037*. Ancestry.com and The Church of Jesus Christ of Latter-day Saints. *1880 United States Federal Census* [database on-line]. Lehi, UT, USA: Ancestry.com Operations Inc, 2010. 1880 U.S. Census Index provided by The Church of Jesus Christ of Latter-day Saints © Copyright 1999 Intellectual Reserve, Inc. Original data: Tenth Census of the United States, 1880. (NARA microfilm publication T9, 1,454 rolls). Records of the Bureau of the Census, Record Group 29. National Archives, Washington, D.C. (**Confirmed as local residents**)

No Author. **Census 1880 for Pedro Antonio Lucero**. Place: *San Miguel, New Mexico*; Roll: *803*; Page: *381B*; Enumeration District: *035*. Ancestry.com and The Church of Jesus Christ of Latter-day Saints. *1880 United States Federal Census* [database on-line]. Lehi, UT, USA: Ancestry.com Operations Inc, 2010. 1880 U.S. Census Index provided by The Church of Jesus Christ of Latter-day Saints © Copyright 1999 Intellectual Reserve, Inc. All rights reserved. Original data: Tenth Census of the United States, 1880. (NARA microfilm publication T9, 1,454 rolls). Records of the Bureau of the Census, Record Group 29. National Archives, Washington, D.C. (**Confirmed as local resident**)

OUTLAW MYTH ARTICLES ABOUT (CHRONOLOGICAL)

GENERAL ARTICLES (CHRONOLOGICAL)

No Author. Grant County *Herald*. **May 10, 1879**. Results of the Lincoln County Grand Jury. (**Also published in the Mesilla** *Thirty Four*. **Confirmation of the Billy's testimony and indictments, from Page 224 of William Kelleher,** *Violence in Lincoln County*.)

Koogler, John H. Editorial. "Desperadoe's Stronghold, An Organized Gang Assisted by Nature and Defiantly Reckless, Who Terrorize the Country to the East of Us." *Las Vegas Morning Gazette*. **December 3, 1880**. Volume 2, Number 120. https://chroniclingamerica.loc.gov. (**Calling Billy an outlaw leader; motivating his denial letter of December 12, 1880 to Governor Lew Wallace.**)

No Author. "Outlaws of New Mexico, The Exploits of a Band Headed by a New York Youth, The Mountain Fastness of the Kid and His Followers - War Against a Gang of Cattle Thieves and Murderers - The Frontier Confederates of Brockway, the Counterfeiter." *The Sun*. New York. **December 22, 1880**. Volume XLVIII, Number 118, Page 3, Columns 1-2.

No Author. "A Big Haul! Billy Kid, Dave Rudabaugh, Billy Wilson and Tom Pickett in the Clutches of the Law." *The Las Vegas Daily Optic.* Monday, **December 27, 1880.** Volume 2, Number. 45. Page 4, Column 2. chroniclingamerica.loc.gov.

No Author. "A Bay-Mare. Everyone who has heard of Billy 'the kid' has heard of his beautiful bay mare." *Las Vegas Morning Gazette.* Tuesday, **January 4, 1881.**

No Author. "The Kid. Billy 'the Kid' and Billy Wilson were on Monday taken to Mesilla for Trial." *Las Vegas Morning Gazette.* Tuesday, **March 15, 1881.**

Newman, Simon. "In the Name of Justice! In the Case of Billy Kid." *Newman's Semi-Weekly.* Saturday, **April 2, 1881.**

No Author. "Billy the Kid. Seems to be having a stormy journey on his trip Southward." *Las Vegas Morning Gazette.* Tuesday, **April 5, 1881.**

No Author. "The Kid." *Santa Fe Daily New Mexican.* **May 1, 1881.** Volume X, Number 32, Page 1, Column 2.

No Author. "Billy Bonney. Advices from Lincoln bring the intelligence of the escape of 'Billy the Kid.'" *Las Vegas Daily Optic.* Monday, **May 2, 1881.**

No Author. "The Kid's Escape." *Santa Fe Daily New Mexican.* Tuesday Morning, **May 3, 1881.** Volume X, Number 33, Page 1, Column 2.

No Author. "The above is the record of as bold a deed ..." *Santa Fe Daily New Mexican.* **May 4, 1881. (About Billy's great escape jailbreak)**

No Author. "Dare Devil Desperado. Pursuit of 'Billy the Kid' has been abandoned." *Las Vegas Daily Optic.* **May 4, 1881.**

No Author. "More Killing by Kid, When But a Short Distance From Lincoln, He Meets one of His Old Enemies, and Kills Him and His Companion. Two More Victims." Editorial. *Santa Fe Daily New Mexican.* **May 4, 1881.** Volume X, No. 34, Page 1, Column 2. Newspaperarchive.com. **(Claims Kid killed Billy Matthews)**

No Author. No headline. "Anything that the imagination can concoct ..." *Santa Fe Daily New Mexican.* **May 5, 1881.** Volume X. Page 4, Column 1. Newspaperarchive.com. **(Claims Kid was in Albuquerque)**

No Author. No headline. Mr. Richard Dunham says ..." *Santa Fe Daily New Mexican,* **May 5, 1881,** Volume X. Page 4, Column 3. Newspaperarchive.com. **(Claims Kid was in Stinking Springs)**

No Author. "Richard Dunham's May 2, 1881 encounter with Billy the Kid.", *Santa Fe Daily New Mexican,* **May 5, 1881,** Page 4, Column 3. (private collection)

No Author. "The question if how to deal with desperados who commit murder has but one solution - kill them." *Las Vegas Daily Optic.* Tuesday, **May 10, 1881.**

No Author. "Billy 'the Kid.'" *Las Vegas Gazette.* Thursday, **May 12, 1881.**

No Author. "The Kid was in Chloride City ..." *Santa Fe Daily New Mexican.* **May 13, 1881.** Page 4, Column 3.

No Author. "Billy 'the Kid' is in the vicinity of Sumner." *Las Vegas Gazette.* Sunday, **May 15, 1881.**

No Author. "The Kid is believed to be in the Black Range ..." *Santa Fe Daily New Mexican.* **May 19, 1881.** Page 4, Column 1.

No Author. "Billy the Kid was last seen in Lincoln County ..." *Santa Fe Daily New Mexican.* **May 19, 1881.** Page 4, Column 1.

No Author. (O.L. Houghton's Conversation with Lew Wallace, before May 26, 1881), *The Las Vegas Daily Optic,* **May 26, 1881,** p.4, c.4. Indiana Historical Society. Lew Wallace Collection. M0292.

No Author. "'Billy the Kid' has been heard from again." *Las Vegas Daily Optic.* Friday, **June 10, 1881.**

No Author. "'Billy the Kid,' He is Reported to Have Been Seen on Our Streets Saturday Night." *Las Vegas Daily Optic.* Monday Evening, **June 13, 1881.** Volume 2, Number 188, Page 4, Column 2.

Wilcox, Lute, Ed. "Billy the Kid would make an ideal newspaper-man in that he always endeavors to 'get even' with his enemies." *Las Vegas Daily Optic.* Monday Evening, **June 13, 1881.** Volume 2, Number 188, Page 4, Column 1.

No Author. "Land of the Petulant Pistol, "Scenes" where Life and Land are Cheap ... 'Billy the Kid' as a Killer." *Las Vegas Daily Optic.* Wednesday Evening, **June 15, 1881.** Front Page. 1, Volume 2, Number 190, Columns 1-2. (Possibly contributed to by Lew Wallace, who published with a similar title in the Crawfordsville *Saturday Evening Journal* on June 18, 1881)

No Author. "Barney Mason at Fort Sumner states the 'Kid' is in Local Sheep Camps." *Las Vegas Morning Gazette.* **June 16, 1881.**

No Author. "The Kid." *Santa Fe Daily New Mexican.* **June 16, 1881.** Volume X, Number 90, Page 4, Column 2.

No Author. "Billy the Kid." *Las Vegas Daily Optic.* Thursday, June 28, 1881.

No Author. " 'The Kid' Killed! He Meets His Death at the Hands of Sheriff Pat Garrett, of Lincoln County. The Particulars of the Affair as Poured into the Ears of Eager Reporters. *The Las Vegas Daily Optic.* **July 18, 1881.** Volume 2, Number 217. Newspaperarchives.com. (**Confirming Pat Garrett's killing of Billy the Kid**)

No Author. "Words of Commendation and Encouragement." *Las Vegas Daily Gazette.* **July 22, 1881.** Volume 3. Number 15. Newspapers.com. (**Confirming Pat Garrett's killing of Billy the Kid**)

No Author. No title. **Thursday, July 28, 1881.** Pueblo, Colorado, *Colorado Chieftain*. www.coloradohistoricnewspapers.org. (**Quoting from the New York *Tribune* on killing of "Tiger in human form known as "Billy the Kid"**)

No Author. "The Life of Billy the Kid. His Name Was Billy McCarthy, and He was Born in New York." *The New York Sun.* (From *The St. Louis Globe-Democrat*) **August 10, 1881.** Volume XLIII, Number 314. Newspapers.com. (**Confirming Pat Garrett's killing of Billy the Kid**)

Gauss, Gottfried. Interview with *Lincoln County Leader.* **November 21, 1889.** (About Billy Bonney's Lincoln jailbreak)

LEW WALLACE'S ARTICLES

Koogler, John H. "Interview with Governor Lew Wallace on 'The Kid.'" *Las Vegas Gazette.* **April 28, 1881.**

No Author. "The Thug's Territory. Stage Robbers and Cut-Throats Have Things Their Own Way in New Mexico. Gen. Lew Wallace Anxious to Punish the Crime That is So Prevalent – A Chapter About 'Billy the Kid' – The Governor has a Narrow Escape From Being Spanked." *St. Louis Daily Globe-Democrat.* Monday Morning, **May 16, 1881.** Page 2, Columns 5 and 6. (private collection)

No Author. (Lew Wallace interview) "Billy the Kid. General Wallace Tells Why the Young Desperado of New Mexico Wanted to Kill Him, A Dashing and Daring Career in the Land of the Petulant Pistol." (Lew Wallace interviewed on June 13, 1881), Crawfordsville *Saturday Evening Journal,* **June 18, 1881.** Indiana Historical Society. The Papers of Lew and Susan Wallace. Microfilm Edition. Indianapolis, Indiana: Indiana Historical Society Press. 2008.

No Author. (Lew Wallace interview) "Lew Wallace's Foe. Threatened by 'Billy the Kid.' The Writing of 'Ben Hur' Interrupted. An Incident of the Soldier-Author's Career in New Mexico. *San Francisco Chronicle.* December 10, 1893. Indiana Historical Society. Lew Wallace Collection. M0292. Box 14. Folder 11. (Lew Wallace creating outlaw myth of outlaw Billy the Kid")

No Author. "Street Pickings," Weekly *Crawfordsville Review - Saturday Edition,* **January 6, 1894.** Indiana Historical Society. The Papers of Lew and Susan Wallace. Microfilm Edition. Series I. Reel 27. Indianapolis, Indiana: Indiana Historical Society Press. 2008.

No Author. "An Old Incident Recalled." Crawfordsville *Weekly News-Review.* **December 20, 1901.** Indiana Historical Society. The Papers of Lew and Susan Wallace. Microfilm Edition. Series I. Reel 27. Indianapolis, Indiana: Indiana Historical Society Press. 2008.

Lewis, E.I. "Gen. Wallace's Feud with Billy the Kid, When the General Was Governor of New Mexico and Billy Bonne Was the Most Dangerous Western Outlaw. He Was a Waif and Was Reared in Indiana. *The Indianapolis Press.* Saturday, **June 23, 1900.** Page 7. Lew Wallace Collection. Indiana Historical Society. M0292. Box 14. Folder 11. (photocopy) (Original article is in OMB 23, Box 1. Folder 5) **(Creating self-serving myth of outlaw Billy the Kid")**

Wallace, Lew. "General Lew Wallace Writes a Romance of 'Billy the Kid' Most Famous Bandit of the Plains: Thrilling Story of the Midnight Meeting Between Gen Wallace, Then Governor of New Mexico, and the Notorious Outlaw, in a Lonesome Hut in Santa Fe." *New York World Magazine.* Sunday, **June 8, 1902.** Lew Wallace Collection. Indiana Historical Society. M0292. . Box 14. Folder 11.

OTHER HISTORICAL FIGURES (PERIOD)

ANGEL, FRANK WARNER

REPORTS BY

Angel, Frank Warner. *Examination of charges against F. C. Godfroy, Indian Agent, Mescalero, N. M.* **October 2, 1878.** (Report 1981, Inspector E.C. Watkins; Cited as Watkins Report). M319-20 and L147, 44-4-8. Record Group 075. National Archives and Records Administration. U.S. Department of Justice. Washington, D. C.

_____. *In the Matter of the Investigation of the Charges Against S.B. Axtell Governor of New Mexico. Report and Testimony.* **October 3, 1878.** Angel Report. Interior Department Papers 1850-1907; Appointments Division and Subsequent Actions. Microfilm Case File No. 44-4-8-3. Record Group 48. Microfilm Roll M750. National Archives and Records Administration. U.S. Department of Interior. Washington, D.C. **(Mentions Santa Fe Ring)**

_____. *In the Matter of the Examination of the Causes and Circumstances of the Death of John H. Tunstall a British Subject.* Report filed **October 4, 1878.** Angel Report. Interior Department Papers 1850-1907; Appointments Division and Subsequent Actions. Microfilm File Case Number 44-4-8-3. Record Group 48. Microfilm No. M750. Roll 1. National Archives and Records Administration. U.S. Department of Justice. Washington, D.C.

_____. *In the Matter of the Lincoln County Troubles. To the Honorable Charles Devens, Attorney General.* **October 4, 1878.** Angel Report. Microfilm Case File No. 44-4-8-3. Record Group 48. Microfilm Roll M750. National Archives and Records Administration. U.S. Department of Justice. Washington, D.C.

NOTEBOOK ON SANTA FE RING MEMBERS BY

Angel, Frank Warner. "To Gov. Lew Wallace / Santa Fe, N. M., 1878." Notebook. **1878.** Indiana Historical Society. Lew Wallace Collection. M0292. Microfilm No. F372. **(Original missing, prepared for Lew Wallace listing Ringites)**

Theisen, Lee Scott. "Frank Warner Angel's Notes on New Mexico Territory, 1878." *Arizona and the West: A Quarterly Journal of History.* Winter 1976. Volume 18. Number 4. Pages 333-370. **(About the Angel notebook)**

AXTELL, SAMUEL BEACH

CONTEMPORARY SOURCES (CHRONOLOGICAL)

No author. "Anarchy at Cimarron." *Santa Fe Weekly New Mexico.* **November 16, 1875.** **(Ring-biased article justifying Governor S.B. Axtell calling in troops in the Colfax County War after murder of Reverend Franklin Tolby)**

Axtell, Samuel B. "The Legislature to Assess Property. *Message of Gov. Samuel B. Axtell to the Legislative Assembly of New Mexico, Twenty-second Session.* Page 4. Manderfield & Tucker, Public Printers: Santa Fe, New Mexico. **1875 or 1876**. Interior Department Papers 1850-1907; Appointments Division and Subsequent Actions. Microfilm File Case Number 44-4-8-3. Record Group 48. Microfilm No. M750. Roll 1. National Archives and Records Administration. U.S. Department of Justice. Washington, D.C.

Elkins, Stephen B. "I trouble you to say a word in behalf of Gov. Axtell …" Letter to President Rutherford B. Hayes. **June 11, 1877**. Interior Department Papers 1850-1907; Appointments Division and Subsequent Actions. Microfilm Roll M750. National Archives and Records Administration Record Group 48. Microfilm Case Number 44-4-8-3. U. S. Department of Interior. Washington D. C. (**Ring head trying to prevent Axtell's removal as governor**)

Axtell, Samuel B. "I have today mailed to you a reply to the charges on file in your Dept against me." Letter to Secretary of the Interior Carl Schurz. **June 15, 1877**. Interior Department Papers 1850-1907; Appointments Division and Subsequent Actions. Microfilm Roll M750. National Archives and Records Administration Record Group 48. Microfilm Case Number 44-4-8-3 U.S. Department of Interior. Washington D.C. (**Refuting charges made in Colfax County**).

Isaacs, I. and G.N. Coe. "Charges Against S.B. Axtell, Governor of New Mexico." **June 22, 1878**. Interior Department Papers 1850-1907; Appointments Division and Subsequent Actions. Microfilm File Case Number 44-4-8-3. Microfilm No. M750. Roll 1. National Archives and Records Administration. Record Group 48. U.S. Department of Justice. Washington, D.C.

Routt, John C. "I am here on a visit to my daughter and have more by accident than otherwise heard statements …" Letter to President Rutherford B. Hayes. **August 29, 1878**. Interior Department Papers 1850-1907; Appointments Division and Subsequent Actions. Microfilm File Case Number 44-4-8-3. Microfilm No. M750. Roll 1. National Archives and Records Administration. U.S. Department of Justice. Washington, D.C. (**Ringite letter opposing removal of Governor Axtell and U.S. Attorney Catron.**)

Schurz, Carl. "I transmit herewith an order from the President …" **September 4, 1878**. Letter to Lew Wallace. Indiana Historical Society. Lew Wallace Collection. M0292. Box 3. Folder 14. (**Suspension of Governor S.B. Axtell and Wallace's appointment as new Governor**)

Elkins, Stephen Benton. "To the President. Referring to a conversation had with you last week …" Letter to President James Abram Garfield. **March 17, 1881**. (Received Executive Mansion April 6, 1881). Interior Department Papers 1850-1907; Appointments Division and Subsequent Actions. Microfilm Roll M750. National Archives and Records Administration Microfilm Roll M750. National Archives and Records Administration Record Group 48. Microfilm Case Number 44-4-8-3. U.S. Department of Interior. Washington D.C. Microfilm Case Number 44-4-8-3. U.S. Department of Interior. Washington D.C. (**Request for re-appointment of Axtell as Territorial New Mexico Governor**)

Bradstreet, George P. "Referring to the nomination of Sam'l B. Axtell of Ohio to be Chief Justice of the Supreme Court of New Mexico … he is alleged to have been removed by President Hayes …" Letter to Judiciary Committee of the U.S. Senate. **June 22, 1882**. Interior Department Papers 1850-1907; Appointments Division and Subsequent Actions. Microfilm Roll M750. National Archives and Records Administration Microfilm Roll M750. National Archives and Records Administration Record Group 48. Microfilm Case Number 44-4-8-3. U.S. Department of Interior. Washington D.C.

No Author. " 'Chief Justice Axtell' is a bitter pill for the Raton *News and Press.*" *Santa Fe New Mexican.* **July 18, 1882.** (**Santa Fe Ring instatement of S.B. Axtell as Chief Justice**)

BACA, SATURNINO

BIOGRAPHICAL SOURCES

Charles, Tom. (Edited by Mrs. Tom Charles) "The Father of Lincoln County." *More Tales of Tularosa*. 1961. (unpublished manuscript)

Jonathan (no last name given). "About Saturnino Baca." July 23, 2001. http://www.genealogy.com/forum/surnames/topics/baca/509/

Nolan, Frederick. "New and Updated Biographies." *The Lincoln County War: A Documentary History. Revised Edition*. .Santa Fe: Sunstone Press. 2009.

LETTERS FROM AND ABOUT (CHRONOLOGICAL)

Baca, Saturnino. "When I sent in my bid for the hay contract ..." Letter to Quartermaster Captain A.J. McGonigle. **July 19, 1871**. University of New Mexico Library. Center for Southwest Studies. Thomas B. Catron Papers, MSS 29, Series 803, Box 1, Folder 25. (**About hay contract to Fort Stanton**)

Kantz, August V. "I learn from Col. Fritz that you are under the impression ..." Letter to Quartermaster Captain A.J. McGonigle. **July 20, 1871**. University of New Mexico Library. Center for Southwest Studies. Thomas B. Catron Papers, MSS 29, Series 803, Box 1, Folder 25. (**Emil Fritz pressures Fort Stanton to take bottom hay - which would allow Baca tp fill his contract - and Kantz warns that Fritz and Murphy will get hay monopoly**)

Carey, A.B. "Letter of Saturnino Baca, dated Fort Stanton ..." Letter to Quartermaster Captain A.J. McGonigle. **July 20, 1871**. University of New Mexico Library. Center for Southwest Studies. Thomas B. Catron Papers, MSS 29, Series 803, Box 1, Folder 25. (**Baca declines his contract to supply grama hay**)

McGonigle, A.J.M. "I have the honor to forward enclosed herewith ..." Letter to Quartermaster General M.C. Meigs. **September 24, 1871**. University of New Mexico Library. Center for Southwest Studies. Thomas B. Catron Papers, MSS 29, Series 803, Box 1, Folder 25. (**Wants Baca barred from hay contracts**)

BONNEY, WILLIAM HENRY

(See History of William Henry Bonney)

BOWDRE, CHARLES

CONTEMPORARY SOURCES (CHRONOLOGICAL)

Wallace, Lew. "Please select ten of your Rangers ..." Letter to Juan Patrón. **March 3, 1879**. Indiana Historical Society. Lew Wallace Collection. M0292. Box 4. Folder 4. (**To arrest "Scurlock and Bowdre"**)

_____. Lew. "I have reliable information that J.G. Scurlock and Charles Bowdre are now at a ranch called Taiban ..." Letter to Edward Hatch. **March 6, 1879**. Indiana Historical Society. Lew Wallace Collection. Box 4, Folder 4.

BRADY, WILLIAM

BIOGRAPHICAL SOURCE

Lavash, Donald R. *Sheriff William Brady. Tragic Hero of the Lincoln County War*. Santa Fe, New Mexico: Sunstone Press. 1986.

CONTEMPORARY SOURCES (CHRONOLOGICAL)

Brady, William. Affidavit of **July 2, 1876** concerning appointment as Administrator for the Emil Fritz Estate. Copied from the original District Court Record. (private collection)

_____. Affidavit of **August 22, 1876** documenting business debts to L. G. Murphy and Co. pertaining to the Emil Fritz Estate. Copied from the original District Court Record. (private collection)

_____. Affidavit of **July _, 1876** of Resignation as Emil Fritz Estate Administrator. Copied from the original District Court Record. (private collection.)

_____. Affidavit of **August 22, 1876** confirming giving Alexander McSween the books of the L.G. Murphy Company for the purpose of making business debt collections. Copied from the original District Court Record. (private collection)

Tunstall, John Henry. "A Taxpayer's Complaint ... January 18, 1878." Mesilla *Independent*. **January 26, 1878**. **(Exposé of William Brady embezzling tax money to buy cattle for "The House;" and Catron then paid that bill)**

Dolan, James J. "Answer to A Taxpayer's Complaint." Mesilla *Independent*. **January 29, 1878**. **(Response to J.H. Tunstall's exposé)**

Bristol, Warren. "Action of Assumpsit to command Sheriff Brady of Lincoln County to attach goods of Alexander A. McSween." **February 7, 1878**. District Court Record. (private collection). **(Used for malicious prosecution of John Tunstall by the false claim that he was McSween's partner)**

_____. Preprinted form for "Writ of Attachment" (Printed and sold at the office of the Mesilla News) filled out to command the Sheriff of Lincoln County to attach goods of Alexander McSween for a suit of damages for ten thousand dollars. **February 7, 1878**. District Court Record. (private collection).

Brady, William. "List of Articles Inventoried by Wm Brady sheriff in the suit of Charles Fritz & Emilie Scholand vs A.A. McSween now in the dwelling house belonging to A.A. McSween." (undated, but in **February of 1878**) (private collection)

BRISTOL, WARREN HENRY

CONTEMPORARY SOURCES (CHRONOLOGICAL)

Bristol Warren. "From sources of information that I deem perfectly reliable I am satisfied that there are public disorders in Lincoln County ..." Letter to Governor Marsh Giddings. **January 10, 1874**. Herman B. Weisner Papers, ca. 1957-1992. New Mexico State University Library at Las Cruces. Rio Grande Historical Collections. Accession No. Weisner Ms 0249. Box 4/39. Folder D-4. Folder Name: "Judge Bristol's letter." **(Creating Ring's outlaw myth)**

_____. "Writ of Embezzlement." **December 21, 1877**. Herman B. Weisner Papers, ca. 1957-1992. New Mexico State University Library at Las Cruces. Rio Grande Historical Collections. Accession No. Ms 0249. Box 10. Folder M-13. Folder Name. "Will and Testament A. McSween."

_____. "Action of Assumpsit to command Sheriff Brady of Lincoln County to attach goods of Alexander A. McSween." **February 7, 1878**. District Court Record. (private collection).

_____. Preprinted form for "Writ of Attachment" (Printed and sold at the office of the Mesilla News) filled out to command the Sheriff of Lincoln County to attach goods of Alexander McSween for a suit of damages for ten thousand dollars. **February 7, 1878**. District Court Record. (private collection).

_____. "My reasons for not holding October term of Court ..." Telegram to U.S. Marshal John Sherman. **October 4, 1878**. Indiana Historical Society. Lew Wallace Collection. M0292. Box 3. Folder 15.

_____. *Instructions to the Jury*. District Court 3rd Judicial. District Doña Ana. Filed **April 9, 1881**. Writ of Embezzlement. New Mexico State University Library at Las Cruces. Rio Grande Historical Collection. Accession No. Ms 0249. Box 1. Folder 14C. Folder Name: "Billy the Kid Legal Documents."

CATRON, THOMAS BENTON

BIBLIOGRAPHICAL SOURCES

Cleaveland, Norman, *A Synopsis of the Great New Mexico Cover-up*. Self-printed. 1989.

_____. *The Great Santa Fe Cover-up. Based on a Talk given Before the Santa Fe Historical Society on November 1, 1978*. Self-printed. 1982.

_____. *The Morleys - Young Upstarts on the Southwest Frontier*. Albuquerque, New Mexico: Calvin Horn Publisher, Inc. 1971. (**Page 93 gives Catron's vindictive indictment of Cleaveland's grandmother, Ada Morley, for mail theft as revenge denying him use of a Maxwell Land Grant buggy.**

Dodge, Andrew R., and Betty K. Koed, eds. *Biographical Directory of the United States Congress 1774-2005*. Washington, D.C.: United States Government Printing Office. 2005

Dunham, Harold H. "New Mexican Land Grants with Special Reference to the Title Papers of the Maxwell Grant." *New Mexico Historical Review*. (January, 1955) Volume 70, Number 1, Pages 1 - 23.

Hefferan, Vioalle Clark. *Thomas Benton Catron*. Albuquerque, New Mexico: University of New Mexico. Zimmerman Library. Unpublished Thesis for the Degree of Master of Arts. 1940. .(**In praise of Catron; includes railroad involvement, Page 35; First National Bank stockholder from 1871 to 1907, Page 28**)

Keleher, William A. *The Maxwell Land Grant. A New Mexico Item*. Albuquerque, New Mexico: University of New Mexico Press. 1964.

Klasner, Lilly. Eve Ball. Ed. *My Girlhood Among Outlaws*. Tucson, Arizona: The University of Arizona Press. 1972.

Lamar, Howard Robert N. *The Far Southwest 1846 - 1912: A Territorial History*. New Haven and London: Yale University Press. 1966. (**Chapter 6 covers the Santa Fe Ring**))

Montoya, María E. *Translating Property. The Maxwell Land Grant and the Conflict Over Land in the American West, 1840-1900*. Berkeley and Los Angeles: University of California Press. 2002.

Mullin, Robert N. "A Specimen of Catron's Dirty Work. Sworn Affidavit of Samuel Davis." October 1, 1878. Binder RNM IV, EE. (Unpublished). Midland, Texas: Nita Stewart Haley Memorial Library and J. Evetts Haley Historical Center.

_____. "Catron Embarrassed Throughout His Life by an Affliction." (Date Unknown). Binder RNM, IV, M. (Unpublished). Midland, Texas: Nita Stewart Haley Memorial Library and J. Evetts Haley Historical Center. Robert Mullin Papers. Binder RNM IV, EE (Unpublished).

_____. "Prior to Lincoln County War Catron Had Defended Colonel Dudley." (No Date). Notes from "Lincoln County War Cast of Characters." Midland, Texas: Nita Stewart Haley Memorial Library and J. Evetts Haley Historical Center.

Murphy, Lawrence R. *Lucien Bonaparte Maxwell. Napoleon of the Southwest*. Norman: University of Oklahoma Press. 1983.

Otero, Miguel A. *My Life on the Frontier, 1882-1897: Incidents and Characters of the period when Kansas, Colorado, and New Mexico were passing through the last of their Wild and Romantic Years*. New York: The Press of the Pioneers. 1935. Pages 232-233. (Quoted by Victor Westphall, *Thomas Benton Catron and His Era*. Page 188*)*

Pearson, Jim Berry. *The Maxwell Land Grant*. Norman: University of Oklahoma Press. 1961.

Sluga, Mary Elizabeth. *Political Life of Thomas Benton Catron 1896-1912*. Albuquerque, New Mexico: University of New Mexico. Zimmerman Library. Unpublished Thesis for the Degree of Master of Arts. 1941.

Taylor, Morris F. *O.P. McMains and the Maxwell Land Grant Conflict*. Tucson, Arizona: The University of Arizona Press. 1979. (**Traces origins of the Santa Fe Ring with T.B. Catron and S.B. Elkins**)

Westphall, Victor. *Thomas Benton Catron and His Era*. Tucson, Arizona: University of Arizona Press. 1973.

_____. "Fraud and Implications of Fraud in the Land Grants of New Mexico." *New Mexico Historical Review*. 1974. Volume XLIX, Number 3, Pages 189 - 218.

Wooden, John Paul. *Thomas Benton Catron and New Mexico Politics 1866-1921*. Albuquerque, New Mexico: University of New Mexico. Zimmerman Library. Unpublished Thesis for the Degree of Master of Arts. 1959. (**M.A. thesis praising Catron**)

GENERAL CONTEMPORARY EXPOSÉS OF(CHRONOLOGICAL)

Middaugh, Asa F. Deposition. **March 31, 1876.** "Exhibit B" in the August 9, 1878 deposition of Frank Springer to Investigator Frank Warner Angel. Frank Warner Angel report titled *In the Matter of the Investigation of the Charges Against S.B. Axtell Governor of New Mexico*. October 3, 1878. Interior Department Papers 1850-1907; Appointments Division and Subsequent Actions. Microfilm Case File No. 44-4-8-3. Record Group 48. Microfilm Roll M750. National Archives and Records Administration. U.S. Department of Interior. Washington, D.C. (**About Catron's malicious prosecution of Ada McPherson Morley**)

Springer, Frank. Deposition to Investigator Frank Warner Angel. **August 9, 1878.** Frank Warner Angel report titled *In the Matter of the Investigation of the Charges Against S.B. Axtell Governor of New Mexico*. October 3, 1878. Interior Department Papers 1850-1907; Appointments Division and Subsequent Actions. Microfilm Case File No. 44-4-8-3. Record Group 48. Microfilm Roll M750. National Archives and Records Administration. U.S. Department of Interior. Washington, D.C. (**Mentions Catron, Elkins, and the Santa Fe Ring, and provided Exhibits of letters exposing Catron's evil.**)

No Author. "The Santa Fe Ring is the most corrupt combination that ever cursed any country or community." Las Cruces *Thirty-Four Newspaper*. **October 27, 1880**. From Victor Westphall, *Thomas Benton Catron and His Era*. Page 186. (**Article summarizing Ring abuses in urging voters to oppose Ring candidates**)

No Author. "The Ring must soon discover that the time has passed in New Mexico when men can be herded like so many sheep ..." *Albuquerque Daily Democrat*. **March 4, 1884**. Quoted by Victor Westphall, *Thomas Benton Catron and His Era*. Page 191. (**About Santa Fe Ring control of appointments to legislature**)

Valdez, Jose and Enrique Mares. "Scorching Letter, The Knights of Labor Send a Communication to Powderly! Politicians Arraigned! The Boldest Document Ever Issued in the Territory." **August 18, 1890**. *Las Vegas Democrat*. Volume 1. Center for Southwest Studies. Thomas B. Catron Papers, MSS 29, Series 102, Box 8, Folder 4. (**Gives history of Santa Fe Ring with T.B. Catron as head**)

No Author. "Catron and the Laboring Men." Unknown newspaper. **1892?** University of New Mexico Library. Center for Southwest Studies. Thomas B. Catron Papers, MSS 29, Series 401, Box 1, Folder 3. (**Opposition to Catron as Delegate to Congress as "the biggest corporation man in New Mexico"**)

Victory, John P. "No Consistent Democrat Should Vote for T.B. Catron, John P. Victory in Forcible and Cogent Language Gives Answerable Reasons." **No month, 1895.** Printed broadside. University of New Mexico Library. Center for Southwest Studies. Thomas B. Catron Papers, MSS 29, Series 409, Box 1, Folder 3.

Wallace, Lew. "I have your several letters, including the last one of the 3rd inst." Letter to Eugene Fiske. **November 6, 1897**. Indiana Historical Society. Lew Wallace Collection. AC233. Box 1. Folder 7. (part of 1981 addition) (**About Catron's control over New Mexicans**)

Cutting, Bronson. "Catron was the boss of the Territory ..." Letter to James Roger Addison. **December 11, 1911**. Cited by Victor Westphall in *Thomas Benton Catron and His Era* from his citation: Lincoln County Manuscripts Division. Box 12. Courtesy of David Stratton. (**Catron as head of the Santa Fe Ring**)

Johnson, E. Dana. "[H]e ruled with a rod of iron ..." Editorial. *Santa Fe New Mexican.* **May 16, 1921.** Catron Papers 801, Box 1. Quoted by Victor Westphall, *Thomas Benton Catron and His Era.* Pages 394-395. (**Tactics of "boss" Catron without using the words Santa Fe Ring**)

(SEE: Santa Fe Ring; Frank Warner Angel)

FEDERAL INDICTMENT OF REGULATORS BY

Catron, Thomas Benton. "Case No. 411. The United States vs. Charles Bowdry [Bowdre], Doc Scurlock, Henry Brown, Henry Antrim alias "Kid," John Middleton, Stephen Stevens, John Scroggins, George Coe and Frederick Waite." **June 21, 1878.** Herman B. Weisner Papers, ca. 1957-1992. New Mexico State University Library at Las Cruces. Rio Grande Historical Collections. Accession No. Ms 0249. Box 1. Folder B-4. Folder Name: Andrew Roberts Indictment.

RESIGNATION AS TERRITORIAL U.S. ATTORNEY BY

Elkins, Stephen Benton. "Elkins – Telegraph Cipher, Cipher with Catron." Sent to T.B. Catron. ___ **1878?** University of New Mexico Library. Center for Southwest Studies. Thomas B. Catron Papers, MSS 29, Series 108, Box 1, Folder 4. (**Ring code-cipher key about T.B. Catron's resignation as U.S. Attorney**)

_____. "Asking delay of action upon charges against U.S. Atty. Catron ..." **September 24, 1878.** Angel Report. Microfilm File Case No. 44-4-8-3. Record Group 48. National Records and Archives Administration. Microfilm No. M750. Roll 1. U.S. Department of Justice. Washington, D. C.

_____. "Regarding Attorney General's decision on T.B. Catron." Letter. **September___, 1878.** Angel Report. Microfilm File Case No. 44-4-8-3. Record Group 48. National Records and Archives Administration. Microfilm No. M750. Roll 1. U.S. Department of Justice. Washington, D.C.

Catron, Thomas Benton. "In accordance with a purpose long entertained ...." Letter to Charles Devens. **October 10, 1878.** Angel Report. Microfilm File Case No. 44-4-8-3. Record Group 48. National Records and Archives Administration. Microfilm No. M750. Roll 1. U.S. Department of Justice. Washington, D.C. (**Resignation as U.S. Attorney**)

Devens, Charles. "Your resignation of the office of United States Attorney ..." Letter to T.B. Catron. **October 19, 1878.** Angel Report. Microfilm File Case No. 44-4-8-3. Record Group 48. National Records and Archives Administration. Microfilm No. M750. Roll 1. U.S. Department of Justice. Washington, D. C.

Catron, Thomas Benton. "Please change my resignation ...." **November 4, 1878.** Telegram to Charles Devens. Angel Report. Microfilm File Case No. 44-4-8-3. Record Group 48. National Records and Archives Administration. Microfilm No. M750. Roll 1. U.S. Department of Justice. Washington, D. C. (**Resignation as U.S. Attorney**)

Devens, Charles. "Your resignation of the office of United States Attorney ..." Letter to T.B. Catron. **November 12, 1878.** Angel Report. Microfilm File Case No. 44-4-8-3. Record Group 48. National Records and Archives Administration. Microfilm No. M750. Roll 1. U.S. Department of Justice. Washington, D.C.

Elkins, Stephen Benton. "Relative to resignation of T. B. Catron U. S. Attorney." Letter to Charles Devens. **November 10, 1878.** Angel Report. Microfilm File Case No. 44-4-8-3. Record Group 48. National Records and Archives Administration. Microfilm No. M750. Roll 1. U.S. Department of Justice. Washington, D.C.

Devens, Charles. "To honorable S. B. Elkins re. T. B. Catron continuing to act as U.S. Attorney ..." Letter to Stephen B. Elkins. **November 12, 1878.** Angel Report. Microfilm File Case No. 44-4-8-3. Record Group 48. National Records and Archives Administration. Microfilm No. M750. Roll 1. U.S. Department of Justice. Washington, D.C.

Barnes, Sidney M.. "I Sidney M. Barnes do solemnly swear ..." Swearing in as U.S. Attorney. **January 20, 1879**. Angel Report. Microfilm File Case No. 44-4-8-3. Record Group 48. National Records and Archives Administration. Microfilm No. M750. Roll 1. U.S. Department of Justice. Washington, D.C. (**Catron replaced**)

Elkins, Stephen Benton. "I have waited some time to reply to your lengthy letter ..." Letter to T.B. Catron. **August 15, 1879**. West Virginia & Regional History Center. West Virginia University Libraries, Morgantown, W. Va. Stephen B. Elkins Papers (A&M 53). Box 1. Folder 1. (**Reveals he prevented Catron's dismissal and indictment from Angel's report**)

Clancy, Frank W. "From something I have heard ..." Letter to T.B. Catron. **September 20, 1892**. University of New Mexico Library. Center for Southwest Studies. Thomas B. Catron Papers, MSS 29, Series 102, Box 16, Folder 2. (**Warning Catron that opponents are seeking the Angel Report to use against his campaign for Delegate, but Elkins is making obstacles**)

_____. "I am much surprised at what you say in your letter ..." Letter to T.B. Catron. **December 2, 1896**. University of New Mexico Library. Center for Southwest Studies. Thomas B. Catron Papers, MSS 29, Series 106, Box 1, Folder 6. (**Surprise that Catron now wants to be U.S. Attorney again**)

PECOS RIVER COW CAMP OF (CHRONOLOGICAL)

Riley, John H. Letter to N.A.M. Dudley. **May 19, 1878.** (**Fabricated Regulator theft of Catron's cattle from the Dolan Pecos Cow Camp**) Cited by Victor Westphall, Page 87.

Catron, Thomas Benton. Catron letter to Governor S. B. Axtell to intervene in Lincoln County. **May 30, 1878**. Midland, Texas: Nita Stewart Haley Memorial Library and J. Evetts Haley Historical Center. Robert Mullin Papers. Binder RNM IV, EE (Unpublished). (**Fabricated attack of Regulators on his cow camp workers**) Cited by Victor Westphall, Page 89-90.

OWNERSHIP FILING ON CARRIZOZO CATTLE COMPANY BY

Catron, Thomas Benton.. Statement of Sole ownership of Carrizozo Ranch in Tax Dispute Case. No date. Herman B. Weisner Papers, ca. 1957-1992. New Mexico State University Library at Las Cruces. Rio Grande Historical Collections. Accession No. Ms 0249. Box. 2. Folder C-8. Folder Name "T.B. Catron Tax Troubles." (**One of Catron's Lincoln County holdings**)

CHAPMAN, HUSTON INGRAM

CONTEMPORARY SOURCES (CHRONOLOGICAL)

Wallace, Lew. "I enclose you a copy of a letter from Las Vegas ..." Letter to Edward Hatch. **October 28, 1878**. Indiana Historical Society. Lew Wallace Collection. M0292. Box 3. Folder 16. (**Forwards Chapman's letter to Hatch**)

_____. "In a communication, dated October 28. inst., I requested, for reasons stated, a safe-guard for Mrs. McSween ..." Letter to Edward Hatch. **November 9, 1878**. Indiana Historical Society. Lew Wallace Collection. M0292. Box 3. Folder 17.

No Author. (signed E.). "Death of Chapman." *Las Vegas Gazette.* **March 1, 1879**. From *Proceedings of a Court of Inquiry in the Case of Lt. Col. N.A.M. Dudley (May 2,1879 – July 5, 1879)*. File No. QQ1284. (Boxes 3304, 3305, 3305A); Court Martial Files 1809-1894. Records of the Office of the Judge Advocate General – Army. Record Group 153. Old Military and Civil Branch. National Archives and Records Administration. Washington, D. C.

No Author. "Wallace and Lincoln County." Grant County *Herald.* **March 1, 1879**. Indiana Historical Society. The Papers of Lew and Susan Wallace. Microfilm Edition. Indianapolis, Indiana: Indiana Historical Society Press. 2008.

Chapman, W.W. "Yours of the 1st inst. came ..." Letter to Ira E. Leonard. **March 20, 1879**. Indiana Historical Society. Lew Wallace Collection. M0292. Box 4. Folder 6.

Rynerson, William. "The Grand Jurors for the Territory of New Mexico taken from the body of the good and lawful men of the County of Lincoln ..." Indictments of the April, Lincoln County Grand Jury. **April 28, 1879**. Herman B. Weisner Papers, ca. 1957-1992. New Mexico State University Library at Las Cruces. Rio Grande Historical Collection. Accession No. Ms 0249. Box 4/39. Folder E-Z. Folder Name: "Jessie Evans Accessory to Murder." (**Billy's testimony indicts J.J. Dolan, Billy Campbell, and Jessie Evans fulfilling his pardon bargain**)

Chapman, W.W. "Since receiving yours of the 1st March ..." Letter to Ira Leonard. **May 8, 1879**. Indiana Historical Society. Lew Wallace Collection. M0292. Box 4. Folder 10.

LETTERS BY

Chapman, Huston I. "You will please pardon me for presuming so much upon your kindness ..." Letter to Lew Wallace. **October 24, 1878**. Indiana Historical Society. Lew Wallace Collection. M0292. Box 3. Folder 16. (**Makes clear N.A.M. Dudley's danger to Susan McSween**)

_____. *'You attach much importance to the awe-inspiring influence of the military ..."* Letter to Lew Wallace. **November 25, 1878**. From Frederick Nolan, *The Lincoln County War,* p. 359.

_____. "You must pardon me for so often presuming upon your kindness ..." Letter to Lew Wallace. **November 29, 1878**. Indiana Historical Society. Lew Wallace Collection. M0292. Box 3. Folder 18.

CHISUM, JOHN SIMPSON

Hinton, Harwood P., Jr. "John Simpson Chisum, 1877-84." *New Mexico Historical Review* 31(3) (July 1956): 177 - 205; 31(4) (October 1956): 310 - 337; 32(1) (January 1957): 53 - 65.

Klasner, Lilly. Eve Ball. Ed. *My Girlhood Among Outlaws.* Tucson, Arizona: The University of Arizona Press. 1972. (**Contains John Chisum's in jail write-up about Santa Fe Ring injustices to himself**)

COE FAMILY

BIOGRAPHICAL SOURCES

Coe, George. Doyce B. Nunis, Jr. Ed. *Frontier Fighter. The Autobiography of George Coe Who Fought and Rode With Billy the Kid.* Chicago: R. R. Donnelley and Sons Company. 1984.

Coe, Wilbur. *Ranch on the Ruidoso. The Story of a Pioneer Family in New Mexico, 1871 - 1968.* New York: Alfred A. Knopf. 1968.

DOLAN, JAMES JOSEPH

BIOGRAPHICAL SOURCE

Slates, Thomas. "The James J. Dolan House, Lincoln New Mexico." *New Mexico Architecture* 11. 8/9 (1969). pp. 17-20.(**With Dolan biography**)

CONTEMPORARY SOURCES BY AND ABOUT (CHRONOLOGICAL)

Tunstall, John Henry. "A Tax-payer's Complaint, Office of John H. Tunstall, Lincoln, Lincoln Co., N.M., January 18, 1878, 'The Present Sheriff of Lincoln County Has Paid Nothing During His Present Term of Office.' Governor's Message for 1878." Mesilla *Independent.* **January 26, 1878**. Volume 1, Number 32. NewspaperArchive.com. (**Exposé of William Brady and John Riley**)

Dolan, James J. "Answer to A Taxpayer's Complaint." Mesilla *Independent*.
McSween, Alexander. "It looks as though the agent were the property of J.J. Dolan & J.H. Riley, known here as Dolan & Co." Letter to Secretary of Interior Carl Schurz. **February 11, 1878**. From Frederick Nolan. *The Life and Death of John Henry Tunstall*. Albuquerque, New Mexico: The University of New Mexico Press. 1965. Page 266.
Rynerson, William. "Friends Riley & Dolan, Lincoln N.M. I have just received letters from you mailed 10th inst." **February 14, 1878**. Letter to James Dolan and John Riley. Copy as Exhibit B in June 6, 1878 deposition of Alexander McSween. Frank Warner Angel report. *In the Matter of the Examination of the Causes and Circumstances of the Death of John H. Tunstall a British Subject*. Report filed October 4, 1878. Frank Warner Angel report. Interior Department Papers 1850-1907; Appointments Division and Subsequent Actions. Microfilm File Case Number 44-4-8-3. Record Group 48. Microfilm No. M750. Roll 1. National Archives and Records Administration. U.S. Department of Justice. Washington, D.C. (James J. Dolan Deposition. June 20, 1878. Pages 235-247.) **(Implying planned killing of J.H. Tunstall)**
Wilson, John, George B. Barker, Robert M. Gilbert, John Newcomb, Samuel Smith, Benjamin Ellis. "We the undersigned Justice of the Peace and Coroners Jury who sat upon the inquest held this 19th day of February 1878 on the body of John H. Tunstall ..." Coroner's Jury Report for John Tunstall. **February 19, 1878**. **(Naming the murderers as, among others, James Dolan, Frank Baker, Jessie Evans, William Morton, and George Hindman)**
Rynerson, William. "The Grand Jurors for the Territory of New Mexico taken from the body of the good and lawful men of the County of Lincoln ..." Indictments of the April, Lincoln County Grand Jury. **April 28, 1879**. Herman B. Weisner Papers, ca. 1957-1992. New Mexico State University Library at Las Cruces. Rio Grande Historical Collection. Accession No. Weisner MS 249. Box 4/39. Folder E-Z. Folder Name: "Jessie Evans Accessory to Murder." **(Billy Bonney's testimony indicts J.J. Dolan, Billy Campbell, and Jessie Evans for pardon bargain)**
Wild, Azariah F. "Daily Reports of U. S. Secret Service Agents, Azariah F. Wild." Microfilm T-915. Record Group 87. Rolls 307 (January 1,1878 - June 30, 1879) and 308 **(July 1, 1879 - June 30, 1881)**. National Archives and Records Department. Department of the Treasury. United States Secret Service. Washington, D. C. **(Dolan as an informer against "the Kid gang")**

DUDLEY, NATHAN AUGUSTUS MONROE

BIOGRAPHICAL SOURCES

Kaye, E. Donald. *Nathan Augustus Monroe Dudley: Rogue, Hero, or Both?* Parker, Colorado: Outskirts Press, Inc. 2007.
Oliva, Leo E., *Fort Union and the Frontier Army in the Southwest*. Southwest Cultural Resource Center, Professional Papers No. 41, National Park Service, 1993, Pages 488-489, 550, 574, 624-626, 656-659 are on Dudley. **(Quoted to E. Donald Kaye from the now-lost letter of Amos Kimball: "I guess you heard that Dudley made Colonel. The army bureaucracy is like a giant cesspool, where the biggest chunks rise to the top.")**

MILITARY COURT OF INQUIRY FOR

Leonard, Ira E. "Charges and specifications against Lieutenant Colonel N.A.M. Dudley, Commander at Fort Stanton, New Mexico." **March 4, 1879**. Letter to Secretary of War George McCrary. *Proceedings of a Court of Inquiry in the Case of Lt. Col. N.A.M. Dudley (May 2,1879 - July 5, 1879)*. File No. QQ1284. (Boxes 3304, 3305, 3305A); Court Martial Files 1809-1894. Records of the Office of the Judge Advocate General - Army. Record Group 153. Old Military and Civil Branch.

National Archives and Records Administration. Washington, D. C. (**Charges against Dudley for murders of A.A. McSween and H.I. Chapman and arson of McSween's house**)

No Author. *Proceedings of a Court of Inquiry in the Case of Lt. Col. N.A.M. Dudley (May 2,1879 – July 5, 1879)*. File No. QQ1284. (Boxes 3304, 3305, 3305A); Court Martial Files 1809-1894. Records of the Office of the Judge Advocate General - Army. Record Group 153. Old Military and Civil Branch. National Archives and Records Administration. Washington, D. C.

OTHER CONTEMPORARY SOURCES FOR (CHRONOLOGICAL)

Dudley, Nathan Augustus Monroe. "I am in receipt of a copy of letter written by one H.I. Chapman, calling himself the Attorney ..." **November 9, 1878**. Letter to Lew Wallace. From *Proceedings of a Court of Inquiry in the Case of Lt. Col. N.A.M. Dudley (May 2,1879 – July 5, 1879)*. File No. QQ1284. (Boxes 3304, 3305, 3305A); Court Martial Files 1809-1894. Records of the Office of the Judge Advocate General – Army. Record Group 153. Old Military and Civil Branch. National Archives and Records Administration. Washington, D.C. (**Forwarding the Susan McSween affidavits in answer to the charges made by Chapman**)

Wallace, Lew. "I am in receipt of Col. Dudley's reply to the charges against him ..." Letter to Edward Hatch. **November 14, 1878**. Indiana Historical Society. Lew Wallace Collection. M0292. Box 3. Folder 17. (**Has quote: "the "reply is perfectly satisfactory"**)

_____. "I am constrained to request that Lieut Col. N.A.M. Dudley, Commanding at Fort Stanton, be relieved ..." Letter to Edward Hatch. **December 7, 1878**. Indiana Historical Society. Lew Wallace Collection. M0292. Box 3. Folder 18.

Dudley, Nathan Augustus Monroe. "An Open Letter, By Lieut. Col. N.A.M. Dudley, 9th Cavalry, to His Excellency Governor Lew Wallace." Letter to Lew Wallace. Santa Fe *Weekly New Mexican*. **December 14, 1878**. Reprinted in *Mesilla News*. December 21, 1878. As Exhibit 13 from *Proceedings of a Court of Inquiry in the Case of Lt. Col. N.A.M. Dudley (May 2,1879 – July 5, 1879)*. File No. QQ1284. (Boxes 3304, 3305, 3305A); Court Martial Files 1809-1894. Records of the Office of the   Judge Advocate General – Army. Record Group 153. Old Military and Civil Branch. National Archives and Records Administration. Washington, D.C.

_____. "I have the honor to repeat the request made on a former occasion that Lt. Col. N.A.M. Dudley be relieved of the command ..." Letter to Edward Hatch. **March 7, 1879**. Indiana Historical Society.   Lew Wallace Collection. M0292. Box 4, Folder 4.

Hatch, Edward. "Lieutenant Colonel N.A.M. Dudley is hereby relieved from command and duty ..." Special Field Order 2. **March 8, 1879**. Indiana Historical Society. Lew Wallace Collection. M0292. Box 4, Folder 4. (**Wallace succeeds in removing Dudley**)

Wallace, Lew. "I have official information that a court of inquiry for Col. Dudley has been ordered ..." Letter to Carl Schurz. **April 4, 1879**. Indiana Historical Society. Lew Wallace Collection. M0292. Box 4. Folder 8.

Purington, George Augustus. "The District Court adjourned on Thursday ..." **May 3, 1879**. Letter to Adjutant General. Indiana Historical Society. Lew Wallace Collection. M0292. Box 4. Folder 10.

No Author. Verdict on Civil Cause 298 for arson of Susan McSween's house. *Mesilla News*. **December 6, 1879**. Unpublished. personal communication from Frederick Nolan. July 29, 2005. (**Dudley exonerated**)

ELLIS, ISAAC

Ellis, Isaac. "We are two residents of Lincoln County ..." Letter written with George Coe to President Rutherford B. Hayes. **June 22, 1878**. In Angel Report papers. Microfilm File Case Number 44-4-8-3. Record Group 48. Microfilm No. M750.

Roll 1. National Archives and Records Administration. U.S. Department of Justice. Washington, D.C.

_____. Affidavit of Isaac Ellis. **March ?, 1879**. Indiana Historical Society. Lew Wallace Collection. M0292. Box 4, Folder 7.

EVANS, JESSIE

BIOGRAPHICAL SOURCE

McCright, Grady E. and James H. Powell. *Jessie Evans: Lincoln County Badman.* College Station, Texas: Creative Publishing Company. 1983.

CONTEMPORARY SOURCES (CHRONOLOGICAL)

Wilson, John, George B. Barker, Robert M. Gilbert, John Newcomb, Samuel Smith, Benjamin Ellis. "We the undersigned Justice of the Peace and Coroners Jury who sat upon the inquest held this 19th day of February 1878 on the body of John H. Tunstall ..." Coroner's Jury Report for John Tunstall. **February 19, 1878**. **(Naming as murderers, among others, James Dolan, Frank Baker, Jessie Evans, William Morton, and George Hindman)**

Wallace, Lew. "I have information that William Campbell, J.B. Matthews, and Jesse Evans were of the party engaged in the killing ..." Letter to Edward Hatch. **March 5, 1879**. Indiana Historical Society. Lew Wallace Collection. M0292. Box 4, Folder 4. **(Murder of Huston Chapman)**

Rynerson, William. "Indictments of the April, Lincoln County Grand Jury." **April 28, 1879**. Herman B. Weisner Papers, ca. 1957-1992. New Mexico State University Library at Las Cruces. Rio Grande Historical Society Collection. Accession No. Ms 0249. Box 4/39. Folder E-Z. Folder Name: "Jessie Evans Accessory to Murder." **(Billy's testimony indicts Dolan, Campbell, and Evans for his pardon)**

FOUNTAIN, ALBERT JENNINGS

BIBLIOGRAPHICAL SOURCE

Gibson, A. M. *The Life and Death of Colonel Albert Jennings Fountain.* Norman: University of Oklahoma Press. 1965.

CONTEMPORARY SOURCE

Fountain, Albert Jennings, Attorney and J.D. Bail. "Instructions Asked for by Defendants Counsel. April 9, 1881. Herman B. Weisner Papers, ca. 1957-1992. New Mexico State University Library at Las Cruces. Rio Grande Historical Society Collection. Accession No. Ms 0249. Box 1. Folder 14-D. Folder Name: "Billy the Kid Legal Documents."

FRITZ FAMILY (EMIL AND CHARLES FRITZ AND EMILIE FRITZ SCHOLAND)

Fritz, Charles. Affidavit of **September 18, 1876** claiming that Emil Fritz had a will. Probate Court Record. (private collection)

_____. Affidavit of **September 26, 1876** Authorizing Alexander McSween to Receive Payments for the Emil Fritz Estate. Probate Court Record. (private collection)

Scholand, Emilie and Charles Fritz. Affidavit of **September 26, 1876** appointing McSween to collect debts for the Emil Fritz Estate. Copied from the original District Court Record. (private collection)

Fritz, Charles. Affidavit of **December 7, 1877** to order Alexander McSween to pay the Emil Fritz insurance policy money. Probate Court Record. (private collection)

Scholand, Emilie. Affidavit of **December 21, 1877** Accusing Alexander McSween of Embezzlement. Copied from the original District Court Record. (private collection)

Bristol Warren. "Writ of Embezzlement." **December 21, 1877.** Herman B. Weisner Papers, ca. 1957-1992. New Mexico State University Library at Las Cruces. Rio Grande Historical Collections. Accession No. Ms 0249. Box 10. Folder M-13. Folder Name. "Will and Testament A. McSween." **(Emilie Fritz Scholand's sworn complaint against Alexander McSween)**

Fritz, Charles. Affidavit sworn before John Crouch, Clerk of Doña Ana District Court, for Writ of Attachment issued against property of Alexander A. McSween. Probate Court Record. **February 6, 1878.** (private collection)

_____ and Emilie Scholand. Attachment Bond sworn before John Crouch, Clerk of Doña Ana District Court, against Alexander A. McSween for indebtedness to them. **February 6, 1878.** (private collection).

No Author. Diagram showing parcels of land to each of the heirs of Emil Fritz. Herman B. Weisner Papers, ca. 1957-1992. New Mexico State University Library at Las Cruces. Rio Grande Historical Collections. Accession No. Ms 0249. Box P1. Folder 11. Folder Name. "Charles Fritz Estate."

GARRETT, PATRICK FLOYD

AUTOBIOGRAPHICAL SOURCE

Garrett, Pat F. *The Authentic Life of Billy the Kid The Noted Desperado of the Southwest, Whose Deeds of Daring and Blood Made His Name a Terror in New Mexico, Arizona, and Northern Mexico.* Santa Fe, New Mexico: New Mexico Printing and Publishing Co. 1882. (Edition used: Edited by Maurice Garland Fulton. New York: The Macmillan Company. 1927)

BIBLIOGRAPHICAL SOURCES

Glen, Skelton. "Pat Garrett As I Knew Him on the Buffalo Ranges." **(1890,** Unpublished). Binder RNM, III B, 20. Nita Stewart Haley Memorial Museum. Haley Library. Midland, Texas. **(His killing of Joe Briscoe is recounted)**

Metz, Leon C. *Pat Garrett. The Story of a Western Lawman.* Norman: University of Oklahoma Press. 1974.

Mullin, Robert N. "Killing of Joe Briscoe." Letter to Eve Ball. January 31, 1964. (Unpublished). Binder RNM, VI, H. Nita Stewart Haley Memorial Museum. Haley Library. Midland, Texas.

_____. "Pat Garrett. Two Forgotten Killings." *Password.* X(2) (Summer 1965). pp. 57 - 65.

REWARD FOR KILLING BILLY THE KID

No Author. No title. *Santa Fe Daily New Mexican.* **July 21, 1881.** Volume X, Number 120, Page 4. Column 1. NewspaperArchive.com. **(Pat Garrett's meeting with Acting-Governor Ritch about the Billy the Kid reward.)**

Ritch, William G. "In the matter of the application by Patrick F. Garrett for a reward claimed to have been offered May-1881 for the capture of Wm Bonney alias "the Kid." *Executive Record Book Number 2.* July 25, 1867-November 8, 1882. **July 21, 1881.** Pages 533-535. New Mexico Secretary of State Records. Collection 1971-001, Series 1; Records of the Secretary of the Territory. (Accessed from Albuquerque Public Library Microfilm, Territorial Archives of New Mexico, Roll 21.) **(Presentation of Garret's bill for the reward, showing that Acting-Governor Ritch agreed with the reward, but legal opinion from Attorney General William Breeden necessitated getting a legislative act to convert Wallace's private reward to Territorial)**

No Author. "Kid the Killer Killed, Wm. Bonney alias Antrim, alias Billy the Kid, Fatally Meets Pat Garrett, the Lincoln County Sheriff." Las Cruces *Rio*

Grande Republican. **July 23, 1881**. Page 2. Volume 1, Number 10. NewspaperArchive.com. **(Copy of Pat Garrett's letter to Acting-Governor William Ritch confirming that the original Coroner's Jury Report was sent to District Attorney of the First Judicial District, and copy of it was included in this letter to the Governor)**

Sheldon, Lionel. "In the Matter of the Claim of Sheriff Pat Garrett." Letter to the Legislature. **February 14, 1882**. Territorial Archives of New Mexico. Microfilm Roll 5, Frame 765. **(As Governor, approving Garrett's reward and stating he would have granted it outright had it not already been sent to the Legislature by Acting-Governor Ritch for an act)**

No Author. "An Act for the Relief of Pat. Garrett." *1882 Acts of the Legislative Assembly of the Territory of New Mexico, Twenty-Fifth Session. Convened at the Capitol, at the City of Santa Fe, on Monday, the 2d day of January, 1882, and adjourned on Thursday, the 2d day of March, 1882*. **February 18, 1882**. Chapter 101. Page 191. **(Granting Pat Garrett's reward for Billy the Kid, confirming it had been withheld on a technicality)**

Fulton, Maurice Garland. "I think I have solved the puzzle of the reward offers ..." October 28, 1951. Letter to Robert N. Mullin. Nita Stewart Haley Memorial Library and J. Evetts Haley History Center, Midland, Texas. Mullin Collection. Series RNM, VI, J, Legal Papers and Documents. "William Bonney, Reward for Death, Lincoln Notes." **(Confirming Attorney General's opinion to Acting-Governor William Ritch about conversion of reward by legislative act)**

_____. "The rewards for the Kid give a clue to Catron's participation ..." **November 26, 1951**. Letter to Robert N. Mullin. Nita Stewart Haley Memorial Library and J. Evetts Haley History Center, Midland, Texas. Mullin Collection. Series RNM, VI, J, Legal Papers and Documents. "William Bonney, Rewards." **(Contemplating Catron's participation for the reward)**

_____. "Ritch was governor for the time-being ..." **March 15, 1953**. Letter to Robert N. Mullin. Nita Stewart Haley Memorial Library and J. Evetts Haley History Center, Midland, Texas. Mullin Collection. Series RNM, VI, J, Legal Papers and Documents. "William Bonney, Rewards." **(Confirming Attorney General's opinion to Acting Governor William Ritch about conversion of reward by legislative act)**

OTHER CONTEMPORARY SOURCES (CHRONOLOGICAL)

No Author. "Garrett Exonerates Maxwell." *Santa Fe Daily New Mexican*. **July 21, 1881**. Volume X, Number 120. NewspaperArchive.com. **(Denial that Peter Maxwell was complicit in Billy Bonney's ambush)**

Wild, Azariah F. "Daily Reports of U. S. Secret Service Agents, Azariah F. Wild." Microfilm T-915. Record Group 87. Roll 308 **(July 1, 1879 - June 30, 1881)**. National Archives and Records Administration. Department of the Treasury. United States Secret Service. Washington, D. C. **(Capture of Billy Bonney)**

GAUSS, GOTTFRIED

Gauss, Gottfried. Interview with *Lincoln County Leader*. **November 21, 1889**. **(About Billy Bonney's Lincoln jailbreak)**

HOYT, HENRY F.

AUTOBIOGRAPHICAL SOURCE

Hoyt, Henry. *A Frontier Doctor*. Boston and New York: Houghton Mifflin Company. 1929. **(Describes Billy Bonney's superior abilities, pp. 93-94.)**

CONTEMPORARY SOURCES (CHRONOLOGICAL)

Bonney, William H. Bill of Sale to Henry Hoyt. **October 24, 1878**. Collection of Panhandle-Plains Historical Museum. Canyon, Texas. (Item No. X1974-98/1)

Hoyt, Henry F. "This time it is me who is apologizing ..." Letter to Lew Wallace Jr. (Lew Wallace's grandson) **April 27, 1927**. Indiana Historical Society. Lew Wallace Collection. M0292. Box 14, Folder 11.

_____. "Copy of a bill of sale written by Wm H. Bonney ..." Letter to Lew Wallace Jr. **April 27, 1927**. Indiana Historical Society. Lew Wallace Collection. M0292. Box 14, Folder 11.

LEONARD, IRA E.

BIOGRAPHICAL SOURCE

Nolan, Frederick. Biography and photograph of Ira Leonard. Unpublished. personal communication. July 29, 2005.

COURT OF INQUIRY OF N.A.M. DUDLEY BY (SEE: Nathan Augustus Monroe Dudley Court of Inquiry)

LETTERS TO AND FROM

LEW WALLACE TO AND FROM

Leonard, Ira E. "Dear Gov. You have undoubtedly learned ere this of the assassination ..." Letter to Lew Wallace. **February 24, 1879**. Indiana Historical Society. Lew Wallace Collection. M0292. Box 4. Folder 3. (**On Chapman murder.**)

Wallace, Lew. "It is important to take steps to protect the coming court ..." Letter to Ira Leonard. **April 6, 1879**. Indiana Historical Society. Lew Wallace Collection. M0292. Box 4. Folder 8.

Leonard, Ira. "The air is filled tonight with 'rumors of wars ... Letter to Lew Wallace. **April 20, 1879**. Indiana Historical Society. Lew Wallace Collection. M0292. Box 4. Folder 9. (**About District Attorney Rynerson: "He is bent on going for the Kid"**)

_____. "When you left here I promised to write you concerning events transpiring here ..." Letter to Lew Wallace. **May 20, 1878 [sic - 79]**. Indiana Historical Society. Lew Wallace Collection. M0292. Box 4. Folder 10. (**Has quote on the Murphy-Dolan party as: "part and parcel of the Santa Fe ring that has been so long an incubus on the government of this territory."**)

_____. "I write to you with pencil because I am laboring for breath ..." Letter to Lew Wallace. **May 23, 1879**. Indiana Historical Society. Lew Wallace Collection. M0292. Box 4. Folder 11. (**With quote "we are pouring the 'hot shot' into Dudley." (With enclosed letter of May 20, 1879)**)

_____. "Dudley commenced on the defense Thursday afternoon ..." Letter to Wallace. **June 6, 1879**, Indiana Historical Society. Lew Wallace Collection. M0292. Box 4. Folder 11. (**About disgust at corrupt Court.**)

_____. "Yours of the 7th inst reached me ..." Letter to Lew Wallace. **June 13, 1879**. Indiana Historical Society. Lew Wallace Collection. M0292. Box 4. Folder 11. (**about Court of Inquiry corruption**)

MATTHEWS, JACOB BASIL "BILLY"

BIOGRAPHICAL SOURCE

Fleming, Elvis E. *J.B. Matthews. Biography of a Lincoln County Deputy*. Las Cruces, New Mexico: Yucca Tree Press. 1999.

MAXWELL, DELUVINA

Maxwell, Deluvina. "I came here after Lucien Maxwell was already here...." Letter to J. Evetts Haley. June 24, 1927. Nita Stewart Haley Memorial Library and J. Evetts Haley History Center, Midland, Texas. J. Evetts Haley Collection, JEH, J-I – Maxwell, Deluvina. (**Confirming Billy Bonney's killing**)

MAXWELL FAMILY

Cleaveland, Agnes Morley. *No Life for a Lady.* Boston: Houghton Mifflin. 1941.
_____. *Satan's Paradise: From Lucien Maxwell to Fred Lambert.* Boston: Houghton Mifflin Company. 1952.
Cleaveland, Norman. *The Morleys - Young Upstarts on the Southwest Frontier.* Albuquerque, New Mexico: Calvin Horn Publisher, Inc. 1971.
Dunham, Harold H. "New Mexican Land Grants with Special Reference to the Title Papers of the Maxwell Grant." *New Mexico Historical Review.* (January 1955) Volume 30, Number 1, Pages 1 - 23.
East, James H. "Jim." "I wish to say that I appreciate your courtesy ..." Letter to William B. Burgess. **May 20, 1926.** C.L. Sonnichsen Papers, MS 141. C.L. Sonnichsen Special Collections Department. University of Texas El Paso Library. Box 92. Folder 386. (**About Paulita Maxwell as Billy's lover**)
Freiberger, Harriet. *Lucien Maxwell: Villain or Visionary.* Santa Fe, New Mexico: Sunstone Press. 1999.
Keleher, William A. *The Maxwell Land Grant. A New Mexico Item.* Albuquerque, New Mexico: University of New Mexico Press. 1964.
Lamar, Howard Roberts. *The Far Southwest 1846 - 1912. A Territorial History.* New Haven and London: Yale University Press. 1966.
Miller, Kenny. Descendant of Lucien Bonaparte Maxwell. Personal communication. 2011 to 2012.
Montoya, María E. *Translating Property. The Maxwell Land Grant and the Conflict Over Land in the American West, 1840-1900.* Berkeley and Los Angeles, California: University of California Press. 2002.
Murphy, Lawrence R. *Lucien Bonaparte Maxwell. Napoleon of the Southwest.* Norman: University of Oklahoma Press. 1983.
Pearson, Jim Berry. *The Maxwell Land Grant.* Norman: University of Oklahoma Press. 1961.
Poe, Sophie. *Buckboard Days.* Albuquerque, New Mexico: University of New Mexico Press. 1964.
Taylor, Morris F. *O. P. McMains and the Maxwell Land Grant Conflict.* Tucson, Arizona: The University of Arizona Press. 1979. (**Origins of Santa Fe Ring**)
No Author. "Mrs. Paula M. Jaramillo, 65 Died Here Tuesday." *The Fort Sumner Leader.* Official Newspaper County of De Baca. December 20, 1929. No. 1158, Page 1, Column 1. (**Billy Bonney's sweetheart, Paulita Maxwell**)

COMMANDING OFFICER'S QUARTERS BEFORE MAXWELL FAMILY CONVERSION

Diagram. "Commanding Officer's Quarters Fort Sumner, New Mexico Territory." National Archives, Microfilm RG 98, Consolidated Files Quartermaster General; with copy in Fort Sumner, New Mexico, State Monument. (**Faked in *Cold Case Billy the Kid* as being the Maxwell house itself**)

MAXWELL FAMILY HOUSE IN FORT SUMNER

Drawing. "As per Burns account." Maxwell family house, and diagram of Peter Maxwell's bedroom with external door. Nita Stewart Haley Memorial Library and J. Evetts Haley History Center, Midland, Texas. Mullin Collection. Series RNM,

IV, Y, Notebook: Places and Events, A-O. (**Debunking** *Cold Case Billy the Kid* **hoax that Peter Maxwell's bedroom had no door to the outside**)

Photograph. "Pete Maxwell's House Fort Sumner." Annotated on back by Robert N. Mullin. **Undated.** Nita Stewart Haley Memorial Library and J. Evetts Haley History Center, Midland, Texas. Mullin Collection. Series RNM, IV, A, 161.0. (**Maxwell family house showing external door in Peter Maxwell's bedroom debunking** *Cold Case Billy the Kid* **that the Maxwell house was one story and that Maxwell's bedroom had no door to the outside**)

Mullin, Robert N. "Pete Maxwell's House Fort Sumner, Prior to Erection of New Home 2 ½ Mi. S.E.[after sale of town]; Originally 1 Story Flat Roof, Officers Quarters. 2nd Floor Added By Maxwell." Annotation on back of photograph of Maxwell house. **Undated.** . Nita Stewart Haley Memorial Library and J. Evetts Haley History Center, Midland, Texas. Mullin Collection. Series RNM, IV, A, 161.0. (**Making clear the distinction between the Officer's Quarters and the later Maxwell house**)

PETER MAXWELL'S HOUSE OUTSIDE OF FORT SUMNER

Photograph. "Peter Maxwell's home near Fort Sumner, post Lincoln County War, presented to Robert N. Mullin by Maurice Garland Fulton, who obtained it from Mrs. Susan McSween Barber. Nita Stewart Haley Memorial Library and J. Evetts Haley History Center, Midland, Texas. Mullin Collection. Series RNM, IV, A-161. (**For debunking** *Cold Case Billy the Kid* **hoax that Peter Maxwell lived as a cook in a San Andres Mountain cow camp instead of Fort Sumner**)

No Author. "Las Vegas." Death Notice of Peter Maxwell. **June 28, 1898.** *The Albuquerque Citizen.* Page 2, Column 3. NewspaperArchive.com. (**Peter Maxwell death notice about Fort Sumner area residence and death**)

MAXWELL FAMILY FURNITURE

Blythe, Dee. "Billy the Kid Landmarks Fast Vanishing: Historic Spots Hard to Find; Markers Needed." *Clovis, New Mexico Evening News-Journal.* **May 31, 1937** Volume 9. Number 2. Section E. Monday,. (**Photo and article about Maxwell family furniture**)

Weddle, Jerry. "The Kid at Old Fort Sumner." *The Outlaw Gazette: Billy the Kid Outlaw Gang New Mexico.* **December, 1992.** (**Louisa Beaubien Barrett, Luz Maxwell's niece, error-filled history as recorded by her daughter Marian Barrett, with claim that Garrett's second shot went through a washstand**)

_____. Statement that he interviewed Stella Abreu Maxwell in Albuquerque in her old age, and she stated she got the carpenter's bench from a man in Fort Sumner for her 1925 Billy the Kid Museum. Author's interview. February 5, 2018. (**The bench had not been kept by the family**)

McSWEEN, ALEXANDER

Bristol Warren. "Writ of Embezzlement." **December 21, 1877.** Writ of Embezzlement. New Mexico State University Library at Las Cruces. Rio Grande Historical Collections. Lincoln County Papers. New Mexico State University Library at Las Cruces. Rio Grande Historical Collections. Accession No. Ms 0249. Box No. 10. Folder M-13. "Will and Testament A. McSween." (**Emilie Fritz Scholand's sworn complaint against Alexander McSween**)

Fritz, Charles. Affidavit sworn before John Crouch, Clerk of Doña Ana District Court, for Writ of Attachment issued against property of Alexander A. McSween. Probate Court Record. **February 6, 1878.** (private collection).

Bristol, Warren. Action of Assumpsit to command Sheriff of Lincoln County to attach goods of Alexander A. McSween. **February 7, 1878.** District Court Record. (private collection).

_____. Preprinted form in his name for "Writ of Attachment" (Printed and sold at the office of the Mesilla News) filled out to command the Sheriff of Lincoln County to attach goods of Alexander McSween for a suit of damages for ten thousand dollars. **February 7, 1878.** (private collection).

McSween, Alexander. "It looks as though the agent were the property of J.J. Dolan & J.H. Riley, known here as Dolan & Co." Letter to Secretary of Interior Carl Schurz. **February 11, 1878.** From Frederick Nolan. *The Life and Death of John Henry Tunstall.* Albuquerque, New Mexico: The University of New Mexico Press. 1965. Page 266.

_____. "Will and Testament A. McSween." **February 25, 1878.** Herman B. Weisner Papers, ca. 1957-1992. New Mexico State University Library at Las Cruces. Rio Grande Historical Collections. Accession No. Ms 0249. Box 10. Folder M15. Folder Name. "Will and Testament A. McSween."

_____. and B.H. Ellis. Secretaries. "The undersigned have the Honor of transmitting you, as requested, a copy of the proceedings of a meeting held by the citizens of Lincoln County ..." Letter to President Rutherford B. Hayes; with attached proceedings of the April 1878 Lincoln Grand Jury. **April 26, 1878.** Microfilm File Case Number 44-4-8-3. Record Group 48. Microfilm No. M750. Roll 1. National Archives and Records Administration. U.S. Department of Justice. Washington, D.C.

_____. Deposition to Frank Warner Angel. **June 6, 1878.** Pages 5-183 of Frank Warner Angel report *In the Matter of the Examination of the Causes and Circumstances of the Death of John H. Tunstall a British Subject.* Report filed **October 4, 1878.** Angel Report. Microfilm File Case Number 44-4-8-3. Record Group 48. Microfilm No. M750. Roll 1. National Archives and Records Administration. U.S. Department of Justice. Washington, D.C. (**Reports secret**

Angel, Frank Warner. *In the Matter of the Lincoln County Troubles.* To the Honorable Charles Devens, Attorney General. **October 4, 1878.** Angel Report. Microfilm File Case Number 44-4-8-3. Record Group 48. Microfilm No. M750. Roll 1. National Archives and Records Administration. U.S. Department of Justice. Washington, D.C.

McSWEEN, SUSAN

BIOGRAPHICAL SOURCE FOR

Chamberlain, Kathleen P. *In the Shadow of Billy the Kid: Susan McSween and the Lincoln County War.* Albuquerque: University of New Mexico Press. 2013.

CONTEMPORARY SOURCES ABOUT (CHRONOLOGICAL)

Dudley, Nathan Augustus Monroe. "I am in receipt of a copy of letter written by one H.I. Chapman, calling himself the Attorney ..." **November 9, 1878.** Letter to Lew Wallace. From *Proceedings of a Court of Inquiry in the Case of Lt. Col. N.A.M. Dudley (May 2,1879 – July 5, 1879).* File No. QQ1284. (Boxes 3304, 3305, 3305A); Court Martial Files 1809-1894. Records of the Office of the Judge Advocate General - Army. Record Group 153. Old Military and Civil Branch. National Archives and Records Administration. Washington, D.C. (**Answer to charges, with attached defamatory affidavits against Susan McSween**)

McSween, Susan. Testimony in Court of Inquiry for Lieutenant Colonel N.A.M. Dudley. **May 23-24, 26, 1879.** *Proceedings of a Court of Inquiry in the Case of Lt. Col. N.A.M. Dudley (May 2,1879 – July 5, 1879).* File No. QQ1284. (Boxes 3304, 3305, 3305A); Court Martial Files 1809-1894. Records of the Office of the Judge Advocate General – Army. Record Group 153. Old Military and Civil Branch. National Archives and Records Administration. Washington, D.C.

No Author. Verdict on Civil Cause 298 for arson of Susan McSween's house. *Mesilla News.* **December 6, 1879.** Unpublished. personal communication from Frederick Nolan. July 29, 2005. (**Dudley exonerated**)

MEADOWS, JOHN P.

Meadows, John P. "Billy the Kid to John P. Meadows on the Peñasco, May 1-2, 1881." *Roswell Daily Record.* **February 16, 1931.** Page 6.

_____. "Story of Billy the Kid, His Life and Death, as Told Here by John Meadows, Friend of the Kid." *Roswell Daily Record.* **March 2, 1931.** Page 6. **(With quote on Billy's roughness)**

_____. "Oldtimer, Friend of the Billy the Kid, Tells of the Kid's Capture After Many Killings." *Roswell Daily Record.* **March 3, 1931.** Page 6.

_____. "Oldtimer Pays Tribute to Sheriff Pat Garrett in Final Chapter of Billy the Kid." *Roswell Daily Record.* **March 4, 1931.** Page 6.

_____. Ed. John P. Wilson. *Pat Garrett and Billy the Kid as I Knew Them: Reminiscences of John P. Meadows.* Albuquerque: University of New Mexico Press. 2004.

Meadows, John P. Ed. John P. Wilson. *Pat Garrett and Billy the Kid as I Knew Them: Reminiscences of John P. Meadows.* Albuquerque: University of New Mexico Press. 2004.

MURPHY, LAWRENCE GUSTAV

Murphy, Lawrence G. "Will of Lawrence G. Murphy." Herman B. Weisner Papers, ca. 1957-1992. New Mexico State University Library at Las Cruces. Rio Grande Historical Collections. Accession No. Ms 0249. Box 11. Folder P15. Folder Name: "Murphy, Lawrence G."

PATRÓN, JUAN

Wallace, Lew. "Be good enough to send word to all your men to turn out soon as possible ..." Letter to Juan Patrón. **March 19, 1879.** Indiana Historical Society. Lew Wallace Collection. M0292. Box 4. Folder 6.

Patrón, Juan. First letter to Lew Wallace on **March 29, 1879.** Indiana Historical Society. Lew Wallace Collection. M0292. Box 4, Folder 7.

_____. Second letter to Lew Wallace on **March 29, 1879.** Indiana Historical Society. Lew Wallace Collection. M0292. Box 4, Folder 7.

POE, JOHN WILLIAM

Poe, John W. "The Killing of Billy the Kid." (a personal letter written at Roswell, New Mexico to Mr. Charles Goodnight, Goodnight P.C., Texas) July 10, 1917.

_____. *The Death of Billy the Kid.* (Introduction by Maurice Garland Fulton). Boston and New York: Houghton Mifflin Company. 1933.

Poe, Sophie. *Buckboard Days.* Albuquerque, New Mexico: University of New Mexico Press. 1964. **(Biographical)**

RILEY, JOHN HENRY

Tunstall, John Henry. "A Tax-payer's Complaint, Office of John H. Tunstall, Lincoln, Lincoln Co., N.M., January 18, 1878, 'The Present Sheriff of Lincoln County Has Paid Nothing During His Present Term of Office.' Governor's Message for 1878." Mesilla *Independent.* **January 26, 1878.** Volume 1, Number 32. NewspaperArchive.com. **(Exposé of William Brady and John Riley for embezzling tax money to buy cattle; and T.B. Catron then paid that bill)**

Dolan, James J. "Answer to A Taxpayer's Complaint." Mesilla *Independent.* **January 29, 1878. (Response to J.H. Tunstall's exposé)**

McSween, Alexander. "It looks as though the [Indian] agent were the property of J.J. Dolan & J.H. Riley, known here as Dolan & Co." Letter to Secretary of Interior Carl Schurz. **February 11, 1878.** From Frederick Nolan. *The Life and Death of John Henry Tunstall.* Albuquerque, New Mexico: The University of New Mexico Press. 1965. Page 266.

RUDULPH, MILNOR

Rudulph, Milnor. " I beg your indulgence for ..." Letter to William G. Ritch. **May 18, 1879.** Albuquerque and Bernalillo County Public Library. Genealogical Center. MS. Territorial Archives of New Mexico Microfilm. Roll 99. Image 10. (**Rudulph's signature matches his signature on the Coroner's Jury Report.**)

Keleher, William A. *Violence in Lincoln County 1869-1881.* Pages 350-351. Albuquerque, New Mexico: University of New Mexico Press. 1957.

(SEE: William H. Bonney Coroner's Jury Report)

RYNERSON, WILLIAM LOGAN

BIOGRAPHICAL SOURCES

Miller, Darlis A. "William Logan Rynerson in New Mexico. 1862-1893." *New Mexico Historical Review* 48 (April 1973) pp. 101-131.

No Author. "A Brief History of the Rynerson House." Las Cruces: Del Valle Design & Imaging. No copyright. https://delvalleprintinglc.com/rynerson-house/.

CONTEMPORARY SOURCES BY AND ABOUT (CHRONOLOGICAL)

Rynerson, William L "Indictments of the April, Lincoln County Grand Jury." **April 28, 1879.** Herman B. Weisner Papers, ca. 1957-1992. New Mexico State University Library at Las Cruces. Rio Grande Historical Society Collection. Accession No. Ms 0249. Box 4/39. Folder E-Z. Folder Name: "Jessie Evans Accessory to Murder." (**Indictments of Dolan, Campbell, and Evans**)

_____. "Friends Riley & Dolan, Lincoln N.M. I have just received letters from you mailed 10th inst." Letter to James Dolan and John Riley. **February 14, 1878.** Copy as Exhibit B in June 6, 1878 deposition of Alexander McSween. Frank Warner Angel report. *In the Matter of the Examination of the Causes and Circumstances of the Death of John H. Tunstall a British Subject.* Report filed October 4, 1878. Interior Department Papers 1850-1907; Appointments Division and Subsequent Actions. Microfilm File Case Number 44-4-8-3. Microfilm No. M750. Roll 1. National Archives and Records Administration. U.S. Department of Justice. Washington, D.C. (James J. Dolan Deposition. June 20, 1878. Pages 235-247.) (**Planned killing of J.H. Tunstall**)

Angel, Frank Warner. "I have just been favored by a call from W.L. Rynerson ..." Letter to Secretary of Interior Carl Schurz. **September 6, 1878.** Microfilm File Case Number 44-4-8-3. Record Group 48. Microfilm No. M750. Roll 1. National Archives and Records Administration. U. S. Department of Justice. Washington, D.C.

Rynerson, William. Venue Change. **April 21, 1879.** Herman B. Weisner Papers, ca. 1957-1992. New Mexico State University Library at Las Cruces. Rio Grande Historical Collection. Accession No. Ms 0249. Box 1. Folder 14-D. Folder Name: "Billy the Kid Legal Documents." (**Change of Billy Bonney's trial venue from Lincoln County to Doña Ana County to insure a hanging trial by prevent Lincoln County citizens knowledgeable about the War being jurors**)

SALAZAR, YGINIO

Wallace, Lew. "I beg to submit to you a list of persons ... to arrest ..." Letter to Henry Carroll. **March 11, 1879.** Indiana Historical Society. Lew Wallace Collection. M0292. Box 4. Folder 5. (**Lists Ygenio Salazar and "the Kid**)

Salazar, Joe. (Grandson of Yginio Salazar). Personal Interviews 1999-2001. (**My interviews about Ygenio**)

TUNSTALL, JOHN HENRY

BIOGRAPHICAL SOURCES

Nolan, Frederick W. *The Life and Death of John Henry Tunstall.* Albuquerque, New Mexico: The University of New Mexico Press. 1965.

CONTEMPORARY SOURCES (CHRONOLOGICAL)

Tunstall, John Henry. "A Tax-payer's Complaint, Office of John H. Tunstall, Lincoln, Lincoln Co., N.M., January 18, 1878, 'The Present Sheriff of Lincoln County Has Paid Nothing During His Present Term of Office.' Governor's Message for 1878." Mesilla *Independent.* **January 26, 1878.** Volume 1, Number 32. NewspaperArchive.com. **(Exposé of William Brady and John Riley for embezzling tax money to buy cattle; and T.B. Catron then paid that bill)**

Dolan, James J. "Answer to A Taxpayer's Complaint." Mesilla *Independent.* **January 29, 1878. (Response to J.H. Tunstall's exposé of embezzlement of tax money to buy cattle)**

Rynerson, William. "Friends Riley & Dolan, Lincoln N.M. I have just received letters from you mailed 10th inst." Letter to James Dolan and John Riley. **February 14, 1878.** Copy as Exhibit B in June 6, 1878 deposition of Alexander McSween. Frank Warner Angel report. *In the Matter of the Examination of the Causes and Circumstances of the Death of John H. Tunstall a British Subject.* Report filed October 4, 1878. Interior Department Papers 1850-1907; Appointments Division and Subsequent Actions. Microfilm File Case Number 44-4-8-3. Record Group 48. Microfilm No. M750. Roll 1. National Archives and Records Administration. U. S. Department of Justice. Washington, D.C. (James J. Dolan Deposition. June 20, 1878. pp. 235-247.) **(Planned killing of J.H. Tunstall)**

Wilson, John, George B. Barker, Robert M. Gilbert, John Newcomb, Samuel Smith, Benjamin Ellis. "We the undersigned Justice of the Peace and Coroners Jury who sat upon the inquest held this 19th day of February 1878 on the body of John H. Tunstall ..." Coroner's Jury Report for John Tunstall. **February 19, 1878. (Naming Tunstall's murderers)**

Springer, Frank. "I hope you have received a full account of the Troubles in Lincoln County from your nephew ..." Letter to Senator Rush Clark. **April 9, 1878.** Herman B. Weisner Papers, ca. 1957-1992. New Mexico State University Library at Las Cruces. Rio Grande Historical Collections. Accession No. Ms 0249. Box 4/39. Folder D-6. Folder Name "Frank Springer Letter to Rush Clark." **(Links Santa Fe Ring to murder of J.H. Tunstall)**

Ealy, Mrs. Taylor. Ed. Haniel Long. "New Mexico Writers: The Lincoln County War Part 1. *The New Mexico Sentinel.* **October 5, 1937.** Volume 1, Number 45, Page 8. New York Public Library. **(Eye-witness of Lincoln County War; describes mutilation of head of murdered Tunstall)**

(SEE: Frank Warner Angel)

WALLACE, LEW

AUTOBIOGRAPHICAL AND BIOGRAPHICAL SOURCES

Governor of Territorial New Mexico. 1878-81." *New Mexico Historical Review.* 59(1) (January, 1984).

Morsberger, Robert E. and Katherine M. Morsberger. *Lew Wallace: Militant Romantic.* New York: McGraw-Hill Book Company. 1980.

Wallace, Lew. *An Autobiography. Vol. I.* New York and London: Harper and Brothers Publishers. 1997.

_____. *An Autobiography. Vol. II.* New York and London: Harper and Brothers Publishers. 1997.

SECRET ANGEL NOTEBOOK ON SANTA FE RING FOR

Angel, Frank Warner. "To Gov. Lew Wallace, Santa Fe, N. M., 1878." Notebook. **1878**. Indiana Historical Society. Lew Wallace Collection. M0292. Microfilm No. F372. (**Original missing, copy on microfilm; secret notebook prepared for Lew Wallace listing names for Lincoln County and the Santa Fe Ring**)

Theisen, Lee Scott. "Frank Warner Angel's Notes on New Mexico Territory, 1878." *Arizona and the West: A Quarterly Journal of History.* Winter 1976. Volume 18. Number 4. Pages 333-370. (**About the Angel notebook**)

AMNESTY PROCLAMATION OF

Wallace, Lew. "Proclamation by the Governor." **November 13, 1878**. Indiana Historical Society. Lew Wallace Collection. M0292. Box 3. Folder 17. (**Amnesty Proclamation for Lincoln County War fighters, but excluding those already indicted, like Billy Bonney**)

DUDLEY COURT OF INQUIRY TESTIMONY BY

Wallace, Lew. Testimony in Court of Inquiry for Lieutenant Colonel N.A.M. Dudley. **May 12-15, 1879**. *Proceedings of a Court of Inquiry in the Case of Lt. Col. N.A.M. Dudley (May 2,1879 – July 5, 1879).* File No. QQ1284. (Boxes 3304, 3305, 3305A); Court Martial Files 1809-1894. Records of the Office of the Judge Advocate General – Army. Record Group 153. Old Military and Civil Branch. National Archives and Records Administration. Washington, D.C.

INTERVIEW NOTES ON BILLY BONNEY BY (SEE: William H. Bonney)

REWARD NOTICES AND POSTERS FOR WILLIAM BONNEY BY
(SEE: William H. Bonney)

LETTERS BY AND TO

TO AND FROM WILLIAM BONNEY
(SEE: History of William H. Bonney)

TO SHERIFF PATRICK F. GARRETT

Wallace, Lew. "To the Sheriff of Lincoln County, New Mexico, Greeting ..." **April 30, 1881**. Indiana Historical Society. Lew Wallace Collection. M0292. Box 9. Folder 11. (**Death Warrant for William Bonney after his Mesilla trial and before his Lincoln jailbreak**)

TO AND FROM JUSTICE OF THE PEACE JOHN B. WILSON

Wallace, Lew. "I hasten to acknowledge receipt of your favor of the 11th Jan. ult. ..." **January 18, 1879**. Indiana Historical Society. Lew Wallace Collection. M0292. Box 4. Folder 1. (**Lincoln County as carrying on a revolution**)

Wallace, Lew. "I enclose a note for Bonney." Letter to John "Squire" Wilson. **March 20, 1879**. Indiana Historical Society. Lew Wallace Collection. M0292. Box 4. Folder 6. (**The pardon negotiation for Billy Bonney**)

Wilson, John B. Signed JBW. **April 8, 1879**. Indiana Historical Society, Lew Wallace Collection. M0292. Box 4, Folder 8. (**Notes on rustling**)

_____. Letter to Lew Wallace. **May 18, 1879**. Indiana Historical Society. Lew Wallace Collection. M0292. Box 4, Folder 5.

ARTICLES ABOUT WILLIAM BONNEY BY (SEE: William H. Bonney)

WALZ, EDGAR A.

No Author. *The American Book of Biography: Men of 1912.* Chicago: American Publishers Association. 1913. Page 614.

No Author. "Edgar A. Walz Dead: Expert on credit, Founder of The Travelers Hotel Credit Corporation – Managed New Mexico Ranch in Youth." *The New York Times.* **April 5, 1935.** Volume LXXXIV, Number 28,195. Page 24.

WILD, AZARIAH

BIOGRAPHICAL SOURCE

Nolan, Frederick. "Biography of Azariah Wild." Unpublished and personal communications, June 11, 2005 and October 9, 2005.

CONTEMPORARY SOURCES (CHRONOLOGICAL)

Brooks, James J. *1877 Report on Secret Service Operatives.* "On Azariah Wild." **September 26, 1877.** Page 392. Department of the Treasury. United States Secret Service. Washington, D.C.

Wild, Azariah F. "Daily Reports of U. S. Secret Service Agents, 1875-1937." Record Group 87. Microfilm T-915. Microfilm Rolls 306 (June 15, 1877 - December 31, 1877), 307 (January 1,1878 - June 30, 1879), 308 (July 1, 1879 - June 30, 1881; October 4, 1880, Pages 330-333; October 5, 1880, Pages 336-339; November 11, 1880, Pages 484-488), 309 (July 1, 1881 - September 30, 1883), 310 (October 1, 1883 - July 31, 1886). National Archives and Records Department. Department of the Treasury. Secret Service Division. Washington, D.C.

WILSON, JOHN B. "SQUIRE"

CORONER'S JURY REPORT FOR JOHN H. TUNSTALL BY

Wilson, John, George B. Barker, Robert M. Gilbert, John Newcomb, Samuel Smith, Benjamin Ellis. "We the undersigned Justice of the Peace and Coroners Jury who sat upon the inquest held this 19th day of February 1878 on the body of John H. Tunstall ..." Coroner's Jury Report for John Tunstall. **February 19, 1878.** (**Naming as murderers, among others, James Dolan, Frank Baker, Jessie Evans, William Morton, and George Hindman**)

LETTERS FROM

Wilson, John B. Letter to Lew Wallace. Unsigned but noted as from "Sqr. Wilson by Wallace. Undated, but likely **March, 1879.** Indiana Historical Society. Lew Wallace Collection. M0292. Box 4, Folder 7. (**On Lady Liberty stationery**)

_____. Affidavit of John Wilson. **March ?, 1879.** Indiana Historical Society. Lew Wallace Collection. M0292. Box 4, Folder 7.

_____. Signed JBW. **April 8, 1879.** Indiana Historical Society, Lew Wallace Collection. M0292. Box 4, Folder 8. (**Notes on rustling**)

_____. Letter to Lew Wallace. **May 18, 1879.** Indiana Historical Society. Lew Wallace Collection. M0292. Box 4, Folder 5.

LETTERS TO

Bonney, W H. "Friend Wilson ..." **March 18, 1879.** Indiana Historical Society. Lew Wallace Collection. M0292. (**For mediating his pardon negotiation with Lew Wallace**)

Wallace, Lew. "I enclose a note for Bonney." Letter to John "Squire" Wilson. **March 20, 1879.** Indiana Historical Society. Lew Wallace Collection. M0292. Box 4. Folder 6. (**The pardon negotiation for Billy Bonney**)

THE ORIGINAL "BRUSHY BILL" ROBERTS BILLY THE KID IMPOSTER HOAX

RELATED PUBLICATIONS

Sonnichsen, C.L. and William V. Morrison. *Alias Billy the Kid*. Albuquerque, New Mexico: University of New Mexico Press. **1955. (Faked as Billy the Kid)**

No Author. "UNM to Combine 3 Publications Under One Head." *Albuquerque Journal*. **June 14, 1956.** Page 22. newspapers.com. **(Firing of *Alias Billy the Kid* publisher, E.B. Mann)**

No Author. "Magazine Editor." *Albuquerque Journal*. **September 8, 1956.** Page 10. newspapers.com. **(E.B. Mann, *Alias Billy the Kid's* fired publisher, becomes managing Editor at *Guns* magazine)**

Coleman, Solon F. Death Certificate Dewitt Travis. **February 26, 1961. (Giving birth date of "Brushy"-backing Travis as March 26, 1888)**

Walker, Dale L. *C.L. Sonnichsen: Grassroots Historian*. El Paso: Texas Western Press. **1972. ("Brushy"-backer writing about co-author of *Alias Billy the Kid*)**

Mann, E.B. "Billy the Kid." *Field & Stream*. **July, 1981.** Volume LXXXVI. Number 3. Pages 104-109. **(Duped past director of University of New Mexico Press still backing "Brushy Bill")**

Sonnichsen, Charles Leland. Interview. Oklahoma City, Oklahoma. **1991. (With Sonnichsen's unrepentant claim that there was not a "shred of evidence" that "Brushy" was not Billy the Kid; from Jameson and Bean's *The Return of the Outlaw Billy the Kid*, Page 200)**

Walker, Dale L. *Legends and Lies: Great Mysteries of the American West*. New York: A Tom Doherty Associates Book. **1997. (Backing Roberts as Billy the Kid)**

Sonnichsen, C.L. *Ten Texas Feuds* with "Foreword by Dale L. Walker. Albuquerque: University of New Mexico Press. **2000. ("Brushy"-backing Sonnichsen biographer, Walker gives insight into Sonnichsen's ambitions)**

Sonnichsen, C.L. and William V. Morrison. *Alias Billy the Kid*. Barto, Pennsylvania: Creative Texts Publishers, LLC. **2015. (Reprint of *Alias Billy the Kid* with back cover misinformation and quote from President Harry S. Truman)**

(See W.C. Jameson's 21st century "Brushy"-backing books)

BIOGRAPHICAL SOURCES AND DEBUNKING

No Author. Roberts family members. Federal Census for Arkansas, Sebastion County, Bates Township. **June 1, 1880.** Lines 27-33. **(Cited in Don Cline's *Brushy Bill Roberts: I Wasn't Billy the Kid* to show "Brushy" was 10 months old at the census – 20 years too young to be Billy Bonney)**

No Author. "Brushy Bill Buried But the Legend He was 'Kid' Lives On." *Lubbock Morning Avalanche*. **December 30, 1950.** Page 2. NewspaperArchive.com. **(Dewitt Travis attending "Brushy's" funeral; Morrison calling himself an attorney at the funeral; saying Mabry ignored the "evidence" "Brushy" was Billy the Kid)**

No Author. "Notorious Character is Buried." *Hico News Review*. **January 5, 1951.** Front Page. Volume LXV, Number 34. Texas Tech University Library. Southwest Collections/Special Collections Library. Microfilm H626 Hico (Texas) News Review 1929-1974 Reel 8. **(Obituary of "Brushy Bill" Roberts)**

Caperton, Thomas J. *Historic Structure Report. Lincoln State Monument.* Lincoln New Mexico. Santa Fe, New Mexico: Office of Cultural Affairs, Department of Finance and Administration, Historic Preservation Division. **1983. (With floor plan of the Lincoln court-house proving "Brushy's" faked armory location)**

Pittmon, Geneva Roberts. "Dear Sir: the reason you are not finding my family ..." **December 16, 1987.** Letter to Joe Bowlin. In collection of Old Fort Sumner Museum, Fort Sumner, New Mexico. (**Roberts's niece using family Bible to prove Roberts was not Billy the Kid**)

_____. "I don't know of any job he held ..." Letter to Don Cline. **April 27, 1988.** (Cited in Don Cline's *Brushy Bill Roberts: I Wasn't Billy the Kid* to show "Brushy" was a mentally disabled farm hand in his real life.)

Cline, Don. *Brushy Bill Roberts: I Wasn't Billy the Kid.* **Undated [1988?].** Unpublished manuscript. New Mexico Commission of Public Records. State Records Center and Archives. Santa Fe. MS Donald Cline Collection. Subseries 5.2, Folder 138. Box 10421. Serial No. 9560 Santa Fe NMSRCA. (**Debunking "Brushy Bill's" claim to be Billy the Kid**)

_____. Interview with "Brushy's" brother, Tom's daughter, Mary June Roberts. January 28, 1988. (**Denying "Brushy's" genealogical claims**)

Kyle, Thomas G. "Computers, Billy the Kid, and Brushy Bill: The Verdict is In." *True West.* **July, 1990.** Pages 16-19. (**Lincoln County Heritage Trust photoanalysis with no match of Billy the Kid tintype and "Brushy Bill"**)

Weathers, Elreeta Crain. "Brushy Bill or Billy the Kid? Ollie L. Roberts." **March, 1998.** *People and Places: Gazetteer of Hamilton County, Texas.* http://freepages.rootsweb.com/~gazetteer2000/genealogy/b/brushy_b/brushy_b.htm. (**Description of "crazy" Hico local "Brushy" claiming to be Billy the Kid; her biography is at Weathers, Elreeta. "Find a Grave." https://findagrave.com/user/profile/47271637**)

Nolan, Frederick. *The West of Billy the Kid.* Norman: University of Oklahoma Press. **1998.** (**See Page 7 for quote on the Eugene Cunningham's hoaxed Catherine Antrim photo, which "Brushy" made-up as Aunt Katherine Bonney; and with Seven Rivers boy's tintype with Marion Turner, who "Brushy" made-up was himself at 17 as Billy the Kid; Page 157**)

Salazar, Joe. (Grandson of Yginio Salazar). Interviews **1999-2001.** (**My interviews about Ygenio Salazar, cited by the hoaxers as believing Billy had survived the Garrett shooting, but stating Ygenio thought surviving Billy was a teacher in Mexico**)

Johnson, Jim. *Billy the Kid: His Real Name Was ..."* Denver, Colorado: Outskirts Press, Inc. **2006.** (**Debunking Roberts as Billy the Kid**)

Haws, Roy L. *Brushy Bill: Proof That His Claim to Be Billy the Kid Was a Hoax.* Santa Fe: Sunstone Press. **2015.** (**Roberts relative debunking him as Billy the Kid**)

(SEE: William H. Bonney's Coroner's Jury Report; Relevant 19th century history, Morrison's pardon attempt)

"BRUSHY BILL'S" WRITINGS, NOTES (WRITTEN BY HIM AND RETYPED BY MORRISON) AND TRANSCRIPTS OF MORRISON'S INTERVIEWS OF HIM
(FROM C.L. SONNICHSEN PAPERS, C.L. SONNICHSEN SPECIAL COLLECTIONS DEPARTMENT, UNIVERSITY OF TEXAS EL PASO LIBRARY, MS 141 – WITH BOX AND FOLDER NUMBERS BELOW)

Roberts, Oliver Pleasant. Typed Note titled "1940." **1940.** Box 92. Folder 386. (**Pre-Morrison coaching; claiming he was in all major Wild West Shows, and had his own for 25 years; and has fake genealogy with grandfather Ben, and father Al**)

_____. "She said she had three affidavits that people knew me in 1887 ..." **May 24, 1949.** Letter to William V. Morrison. Footnote in *Alias Billy the Kid.* (Page 59) (**Proving "Brushy" could write**)

_____. Interview transcript, Hamilton, Texas. **June 16, 1949.** Interview with William V. Morrison. Box 92. Folder 386. (**Revealing out-takes and admission of notes, Pages 6, 9**)

_____. Interview transcript, Lincoln, New Mexico. **August 18, 1949.** Interview with William V. Morrison. Box 92. Folder 386. (**Refers Morrison to his notebook for list of names; thinks President was McKinley; Pages 2, 3**)

_____. Interview transcript, Carrizozo, New Mexico. **August 18, 1949.** Interview with William V. Morrison. Box 92. Folder 386. (**Using Billy letters as a prompts, Pages 4, 6**)

_____. Interview transcript, Carrizozo, New Mexico. **August 18, 1949.** Interview with William V. Morrison. Box 92. Folder 386. (**Using a December 28, 1880, *Las Vegas Gazette* interview of Billy as a prompt, Page 8**)

_____. "Notes for Brushy Bill Roberts 'The Texas Kid.'" **Undated (1949?).** C.L. Box 92. Folder 386. (**Typed notes with added script apparently by "Brushy," and altered dates for corrections**)

_____. "My father moved to Idaho ..." Retyping of "Brushy's" notes. **Undated (1949?).**" Box 92. Folder 386. (**Signed Ollie Roberts, retyped by Morrison, original of it is in print letters**)

_____. "Brushy Bill Roberts." Typed notes. **Undated (1949?).** Box 92. Folder 386. (**Typed notes saying he knew Frank Dalton since 1859**)

_____. Typed notes. **Undated (1949?).** Box 92. Folder 386. (**Claim being invited to England by Queen Victoria**)

_____. Typed notes, with added script by Morrison and "Brushy." **Undated (1949?).** Box 92. Folder 386. (**Example of "Brushy's" cursive handwriting**)

_____. Typed notes, with added script by Morrison and "Brushy." **Undated (1949?).** Box 92. Folder 386. (**Example of "Brushy's" printed handwriting**)

_____. "Affidavit" **April 18, 1951.** C.L. Sonnichsen Papers, MS 141. Box 118. Folder 841. (**Subsequently hidden Affidavit written by Morrison confirming "Brushy's" writings**)

"BRUSHY'S" NON-BILLY THE KID IMPOSTURES

No Author. "'Brushy Bill' Has Come to Hico to Spend the Rest of His Life." *The Hico News Review.* **July 25, 1941.** Volume LVII, Number 9, Front Page. Texas Tech University Library. Southwest Collections/Special Collections Library. Microfilm H626 Hico (Texas) News Review 1929-1974. (**Pre-Morrison hoax "Brushy," with a fake father named Al Roberts**)

No Author. "Jesse James' Friend to Be at Hinton Rodeo July 14-15-16." *The Hinton Record.* **July 8, 1948.** Front Page. Oklahoma Historical Society, Research Center, Microfilm 9335-200. (**"Brushy" as backing imposter J. Frank Dalton as being Jesse James**)

Roberts, Oliver Pleasant. ("Brushy" writing as O.L. Roberts) "Dear Uncle Kit Carson, We got here O.K. ..." Letter to Oran Ardious Woodman. **April 1, 1949.** From Roy L. Haws, *Brushy Bill: Proof His Claim to Be Billy the Kid Was a Hoax.* 2015. (Pages 113-117) (**Calling himself son of Billy the Kid to this Kit Carson imposter**)

No Author. "Latest Jesse Tells of $2,000,000 Loot." *The Whitewright Sun.* **January 12, 1950.** Page 16, Columns 2 and 3. Newspaper Archive.com. (**J. Frank Dalton Jesse James imposter hoax as backed by Dewitt Travis, with "Brushy" as a witness also**)

No Author. "Cornering Jesse James." *Hico News Review.* **February 3, 1950.** Front Page. Volume LXIV, Number 38. Texas Tech University Library. Southwest Collections/Special Collections Library. Microfilm H626 Hico (Texas) News Review 1929-1974 Reel 8. (**"Brushy" claiming to identify J. Frank Dalton as Jesse James**)

Holford, Carolyn. " 'Brushy Bill' Is Back From Gotham." *Hico News Review.* **February 20, 1950.** Front Page. Volume LXIV, Number 36. Texas Tech University Library. Southwest Collections/Special Collections Library. Microfilm H626 Hico (Texas) News Review 1929-1974 Reel 8. **(Reporting on Morrison-backed radio show on January 3, 1950 with J. Frank Dalton as Jesse James; and "Brushy" backing him and having "wild west" tales)**

Turner, Thomas. "Sam Bass' Pistol, Texan Knew Bad Men, Saw Hoss Thieves Hang." *Dallas Morning News.* **September 18, 1950.** Number 353. Part 1, Page 8. **(Only three months before the pardon attempt, "Brushy" tells his tall tales in Hico, but omits his Billy the Kid imposture, gives a different family history, and puts himself in the Dakota Black Hills at 21 – no Fort Sumner shooting scene)**

Cox, Jim. *The Great Radio Soap Operas.* Jefferson, North Carolina: McFarland & Company, Inc. Publishers. **1999.** **(About "We the People" radio show, in which "Brushy" vouched for J. Frank Dalton as Jesse James)**

WILLIAM MORRISON'S BIOGRAPHY (CHRONOLOGICAL)

BIOGRAPHY

Morrison, William V. "Family History." **January 2, 1942.** Missouri Historical Society Archives, St. Louis, Missouri. Morrison, William Vincent V. Family History Sheet. **(Lying that he is an lawyer)**

Sonnichsen, C.L. "I believe, without evidence, that Bill Morrison had a law degree ..." Letter to Don Cline. **June 30, 1988.** (From Cline's 1988 *Brushy Bill Roberts: I Wasn't Billy the Kid,* **Page 73)**

Metz, Leon. "I met William V. Morrison in the early 1970's ..." Letter to Don Cline. **July 2, 1988.** (Cited in Don Cline's *Brushy Bill Roberts: I Wasn't Billy the Kid* to show that Morrison had no real evidence for "Brushy")

No Author. "Memorials." *El Paso Post-Herald.* **September 9, 1977.** Volume XCVII, Number 216. Page 24, Column 5. Newspaperarchive.com **(Obituary for William V. Morrison, showing he was not an attorney)**

COLLECTED PAPERS IN ABRAHAM LINCOLN PRESIDENTIAL LIBRARY AND MUSEUM

No Author. William Vincent Morrison Papers. Abraham Lincoln Presidential Library and Museum. Springfield, Illinois. William Vincent Morrison Papers 1777-1975. Collection BC473. Location M4-4.6. Box 1, Folders: 1-29, 31; Box 2, Folders: 1-27. **(Research on family documents to establish his heirship from Pierre Menard; and the litigation to reclaim Menard land in Texas)**

No Author. William Vincent Morrison Biography. Abraham Lincoln Presidential Library and Museum. Springfield, Illinois. William Vincent Morrison Papers 1777-1975. Collection BC473. Location M4-4.6. Box 1, Folder 30.

PRIMARY DOCUMENTS

No Author. "1850 Census for Kaskaskia, Randolph, Illinois." Ancestry.com. *1850 United States Federal Census.* Provo, Utah, USA: Ancestry.com Operations, Inc., 2009. Roll: M432_125, Page 128A, Image: 510. Images reproduced by FamilySearch. **(Confirming Evelyn Maxwell as a daughter of Ferdinand Maxwell and Evelyn in Kaskaskia)**

No Author. "1860 Census for Kaskaskia, Randolph, Illinois." Ancestry.com. *1860 United States Federal Census.* Provo, Utah, USA: Ancestry.com Operations, Inc., 2009. Roll: M653_221, Page 923, Family History Library Film: 803221. Images reproduced by FamilySearch. **(Confirming Evelyn Maxwell as a newborn daughter of Ferdinand Maxwell and Evelyn in Kaskaskia)**

No Author. "Illinois, County Marriages, 1810-1940." *Family Search* (https://family search.org/ark:/61903/3:1:33S7-9B22-VNK?cc=1803970&wc=326X-T3X%3A145955101:3March2016), 0975010 (005204395) image 151 of 371; county offices, Illinois. **(Confirming marriage of William M. Maxwell and Evelyn Maxwell on January 6, 1859)**

No Author. "Illinois, County Marriages, 1810-1940." *Family Search* (https://family search.org/ark:/61903/3:1:33S7-LB22-93BG?cc=1803970&wc=326X-YWT%3A145956501:3March2016), 0975010 (005204396) image 518 OF 270; county offices, Illinois. **(Confirming marriage of William M. Maxwell to Sophie Hartman in Kaskaskia on August 19, 1884, with William's parents listed as William M. Morrison and Evelyn Maxwell)**

No Author. "1900 Census for Kaskaskia, Randolph, Illinois." Ancestry.com. *1910 United States Federal Census*. Lehi, Utah, USA: Ancestry.com Operations, Inc., 2006. Roll: T624_319, Page 5B, Enumeration District: 0108; FHL microfilm: 1374332. **(Confirming Jarrett Morrison (born 1886) with parents William M. Morrison (1859-1939) and Sophie Morrison in Kaskaskia)**

No Author. "1920 Census for Kaskaskia, Randolph, Illinois." Ancestry.com. *1920 United States Federal Census*. Provo, Utah, USA: Ancestry.com Operations, Inc., 2010. Roll: T625_396, Page 5A, Enumeration District: 116. **(Confirming William V. Morrison as age 13 and living with his parents Jarrett Morrison and Afra Link in Kaskaskia)**

Morrison, William V. "You are hereby notified that a book ..." Letter to legal department of World Press. **June 30, 1955**. C.L. Sonnichsen Papers, MS 141. C.L. Sonnichsen Special Collections Department. University of Texas El Paso Library. Box 118. Folder 841. **(Gives family history)**

No Author. Death Certificate for William Vincent Morrison. Texas Department of State Health Services, Austin, Texas. Ancestry.com. *Texas Death Certificates, 1903-1982*. Provo, Utah, USA: Ancestry.com Operations, Inc., 2013. **(Confirming Morrison's parents as Jarrett Morrison and Afra Link)**

No Author. "Memorial mass for William V. Morrison." *El Paso Herald-Post*. September 9, 1977. Volume XCVII, Number 216. **(Described as a "graduate lawyer," bankruptcy referee, real estate sales associate, and member of historical societies)**

LETTER

Morrison, William V. "You are hereby notified that a book ..." Letter to Legal Department World Press. **June 30, 1955**. C.L. Sonnichsen Papers, MS 141. C.L. Sonnichsen Special Collections Department. University of Texas El Paso Library. Box 118. Folder 841. **(Gives his Maxwell-Menard genealogy)**

PARDON ATTEMPT FOR "BRUSHY" (CHRONOLOGICAL)

Andress, Lipscomb and Peticolas. "Application is herewith respectfully made for a full, unconditional pardon ..." Alleged pardon application to T.J. Mabry for "Brushy Bill." **November 15, 1950**. C.L. Sonnichsen Papers, MS 141. C.L. Sonnichsen Special Collections Department. University of Texas El Paso Library. Box 118. Folder 838. **(Pardon Petition, possibly written by W.V. Morrison, with misstatement of the Lew Wallace pardon agreement with Billy Bonney)**

Humphreys, Sexton. "Pardon Me, I'm Alive," Says Billy the Kid." *Indianapolis News*. **November 25, 1950**. Page 9. Indiana Historical Society. Lew Wallace Collection. M0292. Box 14. Folder 12.

Morrison, William V. "Statement of Facts" with "instruments for reference." **November 30, 1950**. Nita Stewart Haley Memorial Library, Midland, Texas. Robert N. Mullin Collection. RNM, I, Morrison, William V. 1949-1957. **(Copy of Morrison's fake "evidence" for the "Brushy Bill" pardon hearing with Governor Thomas Jewett Mabry)**

Morgan, Art. "Billy the Kid Only a Phony It Turns Out." *Santa Fe New Mexican.* **November 30, 1950.** Issue 6. Front page, Page 3. NewspaperArchive.com.

No Author. "Mabry Terms "Billy" Outright Imposter." *Clovis News Journal.* **November 30, 1950.** Volume 22, Number 208. Newspaperarchive.com. **(Thursday, when interview was held)**

Smylie, Vernon. "Billy the Kid Flunks in Talk With Governor." *El Paso Herald Post.* **November 30, 1950.** Volume LXX, Number 285. Front Page, Page 13. Newspaperarchive.com. **(Thursday, when interview was held)**

United Press. "Pardon Mt 6-Shooters. Billy the Kid? Governor to Decide." *The Indianapolis News.* **November 30, 1950.** Indiana Historical Society. Lew Wallace Collection. M0292. Box 14. Folder 12.

No Author. " 'Billy the Kid' Bubble Bursts as Gov. Mabry Rejects Oldster's Claim." *Albuquerque Journal.* **December 1, 1950.** Volume [illegible], Number 61. Front Page, Page 4. Newspapers.com.

No Author. "Will A. Keleher, History Student, Sure Kid Was Shot." *Albuquerque Journal.* **December 1, 1950.** Volume [illegible], Number 61. Front Page. Newspaperarchive.com. **(Supports Governor Mabry calling "Brushy Bill" a Billy the Kid imposter)**

No Author. "Billy the Kid is Called Imposter by New Mexico Chief." *Lubbock Morning Avalanche.* **December 30, 1950.** Page 12. Newspaperarchive.com.

Hendron, J.W. "No Pardon for Billy." **January 5, 1951.** *Highway Happenings.* Volume 2, Number 2. C.L. Sonnichsen Papers, MS 141. C.L. Sonnichsen Special Collections Department. University of Texas El Paso Library. , "Billy the Kid-Roberts." Box 92. Folder 386. **(Describing "Brushy's" Mabry hearing failure)**

MORRISON'S PROMOTIONAL ATTEMPTS FOR "BRUSHY" (CHRONOLOGICAL)

Autry, Gene via Mr. Schaefer. "Your letter of March 23rd regarding information on Billy the Kid ..." Letter to William V. Morrison. **March 31, 1954.** C.L. Sonnichsen Papers, C.L. Sonnichsen Special Collections Department. University of Texas El Paso Library. MS 141, Box 118. Folder 838. **(Rejection of movie)**

Morrison, William V. Letter to Carl Breihan. **March 17, 1954.** (In Don Cline's *Brushy Bill Roberts: I Wasn't Billy the Kid* to show Morrison's attempt to sell "Brushy's" story for movies or TV)

_____. Letter to Philip Rasch. **April 12, 1954.** Rio Grande Historical Collections./Hobson Huntslinger University Archives. New Mexico State University, Las Cruces. **(Lying about William Keleher backing)**

_____. "I received a nice letter from Mr. Schaefer ..." Letter to Gene Autry. **September 10, 1954.** C.L. Sonnichsen Papers, C.L. Sonnichsen Special Collections Department. University of Texas El Paso Library. MS 141, Box 118. Folder 838. **(Informing that *Alias Billy the Kid* accepted for publication)**

_____. "I am enclosing a list of names of people ..." Letter to Eileen Quinn (at University of New Mexico Press). **December 14, 1954.** C.L. Sonnichsen Papers, C.L. Sonnichsen Special Collections Department. University of Texas El Paso Library. MS 141, Box 118. Folder 840. **(Making-up that William Keleher, Philip Rasch, and Gene Autry would publicize *Alias Billy the Kid*)**

Truman, Harry S. "I can't tell you how very much I appreciate the Number 1 copy of Alias Billy the Kid ..." Letter to William V. Morrison. **May 19, 1955.** C.L. Sonnichsen Papers, C.L. Sonnichsen Special Collections Department. University of Texas El Paso Library. MS 141, Box 118. Folder 839. **(duped Truman)**

Truman, Harry S. "I appreciate your letter ..." Letter to William V. Morrison. **June 8, 1955.** C.L. Sonnichsen Papers, C.L. Sonnichsen Special Collections Department. University of Texas El Paso Library. MS 141, Box 118. Folder 839. **(Truman requesting copy of his microfilm "evidence")**

Morrison, William V. "While recuperating from a three month research project ..." Letter to C. L. Sonnichsen. **March 28, 1977.** Box 136. Folder 1073. **(Reviewing past profit hopes for *Alias Billy the Kid*)**

WILLIAM V. MORRISON CORRESPONDENCE AND TALK IN BLAZER FAMILY PAPERS 1864-1965, NEW MEXICO STATE UNIVERSITY, LAS CRUCES

Morrison, William V. "Regarding Billy the Kid." Correspondence. **October 28, 1949-August 4, 1955.** New Mexico State University Library, Archives and Special Collections Department. Blazer Family Papers, 1864-1965. MS 0110, 15:12 and MS 0110, 15:13, William Vincent Morrison Correspondence, Billy the Kid, regarding and General, August 18, 1952-April 24, 1956, March 31, 1962.

CORRESPONDENCE, BILLY THE KID, MS 0110, 15:12

Morrison, William V. "I certainly enjoyed talking with you ..." Letter to Paul A. Blazer. **August 18, 1952. (Getting information on Billy being ambidextrous)**

_____. "First, I want to thank you for taking me through the cemetery ..." Letter to Paul A. Blazer. **April 27, 1953. (Getting information on the graves of "Buckshot" Roberts and Dick Brewer.)**

_____. "I wish to thank you for your time ..." Letter to Paul A. Blazer. **June 26, 1953. (Trying to convince people that Garrett did not kill the Kid)**

_____. "Your winter issue, 1953, Volume 1, No. 3, was handed to me ..." Letter to Fred Gipson. **April 17, 1954. (Informing editor of *True West* magazine that Garrett did not kill the Kid)**

_____. "Your letter of the first arrived here ..." Letter to Paul A. Blazer. **April 6, 1955. (Announcing publication of *Alias Billy the Kid*)**

CORRESPONDENCE, BILLY THE KID, MS 0110, 15:13

Olyanova, Nadya. "I have your letter of May 13th in which you throw out the challenge ..." Letter to William V. Morrison. **May 18, 1953. (Contact with a handwriting analyst about a Billy the Kid letter)**

Morrison, William V. "I have your letter of the 13th ..." Letter to Carl W. Breihan. **March 17, 1954. (About Dalton being Jesse James, historians, like William Keleher, accepting that "Brushy" was Billy the Kid, that he sought movie and television rights for his work, and that he had sought exhumations)**

_____. "Your comment in the March issue with reference to Corle's 'Billy the Kid' ..." Letter to Raymond Carlson. **March 17, 1954. (Boasting to *Arizona Highway* editor, Carlson, wrongly that Ira Leonard did not represent Billy in Mesilla – revealing where "Brushy" got that error)**

Morrison, William V. "I have your letter of March 24, and wish to thank you ..." Letter to Carl W. Breihan. **April 3, 1954. (Faking reasons for why "Brushy" lost the Governor Mabry pardon)**

_____. "Thanks for your most interesting letter ..." Letter to Philip J. Rasch. **April 19, 1954. (Trying to convince Rasch that "Brushy" matched Billy physically, and the Mabry hearing was affected by the Santa Fe Ring)**

_____. "Thanks for your letter of the first ..." Letter to Philip J. Rasch. **May 7, 1954. (Calling Sonnichsen a Billy the Kid historian)**

Morrison, William V. "I am very grateful for your kind letter ..."Letter to William Waters. **June 29, 1955. (About wanting to exhume Billy the Kid')**

_____. "I have a letter from Doc. Sonnichsen ..." Letter to Robert N. Mullin. **(Claiming "Brushy" could not read)**

WILLIAM VINCENT MORRISON ROTARY CLUB LECTURE, CORRESPONDENCE BILLY THE KID, MS 0110, 15:12

Morrison, William V. "Billy the Kid." Talk to the El Paso, Texas, Rotary Club. December 3, 1953. Text of talk sent to Paul A. Blazer. **(Presenting the full-blown "Brushy Bill" hoax, with introduction by C.L. Sonnichsen)**

C.L. SONNICHSEN PAPERS, C.L. SONNICHSEN SPECIAL SPECIAL COLLECTIONS DEPARTMENT, UNIVERSITY OF TEXAS AT EL PASO LIBRARY, MS 141 (Note that only Box and Folder are listed below; with Box 92 as Billy the Kid - Roberts;" Box 118 as "Alias Billy the Kid Correspondence;" Box 135 as "William J. [sic] Morrison;" and Box 136 as "Morrison-Villa")

DOCUMENTS: PRIMARILY COPIES OF WILLIAM V. MORRISON'S CORRESPONDENCE

McFarland, D.F. Marriage certification. **March 1, 1873.** Box 136. Folder 1073. **(Certified copy of Catherine McCarty marriage with Henry and Josie McCarty as witnesses; and concealed by Morrison and Sonnichsen)**

Bristol, Warren. Quashing of Billy Bonney's Indictment for Andrew "Buckshot" Roberts. **April 6, 1881.** Box 92. Folder 386. **(Morrison prompt research for "Brushy's" special knowledge)**

Ealy, Mrs. Taylor. Ed. Haniel Long. "New Mexico Writers: The Lincoln County War Part 1. *The New Mexico Sentinel.* **October 5, 1937.** Volume 1, Number 45, Page 8. New York Public Library. **(Eye-witness of Lincoln County War as prompt source)**

_____. Ed. Haniel Long. "New Mexico Writers: The Lincoln County War Part 2. *The New Mexico Sentinel.* **October 12, 1937.** Volume 1, Number 46, Page 6. New York Public Library. **(Eye-witness of Lincoln County War as prompt source)**

No Author. "Denies Garrett's Shot Killed Billy the Kid. **November 10, 1937.** *El Paso Times.* Box 92. Folder 386. **(A non-historical old-timer says he saw Billy in Taos after the shooting)**

Romero, Alicia. "This will acknowledge receipt of your recent letter ..." Letter to William Morrison. **November 9, 1949.** Box 92. Folder 386. **(Secretary of State confirming Morrison's requesting a certified copy of the Executive Records Book pages)**

Fulton, Maurice Garland. "Since your visit I have looked into the possible whereabouts ..." Letter to William V. Morrison. **December 7, 1949.** Box 92. Folder 386. **(Informing Morrison that the Coroner's Jury Report was filed in Santa Fe, as the first judicial district; leading Morrison to do a fake search in Las Vegas, the fourth judicial district, to claim no Report existed)**

Morrison, William V. Handwritten notes on Edgar Walz and Jim East. **Undated.** Box 92. Folder 386. **(Prompt notes for "Brushy")**

_____. Handwritten notes about items in Lew Wallace collection, Silver City articles, Tunstall, Chapman killing, Lincoln County War Battle. **Undated.** Box 92. Folder 386. **(Prompt notes for "Brushy")**

_____. "Your letter of the 21st received ..." Letter to Eugene Cunningham. **June 27, 1950.** Box 118. Folder 838. **(Denial of the Coroner's Jury Report)**

_____. "Upon my arrival here I found ..." Letter to Robert E. Lee. **July 10, 1950.** Box 118. Folder 838. **(Acknowledging receipt of Affidavit for "Brushy")**

_____. "It was certainly a pleasure to be able to meet you in person ..." Letter to Bill Jones. **July 4, 1950.** Box 118. Folder 838. **(Failed attempt to get Jones brother, Bill, to sign his pre-written affidavit stating "Brushy" was Billy Bonney; see letter to Sam Jones)

_____. "Although our time was very limited ..." Letter to Sam Jones. **July 4, 1950**. C.L. Sonnichsen Papers, MS 141. Box 118. Folder 838. (**Failed attempt to get Jones brother, Sam, to sign his pre-written affidavit stating "Brushy" was Billy Bonney**)

_____. "Affidavit." **undated, but referenced in letters of July 4, 1950 to Bill and Sam Jones.**" Box 118. Folder 838. (**Fake Affidavit which Jones brothers refused to sign attesting that "Brushy" was Billy the Kid**)

_____. "My dear Friend Billy ..." Letter to "Brushy Bill" Roberts. **August 3, 1950**. Box 118. Folder 840. (**Pumping-up "Brushy," who was not illiterate and could read**)

_____. "I take this opportunity to thank you ..." Letter to W.J. Hooten. **August 3, 1950**. Box 118. Folder 839. (**Claims no Coroner's Jury Report by fake search in Las Vegas, New Mexico**)

_____. "I was delighted to be able to talk to you ..." Letter to G. Wilson. **August 7, 1950**. Box 118. Folder 841. (**Apparent prompt source claiming Garrett shot the wrong man while the Kid was in the "yard."**)

_____. "Your item, Everyday Events ..." Letter to Bill Latham. **August 12, 1950**. Box 118. Folder 841. (**Claiming no Coroner's Jury Report**)

_____. "I enjoyed our chat again ..." Letter to C.L. Sonnichsen. **August 17, 1950**. Box 118. Folder 841. (**Minimizing Coroner's Jury Report, and telling him about interest of Bill Latham, Managing Editor of** *The El Paso Times*)

Andress, Lipscomb and Peticolas. "Application is herewith respectfully made for a full, unconditional pardon ..." Alleged pardon application to T.J. Mabry for "Brushy Bill." **November 15, 1950**. Box 118. Folder 838. (**Pardon Petition, possibly written by W.V. Morrison, with massively erroneous statement of the Lew Wallace pardon agreement with Billy Bonney**)

No Author. "Old Timer Claims He Helped Bury Billy the Kid." **December 1, 1950**. *Albuquerque Journal*. Box 92. Folder 386. (**Old-timer fake claim that Billy was buried on July 16, 1880**)

Morrison, William V. "I mailed you a letter yesterday ..." Letter to "Brushy Bill" Roberts. **December 18, 1950**. Box 118. Folder 838. (**Prompting "Brushy" on Clay Allison**)

_____. "Your letter of the 21st received ..." Letter to Dennis Zimmerman. **December 18, 1950**. Box 118. Folder 838. (**Claiming to have "Brushy's" handwriting**)

_____. "Your communication of November 27th ..." Letter to Carl. W. Breihan. **December 18, 1950**. Box 118. Folder 838. (**Claims two Coroner's Jury Reports - English and Spanish - and death scene in rear yard**)

_____. "You have probably read in the papers where we lost..." Letter to Severo Gallegos. **December 18, 1950**. Box 118. Folder 838. (**Keeping his Affidavit-signing dupe in the loop**)

_____. "We have not relied wholly upon personal identification ..." Letter to C.L. Sonnichsen. **December 31, 1950**. Box 118. Folder 838. (**Sonnichsen in the loop**)

_____. "The file that I submitted ..." Letter to Art Leibson possibly at *Life Magazine*. **January 2, 1951**. Box 118. Folder 838. (**Selling "Brushy" as Billy**)

_____. "Your letter of December 28th received ..." Letter to John S. Mayfield. **January 2, 1951**. Box 118. Folder 838. (**Selling "Brushy" as Billy with fake names and that Ted Andress represented him in the pardon petition**)

_____. "Your letter addressed to Mrs. O.L. Roberts ..." Letter to A. P. Von Blon. **January 3, 1951**. Box 118. Folder 838. (**Impersonating a lawyer**)

Travis, Dewitt. "Your letter received and thanks for the picture ..." Letter to William V. Morrison. **January 23, 1951**. Box 92. Folder 386. (**About "Brushy" having "tusk-like" canine teeth pulled**)

Morrison, William V. "Your letter of the 23rd received ..." Letter to A. P. Von Blon. **January 29, 1951.** Box 118. Folder 841. (**No Coroner's Jury Report, and Wallace never gave Garrett the reward**)

_____. "Your letter of the 30th received ..." Letter to Mrs. Roberts. **January 31, 1951.** Box 118. Folder 841. (**Contents of "Brushy's" trunk; and picture of him and "Brushy" taken in Juarez trip**)

No Author. "Glimpses of History." **February, 1951.** *New Mexico Magazine.* Volume 29, Number 2, Pages 26, 54. Box 92. Folder 386. (**With photostatic copy of Coroner's Jury Report made by Harold Abbott**)

Morrison, William V. "Your most welcome letter of the 9th was received ..." Letter to Ola Eberhard. **February 14, 1951.** Box 118. Folder 841. (**"Brushy's" diaries**)

_____. "Your letter received ..." Letter to Mrs. Roberts. **February 22, 1951.** Box 118. Folder 841. (**Wants sample of "Brushy's" writing in early stage of hoax before illiteracy was faked**)

_____. "Little things show how careful he was not to give himself away ..." Note to C.L Sonnichsen. **Undated (February, 1951?)** Box 92. Folder 386. (**Early phase of hoax claiming "Brushy" hid his handwriting to hide that he was Billy the Kid!**)

_____. "Your letters of the 19th and 20th received ..." Letter to Robert N. Mullin. **March 24, 1951.** Box 118. Folder 841. (**Key source revealed for Morrison's prompting – here an erroneous version of the Dudley Court of Inquiry transcript, which was then parroted by "Brushy" as "shooting [N-word] soldiers; and two Coroner's Jury Reports claim."**)

_____. "Having not heard from you ..." Letter to Dewitt Travis. **March 30, 1951.** Box 118. Folder 841. (**Morrison writing the Affidavit for him**)

_____. "It is my understanding that your society has possession ..." Letter to Colorado State Historical Society. **April 4, 1951.** Box 118. Folder 841. (**Seeking Billy Bonney's letter to Edgar Caypless**)

_____. "We represented Brushy Bill Roberts ..." Letter to Eva Jones. **April 7, 1951.** Box 118. Folder 841. (**Impersonating an attorney**)

_____. "I received your comment today ..." Letter to C.G. Killinger. **April 9, 1951.** Box 118. Folder 841. (**Claiming "Brushy" was Billy the Kid, and had an unfair pardon hearing**)

Travis, Dewitt. "I will write you again ..." Letter to William V. Morrison. **April 9, 1951.** Box 92. Folder 386. (**Repeating new "Brushy's" fake tales about Belle Starr**)

Morrison, William V. "Your letter of the 9th received ..." Letter to Robert N. Mullin. **April 14, 1951.** Box 118. Folder 841. (**With a "Brushy" confabulation that Lincoln County War shooting was from "the Murphy Store Building" at the McSween house; and Morrison's own genealogy**)

Roberts, J. Henry. "I will answer the questions ..." Letter to William V. Morrison. **April 16, 1951.** Box 92. Folder 386. (**Said "brushy" was not the Kid**)

Morrison, William V. "While talking to Mary Neal ..." Letter to Elzey Perry Jr. **April 18, 1951.** Box 118. Folder 841. (**Failed attempt to get a George Coe family affidavit for "Brushy"**)

Morrison, William V. "I received your address ..." Letter to I.A. Adams. **April 23, 1951.** Box 118. Folder 841. (**Confirming Morrison's working on "Brushy's" fake genealogy**)

_____. "I received your address ..." Letter to Tom Roberts. **April 23, 1951.** Box 118. Folder 841. (**Confirming Morrison's working on "Brushy's" fake genealogy**)

_____. "Your letter of the 9th received ..." Letter to Dewitt Travis. **April 23, 1951.** Box 118. Folder 841. (**Confirming Morrison wrote Travis's affidavit on "Brushy"**)

_____. "This will serve to acknowledge ..." Letter Robert N. Mullin. **May 2, 1951.** Box 118. Folder 841. (**Was sent a copy of the Report by Mullin, but fakes its denial**)

Travis, Dewitt. "My father, Elbert Travis and Brushy Bill's father ..." Letter to William V. Morrison. **May 2, 1951.** Box 92. Folder 386. **(Repeating new "Brushy's" fake tales about Belle Starr)**

Morrison, William V. "Your letter of the 2nd received ..." Letter to Dewitt Travis. **May 4, 1951.** Box 118. Folder 841. **(Prompting on what to write in affidavit for "Brushy")**

_____. "Your letter of April 16th received ..." Letter to J. Henry Roberts. **May 4, 1951.** Box 118. Folder 841. **(Getting information for fake "Brushy" genealogy)**

_____. "Your letter and article, "No Pardon For Billy" ..." Letter J.W. Hendron. **May 13, 1951.** C.L. Sonnichsen Papers, MS 141. Box 118. Folder 841. **(List of fake excuses for "Brushy's" pardon hearing failure)**

_____. "I plan to be in Ruidoso ..." Letter to Severo Gallegos. **June 2, 1951.** Box 118. Folder 838. **(Wanting to record him about Billy the Kid)**

_____. "I take this opportunity to thank you ..." Letter to A.S. Gaylord. **July 23, 1951.** Box 118. Folder 838. **(Impersonating an attorney)**

No Author. "Coroner's Report Proves Billy the Kid is Dead, Historian Asserts, Researcher Discovers Document." **August 5, 1951.** *The El Paso Times.* Number 217, Page 13. Box 118. Folder 841. **(Maurice Garland Fulton debunks Morrison's claim that the Report was not authentic)**

Morrison, William V. "With regards to item in your August 5th issue ..." Letter to Editor *El Paso Times.* **August 7, 1951.** Box 118. Folder 841. **(Faking that Fulton did not have copies of the original Coroner's Jury Report)**

_____. "First I was referred to your office ..." Letter to District Attorney of Fourth Judicial District. **August 9, 1951.** Box 118. Folder 841. **(Faking search for Coroner's Jury Report by writing to wrong office in the 4th Judicial District, not the 1st)**

Armijo, Jose E. "I wish to acknowledge receipt of your letter of August 9, 1951 ..." **Undated (but soon after August 9, 1951)** Box 118. Folder 841. **(Stating 4th Judicial District has no requested Coroner's Jury Report)**

Morrison, William V. "First I want to thank you ..." Letter to George Fitzpatrick. **August 24, 1951.** Box 118. Folder 838. **(Getting the A.P. Anaya letter faking two Coroner's Jury Reports)**

Andress, Ted. "Application is herewith respectfully made ..." Letter to Thomas J. Mabry. **November 15, 1951.** Box 92. Folder 386. **(Petition for pardoning "Brushy" as Billy the Kid)**

Morrison, William V. "Your recent letter is not at hand ..." Letter to Carl W. Breihan. **December 8, 1951.** Box 118. Folder 841. **(J. Frank Dalton's J. stood for Jesse)**

Morrison, William V. and C.L. Sonnichsen. "Agreement." **December 27, 1951.** Box 92. Folder 386. **(*Alias Billy the Kid* writing agreement)**

Morrison, William V. Notes on *The Authentic Life of Billy the Kid.*" For C.L. Sonnichsen. **Undated, 1951?** Box 92. Folder 386. **(Showing "Brushy's" prompts and fake claims about no Coroner's Jury Report)**

_____. Notes on John W. Poe's *The Death of Billy the Kid.*" Notes for C.L. Sonnichsen. **Undated, 1951?** Box 92. Folder 386. **(Making fake claims to contradict editor, Maurice Garland Fulton's Coroner's Jury Report claims)**

_____. Notes on Sophie Poe's *Buckboard Days.*" For C.L. Sonnichsen. **Undated, 1951?** Box 92. Folder 386. **(Using a "Brushy" confabulation about Billy the Kid shooting Bob Beckwith to claim she was incorrect that he was killed by friendly fire)**

_____. "Las Vegas Gazette, December 24, 1880." Note for C.L. Sonnichsen. **Undated, 1951?** Box 92. Folder 386. **(Giving incorrect date and incorrect wording of Lew Wallace's reward notice of December 22, 1880 for Billy the Kid; as used by Sonnichsen to deny any notice in *Alias Billy the Kid*)**

_____. "Las Vegas Gazette, November 30, 1880." Note for C.L. Sonnichsen. **Undated, 1951?** Box 92. Folder 386. (**Prompt source "Brushy's" incorrect name-dropping of Regulators - like Dave Rudabaugh and Billy Wilson in** *Alias Billy the Kid*)

_____. "Note on Scarf." For C.L. Sonnichsen. **Undated, 1951?** C.L. Sonnichsen Papers, MS 141. Box 92. Folder 386. (**Giving "Brushy's" fake scarf story in his own words, adding that he has a photo of the scarf**)

_____. "*Alias Billy the* Kid, *Billy the Kid Comes Back* ..." List of possible book titles. **Undated, 1951?** Box 118. Folder 841. (**List of possible book titles for Sonnichsen**)

Richeson, Hawley. "Billy the Kid." "Mr. Morrison - This story, which is almost identical ..." Press release sent to William V. Morrison. **Undated, 1951?** El Paso Sunland News Bureau. Box 118. Folder 841. (**Claiming Sonnichsen vouched for Morrison's "evidence"**)

Fitzpatrick, George. "I am attaching a copy of A.P. Anaya's letter ...." Letter to C.L. Sonnichsen. **January 19, 1952.** Box 92. Folder 386. (**Giving him a copy of "Paco" Anaya's two Coroner's Jury Report letter**)

Morrison, William V. "Sometime after receiving your letter ..." Letter to A.S. Gaylord Jr. **January 12, 1952.** Box 92. Folder 386. (**Claiming the Wallace reward was "suspended;" so Garrett did not get the reward**)

Fulton, Maurice Garland. "I am glad to hear from you directly about your book." Letter to C.L. Sonnichsen. **February 24, 1952.** Box 118. Folder 839. (**Warning Sonnichsen that Morrison coached "Brushy," who is an imposter; and assuming Sonnichsen's *Alias Billy the Kid* would be an exposé**)

Morrison, William V. "Your letter received ..." Letter to Dewitt Travis. **March 15, 1952.** Box 118. Folder 838. (**Confirming Sonnichsen wrote *Alias Billy the Kid***)

_____. "All of your letters have been received ..." Letter to Mrs. Roberts. **March 15, 1952.** Box 118. Folder 839. (**Confirming that Sonnichsen wrote *Alias Billy the Kid***)

_____. "Your letter of the 15th received ..." Letter to J.W. Hendron. **May 19, 1952.** Box 118. Folder 841. (**Presenting his lies that Charles W. Greene was Garrett's layer for the reward and forged the Coroner's Jury Report himself**)

_____. "Some time ago a clipping from the Arizona Republic ..." Letter to Roscoe Wilson. **June 16, 1952.** Box 118. Folder 840. (**Seeking information on Billy's Silver City time and the name "McCartney" for *Alias Billy the Kid***)

_____. "He Said He Was Billy the Kid." Kiwanis Club talk in Silver City. **August 14, 1952.** Box 118. Folder 841; and Box 92, Folder 386. (**Faking "Brushy" as Billy the Kid, and claiming no Coroner's Jury Report**)

_____. "Glen called today saying the members enjoyed ..." Letter to Dr. McCain. **August 15, 1952.** Box 118. Folder 841. (**Responding to his Kiwanis Club talk on "Brushy," and enclosing a copy**)

_____. "I wish you could have been there ..." Letter to C. L. Sonnichsen. **August 15, 1952.** Box 118. Folder 841. (**About Kiwanis Club talk success**)

No Author. "Kiwanis Hear Writer Support Claims of Man Who Said He was 'Kid.'" *Silver City Daily Press.* **August 15, 1952.** Volume LVI. Number 45. Box 118. Folder 841. (**About Morrison's Kiwanis Club talk on "Brushy" being Billy the Kid**)

Morrison, William V. "It was interesting to talk to you yesterday ..." Letter to William A. Keleher. **August 18, 1952.** Box 118. Folder 841. (**Responding to his debunking of "Brushy"**)

_____. "Must give them something to dwarf ..." Letter to C.L. Sonnichsen. **Undated (August, 1952 ?).** Box 118. Folder 841. (**Strategizing manipulative book release**)

_____. "As suggested by you ..." Letter to George G. Swett. **October 8, 1952.** C.L. Sonnichsen Papers, MS 141. Box 118. Folder 840. (**Wanting to compare Billy's and "Brushy's" handwriting; proving "Brushy" literacy**)

_____. "I certainly enjoyed the visit with you ..." Letter to George Fitzpatrick. **October 8, 1952.** Box 118. Folder 839. (**Claiming the Lew Wallace reward was not paid to Garrett; instead Garrett was paid by the Santa Fe Ring**)

_____. "My trip was very pleasant ..." Letter to Henry G. Morris. **October 8, 1952.** Box 118. Folder 840. (**Claiming he has the Executive Record book about Garrett's reward**)

_____. "I am wondering if your old San Miguel County ..." Letter to D.B. McKibbin. **November 9, 1952.** Box 118. Folder 840 (**Fake search for Coroner's Jury Report in University of New Mexico Library!**)

_____. "I have your letter of the 6th ..." Letter to Philip J. Rasch. **November 10, 1952.** Box 118. Folder 841. (**Claims his book has a picture of "Brushy's" "foster mother, Katherine Bonney;" when it was a picture of "Brushy's" real mother, Sara Elizabeth Ferguson Roberts**)

_____. "Your letter of the 5th received ..." Letter to Sollie Nalda. **November 11, 1952.** Box 118. Folder 841. (**Gives his Maxwell-Menard genealogy**)

_____. "Your letter of the 8th received ..." Letter to Ozark Jack. **December 8, 1952.** Box 118. Folder 841. (**Summary of his Coroner's Jury Report hoax**)

_____. "I must declare that I have never seen any legal evidence ..." Letter to Philip J. Rasch. **December 12, 1952.** C.L. Sonnichsen Papers, MS 141. Box 118. Folder 840. (**Claims no interest in the Antrim and Bonney family names as irrelevant to "Brushy," with Mrs. Antrim being his aunt; also claiming he only used facts, not hearsay**)

_____. "Yours of the 20th received today ..." Letter to Philip J. Rasch. **December 23, 1952.** Box 118. Folder 839. (**Admits no proof that Antrim married a Katherine Dunn, but fakes that background was irrelevant, including "McCartney" name**)

_____. "Yours of the 19th received ..." Letter to Paul Sann. **January 23, 1953.** Box 118. Folder 839. (**About seeking a posthumous pardon for "Brushy" and writing a book about it**)

_____. "Since I talked with you ..." Letter to Ted Andress. **January 28, 1953.** Box 118. Folder 839. (**About seeking a posthumous pardon for "Brushy"**)

_____. "Since talking to you Thursday ..." Letter to Lou Blachley. **March 15, 1953.** Box 118. Folder 839. (**Claims "Brushy" as ambidextrous, left-hand favoring**)

_____. "I enjoyed the visit with you ..." Letter to Patience Glennon. **March 15, 1953.** Box 118. Folder 839. (**Daughter of Billy Bonney's Silver City teacher used for ambidextrous claim and possible hand-writing match – before calling "Brushy" illiterate**)

_____. "Thanks for the autograph copy ..." Letter to Peter Hertzog. **March 27, 1953.** Box 118. Folder 839. (**Claiming Charles Greene as Garrett's lawyer for the reward; and William Keleher having no proof of the Coroner's Jury Report**)

Morrison, William V. "During your absence a few weeks ago ..." Letter to Geraldine S. Mathison. **April 1, 1953.** Box 118. Folder 840. (**Requesting "certified copies"**)

_____. "This is to notify you that ..." Letter to Georgia B. Redfield. **August 9, 1953.** Box 118. Folder 841. (**Bullying an opponent of "Brushy Bill"**)

_____. "I certainly enjoyed the wonderful convention ... ..." Letter to Floyd Rigdon. **January 25, 1954.** C.L. Sonnichsen Papers, MS 141. Box 118. Folder 841. (**As a microfilm company salesman**)

_____. "This will confirm our conversation ... ..." Letter to Marcus Griffin. **January 25, 1954.** C.L. Sonnichsen Papers, MS 141. C.L. Sonnichsen Special Collections Department. University of Texas El Paso Library. Box 118. Folder 841. (**As a microfilm company salesman**)

_____. "I have been unable to locate a substantial bidder yet ..." Letter to Henry V. Vance. **January 25, 1954.** Box 118. Folder 841. (**As a bankruptcy collector**)

_____. "I have your letter of March 24 ..." Letter to Carl W. Breihan. **April 3, 1954.** Box 118. Folder 838. (**Rationalizing the pardon failure**)

_____. "Your winter issue, 1953 ..." Letter to Fred Gipson. **April 17, 1954.** C.L. Sonnichsen Papers, MS 141. Box 118. Folder 838. (**About no Coroner's Jury Report**)

Chesley, Hervey. "Thank you very much for the letter ..." Letter to C.L. Sonnichsen. **April 19, 1954.** Box 118. Folder 839. (**About knowing "Brushy" was a fake**)

Morrison, William V. "I want to answer your fine letter ..." Letter to Carl W. Breihan. **April 19, 1954.** Box 118. Folder 838. (**About being a microfilm company salesman**)

_____. "Thanks for your most interesting letter ..." Letter to Philip J. Rasch. **April 19, 1954.** Box 118. Folder 838. (**Faking that "Brushy" used the name "McCarthy," and faking that the legislature was involved in Garrett's reward because of no Coroner's Jury Report**)

Campbell, Edward M.. "Mrs. Brothers showed me the letter you wrote ..." Letter to William M. Morrison. **May 18, 1954.** Box 118. Folder 838. (**As Morrison representing himself as a lawyer from St. Louis**)

Olyanova, Nadya. "I have your letter of May 13th in which you throw out a challenge ..." **May 18, 1953.** Letter to William V. Morrison. Box 118. Folder 838. (**Pressuring her on handwriting analysis of Billy Bonney's letter**)

Corle, Edwin. "The answer to your excited letters ..." Letter to William V. Morrison. **July 26, 1953.** Box 118. Folder 841. (**Informing him his Billy the Kid book was just a novel**)

_____. "A Mr. William V. Morrison states ..." Letter to C.L. Sonnichsen. **July 26, 1953.** Box 118. Folder 841. (**Informing Sonnichsen about Morrison's crazy attacks on him**)

Morrison, William V. "Your letter of July 26 was received ..." Letter to Edwin Corle. **August 11, 1953.** Box 118. Folder 841. (**Crazy harassment of Billy the Kid novelist**)

_____. "Words cannot express my appreciation ..." Letter to C.L. Sonnichsen. **December 3, 1953.** Box 118. Folder 841. (**Thanking for Rotary Club talk introduction**)

_____. "I attended the dedication of the Old Lincoln County Courthouse ..." Letter to Philip J. Rasch. **June 30, 1954.** Box 118. Folder 838. (**Trying to convince Philip Rasch about "Brushy" as Billy**)

_____. "Since just writing to you ..." Letter to Philip J. Rasch. **July 15, 1954.** Box 118. Folder 838. (**Telling Philip Rasch "Brushy" was Billy**)

_____. "I am writing to Homer Croy ..." Letter to Philip J. Rasch. **July 15, 1954.** (Second letter on same date) Box 118. Folder 838. (**Impersonating an attorney**)

_____. "Your most welcome and interesting letter in reply ..." Letter to Raymond Schleede. **September 1, 1954.** Box 118. Folder 838. (***Alias Billy the Kid* accepted for publication**)

_____. "Thanks for your wonderful letter ..." Letter to Robert N. Mullin. **September 10, 1954.** Box 118. Folder 838. (**Sonnichsen wrote *Alias Billy the Kid***)

_____. "In conversation with Doc Sonnichsen today ..." Letter to E.B. Mann. **October 1, 1954.** Box 118. Folder 838. (**Claims Ted Andress was attorney of record for Pardon Petition**)

_____. "A friend forwarded to me a copy ..." Letter to Mary Hudson Brothers. **November 10, 1954.** Box 118. Folder 840. (**Attacking Brothers as not a Billy the Kid expert like himself**)

_____. "I take this opportunity to thank you ..." Letter to J.C. Careaga. **November 10, 1954.** Box 118. Folder 840. (**Printing machine salesman in Mexico**)

_____. "I take this opportunity to thank all of you ..." Letter to L.D. Gaines. **November 10, 1954.** Box 118. Folder 840. **(As a printing machine salesman in Mexico)**

_____. "Thanks for your letter of the first ..." Letter to E.B. Mann. **November 10, 1954.** Box 118. Folder 840. **(About sending microfilmed records pertaining to *Alias Billy the Kid*, which Mann's University of New Mexico Press had accepted)**

_____. "Thanks for your letter of the 16th ..." Letter to Edward M. Campbell. **November 30, 1954.** Box 118. Folder 838. **(Attacking William Keleher's historian authority)**

_____. "I certainly enjoyed the visit ..." Letter to E.B. Mann. **January 7, 1955.** Box 118. Folder 840. **(Flattering Director of University of New Mexico Press)**

_____. "Since most of my time was spent in Mexico ..." Letter to J.C. Dykes. **January 11, 1955.** Box 118. Folder 840. **(Claiming "Brushy" said Billy not indicted for Arizona killing)**

_____. "Thanks for Sagebrush Sleuth on Siringo ..." Letter to George Fitzpatrick. **January 23, 1955.** Box 118. Folder 840. **(Claiming Billy the Kid would not carry a Colt .41)**

_____. "Recently, I have been advised that you may be able to give me information ..." Letter to M.H. Borden. **February 2, 1955.** Box 118. Folder 840. **(Claiming no Coroner's Jury report with fake legalese)**

_____. "I am very grateful for your letter ..." Letter to Marion H. Borden. **February 9, 1955.** Box 118. Folder 838. **(Listing copied records; denying being a practicing attorney)**

_____. "Recently I was advised that you had served on the Ranger Force ..." Letter to J.T. O'Brien. **February 9, 1955.** Box 118. Folder 838. **(Summary of no Coroner's Jury Report and Sheriff Romero not notified - as questioning Pat Garrett's authority)**

_____. "On today's program, I heard you state ..." Letter to a *Texas Star* reporter. **February 14, 1955.** Box 118. Folder 838. **(Attacking him as a liar for saying Garrett killed the Kid)**

_____. "Thanks for your personal letter ..." Letter to Guy W. Bradford. **February 23, 1955.** Box 118. Folder 840. **(Lying that the Legislature denied the Coroner's Jury Report)**

_____. "Last night while checking through ..." Letter to Carl W. Breihan. **February 24, 1955.** Box 118. Folder 840. **(On Jim Hines being William Campbell)**

_____. "Your letter of the first received ..." Letter to Carl W. Breihan. **March 5, 1955.** Box 118. Folder 840. **(Claiming Joe Hines being William Campbell, and claiming Lew Wallace thought Campbell was Jesse James; also references his bankruptcy work)**

_____. "Wile working with the University of New Mexico ..." Letter to Susie Peters. **March 7, 1955.** Box 118. Folder 840. **(Claiming Mabry never gave "Brushy" a hearing)**

_____. "Last night while checking through ..." Letter to Philip J. Rasch. **March 19, 1955.** Box 118. Folder 840. **(On Jim Hines being William Campbell)**

_____. "Thanks for your letter of the 13th ..." Letter to Robert N. Mullin. **March 19, 1955.** Box 118. Folder 840. **(His error that Sabal and Celsa Gutierrez were siblings, which was then parroted by "Brushy")**

_____. "While stopping in Tombstone a few days ago ..." Letter to George Reid. **March 19, 1955.** C.L. Sonnichsen Papers, MS 141. Box 118. Folder 840. **(On no Coroner's Jury Report and no killing of anyone by Garrett)**

_____. "Thanks for your letter of the 23rd ..." Letter to Carl W. Breihan. **March 23, 1955.** Box 118. Folder 839. **(Attacking Coroner's Jury Report)**

_____. "We had a very successful autographing party ..." Letter to Robert N. Mullin. **May 9, 1955.** Box 118. Folder 840. (**Faking the Legislative Act for Garrett's reward as not about the killing of Billy Bonney**)

Morrison, William V. "Thanks for your letter of the 19th ..." Letter to Philip J. Rasch. **May 21, 1955.** Box 118. Folder 840. (**Admitting he could not afford to buy the Dudley Court of Inquiry transcript**)

Morrison, William V. "Thanks for your letter of May 29 ..." Letter to Philip J. Rasch. **June 1, 1955.** Box 118. Folder 840. (**Lying responses to Rasch's debunking of *Alias Billy the Kid***)

_____. "I have just read your letter of the 29 thoroughly ..." Letter to Philip J. Rasch. **June 4, 1955.** Box 118. Folder 840. (**Refusing to accept the McCarty name as Billy's**)

_____. "You are hereby notified that a book ..." Letter to Legal Department World Press. **June 30, 1955.** Box 118. Folder 841. (**Gives his Maxwell-Menard genealogy**)

_____. "I have a letter from Doc. Sonnichsen ..." Letter to Robert N. Mullin. **July 12, 1955.** C.L. Sonnichsen Papers, MS 141. Box 118. Folder 840. (**Stating he has the "Brushy" tapes; and saying "Brushy" could not read**)

_____. "Thanks for the fine book review ..." Letter to Philip J. Rasch. **August 2, 1955.** Box 118. Folder 840. (**Defensive about not having the Court of Inquiry transcript – so "Brushy" was fatally unaware of Billy Bonney's testimony**)

_____. "Your letter came while I ..." Letter to C.L. Sonnichsen. **August 21, 1955.** Box 118. Folder 840. (**Calling Philip Rasch a "rat"**)

_____. "Your letter received after I had written ..." Letter to Carl Breihan. **November 28, 1955.** Box 136. Folder 1073. (**Saying he takes the offensive to push "Brushy"**)

_____. "Thanks for your letter of November 28 ..." Letter to Rick Steinke. **January 6, 1956.** Box 136. Folder 1073. (**Saying Severo Gallegos had denied his affidavit to the press; that no one ever mentioned "Brushy's" Maxwell yard fight; and "Brushy" was illiterate for 25 years**)

_____. "Since talking with you there in December ..." Letter to E.B. Mann. **January 24, 1956.** Box 136. Folder 1073. (**Updating on progress of Pancho Villa book**)

_____. "I have just read a story ..." Letter to Fred Gipson. **March 18, 1956.** C.L. Sonnichsen Papers, MS 141. Box 118. Folder 840. (**Offering reward for Coroner's Jury Report**)

_____. "Today, I met your son, Craig ..." Letter to George J. Hayes. **April 29, 1956.** C.L. Sonnichsen Papers, MS 141. Box 136. Folder 1073. (**Claiming *Alias Billy the Kid* is considered the best book on Billy the Kid**)

_____. "Your letter received the morning following ..." Letter to William Kimble. **May 21, 1956.** Box 136. Folder 1073. (**Advertising himself as an historian**)

_____. "Just a line before I leave for Mexico ..." Letter to C.L. Sonnichsen. **August 20, 1956.** Box 136. Folder 1073. (**Letterhead as "researches, Appraisals, Estates"**)

_____. "I appreciate your interest in our book ..." Letter to E.B. Foewler. **October 3, 1956.** Box 136. Folder 1073. (**Claim that Billy Bonney did not write his letters**)

Dickey, Roland. "Dr. Sonnichsen has informed me of your proposed book on Villa ..." Letter to William V. Morrison. **January 27, 1958.** Box 136. Folder 1073. (**Rejecting the book on Pancho Villa**)

Morrison, William V. "Probably you may recall my efforts ..." Letter to Paul Baker. **May 8, 1961.** Box 118. Folder 839. (**Hope to dig up Billy the Kid, Coroner's Jury Report denial, comment on Lois Telfer case, Cc. to Harry S. Truman**)

_____. "Sorry I do not keep in closer contact ..." Letter to C.L. Sonnichsen. **May 24, 1961.** Box 118. Folder 839. (**Seeking posthumous pardon for "Brushy" and exhuming the Billy the Kid grave**)

Humphrey, John. "Your cousin, Mrs. Michel Nalda, gave me your address..." Letter to William V. Morrison. **January 30, 1962.** Box 118. Folder 839. **(Wanting him as an expert on Billy the Kid genealogy for opposition to the Lois Telfer exhumation case)**

Morrison, William V. "Thanks for your letter of January 30, 1962 ..." Letter to John Humphrey. **February 8, 1962.** Box 118. Folder 839. **(Denying Lois Telfer's claim based on Josie McCarty being missing - though unknown to "Brushy;" and reworking the "Brushy" hoax as done to establish "heirship" of "William Campbell")**

Swann, Tom. "I am very glad that my information ..." Letter to C.L. Sonnichsen. **July 24, 1963.** Box 136. Folder 1073. **(Sending a copy of the song "Billy Barlow")**

Morrison, William V. "Your letter of February 29, 1964 ..." Letter to Mike Francis and John McGinnis. **March 11, 1964.** Box 136. Folder 1073. **(Calling himself a real estate broker; and giving a fake argument that dead Billy could not have a Colt .41 as Garrett claimed in** *The Authentic Life of Billy the Kid***)**

_____. "I enjoyed talking with you ..." Letter to Paul Albright. **April 10, 1966.** C.L. Sonnichsen Papers, MS 141. Box 118. Folder 839. **(His Maxwell-Menard genealogy)**

_____. "I enjoyed talking with you ..." Letter to Paul Albright. **April 11, 1966.** C.L. Sonnichsen Papers, MS 141. Box 118. Folder 839. **(Impersonating an attorney)**

Humphrey, John. "I was sorry that I didn't get to see you ..." Letter to William V. Morrison. **March 14, 1962.** Box 118. Folder 839. **(Confirming that the Telfer case was lost based on uncertain location of the Billy the Kid grave)**

Morrison, William V. "I enjoyed talking to you tonight ..." Letter to C.L. Sonnichsen. **December 11, 1976.** Box 136. Folder 1073. **(Blaming University of New Mexico Press's firing of E.B. Mann on a conspiracy against** *Alias Billy the Kid***)**

_____. "While recuperating from a three month research project ..." Letter to Barbara Franklin. **December 14, 1976.** Box 136. Folder 1073. **(Blaming "Brushy's" pardon failure on Santa Fe Ring politics, and hiding that there was no Coroner's Jury Report)**

_____. "While recently conferring with Dr. Sonnichsen ..." Letter to Director University of New Mexico Press. **March 28, 1977.** Sonnichsen Papers, MS 141. C.L. Sonnichsen Special Collections Department. University of Texas El Paso Library. Box 136. Folder 1073. **(Requesting reprint of** *Alias Billy the Kid***)**

_____. "Thanks for your calls and the letter ..." Letter to Lawrence K. Mooney. **April 12, 1977.** Box 136. Folder 1073. **(Stating that Maurice Garland Fulton made a photostat of the Coroner's Jury Report from Santa Fe, but Morrison denied it was real; Morrison's argument about one photostatic copy being rat chewed showed it was not identical to another copy; saying the name McCarty was not documented; saying he corrected Brushy's" memoirs and letters to him; saying the Legislature claimed the Kid was killed in August, 1881)**

Treadwell, Hugh W. "Copyright on the book entitled ALIAS BILLY THE KID ..." Letter to William V. Morrison and C.L. Sonnichsen. **June 3, 1977.** Box 136. Folder 1073. **(Return of copyright by University of New Mexico Press not republishing** *Alias Billy the Kid***)**

No Author. Obituary for William V. Morrison. **August 31, 1977.** Newspaper name clipped off. Box 136. Folder 1073. **(Claiming he was in real estate and a bankruptcy referee – no mention of lawyer)**

Sonnichsen, C.L. "Last week your letter came in ..." Letter to Hugh W. Treadwell. **September 5, 1977.** Box 136. Folder 1073. **(Claiming no interest in republishing** *Alias Billy the Kid***)**

Haws, Eulaine. "Thanks for your picture ..." Letter to William A. Tunstill. C.L. **February 5, 1983.** Box 118. Folder 839. (**Duped relative helping Tunstill fake a "Brushy" genealogy**)

Cline, Donald. "I am the author of the book ..." Letter to New Mexico Book League. **August 4, 1986.** C.L. Sonnichsen Papers, MS 141. Box 118. Folder 837. (**Accusing Sonnichsen and Morrison of faking "Brushy" as Billy the Kid for the "buck"**)

Yeatman, Ted P. Letter to the Editors. *The Dallas Morning News.* **August 9, 1986.** Box 118. Folder 837. (**About "Brushy" backing J. Frank Dalton as Jesse James**)

Sonnichsen, C.L. "I have on my desk a copy of a letter ..." Letter to Barbara J. Kuchler. **March 23, 1987.** Box 118. Folder 839. (**Trying to make her help genealogy faker William A. Tunstill**)

Tunstill, William A. "Your letter of April 17th at hand ..." Letter to C.L. Sonnichsen. **April 24, 1987.** Box 118. Folder 839. (**Asking for help getting cooperation from Morrison's daughter, Barbara J. Kuchler, for his "Brushy"-backing book; and proving Sonnichsen's helping him for six years**)

Moore, Evan. "A Texas Town's Brush With Billy the Kid.." *Houston Chronicle.* **February 12, 1989.** Pages 21 A - 22 A. Box 118. Folder 837. (**With "Brushy"-backing William A. Tunstill's background**)

Dyer, Robert. "I am a great admirer of your work ..." Letter to C.L. Sonnichsen. **May 26, 1989.** Pages 21 A - 22 A. Box 118. Folder 840. (**Asking if Sonnichsen regretted writing *Alias Billy the Kid***)

Sonnichsen, C.L. "I have your interesting letter ..." Letter to Robert Dyer. **May 30, 1989.** Box 118. Folder 840. (**Denies taking sides in the "Brushy" case, and Morrison was an honest man**)

Haederle, Michael. "Experts in photographic studies unable to picture Hico man as Billy the Kid." *The Dallas Morning News.* **April 22, 1990.** Box 118. Folder 839. (**No match of "Brushy" to Billy the Kid tintype**)

Cline, Donald. "It has been some time since we last corresponded ..." Letter to C.L. Sonnichsen. **April 24, 1990.** Box 118. Folder 839. (**On "Brushy" being a fraud, and Morrison not being a lawyer; making clear that Sonnichsen was perpetrating a hoax by backing them**)

Bean, Frederick. "Please accept my most sincere thanks ..." Letter to C.L. Sonnichsen. **April 27, 1990.** Box 118. Folder 840. (**Asking if Morrison was an attorney**)

Sonnichsen, C.L. "To answer your final question ..." Letter to Frederick Bean. **May 6, 1990.** Box 118. Folder 840. (**Calling Morrison a "non-practicing" lawyer**)

Bean, Frederick. "This letter requires no response ..." Letter to C.L. Sonnichsen. **May 9, 1990.** C.L. Sonnichsen Papers, MS 141. Box 118. Folder 840. (**Decided that Morrison could be called an attorney based on Sonnichsen's answer; showing that Sonnichsen participated in Morrison's imposture**)

Bean, Frederick. "Thanks so very, very much for the copy of Arizona History ..." Letter to C.L. Sonnichsen. **November 15, 1990.** Box 118. Folder 837. (**From the future author of *The Return of the Outlaw Billy the Kid* showing Sonnichsen's encouragement of his backing of "brushy Bill"**)

Sonnichsen, C.L. "I write in reply to your inquiry ...' Letter to Stephanie Ricks. **May 29, 1991.** Box 118. Folder 837. (**Confirming transfer of *Alias Billy the Kid* rights to Morrison**)

Ashton, Sarah. "Biographical Sketch" for "C.L. Sonnichsen Papers. **1996.** C.L. Sonnichsen Papers, MS 141.. (**Donated in 1972 and 1992 for his collected papers**)

Erekson, Keith. A. *Layers of History at the University of Texas at El Paso.* El Paso: UTEP. **2012.** https://academics.utep.edu/.

"BRUSHY BILL'S" PROMPT SOURCES, ALSO APPEARING AS SOURCE FOOTNOTES IN ALIAS BILLY THE KID (CHRONOLOGICAL)

BOOKS

Roberts, Dan W. *Rangers and Sovereignty*. San Antonio: Wood Printing and Engraving. 1914. (Uncited possible source of "Brushy's" faked grandfather Ben Roberts – actually Dan W. Roberts's father, named Alexander; also "Brushy's" apparent source for a Sam Bass tall tale about getting his revolver)

Siringo, Charles A. *History of Billy the Kid*. Printed by Charles A. Siringo. 1920. Page 32. (largely fictionalized, using Garrett's *The Authentic Life of Billy the Kid*, by a Garrett posseman not involved in capturing Billy, for claim that Billy worked for Murphy and Dolan. Also, it contained the Jim East letter used by "Brushy" to confabulate a story about giving an "Indian girl" the Billy the Kid tintype)

Burns, Walter Noble. *The Saga of Billy the Kid*. Stamford, Connecticut: Longmeadow Press. 1992. (Original printing: **1926**, Doubleday.) **(Fictionalized account using Pat Garrett's 1882 edition of *The Authentic Life of Billy the Kid*)**

Garrett, Pat F. *The Authentic Life of Billy the Kid The Noted Desperado of the Southwest, Whose Deeds of Daring and Blood Made His Name a Terror in New Mexico, Arizona, and Northern Mexico*. Santa Fe, New Mexico: New Mexico Printing and Publishing Co. 1882. (Edition used: Edited by Maurice Garland Fulton. New York: The Macmillan Company. **1927)**

Coe, George with Doyce B. Nunis, Jr. Ed. *Frontier Fighter. The Autobiography of George Coe Who Fought and Rode With Billy the Kid*. Chicago: R. R. Donnelley and Sons Company. **1934. (multiple references)**

Poe, John W. *The Death of Billy the Kid*. Boston and New York: Houghton Mifflin Company. **1933**. Page 21. [sic- Page 31 in *Alias Billy the Kid*]. **(cited by Sonnichsen for fake argument that Fort Sumner residents would have hidden Billy's survival of the Garrett shooting)**

King, Frank M. *Wranglin' the Past: Reminiscences of Frank M. King*. "Chapter xix, The Kid's Exit." Pasadena, California: Trail's End Publishing Company. **1935 and 1946. (Uncited but with used claims: Tom O'Folliard and Kip McKinney were cousins, Page 173; Billy had unfair trial, Page 169; shackle-slipping, Page 170)**

Miguel Otero. *The Real Billy the Kid*. Rufus Rockwell Wilson, Inc. **1936**. Page 37. **(for Pat Garrett's statement that Billy tried to shoot Billy Matthews at Sheriff Brady's ambush, then repeated verbatim by "Brushy")**

Hudson, Bell. Ed. Mary Hudson Brothers. *Billy the Kid*. Farmington, New Mexico: The Hustler Press. 1949. Page 47. **(Prompt source footnote from fictional tales used for "Brushy's" claims of being sought by Barney Mason at a sheep camp while he himself was intending to kill Mason; for intending to kill John Chisum, and for Charlie Bowdre dying at rock house doorway)**

Anaya, Paco. *I Buried Billy*. College Station, Texas: Creative Publishing Company. 1991. **(Later published claims of Anaya used by "Brushy" hoaxers as source of the two coroner's jury reports; though concealed was that Anaya confirmed the body was Billy's)**

BILLY THE KID'S WRITINGS
(SEE BILLY'S LETTERS, INTERVIEW, AND HOYT BILL OF SALE)

Morrison, William V. "Urgent need of photostatic copies correspondence ..." **October 6, 1950**. Telegram to Indiana Historical Society, The William Henry Smith Memorial Library. Indiana Historical Society. Collection Number RG6. Box 17, Folder 11.

Dunn, Caroline. "We have microfilm of Bonney-Wallace correspondence ..." Letter to William V. Morrison. **October 7, 1950.** Letter to William V. Morrison. Indiana Historical Society, The William Henry Smith Memorial Library. Collection Number RG6. Box 17, Folder 11.

Morrison, William V. "Upon my return from Lincoln, N.M., today I have your telegram ..." **October 9, 1950. Letter** to The William Henry Smith Memorial Library. Collection Number RG6. Box 17, Folder 11.

Dunn, Caroline. "Your letter of the 9th received ..." **October 13, 1950.** Letter to William V. Morrison. Indiana Historical Society. Collection Number RG6. Box 17, Folder 11.

Morrison, William V. "Your letter of the 13th received ..." **October 17, 1950.** Letter to Caroline Dunn of The William Henry Smith Memorial Library. Indiana Historical Society. Collection Number RG6. Box 17, Folder 11.

No Author. Bill for $9.78 for "17 sheets photostats, Lew Wallace Collection. **October 25, 1950.** Telegram to Indiana Historical Society Memorial Library. Indiana Historical Society. Collection Number RG6. Box 17, Folder 11.

Dunn, Caroline. "Enclosed are the photostats of the documents in the Lew Wallace collection, with certification ..." **October 25, 1950.** Letter to William V. Morrison. Indiana Historical Society. Collection Number RG6. Box 17, Folder 11.

Morrison, William V. "This will serve to acknowledge receipt ..." **October 28, 1950.** Letter to Caroline Dunn of The William Henry Smith Memorial Library. Indiana Historical Society. Collection Number RG6. Box 17, Folder 11.

No Author. Bill for $2.61 for "6 Pstat neg." **October 30, 1950.** Telegram to Indiana Historical Society Memorial Library. Indiana Historical Society. Collection Number RG6. Box 17, Folder 11.

Wallace, Lew Jr. "A photostatic copy is being prepared of the letter in my possession from William H. Bonney ..." **October 30, 1950** . Letter to William V. Morrison. Indiana Historical Society. Lew Wallace Collection. M0292. Box 8. Folder 3. **(Received a copy of actual Billy Bonney pardon plea letter of March 13, 1879)**

_____. "Your letter of November 2 confuses me ..." **November 10, 1950.** Letter to William V. Morrison. Indiana Historical Society. Lew Wallace Collection. M0292. Box 8. Folder 3. **(Expressing suspicion about a Billy the Kid imposter)**

Unnamed Archivist. "Copy of transcript sent by Wm V. Morrison ..." **November 10, 1950.** Indiana Historical Society. Lew Wallace Collection. M0292. Box 8. Folder 3. **(Seeking a copy of original of Billy Bonney's first pardon request letter)**

Dunn, Caroline. "In my letter to you of November 5 I said I was returning the transcripts ..." **November 14, 1950.** Letter to William V. Morrison. Indiana Historical Society. Collection Number RG6. Box 17, Folder 11.

OTHER LETTERS ABOUT BILLY BONNEY

Nevill, C.L. Letter reporting that a party headed by Billy Antum [sic], alias Kid, is on their way to free Jesse Evans. **September, 1880.** Adjutant General's Department Departmental Correspondence at Texas State Archives. Box 401-400, Folder 1. https://legacy.lib.utexas.edu/taro/tslac/30004/tsl-30004.html. **(About Lieutenant Nevill's intercepted letter from Jessie, which never reached Billy; but was a prompt for "Brushy" to claim that he tried to rescue Jessie)**

East, James H. "Jim." "I wish to say that I appreciate your courtesy ..." Letter to William B. Burgess. **May 20, 1926.** C.L. Sonnichsen Papers, MS 141. C.L. Sonnichsen Special Collections Department. University of Texas El Paso Library. "Billy the Kid-Roberts." Box 92. Folder 386. **(Used for "Brushy's" scarf fable by adding it to East's description of Maxwell family wanting to meet with captured Billy; but missing his description of Paulita as Billy's lover)**

Burns, Walter Noble. *"I also know that the Kid and Paulita were sweethearts."* Unpublished letter to Jim East. **June 3, 1926**. Robert N. Mullin Collection. File RNM, IV, NM, 116-117. Nita Stewart Haley Memorial Museum, Haley Library. Midland, Texas.

Anaya, A.P. "Paco." "I have your letter of April 1st in which you tell me many things ..." Letter to George Fitzpatrick. **February 5, 1936**. C.L. Sonnichsen Papers, C.L. Sonnichsen Special Collections Department. University of Texas El Paso Library. MS 141, Box 92. Folder 386. **(Fabricates that Garrett lost the first report and had it rewritten; key source for hoax claim of two Coroner's Jury Reports)**

JOURNALS AND MAGAZINES (CHRONOLOGICAL)

Hunter's Frontier Times Magazine. "A Story of 'Billy the Kid.'" July, 1943, Pages 217-218. (quoting *Laredo Times* for **August 10, 1881**). frontiertimesmagazine.com/. **(source for claiming Billy the Kid as Billy Bonney's alias; and falsely claiming Billy' demanded $5 per day payment from John Chisum)**

Adams, Ramon F. "Billy the Kid's Lost Years: Cyclone Denton Tells of Bonney's Life as a Cowboy in Arizona." *The Texas Monthly*. 4.2. (**August-December, 1929**). Pages 205-211. (Scan courtesy of Cornette Library at West Texas A&M. **source for claiming falsely that Billy worked at the Gila Ranch in Arizona**)

Smith, Wilbur. Interview. "The Amigo of 'Billy the Kid': The Man Who Fought Side by Side With Lincoln County's Outlaw Character Tells About the Days of 'Judge Colt's Rule.'" *New Mexico Magazine* article interview of **April, 1933**. Pages 26-49. University of New Mexico, Albuquerque. Zimmerman Library. Center for Southwest Research Anderson. Call Number F 791 N45. **(gives names of people hoping that Billy was alive, including Ygenio) Salazar)**

Shipman, Jack. "Brief Career of Tom O'Folliard, Billy the Kid's Partner." No Author. *Voice of the Mexican Border*. Volume 1, Number 5. **January, 1934**. Pages 216-219. **(Uncited source with erroneous claim that Tom O'Folliard and Kip McKinney were cousins, as "Brushy" parroted; but Morrison interviewed Shipman's widow on December 6, 1949.)**

Traylor, Leslie. "Facts Regarding the Escape of Billy the Kid." *Frontier Times*. **July, 1936**. Pages 506-513 (on Page 509). FrontierTimesMagazine.com. **(About Billy the Kid's jailbreak being aided by Sam Corbet placing a gun in the latrine, based on a hearsay interview by Traylor in Lincoln in 1933 and 1935; also in article are his Jesus Silva interview on identifying Billy's body and his confirming the erroneous identification of Billy's gravesite in the Fort Sumner cemetery in 1935)**

Ball, Eve. "Billy Strikes the Pecos." *New Mexico Folklore Record*, IV. **1949-50**. Pages 7-10. University of New Mexico, Albuquerque. Zimmerman Library. Call Number GR 1 N 47 Volume 4. **(source for Billy Bonney's crossing the Guadalupe Mountains on foot to the Seven Rivers Jones family)**

Fulton, Maurice Garland. "Billy the Kid in Life and Books." *The New Mexico Folklore Record*. Volume IV, **1949-1950**. Pages 1-6. University of New Mexico, Albuquerque. Zimmerman Library. Call Number GR 1 N 47 Vol 4. **(source for the Greathouse shooting of Jim Carlyle, for the Mesilla trial being unjust to Billy, for a photo claimed to be Billy's mother, and for her name being "Mrs. Antrim")**

Hendron, J.W. "No Pardon for Billy." **January 5, 1951**. *Highway Happenings*. Volume 2, Number 2. C.L. Sonnichsen Papers, C.L. Sonnichsen Special Collections Department. University of Texas El Paso Library, MS 141, Box 92. Folder 386. **("Brushy" debunker falsely cited by the publisher in *Alias Billy the Kid* as backing "Brushy")**

Morrison, William V. and C.L. Sonnichsen. "They Killed Pancho Villa!" *Frontier Times*. **Winter, 1959-1960**. Volume 34, Number 1, New Series Number 9, Pages 6-10,

48-50. (Morrison teamed with C.L. Sonnichsen for this never-completed history of Pancho Villa, possible past source of "Brushy" prompting)

NEWSPAPER ARTICLES

No Author. "Sheriff's Scampering: A Gang Drive Sheriff Kimball Into White Oaks." *Las Vegas Daily Gazette*. November 30, 1880. Page 4. https://chroniclingamerica.loc.gov/ Note about reference for C.L. Sonnichsen by Morrison. Undated, 1951? C.L. Sonnichsen's Papers, C.L. Sonnichsen Special Collections Department. University of Texas El Paso Library. MS 141, Box 92. Folder 386. (**Prompt source for "Brushy's" incorrect name-dropping of Regulators by adding Dave Rudabaugh and Billy Wilson**)

No Author. *Las Vegas Gazette* December 24, 1880, and the *Santa Fe New Mexican* of May 7, 1881. (**Wrong dates used by Sonnichsen for Wallace's reward notices, to claim they were never published**)

Wilcox, Lucius "Lute" M. Interview, at train depot. *Las Vegas Gazette*. December 28, 1880. (**Source for August 18, 1949 interview about dead horse blocking Stinking Springs rock house doorway**)

Newman, Simon N. Ed. Departure from Mesilla. *Newman's Semi-Weekly*. April 20, 1881. Pages 1, 3. https://chroniclingamerica.loc.gov/ (**Reporting for April 16th, listing the transport guards and their positions in the vehicle, which "Brushy" parroted verbatim**)

No Author. "Land of the Petulant Pistol, "Scenes" where Life and Land are Cheap ... 'Billy the Kid' as a Killer." *Las Vegas Daily Optic*. Wednesday Evening, **June 15, 1881**. Front Page. 1, Volume 2, Number 190, Columns 1-2. (Possibly contributed to by Lew Wallace, who published with a similar title in the Crawfordsville *Saturday Evening Journal* on June 18, 1881) (**Uncited source for fake shackle-slipping**)

No Author. (Lew Wallace interview) "Billy the Kid. General Wallace Tells Why the Young Desperado of New Mexico Wanted to Kill Him, A Dashing and Daring Career in the Land of the Petulant Pistol." (Lew Wallace interviewed on June 13, 1881), Crawfordsville *Saturday Evening Journal*, **June 18, 1881**. Indiana Historical Society. The Papers of Lew and Susan Wallace. Microfilm Edition. Indianapolis, Indiana: Indiana Historical Society Press. 2008. (**Source for fakery that Billy was killing Chisum's men for unpaid debt; a source for source footnote's 1943 *Frontier Times* magazine's "A Story of Billy the Kid;" reprinted in an August 10, 1881 *Laredo Times* article titled "Killing of 'Billy the Kid.' "**)

No Author. "Kid the Killer Killed, Wm. Bonney alias Antrim, alias Billy the Kid, Fatally Meets Pat Garrett, the Lincoln County Sheriff." Las Cruces *Rio Grande Republican*. **July 23, 1881**. Page 2. Volume 1, Number 10. NewspaperArchive.com. (**Faked by hoax as denying Garrett the reward ; but actually a copy of Pat Garrett's letter to Acting-Governor William Ritch confirming that the original Coroner's Jury Report was sent to District Attorney of the First Judicial District, and copy of it was included in this letter to the Governor**)

Lewis, E.I. "Gen. Wallace's Feud with Billy the Kid, When the General Was Governor of New Mexico and Billy Bonne Was the Most Dangerous Western Outlaw. He Was a Waif and Was Reared in Indiana. *The Indianapolis Press*. Saturday, **June 23, 1900**. Page 7. Lew Wallace Collection. Indiana Historical Society. M0292. Box 14. Folder 11. (photocopy) (Original article is in OMB 23, Box 1. Folder 5) (**Uncited, but with "Brushy's" lifted "I wasn't born to hang" quote**)

Wallace, Lew. *New York World Magazine*. "General Lew Wallace Writes a Romance of 'Billy the Kid' Most Famous Bandit of the Plains: Thrilling Story of the Midnight Meeting Between Gen Wallace, Then Governor of New Mexico, and the Notorious Outlaw, in a Lonesome Hut in Santa Fe." **June 8, 1902**. Lew Wallace Collection.

Indiana Historical Society. M0292. . Box 14. Folder 11.("**Brushy's**" **source for pardon bargain misinformation, leaving pardon jailing, and shackle-slipping**) Cited by Sonnichsen, but identified as from the Indiana Historical Society, meaning Morrison's research.

No Author. "Billy the Kid, Alive Is Ridiculed by Oldtimers." El Paso *Herald.* **June 23, 1926.** Page 7. Newspapers.com. (**contradicting hearsay reports that Garrett had not killed the Kid; but used by hoax to quote those hearsay reports as proving Billy survived**)

Meadows, John P. "My Association With Pat Garrett, Pioneer Peace Officer of N.M. As Told by John P. Meadows, to a Representative of the Alamogordo News." *Alamogordo News.* **March 8, 1936.** Pages 1 and 4. University of New Mexico. Zimmerman Library. Microfilm AN2 A46. (**Made-up that Garrett killed his buffalo hunter partner, "Glenn," as parroted by "Brushy;" when Garrett actually killed teenager, Joe Briscoe**)

Ealy, Mrs. Taylor. Ed. Haniel Long. "New Mexico Writers: The Lincoln County War Part 1. *The New Mexico Sentinel.* **October 5, 1937.** Volume 1, Number 45, Page 8. New York Public Library. (**Cited in Morrison's notes in Sonnichsen's collected papers as Lincoln County War source; C.L. Sonnichsen's Papers, C.L. Sonnichsen Special Collections Department. University of Texas El Paso Library. MS 141, Box 92. Folder 386**)

_____. "New Mexico Writers: The Lincoln County War Part 2. *The New Mexico Sentinel.* **October 12, 1937.** Volume 1, Number 46, Page 6. New York Public Library. (**Cited in Morrison's notes in Sonnichsen's collected papers as Lincoln County War source; C.L. Sonnichsen's Papers, MS 141. C.L. Sonnichsen Special Collections Department. University of Texas El Paso Library. Box 92. Folder 386**)

No Author. "Frontiersmen Track Reports 'Kid' Is Alive." El Paso *Herald-Post.* **June 22, 1938.** newspaperarchive.com. and El Paso *Times.* **November 10, 1937.** (**article about Pawnee Bill's planned to search for Billy the Kid as being alive as dishonestly misstated in *Alias Billy the Kid* to mean Pawnee Bill was searching for "Brushy;" possible prompt source for "Brushy's" parroting of working for Pawnee Bill's Wild West Show**)

Corbet, Sam. "Sam Corbet Writes of Slayings." *The New Mexico Sentinel.* **July 17, 1938.** Volume 2, Number 33. Angelo State University Library. West Texas Collection, New York Public Library. (**Listed as a source in Sonnichsen's Papers, MS 141. C.L. Sonnichsen Special Collections Department. University of Texas El Paso Library. Box 92. Folder 386.; used by "Brushy" to name-dropping Sam Corbett as wrongly aiding jailbreak**)

_____. "Tunstall's Father Learns of the Raids." *The New Mexico Sentinel.* **July 17, 1938.** Volume 2, Number 33. Angelo State University Library. West Texas Collection,New York Public Library. (**Sam Corbet's letter as eye-witness of Lincoln County War; listed as a source in Sonnichsen's Papers, MS 141. C.L. Sonnichsen Special Collections Department. University of Texas El Paso Library. Box 92. Folder 386.; used by "Brushy" to name-dropping Sam Corbett as wrongly aiding jailbreak**)

Taeger, Mary Nell. "Severo Gallegos Tells His Story and of His Family's Friend, 'Billy the Kid.' " *Ruidoso News.* **July 30, 1948.** Front page, Page 6. Volume II, Number 11. NewspaperArchive.com. (**Used as prompt for "Brushy's" jailbreak tale. Gallegos was then used give a fake affidavit that "Brushy" was Billy**)

_____. No Author. "Severo Gallegos Tells His Story and of His Family's Friend, 'Billy the Kid.' " (continued) *Ruidoso News.* **August 6, 1948.** Page 3. Volume II, Number 12. NewspaperArchive.com. (**Used as prompt for "Brushy's" jailbreak tale. Gallegos was then used give a fake affidavit that "Brushy" was Billy**)

COURT, MILITARY, AND LEGISLATIVE RECORDS

U.S. District Court Minute Book B, Third Judicial District, Indictment 411 for killing "Buckshot" Roberts [1878,], Page 76, quashed.

Lincoln County Grand Jury Minute Book B for **April, 1879**, for Indictments 243, 244; Pages 92-93, 298-299 (**misread and confused with Billy's 1880 Mesilla hanging trial**) (Page 34)

No Author. *Proceedings of a Court of Inquiry in the Case of Lt. Col. N.A.M. Dudley (May 2, 1879 – July 5, 1879)*. File No. QQ1284. (Boxes 3304, 3305, 3305A); Court Martial Files 1809-1894. Records of the Office of the Judge Advocate General - Army. Record Group 153. Old Military and Civil Branch. National Archives and Records Administration. Washington, D. C. (**Used was only a page of Billy 's testimony about escaping the burning McSween house, with a quote**)

Adjutant General's files from the State Library in Austin, Texas, about Jessie Evans's **July 7, 1880** capture near Fort Stockton, Texas. (**about Jessie Evan's 1880 capture in Texas**)

Doña Ana County Court Minutes, "Instructions to the Jury," Cause No. 532. Pages 100-103; (**indictment for Brady ?**)

Doña Ana County Court Minute Book D for Cause No. 532 (verdict and sentence), killing of William Brady. [1881] Page 406.

Ritch, William G. "In the matter of the application by Patrick F. Garrett for a reward claimed to have been offered May-1881 for the capture of Wm Bonney alias "the Kid." *Executive Record Book Number 2*. July 25, 1867-November 8, 1882. **July 21, 1881**. Pages 533-535. New Mexico Secretary of State Records. Collection 1971-001, Series 1; Records of the Secretary of the Territory. (Accessed from Albuquerque Public Library Microfilm, Territorial Archives of New Mexico, Roll 21.) (**Faked as denying Pat Garrett's reward based on no Coroner's Jury Report; actually just Ritch agreeing with reward but delaying its payment until the Legislature converted it to Territorial from Wallace's private offer; also shows that Charles Greene was the printer of the reward notice, not Garrett's attorney as C.L. Sonnichsen wrongly claimed**)

No Author. "An Act for the Relief of Pat. Garrett." *1882 Acts of the Legislative Assembly of the Territory of New Mexico, Twenty-Fifth Session. Convened at the Capitol, at the City of Santa Fe, on Monday, the 2d day of January, 1882, and adjourned on Thursday, the 2d day of March, 1882*. **February 18, 1882**. Chapter 101. Page 191. (**Faked as granting the reward based on a Santa Fe Ring conspiracy, instead of its stated "technicality" of converting Wallace's private offer to a Territorial one; also used to fake no Coroner's Jury Report because it dated the killing to "on or about the month of August, 1881"**)

INTERVIEWS

Mullin, Robert N. cited as having copies of reminiscences of Louis Abraham about Silver City and Billy. No date. (**noted by Sonnichsen as showing the murder at 12 as fictitious, but rest of information was ignored**) (Page 77)

Sonnichsen, C.L. Interview With Jack Fountain. April 15, 1944. (**Source footnote for "Brushy's" parroted back-porch Barlow shooting; from A.J. Fountain's fake hearsay account of Garrett telling him he killed Billy to get a $10,000 reward, and that the side of beef was beside Maxwell's bedroom**)

Morrison, William V. Interview with Severo Gallegos. **October 11, 1949**. Prompt footnote in *Alias Billy the Kid*. Page 45. (**Used for parroted errors about the jailbreak and escape horse**)

_____. "Interview Mrs Jack Shipman." **December 6, 1949**. C.L. Sonnichsen Papers, C.L. Sonnichsen Special Collections Department. University of Texas El Paso Library, MS 141, Box 92. Folder 386. (**Wife of Jack Shipman who falsely** called Tom O'Folliard "Kip" McKinney's cousin – so "Brushy" parroted that) [Shipman, Jack. "Brief Career of Tom O'Folliard, Billy the Kid's Partner." No Author. *Voice of the Mexican Border*. Volume 1, Number 5. January, 1934. Pages 216-219. **(Gives unsubstantiated genealogy of Tom O'Folliard (Page 216), without mention that he and McKinney were cousins)**]

Morrison, William V. Interviews with Oliver "Brushy Bill" Roberts. 1949-1950. (Unpublished)

_____. Interview with G. Wilson, John "Squire" Wilson's grandson. **August 7, 1950. (Hearsay account error that Billy was killed in the Maxwell house yard; then parroted by "Brushy")**

THE "BRUSHY BILL" HOAX IN THE RETURN OF THE OUTLAW BILLY THE KID

BOOK

Jameson, W.C. and Frederic Bean. *The Return of the Outlaw Billy the Kid*. Plano, Texas: Republic of Texas Press. **1998. (Backing Roberts as Billy the Kid)**

FAKE PHOTOANALYSIS FOR

Acton, Scott. "For some reason, I have spent a lot of time on this project ..." Letter to Frederick Bean. Photoanalysis Report. **August 30, 1990.** C.L. Sonnichsen Papers, Sonnichsen Special Collections Department. University of Texas El Paso Library. MS 141, Box 118. Folder 840. **(Acton's fake photo-comparison of "Brushy" and Billy the Kid tintype)**

ASSISTANCE OF C.L. SONNICHSEN FOR

Jameson, W.C. and Frederic Bean. Interview with C.L. Sonnichsen in Oklahoma City, Oklahoma. June 25, 1991. **(Apparent coaching for their "Brushy"-backing, and providing the Ashenfelter fake corpse article)**

SOURCES FOR (SEE ORIGINAL "BRUSHY" HOAX)

Ashenfelter, Singleton M. "Exit 'The Kid', The Fugitive Murderer Hunted Down and Killed by Sheriff Garrett." *The New Southwest, And Grant County Herald*. **July 23, 1881.** Number 30. Page 2. Column 3. University of New Mexico. Zimmerman Library. Microfilm AN2 G71. **(Ashenfelter's fake description of Billy the Kid's body as swarthy and bearded, used by the hoaxers to claim it was not really Billy)**

Branch, Louis Leon. From manuscript of Charles Frederick Rudulph. *"Los Billitos": The Story of "Billy the Kid" and His Gang: As Told by Charles Frederick Rudulph – a Member of Garrett's Historical Posse*. New York: Carleton Press. **1980. (Hearsay claim that the body of Billy the Kid was left in the Maxwell bedroom overnight for the coroner's Jury)**

Tunstill, William A. *Billy the Kid and Me Were the Same: A Documentary on the Life of Billy the Kid*. Roswell, New Mexico: Western History Research Center. **1988. ("Brushy"-backer faking a genealogy)**

JOHN MILLER
BILLY THE KID IMPOSTER HOAX

No Author. Obituary of John Miller. *Prescott Courier.* **November 8, 1937. (Gives date of birth as December, 1850)**

Huff, J. Wesley. "Did Pat Garrett Kill Billy the Kid? Herman Tecklenburg Says No; Billy Lived on Ranch at Ramah 35 Years Ago and Visited Him. *The Gallup Independent.* **August 9, 1944.** Volume 55, Number 185. Newspapers.com. **(Tecklenburg's Billy the Kid confabulations)**

Airy, Helen L. *Whatever Happened to Billy the Kid?* Santa Fe, New Mexico: Sunstone Press. **1993. (John Miller as Billy the Kid)**

Johnson, Jim. *Billy the Kid: His Real Name Was ...* Denver, Colorado: Outskirts Press, Inc. **2006. (Debunking John Miller as Billy the Kid)**

(SEE: "Billy the Kid Case" hoax articles on the exhumation of John Miller)

"BILLY THE KID CASE" HOAX
LINCOLN COUNTY SHERIFF'S
DEPARTMENT
CASE NO. 2003-274

RELEVANT BOOKS FOR DEBUNKING

Althouse, Bill. *Frozen Lightening: Bill Richardson's Strike on the Political Landscape of New Mexico.* Buckman, New Mexico: Thinking Out Loud Press. **2006.**

Bugliosi, Vincent. *Outrage: The Five Reasons Why O.J. Simpson Got Away With Murder.* New York and London: W.W. Norton & Company. **1996. (Exposé of Dr. Henry Lee faking forensics in legal cases, Pages 47-49)**

Cline, Donald. *Alias Billy the Kid: The Man Behind the Legend.* Santa Fe: New Mexico: Sunstone Press. **1986. (Cited by the hoaxers as backing them; unaware of his 1988 manuscript: *Brushy Bill Roberts: I Wasn't Billy the Kid*)**

Cooper, Gale. *Billy the Kid's Pretenders: Brushy Bill and John Miller.* Albuquerque, New Mexico: Gelcour Books. **2012.**

_____. *Billy the Kid's Writings, Words, and Wit.* Albuquerque, New Mexico: Gelcour Books. **2012.**

_____. *MegaHoax: The Strange Plot to Exhume Billy the Kid and Become President.* Albuquerque, New Mexico: Gelcour Books. **2012.**

_____. *Cracking the Billy the Kid Case Hoax: The Strange Plot to Exhume Billy the Kid, Convict Sheriff Pat Garrett of Murder, and Become President of the United States.* Albuquerque, New Mexico: Gelcour Books. **2014.**

_____. *The Billy the Kid Imposter Hoax of Brushy Bill Roberts.* Albuquerque, New Mexico: Gelcour Books. **2019.**

_____. *Billy the Kid's Pretender John Miller.* Albuquerque, New Mexico: Gelcour Books. **2019.**

_____. *The Famous Coroner's Jury Report of Billy the Kid: An Inquest That Made History.* Albuquerque, New Mexico: Gelcour Books. **2019.**

Palast, Greg. *Armed Madhouse.* New York: Penguin Group USA. **2007. (Bill Richardson exposé)**

Richardson, Bill, with Michael Ruby. *Between Worlds: The Making of an American Life.* New York: G.P. Putnam's Sons. **2005. (Bill Richardson autobiography)**

Siringo, Charles. *The History of Billy the Kid.* Santa Fe: New Mexico. Privately Printed. **1920. (Reproduces the Jim East letter on pages 96-107)**

(SEE: William H. Bonney; Pat Garrett, John W. Poe; Oliver "Brushy Bill" Roberts Billy the Kid Imposter Hoax; John Miller Billy the Kid Imposter Hoax)

SOURCES USED FOR THE HOAXING (CHRONOLOGICAL)

No Author. Unpublished account of unnamed grandchildren of Lucien Bonaparte Maxwell making up a quote by Deluvina Maxwell. **Undated. (Hearsay to fake the washstand as part of the shooting scene)**

No Author. No title. About Billy Bonney's jailbreak. **May 21, 1881.** *The National Police Gazette.* **(Invalid tabloid, not an historical source)**

Barnes, Sidney. **May 30, 1881.** Letter to the Attorney General Unnamed). No source given. **(Making-up that Billy killed 15 men)**

No Author. WPA interview of Francisco Trujillo. **May 1937. (Meaningless hearsay about the death scene)**

Tolly [sic - Totty], Frances E. "Early Days in Lincoln County," Charles Remark Interview. **February 14, 1938**, Works Progress Administration, Federal Writer's Project, Folklore-Life Histories, Manuscript Division. Library of Congress.

Sonnichsen, C.L. and William V. Morrison. *Alias Billy the Kid.* Albuquerque, New Mexico: University of New Mexico Press. **1955. (Faked as Billy the Kid)**

Jameson, W.C. and Frederic Bean. *The Return of the Outlaw Billy the Kid.* Plano, Texas: Republic of Texas Press. **1998. (Backing Roberts as Billy the Kid)**

Overton, Homer D. aka Homer D. Kinsworthy. Affidavit that Garrett did not kill Billy the Kid. **December 22, 2003. (Fakery revealed by fabricated dates)**

(SEE: Sources for *Alias Billy the Kid* and *The Return of the Outlaw Billy the Kid*; Azariah Wild, John Miller)

CORONER'S JURY REPORT FOR WILLIAM H. BONNEY (SEE WILLIAM H. BONNEY)

PAT GARRETT'S PROSECUTION IMMUNITY "BILLY THE KID CASE" BY STATUTE OF LIMITATIONS

No Author. "An Act to Provide the Limitation of Criminal Actions." *Acts of the Legislative Assembly of the Territory of New Mexico, Twenty-Second Session, Convened at the Capitol. at the City of Santa Fe on Monday the 6th Day of December, 1875, and Adjourned on Friday the 14th day of January, 1876.* Santa Fe, New Mexico: Manderfield & Tucker, Public Printers. **1876.** Hathitrust Digital Library. **(Providing for a 10 year statute of limitations on murder; so Garrett could not be prosecuted in 2003 for the 1881 killing of Billy Bonney, since that expired in 1891)**

No Author. Ed. L. Bradford Prince. *The General Laws of New Mexico.* "Limitations of Criminal Actions. "Limitation of Criminal Actions, Acts of the Legislative Assembly of the Territory of New Mexico, Twenty-Second Session, Convened at the Capitol, at the City of Santa Fe on Monday the 6th day of December, 1875, and Adjourned on Friday the 14th day of January, 1876." Chapter 13, Section 1. **1882. (Providing for a 10 year statute of limitations on murder; so Garrett could not be prosecuted in 2003 for the 1881 killing of Billy Bonney)**

PAMPHLETS FOR (CHRONOLOGICAL)

Turk, David S. Historian U.S. Marshals Service. "Research Report: The U.S. Marshals Service and Billy the Kid. To Be Added in its Present Entirety, with Exhibits, to Lincoln County, New Mexico Case # 2003-274." U.S. Marshals Service Executive Services Division." **December, 2003. (a major hoax document by "Billy the Kid Case" participant as an addendum to the "Probable Cause Statement")**

Madrid, Patricia A. Attorney General. *Inspection of Public Records Act Compliance Guide. Fourth Edition. The "Inspection of Public Records Act" NMSA 1978, Chapter 14, Article 2: A Compliance Guide for New Mexico Public Officials and Citizens.* Santa Fe: Office of the Attorney General. **January, 2004. (For open records compliance and litigation)**

PRESS RELEASE FOR (GOVERNOR BILL RICHARDSON)

Richardson, Bill. "Governor Bill Richardson Announces State Support of Billy the Kid Investigation." **June 10, 2003. (Announcement at State Capitol of state backing of case # 2003-274 and listing of the participants: Tom Sullivan, Steve Sederwall, Gary Graves, Sherry Tippett, and Paul Hutton)**

_____. "Gov. Bill Richardson Appoints Criminal Defense Lawyer to NM Supreme Court." **November 2, 2007. (Corrupt Charles Daniels, husband of Richardson's attorney Randi McGinn)**

_____. "Governor Bill Richardson to Consider Billy the Kid Pardon Petition." Press release. **December 16, 2010. (The Randi McGinn pardon petition for "Billy the Kid")**

_____. "Governor Richardson to Announce his decision on Billy the Kid Pardon Request Tomorrow." Press release. **December 30, 2010.**

LETTERS ABOUT

Kurtis, Bill. "This letter is provided as official verification ..." Letter to Steve Sederwall. **October 4, 2010.** Entered by Sederwall's Defense Attorney as Exhibit A in Sandoval District Court Case No. D-1329-CV-2007-1364 Hearing on January 17, 2012. **(Paying for Dr. Henry Lee's forensics)**

E-MAILS ABOUT

Saar, Meghan. To Gale Cooper. "BTK Hoax Article." E-Mail To Gale Cooper. **January 31, 2006. (Hoax-backing *True West* magazine rejecting my article proposal to expose the "Billy the Kid Case" hoax)**

Ford, Simon. "Subj. Questions regarding Orchid-Cellmark." E-mail to Gale Cooper. **January 31, 2011. (Consultation on mixed DNA samples and DNA separation costs)**

Miller, Kenny. Personal communication to author about family history and showing Maxwell family objects - including the carpenter's bench, bedstead, and wash stand - and providing photos of them to author. **2011 to 2012. (Information from Maxwell family descendant)**

BLOGS ABOUT

No author. "Fraud Alleged at Cellmark, DNA Testing Firm. TalkLeft: The Politics of Crime. http://www.talkleft.com./new_archives/008809.html. **November 18, 2004.**

Boze Bell, Bob. "The Wild is back in the West." BBB's Blog. **April 24, 2006. (Announcement of invitation of Sullivan and Sederwall to Cannes Film Festival.)** http://www.truewestmagazine.com/weblog/blogger1.htm

WEBSITE FOR:

Sederwall, Steve. "billythekidcase.com" Website. From **October (?) 2010 to 2012(?). (For $25.00 membership selling Case 2003-274 records)**

TELEVISION DOCUMENTARIES PERPETRATING

History Channel. "Investigating History: Billy the Kid." Week **of April 24, 2004 and May 2, 2004.(Co-Producer, writer, narrator was "Billy the Kid Case" hoaxer Paul Hutton)**

National Geographic International Discovery ID Channel. "History Mysteries." **2010**. **(Sederwall presenting the fake Dr. Lee Deputy James Bell top-of-the-stairs murder "investigation")**

ARTICLES ABOUT (CHRONOLOGICAL)

Humphreys, Sexson. "Pardon My 6-Shooters: Billy the Kid? Governor to Decide; 'Pardon Me, I'm Alive,' Says Billy the Kid." *The Indianapolis News*. Thursday, **November 30, 1950**. Indiana Historical Society. Lew Wallace Collection (M292). Box 14. Folder 12.

Hutton, Paul Andrew. "Dreamscape Desperado." *New Mexico Magazine*. Volume 68. Number 6. Pages 44-58. **June, 1990**.

Janofsky, Michael. "122 Years Later, the Lawmen Are Still Chasing Billy the Kid." *The New York Times*. **June 5, 2003**. Volume CLII, Number 52,505, Pages 1, A31. **(First national announcement of Billy the Kid Case)**

No Author. "Lincoln County deputy sheriff sends his own letter to governor." *Silver City Daily Press*. **June 25, 2003**. Pages 1, 13.

DellaFlora, Anthony. "State Not Kidding Around: Governor won't mind if probe of the notorious 19th century N.M. outlaw boosts tourism." *Albuquerque Journal*. **June 11, 2003**. Number 162. Pages 1, A1. **(First big New Mexico announcement of Billy the Kid Case)**

Bommersbach, Jana. "Digging Up Billy: If Pat Garrett didn't kill the Kid, who's buried in his grave?" *True West*. **August/September 2003**. Volume 50. Issue 7. P. 42-45.

No Author. AP. "Authorities call for exhumation of Billy the Kid's mother to solve mystery." *Silver City Sun News*. **October 11, 2003**.

Bommersbach, Jana. "From Shovels to DNA: The inside story of digging up Billy." *True West*. **October/November, 2003**. Volume 50. Issue 7. Pages 42-45.

Jameson, W.C. and Leon Metz. "Was Brushy Bill Really Billy the Kid? Experts face off over new evidence." *True West*. **November/December, 2003**. Volume 50. Issue 10. Pages 32-33.

Murphy, Mary Alice. "Billy the Kid 'Hires' a Lawyer." *Silver City Daily Press Internet Edition*. http://www.thedailypress.com/NewsFolder/11.17.2.html. **November 17, 2003**.

Boyle, Alan. "Billy the Kid gets a lawyer: 122 years after shootout, attorney to gather information for a pardon." msnbc.com. **November 18, 2003**.

Fecteau, Loie. "No Kidding: Governor Taps Lawyer For Billy." *Albuquerque Journal*. Page 1, A6. **November 19, 2003**.

No Author. AP. "Lawyer Appointed to Represent Dead Outlaw." *Silver City Sun News*. http://www.krqe.com/expanded.asp?RECORD_KEY%5bContent. **November 19, 2003**. **(Bill Robins III's appointment by Richardson)**

No Author. "Lawmakers Consider Posthumous Pardon for Billy the Kid." *abqtrib.com News*. **November 21, 2003**.

Boyle, Alan. "Billy the Kid's DNA Sparks Legal Showdown: Sheriffs and mayors face off over digging up remains from the Old West." *msnbc.com*. **November 21, 2003**.

Romo, Rene. "Kid's Mom May Stay Buried: Silver City wins round to block exhumation for outlaw's DNA." *Albuquerque Journal*. **December 9, 2003**. Section D3.

Janna Bommersbach. "Breaking Out More Shovels: Fort Sumner's Sheriff Gary Graves commits to digging up Billy the Kid's Grave." *True West*. **January/February, 2004**. Volume 51. Issue 1. Pages 46-47. **(Hoax-backing article)**

Benke, Richard. AP. "N.M. Re-Opens Case of Billy the Kid." Yahoo! News. **January 13, 2004**.

_____. "Billy the Kid's Life and Death May Be Put to DNA Test: Officials want to examine the body of the outlaw's mother to test a Texas man's claim that he was Bonney. If so, Pat Garrett didn't kill the Kid." *The Nation*. **January 18, 2004**. **(Uses fake Overton Affidavit given by Attorney Sherry Tippett)**

No Author. AP. "Billy the Kid hearing delayed for months: Sheriffs need more time to prepare arguments for exhuming remains of outlaw's mother." **January 23, 2004.**
Miller, Jay. "Digging Up the Latest on Billy the Kid." *Las Cruces Sun-News.* **February 3, 2004.**
Gonzales. Carolyn. "Hutton writes wild frontier stories for History Channel." *University of New Mexico Campus News.* **February 16, 2004.** Volume 39. No. 12. **(Hoaxer Hutton's TV program announced)**
Miller, Jay. "The Billy the Kid Code." *Las Cruces Sun-News.* **March 29, 2004.**
Nathanson, Rick. "Grave Doubts: 'Investigating History' series tries to clear up the mysteries surrounding Billy the Kid." *Albuquerque Journal Weekly TV Guide: Entertainer.* **April 24, 2004.** Pages 3, 5.
Garrett, Wm. F. "Letters to the Editor." *De Baca County News.* Page 4. **May 6, 2004.** **(Garrett family member objects to hoax)**
Murphy, Mary Alice and Melissa St. Aude. "Sederwall, Sullivan uninvited to ball." *Silver City Daily Press Internet Edition.* **June 10, 2004.**
Hill, Levi. "Billy the Kid Stirring Up Dust in Silver City." *Las Cruces Sun-News.* **June 12, 2004.** Section 5A. Pages 1, A2.

No Author. "Attorney Refuses Judge's statements concerning exhumation." *thedailypress.com.* **June 15, 2004. (Attorney Tippett lies about the OMI)**
Richardson, Bill. "Verbatim: I have to decide whether to pardon him. But not right away – after the investigation, after the state gets more publicity." *Time.* **June 21, 2004.** Vol. 163. No. 25. Page 17.
Romo, Rene. "Back off on Billy, Gov. Asked: Silver City says inquiry into death of Kid would harm state tourism. *Albuquerque Journal.* **June 23, 2004.** Section B-1, B-5.
No Author. "Lincoln county deputy sheriff sends his own letter to governor." *Silver City Daily Press.* **June 25, 2004.** Pages 1, 13. **(Letter from Steve Sederwall)**
No Author. "Editorials: New Racing Schedule Tramples Horseman." *Albuquerque Journal.* **June 26, 2004.**
Miller, Jay. "Inside the Capitol. Bizarre case of Billy the Kid." *Roswell Daily Record.* **July 2, 2004.** Page A4.
Romo, Rene. "Forensic Expert on Billy's Case: Questions Remain on Outlaw's Fate." *Albuquerque Journal.* **August 2, 2004.** Page 1. **(Falsely claims blood on bench; says "trace blood")**
No Author. "Forensic expert joins Billy the Kid inquiry in New Mexico." *AP SignOnSanDiego.com.* **August 2, 2004. (Announcing Dr. Henry Lee)**
Miller, Jay. "Inside the Capitol. Sheriffs slippery on Billy the Kid Case." *Roswell Daily Record.* **August 9, 2004.** Page A4.
Cherry, Doris. "Forensics 101 for 'Billy'." *Lincoln County News.* **August 12, 2004.** Pages 2, 10. **(Quotes Sullivan's lie: "a lot" of blood on bench)**
Miller, Jay. "Inside the Capitol. Expert questions Kid probe." *Roswell Daily Record.* **August 20, 2004.** Page A4.
_____. "Inside the Capitol. Hat dance on probe funding." *Roswell Daily Record.* **September 1, 2004.** Page A4.
_____. "Inside the Capitol. Three sheriffs push Kid Case." *Roswell Daily Record.* **September 5, 2004.** Page A4.
_____. "Inside the Capitol. Sheriffs hoax is world-class." *Roswell Daily Record.* **September 8, 2004.** Page A4.
_____. "Inside the Capitol. Kid gets day in court Sept. 27." *Roswell Daily Record.* **September 12, 2004.** Page A4.
_____. "Inside the Capitol. Kid probe making us think." *Roswell Daily Record.* **September 13, 2004.** Page A4.
Stinnett, Scot. "De Baca County Citizens' Committee Files Petition for Recall of Sheriff Gary Graves." *De Baca County News.* **September 14, 2004.**
Miller, Jay. "Inside the Capitol. Who is Attorney Bill Robins?" *Roswell Daily Record.* **September 15, 2004.** Page A4.

Green, Keith. "Mountain Asides: Billy's restless bones are stirred up once again." *RuidosoNews.com*. **September 16, 2004.**

Miller, Jay. "Inside the Capitol. Kid Case: David fights Goliath." *Roswell Daily Record*. **September 17, 2004.** Page A4.

_____. "Inside the Capitol. Many reasons to dig up Kid." *Roswell Daily Record*. **September 19, 2004.** Page A4.

_____. "Inside the Capitol. Nothing to worry about." *Roswell Daily Record*. **September 20, 2004.** Page A4.

Stallings, Dianne. "Showdown in the County Seat." *RuidosoNews.com* **September 21, 2004. (Commissioner Leo Martinez's meeting threatening recall of Sheriff Sullivan for perpetrating a hoax)**

Miller, Jay. "Inside the Capitol. Who speaks for Pat Garrett?" *Roswell Daily Record*. **September 22, 2004.** Page A4.

Stallings, Dianne. "Showdown in the County Seat: shouting match erupts at County Commissioners meeting Tuesday over investigation of Billy the Kid." *Ruidoso News*. **September 22, 2004.**

Cherry, Doris. "Lincoln County 'War' Heats Up Over 'Billy: Capitan Mayor Tracks His Kind of '---' To County Commission Meeting. Tells Jay Miller where to go: wonders why commissioner has his panties in a wad." *Lincoln County News*. **September 23, 2003.** Vol. 99. No. 38. Pages 1-3. **(Commissioner Martinez stops the hoaxers' exhuming Billy the Kid)**

Miller, Jay. "Inside the Capitol. Is there a new Santa Fe Ring?" *Roswell Daily Record*. **September 24, 2004.** Page A4.

Stinnett, Scott. "Rest in Peace, Billy! Exhumation case dismissed." *De Baca County News*. **September 30, 2004.** Vol. 104. No. 2. Pages 1, 5, 6.

Miller, Jay. "Inside the Capitol. Fort Sumner celebrates win." *Roswell Daily Record*. **October 1, 2004.** Page A4.

No author. "Fraud Alleged at Cellmark, DNA Testing Firm. TalkLeft: The Politics of Crime. http://www.talkleft.com./new_archives/008809.html. **November 18, 2004. (Dr. Henry Lee's lab commits DNA faking)**

Jana Bommersbach. "Kid Exhumation Nixed: Billy and his mom to rest in peace. *True West*. **January/February 2005.** Volume 52. Issue 1. Pages 68-69.

Massey, Barry. "Casinos, contracting lawyers fund Madrid." The New Mexican. http://www.freenewmexican.com/news/13746.html **May 14, 2005.**

Stinnett, Scott. "Judge rules Graves recall can proceed: Parker finds probable cause after two-day hearing." *De Baca County News*. **August 25, 2005.** Vol. 104. No. 49. Pages 1, 4, 10. **(The Recall Hearing of Sheriff Gary Graves)**

_____. "Testimony paints Graves as 'above the law': Recall probable cause hearing emotional, contentious." *De Baca County News*. **September 1, 2005.** Vol. 104. No. 50. Pages 1, 5, 6, 8, 9, 10.

Carter, Julie. "Follow the Blood: In the Billy the Kid Case, Miller Exhumed." *RuidosoNews.com*. **October 6, 2005. (Sederwall lies about blood on bench; gives "dead men don't bleed" quote; has the Lonnie Lippman photo of him holding John Miller/William Hudspeth skull)**

Sullivan, Tom. "Letters: Your Opinion." *RuidosoNews.com*. **October 21, 2005. (Sullivan letter to the editor: "Why are they so afraid of the truth?")**

Carter, Julie. "Billy the Kid in Prescott? *New Mexico Stockman*. **November, 2005.** Pages 38, 39, 76.

Romo, Rene. "Billy the Kid Probe May Yield New Twist. *Albuquerque Journal*. *ABQ Journal.com*. **November 6, 2005. (Claims Sullivan and Sederwall have John Miller's DNA)**

Struckman, Robert. "Bitterroot man hopes to uncover truth about Billy the Kid." http://www.helenair.com/articles/2006/03/13/montana/a05031306_01.txt (Missoulian) **March 13, 2006. (Hoaxer Dale Tunnell backing John Miller as Billy the Kid**

Dodder, Joanna. "Officials could face charges for digging up alleged Billy the Kid." *The Daily Courier of Prescott Arizona.* **April 12, 2006. (Sullivan claims DNA in "two months," and fakes Hudspeth skeleton as John Miller's and makes up a left scapula bullet wound)**
Banks, Leo W. "The New Billy the Kid? The mad search for the bones of an American outlaw icon has come to Arizona." *Tucson Weekly.* http://www.tucsonweekly.com/gbase/Currents/Content?oid=oid:81013 **April 13, 2006. (Sullivan lies that bench is "saturated with blood; Dr. Rick Staub says DNA extracted from William Hudspeth not John Miller)**
Carter, Julie. "Digging up bones, Arizona may protest Miller exhumation." jcarter@tularosa.net. **April 19, 2006.**
Dodder, Joanna. "Officials could face charges for digging up alleged Billy the Kid." *The Daily Courier of Prescott Arizona.* **April 12, 2006. (Sullivan claims DNA in "two months," and fakes Hudspeth skeleton as John Miller's with buck teeth and a left scapula bullet wound)**
Banks, Leo W. "The New Billy the Kid? The mad search for the bones of an American outlaw icon has come to Arizona." *Tucson Weekly.* http://www.tucsonweekly.com/gbase/Currents/Content?oid=oid:81013 **April 13, 2006. (Reports exhumation of second man; Sullivan lies that bench is "saturated with blood; Dr. Rick Staub says DNA extracted from William Hudspeth not John Miller)**
Carter, Julie. "Digging up bones, Arizona may protest Miller exhumation." jcarter@tularosa.net. **April 19, 2006.**
Carter, Julie. "Culture Shock: The cowboys and the Kid go to France." jcarter@tulerosa.net. **May 5, 2006. (Sullivan worked on movie 9 months)**
Shafer, Mark. "N.M. pair may face charges in grave case." **May 13, 2006.** markshafer @ArizonaRepublic.com. http://www.azcentral.com/arizonarepublic/local/articles/0513billythekid0513.html
Myers, Amanda Lee. "New Mexicans Dig Up Trouble in Arizona." *Albuquerque Journal, New Mexico and the West.* **May 14, 2006.** Page B4. **(Also in gulfnews.com; states Dallas lab" is doing DNA comparisons)**
_____."Billy the Kid Still 'Wanted.' " **May 16, 2006.** gulfnews.com. http://archive.gulfnews.com/articles/06/05/16/10040234.html.
No author. "Festival de Cannes, **May 17-28, 2006.** Requiem for Billy the Kid." http://www.festival-cannes.fr/films/fiche_film.php?langue=4355535. **(Cannes Film Festival synopsis)**
No author. "Out of Competition/Cannes Classics: Requiem for Billy the Kid. Festival de Cannes May 17-28, 2006." http://www.festival-cannes.fr/films/fiche_film.php?langue=4355535. **May 20, 2006. (Sullivan and Sederwall called two sheriffs)**
McCarthy, Todd. "Requiem for Billy the Kid." **May 21, 2006.** Variety.com. http://www.variety.com/review/VE1117930570?categoryid=2220&cs=1&nid=2562.
McCoy, Dave. "L 'Ouest Américain." **May 25, 2006.** MSN Movies. http://movies.msn.com/movies/canneso6/dispatch8.
Bennett, Ray. "Requiem for Billy the Kid." TheHollywoodReporter.com. **May 26, 2006. (Demonstration of hoax damage to history)**
Carter, Julie. "The cowboys are back in town, film in six months." jcarter@tulerosa.net. **June 9, 2006. (Describes plans for more programs)**
Valdez, Jannay. "Digging Up the Truth About Billy." *RuidosoNews.com.* http://ruidosonews.com/apps/pbcs.dll./article?AID=/2006069/OPINION03/6060903 51/101 **June 9, 2006.**
Dodder, Joanna. "Back at Rest: Bones of Billy the Kid return to Prescott." *The Daily Courier.* **July 9, 2006.** http://prescottdailycourier.com/print.asp?ArticleID=40353&Section ID=1&SubSectionID=1

No Author. AP. "Prescott, Ariz. - Prosecutors won't seek charges against two men who exhumed the remains of a man who claimed to be the outlaw Billy the Kid." AOL News. **October 23, 2006.**

_____. AP. "Billy the Kid Case Dropped." *Albuquerque Journal. Metro.* D3. **October 24, 2006.**

_____. AP. "Men Who Exhumed Billy the Kid Won't Be Charged." **October 24, 2006.** *New York Sun.* http://www.nysun.com/article/42176. **(Claims Sullivan and Sederwall did Arizona exhumation, have Miller DNA, and sent to Orchid for matchings to bench DNA)**

_____. AP. "Arizona: No Charges Sought for Exhuming Remains." *New York Times.* A-26. **October 24, 2006.** http://www.nytimes.com/2006/10/24/us/24brfs-002.html?r=1&oref=slogin. **(Cover-up of illegal John Miller/William Hudspeth exhumations)**

Martínez, Tony and Alison. "Better Days Ahead for New Mexico Highlands University?" *The Hispanic Outlook in Higher Education.* **December 4, 2006.**

Turk, David S. "Billy the Kid and the U.S. Marshals Service." *Wild West.* **February, 2007.** Volume 19. Number 5. Pages 34 – 41. **(Turk's expurgated "U.S. Marshals Service and Billy the Kid")**

Jason Strykowski. "A Tale of Two Governors ... And one Kid." *True West.* **May, 2007.** Vol. 54. Issue 5. Page 64.

No Author. AP. "Billy the Kid Exhumation a Possibility." *Roswell Daily Record.* **May 2, 2007.** From Stephenville, Texas AP on "Brushy Bill" exhumation attempt; Sederwall claims has John Miller's DNA)

Carter, Julie. "Brushy Bill targeted for DNA testing; Billy the Kid workbench goes on display." *Ruidoso News.* **May 3, 2007.**

_____. AP. "Manhunt for Real Billy the Kid Goes On: Deputy hopes DNA will finally reveal outlaw's true identity." *Albuquerque Journal.* **May 4, 2007.** B3.

Zorosec, Thomas. "DNA could solve mystery of Billy the Kid." Chron.com - Houston Chronicle. **May 5, 2007. (From Hamilton, Texas; "Brushy Bill" exhumation attempt)**

Carter, Julie. AP. "Texas town denies request to exhume Billy the Kid claimant." *Houston Chronicle.* **May 11, 2007.**

_____. "Evidence Hidden in Spector Trial." BBC Internet News. May 24, 2007. **(Dr. Henry Lee alleged as destroying evidence)**

_____. AP. "Famed experts credibility takes a hit at Spector trial." CNN.com law center. **May 25, 2007. (Dr. Henry Lee allegedly destroyed evidence)**

Stallings, Dianne. "Billy the Kid case straps county for insurance." *RuidosoNews.com.* **August 13, 2008.**

Carter, Julie. "Lincoln County deputies resign commissions for Kid case." *Ruidosonews.com.* **August 16, 2007. (Start of ploy calling Case 2003-274 a "hobby")**

Romo, Rene. "Seeking the Kid, Minus Badges. Deputies Resign to Hunt for Billy." *Albuquerque Journal.* **August 18, 2007.** No. 230. pp. 1-2.

Concerned Citizens of Lincoln County. "Should Lincoln County Have Grave Concerns Over A Person Like Steve Sederwall Running for Sheriff? *Lincoln County News.* **October 16, 2008.** Page 6.

Miller, Jay. "Kid's Pardon a Publicity Stunt." "Inside the Capitol" syndicated column "Inside the Capitol" and blog, insidethecapitol.blogspot.com. **June 23, 2010.**

Stinnett, Scot. "Billy the Kid historian says pardon all part of the hoax." *De Baca County News.* Pages 3, 9. **June 24, 2010. (Reprint of my Jay Miller article without commentary)**

No Author. "Billy the Kid 'to be pardoned.' " *Press Trust of India (Hindustan Times)* and Pakistan *Daily Express.* **July 11, 2010. (Pardon for "Brushy Bill")**

Romo, Rene. "Gov. Weighs Pardon for Billy the Kid." *Albuquerque Journal.* Saturday, No. 205. Front page, and A6. **July 24, 2010.**

Licón, Adriana Gómez. "Pardon form New Mexico governor unlikely for Billy the Kid." *El Paso Times*. **July 29, 2010.**

Massey, Barry. Associated Press. Santa Fe. "Billy the Kid To Be Pardoned, 130 Years Later? Lawman's Grandchildren Outraged; 'Would You Issue A Pardon For Someone Who Made His Living As A Thief?' National, international, and internet publications. **July 30, 2010.**

Gardner, David. Los Angeles. "Pat Garrett's family plan showdown over plans to finally pardon Billy the Kid." London's *Daily Mail Online*. **July 31, 2010.**

Boardman, Mark. "The Lunacy of Billy the Kid." *True West*. August, 2010. Volume 57. Issue 8. Pages 42-47. **(Defamatory article about me)**

Massey, Barry. Associated Press. Santa Fe. "NM gov meets with lawman Pat Garrett's descendants." **August 4, 2010.** www.wthr.com/global/story.asp?s=12926188.

Vaughn, Chris. "Texas Town seeks New Mexico pardon for Billy the Kid." *Fort Worth Star-Telegram*. **August 14, 2010. (Bid for "Brushy Bill" Roberts pardon.)**

Lacey, Marc. "Old West Showdown Is Revived. *New York Times*. **August 15, 2010. (Richardson shape-shifted to "amateur historian.")**

No Author. "A Tale of Two Billys." *New English Review: The Iconoclast*. (Internet). **August 15, 2010.**

Gordon, Bea. "Examining Legend: The Pardoning of Billy the Kid.. New Mexico Gov. Bill Richardson's talking about exonerating the state's most famous outlaw. But at what cost?" www.newwest.net/topic/article/29850/C37/L37/ **August 17, 2010.**

Massey, Barry. Associated Press. Santa Fe. " 'Billy the Kid' pardon effort draws Wild West showdown." Wilkes-Barre, Pennsylvania. *The Times Leader*. **August 21, 2010. (Introduction of William N. Wallace and Indiana Historical Society opposition. In starpress.com of east central Indiana as "Should Billy the Kid Be Pardoned?")**

Miller, Jay. "When is a promise not a promise?" *Inside the Capitol*. **August 30, 2010.** (Sides, Hampton. "Not-So-Charming Billy." *NY Times Opinion Section Op-Ed Contributor*. September 6, 2010.

Richardson, Bill. "Governor Bill Richardson to Consider Billy the Kid Pardon Petition." Press release. **December 16, 2010. (Floating the Randi McGinn petition)**

Martinez, Edecio. "Billy the Kid to be Pardoned 130 Years Later." CBSNEWS.com. **December 27, 2010.**

Guarino, Mark. "Outgoing New Mexico Gov. Bill Richardson is considering a pardon for celebrated outlaw Billy the Kid. An informal e-mail poll shows support. But time is running out." Associated Press. **December 29, 2010.**

Levy, Glen. "Will Billy the Kid Be Pardoned? Governor Has Until Friday." TIME NewsFeed.com. **December 29, 2010.**

Richardson, Bill. "Governor Richardson to Announce his decision on Billy the Kid Pardon Request Tomorrow." Press release. **December 30, 2010.**

Burke, Kelly David. "Billy the Kid Pardon?" FoxNews.com. **December 30, 2010.**

Hopper, Jessica. "Gov. Bill Richardson: 'I've Decided Not to Pardon Billy the Kid.' " ABCNEWS.com. **December 31, 2010.**

Rojas, Rick. "No Pardon for Billy the Kid. New Mexico Gov. Bill Richardson says, 'The Romanticism appealed to me ... but the facts and evidence did not support it." *Los Angeles Times*. **December 31, 2010.**

Watson, Kathryn. "Alas, no pardon for Billy the Kid: New Mexico's Richardson says close call." washingtontimes.com. **December 31, 2010.**

No Author. "Richardson Declines to Pardon Outlaw Billy the Kid." FoxNews.com. **December 31, 2010.**

Lacey, Marc. "For 2nd Time in 131 Years, Billy the Kid is Denied Pardon." *New York Times*. Page A10. **January 1, 2011.**

Todd, Jeff. "Trial seeks truth in Billy the Kid case." KRQE. **February 17, 2011.**

Romo, Rene. "Fight Won, Questions Remain: Billy the Kid DNA Report Released." *Albuquerque Journal*. Front Page and Page B1. **April 29, 2012.**

Sandlin, Scott. "Billy the Kid case costs taxpayers nearly $200K: Billy the Kid lives on in battle of public records." *Albuquerque Journal.* Front Page, Page A2, Page A8. No. 162. **June 11, 2013. (Fakes blood on carpenter's bench)**

Cherry, Doris. "Modern Billy the Kid 'Cases' Cost Public Plenty: County Shells Out Bucks for Failing to Release Information." *Lincoln County News.* **June 27, 2013.** Volume 109. Number 6. Front Page and Pages 7-8. **(Based on my June 18, 2013 letter to the Lincoln County Commissioners)**

Stallings, Dianne. "Former Lincoln County sheriff dies in Texas: Tom Sullivan died Saturday in Texas." **October 22, 2013.** ruidosonews.com.

"BILLY THE KID CASE" LEGAL DOCUMENTS
CAPITAN, NEW MEXICO
(FIRST ANNOUNCEMENT OF CASE NO. 2003-274)

Sederwall, Steve, "Mayor's Report, **May 5, 2003**." *Village of Capitan: Capitan Village Hall News.* Capitan, New Mexico. **(Announces filed Case 2003-274)**

ALBUQUERQUE, NEW MEXICO
(OPPOSITION OF THE OMI TO EXHUMATIONS)

Zumwalt, Ross E. "Affidavit of Ross E. Zumwalt, MD. In the Matter of Catherine Antrim. Case No. MS 2003-11 Sixth Judicial Court, County of Grant, State of New Mexico. **January 9, 2004. (Exhumation refused based on invalid DNA)**

Komar, Debra. "Affidavit of Debra Komar, PhD. In the Matter of Catherine Antrim. Case No. MS 2003-11 Sixth Judicial Court, County of Grant, State of New Mexico. **January 9, 2004. (Exhumation refused based on invalid DNA)**

Snead, William E. Attorney for Office of Medical Investigator." "In the Matter of Catherine Antrim: Response of Office of Medical Investigator to Petition to Exhume Remains of Catherine Antrim." Case No. MS 2003-11. Sixth Judicial Court, Grant County. **January 13, 2004. (Opposition of OMI to exhumation)**

Komar, Debra. "Deposition of Debra Komar, Ph.D. In the Matter of Catherine Antrim. Case No. MS 2003-11." Sixth Judicial Court, County of Grant, State of New Mexico. Taken by Adam S. Baker, Attorney for Town of Silver City. Signed: Debra Komar, Ph.D. **January 20, 2004. (Exhumation refused based on invalid DNA in Billy the Kid's and mother's graves)**

LINCOLN COUNTY, NEW MEXICO
(LINCOLN COUNTY SHERIFF'S DEPARTMENT
CASE NO. 2003-274, "BILLY THE KID CASE")

Virden, R.E. Lincoln County Undersheriff report. "I participated in the investigative reconstruction ..." **April 28, 2003. (Participation in Case # 2003-274.)**

Sullivan, Tom. Lincoln County Sheriff. "Lincoln County Sheriff's Department is currently conducting an investigation ..." Letter to Charles Ryan, Director Arizona Department of Corrections. **April 30, 2003. (Describes Garrett as murderer and planned exhumations of John Miller and "Brushy Bill" Roberts)**

_____. "Denial Letter." Pre-printed form to my attorney, Randall M. Harris. **October 8, 2003. (Open records denial for the Probable Cause Statement using exception of ongoing law enforcement investigation.)**

Sullivan, Tom. Sheriff, Lincoln County Sheriff's Office, and Steven M. Sederwall. Deputy Sheriff, Lincoln County Sheriff's Office. "Lincoln County Sheriff's Office, Lincoln County, New Mexico, Case: William H. Bonney, a.k.a. William Antrim, a.k.a. The Kid, a.k.a. Billy the Kid: An Investigation into the events of April 28, 1881 through July 14, 1881 – l days of doubt." **No Date. (Rejected Probable Cause Statement for Case No. 2003-274. In Lincoln County Sheriff's Department case file for 2003-274.)**

_____. "Lincoln County Sheriff's Department Case #2003-274 Probable Cause Statement." Filed in Lincoln County Sheriff's Department. Carrizozo, New Mexico. **December 31, 2003. (Became publicly available as "Plaintiff Exhibit 1 in Petitioner's Attorney Sherry Tippett's Silver City "Brief in Chief in Support of the Exhumation of Catherine Antrim." Case No. MS 03-011." Sixth Judicial Court, County of Grant, State of New Mexico." January 5, 2004)**

Overton, Homer D. aka Homer D. Kinsworthy. "Affidavit for Lincoln County Sheriff's Department Case #2003-274 Probable Cause Statement." **December 22, 2003. (Fake swearing that Garrett's widow –dead in 1936 - told him in 1940 that Garrett did not kill the Kid. Became publicly available as "Plaintiff Exhibit 1 in Petitioner's Attorney Sherry Tippett's Silver City "Brief in Chief in Support of the Exhumation of Catherine Antrim." Case No. MS 03-011." Sixth Judicial Court, County of Grant, State of New Mexico." January 5, 2004)**

No Author. "Contact List, William H. Bonney Case # 2003-274, Lincoln County Sheriff's Office & Investigators." No Date. **Probably 2003. (In Lincoln County Sheriff's Department Case file for 2003-274; and obtained by subpoena in my open records act litigation)**

Virden, Rick, Lincoln County Sheriff. "Deputy Sheriff Commission [Card] to Tom Sullivan." **January 1, 2005.**

_____. "Deputy Sheriff Commission [Card] to Steven Sederwall." **February 25, 2005.**

Sederwall, Steven M., Lincoln County Sheriff's Deputy Investigator. "Lincoln County Sheriff's Department Supplemental Report, Case #2003-274. Subject: Exhumation of John Miller. Location: Arizona Pioneers' Cemetery, Prescott, Arizona." **May 19, 2005. (Arizona exhumations John Miller and William Hudspeth)**

Virden, R.E. Lincoln County Sheriff. letter to Jay Miller. "We are interested in the truth surrounding Billy the Kid and are continuing the investigation ..." **November 28, 2005. (Virden confirms continuing Billy the Kid case and deputizing Sullivan and Sederwall for it.)**

Virden, R.E. Lincoln County Sheriff. To Hamilton, Texas, Mayor Roy Ramsey [sic]. "This letter will inform you that Tom Sullivan and Steve Sederwall are both commissioned deputies ..." **No date, but around May 2007. (Virden's attempt to exhume "Brushy" with Sullivan and Sederwall as the Deputies)**

Lee, Henry, Dr. Letter to Jay Miller. "In response to your letter dated March 27, 2006 ..." **May 1, 2006. (Lee confirms sending his carpenter's bench and floorboard report to Lincoln County Sheriff's Department.)**

Sederwall, Steve. "billythekidcase.com." Sederwall's pay for view website with Case 2003-274 records. **October, 2010. (Selling public records online.**

SILVER CITY, NEW MEXICO
(EXHUMATION ATTEMPT ON CATHERINE ANTRIM)

Tippett, Sherry. Attorney. To Richard Gay, Assistant to the Chief of Staff, Governor Richardson's Office. "Memorandum, RE: Exhumation of Catherine Antrim." **July 11, 2003. (Tippett's lie of OMI backing exhumation.)**

Tippett, Sherry. Attorney for Petitioners Sullivan, Sederwall, and Graves. "In the Matter of Catherine Antrim: Petition to Exhume Remains." Case No. MS 03-011. Sixth Judicial Court, County of Grant, State of New Mexico. **October 3, 2003. (Start of exhumation attempts; perjury about permission from OMI)**

Kennedy, Paul J., Adam S. Baker, Thomas F. Stewart, Robert L. Scavron, Attorneys for Mayor Terry Fortenberry on Behalf of the Town of Silver City. "In the Matter of Catherine Antrim: Motion to Intervene." Case No. MS 03-011. Sixth Judicial Court, County of Grant, State of New Mexico. **October 31, 2003. (Start of my exhumation opposition)**

_____. "In the Matter of Catherine Antrim: Response in Opposition to the Petition to Exhume Remains." Case No. MS 03-011. Sixth Judicial Court, County of Grant, State of New Mexico. **October 31, 2003.**

Tippett, Sherry J. Attorney for Petitioners. "State of New Mexico, County of Grant, Sixth Judicial District Court, In the Matter of Catherine Antrim, No. MS. 2003-11. Petitioner's Response in Opposition to the Town of Silver City's Motion to Intervene." (Unfiled) **No Date.**

Baker, Adam S. Attorneys for Mayor Terry Fortenberry on Behalf of Silver City. "In the Matter of Catherine Antrim: Request for Hearing." Case No. MS 03-011. Sixth Judicial Court, County of Grant, State of New Mexico. **November 4, 2003.**

Foy, Jim, District Judge. "In the Matter of Catherine Antrim: Notice of Recusal." Case No. MS 03-011. Sixth Judicial Court, County of Grant, State of New Mexico. **November 14, 2003. (Honest Judge Foy removes himself)**

Miranda, Velia C., District Court Clerk. "In the Matter of Catherine Antrim: Notice of Assignment/Designation of District Judge H.R. Quintero." Case No. MS 03-011. Sixth Judicial Court, County of Grant, State of New Mexico. **November 14, 2003. (Entry of Richardson appointee judge)**

Tippett, Sherry J. Attorney for Petitioners Sullivan, Sederwall and Graves. "In the Matter of Catherine Antrim: Petitioner's Response in Opposition to the Town of Silver City's Motion to Intervene." No. MS. 2003-11. State of New Mexico, County of Grant, Sixth Judicial District Court. (Unfiled) **No Date.**

Robins, Bill III and David Sandoval, Attorneys for Billy the Kid. "In the Matter of Catherine Antrim: Billy the Kid's Unopposed Motion for Intervention and Request for Expedited Disposition." Case No. MS 2003-11. Sixth Judicial Court, County of Grant, State of New Mexico. **November 26, 2003. (First petition with dead Billy the Kid as co-Petitioner to Sullivan, Sederwall, and Graves.)**

Amos-Staats, Joani. "In the Matter of Catherine Antrim: Joani Amos-Staats' [sic] Response in Opposition to the Petition to Exhume." Case No. MS 2003-11. Sixth Judicial Court, County of Grant, State of New Mexico. **December 5, 2003. (Adjacent grave opposition based on disturbing remains)**

_____. "In the Matter of Catherine Antrim: Joani Amos-Staats' [sic] Motion to Intervene and Request for Expedited Hearing." Case No. MS 2003-11. Sixth Judicial Court, County of Grant, State of New Mexico. **December 8, 2003.**

_____. "In the Matter of Catherine Antrim: Joani Amos-Staats' [sic] Response in Opposition to the Petition to Exhume Remains." Case No. MS 2003-11. Sixth Judicial Court, County of Grant, State of New Mexico. **December 8, 2003.**

Kennedy, Paul J., Adam S. Baker, Thomas F. Stewart, Robert L. Scavron, Attorneys for Mayor Terry Fortenberry on Behalf of the Town of Silver City. "In the Matter of Catherine Antrim: Reply in Support of the Town of Silver City's Motion to Intervene." Case No. MS 2003-11. Sixth Judicial Court, County of Grant, State of New Mexico. **December 8, 2003. (Justifying need to protect Antrim grave)**

Tippett, Sherry J. Attorney for Petitioners Sullivan, Sederwall and Graves. "In the Matter of Catherine Antrim: Petitioners Response in Opposition to the Town of Silver City's Motion to Intervene." Case No. MS 2003-11. Sixth Judicial Court, County of Grant, State of New Mexico. **December 8, 2003. (Tippett lies by saying town has no "legal interest" to intervene)**

Quintero, H.R. District Judge. "In the Matter of Catherine Antrim: Order." Case No. MS 03-011. Sixth Judicial Court, County of Grant, State of New Mexico. **December 9, 2003. (Rescheduling hearing from January 6, 2004 to January 27, 2004.)**

Baker, Adam S. Attorneys for Mayor Terry Fortenberry on Behalf of the Town of Silver City. "In the Matter of Catherine Antrim: Intervenor Town of Silver City's Brief on Petition to Exhume." Case No. MS 03-011. Sixth Judicial Court, County of Grant, State of New Mexico. **January 5, 2004. (Arguing 1962 precedent case of Lois Telfer blocking exhumation)**

Tippett, Sherry J. Attorney. To Mayor Steve Sederwall, Sheriff Tom Sullivan, Sheriff Gary Graves. "In the Matter of Catherine Antrim: Petitioners Brief in Chief in Support of Exhumation." Case No. MS 2003-11. Sixth Judicial Court, County of Grant, State of New Mexico. **January 5, 2004. (Using Probable Cause Statement and Homer Overton Affidavit as Plaintiff exhibits)**

Robins, Bill III and David Sandoval. Attorneys for Billy the Kid. "In the Matter of Catherine Antrim: Billy the Kid's Pre-Hearing Brief." Case No. MS 2003-11. Sixth Judicial Court, Grant County. **January 5, 2004. (Linking exhumation and pardon with "Brushy Bill" Roberts as Billy – CRACKED THE HOAX as a "Brushy Bill" scam by using "Brushy's" dark night for July 14, 1881)**

Tippett, Sherry. Attorney for law enforcement Petitioners Tom Sullivan, Steve Sederwall, Gary Graves. "In the Matter of Catherine Antrim: Petitioner's [sic] Brief in Chief in Support of Exhumation." Case No. MS 2003-11. Sixth Judicial Court, Grant County. **January 5, 2004.**

Amos-Staats, Joani. "In the Matter of Catherine Antrim: Intervenor Joani Amos-Staats' [sic] Brief on Petition to Exhume." Case No. MS 2003-11. Sixth Judicial Court, County of Grant, State of New Mexico. **January 6, 2004.**

Kennedy, Paul J., Adam S. Baker, Thomas F. Stewart, Robert L. Scavron, Attorneys for Mayor Terry Fortenberry on Behalf of the Town of Silver City. "In the Matter of Catherine Antrim: Response in Opposition to Petitioners' Brief in Chief." Case No. MS 2003-11. Sixth Judicial Court, County of Grant, State of New Mexico. **January 21, 2004.**

_____. "In the Matter of Catherine Antrim: Silver City's Response in Opposition to Petitioners' Motion for Continuance." Case No. MS 2003-11. Sixth Judicial Court, County of Grant, State of New Mexico. **January 21, 2004.**

Tippett, Sherry J. Attorney. To Mayor Steve Sederwall, Sheriff Tom Sullivan, Sheriff Gary Graves. "Attached is a copy of Judge Quintero's Order of December 9, 2003, ruling on our Hearing ..." **December 17, 2003. (States that they will win on January 27, 2004; urges completing the Probable Cause Statement)**

Quintero, H.R. District Judge, Division 1. "Order of Continuance. In the Matter of Catherine Antrim. Case No. MS 03-011." Filed **January 23, 2004.** Sixth Judicial Court, County of Grant, State of New Mexico. Filed January 23, 2004. **(Tippett sanctioned to pay airfare for witness, Frederick Nolan for changing the hearing date on short notice)**

Robins, Bill III and David Sandoval. Attorneys for Billy the Kid. "In the Matter of Catherine Antrim: Billy the Kid's Brief on the Question of Ripeness." Case No. MS 2003-11. Sixth Judicial Court, Grant County. **February 24, 2004. (Setting up Quintero's sending the exhumation to Fort Sumner)**

Acúna, Mark Anthony and Sherry J. Tippett. Attorneys for Petitioners Sullivan, Sederwall and Graves. "In the Matter of Catherine Antrim: Petitioners' Brief on the Question of Ripeness." Case No. MS 2003-11. Sixth Judicial Court, Grant County. **February 24, 2004.**

Baker, Adam S. and Thomas F. Stewart, Robert L. Scavron, Attorneys for Silver City and Joani Amos-Staats. "In the Matter of Catherine Antrim: Silver City's and Joani Amos-Staats' [sic] Joint Motion to Dismiss on Grounds of Ripeness." Case No. MS 2003-11. Sixth Judicial Court, County of Grant, State of New Mexico. **February 24, 2004.**

Acúna, Mark Anthony. Attorney for Petitioners Sullivan, Sederwall and Graves. "In the Matter of Catherine Antrim: Entry of Appearance." Case No. MS 03-011. Sixth Judicial Court, County of Grant, State of New Mexico. **February 26, 2004. (Replacing Tippett for law enforcement Petitioners)**

Robins, Bill III and David Sandoval. Attorneys for Billy the Kid. "In the Matter of Catherine Antrim: Response to Motion to Dismiss." Case No. MS 2003-11. Sixth Judicial Court, Grant County. **March 10, 2004.**

Quintero, Henry R. "In the Matter of Catherine Antrim: Decision and Order." Case No. MS 03-011." Sixth Judicial Court, County of Grant, State of New Mexico. **April 2, 2004. (Stipulation that case is not ripe, and requires DNA from Fort Sumner Billy the Kid grave first before trying to exhume Catherine Antrim)**

Fortenberry, Terry D, Mayor; Thomas A. Nupp Councilor District 2; Steve May, Councilor District 4; Gary Clauss, Councilor District 3; Judy Ward, Councilor District 1; Alex Brown, Town Manager; Cissy McAndrew, Executive Director Chamber of Commerce; Frank Milan, Director Silver City Mainstreet Project; Susan Berry, Director Silver City Museum. "Open Letter to Governor Bill Richardson." **June 21, 2004. (Request to cease "Billy the Kid Case" exhmations)**

Kemper, Lisa. Kennedy Han, PC. Controller, (via fax). To Gale Cooper. "*In the Matter of Catherine Antrim, 6th Judicial Dist. Ct. Case No. MS 2003-001*, 'This is to confirm our receipt of payment ...'" Baker, Adam. Confirmation of payment of Attorney Sherry Tippett's Judge Henry Quintero sanction by Attorney Bill Robins III. **September 1, 2004.** (See "Order of Continuance. In the Matter of Catherine Antrim. Case No. MS 03-011.") Filed January 23, 2004. Sixth Judicial Court, County of Grant, State of New Mexico. Signed: H.R. Quintero, District Judge, Division 1." April 28, 2004, **(Court sanctions Tippett, and secret donor to case, Bill Robins III pays her sanction.)**

FORT SUMNER, NEW MEXICO
(EXHUMATION ATTEMPT ON WILLIAM H. BONNEY)

De Baca County Commissioners Special Meeting." Minutes. (Powhatan Carter III, Chairman; Joe Steele; Tommy Roybal; Nancy Sparks, County Clerk. To whom it may concern. "The De Baca County Commissioners are in full support of Village of Fort Sumner's stand against exhuming the body of Billy the Kid." **September 25, 2003. (Voted against exhumation of Billy the Kid)**

Robins, Bill III and David Sandoval, Mark Acuña, Attorneys for Co-Petitioner Billy the Kid and Sheriff-Petitioners. "In the Matter of William H. Bonney, aka 'Billy the Kid': Petition for the Exhumation of Billy the Kid's Remains." Case No. CV-04-00005. Tenth Judicial District, County of De Baca, State of New Mexico. **February 26, 2004. (Robins joins Acuña to exhume the Kid)**

Robins, Bill III and David Sandoval, Attorneys for Co-Petitioner Billy the Kid. "In the Matter of William H. Bonney, aka 'Billy the Kid': Notice of Excusal." Case No. CV-2004 [sic]-00005. Tenth Judicial District, County of De Baca, State of New Mexico. **March 5, 2004. (Petitioners' removal of honest Judge Ricky Purcell from hearing the case.)**

Jimenez Maes, Petra, Chief Justice. "In the Matter of William H. Bonney, aka 'Billy the Kid': Order Designating Judge." Case No. CV-2004-00005. Tenth Judicial District, County of De Baca, State of New Mexico. **April 1, 2004. (Richardson's corrupt judge appointee, Ted Hartley, is appointed to case)**

Baker, Adam S. and Herb Marsh, Jr., Attorneys for the Village of Fort Sumner. "In the Matter of William H. Bonney, aka 'Billy the Kid': Village of Fort Sumner's Unopposed Motion to Intervene." Case No. CV-04-00005. Tenth Judicial District, County of De Baca, State of New Mexico. **April 12, 2004.**

_____. "In the Matter of William H. Bonney, aka 'Billy the Kid': Response in Opposition to the Petitioners for the Exhumation of Billy the Kid's Remains. In the Matter of William H. Bonney, aka 'Billy the Kid.' " Case No. CV-04-00005. Tenth Judicial District, County of De Baca, State of New Mexico. **April 12, 2004.**

Hartley, Teddy L. "In the Matter of William H. Bonney, aka 'Billy the Kid': Order." Case No. CV-04-00005. Tenth Judicial District, County of De Baca, State of New Mexico. **April 20, 2004. (Intervention of Village of Fort Sumner granted)**

Baker, Adam S. and Herb Marsh, Jr., Attorneys for the Village of Fort Sumner. "In the Matter of William H. Bonney, aka 'Billy the Kid': Response in Opposition to the Petition for the Exhumation of Billy the Kid's Remains." Case No. CV-04-00005. Tenth Judicial District, County of De Baca, State of New Mexico. **May 6, 2004.**

_____. "In the Matter of William H. Bonney, aka 'Billy the Kid': Village of Fort Sumner's Motion For Proof of Attorneys' Authority To Act On Behalf Of William H. Bonney." Case No. CV-04-00005. Tenth Judicial District, County of De Baca, State of New Mexico. **June 24, 2004. (Confronting Attorney Bill Robins III's fakery of representing Billy the Kid based on dead Billy not being real so he cannot have a lawyer)**

_____. "In the Matter of William H. Bonney, aka 'Billy the Kid': Village of Fort Sumner's Motion to Dismiss Against Petitioners Sullivan, Sederwall, and Graves for Lack of Standing." Case No. CV-04-00005. Tenth Judicial District, County of De Baca, State of New Mexico. **June 24, 2004. (Invalid murder case because Pat Garrett properly killed Billy the Kid)**

Hartley, Teddy L. District Judge. "Notice of Hearing. "In the Matter of William H. Bonney, aka 'Billy the Kid': Notice of Hearing." Case No. CV-04-00005. Tenth Judicial District, County of De Baca, State of New Mexico. **July 6, 2004. (Hearing set for September 27, 2004)**

Acuña, Mark Anthony, Attorney for the Petitioners Sullivan, Sederwall and Graves. "In the Matter of William H. Bonney, aka 'Billy the Kid': Petitioner's Response to the Village of Ft. Sumner's Motion to Dismiss." Case No. CV-04-00005." Tenth Judicial District, State of New Mexico, County of De Baca. **July 29, 2004.(Acuña argues Sheriff-petitioners' Sullivan, Graves, and Sederwall's standing based on law enforcement as Sheriffs and Deputy Sheriff; later Sullivan and Sederwall would lie that they had done the case as private hobbyists to avoid the open records act for public officials to hide their fake DNA documents)**

Robins, Bill III and David Sandoval; Attorneys for the Billy the Kid; and Adam S. Baker and Herb Marsh, Jr., Attorneys for the Village of Fort Sumner. "In the Matter of William H. Bonney, aka 'Billy the Kid': Stipulation of Dismissal." Case No. CV-04-00005. Tenth Judicial District, County of De Baca, State of New Mexico. **August 23, 2004. (Fake dead Billy the Kid petition dismissed with prejudice)**

"In the Matter of De Baca County Sheriff Gary Graves. Petition for Order Allowing Recall Vote." Case No. CV-04-00019. Tenth Judicial District Court, State of New Mexico, County of De Baca. **September 13, 2004. (Recall starts against Sheriff Gary Graves, separate from the exhumation case.)**

Acuña, Mark Anthony and Adam S. Baker, Attorneys for Petitioners Graves, Sullivan and Sederwall; and the Village of Fort Sumner. "In the Matter of William H. Bonney, aka 'Billy the Kid': Stipulation of Dismissal With Prejudice." Case No. CV-04-00005. Tenth Judicial District, County of De Baca, State of New Mexico. **September 24, 2004. (Petitioners withdraw with prejudice at Fort Sumner. Definitive victory against Billy the Kid exhumation.)**

ARIZONA: YAVAPAI (PRESCOTT) AND MARICOPA COUNTIES (EXHUMATIONS OF JOHN MILLER AND WILLIAM HUDSPETH)

Sederwall, Steven M., Lincoln County Sheriff's Deputy Investigator. "Lincoln County Sheriff's Department Supplemental Report, Case #2003-274. Subject: Exhumation of John Miller. Location: Arizona Pioneers' Cemetery, Prescott, Arizona." **May 19, 2005. (Arizona exhumations John Miller and William Hudspeth)**

Cahall, Anna, Detective Prescott Police Department. "CASE REPORT 0600012767." **April 5, 2006. (Concerning the John Miller exhumation)**

Tunnell, Dale. To Jeanine Dike. "Subject: RE: Disinterment of Wm Bonney." **May 3, 2005.**

Dike, Jeanine. To Dale Tunnell. "Subject: Disinterment of Wm Bonney." **May 3, 2005.**
—————. To Dale Sams. "Subject: FW: Disinterment Wm Bonney." **May 3, 2005.**
—————. To Dale Sams. "Subject: FW: Disinterment Wm Bonney." **May 4, 2005.**
Sams, Dale. To George Thompson. "Subject: Disinterment." **May 4, 2005. (Confirms Sams has no idea where the Miller grave is located.)**
Sederwall, Steven M., Lincoln County Sheriff's Deputy Investigator. "Lincoln County Sheriff's Department Supplemental Report, Case #2003-274. Subject: Exhumation of John Miller. Location: Arizona Pioneers' Cemetery, Prescott, Arizona." **May 19, 2005. (Arizona exhumations John Miller and William Hudspeth)**
Fulginiti, Laura C. Ph.D., D-ABFA. Forensic Anthropologist. To Dale L. Tunnell, Ph.D. "RE: Exhumation, Pioneer Home Cemetery, Prescott, Arizona." **June 2, 2005. (Report of the Miller-Hudspeth exhumations revealing fake hoaxer claims of buck teeth and bullet wound to left scapula of John Miller.)**
Sederwall, Steven. To Misty Rodarte. "Subject: Billy the Kid." **July 6, 2005.**
Winter, Anne. "To: Tim Nelson; Alan Stephens. Subject: Pioneer Home, Grave, Billy the Kid and DNA." **August 18, 2005. (Has attachment of Pioneers' Home Supervisor Gary Olson's cover-up letter to her and implied internal cover-up. Also states that Sullivan paid for the exhumation.)**
—————. "To: Tim Nelson; Alan Stephens. Subject: Billy the Kid." **September 8, 2005. ("80% DNA match" with Miller claimed)**
Olson, Gary. Superintendent Arizona Pioneers' Home. To David Snell. "You recently asked the Arizona Pioneers' Home if a body in its cemetery had been exhumed ..." October 3, 2005. **(Confirms original cover-up of John Miller exhumation.)**
Winter, Anne. "To Gary Olson. Subject: RE: the kid." **October 17, 2005.**
Olson, Gary. "To Anne Winter. Subject: RE: the kid." **October 17, 2005. (Reporting on no DNA results yet to him.)**
Winter, Anne. "To: Jeanine L'Ecuyer. Subject: FW: the kid." **October 17, 2005. (Reporting on no DNA results yet to Olson.)**
Olson, Gary. "To: Anne Winter. Subject: FW: re. John Miller." **October 20, 2005. (Cover-up `planned for Romo. "I thought you and the Governor may want to know about this request.")**
Winter, Anne. "To: Tim Nelson; Alan Stephens. Subject: FW: re. John Miller. **October 20, 2005. (Cover-up plan for Romo presentation: "Remember there was the legal issue that they dug up two bodies.")**
—————. "To: Jeanine L'Ecuyer. Subject: FW: re. John Miller." **October 25, 2005. (Planning cover-up for media requests.)**
Sederwall, Steven. "To: Barbara J. Miller; Steve McGregor; Rick Staub; Misty Rodarte; Emily Smith; Bob Boze Bell. Subject: in the Albuquerque Journal." **November 6, 2005. (Copy Romo article.)**
Olson, Gary. "To Anne Winter, Mark Wilson. Subject: FW: in the Albuquerque Journal." **November 7, 2005. (Copy Romo article.)**
Winter, Anne. "To: Jeanine L'Ecuyer; Tim Nelson; Alan Stephens. Subject: Billy the Kid. **November 7, 2005. (About Gary Olson's cover-up in KPNX interview.)**
Snell, David. To Shiela Polk. Yavapai County Attorney. "I feel it is my duty to report to you that graverobbers are plying their trade ..." **March 11, 2006. (Arizona citizen starting criminal investigation of Miller/Hudspeth exhumations.)**
Jacobson, Marcia. "To Anne Winter, Policy Advisor for Health, Office of the Governor, and Chief Randy Oaks, Prescott Police Department. Re: Disinterment of bodies at Arizona Pioneer's [sic] Home Cemetery." **March 30, 2006. (Attempted cover-up of John Miller and William Hudspeth exhumations.)**
Cahall, Anna, Detective Prescott Police Department. "CASE REPORT 0600012767." **April 5, 2006. (Concerning the John Miller exhumation; interviews with Sullivan, Sederwall, Tunnell)**
Savona, Glenn A. Prescott City Prosecutor. To Shiela Sullivan Polk, Yavapai County Attorney. "Re: Police Department DR# 2006-12767 Arizona Pioneers' Home Cemetery." **April 13, 2006. (Calls exhumations potential felonies)**

Cooper, Gale. To Detective Anna Cahall. Prescott Police Department. "Re: Exhumation of John Miller and adjacent grave for pursuing the New Mexico Billy the Kid Case." **April 13, 2006.**

_____. To Detective Anna Cahall. Prescott Police Department. "Re: Pertinent articles regarding exhumation of John Miller and remains from adjacent grave for alleged promulgation of the New Mexico Billy the Kid Case, a murder investigation." **April 17, 2006.**

_____. To Deputy County Attorney Steve Jaynes and County Attorney Dennis McGrane. (via fax) "Re: Information on the New Mexico Billy the Kid Case pertinent to the Arizona John Miller exhumations." **May 2, 2006.**

Sederwall, Steve. To confidential recipient. "Well we have the governor reaching out to the Arizona to stop this investigation." **May 16, 2006.**

Cooper, Gale. To Attorney Jonell Lucca (via fax). "Re: Case # CA20006020516. Follow-up to our telephone conversation of June 9, 2006, to address the issue of Permit for the exhumations of John Miller and the remains from an adjacent grave for promulgation of the New Mexico Billy the Kid Case, a murder investigation." **June 12, 2006.**

_____. To Attorney Jonell Lucca (via fax). "Re: Case # CA20006020516. Follow-up to my fax of June 12, 2006, to address additional issues pertinent to the exhumations of John Miller and William Hudspeth, done for promulgation of the New Mexico Billy the Kid Case, an alleged murder investigation." July 11, 2006.

Sams, Dale. Arizona Pioneers' Home Administrator. To Gale Cooper. Confirming approximate date of John Miller's birth as 1850. **August 8, 2006.**

Cooper, Gale. To Attorney Jonell Lucca (via fax). "Re: Case # CA20006020516. Follow-up to my fax of July 11, 2006, to address issues pertinent to the promulgators of the New Mexico Billy the Kid Case (which resulted in the exhumations of John Miller and William Hudspeth); with added focus on its alleged forensic experts and co-participants." **August 11, 2006.**

_____. To Attorney Jonell Lucca. "Re: Enclosed reference copy of Freedom of Information Act (FOIA) to Governor Janet Napolitano regarding her possible participation in the Prescott, Arizona exhumations of John Miller and William Hudspeth, and their legal issues related to Maricopa County Prosecutor's Office Case # CA20006020516." **September 22, 2006.**

_____. To Attorney Jonell Lucca. "Re: Information pertaining to Case # CA20006020516 (exhumations of John Miller and William Hudspeth) - American Academy of Forensic Science Ethics and Conduct Complaint against Dr. Henry Lee." **October 2, 2006.**

Lucca, Jonell L. To Dr. Gale Cooper. "This letter is to inform you that the Maricopa County Attorney's Office has declined to file charges ..." **October 17, 2006. (Corrupt claim that the only suspects were Jeanine Dike and Dale Tunnell to shield Sullivan and Sederwall)**

Cooper, Gale. To Attorney Jonell Lucca. "Re: Maricopa County Case # CA20006020516." **October 30, 2006. (Confirmation of getting her case termination letter, and asking why she changed suspects. Never answered.)**

Cooper, Gale. To Detective Anna. Prescott Police Department. "Re: Freedom of Information Act Request for Records of Prescott Police Department Case No. 06-12767. **September 11, 2008. (No response)**

HAMILTON, TEXAS
(EXHUMATION ATTEMPT ON "BRUSHY BILL" ROBERTS)

Cooper, Gale. "Billy the Kid Case in a Nutshell." Faxed letter to Hamilton, Texas, Mayor Roy Rumsey. **May 3, 2007. (About hoax to dig up "Brushy Bill")**

Virden, R.E. Lincoln County Sheriff. To Hamilton, Texas, Mayor Roy Ramsey [sic]. "This letter will inform you that Tom Sullivan and Steve Sederwall are both commissioned deputies ..." **No date, but around May 2007. (Virden's attempt to exhume "Brushy Bill" Roberts.)**

Cooper, Gale. "RE: Lincoln County Sheriff's Department's 2007 attempt to exhume Oliver "Brushy Bill" Roberts. Faxed letter to Hamilton, Texas, Mayor Roy Rumsey. **September 11, 2008.**

Rumsey, Roy. Hamilton Mayor. "RE: Lincoln County Sheriff's Department's 2007 attempt to exhume Oliver Roberts." Faxed letter to Gale Cooper. **September 12, 2008. (Confirmation that the case is closed)**

PAST ATTEMPT TO EXHUME WILLIAM H. BONNEY

"Motion to Intervene. In Re Application of Lois Telfer, Petitioner for the Removal of the Body of William H. Bonney, Deceased, From the Ft. Sumner Cemetery in Which He is Interred for Reinterment in the Lincoln, New Mexico, Cemetery. Case No. 3255." **December 5, 1961.** In the District Court of the Tenth Judicial District Within and For the County of De Baca. Signed: Victor C. Breen and John Humphrey, Jr., Attorneys for Louis A Bowdre. **(Louis Bowdre was the relative of Charles Bowdre whose grave is contiguous to William Bonney's.)**

Breen, Victor C. and John Humphrey, Jr., Attorneys for Louis A Bowdre. "Motion to Intervene. In Re Application of Lois Telfer, Petitioner for the Removal of the Body of William H. Bonney, Deceased, From the Ft. Sumner Cemetery in Which He is Interred for Reinterment in the Lincoln, New Mexico, Cemetery." Case No. 3255. In the District Court of the Tenth Judicial District, County of De Baca. **December 5, 1961. (Louis Bowdre was the relative of Charles Bowdre whose grave is contiguous to William Bonney's.)**

Kinsley, E.T. District Judge. "Decree. In Re Application of Lois Telfer, Petitioner for the Removal of the Body of William H. Bonney, Deceased, From the Ft. Sumner Cemetery in Which He is Interred for Reinterment in the Lincoln, New Mexico, Cemetery." Case No. 3255." In the District Court of the Tenth Judicial District Within and For the County of De Baca. **April 6, 1962. (Petition for exhumation Billy the Kid denied on basis that his grave could not be located and the search would disturb Bowdre's remains. That precedent was ignored by the current Petitioners and their attorneys.)**

OPEN RECORDS REQUESTS FOR CASE 2003-274
(For listings see my 2014 book, *Cracking the Billy the Kid Case Hoax: The Strange Plot to Exhume Billy the Kid, Convict Sheriff Pat Garrett of Murder, and become President of the United States*)

INVESTIGATIONS OF DR. HENRY LEE AND ORCHID CELLMARK LAB (CHRONOLOGICAL)

BACKGROUND

Bugliosi, Vincent. *Outrage: The Five Reasons Why O.J. Simpson Got Away With Murder.* New York and London: W.W. Norton & Company. **1996. (Exposé of Dr. Henry Lee forensic scams, Pages 47-49.)**

No author. "Fraud Alleged at Cellmark, DNA Testing Firm." TalkLeft: The Politics of Crime. http://www.talkleft.com./new_archives/008809.html. **November 18, 2004.**

Bailey, James A. and Margaret B. Bailey. "Billy the Kid Death Scene: Reviewing Ballistic Evidence. *Wild West History Association.* **September, 2016.** Volume 9, Number 3, Pages 30-46. **(Using Lee's forensic fakery of the washstand to create a death scene; also traces is furniture 's provenance (Pages 31-32))**

Shen, Maxine. "CBS and the brother of JonBenet Ramsey settle their $750m defamation lawsuit to the 'satisfaction of both parties' after he claimed their documentary implied he killed his sister." **January 5, 2019.** DailyMailOnline.com. **(Defamation case involving Dr. Henry Lee's forensics)**

RECORDS REQUESTS BY JAY MILLER AS MY PROXY

Miller, Jay. To Dr. Henry Lee. "Re: Forensic consultation in the New Mexico Billy the Kid Case." **March 27, 2006. (Included all the articles with Lee's forensic claims)**

Lee, Henry, Dr. To Jay Miller. "In response to your letter dated March 27, 2006 ..." **May 1, 2006. (Says sent his single forensic report for Case No. 2003-274 to the Lincoln County Sheriff's Department directly)**

Miller, Jay. To Dr. Henry Lee. "Re: Follow-up on your letter of May 1, 2006 responding to my request of March 27, 2006 for information on your forensic consultation in the New Mexico Billy the Kid Case." **June 15, 2006.**

_____. To Dr. Henry Lee. "Re: Follow-up to my letter of June 15, 2006 with regard to your forensic consultation in the New Mexico Billy the Kid Case." **August 8, 2006.**

_____. To Dr. Rick Staub. "Re: The participation by you and Orchid Cellmark in the New Mexico Billy the Kid Case." **August 8, 2006. (No response)**

ETHICS COMPLAINT AGAINST

Cooper, Gale. To Haskell Pitluck, AAFS Ethics Committee Chairman and members of the AAFS Ethics Committee. "Re: Formal Ethics Complaint against Dr. Henry Lee for his work as a forensic expert in Lincoln County, New Mexico, Sheriff's Department Case # 2003-274 ('the Billy the Kid Case')." **October 2, 2006.**

Cooper, Gale. To Haskell Pitluck, AAFS Ethics Committee Chairman. "Re: Follow-up on my October 2, 2006 complaint on Dr. Henry Lee to the Ethics Committee of the American Academy of Forensic Sciences." **March 5, 2007.**

_____. To Dr. Bruce Goldberger. President AAFS. "Re: Informing of non-action to date on my American Academy of Forensic Sciences Ethics Committee complaint filed October 2, 2006 against Dr. Henry Lee." **April 10, 2007.**

Goldberger, Bruce. Dr. and President AAFS. To Gale Cooper. (via fax) "I have received the complaint today ..." **April 12,, 2007.**

_____. To Gale Cooper. (via fax) "You should receive a letter from Mr. Pitluck in the coming week or two ..." **May 4, 2007.**

Pitluck, Haskell M. AAFS Ethics Committee Chairman. To Gale Cooper, M.D. "Ethics Committee has completed its investigation ..." **May 9, 2007. (Corrupt denial)**

RICHARDSON'S PARDON THRUST AND OPPOSITION TO

Cooper, Gale. "Re: Referred by Bob McCubbin." E-mail to Susannah Garrett. **June 13, 2010.**

Miller, Jay. "Kid's Pardon a Publicity Stunt." "Inside the Capitol" syndicated column and blog, insidethecapitol.blogspot.com. **June 23, 2010. (Papers refused to print; on blog only)**

Garrett, Jarvis Patrick "JP." "RE: Meeting" "... I would like el pinto." E-mail to Gale Cooper. **June 29, 2010. (Meeting with JP in which he suggested a meeting with Richardson)**

Cooper, Gale. "Lunch with Tourism Secretary." E-mail to JP and Susannah Garrett. **July 9, 2010. (I set up lunch with Mike Cerletti, Jay Miller, and the Garretts at La Fonda)**

_____. "Subj: Listing of Garrett Damages." E-mail to JP Garrett. July 10, 2010.

No Author. "Billy the Kid 'to be pardoned.'" *Press Trust of India* (*Hindustan Times*) and Pakistan *Daily Express*. **July 11, 2010. (Richardson's pardon publicity move - with "Brushy" as Billy.)**

Garrett, Jarvis Patrick "JP." "Petition in Opposition to Pardon of Billy the Kid." July 20, 2010. **(Made for signings at the Ruidoso Wild West Round-up)**

Romo, Rene. "Gov. Weighs Pardon for Billy the Kid." *Albuquerque Journal.* Saturday, No. 205. Front page, lead story, cont. A6. **July 24, 2010.**

Garrett, Jarvis Patrick "JP," Susan Floyd Garrett, and Pauline Garrett Tillinghast. "Representatives of the Garrett Family. "As grandchildren of Pat Garrett, we have watched with outrage and sadness ..." Letter to Governor Richardson. **July 25, 2010. (Prepared with my input)**

Licón, Adriana Gómez. "Pardon form New Mexico governor unlikely for Billy the Kid." *El Paso Times.* **July 29, 2010.**

Sharpe, Tom. "English kin trace path of 'Billy the Kid's' ex-boss: Tunstall's murder sparked Lincoln County War." *The New Mexican.* **July 29, 2010.**

Massey, Barry. AP. "Billy the Kid To Be Pardoned, 130 Years Later? Lawman's Grandchildren Outraged; 'Would You Issue A Pardon For Someone Who Made His Living As A Thief?' National, international, and internet publications. **July 30, 2010.**

Cooper, Gale. Re: Old West Royalty." "Don't forget that you are all Old West royalty." E-mail to Garrett family. **July 31, 2010.**

Gardner, David. Los Angeles. "Pat Garrett's family plan showdown over plans to finally pardon Billy the Kid." London's *Daily Mail Online.* **July 31, 2010.**

Garrett, Jarvis Patrick "JP," Susan Floyd Garrett, and Pauline Garrett Tillinghast. "Representatives of the Garrett Family. "Re. August 2, 2010 meeting with you concerning your possible pardon of Billy the Kid ..." Letter to Governor Richardson. **August 2, 2010.**

Cooper, Gale. "Garrett Family Statement to Governor Bill Richardson." **August 4, 2010.**

Massey, Barry. Associated Press. Santa Fe. "NM gov meets with lawman Pat Garrett's descendants." **August 4, 2010.** www.wthr.com/global/story.asp?s=12926188.

Cooper, Gale. "Re: Thanks." "I want to thank you and your children for the tremendous effort and grace that went into the Richardson meeting." E-mail to Garrett family. **August 5, 2010.**

Garrett, Susannah. "Re: Thanks." "Thanks for all your valuable and supportive presence through all this." E-mail to Gale Cooper. **August 5, 2010.**

Richardson, Bill. "Dear Garrett Family, Thank you for meeting with me ..." Letter to the Garretts. **August 9, 2010. (Follow-up to the August 4, 2010 meeting)**

Cooper, Gale. "Subj: Sample Wallace Family Statement." E-mail to William N. Wallace. **August 10, 2010.**

Wallace, William N. "Re: Sample Wallace Family Statement." ... "I have sent Governor Richardson by e-mail a modified version of the proposed 'Wallace Family' letter. E-mail to Gale Cooper. **August 10, 2010. (Lew Wallace's great-grandson)**

Cooper, Gale. "Re: Talking Points on Pardon Issue." E-mail to William N. Wallace. **August 14, 2010.**

Vaughn, Chris. "Texas Town seeks New Mexico pardon for Billy the Kid." *Fort Worth Star-Telegram.* **August 14, 2010. (Bid for "Brushy Bill" Roberts pardon.)**

Lacey, Marc. "Old West Showdown Is Revived. *New York Times.* **August 15, 2010. (Richardson shape-shifted to "amateur historian.")**

No Author. "A Tale of Two Billys." *New English Review: The Iconoclast.* (Internet). **August 15, 2010.**

Gordon, Bea. "Examining Legend: The Pardoning of Billy the Kid.. New Mexico Gov. Bill Richardson's talking about exonerating the state's most famous outlaw. But at what cost?" www.newwest.net/topic/article/29850/C37/L37/ **August 17, 2010.**

Massey, Barry. Associated Press. Santa Fe. " 'Billy the Kid' pardon effort draws Wild West showdown." Wilkes-Barre, Pennsylvania. *The Times Leader.* **August 21, 2010. (Introduction of William N. Wallace opposition)**

Wallace, William N. . "Re: Reply wnwallace: "Barry Massey of the AP has ready from me a reaction quote should Gov. Richardson go ahead with the pardon. E-mail to Gale Cooper. **September 16, 2010.**

Cooper, Gale. "Re: Reply wnwallace: 'That powerful stance of yours gives me hope that it can deter Governor Richardson's pardon publicity stunt." E-Mail to William N. Wallace. **September 16, 2010.**

McGinn, Randi. "RE: Application for Pardon for Henry McCarty, AKA William Bonney or Billy the Kid." Letter to Shammara Henderson, Legal Counsel Governor Richardson. **December 14, 2010. (Secret Richardson attorney for a lost pay-to-play Grand Jury case; wife of Charlie Daniels, appointed by Richardson in 2007 as Chief Justice of the state Supreme Court; with both major Richardson donors)**

Richardson, Bill. "Governor Bill Richardson to Consider Billy the Kid Pardon Petition." Press release. **December 16, 2010. (Floating the Randi McGinn petition)**

Garrett, Jarvis Patrick "JP." "No Subject." "... the petitioner for the pardon is Randi McGinn, so what's her link to Richardson ..." E-mail to Gale Cooper. **December 16, 2010.**

Wallace, William N. "Governor Richardson - Your imminent action ..." Letter to Bill Richardson. **December 21, 2010. (Opposition to Billy the Kid pardon)**

_____. "Subject: BtK/WnWallace." ... Ms. Cooper: I have sent the following to governor ..." E-mail to Gale Cooper. **December 21, 2010. (Copy of opposition letter)**

Garrett, Jarvis Patrick, JP. "Subj: Wallace draft." "I'm just sending you my thoughts ..." E-mail to William N. Wallace. **December 26, 2010. (I put the Garretts and Wallace together)**

Martinez, Edecio. "Billy the Kid to be Pardoned 130 Years Later." CBSNEWS.com. **December 27, 2010.**

Guarino, Mark. "Outgoing New Mexico Gov. Bill Richardson is considering a pardon for celebrated outlaw Billy the Kid. An informal e-mail poll shows support. But time is running out." Associated Press. **December 29, 2010.**

Levy, Glen. "Will Billy the Kid Be Pardoned? Governor Has Until Friday." TIME NewsFeed.com. December 29, 2010.

Garrett, Jarvis Patrick, JP. "RE: CNN Comment ... press letter revised." E-mail to Gale Cooper. **December 30, 2010.**

Ray, Alarie. "Subj: FW: Governor Bill Richardson to Announce Decision on Billy the Kid Pardon Request Tomorrow." E-mail forwarded to Gale Cooper. **December 30, 2013.**

Richardson, Bill. "Governor Richardson to Announce his decision on Billy the Kid Pardon Request Tomorrow." Press release. **December 30, 2010.**

Burke, Kelly David. "Billy the Kid Pardon?" FoxNews.com. **December 30, 2010.**

Garrett, Jarvis Patrick "JP." "No Subject" "yea!!! no pardon!!! =" E-mail to Gale Cooper. **December 31, 2010.**

Hopper, Jessica. "Gov. Bill Richardson: 'I've Decided Not to Pardon Billy the Kid.'" ABCNEWS.com. **December 31, 2010.**

Rojas, Rick. "No Pardon for Billy the Kid. New Mexico Gov. Bill Richardson says, 'The Romanticism appealed to me ... but the facts and evidence did not support it." *Los Angeles Times*. **December 31, 2010.**

Watson, Kathryn. "Alas, no pardon for Billy the Kid: New Mexico's Richardson says close call." washingtontimes.com. **December 31, 2010. (With "waste time" quote by Governor Susana Martinez)**

No Author. "Richardson Declines to Pardon Outlaw Billy the Kid." FoxNews.com. **December 31, 2010.**

Wallace, William N. "Your persistence ... enabled common sense." E-mail To Gale Cooper. **December 31, 2010.**

Lacey, Marc. "For 2nd Time in 131 Years, Billy the Kid is Denied Pardon." *New York Times*. Page A10. **January 1, 2011.**

OPEN RECORDS VIOLATION CASE:
Sandoval County District Cause No. D-1329-CV-2007-1364, Gale Cooper and De Baca County News, a New Mexico Corporation, PLAINTIFFS, vs. Rick Virden, Lincoln County Sheriff and Custodian of Records; and Steven M. Sederwall, Former Lincoln County Deputy Sheriff; and Thomas T. Sullivan, Former Lincoln County Sheriff and Former Lincoln County Deputy Sheriff, DEFENDANTS.

(For full listings see my 2014 book, Cracking the Billy the Kid Case Hoax: The Strange Plot to Exhume Billy the Kid, Convict Sheriff Pat Garrett of Murder, and become President of the United States)
THE FORGED DR. HENRY LEE REPORTS

Brown, Kevin. "I am enclosing the document Mr. Sederwall received from Dr. Lee ..." Letter. **February 18, 2010. (Unrequested Lee floorboard report which was a forgery)**

Lee, Henry and Calvin Ostler. "Forensic Research and Training Center Forensic Examination Report: "Examination of Lincoln County Court House." February 25, 2005. **(Given to me on February 18, 2010 by Kevin Brown and on April 6, 2010 by Nicole Werkmeister as a requested Lee report – but was Version I (9 pages) of an unrequested and forged floorboard report)**

Threet, Martin E. "I am returning the Lee report ..." Letter to Brown. (Rejecting and returning the Lee floorboard report) **February 25, 2010. (Not knowing it was a forgery, I returned it merely as unrequested)**

"Presentment Hearing." Transcript. **March 9, 2010. (Defendants gave the judge the unrequested (forged) Lee floorboard report as fulfilling records turnover; and lied that was the only record in Sederwall's possession)**

Werkmeister, Nicole. "Attached is the Forensic Examination Report From Dr. Henry Lee ..." Fax cover letter. **April 6, 2010. (Copy faxed of same unrequested (forged) Lee floorboard report from Brown)**

Brown, Kevin. "Enclosed please find a copy of another report dated February 25, 2005 which deals with the examination of furniture by Dr. Lee." Letter to Threet. **November 10, 2010. (Sending Lee's (forged) bench report; different font than the (forged) floorboard report)**

Lee, Henry and Calvin Ostler. "Forensic Research and Training Center Forensic Examination Report: "Examination of furniture from Pete Maxwell's of July 15, 1881." February 25, 2005. **(Given to me on November 10, 2010 as Lee bench report (16 pages) – but was forged)**

"Evidentiary Hearing on Plaintiff's Motion for Mandatory Order of Disclosure and Production." Transcript. **January 21, 2011. (Defendants gave forged Lee Floorboard report (9 pages) Version II as Exhibit F; and forged Lee bench report (16 pages) as Exhibit E)**

Lee, Henry and Calvin Ostler. "Forensic Research and Training Center Forensic Examination Report: "Examination of furniture from Pete Maxwell's of July 15, 1881." February 25, 2005. **(Given to Court on January 21, 2011 as Lee bench report (16 pages), Exhibit E – but was a forgery)**

Lee, Henry and Calvin Ostler. "Forensic Research and Training Center Forensic Examination Report: "Examination of Lincoln County Court House." February 25, 2005. **(Given to Court on January 21, 2011 as Lee floorboard report (9 pages), Exhibit F – but was its forged Version II)**

"Presentment Hearing." Transcript. **September 23, 2011. (I realized forgery was taking place and presented discrepancies in the Lee reports)**

Hearing on "Plaintiffs' Motion to Supplement the Record and a Request for Sanctions, and Co-Plaintiff's Motion For Attorney Fees." January 17, 2012 **(Sanctions** against Defendants requested for forged reports; and co-plaintiff requested fees for past attorneys. Judge granted 100% fees)

Eichwald, George P., District Judge. "Order on Plaintiffs Motion to Supplement the Record and Request for Award of Sanctions against Defendants." February 23, 2012. **(Ordered Sederwall to produce authentic Lee report)**

Lee, Henry and Calvin Ostler. "Forensic Research and Training Center Forensic Examination Report." February 25, 2005. **(Court-ordered turn-over to Plaintiffs on January 31, 2012 as "original," authentic, sole Lee report (25 pages) combining bench, floorboards, and wash stand)**

Hearing on "Plaintiffs' Second Motion to Supplement the Record and a Request for Sanctions." **May 31, 2012 (Sanctions requested for forged Lee reports)**

ORCHID CELLMARK RECORDS SUBPOENAED (RECEIVED 133 PAGES ON APRIL 20, 2012)

Griebel, Patrick J. Attorney for Scot Stinnett. "Subpoena for Production or Inspection to Laboratory Corporation of America." **March 29, 2012. (Non-IPRA subpoena of records from Orchid Cellmark parent company; got 133 pages of results of Lee's floorboards and bench, and Arizona exhumations; missing DNA matching results of bench to remains)**

SELECT RECORDS

Evidence Bag Photo. Chain of Custody Label: "Case No. 2003-274, Underside Bench 4. Date: 07,31,04." Below is written Orchid Cellmark Case and Specimen No. 4444-002B. **July 31, 2004. (Case 2003-274 was made Orchid Cellmark Case No. 4444)**

Ostler, Calvin D. "FedEx Mailing Envelope and tracking information to "Rick Staub, Orchid Cellmark." **August 3, 2004. (Specimens delivered August 4, 2004)**

"Orchid Cellmark Evidence Evaluation Worksheet Case No. 4444 A and B." **August 16, 2004. (Identifying Calvin Ostler as client; listing Lee's floorboard and bench specimens)**

"Orchid Cellmark Evidence Evaluation Worksheet Case No. 4444." **April 13, 2006. (Listing specimens from John Miller-William Hudspeth exhumations.**

"Orchid Cellmark Chain of Custody for Case No. 4444." **May 19, 2005. (On date of John Miller exhumation and signed by Orchid Cellmark Director Rick Staub with the south and north grave specimens he collected listed)**

"Orchid Cellmark Laboratory Report - Forensic Identity - Mitochondrial Analysis for 4444." **January 26, 2009. (Listing specimens for reports requested by me: Lee's from bench and Orchid Cellmark's from the Arizona graves.)**

GALE COOPER AS PRO SE (For full listings see my 2014 book, *Cracking the Billy the Kid Case Hoax: The Strange Plot to Exhume Billy the Kid, Convict Sheriff Pat Garrett of Murder, and become President of the United States*)

No Author. Hearing for Plaintiff Gale Cooper's Motion to Request Award of Her Costs and Damages From Defendants and to Request Award of Sanctions Against Defendants." Transcript. December 18, 2013. **(I won!)**

Eichwald, George P. Judge. "Findings of Fact and Conclusions of Law and Order of the Court." **May 15, 2014. (Plaintiff Gale Cooper prevailed)**

_____ "Final Judgment." **March 8, 2017. (Plaintiff Gale Cooper prevailed)**

W.C. JAMESON'S 21st CENTURY "BRUSHY BILL" BACKING BOOKS

THE JAMESON BOOKS (CHRONOLOGICAL)

Jameson, W.C. *Billy the Kid: Beyond the Grave.* Boulder, Lanham, Maryland: Taylor Trade Publishing. **2005**. **(A repeat of the "Brushy Bill" imposter hoax)**

_____. *Billy the Kid: The Lost Interviews.* Clearwater, Florida: Garlic Press Publishing. **2012**. (Reprint 2017). **(Forged rewriting of the 1949 Morrison transcript of "Brushy" to fake dialogue to update the hoax)**

_____. *Pat Garrett: The Man Behind the Badge.* Boulder, Colorado: Taylor Trade Publishing. **2016**. **(Defamation of Pat Garrett, "Brushy Bill" as a quoted authority, and "Billy the Kid Case" hoaxing as evidence to claim Garrett murdered an innocent victim instead of Billy the Kid)**

_____. *Cold Case Billy the Kid: Investigating History's Mysteries.* Guilford, Connecticut: Twodot. **2018**. **(Fusing the "Brushy" hoax and "Billy the Kid Case" hoax to argue for "Brushy" as Billy the Kid)**

SOURCES FOR DEBUNKING CLAIMS (CHRONOLOGICAL)

(SEE: sources debunking "Brushy Bill" Roberts; see "Billy the Kid Case" hoax)

RELEVANT TO "BRUSHY BILL'S" FAKE GENEALOGY

Tunstill, William A. *Billy the Kid and Me Were the Same: A Documentary on the Life of Billy the Kid.* Roswell, New Mexico: Western History Research Center. **1988**. **("Brushy"-backer faking a genealogy)**

RELEVANT TO DENYING WILLIAM H. BONNEY'S CORONER'S JURY REPORT'S EXISTENCE

(SEE: William H. Bonney, Coroner's Jury Report; and Patrick F. Garrett, Reward)

RELEVANT TO FAKING BILLY THE KID'S LETTERS AS WRITTEN BY OTHERS

Cooper, Gale. *Billy the Kid's Writings, Words, and Wit.* Gelcour Books: Albuquerque: New Mexico. **2012**. **(Analysis of Billy Bonney's handwriting to show same person wrote all of them)**

RELEVANT TO FAKING "INVESTIGATION" OF JOHN TUNSTALL'S MURDER

Gonzales, Florencio. Deposition to Frank Warner Angel. **June 8, 1878**. Frank Warner Angel report, Pages 314-319 from *In the Matter of the Examination of the Causes and Circumstances of the Death of John H. Tunstall a British Subject.* Report filed October 4, 1878. Angel Report. Records of the Justice Department. Record Group 60. Class 44 Litigation Files. Container 21. National Archives and Records Administration. U.S. Department of Justice. Washington, D.C. or Angel Report in Interior Department Papers 1850-1907; Appointments Division and Subsequent Actions. Microfilm File Case Number 44-4-8-3. Record Group 48. Microfilm No. M750. Roll 1. National Archives and Records Administration. U.S. Department of Justice. Washington, D.C. **(Showing that Steve Sederwall's claim that Gonzales was involved in a cover-up of Tunstall's murder was wrong)**

Appel, Daniel M. Deposition to Frank Warner Angel. **July 1, 1878**. Frank Warner

Angel report, Pages 314-319 from *In the Matter of the Examination of the Causes and Circumstances of the Death of John H. Tunstall a British Subject*. Report filed October 4, 1878. Angel Report. Records of the Justice Department. Record Group 60. Class 44 Litigation Files. Container 21. National Archives and Records Administration. U.S. Department of Justice. Washington, D.C. or Angel Report in Interior Department Papers 1850-1907; Appointments Division and Subsequent Actions. Microfilm File Case Number 44-4-8-3. Record Group 48. Microfilm No. M750. Roll 1. National Archives and Records Administration. U.S. Department of Justice. Washington, D.C. **(Contradicting Steve Sederwall's description of Appel's autopsy report on John Tunstall)**

Nolan, Frederick W. *The Life and Death of John Henry Tunstall*. Albuquerque, New Mexico: The University of New Mexico Press. **1965**. **(With Tunstall's Coroner's Jury Report, page 285; and Daniel Appel's autopsy report, pages 286-287)**

RELEVANT TO FAKING "BUCKSHOT" ROBERTS KILLING

Catron, Thomas Benton. "Case No. 411. The United States vs. Charles Bowdry [Bowdre], Doc Scurlock, Henry Brown, Henry Antrim alias "Kid," John Middleton, Stephen Stevens, John Scroggins, George Coe and Frederick Waite." **June 21, 1878**. Herman B. Weisner Papers, ca. 1957-1992. New Mexico State University Library at Las Cruces. Rio Grande Historical Collections. Accession No. Ms 0249. Box 1. B-Folder 4. Name: Andrew Roberts Indictment. **(Describes the "Buckshot" Roberts killing and his single fatal would, contradicting the fabrication used of A.N. Blazer)**

RELEVANT TO FAKING PAT GARRETT AS A NON-LEGITIMATE DEPUTY U.S. MARSHAL

Wild, Azariah F. "Daily Reports of U. S. Secret Service Agents, 1875-1937." Microfilm T-915. Record Group 87. Microfilm Roll 308 (July 1, 1879 - June 30, 1881; October 13, 1880; October 21, 1880; October 29, 1880; January 3, 1881 (replacing his name with crossed-out John Hurley); January 25, 1881 (letter praising Garrett's service). National Archives and Records Department. Department of the Treasury. Secret Service Division. Washington, D.C. **(Showing legal appointment)**

RELEVANT TO FAKING THE LOCATION OF THE COURTHOUSE-JAIL'S ARMORY

Caperton, Thomas J. *Historic Structure Report. Lincoln State Monument. Lincoln New Mexico*. Santa Fe, New Mexico: Office of Cultural Affairs, Historic Preservation Division. **1983**. **(Its Lincoln courthouse's second floor diagram (Page 252) is used as a fix-up to place the armory correctly, instead of "Brushy's" confabulated location opposite Garrett's office)**

RELEVANT TO FAKING DEPUTY BELL'S BLOOD AT TOP OF STAIRS

Poe, Sophie. *Buckboard Days*. Albuquerque, New Mexico: University of New Mexico Press. **1964**. **(Making up her location of blood)**

RELEVANT TO FAKING PETER MAXWELL'S EXTERNAL BEDROOM DOOR AS ABSENT

Armstrong, Mel and John McCarty. "Kid Dobbs Interviews: An Interview with Garrett H. 'Kid' Dobbs at Farmington, New Mexico," on September 12, 1942, with Mel Armstrong and John McCarty [with] Garrett H. Kid Dobbs in his Home in Farmington, New Mexico, Thursday Morning, October 22, 1942, In the Presence of

Mrs. Dobbs and Pat Flynn. J.D. White, Amarillo, Heard Part of the Final Statements of this Interview Re. Billy the Kid's Death." **October 22, 1942.** John L. McCarty Papers. Amarillo Public Library. (**Old-timer malarkey claiming no outside door in Maxwell bedroom used as a source**)

Author Unknown. (Falsely attributed to Gregory Scott Smith). "The Death of Billy the Kid: A New Scenario?" Using "Kid Dobbs Interviews: An Interview with Garrett H. 'Kid' Dobbs at Farmington, New Mexico," on September 12, 1942, with Mel Armstrong and John McCarty" with undated commentary attributed incorrectly to Gregory Scott Smith, Monument Manager at the Fort Sumner State Monument, and using mislabeled diagram of Fort Sumner Commanding Officer's Quarters as the Maxwell house. Fort Sumner, New Mexico, State Monument files. (**Article using Kid Dobbs's fakery with added mislabeled diagram of Fort Sumner's Commanding Officer's Quarters as being the Maxwell house, to fabricate no outside door to the Maxwell bedroom**)

Boze Bell, Bob. (With Steve Sederwall) "Caught With His Pants Down? Billy the Kid Vs Pat Garrett. One Door Closes." **August, 2010.** *True West.* Volume 57. (**Using wrongly alleged author, Gregory Scott Smith's, "Death of Billy the Kid" article to claim no outside door, plus Sederwall hoaxing "CSI" proof of it by Dr. Henry Lee's fake washstand investigation. It was recycled by Sederwall in W.C. Jameson's *Cold Case Billy the Kid*)**

RELEVANT TO FAKING FACE DOWN CORPSE

Traylor, Leslie. "Facts Regarding the Escape of Billy the Kid." *Frontier Times.* **July, 1936.** Pages 506-513 (on Page 509). FrontierTimesMagazine.com. (**About his Jesus Silva interview on identifying Billy's body**)

Otero, Miguel, *The Real Billy the Kid.* New York: Rufus Rockwell Wilson. **1936.** (**Claim that Jesus Silva for shot Billy Bonney face down. But Otero had no first-hand knowledge, and the book was 55 years after the event.**)

RELEVANT TO FAKING OLD PETER MAXWELL AS A COOK DENYING GARRETT SHOT BILLY

Avant, Bundy. (Told to Arthur Clements). "The Bundy Avant Story: New Mexico in the days when a thin population was intent on bettering itself and each man could devise his own method for 'getting' while getting' was good.' " (Part One) *True West.* **May-June, 1978,** Volume 25, Number 5. (**Old-timer malarkey about a "Peter Maxwell" in the San Andres Mountains telling Avant that Garrett did not kill Billy the Kid**)

No Author. "Las Vegas." *The Albuquerque Citizen.* **June 28, 1898.** Page 2, Column 3. NewspaperArchive.com. (**Peter Maxwell death notice about his Fort Sumner area residence and death**)

INDEX

Abbott, E.C. "Teddy Blue" – 92, 128, 227
Abbott, George – 29, 33
Abbott, Harold – 29-30, 32-33, 36-38, 54, 246, 390, 462
"ABC Good Morning America" – 612-613
Abeline, Kansas – 203
Able, John – 380
Able, Martile – 238, 248, 251, 380
Abraham Lincoln Library and Museum – 182-183
Abraham, Louis – 385
Abreu, Manuel – 46, 58, 514, 569
Abreu, Odelia – 403, 702
Abreu, Stella – 514-515, 569, 576; **Billy the Kid Museum with alleged Peter Maxwell furniture of:** 514-515, 569, 576, 578-580, 721; with carpenter's bench gotten from a local man by: 514, 569h
Acton, Scott – 199, 454, 457-459, 483, 646, 633
Acuña, Mark Anthony – 546, 556-557, 625, 728
Adams, I.A. – 308
Adams, Ramon F. - 317
Agler, Don – 528
Airy, Helen – 383, 532, 586; *Whatever Happened to Billy the Kid?* **by** (See Helen Airy)
Alamogordo, New Mexico – 29, 33, 35, 375, 476
Alamogordo News – 29, 37-38, 54, 92, 246, 248, 346
Albuquerque Citizen – 710
Albuquerque Genealogical Library – 15
Albuquerque Journal – 50, 188, 249-250, 256, 259, 292, 481, 496, 533, 572-573, 577, 579, 581, 590, 596, 598, 727
Albuquerque Museum of Art and History – 562, 570

Albuquerque, New Mexico – 66, 191, 237, 248, 255, 259, 285, 514, 533, 558, 562-563, 569, 599-600, 613, 632, 635, 721
Allison, Malinda E. – 168
Allison, William E. "Bill" – 168, 417, 424, 428, 440, 536, 646, 648, 656-657
Amarillo, Texas – 704
Amos, Donna Jenice – 489
Amos-Staats, Joani – 489
Analla, Pablo – 151
Anaya, A.P. "Paco" – 44-47, 62, 211, 389-390, 462, 516-517, 714; **two Coroner's Jury Reports faked by:** 44-47, 389, 462, 517, 670, 714; *I Buried Billy* **by:** 62, 211, 389-390, 517
Anaya, Louis – 516
Andress, Lipscomb, and Peticolas Law Firm – 44, 239-240, 255, 307
Andress, Ted – 239-240, 250, 407, 460
Angel, Frank Warner – 93-95, 97, 109, 111-112, 126, 131-132, 219, 226, 246, 323, 330, 378, 398, 432, 497, 678-679, 681, 684; **reports of:** 93 (See William H. Bonney deposition)
Anti-Horse Thief Association – 179, 249, 254, 369, 372, 651
Antrim, Catherine McCarty – 276-277, 281, 314-315, 371, 409, 464, 477, 480, 487-492, 494, 502, 519, 549, 552, 557, 592, 596, 598, 619-620, 623, 628, 727; **fake photograph of:** 371; **exhumation attempt on** (See "Billy the Kid Case" hoax)
Antrim, Henry - (see William H. Bonney)
Antrim, William Henry (see William H. Bonney)
Antrim, Joseph "Josie" – 104, 277, 409

Antrim, William Henry
  Harrison – 104, 276, 314, 317, 428
Appel, Daniel – 678, 684-686
Arenso, Cabra – 16
Argentina – 164, 369
Arizona Highway – 352
Arizona Pioneers' Home – 588
Arizona Pioneers' Home
  Cemetery – 586-587, 589
Arkinda, Arkansas – 165
Armijo, Jose E. – 42-43, 462
armory (see Lincoln County
  courthouse-jail)
Ashenfelter, Singleton M. – 446-448, 450, 463-464, 655; **article by with fake Billy the Kid corpse description:** 447-448
Ashton, Sarah – 192
Atkin, George – 523
Autry, Gene – 284-285
Avant, Bundy – 709-712, 721
Awly, J. – 131
Axtell, Samuel Beach – 93-94, 108, 110-112, 132, 243, 398, 412, 601-602, 680-682, 719-720
Baca, Bonificio – 357
Baca, Saturnino – 111, 158, 357, 684-685
Bailey, David – 730
Baker, Frank – 108, 116, 121, 130-133, 142-143, 320, 682
Baker, Paul – 53, 408, 472, 486
Ball, Eve – 320, 372
Bank of Roswell – 59
Banks, Leo W. – 574, 586, 589, 591
Barlow Billy – 245, 249, 252-253, 255, 258-259, 262, 269, 284, 364-368, 388, 403, 408, 423, 440-444, 448, 450, 463, 468, 472, 476, 482, 487, 494-496, 522, 536-539, 541-542, 544, 583, 646-647, 650, 655, 666-670, 676, 712, 719, 739
Barnes, Seba – 177
Barnes, Sidney – 116, 564
Barrow-Rutledge Funeral
  Chapel – 263

Barnum, P.T. – 163, 263, 287
Barrier, Adolph – 97, 107
Barto, Pennsylvania – 413, 654
Bass, Sam – 177-179
Bataan Memorial Building – 32
Bates, Sebrian – 687
Baton Rouge, Louisiana – 383-384
Bean, Frederick – 197-199, 217, 232, 293-294, 428-430, 458, 468, 473, 522, 536, 648, 653, 656; **informing C.L. Sonnichsen about the Acton photoanalysis by:** 458; *The Return of the Outlaw Billy the Kid* **co-authored by (See W.C. Jameson); alleged locating and transcribing of Morrison's "Brushy" tapes by:** 217, 232, 293, 536, 653, 656; **alternate claim that transcribing Morrison's tapes was by Bill Allison:** 536; **W.C. Jameson's claim that Bean found the Roberts family Bible in "Brushy's" trunk:** 428-430 (See Oliver Pleasant "Brushy Bill" Roberts, William V. Morrison, C.L. Sonnichsen)
Beaver Smith's Saloon – 114
Beckwith family – 143
Beckwith, Henry – 143
Beckwith, John – 143
Beckwith, Robert W. "Bob" – 92, 143, 147, 337-338, 452, 661, 688
Bell, James W. – 104, 120-121, 126-127, 244, 256-257, 269, 291, 303-304, 344, 357, 360, 379, 422, 452, 476, 479, 482, 494, 498, 500-501, 525-528, 539, 540-541, 544-545, 561, 563, 566-567, 579, 581-585, 601, 606, 618, 625, 639-630, 638; 665; 715-719; **"Case 2003-274 Probable Cause Statement" sub-investigation for killing of** (See "Billy the Kid Case" hoax); **Dr. Henry Lee's fake**

forensics for shooting of
(See Henry Lee, "Billy the Kid
Case" hoax)
Bennett, Ray – 594
Bernstein, Morris – 351, 386
"Big Casino" – 114
Bill Kurtis Productions (See Bill
Kurtis)
Billy the Kid (see William H.
Bonney)
BillytheKidCase.com website (See
Steve Sederwall)
"Billy the Kid Case" (See "Billy
the Kid Case" hoax)
"Billy the Kid Case" hoax (Lincoln
County Sheriff's Department
Case No. 2003-274, De Baca
County Sheriff's Department
Case No. 03-06-136-01) – 7-8,
103, 284, 346, 365, 370, 463-
464, 467-468, 471-642, 645,
647, 652, 666-667, 669-672,
675-676, 687, 690-691, 694,
698, 706, 708, 712-713, 715,
718-719, 723-724, 730-731, 743;
summary of: 471-473, 480-
487; **fake announcement
news for:** 473-479; **OMI
exhumation permit refusals
for:** 488-493; **hoax documents
for:** "Mayor's Report" for: 494-
496; "Case 2003-274: "Probable
Cause Statement" for Pat
Garrett as a murderer for: 497-
519, 563, 567-568, 573, 576-
577, 579, 586, 618, 621, 645,
681, 684, 698, 712-713, 715;
sub-investigation in: 500-501,
579, 618, 638; fake Overton
Affidavit for: 520-521, 712;
abandoned "Probable Cause
Statement" for: 522-545, 645,
647, 657; "U.S. Marshals
Service and Billy the Kid"
Addendum for: 563-568;
exhumation petitions for: 546-
557; **hoax TV documentary
"Investigating History: Billy
the Kid" for:** 558-562; **fake
forensics for:** 568-584; faking
carpenter's bench blood of Billy
the Kid for: 569-576, 743-744;
faking Billy the Kid shooting
scene for: 576-579; faking
Deputy Bell shooting for: 579-
582; faking DNA results for:
582-584; **illegal exhumations
of John Miller and William
Hudspeth for:** 585-592;
**"Requiem for Billy the Kid"
movie using:** 593-594;
**attempt to exhume "Brushy
Bill" for:** 595-596; **stopping
pardon of "Brushy Bill" for:**
597-614; Pardon Petition in:
600-608; **open records act
litigation against:** 615-640;
hoaxers' "Memorandum" for:
617-629; hoaxer's forging of Dr.
Lee reports for: 630-637, 675,
715-716, 721-723; judge's ruling
on: 638-640 (See hoaxers: Bill
Richardson, Bill Robins III,
Paul Hutton, Henry Lee, Tom
Sullivan, Gary Graves, Steve
Sederwall, David Turk, Alan
Morel, Sherry Tippett, Henry
Quintero, Ted Hartley, Rick
Staub, Randi McGinn) (See
Orchid Cellmark Laboratory)
Billy the Kid Museum in Canton,
Texas – 476
Billy the Kid Outlaw Gang – 166,
197, 516, 728
Bingham, George "Red" – 322
Blachley, Lou – 649
Black Hills of South Dakota –
175-176, 179, 208, 317, 369
Blandano, Manuel – 359
Blazer, A.N. – 683
Blazer, Joseph – 195, 209-210,
273, 332, 352, 683
Blazer, Paul – 195, 209-210, 229,
236, 265, 273-274, 282-285,
287, 352, 406, 471, 649
Blazer's Mill – 84, 119, 229, 244,
273, 331-332, 421, 683
Bommersbach, Jana – 468

Bonita, Arizona – 105, 318
Bonito River – 111, 290, 337
Bonney, William H. "Billy" (William Henry McCarty, Henry Antrim, Billy Bonney, Billy the Kid) – 6, 9-18, 20-30, 32-36, 53, 67-92, 96, 98, 100, 103-160, 163, 197, 211-214, 216, 219-224, 227-228, 236, 239, 243, 247, 258, 290, 299-300, 303-304, 307, 310, 321, 331, 334, 340-341, 344, 348-349, 372, 378, 386, 391, 399-400, 405, 411, 417, 422, 424, 435, 446, 451, 454-459, 542, 603, 607, 648-649, 652, 672, 680, 690, 698-699, 735, 739, 742; **history of:** 103-122; **contemporary champions of:** 123-128; **writings, deposition, testimonies, and words of:** 85, 129-160, 219-224, 648;   **bilingual in Spanish:** 104, 123, 127, 219, 227-228, 405, 424, 698-699; **outlaw myth of:** 67-84, 86, 91, 100, 116-117, 121-123, 128, 155, 163, 211, 236, 299-300, 303, 307, 334, 341, 386, 411, 542, 603, 680, 690, 735; **"Billy the Kid" moniker of:** 85-92; **tintype of :** 53, 98, 100, 109, 116-117, 197, 212, 244, 258, 290, 303-304, 321, 348-349, 372, 417, 446, 451, 454-459, 649, 652, 672, 739, 742; **Paulita Maxwell as sweetheart of** (See Paulita Maxwell); **pardon bargain with Lew Wallace:** 6, 74, 85, 94-95, 113, 117-118, 124, 129, 139, 144, 149, 153, 211, 213-214, 216, 227, 239, 243, 247, 310, 331, 340-341, 344, 378, 405, 422, 435, 607, 648; **pardon bargain with Secret Service by:** 96, 117; **Wallace rewards for:** 20-28, 87-88, 391, 399-400; **Coroner's Jury Report of:** 9-18, 20, 22, 29-30, 32-36; **1961-1962 exhumation attempt on** (See Lois Telfer); **2003-2004 exhumation attempt on** (See "Billy the Kid Case" hoax)

Borden, Marion H. – 188, 212, 471
Bordley, William – 563
Bosque Grande – 69-70, 112, 321
Bosque Redondo – 115, 321, 431, 701
Bowdre, Charles "Charlie" – 58, 86, 104, 108-109, 112, 115-116, 118-119, 121, 127, 136, 150, 157, 243, 331-332, 348, 361, 363, 372, 422, 438-439, 446, 467, 472, 491, 500, 543, 683
Bowdre, Manuela – 112, 361, 543
Bowlin, Joe – 166, 516
Bowlin, Marlyn Estes Perez – 166, 516, 728, 730
Boyle, Andrew "Andy" – 337, 687
Boze Bell, Bob – 284, 481, 483, 559, 560, 645, 691, 706; *True West* magazine of See Bob Boze Bell; "Billy the Kid Case" hoax)
Brady, Arcadio – 248, 256
Brady, Nadine – 533
Brady, William – 82, 97, 106-112, 116, 119-121, 126-127, 130-131, 135, 137-138, 154, 158, 195, 217, 224, 242, 244, 248, 250-251, 253, 256, 251, 269-270, 290-291, 295, 304, 326-327, 329-331, 340, 346, 353-354, 372, 378, 382, 386, 402, 419-422, 431-433, 436-437, 439, 475, 497, 524, 533, 550, 552, 560-561, 593, 601-603, 606-607, 659-660, 664-665, 679, 681-682, 685, 688, 720, 740
Brady, William E. – 248
Bradford, Guy W. – 49
Ballard, Luticia – 168
Branch, Tom – 478
Brazel, Wayne – 284
Breeden, William – 10, 18, 20, 22-25, 29-32, 37, 39-40, 42-43, 47-48, 51, 54, 80, 388, 392-394, 396-399, 462, 517 (See Coroner's Jury Report)
Breihan, Carl W. – 39, 43-44, 186-187, 189, 205, 209, 265-266, 285, 352, 410-411

Brewer, Richard "Dick" – 84, 108-109, 121, 124, 126, 130-131, 133-135, 242, 274, 290, 332, 420, 659, 684
Brininstool, E.A. – 59, 505
Briscoe, Joe – 42, 114, 346, 437
Bristol, Warren H. – 107, 113-114, 119-120, 154, 247, 353, 386, 422, 524, 664, 677, 740
Brockway, William E. – 67-68, 71, 672, 675, 689-691
Brooks, James J. – 96, 116-117, 500, 695-696 (See Azariah Wild)
Brothers, Mary Hudson – 187
Brown, "Hank" – 353-354
Brown, Henry Newton – 119, 126, 135, 601
Brown, Kevin – 630-631, 633-634
Brown, Mollie – 168
Brownsville, Texas – 370, 379, 742
Brunswick, M. – 22
"Brushy Bill" hoax (See Oliver Pleasant Roberts, William V. Morrison, C.L. Sonnichsen, W.C. Jameson, Frederick Bean)
"Brushy Bill" Roberts - (see Oliver Pleasant Roberts)
Buffalo Gap, Texas – 172, 175, 178, 206, 208, 253, 255, 257, 260-261, 264, 269, 309, 313, 425
Bugliosi, Vincent – 571; *Outrage: The Five Reasons that O.J. Simpson Got Away With Murder* by: 571
Burgess, William B. – 98, 350, 407
Burgess, W.H. – 349
Burns, Walter Noble – 67, 83-85, 97-98, 189, 211, 218-219, 222, 244, 247, 260, 303-304, 306, 309, 316-317, 319-320, 324-331, 333-334, 336-338, 341-342, 349-352, 358-361, 363-364, 368, 404, 407, 452-453, 738, 751; *The Saga of Billy the Kid* by (See Walter Noble Burns)
Burt, Billy – 127, 360-361, 379, 526, 719

Cahill, Frank "Windy" – 105, 108-109, 116, 120-121, 318, 344, 419, 523
Campbell, Billy – 113, 140, 144, 213, 243, 340, 409-412, 422, 434, 561, 603-605, 661-662
Campbell, Edward M. – 187
Campbell, Nell – 188
Cannes Film Festival – 484, 593, 676
Canton, Texas – 165, 172-173, 313, 370, 474, 476
Capitan Mountains – 121, 141, 329, 360, 381, 433, 680
Capitan, New Mexico – 475, 478, 481, 494, 559, 565, 590, 626, 632, 634, 709, 725
"Capitan Village Hall News" – 494
Caplan, Sara – 571
Cardon, Bill – 185; **Dautrich Reality Company of:** 185
Careage, J.C. – 187
Carlsbad Current Argus – 187
Carlsbad, New Mexico – 187, 253, 309, 377, 380, 739-740
Carlson, Raymond – 352
Carlyle, Jim – 70-71, 118, 121, 150-151, 218, 235, 243, 297, 306, 345-346, 386, 422, 437, 453
Carrizozo, New Mexico Territory – 141, 238, 298, 356, 381, 520
Carson, Kit – 176, 178, 181, 232
Carter, Julie – 570, 574, 579, 588, 590, 592, 690
Casey, Robert – 106
Catron, Thomas Benton – 22, 63, 80, 99-100, 104, 106-107, 109-112, 114-116, 119-120, 128, 136-137, 213, 225, 283, 324, 326, 352-353, 393, 397, 399, 432, 606, 662, 664, 682-683, 685-686; **Federal indictment No. 411 of Regulators by:** 119, 242, 244, 447 (See Santa Fe Ring)
Caypless, Edgar – 120, 154, 211, 213, 226, 244, 247, 301, 351-353, 453
"CBS News" – 612

Cedric, Nikki – 570
Chandler, Howard – 648
Chapman, Huston – 74-76, 94, 112-114, 138-139, 144, 213, 240, 243, 295, 322, 328, 340-343, 353, 386, 404, 410-412, 422, 434-436, 499, 561, 602-603, 605, 662-664
Chávez, Florencio – 110
Chávez y Chávez, José – 110, 145, 148-149, 339
Cherry, Doris – 570, 572, 574-575, 582
Chesley, Hervey – 202
Chisum, John Simpson – 79, 106-109, 143, 151, 157, 181, 201, 225, 236, 242-243, 249, 258, 262, 290, 321, 323-326, 332-334, 343, 346, 361-363, 375, 431, 435, 468, 602, 677, 691, 710, 739
Cisneros, Ben – 251
Cisneros house – 304, 331, 433
Citizens Bank of Roswell – 59
Claiborne Parish, Louisiana – 114
Clanin, Doug – 611
Clarkson, Lana – 571
Clifford, Frank – 693-694; *Deep Trials in the Old Southwest* by (See Frank Clifford)
Cline, Donald – 164-167, 169, 172-173, 180-181, 185-186, 190-191, 198-199, 204-207, 228, 241, 264, 309-310, 313-314, 317, 369, 381, 425, 651; *Brushy Bill Roberts: I Wasn't Billy the Kid* by (See Don Cline)
Cody, Buffalo Bill – 164, 174-175, 208, 369, 374; **Buffalo Bill Cody Wild West Show of** (See Buffalo Bill Cody)
Coe, Frank – 108-109, 123-124, 219, 248, 259, 431, 533
Coe, George – 92, 109, 119, 123-124, 211, 259, 323, 329, 332, 375, 377-378, 709; *Frontier Fighter* by (See George Coe)
Coe, Wilbur – 248
Coghlan, Pat – 112

Colfax County War – 5, 218
Conovair, J. – 131
Cook, David – 692-694
Cook, Eliza Jane (See Eliza Jane McKinney Cook)
Cook, Eliza Jane McKinney – 694
Cook, Jim (Lane) – 691-692; *Lane of the Llano: Being the Story of Jim (Lane) Cook as Told to T.M. Pearce* by (See Jim (Lane) Cook
Cook, John – 692-693
Cook, John Enoch – 694
Cook, Margaret Jane – 693
Cook, Sarah – 692-693
Copeland, John – 110, 719
Corbet, Sam R. – 141, 213, 357
Corle, Edwin – 271-272
Corn, Robert – 719
Coroner's Jury Report (see William H. Bonney)
Cosgrove, Michael "Mike" – 155, 690
Coyote Spring – 70, 118, 297
Crawford, Charles "Charlie" – 686
Crawfordsville, Indiana – 89, 250
Crawfordsville Review – 90
Crawfordsville Saturday Evening Journal – 334, 411
Croy, Homer – 209
Cuba – 370-371, 651
Cuellar, Kathyrn – 233, 737
Cunningham, Eugene – 41, 371; *Triggernometry* by (See Eugene Cunningham)
Cureton Brothers Ranch – 362
Cureton, Jim – 362
Dalton gang – 178, 369
Dalton, J. Frank – 174, 205-210, 212, 295, 309, 381, 384, 411, 423, 646; **as impersonating Jesse James** (See J. Frank Dalton)
Daniels, Charles "Charlie" – 617
Davidson, Morrey – 207
Davis, George – 130-131, 143
De Baca County, New Mexico – 7, 41-42, 247, 390, 409, 477, 480-481, 488, 494, 546, 556-557,

565, 620, 641, 728, 730
De Baca County Sheriff's Department Case No. 03-06-136-01 (See "Billy the Kid Case" hoax)
Dedrick brothers livery – 112, 117-118
Dedrick, Dan – 112, 117, 119, 321, 349, 690
Dedrick, Mose – 117
Dedrick, Sam – 117
Denton, Cyclone – 317
DeZulovich, Marvis – 563
Diaz, Porfiro – 370, 650
Dike, Jeanine – 587, 591-592
Dillon, Matt – 474
Dills, Lucius – 680
Dobbs, Garrett H. "Kid" – 704
Dodge City, Kansas – 317, 321, 372, 739
Dolan, James – 94, 100, 106, 108, 110-114, 116-117, 120, 130-131, 133, 138, 140, 143-144, 158, 243, 290, 322-324, 326, 337, 340, 353, 356, 397, 410, 419-422, 431-432, 434-435, 498, 524, 560-561, 601-605, 661-664, 678, 680-681, 686, 692
Donaldson, Sam – 464
Doña Ana County, New Mexico – 113, 186, 213, 243, 247, 354-355, 524
Dudley, Nathan Augustus Monroe – 85-86, 94-95, 111-114, 129, 144-149, 168, 211, 219, 225-226, 242, 290, 328, 334-339, 342, 386, 422, 425-426, 434, 436, 452, 602, 660, 662-663, 684-687; **Court of Inquiry for:** 85-86, 94-95, 114, 129, 211, 219, 225-226, 242, 306, 328, 335, 338-339, 342, 386, 452, 684, 687 (See Lincoln County War Battle; William H. Bonney prosecution testimony)
Dyer, Robert – 197, 199
Dykes, J.C. – 318
Ealy, Taylor – 331, 678
East, James H. "Jim" – 98, 211, 243-244, 247, 348-350, 404, 407, 438
Eberhard, Ola – 181, 229, 655
Eddy County News – 187
Ellis, Benjamin J. "Ben" – 686
Ellis, Isaac – 158, 305, 354
El Paso Herald – 374-375
El Paso Herald Post – 191, 249, 254, 533
El Paso Historical Society – 192
El Paso Rotary Club – 282, 323, 340, 342, 351, 387
El Paso Sunland News Bureau – 196
El Paso, Texas – 30, 185, 189, 250-251, 254-256, 287, 307, 376, 381, 410, 737
El Paso Times – 33, 37-38, 40, 42, 54, 66, 124, 189, 191, 194, 238, 272, 533, 719, 738
Emerson, Joseph – 168, 171
Emerson, Paul – 168, 171
Ervin, Robert P. – 32
Evans, Jessie – 105, 108, 113, 130-131, 144, 181, 205, 295, 318-320, 322, 340, 404, 410-411, 423, 497, 535, 560, 603, 685
Executive Record Book – 23, 25-26, 47, 388, 391, 393-395, 398, 400
Farmington, New Mexico Territory – 123, 707
Fecteau, Louie – 496
Feinsilber, Anne – 593-594; **"Requiem for Billy the Kid" by** (See Anne Feinsilber)
Feliz River (Rio) – 106-107, 323, 431
Feliz River Ranch (See John H. Tunstall)
Ferguson, Sara Elizabeth – 165-168, 313, 315, 372, 425 (See Henry Oliver Roberts)
Fidler, Larry Paul –571
First National Bank of Santa Fe – 100
First Presbyterian Church of Santa Fe – 276-277

Fitzpatrick, George – 44-46, 286, 389, 517, 668
Flynn, Pat – 704
Forensitec – 587, 591
Fort Grant, Arizona – 105, 318
Fort Sill, Texas – 209, 586
Fort Smith, Arkansas – 369, 739
Fort Stanton, New Mexico Territory – 94-95, 106, 139-142, 144, 194, 228, 242, 306-307, 336, 342, 354-355, 404, 411, 421, 436, 452, 523, 604, 664, 678, 684, 686, 740-741
Fort Stockton – 322
Fort Sumner, New Mexico Territory – 3-4, 6, 9-11, 16, 18-19, 23, 27, 30, 35, 38, 42, 44-46, 49-50, 57-60, 62-63, 65, 68-69, 71, 78-79, 86-87, 97-98, 103-104, 112, 114-118, 121, 150, 166, 182-183, 212, 214, 224, 232, 239, 244-245, 247-249, 252-256, 259, 262-263, 265-266, 269, 288, 290-291, 293, 295, 306, 308, 321, 343-344, 346-350, 357, 361-364, 366-368, 375, 383, 387, 390, 396, 401-403, 418, 422, 431, 439-442, 444-447, 449, 454-455, 462-464, 471-472, 475, 477-480, 482, 487, 492-494, 499-503, 505-506, 510-513, 515, 517, 519, 521-522, 524, 529-533, 536-546, 549-550, 556-557, 559-562, 568-570, 577-578, 580, 594, 596-597, 599-600, 606, 611, 617-618, 620-625, 629, 642, 647, 663, 666, 670, 672, 690, 697-698, 700-701, 704-705, 709-713, 715, 721, 724, 726-730, 738-739, 742
Fort Sumner State Monument – 700-701, 704
Fountain, Albert Jennings – 119, 154, 213, 226, 343, 352-353, 366, 436, 606, 663-664, 710
Fountain, Jack – 366-367, 440, 450, 667
Fowler, E.B. – 226

FoxNews.com – 612-613
Franklin, Barbara – 292
French, Jim "Frenchie" – 86, 109-110, 601, 681
Fritz, Charles "Charlie" – 420, 682
Fritz, Emil – 94, 97, 106, 419-420, 431-432, 678; **life insurance policy of** (See Emil Fritz)
Fulginiti, Laura – 484, 587-588, 591, 724; **denial of John Miller buck teeth by:** 494, 591, 724; **denial John miller Scapula wound by:** 494, 591, 724; **forensic report of:** 484, 587, 591, 724
Fulton, Maurice Garland – 33-38, 40, 54, 80, 99, 125, 136, 194-195, 200, 202, 211, 214, 222, 268, 302, 324, 326, 345, 353, 371, 388, 390-391, 398, 462, 526, 570, 624, 629, 683, 702, 715; **relocating and certifying Coroner's Jury Report of William H. Bonney by:** 33-34
Fusco, John – 467-468, 593; **"Young Guns II" by** (See John Fusco)
Gaines, L.D. – 187
Gallegos, Pantaleon – 130
Gallegos, Severo – 248, 356, 358-360, 378-381, 439, 712, 719; **Affidavit for "Brushy Bill" of:** 248, 356, 378-380
Garcia, Alarie Ray – 612
Garrett, Apolinaria (see Apolinaria Gutierrez)
Garrett,, Juanita (see Juanita Gutierrez)
Garrett, Jarvis – 189, 248, 253, 256
Garrett, Jarvis Patrick "J.P." – 486, 597, 613
Garrett, Oscar – 249, 253, 255, 258, 292, 302, 410
Garrett, Patrick Floyd "Pat" – 3-4, 6-7, 9-11, 18-30, 32m 34, 36-37, 39-67, 70-84, 96, 98-100, 104, 114-116, 118-122, 150-151, 154,

167, 180, 188-190, 194, 197, 201, 205, 211-214, 217-218, 226-227, 236-239, 241, 243-260, 262-263, 265-267, 269-271, 276, 279-284, 288-293, 301-306, 308-309, 316-320, 322, 324-333, 337-338, 340, 342-351, 353-356, 361-368, 370, 372-378, 382, 385-394, 397-405, 410, 418, 422-424, 437-450, 452-455, 460-464, 468, 472-478, 480, 482-484, 486-488, 494-511, 513-522, 524-548, 550, 553-554, 556, 559-561, 563-570, 573, 576-577, 579, 581-582, 586, 590-591, 593-594, 597-599, 601, 6060606, 610-612, 615, 618-622, 624, 638, 641-642, 445-648, 650-651, 654, 663-664, 666-672, 675-676, 680, 688-691, 694-701, 704-709, 711-723, 725-726, 738-741; *The Authentic Life of Billy the Kid* by: 47, 52, 57-59, 80, 83, 89, 99, 116, 211, 213, 218, 227, 303, 309, 316-320, 322, 324-333, 337, 340, 342-344, 347-348, 351, 355-356, 385, 389, 398, 460, 498, 506, 527, 531, 542, 545, 564, 606, 683, 690, 694, 716, 739; **killing of Joe Briscoe by:** 114, 346, 437; **elected as Lincoln County Sheriff:** 118; **Territory-wide jurisdiction as Deputy U.S. Marshal:** 96, 118, 344, 387, 668, 695-696; **collecting the Billy the Kid reward by:** 9, 18-28; **Statute of Limitations for murder applicable to:** 402, 472, 477, 480, 487, 495, 545 (See Coroner's Jury Report for William H. Bonney)

Gatling gun – 111, 334, 339, 453, 687

Gatti, Kathleen M. – 191

Gauss, Gottfried – 90, 120, 125-126, 133-134, 357-358, 360, 379, 439, 498, 525, 527, 540-541, 581, 665, 717, 719-720

Gay, Richard – 488

Gaylord, A.S. – 49, 51, 186

Gazateer of Hamilton County, Texas – 176

George Hervey Real Estate Company – 191

Gila Ranch – 317-318, 431

Gila River – 317, 431

Gipson, Fred – 38, 284

Gladewater, Texas – 174-175, 179-180, 208, 218, 370, 381, 451, 656

Glen, Willis Skelton – 346

Glennon, Patience – 229, 274

Godfroy, Frederick – 93, 273

Goff, D.L. – 168, 171, 425

Gomber, Drew – 606

Gomber, Elise – 606

Gonzales, Florencio – 420, 678-679

Gonzales, Ignacio – 110

Grand Saline, Texas – 369

Grant County Herald – 144, 446

Grant County, New Mexico – 463, 478, 480-481, 488, 494, 549, 620, 727-728

Grant County Rebellion of 1876 – 5

Grant, Joe – 116, 120, 343-344, 405-422

Graves, Arthur – 185, 205

Graves, Gary Wayne – 477, 481, 488, 494, 546, 556-557, 565, 619-620, 627, 629, 641, 675, 728, 730; **De Baca County Case No. 03-06-136-01 for exhumation of Billy the Kid by:** 480, 488, 494, 546 (See "Billy the Kid Case" hoax)

Greathouse, Jim "Whiskey Jim" – 69-71, 118, 150-151, 218, 243, 297, 306, 345, 422, 437; **Greathouse ranch of** (See Jim Greathouse)

Greene, Charles W. – 23, 80, 391, 398-399; **printer of** *Santa Fe Daily New Mexican*: 23, 80, 391; **affidavit about printing**

Billy the Kid reward notices by: 23, 391; **faked as Pat Garrett's lawyer in Brushy" hoax:** 284, 391-393, 397-398
Green, T. – 131
Griffin, Marcus – 187, 285
Griffin, Willie E. – 493
Griggs, George – 371
Guadalupe Mountains – 320, 431
Guarino, Mark – 612
Gutierrez, Apolinaria – 115-116, 363, 520
Gutierrez, Celsa – 46, 115, 122, 214, 244-245, 253, 259, 269, 350, 462-363, 366, 368, 423, 439-440, 443-444, 503, 529, 538, 647, 667, 669; **sister-of-Saval error in "Brushy" hoax for:** 362-363, 439, 443, 667; **pseudo-Celsa in hoax:** 443-444, 647, 667
Gutierrez, Juanita – 43, 189, 565
Gutierrez, Saval (Sabal) – 10-11, 16, 20, 45-46, 115, 122, 362-363, 365-366, 439-441, 443, 445, 510, 517, 536, 647, 667, 713
Haag, Mike – 632, 635, 672
Haederle, Michael – 455
Haley, J. Evetts – 63, 504, 576
Hamilton, Texas – 174, 176, 178-180, 202, 205, 226, 228, 257, 264, 272, 302, 382, 404, 423, 477, 480, 483, 493, 534-535, 545, 549, 590, 595-596, 598, 625, 627-629
Harbert, Ben – 66
Hargrove's Saloon – 114-116, 343
Harris, David – 488
Hart, Bob – 455, 464
Hartley, Ted – 481, 493, 550, 557
Haws, Eulaine Faye Goff – 167-168, 425-427, 430 (See William A. Tunstill)
Haws, Leonard – 168, 425
Haws, Roy L. – 165, 167-171, 176, 180-181, 207, 232, 312-313, 316, 365, 370, 372-373, 425, 649; *Brushy Bill: Proof That His Claim to Be Billy the Kid Was a Hoax* by (See Roy L. Haws)
Hayes, George J. – 287
Hayes, Rutherford B. – 5, 93, 109, 295
Heard, Robins, Cloud, Lubel & Greenwood LLP - 549, 551, 555
Heath, Cora – 171
Heath, Dudley – 168, 425-426
Heath, Martha Vada Roberts – 168, 171, 425-426, 428, 656-657
Heath, Vada Bell Roberts – 168, 171, 425
Hefner, Bob – 181, 199
Hendron, J.W. – 248, 257, 261, 268, 270, 301, 391
Herrera, Fernando - 686
Hertzog, Peter – 392
Hico News Review – 172, 174, 207-208, 241, 263, 309, 312
Hico, Texas – 3, 33, 172, 174-175, 178-181, 185, 189, 202-203, 205-208, 210, 264-265, 272, 298, 312, 453, 455, 476-477, 549, 556
Hill, Thomas "Tom" – 131-133, 143, 497
Hindman, George – 109, 112, 116, 119, 121, 130-132, 138, 247, 330, 340, 346, 422, 437, 601-602, 681-682
Hines, Jim – **as Jessie Evans:** 205, 212, 295, 302, 423, 535, 646; **as Billy Campbell:** 410-412
Holford, Carolyn – 207
Holguin, Raul – 494
Hooker Ranch – 318
Hooten, W.J. – 42, 238
Hopper, Jessica – 613
Hotel de Luna – 318
Hough, Emmerson – 260
Howard, George J. – 137, 222
howitzer cannon – 111, 334, 339, 453, 686-687
Hoyt, Henry F. – 112, 127, 129, 137, 222-225, 227, 229, 349, 650, 682, 691; **W.H. Bonney's**

bill of sale to: 129, 137, 222-225, 229, 349, 682; *A Frontier Doctor* by: 127, 211, 227, 691; **confirming Billy's writing by:** 222-224; confirming Billy's Spanish proficiency by: 227, 650

Hudson, Bell – 348, 362; *Billy the Kid* by (See Bell Hudson)

Hudspeth, William – 484-485, 494, 584-592, 616, 626, 638, 641, 723-724 (See "Billy the Kid Case" hoax)

Huff, J. Wesley – 363

Hughes, Howard – 285

Humphrey, John – 409

Hunter and Evans – 321

Hurley, John – 132, 134, 146, 267, 500, 694, 696

Hurley, Johnnie – 379

Hutton, Paul – 477-479, 481, 483, 558-562, 568, 571, 573, 641, 726; **official historian for "Billy the Kid Case" as:** 477, 479, 481; confirmed as official historian by Robert Utley: 562; **"Investigating History: Billy the Kid" History Channel TV by:** 481, 483, 558-562, 645; **helping to bring in Dr. Henry Lee by:** 57; **fake carpenter's bench authentication by:** 562, 570; **Albuquerque Museum of Art and History Billy the Kid show of:** 562, 570; **backing Bill Richardson's fake "Billy the Kid" pardon by:** 612 (See "Billy the Kid Case" hoax)

Iglesias, David – 484

Jacobsen, Joel – 606; *Such Men as Billy the Kid: The Lincoln County War Revisited* (See Joel Jacobson)

Jaffe Law Firm – 546, 548

James, Frank – 164, 173, 207

James, Jesse – 7, 75, 164, 174, 178-179, 181, 191, 205-209, 213, 295, 302, 309, 381, 383-384, 410-412, 423, 430, 646, 675, 691

Jameson, William Carl "W.C." – 8, 197, 200, 217-218, 232, 293-294, 298, 417-464, 468, 471, 473, 483, 486, 496, 500, 507-508, 512, 517, 522, 535-536, 559-560, 645-672, 675-731; **"Brushy"-backing of encouraged by C.L. Sonnichsen:** 200, 298; **aware of "Brushy's" literacy:** 217, 232; **debunking of *The Return of the Outlaw Billy the Kid* by:** 417-464, 496, 522, 536; **in "Billy the Kid Case" hoax:** 468, 471, 496, 522, 535-536; debating Leon Metz for: 483; participating in TV "Investigating History Billy the Kid": 481, 483, 559-560; **promoting the "Brushy" hoax in 21st century books:** 486, 500, 507-508, 512, 517, 563, 645-672, 675-731; forging "Brushy's" words for: 645-648; debunking *Billy the Kid: Beyond the Grave* by: 645-652, debunking *Billy the Kid: The Lost Interviews* by: 653-670; debunking *Pat Garrett: The Man Behind the Badge* by: 671-672; *Cold Case Billy the Kid: Investigating History's Mysteries* by: 675-731; repeating "Billy the Kid Case" fake forensics in: 715-724 (See Frederick Bean, Steve Sederwall, "Billy the Kid Case" hoax)

Janofsky, Michael – 474

Jaramillo, Lorenzo – 10-11, 16, 20, 445, 510, 713

Jennings, Al – 209

Jim Vance Microfilm Company – 187

J.J. Vance Microfilm Service (Company) – 185, 187

Johnson, Jim – 383, 586, 650-651;

Billy the Kid: His Real Name Was ... by (See Jim Johnson)
Jones, Bill – 321-322, 375-376
Jones, Eva – 186
Jones, Heiskell – 321
Jones, Jim – 142, 321, 375, 431
Jones, John – 142, 146, 148, 321, 431
Jones, Sam – 372, 376, 739
Jones, Tom – 143 (See George Davis)
Kearny Code – 317, 386
Keleher, William – 35-36, 198, 248, 259-260, 268, 270, 284-286, 292, 352, 388, 462, 714; *Violence in Lincoln County 1869-1881* by (See William Keleher)
Killinger, C.G. – 265
Kimbrell, George – 112, 117-118, 140, 605, 646, 662
King, Frank M. – 29, 32, 304, 347, 353, 694; *Wranglin' the Past: Reminiscences of Frank M. King* (See Frank M. King)
Kinney, John – 99, 110, 136, 160, 332, 354-355, 665, 684-686
Kistler, Russ – 304
Komar, Debra – 488-493, 557, 617, 619, 622-623, 729-730; **Affidavit opposing exhumations by:** 490-491, 557; **Deposition opposing exhumations by:** 491-493, 557 (See "Billy the Kid Case" hoax)
Kristopherson, Cris – 484
Kuchler, Barbara J. – 189, 191, 427
Kurtis, Bill – 483-484, 558, 571-574, 576, 581-582, 587-589, 630, 632, 634-635; **funding Dr. Henry Lee by:** 558, 572, 582; **Kurtis Productions of** (See Bill Kurtis)
Kyle, Thomas G. – 455-458, 652
Lacey, Marc – 614
LaRue, Lash – 180; "Son of Billy the Kid" movie in (See Lash LaRue)

Las Cruces, New Mexico – 78, 88, 142, 158, 256, 454, 520, 563
Las Cruces *Rio Grande Republican* – 18, 64, 446, 708
Las Cruces *Thirty-Four* – 213
Las Vegas (Daily) Gazette – 21, 65, 82, 85-87, 118, 149-150, 155, 157, 219, 225, 297, 300, 323, 345, 348, 383, 398, 437, 458, 605, 690
Las Vegas Daily Optic – 64-65, 304, 503
Las Vegas, New Mexico Territory – 71, 73, 86, 97, 154, 345, 437, 458, 690
Anna Lee – 168
Lee, Henry C. – 473, 481-482, 485, 501, 558, 563, 568-579, 582-584, 586, 595-596, 616, 626, 630, 623, 634-635, 638, 672, 675, 706, 708, 715-716, 721-723; **background of:** 571-573; **Orchid Cellmark Lab of** (See Orchid Cellmark Lab); **subpoenaed DNA findings of:** 485, 582, 639; **brought in for "Billy the Kid Case" by Paul Hutton:** 558; **funded by Bill Kurtis:** 558, 572, 582; **fake forensics for carpenter's workbench by:** 482, 563, 568-571, 573-576, 616; **no DNA recovered from:** 485, 583-584, 743-744; **fake forensics on courthouse floorboards for Deputy Bell killing by:** 482, 501, 579, 581-582, 616; **fake shooting scene investigation with washstand and headboard by:** 482-483, 576-580; **single forensic report for Case 2003-274 by:** 485, 582; **American Academy of Forensic Sciences Ethics Committee complaint against:** 485, 595 (See "Billy the Kid Case" hoax)
Lee, John Doyle – 50

847

Lee, Robert E. – 180, 383
Legislature Revolt of 1872 – 63, 461
Leonard, Ira – 96, 99, 113-114, 117, 119, 158, 343, 352-353, 436, 663, 719
Levy, Glen – 612
Lexigen – 583
Liebson, Al – 279
Life Magazine – 279
Lillie, Gorden W. "Pawnee Bill" – 66, 164, 179, 181, 234, 296, 370-371; **Pawnee Bill's Wild West Show of** (See Gordon Lillie)
Lincoln Bank – 106
Lincoln County courthouse-jail – 291, 300, 354, 356, 372, 378-380, 446, 448, 452, 475, 479, 482, 523, 561, 563, 581-582, 598, 601, 611, 630, 635, 648, 664, 715-716; **outhouse of**: 120, 357, 422, 476, 527-528, 539-541, 561, 717, 719-720; **armory of**: 291, 356, 360, 379, 452, 527, 539, 648, 716, 718, 741
Lincoln County Grand Jury – **of 1878**: 109; **of 1879**: 144, 243, 343, 436
Lincoln County Heritage Trust – 197, 455-456, 458, 464, 652
Lincoln County Leader – 90, 126, 525
Lincoln County, New Mexico – 18, 21, 23, 25-28, 34, 41, 49-50, 64-65, 70, 72, 82, 85, 92, 96, 99, 106, 108, 111-114, 116, 118, 120, 125, 128, 131, 139, 155, 158, 212, 225, 239-240, 242-243, 246-247, 256, 260-261, 280, 290, 300, 321, 323-324, 342, 344, 356, 359, 374, 378, 381, 387, 401, 410-411, 419, 431, 447, 464, 474-475, 478-479, 483-485, 488, 497-498, 522-523, 535-536, 543, 545, 556, 564-565, 574, 581, 585, 592, 594-596, 598, 601-602, 618, 626, 629, 631-632, 635, 649, 690, 694-696, 720, 742
Lincoln County News – 53, 408, 472, 486, 570, 572, 574, 582
Lincoln County Sheriff's Department Case No. 2003-274 (see "Billy the Kid Case" hoax)
Lincoln County Sheriff's Department Supplemental Report for Case No. 2003-274 (See John Miller)
Lincoln County War – 5, 7, 67, 73, 80, 82, 85, 99, 103-104, 106, 108, 113, 115, 118-121, 123-125, 128, 132, 136-138, 140, 143, 181, 194-195, 205, 209-210, 224, 242-243, 249, 252, 255, 257-258, 260-261, 273, 282-283, 293, 301-302, 307, 318, 323, 325, 328, 333, 335, 340-341, 346, 354, 358, 378, 405, 411, 421, 423, 431, 434, 447, 454, 464, 473, 475, 497, 499, 524, 533, 535, 561, 564-565, 590, 597-598, 601-603, 608, 610-611, 646, 666, 678, 680-681, 684; **as a freedom fight**: 4-6, 62-63, 67, 85, 96, 98-99, 103, 108, 121, 123-124, 305, 328, 333, 405, 473, 678, 684; **Battle in**: 4-5, 94, 99, 112, 123, 125, 127, 136, 144, 212, 227-228, 306, 328, 332-335, 357, 375, 434, 452, 646, 684, 704, 720; white soldiers firing a volley in: 95, 111, 114, 144, 149, 336, 339, 452, 688 (See testimony of William H. Bonney, N.A.M. Dudley)
Lincoln Museum – 35, 211, 214, 296, 301, 306
Lincoln, New Mexico – 59, 61, 72, 75, 82, 85-86, 89, 94, 97, 106-108, 110-113, 116-117, 119-120, 124-126, 131-135, 138, 140, 144-145, 150-151, 154, 157-160, 191, 201, 211-214, 217, 226, 338, 238, 240, 243-244, 249, 253, 256, 261, 280, 286, 290, 295, 298, 303-305, 309, 324-

325, 327-330, 333-334, 340, 342, 344, 354-359, 364, 367, 372, 375, 378, 381, 386, 408, 412, 420-421, 431-434, 436, 439, 447, 451-452, 455-456, 463, 467, 474-475, 479, 494-495, 498-500, 518, 523-525, 528-529, 533, 539-540, 542, 544-545, 560, 563, 566-567, 573, 601, 603, 605-606, 611, 646, 648, 659, 662-665, 678, 682-687, 696, 709, 716, 719, 740-741
Lincoln pit jail – 108, 131-132, 328, 378
Link, Afra – 182
"Little Casino" – 114
Lobato, Frank – 440-441, 443, 502, 538, 670
Long, Jack – 146, 685
"Long Rail Brand" – 710
"Long S Brand" – 710
Longview, Texas – 209, 264, 381
Lopez, Raymond – 619-620, 629, 726-728
Los Alamos Laboratory – 455-456, 479
Los Angeles Times – 613
Lucca, Jonnell – 592
Lucero, Pedro Antonio – 10-11, 16, 20, 445, 510, 713
Luminol – 574, 581, 632
Luna, Miguel – 359-360
Mabry, Thomas Jewett – 30, 34-35, 174, 176, 186, 189, 232, 235, 237, 239-240, 248-257, 260-261, 263, 265, 268-270, 280-283, 287-288, 292, 294, 301-302, 357, 365, 370, 373, 377-378, 382, 384, 401, 404, 410, 418, 439, 448, 464, 471, 486, 549, 597, 646, 648-650, 654-655, 675, 737, 740; **biography:** 237
Mackie, John – 105, 318
MacNab, Frank – 108, 110, 121, 321-322, 601, 680
Mann, Edward Beverly "E.B." – 203, 288, 292, 301, 334, 351, 404

Markland, Absalom – 99
Martinez, Atanacio – 108, 131, 295, 433
Martinez, Edecio – 612
Martinez, Leo – 557, 624-625, 728
Martz, Martin "Dutch" – 126, 133-134
Mason, Barney – 115, 121, 214, 361-362, 439, 690
Massey, Barry – 599, 609, 611
Master Bank of Kansas City – 691
Mastin Bank of Kansas City – 691
Mathison, Geraldine S. – 186
Matthews, Jacob Basil "Billy" – 109, 114, 131-134, 158, 270, 304, 327
Maxwell, Deluvina – 63-64, 103, 289, 291, 349, 445, 462, 504, 514-515, 569, 576, 647, 650
Maxwell family – 9, 58, 62, 482, 513, 570, 721
Maxwell, Ferdinand – 182, 189, 302, 423, 534 (See William V. Morrison)
Maxwell house (mansion) – 244-245, 255, 258, 348-350, 364, 438, 441-442, 444, 453, 512, 514, 537, 599, 576, 606, 667, 700-703, 705, 713; **floor plan of:** 701-703; **Peter Maxwell's bedroom in:** 9, 58, 103, 122, 244, 262, 364, 366-367, 418, 423, 440, 460, 513-516, 542, 564, 569, 576-577, 579, 650, 672, 697-709; **sale of:** 513-514
Maxwell Land Grant – 63, 97, 104, 115, 182, 710
Maxwell, Lucien Bonaparte – 63, 97, 103-104, 115, 182-183, 189, 205, 302, 321, 423, 431, 514, 534, 576, 701, 705-706, 710
Maxwell, Luz Trotier de Beaubien – 11, 89, 115, 445, 510, 512, 514, 706, 713
Maxwell, Paulita – 62, 97-98, 103-104, 115, 121, 224, 244-245, 259, 262, 269, 350, 361-362, 405, 522, 528-529, 706-707; **hoaxers' Paulita as Peter**

Maxwell's "daughter" error: 522, 528-529
Maxwell, Peter "Pete" – 10-11, 21, 50, 57-59, 61, 63-64, 68, 115, 122, 238, 242, 249, 252-253, 258-259, 262, 288-291, 295, 364-365, 386, 422-423, 431, 444-445, 447, 449, 460, 462, 475, 495, 503, 513-515, 518, 522, 528-529, 533-534, 537-538, 543-544, 560, 567, 569, 576-577, 579, 632, 650, 655; **as witness to William Bonney's killing:** 21, 57, 59, 65, 291, 445, 462, 650, 709, 714; **as hoaxed pseudo-Pete Maxwell:** 672, 709-712
Mayfield, John S. – 239, 315
McCarthy, Todd – 594
McCarty, Catherine (See Catherine Antrim)
McCarty, John L. – 704
McCarty, Joseph "Josie" – 104, 277, 409
McCarty, Michael – 428
McCarty, William Henry (see William H. Bonney)
McCloskey, William – 680
McCoy, Dave – 594
McDaniels, Jim (James) – 142, 174, 320, 322
McFarland, David F. – 277, 409
McGinn, Carpenter, Montoya & Love P.A. – 600
McGinn, Randi – 486, 600-609, 612-613, 617, 682; **Pardon Petition by:** 600-606 (See Charles Daniels)
McGinnis, John – 52
McIntosh, Jim – 704
McKibbin, D.B. – 43
McKinney, Cliff – 248, 253, 255
McKinney, Elizabeth Francis – 694
McKinney, Thalis – 694
McKinney, Thomas Christopher "Kip" – 248, 255, 259, 347, 438, 447, 508, 663, 692, 694, 740

McMasters, James E. – 137, 222, 224
McNatt, C.C. – 375
McSween, Alexander – 94, 97, 99, 106-111, 113, 121, 133, 137, 141, 143-149, 219, 242, 290, 325-326, 330, 338, 386, 397, 419-421, 431-434, 523, 560, 659, 661, 677-678, 681-682, 684-686, 688, 720
McSweens (followers) – 82, 110-111, 149, 242-243, 306, 561, 602, 685
McSween, Susan – 86, 94-95, 112, 114, 290, 334, 340, 422, 434, 602-603, 662, 687
Meadows, John – 91-92, 121, 128, 346
Memory Lane Cemetery – 488, 490-491
Mescalero Indian Reservation – 106, 109, 140, 273, 352, 386, 431
Mesilla, New Mexico Territory – 73, 88, 95, 107, 110, 114, 119-120, 125, 144, 151, 153, 155, 158-159, 213, 225, 244, 318, 320, 343, 351-352, 354-355, 366, 378, 386, 404, 422, 432, 436, 438, 451, 479, 524, 540, 564, 568, 614, 659, 663-664, 685-686, 740
Mesilla News – 158, 225, 540, 614
Metz, Leon – 96, 190, 197-198, 212, 241, 345, 463, 483, 645, 695; *Pat Garrett: The Story of a Western Lawman* by (See Leon Metz)
Middleton, John – 108-109, 119, 126, 130, 133-135, 332, 601
Miller, Isadora – 529
Miller, Jay – 562, 570, 585, 615, 617, 626-627, 630, 634
Miller, John – 7-8, 269, 383, 474, 477, 481, 483-485, 522, 529, 532-533, 553, 556, 576, 584-593, 598, 616, 625, 638, 641, 676, 723-724, 726, 728-731; **birth date of:** 586, 724;

Lincoln County Sheriff's Department Supplemental Report for exhumation of: 588; illegal exhumation of: 494, 584-593, 616, 723-724; **hoax buck teeth and shot scapula of:** 484, 590-591, 724 (See Helen Airy, "Billy the Kid Case" hoax, Laura Fulginiti)

Miller, Kenneth "Kenny" – 569-570, 580

Miller, Manuel "Mannie" – 514, 516, 569-570, 632, 721

Miller, Stella Abreu (See Stella Abreu)

Mills, A.H. – 130-131

Missouri Historical Society – 183-184, 190, 214, 302, 423, 534

Monclova, Coahuila, Mexico – 692

Montaño, José – 140, 604, 660, 687

Mooney, Lawrence K. – 35, 50, 233, 277

Moore, K. – 185

Moore Scott – 154, 352-353

Moore's Hotsprings Hotel – 353

Moore, Tex – 374

Moore, William – 130

Morel, Alan – 481, 485, 616-617, 626 (See "Billy the Kid Case" hoax)

Morgan, Art – 252

Morris, Henry G. – 388

Morrison, Ruth – 191

Morrison, William Vincent "Bill" – 3-4, 36-56, 67, 95, 129, 163, 175, 177, 181-191, 193-204, 206-219, 224, 226, 228-237, 241-248, 265-272, 276-278, 280-284, 286, 288-408, 410-413, 417-418, 423-425, 427, 430, 433-435, 438, 440, 444-446, 450-452, 459-460, 462, 467-468, 471-472, 481, 483, 486, 494-495, 520, 522, 534-536, 542-543, 597, 645-646, 649-658, 664-666, 668, 670-672, 675, 737-742; **background of:** 3, 183-191, 423, 534-536, 654; **as a traveling salesman:** 3, 7, 182-183, 187-188, 190, 192, 194, 198, 205, 250, 252, 254, 256-257, 268, 272, 286, 418, 468, 472; **impersonating a lawyer by:** 3, 183-190, 194, 198, 418, 495, 534, 542-543, 651-652, 654; **impersonating an historian by:** 190-191; **faking no Coroner's Jury Report by:** 36-56, 194, 446, 462, 670; **promotion of J. Frank Dalton as Jesse James by:** 206-209; **research, touring, promoting, and fixing-up "Brushy" for Billy the Kid impersonation by:** 98, 163, 174, 181, 193, 210-218, 276-278, 296-298, 430, 433-435, 438, 445, 451-452, 665, 718; **rehearsal tapes and transcripts of "Brushy" by:** 217, 228, 417, 424, 440, 534, 649, 653, 656-658, 671; **tintype reversal error by:** 100, 303, 451, 649, 742; **seeking pardon for "Brushy" as Billy the Kid:** 237-260, 262, 675; Pardon Petition by: 239-240; fake evidence packet for: 241-248; rationalizing failed pardon by: 265-272, 448, 646; **posthumous pardon thrust by:** 407-408; Colt .41 misinformation scam by: 450; *Alias Billy the Kid* debunking of: 288-406; fake Affidavits in: 123, 180, 248, 375-384, 404, 451, 520, 651; secret Parkinson Affidavit for: 232-235, 737-742; fake conspiracy theories in (See C.L. Sonnichsen); **promoting "Brushy" and book by:** 280-285, 286, 468; attempting to dupe Gene Autry by: 284-285; Harry S, Truman duped by: 416, 471, 597; **failed attempt to exhume Billy the Kid by:**

408, 471-472; **promoting Jim Hines as Billy Campbell by:** 410-412 (See Oliver Pleasant Roberts, C.L. Sonnichsen, T.J. Mabry, W.C. Jameson, Frederick Bean)

Morton, William "Buck" – 108, 116, 121, 130-131, 290-291, 320, 326-329, 433, 497, 679-680, 682

"MSNBC News" – 620

"MSN Movies" – 594

Mullin, Robert N. – 38-39, 44, 51, 55, 98, 183, 195-196, 211, 213, 236, 241, 268, 298, 302, 335-336, 338, 349, 363, 385, 424, 624, 629, 701-703, 711

Murphy-Kinney party – 99, 136

Murphy, Lawrence G. – 106, 677; **L.G. Murphy & Co. of:** 523

Myres, Tio Sam – 407

Napolitano, Janet – 481, 483, 485, 586, 592

National Cemetery of Santa Fe – 493

National Frontiersmen's Association – 374

Nation, Arleigh – 533

Nevill, C.L. – 322

Newcomb, John – 158

Newman, Simon – 386

Newman's Semi-Weekly – 73, 159, 355, 386

New Mexico Magazine – 33, 38, 44-45, 51, 285-286, 375, 385, 389, 517, 658, 668

New Mexico Sentinel – 213

New York Children's Aid Society – 419

New York Post – 407

New York Sun – 66-67, 87, 117, 278, 543, 690

New York Times – 280, 408, 473, 486, 542-543, 549, 593, 596, 608-610, 614

New York World Magazine – 73, 91, 213, 304, 341, 348, 362, 411, 603

Nicholi, Bill – 567

Nolan, Frederick – 94, 99, 268, 277, 314, 323, 344, 347, 367, 371-372, 527, 557, 606, 611, 621-622, 625, 653, 679, 693-694, 707, 726, 728; *The Life and Death of John Henry Tunstall* by, *The Lincoln County War: A Documentary History* by, *The West of Billy the Kid* by (See Frederick Nolan)

Nusbaum, Jesse – 32

Nusbaum, Rosemary – 32

O'Brien, J.T. – 387

Office of the Medical Investigator (OMI), Albuquerque, New Mexico – 480, 482, 487-491, 493, 549, 556, 562, 617, 619-620, 622-623, 629, 729 (See Ross Zumwalt, Debra Komar)

O'Folliard, Tom – 57, 104, 110, 112-113, 115-118, 127, 150, 243, 291, 347, 372, 422, 437-438, 446, 467, 472, 491, 500, 661, 691-694, 704, 740

O'Keffe, Tom – 320

Oklahoma Indian Territory – 179, 232, 313

Olinger, Robert "Bob" – 104, 120-121, 126-127, 143, 160, 244, 256-257, 269, 291, 344, 354-355, 357-359, 379, 422, 476, 479, 498, 501, 525-528, 539, 541, 545, 561, 565-567, 585, 601, 606, 618, 625, 629, 638, 696, 716, 718, 741

Orchid Cellmark Laboratory – 483, 485, 575-576, 582-583, 587-589, 596, 616, 625-627, 633, 637-640, 716, 721, 743; **DNA faking scandal of:** 575-576, 589; **no testing for blood by:** 575, 716, 721; **no DNA from carpenter's bench by:** 485, 576, 583, 627, 743; **participating in Miller/Hudspeth exhumation by:** 587-588;

subpoenaed Case 2003-274 records of: 485, 582, 588-589, 616, 633, 639 (See "Billy the Kid Case" hoax)
Ostler, Calvin – 573-574, 577, 581, 632, 635, 637; **business partner of Henry Lee:** 573
Ostler, Kim – 632, 635
Otero, Miguel – 439, 450, 709; *The Real Billy the Kid* by (See Miguel Otero)
Otero, Vincinte – 505
Ortho-tolidine (O-tolidine) – 581, 630, 632, 716, 721
Overton, Homer D. aka Homer D. Kinsworthy – 496, 520-521; **Affidavit of:** 520-521 (See "Billy the Kid Case" hoax)
Pakistan Daily Express – 597
Parker, Isaac C. – 369, 374
Parkinson, S.N. – 232-233, 737-742; **Affidavit of:** 334-335, 737-742
Patrón, Juan – 106, 113, 140, 342, 354, 378, 436, 603
"Pawnee Bill" (See Gorden W. Lillie)
Pawnee Bill's Wild West Show (See Gorden W. Lillie)
Peckinpah, Sam – 593-594
Pecos River – 65, 70, 106, 115, 319-322, 421
Peñasco River – 105, 114, 132, 323, 405, 421, 434
Peppin, George – 99, 110-112, 141, 143-145, 147, 226, 242, 290, 295, 306, 330, 332-335, 337-339, 359, 421, 660, 664, 684-687, 719
Perry, Elzet Jr. – 377
Peters, Susie – 268
Picacho, New Mexico – 110, 333
Pickett, Tom – 118, 155, 291, 323, 374
Pittmon, Geneva Roberts – 164-168, 171, 173, 425-426, 430, 649, 654
Poe, Frank – 704

Poe, John William – 19, 44, 58-59, 61-62, 64, 114, 121-122, 211, 214, 244-245, 259, 276, 361, 364, 367-368, 391, 402-403, 418, 423, 440-444, 449-450, 460-462, 502-515, 518-519, 529, 531, 542, 560, 567, 576, 579, 650-651, 670, 697-699, 701, 704, 706-709, 711-712, 717, 722; *The Death of Billy the Kid* by (See John William Poe)
Poe, Sophie – 211, 717; *Buckboard Days* by (See Sophie Poe)
Poling, Mike – 588, 591
Posse Comitatus Act – 111, 114, 144, 336, 339, 685-687
Prescott, Arizona – 477, 481, 532-533, 588, 590-591
Prescott Police Department – 587, 591
Press Trust of India Hindustan Times – 597
"Prime Time Live" – 464
Prince, L. Bradford – 16
Purington, George – 686
Quantrill, William – 310, 313, 382
Quinn, Eileen – 284
Quintero, Henry – 481, 488, 493, 550, 555, 557, 592, 596, 607, 623, 727-728
Raffe, Jerry – 521
Ramath, Arizona – 383
Ramsey, JonBenet – 572
Ramsey, Burke – 572
Rasch, Philip J. – 50, 186-187, 191, 195, 211, 266-267, 274-278, 283-284, 286, 303, 314, 335, 338, 343-344, 411, 502, 504-505, 693; *Trailing Billy the Kid by*: 505, 693
Redfield, Georgia B. – 272
Regulators – 97, 108-113, 116-117, 119, 121, 123, 127, 132, 137, 154, 242, 291, 304, 328-329, 331-333, 378, 386, 405, 418, 420-421, 431, 433-434, 436, 438, 464, 468, 560, 601, 659, 680-685, 720

Richardson, William Blaine III
"Bill" – 7, 293, 464, 471-475,
477-478, 480-484, 486, 488,
490, 493-494, 549, 550, 552,
555, 557-559, 561-562, 573,
586, 592-593, 595-600, 607-614,
617-619, 621, 626, 629, 641,
675, 725-727, 729, 730 (See
"Billy the Kid Case" hoax)
Richeson, Hawley – 196
RICO – 484
Rigdon, Floyd – 187
Riley, John – 106, 140, 143, 681
Rio Grande Republican (see Las
Cruces *Rio Grande Republican*)
Ritch, William – 15, 18, 20-26, 28-
29, 32, 40, 48, 51, 55, 388, 390-
400, 708 (See Coroner's Jury
Report of William H. Bonney,
Reward of Pat Garrett)
Rivers, Frank – 601
Roberts, Al (See Oliver Pleasant
"Brushy Bill" Roberts)
Roberts, Andrew Berry – 168
Roberts, Andrew "Buckshot" – 82,
92, 95, 109, 116, 119, 121, 131,
138, 213, 242, 244, 247, 273,
331-332, 340, 343, 352, 358,
386, 421-422, 433-434, 438,
526, 528, 602, 664, 683-684,
696, 741 (See T.B. Catron's
federal indictment for killing)
Roberts, Caroline Dunn – 168-
169, 171, 313, 425 (See Oliver
Pleasant "Brushy Bill" Roberts
for a faked Caroline Dunn)
Roberts, Cordelia – 164, 167-168,
172-173
Roberts, Dan Webster – 177, 310;
Rangers and Sovereignty by
(See Dan Webster Roberts)
Roberts, John Henry – 308 (See
Oliver Pleasant "Brushy Bill"
Roberts for a faked John Henry
Roberts)
Roberts, John W. – 168
Roberts, Henry Oliver "H.O." –
165-169, 172-173, 199, 312-313,
315, 372-373, 425-428, 656;

**first marriage to Caroline
Dunn by:** 168-169, 171, 313,
425; **second marriage to
Sara Elizabeth Ferguson
(mother of "Brushy Bill")
by:** 165-168, 313, 315, 372, 425
Roberts, Joseph Irvin – 168
Roberts, Lonnie V. – 168
Roberts, Martha Vada (See
Martha Vada Roberts Heath)
Roberts, Mary C. – 168
Roberts, Mary June – 166
Roberts, Nora – 168
Roberts, Oliver L. "Ollie" " Brushy
Bill" (see Oliver Pleasant
Roberts)
Roberts, Oliver Pleasant "Brushy
Bill" – 3-4, 6-7, 15-16, 29-30, 33,
36-38, 42, 44-46, 49-50, 53, 55-
57, 66-95, 97-100, 103, 123,
125, 127-129, 160, 163-183,
185-191, 193-218, 224, 226-228,
230-231, 235-262, 265-268, 270-
281, 283, 285, 287-404, 417,
419, 423-446, 448, 450-454,
457-464, 471-614, 617, 620-621,
623, 625, 629, 638, 641-642,
645-671, 677-696, 724, 731,
735, 737-742; **biography of:**
164-181, 262-263, 268;
birthday of: 167-168, 172, 199,
308, 425, 649; **genealogy of:**
165-171; provided by family of:
164-171; **confabulation by:**
180, 210, 218, 245, 254, 273-
274, 294, 299, 305, 307, 316,
335-336, 341, 350, 353, 364-
365, 374, 405, 431, 433-436,
441, 451, 453, 538, 556, 658,
669, 679, 688, 712, 735; **age
faking by:** adding 10 years for
Social Security benefits fraud
as "Oliver L. Roberts" by: 171-
172, 175, 181, 206, 308-310,
315; miscellaneous age faking
by: 172; adding 20 years for
Billy the Kid impersonation by:
171, 174, 200, 219, 308, 425;
fake genealogy for: 174-176,

181, 206, 296, 310-316, 373, 429; **impersonating Frank James by:** 164, 173; **backing J. Frank Dalton as Jesse James by:** 203, 205-209; **fake William Henry name of:** 164, 200, 236, 239-240, 242, 250, 261, 275, 279, 308-309, 313, 315-316, 377, 417, 423, 426, 428, 440-441, 444, 448-450, 453-454, 483, 534, 646-647, 649, 658, 715, 725; **other fake aliases by (Kid Roberts, Texas Kid, Hugo Kid, Rattlesnake Bill):** 164, 207, 228, 233, 235, 306, 315, 317, 369-370, 430, 737-738; **other fake personas of:** 164, 174-179, 202-203, 207, 369-371; **faking physical match to Billy the Kid by:** 53, 100, 164, 238, 267-268, 270, 281-282, 303-304, 357, 381-382, 419, 423, 451-452, 536, 649, 654, 715, 742; **faking special knowledge:** 163, 193-194, 210-218, 229, 233, 235-236, 242, 268, 281, 285, 293, 296, 299, 304-305, 334, 341, 346-347, 351, 354, 373, 384-385, 403-405, 417, 419, 437-439, 451-453, 468, 646, 658, 669, 672, 675, 688, 720, 724, 740; **admission of "Brushy's" literacy by autobiography, diaries, notebooks, correspondence of:** 207, 229, 232-235, 307, 317, 373, 435, 451; **"Brushy's" handwriting:** 224, 228, 230-231, 737-742; admitted by "Brushy": 235; **faking illiteracy for:** for illiterate for past 25-30 years scam: 235, 281; admitted by "Brushy" to pretending illiteracy: 435; for semi-literate scam: 424, 434, 648-649; **no Spanish fluency of:** 128, 227; **sources used for Billy the Kid impersonation by:** 67-92, 211-218, 802-808 (See William V. Morrison and C.L. Sonnichsen); **failed Billy the Kid pardon attempt by:** 7, 29-30, 33, 37-38, 44, 50, 237-262, 265-268, 270, 281-282, 424, 471: **DEBUNKED IN *ALIAS BILLY THE KID*: 299-405; fix-ups and transcript forgeries for "Brushy's" words in:** 293-298; **major fatal errors in:** ignorance of Antrim, Bonney, and McCarty names in: 274-278, 309, 314; unaware of Paulita Maxwell as sweetheart in: 97-98, 224, 245, 262, 269, 349-350, 361-362, 405; Celsa Gutierrez sweetheart error by: 244-245, 269, 350, 362-363, 443, 529, 667; Celsa Gutierrez sister of Saval Gutierrez error by: 362-363, 439, 443, 667; "cattle war" error: 242, 249, 257-258, 260, 323-324, 326, 331, 333, 464; unaware of San Patricio massacre: 99, 110, 136, 332-333, 405, 684; racism and Lincoln County War Battle shooting "[N-word]" soldiers by: 95, 226, 228, 294, 306, 334-335, 337, 339, 418, 434, 451-452, 464, 642, 646, 658, 660-661, 687-688, 735; unaware of Secret Service intervention in: 95-96, 211-212, 343-346; unaware of Secret Service possible pardon: 96, 117, 344; unaware of courthouse-jail armory location: 356, 452, 648; back porch killing scene in: 262, 364, 366-367, 423, 442, 450, 537, 666; dark night moon error for July 14, 1881 in: 244, 441, 444-445, 522, 537, 550, 556, 645, 647, 666, 671, 735; **fake Affidavits for** (See William V. Morrison and C.L. Sonnichsen);

failed posthumous pardon attempt for: 473-474, 477, 480, 486, 597-614 (See "Billy the Kid Case" hoax); LATER FIX-UPS AND FORGERIES OF "BRUSHY'S" WORDS (See Frederick Bean, W.C. Jameson): **added fake genealogy for:** 425-430; **fake photo-comparison:** 454, 457-459; **fake conspiracy theories for:** 459-464; **forging "Brushy's" interview transcript:** 657-670; **fake forensic exhumation case for** (See "Billy the Kid Case" hoax); **inadvertent "Brushy"-bashing by:** 672, 689-696, 724, 731; **"BRUSHY"-BACKING FILMS AND DOCUMENTARY ABOUT: "Young Guns II":** 467-468, 471; **"Investigating History: Billy the Kid":** 483, 558-562, 572, 612, 641, 643; **"Requiem for Billy the Kid":** 593-594 (See William V. Morrison, C.L. Sonnichsen, W.C. Jameson, "Billy the Kid Case" hoax)

Roberts, Samantha Belle – 168

Roberts, Tom Ulce – 164-168, 173

Roberts, Vada Bell (See Vada Bell Roberts Heath)

Roberts, William Henry (see Oliver Pleasant Roberts)

Robins, Bill III – 472, 474, 480, 491-493, 496, 522, 535, 549-550, 555, 557, 559, 596, 613, 617, 623, 641, 726-729 (See "Billy the Kid Case" hoax)

Robinson, Berry – 111, 686

Robinson, Will – 428, 455, 458

Rodarte, Misty – 588

Rojas, Rick – 613

Romero, Alicia – 41, 47-48, 246-248, 388

Romero, Vincente – 110-111, 113, 144-145, 339, 688

Romney, Pearl Tenney – 430

Romo, Rene – 572-574, 577, 579, 581, 590-591, 598-599, 724

Roosevelt, Theodore – 164, 370-371; **Rough Riders of:** 181, 650-651

R.R. Roberts Accounting and Law Firm – 269

Rose, Noah H. – 209, 371

Roswell Daily Record – 91, 596

Roswell Museum – 35-36

Roswell, New Mexico Territory – 34, 59, 65, 91, 116, 142, 166, 186, 200, 222, 259, 321, 709, 711

Rudabaugh, Dave "Dirty Dave" – 68, 70, 72-73, 86-87, 98, 117-118, 155, 323, 349-350, 431, 438

Rudulph, Charles Frederick "Charlie" – 445, 450; *Los Billitos: The Story of Billy the Kid and His Gang* by (See Charles Frederick Rudulph)

Rudulph, Milnor – 10-11, 15-16, 45-46, 63, 122, 289, 393, 410, 445, 461, 502, 506, 510, 670, 713 (See Legislature Revolt, Coroner's Jury Report for William H. Bonney)

Ruidoso, New Mexico – 251, 377-378, 380, 420-421, 598

Ruidoso News – 359, 378-380, 590, 592, 622, 690

RuidosoNews.com – 570, 588

Ruidoso River – 124, 135, 242, 281, 331, 431, 563

Rumsey, Roy – 595-596

Rynerson, William Logan – 94, 107, 113-114, 386, 422, 498, 605

Salazar, Francisco – 357

Salazar, Yginio – 125, 361, 375, 439, 665, 719

Sampson, Michael – 690

San Andres Mountains – 710-711, 721

Sanches, Arley – 533

Sandia Laboratory – 479, 620

Sandoval, David – 551, 555-556, 728

San Miguel County, New Mexico Territory – 9-11, 16, 18, 20, 23, 27, 29-30, 32-33, 35, 38, 40-43, 55, 118, 155, 239, 245-247, 283, 363, 387-388, 390, 393, 396, 409, 446, 462, 543, 668, 714

Sann, Paul – 407

San Patricio, New Mexico Territory – 99, 108, 110, 136, 139-140, 226, 331- 333, 378, 405, 433, 604, 661, 679, 684; **massacre at:** 99, 110, 136, 332-333, 405, 684

Santa Fe Daily New Mexican – 21-22, 65, 88, 155, 158, 385, 391-392, 394, 397-400, 503

Santa Fe County – 42-43, 55, 276

Santa Fe jail – 88, 119, 151-153, 221, 226-227, 235, 244, 350-351, 384, 422, 436, 438, 561, 646, 649

Santa Fe Museum of New Mexico – 49, 51

Santa Fe, New Mexico – 5, 9, 25, 28-29, 32, 35, 37, 40, 42-43, 47, 74, 80, 90-91, 153, 156-157, 186, 203, 213, 239, 246-248, 251-252, 254, 256-257, 259-261, 266, 270, 276-277, 279-280, 282, 290, 314, 324, 341, 384, 390, 398, 409, 412, 428, 430, 462, 478-479, 524, 563, 598-599, 603, 605, 607, 611, 627, 662, 670, 694, 725, 737, 740

Santa Fe Ring (the Ring) – 4-6, 9, 36, 51-52, 54, 63, 67, 80, 82, 85-86, 93-94, 96-100, 103-105, 112, 115, 121-123, 128-129, 136, 140, 144, 158, 163, 211, 236, 243, 266-267, 282-283, 292, 323-325, 344, 386, 392-393, 397, 403, 421, 431-432, 472-473, 481, 523, 561, 607, 614, 617, 641, 664, 677-678, 680, 684

Savona, Glen – 591

Segura, Melquiadez – 319

Schleede, Raymond – 195

Scholand, Emilie Fritz – 420

Scurlock, Josiah "Doc" – 110, 113, 117, 119

Sebastion County, Arkansas – 168

Secret Service – 86, 95-96, 116-117, 121, 150, 211-212, 343-346, 387, 405, 422, 437, 500, 542, 561, 563-564, 566, 672, 689-690, 694-695 (See Azariah F. Wild)

Second National Bank of Santa Fe – 80

Sederwall, Steven M. "Steve" – 71, 474-478, 481, 484-485, 488, 494-519, 522-548, 550-551, 556, 558-560, 565, 570-574, 577, 579, 581, 583, 586-588, 590-593, 595-596, 616-641, 652, 661, 670-672, 675-676, 678-731; **Capitan Mayor's Report of:** 494-496; **deputized for Case No. 2003-274:** 474, 477, 481, 484-485, 494, 585; **authorship of "Case 2003-274 Probable Cause Statement" claimed by:** 494, 496-519; reported locating carpenter's bench as a deputy in: 568; **listed as co-signer for abandoned "Case 2003-274 Probable Cause Statement":** 522-545; with David Turk claiming Sederwall contacted him as a deputy for participation in Case 2003-274: 565; **exhumation petitions and exhumation involvement for Case 2003-274 as a Deputy Sheriff for:** for Catherine Antrim and William Bonney by: 477, 484, 488, 545-548, 550-551, 556; for John Miller and William Hudspeth by: 587-588, 590-593; wrote "Lincoln County Sheriff's Department Supplemental Report" for: 587-588; faked John Miller's skeleton as matching Billy the Kid's for: 590-591; criminally investigated for exhumations:

591-592; **attempt to exhume "Brushy Bill" as a Case 2003-274 Deputy by:** 595-596; in "Brushy" hoax TV documentary "Investigating History: Billy the Kid": 558-560; **billythekidcase.com website of:** 640; **participating in fake forensics for:** 570-574, 577, 583; contacting Dr. Henry Lee through Paul Hutton by: 571; communicating with Bill Kurtis about paying Dr. Lee by: 572; lying about blood on the carpenter's bench by: 573-574, 583; listed as a Deputy in Dr. Lee's report: 574; in Lee's fake Billy the Kid killing investigation: 577, 579; in Lee's fake Deputy Bell killing investigation: 581; **open records act litigation against:** 485, 616-617; "Memorandum: Billy the Kid Investigation" by: 618-629; forging Dr. Henry Lee reports to fake a private hobby by: 630-637; judge's ruling on forgeries: 637; judge's final ruling on: 638-640; **allying with W.C. Jameson by:** 652-654, 661, 670, 672, 675-676, 678-730; hoaxing Tom O'Folliard's name as "Folliard" by: 661, 691-694; defaming Pat Garrett by; 672; fake investigation of Tunstall murder by: 678-679; fake investigation of Morton/Baker killing by: 680; fake investigation of Sheriff Brady killing by: 681-682; fake investigation of "Buckshot" Roberts killing by: 683-684; faking the Lincoln County War Battle by: 684-688; faking Billy the Kid as a counterfeiter by: 689-691; faking Pat Garrett's lack of authority by: 694-696; FAKING DISCREPANCIES IN THE DEATH SCENE BY: 697-705; faking Maxwell's bedroom as lacking an outside door by: 700-705; faking death scene doubts by: 707-708; faking the body's permanent removal by: 708-709; faking a "Pete Maxwell" denying the shooting by: 709-712, faking no Coroner's Jury Report by: 713-714; RECYCLING AND ADDING TO DR. HENRY LEE'S FAKE FORENSICS BY: 715-723; carpenter's bench forensics faked: 721-722; Garrett shooting scene faked: 722-723; FAKING THE JOHN MILLER EXHUMATION BY: 723-724; faking Miller's skeletal Match to Billy the Kid by: 724; faking a conspiracy against himself by: 725-730 (See "Billy the Kid Case" hoax)

Segura, Alejandro – 10-11, 16, 18, 41, 43, 389-390, 392, 445, 463, 504, 510-511, 517 (See Coroner's Jury Report of William H. Bonney)

Segura, Melquiadez "Mel" – 319

Selman, John – 142, 213, 295, 374

Seven Rivers boys (rustlers) – 110, 121, 137, 322, 329, 372, 376, 684-685, 739

Seven Rivers, New Mexico Territory – 120, 140-143, 295, 322, 329, 374, 431

"Seven Rivers Warriors" – 685

Sexual Maturity Ratings – 463

Shedd's Ranch – 142

Shen, Maxine – 572

Sherman, John – 385, 500, 606, 694

Shetland Islands – 164, 295, 369

Shipman, Jack – 347, 693

Silva, Jesus – 45-46, 365, 440-441, 450, 505, 536-537, 669, 709

Silver City Daily Press – 282

Silver City Independent – 213, 385

Silver City, New Mexico Territory – 49, 57, 80-81, 83,

104-105, 141-142, 203, 213-214, 229, 241, 253, 261, 270, 274-277, 281-282, 309, 314-319, 371, 385, 400, 409, 419, 430, 446, 454, 472, 477, 479-480, 482, 488-489, 491, 493, 544, 549-550, 553-555, 557, 562-563, 568, 592, 598-600, 617, 619-621, 623-625, 627-628, 646, 654, 658, 727

Simpson, Nicole – 571
Simpson, O.J. – 571
Siringo, Charles "Charlie" – 211, 213, 259, 322; *History of Billy the Kid* by (See Charles Siringo)
Smith, Gregory Scott – 704
Smith, Henry Street – 553
Smith, Sam – 690
Smith, Wilbur – 375
Smylie, Vernon – 254
Snead, William – 490, 493
Snow, Clyde – 455, 464, 652
Sonnichsen, Charles Leland – 3-4, 8, 33, 37-39, 45-56, 66-67, 98, 163, 185, 187, 190-204, 207, 210, 212-214, 218, 224, 226, 228-236, 238-239, 241, 244, 261-263, 267-268, 271-278, 281-286, 289, 292-405, 426-427; **background of:** 191-204; **profiteering motive of:** 285, 401; **faking neutrality about "Brushy" by:** 271; **"Brushy"-backing by:** 190, 196-200, 203-204, 282-283, 426-427, 458; ignoring warnings that "Brushy" was an imposter by: 200-203, 261-262; introducing William V. Morrison's El Paso Rotary Club "Brushy" talk by: 282-283; **shoddy historical research by:** 66, 196, 200, 212, 263, 350, 362, 367, 373-385, 401; responsible for "Brushy's" prompt about the back porch killing scene: 244, 262, 364, 366-367, 423, 442, 450, 537, 666-667 (See *Alias Billy the Kid* source footnotes by); **as charlatan:** 401; example of hiding "Brushy's" literacy by: 207, 224, 226, 228-235; example of lying that "Brushy" was illiterate by: 236; *Alias Billy the Kid* **written by:** 190, 195, 200, 268, 272-273, 279, 281, 287-289, 292-405; debunking of: 299-405; using William V. Morrison's notes and interview recordings by: 298; secretly fixing-up "Brushy's" words by: 200, 262, 273-278, 293-298; prompt sources and source footnotes for: 98, 210, 213-214, 218, 299-300, 307, 317, 320-323, 329-330, 333, 341, 343, 345-346, 348-354, 357-359, 2362, 366, 371-372, 386, 388, 393, 397-398, 430, 439; fake conspiracy theories by: 36, 38-39, 45-55, 385-401 (See Oliver Pleasant "Brushy Bill" Roberts, William V. Morrison)

South Spring River Ranch – 321, 361
Sparks, Billy – 474, 478, 562, 619, 624, 629, 725-726, 728-729
Spector, Phil – 571
Speer, Lucas – 629
Spencerian penmanship – 15, 104, 113, 219-220, 227, 229, 648
Spitz, Werner – 572
Starr, Bell aka Myra Belle Shirley Reed – 164, 317
State Land Office, Santa Fe, New Mexico – 29-30, 32-33, 35, 246, 248
Staub, Rick – 483-484, 576, 587-589, 596, 625, 675
Steinke, Rick – 235, 368, 380
Stewart, Frank – 70, 88, 120, 154, 353
Stinking Springs – 58, 87, 98, 104, 118, 120, 150, 154-155, 218, 243, 258, 291, 297, 348-349, 353, 379, 404, 422, 438, 458, 499, 524, 561, 605, 690, 738

St. Louis (Daily) Globe-Democrat – 66, 89
St. Louis, Missouri – 34, 107, 183-185, 187, 190, 209, 214, 226-227, 250, 252-254, 257, 260, 408
Stolorow, Mark – 575
Sullivan, Lawrence – 312
Sullivan, Thomas T. "Tom" – 474, 478, 481, 484, 488, 494-496, 519-522, 545-548, 550-551, 556-559, 561-562, 565, 572, 574-575, 577, 581, 585-586, 588, 590-595, 616-619, 622-624, 626-630, 632-633, 635, 638, 640-641, 672, 712, 725, 728; **deputizing Steve Sederwall for Case 2003-274 by:** 494, 585; **"Probable Cause Statement for Case 2003-274" signer:** 496, 519, 522, 545; **fake Overton Affidavit made to:** 520-521, 712; **deputizing for Case 2003-274 by Sheriff Virden of:** 485, 595; **faking blood on the carpenter's bench by:** 574; **faking courthouse investigation by:** 582; **backing John Miller by:** 586; **involvement in Miller/Hudspeth exhumation of:** 588, 590; **faking John Miller's bones matching Billy the Kid by:** 591; **playing Sheriff Brady in "Requiem for Billy the Kid" by:** 593; **trying the exhume "Brushy Bill" by:** 595; **open records act violation by:** 606-619, 622-624, 626-630, 632-633, 635, 638, 640-641, 725 (See Lincoln County Sheriff's Department Case 2003-274, "Billy the Kid Case" hoax)
Struckman, Robert – 586
Sulphur Springs, Texas – 172, 316, 369, 371
Sunnyside, New Mexico Territory – 16, 46, 63, 122, 389, 461, 502, 505-506, 511
Swett, George G. – 229
Taeger, Mary Nell – 359, 378
TalkLeft.com – 575, 589
Tascosa, Texas – 112, 127, 137, 224, 348-349, 682
Taylor, Daniel – 513
Taylor, Manuel – 374
Tecklenburg, Herman – 383
Telfer, Lois – 408-409, 480, 482, 487, 549
Texas Ranger Museum (Hall of Fame) – 528
"The House" – 97, 99, 106-107, 126, 140, 244, 325, 336-337, 432, 606, 681, 684-685, 720, 741
The Daily Courier of Prescott – 590
The Dallas Morning News – 176, 209, 370, 455
The El Paso Times – 33, 37-38, 40, 42, 54, 66, 124, 189, 194, 238, 272, 533, 719, 738
The Hollywood Reporter – 594
The Indianapolis Press – 90
The New Mexico Folklore Record – 278, 320, 345, 353, 371
The New Southwest – 446, 463
The Texaco Star Reporter – 49, 188
Thunderer (Colt .41) – 53, 291, 450, 668
Tippett, Sherry – 477-478, 488-491, 493, 549
Totty, Frances E. – 518, 564
Traylor, Leslie – 357, 533, 709
Travis, Dewitt – 174, 180, 195, 208-209, 381-384, 451, 651, 656; **backing J. Frank Dalton was Jesse James by:** 208-209; **Affidavit for "Brushy Bill" as Billy the Kid by:** 195, 381-383, 451, 651
Treadwell, Hugh W. – 293
Trinidad, Colorado – 314

Truesdell, Chauncey – 275, 277, 319
True West magazine (See Bob Boze Bell)
Trujillo, Francisco – 567, 681
Truman, Harry S. – 293, 406, 413, 471, 597
Tucson Weekly – 573-574, 586, 588-589, 591
Tularosa Ditch War – 356
Tularosa, New Mexico Territory – 142
Tunnell, Dale – 588, 592, 675
Tunstall, John Henry – 82, 85, 93-94, 97, 99, 105-110, 112-114, 116, 120-121, 123-126, 129-136, 141, 144-145, 147-148, 201, 225, 236, 242, 262, 267, 277, 290, 295, 304, 322-332, 336, 339, 354, 357, 378, 419-421, 431-434, 497-498, 523-524, 532, 540, 560, 601-602, 606, 646, 659-661, 677-682, 684, 688, 710, 720
Tunstall, John Partridge – 99
Tunstill, William A. – 166-167, 171, 196-199, 418, 425-430, 646, 656-657; **fake "Brushy" Bill genealogy by:** 315-316, 373, 429; *Billy the Kid and Me Were the Same* by (See William Tunstill)
Turk, David S. – 481, 485, 496, 499, 518, 522, 563-568, 570, 573-574, 581, 630, 632, 635, 641, 672, 675, 678, 687, 690; **input for Case 2003-274 "Probable Cause Statement" by:** 496, 499, 518, 563; **"The U.S. Marshals Service and Billy the Kid" by:** 522, 563-568; **vouching for Dr. Henry Lee by:** 573; **fake authentication of carpenter's bench by:** 563, 568, 570 (See "Billy the Kid Case" hoax)
Turner, Marion F. – 142, 188, 212, 322, 372, 376, 471, 739

Turner, Thomas – 176, 178, 370
University of Texas at El Paso, (College of Mines and Metallurgy; UTEP) – 192, 230-231, 454
Upson, Ashmun "Ash" – 57, 67, 79-80, 116, 260, 269, 303, 309, 319-320, 498, 543, 621
Utley, Robert M. – 498, 562, 621; *Billy the Kid: A Short and Violent Life* (See Robert Utley)
Valdez, Jannay P. – 474, 476, 593, 596
Vance, Jim – 187
Van Zant County, Texas – 168
Variety magazine – 594
Villa, Pancho – 164, 191, 203, 370-371, 596, 741
Virden, Rick E. – 481, 484-485, 564, 585, 595-596, 615-618, 631, 634, 638-640; **deputizing Tom Sullivan and Steve Sederwall foe Case 2003-274 by:** 485, 494, 585, 638; **exhumations of John Miller/William Hudspeth under:** 484-485, 587, 638; **attempted exhumation of "Brushy Bill" Roberts by:** 595-596; **open records violation case against:** 615-618, 631, 634, 638-640 (See "Billy the Kid Case" hoax)
Von Blon, A.F. – 51
Waggoner, Tom – 374
Waite, Fred Tecumseh – 105, 108-109, 119, 126, 131-132, 134-135, 295, 304, 327, 331, 372, 421, 433, 601, 678
Waldo, Henry – 80, 114
Walker, Charlie – 532
Walker, Dale L. – 192-193, 195, 204, 236-237, 676; *C.L. Sonnichsen: Grassroots Historian* by, and *Legends and Lies: Great Mysteries of the American West* by (See Dale L. Walker)

Wallace, Lew – 6, 20-27, 37, 39, 44, 48-49, 51-52, 54-56, 66-67, 72-79, 85, 87-91, 93-95, 99, 104, 112-114, 116-119, 124, 129, 137-144, 149-153, 159, 204, 211, 213-216, 218-222, 224-227, 235, 238-240, 243-244, 246-248, 250, 258, 268-269, 279-280, 283, 289, 291, 295-297, 300, 302-303, 305-306, 310, 331, 334, 340-343, 345, 348, 350, 361, 363, 376, 378, 384, 386, 388, 391-400, 404-405, 407, 411, 422, 424, 435-437, 451, 453, 463, 474-475, 479, 486, 552, 561, 597-598, 600, 602-605, 607-612, 662, 664, 680, 740; **Amnesty Proclamation by:** 112, 138, 243, 246, 291, 404, 495, 602; **secret letter on Santa Fe Ring by:** 99; *Ben-Hur* **by:** 90, 250; **pardon bargain with Billy Bonney of:** 6, 37, 94-95, 104, 113, 116-117, 119, 138-144, 149-153, 159-204, 216, 238-240, 243-240, 243, 250, 268, 279-280, 283, 296, 302-303, 305, 310, 331, 340-343, 378, 386, 422, 424, 435-436, 474-475, 479, 486, 495, 499, 550, 552, 561, 597-598, 600, 602-605, 607, 609-611, 662, 664, 740; **reward for Billy the Kid by:** 20-27, 39, 44, 48-49, 51-52, 54-56, 87-88, 118, 246, 258, 388, 391-396, 398-400, 404, 463, 605; **outlaw myth of Billy the Kid by:** 6, 66-67, 73-79, 89-91, 211, 213, 303, 305, 334, 348, 361, 386, 411-412, 603 (See William H. Bonney's letters and interview)

Wallace, Lew Jr. – 137, 211, 214-217, 222, 244, 608

Wallace, William N. – 486, 608-611, 613

Walz, Edgar – 99, 106, 116-117, 136, 213, 324

Walz, Kent – 481

Washington Times – 128, 613

Wastman Verifax Printer – 187

Waters, William – 210, 284, 471, 650

Watson, Kathryn – 613

Weathers, Elreeta Crain – 176

Weddle, Jerry (Richard) – 275, 316, 514, 654; *Antrim is my Stepfather's Name* **by:** 275, 316, 654; **consultation on carpenter's bench by:** 514, 569

"We the People" radio – 207-209

Whipple, Arizona Veterans' Hospital – 374

White, J.D. – 704

Whitehill, Harvey – 105

White Oaks livery – 112, 117-118

White Oaks, New Mexico – 59, 70, 72, 112, 117, 120, 160, 260, 498, 525, 541, 709, 716, 719

White Oaks posse – 118, 121, 150, 345, 422, 437

Widenmann, Robert – 126, 132-135, 601

Wilcox, Lucius "Lute" – 87, 155, 225, 458, 680, 690

Wild, Azariah F. – 86, 95-95, 117-119, 121, 212, 344, 500, 542, 563-564, 566, 690, 693; **pardon bargain for Billy the Kid by:** 96, 117, 344; **appointment Pat Garrett as Deputy U.S. Marshal by:** 118, 344, 694-696

Wild World Magazine – 505

William Henry Smith Memorial Library – 214, 247

Williams, Cecil W. – 247

Wilson, Gorgonio – 367, 719

Wilson, John B. "Squire" – 108, 130-132, 139, 243, 327, 342, 354, 367, 421, 436, 603-604, 659

Wilson, Roscoe – 275, 318

Wilson, William "Billy" – 68, 72, 87-88, 117-118, 155, 158, 323

Winchester '73 carbine – 53, 71-72, 75, 87, 108-109, 130-131, 157, 175, 295, 304, 329-330, 332, 433, 561, 660, 739, 742

Wood, Miles – 523
Woodman, Oran Ardious "Uncle Kit Carson, Father of Billy the Kid" – 181, 232
Wortley Hotel – 120, 147, 337, 495, 525-526
Yaqui Indians – 255
Yeatman, Ted P. – 209
Yerby Ranch – 363, 536
Yerby, Thomas – 363
"Young Guns II" (See John Fusco)
Zamora, Francisco – 110-111, 113, 144-145, 339, 688
Zuber, Hugo – 151
Zumwalt, Ross – 488;
   Affidavit opposing exhumations by: 490-491, 557

www.ingramcontent.com/pod-product-compliance
Lightning Source LLC
Chambersburg PA
CBHW031246230426
43670CB00005B/61